Quantitative Analysis for Management

TWELFTH EDITION

BARRY RENDER

Charles Harwood Professor of Management Science
Crummer Graduate School of Business, Rollins College

RALPH M. STAIR, JR.

Professor of Information and Management Sciences,
Florida State University

MICHAEL E. HANNA

Professor of Decision Sciences,
University of Houston–Clear Lake

TREVOR S. HALE

Associate Professor of Management Sciences,
University of Houston–Downtown

PEARSON

Boston Columbus Indianapolis New York San Francisco Upper Saddle River
Amsterdam Cape Town Dubai London Madrid Milan Munich Paris Montréal Toronto
Delhi Mexico City São Paulo Sydney Hong Kong Seoul Singapore Taipei Tokyo

To my wife and sons—BR

To Lila and Leslie—RMS

To Zoe and Gigi—MEH

To Valerie and Lauren—TSH

Editor in Chief: Donna Battista
Editorial Project Manager: Mary Kate Murray
Editorial Assistant: Elissa Senra-Sargent
Director of Marketing: Maggie Moylan
Senior Marketing Manager: Anne Fahlgren
Managing Editor: Jeff Holcomb
Senior Production Project Manager: Kathryn Dinovo
Manufacturing Buyer/Procurement Specialist: Carol Melville
Art Director, Cover: Jayne Conte

Cover Designer: Bruce Kenselaar
Cover Art: Ocean/Corbis
Media Project Manager: Lisa Rinaldi
Full-Service Project Management: PreMediaGlobal
Composition: PreMediaGlobal
Printer/Binder: Courier/Kendallville
Cover Printer: Lehigh-Phoenix Color/Hagerstown
Text Font: 10/12 Times Roman

Credits and acknowledgments borrowed from other sources and reproduced, with permission, in this textbook appear on the appropriate page within text.

Microsoft and/or its respective suppliers make no representations about the suitability of the information contained in the documents and related graphics published as part of the services for any purpose. All such documents and related graphics are provided "as is" without warranty of any kind. Microsoft and/or its respective suppliers hereby disclaim all warranties and conditions with regard to this information, including all warranties and conditions of merchantability, whether express, implied or statutory, fitness for a particular purpose, title and non-infringement. In no event shall Microsoft and/or its respective suppliers be liable for any special, indirect or consequential damages or any damages whatsoever resulting from loss of use, data or profits, whether in an action of contract, negligence or other tortious action, arising out of or in connection with the use or performance of information available from the services.

The documents and related graphics contained herein could include technical inaccuracies or typographical errors. Changes are periodically added to the information herein. Microsoft and/or its respective suppliers may make improvements and/or changes in the product(s) and/or the program(s) described herein at any time. Partial screen shots may be viewed in full within the software version specified.

Microsoft® and Windows® and Excel® are registered trademarks of the Microsoft Corporation in the U.S.A. and other countries. This book is not sponsored or endorsed by or affiliated with the Microsoft Corporation.

Many of the designations by manufacturers and sellers to distinguish their products are claimed as trademarks. Where those designations appear in this book, and the publisher was aware of a trademark claim, the designations have been printed in initial caps or all caps.

Library of Congress Cataloging-in-Publication Data
Render, Barry.
 Quantitative analysis for management / Barry Render, Charles Harwood professor of management science, Crummer Graduate School of Business, Rollins College, Ralph M. Stair, Jr., professor of information and management sciences, Florida State University, Michael E. Hanna, professor of decision sciences, University of Houston–Clear Lake, Trevor S. Hale, associate professor of management sciences, University of Houston–Downtown.—Twelfth edition.
    pages cm
 Includes bibliographical references and index.
 ISBN-13: 978-0-13-350733-1
 ISBN-10: 0-13-350733-5
 1. Management science—Case studies. 2. Operations research—Case studies. I. Title.
 T56.R543 2015
 658.4'033—dc23

2013037583

10 9 8 7 6 5 4 3 2
V011

ISBN-13: 978-0-13-350733-1
ISBN-10:   0-13-350733-5

Barry Render is Professor Emeritus, the Charles Harwood Distinguished Professor of Operations Management, Crummer Graduate School of Business, Rollins College, Winter Park, Florida. He received his B.S. in Mathematics and Physics at Roosevelt University and his M.S. in Operations Research and his Ph.D. in Quantitative Analysis at the University of Cincinnati. He previously taught at George Washington University, the University of New Orleans, Boston University, and George Mason University, where he held the Mason Foundation Professorship in Decision Sciences and was Chair of the Decision Science Department. Dr. Render has also worked in the aerospace industry for General Electric, McDonnell Douglas, and NASA.

Dr. Render has coauthored 10 textbooks published by Pearson, including *Managerial Decision Modeling with Spreadsheets, Operations Management, Principles of Operations Management, Service Management, Introduction to Management Science,* and *Cases and Readings in Management Science.* More than 100 articles of Dr. Render on a variety of management topics have appeared in *Decision Sciences, Production and Operations Management, Interfaces, Information and Management, Journal of Management Information Systems, Socio-Economic Planning Sciences, IIE Solutions,* and *Operations Management Review,* among others.

Dr. Render has been honored as an AACSB Fellow and was named twice as a Senior Fulbright Scholar. He was Vice President of the Decision Science Institute Southeast Region and served as software review editor for *Decision Line* for six years and as Editor of the *New York Times* Operations Management special issues for five years. From 1984 to 1993, Dr. Render was President of Management Service Associates of Virginia, Inc., whose technology clients included the FBI, the U.S. Navy, Fairfax County, Virginia, and C&P Telephone. He is currently Consulting Editor to *Financial Times Press.*

Dr. Render has taught operations management courses at Rollins College for MBA and Executive MBA programs. He has received that school's Welsh Award as leading professor and was selected by Roosevelt University as the 1996 recipient of the St. Claire Drake Award for Outstanding Scholarship. In 2005, Dr. Render received the Rollins College MBA Student Award for Best Overall Course, and in 2009 was named Professor of the Year by full-time MBA students.

Ralph Stair is Professor Emeritus at Florida State University. He earned a B.S. in chemical engineering from Purdue University and an M.B.A. from Tulane University. Under the guidance of Ken Ramsing and Alan Eliason, he received a Ph.D. in operations management from the University of Oregon. He has taught at the University of Oregon, the University of Washington, the University of New Orleans, and Florida State University.

He has taught twice in Florida State University's Study Abroad Program in London. Over the years, his teaching has been concentrated in the areas of information systems, operations research, and operations management.

Dr. Stair is a member of several academic organizations, including the Decision Sciences Institute and INFORMS, and he regularly participates in national meetings. He has published numerous articles and books, including *Managerial Decision Modeling with Spreadsheets, Introduction to Management Science, Cases and Readings in Management Science, Production and Operations Management: A Self-Correction Approach, Fundamentals of Information Systems, Principles of Information Systems, Introduction to Information Systems, Computers in Today's World, Principles of Data Processing, Learning to Live with Computers, Programming in BASIC, Essentials of BASIC Programming, Essentials of FORTRAN Programming,* and *Essentials of COBOL Programming.* Dr. Stair divides his time between Florida and Colorado. He enjoys skiing, biking, kayaking, and other outdoor activities.

Michael E. Hanna is Professor of Decision Sciences at the University of Houston–Clear Lake (UHCL). He holds a B.A. in Economics, an M.S. in Mathematics, and a Ph.D. in Operations Research from Texas Tech University. For more than 25 years, he has been teaching courses in statistics, management science, forecasting, and other quantitative methods. His dedication to teaching has been recognized with the Beta Alpha Psi teaching award in 1995 and the Outstanding Educator Award in 2006 from the Southwest Decision Sciences Institute (SWDSI).

Dr. Hanna has authored textbooks in management science and quantitative methods, has published numerous articles and professional papers, and has served on the Editorial Advisory Board of *Computers and Operations Research.* In 1996, the UHCL Chapter of Beta Gamma Sigma presented him with the Outstanding Scholar Award.

Dr. Hanna is very active in the Decision Sciences Institute, having served on the Innovative Education Committee, the Regional Advisory Committee, and the Nominating Committee. He has served on the board of directors of the Decision Sciences Institute (DSI) for two terms and also as regionally elected vice president of DSI. For SWDSI, he has held several positions, including president, and he received the SWDSI Distinguished Service Award in 1997. For overall service to the profession and to the university, he received the UHCL President's Distinguished Service Award in 2001.

Trevor S. Hale is Associate Professor of Management Science at the University of Houston–Downtown (UHD). He received a B.S. in Industrial Engineering from Penn State University, an M.S. in Engineering Management from Northeastern University, and a Ph.D. in Operations Research from Texas A&M University. He was previously on the faculty of both Ohio University–Athens, and Colorado State University–Pueblo.

Dr. Hale was honored three times as an Office of Naval Research Senior Faculty Fellow. He spent the summers of 2009, 2011, and 2013 performing energy security/cyber security research for the U.S. Navy at Naval Base Ventura County in Port Hueneme, California.

Dr. Hale has published dozens of articles in the areas of operations research and quantitative analysis in journals such as the *International Journal of Production Research,* the *European Journal of Operational Research, Annals of Operations Research,* the *Journal of the Operational Research Society,* and the *International Journal of Physical Distribution and Logistics Management* among several others. He teaches quantitative analysis courses in the University of Houston–Downtown MBA program and Masters of Security Management for Executives program. He is a senior member of both the Decision Sciences Institute and INFORMS.

BRIEF CONTENTS

CONTENTS

PREFACE

OVERVIEW

Welcome to the twelfth edition of *Quantitative Analysis for Management*. Our goal is to provide undergraduate and graduate students with a genuine foundation in business analytics, quantitative methods, and management science. In doing so, we owe thanks to the hundreds of users and scores of reviewers who have provided invaluable counsel and pedagogical insight for more than 30 years.

To help students connect how the techniques presented in this book apply in the real world, computer-based applications and examples are a major focus of this edition. Mathematical models, with all the necessary assumptions, are presented in a clear and "plain-English" manner. The ensuing solution procedures are then applied to example problems alongside step-by-step "how-to" instructions. We have found this method of presentation to be very effective and students are very appreciative of this approach. In places where the mathematical computations are intricate, the details are presented in such a manner that the instructor can omit these sections without interrupting the flow of material. The use of computer software enables the instructor to focus on the managerial problem and spend less time on the details of the algorithms. Computer output is provided for many examples throughout the book.

The only mathematical prerequisite for this textbook is algebra. One chapter on probability and another on regression analysis provide introductory coverage on these topics. We employ standard notation, terminology, and equations throughout the book. Careful explanation is provided for the mathematical notation and equations that are used.

NEW TO THIS EDITION

- An introduction to business analytics is provided.
- Excel 2013 is incorporated throughout the chapters.
- The transportation, assignment, and network models have been combined into one chapter focused on modeling with linear programming.
- Specialized algorithms for the transportation, assignment, and network methods have been combined into Online Module 8.
- New examples, over 25 problems, 8 QA in Action applications, 4 Modeling in the Real World features, and 3 new Case Studies have been added throughout the textbook. Other problems and Case Studies have been updated.

SPECIAL FEATURES

Many features have been popular in previous editions of this textbook, and they have been updated and expanded in this edition. They include the following:

- *Modeling in the Real World* boxes demonstrate the application of the quantitative analysis approach to every technique discussed in the book. Four new ones have been added.

- *Procedure* boxes summarize the more complex quantitative techniques, presenting them as a series of easily understandable steps.

- *Margin notes* highlight the important topics in the text.

- *History* boxes provide interesting asides related to the development of techniques and the people who originated them.

- *QA in Action* boxes illustrate how real organizations have used quantitative analysis to solve problems. Several new QA in Action boxes have been added.

- *Solved Problems*, included at the end of each chapter, serve as models for students in solving their own homework problems.

- *Discussion Questions* are presented at the end of each chapter to test the student's understanding of the concepts covered and definitions provided in the chapter.

- *Problems* included in every chapter are applications oriented and test the student's ability to solve exam-type problems. They are graded by level of difficulty: introductory (one bullet), moderate (two bullets), and challenging (three bullets). More than 40 new problems have been added.

- *Internet Homework Problems* provide additional problems for students to work. They are available on the Companion Website.

- *Self-Tests* allow students to test their knowledge of important terms and concepts in preparation for quizzes and examinations.

- *Case Studies*, at the end of each chapter, provide additional challenging managerial applications.

- *Glossaries*, at the end of each chapter, define important terms.

- *Key Equations*, provided at the end of each chapter, list the equations presented in that chapter.

- *End-of-chapter bibliographies* provide a current selection of more advanced books and articles.

- *The software POM-QM for Windows* uses the full capabilities of Windows to solve quantitative analysis problems.

- *Excel QM* and *Excel 2013* are used to solve problems throughout the book.

- Data files with Excel spreadsheets and POM-QM for Windows files containing all the examples in the textbook are available for students to download from the Companion Website. Instructors can download these plus additional files containing computer solutions to the relevant end-of-chapter problems from the Instructor Resource Center Web site.

- *Online modules* provide additional coverage of topics in quantitative analysis.

- The Companion Website, at www.pearsonhighered.com/render, provides the online modules, additional problems, cases, and other material for almost every chapter.

SIGNIFICANT CHANGES TO THE TWELFTH EDITION

In the twelfth edition, we have introduced Excel 2013 in all of the chapters. Screenshots are integrated in the appropriate sections so that students can easily learn how to use Excel for the calculations. The Excel QM add-in is used with Excel 2013 allowing students with limited Excel experience to easily perform the necessary calculations. This also allows students to improve their Excel skills as they see the formulas automatically written in Excel QM.

From the Companion Website, students can access files for all of the examples used in the textbook in Excel 2013, QM for Windows, and Excel QM. Other files with all of the end-of-chapter problems involving these software tools are available to the instructors.

Business analytics, one of the hottest topics in the business world, makes extensive use of the models in this book. A discussion of the business analytics categories is provided, and the relevant management science techniques are placed into the appropriate category.

The transportation, transshipment, assignment, and network models have been combined into one chapter focused on modeling with linear programming. The specialized algorithms for these models have been combined into a new online module.

Examples and problems have been updated, and many new ones have been added. New screenshots are provided for almost all of the examples in the book. A brief summary of the other changes in each chapter are presented here.

Chapter 1 *Introduction to Quantitative Analysis.* A section on business analytics has been added, the self-test has been modified, and two new problems were added.

Chapter 2 *Probability Concepts and Applications.* The presentation of the fundamental concepts of probability has been significantly modified and reorganized. Two new problems have been added.

Chapter 3 *Decision Analysis.* A more thorough discussion of minimization problems with payoff tables has been provided in a new section. The presentation of software usage with payoff tables was expanded. Two new problems were added.

Chapter 4 *Regression Models.* The use of different software packages for regression analysis has been moved to the body of the textbook instead of the appendix. Five new problems and one new QA in Action item have been added.

Chapter 5 *Forecasting.* The presentation of time-series forecasting models was significantly revised to bring the focus on identifying the appropriate technique to use based on which time-series components are present in the data. Five new problems were added, and the cases have been updated.

Chapter 6 *Inventory Control Models.* The four steps of the Kanban production process have been updated and clarified. Two new QA in Action boxes, four new problems, and one new Modeling in the Real World have been added.

Chapter 7 *Linear Programming Models: Graphical and Computer Methods.* More discussion of Solver is presented. A new Modeling in the Real World item was added, and the solved problems have been revised.

Chapter 8 *Linear Programming Applications.* The transportation model was moved to Chapter 9, and a new section describing other models has been added. The self-test questions were modified; one new problem, one new QA in Action summary, and a new case study have been added.

Chapter 9 *Transportation, Assignment, and Network Models.* This new chapter presents all of the distribution, assignment, and network models that were previously in two separate chapters. The modeling approach is emphasized, while the special-purpose algorithms were moved to a new online module. A new case study, Northeastern Airlines, has also been added.

Chapter 10 *Integer Programming, Goal Programming, and Nonlinear Programming.* The use of Excel 2013 and the new screen shots were the only changes to this chapter.

Chapter 11 *Project Management.* Two new end-of-chapter problems and three new QA in Action boxes have been added.

Chapter 12 *Waiting Lines and Queuing Theory Models.* Two new end-of-chapter problems were added.

Chapter 13 *Simulation Modeling.* One new Modeling in the Real World vignette, one new QA in Action box, and a new case study have been added.

Chapter 14 *Markov Analysis.* One new QA in Action box and two new end-of-chapter problems have been added.

Chapter 15 *Statistical Quality Control.* One new Modeling in the Real World vignette, one new QA in Action box, and two new end-of-chapter problems have been added.

Modules 1–8 The only significant change to the modules is the addition of Module 8: *Transportation, Assignment, and Network Algorithms.* This includes the special-purpose algorithms for the transportation, assignment, and network models.

ONLINE MODULES

To streamline the book, eight topics are contained in modules available on the Companion Website for the book.

1. Analytic Hierarchy Process
2. Dynamic Programming
3. Decision Theory and the Normal Distribution
4. Game Theory
5. Mathematical Tools: Determinants and Matrices
6. Calculus-Based Optimization
7. Linear Programming: The Simplex Method
8. Transportation, Assignment, and Network Algorithms

SOFTWARE

Excel 2013 Instructions and screen captures are provided for, using Excel 2013, throughout the book. Instructions for activating the Solver and Analysis ToolPak add-ins in Excel 2013 are provided in an appendix. The use of Excel is more prevalent in this edition of the book than in previous editions.

Excel QM Using the Excel QM add-in that is available on the Companion Website makes the use of Excel even easier. Students with limited Excel experience can use this and learn from the formulas that are automatically provided by Excel QM. This is used in many of the chapters.

POM-QM for Windows This software, developed by Professor Howard Weiss, is available to students at the Companion Website. This is very user-friendly and has proven to be a very popular software tool for users of this textbook. Modules are available for every major problem type presented in the textbook.

COMPANION WEBSITE

The Companion Website, located at www.pearsonhighered.com/render, contains a variety of materials to help students master the material in this course. These include the following:

Modules There are eight modules containing additional material that the instructor may choose to include in the course. Students can download these from the Companion Website.

Files for Examples in Excel, Excel QM, and POM-QM for Windows Students can download the files that were used for examples throughout the book. This helps them become familiar with the software, and it helps them understand the input and formulas necessary for working the examples.

Internet Homework Problems In addition to the end-of-chapter problems in the textbook, there are additional problems that instructors may assign. These are available for download at the Companion Website.

Internet Case Studies Additional case studies are available for most chapters.

POM-QM for Windows Developed by Howard Weiss, this very user-friendly software can be used to solve most of the homework problems in the text.

Excel QM This Excel add-in will automatically create worksheets for solving problems. This is very helpful for instructors who choose to use Excel in their classes but who may have students with limited Excel experience. Students can learn by examining the formulas that have been created, and by seeing the inputs that are automatically generated for using the Solver add-in for linear programming.

INSTRUCTOR RESOURCES

- *Instructor Resource Center:* The Instructor Resource Center contains the electronic files for the test bank, PowerPoint slides, the Solutions Manual, and data files for both Excel and POM-QM for Windows for all relevant examples and end-of-chapter problems. (www.pearsonhighered.com/render).

- *Register, Redeem, Login:* At www.pearsonhighered.com/irc, instructors can access a variety of print, media, and presentation resources that are available with this text in downloadable, digital format. For most texts, resources are also available for course management platforms such as Blackboard, WebCT, and Course Compass.

- *Need help?* Our dedicated technical support team is ready to assist instructors with questions about the media supplements that accompany this text. Visit http://247pearsoned.custhelp .com/ for answers to frequently asked questions and toll-free user support phone numbers. The supplements are available to adopting instructors. Detailed descriptions are provided on the Instructor Resource Center.

Instructor's Solutions Manual The Instructor's Solutions Manual, updated by the authors, is available for download from the Instructor Resource Center. Solutions to all Internet Homework Problems and Internet Case Studies are also included in the manual.

PowerPoint Presentation An extensive set of PowerPoint slides is available for download from the Instructor Resource Center.

Test Bank The updated test bank is available for download from the Instructor Resource Center.

TestGen The computerized TestGen package allows instructors to customize, save, and generate classroom tests. The test program permits instructors to edit, add, or delete questions from the test bank; edit existing graphics and create new graphics; analyze test results; and organize a database of test and student results. This software allows the instructors to benefit from the extensive flexibility and ease of use. It provides many options for organizing and displaying tests, along with search and sort features. The software and the test banks can be downloaded at www.pearsonhighered.com/render.

ACKNOWLEDGMENTS

We gratefully thank the users of previous editions and the reviewers who provided valuable suggestions and ideas for this edition. Your feedback is valuable in our efforts for continuous improvement. The continued success of *Quantitative Analysis for Management* is a direct result of instructor and student feedback, which is truly appreciated.

The authors are indebted to many people who have made important contributions to this project. Special thanks go to Professors Faizul Huq, F. Bruce Simmons III, Khala Chand Seal, Victor E. Sower, Michael Ballot, Curtis P. McLaughlin, and Zbigniew H. Przanyski for their contributions to the excellent cases included in this edition.

We thank Howard Weiss for providing Excel QM and POM-QM for Windows, two of the most outstanding packages in the field of quantitative methods. We would also like to thank the reviewers who have helped to make this textbook the most widely used one in the field of quantitative analysis:

Stephen Achtenhagen, *San Jose University*

M. Jill Austin, *Middle Tennessee State University*

Raju Balakrishnan, *Clemson University*

Hooshang Beheshti, *Radford University*

Jason Bergner, *University of Central Missouri*

Bruce K. Blaylock, *Radford University*

Rodney L. Carlson, *Tennessee Technological University*

Edward Chu, *California State University, Dominguez Hills*

John Cozzolino, *Pace University–Pleasantville*

Ozgun C. Demirag, *Penn State–Erie*

Shad Dowlatshahi, *University of Wisconsin, Platteville*

Ike Ehie, *Southeast Missouri State University*

Richard Ehrhardt, *University of North Carolina–Greensboro*

Sean Eom, *Southeast Missouri State University*

Ephrem Eyob, *Virginia State University*

Mira Ezvan, *Lindenwood University*

Wade Ferguson, *Western Kentucky University*

Robert Fiore, *Springfield College*

Frank G. Forst, *Loyola University of Chicago*

Ed Gillenwater, *University of Mississippi*

Stephen H. Goodman, *University of Central Florida*

Irwin Greenberg, *George Mason University*

Nicholas G. Hall, *Ohio State University*

Robert R. Hill, *University of Houston–Clear Lake*

Gordon Jacox, *Weber State University*

Bharat Jain, *Towson University*

Vassilios Karavas, *University of Massachusetts Amherst*

Darlene R. Lanier, *Louisiana State University*

Kenneth D. Lawrence, *New Jersey Institute of Technology*

Jooh Lee, *Rowan College*

Richard D. Legault, *University of Massachusetts–Dartmouth*

Douglas Lonnstrom, *Siena College*

Daniel McNamara, *University of St. Thomas*

Peter Miller, *University of Windsor*

Ralph Miller, *California State Polytechnic University*

Shahriar Mostashari, *Campbell University*

David Murphy, *Boston College*

Robert C. Myers, *University of Louisville*

Barin Nag, *Towson State University*

Nizam S. Najd, *Oklahoma State University*

Harvey Nye, *Central State University*

Alan D. Olinsky, *Bryant College*

Savas Ozatalay, *Widener University*

Young Park, *California University of Pennsylvania*

Cy Peebles, *Eastern Kentucky University*

Yusheng Peng, *Brooklyn College*

Dane K. Peterson, *Southwest Missouri State University*

Sanjeev Phukan, *Bemidji State University*

Ranga Ramasesh, *Texas Christian University*

William Rife, *West Virginia University*

Bonnie Robeson, *Johns Hopkins University*

Grover Rodich, *Portland State University*

Vijay Shah, *West Virginia University–Parkersburg*

L. Wayne Shell, *Nicholls State University*

Thomas Sloan, *University of Massachusetts–Lowell*

Richard Slovacek, *North Central College*

Alan D. Smith, *Robert Morris University*

John Swearingen, *Bryant College*

F. S. Tanaka, *Slippery Rock State University*

Jack Taylor, *Portland State University*

Madeline Thimmes, *Utah State University*

M. Keith Thomas, *Olivet College*

Andrew Tiger, *Southeastern Oklahoma State University*

Chris Vertullo, *Marist College*

James Vigen, *California State University, Bakersfield*

William Webster, *University of Texas at San Antonio*

Larry Weinstein, *Eastern Kentucky University*

Fred E. Williams, *University of Michigan–Flint*

Mela Wyeth, *Charleston Southern University*

Oliver Yu, *San Jose State University*

We are very grateful to all the people at Pearson who worked so hard to make this book a success. These include Donna Battista, editor in chief; Mary Kate Murray, senior project manager; and Kathryn Dinovo, senior production project manager. We are also grateful to Tracy Duff, our project manager at PreMediaGlobal. We are extremely thankful to Annie Puciloski for her tireless work in error checking the textbook. Thank you all!

Barry Render
brender@rollins.edu

Ralph Stair

Michael Hanna
hanna@uhcl.edu

Trevor S. Hale
halet@uhd.edu

CHAPTER 1

Introduction to Quantitative Analysis

LEARNING OBJECTIVES

After completing this chapter, students will be able to:

1. Describe the quantitative analysis approach.
2. Understand the application of quantitative analysis in a real situation.
3. Describe the three categories of business analytics.
4. Describe the use of modeling in quantitative analysis.
5. Use computers and spreadsheet models to perform quantitative analysis.
6. Discuss possible problems in using quantitative analysis.
7. Perform a break-even analysis.

CHAPTER OUTLINE

Summary • Glossary • Key Equations • Self-Test • Discussion Questions and Problems • Case Study: Food and Beverages at Southwestern University Football Games • Bibliography

1.1   Introduction

People have been using mathematical tools to help solve problems for thousands of years; however, the formal study and application of quantitative techniques to practical decision making is largely a product of the twentieth century. The techniques we study in this book have been applied successfully to an increasingly wide variety of complex problems in business, government, health care, education, and many other areas. Many such successful uses are discussed throughout this book.

It isn't enough, though, just to know the mathematics of how a particular quantitative technique works; you must also be familiar with the limitations, assumptions, and specific applicability of the technique. The successful use of quantitative techniques usually results in a solution that is timely, accurate, flexible, economical, reliable, and easy to understand and use.

In this and other chapters, there are *QA (Quantitative Analysis) in Action* boxes that provide success stories on the applications of management science. They show how organizations have used quantitative techniques to make better decisions, operate more efficiently, and generate more profits. Taco Bell has reported saving over $150 million with better forecasting of demand and better scheduling of employees. NBC television increased advertising revenue by over $200 million between 1996 and 2000 by using a model to help develop sales plans for advertisers. Continental Airlines saves over $40 million per year by using mathematical models to quickly recover from disruptions caused by weather delays and other factors. These are but a few of the many companies discussed in *QA in Action* boxes throughout this book.

To see other examples of how companies use quantitative analysis or operations research methods to operate better and more efficiently, go to the website www.scienceofbetter.org. The success stories presented there are categorized by industry, functional area, and benefit. These success stories illustrate how operations research is truly the "science of better."

1.2   What Is Quantitative Analysis?

Quantitative analysis uses a scientific approach to decision making.

Quantitative analysis is the scientific approach to managerial decision making. This field of study has several different names including quantitative analysis, **management science**, and operations research. These terms are used interchangeably in this book. Also, many of the quantitative analysis methods presented in this book are used extensively in business analytics.

Whim, emotions, and guesswork are not part of the quantitative analysis approach. The approach starts with data. Like raw material for a factory, these data are manipulated or processed into information that is valuable to people making decisions. This processing and manipulating of raw data into meaningful information is the heart of quantitative analysis. Computers have been instrumental in the increasing use of quantitative analysis.

In solving a problem, managers must consider both qualitative and quantitative factors. For example, we might consider several different investment alternatives, including certificates of deposit at a bank, investments in the stock market, and an investment in real estate. We can use quantitative analysis to determine how much our investment will be worth in the future when deposited at a bank at a given interest rate for a certain number of years. Quantitative analysis can also be used in computing financial ratios from the balance sheets for several companies whose stock we are considering. Some real estate companies have developed computer programs that use quantitative analysis to analyze cash flows and rates of return for investment property.

Both qualitative and quantitative factors must be considered.

In addition to quantitative analysis, *qualitative* factors should also be considered. The weather, state and federal legislation, new technological breakthroughs, the outcome of an election, and so on may all be factors that are difficult to quantify.

Because of the importance of qualitative factors, the role of quantitative analysis in the decision-making process can vary. When there is a lack of qualitative factors and when the problem, model, and input data remain the same, the results of quantitative analysis can *automate* the decision-making process. For example, some companies use quantitative inventory models to determine automatically *when* to order additional new materials. In most cases, however, quantitative analysis will be an *aid* to the decision-making process. The results of quantitative analysis will be combined with other (qualitative) information in making decisions.

Quantitative analysis has been particularly important in many areas of management. The field of production management, which evolved into **production/operations management (POM)** as society became more service oriented, uses quantitative analysis extensively. While POM focuses on internal operations of a company, the field of supply chain management takes a more complete view of the business and considers the entire process of obtaining materials from suppliers, using the materials to develop products, and distributing these products to the final consumers. Supply chain management makes extensive use of many management science models. Another area of management that could not exist without the quantitative analysis methods presented in this book, and perhaps the hottest discipline in business today, is business analytics.

1.3 Business Analytics

Business analytics is a data-driven approach to decision making that allows companies to make better decisions. The study of business analytics involves the use of large amounts of data, which means that information technology related to the management of the data is very important. Statistical and quantitative analysis are used to analyze the data and provide useful information to the decision maker.

Business analytics is often broken into three categories: descriptive, predictive, and prescriptive. **Descriptive analytics** involves the study and consolidation of historical data for a business and an industry. It helps a company measure how it has performed in the past and how it is performing now. **Predictive analytics** is aimed at forecasting future outcomes based on patterns in the past data. Statistical and mathematical models are used extensively for this purpose. **Prescriptive analytics** involves the use of optimization methods to provide new and better ways to operate based on specific business objectives. The optimization models presented in this book are very important to prescriptive analytics. While there are only three business analytics categories, many business decisions are made based on information obtained from two or three of these categories.

Many of the quantitative analysis techniques presented in the chapters of this book are used extensively in business analytics. Table 1.1 highlights the three categories of business analytics, and it places many of the topics and chapters in this book in the most relevant category. Keep in mind that some topics (and certainly some chapters with multiple concepts and models) could possibly be placed in a different category. Some of the material in this book could overlap two or even three of these categories. Nevertheless, all of these quantitative analysis techniques are very important tools in business analytics.

The three categories of business analytics are descriptive, predictive, and prescriptive.

TABLE 1.1

Business Analytics and Quantitative Analysis Models

BUSINESS ANALYTICS CATEGORY	QUANTITATIVE ANALYSIS TECHNIQUE (CHAPTER)
Descriptive analytics	• Statistical measures such as means and standard deviations (Chapter 2)
	• Statistical quality control (Chapter 15)
Predictive analytics	• Decision analysis and decision trees (Chapter 3)
	• Regression models (Chapter 4)
	• Forecasting (Chapter 5)
	• Project scheduling (Chapter 11)
	• Waiting line models (Chapter 12)
	• Simulation (Chapter 13)
	• Markov analysis (Chapter 14)
Prescriptive analytics	• Inventory models such as the economic order quantity (Chapter 6)
	• Linear programming (Chapters 7, 8)
	• Transportation and assignment models (Chapter 9)
	• Integer programming, goal programming, and nonlinear programming (Chapter 10)
	• Network models (Chapter 9)

1.4   The Quantitative Analysis Approach

Defining the problem can be the most important step.

Concentrate on only a few problems.

FIGURE 1.1

The Quantitative Analysis Approach

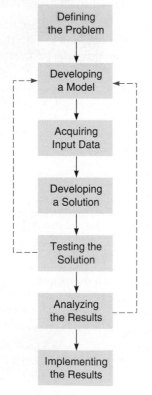

The types of models include physical, scale, schematic, and mathematical models.

The quantitative analysis approach consists of defining a problem, developing a model, acquiring input data, developing a solution, testing the solution, analyzing the results, and implementing the results (see Figure 1.1). One step does not have to be finished completely before the next is started; in most cases, one or more of these steps will be modified to some extent before the final results are implemented. This would cause all of the subsequent steps to be changed. In some cases, testing the solution might reveal that the model or the input data are not correct. This would mean that all steps that follow defining the problem would need to be modified.

Defining the Problem

The first step in the quantitative approach is to develop a clear, concise statement of the **problem**. This statement will give direction and meaning to the following steps.

In many cases, defining the problem is the most important and the most difficult step. It is essential to go beyond the symptoms of the problem and identify the true causes. One problem may be related to other problems; solving one problem without regard to other related problems can make the entire situation worse. Thus, it is important to analyze how the solution to one problem affects other problems or the situation in general.

It is likely that an organization will have several problems. However, a quantitative analysis group usually cannot deal with all of an organization's problems at one time. Thus, it is usually necessary to concentrate on only a few problems. For most companies, this means selecting those problems whose solutions will result in the greatest increase in profits or reduction in costs to the company. The importance of selecting the right problems to solve cannot be overemphasized. Experience has shown that bad problem definition is a major reason for failure of management science or operations research groups to serve their organizations well.

When the problem is difficult to quantify, it may be necessary to develop *specific, measurable* objectives. A problem might be inadequate health care delivery in a hospital. The objectives might be to increase the number of beds, reduce the average number of days a patient spends in the hospital, increase the physician-to-patient ratio, and so on. When objectives are used, however, the real problem should be kept in mind. It is important to avoid obtaining specific and measurable objectives that may not solve the real problem.

Developing a Model

Once we select the problem to be analyzed, the next step is to develop a **model**. Simply stated, a model is a representation (usually mathematical) of a situation.

Even though you might not have been aware of it, you have been using models most of your life. You may have developed models about people's behavior. Your model might be that friendship is based on reciprocity, an exchange of favors. If you need a favor such as a small loan, your model would suggest that you ask a good friend.

Of course, there are many other types of models. Architects sometimes make a *physical model* of a building that they will construct. Engineers develop *scale models* of chemical plants, called pilot plants. A *schematic model* is a picture, drawing, or chart of reality. Automobiles, lawn mowers, gears, fans, typewriters, and numerous other devices have schematic models (drawings and

IN ACTION   Operations Research and Oil Spills

Operations researchers and decision scientists have been investigating oil spill response and alleviation strategies since long before the BP oil spill disaster of 2010 in the Gulf of Mexico. A four-phase classification system has emerged for disaster response research: mitigation, preparedness, response, and recovery. *Mitigation* means reducing the probability that a disaster will occur and implementing robust, forward-thinking strategies to reduce the effects of a disaster that does occur. *Preparedness* is any and all organization efforts that happen *a priori* to a disaster. *Response* is the location, allocation, and overall coordination of resources and procedures during the disaster that are aimed at preserving life and property. *Recovery* is the set of actions taken to minimize the long-term impacts of a particular disaster after the immediate situation has stabilized.

Many quantitative tools have helped in areas of risk analysis, insurance, logistical preparation and supply management, evacuation planning, and development of communication systems. Recent research has shown that while many strides and discoveries have been made, much research is still needed. Certainly each of the four disaster response areas could benefit from additional research, but recovery seems to be of particular concern and perhaps the most promising for future research.

Source: Based on N. Altay and W. Green. "OR/MS Research in Disaster Operations Management," *European Journal of Operational Research* 175, 1 (2006): 475–493.

---

pictures) that reveal how these devices work. What sets quantitative analysis apart from other techniques is that the models that are used are mathematical. A **mathematical model** is a set of mathematical relationships. In most cases, these relationships are expressed in equations and inequalities, as they are in a spreadsheet model that computes sums, averages, or standard deviations.

Although there is considerable flexibility in the development of models, most of the models presented in this book contain one or more variables and parameters. A **variable**, as the name implies, is a measurable quantity that may vary or is subject to change. Variables can be *controllable* or *uncontrollable*. A controllable variable is also called a *decision variable.* An example would be how many inventory items to order. A **parameter** is a measurable quantity that is inherent in the problem. The cost of placing an order for more inventory items is an example of a parameter. In most cases, variables are unknown quantities, while parameters are known quantities. All models should be developed carefully. They should be solvable, realistic, and easy to understand and modify, and the required **input data** should be obtainable. The model developer has to be careful to include the appropriate amount of detail to be solvable yet realistic.

Acquiring Input Data

Garbage in, garbage out means that improper data will result in misleading results.

Once we have developed a model, we must obtain the data that are used in the model (*input data*). Obtaining accurate data for the model is essential; even if the model is a perfect representation of reality, improper data will result in misleading results. This situation is called *garbage in, garbage out.* For a larger problem, collecting accurate data can be one of the most difficult steps in performing quantitative analysis.

There are a number of sources that can be used in collecting data. In some cases, company reports and documents can be used to obtain the necessary data. Another source is interviews with employees or other persons related to the firm. These individuals can sometimes provide excellent information, and their experience and judgment can be invaluable. A production supervisor, for example, might be able to tell you with a great degree of accuracy the amount of time it takes to produce a particular product. Sampling and direct measurement provide other sources of data for the model. You may need to know how many pounds of raw material are used in producing a new photochemical product. This information can be obtained by going to the plant and actually measuring with scales the amount of raw material that is being used. In other cases, statistical sampling procedures can be used to obtain data.

Developing a Solution

Developing a solution involves manipulating the model to arrive at the best (optimal) solution to the problem. In some cases, this requires that an equation be solved for the best decision. In other cases, you can use a *trial and error* method, trying various approaches and picking the one that results in the best decision. For some problems, you may wish to try all possible values for the variables in the model to arrive at the best decision. This is called *complete enumeration.* This book also shows you how to solve very difficult and complex problems by repeating a few simple steps until you find the best solution. A series of steps or procedures that are repeated is called an **algorithm**, named after Algorismus, an Arabic mathematician of the ninth century.

The input data and model determine the accuracy of the solution.

The accuracy of a solution depends on the accuracy of the input data and the model. If the input data are accurate to only two significant digits, then the results can be accurate to only two significant digits. For example, the results of dividing 2.6 by 1.4 should be 1.9, not 1.857142857.

Testing the Solution

Testing the data and model is done before the results are analyzed.

Before a solution can be analyzed and implemented, it needs to be tested completely. Because the solution depends on the input data and the model, both require testing.

Testing the input data and the model includes determining the accuracy and completeness of the data used by the model. Inaccurate data will lead to an inaccurate solution. There are several ways to test input data. One method of testing the data is to collect additional data from a different source. If the original data were collected using interviews, perhaps some additional data can be collected by direct measurement or sampling. These additional data can then be compared with the original data, and statistical tests can be employed to determine whether there are differences between the original data and the additional data. If there are significant differences, more effort is required to obtain accurate input data. If the data are accurate but the results are inconsistent with the problem, the model may not be appropriate. The model can be checked to make sure that it is logical and represents the real situation.

Although most of the quantitative techniques discussed in this book have been computerized, you will probably be required to solve a number of problems by hand. To help detect both logical and computational mistakes, you should check the results to make sure that they are consistent with the structure of the problem. For example, (1.96)(301.7) is close to (2)(300), which is equal to 600. If your computations are significantly different from 600, you know you have made a mistake.

Analyzing the Results and Sensitivity Analysis

Analyzing the results starts with determining the implications of the solution. In most cases, a solution to a problem will result in some kind of action or change in the way an organization is operating. The implications of these actions or changes must be determined and analyzed before the results are implemented.

Sensitivity analysis determines how the solutions will change with a different model or input data.

Because a model is only an approximation of reality, the sensitivity of the solution to changes in the model and input data is a very important part of analyzing the results. This type of analysis is called **sensitivity analysis** or *postoptimality analysis.* It determines how much the solution will change if there were changes in the model or the input data. When the solution is sensitive to changes in the input data and the model specification, additional testing should be performed to make sure that the model and input data are accurate and valid. If the model or data are wrong, the solution could be wrong, resulting in financial losses or reduced profits.

The importance of sensitivity analysis cannot be overemphasized. Because input data may not always be accurate or model assumptions may not be completely appropriate, sensitivity analysis can become an important part of the quantitative analysis approach. Most of the chapters in the book cover the use of sensitivity analysis as part of the decision-making and problem-solving process.

Implementing the Results

The final step is to *implement* the results. This is the process of incorporating the solution into the company. This can be much more difficult than you would imagine. Even if the solution is optimal and will result in millions of dollars in additional profits, if managers resist the new solution, all of the efforts of the analysis are of no value. Experience has shown that a large number of quantitative analysis teams have failed in their efforts because they have failed to implement a good, workable solution properly.

After the solution has been implemented, it should be closely monitored. Over time, there may be numerous changes that call for modifications of the original solution. A changing economy, fluctuating demand, and model enhancements requested by managers and decision makers are only a few examples of changes that might require the analysis to be modified.

MODELING IN THE REAL WORLD   Railroad Uses Optimization Models to Save Millions

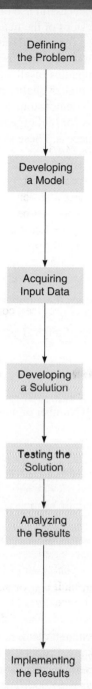

Defining the Problem

CSX Transportation, Inc., has 35,000 employees and annual revenue of $11 billion. It provides rail freight services to 23 states east of the Mississippi River, as well as parts of Canada. CSX receives orders for rail delivery service and must send empty railcars to customer locations. Moving these empty railcars results in hundreds of thousands of empty-car miles every day. If allocations of railcars to customers is not done properly, problems arise from excess costs, wear and tear on the system, and congestion on the tracks and at rail yards.

Developing a Model

In order to provide a more efficient scheduling system, CSX spent 2 years and $5 million developing its Dynamic Car-Planning (DCP) system. This model will minimize costs, including car travel distance, car handling costs at the rail yards, car travel time, and costs for being early or late. It does this while at the same time filling all orders, making sure the right type of car is assigned to the job, and getting the car to the destination in the allowable time.

Acquiring Input Data

In developing the model, the company used historical data for testing. In running the model, the DCP uses three external sources to obtain information on the customer car orders, the available cars of the type needed, and the transit-time standards. In addition to these, two internal input sources provide information on customer priorities and preferences and on cost parameters.

Developing a Solution

This model takes about 1 minute to load but only 10 seconds to solve. Because supply and demand are constantly changing, the model is run about every 15 minutes. This allows final decisions to be delayed until absolutely necessary.

Testing the Solution

The model was validated and verified using existing data. The solutions found using the DCP were found to be very good compared to assignments made without DCP.

Analyzing the Results

Since the implementation of DCP in 1997, more than $51 million has been saved annually. Due to the improved efficiency, it is estimated that CSX avoided spending another $1.4 billion to purchase an additional 18,000 railcars that would have been needed without DCP. Other benefits include reduced congestion in the rail yards and reduced congestion on the tracks, which are major concerns. This greater efficiency means that more freight can ship by rail rather than by truck, resulting in significant public benefits. These benefits include reduced pollution and greenhouse gases, improved highway safety, and reduced road maintenance costs.

Implementing the Results

Both senior-level management who championed DCP and key car-distribution experts who supported the new approach were instrumental in gaining acceptance of the new system and overcoming problems during the implementation. The job description of the car distributors was changed from car allocators to cost technicians. They are responsible for seeing that accurate cost information is entered into DCP, and they also manage any exceptions that must be made. They were given extensive training on how DCP works so they could understand and better accept the new system. Due to the success of DCP, other railroads have implemented similar systems and achieved similar benefits. CSX continues to enhance DCP to make DCP even more customer friendly and to improve car-order forecasts.

Source: Based on M. F. Gorman, et al. "CSX Railway Uses OR to Cash in on Optimized Equipment Distribution," *Interfaces* 40, 1 (January–February 2010): 5–16.

The Quantitative Analysis Approach and Modeling in the Real World

The quantitative analysis approach is used extensively in the real world. These steps, first seen in Figure 1.1 and described in this section, are the building blocks of any successful use of quantitative analysis. As seen in our first *Modeling in the Real World* box, the steps of the quantitative analysis approach can be used to help a large company such as CSX plan for critical scheduling needs now and for decades into the future. Throughout this book, you will see how the steps of the quantitative analysis approach are used to help countries and companies of all sizes save millions of dollars, plan for the future, increase revenues, and provide higher-quality products and services. The *Modeling in the Real World* boxes in every chapter will demonstrate to you the power and importance of quantitative analysis in solving real problems for real organizations. Using the steps of quantitative analysis, however, does not guarantee success. These steps must be applied carefully.

1.5   How to Develop a Quantitative Analysis Model

Developing a model is an important part of the quantitative analysis approach. Let's see how we can use the following mathematical model, which represents profit:

$$\text{Profit} = \text{Revenue} - \text{Expenses}$$

Expenses include fixed and variable costs.

In many cases, we can express revenues as price per unit multiplied times the number of units sold. Expenses can often be determined by summing fixed costs and variable cost. Variable cost is often expressed as variable cost per unit multiplied times the number of units. Thus, we can also express profit in the following mathematical model:

$$\text{Profit} = \text{Revenue} - (\text{Fixed cost} + \text{Variable cost})$$
$$\text{Profit} = (\text{Selling price per unit})(\text{Number of units sold})$$
$$- [\text{Fixed cost} + (\text{Variable cost per unit})(\text{Number of units sold})]$$
$$\text{Profit} = sX - [f + vX]$$
$$\text{Profit} = sX - f - vX \tag{1-1}$$

where

$$s = \text{selling price per unit}$$
$$f = \text{fixed cost}$$
$$v = \text{variable cost per unit}$$
$$X = \text{number of units sold}$$

The parameters in this model are f, v, and s, as these are inputs that are inherent in the model. The number of units sold (X) is the decision variable of interest.

EXAMPLE: PRITCHETT'S PRECIOUS TIME PIECES We will use the Bill Pritchett clock repair shop example to demonstrate the use of mathematical models. Bill's company, Pritchett's Precious Time Pieces, buys, sells, and repairs old clocks and clock parts. Bill sells rebuilt springs for a price per unit of $8. The fixed cost of the equipment to build the springs is $1,000. The variable cost per unit is $3 for spring material. In this example,

$$s = 8$$
$$f = 1,000$$
$$v = 3$$

The number of springs sold is X, and our profit model becomes

$$\text{Profit} = \$8X - \$1,000 - \$3X$$

If sales are 0, Bill will realize a $1,000 loss. If sales are 1,000 units, he will realize a profit of $4,000 ($4,000 = ($8)(1,000) - $1,000 - ($3)(1,000)). See if you can determine the profit for other values of units sold.

The BEP results in $0 profits.

In addition to the profit models shown here, decision makers are often interested in the **break-even point** (BEP). The BEP is the number of units sold that will result in $0 profits. We set profits equal to $0 and solve for X, the number of units at the BEP:

$$0 = sX - f - \nu X$$

This can be written as

$$0 = (s - \nu)X - f$$

Solving for X, we have

$$f = (s - \nu)X$$

$$X = \frac{f}{s - \nu}$$

This quantity (X) that results in a profit of zero is the BEP, and we now have this model for the BEP:

$$BEP = \frac{Fixed\ cost}{(Selling\ price\ per\ unit) - (Variable\ cost\ per\ unit)}$$

$$BEP = \frac{f}{s - \nu} \tag{1-2}$$

For the Pritchett's Precious Time Pieces example, the BEP can be computed as follows:

$$BEP = \$1,000/(\$8 - \$3) = 200 \text{ units, or springs, at the BEP.}$$

The Advantages of Mathematical Modeling

There are a number of advantages of using mathematical models:

1. Models can accurately represent reality. If properly formulated, a model can be extremely accurate. A valid model is one that is accurate and correctly represents the problem or system under investigation. The profit model in the example is accurate and valid for many business problems.

2. Models can help a decision maker formulate problems. In the profit model, for example, a decision maker can determine the important factors or contributors to revenues and expenses, such as sales, returns, selling expenses, production costs, and transportation costs.

3. Models can give us insight and information. For example, using the profit model from the preceding section, we can see what impact changes in revenues and expenses will have on profits. As discussed in the previous section, studying the impact of changes in a model, such as a profit model, is called *sensitivity analysis.*

4. Models can save time and money in decision making and problem solving. It usually takes less time, effort, and expense to analyze a model. We can use a profit model to analyze the impact of a new marketing campaign on profits, revenues, and expenses. In most cases, using models is faster and less expensive than actually trying a new marketing campaign in a real business setting and observing the results.

5. A model may be the only way to solve some large or complex problems in a timely fashion. A large company, for example, may produce literally thousands of sizes of nuts, bolts, and fasteners. The company may want to make the highest profits possible given its manufacturing constraints. A mathematical model may be the only way to determine the highest profits the company can achieve under these circumstances.

6. A model can be used to communicate problems and solutions to others. A decision analyst can share his or her work with other decision analysts. Solutions to a mathematical model can be given to managers and executives to help them make final decisions.

Mathematical Models Categorized by Risk

Deterministic means with complete certainty.

Some mathematical models, like the profit and break-even models previously discussed, do not involve risk or chance. We assume that we know all values used in the model with complete certainty. These are called **deterministic models**. A company, for example, might want to minimize manufacturing costs while maintaining a certain quality level. If we know all these values with certainty, the model is deterministic.

Other models involve risk or chance. For example, the market for a new product might be "good" with a chance of 60% (a probability of 0.6) or "not good" with a chance of 40% (a probability of 0.4). Models that involve chance or risk, often measured as a probability value, are called **probabilistic models**. In this book, we will investigate both deterministic and probabilistic models.

1.6   The Role of Computers and Spreadsheet Models in the Quantitative Analysis Approach

Developing a solution, testing the solution, and analyzing the results are important steps in the quantitative analysis approach. Because we will be using mathematical models, these steps require mathematical calculations. Excel 2013 can be used to help with these calculations, and some spreadsheets developed in Excel will be shown in some chapters. However, some of the techniques presented in this book require sophisticated spreadsheets and are quite tedious to develop. Fortunately, there are two software programs available from the Companion Website for this book that makes this much easier. These are:

1. POM-QM for Windows is an easy-to-use decision support program that was developed POM and quantitative methods (QM) courses. POM for Windows and QM for Windows were originally separate software packages for each type of course. These are now combined into one program called POM-QM for Windows. As seen in Program 1.1, it is possible to display all the modules, only the POM modules, or only the QM modules. The images shown in this textbook will typically display only the QM modules. Hence, in this book, reference will usually be made to QM for Windows. Appendix E at the end of the book provides more information about QM for Windows.

   To use QM for Windows to solve the break-even problem presented earlier, from the Module drop-down menu select Breakeven/Cost-Volume Analysis. Then select New-Breakeven Analysis to enter the problem. When the window opens, enter a name for the problem and select OK. Upon doing this, you will see the screen shown in Program 1.2A. The solution is shown in Program 1.2B. Notice the additional output available from the Window drop-down menu.

PROGRAM 1.1

The QM for Windows Main Menu

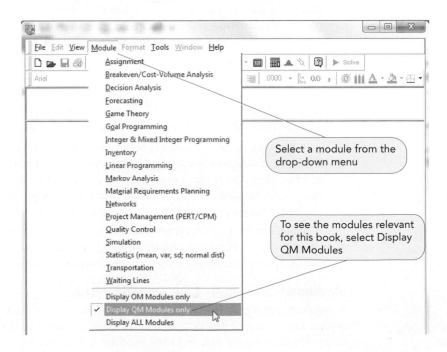

PROGRAM 1.2A

Entering the Data for Pritchett's Precious Time Pieces Example into QM for Windows

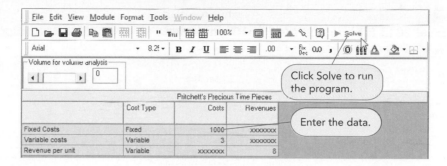

PROGRAM 1.2B

QM for Windows Solution Screen for Pritchett's Precious Time Pieces Example

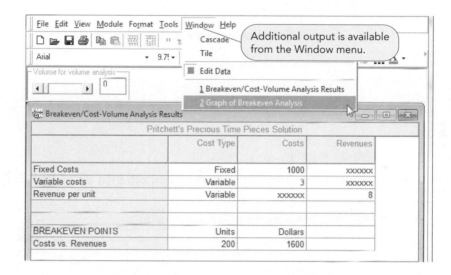

Files for the QM for Windows examples throughout the book can be downloaded from the Companion Website. Opening these files will demonstrate how data are input for the various modules of QM for Windows.

2. Excel QM, an add-in for Excel, can also be used to perform the mathematical calculations for the techniques discussed in each chapter. When installed, in Excel 2013, Excel QM will appear as a tab on the ribbon. From this tab, the appropriate model can be selected from a menu as shown in Program 1.3. Appendix F has more information about this. Excel files with the example problems shown can be downloaded from the Companion Website.

To use Excel QM in Excel 2013 to solve the break-even problem presented earlier, from the Alphabetical Menu (see Program 1.3) select Breakeven Analysis. When this is done, a worksheet is prepared automatically and the user simply inputs the fixed cost, variable cost, and revenue (selling price per unit) as shown in Program 1.4. The solution is calculated when all the inputs have been entered.

Excel 2013 contains some functions, special features, formulas, and tools that help with some of the questions that might be posed in analyzing a business problem. Once such feature, Goal Seek, is shown in Program 1.5 as it is applied to the break-even example. Excel 2013 also has some add-ins that must be activated before using them the first time. These include the Data Analysis add-in and the Solver add-in, which will be discussed in later chapters.

PROGRAM 1.3

Excel QM in Excel 2013 Ribbon and Menu of Techniques

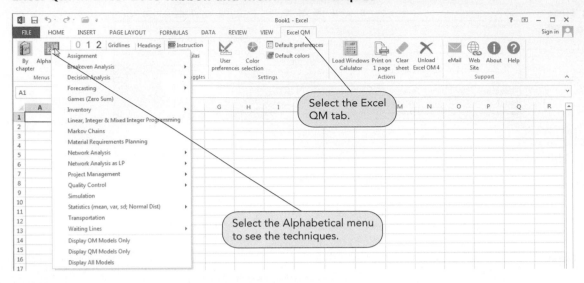

PROGRAM 1.4

Entering the Data for Pritchett's Precious Time Pieces Example into Excel QM in Excel 2013

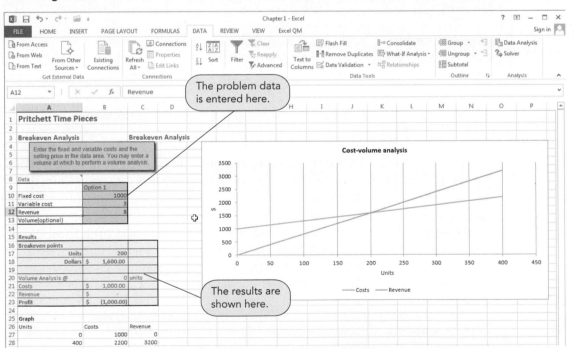

PROGRAM 1.5

Using Goal Seek in the Break-Even Problem to Achieve a Specified Profit

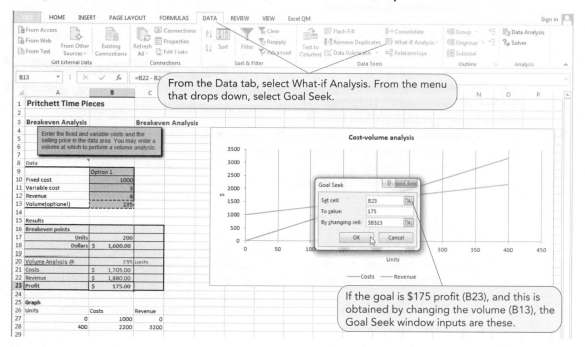

From the Data tab, select What-if Analysis. From the menu that drops down, select Goal Seek.

If the goal is $175 profit (B23), and this is obtained by changing the volume (B13), the Goal Seek window inputs are these.

IN ACTION   Major League Operations Research at the Department of Agriculture

In 1997, the Pittsburgh Pirates signed Ross Ohlendorf because of his 95-mph sinking fastball. Little did they know that Ross possessed operations research skills also worthy of national merit. Ross Ohlendorf had graduated from Princeton University with a 3.8 GPA in operations research and financial engineering.

Indeed, after the 2009 baseball season, when Ross applied for an 8-week unpaid internship with the U.S. Department of Agriculture, he didn't need to mention his full-time employer because the Secretary of the Department of Agriculture at the time, Tom Vilsack, was born and raised in Pittsburgh and was an

avid Pittsburgh Pirates fan. Ross spent 2 months of the ensuing off-season utilizing his educational background in operations research, helping the Department of Agriculture track disease migration in livestock, a subject Ross has a vested interest in as his family runs a cattle ranch in Texas. Moreover, when ABC News asked Ross about his off-season unpaid internship experience, he replied, "This one's been, I'd say, the most exciting off-season I've had."

Source: Rick Klein, "Ross Ohlendorf: From Major League Pitcher to Unpaid Intern," ABCnews.go.com, December 15, 2009.

1.7   Possible Problems in the Quantitative Analysis Approach

We have presented the quantitative analysis approach as a logical, systematic means of tackling decision-making problems. Even when these steps are followed carefully, there are many difficulties that can hurt the chances of implementing solutions to real-world problems. We now take a look at what can happen during each of the steps.

Defining the Problem

One view of decision makers is that they sit at a desk all day long, waiting until a problem arises, and then stand up and attack the problem until it is solved. Once it is solved, they sit down, relax, and wait for the next big problem. In the worlds of business, government, and education, problems are, unfortunately, not easily identified. There are four potential roadblocks that quantitative analysts face in defining a problem. We use an application, inventory analysis, throughout this section as an example.

All viewpoints should be considered before formally defining the problem.

CONFLICTING VIEWPOINTS   The first difficulty is that quantitative analysts must often consider conflicting viewpoints in defining the problem. For example, there are at least two views that managers take when dealing with inventory problems. Financial managers usually feel that inventory is too high, as inventory represents cash not available for other investments. Sales managers, on the other hand, often feel that inventory is too low, as high levels of inventory may be needed to fill an unexpected order. If analysts assume either one of these statements as the problem definition, they have essentially accepted one manager's perception and can expect resistance from the other manager when the "solution" emerges. So it's important to consider both points of view before stating the problem. Good mathematical models should include all pertinent information. As we shall see in Chapter 6, both of these factors are included in inventory models.

IMPACT ON OTHER DEPARTMENTS   The next difficulty is that problems do not exist in isolation and are not owned by just one department of a firm. Inventory is closely tied with cash flows and various production problems. A change in ordering policy can seriously hurt cash flows and upset production schedules to the point that savings on inventory are more than offset by increased costs for finance and production. The problem statement should thus be as broad as possible and include input from all departments that have a stake in the solution. When a solution is found, the benefits to all areas of the organization should be identified and communicated to the people involved.

BEGINNING ASSUMPTIONS   The third difficulty is that people have a tendency to state problems in terms of solutions. The statement that inventory is too low implies a solution that inventory levels should be raised. The quantitative analyst who starts off with this assumption will probably indeed find that inventory should be raised. From an implementation standpoint, a "good" solution to the *right* problem is much better than an "optimal" solution to the *wrong* problem. If a problem has been defined in terms of a desired solution, the quantitative analyst should ask questions about why this solution is desired. By probing further, the true problem will surface and can be defined properly.

An optimal solution to the wrong problem leaves the real problem unsolved.

SOLUTION OUTDATED   Even with the best of problem statements, however, there is a fourth danger. The problem can change as the model is being developed. In our rapidly changing business environment, it is not unusual for problems to appear or disappear virtually overnight. The analyst who presents a solution to a problem that no longer exists can't expect credit for providing timely help. However, one of the benefits of mathematical models is that once the original model has been developed, it can be used over and over again whenever similar problems arise. This allows a solution to be found very easily in a timely manner.

Developing a Model

FITTING THE TEXTBOOK MODELS   One problem in developing quantitative models is that a manager's perception of a problem won't always match the textbook approach. Most inventory models involve minimizing the total of holding and ordering costs. Some managers view these costs as unimportant; instead, they see the problem in terms of cash flow, turnover, and levels of customer satisfaction. Results of a model based on holding and ordering costs are probably not acceptable to such managers. This is why the analyst must completely understand the model and not simply use the computer as a "black box" where data are input and results are given with no understanding of the process. The analyst who understands the process can explain to the manager how the model does consider these other factors when estimating the different types of inventory costs. If other factors are important as well, the analyst can consider these and use sensitivity analysis and good judgment to modify the computer solution before it is implemented.

UNDERSTANDING THE MODEL   A second major concern involves the trade-off between the complexity of the model and ease of understanding. Managers simply will not use the results of a model they do not understand. Complex problems, though, require complex models. One trade-off is to simplify assumptions in order to make the model easier to understand. The model loses some of its reality but gains some acceptance by management.

One simplifying assumption in inventory modeling is that demand is known and constant. This means that probability distributions are not needed and it allows us to build simple, easy-to-understand models. Demand, however, is rarely known and constant, so the model we build lacks some reality. Introducing probability distributions provides more realism but may put comprehension beyond all but the most mathematically sophisticated managers. One approach is for the quantitative analyst to start with the simple model and make sure that it is completely understood. Later, more complex models can be introduced slowly as managers gain more confidence in using the new approach. Explaining the impact of the more sophisticated models (e.g., carrying extra inventory called safety stock) without going into complete mathematical details is sometimes helpful. Managers can understand and identify with this concept, even if the specific mathematics used to find the appropriate quantity of safety stock is not totally understood.

Acquiring Input Data

Gathering the data to be used in the quantitative approach to problem solving is often not a simple task. One-fifth of all firms in a recent study had difficulty with data access.

Obtaining accurate input data can be very difficult.

USING ACCOUNTING DATA   One problem is that most data generated in a firm come from basic accounting reports. The accounting department collects its inventory data, for example, in terms of cash flows and turnover. But quantitative analysts tackling an inventory problem need to collect data on holding costs and ordering costs. If they ask for such data, they may be shocked to find that the data were simply never collected for those specified costs.

Professor Gene Woolsey tells a story of a young quantitative analyst sent down to accounting to get "the inventory holding cost per item per day for part 23456/AZ." The accountant asked the young man if he wanted the first-in, first-out figure, the last-in, first-out figure, the lower of cost or market figure, or the "how-we-do-it" figure. The young man replied that the inventory model required only one number. The accountant at the next desk said, "Hell, Joe, give the kid a number." The kid was given a number and departed.

VALIDITY OF DATA   A lack of "good, clean data" means that whatever data are available must often be distilled and manipulated (we call it "fudging") before being used in a model. Unfortunately, the validity of the results of a model is no better than the validity of the data that go into the model. You cannot blame a manager for resisting a model's "scientific" results when he or she knows that questionable data were used as input. This highlights the importance of the analyst understanding other business functions so that good data can be found and evaluated by the analyst. It also emphasizes the importance of sensitivity analysis, which is used to determine the impact of minor changes in input data. Some solutions are very robust and would not change at all for certain changes in the input data.

Developing a Solution

Hard-to-understand mathematics and one answer can be a problem in developing a solution.

HARD-TO-UNDERSTAND MATHEMATICS   The first concern in developing solutions is that although the mathematical models we use may be complex and powerful, they may not be completely understood. Fancy solutions to problems may have faulty logic or data. The aura of mathematics often causes managers to remain silent when they should be critical. The well-known operations researcher C. W. Churchman cautions that "because mathematics has been so revered a discipline in recent years, it tends to lull the unsuspecting into believing that he who thinks elaborately thinks well."[1]

ONLY ONE ANSWER IS LIMITING   The second problem is that quantitative models usually give just one answer to a problem. Most managers would like to have a *range* of options and not be

---

[1] C. W. Churchman. "Relativity Models in the Social Sciences," *Interfaces* 4, 1 (November 1973).

put in a take-it-or-leave-it position. A more appropriate strategy is for an analyst to present a range of options, indicating the effect that each solution has on the objective function. This gives managers a choice as well as information on how much it will cost to deviate from the optimal solution. It also allows problems to be viewed from a broader perspective, since nonquantitative factors can be considered.

Testing the Solution

The results of quantitative analysis often take the form of predictions of how things will work in the future if certain changes are made now. To get a preview of how well solutions will really work, managers are often asked how good the solution looks to them. The problem is that complex models tend to give solutions that are not intuitively obvious. Such solutions tend to be rejected by managers. The quantitative analyst now has the chance to work through the model and the assumptions with the manager in an effort to convince the manager of the validity of the results. In the process of convincing the manager, the analyst will have to review every assumption that went into the model. If there are errors, they may be revealed during this review. In addition, the manager will be casting a critical eye on everything that went into the model, and if he or she can be convinced that the model is valid, there is a good chance that the solution results are also valid.

Assumptions should be reviewed.

Analyzing the Results

Once a solution has been tested, the results must be analyzed in terms of how they will affect the total organization. You should be aware that even small changes in organizations are often difficult to bring about. If the results indicate large changes in organization policy, the quantitative analyst can expect resistance. In analyzing the results, the analyst should ascertain who must change and by how much, if the people who must change will be better or worse off, and who has the power to direct the change.

IN ACTION   PLATO Helps 2004 Olympic Games in Athens

The 2004 Olympic Games were held in Athens, Greece, over a period of 16 days. More than 2,000 athletes competed in 300 events in 28 sports. The events were held in 36 different venues (stadia, competition centers, etc.), and 3.6 million tickets were sold to people who would view these events. In addition, 2,500 members of international committees and 22,000 journalists and broadcasters attended these games. Home viewers spent more than 34 billion hours watching these sporting events. The 2004 Olympic Games was the biggest sporting event in the history of the world up to that point.

In addition to the sporting venues, other noncompetitive venues, such as the airport and Olympic village, had to be considered. A successful Olympics requires tremendous planning for the transportation system that will handle the millions of spectators. Three years of work and planning were needed for the 16 days of the Olympics.

The Athens Olympic Games Organizing Committee (ATHOC) had to plan, design, and coordinate systems that would be delivered by outside contractors. ATHOC personnel would later be responsible for managing the efforts of volunteers and paid staff during the operations of the games. To make the Athens Olympics run efficiently and effectively, the Process Logistics Advanced Technical Optimization (PLATO) project was begun. Innovative techniques from management science, systems engineering, and information technology were used to change the planning, design, and operations of venues.

The objectives of PLATO were to (1) facilitate effective organizational transformation, (2) help plan and manage resources in a cost-effective manner, and (3) document lessons learned so future Olympic committees could benefit. The PLATO project developed business-process models for the various venues, developed simulation models that enable the generation of what-if scenarios, developed software to aid in the creation and management of these models, and developed process steps for training ATHOC personnel in using these models. Generic solutions were developed so that this knowledge and approach could be made available to other users.

PLATO was credited with reducing the cost of the 2004 Olympics by over $69 million. Perhaps even more important is the fact that the Athens games were universally deemed an unqualified success. The resulting increase in tourism is expected to result in economic benefit to Greece for many years in the future.

Source: Based on D. A. Beis et al. PLATO Helps Athens Win Gold: Olympic Games Knowledge Modeling for Organizational Change and Resource Management," *Interfaces* 36, 1 (January–February 2006): 26–42.

1.8   Implementation—Not Just the Final Step

We have just presented some of the many problems that can affect the ultimate acceptance of the quantitative analysis approach and use of its models. It should be clear now that implementation isn't just another step that takes place after the modeling process is over. Each one of these steps greatly affects the chances of implementing the results of a quantitative study.

Lack of Commitment and Resistance to Change

Even though many business decisions can be made intuitively, based on hunches and experience, there are more and more situations in which quantitative models can assist. Some managers, however, fear that the use of a formal analysis process will reduce their decision-making power. Others fear that it may expose some previous intuitive decisions as inadequate. Still others just feel uncomfortable about having to reverse their thinking patterns with formal decision making. These managers often argue against the use of quantitative methods.

Many action-oriented managers do not like the lengthy formal decision-making process and prefer to get things done quickly. They prefer "quick and dirty" techniques that can yield immediate results. Once managers see some QA results that have a substantial payoff, the stage is set for convincing them that quantitative analysis is a beneficial tool.

Management support and user involvement are important.

We have known for some time that management support and user involvement are critical to the successful implementation of quantitative analysis projects. A Swedish study found that only 40% of projects suggested by quantitative analysts were ever implemented. But 70% of the quantitative projects initiated by users, and fully 98% of projects suggested by top managers, *were* implemented.

Lack of Commitment by Quantitative Analysts

Just as managers' attitudes are to blame for some implementation problems, analysts' attitudes are to blame for others. When the quantitative analyst is not an integral part of the department facing the problem, he or she sometimes tends to treat the modeling activity as an end in itself. That is, the analyst accepts the problem as stated by the manager and builds a model to solve only that problem. When the results are computed, he or she hands them back to the manager and considers the job done. The analyst who does not care whether these results help make the final decision is not concerned with implementation.

Successful implementation requires that the analyst not *tell* the users what to do, but work with them and take their feelings into account. An article in *Operations Research* describes an inventory control system that calculated reorder points and order quantities. But instead of insisting that computer-calculated quantities be ordered, a manual override feature was installed. This allowed users to disregard the calculated figures and substitute their own. The override was used quite often when the system was first installed. Gradually, however, as users came to realize that the calculated figures were right more often than not, they allowed the system's figures to stand. Eventually, the override feature was used only in special circumstances. This is a good example of how good relationships can aid in model implementation.

Summary

Quantitative analysis is a scientific approach to decision making. The quantitative analysis approach includes defining a problem, developing a model, acquiring input data, developing a solution, testing the solution, analyzing the results, and implementing the results. In using the quantitative approach, however, there can be potential problems, including conflicting viewpoints, the impact of quantitative analysis models on other departments, beginning assumptions, outdated solutions, fitting textbook models, understanding the model, acquiring good input data, hard-to-understand mathematics, obtaining only one answer, testing the solution, and analyzing the results. In using the quantitative analysis approach, implementation is not the final step. There can be a lack of commitment to the approach and resistance to change.

Glossary

Algorithm   A set of logical and mathematical operations performed in a specific sequence.

Break-Even Point   The quantity of sales that results in zero profit.

Business Analytics   A data-driven approach to decision making that allows companies to make better decisions.

Descriptive Analytics   The study and consolidation of historical data to describe how a company has performed in the past is performing now.

Deterministic Model   A model in which all values used in the model are known with complete certainty.

Input Data   Data that are used in a model in arriving at the final solution.

Mathematical Model   A model that uses mathematical equations and statements to represent the relationships within the model.

Model   A representation of reality or of a real-life situation.

Parameter   A measurable input quantity that is inherent in a problem.

Predictive Analytics   The use of techniques to forecast how things will be in the future based on patterns of past data.

Prescriptive Analytics   The use of optimization methods to provide new and better ways to operate based on specific business objectives.

Probabilistic Model   A model in which all values used in the model are not known with certainty but rather involve some chance or risk, often measured as a probability value.

Problem   A statement, which should come from a manager, that indicates a problem to be solved or an objective or a goal to be reached.

Quantitative Analysis or Management Science   A scientific approach that uses quantitative techniques as a tool in decision making.

Sensitivity Analysis   A process that involves determining how sensitive a solution is to changes in the formulation of a problem.

Variable   A measurable quantity that is subject to change.

Key Equations

(1-1) $\text{Profit} = sX - f - vX$

where

s = selling price per unit

f = fixed cost

v = variable cost per unit

X = number of units sold

An equation to determine profit as a function of the selling price per unit, fixed costs, variable costs, and number of units sold.

(1-2) $\text{BEP} = \dfrac{f}{s - v}$

An equation to determine the break-even point (BEP) in units as a function of the selling price per unit (s), fixed costs (f), and variable costs (v).

Self-Test

- Before taking the self-test, refer to the learning objectives at the beginning of the chapter, the notes in the margins, and the glossary at the end of the chapter.
- Use the key at the back of the book to correct your answers.
- Restudy pages that correspond to any questions that you answered incorrectly or material you feel uncertain about.

1. In analyzing a problem, you should normally study
   a. the qualitative aspects.
   b. the quantitative aspects.
   c. both a and b.
   d. neither a nor b.
2. Quantitative analysis is
   a. a logical approach to decision making.
   b. a rational approach to decision making.
   c. a scientific approach to decision making.
   d. all of the above.
3. Frederick Winslow Taylor
   a. was a military researcher during World War II.
   b. pioneered the principles of scientific management.
   c. developed the use of the algorithm for QA.
   d. all of the above.
4. An input (such as variable cost per unit or fixed cost) for a model is an example of
   a. a decision variable.
   b. a parameter.
   c. an algorithm.
   d. a stochastic variable.

5. The point at which the total revenue equals total cost (meaning zero profit) is called the
   a. zero-profit solution.
   b. optimal-profit solution.
   c. break-even point.
   d. fixed-cost solution.
6. Quantitative analysis is typically associated with the use of
   a. schematic models.
   b. physical models.
   c. mathematical models.
   d. scale models.
7. Sensitivity analysis is most often associated with which step of the quantitative analysis approach?
   a. defining a problem
   b. acquiring input data
   c. implementing the results
   d. analyzing the results
8. A deterministic model is one in which
   a. there is some uncertainty about the parameters used in the model.
   b. there is a measurable outcome.
   c. all parameters used in the model are known with complete certainty.
   d. there is no available computer software.
9. The term *algorithm*
   a. is named after Algorismus.
   b. is named after a ninth-century Arabic mathematician.
   c. describes a series of steps or procedures to be repeated.
   d. all of the above.
10. An analysis to determine how much a solution would change if there were changes in the model or the input data is called
    a. sensitivity or postoptimality analysis.
    b. schematic or iconic analysis.
    c. futurama conditioning.
    d. both b and c.
11. Decision variables are
    a. controllable.
    b. uncontrollable.
    c. parameters.
    d. constant numerical values associated with any complex problem.
12. Which of the following categories of business analytics involves the use of optimization models?
    a. descriptive
    b. predictive
    c. prescriptive
    d. none of the above

Discussion Questions and Problems

Discussion Questions

1-1 What is the difference between quantitative and qualitative analysis? Give several examples.

1-2 Define *quantitative analysis*. What are some of the organizations that support the use of the scientific approach?

1-3 What are the three categories of business analytics?

1-4 What is the quantitative analysis process? Give several examples of this process.

1-5 Briefly trace the history of quantitative analysis. What happened to the development of quantitative analysis during World War II?

1-6 Give some examples of various types of models. What is a mathematical model? Develop two examples of mathematical models.

1-7 List some sources of input data.

1-8 What is implementation, and why is it important?

1-9 Describe the use of sensitivity analysis and postoptimality analysis in analyzing the results.

1-10 Managers are quick to claim that quantitative analysts talk to them in a jargon that does not sound like English. List four terms that might not be understood by a manager. Then explain in nontechnical terms what each term means.

1-11 Why do you think many quantitative analysts don't like to participate in the implementation process? What could be done to change this attitude?

1-12 Should people who will be using the results of a new quantitative model become involved in the technical aspects of the problem solving procedure?

1-13 C. W. Churchman once said that "mathematics … tends to lull the unsuspecting into believing that he who thinks elaborately thinks well." Do you think that the best QA models are the ones that are most elaborate and complex mathematically? Why?

1-14 What is the break-even point? What parameters are necessary to find it?

Problems

1-15 Gina Fox has started her own company, Foxy Shirts, which manufactures imprinted shirts for special occasions. Since she has just begun this operation, she rents the equipment from a local printing shop when necessary. The cost of using the equipment is $350. The materials used in one shirt cost $8, and Gina can sell these for $15 each.

(a) If Gina sells 20 shirts, what will her total revenue be? What will her total variable cost be?

(b) How many shirts must Gina sell to break even? What is the total revenue for this?

1-16 Ray Bond sells handcrafted yard decorations at county fairs. The variable cost to make these is $20 each, and he sells them for $50. The cost to rent a booth at the fair is $150. How many of these must Ray sell to break even?

1-17 Ray Bond, from Problem 1-16, is trying to find a new supplier that will reduce his variable cost of production to $15 per unit. If he was able to succeed in reducing this cost, what would the break-even point be?

1-18 Katherine D'Ann is planning to finance her college education by selling programs at the football games for State University. There is a fixed cost of $400 for printing these programs, and the variable cost is $3. There is also a $1,000 fee that is paid to the university for the right to sell these programs. If Katherine was able to sell programs for $5 each, how many would she have to sell in order to break even?

1-19 Katherine D'Ann, from Problem 1-18, has become concerned that sales may fall, as the team is on a terrible losing streak, and attendance has fallen off. In fact, Katherine believes that she will sell only 500 programs for the next game. If it was possible to raise the selling price of the program and still sell 500, what would the price have to be for Katherine to break even by selling 500?

1-20 Farris Billiard Supply sells all types of billiard equipment, and is considering manufacturing their own brand of pool cues. Mysti Farris, the production manager, is currently investigating the production of a standard house pool cue that should be very popular. Upon analyzing the costs, Mysti determines that the materials and labor cost for each cue is $25, and the fixed cost that must be covered is $2,400 per week. With a selling price of $40 each, how many pool cues must be sold to break even? What would the total revenue be at this break-even point?

1-21 Mysti Farris (see Problem 1-20) is considering raising the selling price of each cue to $50 instead of $40. If this is done while the costs remain the same, what would the new break-even point be? What would the total revenue be at this break-even point?

1-22 Mysti Farris (see Problem 1-20) believes that there is a high probability that 120 pool cues can be sold if the selling price is appropriately set. What selling price would cause the break-even point to be 120?

1-23 Golden Age Retirement Planners specializes in providing financial advice for people planning for a comfortable retirement. The company offers seminars on the important topic of retirement planning. For a typical seminar, the room rental at a hotel is $1,000, and the cost of advertising and other incidentals is about $10,000 per seminar. The cost of the materials and special gifts for each attendee is $60 per person attending the seminar. The company charges $250 per person to attend the seminar as this seems to be competitive with other companies in the same business. How many people must attend each seminar for Golden Age to break even?

1-24 A couple of entrepreneurial business students at State University decided to put their education into practice by developing a tutoring company for business students. While private tutoring was offered, it was determined that group tutoring before tests in the large statistics classes would be most beneficial. The students rented a room close to campus for $300 for 3 hours. They developed handouts based on past tests, and these handouts (including color graphs) cost $5 each. The tutor was paid $25 per hour, for a total of $75 for each tutoring session.

   (a) If students are charged $20 to attend the session, how many students must enroll for the company to break even?
   (b) A somewhat smaller room is available for $200 for 3 hours. The company is considering this possibility. How would this affect the break-even point?

1-25 Zoe Garcia is the manager of a small office support business that supplies copying, binding, and other services for local companies. Zoe must replace a worn-out copy machine that is used for black and white copying. Two machines are being considered, and each of these has a monthly lease cost plus a cost for each page that is copied. Machine 1 has a monthly lease cost of $600, and there is a cost of $0.010 per page copied. Machine 2 has a monthly lease cost of $400, and there is a cost of $0.015 per page copied. Customers are charged $0.05 per page for copies.

   (a) What is the break-even point for each machine?
   (b) If Zoe expects to make 10,000 copies per month, what would be the cost for each machine?
   (c) If Zoe expects to make 30,000 copies per month, what would be the cost for each machine?
   (d) At what volume (the number of copies) would the two machines have the same monthly cost? What would the total revenue for this number of copies?

Case Study

Food and Beverages at Southwestern University Football Games

Southwestern University (SWU), a large state college in Stephenville, Texas, 30 miles southwest of the Dallas/Fort Worth metroplex, enrolls close to 20,000 students. The school is the dominant force in the small city, with more students during fall and spring than permanent residents.

A longtime football powerhouse, SWU is a member of the Big Eleven conference and is usually in the top 20 in college football rankings. To bolster its chances of reaching the elusive and long-desired number-one ranking, in 2013 SWU hired the legendary Billy Bob Dillon as its head coach. Although the number-one ranking remained out of reach, attendance at the five Saturday home games each year increased. Prior to Dillon's arrival, attendance generally averaged 25,000–29,000. Season ticket sales bumped up by 10,000 just with the announcement of the new coach's arrival. Stephenville and SWU were ready to move to the big time!

With the growth in attendance came more fame, the need for a bigger stadium, and more complaints about seating, parking, long lines, and concession stand prices. Southwestern University's president, Dr. Marty Starr, was concerned not only about the cost of expanding the existing stadium versus building a new stadium but also about the ancillary activities. He wanted to be sure that these various support activities generated revenue adequate to pay for themselves. Consequently, he wanted the parking lots, game programs, and food service to all be handled as profit centers. At a recent meeting discussing the new stadium, Starr told the stadium manager, Hank Maddux, to develop a break-even chart and related data for each of the centers. He instructed Maddux to have the food service area break-even report ready for the next meeting. After discussion with other facility managers and his subordinates, Maddux developed the following table showing the suggested selling prices, and his estimate of variable costs, and the percent revenue by item. It also provides an estimate of the percentage of the total revenues that would be expected for each of the items based on historical sales data.

Maddux's fixed costs are interesting. He estimated that the prorated portion of the stadium cost would be as follows: salaries for food services at $100,000 ($20,000 for each of the five home games); 2,400 square feet of stadium space at $2 per

ITEM	SELLING PRICE/UNIT	VARIABLE COST/UNIT	PERCENT REVENUE
Soft drink	$1.50	$0.75	25%
Coffee	2.00	0.50	25
Hot dogs	2.00	0.80	20
Hamburgers	2.50	1.00	20
Misc. snacks	1.00	0.40	10

square foot per game; and six people per booth in each of the six booths for 5 hours at $7 an hour. These fixed costs will be proportionately allocated to each of the products based on the percentages provided in the table. For example, the revenue from soft drinks would be expected to cover 25% of the total fixed costs.

Maddux wants to be sure that he has a number of things for President Starr: (1) the total fixed cost that must be covered at each of the games; (2) the portion of the fixed cost allocated to each of the items; (3) what his unit sales would be at break-even for each item—that is, what sales of soft drinks, coffee, hot dogs, and hamburgers are necessary to cover the portion of the fixed cost allocated to each of these items; (4) what the dollar sales for each of these would be at these break-even points; and (5) realistic sales estimates per attendee for attendance of 60,000 and 35,000. (In other words, he wants to know how many dollars each attendee is spending on food at his projected break-even sales at present and if attendance grows to 60,000.) He felt this last piece of information would be helpful to understand how realistic the assumptions of his model are, and this information could be compared with similar figures from previous seasons.

Discussion Question

1. Prepare a brief report with the items noted so it is ready for Dr. Starr at the next meeting.

Adapted from J. Heizer and B. Render. *Operations Management*, 6th ed. Upper Saddle River, NJ: Prentice Hall, 2000, pp. 274–275.

Bibliography

Ackoff, R. L. *Scientific Method: Optimizing Applied Research Decisions*. New York: John Wiley & Sons, Inc., 1962.

Beam, Carrie. "ASP, the Art and Science of Practice: How I Started an OR/MS Consulting Practice with a Laptop, a Phone, and a PhD," *Interfaces* 34 (July–August 2004): 265–271.

Board, John, Charles Sutcliffe, and William T. Ziemba. "Applying Operations Research Techniques to Financial Markets," *Interfaces* 33 (March–April 2003): 12–24.

Churchman, C. W. "Relativity Models in the Social Sciences," *Interfaces* 4, 1 (November 1973).

Churchman, C. W. *The Systems Approach*. New York: Delacort Press, 1968.

Dekker, Rommert, Jacqueline Bloemhof, and Ioannis Mallidis . "Operations Research for Green Logistics—An Overview of Aspects, Issues, Contributions and Challenges," *European Journal of Operational Research* 219, 3 (June 2012): 671–679.

Dutta, Goutam. "Lessons for Success in OR/MS Practice Gained from Experiences in Indian and U.S. Steel Plants," *Interfaces* 30, 5 (September October 2000): 23–30.

Eom, Sean B., and Eyong B. Kim. "A Survey of Decision Support System Applications (1995–2001)," *Journal of the Operational Research Society* 57, 11 (2006): 1264–1278.

Evans, James. R. "Business Analytics: The Next Frontier for Decision Sciences," *Decision Line* 43, 2 (March 2012).

Horowitz, Ira. "Aggregating Expert Ratings Using Preference-Neutral Weights: The Case of the College Football Polls," *Interfaces* 34 (July–August 2004): 314–320.

Keskinocak, Pinar, and Sridhar Tayur. "Quantitative Analysis for Internet-Enabled Supply Chains," *Interfaces* 31, 2 (March–April 2001): 70–89.

Laval, Claude, Marc Feyhl, and Steve Kakouros. "Hewlett-Packard Combined OR and Expert Knowledge to Design Its Supply Chains," *Interfaces* 35 (May–June 2005): 238–247.

Pidd, Michael. "Just Modeling Through: A Rough Guide to Modeling," *Interfaces* 29, 2 (March–April 1999): 118–132.

Saaty, T. L. "Reflections and Projections on Creativity in Operations Research and Management Science: A Pressing Need for a Shifting Paradigm," *Operations Research* 46, 1 (1998): 9–16.

Salveson, Melvin. "The Institute of Management Science: A Prehistory and Commentary," *Interfaces* 27, 3 (May–June 1997): 74–85.

Wright, P. Daniel, Matthew J. Liberatore, and Robert L. Nydick. "A Survey of Operations Research Models and Applications in Homeland Security," *Interfaces* 36 (November–December 2006): 514–529.

CHAPTER 2

Probability Concepts and Applications

LEARNING OBJECTIVES

After completing this chapter, students will be able to:

1. Understand the basic foundations of probability analysis.
2. Describe statistically dependent and independent events.
3. Use Bayes' theorem to establish posterior probabilities.
4. Describe and provide examples of both discrete and continuous random variables.
5. Explain the difference between discrete and continuous probability distributions.
6. Calculate expected values and variances and use the normal table.

CHAPTER OUTLINE

Summary • Glossary • Key Equations • Solved Problems • Self-Test • Discussion Questions and Problems • Internet Homework Problems • Case Study: WTVX • Bibliography

Appendix 2.1: Derivation of Bayes' Theorem

2.1 Introduction

Life would be simpler if we knew without doubt what was going to happen in the future. The outcome of any decision would depend only on how logical and rational the decision was. If you lost money in the stock market, it would be because you failed to consider all the information or to make a logical decision. If you got caught in the rain, it would be because you simply forgot your umbrella. You could always avoid building a plant that was too large, investing in a company that would lose money, running out of supplies, or losing crops because of bad weather. There would be no such thing as a risky investment. Life would be simpler, but boring.

It wasn't until the sixteenth century that people started to quantify risks and to apply this concept to everyday situations. Today, the idea of risk or probability is a part of our lives. "There is a 40% chance of rain in Omaha today." "The Florida State University Seminoles are favored 2 to 1 over the Louisiana State University Tigers this Saturday." "There is a 50–50 chance that the stock market will reach an all-time high next month."

A probability is a numerical statement about the chance that an event will occur.

A **probability** *is a numerical statement about the likelihood that an event will occur.* In this chapter, we examine the basic concepts, terms, and relationships of probability and probability distributions that are useful in solving many quantitative analysis problems. Table 2.1 lists some of the topics covered in this book that rely on probability theory. You can see that the study of quantitative analysis and business analytics would be quite difficult without it.

2.2 Fundamental Concepts

There are several rules, definitions, and concepts associated with probability that are very important in understanding the use of probability in decision making. These will be briefly presented with some examples to help clarify them.

Two Basic Rules of Probability

There are two basic rules regarding the mathematics of probability:

People often misuse the two basic rules of probabilities when they use statements such as, "I'm 110% sure we're going to win the big game."

1. The probability, *P*, of any event or state of nature occurring is greater than or equal to 0 and less than or equal to 1. That is,

$$0 \leq P(\text{event}) \leq 1 \qquad (2\text{-}1)$$

   A probability of 0 indicates that an event is never expected to occur. A probability of 1 means that an event is always expected to occur.
2. The sum of the simple probabilities for all possible outcomes of an activity must equal 1. Regardless of how probabilities are determined, they must adhere to these two rules.

TABLE 2.1

Chapters in This Book That Use Probability

CHAPTER	TITLE
3	Decision Analysis
4	Regression Models
5	Forecasting
6	Inventory Control Models
11	Project Management
12	Waiting Lines and Queuing Theory Models
13	Simulation Modeling
14	Markov Analysis
15	Statistical Quality Control
Module 3	Decision Theory and the Normal Distribution
Module 4	Game Theory

TABLE 2.2

Relative Frequency Approach to Probability for Paint Sales

QUANTITY DEMANDED (GALLONS)	NUMBER OF DAYS	PROBABILITY
0	40	0.20 (= 40/200)
1	80	0.40 (= 80/200)
2	50	0.25 (= 50/200)
3	20	0.10 (= 20/200)
4	10	0.05 (= 10/200)
	Total 200	1.00 (= 200/200)

Types of Probability

There are two different ways to determine probability: the **objective approach** and the **subjective approach**.

The **relative frequency approach** is an objective probability assessment. The probability assigned to an event is the relative frequency of that occurrence. In general,

$$P(\text{event}) = \frac{\text{Number of occurrences of the event}}{\text{Total number of trials or outcomes}}$$

Here is an example. Demand for white latex paint at Diversey Paint and Supply has always been 0, 1, 2, 3, or 4 gallons per day. (There are no other possible outcomes and when one occurs, no other can.) Over the past 200 working days, the owner notes the frequencies of demand as shown in Table 2.2. If this past distribution is a good indicator of future sales, we can find the probability of each possible outcome occurring in the future by converting the data into percentages.

Thus, the probability that sales are 2 gallons of paint on any given day is $P(2 \text{ gallons}) = 0.25 = 25\%$. The probability of any level of sales must be greater than or equal to 0 and less than or equal to 1. Since 0, 1, 2, 3, and 4 gallons exhaust all possible events or outcomes, the sum of their probability values must equal 1.

Objective probability can also be set using what is called the **classical** or **logical method**. Without performing a series of trials, we can often logically determine what the probabilities of various events should be. For example, the probability of tossing a fair coin once and getting a head is

$$P(\text{head}) = \frac{1}{2} \begin{matrix} \leftarrow \textit{Number of ways of getting a head} \\ \leftarrow \textit{Number of possible outcomes (head or tail)} \end{matrix}$$

Similarly, the probability of drawing a spade out of a deck of 52 playing cards can be logically set as

$$P(\text{spade}) = \frac{13}{52} \begin{matrix} \leftarrow \textit{Number of chances of drawing a spade} \\ \leftarrow \textit{Number of possible outcomes} \end{matrix}$$
$$= {}^1\!/_4 = 0.25 = 25\%$$

When logic and past history are not available or appropriate, probability values can be assessed *subjectively*. The accuracy of subjective probabilities depends on the experience and judgment of the person making the estimates. A number of probability values cannot be determined unless the subjective approach is used. What is the probability that the price of gasoline will be more than $4 in the next few years? What is the probability that our economy will be in a severe depression in 2020? What is the probability that you will be president of a major corporation within 20 years?

There are several methods for making subjective probability assessments. Opinion polls can be used to help in determining subjective probabilities for possible election returns and potential political candidates. In some cases, experience and judgment must be used in making subjective assessments of probability values. A production manager, for example, might believe that the probability of manufacturing a new product without a single defect is 0.85. In the Delphi method, a panel of experts is assembled to make their predictions of the future. This approach is discussed in Chapter 5.

Where do probabilities come from? Sometimes they are subjective and based on personal experiences. Other times they are objectively based on logical observations such as the roll of a die. Often, probabilities are derived from historical data.

Mutually Exclusive and Collectively Exhaustive Events

Events are said to be **mutually exclusive** if only one of the events can occur on any one trial. They are called **collectively exhaustive** if the list of outcomes includes every possible outcome. Many common experiences involve events that have both of these properties.

In tossing a coin, the possible outcomes are a head or a tail. Since both of them cannot occur on any one toss, the outcomes head and tail are mutually exclusive. Since obtaining a head and obtaining a tail represent every possible outcome, they are also collectively exhaustive.

Figure 2.1 provides a Venn diagram representation of mutually exclusive events. Let A be the event that a head is tossed, and let B be the event that a tail is tossed. The circles representing these events do not overlap, so the events are mutually exclusive.

The following situation provides an example of events that are not mutually exclusive. You are asked to draw one card from a standard deck of 52 playing cards. The following events are defined:

$$A = \text{event that a 7 is drawn}$$
$$B = \text{event that a heart is drawn}$$

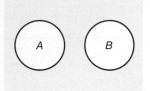

FIGURE 2.1

Venn Diagram for Events That Are Mutually Exclusive

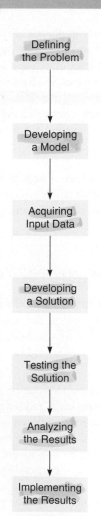

MODELING IN THE REAL WORLD — Liver Transplants in the United States

Defining the Problem → Developing a Model → Acquiring Input Data → Developing a Solution → Testing the Solution → Analyzing the Results → Implementing the Results

Defining the Problem

The scarcity of liver organs for transplants has reached critical levels in the United States; 1,131 individuals died in 1997 while waiting for a transplant. With only 4,000 liver donations per year, there are 10,000 patients on the waiting list, with 8,000 being added each year. There is a need to develop a model to evaluate policies for allocating livers to terminally ill patients who need them.

Developing a Model

Doctors, engineers, researchers, and scientists worked together with Pritsker Corp. consultants in the process of creating the liver allocation model, called ULAM. One of the model's jobs would be to evaluate whether to list potential recipients on a national basis or regionally.

Acquiring Input Data

Historical information was available from the United Network for Organ Sharing (UNOS), from 1990 to 1995. The data were then stored in ULAM. "Poisson" probability processes described the arrivals of donors at 63 organ procurement centers and arrival of patients at 106 liver transplant centers.

Developing a Solution

ULAM provides probabilities of accepting an offered liver, where the probability is a function of the patient's medical status, the transplant center, and the quality of the offered liver. ULAM also models the daily probability of a patient changing from one status of criticality to another.

Testing the Solution

Testing involved a comparison of the model output to actual results over the 1992–1994 time period. Model results were close enough to actual results that ULAM was declared valid.

Analyzing the Results

ULAM was used to compare more than 100 liver allocation policies and was then updated in 1998, with more recent data, for presentation to Congress.

Implementing the Results

Based on the projected results, the UNOS committee voted 18–0 to implement an allocation policy based on regional, not national, waiting lists. This decision is expected to save 2,414 lives over an 8-year period.

Source: Based on A. A. B. Pritsker. "Life and Death Decisions," *OR/MS Today* (August 1998): 22–28.

FIGURE 2.2

Venn Diagram for Events That Are Not Mutually Exclusive

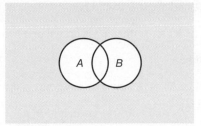

The probabilities can be assigned to these using the relative frequency approach. There are four 7s in the deck and thirteen hearts in the deck. Thus, we have

$$P(\text{a 7 is drawn}) = P(A) = {}^{4}/_{52}$$
$$P(\text{a heart is drawn}) = P(B) = {}^{13}/_{52}$$

These events are not mutually exclusive as the 7 of hearts is common to both event A and event B. Figure 2.2 provides a Venn diagram representing this situation. Notice that the two circles intersect, and this intersection is whatever is in common to both. In this example, the intersection would be the 7 of hearts.

Unions and Intersections of Events

The **intersection** of two events is the set of all outcomes that are common to both events. The word *and* is commonly associated with the intersection, as is the symbol ∩. There are several notations for the intersection of two events:

$$\text{Intersection of event } A \text{ and event } B = A \text{ and } B$$
$$= A \cap B$$
$$= AB$$

The notation for the probability would be

$$P(\text{Intersection of event } A \text{ and event } B) = P(A \text{ and } B)$$
$$= P(A \cap B)$$
$$= P(AB)$$

The probability of the intersection is sometimes called a **joint probability**, which implies that both events are occurring at the same time or jointly.

The **union** of two events is the set of all outcomes that are contained in either of these two events. Thus, any outcome that is in event A is in the union of the two events, and any outcome that is in event B is also in the union of the two events. The word *or* is commonly associated with the union, as is the symbol ∪. Typical notation for the union of two events would be

$$\text{Union of event } A \text{ and event } B = (A \text{ or } B)$$

The notation for the probability of the union of events would be

$$P(\text{Union of event } A \text{ and event } B) = P(A \text{ or } B)$$
$$= P(A \cup B)$$

In the previous example, the intersection of event A and event B would be

$$(A \text{ and } B) = \text{the 7 of hearts is drawn}$$

The notation for the probability would be

$$P(A \text{ and } B) = P(7 \text{ of hearts is drawn}) = {}^{1}/_{52}$$

Also, the union of event A and event B would be

$$(A \text{ or } B) = (\text{either a 7 is drawn or a heart is drawn})$$

and the probability would be

$$P(A \text{ or } B) = P(\text{any 7 or any heart is drawn}) = {}^{16}/_{52}$$

To see why $P(A \text{ or } B) = {}^{16}/_{52}$ and not ${}^{17}/_{52}$ (which is $P(A) + P(B)$), count all of the cards that are in the union, and you will see there are 16. This will help you understand the general rule for the probability of the union of two events that is presented next.

Probability Rules for Unions, Intersections, and Conditional Probabilities

The general rule for the probability of the union of two events (sometimes called the additive rule) is the following:

$$P(A \text{ or } B) = P(A) + P(B) - P(A \text{ and } B) \tag{2-2}$$

To illustrate this with the example we have been using, to find the probability of the union of the two events (a 7 or a heart is drawn), we have

$$\begin{aligned} P(A \text{ or } B) &= P(A) + P(B) - P(A \text{ and } B) \\ &= {}^{4}/_{52} + {}^{13}/_{52} - {}^{1}/_{52} \\ &= {}^{16}/_{52} \end{aligned}$$

One of the most important probability concepts in decision making is the concept of a conditional probability. A **conditional probability** is the probability of an event occurring given that another event has already happened. The probability of event A given that event B has occurred is written as $P(A|B)$. When businesses make decisions, they often use market research of some type to help determine the likelihood of success. Given a good result from the market research, the probability of success would increase.

The probability that A will occur given that event B has occurred can be found by dividing the probability of the intersection of the two events (A and B) by the probability of the event that has occurred (B):

$$P(A|B) = \frac{P(AB)}{P(B)} \tag{2-3}$$

From this, the formula for the intersection of two events can be easily derived and written as

$$P(AB) = P(A|B)P(B) \tag{2-4}$$

In the card example, what is the probability that a 7 is drawn (event A) given that we know that the card drawn is a heart (event B)? With what we already know, and given the formula for conditional probability, we have

$$P(A|B) = \frac{P(AB)}{P(B)} = \frac{{}^{1}/_{52}}{{}^{13}/_{52}} = {}^{1}/_{13}$$

With this card example, it might be possible to determine this probability without using the formula. Given that a heart was drawn and there are 13 hearts with only one of these being a 7, we can determine that the probability is $^{1}/_{13}$. In business, however, we sometimes do not have this complete information and the formula is absolutely essential.

Two events are said to be **independent** if the occurrence of one has no impact on the occurrence of the other. Otherwise, the events are dependent.

For example, suppose a card is drawn from a deck of cards and it is then returned to the deck and a second drawing occurs. The probability of drawing a seven on the second draw is $^{4}/_{52}$ regardless of what was drawn on the first draw because the deck is exactly the same as it was on the first draw. Now contrast to a similar situation with two draws from a deck of cards, but the first card is not returned to the deck. Now there are only 51 cards left in the deck, and there are either three or four 7s in the deck depending on what the first card drawn happens to be.

A more precise definition of statistical independence would be the following: Event A and event B are independent if

$$P(A|B) = P(A)$$

Independence is a very important condition in probability as many calculations are simplified. One of these is the formula for the intersection of two events. If A and B are independent, then the probability of the intersection is

$$P(A \text{ and } B) = P(A)P(B)$$

Suppose a fair coin is tossed twice. The events are defined as:

A = event that a head is the result of the first toss

B = event that a head is the result of the second toss

These events are independent because the probability of a head on the second toss will be the same regardless of the result on the first toss. Because it is a fair coin, we know there are two equally likely outcomes on each toss (head or tail), so

$$P(A) = 0.5$$

and

$$P(B) = 0.5$$

Because A and B are independent,

$$P(AB) = P(A)P(B) = 0.5(0.5) = 0.25$$

Thus, there is a 0.25 probability that two tosses of a coin will result in two heads.

If events are not independent, then finding probabilities may be a bit more difficult. However, the results may be very valuable to a decision maker. A market research study about opening a new store in a particular location may have a positive outcome, and this would cause a revision of our probability assessment that the new store would be successful. The next section provides a means of revising probabilities based on new information.

2.3 Revising Probabilities with Bayes' Theorem

Bayes' theorem is used to incorporate additional information as it is made available and help create revised or *posterior probabilities* from the original or *prior probabilities*. This means that we can take new or recent data and then revise and improve upon our old probability estimates for an event (see Figure 2.3). Let us consider the following example.

A cup contains two dice identical in appearance. One, however, is fair (unbiased) and the other is loaded (biased). The probability of rolling a 3 on the fair die is $\frac{1}{6}$, or 0.166. The probability of tossing the same number on the loaded die is 0.60.

We have no idea which die is which, but select one by chance and toss it. The result is a 3. Given this additional piece of information, can we find the (revised) probability that the die rolled was fair? Can we determine the probability that it was the loaded die that was rolled?

FIGURE 2.3
Using Bayes' Process

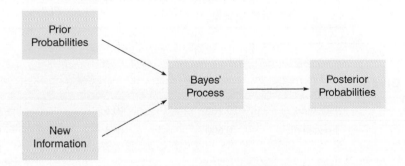

The answer to these questions is yes, and we do so by using the formula for joint probability under statistical dependence and Bayes' theorem. First, we take stock of the information and probabilities available. We know, for example, that since we randomly selected the die to roll, the probability of it being fair or loaded is 0.50:

$$P(\text{fair}) = 0.50 \quad P(\text{loaded}) = 0.50$$

We also know that

$$P(3\,|\,\text{fair}) = 0.166 \quad P(3\,|\,\text{loaded}) = 0.60$$

Next, we compute joint probabilities $P(3 \text{ and fair})$ and $P(3 \text{ and loaded})$ using the formula $P(AB) = P(A\,|\,B) \times P(B)$:

$$P(3 \text{ and fair}) = P(3\,|\,\text{fair}) \times P(\text{fair})$$
$$= (0.166)(0.50) = 0.083$$

$$P(3 \text{ and loaded}) = P(3\,|\,\text{loaded}) \times P(\text{loaded})$$
$$= (0.60)(0.50) = 0.300$$

A 3 can occur in combination with the state "fair die" or in combination with the state "loaded die." The sum of their probabilities gives the unconditional or marginal probability of a 3 on the toss, namely, $P(3) = 0.083 + 0.300 = 0.383$.

If a 3 does occur, and if we do not know which die it came from, the probability that the die rolled was the fair one is

$$P(\text{fair}\,|\,3) = \frac{P(\text{fair and }3)}{P(3)} = \frac{0.083}{0.383} = 0.22$$

The probability that the die rolled was loaded is

$$P(\text{loaded}\,|\,3) = \frac{P(\text{loaded and }3)}{P(3)} = \frac{0.300}{0.383} = 0.78$$

These two conditional probabilities are called the **revised** or **posterior probabilities** for the next roll of the die.

Before the die was rolled in the preceding example, the best we could say was that there was a 50–50 chance that it was fair (0.50 probability) and a 50–50 chance that it was loaded. After one roll of the die, however, we are able to revise our **prior probability** estimates. The new posterior estimate is that there is a 0.78 probability that the die rolled was loaded and only a 0.22 probability that it was not.

Using a table is often helpful in performing the calculations associated with Bayes' theorem. Table 2.3 provides the general layout for this, and Table 2.4 provides this specific example.

TABLE 2.3

Tabular Form of Bayes' Calculations Given That Event B Has Occurred

STATE OF NATURE	$P(B\,|\,$ STATE OF NATURE)	PRIOR PROBABILITY	JOINT PROBABILITY	POSTERIOR PROBABILITY
A	$P(B\,|\,A)$	$\times P(A)$	$= P(B \text{ and } A)$	$P(B \text{ and } A)/P(B) = P(A\,|\,B)$
A'	$P(B\,|\,A')$	$\times P(A')$	$= P(B \text{ and } A')$	$P(B \text{ and } A')/P(B) = P(A'\,|\,B)$
			$P(B)$	

TABLE 2.4

Bayes' Calculations Given That a 3 Is Rolled in Example 7

STATE OF NATURE	$P(3\,|\,$ STATE OF NATURE)	PRIOR PROBABILITY	JOINT PROBABILITY	POSTERIOR PROBABILITY
Fair die	0.166	$\times 0.5$	$= 0.083$	$0.083/0.383 = 0.22$
Loaded die	0.600	$\times 0.5$	$= 0.300$	$0.300/0.383 = 0.78$
			$P(3) = 0.383$	

General Form of Bayes' Theorem

Another way to compute revised probabilities is with Bayes' theorem.

Revised probabilities can also be computed in a more direct way using a general form for **Bayes' theorem**:

$$P(A|B) = \frac{P(B|A)P(A)}{P(B|A)P(A) + P(B|A')P(A')} \tag{2-5}$$

where

A' = the complement of the event A;

for example, if A is the event "fair die," then A' is "loaded die"

We originally saw in Equation 2-3 the conditional probability of event A, given event B, is

$$P(A|B) = \frac{P(AB)}{P(B)}$$

A Presbyterian minister, Thomas Bayes (1702–1761), did the work leading to this theorem.

Thomas Bayes derived his theorem from this. Appendix 2.1 shows the mathematical steps leading to Equation 2-5. Now let's return to the example.

Although it may not be obvious to you at first glance, we used this basic equation to compute the revised probabilities. For example, if we want the probability that the fair die was rolled given the first toss was a 3, namely, P(fair die | 3 rolled), we can let

event "fair die" replace A in Equation 2-5

event "loaded die" replace A' in Equation 2-5

event "3 rolled" replace B in Equation 2-5

We can then rewrite Equation 2-5 and solve as follows:

$$P(\text{fair die} | 3 \text{ rolled})$$

$$= \frac{P(3|\text{fair})P(\text{fair})}{P(3|\text{fair})P(\text{fair}) + P(3|\text{loaded})P(\text{loaded})}$$

$$= \frac{(0.166)(0.50)}{(0.166)(0.50) + (0.60)(0.50)}$$

$$= \frac{0.083}{0.383} = 0.22$$

This is the same answer that we computed earlier. Can you use this alternative approach to show that P(loaded die | 3 rolled) = 0.78? Either method is perfectly acceptable, but when we deal with probability revisions again in Chapter 3, we may find that Equation 2-5 or the tabular approach is easier to apply.

2.4 Further Probability Revisions

Although one revision of prior probabilities can provide useful posterior probability estimates, additional information can be gained from performing the experiment a second time. If it is financially worthwhile, a decision maker may even decide to make several more revisions.

Returning to the previous example, we now attempt to obtain further information about the posterior probabilities as to whether the die just rolled is fair or loaded. To do so, let us toss the die a second time. Again, we roll a 3. What are the further revised probabilities?

To answer this question, we proceed as before, with only one exception. The probabilities P(fair) = 0.50 and P(loaded) = 0.50 remain the same, but now we must compute $P(3, 3 | \text{fair})$ = $(0.166)(0.166) = 0.027$ and $P(3, 3 | \text{loaded}) = (0.6)(0.6) = 0.36$. With these joint probabilities of two 3s on successive rolls, given the two types of dice, we may revise the probabilities:

$$P(3, 3 \text{ and fair}) = P(3, 3 | \text{fair}) \times P(\text{fair})$$

$$= (0.027)(0.5) = 0.013$$

$$P(3, 3 \text{ and loaded}) = P(3, 3 | \text{loaded}) \times P(\text{loaded})$$

$$= (0.36)(0.5) = 0.18$$

IN ACTION   Flight Safety and Probability Analysis

With the horrific events of September 11, 2001, and the use of airplanes as weapons of mass destruction, airline safety has become an even more important international issue. How can we reduce the impact of terrorism on air safety? What can be done to make air travel safer overall? One answer is to evaluate various air safety programs and to use probability theory in the analysis of the costs of these programs.

Determining airline safety is a matter of applying the concepts of objective probability analysis. The chance of getting killed in a scheduled domestic flight is about 1 in 5 million. This is probability of about .0000002. Another measure is the number of deaths per passenger mile flown. The number is about 1 passenger per billion passenger miles flown, or a probability of about .000000001. Without question, flying is safer than many other forms of transportation, including driving. For a typical weekend, more people are killed in car accidents than a typical air disaster.

Analyzing new airline safety measures involves costs and the subjective probability that lives will be saved. One airline expert proposed a number of new airline safety measures. When the costs involved and probability of saving lives were taken into account, the result was about a $1 billion cost for every life saved on average. Using probability analysis will help determine which safety programs will result in the greatest benefit, and these programs can be expanded.

In addition, some proposed safety issues are not completely certain. For example, a Thermal Neutron Analysis device to detect explosives at airports had a probability of .15 of giving a false alarm, resulting in a high cost of inspection and long flight delays. This would indicate that money should be spent on developing more reliable equipment for detecting explosives. The result would be safer air travel with fewer unnecessary delays.

Without question, the use of probability analysis to determine and improve flight safety is indispensable. Many transportation experts hope that the same rigorous probability models used in the airline industry will some day be applied to the much more deadly system of highways and the drivers who use them.

Sources: Based on Robert Machol. "Flying Scared," *OR/MS Today* (October 1997): 32–37; and Arnold Barnett. "The Worst Day Ever," *OR/MS Today* (December 2001): 28–31.

Thus, the probability of rolling two 3s, a marginal probability, is $0.013 + 0.18 = 0.193$, the sum of the two joint probabilities:

$$P(\text{fair}\,|\,3, 3) = \frac{P(3, 3 \text{ and fair})}{P(3, 3)}$$

$$= \frac{0.013}{0.193} = 0.067$$

$$P(\text{loaded}\,|\,3, 3) = \frac{P(3, 3 \text{ and loaded})}{P(3, 3)}$$

$$= \frac{0.18}{0.193} = 0.933$$

What has this second roll accomplished? Before we rolled the die the first time, we knew only that there was a 0.50 probability that it was either fair or loaded. When the first die was rolled in the previous example, we were able to revise these probabilities:

$$\text{probability the die is fair} = 0.22$$
$$\text{probability the die is loaded} = 0.78$$

Now, after the second roll in this example, our refined revisions tell us that

$$\text{probability the die is fair} = 0.067$$
$$\text{probability the die is loaded} = 0.933$$

This type of information can be extremely valuable in business decision making.

2.5   Random Variables

We have just discussed various ways of assigning probability values to the outcomes of an experiment. Let us now use this probability information to compute the expected outcome, variance, and standard deviation of the experiment. This can help select the best decision among a number of alternatives.

TABLE 2.5   Examples of Random Variables

EXPERIMENT	OUTCOME	RANDOM VARIABLES	RANGE OF RANDOM VARIABLES
Stock 50 Christmas trees	Number of Christmas trees sold	X = number of Christmas trees sold	0, 1, 2, . . . , 50
Inspect 600 items	Number of acceptable items	Y = number of acceptable items	0, 1, 2, . . . , 600
Send out 5,000 sales letters	Number of people responding to the letters	Z = number of people responding to the letters	0, 1, 2, . . . , 5,000
Build an apartment building	Percent of building completed after 4 months	R = percent of building completed after 4 months	$0 \leq R \leq 100$
Test the lifetime of a lightbulb (minutes)	Length of time the bulb lasts up to 80,000 minutes	S = time the bulb burns	$0 \leq S \leq 80,000$

A **random variable** assigns a real number to every possible outcome or event in an experiment. It is normally represented by a letter such as X or Y. When the outcome itself is numerical or quantitative, the outcome numbers can be the random variable. For example, consider refrigerator sales at an appliance store. The number of refrigerators sold during a given day can be the random variable. Using X to represent this random variable, we can express this relationship as follows:

$$X = \text{number of refrigerators sold during the day}$$

In general, whenever the experiment has quantifiable outcomes, it is beneficial to define these quantitative outcomes as the random variable. Examples are given in Table 2.5.

When the outcome itself is not numerical or quantitative, it is necessary to define a random variable that associates each outcome with a unique real number. Several examples are given in Table 2.6.

There are two types of random variables: *discrete random variables* and *continuous random variables*. Developing probability distributions and making computations based on these distributions depends on the type of random variable.

A random variable is a **discrete random variable** if it can assume only a finite or limited set of values. Which of the random variables in Table 2.5 are discrete random variables? Looking at Table 2.5, we can see that the variables associated with stocking 50 Christmas trees, inspecting 600 items, and sending out 5,000 letters are all examples of discrete random variables. Each of these random variables can assume only a finite or limited set of values. The number of Christmas trees sold, for example, can only be integer numbers from 0 to 50. There are 51 values that the random variable X can assume in this example.

A **continuous random variable** is a random variable that has an infinite or an unlimited set of values. Are there any examples of continuous random variables in Table 2.5 or 2.6? Looking

Try to develop a few more examples of discrete random variables to be sure you understand this concept.

TABLE 2.6

Random Variables for Outcomes That Are Not Numbers

EXPERIMENT	OUTCOME	RANDOM VARIABLES	RANGE OF RANDOM VARIABLES
Students respond to a questionnaire	Strongly agree (SA) Agree (A) Neutral (N) Disagree (D) Strongly disagree (SD)	$X = \begin{cases} 5 \text{ if SA} \\ 4 \text{ if A} \\ 3 \text{ if N} \\ 2 \text{ if D} \\ 1 \text{ if SD} \end{cases}$	1, 2, 3, 4, 5
One machine is inspected	Defective Not defective	$Y = \begin{cases} 0 \text{ if defective} \\ 1 \text{ if not defective} \end{cases}$	0, 1
Consumers respond to how they like a product	Good Average Poor	$Z = \begin{cases} 3 \text{ if good} \\ 2 \text{ if average} \\ 1 \text{ if poor} \end{cases}$	1, 2, 3

at Table 2.5, we can see that testing the lifetime of a lightbulb is an experiment whose results can be described with a continuous random variable. In this case, the random variable, S, is the time the bulb burns. It can last for 3,206 minutes, 6,500.7 minutes, 251.726 minutes, or any other value between 0 and 80,000 minutes. In most cases, the range of a continuous random variable is stated as: lower value $\leq S \leq$ upper value, such as $0 \leq S \leq 80{,}000$. The random variable R in Table 2.5 is also continuous. Can you explain why?

2.6 Probability Distributions

Earlier we discussed the probability values of an event. We now explore the properties of **probability distributions**. We see how popular distributions, such as the normal, Poisson, binomial, and exponential probability distributions, can save us time and effort. Since a random variable may be *discrete* or *continuous*, we consider **discrete probability distributions** and **continuous probability distributions** seperately.

Probability Distribution of a Discrete Random Variable

When we have a *discrete random variable*, there is a probability value assigned to each event. These values must be between 0 and 1, and they must sum to 1. Let's look at an example.

The 100 students in Pat Shannon's statistics class have just completed a math quiz that he gives on the first day of class. The quiz consists of five very difficult algebra problems. The grade on the quiz is the number of correct answers, so the grades theoretically could range from 0 to 5. However, no one in this class received a score of 0, so the grades ranged from 1 to 5. The random variable X is defined to be the grade on this quiz, and the grades are summarized in Table 2.7. This discrete probability distribution was developed using the relative frequency approach presented earlier.

The distribution follows the three rules required of all probability distributions: (1) the events are mutually exclusive and collectively exhaustive, (2) the individual probability values are between 0 and 1 inclusive, and (3) the total of the probability values sum to 1.

Although listing the probability distribution as we did in Table 2.7 is adequate, it can be difficult to get an idea about characteristics of the distribution. To overcome this problem, the probability values are often presented in graph form. The graph of the distribution in Table 2.7 is shown in Figure 2.4.

The graph of this probability distribution gives us a picture of its shape. It helps us identify the central tendency of the distribution, called the mean or **expected value**, and the amount of variability or spread of the distribution, called the **variance**.

Expected Value of a Discrete Probability Distribution

Once we have established a probability distribution, the first characteristic that is usually of interest is the *central tendency* of the distribution. The expected value, a measure of central tendency, is computed as the weighted average of the values of the random variable:

The expected value of a discrete distribution is a weighted average of the values of the random variable.

$$
\begin{aligned}
E(X) &= \sum_{i=1}^{n} X_i P(X_i) \\
&= X_1 P(X_1) + X_2 P(X_2) + \cdots + X_n P(X_n)
\end{aligned}
\tag{2-6}
$$

TABLE 2.7

Probability Distribution for Quiz Scores

RANDOM VARIABLE (X)-SCORE	NUMBER	PROBABILITY $P(X)$
5	10	$0.1 = 10/100$
4	20	$0.2 = 20/100$
3	30	$0.3 = 30/100$
2	30	$0.3 = 30/100$
1	10	$0.1 = 10/100$
	Total 100	$1.0 = 100/100$

FIGURE 2.4

Probability Distribution for Dr. Shannon's Class

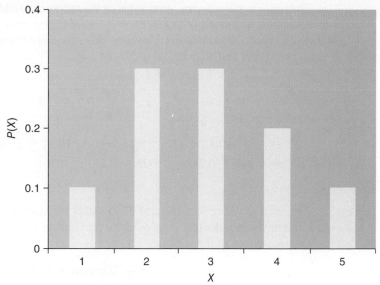

where

$$X_i = \text{random variable's possible values}$$

$$P(X_i) = \text{probability of each of the random variable's possible values}$$

$$\sum_{i=1}^{n} = \text{summation sign indicating we are adding all } n \text{ possible values}$$

$$E(X) = \text{expected value or mean of the random variable}$$

The expected value or mean of any discrete probability distribution can be computed by multiplying each possible value of the random variable, X_i, times the probability, $P(X_i)$, that outcome will occur and summing the results, $\sum$. Here is how the expected value can be computed for the quiz scores:

$$
\begin{aligned}
E(X) &= \sum_{i=1}^{5} X_i P(X_i) \\
&= X_1 P(X_1) + X_2 P(X_2) + X_3 P(X_3) + X_4 P(X_4) + X_5 P(X_5) \\
&= (5)(0.1) + (4)(0.2) + (3)(0.3) + (2)(0.3) + (1)(0.1) \\
&= 2.9
\end{aligned}
$$

The expected value of 2.9 is the mean score on the quiz.

Variance of a Discrete Probability Distribution

In addition to the central tendency of a probability distribution, most people are interested in the variability or the spread of the distribution. If the variability is low, it is much more likely that the outcome of an experiment will be close to the average or expected value. On the other hand, if the variability of the distribution is high, which means that the probability is spread out over the various random variable values, there is less chance that the outcome of an experiment will be close to the expected value.

A probability distribution is often described by its mean and variance. Even if most of the men in class (or the United States) have heights between 5 feet 6 inches and 6 feet 2 inches, there is still some small probability of outliers.

The *variance* of a probability distribution is a number that reveals the overall spread or dispersion of the distribution. For a discrete probability distribution, it can be computed using the following equation:

$$\sigma^2 = \text{Variance} = \sum_{i=1}^{n} [X_i - E(X)]^2 P(X_i) \tag{2-7}$$

where

$$X_i = \text{random variable's possible values}$$

$$E(X) = \text{expected value of the random variable}$$

$$[X_i - E(X)] = \text{difference between each value of the random variable and the expected value}$$

$$P(X_i) = \text{probability of each possible value of the random variable}$$

To compute the variance, each value of the random variable is subtracted from the expected value, squared, and multiplied times the probability of occurrence of that value. The results are then summed to obtain the variance. Here is how this procedure is done for Dr. Shannon's quiz scores:

$$\text{Variance} = \sum_{i=1}^{5} [X_i - E(X)]^2 P(X_i)$$

$$\text{Variance} = (5 - 2.9)^2(0.1) + (4 - 2.9)^2(0.2) + (3 - 2.9)^2(0.3) + (2 - 2.9)^2(0.3)$$
$$+ (1 - 2.9)^2(0.1)$$
$$= (2.1)^2(0.1) + (1.1)^2(0.2) + (0.1)^2(0.3) + (-0.9)^2(0.3) + (-1.9)^2(0.1)$$
$$= 0.441 + 0.242 + 0.003 + 0.243 + 0.361$$
$$= 1.29$$

A related measure of dispersion or spread is the **standard deviation**. This quantity is also used in many computations involved with probability distributions. The standard deviation is just the square root of the variance:

$$\sigma = \sqrt{\text{Variance}} = \sqrt{\sigma^2} \tag{2-8}$$

where

$$\sqrt{} = \text{square root}$$
$$\sigma = \text{standard deviation}$$

The standard deviation for the random variable X in the example is

$$\sigma = \sqrt{\text{Variance}}$$
$$= \sqrt{1.29} = 1.14$$

These calculations are easily performed in Excel. Program 2.1A provides the output for this example. Program 2.1B shows the inputs and formulas in Excel for calculating the mean, variance, and standard deviation in this example.

Probability Distribution of a Continuous Random Variable

There are many examples of *continuous random variables*. The time it takes to finish a project, the number of ounces in a barrel of butter, the high temperature during a given day, the exact length of a given type of lumber, and the weight of a railroad car of coal are all examples of continuous random variables. Since random variables can take on an infinite number of values, the fundamental probability rules for continuous random variables must be modified.

As with discrete probability distributions, the sum of the probability values must equal 1. Because there are an infinite number of values of the random variables, however, the probability of each value of the random variable must be 0. If the probability values for the random variable values were greater than 0, the sum would be infinitely large.

PROGRAM 2.1A

Excel 2013 Output for the Dr. Shannon Example

	A	B	C	D
1	X	P(X)	XP(X)	(X - E(X))²P(X)
2	5	0.1	0.5	0.441
3	4	0.2	0.8	0.242
4	3	0.3	0.9	0.003
5	2	0.3	0.6	0.243
6	1	0.1	0.1	0.361
7		E(X) = ΣXP(X) =	2.9	1.290
8				1.136

PROGRAM 2.1B

Formulas in an Excel Spreadsheet for the Dr. Shannon Example

	C	D
2	=A2*B2	=(A2-$C$7)^2*B2
3	=A3*B3	=(A3-$C$7)^2*B3
4	=A4*B4	=(A4-$C$7)^2*B4
5	=A5*B5	=(A5-$C$7)^2*B5
6	=A6*B6	=(A6-$C$7)^2*B6
7	=SUM(C2:C6)	=SUM(D2:D6)
8		=SQRT(D7)

FIGURE 2.5

Graph of Sample Density Function

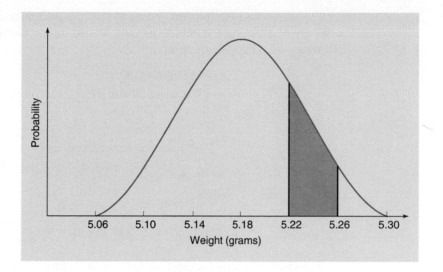

A probability density function, f(X), is a mathematical way of describing the probability distribution.

With a continuous probability distribution, there is a continuous mathematical function that describes the probability distribution. This function is called the **probability density function** or simply the **probability function**. It is usually represented by $f(X)$. When working with continuous probability distributions, the probability function can be graphed, and the area underneath the curve represents probability. Thus, to find any probability, we simply find the area under the curve associated with the range of interest.

We now look at the sketch of a sample density function in Figure 2.5. This curve represents the probability density function for the weight of a particular machined part. The weight could vary from 5.06 to 5.30 grams, with weights around 5.18 grams being the most likely. The shaded area represents the probability the weight is between 5.22 and 5.26 grams.

If we wanted to know the probability of a part weighing exactly 5.1300000 grams, for example, we would have to compute the area of a line of width 0. Of course, this would be 0. This result may seem strange, but if we insist on enough decimal places of accuracy, we are bound to find that the weight differs from 5.1300000 grams *exactly*, be the difference ever so slight.

This is important because it means that, for any continuous distribution, the probability does not change if a single point is added to the range of values that is being considered. In Figure 2.5, this means the following probabilities are all exactly the same:

$$P(5.22 < X < 5.26) = P(5.22 < X \le 5.26) = P(5.22 \le X < 5.26)$$
$$= P(5.22 \le X \le 5.26)$$

The inclusion or exclusion of either endpoint (5.22 or 5.26) has no impact on the probability.

In this section, we have investigated the fundamental characteristics and properties of probability distributions in general. In the next three sections, we introduce three important continuous distributions—the normal distribution, the F distribution, and the exponential distribution—and two discrete distributions—the Poisson distribution and the binomial distribution.

2.7   The Binomial Distribution

Many business experiments can be characterized by the **Bernoulli process**. The probability of obtaining specific outcomes in a Bernoulli process is described by the binomial probability distribution. In order to be a Bernoulli process, an experiment must have the following characteristics:

1. Each trial in a Bernoulli process has only two possible outcomes. These are typically called a success and a failure, although examples might be yes or no, heads or tails, pass or fail, defective or good, and so on.
2. The probability stays the same from one trial to the next.
3. The trials are statistically independent.
4. The number of trials is a positive integer.

A common example of this process is tossing a coin.

The **binomial distribution** is used to find the probability of a specific number of successes out of n trials of a Bernoulli process. To find this probability, it is necessary to know the following:

$$n = \text{the number of trials}$$
$$p = \text{the probability of a success on any single trial}$$

We let

$$r = \text{the number of successes}$$
$$q = 1 - p = \text{the probability of a failure}$$

The binomial formula is

$$\text{Probability of } r \text{ successes in } n \text{ trials} = \frac{n!}{r!(n-r)!} p^r q^{n-r} \qquad (2\text{-}9)$$

The symbol ! means factorial, and $n! = n(n-1)(n-2) \ldots (1)$. For example,

$$4! = (4)(3)(2)(1) = 24$$

Also, $1! = 1$, and $0! = 1$ by definition.

Solving Problems with the Binomial Formula

A common example of a binomial distribution is the tossing of a coin and counting the number of heads. For example, if we wished to find the probability of 4 heads in 5 tosses of a coin, we would have

$$n = 5, r = 4, p = 0.5, \quad \text{and} \quad q = 1 - 0.5 = 0.5$$

Thus,

$$P(4 \text{ successes in 5 trials}) = \frac{5!}{4!(5-4)!} 0.5^4 0.5^{5-4}$$

$$= \frac{5(4)(3)(2)(1)}{4(3)(2)(1)(1!)} (0.0625)(0.5) = 0.15625$$

Thus, the probability of 4 heads in 5 tosses of a coin is 0.15625 or about 16%.

Using Equation 2-9, it is also possible to find the entire probability distribution (all the possible values for r and the corresponding probabilities) for a binomial experiment. The probability distribution for the number of heads in 5 tosses of a fair coin is shown in Table 2.8 and then graphed in Figure 2.6.

TABLE 2.8

Binomial Probability Distribution for $n = 5$ and $p = 0.50$

NUMBER OF HEADS (r)	PROBABILITY $= \dfrac{5!}{r!(5-r)!}(0.5)^r (0.5)^{5-r}$
0	$0.03125 = \dfrac{5!}{0!(5-0)!}(0.5)^0 (0.5)^{5-0}$
1	$0.15625 = \dfrac{5!}{1!(5-1)!}(0.5)^1 (0.5)^{5-1}$
2	$0.31250 = \dfrac{5!}{2!(5-2)!}(0.5)^2 (0.5)^{5-2}$
3	$0.31250 = \dfrac{5!}{3!(5-3)!}(0.5)^3 (0.5)^{5-3}$
4	$0.15625 = \dfrac{5!}{4!(5-4)!}(0.5)^4 (0.5)^{5-4}$
5	$0.03125 = \dfrac{5!}{5!(5-5)!}(0.5)^5 (0.5)^{5-5}$

FIGURE 2.6

Binomial Probability Distribution for n = 5 and p = 0.50

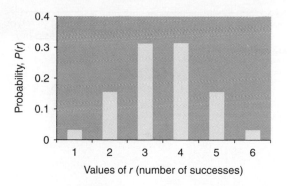

Solving Problems with Binomial Tables

MSA Electronics is experimenting with the manufacture of a new type of transistor that is very difficult to mass produce at an acceptable quality level. Every hour a supervisor takes a random sample of 5 transistors produced on the assembly line. The probability that any one transistor is defective is considered to be 0.15. MSA wants to know the probability of finding 3, 4, or 5 defectives if the true percentage defective is 15%.

For this problem, $n = 5, p = 0.15$, and $r = 3, 4,$ or 5. Although we could use the formula for each of these values, it is easier to use binomial tables for this. Appendix B gives a binomial table for a broad range of values for $n, r,$ and p. A portion of this appendix is shown in Table 2.9. To find these probabilities, we look through the $n = 5$ section and find the

TABLE 2.9   A Sample Table for the Binomial Distribution

						P					
n	r	0.05	0.10	0.15	0.20	0.25	0.30	0.35	0.40	0.45	0.50
1	0	0.9500	0.9000	0.8500	0.8000	0.7500	0.7000	0.6500	0.6000	0.5500	0.5000
	1	0.0500	0.1000	0.1500	0.2000	0.2500	0.3000	0.3500	0.4000	0.4500	0.5000
2	0	0.9025	0.8100	0.7225	0.6400	0.5625	0.4900	0.4225	0.3600	0.3025	0.2500
	1	0.0950	0.1800	0.2500	0.3200	0.3750	0.4200	0.4550	0.4800	0.4950	0.5000
	2	0.0025	0.0100	0.0225	0.0400	0.0625	0.0900	0.1225	0.1600	0.2025	0.2500
3	0	0.8574	0.7290	0.6141	0.5120	0.4219	0.3430	0.2746	0.2160	0.1664	0.1250
	1	0.1354	0.2430	0.3251	0.3840	0.4219	0.4410	0.4436	0.4320	0.4084	0.3750
	2	0.0071	0.0270	0.0574	0.0960	0.1406	0.1890	0.2389	0.2880	0.3341	0.3750
	3	0.0001	0.0010	0.0034	0.0080	0.0156	0.0270	0.0429	0.0640	0.0911	0.1250
4	0	0.8145	0.6561	0.5220	0.4096	0.3164	0.2401	0.1785	0.1296	0.0915	0.0625
	1	0.1715	0.2916	0.3685	0.4096	0.4219	0.4116	0.3845	0.3456	0.2995	0.2500
	2	0.0135	0.0486	0.0975	0.1536	0.2109	0.2646	0.3105	0.3456	0.3675	0.3750
	3	0.0005	0.0036	0.0115	0.0256	0.0469	0.0756	0.1115	0.1536	0.2005	0.2500
	4	0.0000	0.0001	0.0005	0.0016	0.0039	0.0081	0.0150	0.0256	0.0410	0.0625
5	0	0.7738	0.5905	0.4437	0.3277	0.2373	0.1681	0.1160	0.0778	0.0503	0.0313
	1	0.2036	0.3281	0.3915	0.4096	0.3955	0.3602	0.3124	0.2592	0.2059	0.1563
	2	0.0214	0.0729	0.1382	0.2048	0.2637	0.3087	0.3364	0.3456	0.3369	0.3125
	3	0.0011	0.0081	0.0244	0.0512	0.0879	0.1323	0.1811	0.2304	0.2757	0.3125
	4	0.0000	0.0005	0.0022	0.0064	0.0146	0.0284	0.0488	0.0768	0.1128	0.1563
	5	0.0000	0.0000	0.0001	0.0003	0.0010	0.0024	0.0053	0.0102	0.0185	0.0313
6	0	0.7351	0.5314	0.3771	0.2621	0.1780	0.1176	0.0754	0.0467	0.0277	0.0156
	1	0.2321	0.3543	0.3993	0.3932	0.3560	0.3025	0.2437	0.1866	0.1359	0.0938
	2	0.0305	0.0984	0.1762	0.2458	0.2966	0.3241	0.3280	0.3110	0.2780	0.2344
	3	0.0021	0.0146	0.0415	0.0819	0.1318	0.1852	0.2355	0.2765	0.3032	0.3125
	4	0.0001	0.0012	0.0055	0.0154	0.0330	0.0595	0.0951	0.1382	0.1861	0.2344
	5	0.0000	0.0001	0.0004	0.0015	0.0044	0.0102	0.0205	0.0369	0.0609	0.0938
	6	0.0000	0.0000	0.0000	0.0001	0.0002	0.0007	0.0018	0.0041	0.0083	0.0156

PROGRAM 2.2A

Excel Output for the Binomial Example

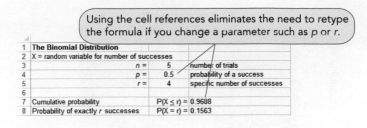

Using the cell references eliminates the need to retype the formula if you change a parameter such as *p* or *r*.

	The Binomial Distribution		
1	The Binomial Distribution		
2	X = random variable for number of successes		
3	n =	5	number of trials
4	p =	0.5	probability of a success
5	r =	4	specific number of successes
6			
7	Cumulative probability	P(X ≤ r) =	0.9688
8	Probability of exactly r successes	P(X = r) =	0.1563

PROGRAM 2.2B

Function in an Excel 2013 Spreadsheet for Binomial Probabilities

The function BINOM.DIST (*r*,*n*,*p*,TRUE) returns the cumulative probability.

	C
7	=BINOMDIST(B5,B3,B4,TRUE)
8	=BINOMDIST(B5,B3,B4,FALSE)

$p = 0.15$ column. In the row where $r = 3$, we see 0.0244. Thus, $P(r = 3) = 0.0244$. Similarly, $P(r = 4) = 0.0022$, and $P(r = 5) = 0.0001$. By adding these three probabilities, we have the probability that the number of defects is 3 or more:

$$P(3 \text{ or more defects}) = P(3) + P(4) + P(5)$$
$$= 0.0244 + 0.0022 + 0.0001 = 0.0267$$

The expected value (or mean) and the variance of a binomial random variable may be easily found. These are

$$\text{Expected value (mean)} = np \tag{2-10}$$

$$\text{Variance} = np(1 - p) \tag{2-11}$$

The expected value and variance for the MSA Electronics example are computed as follows:

$$\text{Expected value} = np = 5(0.15) = 0.75$$
$$\text{Variance} = np(1 - p) = 5(0.15)(0.85) = 0.6375$$

Programs 2.2A and 2.2B illustrate how Excel is used for binomial probabilities.

2.8 The Normal Distribution

The normal distribution affects a large number of processes in our lives (e.g., filling boxes of cereal with 32 ounces of corn flakes). Each normal distribution depends on the mean and standard deviation.

One of the most popular and useful continuous probability distributions is the **normal distribution**. The probability density function of this distribution is given by the rather complex formula

$$f(X) = \frac{1}{\sigma\sqrt{2\pi}} e^{\frac{-(x-\mu)^2}{2\sigma^2}} \tag{2-12}$$

The normal distribution is specified completely when values for the mean, μ, and the standard deviation, σ, are known. Figure 2.7 shows several different normal distributions with the same standard deviation and different means. As shown, differing values of μ will shift the average or center of the normal distribution. The overall shape of the distribution remains the same. On the other hand, when the standard deviation is varied, the normal curve either flattens out or becomes steeper. This is shown in Figure 2.8.

As the standard deviation, σ, becomes smaller, the normal distribution becomes steeper. When the standard deviation becomes larger, the normal distribution has a tendency to flatten out or become broader.

FIGURE 2.7

Normal Distribution with Different Values for μ

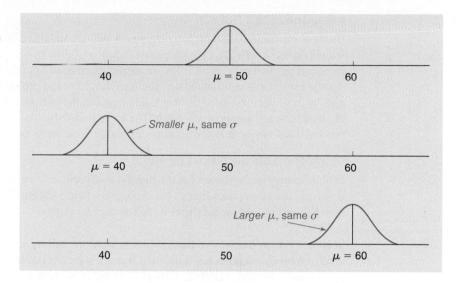

FIGURE 2.8

Normal Distribution with Different Values for σ

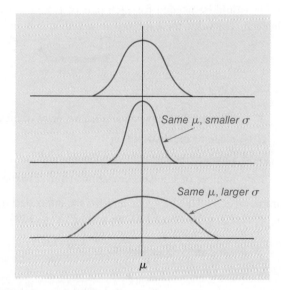

IN ACTION   Probability Assessments of Curling Champions

Probabilities are used every day in sporting activities. In many sporting events, there are questions involving strategies that must be answered to provide the best chance of winning the game. In baseball, should a particular batter be intentionally walked in key situations at the end of the game? In football, should a team elect to try for a two-point conversion after a touchdown? In soccer, should a penalty kick ever be aimed directly at the goal keeper? In curling, in the last round, or "end" of a game, is it better to be behind by one point and have the hammer or is it better to be ahead by one point and not having the hammer? An attempt was made to answer this last question.

In curling, a granite stone, or "rock," is slid across a sheet of ice 14 feet wide and 146 feet long. Four players on each of two teams take alternating turns sliding the rock, trying to get it as close as possible to the center of a circle called the "house." The team with the rock closest to this scores points. The team that is behind at the completion of a round or end has the advantage in

the next end by being the last team to slide the rock. This team is said to "have the hammer." A survey was taken of a group of experts in curling, including a number of former world champions. In this survey, about 58% of the respondents favored having the hammer and being down by one going into the last end. Only about 42% preferred being ahead and not having the hammer.

Data were also collected from 1985 to 1997 at the Canadian Men's Curling Championships (also called the Brier). Based on the results over this time period, it is better to be ahead by one point and not have the hammer at the end of the ninth end rather than be behind by one and have the hammer, as many people prefer. This differed from the survey results. Apparently, world champions and other experts preferred to have more control of their destiny by having the hammer even though it put them in a worse situation.

Source: Based on Keith A. Willoughby and Kent J. Kostuk. "Preferred Scenarios in the Sport of Curling," *Interfaces* 34, 2 (March–April 2004): 117–122.

Area Under the Normal Curve

Because the normal distribution is symmetrical, its midpoint (and highest point) is at the mean. Values on the X axis are then measured in terms of how many standard deviations they lie from the mean. As you may recall from our earlier discussion of probability distributions, the area under the curve (in a continuous distribution) describes the probability that a random variable has a value in a specified interval. When dealing with the uniform distribution, it is easy to compute the area between any points a and b. The normal distribution requires mathematical calculations beyond the scope of this book, but tables that provide areas or probabilities are readily available.

Using the Standard Normal Table

When finding probabilities for the normal distribution, it is best to draw the normal curve and shade the area corresponding to the probability being sought. The normal distribution table can then be used to find probabilities by following two steps.

Step 1. Convert the normal distribution to what we call a *standard normal distribution*. A standard normal distribution has a mean of 0 and a standard deviation of 1. All normal tables are set up to handle random variables with $\mu = 0$ and $\sigma = 1$. Without a standard normal distribution, a different table would be needed for each pair of μ and σ values. We call the new standard random variable Z. The value for Z for any normal distribution is computed from this equation:

$$Z = \frac{X - \mu}{\sigma} \tag{2-13}$$

where

$X =$ value of the random variable we want to measure

$\mu =$ mean of the distribution

$\sigma =$ standard deviation of the distribution

$Z =$ number of standard deviations from X to the mean, μ

For example, if $\mu = 100$, $\sigma = 15$, and we are interested in finding the probability that the random variable X (IQ) is less than 130, we want $P(X < 130)$:

$$Z = \frac{X - \mu}{\sigma} = \frac{130 - 100}{15}$$

$$= \frac{30}{15} = 2 \text{ standard deviations}$$

This means that the point X is 2.0 standard deviations to the right of the mean. This is shown in Figure 2.9.

FIGURE 2.9

Normal Distribution Showing the Relationship Between Z Values and X Values

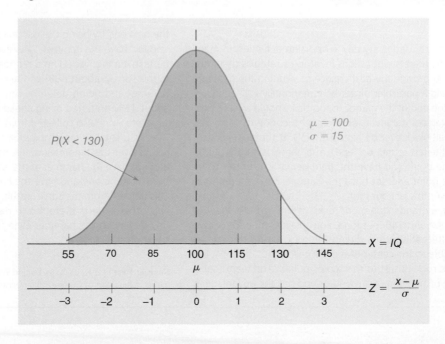

Step 2. Look up the probability from a table of normal curve areas. Table 2.10, which also appears as Appendix A, is such a table of areas for the standard normal distribution. It is set up to provide the area under the curve to the left of any specified value of Z.

Let's see how Table 2.10 can be used. The column on the left lists values of Z, with the second decimal place of Z appearing in the top row. For example, for a value of $Z = 2.00$ as just computed, find 2.0 in the left-hand column and 0.00 in the top row. In the body of the table, we find that the area sought is 0.97725, or 97.7%. Thus,

$$P(X < 130) = P(Z < 2.00) = 97.7\%$$

This suggests that if the mean IQ score is 100, with a standard deviation of 15 points, the probability that a randomly selected person's IQ is less than 130 is 97.7%. This is also the probability that the IQ is less than or equal to 130. To find the probability that the IQ is greater than 130, we simply note that this is the complement of the previous event and the total area under the curve (the total probability) is 1. Thus,

$$P(X > 130) = 1 - P(X \le 130) = 1 - P(Z \le 2) = 1 - 0.97725 = 0.02275$$

To be sure you understand the concept of symmetry in Table 2.10, try to find the probability such as $P(X < 85)$. Note that the standard normal table shows only positive Z values.

While Table 2.10 does not give negative Z values, the symmetry of the normal distribution can be used to find probabilities associated with negative Z values. For example, $P(Z < -2) = P(Z > 2)$.

To feel comfortable with the use of the standard normal probability table, we need to work a few more examples. We now use the Haynes Construction Company as a case in point.

Haynes Construction Company Example

Haynes Construction Company builds primarily three- and four-unit apartment buildings (called triplexes and quadraplexes) for investors, and it is believed that the total construction time in days follows a normal distribution. The mean time to construct a triplex is 100 days, and the standard deviation is 20 days. Recently, the president of Haynes Construction signed a contract to complete a triplex in 125 days. Failure to complete the triplex in 125 days would result in severe penalty fees. What is the probability that Haynes Construction will not be in violation of their construction contract? The normal distribution for the construction of triplexes is shown in Figure 2.10.

To compute this probability, we need to find the shaded area under the curve. We begin by computing Z for this problem:

$$Z = \frac{X - \mu}{\sigma}$$

$$= \frac{125 - 100}{20}$$

$$= \frac{25}{20} = 1.25$$

Looking in Table 2.10 for a Z value of 1.25, we find an area under the curve of 0.89435. (We do this by looking up 1.2 in the left-hand column of the table and then moving to the 0.05 column to find the value for $Z = 1.25$.) Therefore, the probability of not violating the contract is 0.89435, or about an 89% chance.

FIGURE 2.10

Normal Distribution for Haynes Construction

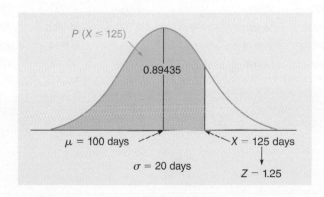

$P(X < 125)$

0.89435

$\mu = 100$ days

$\sigma = 20$ days

$X = 125$ days

$Z = 1.25$

TABLE 2.10 Standardized Normal Distribution Function

	AREA UNDER THE NORMAL CURVE									
Z	0.00	0.01	0.02	0.03	0.04	0.05	0.06	0.07	0.08	0.09
0.0	.50000	.50399	.50798	.51197	.51595	.51994	.52392	.52790	.53188	.53586
0.1	.53983	.54380	.54776	.55172	.55567	.55962	.56356	.56749	.57142	.57535
0.2	.57926	.58317	.58706	.59095	.59483	.59871	.60257	.60642	.61026	.61409
0.3	.61791	.62172	.62552	.62930	.63307	.63683	.64058	.64431	.64803	.65173
0.4	.65542	.65910	.66276	.66640	.67003	.67364	.67724	.68082	.68439	.68793
0.5	.69146	.69497	.69847	.70194	.70540	.70884	.71226	.71566	.71904	.72240
0.6	.72575	.72907	.73237	.73565	.73891	.74215	.74537	.74857	.75175	.75490
0.7	.75804	.76115	.76424	.76730	.77035	.77337	.77637	.77935	.78230	.78524
0.8	.78814	.79103	.79389	.79673	.79955	.80234	.80511	.80785	.81057	.81327
0.9	.81594	.81859	.82121	.82381	.82639	.82894	.83147	.83398	.83646	.83891
1.0	.84134	.84375	.84614	.84849	.85083	.85314	.85543	.85769	.85993	.86214
1.1	.86433	.86650	.86864	.87076	.87286	.87493	.87698	.87900	.88100	.88298
1.2	.88493	.88686	.88877	.89065	.89251	.89435	.89617	.89796	.89973	.90147
1.3	.90320	.90490	.90658	.90824	.90988	.91149	.91309	.91466	.91621	.91774
1.4	.91924	.92073	.92220	.92364	.92507	.92647	.92785	.92922	.93056	.93189
1.5	.93319	.93448	.93574	.93699	.93822	.93943	.94062	.94179	.94295	.94408
1.6	.94520	.94630	.94738	.94845	.94950	.95053	.95154	.95254	.95352	.95449
1.7	.95543	.95637	.95728	.95818	.95907	.95994	.96080	.96164	.96246	.96327
1.8	.96407	.96485	.96562	.96638	.96712	.96784	.96856	.96926	.96995	.97062
1.9	.97128	.97193	.97257	.97320	.97381	.97441	.97500	.97558	.97615	.97670
2.0	.97725	.97778	.97831	.97882	.97932	.97982	.98030	.98077	.98124	.98169
2.1	.98214	.98257	.98300	.98341	.98382	.98422	.98461	.98500	.98537	.98574
2.2	.98610	.98645	.98679	.98713	.98745	.98778	.98809	.98840	.98870	.98899
2.3	.98928	.98956	.98983	.99010	.99036	.99061	.99086	.99111	.99134	.99158
2.4	.99180	.99202	.99224	.99245	.99266	.99286	.99305	.99324	.99343	.99361
2.5	.99379	.99396	.99413	.99430	.99446	.99461	.99477	.99492	.99506	.99520
2.6	.99534	.99547	.99560	.99573	.99585	.99598	.99609	.99621	.99632	.99643
2.7	.99653	.99664	.99674	.99683	.99693	.99702	.99711	.99720	.99728	.99736
2.8	.99744	.99752	.99760	.99767	.99774	.99781	.99788	.99795	.99801	.99807
2.9	.99813	.99819	.99825	.99831	.99836	.99841	.99846	.99851	.99856	.99861
3.0	.99865	.99869	.99874	.99878	.99882	.99886	.99889	.99893	.99896	.99900
3.1	.99903	.99906	.99910	.99913	.99916	.99918	.99921	.99924	.99926	.99929
3.2	.99931	.99934	.99936	.99938	.99940	.99942	.99944	.99946	.99948	.99950
3.3	.99952	.99953	.99955	.99957	.99958	.99960	.99961	.99962	.99964	.99965
3.4	.99966	.99968	.99969	.99970	.99971	.99972	.99973	.99974	.99975	.99976
3.5	.99977	.99978	.99978	.99979	.99980	.99981	.99981	.99982	.99983	.99983
3.6	.99984	.99985	.99985	.99986	.99986	.99987	.99987	.99988	.99988	.99989
3.7	.99989	.99990	.99990	.99990	.99991	.99991	.99992	.99992	.99992	.99992
3.8	.99993	.99993	.99993	.99994	.99994	.99994	.99994	.99995	.99995	.99995
3.9	.99995	.99995	.99996	.99996	.99996	.99996	.99996	.99996	.99997	.99997

FIGURE 2.11

Probability That Haynes Will Receive the Bonus by Finishing in 75 Days or Less

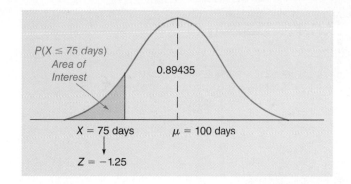

$P(X \leq 75 \text{ days})$
Area of
Interest

0.89435

$X = 75$ days $\mu = 100$ days

$Z = -1.25$

Now let us look at the Haynes problem from another perspective. If the firm finishes this triplex in 75 days or less, it will be awarded a bonus payment of $5,000. What is the probability that Haynes will receive the bonus?

Figure 2.11 illustrates the probability we are looking for in the shaded area. The first step is again to compute the Z value:

$$Z = \frac{X - \mu}{\sigma}$$

$$= \frac{75 - 100}{20}$$

$$= \frac{-25}{20} = -1.25$$

This Z value indicates that 75 days is -1.25 standard deviations to the left of the mean. But the standard normal table is structured to handle only positive Z values. To solve this problem, we observe that the curve is symmetric. The probability that Haynes will finish in *75 days or less is equivalent* to the probability that it will finish in *more than 125 days*. A moment ago (in Figure 2.10) we found the probability that Haynes will finish in less than 125 days. That value is 0.89435. So the probability it takes more than 125 days is

$$P(X > 125) = 1.0 - P(X \leq 125)$$
$$= 1.0 - 0.89435 = 0.10565$$

Thus, the probability of completing the triplex in 75 days or less is 0.10565, or about 11%.

One final example: What is the probability that the triplex will take between 110 and 125 days? We see in Figure 2.12 that

$$P(110 < X < 125) = P(X \leq 125) - P(X < 110)$$

That is, the shaded area in the graph can be computed by finding the probability of completing the building in 125 days or less *minus* the probability of completing it in 110 days or less.

FIGURE 2.12

Probability That Haynes Will Complete in 110 to 125 Days

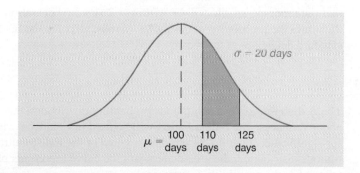

$\sigma = 20$ days

100   110   125
$\mu =$ days   days   days

PROGRAM 2.3A

Excel 2013 Output for the Normal Distribution Example

	A	B
1	X is a normal random variable	
2	with mean, μ, and standard deviation, σ.	
3	μ =	100
4	σ =	20
5	x =	75
6	P(X ≤ x) =	0.10565
7	P(X > x) =	0.89435

PROGRAM 2.3B

Function in an Excel 2013 Spreadsheet for the Normal Distribution Example

	B
6	=NORMDIST(B5,B3,B4,TRUE)
7	=1-B6

Recall that $P(X \leq 125 \text{ days})$ is equal to 0.89435. To find $P(X < 110 \text{ days})$, we follow the two steps developed earlier:

1.
$$Z = \frac{X - \mu}{\sigma} = \frac{110 - 100}{20} = \frac{10}{20}$$
$$= 0.5 \text{ standard deviations}$$

2. From Table 2.10, the area for $Z = 0.50$ is 0.69146. So the probability the triplex can be completed in less than 110 days is 0.69146. Finally,

$$P(110 \leq X \leq 125) = 0.89435 - 0.69146 = 0.20289$$

The probability that it will take between 110 and 125 days is about 20%. Programs 2.3A and 2.3B show how Excel can be used for this.

The Empirical Rule

While the probability tables for the normal distribution can provide precise probabilities, many situations require less precision. The empirical rule was derived from the normal distribution and is an easy way to remember some basic information about normal distributions. The empirical rule states that for a normal distribution

approximately 68% of the values will be within ± 1 standard deviation of the mean

approximately 95% of the values will be within ± 2 standard deviations of the mean

almost all (about 99.7%) of the values will be within ± 3 standard deviations of the mean

Figure 2.13 illustrates the empirical rule. The area from point a to point b in the first drawing represents the probability, approximately 68%, that the random variable will be within ± 1 standard deviation of the mean. The middle drawing illustrates the probability, approximately 95%, that the random variable will be within ± 2 standard deviations of the mean. The last drawing illustrates the probability, about 99.7% (almost all), that the random variable will be within ± 3 standard deviations of the mean.

2.9   The *F* Distribution

The ***F* distribution** is a continuous probability distribution that is helpful in testing hypotheses about variances. The *F* distribution will be used in Chapter 4 when regression models are tested for significance. Figure 2.14 provides a graph of the *F* distribution. As with a graph for any continuous distribution, the area underneath the curve represents probability. Note that for a large value of *F*, the probability is very small.

The *F* statistic is the ratio of two sample variances from independent normal distributions. Every *F* distribution has two sets of degrees of freedom associated with it. One of the degrees of freedom is associated with the numerator of the ratio, and the other is associated with the denominator of the ratio. The degrees of freedom are based on the sample sizes used in calculating the numerator and denominator.

FIGURE 2.13
Approximate Probabilities from the Empirical Rule

Figure 2.13 is very important, and you should comprehend the meanings of ±1, 2, and 3 standard deviation symmetrical areas.

Managers often speak of 95% and 99% confidence intervals, which roughly refer to ±2 and 3 standard deviation graphs.

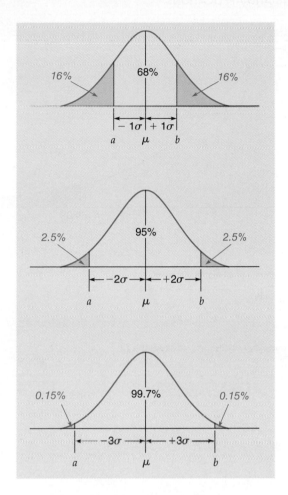

Appendix D provides values of F associated with the upper tail of the distribution for certain probabilities (denoted by α) and degrees of freedom for the numerator (df_1) and degrees of freedom for the denominator (df_2).

To find the F value that is associated with a particular probability and degrees of freedom, refer to Appendix D. The following notation will be used:

$$df_1 = \text{degrees of freedom for the numerator}$$

$$df_2 = \text{degrees of freedom for the denominator}$$

Consider the following example:

$$df_1 = 5$$
$$df_2 = 6$$
$$\alpha = 0.05$$

FIGURE 2.14
The F Distribution

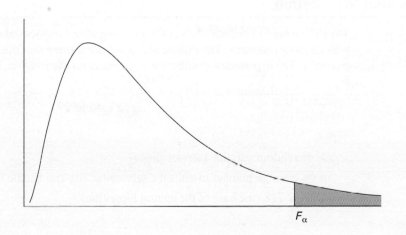

FIGURE 2.15

F Value for 0.05
Probability with 5 and
6 Degrees of Freedom

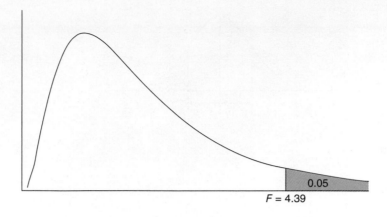

F = 4.39

PROGRAM 2.4A

Excel 2013 Output for
the *F* Distribution

	A	B	C	D
1	F Distribution with df1 and df2 degrees of freedom			
2	To find F given α			
3	df1 =	5		
4	df2 =	6		
5	α =	0.05		
6	F-value =	4.39		
7				
8	To find the probability to the right of a calculated value, *f*			
9	df1 =	5		
10	df2 =	6		
11	*f* =	4.2		
12	P(F > f) =	0.0548		

PROGRAM 2.4B

Functions in an Excel
2013 Spreadsheet for
the *F* Distribution

	B
6	=FINV(B5,B3,B4)
12	=FDIST(B11,B9,B10)

From Appendix D, we get

$$F_{\alpha,\,df1,\,df2} = F_{0.05,\,5,\,6} = 4.39$$

This means

$$P(F > 4.39) = 0.05$$

The probability is very low (only 5%) that the *F* value will exceed 4.39. There is a 95% probability that it will not exceed 4.39. This is illustrated in Figure 2.15. Appendix D also provides *F* values associated with $\alpha = 0.01$. Programs 2.4A and 2.4B illustrate Excel functions for the *F* distribution.

2.10   The Exponential Distribution

The *exponential distribution*, also called the **negative exponential distribution**, is used in dealing with queuing problems. The exponential distribution often describes the time required to service a customer. The exponential distribution is a continuous distribution. Its probability function is given by

$$f(X) = \mu e^{-\mu x} \tag{2-14}$$

where

$\qquad X = $ random variable (service times)

$\qquad \mu = $ average number of units the service facility can handle in a specific period of time

$\qquad e = 2.718$ (the base of the natural logarithm)

FIGURE 2.16
Exponential Distribution

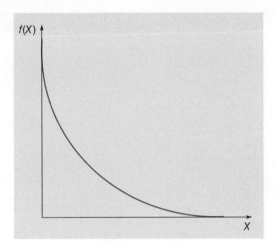

The general shape of the exponential distribution is shown in Figure 2.16. Its expected value and variance can be shown to be

$$\text{Expected value} = \frac{1}{\mu} = \text{Average service time} \qquad (2\text{-}15)$$

$$\text{Variance} = \frac{1}{\mu^2} \qquad (2\text{-}16)$$

As with any other continuous distribution, probabilities are found by determining the area under the curve. For the normal distribution, we found the area by using a table of probabilities. For the exponential distribution, the probabilities can be found using the exponent key on a calculator with the formula below. The probability that an exponentially distributed time (X) required to serve a customer is less than or equal to time t is given by the formula

$$P(X \le t) = 1 - e^{-\mu t} \qquad (2\text{-}17)$$

The time period used in describing μ determines the units for the time t. For example, if μ is the average number served per hour, the time t must be given in hours. If μ is the average number served per minute, the time t must be given in minutes.

Arnold's Muffler Example

Arnold's Muffler Shop installs new mufflers on automobiles and small trucks. The mechanic can install new mufflers at a rate of about three per hour, and this service time is exponentially distributed. What is the probability that the time to install a new muffler would be $^1/_2$ hour or less? Using Equation 2-17, we have

$$X = \text{exponentially distributed service time}$$
$$\mu = \text{average number that can be served per time period} = 3 \text{ per hour}$$
$$t = ^1/_2 \text{ hour} = 0.5 \text{ hour}$$

$$P(X \le 0.5) = 1 - e^{-3(0.5)} = 1 - e^{-1.5} = 1 - 0.2231 = 0.7769$$

Figure 2.17 shows the area under the curve from 0 to 0.5 to be 0.7769. Thus, there is about a 78% chance the time will be no more than 0.5 hour and about a 22% chance that the time will be longer than this. Similarly, we could find the probability that the service time is no more $^1/_3$ hour or $^2/_3$ hour, as follows:

$$P\left(X \le \frac{1}{3}\right) = 1 - e^{-3\left(\frac{1}{3}\right)} = 1 - e^{-1} = 1 - 0.3679 = 0.6321$$

$$P\left(X \le \frac{2}{3}\right) = 1 - e^{-3\left(\frac{2}{3}\right)} = 1 - e^{-2} = 1 - 0.1353 = 0.8647$$

FIGURE 2.17

Probability That the Mechanic Will Install a Muffler in 0.5 Hour

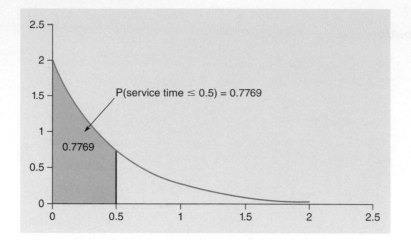

PROGRAM 2.5A

Excel 2013 Output for the Exponential Distribution

	A	B	C
1	Exponential distribution - the random variable (X) is time		
2	Average number per time period = μ =	3	per hour
3	t =	0.5000	hours
4	P(X ≤ t) =	0.7769	
5	P(X > t) =	0.2231	

Program 2.5B

Function in an Excel 2013 Spreadsheet for the Exponential Distribution

	B
4	=EXPONDIST(B3,B2,TRUE)
5	=1-B4

While Equation 2-17 provides the probability that the time (X) is less than or equal to a particular value t, the probability that the time is greater than a particular value t is found by observing that these two events are complementary. For example, to find the probability that the mechanic at Arnold's Muffler Shop would take longer than 0.5 hour, we have

$$P(X > 0.5) = 1 - P(X \le 0.5) = 1 - 0.7769 = 0.2231$$

Programs 2.5A and 2.5B illustrate how a function in Excel can find exponential probabilities.

2.11 The Poisson Distribution

An important **discrete probability distribution** is the **Poisson distribution**.[1] We examine it because of its key role in complementing the exponential distribution in queuing theory in Chapter 12. The distribution describes situations in which customers arrive independently during a certain time interval, and the number of arrivals depends on the length of the time interval. Examples are patients arriving at a health clinic, customers arriving at a bank window, passengers arriving at an airport, and telephone calls going through a central exchange.

The Poisson probability distribution is used in many queuing models to represent arrival patterns.

The formula for the Poisson distribution is

$$P(X) = \frac{\lambda^x e^{-\lambda}}{X!} \tag{2-18}$$

---

[1]This distribution, derived by Siméon Denis Poisson in 1837, is pronounced "pwah-sahn."

where

$P(X)$ = probability of exactly X arrivals or occurrences

λ = average number of arrivals per unit of time (the mean arrival rate), pronounced "lambda"

e = 2.718, the base of the natural logarithm

X = number of occurrences $(0, 1, 2, \ldots)$

The mean and variance of the Poisson distribution are equal and are computed simply as

$$\text{Expected value} = \lambda \qquad (2\text{-}19)$$

$$\text{Variance} = \lambda \qquad (2\text{-}20)$$

With the help of the table in Appendix C, the values of $e^{-\lambda}$ are easy to find. We can use these in the formula to find probabilities. For example, if $\lambda = 2$, from Appendix C we find $e^{-2} = 0.1353$. The Poisson probabilities that X is 0, 1, and 2 when $\lambda = 2$ are as follows:

$$P(X) = \frac{e^{-\lambda}\lambda^{x}}{X!}$$

$$P(0) = \frac{e^{-2}2^{0}}{0!} = \frac{(0.1353)1}{1} = 0.1353 \approx 14\%$$

$$P(1) = \frac{e^{-2}2^{1}}{1!} = \frac{e^{-2}2}{1} = \frac{0.1353(2)}{1} = 0.2706 \approx 27\%$$

$$P(2) = \frac{e^{-2}2^{2}}{2!} = \frac{e^{-2}4}{2(1)} = \frac{0.1353(4)}{2} = 0.2706 \approx 27\%$$

These probabilities, as well as others for $\lambda = 2$ and $\lambda = 4$, are shown in Figure 2.18. Notice that the chances that 9 or more customers will arrive in a particular time period are virtually nil. Programs 2.6A and 2.6B illustrate how Excel can be used to find Poisson probabilities.

It should be noted that the exponential and Poisson distributions are related. If the number of occurrences per time period follows a Poisson distribution, then the time between occurrences follows an exponential distribution. For example, if the number of phone calls arriving at a customer service center followed a Poisson distribution with a mean of 10 calls per hour, the time between each phone call would be exponentially distributed with a mean time between calls of $^{1}/_{10}$ hour (6 minutes).

FIGURE 2.18
Sample Poisson Distributions with $\lambda = 2$ and $\lambda = 4$

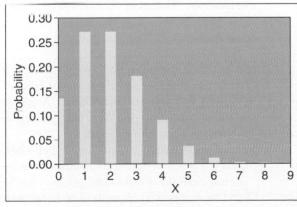

$\lambda = 2$ Distribution

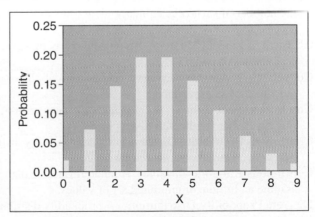

$\lambda = 4$ Distribution

PROGRAM 2.6A

Excel 2013 Output for the Poisson Distribution

	A	B	C	D	E	F	G	H
1	Poisson distribution - the random variable is the number of occurrences per time period							
2	λ =	2						
3	x	P(X)	P(X ≤ x)					
4	0	0.1353	0.1353					
5	1	0.2707	0.4060					
6	2	0.7293	0.6767					

PROGRAM 2.6B

Functions in an Excel 2013 Spreadsheet for the Poisson Distribution

	B	C
4	=POISSON(A4,$B$2,FALSE)	=POISSON(A4,$B$2,TRUE)
5	=POISSON(A5,$B$2,FALSE)	=POISSON(A5,$B$2,TRUE)
6	=1-B5	=POISSON(A6,$B$2,TRUE)

Summary

This chapter presents the fundamental concepts of probability and probability distributions. Probability values can be obtained objectively or subjectively. A single probability value must be between 0 and 1, and the sum of all probability values for all possible outcomes must be equal to 1. In addition, probability values and events can have a number of properties. These properties include mutually exclusive, collectively exhaustive, statistically independent, and statistically dependent events. Rules for computing probability values depend on these fundamental properties. It is also possible to revise probability values when new information becomes available. This can be done using Bayes' theorem.

We also covered the topics of random variables, discrete probability distributions (such as Poisson and binomial), and continuous probability distributions (such as normal, *F*, and exponential). A probability distribution is any statement of a probability function having a set of collectively exhaustive and mutually exclusive events. All probability distributions follow the basic probability rules mentioned previously.

The topics presented here will be very important in many of the chapters to come. Basic probability concepts and distributions are used for decision theory, inventory control, Markov analysis, project management, simulation, and statistical quality control.

Glossary

Bayes' Theorem   A formula that is used to revise probabilities based on new information.

Bernoulli Process   A process with two outcomes in each of a series of independent trials in which the probabilities of the outcomes do not change.

Binomial Distribution   A discrete distribution that describes the number of successes in independent trials of a Bernoulli process.

Classical or **Logical Method**   An objective way of assessing probabilities based on logic.

Collectively Exhaustive Events   A collection of all possible outcomes of an experiment.

Conditional Probability   The probability of one event occurring given that another has taken place.

Continuous Probability Distribution   A probability distribution with a continuous random variable.

Continuous Random Variable   A random variable that can assume an infinite or unlimited set of values.

Discrete Probability Distribution   A probability distribution with a discrete random variable.

Discrete Random Variable   A random variable that can only assume a finite or limited set of values.

Expected Value   The (weighted) average of a probability distribution.

***F* Distribution**   A continuous probability distribution that is the ratio of the variances of samples from two independent normal distributions.

Independent Events   The situation in which the occurrence of one event has no effect on the probability of occurrence of a second event.

Intersection   The set of all outcomes that are common to both events.

Joint Probability   The probability of events occurring together (or one after the other).

Mutually Exclusive Events   A situation in which only one event can occur on any given trial or experiment.

Negative Exponential Distribution   A continuous probability distribution that describes the time between customer arrivals in a queuing situation.

Normal Distribution   A continuous bell-shaped distribution that is a function of two parameters, the mean and standard deviation of the distribution.

Objective Approach   A method of determining probability values based on historical data or logic.

Poisson Distribution   A discrete probability distribution used in queuing theory.

Prior Probability   A probability value determined before new or additional information is obtained. It is sometimes called an a priori probability estimate.

Probability   A statement about the likelihood of an event occurring. It is expressed as a numerical value between 0 and 1, inclusive.

Probability Density Function   The mathematical function that describes a continuous probability distribution. It is represented by $f(X)$.

Probability Distribution   The set of all possible values of a random variable and their associated probabilities.

Random Variable   A variable that assigns a number to every possible outcome of an experiment.

Relative Frequency Approach   An objective way of determining probabilities based on observing frequencies over a number of trials.

Revised or **Posterior Probability**   A probability value that results from new or revised information and prior probabilities.

Standard Deviation   The square root of the variance.

Subjective Approach   A method of determining probability values based on experience or judgment.

Union   The set of all outcomes that are contained in either of these two events.

Variance   A measure of dispersion or spread of the probability distribution.

Key Equations

(2-1) $0 \le P(\text{event}) \le 1$

A basic statement of probability.

(2-2) $P(A \text{ or } B) = P(A) + P(B) - P(A \text{ and } B)$

Probability of the union of two events.

(2-3) $P(A|B) = \dfrac{P(AB)}{P(B)}$

Conditional probability.

(2-4) $P(AB) = P(A|B)P(B)$

Probability of the intersection of two events.

(2-5) $P(A|B) = \dfrac{P(B|A)P(A)}{P(B|A)P(A) + P(B|A')P(A')}$

Bayes' theorem in general form.

(2-6) $E(X) = \sum\limits_{i=1}^{n} X_i P(X_i)$

An equation that computes the expected value (mean) of a discrete probability distribution.

(2-7) $\sigma^2 = \text{Variance} = \sum\limits_{i=1}^{n} [X_i - E(X)]^2 P(X_i)$

An equation that computes the variance of a discrete probability distribution.

(2-8) $\sigma = \sqrt{\text{Variance}} = \sqrt{\sigma^2}$

An equation that computes the standard deviation from the variance.

(2-9)   Probability of r successes in n trials $= \dfrac{n!}{r!(n-r)!} p^r q^{n-r}$

A formula that computes probabilities for the binomial probability distribution.

(2-10) Expected value (mean) $= np$

The expected value of the binomial distribution.

(2-11) Variance $= np(1-p)$

The variance of the binomial distribution.

(2-12) $f(X) = \dfrac{1}{\sigma\sqrt{2\pi}} e^{\frac{-(x-\mu)^2}{2\sigma^2}}$

The density function for the normal probability distribution.

(2-13) $Z = \dfrac{X - \mu}{\sigma}$

An equation that computes the number of standard deviations, Z, the point X is from the mean μ.

(2-14) $f(X) = \mu e^{-\mu x}$

The exponential distribution.

(2-15) Expected value $= \dfrac{1}{\mu}$

The expected value of an exponential distribution

(2-16) Variance $= \dfrac{1}{\mu^2}$

The variance of an exponential distribution.

(2-17) $P(X \le t) = 1 - e^{-\mu t}$

Formula to find the probability that an exponential random variable (X) is less than or equal to time t.

(2-18) $P(X) = \dfrac{\lambda^x e^{-\lambda}}{X!}$

The Poisson distribution.

(2-19) Expected value $= \lambda$

The mean of a Poisson distribution.

(2-20) Variance $= \lambda$

The variance of a Poisson distribution.

Solved Problems

Solved Problem 2-1

In the past 30 days, Roger's Rural Roundup has sold 8, 9, 10, or 11 lottery tickets. It never sold fewer than 8 or more than 11. Assuming that the past is similar to the future, find the probabilities for the number of tickets sold if sales were 8 tickets on 10 days, 9 tickets on 12 days, 10 tickets on 6 days, and 11 tickets on 2 days.

Solution

SALES	NO. DAYS	PROBABILITY
8	10	0.333
9	12	0.400
10	6	0.200
11	2	0.067
Total	30	1.000

Solved Problem 2-2

A class contains 30 students. Ten are female (F) and U.S. citizens (U); 12 are male (M) and U.S. citizens; 6 are female and non-U.S. citizens (N); 2 are male and non-U.S. citizens.

A name is randomly selected from the class roster and it is female. What is the probability that the student is a U.S. citizen?

Solution

$$P(FU) = {}^{10}/_{30} = 0.333$$
$$P(FN) = {}^{6}/_{30} = 0.200$$
$$P(MU) = {}^{12}/_{30} = 0.400$$
$$P(MN) = {}^{2}/_{30} = 0.067$$
$$P(F) = P(FU) + P(FN) = 0.333 + 0.200 = 0.533$$
$$P(M) = P(MU) + P(MN) = 0.400 + 0.067 = 0.467$$
$$P(U) = P(FU) + P(MU) = 0.333 + 0.400 = 0.733$$
$$P(N) = P(FN) + P(MN) = 0.200 + 0.067 = 0.267$$
$$P(U|F) = \frac{P(FU)}{P(F)} = \frac{0.333}{0.533} = 0.625$$

Solved Problem 2-3

Your professor tells you that if you score an 85 or better on your midterm exam, then you have a 90% chance of getting an A for the course. You think you have only a 50% chance of scoring 85 or better. Find the probability that *both* your score is 85 or better *and* you receive an A in the course.

Solution

$$P(A \text{ and } 85) = P(A|85) \times P(85) = (0.90)(0.50)$$
$$= 45\%$$

Solved Problem 2-4

A statistics class was asked if it believed that all tests on the Monday following the football game win over their archrival should be postponed automatically. The results were as follows:

Strongly agree	40
Agree	30
Neutral	20
Disagree	10
Strongly disagree	0
	100

Transform this into a numeric score, using the following random variable scale, and find a probability distribution for the results:

Strongly agree	5
Agree	4
Neutral	3
Disagree	2
Strongly disagree	1

Solution

OUTCOME	PROBABILITY, $P(X)$
Strongly agree (5)	$0.4 = 40/100$
Agree (4)	$0.3 = 30/100$
Neutral (3)	$0.2 = 20/100$
Disagree (2)	$0.1 = 10/100$
Strongly disagree (1)	$0.0 = 0/100$
Total	$1.0 = 100/100$

Solved Problem 2-5

For Solved Problem 2-4, let X be the numeric score. Compute the expected value of X.

Solution

$$E(X) = \sum_{i=1}^{5} X_i P(X_i) = X_1 P(X_1) + X_2 P(X_2)$$
$$+ X_3 P(X_3) + X_4 P(X_4) + X_5 P(X_5)$$
$$= 5(0.4) + 4(0.3) + 3(0.2) + 2(0.1) + 1(0)$$
$$= 4.0$$

Solved Problem 2-6

Compute the variance and standard deviation for the random variable X in Solved Problems 2-4 and 2-5.

Solution

$$\text{Variance} = \sum_{i=1}^{5} (X_i - E(X))^2 P(X_i)$$
$$= (5 - 4)^2(0.4) + (4 - 4)^2(0.3) + (3 - 4)^2(0.2) + (2 - 4)^2(0.1) + (1 - 4)^2(0.0)$$
$$= (1)^2(0.4) + (0)^2(0.3) + (-1)^2(0.2) + (-2)^2(0.1) + (-3)^2(0.0)$$
$$= 0.4 + 0.0 + 0.2 + 0.4 + 0.0 = 1.0$$

The standard deviation is
$$\sigma = \sqrt{\text{Variance}} = \sqrt{1} = 1$$

Solved Problem 2-7

A candidate for public office has claimed that 60% of voters will vote for her. If 5 registered voters were sampled, what is the probability that exactly 3 would say they favor this candidate?

Solution

We use the binomial distribution with $n = 5$, $p = 0.6$, and $r = 3$:

$$P(\text{exactly 3 successes in 5 trials}) = \frac{n!}{r!(n-r)!} p^r q^{n-r} = \frac{5!}{3!(5-3)!}(0.6)^3(0.4)^{5-3} = 0.3456$$

Solved Problem 2-8

The length of the rods coming out of our new cutting machine can be said to approximate a normal distribution with a mean of 10 inches and a standard deviation of 0.2 inch. Find the probability that a rod selected randomly will have a length

(a) of less than 10.0 inches
(b) between 10.0 and 10.4 inches
(c) between 10.0 and 10.1 inches
(d) between 10.1 and 10.4 inches
(e) between 9.6 and 9.9 inches
(f) between 9.9 and 10.4 inches
(g) between 9.886 and 10.406 inches

Solution

First, compute the standard normal distribution, the Z value:

$$Z = \frac{X - \mu}{\sigma}$$

Next, find the area under the curve for the given Z value by using a standard normal distribution table.

(a) $P(X < 10.0) = 0.50000$
(b) $P(10.0 < X < 10.4) = 0.97725 - 0.50000 = 0.47725$
(c) $P(10.0 < X < 10.1) = 0.69146 - 0.50000 = 0.19146$
(d) $P(10.1 < X < 10.4) = 0.97725 - 0.69146 = 0.28579$
(e) $P(9.6 < X < 9.9) = 0.97725 - 0.69146 = 0.28579$
(f) $P(9.9 < X < 10.4) = 0.19146 + 0.47725 = 0.66871$
(g) $P(9.886 < X < 10.406) = 0.47882 + 0.21566 = 0.69448$

Self-Test

- Before taking the self-test, refer to the learning objectives at the beginning of the chapter, the notes in the margins, and the glossary at the end of the chapter.
- Use the key at the back of the book to correct your answers.
- Restudy pages that correspond to any questions that you answered incorrectly or material you feel uncertain about.

1. If only one event may occur on any one trial, then the events are said to be
   a. independent.
   b. exhaustive.
   c. mutually exclusive.
   d. continuous.
2. New probabilities that have been found using Bayes' theorem are called
   a. prior probabilities.
   b. posterior probabilities.
   c. Bayesian probabilities.
   d. joint probabilities.
3. A measure of central tendency is
   a. expected value.
   b. variance.
   c. standard deviation.
   d. all of the above.

4. To compute the variance, of a discrete random variable you need to know the
   a. variable's possible values.
   b. expected value of the variable.
   c. probability of each possible value of the variable.
   d. all of the above.
5. The square root of the variance is the
   a. expected value.
   b. standard deviation.
   c. area under the normal curve.
   d. all of the above.
6. Which of the following is an example of a discrete distribution?
   a. the normal distribution
   b. the exponential distribution
   c. the Poisson distribution
   d. the Z distribution

7. The total area under the curve for any continuous distribution must equal
   a. 1.
   b. 0.
   c. 0.5.
   d. none of the above.
8. Probabilities for all the possible values of a discrete random variable
   a. may be greater than 1.
   b. may be negative on some occasions.
   c. must sum to 1.
   d. are represented by area underneath the curve.
9. In a standard normal distribution, the mean is equal to
   a. 1.
   b. 0.
   c. the variance.
   d. the standard deviation.
10. The probability of two or more independent events occurring is the
   a. marginal probability.
   b. simple probability.
   c. conditional probability.
   d. joint probability.
   e. all of the above.
11. In the normal distribution, 95.45% of the population lies within
   a. 1 standard deviation of the mean.
   b. 2 standard deviations of the mean.
   c. 3 standard deviations of the mean.
   d. 4 standard deviations of the mean.
12. If a normal distribution has a mean of 200 and a standard deviation of 10, 99.7% of the population falls within what range of values?
   a. 170–230
   b. 180–220
   c. 190–210
   d. 175–225
   e. 170–220
13. If two events are mutually exclusive, then the probability of the intersection of these two events will equal
   a. 0.
   b. 0.5.
   c. 1.0.
   d. cannot be determined without more information.
14. If $P(A) = 0.4$ and $P(B) = 0.5$ and $P(A \text{ and } B) = 0.2$, then $P(B|A) =$
   a. 0.80.
   b. 0.50.
   c. 0.10.
   d. 0.40.
   e. none of the above.
15. If $P(A) = 0.4$ and $P(B) = 0.5$ and $P(A \text{ and } B) = 0.2$, then $P(A \text{ or } B) =$
   a. 0.7.
   b. 0.9.
   c. 1.1.
   d. 0.2.
   e. none of the above.

Discussion Questions and Problems

Discussion Questions

2-1 What are the two basic laws of probability?

2-2 What is the meaning of mutually exclusive events? What is meant by collectively exhaustive? Give an example of each.

2-3 Describe the various approaches used in determining probability values.

2-4 Why is the probability of the intersection of two events subtracted in the sum of the probability of two events?

2-5 Describe what it means for two events to be independent.

2-6 What is Bayes' theorem, and when can it be used?

2-7 Describe the characteristics of a Bernoulli process. How is a Bernoulli process associated with the binomial distribution?

2-8 What is a random variable? What are the various types of random variables?

2-9 What is the difference between a discrete probability distribution and a continuous probability distribution? Give your own example of each.

2-10 What is the expected value, and what does it measure? How is it computed for a discrete probability distribution?

2-11 What is the variance, and what does it measure? How is it computed for a discrete probability distribution?

2-12 Name three business processes that can be described by the normal distribution.

2-13 A card is drawn from a standard deck of playing cards. For each of the following pairs of events, indicate if the events are mutually exclusive and indicate if the events are exhaustive.
   (a) Draw a spade and draw a club.
   (b) Draw a face card and draw a number card.
   (c) Draw an ace and draw a three.

(d) Draw a red card and draw a black card.

(e) Draw a five and draw a diamond.

(f) Draw a red card and draw a diamond.

Problems

• 2-14   A student taking Management Science 301 at East Haven University will receive one of the five possible grades for the course: A, B, C, D, or F. The distribution of grades over the past 2 years is as follows:

GRADE	NUMBER OF STUDENTS
A	80
B	75
C	90
D	30
F	25
	Total 300

If this past distribution is a good indicator of future grades, what is the probability of a student receiving a C in the course?

• 2-15   A silver dollar is flipped twice. Calculate the probability of each of the following occurring:

(a) a head on the first flip

(b) a tail on the second flip given that the first toss was a head

(c) two tails

(d) a tail on the first and a head on the second

(e) a tail on the first and a head on the second or a head on the first and a tail on the second

(f) at least one head on the two flips

• 2-16   An urn contains 8 red chips, 10 green chips, and 2 white chips. A chip is drawn and replaced, and then a second chip drawn. What is the probability of

(a) a white chip on the first draw?

(b) a white chip on the first draw and a red on the second?

(c) two green chips being drawn?

(d) a red chip on the second, given that a white chip was drawn on the first?

• 2-17   Evertight, a leading manufacturer of quality nails, produces 1-, 2-, 3-, 4-, and 5-inch nails for various uses. In the production process, if there is an overrun or the nails are slightly defective, they are placed in a common bin. Yesterday, 651 of the 1-inch nails, 243 of the 2-inch nails, 41 of the 3-inch nails, 451 of the 4-inch nails, and 333 of the 5-inch nails were placed in the bin.

(a) What is the probability of reaching into the bin and getting a 4-inch nail?

(b) What is the probability of getting a 5-inch nail?

(c) If a particular application requires a nail that is 3 inches or shorter, what is the probability of getting a nail that will satisfy the requirements of the application?

⁞ 2-18   Last year, at Northern Manufacturing Company, 200 people had colds during the year. One hundred fifty-five people who did no exercising had colds, and the remainder of the people with colds were involved in a weekly exercise program. Half of the 1,000 employees were involved in some type of exercise.

(a) What is the probability that an employee will have a cold next year?

(b) Given that an employee is involved in an exercise program, what is the probability that he or she will get a cold next year?

(c) What is the probability that an employee who is not involved in an exercise program will get a cold next year?

(d) Are exercising and getting a cold independent events? Explain your answer.

⁞ 2-19   The Springfield Kings, a professional basketball team, has won 12 of its last 20 games and is expected to continue winning at the same percentage rate. The team's ticket manager is anxious to attract a large crowd to tomorrow's game but believes that depends on how well the Kings perform tonight against the Galveston Comets. He assesses the probability of drawing a large crowd to be 0.90 should the team win tonight. What is the probability that the team wins tonight and that there will be a large crowd at tomorrow's game?

⁞ 2-20   David Mashley teaches two undergraduate statistics courses at Kansas College. The class for Statistics 201 consists of 7 sophomores and 3 juniors. The more advanced course, Statistics 301, has 2 sophomores and 8 juniors enrolled. As an example of a business sampling technique, Professor Mashley randomly selects, from the stack of Statistics 201 registration cards, the class card of one student and then places that card back in the stack. If that student was a sophomore, Mashley draws another card from the Statistics 201 stack; if not, he randomly draws a card from the Statistics 301 group. Are these two draws independent events? What is the probability of

(a) a junior's name on the first draw?

(b) a junior's name on the second draw, given that a sophomore's name was drawn first?

(c) a junior's name on the second draw, given that a junior's name was drawn first?

(d) a sophomore's name on both draws?

(e) a junior's name on both draws?

(f) one sophomore's name and one junior's name on the two draws, regardless of order drawn?

Note: ℺ means the problem may be solved with QM for Windows; ✘ means the problem may be solved with Excel QM; and ℺ means the problem may be solved with QM for Windows and/or Excel QM.

: 2-21 The oasis outpost of Abu Ilan, in the heart of the Negev desert, has a population of 20 Bedouin tribesmen and 20 Farima tribesmen. El Kamin, a nearby oasis, has a population of 32 Bedouins and 8 Farima. A lost Israeli soldier, accidentally separated from his army unit, is wandering through the desert and arrives at the edge of one of the oases. The soldier has no idea which oasis he has found, but the first person he spots at a distance is a Bedouin. What is the probability that he wandered into Abu Ilan? What is the probability that he is in El Kamin?

: 2-22 The lost Israeli soldier mentioned in Problem 2-21 decides to rest for a few minutes before entering the desert oasis he has just found. Closing his eyes, he dozes off for 15 minutes, wakes, and walks toward the center of the oasis. The first person he spots this time he again recognizes as a Bedouin. What is the posterior probability that he is in El Kamin?

: 2-23 Ace Machine Works estimates that the probability its lathe tool is properly adjusted is 0.8. When the lathe is properly adjusted, there is a 0.9 probability that the parts produced pass inspection. If the lathe is out of adjustment, however, the probability of a good part being produced is only 0.2. A part randomly chosen is inspected and found to be acceptable. At this point, what is the posterior probability that the lathe tool is properly adjusted?

: 2-24 The Boston South Fifth Street Softball League consists of three teams: Mama's Boys, team 1; the Killers, team 2; and the Machos, team 3. Each team plays the other teams just once during the season. The win–loss record for the past 5 years is as follows:

WINNER	(1)	(2)	(3)
Mama's Boys (1)	X	3	4
The Killers (2)	2	X	1
The Machos (3)	1	4	X

Each row represents the number of wins over the past 5 years. Mama's Boys beat the Killers 3 times, beat the Machos 4 times, and so on.

(a) What is the probability that the Killers will win every game next year?

(b) What is the probability that the Machos will win at least one game next year?

(c) What is the probability that Mama's Boys will win exactly one game next year?

(d) What is the probability that the Killers will win fewer than two games next year?

: 2-25 The schedule for the Killers next year is as follows (refer to Problem 2-24):

Game 1: The Machos

Game 2: Mama's Boys

(a) What is the probability that the Killers will win their first game?

(b) What is the probability that the Killers will win their last game?

(c) What is the probability that the Killers will break even—win exactly one game?

(d) What is the probability that the Killers will win every game?

(e) What is the probability that the Killers will lose every game?

(f) Would you want to be the coach of the Killers?

: 2-26 The Northside Rifle team has two markspersons, Dick and Sally. Dick hits a bull's-eye 90% of the time, and Sally hits a bull's-eye 95% of the time.

(a) What is the probability that either Dick or Sally or both will hit the bull's-eye if each takes one shot?

(b) What is the probability that Dick and Sally will both hit the bull's-eye?

(c) Did you make any assumptions in answering the preceding questions? If you answered yes, do you think that you are justified in making the assumption(s)?

: 2-27 In a sample of 1,000 representing a survey from the entire population, 650 people were from Laketown, and the rest of the people were from River City. Out of the sample, 19 people had some form of cancer. Thirteen of these people were from Laketown.

(a) Are the events of living in Laketown and having some sort of cancer independent?

(b) Which city would you prefer to live in, assuming that your main objective was to avoid having cancer?

: 2-28 Compute the probability of "loaded die, given that a 3 was rolled," as shown in the example in Section 2.3, this time using the general form of Bayes' theorem from Equation 2-5.

• 2-29 Which of the following are probability distributions? Why?

(a)

RANDOM VARIABLE X	PROBABILITY
2	0.1
−1	0.2
0	0.3
1	0.25
2	0.15

(b)

RANDOM VARIABLE Y	PROBABILITY
1	1.1
1.5	0.2
2	0.3
2.5	0.25
3	−1.25

(c)

RANDOM VARIABLE Z	PROBABILITY
1	0.1
2	0.2
3	0.3
4	0.4
5	0.0

• 2-30 Harrington Health Food stocks 5 loaves of Neutro-Bread. The probability distribution for the sales of Neutro-Bread is listed in the following table. How many loaves will Harrington sell on average?

NUMBER OF LOAVES SOLD	PROBABILITY
0	0.05
1	0.15
2	0.20
3	0.25
4	0.20
5	0.15

• 2-31 What are the expected value and variance of the following probability distribution?

RANDOM VARIABLE X	PROBABILITY
1	0.05
2	0.05
3	0.10
4	0.10
5	0.15
6	0.15
7	0.25
8	0.15

X:2-32 There are 10 questions on a true–false test. A student feels unprepared for this test and randomly guesses the answer for each of these.

(a) What is the probability that the student gets exactly 7 correct?

(b) What is the probability that the student gets exactly 8 correct?

(c) What is the probability that the student gets exactly 9 correct?

(d) What is the probability that the student gets exactly 10 correct?

(e) What is the probability that the student gets more than 6 correct?

X:2-33 Gary Schwartz is the top salesman for his company. Records indicate that he makes a sale on 70% of his sales calls. If he calls on four potential clients, what is the probability that he makes exactly 3 sales? What is the probability that he makes exactly 4 sales?

X:2-34 If 10% of all disk drives produced on an assembly line are defective, what is the probability that there will be exactly one defect in a random sample of 5 of these? What is the probability that there will be no defects in a random sample of 5?

X:2-35 Trowbridge Manufacturing produces cases for personal computers and other electronic equipment. The quality control inspector for this company believes that a particular process is out of control. Normally, only 5% of all cases are deemed defective due to discolorations. If 6 such cases are sampled, what is the probability that there will be 0 defective cases if the process is operating correctly? What is the probability that there will be exactly 1 defective case?

X:2-36 Refer to the Trowbridge Manufacturing example in Problem 2-35. The quality control inspection procedure is to select 6 items, and if there are 0 or 1 defective cases in the group of 6, the process is said to be in control. If the number of defects is more than 1, the process is out of control. Suppose that the true proportion of defective items is 0.15. What is the probability that there will be 0 or 1 defects in a sample of 6 if the true proportion of defects is 0.15?

X:2-37 An industrial oven used to cure sand cores for a factory manufacturing engine blocks for small cars is able to maintain fairly constant temperatures. The temperature range of the oven follows a normal distribution with a mean of 450°F and a standard deviation of 25°F. Leslie Larsen, president of the factory, is concerned about the large number of defective cores that have been produced in the past several months. If the oven gets hotter than 475°F, the core is defective. What is the probability that the oven will cause a core to be defective? What is the probability that the temperature of the oven will range from 460° to 470°F?

X:2-38 Steve Goodman, production foreman for the Florida Gold Fruit Company, estimates that the average sale of oranges is 4,700 and the standard deviation is 500 oranges. Sales follow a normal distribution.

(a) What is the probability that sales will be greater than 5,500 oranges?

(b) What is the probability that sales will be greater than 4,500 oranges?

(c) What is the probability that sales will be less than 4,900 oranges?

(d) What is the probability that sales will be less than 4,300 oranges?

X:2-39 Susan Williams has been the production manager of Medical Suppliers, Inc., for the past 17 years. Medical Suppliers, Inc., is a producer of bandages and arm slings. During the past 5 years, the demand for No-Stick bandages has been fairly constant. On the average, sales have been about 87,000 packages of No-Stick. Susan has reason to believe that the distribution of No-Stick follows a normal curve, with a standard deviation of 4,000 packages. What is the probability that sales will be less than 81,000 packages?

2-40 Armstrong Faber produces a standard number-two pencil called Ultra-Lite. Since Chuck Armstrong started Armstrong Faber, sales have grown steadily. With the increase in the price of wood products, however, Chuck has been forced to increase the price of the Ultra-Lite pencils. As a result, the demand for Ultra-Lite has been fairly stable over the past 6 years. On the average, Armstrong Faber has sold 457,000 pencils each year. Furthermore, 90% of the time sales have been between 454,000 and 460,000 pencils. It is expected that the sales follow a normal distribution with a mean of 457,000 pencils. Estimate the standard deviation of this distribution. (*Hint:* Work backward from the normal table to find Z. Then apply Equation 2-13.)

2-41 The time to complete a construction project is normally distributed with a mean of 60 weeks and a standard deviation of 4 weeks.

(a) What is the probability the project will be finished in 62 weeks or less?

(b) What is the probability the project will be finished in 66 weeks or less?

(c) What is the probability the project will take longer than 65 weeks?

2-42 A new integrated computer system is to be installed worldwide for a major corporation. Bids on this project are being solicited, and the contract will be awarded to one of the bidders. As a part of the proposal for this project, bidders must specify how long the project will take. There will be a significant penalty for finishing late. One potential contractor determines that the average time to complete a project of this type is 40 weeks with a standard deviation of 5 weeks. The time required to complete this project is assumed to be normally distributed.

(a) If the due date of this project is set at 40 weeks, what is the probability that the contractor will have to pay a penalty (i.e., the project will not be finished on schedule)?

(b) If the due date of this project is set at 43 weeks, what is the probability that the contractor will have to pay a penalty (i.e., the project will not be finished on schedule)?

(c) If the bidder wishes to set the due date in the proposal so that there is only a 5% chance of being late (and consequently only a 5% chance of having to pay a penalty), what due date should be set?

2-43 Patients arrive at the emergency room of Costa Valley Hospital at an average of 5 per day. The demand for emergency room treatment at Costa Valley follows a Poisson distribution.

(a) Using Appendix C, compute the probability of exactly 0, 1, 2, 3, 4, and 5 arrivals per day.

(b) What is the sum of these probabilities, and why is the number less than 1?

2-44 Using the data in Problem 2-43, determine the probability of more than 3 visits for emergency room service on any given day.

2-45 Cars arrive at Carla's Muffler shop for repair work at an average of 3 per hour, following an exponential distribution.

(a) What is the expected time between arrivals?

(b) What is the variance of the time between arrivals?

2-46 A particular test for the presence of steroids is to be used after a professional track meet. If steroids are present, the test will accurately indicate this 95% of the time. However, if steroids are not present, the test will indicate this 90% of the time (so it is wrong 10% of the time and predicts the presence of steroids). Based on past data, it is believed that 2% of the athletes do use steroids. This test is administered to one athlete, and the test is positive for steroids. What is the probability that this person actually used steroids?

2-47 Market Researchers, Inc., has been hired to perform a study to determine if the market for a new product will be good or poor. In similar studies performed in the past, whenever the market actually was good, the market research study indicated that it would be good 85% of the time. On the other hand, whenever the market actually was poor, the market study incorrectly predicted it would be good 20% of the time. Before the study is performed, it is believed there is a 70% chance the market will be good. When Market Researchers, Inc., performs the study for this product, the results predict the market will be good. Given the results of this study, what is the probability that the market actually will be good?

2-48 Policy Pollsters is a market research firm specializing in political polls. Records indicate in past elections, when a candidate was elected, Policy Pollsters had accurately predicted this 80% of the time and they were wrong 20% of the time. Records also show, for losing candidates, Policy Pollsters accurately predicted they would lose 90% of the time and they were only wrong 10% of the time. Before the poll is taken, there is a 50% chance of winning the election. If Policy Pollsters predicts a candidate will win the election, what is the probability that the candidate will actually win? If Policy Pollsters predicts that a candidate will lose the election, what is the probability that the candidate will actually lose?

2-49 Burger City is a large chain of fast-food restaurants specializing in gourmet hamburgers. A mathematical model is now used to predict the success of new restaurants based on location and demographic information for that area. In the past, 70% of all restaurants that were opened were successful. The mathematical model has been tested in the existing restaurants to determine how effective it is. For the restaurants that were successful, 90% of the time the model predicted they would be, while 10% of the time the model predicted a failure. For the restaurants that were not successful, when the mathematical model was applied, 20% of the time it incorrectly predicted a successful restaurant while 80% of the time it was accurate and predicted an unsuccessful restaurant. If the model is used on a new location and predicts the restaurant will be successful, what is the probability that it actually is successful?

2-50 A mortgage lender attempted to increase its business by marketing its subprime mortgage. This mortgage is designed for people with a less-than-perfect credit rating, and the interest rate is higher to offset the extra risk. In the past year, 20% of these mortgages resulted in foreclosure as customers defaulted on their loans. A new screening system has been developed to determine whether to approve customers for the subprime loans. When the system is applied to a credit application, the system will classify the application as "Approve for loan" or "Reject for loan." When this new system was applied to recent customers who had defaulted on their loans, 90% of these customers were classified as "Reject." When this same system was applied to recent loan customers who had not defaulted on their loan payments, 70% of these customers were classified as "Approve for loan."

(a) If a customer did not default on a loan, what is the probability that the rating system would have classified the applicant in the reject category?

(b) If the rating system had classified the applicant in the reject category, what is the probability that the customer would not default on a loan?

2-51 Use the F table in Appendix D to find the value of F for the upper 5% of the F distribution with

(a) $df_1 = 5, df_2 = 10$
(b) $df_1 = 8, df_2 = 7$
(c) $df_1 = 3, df_2 = 5$
(d) $df_1 = 10, df_2 = 4$

2-52 Use the F table in Appendix D to find the value of F for the upper 1% of the F distribution with

(a) $df_1 = 15, df_2 = 6$
(b) $df_1 = 12, df_2 = 8$
(c) $df_1 = 3, df_2 = 5$
(d) $df_1 = 9, df_2 = 7$

2-53 For each of the following F values, determine whether the probability indicated is greater than or less than 5%:

(a) $P(F_{3,4} > 6.8)$
(b) $P(F_{7,3} > 3.6)$
(c) $P(F_{20,20} > 2.6)$
(d) $P(F_{7,5} > 5.1)$
(e) $P(F_{7,5} < 5.1)$

2-54 For each of the following F values, determine whether the probability indicated is greater than or less than 1%:

(a) $P(F_{5,4} > 14)$
(b) $P(F_{6,3} > 30)$
(c) $P(F_{10,12} > 4.2)$
(d) $P(F_{2,3} > 35)$
(e) $P(F_{2,3} < 35)$

2-55 Nite Time Inn has a toll-free telephone number so that customers can call at any time to make a reservation. A typical call takes about 4 minutes to complete, and the time required follows an exponential distribution. Find the probability that a call takes

(a) 3 minutes or less
(b) 4 minutes or less
(c) 5 minutes or less
(d) longer than 5 minutes

2-56 During normal business hours on the east coast, calls to the toll-free reservation number of the Nite Time Inn arrive at a rate of 5 per minute. It has been determined that the number of calls per minute can be described by the Poisson distribution. Find the probability that in the next minute, the number of calls arriving will be

(a) exactly 5
(b) exactly 4
(c) exactly 3
(d) exactly 6
(e) less than 2

2-57 In the Arnold's Muffler example for the exponential distribution in this chapter, the average rate of service was given as 3 per hour, and the times were expressed in hours. Convert the average service rate to the number per minute and convert the times to minutes. Find the probabilities that the service times will be less than $1/2$ hour, $1/3$ hour, and $2/3$ hour. Compare these probabilities to the probabilities found in the example.

Internet Homework Problems

See our Internet home page, at **www.pearsonhighered.com/render**, for additional homework problems, Problems 2-58 to 2-65.

Case Study

WTVX

WTVX, Channel 6, is located in Eugene, Oregon, home of the University of Oregon's football team. The station was owned and operated by George Wilcox, a former Duck (University of Oregon football player). Although there were other television stations in Eugene, WTVX was the only station that had a weatherperson who was a member of the American Meteorological Society (AMS). Every night, Joe Hummel would be introduced as the only weatherperson in Eugene who was a member of the AMS. This was George's idea, and he believed that this gave his station the mark of quality and helped with market share.

In addition to being a member of AMS, Joe was also the most popular person on any of the local news programs. Joe was always trying to find innovative ways to make the weather interesting, and this was especially difficult during the winter months when the weather seemed to remain the same over long periods of time. Joe's forecast for next month, for example, was that there would be a 70% chance of rain *every* day, and that what happens on one day (rain or shine) was not in any way dependent on what happened the day before.

One of Joe's most popular features of the weather report was to invite questions during the actual broadcast. Questions would be phoned in, and they were answered on the spot by Joe. Once a 10-year-old boy asked what caused fog, and Joe did an excellent job of describing some of the various causes.

Occasionally, Joe would make a mistake. For example, a high school senior asked Joe what the chances were of getting 15 days of rain in the next month (30 days). Joe made a quick calculation: $(70\%) \times (15 \text{ days}/30 \text{ days}) = (70\%)(1/2) = 35\%$. Joe quickly found out what it was like being wrong in a university town. He had over 50 phone calls from scientists, mathematicians, and other university professors, telling him that he had made a big mistake in computing the chances of getting 15 days of rain during the next 30 days. Although Joe didn't understand all of the formulas the professors mentioned, he was determined to find the correct answer and make a correction during a future broadcast.

Discussion Questions

1. What are the chances of getting 15 days of rain during the next 30 days?
2. What do you think about Joe's assumptions concerning the weather for the next 30 days?

Bibliography

Berenson, Mark, David Levine, and Timothy Krehbiel. *Basic Business Statistics*, 10th ed. Upper Saddle River, NJ: Prentice Hall, 2006.

Campbell, S. *Flaws and Fallacies in Statistical Thinking*. Upper Saddle River, NJ: Prentice Hall, 1974.

Feller, W. *An Introduction to Probability Theory and Its Applications*, Vols. 1 and 2. New York: John Wiley & Sons, Inc., 1957 and 1968.

Groebner, David, Patrick Shannon, Phillip Fry, and Kent Smith. *Business Statistics*, 8th ed. Upper Saddle River, NJ: Prentice Hall, 2011.

Hanke, J. E., A. G. Reitsch, and D. W. Wichern. *Business Forecasting*, 9th ed. Upper Saddle River, NJ: Prentice Hall, 2008.

Huff, D. *How to Lie with Statistics*. New York: W. W. Norton & Company, Inc., 1954.

Newbold, Paul, William Carlson, and Betty Thorne. *Statistics for Business and Economics*, 6th ed. Upper Saddle River, NJ: Prentice Hall, 2007.

Appendix 2.1: Derivation of Bayes' Theorem

We know that the following formulas are correct:

$$P(A \mid B) = \frac{P(AB)}{P(B)} \tag{1}$$

$$P(B \mid A) = \frac{P(AB)}{P(A)}$$

[which can be rewritten as $P(AB) = P(B|A)P(A)$] and (2)

$$P(B|A') = \frac{P(A'B)}{P(A')}$$

[which can be rewritten as $P(A'B) = P(B|A')P(A')$]. (3)

Furthermore, by definition, we know that

$$P(B) = P(AB) + P(A'B)$$
$$= P(B|A)P(A) + P(B|A')P(A') \qquad (4)$$

from (2)   from (3)

Substituting Equations 2 and 4 into Equation 1, we have

$$P(A|B) = \frac{P(AB)}{P(B)} \qquad \text{from (2)}$$

$$= \frac{P(B|A)P(A)}{P(B|A)P(A) + P(B|A')P(A')} \qquad (5)$$

from (4)

This is the general form of Bayes' theorem, shown as Equation 2-5 in this chapter.

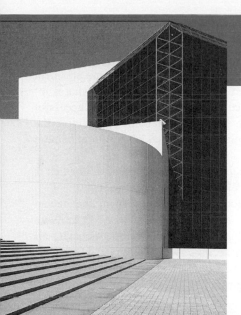

Decision Analysis

LEARNING OBJECTIVES

After completing this chapter, students will be able to:

1. List the steps of the decision-making process.
2. Describe the types of decision-making environments.
3. Make decisions under uncertainty.
4. Use probability values to make decisions under risk.
5. Develop accurate and useful decision trees.
6. Revise probability estimates using Bayesian analysis.
7. Use computers to solve basic decision making problems.
8. Understand the importance and use of utility theory in decision making.

CHAPTER OUTLINE

Summary • Glossary • Key Equations • Solved Problems • Self-Test • Discussion Questions and Problems • Internet Homework Problems • Case Study: Starting Right Corporation • Case Study: Blake Electronics • Internet Case Studies Bibliography

3.1 Introduction

Decision theory is an analytic and systematic way to tackle problems.

A good decision is based on logic.

To a great extent, the successes or failures that a person experiences in life depend on the decisions that he or she makes. The person who managed the ill-fated space shuttle *Challenger* is no longer working for NASA. The person who designed the top-selling Mustang became president of Ford. Why and how did these people make their respective decisions? In general, what is involved in making good decisions? One decision may make the difference between a successful career and an unsuccessful one. **Decision theory** is an analytic and systematic approach to the study of decision making. In this chapter, we present the mathematical models useful in helping managers make the best possible decisions.

What makes the difference between good and bad decisions? A good decision is one that is based on logic, considers all available data and possible alternatives, and applies the quantitative approach we are about to describe. Occasionally, a good decision results in an unexpected or unfavorable outcome. But if it is made properly, it is *still* a good decision. A bad decision is one that is not based on logic, does not use all available information, does not consider all alternatives, and does not employ appropriate quantitative techniques. If you make a bad decision but are lucky and a favorable outcome occurs, you have *still* made a bad decision. Although occasionally good decisions yield bad results, in the long run, using decision theory will result in successful outcomes.

3.2 The Six Steps in Decision Making

Whether you are deciding about getting a haircut today, building a multimillion-dollar plant, or buying a new camera, the steps in making a good decision are basically the same:

Six Steps in Decision Making

1. Clearly define the problem at hand.
2. List the possible alternatives.
3. Identify the possible outcomes or states of nature.
4. List the payoff (typically profit) of each combination of alternatives and outcomes.
5. Select one of the mathematical decision theory models.
6. Apply the model and make your decision.

We use the Thompson Lumber Company case as an example to illustrate these decision theory steps. John Thompson is the founder and president of Thompson Lumber Company, a profitable firm located in Portland, Oregon.

The first step is to define the problem.

Step 1. The problem that John Thompson identifies is whether to expand his product line by manufacturing and marketing a new product, backyard storage sheds.

Thompson's second step is to generate the alternatives that are available to him. In decision theory, an **alternative** is defined as a course of action or a strategy that the decision maker can choose.

The second step is to list alternatives.

Step 2. John decides that his alternatives are to construct (1) a large new plant to manufacture the storage sheds, (2) a small plant, or (3) no plant at all (i.e., he has the option of not developing the new product line).

One of the biggest mistakes that decision makers make is to leave out some important alternatives. Although a particular alternative may seem to be inappropriate or of little value, it might turn out to be the best choice.

The next step involves identifying the possible outcomes of the various alternatives. A common mistake is to forget about some of the possible outcomes. Optimistic decision makers tend to ignore bad outcomes, whereas pessimistic managers may discount a favorable outcome. If you don't consider all possibilities, you will not be making a logical decision, and the results may be undesirable. If you do not think the worst can happen, you may design another Edsel automobile. In decision theory, those outcomes over which the decision maker has little or no control are called **states of nature**.

TABLE 3.1

Decision Table with Conditional Values for Thompson Lumber

ALTERNATIVE	STATE OF NATURE	
	FAVORABLE MARKET ($)	UNFAVORABLE MARKET ($)
Construct a large plant	200,000	−180,000
Construct a small plant	100,000	−20,000
Do nothing	0	0

Note: It is important to include all alternatives, including "do nothing."

The third step is to identify possible outcomes.

Step 3. Thompson determines that there are only two possible outcomes: the market for the storage sheds could be favorable, meaning that there is a high demand for the product, or it could be unfavorable, meaning that there is a low demand for the sheds.

Once the alternatives and states of nature have been identified, the next step is to express the payoff resulting from each possible combination of alternatives and outcomes. In decision theory, we call such payoffs or profits **conditional values**. Not every decision, of course, can be based on money alone—any appropriate means of measuring benefit is acceptable.

The fourth step is to list payoffs.

During the fourth step, the decision maker can construct decision or payoff tables.

Step 4. Because Thompson wants to maximize his profits, he can use *profit* to evaluate each consequence.

John Thompson has already evaluated the potential profits associated with the various outcomes. With a favorable market, he thinks a large facility would result in a net profit of $200,000 to his firm. This $200,000 is a *conditional value* because Thompson's receiving the money is conditional upon both his building a large factory and having a good market. The conditional value if the market is unfavorable would be a $180,000 net loss. A small plant would result in a net profit of $100,000 in a favorable market, but a net loss of $20,000 would occur if the market was unfavorable. Finally, doing nothing would result in $0 profit in either market. The easiest way to present these values is by constructing a **decision table**, sometimes called a **payoff table**. A decision table for Thompson's conditional values is shown in Table 3.1. All of the alternatives are listed down the left side of the table, and all of the possible outcomes or states of nature are listed across the top. The body of the table contains the actual payoffs.

The last two steps are to select and apply the decision theory model.

Steps 5 and 6. The last two steps are to select a decision theory model and apply it to the data to help make the decision. Selecting the model depends on the environment in which you're operating and the amount of risk and uncertainty involved.

3.3 Types of Decision-Making Environments

The types of decisions people make depend on how much knowledge or information they have about the situation. There are three decision-making environments:

- Decision making under certainty
- Decision making under uncertainty
- Decision making under risk

In the environment of **decision making under certainty**, decision makers know with certainty the consequence of every alternative or decision choice. Naturally, they will choose the alternative that will maximize their well-being or will result in the best outcome. For example, let's say that you have $1,000 to invest for a 1-year period. One alternative is to open a savings account paying 4% interest and another is to invest in a government Treasury bond paying 6% interest. If both investments are secure and guaranteed, there is a certainty that the Treasury bond will pay a higher return. The return after 1 year will be $60 in interest.

In **decision making under uncertainty**, there are several possible outcomes for each alternative, and the decision maker does not know the probabilities of the various outcomes. As

Probabilities are not known.

an example, the probability that a Democrat will be president of the United States 25 years from now is not known. Sometimes it is impossible to assess the probability of success of a new undertaking or product. The criteria for decision making under uncertainty are explained in Section 3.4.

Probabilities are known.

In **decision making under risk**, there are several possible outcomes for each alternative, and the decision maker knows the probability of occurrence of each outcome. We know, for example, that when playing cards using a standard deck, the probability of being dealt a club is 0.25. The probability of rolling a 5 on a die is 1/6. In decision making under risk, the decision maker usually attempts to maximize his or her expected well-being. Decision theory models for business problems in this environment typically employ two equivalent criteria: maximization of expected monetary value and minimization of expected opportunity loss.

In the Thompson Lumber example, John Thompson is faced with decision making under uncertainty. If either a large plant or a small plant is constructed, the actual payoff depends on the state of nature, and probabilities are not known. If probabilities for a favorable market and for an unfavorable market were known, the environment would change from uncertainty to risk. For the third alternative, do nothing, the payoff does not depend on the state of nature and is known with certainty.

3.4 Decision Making Under Uncertainty

The presentation in this section of the criteria for decision making under uncertainty (and also for decision making under risk) is based on the assumption that the payoff is something in which larger values are better and high values are desirable. For payoffs such as profit, total sales, total return on investment, and interest earned, the best decision would be one that resulted in some type of maximum payoff. However, there are situations in which lower payoff values (e.g., cost) are better, and these payoffs would be minimized rather than maximized. The statement of the decision criteria would be modified slightly for such minimization problems. These differences will be mentioned in this section, and an example will be provided in a later section.

Several criteria exist for making decisions under conditions of uncertainty. The ones that we cover in this section are as follows:

1. Optimistic
2. Pessimistic
3. Criterion of realism (Hurwicz)
4. Equally likely (Laplace)
5. Minimax regret

The first four criteria can be computed directly from the decision (payoff) table, whereas the minimax regret criterion requires use of the opportunity loss table. Let's take a look at each of the five models and apply them to the Thompson Lumber example.

Optimistic

Maximax is an optimistic approach.

In using the **optimistic** criterion, the best (maximum) payoff for each alternative is considered and the alternative with the best (maximum) of these is selected. Hence, the optimistic criterion is sometimes called the **maximax** criterion. In Table 3.2, we see that Thompson's optimistic choice is the first alternative, "construct a large plant." By using this criterion, the highest of all possible payoffs ($200,000 in this example) may be achieved, while if any other alternative were selected, it would be impossible to achieve a payoff this high.

In using the optimistic criterion for minimization problems in which lower payoffs (e.g., cost) are better, you would look at the best (minimum) payoff for each alternative and choose the alternative with the best (minimum) of these.

TABLE 3.2

Thompson's Maximax Decision

| ALTERNATIVE | STATE OF NATURE | | MAXIMUM IN A ROW ($) |
	FAVORABLE MARKET ($)	UNFAVORABLE MARKET ($)	
Construct a large plant	200,000	−180,000	200,000 ◄ Maximax
Construct a small plant	100,000	−20,000	100,000
Do nothing	0	0	0

TABLE 3.3
Thompson's Maximin
Decision

	STATE OF NATURE		
ALTERNATIVE	FAVORABLE MARKET ($)	UNFAVORABLE MARKET ($)	MINIMUM IN A ROW ($)
Construct a large plant	200,000	−180,000	−180,000
Construct a small plant	100,000	−20,000	−20,000
Do nothing	0	0	⓪ ← Maximin

Pessimistic

Maximin is a pessimistic approach.

In using the *pessimistic* criterion, the worst (minimum) payoff for each alternative is considered and the alternative with the best (maximum) of these is selected. Hence, the pessimistic criterion is sometimes called the **maximin** criterion. This criterion guarantees the payoff will be at least the maximin value (the best of the worst values). Choosing any other alternative may allow a worse (lower) payoff to occur.

Thompson's maximin choice, "do nothing," is shown in Table 3.3. This decision is associated with the maximum of the minimum number within each row or alternative.

In using the pessimistic criterion for minimization problems in which lower payoffs (e.g., cost) are better, you would look at the worst (maximum) payoff for each alternative and choose the alternative with the best (minimum) of these.

Both the maximax and maximin criteria consider only one extreme payoff for each alternative, while all other payoffs are ignored. The next criterion considers both of these extremes.

Criterion of Realism (Hurwicz Criterion)

Criterion of realism uses the weighted average approach.

Often called the **weighted average**, the **criterion of realism** (the **Hurwicz criterion**) is a compromise between an optimistic and a pessimistic decision. To begin, a **coefficient of realism**, α, is selected. This measures the degree of optimism of the decision maker and is between 0 and 1. When α is 1, the decision maker is 100% optimistic about the future. When α is 0, the decision maker is 100% pessimistic about the future. The advantage of this approach is that it allows the decision maker to build in personal feelings about relative optimism and pessimism. The weighted average is computed as follows:

$$\text{Weighted average} = \alpha(\text{best in row}) + (1 - \alpha)(\text{worst in row})$$

For a maximization problem, the best payoff for an alternative is the highest value, and the worst payoff is the lowest value. Note that when $\alpha = 1$, this is the same as the optimistic criterion, and when $\alpha = 0$ this is the same as the pessimistic criterion. This value is computed for each alternative, and the alternative with the highest weighted average is then chosen.

If we assume that John Thompson sets his coefficient of realism, α, to be 0.80, the best decision would be to construct a large plant. As seen in Table 3.4, this alternative has the highest weighted average: $124,000 = (0.80)(\$200,000) = (0.20)(-\$180,000)$.

In using the criterion of realism for minimization problems, the best payoff for an alternative would be the lowest payoff in the row and the worst would be the highest payoff in the row. The alternative with the lowest weighted average is then chosen.

TABLE 3.4
Thompson's Criterion
of Realism Decision

	STATE OF NATURE		
ALTERNATIVE	FAVORABLE MARKET ($)	UNFAVORABLE MARKET ($)	CRITERION OF REALISM OR WEIGHTED AVERAGE ($\alpha = 0.8$) $
Construct a large plant	200,000	−180,000	⟨124,000⟩ ← Realism
Construct a small plant	100,000	−20,000	76,000
Do nothing	0	0	0

TABLE 3.5
Thompson's Equally Likely Decision

	STATE OF NATURE		
ALTERNATIVE	FAVORABLE MARKET ($)	UNFAVORABLE MARKET ($)	ROW AVERAGE ($)
Construct a large plant	200,000	−180,000	10,000
Construct a small plant	100,000	−20,000	40,000 ← Equally likely
Do nothing	0	0	0

Because there are only two states of nature in the Thompson Lumber example, only two payoffs for each alternative are present and both are considered. However, if there are more than two states of nature, this criterion will ignore all payoffs except the best and the worst. The next criterion will consider all possible payoffs for each decision.

Equally Likely (Laplace)

Equally likely criterion uses the average outcome.

One criterion that uses all the payoffs for each alternative is the **equally likely**, also called **Laplace**, decision criterion. This involves finding the average payoff for each alternative, and selecting the alternative with the best or highest average. The equally likely approach assumes that all probabilities of occurrence for the states of nature are equal, and thus each state of nature is equally likely.

The equally likely choice for Thompson Lumber is the second alternative, "construct a small plant." This strategy, shown in Table 3.5, is the one with the maximum average payoff.

In using the equally likely criterion for minimization problems, the calculations are exactly the same, but the best alternative is the one with the lowest average payoff.

Minimax Regret

Minimax regret criterion is based on opportunity loss.

The next decision criterion that we discuss is based on **opportunity loss** or **regret**. Opportunity loss refers to the difference between the optimal profit or payoff for a given state of nature and the actual payoff received for a particular decision for that state of nature. In other words, it's the amount lost by not picking the best alternative in a given state of nature.

The first step is to create the opportunity loss table by determining the opportunity loss for not choosing the best alternative for each state of nature. Opportunity loss for any state of nature, or any column, is calculated by subtracting each payoff in the column from the *best* payoff in the same column. For a favorable market, the best payoff is $200,000 as a result of the first alternative, "construct a large plant." The opportunity loss is 0, meaning that it is impossible to achieve a higher payoff in this state of nature. If the second alternative is selected, a profit of $100,000 would be realized in a favorable market, and this is compared to the best payoff of $200,000. Thus, the opportunity loss is 200,000 − 100,000 = 100,000. Similarly, if "do nothing" is selected, the opportunity loss would be 200,000 − 0 = 200,000.

For an unfavorable market, the best payoff is $0 as a result of the third alternative, "do nothing," so this has 0 opportunity loss. The opportunity losses for the other alternatives are found by subtracting the payoffs from this best payoff ($0) in this state of nature as shown in Table 3.6. Thompson's opportunity loss table is shown as Table 3.7.

TABLE 3.6
Determining Opportunity Losses for Thompson Lumber

STATE OF NATURE	
FAVORABLE MARKET ($)	UNFAVORABLE MARKET ($)
200,000 − 200,000	0 − (−180,000)
200,000 − 100,000	0 − (−20,000)
200,000 − 0	0 − 0

TABLE 3.7
Opportunity Loss Table for Thompson Lumber

	STATE OF NATURE	
ALTERNATIVE	FAVORABLE MARKET ($)	UNFAVORABLE MARKET ($)
Construct a large plant	0	180,000
Construct a small plant	100,000	20,000
Do nothing	200,000	0

IN ACTION   Ford Uses Decision Theory to Choose Parts Suppliers

Ford Motor Company manufactures about 5 million cars and trucks annually and employs more than 200,000 people at about 100 facilities around the globe. Such a large company often needs to make large supplier decisions under tight deadlines.

This was the situation when researchers at MIT teamed up with Ford management and developed a data-driven supplier selection tool. This computer program aids in decision making by applying some of the decision-making criteria presented in this

chapter. Decision makers at Ford are asked to input data about their suppliers (part costs, distances, lead times, supplier reliability, etc.) as well as the type of decision criterion they want to use. Once these are entered, the model outputs the best set of suppliers to meet the specified needs. The result is a system that is now saving Ford Motor Company over $40 million annually.

Source: Based on E. Klampfl, Y. Fradkin, C. McDaniel, and M. Wolcott. "Ford Uses OR to Make Urgent Sourcing Decisions in a Distressed Supplier Environment," *Interfaces* 39, 5 (2009): 428–442.

TABLE 3.8

Thompson's Minimax Decision Using Opportunity Loss

	STATE OF NATURE		
ALTERNATIVE	FAVORABLE MARKET ($)	UNFAVORABLE MARKET ($)	MAXIMUM IN A ROW ($)
Construct a large plant	0	180,000	180,000
Construct a small plant	100,000	20,000	100,000 ← Minimax
Do nothing	200,000	0	200,000

Using the opportunity loss (regret) table, the **minimax regret** criterion first consider the maximum (worst) opportunity loss for each alternative. Next, looking at these maximum values, pick that alternative with the minimum (or best) number. By doing this, the opportunity loss actually realized is guaranteed to be no more than this minimax value. In Table 3.8, we can see that the minimax regret choice is the second alternative, "construct a small plant." When this alternative is selected, we know the maximum opportunity loss cannot be more than 100,000 (the *mini*mum of the *maxi*mum regrets).

In calculating the opportunity loss for minimization problems such as those involving costs, the best (lowest) payoff or cost in a column is subtracted from each payoff in that column. Once the opportunity loss table has been constructed, the minimax regret criterion is applied in exactly the same way as just described. The maximum opportunity loss for each alternative is found, and the alternative with the minimum of these maximums is selected. As with maximization problems, the opportunity loss can never be negative.

We have considered several decision-making criteria to be used when probabilities of the states of nature are not known and cannot be estimated. Now we will see what to do if the probabilities are available.

3.5   Decision Making Under Risk

Decision making under risk is a decision situation in which several possible states of nature may occur, and the probabilities of these states of nature are known. In this section, we consider one of the most popular methods of making decisions under risk: selecting the alternative with the highest expected monetary value (or simply expected value). We also use the probabilities with the opportunity loss table to minimize the expected opportunity loss.

Expected Monetary Value

Given a decision table with conditional values (payoffs) that are monetary values, and probability assessments for all states of nature, it is possible to determine the **expected monetary value (EMV)** for each alternative. The *expected value*, or the *mean value*, is the long-run average value of that decision. The EMV for an alternative is just the sum of possible payoffs of the alternative, each weighted by the probability of that payoff occurring.

EMV is the weighted sum of possible payoffs for each alternative.

This could also be expressed simply as the expected value of X, or $E(X)$, which was discussed in Section 2.6 of Chapter 2.

$$\text{EMV(alternative)} = \sum X_i P(X_i) \tag{3-1}$$

TABLE 3.9

Decision Table with Probabilities and EMVs for Thompson Lumber

| | STATE OF NATURE | | |
ALTERNATIVE	FAVORABLE MARKET ($)	UNFAVORABLE MARKET ($)	EMV ($)
Construct a large plant	200,000	−180,000	10,000
Construct a small plant	100,000	−20,000	40,000 ← Best EMV
Do nothing	0	0	0
Probabilities	0.50	0.50	

where

$$X_i = \text{payoff for the alternative in state of nature } i$$
$$P(X_i) = \text{probability of achieving payoff } X_i \text{ (i.e., probability of state of nature } i)$$
$$\Sigma = \text{summation symbol}$$

If this were expanded, it would become

EMV (alternative)

    = (payoff in first state of nature) × (probability of first state of nature)

        + (payoff in second state of nature) × (probability of second state of nature)

        + ··· + (payoff in last state of nature) × (probability of last state of nature)

The alternative with the maximum EMV is then chosen.

    Suppose that John Thompson now believes that the probability of a favorable market is exactly the same as the probability of an unfavorable market; that is, each state of nature has a 0.50 probability. Which alternative would give the greatest EMV? To determine this, John has expanded the decision table, as shown in Table 3.9. His calculations follow:

$$\text{EMV (large plant)} = (\$200,000)(0.50) + (-\$180,000)(0.50) = \$10,000$$
$$\text{EMV (small plant)} = (\$100,000)(0.50) + (-\$20,000)(0.50) = \$40,000$$
$$\text{EMV (do nothing)} = (\$0)(0.50) + (\$0)(0.50) = \$0$$

The largest expected value ($40,000) results from the second alternative, "construct a small plant." Thus, Thompson should proceed with the project and put up a small plant to manufacture storage sheds. The EMVs for the large plant and for doing nothing are $10,000 and $0, respectively.

    When using the EMV criterion with minimization problems, the calculations are the same, but the alternative with the smallest EMV is selected.

Expected Value of Perfect Information

John Thompson has been approached by Scientific Marketing, Inc., a firm that proposes to help John make the decision about whether to build the plant to produce storage sheds. Scientific Marketing claims that its technical analysis will tell John with certainty whether the market is favorable for his proposed product. In other words, it will change his environment from one of decision making under risk to one of decision making under certainty. This information could prevent John from making a very expensive mistake. Scientific Marketing would charge Thompson $65,000 for the information. What would you recommend to John? Should he hire the firm to make the marketing study? Even if the information from the study is perfectly accurate, is it worth $65,000? What would it be worth? Although some of these questions are difficult to answer, determining the value of such *perfect information* can be very useful. It places an upper bound on what you should be willing to spend on information such as that being sold by Scientific Marketing. In this section, two related terms are investigated: the **expected value of perfect information (EVPI)** and the **expected value with perfect information (EVwPI)**. These techniques can help John make his decision about hiring the marketing firm.

    The expected value *with* perfect information is the expected or average return, in the long run, if we have perfect information before a decision has to be made. To calculate this value, we

EVPI places an upper bound on what to pay for information.

choose the best alternative for each state of nature and multiply its payoff times the probability of occurrence of that state of nature.

$$\text{EVwPI} = \sum(\text{best payoff in state of nature } i)(\text{probability of state of nature } i) \qquad (3\text{-}2)$$

If this were expanded, it would become

EVwPI

$= (\text{best payoff in first state of nature}) \times (\text{probability of first state of nature})$

$+ (\text{best payoff in second state of nature}) \times (\text{probability of second state of nature})$

$+ \cdots + (\text{best payoff in last state of nature}) \times (\text{probability of last state of nature})$

The EVPI is the expected value *with* perfect information minus the expected value *without* perfect information (i.e., the best or maximum EMV). Thus, the EVPI is the improvement in EMV that results from having perfect information.

$$\text{EVPI} = \text{EVwPI} - \text{Best EMV} \qquad (3\text{-}3)$$

EVPI is the expected value with perfect information minus the maximum EMV.

By referring to Table 3.9, Thompson can calculate the maximum that he would pay for information, that is, the EVPI. He follows a three-stage process. First, the best payoff in each state of nature is found. If the perfect information says the market will be favorable, the large plant will be constructed, and the profit will be $200,000. If the perfect information says the market will be unfavorable, the "do nothing" alternative is selected, and the profit will be 0. These values are shown in the "with perfect information" row in Table 3.10. Second, the expected value *with* perfect information is computed. Then, using this result, EVPI is calculated.

The expected value with perfect information is

$$\text{EVwPI} = (\$200,000)(0.50) + (\$0)(0.50) = \$100,000$$

Thus, if we had perfect information, the payoff would average $100,000.

The maximum EMV without additional information is $40,000 (from Table 3.9). Therefore, the increase in EMV is

$$\begin{aligned} \text{EVPI} &= \text{EVwPI} - \text{maximum EMV} \\ &= \$100,000 - \$40,000 \\ &= \$60,000 \end{aligned}$$

Thus, the *most* Thompson would be willing to pay for perfect information is $60,000. This, of course, is again based on the assumption that the probability of each state of nature is 0.50.

This EVPI also tells us that the most we would pay for any information (perfect or imperfect) is $60,000. In a later section, we'll see how to place a value on imperfect or sample information.

In finding the EVPI for minimization problems, the approach is similar. The best payoff in each state of nature is found, but this is the lowest payoff for that state of nature rather than the highest. The EVwPI is calculated from these lowest payoffs, and this is compared to the best (lowest) EMV without perfect information. The EVPI is the improvement that results, and this is the best EMV − EVwPI.

TABLE 3.10

Decision Table with Perfect Information

ALTERNATIVE	STATE OF NATURE		EMV ($)
	FAVORABLE MARKET ($)	UNFAVORABLE MARKET ($)	
Construct a large plant	200,000	−180,000	10,000
Construct a small plant	100,000	−20,000	40,000
Do nothing	0	0	0
With perfect information	200,000	0	100,000 ← EVwPI
Probabilities	0.50	0.50	

TABLE 3.11

EOL Table for Thompson Lumber

| | STATE OF NATURE | | |
ALTERNATIVE	FAVORABLE MARKET ($)	UNFAVORABLE MARKET ($)	EOL
Construct a large plant	0	180,000	90,000
Construct a small plant	100,000	20,000	60,000 ← Best EOL
Do nothing	200,000	0	100,000
Probabilities	0.50	0.50	

Expected Opportunity Loss

EOL is the cost of not picking the best solution.

An alternative approach to maximizing EMV is to minimize *expected opportunity loss* (EOL). First, an opportunity loss table is constructed. Then the EOL is computed for each alternative by multiplying the opportunity loss by the probability and adding these together. In Table 3.7, we presented the opportunity loss table for the Thompson Lumber example. Using these opportunity losses, we compute the EOL for each alternative by multiplying the probability of each state of nature times the appropriate opportunity loss value and adding these together:

$$\text{EOL(construct large plant)} = (0.5)(\$0) + (0.5)(\$180,000)$$
$$= \$90,000$$

$$\text{EOL(construct small plant)} = (0.5)(\$100,000) + (0.5)(\$20,000)$$
$$= \$60,000$$

$$\text{EOL(do nothing)} = (0.5)(\$200,000) + (0.5)(\$0)$$
$$= \$100,000$$

Table 3.11 gives these results. Using minimum EOL as the decision criterion, the best decision would be the second alternative, "construct a small plant."

EOL will always result in the same decision as the maximum EMV.

It is important to note that minimum EOL will always result in the same decision as maximum EMV, and that the EVPI will always equal the minimum EOL. Referring to the Thompson case, we used the payoff table to compute the EVPI to be $60,000. Note that this is the minimum EOL we just computed.

Sensitivity Analysis

In previous sections, we determined that the best decision (with the probabilities known) for Thompson Lumber was to construct the small plant, with an expected value of $40,000. This conclusion depends on the values of the economic consequences and the two probability values of a favorable and an unfavorable market. *Sensitivity analysis* investigates how our decision might change given a change in the problem data. In this section, we investigate the impact that a change in the probability values would have on the decision facing Thompson Lumber. We first define the following variable:

Sensitivity analysis investigates how our decision might change with different input data.

$$P = \text{probability of a favorable market}$$

Because there are only two states of nature, the probability of an unfavorable market must be $1 - P$.

We can now express the EMVs in terms of P, as shown in the following equations. A graph of these EMV values is shown in Figure 3.1.

$$\text{EMV(large plant)} = \$200,000P - \$180,000(1 - P)$$
$$= \$200,000P - \$180,000 + 180,000P$$
$$= \$380,000P - \$180,000$$

$$\text{EMV(small plant)} = \$100,000P - \$20,000(1 - P)$$
$$= \$100,000P - \$20,000 + 20,000P$$
$$= \$120,000P - \$20,000$$

$$\text{EMV(do nothing)} = \$0P + \$0(1 - P) = \$0$$

FIGURE 3.1
Sensitivity Analysis

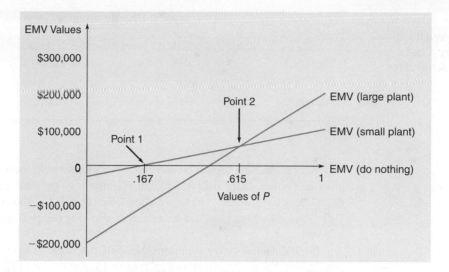

As you can see in Figure 3.1, the best decision is to do nothing as long as P is between 0 and the probability associated with point 1, where the EMV for doing nothing is equal to the EMV for the small plant. When P is between the probabilities for points 1 and 2, the best decision is to build the small plant. Point 2 is where the EMV for the small plant is equal to the EMV for the large plant. When P is greater than the probability for point 2, the best decision is to construct the large plant. Of course, this is what you would expect as P increases. The value of P at points 1 and 2 can be computed as follows:

$$\text{Point 1: EMV (do nothing)} = \text{EMV (small plant)}$$

$$0 = \$120,000P - \$20,000 \quad P = \frac{20,000}{120,000} = 0.167$$

$$\text{Point 2: EMV (small plant)} = \text{EMV (large plant)}$$

$$\$120,000P - \$20,000 = \$380,000P - \$180,000$$

$$260,000P - 160,000 \quad P = \frac{160,000}{260,000} = 0.615$$

The results of this sensitivity analysis are displayed in the following table:

BEST ALTERNATIVE	RANGE OF P VALUES
Do nothing	Less than 0.167
Construct a small plant	0.167 – 0.615
Construct a large plant	Greater than 0.615

3.6 A Minimization Example

The previous examples have illustrated how to apply the decision-making criterion when the payoffs are to be maximized. The following example illustrates how the criteria are applied to problems in which the payoffs are costs that should be minimized.

The Decision Sciences department at State University will be signing a 3-year lease for a new copy machine, and three different machines are being considered. For each of these, there is a monthly fee, which includes service on the machine, plus a charge for each copy. The number of copies that would be made each month is uncertain, but the department has estimated that the number of copies per month could be 10,000 or 20,000 or 30,000 per month. The monthly cost for each machine based on each of the three levels of activity is shown in Table 3.12.

TABLE 3.12

Payoff Table with Monthly Copy Costs for Business Analytics Department

	10,000 COPIES PER MONTH	20,000 COPIES PER MONTH	30,000 COPIES PER MONTH
Machine A	950	1,050	1,150
Machine B	850	1,100	1,350
Machine C	700	1,000	1,300

Which machine should be selected? To determine the best alternative, a specific criterion must be chosen. If the decision maker is optimistic, only the best (minimum) payoff for each decision is considered. These are shown in Table 3.13, and the best (minimum) of these is 700. Thus, Machine C would be selected, allowing the possibility of achieving this best cost of $700.

If the decision maker is pessimistic, only the worst (maximum) payoff for each decision is considered. These are also shown in Table 3.13, and the best (minimum) of these is 1,150. Thus, Machine A would be selected based on the pessimistic criterion. This would guarantee that the cost would be no more than 1,150, regardless of which state of nature occurred.

Using Hurwicz criterion, if we assume that the decision maker is 70% optimistic (the coefficient of realism is 0.7), the weighted average of the best and the worst payoff for each alternative would be calculated using the formula:

$$\text{Weighted average} = 0.7(\text{best payoff}) + (1 - 0.7)(\text{worst payoff})$$

For each of the three copy machines, we would get the following values.

$$\text{Machine A: } 0.7(950) + 0.3(1,150) = 1,010$$
$$\text{Machine B: } 0.7(850) + 0.3(1,350) = 1,000$$
$$\text{Machine C: } 0.7(700) + 0.3(1,300) = 880$$

The decision would be to select Machine C based on this criterion because it has the lowest weighted average cost.

For the equally likely criterion, the average payoff for each machine would be calculated.

$$\text{Machine A: } (950 + 1,050 + 1,150)/3 = 1,050$$
$$\text{Machine B: } (850 + 1,100 + 1,350)/3 = 1,100$$
$$\text{Machine C: } (700 + 1,000 + 1,300)/3 = 1,000$$

Based on the equally likely criterion, Machine C would be selected because it has the lowest average cost.

To apply EMV criterion, probabilities must be known for each state of nature. Past records indicate that 40% of the time the number of copies made in a month was 10,000, while 30% of the time it was 20,000 and 30% of the time it was 30,000. The probabilities for the three states of nature would be 0.4, 0.3, and 0.3. We can use these to calculate the EMVs, and the results are shown in Table 3.14. Machine C would be selected because it has the lowest EMV. The monthly cost would average $970 with this machine, while the other machines would average a higher cost.

TABLE 3.13

Best and Worst Payoffs (Costs) for Business Analytics Department

	10,000 COPIES PER MONTH	20,000 COPIES PER MONTH	30,000 COPIES PER MONTH	BEST PAYOFF (MINIMUM)	WORST PAYOFF (MAXIMUM)
Machine A	950	1,050	1,150	950	1,150
Machine B	850	1,100	1,350	850	1,350
Machine C	700	1,000	1,300	700	1,300

TABLE 3.14

Expected Monetary Values and Expected Value with Perfect Information for Business Analytics Department

	10,000 COPIES PER MONTH	20,000 COPIES PER MONTH	30,000 COPIES PER MONTH	EMV
Machine A	950	1,050	1,150	1,040
Machine B	850	1,100	1,350	1,075
Machine C	700	1,000	1,300	970
With perfect information	700	1,000	1,150	925
Probability	0.4	0.3	0.3	

TABLE 3.15

Opportunity Loss Table for Business Analytics Department

	10,000 COPIES PER MONTH	20,000 COPIES PER MONTH	30,000 COPIES PER MONTH	MAXIMUM	EOL
Machine A	250	50	0	250	115
Machine B	150	100	200	200	150
Machine C	0	0	150	150	45
Probability	0.4	0.3	0.3		

To find EVPI, we first find the payoffs (costs) that would be experienced with perfect information. The best payoff in each state of nature is the lowest value (cost) in that state of nature, as shown in the bottom row of Table 3.14. These values are used to calculate EVwPI. With these costs, we find

$$EVwPI = \$925$$
$$\text{Best EMV without perfect information} = \$970$$
$$EVPI = 970 - 925 = \$45$$

Perfect information would lower the expected value by $45.

To apply criteria based on opportunity loss, we must first develop the opportunity loss table. In each state of nature, the opportunity loss indicates how much worse each payoff is than the best possible payoff in that state of nature. The best payoff (cost) would be the lowest cost. Thus, to get the opportunity loss in this case, we subtract the lowest value in each column from all the values in that column and we obtain the opportunity loss table.

Once the opportunity loss table has been developed, the minimax regret criterion is applied exactly as it was for the Thompson Lumber example. The maximum regret for each alternative is found and the alternative with the minimum of these maximums is selected. As seen in Table 3.15, the minimum of these maximums is 150 so Machine C would be selected based on this criterion.

The probabilities are used to compute the expected opportunity losses as shown in Table 3.15. Machine C has the lowest EOL of $45, so it would be selected based on the minimum EOL criterion. As previously noted, the minimum EOL is equal to the expected value of perfect information.

3.7 Using Software for Payoff Table Problems

It is easy to use QM for Windows or Excel QM or even Excel 2013 without any add-ins to perform the calculations associated with payoff tables. The Thompson Lumber example is used in the following examples for illustration.

QM for Windows

To use QM for Windows for the Thompson Lumber example, select Modules – Decision Theory. Then enter New-Payoff Tables, and a window appears allowing you to set up the problem. Enter a title, the number of options (alternatives), the number of scenarios (states of nature),

PROGRAM 3.1A

QM for Windows Input for Thompson Lumber Example

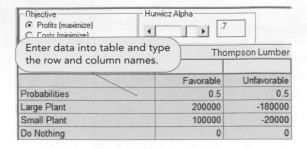

PROGRAM 3.1B

QM for Windows Output Screen for Thompson Lumber Example

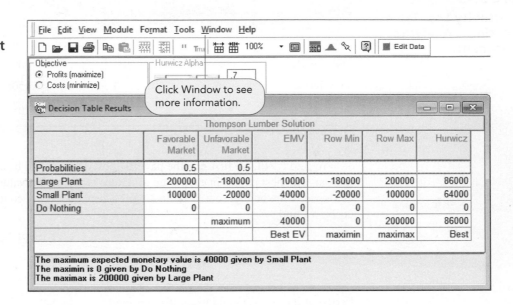

and specify if it is to be maximized or minimized. In this example, there are three alternatives or options, and two states of nature or scenarios. When these are entered, click OK and a window appears (Program 3.1A) allowing you to enter the probabilities and payoffs. You can also change the names of the alternatives and states of nature by simply typing over the default names. When you click *Solve*, the output in Program 3.1B appears. Additional output such as EVPI and opportunity loss results are available by clicking Window on the screen where the output is displayed.

Excel QM

To use Excel QM for the Thompson Lumber example, from the Excel QM ribbon in Excel 2013, click *Alphabetical* Menu and select *Decision Analysis – Decision Tables*. When the window opens to enter the parameters of the problem, you should enter a title, the number of alternatives, the number of states of nature, and specify if it is to be maximized or minimized. Click OK and an empty payoff table is created. You simply enter the probabilities, payoffs, and names for the rows and columns. The calculations are performed automatically and the results are shown in Program 3.2A. While the formulas are automatically developed in Excel QM, Program 3.2B shows the important formulas in this example. To see the formulas in Excel, simply hold down the control key and press the grave accent (`) key (usually found above the Tab key). To return Excel 2013 spreadsheet display to the numbers instead of the formulas, simply press the keys again.

PROGRAM 3.2A

Excel QM Results for Thompson Lumber Example

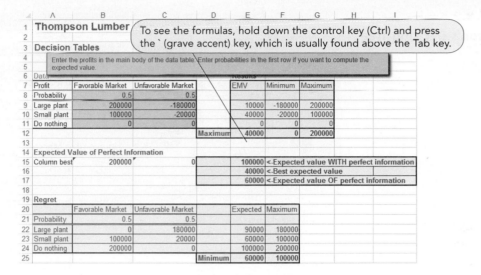

PROGRAM 3.2B

Key Formulas in Excel QM for Thompson Lumber Example

	E	F	G
9	=SUMPRODUCT($B$8:$C$8,B9:C9)	=MIN(B9:C9)	=MAX(B9:C9)
10	=SUMPRODUCT($B$8:$C$8,B10:C10)	=MIN(B10:C10)	=MAX(B10:C10)
11	=SUMPRODUCT($B$8:$C$8,B11:C11)	=MIN(B11:C11)	=MAX(B11:C11)
12	=MAX(E9:E11)	=MAX(F9:F11)	=MAX(G9:G11)
13			
14			
15	=SUMPRODUCT($B$8:$C$8,B15:C15)	<-Expected value W	
16	=F12	<-Best expected val	
17	=E15-E12	< Expected value O	
18			
19			
20	Expected	Maximum	
21			
22	=SUMPRODUCT($B$8:$C$8,B22:C22)	=MAX(B22:C22)	
23	=SUMPRODUCT($B$8:$C$8,B23:C23)	=MAX(B23:C23)	
24	=SUMPRODUCT(B0:$C$8,B24:C24)	=MAX(B24:C24)	
25	=MIN(E22:E24)	=MIN(F22:F24)	

3.8   Decision Trees

Any problem that can be presented in a decision table can also be graphically illustrated in a **decision tree**. All decision trees are similar in that they contain *decision points* or **decision nodes** and *state-of-nature points* or **state-of-nature nodes**:

- A decision node from which one of several alternatives may be chosen
- A state-of-nature node out of which one state of nature will occur

In drawing the tree, we begin at the left and move to the right. Thus, the tree presents the decisions and outcomes in sequential order. Lines or branches from the squares (decision nodes) represent alternatives, and branches from the circles represent the states of nature. Figure 3.2 gives the basic decision tree for the Thompson Lumber example. First, John decides whether to construct a large plant, a small plant, or no plant. Then, once that decision is made, the possible states of nature or outcomes (favorable or unfavorable market) will occur. The next step is to put the payoffs and probabilities on the tree and begin the analysis.

FIGURE 3.2

Thompson's Decision Tree

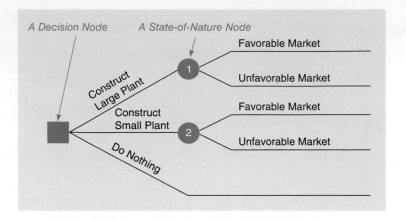

Analyzing problems with decision trees involves five steps:

Five Steps of Decision Tree Analysis

1. Define the problem.
2. Structure or draw the decision tree.
3. Assign probabilities to the states of nature.
4. Estimate payoffs for each possible combination of alternatives and states of nature.
5. Solve the problem by computing EMVs for each state-of-nature node. This is done by working backward, that is, starting at the right of the tree and working back to decision nodes on the left. Also, at each decision node, the alternative with the best EMV is selected.

The final decision tree with the payoffs and probabilities for John Thompson's decision situation is shown in Figure 3.3. Note that the payoffs are placed at the right side of each of the tree's branches. The probabilities are shown in parentheses next to each state of nature. Beginning with the payoffs on the right of the figure, the EMVs for each state-of-nature node are then calculated and placed by their respective nodes. The EMV of the first node is $10,000. This represents the branch from the decision node to construct a large plant. The

FIGURE 3.3

Completed and Solved Decision Tree for Thompson Lumber

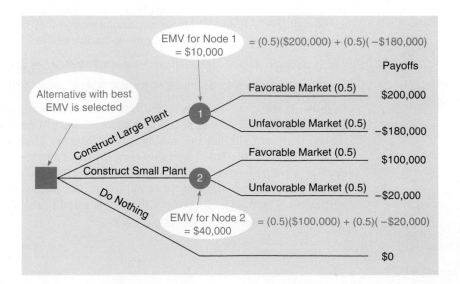

EMV for node 2, to construct a small plant, is $40,000. Building no plant or doing nothing has, of course, a payoff of $0. The branch leaving the decision node leading to the state-of-nature node with the highest EMV should be chosen. In Thompson's case, a small plant should be built.

A MORE COMPLEX DECISION FOR THOMPSON LUMBER—SAMPLE INFORMATION   When **sequential decisions** need to be made, decision trees are much more powerful tools than decision tables. Let's say that John Thompson has two decisions to make, with the second decision dependent on the outcome of the first. Before deciding about building a new plant, John has the option of conducting his own marketing research survey, at a cost of $10,000. The information from his survey could help him decide whether to construct a large plant, a small plant, or not to build at all. John recognizes that such a market survey will not provide him with *perfect* information, but it may help quite a bit nevertheless.

All outcomes and alternatives must be considered.

John's new decision tree is represented in Figure 3.4. Let's take a careful look at this more complex tree. Note that *all possible outcomes and alternatives* are included in their logical sequence. This is one of the strengths of using decision trees in making decisions. The user is forced to examine all possible outcomes, including unfavorable ones. He or she is also forced to make decisions in a logical, sequential manner.

FIGURE 3.4

Larger Decision Tree with Payoffs and Probabilities for Thompson Lumber

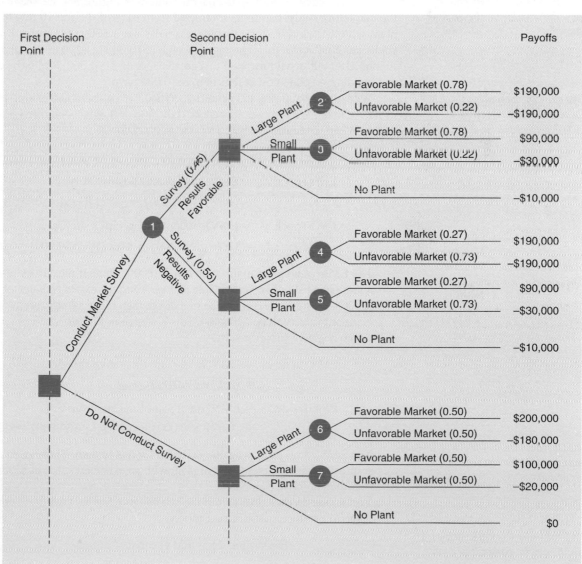

Examining the tree, we see that Thompson's first decision point is whether to conduct the $10,000 market survey. If he chooses not to do the study (the lower part of the tree), he can either construct a large plant, a small plant, or no plant. This is John's second decision point. The market will be either favorable (0.50 probability) or unfavorable (also 0.50 probability) if he builds. The payoffs for each of the possible consequences are listed along the right side. As a matter of fact, the lower portion of John's tree is *identical* to the simpler decision tree shown in Figure 3.3. Why is this so?

The upper part of Figure 3.4 reflects the decision to conduct the market survey. State-of-nature node 1 has two branches. There is a 45% chance that the survey results will indicate a favorable market for storage sheds. We also note that the probability is 0.55 that the survey results will be negative. The derivation of this probability will be discussed in the next section.

Most of the probabilities are conditional probabilities.

The rest of the probabilities shown in parentheses in Figure 3.4 are all **conditional probabilities** or **posterior probabilities** (these probabilities will also be discussed in the next section). For example, 0.78 is the probability of a favorable market for the sheds given a favorable result from the market survey. Of course, you would expect to find a high probability of a favorable market given that the research indicated that the market was good. Don't forget, though, there is a chance that John's $10,000 market survey didn't result in perfect or even reliable information. Any market research study is subject to error. In this case, there is a 22% chance that the market for sheds will be unfavorable given that the survey results are positive.

We note that there is a 27% chance that the market for sheds will be favorable given that John's survey results are negative. The probability is much higher, 0.73, that the market will actually be unfavorable given that the survey was negative.

The cost of the survey had to be subtracted from the original payoffs.

Finally, when we look to the payoff column in Figure 3.4, we see that $10,000, the cost of the marketing study, had to be subtracted from each of the top 10 tree branches. Thus, a large plant with a favorable market would normally net a $200,000 profit. But because the market study was conducted, this figure is reduced by $10,000 to $190,000. In the unfavorable case, the loss of $180,000 would increase to a greater loss of $190,000. Similarly, conducting the survey and building no plant now results in a −$10,000 payoff.

We start by computing the EMV of each branch.

With all probabilities and payoffs specified, we can start calculating the EMV at each state-of-nature node. We begin at the end, or right side of the decision tree and work back toward the origin. When we finish, the best decision will be known.

1. Given favorable survey results,

$$\text{EMV(node 2)} = \text{EMV(large plant} \mid \text{positive survey)}$$
$$= (0.78)(\$190,000) + (0.22)(-\$190,000) = \$106,400$$

$$\text{EMV(node 3)} = \text{EMV(small plant} \mid \text{positive survey)}$$
$$= (0.78)(\$90,000) + (0.22)(-\$30,000) = \$63,600$$

EMV calculations for favorable survey results are made first.

The EMV of no plant in this case is −$10,000. Thus, if the survey results are favorable, a large plant should be built. Note that we bring the expected value of this decision ($106,400) to the decision node to indicate that, if the survey results are positive, our expected value will be $106,400. This is shown in Figure 3.5.

2. Given negative survey results,

$$\text{EMV(node 4)} = \text{EMV(large plant} \mid \text{negative survey)}$$
$$= (0.27)(\$190,000) + (0.73)(-\$190,000) = -\$87,400$$

$$\text{EMV(node 5)} = \text{EMV(small plant} \mid \text{negative survey)}$$
$$= (0.27)(\$90,000) + (0.73)(-\$30,000) = \$2,400$$

EMV calculations for unfavorable survey results are done next.

The EMV of no plant is again −$10,000 for this branch. Thus, given a negative survey result, John should build a small plant with an expected value of $2,400, and this figure is indicated at the decision node.

3. Continuing on the upper part of the tree and moving backward, we compute the expected value of conducting the market survey:

We continue working backward to the origin, computing EMV values.

$$\text{EMV(node 1)} = \text{EMV(conduct survey)}$$
$$= (0.45)(\$106,400) + (0.55)(\$2,400)$$
$$= \$47,880 + \$1,320 = \$49,200$$

FIGURE 3.5

Thompson's Decision Tree with EMVs Shown

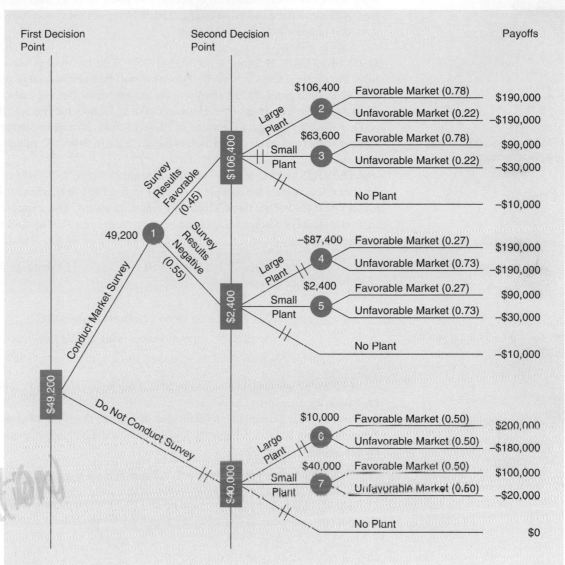

Calculation Node

4. If the market survey is *not* conducted,

$$EMV(\text{node } 6) = EMV(\text{large plant})$$
$$= (0.50)(\$200,000) + (0.50)(-\$180,000)$$
$$= \$10,000$$

$$EMV(\text{node } 7) = EMV(\text{small plant})$$
$$= (0.50)(\$100,000) + (0.50)(-\$20,000)$$
$$= \$40,000$$

The EMV of no plant is $0.

Thus, building a small plant is the best choice, given that the marketing research is not performed, as we saw earlier.

5. We move back to the first decision node and choose the best alternative. The EMV of conducting the survey is $49,200, versus an EMV of $40,000 for not conducting the study, so the best choice is to *seek* marketing information. If the survey results are favorable, John should construct a large plant, but if the research is negative, John should construct a small plant.

In Figure 3.5, these expected values are placed on the decision tree. Notice on the tree that a pair of slash lines / / through a decision branch indicates that a particular alternative is dropped from further consideration. This is because its EMV is lower than the EMV for the best alternative. After you have solved several decision tree problems, you may find it easier to do all of your computations on the tree diagram.

EVSI measures the value of sample information.

EXPECTED VALUE OF SAMPLE INFORMATION   With the market survey he intends to conduct, John Thompson knows that his best decision will be to build a large plant if the survey is favorable or a small plant if the survey results are negative. But John also realizes that conducting the market research is not free. He would like to know what the actual value of doing a survey is. One way of measuring the value of market information is to compute the **expected value of sample information** (EVSI) which is the increase in expected value resulting from the sample information.

The expected value *with* sample information (EV with SI) is found from the decision tree, and the cost of the sample information is added to this since this was subtracted from all the payoffs before the EV with SI was calculated. The expected value *without* sample information (EV without SI) is then subtracted from this to find the value of the sample information.

$$\text{EVSI} = (\text{EV with SI} + \text{cost}) - (\text{EV without SI}) \tag{3-4}$$

where

EVSI = expected value of sample information

EV with SI = expected value with sample information

EV without SI = expected value without sample information

In John's case, his EMV would be $59,200 *if* he hadn't already subtracted the $10,000 study cost from each payoff. (Do you see why this is so? If not, add $10,000 back into each payoff, as in the original Thompson problem, and recompute the EMV of conducting the market study.) From the lower branch of Figure 3.5, we see that the EMV of *not* gathering the sample information is $40,000. Thus,

$$\text{EVSI} = (\$49,200 + \$10,000) - \$40,000 = \$59,200 - \$40,000 = \$19,200$$

This means that John could have paid up to $19,200 for a market study and still come out ahead. Since it costs only $10,000, the survey is indeed worthwhile.

Efficiency of Sample Information

There may be many types of sample information available to a decision maker. In developing a new product, information could be obtained from a survey, from a focus group, from other market research techniques, or from actually using a test market to see how sales will be. While none of these sources of information are perfect, they can be evaluated by comparing the EVSI with the EVPI. If the sample information was perfect, then the efficiency would be 100%. The **efficiency of sample information** is

$$\text{Efficiency of sample information} = \frac{\text{EVSI}}{\text{EVPI}}100\% \tag{3-5}$$

In the Thompson Lumber example,

$$\text{Efficiency of sample information} = \frac{19,200}{60,000}100\% = 32\%$$

Thus, the market survey is only 32% as efficient as perfect information.

Sensitivity Analysis

As with payoff tables, sensitivity analysis can be applied to decision trees as well. The overall approach is the same. Consider the decision tree for the expanded Thompson Lumber problem shown in Figure 3.5. How sensitive is our decision (to conduct the marketing survey) to the probability of favorable survey results?

Let p be the probability of favorable survey results. Then $(1 - p)$ is the probability of negative survey results. Given this information, we can develop an expression for the EMV of conducting the survey, which is node 1:

$$\text{EMV(node 1)} = (\$106,400)p + (\$2,400)(1 - p)$$
$$= \$104,000p + \$2,400$$

We are indifferent when the EMV of conducting the marketing survey, node 1, is the same as the EMV of not conducting the survey, which is $40,000. We can find the indifference point by equating EMV(node 1) to $40,000:

$$\$104,000p + \$2,400 = \$40,000$$
$$\$104,000p = \$37,600$$
$$p = \frac{\$37,600}{\$104,000} = 0.36$$

As long as the probability of favorable survey results, p, is greater than 0.36, our decision will stay the same. When p is less than 0.36, our decision will be not to conduct the survey.

We could also perform sensitivity analysis for other problem parameters. For example, we could find how sensitive our decision is to the probability of a favorable market given favorable survey results. At this time, this probability is 0.78. If this value goes up, the large plant becomes more attractive. In this case, our decision would not change. What happens when this probability goes down? The analysis becomes more complex. As the probability of a favorable market given favorable survey results goes down, the small plant becomes more attractive. At some point, the small plant will result in a higher EMV (given favorable survey results) than the large plant. This, however, does not conclude our analysis. As the probability of a favorable market given favorable survey results continues to fall, there will be a point where not conducting the survey, with an EMV of $40,000, will be more attractive than conducting the marketing survey. We leave the actual calculations to you. It is important to note that sensitivity analysis should consider *all* possible consequences.

3.9   How Probability Values Are Estimated by Bayesian Analysis

Bayes' theorem allows decision makers to revise probability values.

There are many ways of getting probability data for a problem such as Thompson's. The numbers (such as 0.78, 0.22, 0.27, 0.73 in Figure 3.4) can be assessed by a manager based on experience and intuition. They can be derived from historical data, or they can be computed from other available data using Bayes' theorem. The advantage of Bayes' theorem is that it incorporates both our initial estimates of the probabilities and information about the accuracy of the information source (e.g., market research survey).

The Bayes' theorem approach recognizes that a decision maker does not know with certainty what state of nature will occur. It allows the manager to revise his or her initial or prior probability assessments based on new information. The revised probabilities are called posterior probabilities. (Before continuing, you may wish to review Bayes' theorem in Chapter 2.)

Calculating Revised Probabilities

In the Thompson Lumber case solved in Section 3.8, we made the assumption that the following four conditional probabilities were known:

$$P(\text{favorable market(FM)} \mid \text{survey results positive}) = 0.78$$
$$P(\text{unfavorable market(UM)} \mid \text{survey results positive}) = 0.22$$
$$P(\text{favorable market(FM)} \mid \text{survey results negative}) = 0.27$$
$$P(\text{unfavorable market(UM)} \mid \text{survey results negative}) = 0.73$$

TABLE 3.16

Market Survey Reliability in Predicting States of Nature

	STATE OF NATURE	
RESULT OF SURVEY	FAVORABLE MARKET (FM)	UNFAVORABLE MARKET (UM)
Positive (predicts favorable market for product)	$P(\text{survey positive} \mid \text{FM}) = 0.70$	$P(\text{survey positive} \mid \text{UM}) = 0.20$
Negative (predicts unfavorable market for product)	$P(\text{survey negative} \mid \text{FM}) = 0.30$	$P(\text{survey negative} \mid \text{UM}) = 0.80$

We now show how John Thompson was able to derive these values with Bayes' theorem. From discussions with market research specialists at the local university, John knows that special surveys such as his can either be positive (i.e., predict a favorable market) or be negative (i.e., predict an unfavorable market). The experts have told John that, statistically, of all new products with a *favorable market* (FM), market surveys were positive and predicted success correctly 70% of the time. Thirty percent of the time the surveys falsely predicted negative results or an *unfavorable market* (UM). On the other hand, when there was actually an unfavorable market for a new product, 80% of the surveys correctly predicted negative results. The surveys incorrectly predicted positive results the remaining 20% of the time. These conditional probabilities are summarized in Table 3.16. They are an indication of the accuracy of the survey that John is thinking of undertaking.

Recall that without any market survey information, John's best estimates of a favorable and unfavorable market are

$$P(\text{FM}) = 0.50$$
$$P(\text{UM}) = 0.50$$

These are referred to as the *prior probabilities*.

We are now ready to compute Thompson's revised or posterior probabilities. These desired probabilities are the reverse of the probabilities in Table 3.16. We need the probability of a favorable or unfavorable market given a positive or negative result from the market study. The general form of Bayes' theorem presented in Chapter 2 is

$$P(A \mid B) = \frac{P(B \mid A)P(A)}{P(B \mid A)P(A) + P(B \mid A')P(A')} \tag{3-6}$$

where

$$A, B = \text{any two events}$$
$$A' = \text{complement of } A$$

We can let A represent a favorable market and B represent a positive survey. Then, substituting the appropriate numbers into this equation, we obtain the conditional probabilities, given that the market survey is positive:

$$P(\text{FM} \mid \text{survey positive}) = \frac{P(\text{survey positive} \mid \text{FM})P(\text{FM})}{P(\text{survey positive} \mid \text{FM})P(\text{FM}) + P(\text{survey positive} \mid \text{UM})P(\text{UM})}$$

$$= \frac{(0.70)(0.50)}{(0.70)(0.50) + (0.20)(0.50)} = \frac{0.35}{0.45} = 0.78$$

$$P(\text{UM} \mid \text{survey positive}) = \frac{P(\text{survey positive} \mid \text{UM})P(\text{UM})}{P(\text{survey positive} \mid \text{UM})P(\text{UM}) + P(\text{survey positive} \mid \text{FM})P(\text{FM})}$$

$$= \frac{(0.20)(0.50)}{(0.20)(0.50) + (0.70)(0.50)} = \frac{0.10}{0.45} = 0.22$$

Note that the denominator (0.45) in these calculations is the probability of a positive survey. An alternative method for these calculations is to use a probability table as shown in Table 3.17.

TABLE 3.17

Probability Revisions Given a Positive Survey

STATE OF NATURE	CONDITIONAL PROBABILITY P(SURVEY POSITIVE | STATE OF NATURE)	PRIOR PROBABILITY	JOINT PROBABILITY	POSTERIOR PROBABILITY P(STATE OF NATURE | SURVEY POSITIVE)
FM	0.70	× 0.50	= 0.35	0.35/0.45 = 0.78
UM	0.20	× 0.50	= 0.10	0.10/0.45 = 0.22
		P(survey results positive)	= 0.45	1.00

The conditional probabilities, given that the market survey is negative, are

$$P(\text{FM} \mid \text{survey negative}) = \frac{P(\text{survey negative} \mid \text{FM})P(\text{FM})}{P(\text{survey negative} \mid \text{FM})P(\text{FM}) + P(\text{survey negative} \mid \text{UM})P(\text{UM})}$$

$$= \frac{(0.30)(0.50)}{(0.30)(0.50) + (0.80)(0.50)} = \frac{0.15}{0.55} = 0.27$$

$$P(\text{UM} \mid \text{survey negative}) = \frac{P(\text{survey negative} \mid \text{UM})P(\text{UM})}{P(\text{survey negative} \mid \text{UM})P(\text{UM}) + P(\text{survey negative} \mid \text{FM})P(\text{FM})}$$

$$= \frac{(0.80)(0.50)}{(0.80)(0.50) + (0.30)(0.50)} = \frac{0.40}{0.55} = 0.73$$

Note that the denominator (0.55) in these calculations is the probability of a negative survey. These computations given a negative survey could also have been performed in a table instead, as in Table 3.18.

The calculations shown in Tables 3.17 and 3.18 can easily be performed in Excel spreadsheets. Programs 3.3A and 3.3B show the final output for this example and the formulas.

New probabilities provide valuable information.

The posterior probabilities now provide John Thompson with estimates for each state of nature if the survey results are positive or negative. As you know, John's **prior probability** of success without a market survey was only 0.50. Now he is aware that the probability of successfully marketing storage sheds will be 0.78 if his survey shows positive results. His chances of success drop to 27% if the survey report is negative. This is valuable management information, as we saw in the earlier decision tree analysis.

Potential Problem in Using Survey Results

In many decision-making problems, survey results or pilot studies are done before an actual decision (such as building a new plant or taking a particular course of action) is made. As discussed earlier in this section, Bayes' analysis is used to help determine the correct

TABLE 3.18

Probability Revisions Given a Negative Survey

STATE OF NATURE	CONDITIONAL PROBABILITY P(SURVEY NEGATIVE | STATE OF NATURE)	PRIOR PROBABILITY	JOINT PROBABILITY	POSTERIOR PROBABILITY P(STATE OF NATURE | SURVEY NEGATIVE)
FM	0.30	× 0.50	= 0.15	0.15/0.55 = 0.27
UM	0.80	× 0.50	= 0.40	0.40/0.55 = 0.73
		P(survey results negative)	= 0.55	1.00

PROGRAM 3.3A

Results of Bayes' Calculations in Excel 2013

	A	B	C	D	E
1	Bayes Theorem for Thompson Lumber Example				
2					
3	Fill in cells B7, B8, and C7				
4					
5	Probability Revisions Given a Positive Survey				
6	State of Nature	P(Sur.Pos.|state of nature)	Prior Prob.	Joint Prob.	Posterior Probability
7	FM	0.7	0.5	0.35	0.78
8	UM	0.2	0.5	0.1	0.22
9			P(Sur.pos.)=	0.45	
10					
11	Probability Revisions Given a Negative Survey				
12	State of Nature	P(Sur.Pos.|state of nature)	Prior Prob.	Joint Prob.	Posterior Probability
13	FM	0.3	0.5	0.15	0.27
14	UM	0.8	0.5	0.4	0.73
15			P(Sur.neg.)=	0.55	

PROGRAM 3.3B

Formulas Used for Bayes' Calculations in Excel 2013

	B	C	D	E
7	0.7	0.5	=B7*C7	=D7/$D$9
8	0.2	=1-C7	=B8*C8	=D8/$D$9
9		P(Sur.pos.)=	=SUM(D7:D8)	
11				
13	=1-B7	=C7	=B13*C13	=D13/$D$15
14	=1-B8	=C8	=B14*C14	=D14/$D$15
15		P(Sur.neg.)=	=SUM(D13:D14)	

conditional probabilities that are needed to solve these types of decision theory problems. In computing these conditional probabilities, we need to have data about the surveys and their accuracies. If a decision to build a plant or to take another course of action is actually made, we can determine the accuracy of our surveys. Unfortunately, we cannot always get data about those situations in which the decision was not to build a plant or not to take some course of action. Thus, sometimes when we use survey results, we are basing our probabilities only on those cases in which a decision to build a plant or take some course of action is actually made. This means that, in some situations, conditional probability information may not be not quite as accurate as we would like. Even so, calculating conditional probabilities helps to refine the decision-making process and, in general, to make better decisions.

3.10 Utility Theory

We have focused on the EMV criterion for making decisions under risk. However, there are many occasions in which people make decisions that would appear to be inconsistent with the EMV criterion. When people buy insurance, the amount of the premium is greater than the expected payout to them from the insurance company because the premium includes the expected payout, the overhead cost, and the profit for the insurance company. A person involved in a lawsuit may choose to settle out of court rather than go to trial even if the expected value of going to trial is greater than the proposed settlement. A person buys a lottery ticket even though the expected return is negative. Casino games of all types have negative expected returns for the player, and yet millions of people play these games. A businessperson may rule out one potential decision because it could bankrupt the firm if things go bad, even though the expected return for this decision is better than that of all other alternatives.

Why do people make decisions that don't maximize their EMV? They do this because the monetary value is not always a true indicator of the overall value of the result of the

FIGURE 3.6

Your Decision Tree for the Lottery Ticket

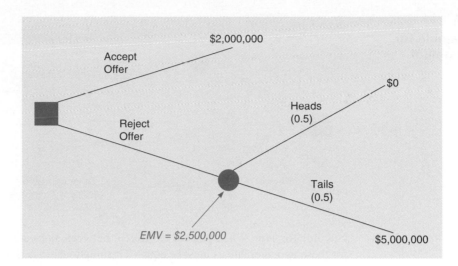

decision. The overall worth of a particular outcome is called **utility**, and rational people make decisions that maximize the expected utility. Although at times the monetary value is a good indicator of utility, there are other times when it is not. This is particularly true when some of the values involve an extremely large payoff or an extremely large loss. Suppose that you are the lucky holder of a lottery ticket. Five minutes from now a fair coin could be flipped, and if it comes up tails, you would win $5 million. If it comes up heads, you would win nothing. Just a moment ago a wealthy person offered you $2 million for your ticket. Let's assume that you have no doubts about the validity of the offer. The person will give you a certified check for the full amount, and you are absolutely sure the check would be good.

The overall value of the result of a decision is called utility.

A decision tree for this situation is shown in Figure 3.6. The EMV for rejecting the offer indicates that you should hold on to your ticket, but what would you do? Just think, $2 million for *sure* instead of a 50% chance at nothing. Suppose you were greedy enough to hold on to the ticket, and then lost. How would you explain that to your friends? Wouldn't $2 million be enough to be comfortable for a while?

Most people would choose to sell the ticket for $2 million. Most of us, in fact, would probably be willing to settle for a lot less. Just how low we would go is, of course, a matter of personal preference. People have different feelings about seeking or avoiding risk. Using the EMV alone is not always a good way to make these types of decisions.

EMV is not always the best approach.

One way to incorporate your own attitudes toward risk is through **utility theory**. In the next section, we explore first how to measure utility and then how to use utility measures in decision making.

Measuring Utility and Constructing a Utility Curve

The first step in using utility theory is to assign utility values to each monetary value in a given situation. It is convenient to begin **utility assessment** by assigning the worst outcome a utility of 0 and the best outcome a utility of 1. Although any values may be used as long as the utility for the best outcome is greater than the utility for the worst outcome, using 0 and 1 has some benefits. Because we have chosen to use 0 and 1, all other outcomes will have a utility value between 0 and 1. In determining the utilities of all outcomes, other than the best or worst outcome, a **standard gamble** is considered. This gamble is shown in Figure 3.7.

Utility assessment assigns the worst outcome a utility of 0 and the best outcome a utility of 1.

In Figure 3.7, p is the probability of obtaining the best outcome, and $(1 - p)$ is the probability of obtaining the worst outcome. Assessing the utility of any other outcome involves determining the probability (p), which makes you indifferent between alternative 1, which is the gamble between the best and worst outcomes, and alternative 2, which is obtaining the other

When you are indifferent, the expected utilities are equal.

FIGURE 3.7

Standard Gamble for Utility Assessment

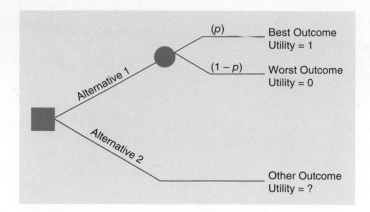

outcome for sure. When you are indifferent between alternatives 1 and 2, the expected utilities for these two alternatives must be equal. This relationship is shown as

Expected utility of alternative 2 = Expected utility of alternative 1

Utility of other outcome = (p)(utility of *best* outcome, which is 1)

+ $(1 - p)$(utility of the *worst* outcome, which is 0)

Utility of other outcome = $(p)(1) + (1 - p)(0) = p$ (3-7)

Now all you have to do is to determine the value of the probability (p) that makes you indifferent between alternatives 1 and 2. In setting the probability, you should be aware that utility assessment is completely subjective. It's a value set by the decision maker that can't be measured on an objective scale. Let's take a look at an example.

Once utility values have been determined, a utility curve can be constructed.

Jane Dickson would like to construct a utility curve revealing her preference for money between $0 and $10,000. A **utility curve** is a graph that plots utility value versus monetary value. She can invest her money either in a bank savings account or in a real estate deal.

If the money is invested in the bank, in 3 years Jane would have $5,000. If she invested in the real estate, after 3 years she could either have nothing or $10,000. Jane, however, is very conservative. Unless there is an 80% chance of getting $10,000 from the real estate deal, Jane would prefer to have her money in the bank, where it is safe. What Jane has done here is to assess her utility for $5,000. When there is an 80% chance (this means that p is 0.8) of getting $10,000, Jane is indifferent between putting her money in real estate and putting it in the bank. Jane's utility for $5,000 is thus equal to 0.8, which is the same as the value for p. This utility assessment is shown in Figure 3.8.

Other utility values can be assessed in the same way. For example, what is Jane's utility for $7,000? What value of p would make Jane indifferent between $7,000 and the gamble that would result in either $10,000 or $0? For Jane, there must be a 90% chance of getting the $10,000. Otherwise, she would prefer the $7,000 for sure. Thus, her utility for $7,000 is 0.90. Jane's utility for $3,000 can be determined in the same way. If there were a 50% chance of obtaining the $10,000, Jane would be indifferent between having $3,000 for sure and taking the gamble of either winning

FIGURE 3.8

Utility of $5,000

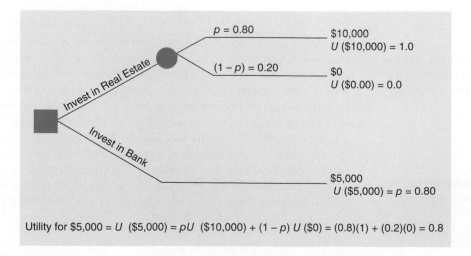

Utility for $5,000 = U ($5,000) = pU ($10,000) + (1 − p) U ($0) = (0.8)(1) + (0.2)(0) = 0.8

FIGURE 3.9

Utility Curve for Jane Dickson

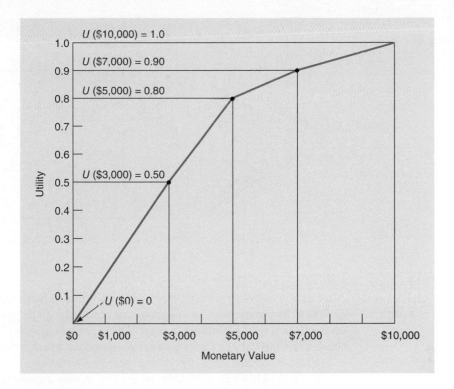

the $10,000 or getting nothing. Thus, the utility of $3,000 for Jane is 0.5. Of course, this process can be continued until Jane has assessed her utility for as many monetary values as she wants. These assessments, however, are enough to get an idea of Jane's feelings toward risk. In fact, we can plot these points in a utility curve, as is done in Figure 3.9. In the figure, the assessed utility points of $3,000, $5,000, and $7,000 are shown by dots, and the rest of the curve is inferred from these.

Jane's utility curve is typical of a **risk avoider**. A risk avoider is a decision maker who gets less utility or pleasure from a greater risk and tends to avoid situations in which high losses might occur. As monetary value increases on her utility curve, the utility increases at a slower rate.

The shape of a person's utility curve depends on many factors.

Figure 3.10 illustrates that a person who is a **risk seeker** has an opposite-shaped utility curve. This decision maker gets more utility from a greater risk and higher potential payoff. As monetary value increases on his or her utility curve, the utility increases at an increasing rate. A person who is *indifferent* to risk has a utility curve that is a straight line. The shape of a person's utility curve depends on the specific decision being considered, the monetary values involved in the situation, the person's psychological frame of mind, and how the person feels about the future. It may well be that you have one utility curve for some situations you face and completely different curves for others.

FIGURE 3.10

Preferences for Risk

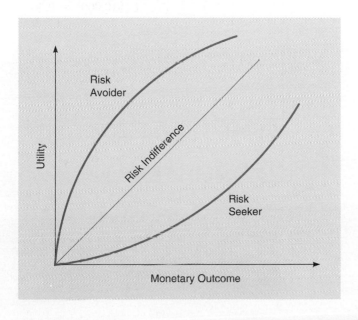

FIGURE 3.11

Decision Facing Mark Simkin

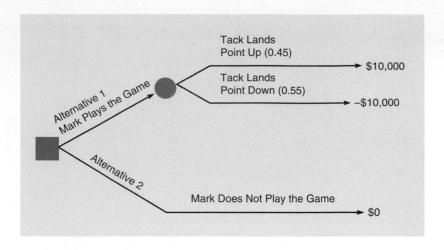

Utility as a Decision-Making Criterion

Utility values replace monetary values.

After a utility curve has been determined, the utility values from the curve are used in making decisions. Monetary outcomes or values are replaced with the appropriate utility values and then decision analysis is performed as usual. The expected utility for each alternative is computed instead of the EMV. Let's take a look at an example in which a decision tree is used and expected utility values are computed in selecting the best alternative.

Mark Simkin loves to gamble. He decides to play a game that involves tossing thumbtacks in the air. If the point on the thumbtack is facing up after it lands, Mark wins $10,000. If the point on the thumbtack is down, Mark loses $10,000. Should Mark play the game (alternative 1) or should he not play the game (alternative 2)?

Alternatives 1 and 2 are displayed in the tree shown in Figure 3.11. As can be seen, alternative 1 is to play the game. Mark believes that there is a 45% chance of winning $10,000 and a 55% chance of suffering the $10,000 loss. Alternative 2 is not to gamble. What should Mark do? Of course, this depends on Mark's utility for money. As stated previously, he likes to gamble. Using the procedure just outlined, Mark was able to construct a utility curve showing his preference for money. Mark has a total of $20,000 to gamble, so he has constructed the utility curve based on a best payoff of $20,000 and a worst payoff of a $20,000 loss. This curve appears in Figure 3.12.

Mark's objective is to maximize expected utility.

We see that Mark's utility for −$10,000 is 0.05, his utility for not playing ($0) is 0.15, and his utility for $10,000 is 0.30. These values can now be used in the decision tree. Mark's objective is to maximize his expected utility, which can be done as follows:

Step 1.
$$U(-\$10,000) = 0.05$$
$$U(\$0) = 0.15$$
$$U(\$10,000) = 0.30$$

FIGURE 3.12

Utility Curve for Mark Simkin

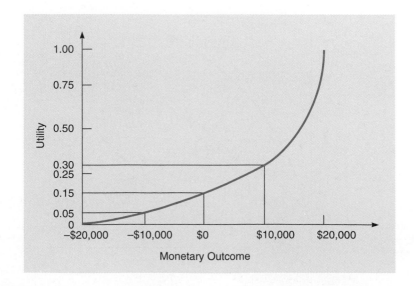

IN ACTION

Multiattribute Utility Model Aids in Disposal of Nuclear Weapons

When the Cold War between the United States and the USSR ended, the two countries agreed to dismantle a large number of nuclear weapons. The exact number of weapons is not known, but the total number has been estimated to be over 40,000. The plutonium recovered from the dismantled weapons presented several concerns. The National Academy of Sciences characterized the possibility that the plutonium could fall into the hands of terrorists as a very real danger. Also, plutonium is very toxic to the environment, so a safe and secure disposal process was critical. Deciding what disposal process would be used was no easy task.

Due to the long relationship between the United States and the USSR during the Cold War, it was necessary that the plutonium disposal process for each country occur at approximately the same time. Whichever method was selected by one country would have to be approved by the other country. The U.S. Department of Energy (DOE) formed the Office of Fissile Materials Disposition (OFMD) to oversee the process of selecting the approach to use for disposal of the plutonium. Recognizing that the decision could be controversial, the OFMD used a team of operations research analysts associated with the Amarillo National Research Center. This OR group used a multiattribute utility (MAU) model to combine several performance measures into one single measure.

A total of 37 performance measures were used in evaluating 13 different possible alternatives. The MAU model combined these measures and helped to rank the alternatives as well as identify the deficiencies of some alternatives. The OFMD recommended two of the alternatives with the highest rankings, and development was begun on both of them. This parallel development permitted the United States to react quickly when the USSR's plan was developed. The USSR used an analysis based on this same MAU approach. The United States and the USSR chose to convert the plutonium from nuclear weapons into mixed oxide fuel, which is used in nuclear reactors to make electricity. Once the plutonium is converted to this form, it cannot be used in nuclear weapons.

The MAU model helped the United States and the USSR deal with a very sensitive and potentially hazardous issue in a way that considered economic, nonproliferation, and ecology issues. The framework is now being used by Russia to evaluate other policies related to nuclear energy.

Source: Based on John C. Butler et al. "The United States and Russia Evaluate Plutonium Disposition Options with Multiattribute Utility Theory," *Interfaces* 35, 1 (January–February 2005): 88–101.

Step 2. Replace monetary values with utility values. Refer to Figure 3.13. Here are the expected utilities for alternatives 1 and 2:

$$E(\text{alternative 1; play the game}) = (0.45)(0.30) + (0.55)(0.05)$$
$$= 0.135 + 0.027 = 0.162$$

$$E(\text{alternative 2: don't play the game}) = 0.15$$

Therefore, alternative 1 is the best strategy using utility as the decision criterion. If EMV had been used, alternative 2 would have been the best strategy. The utility curve is a risk-seeker utility curve, and the choice of playing the game certainly reflects this preference for risk.

FIGURE 3.13

Using Expected Utilities in Decision Making

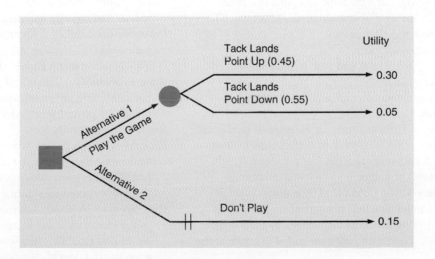

Summary

Decision theory is an analytic and systematic approach to studying decision making. Six steps are usually involved in making decisions in three environments: decision making under certainty, uncertainty, and risk. In decision making under uncertainty, decision tables are constructed to compute criteria such as maximax, maximin, criterion of realism, equally likely, and minimax regret. Methods such as determining expected monetary value (EMV), expected value of perfect information (EVPI), expected opportunity loss (EOL), and sensitivity analysis are used in decision making under risk.

Decision trees are another option, particularly for larger decision problems, when one decision must be made before other decisions can be made. For example, a decision to take a sample or to perform market research is made before we decide to construct a large plant, a small one, or no plant. In this case, we can also compute the expected value of sample information (EVSI) to determine the value of the market research. The efficiency of sample information compares the EVSI to the EVPI. Bayesian analysis can be used to revise or update probability values using both the prior probabilities and other probabilities related to the accuracy of the information source.

Glossary

Alternative   A course of action or a strategy that may be chosen by a decision maker.

Coefficient of Realism (α)   A number from 0 to 1. When the coefficient is close to 1, the decision criterion is optimistic. When the coefficient is close to 0, the decision criterion is pessimistic.

Conditional Probability   A posterior probability.

Conditional Value or Payoff   A consequence, normally expressed in a monetary value, that occurs as a result of a particular alternative and state of nature.

Criterion of Realism   A decision-making criterion that uses a weighted average of the best and worst possible payoffs for each alternative.

Decision Making under Certainty   A decision-making environment in which the future outcomes or states of nature are known.

Decision Making under Risk   A decision-making environment in which several outcomes or states of nature may occur as a result of a decision or alternative. The probabilities of the outcomes or states of nature are known.

Decision Making under Uncertainty   A decision-making environment in which several outcomes or states of nature may occur. The probabilities of these outcomes, however, are not known.

Decision Node (Point)   In a decision tree, this is a point where the best of the available alternatives is chosen. The branches represent the alternatives.

Decision Table   A payoff table.

Decision Theory   An analytic and systematic approach to decision making.

Decision Tree   A graphical representation of a decision-making situation.

Efficiency of Sample Information   A measure of how good the sample information is relative to perfect information.

Equally Likely   A decision criterion that places an equal weight on all states of nature.

Expected Monetary Value (EMV)   The average value of a decision if it can be repeated many times. This is determined by multiplying the monetary values by their respective probabilities. The results are then added to arrive at the EMV.

Expected Value of Perfect Information (EVPI)   The average or expected value of information if it were completely accurate. The increase in EMV that results from having perfect information.

Expected Value of Sample Information (EVSI)   The increase in EMV that results from having sample or imperfect information.

Expected Value with Perfect Information (EVwPI)   The average or expected value of a decision if perfect knowledge of the future is available.

Hurwicz Criterion   The criterion of realism.

Laplace Criterion   The equally likely criterion.

Maximax   An optimistic decision-making criterion. This selects the alternative with the highest possible return.

Maximin   A pessimistic decision-making criterion. This alternative maximizes the minimum payoff. It selects the alternative with the best of the worst possible payoffs.

Minimax Regret   A criterion that minimizes the maximum opportunity loss.

Opportunity Loss   The amount you would lose by not picking the best alternative. For any state of nature, this is the difference between the consequences of any alternative and the best possible alternative.

Optimistic Criterion   The maximax criterion.

Payoff Table   A table that lists the alternatives, states of nature, and payoffs in a decision-making situation.

Posterior Probability   A conditional probability of a state of nature that has been adjusted based on sample information. This is found using Bayes' theorem.

Prior Probability   The initial probability of a state of nature before sample information is used with Bayes' theorem to obtain the posterior probability.

Regret   Opportunity loss.

Risk Avoider   A person who avoids risk. On the utility curve, as the monetary value, the utility increases at a decreasing rate. This decision maker gets less utility for a greater risk and higher potential returns.

Risk Seeker   A person who seeks risk. On the utility curve, as the monetary value increases, the utility increases at an increasing rate. This decision maker gets more pleasure for a greater risk and higher potential returns.

Sequential Decisions Decisions in which the outcome of one decision influences other decisions.

Standard Gamble The process used to determine utility values.

State of Nature An outcome or occurrence over which the decision maker has little or no control.

State-of-Nature Node In a decision tree, a point where the EMV is computed. The branches coming from this node represent states of nature.

Utility The overall value or worth of a particular outcome.

Utility Assessment The process of determining the utility of various outcomes. This is normally done using a standard gamble between any outcome for sure and a gamble between the worst and best outcomes.

Utility Curve A graph or curve that reveals the relationship between utility and monetary values. When this curve has been constructed, utility values from the curve can be used in the decision-making process.

Utility Theory A theory that allows decision makers to incorporate their risk preference and other factors into the decision-making process.

Weighted Average Criterion Another name for the criterion of realism.

Key Equations

(3-1) $\text{EMV}(\text{alternative } i) = \Sigma X_i P(X_i)$

An equation that computes expected monetary value.

(3-2) $\text{EVwPI} = \Sigma(\text{best payoff in state of nature } i)$
$\times (\text{probability of state of nature } i)$

An equation that computes the expected value with perfect information.

(3-3) $\text{EVPI} = \text{EVwPI} - \text{Best EMV}$

An equation that computes the expected value of perfect information.

(3-4) $\text{EVSI} = (\text{EV with SI} + \text{cost}) - (\text{EV without SI})$

An equation that computes the expected value (EV) of sample information (SI).

(3-5) $\text{Efficiency of sample information} = \dfrac{\text{EVSI}}{\text{EVPI}} 100\%$

An equation that compares sample information to perfect information.

(3-6) $P(A|B) = \dfrac{P(B|A)P(A)}{P(B|A)P(A) + P(B|A')P(A')}$

Bayes' theorem—the conditional probability of event A given that event B has occurred.

(3-7) $\text{Utility of other outcome} = (p)(1) + (1 - p)(0) = p$

An equation that determines the utility of an intermediate outcome.

Solved Problems

Solved Problem 3-1

Maria Rojas is considering the possibility of opening a small dress shop on Fairbanks Avenue, a few blocks from the university. She has located a good mall that attracts students. Her options are to open a small shop, a medium-sized shop, or no shop at all. The market for a dress shop can be good, average, or bad. The probabilities for these three possibilities are 0.2 for a good market, 0.5 for an average market, and 0.3 for a bad market. The net profit or loss for the medium-sized and small shops for the various market conditions are given in the following table. Building no shop at all yields no loss and no gain.

a. What do you recommend?
b. Calculate the EVPI.
c. Develop the opportunity loss table for this situation. What decisions would be made using the minimax regret criterion and the minimum EOL criterion?

ALTERNATIVE	GOOD MARKET ($)	AVERAGE MARKET ($)	BAD MARKET ($)
Small shop	75,000	25,000	−40,000
Medium-sized shop	100,000	35,000	−60,000
No shop	0	0	0

Solution

a. Since the decision-making environment is risk (probabilities are known), it is appropriate to use the EMV criterion. The problem can be solved by developing a payoff table that contains all alternatives, states of nature, and probability values. The EMV for each alternative is also computed, as in the following table:

ALTERNATIVE	GOOD MARKET ($)	AVERAGE MARKET ($)	BAD MARKET ($)	EMV ($)
Small shop	75,000	25,000	−40,000	15,500
Medium-sized shop	100,000	35,000	−60,000	19,500
No shop	0	0	0	0
Probabilities	0.20	0.50	0.30	

$$\text{EMV(small shop)} = (0.2)(\$75,000) + (0.5)(\$25,000) + (0.3)(-\$40,000) = \$15,500$$
$$\text{EMV(medium shop)} = (0.2)(\$100,000) + (0.5)(\$35,000) + (0.3)(-\$60,000) = \$19,500$$
$$\text{EMV(no shop)} = (0.2)(\$0) + (0.5)(\$0) + (0.3)(\$0) = \$0$$

As can be seen, the best decision is to build the medium-sized shop. The EMV for this alternative is $19,500.

b. $\text{EVwPI} = (0.2)\$100,000 + (0.5)\$35,000 + (0.3)\$0 = \$37,500$

$\text{EVPI} = \$37,500 - \$19,500 = \$18,000$

c. The opportunity loss table is shown here.

ALTERNATIVE	GOOD MARKET ($)	AVERAGE MARKET ($)	BAD MARKET ($)	MAXIMUM ($)	EOL ($)
Small shop	25,000	10,000	40,000	40,000	22,000
Medium-sized shop	0	0	60,000	60,000	18,000
No shop	100,000	35,000	0	100,000	37,500
Probabilities	0.20	0.50	0.30		

The best payoff in a good market is 100,000, so the opportunity losses in the first column indicate how much worse each payoff is than 100,000. The best payoff in an average market is 35,000, so the opportunity losses in the second column indicate how much worse each payoff is than 35,000. The best payoff in a bad market is 0, so the opportunity losses in the third column indicate how much worse each payoff is than 0.

The minimax regret criterion considers the maximum regret for each decision, and the decision corresponding to the minimum of these is selected. The decision would be to build a small shop since the maximum regret for this is 40,000, while the maximum regret for each of the other two alternatives is higher as shown in the opportunity loss table.

The decision based on the EOL criterion would be to build the medium shop. Note that the minimum EOL ($18,000) is the same as the EVPI computed in part *b*. The calculations are

$$\text{EOL(small)} = (0.2)25,000 + (0.5)10,000 + (0.3)40,000 = 22,000$$
$$\text{EOL(medium)} = (0.2)0 + (0.5)0 + (0.3)60,000 = 18,000$$
$$\text{EOL(no shop)} = (0.2)100,000 + (0.5)35,000 + (0.3)0 = 37,500$$

Solved Problem 3-2

Cal Bender and Becky Addison have known each other since high school. Two years ago they entered the same university and today they are taking undergraduate courses in the business school. Both hope to graduate with degrees in finance. In an attempt to make extra money and to use some of the knowledge gained from their business courses, Cal and Becky have decided to look into the possibility of starting a small company that would provide word processing services to students who needed term papers or other reports prepared in a professional manner. Using a systems approach, Cal and Becky have identified three strategies. Strategy 1 is to invest in a fairly expensive microcomputer system with a high-quality laser printer. In a favorable market, they should be able to obtain a net profit of $10,000 over the next 2 years. If the market is unfavorable, they can lose $8,000. Strategy 2 is to purchase a less expensive system. With a favorable market, they could get a return during the next 2 years of $8,000. With an unfavorable market, they would incur a loss of $4,000. Their final strategy, strategy 3, is to do nothing. Cal is basically a risk taker, whereas Becky tries to avoid risk.

a. What type of decision procedure should Cal use? What would Cal's decision be?
b. What type of decision maker is Becky? What decision would Becky make?
c. If Cal and Becky were indifferent to risk, what type of decision approach should they use? What would you recommend if this were the case?

Solution

The problem is one of decision making under uncertainty. Before answering the specific questions, a decision table should be developed showing the alternatives, states of nature, and related consequences.

ALTERNATIVE	FAVORABLE MARKET ($)	UNFAVORABLE MARKET ($)
Strategy 1	10,000	−8,000
Strategy 2	8,000	−4,000
Strategy 3	0	0

a. Since Cal is a risk taker, he should use the maximax decision criteria. This approach selects the row that has the highest or maximum value. The $10,000 value, which is the maximum value from the table, is in row 1. Thus, Cal's decision is to select strategy 1, which is an optimistic decision approach.
b. Becky should use the maximin decision criteria because she wants to avoid risk. The minimum or worst outcome for each row, or strategy, is identified. These outcomes are −$8,000 for strategy 1, −$4,000 for strategy 2, and $0 for strategy 3. The maximum of these values is selected. Thus, Becky would select strategy 3, which reflects a pessimistic decision approach.
c. If Cal and Becky are indifferent to risk, they could use the equally likely approach. This approach selects the alternative that maximizes the row averages. The row average for strategy 1 is $1,000 [i.e., $1,000 = ($10,000 − $8,000)/2]. The row average for strategy 2 is $2,000, and the row average for strategy 3 is $0. Thus, using the equally likely approach, the decision is to select strategy 2, which maximizes the row averages.

Solved Problem 3-3

Monica Britt has enjoyed sailing small boats since she was 7 years old, when her mother started sailing with her. Today, Monica is considering the possibility of starting a company to produce small sailboats for the recreational market. Unlike other mass-produced sailboats, however, these boats will be made specifically for children between the ages of 10 and 15. The boats will be of the highest quality and extremely stable, and the sail size will be reduced to prevent problems of capsizing.

Her basic decision is whether to build a large manufacturing facility, a small manufacturing facility, or no facility at all. With a favorable market, Monica can expect to make $90,000 from the large facility or $60,000 from the smaller facility. If the market is unfavorable, however, Monica estimates that she would lose $30,000 with a large facility, and she would lose only $20,000 with the small facility. Because of the expense involved in developing the initial molds and acquiring the necessary equipment

FIGURE 3.14

Monica's Decision Tree, Listing Alternatives, States of Nature, Probability Values, and Financial Outcomes for Solved Problem 3-3

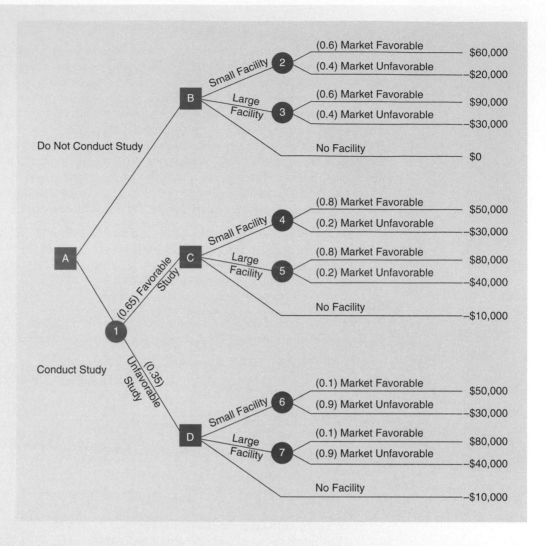

to produce fiberglass sailboats for young children, Monica has decided to conduct a pilot study to make sure that the market for the sailboats will be adequate. She estimates that the pilot study will cost her $10,000. Furthermore, the pilot study can be either favorable or unfavorable. Monica estimates that the probability of a favorable market given a favorable pilot study is 0.8. The probability of an unfavorable market given an unfavorable pilot study result is estimated to be 0.9. Monica feels that there is a 0.65 chance that the pilot study will be favorable. Of course, Monica could bypass the pilot study and simply make the decision as to whether to build a large plant, small plant, or no facility at all. Without doing any testing in a pilot study, she estimates that the probability of a favorable market is 0.6. What do you recommend? Compute the EVSI.

Solution

Before Monica starts to solve this problem, she should develop a decision tree that shows all alternatives, states of nature, probability values, and economic consequences. This decision tree is shown in Figure 3.14.

The EMV at each of the numbered nodes is calculated as follows:

$$\text{EMV(node 2)} = 60{,}000(0.6) + (-20{,}000)0.4 = 28{,}000$$
$$\text{EMV(node 3)} = 90{,}000(0.6) + (-30{,}000)0.4 = 42{,}000$$
$$\text{EMV(node 4)} = 50{,}000(0.8) + (-30{,}000)0.2 = 34{,}000$$
$$\text{EMV(node 5)} = 80{,}000(0.8) + (-40{,}000)0.2 = 56{,}000$$
$$\text{EMV(node 6)} = 50{,}000(0.1) + (-30{,}000)0.9 = -22{,}000$$
$$\text{EMV(node 7)} = 80{,}000(0.1) + (-40{,}000)0.9 = -28{,}000$$
$$\text{EMV(node 1)} = 56{,}000(0.65) + (-10{,}000)0.35 = 32{,}900$$

At each of the square nodes with letters, the decisions would be:

> Node B: Choose Large Facility since the EMV = $42,000.
>
> Node C: Choose Large Facility since the EMV = $56,000.
>
> Node D: Choose No Facility since the EMV = −$10,000.
>
> Node A: Choose Do Not Conduct Study since the EMV ($42,000) for this is higher than EMV(node 1), which is $32,900.

Based on the EMV criterion, Monica would select Do Not Conduct Study and then select Large Facility. The EMV of this decision is $42,000. Choosing to conduct the study would result in an EMV of only $32,900. Thus, the expected value of sample information is

$$\text{EVSI} = \$32,900 + \$10,000 - \$42,000$$
$$= \$900$$

Solved Problem 3-4

Developing a small driving range for golfers of all abilities has long been a desire of John Jenkins. John, however, believes that the chance of a successful driving range is only about 40%. A friend of John's has suggested that he conduct a survey in the community to get a better feeling of the demand for such a facility. There is a 0.9 probability that the research will be favorable if the driving range facility will be successful. Furthermore, it is estimated that there is a 0.8 probability that the marketing research will be unfavorable if indeed the facility will be unsuccessful. John would like to determine the chances of a successful driving range given a favorable result from the marketing survey.

Solution

This problem requires the use of Bayes' theorem. Before we start to solve the problem, we will define the following terms:

$P(\text{SF})$ = probability of successful driving range facility

$P(\text{UF})$ = probability of unsuccessful driving range facility

$P(\text{RF}|\text{SF})$ = probability that the research will be favorable given a successful driving range facility

$P(\text{RU}|\text{SF})$ = probability that the research will be unfavorable given a successful driving range facility

$P(\text{RU}|\text{UF})$ = probability that the research will be unfavorable given an unsuccessful driving range facility

$P(\text{RF}|\text{UF})$ = probability that the research will be favorable given an unsuccessful driving range facility

Now, we can summarize what we know:

$$P(\text{SF}) = 0.4$$
$$P(\text{RF}|\text{SF}) = 0.9$$
$$P(\text{RU}|\text{UF}) = 0.8$$

From this information we can compute three additional probabilities that we need to solve the problem:

$$P(\text{UF}) = 1 - P(\text{SF}) = 1 - 0.4 = 0.6$$
$$P(\text{RU}|\text{SF}) = 1 - P(\text{RF}|\text{SF}) = 1 - 0.9 = 0.1$$
$$P(\text{RF}|\text{UF}) = 1 - P(\text{RU}|\text{UF}) = 1 - 0.8 = 0.2$$

Now we can put these values into Bayes' theorem to compute the desired probability:

$$P(\text{SF}|\text{RF}) = \frac{P(\text{RF}|\text{SF}) \times P(\text{SF})}{P(\text{RF}|\text{SF}) \times P(\text{SF}) + P(\text{RF}|\text{UF}) \times P(\text{UF})}$$

$$= \frac{(0.9)(0.4)}{(0.9)(0.4) + (0.2)(0.6)}$$

$$= \frac{0.36}{(0.36 + 0.12)} = \frac{0.36}{0.48} = 0.75$$

In addition to using formulas to solve John's problem, it is possible to perform all calculations in a table:

Revised Probabilities Given a Favorable Research Result

STATE OF NATURE	CONDITIONAL PROBABILITY		PRIOR PROBABILITY		JOINT PROBABILITY	POSTERIOR PROBABILITY
Favorable market	0.9	×	0.4	=	0.36	0.36/0.48 = 0.75
Unfavorable market	0.2	×	0.6	=	0.12	0.12/0.48 = 0.25
					0.48	

As you can see from the table, the results are the same. The probability of a successful driving range given a favorable research result is 0.36/0.48, or 0.75.

Self-Test

- Before taking the self-test, refer to the learning objectives at the beginning of the chapter, the notes in the margins, and the glossary at the end of the chapter.
- Use the key at the back of the book to correct your answers.
- Restudy pages that correspond to any questions that you answered incorrectly or material you feel uncertain about.

1. In decision theory terminology, a course of action or a strategy that may be chosen by a decision maker is called
   a. a payoff.
   b. an alternative.
   c. a state of nature.
   d. none of the above.
2. In decision theory, probabilities are associated with
   a. payoffs.
   b. alternatives.
   c. states of nature.
   d. none of the above.
3. If probabilities are available to the decision maker, then the decision-making environment is called
   a. certainty.
   b. uncertainty.
   c. risk.
   d. none of the above.
4. Which of the following is a decision-making criterion that is used for decision making under risk?
   a. expected monetary value criterion
   b. Hurwicz criterion (criterion of realism)
   c. optimistic (maximax) criterion
   d. equally likely criterion
5. The minimum expected opportunity loss is
   a. equal to the highest expected payoff.
   b. greater than the expected value with perfect information.
   c. equal to the expected value of perfect information.
   d. computed when finding the minimax regret decision.
6. In using the criterion of realism (Hurwicz criterion), the coefficient of realism (α)
   a. is the probability of a good state of nature.

   b. describes the degree of optimism of the decision maker.
   c. describes the degree of pessimism of the decision maker.
   d. is usually less than zero.
7. The most that a person should pay for perfect information is
   a. the EVPI.
   b. the maximum EMV minus the minimum EMV.
   c. the maximum EOL.
   d. the maximum EMV.
8. The minimum EOL criterion will always result in the same decision as
   a. the maximax criterion.
   b. the minimax regret criterion.
   c. the maximum EMV criterion.
   d. the equally likely criterion.
9. A decision tree is preferable to a decision table when
   a. a number of sequential decisions are to be made.
   b. probabilities are available.
   c. the maximax criterion is used.
   d. the objective is to maximize regret.
10. Bayes' theorem is used to revise probabilities. The new (revised) probabilities are called
   a. prior probabilities.
   b. sample probabilities.
   c. survey probabilities.
   d. posterior probabilities.
11. On a decision tree, at each state-of-nature node,
   a. the alternative with the greatest EMV is selected.
   b. an EMV is calculated.
   c. all probabilities are added together.
   d. the branch with the highest probability is selected.

12. The EVSI
    a. is found by subtracting the EMV without sample information from the EMV with sample information.
    b. is always equal to the expected value of perfect information.
    c. equals the EMV with sample information assuming no cost for the information minus the EMV without sample information.
    d. is usually negative.

13. The efficiency of sample information
    a. is the EVSI/(maximum EMV without SI) expressed as a percentage.
    b. is the EVPI/EVSI expressed as a percentage.
    c. would be 100% if the sample information were perfect.
    d. is computed using only the EVPI and the maximum EMV.

14. On a decision tree, once the tree has been drawn and the payoffs and probabilities have been placed on the tree, the analysis (computing EMVs and selecting the best alternative)
    a. working backward (starting on the right and moving to the left).
    b. working forward (starting on the left and moving to the right).
    c. starting at the top of the tree and moving down.
    d. starting at the bottom of the tree and moving up.

15. In assessing utility values,
    a. the worst outcome is given a utility of -1.
    b. the best outcome is given a utility of 0.
    c. the worst outcome is given a utility of 0.
    d. the best outcome is given a value of -1.

16. If a rational person selects an alternative that does not maximize the EMV, we would expect that this alternative
    a. minimizes the EMV.
    b. maximizes the expected utility.
    c. minimizes the expected utility.
    d. has zero utility associated with each possible payoff.

Discussion Questions and Problems

Discussion Questions

3-1 Give an example of a good decision that you made that resulted in a bad outcome. Also give an example of a bad decision that you made that had a good outcome. Why was each decision good or bad?

3-2 Describe what is involved in the decision process.

3-3 What is an alternative? What is a state of nature?

3-4 Discuss the differences among decision making under certainty, decision making under risk, and decision making under uncertainty.

3-5 What techniques are used to solve decision-making problems under uncertainty? Which technique results in an optimistic decision? Which technique results in a pessimistic decision?

3-6 Define *opportunity loss*. What decision-making criteria are used with an opportunity loss table?

3-7 What information should be placed on a decision tree?

3-8 Describe how you would determine the best decision using the EMV criterion with a decision tree.

3-9 What is the difference between prior and posterior probabilities?

3-10 What is the purpose of Bayesian analysis? Describe how you would use Bayesian analysis in the decision-making process.

3-11 What is the EVSI? How is this computed?

3-12 How is the efficiency of sample information computed?

3-13 What is the overall purpose of utility theory?

3-14 Briefly discuss how a utility function can be assessed. What is a standard gamble, and how is it used in determining utility values?

3-15 How is a utility curve used in selecting the best decision for a particular problem?

3-16 What is a risk seeker? What is a risk avoider? How does the utility curve for these types of decision makers differ?

Problems

Q·3-17 Kenneth Brown is the principal owner of Brown Oil, Inc. After quitting his university teaching job, Ken has been able to increase his annual salary by a factor of over 100. At the present time, Ken is forced to consider purchasing some more equipment for Brown Oil because of competition. His alternatives are shown in the following table:

EQUIPMENT	FAVORABLE MARKET ($)	UNFAVORABLE MARKET ($)
Sub 100	300,000	$-200,000$
Oiler J	250,000	$-100,000$
Texan	75,000	$-18,000$

For example, if Ken purchases a Sub 100 and if there is a favorable market, he will realize a profit of $300,000. On the other hand, if the market is

 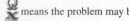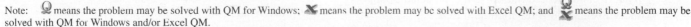

unfavorable, Ken will suffer a loss of $200,000. But Ken has always been a very optimistic decision maker.

(a) What type of decision is Ken facing?
(b) What decision criterion should he use?
(c) What alternative is best?

3-18 Although Ken Brown (discussed in Problem 3-17) is the principal owner of Brown Oil, his brother Bob is credited with making the company a financial success. Bob is vice president of finance. Bob attributes his success to his pessimistic attitude about business and the oil industry. Given the information from Problem 3-17, it is likely that Bob will arrive at a different decision. What decision criterion should Bob use, and what alternative will he select?

3-19 The *Lubricant* is an expensive oil newsletter to which many oil giants subscribe, including Ken Brown (see Problem 3-17 for details). In the last issue, the letter described how the demand for oil products would be extremely high. Apparently, the American consumer will continue to use oil products even if the price of these products doubles. Indeed, one of the articles in the *Lubricant* states that the chances of a favorable market for oil products was 70%, while the chance of an unfavorable market was only 30%. Ken would like to use these probabilities in determining the best decision.

(a) What decision model should be used?
(b) What is the optimal decision?
(c) Ken believes that the $300,000 figure for the Sub 100 with a favorable market is too high. How much lower would this figure have to be for Ken to change his decision made in part *b*?

3-20 Mickey Lawson is considering investing some money that he inherited. The following payoff table gives the profits that would be realized during the next year for each of three investment alternatives Mickey is considering:

DECISION ALTERNATIVE	STATE OF NATURE	
	GOOD ECONOMY	POOR ECONOMY
Stock market	80,000	−20,000
Bonds	30,000	20,000
CDs	23,000	23,000
Probability	0.5	0.5

(a) What decision would maximize expected profits?
(b) What is the maximum amount that should be paid for a perfect forecast of the economy?

3-21 Develop an opportunity loss table for the investment problem that Mickey Lawson faces in Problem 3-20. What decision would minimize the expected opportunity loss? What is the minimum EOL?

3-22 Allen Young has always been proud of his personal investment strategies and has done very well over the past several years. He invests primarily in the stock market. Over the past several months, however, Allen has become very concerned about the stock market as a good investment. In some cases, it would have been better for Allen to have his money in a bank than in the market. During the next year, Allen must decide whether to invest $10,000 in the stock market or in a certificate of deposit (CD) at an interest rate of 9%. If the market is good, Allen believes that he could get a 14% return on his money. With a fair market, he expects to get an 8% return. If the market is bad, he will most likely get no return at all—in other words, the return would be 0%. Allen estimates that the probability of a good market is 0.4, the probability of a fair market is 0.4, and the probability of a bad market is 0.2, and he wishes to maximize his long-run average return.

(a) Develop a decision table for this problem.
(b) What is the best decision?

3-23 In Problem 3-22, you helped Allen Young determine the best investment strategy. Now, Young is thinking about paying for a stock market newsletter. A friend of Young said that these types of letters could predict very accurately whether the market would be good, fair, or poor. Then, based on these predictions, Allen could make better investment decisions.

(a) What is the most that Allen would be willing to pay for a newsletter?
(b) Young now believes that a good market will give a return of only 11% instead of 14%. Will this information change the amount that Allen would be willing to pay for the newsletter? If your answer is yes, determine the most that Allen would be willing to pay, given this new information.

3-24 Today's Electronics specializes in manufacturing modern electronic components. It also builds the equipment that produces the components. Phyllis Weinberger, who is responsible for advising the president of Today's Electronics on electronic manufacturing equipment, has developed the following table concerning a proposed facility:

	PROFIT ($)		
	STRONG MARKET	FAIR MARKET	POOR MARKET
Large facility	550,000	110,000	−310,000
Medium-sized facility	300,000	129,000	−100,000
Small facility	200,000	100,000	−32,000
No facility	0	0	0

(a) Develop an opportunity loss table.
(b) What is the minimax regret decision?

3-25 Brilliant Color is a small supplier of chemicals and equipment that are used by some photographic stores to process 35mm film. One product that Brilliant Color supplies is BC-6. John Kubick, president of Brilliant Color, normally stocks 11, 12, or 13 cases of BC-6 each week. For each case that John sells, he receives a profit of $35. Like many photographic chemicals, BC-6 has a very short shelf life, so if a case is not sold by the end of the week, John must discard it. Since each case costs John $56, he loses $56 for every case that is not sold by the end of the week. There is a probability of 0.45 of selling 11 cases, a probability of 0.35 of selling 12 cases, and a probability of 0.2 of selling 13 cases.

(a) Construct a decision table for this problem. Include all conditional values and probabilities in the table.

(b) What is your recommended course of action?

(c) If John is able to develop BC-6 with an ingredient that stabilizes it so that it no longer has to be discarded, how would this change your recommended course of action?

3-26 Megley Cheese Company is a small manufacturer of several different cheese products. One of the products is a cheese spread that is sold to retail outlets. Jason Megley must decide how many cases of cheese spread to manufacture each month. The probability that the demand will be six cases is 0.1, seven cases is 0.3, eight cases is 0.5, and nine cases is 0.1. The cost of every case is $45, and the price that Jason gets for each case is $95. Unfortunately, any cases not sold by the end of the month are of no value, due to spoilage. How many cases of cheese should Jason manufacture each month?

3-27 Farm Grown, Inc., produces cases of perishable food products. Each case contains an assortment of vegetables and other farm products. Each case costs $5 and sells for $15. If there are any cases not sold by the end of the day, they are sold to a large food processing company for $3 a case. The probability that daily demand will be 100 cases is 0.3, the probability that daily demand will be 200 cases is 0.4, and the probability that daily demand will be 300 cases is 0.3. Farm Grown has a policy of always satisfying customer demands. If its own supply of cases is less than the demand, it buys the necessary vegetables from a competitor. The estimated cost of doing this is $16 per case.

(a) Draw a decision table for this problem.

(b) What do you recommend?

3-28 In Problem 3-27, Farm Grown, Inc. has reason to believe the probabilities may not be reliable due to changing conditions. If these probabilities are ignored, what decision would be made using the optimistic criterion? What decision would be made using the pessimistic criterion?

3-29 Mick Karra is the manager of MCZ Drilling Products, which produces a variety of specialty valves for oil field equipment. Recent activity in the oil fields has caused demand to increase drastically, and a decision has been made to open a new manufacturing facility. Three locations are being considered, and the size of the facility would not be the same in each location. Thus, overtime might be necessary at times. The following table gives the total monthly cost (in $1,000s) for each possible location under each demand possibility. The probabilities for the demand levels have been determined to be 20% for low demand, 30% for medium demand, and 50% for high demand.

	DEMAND IS LOW	DEMAND IS MEDIUM	DEMAND IS HIGH
Ardmore, OK	85	110	150
Sweetwater, TX	90	100	120
Lake Charles, LA	110	120	130

(a) Which location would be selected based on the optimistic criterion?

(b) Which location would be selected based on the pessimistic criterion?

(c) Which location would be selected based on the minimax regret criterion?

(d) Which location should be selected to minimize the expected cost of operation?

(e) How much is a perfect forecast of the demand worth?

(f) Which location would minimize the expected opportunity loss?

(g) What is the expected value of perfect information in this situation?

3-30 Even though independent gasoline stations have been having a difficult time, Susan Solomon has been thinking about starting her own independent gasoline station. Susan's problem is to decide how large her station should be. The annual returns will depend on both the size of her station and a number of marketing factors related to the oil industry and demand for gasoline. After a careful analysis, Susan developed the following table:

SIZE OF FIRST STATION	GOOD MARKET ($)	FAIR MARKET ($)	POOR MARKET ($)
Small	50,000	20,000	−10,000
Medium	80,000	30,000	−20,000
Large	100,000	30,000	−40,000
Very large	300,000	25,000	−160,000

For example, if Susan constructs a small station and the market is good, she will realize a profit of $50,000.

(a) Develop a decision table for this decision.
(b) What is the maximax decision?
(c) What is the maximin decision?
(d) What is the equally likely decision?
(e) What is the criterion of realism decision? Use an α value of 0.8.
(f) Develop an opportunity loss table.
(g) What is the minimax regret decision?

Q: 3-31 Beverly Mills has decided to lease a hybrid car to save on gasoline expenses and to do her part to help keep the environment clean. The car she selected is available from only one dealer in the local area, but that dealer has several leasing options to accommodate a variety of driving patterns. All the leases are for 3 years and require no money at the time of signing the lease. The first option has a monthly cost of $330, a total mileage allowance of 36,000 miles (an average of 12,000 miles per year), and a cost of $0.35 per mile for any miles over 36,000. The following table summarizes each of the three lease options:

3-YEAR LEASE	MONTHLY COST	MILEAGE ALLOWANCE	COST PER EXCESS MILE
Option 1	$330	36,000	$0.35
Option 2	$380	45,000	$0.25
Option 3	$430	54,000	$0.15

Beverly has estimated that, during the 3 years of the lease, there is a 40% chance she will drive an average of 12,000 miles per year, a 30% chance she will drive an average of 15,000 miles per year, and a 30% chance that she will drive 18,000 miles per year. In evaluating these lease options, Beverly would like to keep her costs as low as possible.

(a) Develop a payoff (cost) table for this situation.
(b) What decision would Beverly make if she were optimistic?
(c) What decision would Beverly make if she were pessimistic?
(d) What decision would Beverly make if she wanted to minimize her expected cost (monetary value)?
(e) Calculate the expected value of perfect information for this problem.

Q: 3-32 Refer to the leasing decision facing Beverly Mills in Problem 3-31. Develop the opportunity loss table for this situation. Which option would be chosen based on the minimax regret criterion? Which alternative would result in the lowest expected opportunity loss?

Q: 3-33 The game of roulette is popular in many casinos around the world. In Las Vegas, a typical roulette wheel has the numbers 1–36 in slots on the wheel. Half of these slots are red, and the other half are black. In the United States, the roulette wheel typically also has the numbers 0 (zero) and 00 (double zero), and both of these are on the wheel in green slots. Thus, there are 38 slots on the wheel. The dealer spins the wheel and sends a small ball in the opposite direction of the spinning wheel. As the wheel slows, the ball falls into one of the slots, and that is the winning number and color. One of the bets available is simply red or black, for which the odds are 1 to 1. If the player bets on either red or black, and that happens to be the winning color, the player wins the amount of her bet. For example, if the player bets $5 on red and wins, she is paid $5 and she still has her original bet. On the other hand, if the winning color is black or green when the player bets red, the player loses the entire bet.

(a) What is the probability that a player who bets red will win the bet?
(b) If a player bets $10 on red every time the game is played, what is the expected monetary value (expected win)?
(c) In Europe, there is usually no 00 on the wheel, just the 0. With this type of game, what is the probability that a player who bets red will win the bet? If a player bets $10 on red every time in this game (with no 00), what is the expected monetary value?
(d) Since the expected profit (win) in a roulette game is negative, why would a rational person play the game?

Q: 3-34 Refer to the Problem 3-33 for details about the game of roulette. Another bet in a roulette game is called a "straight up" bet, which means that the player is betting that the winning number will be the number that she chose. In a game with 0 and 00, there are a total of 38 possible outcomes (the numbers 1 to 36 plus 0 and 00), and each of these has the same chance of occurring. The payout on this type of bet is 35 to 1, which means the player is paid 35 and gets to keep the original bet. If a player bets $10 on the number 7 (or any single number), what is the expected monetary value (expected win)?

Q: 3-35 The Technically Techno company has several patents for a variety of different Flash memory devices that are used in computers, cell phones, and a variety of other things. A competitor has recently introduced a product based on technology very similar to something patented by Technically Techno last year. Consequently, Technically Techno has sued the other company for copyright infringement. Based on the facts in the case as well as the record of the lawyers involved, Technically Techno believes there is a 40%

chance that it will be awarded $300,000 if the lawsuit goes to court. There is a 30% chance that they would be awarded only $50,000 if they go to court and win, and there is a 30% chance they would lose the case and be awarded nothing. The estimated cost of legal fees if they go to court is $50,000. However, the other company has offered to pay Technically Techno $75,000 to settle the dispute without going to court. The estimated legal cost of this would only be $10,000. If Technically Techno wished to maximize the expected gain, should they accept the settlement offer?

3-36 A group of medical professionals is considering the construction of a private clinic. If the medical demand is high (i.e., there is a favorable market for the clinic), the physicians could realize a net profit of $100,000. If the market is not favorable, they could lose $40,000. Of course, they don't have to proceed at all, in which case there is no cost. In the absence of any market data, the best the physicians can guess is that there is a 50–50 chance the clinic will be successful. Construct a decision tree to help analyze this problem. What should the medical professionals do?

3-37 The physicians in Problem 3-36 have been approached by a market research firm that offers to perform a study of the market at a fee of $5,000. The market researchers claim their experience enables them to use Bayes' theorem to make the following statements of probability:

probability of a favorable market given
a favorable study = 0.82

probability of an unfavorable market given
a favorable study = 0.18

probability of a favorable market given
an unfavorable study = 0.11

probability of an unfavorable market given
an unfavorable study = 0.89

probability of a favorable research study = 0.55

probability of an unfavorable research study = 0.45

(a) Develop a new decision tree for the medical professionals to reflect the options now open with the market study.
(b) Use the EMV approach to recommend a strategy.
(c) What is the expected value of sample information? How much might the physicians be willing to pay for a market study?
(d) Calculate the efficiency of this sample information.

3-38 Jerry Smith is thinking about opening a bicycle shop in his hometown. Jerry loves to take his own bike on 50-mile trips with his friends, but he believes that any small business should be started only if there is

a good chance of making a profit. Jerry can open a small shop, a large shop, or no shop at all. The profits will depend on the size of the shop and whether the market is favorable or unfavorable for his products. Because there will be a 5-year lease on the building that Jerry is thinking about using, he wants to make sure that he makes the correct decision. Jerry is also thinking about hiring his old marketing professor to conduct a marketing research study. If the study is conducted, the study could be favorable (i.e., predicting a favorable market) or unfavorable (i.e., predicting an unfavorable market). Develop a decision tree for Jerry.

3-39 Jerry Smith (see Problem 3-38) has done some analysis about the profitability of the bicycle shop. If Jerry builds the large bicycle shop, he will earn $60,000 if the market is favorable, but he will lose $40,000 if the market is unfavorable. The small shop will return a $30,000 profit in a favorable market and a $10,000 loss in an unfavorable market. At the present time, he believes that there is a 50–50 chance that the market will be favorable. His old marketing professor will charge him $5,000 for the marketing research. It is estimated that there is a 0.6 probability that the survey will be favorable. Furthermore, there is a 0.9 probability that the market will be favorable given a favorable outcome from the study. However, the marketing professor has warned Jerry that there is only a probability of 0.12 of a favorable market if the marketing research results are not favorable. Jerry is confused.

(a) Should Jerry use the marketing research?
(b) Jerry, however, is unsure the 0.6 probability of a favorable marketing research study is correct. How sensitive is Jerry's decision to this probability value? How far can this probability value deviate from 0.6 without causing Jerry to change his decision?

3-40 Bill Holliday is not sure what she should do. He can build a quadplex (i.e., a building with four apartments), build a duplex, gather additional information, or simply do nothing. If he gathers additional information, the results could be either favorable or unfavorable, but it would cost him $3,000 to gather the information. Bill believes that there is a 50–50 chance that the information will be favorable. If the rental market is favorable, Bill will earn $15,000 with the quadplex or $5,000 with the duplex. Bill doesn't have the financial resources to do both. With an unfavorable rental market, however, Bill could lose $20,000 with the quadplex or $10,000 with the duplex. Without gathering additional information, Bill estimates that the probability of a favorable rental market is 0.7. A favorable report from the study would increase the probability of a favorable rental market to 0.9. Furthermore, an unfavorable report from the additional information would decrease the probability of a favorable rental market to 0.4. Of course, Bill could forget all of these numbers and do nothing. What is your advice to Bill?

: 3-41 Peter Martin is going to help his brother who wants to open a food store. Peter initially believes that there is a 50–50 chance that his brother's food store would be a success. Peter is considering doing a market research study. Based on historical data, there is a 0.8 probability that the marketing research will be favorable given a successful food store. Moreover, there is a 0.7 probability that the marketing research will be unfavorable given an unsuccessful food store.

  (a) If the marketing research is favorable, what is Peter's revised probability of a successful food store for his brother?

  (b) If the marketing research is unfavorable, what is Peter's revised probability of a successful food store for his brother?

  (c) If the initial probability of a successful food store is 0.60 (instead of 0.50), find the probabilities in parts *a* and *b*.

: 3-42 Mark Martinko has been a class A racquetball player for the past 5 years, and one of his biggest goals is to own and operate a racquetball facility. Unfortunately, Mark's thinks that the chance of a successful racquetball facility is only 30%. Mark's lawyer has recommended that he employ one of the local marketing research groups to conduct a survey concerning the success or failure of a racquetball facility. There is a 0.8 probability that the research will be favorable given a successful racquetball facility. In addition, there is a 0.7 probability that the research will be unfavorable given an unsuccessful facility. Compute revised probabilities of a successful racquetball facility given a favorable and given an unfavorable survey.

: 3-43 A financial advisor has recommended two possible mutual funds for investment: Fund A and Fund B. The return that will be achieved by each of these depends on whether the economy is good, fair, or poor. A payoff table has been constructed to illustrate this situation:

	STATE OF NATURE		
INVESTMENT	GOOD ECONOMY	FAIR ECONOMY	POOR ECONOMY
Fund A	$10,000	$2,000	−$5,000
Fund B	$6,000	$4,000	0
Probability	0.2	0.3	0.5

  (a) Draw the decision tree to represent this situation.

  (b) Perform the necessary calculations to determine which of the two mutual funds is better. Which one should you choose to maximize the expected value?

  (c) Suppose there is question about the return of Fund A in a good economy. It could be higher or

lower than $10,000. What value for this would cause a person to be indifferent between Fund A and Fund B (i.e., the EMVs would be the same)?

: 3-44 Jim Sellers is thinking about producing a new type of electric razor for men. If the market were favorable, he would get a return of $100,000, but if the market for this new type of razor were unfavorable, he would lose $60,000. Since Ron Bush is a good friend of Jim Sellers, Jim is considering the possibility of using Bush Marketing Research to gather additional information about the market for the razor. Ron has suggested that Jim use either a survey or a pilot study to test the market. The survey would be a sophisticated questionnaire administered to a test market. It will cost $5,000. Another alternative is to run a pilot study. This would involve producing a limited number of the new razors and trying to sell them in two cities that are typical of American cities. The pilot study is more accurate but is also more expensive. It will cost $20,000. Ron Bush has suggested that it would be a good idea for Jim to conduct either the survey or the pilot before Jim makes the decision concerning whether to produce the new razor. But Jim is not sure if the value of the survey or the pilot is worth the cost.

Jim estimates that the probability of a successful market without performing a survey or pilot study is 0.5. Furthermore, the probability of a favorable survey result given a favorable market for razors is 0.7, and the probability of a favorable survey result given an unsuccessful market for razors is 0.2. In addition, the probability of an unfavorable pilot study given an unfavorable market is 0.9, and the probability of an unsuccessful pilot study result given a favorable market for razors is 0.2.

  (a) Draw the decision tree for this problem without the probability values.

  (b) Compute the revised probabilities needed to complete the decision, and place these values in the decision tree.

  (c) What is the best decision for Jim? Use EMV as the decision criterion.

: 3-45 Jim Sellers has been able to estimate his utility for a number of different values. He would like to use these utility values in making the decision in Problem 3-44: $U(-\$80,000) = 0$, $U(-\$65,000) = 0.5$, $U(-\$60,000) = 0.55$, $U(-\$20,000) = 0.7$, $U(-\$5,000) = 0.8$, $U(\$0) = 0.81$, $U(\$80,000) = 0.9$, $U(\$95,000) = 0.95$, and $U(\$100,000) = 1$. Resolve Problem 3-44 using utility values. Is Jim a risk avoider?

: 3-46. Two states of nature exist for a particular situation: a good economy and a poor economy. An economic study may be performed to obtain more information about which of these will actually occur in the coming year. The study may forecast either a good economy or a poor economy. Currently there is a 60% chance that the economy will be good and a 40% chance that it will be poor. In the past, whenever the economy was good, the economic study predicted it would be good 80% of the time. (The other 20% of the time the prediction was wrong.) In the past, whenever the economy was poor, the economic study predicted it would be poor 90% of the time. (The other 10% of the time the prediction was wrong.)

(a) Use Bayes' theorem and find the following:

P(good economy | prediction of good economy)

P(poor economy | prediction of good economy)

P(good economy | prediction of poor economy)

P(poor economy | prediction of poor economy)

(b) Suppose the initial (prior) probability of a good economy is 70% (instead of 60%), and the probability of a poor economy is 30% (instead of 40%). Find the posterior probabilities in part *a* based on these new values.

Q: 3-47 The Long Island Life Insurance Company sells a term life insurance policy. If the policy holder dies during the term of the policy, the company pays $100,000. If the person does not die, the company pays out nothing and there is no further value to the policy. The company uses actuarial tables to determine the probability that a person with certain characteristics will die during the coming year. For a particular individual, it is determined that there is a 0.001 chance that the person will die in the next year and a 0.999 chance that the person will live and the company will pay out nothing. The cost of this policy is $200 per year. Based on the EMV criterion, should the individual buy this insurance policy? How would utility theory help explain why a person would buy this insurance policy?

Q: 3-48 In Problem 3-37, you helped the medical professionals analyze their decision using expected monetary value as the decision criterion. This group has also assessed their utility for money: $U(-\$45,000) = 0$, $U(-\$40,000) = 0.1$, $U(-\$5,000) = 0.7$, $U(\$0) = 0.9$, $U(\$95,000) = 0.99$, and $U(\$100,000) = 1$. Use expected utility as the decision criterion, and determine the best decision for the medical professionals. Are the medical professionals risk seekers or risk avoiders?

Q: 3-49 In this chapter, a decision tree was developed for John Thompson (see Figure 3.5 for the complete decision tree analysis). After completing the analysis, John was not completely sure that he is indifferent to risk. After going through a number of standard gambles, John was able to assess his utility for money. Here are some of the utility assessments: $U(-\$190,000) = 0$, $U(-\$180,000) = 0.05$, $U(-\$30,000) = 0.10$, $U(-\$20,000) = 0.15$, $U(-\$10,000) = 0.2$, $U(\$0) = 0.3$, $U(\$90,000) =$

0.15, $U(\$100,000) = 0.6$, $U(\$190,000) = 0.95$, and $U(\$200,000) = 1.0$. If John maximizes his expected utility, does his decision change?

Q: 3-50 In the past few years, the traffic problems in Lynn McKell's hometown have gotten worse. Now, Broad Street is congested about half the time. The normal travel time to work for Lynn is only 15 minutes when Broad Street is used and there is no congestion. With congestion, however, it takes Lynn 40 minutes to get to work. If Lynn decides to take the expressway, it will take 30 minutes regardless of the traffic conditions. Lynn's utility for travel time is: $U(15 \text{ minutes}) = 0.9$, $U(30 \text{ minutes}) = 0.7$, and $U(40 \text{ minutes}) = 0.2$.

(a) Which route will minimize Lynn's expected travel time?

(b) Which route will maximize Lynn's utility?

(c) When it comes to travel time, is Lynn a risk seeker or a risk avoider?

Q: 3-51 Coren Chemical, Inc., develops industrial chemicals that are used by other manufacturers to produce photographic chemicals, preservatives, and lubricants. One of their products, K-1000, is used by several photographic companies to make a chemical that is used in the film-developing process. To produce K-1000 efficiently, Coren Chemical uses the batch approach, in which a certain number of gallons is produced at one time. This reduces setup costs and allows Coren Chemical to produce K-1000 at a competitive price. Unfortunately, K-1000 has a very short shelf life of about 1 month.

Coren Chemical produces K-1000 in batches of 500 gallons, 1,000 gallons, 1,500 gallons, and 2,000 gallons. Using historical data, David Coren was able to determine that the probability of selling 500 gallons of K-1000 is 0.2. The probabilities of selling 1,000, 1,500, and 2,000 gallons are 0.3, 0.4, and 0.1, respectively. The question facing David is how many gallons to produce of K-1000 in the next batch run. K-1000 sells for $20 per gallon. Manufacturing cost is $12 per gallon, and handling costs and warehousing costs are estimated to be $1 per gallon. In the past, David has allocated advertising costs to K-1000 at $3 per gallon. If K-1000 is not sold after the batch run, the chemical loses much of its important properties as a developer. It can, however, be sold at a salvage value of $13 per gallon. Furthermore, David has guaranteed to his suppliers that there will always be an adequate supply of K-1000. If David does run out, he has agreed to purchase a comparable chemical from a competitor at $25 per gallon. David sells all of the chemical at $20 per gallon, so his shortage means that David loses the $5 to buy the more expensive chemical.

(a) Develop a decision tree of this problem.

(b) What is the best solution?

(c) Determine the expected value of perfect information.

⊘: 3-52 The Jamis Corporation is involved with waste management. During the past 10 years it has become one of the largest waste disposal companies in the Midwest, serving primarily Wisconsin, Illinois, and Michigan. Bob Jamis, president of the company, is considering the possibility of establishing a waste treatment plant in Mississippi. From past experience, Bob believes that a small plant in northern Mississippi would yield a $500,000 profit regardless of the market for the facility. The success of a medium-sized waste treatment plant would depend on the market. With a low demand for waste treatment, Bob expects a $200,000 return. A medium demand would yield a $700,000 return in Bob's estimation, and a high demand would return $800,000. Although a large facility is much riskier, the potential return is much greater. With a high demand for waste treatment in Mississippi, the large facility should return a million dollars. With a medium demand, the large facility will return only $400,000. Bob estimates that the large facility would be a big loser if there were a low demand for waste treatment. He estimates that he would lose approximately $200,000 with a large treatment facility if demand were indeed low. Looking at the economic conditions for the upper part of the state of Mississippi and using his experience in the field, Bob estimates that the probability of a low demand for treatment plants is 0.15. The probability for a medium-demand facility is approximately 0.40, and the probability of a high demand for a waste treatment facility is 0.45.

Because of the large potential investment and the possibility of a loss, Bob has decided to hire a market research team that is based in Jackson, Mississippi. This team will perform a survey to get a better feeling for the probability of a low, medium, or high demand for a waste treatment facility. The cost of the survey is $50,000. To help Bob determine whether to go ahead with the survey, the marketing research firm has provided Bob with the following information:

P(survey results | possible outcomes)

POSSIBLE OUTCOME	SURVEY RESULTS		
	LOW SURVEY RESULTS	MEDIUM SURVEY RESULTS	HIGH SURVEY RESULTS
Low demand	0.7	0.2	0.1
Medium demand	0.4	0.5	0.1
High demand	0.1	0.3	0.6

As you see, the survey could result in three possible outcomes. Low survey results mean that a low demand is likely. In a similar fashion, medium survey results or high survey results would mean a medium or a high demand, respectively. What should Bob do?

⊘: 3-53 Mary is considering opening a new grocery store in town. She is evaluating three sites: downtown, the mall, and out at the busy traffic circle. Mary calculated the value of successful stores at these locations as follows: downtown, $250,000; the mall, $300,000; the circle, $400,000. Mary calculated the losses if unsuccessful to be $100,000 at either downtown or the mall and $200,000 at the circle. Mary figures her chance of success to be 50% downtown, 60% at the mall, and 75% at the traffic circle.

(a) Draw a decision tree for Mary and select her best alternative.

(b) Mary has been approached by a marketing research firm that offers to study the area to determine if another grocery store is needed. The cost of this study is $30,000. Mary believes there is a 60% chance that the survey results will be positive (show a need for another grocery store). SRP = survey results positive, SRN = survey results negative, SD = success downtown, SM = success at mall, SC = success at circle, SD' = don't succeed downtown, and so on. For studies of this nature:
$P(\text{SRP} \mid \text{success}) = 0.7$,
$P(\text{SRN} \mid \text{success}) = 0.3$,
$P(\text{SRP} \mid \text{not success}) = 0.2$; and
$P(\text{SRN} \mid \text{not success}) = 0.8$.
Calculate the revised probabilities for success (and not success) for each location, depending on survey results.

(c) How much is the marketing research worth to Mary? Calculate the EVSI.

⊘:3-54. Sue Reynolds has to decide if she should get information (at a cost of $20,000) to invest in a retail store. If she gets the information, there is a 0.6 probability that the information will be favorable and a 0.4 probability that the information will not be favorable. If the information is favorable, there is a 0.9 probability that the store will be a success. If the information is not favorable, the probability of a successful store is only 0.2. Without any information, Sue estimates that the probability of a successful store will be 0.6. A successful store will give a return of $100,000. If the store is built but is not successful, Sue will see a loss of $80,000. Of course, she could always decide not to build the retail store.

(a) What do you recommend?

(b) What impact would a 0.7 probability of obtaining favorable information have on Sue's decision? The probability of obtaining unfavorable information would be 0.3.

(c) Sue believes that the probabilities of a successful and an unsuccessful retail store given favorable information might be 0.8 and 0.2, respectively, instead of 0.9 and 0.1, respectively. What impact, if any, would this have on Sue's decision and the best EMV?

(d) Sue had to pay $20,000 to get information. Would her decision change if the cost of the information increased to $30,000?

(c) Using the data in this problem and the following utility table, compute the expected utility. Is this the curve of a risk seeker or a risk avoider?

MONETARY VALUE	UTILITY
$100,000	1
$80,000	0.4
$0	0.2
−$20,000	0.1
−$80,000	0.05
−$100,000	0

(f) Compute the expected utility given the following utility table. Does this utility table represent a risk seeker or a risk avoider?

MONETARY VALUE	UTILITY
$100,000	1
$80,000	0.9
$0	0.8
−$20,000	0.6
−$80,000	0.4
−$100,000	0

Internet Homework Problems

See our Internet home page, at **www.pearsonhighered.com/render**, for additional homework problems, Problems 3-55 to 3-60.

Case Study

Starting Right Corporation

After watching a movie about a young woman who quit a successful corporate career to start her own baby food company, Julia Day decided that she wanted to do the same. In the movie, the baby food company was very successful. Julia knew, however, that it is much easier to make a movie about a successful woman starting her own company than to actually do it. The product had to be of the highest quality, and Julia had to get the best people involved to launch the new company. Julia resigned from her job and launched her new company—Starting Right.

Julia decided to target the upper end of the baby food market by producing baby food that contained no preservatives but had a great taste. Although the price would be slightly higher than for existing baby food, Julia believed that parents would be willing to pay more for a high-quality baby food. Instead of putting baby food in jars, which would require preservatives to stabilize the food, Julia decided to try a new approach. The baby food would be frozen. This would allow for natural ingredients, no preservatives, and outstanding nutrition.

Getting good people to work for the new company was also important. Julia decided to find people with experience in finance, marketing, and production to get involved with Starting Right. With her enthusiasm and charisma, Julia was able to find such a group. Their first step was to develop prototypes of the new frozen baby food and to perform a small pilot test of the new product. The pilot test received rave reviews.

The final key to getting the young company off to a good start was to raise funds. Three options were considered: corporate bonds, preferred stock, and common stock. Julia decided that each investment should be in blocks of $30,000. Furthermore, each investor should have an annual income of at least $40,000 and a net worth of $100,000 to be eligible to invest in Starting Right. Corporate bonds would return 13% per year for the next 5 years. Julia furthermore guaranteed that investors in the corporate bonds would get at least $20,000 back at the end of 5 years. Investors in preferred stock should see their initial investment increase by a factor of 4 with a good market or see the investment worth only half of the initial investment with an unfavorable market. The common stock had the greatest potential. The initial investment was expected to increase by a factor of 8 with a good market, but investors would lose everything if the market was unfavorable. During the next 5 years, it was expected that inflation would increase by a factor of 4.5% each year.

Discussion Questions

1. Sue Pansky, a retired elementary school teacher, is considering investing in Starting Right. She is very conservative and is a risk avoider. What do you recommend?
2. Ray Cahn, who is currently a commodities broker, is also considering an investment, although he believes that there is only an 11% chance of success. What do you recommend?
3. Lila Battle has decided to invest in Starting Right. While she believes that Julia has a good chance of being

successful, Lila is a risk avoider and very conservative. What is your advice to Lila?

4. George Yates believes that there is an equally likely chance for success. What is your recommendation?

5. Peter Metarko is extremely optimistic about the market for the new baby food. What is your advice for Pete?

6. Julia Day has been told that developing the legal documents for each fundraising alternative is expensive. Julia would like to offer alternatives for both risk-averse and risk-seeking investors. Can Julia delete one of the financial alternatives and still offer investment choices for risk seekers and risk avoiders?

Case Study

Blake Electronics

In 1979, Steve Blake founded Blake Electronics in Long Beach, California, to manufacture resistors, capacitors, inductors, and other electronic components. During the Vietnam War, Steve was a radio operator, and it was during this time that he became proficient at repairing radios and other communications equipment. Steve viewed his 4-year experience with the army with mixed feelings. He hated army life, but this experience gave him the confidence and the initiative to start his own electronics firm.

Over the years, Steve kept the business relatively unchanged. By 1992, total annual sales were in excess of $2 million. In 1996, Steve's son, Jim, joined the company after finishing high school and 2 years of courses in electronics at Long Beach Community College. Jim was always aggressive in high school athletics, and he became even more aggressive as general sales manager of Blake Electronics. This aggressiveness bothered Steve, who was more conservative. Jim would make deals to supply companies with electronic components before he bothered to find out if Blake Electronics had the ability or capacity to produce the components. On several occasions this behavior caused the company some embarrassing moments when Blake Electronics was unable to produce the electronic components for companies with which Jim had made deals.

In 2000, Jim started to go after government contracts for electronic components. By 2002, total annual sales had increased to more than $10 million, and the number of employees exceeded 200. Many of these employees were electronic specialists and graduates of electrical engineering programs from top colleges and universities. But Jim's tendency to stretch Blake Electronics to contracts continued as well, and by 2007, Blake Electronics had a reputation with government agencies as a company that could not deliver what it promised. Almost overnight, government contracts stopped, and Blake Electronics was left with an idle workforce and unused manufacturing equipment. This high overhead started to melt away profits, and in 2009, Blake Electronics was faced with the possibility of sustaining a loss for the first time in its history.

In 2010, Steve decided to look at the possibility of manufacturing electronic components for home use. Although this was a totally new market for Blake Electronics, Steve was convinced that this was the only way to keep Blake

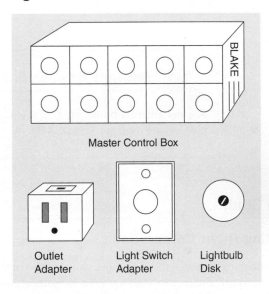

Figure 3.15   Master Control Center

Electronics from dipping into the red. The research team at Blake Electronics was given the task of developing new electronic devices for home use. The first idea from the research team was the Master Control Center. The basic components for this system are shown in Figure 3.15.

The heart of the system is the master control box. This unit, which would have a retail price of $250, has two rows of five buttons. Each button controls one light or appliance and can be set as either a switch or a rheostat. When set as a switch, a light finger touch on the button turns a light or appliance on or off. When set as a rheostat, a finger touching the button controls the intensity of the light. Leaving your finger on the button makes the light go through a complete cycle ranging from off to bright and back to off again.

To allow for maximum flexibility, each master control box is powered by two D-sized batteries that can last up to a year, depending on usage. In addition, the research team has developed three versions of the master control box—versions A, B, and C. If a family wants to control more than 10 lights or appliances, another master control box can be purchased.

The lightbulb disk, which would have a retail price of $2.50, is controlled by the master control box and is used to control the intensity of any light. A different disk is available for each button position for all three master control boxes. By inserting the lightbulb disk between the lightbulb and the socket, the appropriate button on the master control box can completely control the intensity of the light. If a standard light switch is used, it must be on at all times for the master control box to work.

One disadvantage of using a standard light switch is that only the master control box can be used to control the particular light. To avoid this problem, the research team developed a special light switch adapter that would sell for $15. When this device is installed, either the master control box or the light switch adapter can be used to control the light.

When used to control appliances other than lights, the master control box must be used in conjunction with one or more outlet adapters. The adapters are plugged into a standard wall outlet, and the appliance is then plugged into the adapter. Each outlet adapter has a switch on top that allows the appliance to be controlled from the master control box or the outlet adapter. The price of each outlet adapter would be $25.

The research team estimated that it would cost $500,000 to develop the equipment and procedures needed to manufacture the master control box and accessories. If successful, this venture could increase sales by approximately $2 million. But will the master control boxes be a successful venture? With a 60% chance of success estimated by the research team, Steve had serious doubts about trying to market the master control boxes even though he liked the basic idea. Because of his reservations, Steve decided to send requests for proposals (RFPs) for additional marketing research to 30 marketing research companies in southern California.

The first RFP to come back was from a small company called Marketing Associates, Inc. (MAI), which would charge $100,000 for the survey. According to its proposal, MAI has been in business for about 3 years and has conducted about 100 marketing research projects. MAI's major strengths appeared to be individual attention to each account, experienced staff, and

TABLE 3.19 Success Figures for MAI

| | SURVEY RESULTS | | |
OUTCOME	FAVORABLE	UNFAVORABLE	TOTAL
Successful venture	35	20	55
Unsuccessful venture	15	30	45

fast work. Steve was particularly interested in one part of the proposal, which revealed MAI's success record with previous accounts. This is shown in Table 3.19.

The only other proposal to be returned was by a branch office of Iverstine and Walker, one of the largest marketing research firms in the country. The cost for a complete survey would be $300,000. While the proposal did not contain the same success record as MAI, the proposal from Iverstine and Walker did contain some interesting information. The chance of getting a favorable survey result, given a successful venture, was 90%. On the other hand, the chance of getting an unfavorable survey result, given an unsuccessful venture, was 80%. Thus, it appeared to Steve that Iverstine and Walker would be able to predict the success or failure of the master control boxes with a great amount of certainty.

Steve pondered the situation. Unfortunately, both marketing research teams gave different types of information in their proposals. Steve concluded that there would be no way that the two proposals could be compared unless he got additional information from Iverstine and Walker. Furthermore, Steve wasn't sure what he would do with the information, and if it would be worth the expense of hiring one of the marketing research firms.

Discussion Questions

1. Does Steve need additional information from Iverstine and Walker?
2. What would you recommend?

 Internet Case Studies

See our Internet home page, at **www.pearsonhighered.com/render**, for these additional case studies:

(1) **Drink-At-Home, Inc.:** This case involves the development and marketing of a new beverage.
(2) **Ruth Jones' Heart Bypass Operation:** This case deals with a medical decision regarding surgery.
(3) **Ski Right:** This case involves the development and marketing of a new ski helmet.
(4) **Study Time:** This case is about a student who must budget time while studying for a final exam.

Bibliography

Abbas, Ali E. "Invariant Utility Functions and Certain Equivalent Transformations," *Decision Analysis* 4, 1(March 2007): 17–31.

Carassus, Laurence, and Miklós Rásonyi. "Optimal Strategies and Utility-Based Prices Converge When Agents' Preferences Do," *Mathematics of Operations Research* 32, 1 (February 2007): 102–117.

Congdon, Peter. *Bayesian Statistical Modeling.* New York: John Wiley & Sons, Inc., 2001.

Ewing, Paul L., Jr. "Use of Decision Analysis in the Army Base Realignment and Closure (BRAC) 2005 Military Value Analysis," *Decision Analysis* 3 (March 2006): 33–49.

Hammond, J. S., R. L. Kenney, and H. Raiffa. "The Hidden Traps in Decision Making," *Harvard Business Review* (September–October 1998): 47–60.

Hurley, William J. "The 2002 Ryder Cup: Was Strange's Decision to Put Tiger Woods in the Anchor Match a Good One?" *Decision Analysis* 4, 1 (March 2007): 41–45.

Kirkwood, C. W. "An Overview of Methods for Applied Decision Analysis," *Interfaces* 22, 6 (November–December 1992): 28–39.

Kirkwood, C. W. "Approximating Risk Aversion in Decision Analysis Applications," *Decision Analysis* 1 (March 2004): 51–67.

Luce, R., and H. Raiffa. *Games and Decisions.* New York: John Wiley & Sons, Inc., 1957.

Maxwell, Daniel T. "Improving Hard Decisions," *OR/MS Today* 33, 6 (December 2006): 51–61.

Patchak, William M. "Software Survey: Decision Analysis." *OR/MS Today* 39, 5 (October 2012).

Paté-Cornell, M. Elisabeth, and Robin L. Dillon. "The Respective Roles of Risk and Decision Analyses in Decision Support," *Decision Analysis* 3 (December 2006): 220–232.

Pennings, Joost M. E., and Ale Smidts. "The Shape of Utility Functions and Organizational Behavior," *Management Science* 49, 9 (September 2003): 1251–1263.

Raiffa, Howard, John W. Pratt, and Robert Schlaifer. *Introduction to Statistical Decision Theory.* Boston: MIT Press, 1995.

Raiffa, Howard, and Robert Schlaifer. *Applied Statistical Decision Theory.* New York: John Wiley & Sons, Inc., 2000.

Render, B., and R. M. Stair. *Cases and Readings in Management Science,* 2nd ed. Boston: Allyn & Bacon, Inc., 1988.

Schlaifer, R. *Analysis of Decisions Under Uncertainty.* New York: McGraw-Hill Book Company, 1969.

Smith, James E., and Robert L. Winkler. "The Optimizer's Curse: Skepticism and Postdecision Surprise in Decision Analysis," *Management Science* 52 (March 2006): 311–322.

van Binsbergen, Jules H., and Leslie M. Marx. "Exploring Relations Between Decision Analysis and Game Theory," *Decision Analysis* 4, 1 (March 2007): 32–40.

Wallace, Stein W. "Decision Making Under Uncertainty: Is Sensitivity Analysis of Any Use?" *Operations Research* 48, 1 (2000): 20–25.

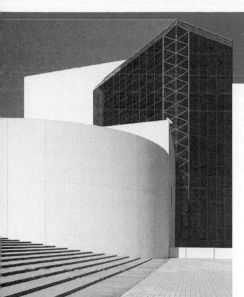

CHAPTER 4

Regression Models

LEARNING OBJECTIVES

After completing this chapter, students will be able to:

1. Identify variables and use them in a regression model.
2. Develop simple linear regression equations from sample data and interpret the slope and intercept.
3. Compute the coefficient of determination and the coefficient of correlation and interpret their meanings.
4. Interpret the F test in a linear regression model.
5. List the assumptions used in regression and use residual plots to identify problems.

6. Develop a multiple regression model and use it for prediction purposes.
7. Use dummy variables to model categorical data.
8. Determine which variables should be included in a multiple regression model
9. Transform a nonlinear function into a linear one for use in regression.
10. Understand and avoid mistakes commonly made in the use of regression analysis.

CHAPTER OUTLINE

4.1   Introduction

Two purposes of regression analysis are to understand the relationship between variables and to predict the value of one based on the other.

Regression analysis is a very valuable tool for today's manager. Regression has been used to model things such as the relationship between level of education and income, the price of a house and the square footage, and the sales volume for a company relative to the dollars spent on advertising. When businesses are trying to decide which location is best for a new store or branch office, regression models are often used. Cost estimation models are often regression models. The applicability of regression analysis is virtually limitless.

There are generally two purposes for regression analysis. The first is to understand the relationship between variables such as advertising expenditures and sales. The second purpose is to predict the value of one variable based on the value of the other. Because of this, regression is a very important forecasting technique and will be mentioned again in Chapter 5.

In this chapter, the simple linear regression model will first be developed, and then a more complex multiple regression model will be used to incorporate even more variables into our model. In any regression model, the variable to be predicted is called the **dependent variable** or **response variable**. The value of this is said to be dependent upon the value of an **independent variable**, which is sometimes called an **explanatory variable** or a **predictor variable**.

4.2   Scatter Diagrams

A scatter diagram is a graph of the data.

To investigate the relationship between variables, it is helpful to look at a graph of the data. Such a graph is often called a **scatter diagram** or a **scatter plot**. Normally the independent variable is plotted on the horizontal axis and the dependent variable is plotted on the vertical axis. The following example will illustrate this.

Triple A Construction Company renovates old homes in Albany. Over time, the company has found that its dollar volume of renovation work is dependent on the Albany area payroll. The figures for Triple A's revenues and the amount of money earned by wage earners in Albany for the past 6 years are presented in Table 4.1. Economists have predicted the local area payroll to be $600 million next year, and Triple A wants to plan accordingly.

Figure 4.1 provides a scatter diagram for the Triple A Construction data given in Table 4.1. This graph indicates that higher values for the local payroll seem to result in higher sales for the company. There is not a perfect relationship because not all the points lie in a straight line, but there is a relationship. A line has been drawn through the data to help show the relationship that exists between the payroll and sales. The points do not all lie on the line, so there would be some error involved if we tried to predict sales based on payroll using this or any other line. Many lines could be drawn through these points, but which one best represents the true relationship? Regression analysis provides the answer to this question.

TABLE 4.1

Triple A Construction Company Sales and Local Payroll

TRIPLE A'S SALES ($100,000s)	LOCAL PAYROLL ($100,000,000s)
6	3
8	4
9	6
5	4
4.5	2
9.5	5

FIGURE 4.1

Scatter Diagram of Triple A Construction Company Data

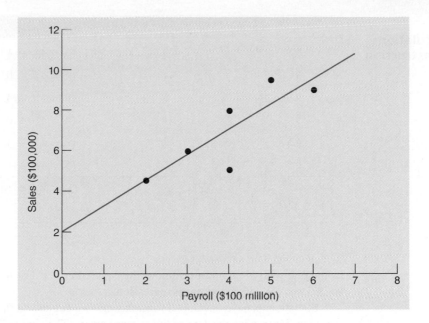

4.3 Simple Linear Regression

In any regression model, there is an implicit assumption (which can be tested) that a relationship exists between the variables. There is also some random error that cannot be predicted. The underlying simple linear regression model is

$$Y = \beta_0 + \beta_1 X + \epsilon \tag{4-1}$$

where

The dependent variable is Y and the independent variable is X.

Y = dependent variable (response variable)

X = independent variable (predictor variable or explanatory variable)

β_0 = intercept (value of Y when $X = 0$)

β_1 = slope of regression line

ϵ = random error

Estimates of the slope and intercept are found from sample data.

The true values for the intercept and slope are not known, and therefore they are estimated using sample data. The regression equation based on sample data is given as

$$\hat{Y} = b_0 + b_1 X \tag{4-2}$$

where

$\hat{Y}$ = predicted value of Y

b_0 = estimate of β_0, based on sample results

b_1 = estimate of β_1, based on sample results

In the Triple A Construction example, we are trying to predict the sales, so the dependent variable (Y) would be sales. The variable we use to help predict sales is the Albany area payroll, so this is the independent variable (X). Although any number of lines can be drawn through these points to show a relationship between X and Y in Figure 4.1, the line that will be chosen is the one that in some way minimizes the errors. **Error** is defined as

$$\text{Error} = (\text{Actual value}) - (\text{Predicted value})$$

$$e = Y - \hat{Y} \tag{4-3}$$

The regression line minimizes the sum of the squared errors.

Since errors may be positive or negative, the average error could be zero even though there are extremely large errors—both positive and negative. To eliminate the difficulty of negative errors canceling positive errors, the errors can be squared. The best regression line will be defined

TABLE 4.2

Regression Calculations for Triple A Construction

Y	X	$(X - \bar{X})^2$	$(X - \bar{X})(Y - \bar{Y})$
6	3	$(3 - 4)^2 = 1$	$(3 - 4)(6 - 7) = 1$
8	4	$(4 - 4)^2 = 0$	$(4 - 4)(8 - 7) = 0$
9	6	$(6 - 4)^2 = 4$	$(6 - 4)(9 - 7) = 4$
5	4	$(4 - 4)^2 = 0$	$(4 - 4)(5 - 7) = 0$
4.5	2	$(2 - 4)^2 = 4$	$(2 - 4)(4.5 - 7) = 5$
9.5	5	$(5 - 4)^2 = 1$	$(5 - 4)(9.5 - 7) = 2.5$
$\sum Y = 42$	$\sum X = 24$	$\sum (X - \bar{X})^2 = 10$	$\sum (X - \bar{X})(Y - \bar{Y}) = 12.5$
$\bar{Y} = 42/6 = 7$	$\bar{X} = 24/6 = 4$		

as the one with the minimum sum of the squared errors. For this reason, regression analysis is sometimes called **least-squares** regression.

Statisticians have developed formulas that we can use to find the equation of a straight line that would minimize the sum of the squared errors. The simple linear regression equation is

$$\hat{Y} = b_0 + b_1 X$$

The following formulas can be used to compute the intercept and the slope:

$$\bar{X} = \frac{\sum X}{n} = \text{average (mean) of } X \text{ values}$$

$$\bar{Y} = \frac{\sum Y}{n} = \text{average (mean) of } Y \text{ values}$$

$$b_1 = \frac{\sum (X - \bar{X})(Y - \bar{Y})}{\sum (X - \bar{X})^2} \tag{4-4}$$

$$b_0 = \bar{Y} - b_1 \bar{X} \tag{4-5}$$

The preliminary calculations are shown in Table 4.2. There are other "shortcut" formulas that are helpful when doing the computations on a calculator, and these are presented in Appendix 4.1. They will not be shown here, as computer software will be used for most of the other examples in this chapter.

Computing the slope and intercept of the regression equation for the Triple A Construction Company example, we have

$$\bar{X} = \frac{\sum X}{6} = \frac{24}{6} = 4$$

$$\bar{Y} = \frac{\sum X}{6} = \frac{42}{6} = 7$$

$$b_1 = \frac{\sum (X - \bar{X})(Y - \bar{Y})}{\sum (X - \bar{X})^2} = \frac{12.5}{10} = 1.25$$

$$b_0 = \bar{Y} - b_1 \bar{X} = 7 - (1.25)(4) = 2$$

The estimated regression equation therefore is

$$\hat{Y} = 2 + 1.25X$$

or

$$\text{sales} = 2 + 1.25(\text{payroll})$$

If the payroll next year is $600 million ($X = 6$), then the predicted value would be

$$\hat{Y} = 2 + 1.25(6) = 9.5$$

or $950,000.

One of the purposes of regression is to understand the relationship among variables. This model tells us that for each $100 million (represented by X) increase in the payroll, we would expect the sales to increase by $125,000 since $b_1 = 1.25$ ($100,000s). This model helps Triple A Construction see how the local economy and company sales are related.

4.4 Measuring the Fit of the Regression Model

Deviations (errors) may be positive or negative.

A regression equation can be developed for any variables X and Y, even random numbers. We certainly would not have any confidence in the ability of one random number to predict the value of another random number. How do we know that the model is actually helpful in predicting Y based on X? Should we have confidence in this model? Does the model provide better predictions (smaller errors) than simply using the average of the Y values?

In the Triple A Construction example, sales figures (Y) varied from a low of 4.5 to a high of 9.5, and the mean was 7. If each sales value is compared with the mean, we see how far they deviate from the mean and we could compute a measure of the total variability in sales. Because Y is sometimes higher and sometimes lower than the mean, there may be both positive and negative deviations. Simply summing these values would be misleading because the negatives would cancel out the positives, making it appear that the numbers are closer to the mean than they actually are. To prevent this problem, we will use the **sum of squares total (SST)** to measure the total variability in Y:

The SST measures the total variability in Y about the mean.

$$\text{SST} = \Sigma(Y - \bar{Y})^2 \qquad (4\text{-}6)$$

If we did not use X to predict Y, we would simply use the mean of Y as the prediction, and the SST would measure the accuracy of our predictions. However, a regression line may be used to predict the value of Y, and while there are still errors involved, the sum of these squared errors will be less than the total sum of squares just computed. The **sum of squares error (SSE)** is

The SSE measures the variability in Y about the regression line.

$$\text{SSE} = \Sigma e^2 = \Sigma(Y - \hat{Y})^2 \qquad (4\text{-}7)$$

Table 4.3 provides the calculations for the Triple A Construction example. The mean ($\bar{Y} = 7$) is compared to each value and we get

$$\text{SST} = 22.5$$

The prediction ($\hat{Y}$) for each observation is computed and compared to the actual value. This results in

$$\text{SSE} = 6.875$$

The SSE is much lower than the SST. Using the regression line has reduced the variability in the sum of squares by $22.5 - 6.875 = 15.625$. This is called the **sum of squares regression (SSR)** and indicates how much of the total variability in Y is explained by the regression model. Mathematically, this can be calculated as

$$\text{SSR} = \Sigma(\hat{Y} - \bar{Y})^2 \qquad (4\text{-}8)$$

TABLE 4.3 Sum of Squares for Triple A Construction

Y	X	$(Y - \bar{Y})^2$	$\hat{Y}$	$(Y - \hat{Y})^2$	$(\hat{Y} - \bar{Y})^2$
6	3	$(6 - 7)^2 = 1$	$2 + 1.25(3) = 5.75$	0.0625	1.563
8	4	$(8 - 7)^2 = 1$	$2 + 1.25(4) = 7.00$	1	0
9	6	$(9 - 7)^2 = 4$	$2 + 1.25(6) = 9.50$	0.25	6.25
5	4	$(5 - 7)^2 = 4$	$2 + 1.25(4) = 7.00$	4	0
4.5	2	$(4.5 - 7)^2 = 6.25$	$2 + 1.25(2) = 4.50$	0	6.25
9.5	5	$(9.5 - 7)^2 = 6.25$	$2 + 1.25(5) = 8.25$	1.5625	1.563
		$\Sigma(Y - \bar{Y})^2 = 22.5$		$\Sigma(Y - \hat{Y})^2 = 6.875$	$\Sigma(\hat{Y} - \bar{Y})^2 = 15.625$
$\bar{Y} = 7$		$\text{SST} = 22.5$		$\text{SSE} = 6.875$	$\text{SSR} = 15.625$

FIGURE 4.2

Deviations from the Regression Line and from the Mean

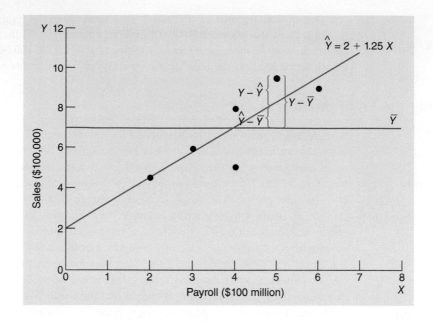

Table 4.3 indicates

$$SSR = 15.625$$

There is a very important relationship between the sums of squares that we have computed:

$$(\text{Sum of squares total}) = (\text{Sum of squares due to regression}) + (\text{Sum of squares error})$$

$$SST = SSR + SSE \tag{4-9}$$

Figure 4.2 displays the data for Triple A Construction. The regression line is shown, as is a line representing the mean of the Y values. The errors used in computing the sums of squares are shown on this graph. Notice how the sample points are closer to the regression line than they are to the mean.

Coefficient of Determination

The SSR is sometimes called the explained variability in Y while the SSE is the unexplained variability in Y. The proportion of the variability in Y that is explained by the regression equation is called the **coefficient of determination** and is denoted by r^2. Thus,

r^2 is the proportion of variability in Y that is explained by the regression equation.

$$r^2 = \frac{SSR}{SST} = 1 - \frac{SSE}{SST} \tag{4-10}$$

Thus, r^2 can be found using either the SSR or the SSE. For Triple A Construction, we have

$$r^2 = \frac{15.625}{22.5} = 0.6944$$

This means that about 69% of the variability in sales (Y) is explained by the regression equation based on payroll (X).

If every point in the sample were on the regression line (meaning all errors are 0), then 100% of the variability in Y could be explained by the regression equation, so $r^2 = 1$ and SSE = 0. The lowest possible value of r^2 is 0, indicating that X explains 0% of the variability in Y. Thus, r^2 can range from a low of 0 to a high of 1. In developing regression equations, a good model will have an r^2 value close to 1.

If every point lies on the regression line, $r^2 = 1$ and SSE = 0.

Correlation Coefficient

Another measure related to the coefficient of determination is the **coefficient of correlation**. This measure also expresses the degree or strength of the linear relationship. It is usually expressed as **r** and can be any number between and including +1 and −1. Figure 4.3 illustrates

The correlation coefficient ranges from −1 to +1.

FIGURE 4.3

Four Values of the Correlation Coefficient

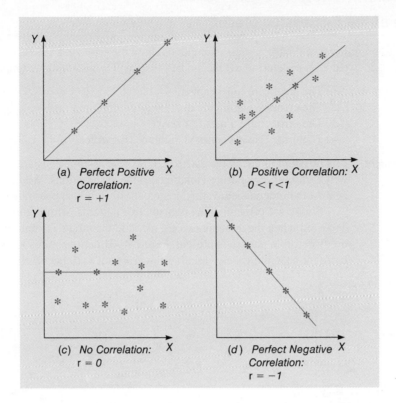

(a) Perfect Positive Correlation: $r = +1$

(b) Positive Correlation: $0 < r < 1$

(c) No Correlation: $r = 0$

(d) Perfect Negative Correlation: $r = -1$

possible scatter diagrams for different values of r. The value of r is the square root of r^2. It is negative if the slope is negative, and it is positive if the slope is positive. Thus,

$$r = \pm\sqrt{r^2} \tag{4-11}$$

For the Triple A Construction example with $r^2 = 0.6944$,

$$r = \sqrt{0.6944} = 0.8333$$

We know it is positive because the slope is $+1.25$.

IN ACTION   Using Regression as Part of Improvement Initiative at Trane/Ingersoll Rand

Trane U.S. Inc. is a brand of Ingersoll Rand and is a leader in both home and commercial air conditioning. In an effort to improve quality and efficiency, the company consolidated its manufacturing of evaporator and condenser coils into one location in South Carolina. A key part of the coil unit is a header, which controls the flow of water or refrigerant through the coil. With about 120 unique headers produced on each shift, with increased demand for their air conditioners due to federal refrigerant standards, and with growing pressure to reduce costs, Trane began an improvement initiative in 2010.

Value stream mapping, a lean manufacturing technique, was used to visualize the entire process and identify waste in the system. A new layout was suggested to improve processing and reduce the overall time of production. To predict how well the new layout would perform in the manufacture of the headers, data was collected about the time to move materials into position, time to set up a job, time to set up a machine, and time to process a job. Several regression models were developed to

determine which job characteristics were most significant in the various times involved in processing, and to measure the variability in times. These were used in simulation models that were developed to determine the overall impact of the new layout and to determine where bottlenecks might occur. One of the bottlenecks, at a robotic machine for welding, was eliminated by retooling the robot to allow the machine operator to operate both sides of the robot. This enables the robot to process two headers simultaneously.

The improvement initiatives from this project are estimated to save over $700,000 per year. This project highlighted the importance of data-based analytics and lean manufacturing tools in identifying the improvement tactics for complex value streams. The company plans similar improvement initiatives for other value streams in the future.

Source: Based on John B. Jensen, Sanjay L. Ahire, and Manoj K. Malhotra. "Trane/Ingersoll Rand Combines Lean and Operations Research Tools to Redesign Feeder Manufacturing Operations," *Interfaces* 43, 4 (July–August 2013): 325–340.

4.5 Assumptions of the Regression Model

If we can make certain assumptions about the errors in a regression model, we can perform statistical tests to determine if the model is useful. The following assumptions are made about the errors:

1. The errors are independent.
2. The errors are normally distributed.
3. The errors have a mean of zero.
4. The errors have a constant variance (regardless of the value of X).

A plot of the errors may highlight problems with the model.

It is possible to check the data to see if these assumptions are met. Often a plot of the residuals will highlight any glaring violations of the assumptions. When the errors (residuals) are plotted against the independent variable, the pattern should appear random.

Figure 4.4 presents some typical error patterns, with Figure 4.4A displaying a pattern that is expected when the assumptions are met and the model is appropriate. The errors are random and no discernible pattern is present. Figure 4.4B demonstrates an error pattern in which the errors increase as X increases, violating the constant variance assumption. Figure 4.4C shows errors

FIGURE 4.4A

Pattern of Errors Indicating Randomness

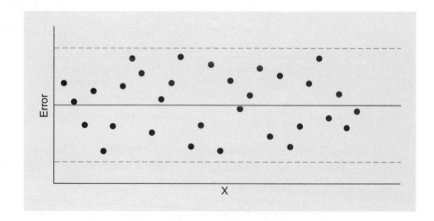

FIGURE 4.4B

Nonconstant Error Variance

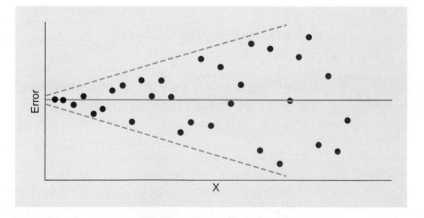

FIGURE 4.4C

Errors Indicate Relationship Is Not Linear

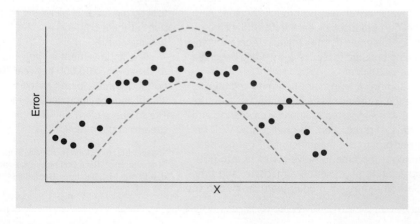

consistently increasing at first, and then consistently decreasing. A pattern such as this would indicate that the model is not linear and some other form (perhaps quadratic) should be used. In general, patterns in the plot of the errors indicate problems with the assumptions or the model specification.

Estimating the Variance

The error variance is estimated by the MSE.

While the errors are assumed to have constant variance (σ^2), this is usually not known. It can be estimated from the sample results. The estimate of σ^2 is the **mean squared error (MSE)** and is denoted by s^2. The MSE is the sum of squares due to error divided by the degrees of freedom:[1]

$$s^2 = \text{MSE} = \frac{\text{SSE}}{n - k - 1} \tag{4-12}$$

where

$$n = \text{number of observations in the sample}$$
$$k = \text{number of independent variables}$$

In the Triple A Construction example, $n = 6$ and $k = 1$. So

$$s^2 = \text{MSE} = \frac{\text{SSE}}{n - k - 1} = \frac{6.8750}{6 - 1 - 1} = \frac{6.8750}{4} = 1.7188$$

From this we can estimate the standard deviation as

$$s = \sqrt{\text{MSE}} \tag{4-13}$$

This is called the **standard error of the estimate** or the *standard deviation of the regression*. In this example,

$$s = \sqrt{\text{MSE}} = \sqrt{1.7188} = 1.31$$

This is used in many of the statistical tests about the model. It is also used to find interval estimates for both Y and regression coefficients.[2]

4.6   Testing the Model for Significance

Both the MSE and r^2 provide a measure of accuracy in a regression model. However, when the sample size is too small, it is possible to get good values for both of these even if there is no relationship between the variables in the regression model. To determine whether these values are meaningful, it is necessary to test the model for significance.

To see if there is a linear relationship between X and Y, a statistical hypothesis test is performed. The underlying linear model was given in Equation 4-1 as

$$Y = \beta_0 + \beta_1 X + \epsilon$$

*An **F** test is used to determine if there is a relationship between **X** and **Y**.*

If $\beta_1 = 0$, then Y does not depend on X in any way. The null hypothesis says there is no linear relationship between the two variables (i.e., $\beta_1 = 0$). The alternate hypothesis is that there is a linear relationship (i.e., $\beta_1 \neq 0$). If the null hypothesis can be rejected, then we have proven that a linear relationship does exist, so X is helpful in predicting Y. The F distribution is used for testing this hypothesis. Appendix D contains values for the F distribution that can be used when calculations are performed by hand. See Chapter 2 for a review of the F distribution. The results of the test can also be obtained from both Excel and QM for Windows.

The F statistic used in the hypothesis test is based on the MSE (seen in the previous section) and the mean squared regression (MSR). The MSR is calculated as

$$\text{MSR} = \frac{\text{SSR}}{k} \tag{4-14}$$

---

[1] See bibliography at end of this chapter for books with further details.
[2] The MSE is a common measure of accuracy in forecasting. When used with techniques besides regression, it is common to divide the SSE by n rather than $n - k - 1$.

where

$$k = \text{number of independent variables in the model}$$

The F statistic is

$$F = \frac{\text{MSR}}{\text{MSE}} \tag{4-15}$$

Based on the assumptions regarding the errors in a regression model, this calculated F statistic is described by the F distribution with

$$\text{degrees of freedom for the numerator} = \text{df}_1 = k$$
$$\text{degrees of freedom for the denominator} = \text{df}_2 = n - k - 1$$

where

$$k = \text{the number of independent } (X) \text{ variables}$$

If the significance level for the F test is low, there is a relationship between X and Y.

If there is very little error, the denominator (MSE) of the F statistic is very small relative to the numerator (MSR), and the resulting F statistic would be large. This would be an indication that the model is useful. A significance level related to the value of the F statistic is then found. Whenever the F value is large, the observed significance level (p-value) will be low, indicating that it is extremely unlikely that this could have occurred by chance. When the F value is large (with a resulting small significance level), we can reject the null hypothesis that there is no linear relationship. This means that there is a linear relationship and the values of MSE and r^2 are meaningful.

The hypothesis test just described is summarized here:

Steps in Hypothesis Test for a Significant Regression Model

1. Specify null and alternative hypotheses:

$$H_0 : \beta_1 = 0$$
$$H_1 : \beta_1 \neq 0$$

2. Select the level of significance (α). Common values are 0.01 and 0.05.
3. Calculate the value of the test statistic using the formula

$$F = \frac{\text{MSR}}{\text{MSE}}$$

4. Make a decision using one of the following methods:
   (a) Reject the null hypothesis if the test statistic is greater than the F value from the table in Appendix D. Otherwise, do not reject the null hypothesis:

$$\text{Reject if } F_{\text{calculated}} > F_{\alpha, \text{df}_1, \text{df}_2}$$
$$\text{df}_1 = k$$
$$\text{df}_2 = n - k - 1$$

   (b) Reject the null hypothesis if the **observed significance level**, or **p-value**, is less than the level of significance (α). Otherwise, do not reject the null hypothesis:

$$p\text{-value} = P(F > \text{calculated test statistic})$$
$$\text{Reject if } p\text{-value} < \alpha$$

Triple A Construction Example

To illustrate the process of testing the hypothesis about a significant relationship, consider the Triple A Construction example. Appendix D will be used to provide values for the F distribution.

Step 1.

$$H_0 : \beta_1 = 0 \quad \text{(no linear relationship between } X \text{ and } Y)$$
$$H_1 : \beta_1 \neq 0 \quad \text{(linear relationship exists between } X \text{ and } Y)$$

Step 2.

$$\text{Select } \alpha = 0.05$$

Step 3. Calculate the value of the test statistic. The MSE was already calculated to be 1.7188. The MSR is then calculated so that F can be found:

$$\text{MSR} = \frac{\text{SSR}}{k} = \frac{15.6250}{1} = 15.6250$$

$$F = \frac{\text{MSR}}{\text{MSE}} = \frac{15.6250}{1.7188} = 9.09$$

Step 4. (a) Reject the null hypothesis if the test statistic is greater than the F value from the table in Appendix D:

$$\text{df}_1 = k = 1$$
$$\text{df}_2 = n - k - 1 = 6 - 1 - 1 = 4$$

The value of F associated with a 5% level of significance and with degrees of freedom 1 and 4 is found in Appendix D. Figure 4.5 illustrates this:

$$F_{0.05,1,4} = 7.71$$
$$F_{\text{calculated}} = 9.09$$
$$\text{Reject H}_0 \text{ because } 9.09 > 7.71$$

Thus, there is sufficient data to conclude that there is a statistically significant relationship between X and Y, so the model is helpful. The strength of this relationship is measured by $r^2 = 0.69$. Thus, we can conclude that about 69% of the variability in sales (Y) is explained by the regression model based on local payroll (X).

The Analysis of Variance (ANOVA) Table

When software such as Excel or QM for Windows is used to develop regression models, the output provides the observed significance level, or p-value, for the calculated F value. This is then compared to the level of significance (α) to make the decision.

FIGURE 4.5

F **Distribution for Triple A Construction Test for Significance**

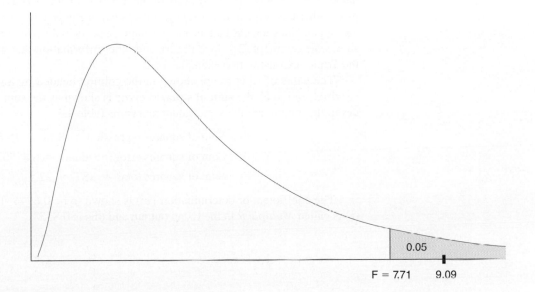

F = 7.71   9.09

TABLE 4.4

Analysis of Variance Table for Regression

	DF	SS	MS	F	SIGNIFICANCE F
Regression	k	SSR	$MSR = SSR/k$	MSR/MSE	$P(F > MSR/MSE)$
Residual	$n - k - 1$	SSE	$MSE = SSE/(n - k - 1)$		
Total	$n - 1$	SST			

Table 4.4 provides summary information about the ANOVA table. This shows how the numbers in the last three columns of the table are computed. The last column of this table, labeled Significance F, is the p-value, or observed significance level, which can be used in the hypothesis test about the regression model.

Triple A Construction ANOVA Example

The Excel output that includes the ANOVA table for the Triple A Construction data is shown in the next section. The observed significance level for $F = 9.0909$ is given to be 0.0394. This means

$$P(F > 9.0909) = 0.0394$$

Because this probability is less than 0.05 (α), we would reject the hypothesis of no linear relationship and conclude that there is a linear relationship between X and Y. Note in Figure 4.5 that the area under the curve to the right of 9.09 is clearly less than 0.05, which is the area to the right of the F value associated with a 0.05, level of significance.

4.7 Using Computer Software for Regression

Software such as Excel 2013, Excel QM, and QM for Windows is usually used for the regression calculations. All of these will be illustrated using the Triple A Construction example.

Excel 2013

To use Excel 2013 for regression, enter the data in columns. Click the *Data* tab to access the data ribbon. Then select *Data Analysis*, as shown in Program 4.1A. If *Data Analysis* does not appear on the Data ribbon, the Excel add-in for this has not yet been activated. See Appendix F at the end of the book for instructions on how to activate this. Once this add-in is activated, it will remain on the *Data* ribbon for future use.

When the *Data Analysis* window opens, scroll down to and highlight *Regression* and click *OK*, as illustrated in Program 4.1A. The Regression window will open, as shown in Program 4.1B, and you can input the X and Y ranges. Check the *Labels* box because the cells with the variable name were included in the first row of the X and Y ranges. To have the output presented on this page rather than on a new worksheet, select *Output Range* and give a cell address for the start of the output. Click the *OK* button, and the output appears in the output range specified. Program 4.1C shows the intercept (2), slope (1.25), and other information that was previously calculated for the Triple A Construction example.

The sums of squares are shown in the column headed by SS. Another name for *error* is **residual**. In Excel, the **sum of squares error** is shown as the sum of squares residual. The values in this output are the same values shown in Table 4.3:

$$\text{Sum of squares regression} = \text{SSR} = 15.625$$
$$\text{Sum of squares error (residual)} = 6.8750$$
$$\text{Sum of squares total} = \text{SST} = 22.5$$

The coefficient of determination (r^2) is shown to be 0.6944. The coefficient of correlation (r) is called *Multiple R* in the Excel output, and this is 0.8333.

PROGRAM 4.1A

Accessing the Regression Option in Excel 2013

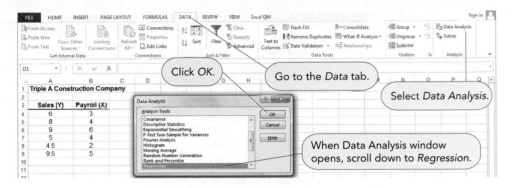

PROGRAM 4.1B

Data Input for Regression in Excel 2013

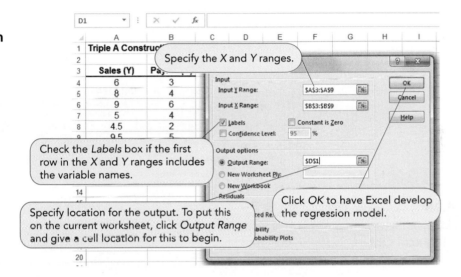

PROGRAM 4.1C

Excel 2013 Output for Triple A Construction Example

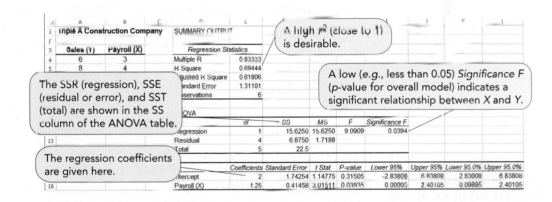

Excel QM

To use Excel QM for regression, from the Excel QM ribbon select the module by clicking *Alphabetical - Forecasting - Multiple Regression* as shown in Program 4.2A. A window will open to allow you to specify the size of the problem, as shown in Program 4.2B. Enter a name or title for the problem, the number of past observations, and the number of independent (*X*) variables. For the Triple A Construction example, there are 6 past periods of data and 1 independent variable. When you click *OK*, a spreadsheet will appear for you to enter the *X* and *Y* data in the shaded area. The calculations are automatically performed, so there is nothing to do after entering the data. The results are seen in Program 4.2C.

PROGRAM 4.2A   Using Excel QM for Regression

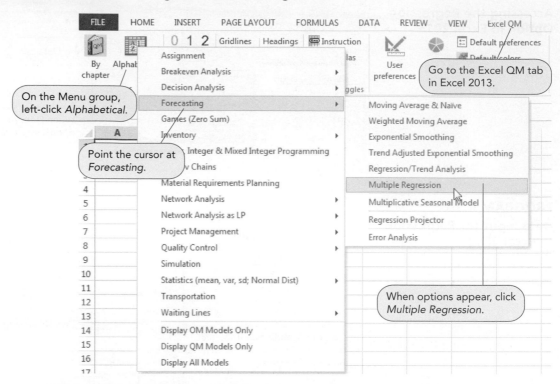

PROGRAM 4.2B

Initializing the Spreadsheet in Excel QM

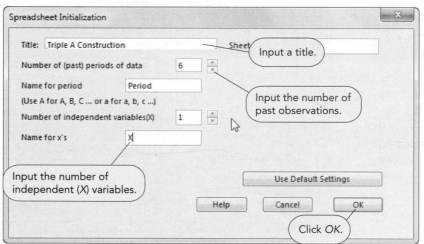

PROGRAM 4.2C

Input and Results for Regression in Excel QM

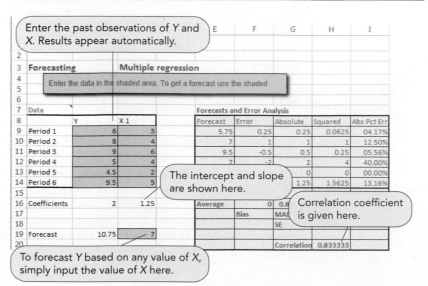

QM for Windows

To develop a regression equation using QM for Windows for the Triple A Construction Company data, select the *Forecasting* module and select *New*. Then choose *Least Squares— Simple and Multiple Regression*, as illustrated in Program 4.3A. This opens the window shown in Program 4.3B. Enter the number of observations (6 in this example) and specify the number of independent variables (1 in this example). Left-click *OK* and a window opens allowing you to input the data as shown in Program 4.3C. After entering the data, click *Solve*, and the forecasting results shown in Program 4.3D are displayed. The equation as well as other information is provided on this screen. Note the regression equation is displayed across two lines. Additional output, including the ANOVA table, is available by clicking the *Window* option on the toolbar.

PROGRAM 4.3A

QM for Windows Regression Option in Forecasting Module

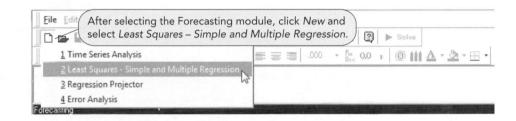

PROGRAM 4.3B

QM for Windows Screen to Initialize the Problem

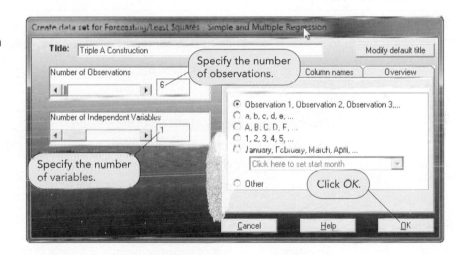

PROGRAM 4.3C

Data Input for Triple A Construction Example

	Triple A Construction	
	Dpndnt var, Y	X1
Observation 1	6	3
Observation 2	8	4
Observation 3	9	6
Observation 4	5	4
Observation 5	4.5	2
Observation 6	9.5	5

PROGRAM 4.3D

QM for Windows Output for Triple A Construction Example

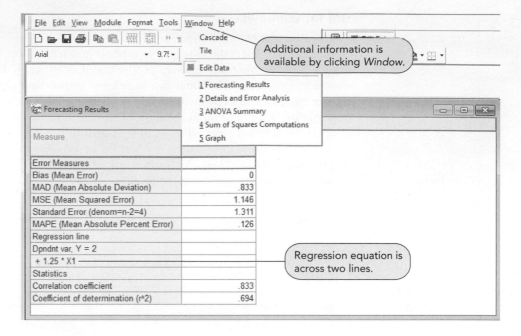

4.8 Multiple Regression Analysis

A multiple regression model has more than one independent variable.

The **multiple regression model** is a practical extension of the model we just observed. It allows us to build a model with several independent variables. The underlying model is

$$Y = \beta_0 + \beta_1 X_1 + \beta_2 X_2 + \cdots + \beta_k X_k + \epsilon \tag{4-16}$$

where

$$
\begin{aligned}
Y &= \text{dependent variable (response variable)} \\
X_i &= i\text{th independent variable (predictor variable or explanatory variable)} \\
\beta_0 &= \text{intercept (value of } Y \text{ when all } X_i = 0) \\
\beta_i &= \text{coefficient of the } i\text{th independent variable} \\
k &= \text{number of independent variables} \\
\epsilon &= \text{random error}
\end{aligned}
$$

To estimate the values of these coefficients, a sample is taken and the following equation is developed:

$$\hat{Y} = b_0 + b_1 X_1 + b_2 X_2 + \cdots + b_k X_k \tag{4-17}$$

where

$$
\begin{aligned}
\hat{Y} &= \text{predicted value of } Y \\
b_0 &= \text{sample intercept (and is an estimate of } \beta_0) \\
b_i &= \text{sample coefficient of } i\text{th variable (and is an estimate of } \beta_i)
\end{aligned}
$$

Consider the case of Jenny Wilson Realty, a real estate company in Montgomery, Alabama. Jenny Wilson, owner and broker for this company, wants to develop a model to determine a suggested listing price for houses based on the size of the house and the age of the house. She selects a sample of houses that have sold recently in a particular area, and she records the selling price, the square footage of the house, the age of the house, and also the

TABLE 4.5

Jenny Wilson Real
Estate Data

SELLING PRICE ($)	SQUARE FOOTAGE	AGE	CONDITION
95,000	1,926	30	Good
119,000	2,069	40	Excellent
124,800	1,720	30	Excellent
135,000	1,396	15	Good
142,800	1,706	32	Mint
145,000	1,847	38	Mint
159,000	1,950	27	Mint
165,000	2,323	30	Excellent
182,000	2,285	26	Mint
183,000	3,752	35	Good
200,000	2,300	18	Good
211,000	2,525	17	Good
215,000	3,800	40	Excellent
219,000	1,740	12	Mint

condition (good, excellent, or mint) of each house as shown in Table 4.5. Initially Jenny plans to use only the square footage and age to develop a model, although she wants to save the information on condition of the house to use later. She wants to find the coefficients for the following multiple regression model:

$$\hat{Y} = b_0 + b_1X_1 + b_2X_2$$

where

$\hat{Y}$ = predicted value of dependent variable (selling price)

b_0 = Y intercept

X_1 and X_2 = value of the two independent variables (square footage and age), respectively

b_1 and b_2 = slopes for X_1 and X_2, respectively

Excel can be used to develop multiple regression models.

The mathematics of multiple regression becomes quite complex, so we leave formulas for b_0, b_1, and b_2 to regression textbooks.[3] Excel can be used to develop a multiple regression model just as it was used for a simple linear regression model. When entering the data in Excel, it is important that all of the independent variables are in adjoining columns to facilitate the input. From the *Data* tab in Excel, select *Data Analysis* and then *Regression*, as shown earlier, in Program 4.1A. This opens the regression window to allow the input, as shown in Program 4.4A. Note that the *X Range* includes the data in two columns (B and C) because there are two independent variables. The Excel output that Jenny Wilson obtains is shown in Program 4.4B, and it provides the following equation:

$$\hat{Y} = b_0 + b_1X_1 + b_2X_2$$
$$= 146,630.89 + 43.82\,X_1 - 2898.69\,X_2$$

Evaluating the Multiple Regression Model

A multiple regression model can be evaluated in a manner similar to the way a simple linear regression model is evaluated. Both the *p*-value for the *F* test and r^2 can be interpreted the same with multiple regression models as they are with simple linear regression

[3]See, for example, Norman R. Draper and Harry Smith. *Applied Regression Analysis*, 3rd ed. New York: John Wiley & Sons, Inc., 1998.

PROGRAM 4.4A

Input Screen for Jenny Wilson Realty Multiple Regression in Excel 2013

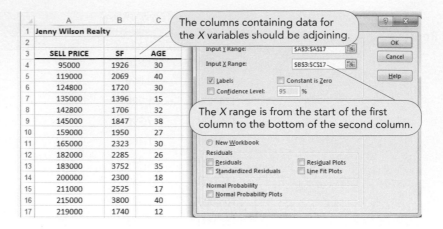

PROGRAM 4.4B

Excel 2013 Output Screen for Jenny Wilson Realty Multiple Regression Example

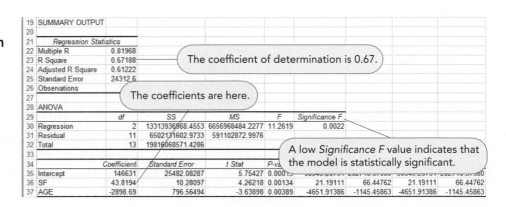

models. However, as there is more than one independent variable, the hypothesis that is being tested with the F test is that all the coefficients are equal to 0. If all these are 0, then none of the independent variables in the model is helpful in predicting the dependent variable.

To determine which of the independent variables in a multiple regression model is significant, a significance test on the coefficient for each variable is performed. While statistics textbooks can provide the details of these tests, the results of these tests are automatically displayed in the Excel output. The null hypothesis is that the coefficient is 0 ($H_0:\beta_i = 0$) and the alternate hypothesis is that it is not 0 ($H_1:\beta_i \neq 0$). The test statistic is calculated in Excel, and the p-value is given. If the p-value is lower than the level of significance (α), then the null hypothesis is rejected and it can be concluded that the variable is significant.

Jenny Wilson Realty Example

In the Jenny Wilson Realty example in Program 4.4B, the overall model is statistically significant and useful in predicting the selling price of the house because the p-value for the F test is 0.002. The r^2 value is 0.6719, so 67% of the variability in selling price for these houses can be explained by the regression model. However, there were two independent variables in the model—square footage and age. It is possible that one of these is significant and the other is not. The F test simply indicates that the model as a whole is significant.

Two significance tests can be performed to determine if square footage or age (or both) are significant. In Program 4.4B, the results of two hypothesis tests are provided. The first test for variable X_1 (square footage) is

$$H_0{:}\beta_1 = 0$$
$$H_1{:}\beta_1 \neq 0$$

Using a 5% level of significance ($\alpha = 0.05$), the null hypothesis is rejected because the p-value for this is 0.0013. Thus, square footage is helpful in predicting the price of a house.

Similarly, the variable X_2 (age) is tested using the Excel output, and the p-value is 0.0039. The null hypothesis is rejected because this is less than 0.05. Thus, age is also helpful in predicting the price of a house.

4.9 Binary or Dummy Variables

A dummy variable is also called an indicator variable or a binary variable.

All of the variables we have used in regression examples have been quantitative variables such as sales figures, payroll numbers, square footage, and age. These have all been easily measurable and have had numbers associated with them. There are many times when we believe a qualitative variable rather than a quantitative variable would be helpful in predicting the dependent variable Y. For example, regression may be used to find a relationship between annual income and certain characteristics of the employees. Years of experience at a particular job would be a quantitative variable. However, information regarding whether or not a person has a college degree might also be important. This would not be a measurable value or quantity, so a special variable called a **dummy variable** (or a **binary variable** or an **indicator variable**) would be used. A dummy variable is assigned a value of 1 if a particular condition is met (e.g., a person has a college degree), and a value of 0 otherwise.

Return to the Jenny Wilson Realty example. Jenny believes that a better model can be developed if the condition of the property is included. To incorporate the condition of the house into the model, Jenny looks at the information available (see Table 4.5), and sees that the three categories are good condition, excellent condition, and mint condition. Since these are not quantitative variables, she must use dummy variables. These are defined as

$$X_3 = 1 \text{ if house is in excellent condition}$$
$$= 0 \text{ otherwise}$$
$$X_4 = 1 \text{ if house is in mint condition}$$
$$= 0 \text{ otherwise}$$

The number of dummy variables must equal 1 less than the number of categories of a qualitative variable.

Notice there is no separate variable for "good" condition. If X_3 and X_4 are both 0, then the house cannot be in excellent or mint condition, so it must be in good condition. When using dummy variables, the number of variables must be 1 less than the number of categories. In this problem, there were three categories (good, excellent, and mint condition) so we must have two dummy variables. If we had mistakenly used too many variables and the number of dummy variables equaled the number of categories, then the mathematical computations could not be performed or would not give reliable values.

These dummy variables will be used with the two previous variables (X_1 - square footage, and X_2 - age) to try to predict the selling prices of houses for Jenny Wilson. Programs 4.5A and 4.5B provide the Excel input and output for this new data, and this shows how the dummy variables were coded. The significance level for the F test is 0.00017, so this model is statistically significant. The coefficient of determination (r^2) is 0.898, so this is a much better model than the previous one. The regression equation is

$$\hat{Y} = 121{,}658 + 56.43X_1 - 3{,}962X_2 + 33{,}162X_3 + 47{,}369X_4$$

PROGRAM 4.5A

Input Screen for Jenny Wilson Realty Example with Dummy Variables in Excel 2013

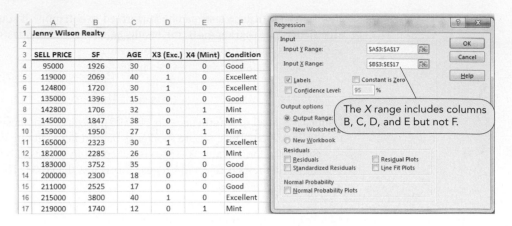

PROGRAM 4.5B

Output Screen for Jenny Wilson Realty Example with Dummy Variables in Excel 2013

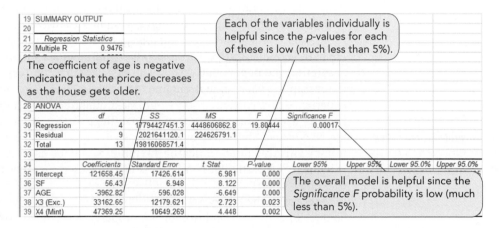

This indicates that a house in excellent condition ($X_3 = 1, X_4 = 0$) would sell for about $33,162 more than a house in good condition ($X_3 = 0, X_4 = 0$). A house in mint condition ($X_3 = 0, X_4 = 1$) would sell for about $47,369 more than a house in good condition.

4.10 Model Building

In developing a good regression model, possible independent variables are identified and the best ones are selected to be used in the model. The best model is a statistically significant model with a high r^2 and few variables.

The value of r^2 can never decrease when more variables are added to the model.

As more variables are added to a regression model, r^2 will usually increase, and it cannot decrease. It is tempting to keep adding variables to a model to try to increase r^2. However, if too many independent variables are included in the model, problems can arise. For this reason, the **adjusted r^2** value is often used (rather than r^2) to determine if an additional independent variable is beneficial. The adjusted r^2 takes into account the number of independent variables in the model, and it is possible for the adjusted r^2 to decrease. The formula for r^2 is

The adjusted r^2 may decrease when more variables are added to the model.

$$r^2 = \frac{SSR}{SST} = 1 - \frac{SSE}{SST}$$

The adjusted r^2 is

$$\text{Adjusted } r^2 = 1 - \frac{SSE/(n - k - 1)}{SST/(n - 1)} \tag{4-18}$$

Notice that as the number of variables (k) increases, $n - k - 1$ will decrease. This causes $SSE/(n - k - 1)$ to increase, and consequently the adjusted r^2 will decrease unless the extra variable in the model causes a significant decrease in the SSE. Thus, the reduction in error (and SSE) must be sufficient to offset the change in k.

As a general rule of thumb, if the adjusted r^2 increases when a new variable is added to the model, the variable should probably remain in the model. If the adjusted r^2 decreases when a new variable is added, the variable should not remain in the model. Other factors should also be considered when trying to build the model, but they are beyond the introductory level of this chapter.

A variable should not be added to the model if it causes the adjusted r^2 *to decrease.*

Stepwise Regression

While the process of model building may be tedious, there are many statistical software packages that include stepwise regression procedures to do this. **Stepwise regression** is an automated process to systematically add or delete independent variables from a regression model. A *forward stepwise procedure* puts the most significant variable in the model first and then adds the next variable that will improve the model the most, given that the first variable is already in the model. Variables continue to be added in this fashion until all the variables are in the model or until any remaining variables do not significantly improve the model. A *backward stepwise procedure* begins with all independent variables in the model, and one by one the least helpful variables are deleted. This continues until only significant variables remain. Many variations of these stepwise models exist.

Multicollinearity

In the Jenny Wilson Realty example illustrated in Program 4.5B, we saw an r^2 of about 0.90 and an adjusted r^2 of 0.85. While other variables such as the size of the lot, the number of bedrooms, and the number of bathrooms might be related to the selling price of a house, we may not want to include these in the model. It is likely that these variables would be correlated with the square footage of the house (e.g., more bedrooms usually means a larger house), which is already included in the model. Thus, the information provided by these additional variables might be duplication of information already in the model.

Multicollinearity exists when a variable is correlated to other variables.

When an independent variable is correlated with one other independent variable, the variables are said to be **collinear**. If an independent variable is correlated with a combination of other independent variables, the condition of **multicollinearity** exists. This can create problems in interpreting the coefficients of the variables as several variables are providing duplicate information. For example, if two independent variables were monthly salary expenses for a company and annual salary expenses for a company, the information provided in one is also provided in the other. Several sets of regression coefficients for these two variables would yield exactly the same results. Thus, individual interpretation of these variables would be questionable, although the model itself is still good for prediction purposes. When multicollinearity exists, the overall F test is still valid, but the hypothesis tests related to the individual coefficients are not. A variable may appear to be significant when it is insignificant, or a variable may appear to be insignificant when it is significant.

4.11 Nonlinear Regression

The regression models we have seen are linear models. However, at times there exist nonlinear relationships between variables. Some simple variable transformations can be used to create an apparently linear model from a nonlinear relationship. This allows us to use Excel and other linear regression programs to perform the calculations. We will demonstrate this in the following example.

Transformations may be used to turn a nonlinear model into a linear model.

On every new automobile sold in the United States, the fuel efficiency (as measured by miles per gallon [MPG] of gasoline) of the automobile is prominently displayed on the

TABLE 4.6
**Automobile Weight
Versus MPG**

MPG	WEIGHT (1,000 LB.)	MPG	WEIGHT (1,000 LB.)
12	4.58	20	3.18
13	4.66	23	2.68
15	4.02	24	2.65
18	2.53	33	1.70
19	3.09	36	1.95
19	3.11	42	1.92

window sticker. The MPG is related to several factors, one of which is the weight of the automobile. Engineers at Colonel Motors, in an attempt to improve fuel efficiency, have been asked to study the impact of weight on MPG. They have decided that a regression model should be used to do this.

A sample of 12 new automobiles was selected, and the weight and MPG rating were recorded. Table 4.6 provides this data. A scatter diagram of this data in Figure 4.6A shows the weight and MPG. A linear regression line is drawn through the points. Excel was used to develop a simple linear regression equation to relate the MPG (Y) to the weight in 1,000 lb. (X_1) in the form

$$\hat{Y} = b_0 + b_1 X_1$$

The Excel output is shown in Program 4.6. From this we get the equation

$$\hat{Y} = 47.6 - 8.2 X_1$$

or

$$MPG = 47.6 - 8.2(\text{weight in } 1,000 \text{ lb.})$$

The model is useful since the significance level for the F test is small and $r^2 = 0.7446$. However, further examination of the graph in Figure 4.6A brings into question the use of a linear model. Perhaps a nonlinear relationship exists, and maybe the model should be modified

FIGURE 4.6A

**Linear Model for
MPG Data**

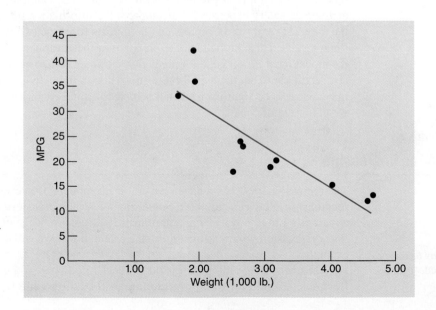

FIGURE 4.6B

Nonlinear Model for MPG Data

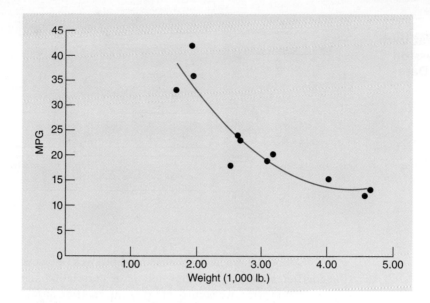

to account for this. A quadratic model is illustrated in Figure 4.6B. This model would be of the form

$$MPG = b_0 + b_1(\text{weight}) + b_2(\text{weight})^2$$

The easiest way to develop this model is to define a new variable

$$X_2 = (\text{weight})^2$$

This gives us the model

$$\hat{Y} = b_0 + b_1 X_1 + b_2 X_2$$

We can create another column in Excel, and again run the regression tool. The output is shown in Program 4.7. The new equation is

$$\hat{Y} = 79.8 - 30.2X_1 + 3.4X_2$$

*A low significance value for **F** and a high r² are indications of a good model.*

The significance level for F is low (0.0002) so the model is useful, and $r^2 = 0.8478$. The adjusted r^2 increased from 0.719 to 0.814, so this new variable definitely improved the model.

PROGRAM 4.6

Excel 2013 Output with Linear Regression Model for MPG Data

	A	B	C	D	E	F	G	H	I	J	K	L
1	Automobile Weight vs. MPG			SUMMARY OUTPUT								
2												
3	MPG (Y)	Weight (X1)		*Regression Statistics*								
4	12	4.58		Multiple R	0.8629							
5	13	4.66		R Square	0.7446							
6	15	4.02		Adjusted R Squ	0.7190							
7	18	2.53		Standard Error	5.0078							
8	19	3.09		Observations	12							
9	19	3.11										
10	20	3.18		ANOVA								
11	23	2.68			df	SS	MS	F	Significance F			
12	24	2.65		Regression	1	730.9090	730.9090	29.1480	0.0003			
13	33	1.70		Residual	10	250.7577	25.0758					
14	36	1.95		Total	11	981.6667						
15	42	1.92										
16					Coefficients	Standard Error	t Stat	P-value	Lower 95%	Upper 95%	Lower 95.0%	Upper 95.0%
17				Intercept	47.619	4.813	9.894	0.000	36.895	58.344	36.895	58.344
18				Weight (X1)	-8.246	1.527	-5.399	0.000	-11.649	-4.843	-11.649	-4.843

PROGRAM 4.7

Excel 2013 Output with Nonlinear Regression Model for MPG Data

	A	B	C	D	E	F	G	H	I	J	K	L
1	Automobile Weight vs. MPG			SUMMARY OUTPUT								
2												
3	MPG (Y)	Weight (X1)	WeightSq.(X2)	Regression Statistics								
4	12	4.58	20.98	Multiple R	0.9208							
5	13	4.66	21.72	R Square	0.8478							
6	15	4.02	16.16	Adjusted R Square	0.8140							
7	18	2.53	6.40	Standard Error	4.0745							
8	19	3.09	9.55	Observations	12.0000							
9	19	3.11	9.67									
10	20	3.18	10.11	ANOVA								
11	23	2.68	7.18		df	SS	MS	F	Significance F			
12	24	2.65	7.02	Regression	2	832.2557	416.1278	25.0661	0.0002			
13	33	1.70	2.89	Residual	9	149.4110	16.6012					
14	36	1.95	3.80	Total	11	981.6667						
15	42	1.92	3.69									
16					Coefficients	Standard Error	t Stat	P-value	Lower 95%	Upper 95%	Lower 95.0%	Upper 95.0%
17				Intercept	79.7888	13.5962	5.8685	0.0002	49.0321	110.5454	49.0321	110.5454
18				Weight (X1)	-30.2224	8.9809	-3.3652	0.0083	-50.5386	-9.9062	-50.5386	-9.9062
19				WeightSq.(X2)	3.4124	1.3811	2.4708	0.0355	0.2881	6.5367	0.2881	6.5367

This model is good for prediction purposes. However, we should not try to interpret the coefficients of the variables due to the correlation between X_1 (weight) and X_2 (weight squared). Normally we would interpret the coefficient for X_1 as the change in Y that results from a 1-unit change in X_1, while holding all other variables constant. Obviously holding one variable constant while changing the other is impossible in this example since $X_2 = X_1^2$. If X_1 changes, then X_2 must change also. This is an example of a problem that exists when multicollinearity is present.

Other types of nonlinearities can be handled using a similar approach. A number of transformations exist that may help to develop a linear model from variables with nonlinear relationships.

4.12 Cautions and Pitfalls in Regression Analysis

This chapter has provided a brief introduction into regression analysis, one of the most widely used quantitative techniques in business. However, some common errors are made with regression models, so caution should be observed when using this.

If the assumptions are not met, the statistical tests may not be valid. Any interval estimates are also invalid, although the model can still be used for prediction purposes.

A high correlation does not mean one variable is causing a change in the other.

Correlation does not necessarily mean causation. Two variables (such as the price of automobiles and your annual salary) may be highly correlated to one another, but one is not causing the other to change. They may both be changing due to other factors such as the economy in general or the inflation rate.

If multicollinearity is present in a multiple regression model, the model is still good for prediction, but interpretation of individual coefficients is questionable. The individual tests on the regression coefficients are not valid.

The regression equation should not be used with values of X that are below the lowest value of X or above the highest value of X found in the sample.

Using a regression equation beyond the range of X is very questionable. A linear relationship may exist within the range of values of X in the sample. What happens beyond this range is unknown; the linear relationship may become nonlinear at some point. For example, there is usually a linear relationship between advertising and sales within a limited range. As more money is spent on advertising, sales tend to increase even if everything else is held constant. However, at some point, increasing advertising expenditures will have less impact on sales unless the company does other things to help, such as opening new markets or expanding the product offerings. If advertising is increased and nothing else changes, the sales will probably level off at some point.

Related to the limitation regarding the range of X is the interpretation of the intercept (b_0). Since the lowest value for X in a sample is often much greater than 0, the intercept is a point on the regression line beyond the range of X. Therefore, we should not be concerned if the t-test for this coefficient is not significant as we should not be using the regression equation to predict a value of Y when $X = 0$. This intercept is merely used in defining the line that fits the sample points the best.

Using the F test and concluding a linear regression model is helpful in predicting Y does not mean that this is the best relationship. While this model may explain much of the variability in Y, it is possible that a nonlinear relationship might explain even more. Similarly, if it is concluded that no linear relationship exists, another type of relationship could exist.

A significant F value may occur even when the relationship is not strong.

A statistically significant relationship does not mean it has any practical value. With large enough samples, it is possible to have a statistically significant relationship, but r^2 might be 0.01. This would normally be of little use to a manager. Similarly, a high r^2 could be found due to random chance if the sample is small. The F test must also show significance to place any value in r^2.

Summary

Regression analysis is an extremely valuable quantitative tool. Using scatter diagrams helps to see relationships between variables. The F test is used to determine if the results can be considered useful. The coefficient of determination (r^2) is used to measure the proportion of variability in Y that is explained by the regression model. The correlation coefficient measures the relationship between two variables.

Multiple regression involves the use of more than one independent variable. Dummy variables (binary or indicator variables) are used with qualitative or categorical data. Nonlinear models can be transformed into linear models.

We saw how to use Excel to develop regression models. Interpretation of computer output was presented, and several examples were provided.

Glossary

Adjusted r^2   A measure of the explanatory power of a regression model that takes into consideration the number of independent variables in the model.

Binary Variable   See Dummy Variable.

Coefficient of Correlation (r)   A measure of the strength of the relationship between two variables.

Coefficient of Determination (r^2)   The percent of the variability in the dependent variable (Y) that is explained by the regression equation.

Collinearity   A condition that exists when one independent variable is correlated with another independent variable.

Dependent Variable   The Y variable in a regression model. This is what is being predicted.

Dummy Variable   A variable used to represent a qualitative factor or condition. Dummy variables have values of 0 or 1. This is also called a binary variable or an indicator variable.

Error   The difference between the actual value (Y) and the predicted value ($\hat{Y}$).

Explanatory Variable   The independent variable in a regression equation.

Independent Variable   The X variable in a regression equation. This is used to help predict the dependent variable.

Least Squares   A reference to the criterion used to select the regression line, to minimize the squared distances between the estimated straight line and the observed values.

Mean Squared Error (MSE)   An estimate of the error variance.

Multicollinearity   A condition that exists when one independent variable is correlated with other independent variables.

Multiple Regression Model   A regression model that has more than one independent variable.

Observed Significance Level   Another name for p-value.

p-Value   A probability value that is used when testing a hypothesis. The hypothesis is rejected when this is low.

Predictor Variable   Another name for explanatory variable.

Regression Analysis   A forecasting procedure that uses the least-squares approach on one or more independent variables to develop a forecasting model.

Residual   Another term for error.

Response Variable The dependent variable in a regression equation.

Scatter Diagrams or **Scatter Plot** Diagrams of the variable to be forecasted, plotted against another variable, such as time. Also called scatter plots.

Standard Error of the Estimate An estimate of the standard deviation of the errors and is sometimes called the standard deviation of the regression.

Stepwise Regression An automated process to systematically add or delete independent variables from a regression model.

Sum of Squares Error (SSE) The total sum of the squared differences between each observation (Y) and the predicted value ($\hat{Y}$).

Sum of Squares Regression (SSR) The total sum of the squared differences between each predicted value ($\hat{Y}$) and the mean ($\overline{Y}$).

Sum of Squares Total (SST) The total sum of the squared differences between each observation (Y) and the mean ($\overline{Y}$).

Key Equations

(4-1) $Y = \beta_0 + \beta_1 X + \epsilon$

Underlying linear model for simple linear regression.

(4-2) $\hat{Y} = b_0 + b_1 X$

Simple linear regression model computed from a sample.

(4-3) $e = Y - \hat{Y}$

Error in regression model.

(4-4) $b_1 = \dfrac{\Sigma(X - \overline{X})(Y - \overline{Y})}{\Sigma(X - \overline{X})^2}$

Slope in the regression line.

(4-5) $b_0 = \overline{Y} - b_1\overline{X}$

The intercept in the regression line.

(4-6) $\text{SST} = \Sigma(Y - \overline{Y})^2$

Total sums of squares.

(4-7) $\text{SSE} = \Sigma e^2 = \Sigma(Y - \hat{Y})^2$

Sum of squares due to error.

(4-8) $\text{SSR} = \Sigma(\hat{Y} - \overline{Y})^2$

Sum of squares due to regression.

(4-9) $\text{SST} = \text{SSR} + \text{SSE}$

Relationship among sums of squares in regression.

(4-10) $r^2 = \dfrac{\text{SSR}}{\text{SST}} = 1 - \dfrac{\text{SSE}}{\text{SST}}$

Coefficient of determination.

(4-11) $r = \pm\sqrt{r^2}$

Coefficient of correlation. This has the same sign as the slope.

(4-12) $s^2 = \text{MSE} = \dfrac{\text{SSE}}{n - k - 1}$

An estimate of the variance of the errors in regression; n is the sample size and k is the number of independent variables.

(4-13) $s = \sqrt{\text{MSE}}$

An estimate of the standard deviation of the errors. Also called the standard error of the estimate.

(4-14) $\text{MSR} = \dfrac{\text{SSR}}{k}$

Mean square regression. k is the number of independent variables.

(4-15) $F = \dfrac{\text{MSR}}{\text{MSE}}$

F statistic used to test significance of overall regression model.

(4-16) $Y = \beta_0 + \beta_1 X_1 + \beta_2 X_2 + \cdots + \beta_k X_k + \epsilon$

Underlying model for multiple regression model.

(4-17) $\hat{Y} = b_0 + b_1 X_1 + b_2 X_2 + \cdots + b_k X_k$

Multiple regression model computed from a sample.

(4-18) Adjusted $r^2 = 1 - \dfrac{\text{SSE}/(n - k - 1)}{\text{SST}/(n - 1)}$

Adjusted r^2 used in building multiple regression models.

Solved Problems

Solved Problem 4-1

Judith Thompson runs a florist shop on the Gulf Coast of Texas, specializing in floral arrangements for weddings and other special events. She advertises weekly in the local newspapers and is considering increasing her advertising budget. Before doing so, she decides to evaluate the past effectiveness of these ads. Five weeks are sampled, and the advertising dollars and sales volume for each of these are shown in the following table. Develop a regression equation that would help Judith evaluate her advertising. Find the coefficient of determination for this model.

SALES ($1,000)	ADVERTISING ($100)
11	5
6	3
10	7
6	2
12	8

Solution

SALES Y	ADVERTISING X	$(X - \bar{X})^2$	$(X - \bar{X})(Y - \bar{Y})$
11	5	$(5 - 5)^2 = 0$	$(5 - 5)(11 - 9) = 0$
6	3	$(3 - 5)^2 = 4$	$(3 - 5)(6 - 9) = 6$
10	7	$(7 - 5)^2 = 4$	$(7 - 5)(10 - 9) = 2$
6	2	$(2 - 5)^2 = 9$	$(2 - 5)(6 - 9) = 9$
12	8	$(8 - 5)^2 = 9$	$(8 - 5)(12 - 9) = 9$
$\Sigma Y = 45$	$\Sigma X = 25$	$\Sigma(X - \bar{X})^2 = 26$	$\Sigma(X - \bar{X})(Y - \bar{Y}) = 26$
$\bar{Y} = 45/5$	$\bar{X} = 25/5$		
$= 9$	$= 5$		

$$b_1 = \frac{\Sigma(X - \bar{X})(Y - \bar{Y})}{\Sigma(X - \bar{X})^2} = \frac{26}{26} = 1$$

$$b_0 = \bar{Y} - b_1\bar{X} = 9 - (1)(5) = 4$$

The regression equation is

$$\hat{Y} = 4 + 1X$$

To compute r^2, we use the following table:

Y	X	$\hat{Y} = 4 + 1X$	$(\hat{Y} - \bar{Y})^2$	$(Y - \bar{Y})^2$
11	5	9	$(11 - 9)^2 = 4$	$(11 - 9)^2 = 4$
6	3	7	$(6 - 7)^2 = 1$	$(6 - 9)^2 = 9$
10	7	11	$(10 - 11)^2 = 1$	$(10 - 9)^2 = 1$
6	2	6	$(6 - 6)^2 = 0$	$(6 - 9)^2 = 9$
12	8	12	$(12 - 12)^2 = 0$	$(12 - 9)^2 = 9$
$\Sigma Y = 45$	$\Sigma X = 25$		$\Sigma (Y - \hat{Y})^2 = 6$	$\Sigma (Y - \bar{Y})^2 = 32$
$\bar{Y} = 9$	$\bar{X} = 5$		SSE	SST

The slope $(b_1 = 1)$ tells us that for each 1 unit increase in X (or $100 in advertising), sales increase by 1 unit (or $1,000). Also, $r^2 = 0.8125$ indicating that about 81% of the variability in sales can be explained by the regression model with advertising as the independent variable.

Solved Problem 4-2

Use Excel with the data in Solved Problem 4-1 to find the regression model. What does the F test say about this model?

Solution

Program 4.8 provides the Excel output for this problem. We see the equation is

$$\hat{Y} = 4 + 1X$$

The coefficient of determination (r^2) is shown to be 0.8125. The significance level for the F test is 0.0366, which is less than 0.05. This indicates the model is statistically significant. Thus, there is sufficient evidence in the data to conclude that the model is useful, and there is a relationship between X (advertising) and Y (sales).

PROGRAM 4.8

Excel 2013 Output for Solved Problem 4-2

17	SUMMARY OUTPUT								
18									
19	*Regression Statistics*								
20	Multiple R	0.9014							
21	R Square	0.8125							
22	Adjusted R Square	0.7500							
23	Standard Error	1.4142							
24	Observations	5							
25									
26	ANOVA								
27		*df*	*SS*	*MS*	*F*	*Significance F*			
28	Regression	1	26	26	13	0.03662			
29	Residual	3	6	2					
30	Total	4	32						
31									
32		*Coefficients*	*Standard Error*	*t Stat*	*P-value*	*Lower 95%*	*Upper 95%*	*Lower 95.0%*	*Upper 95.0%*
33	Intercept	4	1.5242	2.6244	0.0787	-0.8506	8.8506	-0.8506	8.8506
34	Advertising ($100) X	1	0.2774	3.6056	0.0366	0.1173	1.8827	0.1173	1.8827

Self-Test

- Before taking the self-test, refer to the learning objectives at the beginning of the chapter, the notes in the margins, and the glossary at the end of the chapter.
- Use the key at the back of the book to correct your answers.
- Restudy pages that correspond to any questions that you answered incorrectly or material you feel uncertain about.

1. One of the assumptions in regression analysis is that
   a. the errors have a mean of 1.
   b. the errors have a mean of 0.
   c. the observations (Y) have a mean of 1.
   d. the observations (Y) have a mean of 0.
2. A graph of the sample points that will be used to develop a regression line is called
   a. a sample graph.
   b. a regression diagram.
   c. a scatter diagram.
   d. a regression plot.
3. When using regression, an error is also called
   a. an intercept.
   b. a prediction.
   c. a coefficient.
   d. a residual.
4. In a regression model, Y is called
   a. the independent variable.
   b. the dependent variable.
   c. the regression variable.
   d. the predictor variable.
5. A quantity that provides a measure of how far each sample point is from the regression line is
   a. the SSR.
   b. the SSE.
   c. the SST.
   d. the MSR.
6. The percentage of the variation in the dependent variable that is explained by a regression equation is measured by
   a. the coefficient of correlation.
   b. the MSE.
   c. the coefficient of determination.
   d. the slope.
7. In a regression model, if every sample point is on the regression line (all errors are 0), then
   a. the correlation coefficient would be 0.
   b. the correlation coefficient would be −1 or 1.

   c. the coefficient of determination would be −1.
   d. the coefficient of determination would be 0.
8. When using dummy variables in a regression equation to model a qualitative or categorical variable, the number of dummy variables should equal
   a. the number of categories.
   b. 1 more than the number of categories.
   c. 1 less than the number of categories.
   d. the number of other independent variables in the model.
9. A multiple regression model differs from a simple linear regression model because the multiple regression model has more than one
   a. independent variable.
   b. dependent variable.
   c. intercept.
   d. error.
10. The overall significance of a regression model is tested using an F test. The model is significant if
    a. the F value is low.
    b. the significance level of the F value is low.
    c. the r^2 value is low.
    d. the slope is lower than the intercept.
11. A new variable should not be added to a multiple regression model if that variable causes
    a. r^2 to decrease.
    b. the adjusted r^2 to decrease.
    c. the SST to decrease.
    d. the intercept to decrease.
12. A good regression model should have
    a. a low r^2 and a low significance level for the F test.
    b. a high r^2 and a high significance level for the F test.
    c. a high r^2 and a low significance level for the F test.
    d. a low r^2 and a high significance level for the F test.

Discussion Questions and Problems

Discussion Questions

4-1 What is the meaning of least squares in a regression model?

4-2 Discuss the use of dummy variables in regression analysis.

4-3 Discuss how the coefficient of determination and the coefficient of correlation are related and how they are used in regression analysis.

4-4 Explain how a scatter diagram can be used to identify the type of regression to use.

4-5 Explain how the adjusted r^2 value is used in developing a regression model.

4-6 Explain what information is provided by the F test.

4-7 What is the SSE? How is this related to the SST and the SSR?

4-8 Explain how a plot of the residuals can be used in developing a regression model.

Problems

- 4-9 John Smith has developed the following forecasting model:

$$\hat{Y} = 36 + 4.3X_1$$

where

$\hat{Y}$ = Demand for K10 air conditioners

X_1 = the outside temperature (°F)

  (a) Forecast the demand for K10 when the temperature is 70°F.
  (b) What is the demand for a temperature of 80°F?
  (c) What is the demand for a temperature of 90°F?

- 4-10 The operations manager of a musical instrument distributor feels that demand for a particular type of guitar may be related to the number of YouTube views for a music video by the popular rock group Marble Pumpkins during the preceding month. The manager has collected the data shown in the following table:

YouTube VIEWS (1,000s)	GUITAR SALES
30	8
40	11
70	12
60	10
80	15
50	13

  (a) Graph these data to see whether a linear equation might describe the relationship between the views on YouTube and guitar sales.
  (b) Using the equations presented in this chapter, compute the SST, SSE, and SSR. Find the least-squares regression line for these data.
  (c) Using the regression equation, predict guitar sales if there were 40,000 views last month.

- 4-11 Using the data in Problem 4-10, test to see if there is a statistically significant relationship between sales and YouTube views at the 0.05 level of significance. Use the formulas in this chapter and Appendix D.

- 4-12 Using computer software, find the least-squares regression line for the data in Problem 4-10. Based on the F test, is there a statistically significant relationship between the demand for guitars and the number of YouTube views?

- 4-13 Students in a management science class have just received their grades on the first test. The instructor has provided information about the first test grades in some previous classes as well as the final average

for the same students. Some of these grades have been sampled and are as follows:

STUDENT	1	2	3	4	5	6	7	8	9
1st test grade	98	77	88	80	96	61	66	95	69
Final average	93	78	84	73	84	64	64	95	76

  (a) Develop a regression model that could be used to predict the final average in the course based on the first test grade.
  (b) Predict the final average of a student who made an 83 on the first test.
  (c) Give the values of r and r^2 for this model. Interpret the value of r^2 in the context of this problem.

- 4-14 Using the data in Problem 4-13, test to see if there is a statistically significant relationship between the grade on the first test and the final average at the 0.05 level of significance. Use the formulas in this chapter and Appendix D.

- 4-15 Using computer software, find the least-squares regression line for the data in Problem 4-13. Based on the F test, is there a statistically significant relationship between the first test grade and the final average in the course?

- 4-16 Steve Caples, a real estate appraiser in Lake Charles, Louisiana, has developed a regression model to help appraise residential housing in the Lake Charles area. The model was developed using recently sold homes in a particular neighborhood. The price (Y) of the house is based on the square footage (X) of the house. The model is

$$\hat{Y} = 33,478 + 62.4X$$

The coefficient of correlation for the model is 0.63.

  (a) Use the model to predict the selling price of a house that is 1,860 square feet.
  (b) A house with 1,860 square feet recently sold for $165,000. Explain why this is not what the model predicted.
  (c) If you were going to use multiple regression to develop an appraisal model, what other quantitative variables might be included in the model?
  (d) What is the coefficient of determination for this model?

- 4-17 Accountants at the firm Walker and Walker believed that several traveling executives submit unusually high travel vouchers when they return from business trips. The accountants took a sample of 200 vouchers submitted from the past year; they then developed the following multiple regression equation relating expected travel cost (Y) to number of days on the road (X_1) and distance traveled (X_2) in miles:

$$\hat{Y} = \$90.00 + \$48.50X_1 + \$0.40X_2$$

Note: ⍾ means the problem may be solved with QM for Windows; ✖ means the problem may be solved with Excel QM; and ⍾ means the problem may be solved with QM for Windows and/or Excel QM.

The coefficient of correlation computed was 0.68.

(a) If Thomas Williams returns from a 300-mile trip that took him out of town for 5 days, what is the expected amount that he should claim as expenses?

(b) Williams submitted a reimbursement request for $685; what should the accountant do?

(c) Comment on the validity of this model. Should any other variables be included? Which ones? Why?

:4-18 Thirteen students entered the undergraduate business program at Rollins College 2 years ago. The following table indicates what their grade-point averages (GPAs) were after being in the program for 2 years and what each student scored on the SAT exam (maximum 2400) when he or she was in high school. Is there a meaningful relationship between grades and SAT scores? If a student scores a 1200 on the SAT, what do you think his or her GPA will be? What about a student who scores 2400?

STUDENT	SAT SCORE	GPA	STUDENT	SAT SCORE	GPA
A	1263	2.90	H	1443	2.53
B	1131	2.93	I	2187	3.22
C	1755	3.00	J	1503	1.99
D	2070	3.45	K	1839	2.75
E	1824	3.66	L	2127	3.90
F	1170	2.88	M	1098	1.60
G	1245	2.15			

:4-19 Bus and subway ridership in Washington, D.C., during the summer months is believed to be heavily tied to the number of tourists visiting the city. During the past 12 years, the following data have been obtained:

YEAR	NUMBER OF TOURISTS (1,000,000s)	RIDERSHIP (100,000s)
1	7	15
2	2	10
3	6	13
4	4	15
5	14	25
6	15	27
7	16	24
8	12	20
9	14	27
10	20	44
11	15	34
12	7	17

(a) Plot these data and determine whether a linear model is reasonable.

(b) Develop a regression model.

(c) What is expected ridership if 10 million tourists visit the city?

(d) If there are no tourists at all, explain the predicted ridership.

:4-20 Use computer software to develop a regression model for the data in Problem 4-19. Explain what this output indicates about the usefulness of this model.

:4-21 The following data give the starting salary for students who recently graduated from a local university and accepted jobs soon after graduation. The starting salary, grade-point average (GPA), and major (business or other) are provided.

SALARY	$29,500	$46,000	$39,800	$36,500
GPA	3.1	3.5	3.8	2.9
Major	Other	Business	Business	Other

SALARY	$42,000	$31,500	$36,200
GPA	3.4	2.1	2.5
Major	Business	Other	Business

(a) Using a computer, develop a regression model that could be used to predict starting salary based on GPA and major.

(b) Use this model to predict the starting salary for a business major with a GPA of 3.0.

(c) What does the model say about the starting salary for a business major compared to a nonbusiness major?

(d) Do you believe this model is useful in predicting the starting salary? Justify your answer, using information provided in the computer output.

:4-22 The following data give the selling price, square footage, number of bedrooms, and age of houses that have sold in a neighborhood in the past 6 months. Develop three regression models to predict the selling price based upon each of the other factors individually. Which of these is best?

SELLING PRICE ($)	SQUARE FOOTAGE	BEDROOMS	AGE (YEARS)
84,000	1,670	2	30
79,000	1,339	2	25
91,500	1,712	3	30
120,000	1,840	3	40
127,500	2,300	3	18
132,500	2,234	3	30
145,000	2,311	3	19
164,000	2,377	3	7
155,000	2,736	4	10
168,000	2,500	3	1
172,500	2,500	4	3
174,000	2,479	3	3
175,000	2,400	3	1
177,500	3,124	4	0
184,000	2,500	3	2
195,500	4,062	4	10
195,000	2,854	3	3

4-23 Use the data in Problem 4-22 and develop a regression model to predict selling price based on the square footage and number of bedrooms. Use this to predict the selling price of a 2,000-square-foot house with three bedrooms. Compare this model with the models in Problem 4-22. Should the number of bedrooms be included in the model? Why or why not?

4-24 Use the data in Problem 4-22 and develop a regression model to predict selling price based on the square footage, number of bedrooms, and age. Use this to predict the selling price of a 10-year-old, 2,000-square-foot house with three bedrooms.

4-25 The total expenses of a hospital are related to many factors. Two of these factors are the number of beds in the hospital and the number of admissions. Data were collected on 14 hospitals, as shown in the following table:

HOSPITAL	NUMBER OF BEDS	ADMISSIONS (100s)	TOTAL EXPENSES (MILLIONS)
1	215	77	57
2	336	160	127
3	520	230	157
4	135	43	24
5	35	9	14
6	210	155	93
7	140	53	45
8	90	6	6
9	410	159	99
10	50	18	12
11	65	16	11
12	42	29	15
13	110	28	21
14	305	98	63

Find the best regression model to predict the total expenses of a hospital. Discuss the accuracy of this model. Should both variables be included in the model? Why or why not?

4-26 A sample of 20 automobiles was taken, and the miles per gallon (MPG), horsepower, and total weight were recorded. Develop a linear regression model to predict MPG, using horsepower as the only independent variable. Develop another model with weight as the independent variable. Which of these two models is better? Explain.

MPG	HORSEPOWER	WEIGHT
44	67	1,844
44	50	1,998
40	62	1,752

MPG	HORSEPOWER	WEIGHT
37	69	1,980
37	66	1,797
34	63	2,199
35	90	2,404
32	99	2,611
30	63	3,236
28	91	2,606
26	94	2,580
26	88	2,507
25	124	2,922
22	97	2,434
20	114	3,248
21	102	2,812
18	114	3,382
18	142	3,197
16	153	4,380
16	139	4,036

4-27 Use the data in Problem 4-26 to develop a multiple linear regression model. How does this compare with each of the models in Problem 4-26?

4-28 Use the data in Problem 4-26 to find the best quadratic regression model. (There is more than one to consider.) How does this compare to the models in Problems 4-26 and 4-27?

4-29 A sample of nine public universities and nine private universities was taken. The total cost for the year (including room and board) and the median SAT score (maximum total is 2400) at each school were recorded. It was felt that schools with higher median SAT scores would have a better reputation and would charge more tuition as a result of that. The data are in the following table. Use regression to help answer the following questions based on this sample data. Do schools with higher SAT scores charge more in tuition and fees? Are private schools more expensive than public schools when SAT scores are taken into consideration? Discuss how accurate you believe these results are using information related to the regression models.

CATEGORY	TOTAL COST ($)	MEDIAN SAT
Public	21,700	1990
Public	15,600	1620
Public	16,900	1810
Public	15,400	1540
Public	23,100	1540
Public	21,400	1600
Public	16,500	1560
Public	23,500	1890

(Continued on next page)

CATEGORY	TOTAL COST ($)	MEDIAN SAT
Public	20,200	1620
Private	30,400	1630
Private	41,500	1840
Private	36,100	1980
Private	42,100	1930
Private	27,100	2130
Private	34,800	2010
Private	32,100	1590
Private	31,800	1720
Private	32,100	1770

4-30 In 2012, the total payroll for the New York Yankees was almost $200 million, while the total payroll for the Oakland Athletics (a team known for using baseball analytics or sabermetrics) was about $55 million, less than one-third of the Yankees payroll. In the following table, you will see the payrolls (in millions) and the total number of victories for the baseball teams in the American League in the 2012 season. Develop a regression model to predict the total number of victories based on the payroll. Use the model to predict the number of victories for a team with a payroll of $79 million. Based on the results of the computer output, discuss the relationship between payroll and victories.

TEAM	PAYROLL ($MILLIONS)	NUMBER OF VICTORIES
Baltimore Orioles	81.4	93
Boston Red Sox	173.2	69
Chicago White Sox	96.9	85
Cleveland Indians	78.4	68
Detroit Tigers	132.3	88
Kansas City Royals	60.9	72
Los Angeles Angels	154.5	89
Minnesota Twins	94.1	66
New York Yankees	198.0	95
Oakland Athletics	55.4	94
Seattle Mariners	82.0	75
Tampa Bay Rays	64.2	90
Texas Rangers	120.5	93
Toronto Blue Jays	75.5	73

4-31 The number of victories (W), earned run average (ERA), runs scored (R), batting average (AVG), and on-base percentage (OBP) for each team in the American League in the 2012 season are provided in the following table. The ERA is one measure of the effectiveness of the pitching staff, and a lower number is better. The other statistics are measures of effectiveness of the hitters, and higher numbers are better for each of these.

TEAM	W	ERA	R	AVG	OBP
Baltimore Orioles	93	3.90	712	0.247	0.311
Boston Red Sox	69	4.70	734	0.260	0.315
Chicago White Sox	85	4.02	748	0.255	0.318
Cleveland Indians	68	4.78	667	0.251	0.324
Detroit Tigers	88	3.75	726	0.268	0.335
Kansas City Royals	72	4.30	676	0.265	0.317
Los Angeles Angels	89	4.02	767	0.274	0.332
Minnesota Twins	66	4.77	701	0.260	0.325
New York Yankees	95	3.85	804	0.265	0.337
Oakland Athletics	94	3.48	713	0.238	0.310
Seattle Mariners	75	3.76	619	0.234	0.296
Tampa Bay Rays	90	3.19	697	0.240	0.317
Texas Rangers	93	3.99	808	0.273	0.334
Toronto Blue Jays	73	4.64	716	0.245	0.309

(a) Develop a regression model that could be used to predict the number of victories based on the ERA.
(b) Develop a regression model that could be used to predict the number of victories based on the runs scored.
(c) Develop a regression model that could be used to predict the number of victories based on the batting average.
(d) Develop a regression model that could be used to predict the number of victories based on the on-base percentage.
(e) Which of the four models is better for predicting the number of victories?
(f) Find the best multiple regression model to predict the number of wins. Use any combination of the variables to find the best model.

4-32 The closing stock price for each of two stocks was recorded over a 12-month period. The closing price for the Dow Jones Industrial Average (DJIA) was also recorded over this same time period. These values are shown in the following table:

MONTH	DJIA	STOCK 1	STOCK 2
1	11,168	48.5	32.4
2	11,150	48.2	31.7
3	11,186	44.5	31.9
4	11,381	44.7	36.6
5	11,679	49.3	36.7
6	12,081	49.3	38.7
7	12,222	46.1	39.5
8	12,463	46.2	41.2
9	12,622	47.7	43.3
10	12,269	48.3	39.4
11	12,354	47.0	40.1
12	13,063	47.9	42.1
13	13,326	47.8	45.2

(a) Develop a regression model to predict the price of stock 1 based on the Dow Jones Industrial Average.

(b) Develop a regression model to predict the price of stock 2 based on the Dow Jones Industrial Average.

(c) Which of the two stocks is most highly correlated to the Dow Jones Industrial Average over this time period?

Case Study

North–South Airline

In January 2012, Northern Airlines merged with Southeast Airlines to create the fourth largest U.S. carrier. The new North–South Airline inherited both an aging fleet of Boeing 727-300 aircraft and Stephen Ruth. Stephen was a tough former Secretary of the Navy who stepped in as new president and chairman of the board.

Stephen's first concern in creating a financially solid company was maintenance costs. It was commonly surmised in the airline industry that maintenance costs rise with the age of the aircraft. He quickly noticed that historically there had been a significant difference in the reported B727-300 maintenance costs (from ATA Form 41s) in both the airframe and engine areas between Northern Airlines and Southeast Airlines, with Southeast having the newer fleet.

On February 12, 2012, Peg Jones, vice president for operations and maintenance, was called into Stephen's office and asked to study the issue. Specifically, Stephen wanted to know whether the average fleet age was correlated to direct airframe maintenance costs, and whether there was a relationship between average fleet age and direct engine maintenance costs. Peg was to report back by February 26 with the answer, along with quantitative and graphical descriptions of the relationship.

Peg's first step was to have her staff construct the average age of Northern and Southeast B727-300 fleets, by quarter,

since the introduction of that aircraft to service by each airline in late 1993 and early 1994. The average age of each fleet was calculated by first multiplying the total number of calendar days each aircraft had been in service at the pertinent point in time by the average daily utilization of the respective fleet to total fleet hours flown. The total fleet hours flown was then divided by the number of aircraft in service at that time, giving the age of the "average" aircraft in the fleet.

The average utilization was found by taking the actual total fleet hours flown on September 30, 2011, from Northern and Southeast data, and dividing by the total days in service for all aircraft at that time. The average utilization for Southeast was 8.3 hours per day, and the average utilization for Northern was 8.7 hours per day. Because the available cost data were calculated for each yearly period ending at the end of the first quarter, average fleet age was calculated at the same points in time. The fleet data are shown in the following table. Airframe cost data and engine cost data are both shown paired with fleet average age in that table.

Discussion Question

1. Prepare Peg Jones's response to Stephen Ruth.

Note: Dates and names of airlines and individuals have been changed in this case to maintain confidentiality. The data and issues described here are real.

North–South Airline Data for Boeing 727-300 Jets

	NORTHERN AIRLINE DATA				SOUTHEAST AIRLINE DATA		
YEAR	AIRFRAME COST PER AIRCRAFT ($)	ENGINE COST PER AIRCRAFT ($)	AVERAGE AGE (HOURS)		AIRFRAME COST PER AIRCRAFT ($)	ENGINE COST PER AIRCRAFT ($)	AVERAGE AGE (HOURS)
2001	51.80	43.49	6,512		13.29	18.86	5,107
2002	54.92	38.58	8,404		25.15	31.55	8,145
2003	69.70	51.48	11,077		32.18	40.43	7,360
2004	68.90	58.72	11,717		31.78	22.10	5,773
2005	63.72	45.47	13,275		25.34	19.69	7,150
2006	84.73	50.26	15,215		32.78	32.58	9,364
2007	78.74	79.60	18,390		35.56	38.07	8,259

Bibliography

Berenson, Mark L., David M. Levine, and Timothy C. Kriehbiel. *Basic Business Statistics*, 12th ed. Upper Saddle River, NJ: Prentice Hall, 2012.

Black, Ken. *Business Statistics: For Contemporary Decision Making*, 7th ed. John Wiley & Sons, Inc., 2012.

Draper, Norman R., and Harry Smith. *Applied Regression Analysis*, 3rd ed. New York: John Wiley & Sons, Inc., 1998.

Kutner, Michael, John Neter, and Chris J. Nachtsheim. *Applied Linear Regression Models*, 4th ed. Boston; New York: McGraw-Hill/Irwin, 2004.

Mendenhall, William, and Terry L. Sincich. *A Second Course in Statistics: Regression Analysis*, 7th ed. Upper Saddle River, NJ: Prentice Hall, 2012.

Appendix 4.1: Formulas for Regression Calculations

When performing regression calculations by hand, there are other formulas that can make the task easier and are mathematically equivalent to the ones presented in the chapter. These, however, make it more difficult to see the logic behind the formulas and to understand what the results actually mean.

When using these formulas, it helps to set up a table with the columns shown in Table 4.7, which has the Triple A Construction Company data that were used earlier in the chapter. The sample size (n) is 6. The totals for all columns are shown, and the averages for X and Y are calculated. Once this is done, we can use the following formulas for computations in a simple linear regression model (one independent variable). The simple linear regression equation is again given as

$$\hat{Y} = b_0 + b_1 X$$

Slope of regression equation:

$$b_1 = \frac{\sum XY - n\overline{X}\overline{Y}}{\sum X^2 - n\overline{X}^2}$$

$$b_1 = \frac{180.5 - 6(4)(7)}{106 - 6(4^2)} = 1.25$$

Intercept of regression equation:

$$b_0 = \overline{Y} - b_1\overline{X}$$
$$b_0 = 7 - 1.25(4) = 2$$

Sum of squares of the error:

$$SSE = \sum Y^2 - b_0\sum Y - b_1\sum XY$$
$$SSE = 316.5 - 2(42) - 1.25(180.5) = 6.875$$

TABLE 4.7 Preliminary Calculations for Triple A Construction

Y	X	Y^2	X^2	XY
6	3	$6^2 = 36$	$3^2 = 9$	$3(6) = 18$
8	4	$8^2 = 64$	$4^2 = 16$	$4(8) = 32$
9	6	$9^2 = 81$	$6^2 = 36$	$6(9) = 54$
5	4	$5^2 = 25$	$4^2 = 16$	$4(5) = 20$
4.5	2	$4.5^2 = 20.25$	$2^2 = 4$	$2(4.5) = 9$
9.5	5	$9.5^2 = 90.25$	$5^2 = 25$	$5(9.5) = 47.5$
$\sum Y = 42$	$\sum X = 24$	$\sum Y^2 = 316.5$	$\sum X^2 = 106$	$\sum XY = 180.5$

$\overline{Y} = 42/6 = 7$ $\overline{X} = 24/6 = 4$

Estimate of the error variance:

$$s^2 = \text{MSE} = \frac{\text{SSE}}{n - 2}$$

$$s^2 = \frac{6.875}{6 - 2} = 1.71875$$

Estimate of the error standard deviation:

$$s = \sqrt{\text{MSE}}$$

$$s = \sqrt{1.71875} = 1.311$$

Coefficient of determination:

$$r^2 = 1 - \frac{\text{SSE}}{\sum Y^2 - n\bar{Y}^2}$$

$$r^2 = 1 - \frac{6.875}{316.5 - 6(7^2)} = 0.6944$$

This formula for the correlation coefficient automatically determines the sign of r. This could also be found by taking the square root of r^2 and giving it the same sign as the slope:

$$r = \frac{n\sum XY - \sum X \sum Y}{\sqrt{[n\sum X^2 - (\sum X)^2][n\sum Y^2 - (\sum Y)^2]}}$$

$$r = \frac{6(180.5) - (24)(42)}{\sqrt{[6(106) - 24^2][6(316.5) - 42^2]}} = 0.833$$

Forecasting

LEARNING OBJECTIVES

After completing this chapter, students will be able to:

1. Understand and know when to use various families of forecasting models.
2. Compare moving averages, exponential smoothing, and other time-series models.
3. Seasonally adjust data.
4. Understand Delphi and other qualitative decision-making approaches.
5. Compute a variety of error measures.

CHAPTER OUTLINE

Summary • Glossary • Key Equations • Solved Problems • Self-Test • Discussion Questions and Problems • Internet Homework Problems • Case Study: Forecasting Attendance at SWU Football Games • Case Study: Forecasting Monthly Sales • Internet Case Study • Bibliography

5.1   Introduction

Every day, managers make decisions without knowing what will happen in the future. Inventory is ordered though no one knows what sales will be, new equipment is purchased though no one knows the demand for products, and investments are made though no one knows what profits will be. Managers are always trying to reduce this uncertainty and to make better estimates of what will happen in the future. Accomplishing this is the main purpose of forecasting.

There are many ways to forecast the future. In numerous firms (especially smaller ones), the entire process is subjective, involving seat-of-the-pants methods, intuition, and years of experience.

There are also more formal forecasting techniques, both quantitative and qualitative in nature. The primary focus of this chapter will be understanding time-series models and determining which model works best with a particular set of data.

5.2   Types of Forecasting Models

Figure 5.1 lists some of the more common forecasting models, and these are categorized by the type of model. The first category involves qualitative models, while the others are quantitative in nature and use mathematical models to develop better forecasts.

Qualitative Models

Qualitative models are forecasting techniques based on judgmental or subjective factors. When a totally new product such as the iPad is introduced, forecasting demand is very difficult due to the lack of any historical sales data on that particular product or on similar products. The company must rely on expert opinion, individual experiences and judgment, and other subjective factors.

Here is a brief overview of four different qualitative forecasting techniques:

1. *Delphi method.* This iterative group process allows experts, who may be located in different places, to make forecasts. There are three different types of participants in the **Delphi** process: decision makers, staff personnel, and respondents. The **decision-making group** usually consists of 5 to 10 experts who will be making the actual forecast. The staff personnel assist the decision makers by preparing, distributing, collecting, and summarizing a series of questionnaires and survey results. The respondents are a group of people whose judgments are valued and are being sought. This group provides inputs to the decision makers before the forecast is made.

FIGURE 5.1
Forecasting Models

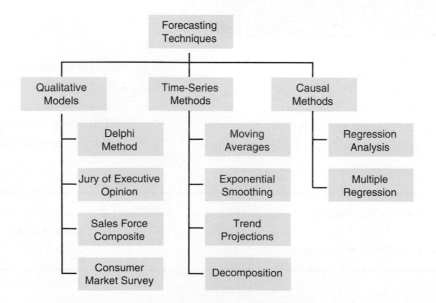

Overview of four qualitative or judgmental approaches: Delphi, jury of executive opinion, sales force composite, and consumer market survey.

In the Delphi method, when the results of the first questionnaire are obtained, the results are summarized and the questionnaire is modified. Both the summary of the results and the new questionnaire are then sent to the same respondents for a new round of responses. The respondents, upon seeing the results from the first questionnaire, may view things differently and may modify their original responses. This process is repeated with the hope that a consensus is reached.

2. *Jury of executive opinion.* This method takes the opinions of a small group of high-level managers, often in combination with statistical models, and results in a group estimate of demand.

3. *Sales force composite.* In this approach, each salesperson estimates what sales will be in his or her region; these forecasts are reviewed to ensure that they are realistic and are then combined at the district and national levels to reach an overall forecast.

4. *Consumer market survey.* This method solicits input from customers or potential customers regarding their future purchasing plans. It can help not only in preparing a forecast but also in improving product design and planning for new products.

Causal Models

A variety of quantitative forecasting models are available when past numerical data are available. Forecasting models are identified as **causal models** if the variable to be forecast is influenced by or correlated with other variables included in the model. For example, daily sales of bottled water might depend on the average temperature, the average humidity, and so on. A causal model would include factors such as these in the mathematical model. Regression models (see Chapter 4) and other more complex models would be classified as causal models.

Time-Series Models

Time series are also quantitative models, and many time-series methods are available. A **time-series model** is a forecasting technique that attempts to predict the future values of a variable by using only historical data on that one variable. These models are extrapolations of past values of that series. While other factors may have influenced these past values, the impact of those other factors is captured in the previous values of the variable being predicted. Thus, if we are forecasting weekly sales for lawn mowers, we use the past weekly sales for lawn mowers in making the forecast for future sales, ignoring other factors such as the economy, competition, and even the selling price of the lawn mowers.

5.3 Components of a Time-Series

A time series is sequence of values recorded at successive intervals of time. The intervals can be days, weeks, months, years, or other time unit. Examples include weekly sales of IIP personal computers, quarterly earnings reports of Microsoft Corporation, daily shipments of Eveready batteries, and annual U.S. consumer price indices. A time series may consist of four possible components—trend, seasonal, cyclical, and random.

The **trend (T) component** is the general upward or downward movement of the data over a relatively long period of time. For example, total sales for a company may be increasing consistently over time. The consumer price index, one measure of inflation, is increasing over time. While consistent upward (or downward) movements are indicative of a trend, there may be a positive (or negative) trend present in a time series and yet the values do not increase (or decrease) in every time period. There may be an occasional movement that seems inconsistent with the trend due to random or other fluctuations.

Figure 5.2 shows scatter diagrams for several time series. The data for all the series are quarterly, and there are four years of data. Series 3 has both trend and random components present.

The **seasonal (S) component** is a pattern of fluctuations above or below an average value that repeats at regular intervals. For example, with monthly sales data on snow blowers, sales tend to be high in December and January and lower in summer months and this pattern is expected to repeat every year. Quarterly sales for a consumer electronics store may be higher in the fourth quarter of every year and lower in other quarters. Daily sales in a retail store may be higher on Saturdays than on other days of the week. Hourly sales in a fast-food restaurant are usually expected to be higher around the lunch hour and the dinner hour, while other times are not as busy. Series 2 in Figure 5.2 illustrates seasonal variations for quarterly data.

FIGURE 5.2

Scatter Diagram for Four Time Series of Quarterly Data

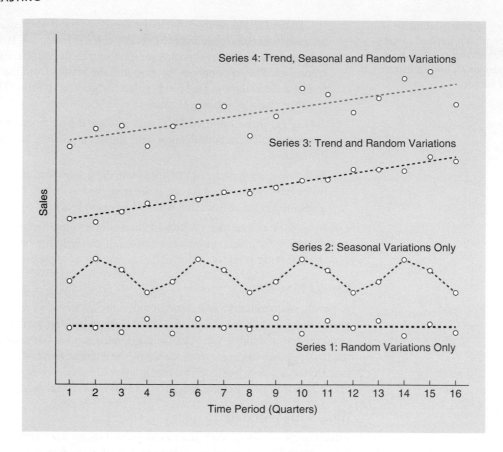

If a seasonal component is present in a set of data, the number of seasons depends on the type of data. With quarterly data, there are four seasons because there are four quarters in a year. With monthly data, there would be 12 seasons because there are 12 months in a year. With daily sales data for a retail store that is open seven days a week, there would be seven seasons. With hourly data, there could be 24 seasons if the business is open 24 hours a day.

A **cyclical (C) component** of a time series is a pattern in annual data that tends to repeat every several years. The cyclical component of a time series is only used when making very long-range forecasts, and it is usually associated with the business cycle. Sales or economic activity might reach a peak and then begin to recede and contract, reaching a bottom or trough. At some point after the trough is reached, activity would pick up as recovery and expansion takes place. A new peak would be reached and the cycle would begin again. Figure 5.3 shows 16 years of annual data for a time series that has a cyclical as well as a random component.

While a time series with cyclical variations and a time series with seasonal variations may look similar on a graph, cyclical variations tend to be irregular in length (from a few years to

FIGURE 5.3

Scatter Diagram of a Times Series with Cyclical and Random Components

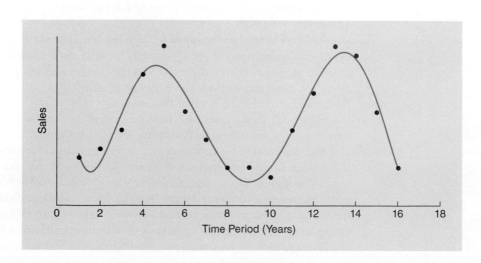

10 or more years) and magnitude, and they are very difficult to predict. Seasonal variations are very consistent in length and magnitude, are much shorter as the seasons repeat in a year or less, and are much easier to predict. The forecasting models presented in this chapter will be for short-range or medium-range forecasts and the cyclical component will not be included in these models.

The **random (R) component** consists of irregular, unpredictable variations in a time series. Any variation in a times series that cannot be attributed to trend, seasonal, or cyclical variations would fall into this category. If data for a time series tends to be level with no discernible trend or seasonal pattern, random variations would be the cause for any changes from one time period to the next. Series 1 in Figure 5.2 is an example of a time series with only a random component.

There are two general forms of time-series models in statistics. The first is a multiplicative model, which assumes that demand is the product of the four components. It is stated as follows:

$$\text{Demand} = T \times S \times C \times R$$

An additive model adds the components together to provide an estimate. Multiple regression is often used to develop additive models. This additive relationship is stated as follows:

$$\text{Demand} = T + S + C + R$$

There are other models that may be a combination of these. For example, one of the components (such as trend) might be additive while another (such as seasonality) could be multiplicative. Understanding the components of a time series will help in selecting an appropriate forecasting technique to use. The methods presented in this chapter will be grouped according to the components considered when the forecast is developed.

5.4 Measures of Forecast Accuracy

We discuss several different forecasting models in this chapter. To see how well one model works, or to compare that model with other models, the forecast values are compared with the actual or observed values. The **forecast error** (or **deviation**) is defined as follows:

$$\text{Forecast error} = \text{Actual value} - \text{Forecast value}$$

One measure of accuracy is the **mean absolute deviation (MAD)**. This is computed by taking the sum of the absolute values of the individual forecast errors and dividing by the numbers of errors (n):

$$\text{MAD} = \frac{\sum |\text{forecast error}|}{n} \qquad (5\text{-}1)$$

TABLE 5.1

Computing the Mean Absolute Deviation (MAD)

MONTH	ACTUAL SALES OF WIRELESS SPEAKERS	FORECAST SALES	ABSOLUTE VALUE OF ERRORS (DEVIATION), |ACTUAL−FORECAST|
1	110	—	—
2	100	110	$\|100 - 110\| = 10$
3	120	100	$\|120 - 100\| = 20$
4	140	120	$\|140 - 120\| = 20$
5	170	140	$\|170 - 140\| = 30$
6	150	170	$\|150 - 170\| = 20$
7	160	150	$\|160 - 150\| = 10$
8	190	160	$\|190 - 160\| = 30$
9	200	190	$\|200 - 190\| = 10$
10	190	200	$\|190 - 200\| = 10$
11	—	190	—

Sum of |errors| = 160

MAD = 160/9 = 17.8

To illustrate how to compute the measures of accuracy, the **naïve model** will be used to forecast one period into the future. The naïve model does not attempt to address any of the components of a time series, but it is very quick and easy to use. A naïve forecast for the next time period is the actual value that was observed in the current time period. For example, suppose someone asked you to forecast the high temperature in your city for tomorrow. If you forecast the temperature to be whatever the high temperature is today, your forecast would be a naïve forecast. This technique is often used if a forecast is needed quickly and accuracy is not a major concern.

Consider the Walker Distributors sales of wireless speakers shown in Table 5.1. Suppose that in the past, Walker had forecast sales for each month to be the sales that were actually achieved in

IN ACTION
Hurricane Landfall Location Forecasts and the Mean Absolute Deviation

Scientists at the National Hurricane Center (NHC) of the National Weather Service have the very difficult job of predicting where the eye of a hurricane will hit land. Accurate forecasts are extremely important to coastal businesses and residents who need to prepare for a storm or perhaps even evacuate. They are also important to local government officials, law enforcement agencies, and other emergency responders who will provide help once a storm has passed. Over the years, the NHC has tremendously improved the forecast accuracy (measured by the mean absolute deviation [MAD]) in predicting the actual landfall location for hurricanes that originate in the Atlantic Ocean.

The NHC provides forecasts and periodic updates of where the hurricane eye will hit land. Such landfall location predictions are recorded when a hurricane is 72 hours, 48 hours, 36 hours, 24 hours, and 12 hours away from actually reaching land. Once the hurricane has come ashore, these forecasts are compared to the actual landfall location, and the error (in miles) is recorded. At the end of the hurricane season, the errors for all the hurricanes in that year are used to calculate the MAD for each type of forecast (12 hours away, 24 hours away, etc.). The graph below shows how the landfall location forecast has improved since 1989. During the early 1990s, the landfall forecast when the hurricane was 48 hours away had an MAD close to 200 miles; in 2009, this number was down to about 75 miles. Clearly, there has been vast improvement in forecast accuracy, and this trend is continuing.

Source: Based on National Hurricane Center, http://www.nhc.noaa.gov.

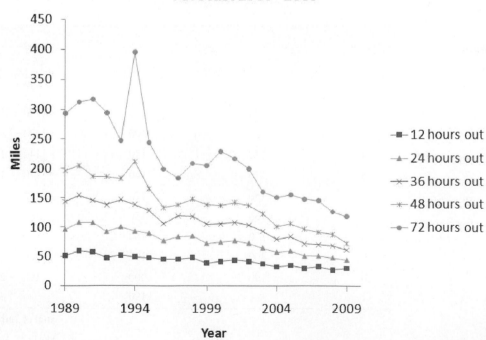

MODELING IN THE REAL WORLD

Forecasting at Tupperware International

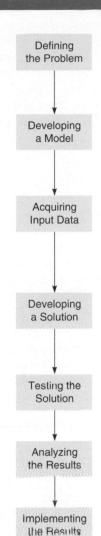

Defining the Problem

Defining the Problem

To drive production at each of Tupperware's 15 plants in the United States, Latin America, Africa, Europe, and Asia, the firm needs accurate forecasts of demand for its products.

Developing a Model

Developing a Model

A variety of statistical models are used, including moving averages, exponential smoothing, and regression analysis. Qualitative analysis is also employed in the process.

Acquiring Input Data

Acquiring Input Data

At world headquarters in Orlando, Florida, huge databases are maintained that map the sales of each product, the test market results of each new product (since 20% of the firm's sales come from products less than 2 years old), and where each product falls in its own life cycle.

Developing a Solution

Developing a Solution

Each of Tupperware's 50 profit centers worldwide develops computerized monthly, quarterly, and 12-month sales projections. These are aggregated by region and then globally.

Testing the Solution

Testing the Solution

Reviews of these forecasts take place in sales, marketing, finance, and production departments.

Analyzing the Results

Analyzing the Results

Participating managers analyze forecasts with Tupperware's version of a "jury of executive opinion."

Implementing the Results

Implementing the Results

Forecasts are used to schedule materials, equipment, and personnel at each plant.

Source: Interviews by the authors with Tupperware executives.

The naïve forecast for the next period is the actual value observed in the current period.

the previous month. Table 5.1 gives these forecasts as well as the absolute value of the errors. In forecasting for the next time period (month 11), the forecast would be 190. Notice that there is no error computed for month 1 since there was no forecast for this month, and there is no error for month 11 since the actual value of this is not yet known. Thus, the number of errors (n) is 9.

From this, we see the following:

$$\text{MAD} = \frac{\Sigma \,|\,\text{forecast error}\,|}{n} = \frac{160}{9} = 17.8$$

This means that on the average, each forecast missed the actual value by 17.8 units.

Other measures of the accuracy of historical errors in forecasting are sometimes used besides the MAD. One of the most common is the **mean squared error (MSE)**, which is the average of the squared errors:[*]

$$\text{MSE} = \frac{\Sigma (\text{error})^2}{n} \tag{5-2}$$

---

[*]In regression analysis, the MSE formula is usually adjusted to provide an unbiased estimator of the error variance. Throughout this chapter, we will use the formula provided here.

Besides the MAD and MSE, the **mean absolute percent error (MAPE)** is sometimes used. The MAPE is the average of the absolute values of the errors expressed as percentages of the actual values. This is computed as follows:

$$\text{MAPE} = \frac{\sum \left| \frac{\text{error}}{\text{actual}} \right|}{n} 100\% \tag{5-3}$$

Three common measures of error are MAD, MSE, and MAPE. Bias gives the average error and may be positive or negative.

There is another common term associated with error in forecasting. **Bias** is the average error and tells whether the forecast tends to be too high or too low and by how much. Thus, bias may be negative or positive. It is not a good measure of the actual size of the errors because the negative errors can cancel out the positive errors.

5.5 Forecasting Models—Random Variations Only

If all variations in a time series are due to random variations, with no trend, seasonal, or cyclical component, some type of averaging or smoothing model would be appropriate. The averaging techniques in this chapter are moving average, weighted moving average, and exponential smoothing. These methods will smooth out the forecasts and not be too heavily influenced by random variations. However, if there is a trend or seasonal pattern present in the data, then a technique which incorporates that particular component into the forecast should be used.

Moving Averages

Moving averages smooth out variations when forecasting demands are fairly steady.

Moving averages are useful if we can assume that market demands will stay fairly steady over time. For example, a four-month moving average is found simply by summing the demand during the past four months and dividing by 4. With each passing month, the most recent month's data are added to the sum of the previous three months' data, and the earliest month is dropped. This tends to smooth out short-term irregularities in the data series.

An *n*-period moving average forecast, which serves as an estimate of the next period's demand, is expressed as follows:

$$\text{Moving average forecast} = \frac{\text{Sum of demands in previous } n \text{ periods}}{n} \tag{5-4}$$

Mathematically, this is written as

$$F_{t+1} = \frac{Y_t + Y_{t-1} + \cdots + Y_{t-n+1}}{n} \tag{5-5}$$

where

$$F_{t+1} = \text{forecast for time period } t + 1$$
$$Y_t = \text{actual value in time period } t$$
$$n = \text{number of periods to average}$$

A 4-month moving average has $n = 4$; a 5-month moving average has $n = 5$.

WALLACE GARDEN SUPPLY EXAMPLE Storage shed sales at Wallace Garden Supply are shown in the middle column of Table 5.2. A 3-month moving average is indicated on the right. The forecast for the next January, using this technique, is 16. Were we simply asked to find a forecast for next January, we would only have to make this one calculation. The other forecasts are necessary only if we wish to compute the MAD or another measure of accuracy.

Weighted Moving Averages

Weights can be used to put more emphasis on recent periods.

A simple moving average gives the same weight $(1/n)$ to each of the past observations being used to develop the forecast. On the other hand, a **weighted moving average** allows different weights to be assigned to the previous observations. As the weighted moving average method typically assigns greater weight to more recent observations, this forecast is more responsive to changes in the pattern of the data that occur. However, this is also a potential drawback to this method because the heavier weight would also respond just as quickly to random fluctuations.

TABLE 5.2

Wallace Garden Supply Shed Sales

MONTH	ACTUAL SHED SALES	3-MONTH MOVING AVERAGE
January	10	
February	12	
March	13	
April	16	$(10 + 12 + 13)/3 = 11.67$
May	19	$(12 + 13 + 16)/3 = 13.67$
June	23	$(13 + 16 + 19)/3 = 16.00$
July	26	$(16 + 19 + 23)/3 = 19.33$
August	30	$(19 + 23 + 26)/3 = 22.67$
September	28	$(23 + 26 + 30)/3 = 26.33$
October	18	$(26 + 30 + 28)/3 = 28.00$
November	16	$(30 + 28 + 18)/3 = 25.33$
December	14	$(28 + 18 + 16)/3 = 20.67$
January	—	$(18 + 16 + 14)/3 = 16.00$

A *weighted moving average* may be expressed as

$$F_{t+1} = \frac{\Sigma(\text{Weight in period } i)(\text{Actual value in period } i)}{\Sigma(\text{Weights})} \tag{5-6}$$

Mathematically, this is

$$F_{t+1} = \frac{w_1 Y_t + w_2 Y_{t-1} + \cdots + w_n Y_{t-n+1}}{w_1 + w_2 + \cdots + w_n} \tag{5-7}$$

where

$$w_i = \text{weight for } i\text{th observation}$$

Wallace Garden Supply decides to use a 3-month weighted moving average forecast with weights of 3 for the most recent observation, 2 for the next observation, and 1 for the most distant observation. This would be implemented as follows:

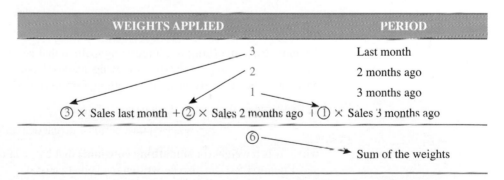

WEIGHTS APPLIED	PERIOD
3	Last month
2	2 months ago
1	3 months ago

③ × Sales last month + ② × Sales 2 months ago + ① × Sales 3 months ago

⑥ Sum of the weights

The results of the Wallace Garden Supply weighted average forecast are shown in Table 5.3. In this particular forecasting situation, you can see that weighting the latest month more heavily provides a much more accurate projection, and calculating the MAD for each of these would verify this.

Choosing the weights obviously has an important impact on the forecasts. One way to choose weights is to try various combinations of weights, calculate the MAD for each, and select the set of weights that results in the lowest MAD. Some forecasting software has an option to search for the best set of weights, and forecasts using these weights are then provided. The best set of weights can also be found by using nonlinear programming, as will be seen in a later chapter.

TABLE 5.3

Weighted Moving Average Forecast for Wallace Garden Supply

MONTH	ACTUAL SHED SALES	3-MONTH WEIGHTED MOVING AVERAGE
January	10	
February	12	
March	13	
April	16	$[(3 \times 13) + (2 \times 12) + (10)]/6 = 12.17$
May	19	$[(3 \times 16) + (2 \times 13) + (12)]/6 = 14.33$
June	23	$[(3 \times 19) + (2 \times 16) + (13)]/6 = 17.00$
July	26	$[(3 \times 23) + (2 \times 19) + (16)]/6 = 20.5$
August	30	$[(3 \times 26) + (2 \times 23) + (19)]/6 = 23.83$
September	28	$[(3 \times 30) + (2 \times 26) + (23)]/6 = 27.5$
October	18	$[(3 \times 28) + (2 \times 30) + (26)]/6 = 28.33$
November	16	$[(3 \times 18) + (2 \times 28) + (30)]/6 = 23.33$
December	14	$[(3 \times 16) + (2 \times 18) + (28)]/6 = 18.67$
January	—	$[(3 \times 14) + (2 \times 16) + (18)]/6 = 15.33$

Some software packages require that the weights add to 1, and this would simplify Equation 5-7 because the denominator would be 1. Forcing the weights to sum to 1 is easily achieved by dividing each of the weights by the sum of the weights. In the Wallace Garden Supply example in Table 5.3, the weights are 3, 2, and 1, which add to 6. These weights could be revised to the new weights 3/6, 2/6, and 1/6, which add to 1. Using these weights gives the same forecasts shown in Table 5.4.

Both simple and weighted moving averages are effective in smoothing out sudden fluctuations in the demand pattern in order to provide stable estimates. Moving averages do, however, have two problems. First, increasing the size of n (the number of periods averaged) does smooth out fluctuations better, but it makes the method less sensitive to *real* changes in the data should they occur. Second, moving averages cannot pick up trends very well. Because they are averages, they will always stay within past levels and will not predict a change to either a higher or a lower level.

Moving averages have two problems: the larger number of periods may smooth out real changes, and they don't pick up trend.

Exponential Smoothing

Exponential smoothing is a forecasting method that is easy to use and is handled efficiently by computers. Although it is a type of moving average technique, it involves little record keeping of past data. The basic exponential smoothing formula can be shown as follows:

$$\text{New forecast} = \text{Last period's forecast} \tag{5-8}$$
$$+ \alpha(\text{Last period's actual demand} - \text{Last period's forecast})$$

where α is a weight (or **smoothing constant**) that has a value between 0 and 1, inclusive.

Equation 5-8 can also be written mathematically as

$$F_{t+1} = F_t + \alpha(Y_t - F_t) \tag{5-9}$$

where

$$F_{t+1} = \text{new forecast (for time period } t + 1)$$
$$F_t = \text{previous forecast (for time period } t)$$
$$\alpha = \text{smoothing constant } (0 \le \alpha \le 1)$$
$$Y_t = \text{previous period's actual demand}$$

The concept here is not complex. The latest estimate of demand is equal to the old estimate adjusted by a fraction of the error (last period's actual demand minus the old estimate).

The smoothing constant, α, allows managers to assign weight to recent data.

The smoothing constant, α, can be changed to give more weight to recent data when the value is high or more weight to past data when it is low. For example, when $\alpha = 0.5$, it can be shown mathematically that the new forecast is based almost entirely on demand in the past three periods. When $\alpha = 0.1$, the forecast places little weight on any single period, even the most recent, and it takes many periods (about 19) of historic values into account.[*]

For example, in January, a demand for 142 of a certain car model for February was predicted by a dealer. Actual February demand was 153 autos, so the forecast error was $153 - 142 = 9$. Using a smoothing constant $\alpha = 0.20$, the exponential smoothing forecast for March demand would be found by adding 20% of this error to the previous forecast of 142. Substituting into the formula, we obtain

$$\text{New forecast (for March demand)} = 142 + 0.2(153 - 142)$$
$$= 144.2$$

Thus, the forecast for the demand for cars in March would be 144 after being rounded by the dealer.

Suppose that actual demand for the cars in March was 136. A forecast for the demand in April, using the exponential smoothing model with a constant of $\alpha = 0.20$, can be made:

$$\text{New forecast (for April demand)} = 144.2 + 0.2(136 - 144.2)$$
$$= 142.6, \text{ or } 143 \text{ autos}$$

GETTING STARTED The exponential smoothing approach is easy to use and has been applied successfully by banks, manufacturing companies, wholesalers, and other organizations. To develop a forecast with this method, a smoothing constant must be selected and a previous forecast must be known or assumed. If a company has been routinely using this method, there is no problem. However, if a company is just beginning to use the method, these issues must be addressed.

The appropriate value of the smoothing constant, α, can make the difference between an accurate forecast and an inaccurate forecast. In picking a value for the smoothing constant, the objective is to obtain the most accurate forecast. Several values of the smoothing constant may be tried, and the one with the lowest MAD could be selected. This is analogous to how weights are selected for a weighted moving average forecast. Some forecasting software will automatically select the best smoothing constant. QM for Windows will display the MAD that would be obtained with values of α ranging from 0 to 1 in increments of 0.01.

When the exponential smoothing model is used for the first time, there is no prior forecast for the current time period to use in developing a forecast for the next time period. Therefore, a previous value for a forecast must be assumed. It is common practice to assume a forecast for time period 1, and to use this to develop a forecast for time period 2. The time period 2 forecast is then used to forecast time period 3, and this continues until the forecast for the current time period is found. Unless there is reason to assume another value, the forecast for time period 1 is assumed to be equal to the actual value in time period 1 (*i.e.*, the error is zero). The value of the forecast for time period 1 usually has very little impact on the value of forecasts many time periods into the future.

PORT OF BALTIMORE EXAMPLE Let us apply this concept with a trial-and-error testing of two values of α in an example. The port of Baltimore has unloaded large quantities of grain from ships during the past eight quarters. The port's operations manager wants to test the use of exponential smoothing to see how well the technique works in predicting tonnage unloaded. He assumes that the forecast of grain unloaded in the first quarter was 175 tons. Two values of α are examined: $\alpha = 0.10$ and $\alpha = 0.50$. Table 5.4 shows the *detailed* calculations for $\alpha = 0.10$ only.

To evaluate the accuracy of each smoothing constant, we can compute the absolute deviations and MADs (see Table 5.5). Based on this analysis, a smoothing constant of $\alpha = 0.10$ is preferred to $\alpha = 0.50$ because its MAD is smaller.

---

[*]The term *exponential smoothing* is used because the weight of any one period's demand in a forecast decreases exponentially over time. See an advanced forecasting book for algebraic proof.

TABLE 5.4

Port of Baltimore Exponential Smoothing Forecasts for $\alpha = 0.10$ and $\alpha = 0.50$

QUARTER	ACTUAL TONNAGE UNLOADED	FORECAST USING $\alpha = 0.10$	FORECAST USING $\alpha = 0.50$
1	180	175	175
2	168	$175.5 = 175.00 + 0.10(180 - 175)$	177.5
3	159	$174.75 = 175.50 + 0.10(168 - 175.50)$	172.75
4	175	$173.18 = 174.75 + 0.10(159 - 174.75)$	165.88
5	190	$173.36 = 173.18 + 0.10(175 - 173.18)$	170.44
6	205	$175.02 = 173.36 + 0.10(190 - 173.36)$	180.22
7	180	$178.02 = 175.02 + 0.10(205 - 175.02)$	192.61
8	182	$178.22 = 178.02 + 0.10(180 - 178.02)$	186.30
9	?	$178.60 = 178.22 + 0.10(182 - 178.22)$	184.15

TABLE 5.5

Absolute Deviations and MADs for the Port of Baltimore Example

QUARTER	ACTUAL TONNAGE UNLOADED	FORECAST WITH $\alpha = 0.10$	ABSOLUTE DEVIATIONS FOR $\alpha = 0.10$	FORECAST WITH $\alpha = 0.50$	DEVIATIONS ABSOLUTE FOR $\alpha = 0.50$
1	180	175	5	175	5
2	168	175.5	7.5	177.5	9.5
3	159	174.75	15.75	172.75	13.75
4	175	173.18	1.82	165.88	9.12
5	190	173.36	16.64	170.44	19.56
6	205	175.02	29.98	180.22	24.78
7	180	178.02	1.98	192.61	12.61
8	182	178.22	3.78	186.30	4.3
Sum of absolute deviations			82.45		98.63

$$\text{MAD} = \frac{\sum |\text{deviation}|}{n} = 10.31 \qquad \text{MAD} = 12.33$$

Using Software for Forecasting Time Series

The two software packages available with this book, Excel QM and QM for Windows, are very easy to use for forecasting. The previous examples will be solved using these.

In using Excel QM with Excel 2013 for forecasting, from the Excel QM ribbon, select *Alphabetical* as shown in Program 5.1A. Then simply select whichever method you wish to use, and an initialization window opens to allow you to set the size of the problem. Program 5.1B shows this window for the Wallace Garden Supply weighted moving average example with the number of past periods and the number of periods in the weighted average already entered. Clicking OK results in the screen shown in Program 5.1C to appear allowing you to enter the data and the weights. Once all numbers are entered, the calculations are automatically performed as you see in Program 5.1C.

To use QM for Windows to forecast, under Modules select *Forecasting*. Then select *New* and *Time Series Analysis* as shown in Program 5.2A. This would be for all of the models presented in this chapter. In the window that opens (Program 5.2B), specify the number of past periods of data. For the Port of Baltimore example, this is 8. Click *OK* and an input screen appears allowing you to enter the data and select the forecasting technique as shown in Program 5.2C. Based on the method you choose, other windows may open to allow you to specify the necessary parameters for that model. In this example, the exponential smoothing model is selected, so the smoothing constant must be specified. After entering the data, click Solve and the output shown in Program 5.2D appears. From this output screen, you can select Window to see additional information such as the details of the calculations and a graph of the time series and the forecasts.

PROGRAM 5.1A

Selecting the Forecasting Model in Wallace Garden Supply Problem

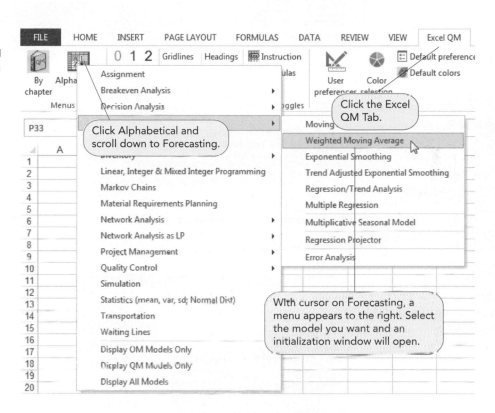

PROGRAM 5.1B

Initializing Excel QM Spreadsheet for Wallace Garden Supply Problem

PROGRAM 5.1C

Excel QM Output for Wallace Garden Supply Problem

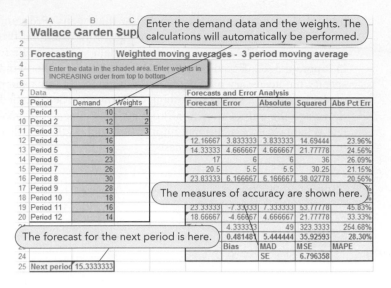

Enter the demand data and the weights. The calculations will automatically be performed.

Enter the data in the shaded area. Enter weights in INCREASING order from top to bottom.

The measures of accuracy are shown here.

The forecast for the next period is here.

PROGRAM 5.2A

Selecting Time-Series Analysis in QM for Windows in the Forecasting Module

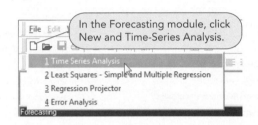

In the Forecasting module, click New and Time-Series Analysis.

PROGRAM 5.2B

Entering Data for Port of Baltimore Example in QM for Windows

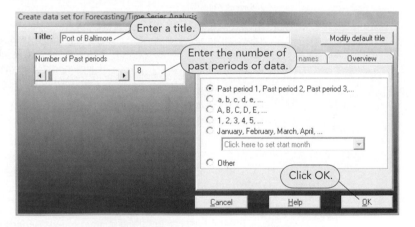

Enter a title.

Enter the number of past periods of data.

Click OK.

PROGRAM 5.2C

Selecting the Model and Entering Data for Port of Baltimore Example in QM for Windows

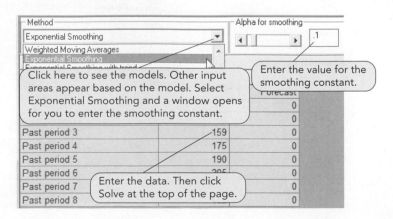

Click here to see the models. Other input areas appear based on the model. Select Exponential Smoothing and a window opens for you to enter the smoothing constant.

Enter the value for the smoothing constant.

Enter the data. Then click Solve at the top of the page.

PROGRAM 5.2D

Output for Port of Baltimore Example in QM for Windows

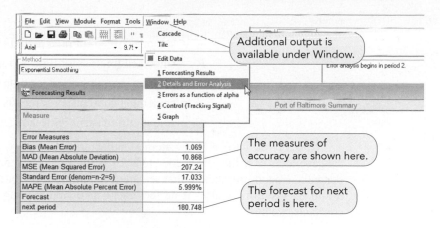

The measures of accuracy are shown here.

The forecast for next period is here.

5.6 Forecasting Models—Trend and Random Variations

If there is trend present in a time series, the forecasting model must account for this and cannot simply average past values. Two very common techniques will be presented here. The first is exponential smoothing with trend, and the second is called trend projection or simply a trend line.

Exponential Smoothing with Trend

An extension of the exponential smoothing model that will explicitly adjust for trend is called the exponential smoothing with trend model. The idea is to develop an exponential smoothing forecast and then adjust this for trend. Two smoothing constants, α and β, are used in this model, and both of these values must be between 0 and 1. The level of the forecast is adjusted by multiplying the first smoothing constant, α, by the most recent forecast error and adding it to the previous forecast. The trend is adjusted by multiplying the second smoothing constant, β, by the most recent error or excess amount in the trend. A higher value gives more weight to recent observations and thus responds more quickly to changes in the patterns.

Two smoothing constants are used.

As with simple exponential smoothing, the first time a forecast is developed, a previous forecast (F_t) must be given or estimated. If none is available, often the initial forecast is assumed to be perfect. In addition, a previous trend (T_t) must be given or estimated. This is often estimated using other past data, if available, or by using subjective means, or by calculating the increase (or decrease) observed during the first few time periods of the data available. Without such an estimate available, the trend is sometimes assumed to be 0 initially, although this may lead to poor forecasts if the trend is large and β is small. Once these initial conditions have been set, the exponential smoothing forecast including trend (FIT_t) is developed using three steps:

Estimate or assume initial values for F_t and T_t

Step 1. Compute the smoothed forecast (F_{t+1}) for time period $t + 1$ using the equation

Smoothed forecast = Previous forecast including trend + α(Last error)

$$F_{t+1} = FIT_t + \alpha(Y_t - FIT_t) \tag{5-10}$$

Step 2. Update the trend (T_{t+1}) using the equation

Smoothed trend = Previous trend + β(Error or excess in trend)

$$T_{t+1} = T_t + \beta(F_{t+1} - FIT_t) \tag{5-11}$$

Step 3. Calculate the trend-adjusted exponential smoothing forecast (FIT_{t+1}) using the equation

Forecast including trend (FIT_{t+1}) = Smoothed forecast (F_{t+1}) + Smoothed trend (T_{t+1})

$$FIT_{t+1} = F_{t+1} + T_{t+1} \tag{5-12}$$

where

$$T_t = \text{smoothed trend for time period } t$$
$$F_t = \text{smoothed forecast for time period } t$$
$$FIT_t = \text{forecast including trend for time period } t$$
$$\alpha = \text{smoothing constant for forecasts}$$
$$\beta = \text{smoothing constant for trend}$$

Consider the case of Midwestern Manufacturing Company, which has a demand for electrical generators over the period 2007 to 2013 as shown in Table 5.6. To use the trend-adjusted exponential smoothing method, first set initial conditions (previous values for F and T) and choose α and β. Assuming that F_1 is perfect and T_1 is 0, and picking 0.3 and 0.4 for the smoothing constants, we have

$$F_1 = 74 \quad T_1 = 0 \quad \alpha = 0.3 \quad \beta = 0.4$$

This results in

$$FIT_1 = F_1 + T_1 = 74 + 0 = 74$$

Following the three steps to get the forecast for 2008 (time period 2), we have

Step 1. Compute F_{t+1} using the equation

$$F_{t+1} = FIT_t + \alpha(Y_t - FIT_t)$$
$$F_2 = FIT_1 + 0.3(Y_1 - FIT_1) = 74 + 0.3(74 - 74) = 74$$

Step 2. Update the trend (T_{t+1}) using the equation

$$T_{t+1} = T_t + \beta(F_{t+1} - FIT_t)$$
$$T_2 = T_1 + 0.4(F_2 - FIT_1) = 0 + 0.4(74 - 74) = 0$$

Step 3. Calculate the trend-adjusted exponential smoothing forecast (FIT_{t+1}) using the equation

$$FIT_2 = F_2 + T_2 = 74 + 0 = 74$$

For 2009 (time period 3) we have

Step 1.

$$F_3 = FIT_2 + 0.3(Y_2 - FIT_2) = 74 + 0.3(79 - 74) = 75.5$$

Step 2.

$$T_3 = T_2 + 0.4(F_3 - FIT_2) = 0 + 0.4(75.5 - 74) = 0.6$$

Step 3.

$$FIT_3 = F_3 + T_3 = 75.5 + 0.6 = 76.1$$

The other results are shown in Table 5.7. The forecast for 2014 would be about 131.35.

TABLE 5.6

Midwestern
Manufacturing's
Demand

YEAR	ELECTRICAL GENERATORS SOLD
2007	74
2008	79
2009	80
2010	90
2011	105
2012	142
2013	122

TABLE 5.7 Midwestern Manufacturing Exponential Smoothing with Trend Forecasts

TIME (t)	DEMAND (Y_t)	$F_{t+1} = FIT_t + 0.3(Y_t - FIT_t)$	$T_{t+1} = T_t + 0.4(F_{t+1} - FIT_t)$	$FIT_{t+1} = F_{t+1} + T_{t+1}$
1	74	74	0	74
2	79	$74 = 74 + 0.3(74 - 74)$	$0 = 0 + 0.4(74 - 74)$	$74 = 74 + 0$
3	80	$75.5 = 74 + 0.3(79 - 74)$	$0.6 = 0 + 0.4(75.5 - 74)$	$76.1 = 75.5 + 0.6$
4	90	77.270 $= 76.1 + 0.3(80 - 76.1)$	1.068 $= 0.6 + 0.4(77.27 - 76.1)$	$78.338 = 77.270 + 1.068$
5	105	81.837 $= 78.338 + 0.3(90 - 78.338)$	2.468 $= 1.068 + 0.4(81.837 - 78.338)$	$84.305 = 81.837 + 2.468$
6	142	90.514 $= 84.305 + 0.3(105 - 84.305)$	4.952 $= 2.468 + 0.4(90.514 - 84.305)$	$95.466 = 90.514 + 4.952$
7	122	109.426 $= 95.466 + 0.3(142 - 95.466)$	10.536 $= 4.952 + 0.4(109.426 - 95.466)$	$119.962 = 109.426 + 10.536$
8		120.573 $= 119.962 + 0.3(122 - 119.962)$	10.780 $= 10.536 + 0.4(120.573 - 119.962)$	$131.353 = 120.573 + 10.780$

To have Excel QM perform the calculations in Excel 2013, from the Excel QM ribbon, select the alphabetical list of techniques and choose *Forecasting* and then *Trend Adjusted Exponential Smoothing*. After specifying the number of past observations, enter the data and the values for α and β as shown in Program 5.3.

Trend Projections

A trend line is a regression equation with time as the independent variable.

Another method for forecasting time series with trend is called **trend projection**. This technique fits a trend line to a series of historical data points and then projects the line into the future for medium- to long-range forecasts. There are several mathematical trend equations that can be developed (e.g., exponential and quadratic), but in this section we look at linear (straight line) trends only. A trend line is simply a linear regression equation in which the independent

PROGRAM 5.3

Output from Excel QM in Excel 2013 for Trend Adjusted Exponential Smoothing Example

	A	B	C	D	E	F	G	H	I	J
1	Midwestern Manufacturing Company Example									
2										
3	Forecasting			Trend adjusted exponential smoothing						
4	Enter alpha and beta (between 0 and 1), enter the past demands in the shaded column then enter									
5	a starting forecast. If the starting forecast is not in the first period then delete the error analysis for									
6										
7	Alpha	0.3								
8	Beta	0.4								
9	Data			Forecasts and Error Analysis						
10	Period	Demand		Smoothed Forecast, F_t	Smoothed Trend, T_t	Forecast Including Trend, FIT_t	Error	Absolute	Squared	Abs Pct Err
11	Period 1	74		74		74	0	0	0	00.00%
12	Period 2	79		74	0	74	5	5	25	06.33%
13	Period 3	80		76.6	0.6	76.1	3.9	3.9	15.21	04.88%
14	Period 4	90		77.27	1.068	78.338	11.662	11.662	136.0022	12.96%
15	Period 5	105		81.8366	2.46744	84.30404	20.69596	20.696	428.3228	19.71%
16	Period 6	142		90.512828	4.950955	95.4637832	46.53622	46.5362	2165.619	32.77%
17	Period 7	122		109.4246482	10.5353	119.959949	2.040051	2.04005	4.161806	0.016722
18		Next period		120.5719646	10.78011	131.352072				
19		Total					89.83423	89.8342	2774.316	78.32%
20							12.83346	12.8335	396.3309	11.19%
21							Bias	MAD	MSE	MAPE
22								SE	23.55554	

The forecast for next period is here.

variable (X) is the time period. The first time period will be time period 1. The second time period will be time period 2, and so forth. The last time period will be time period n. The form of this is

$$\hat{Y} = b_0 + b_1 X$$

where

$$\hat{Y} = \text{predicted value}$$
$$b_0 = \text{intercept}$$
$$b_1 = \text{slope of the line}$$
$$X = \text{time period (i.e., } X = 1, 2, 3, \ldots, n)$$

The **least squares** regression method may be applied to find the coefficients that minimize the sum of the squared errors, thereby also minimizing the mean squared error (MSE). Chapter 4 provides detailed explanation of least squares regression and formulas to calculate the coefficients by hand. In this section, we use computer software to perform the calculations.

Let us consider the case of Midwestern Manufacturing's demand for generators that was presented in Table 5.6. A trend line can be used to predict demand (Y) based on the time period using a regression equation. For the first time period, which was 2007, we let $X = 1$. For 2008, we let $X = 2$, and so forth. Using computer software to develop a regression equation as we did in Chapter 4, we get the following equation:

$$\hat{Y} = 56.71 + 10.54X$$

To project demand in 2014, we first denote the year 2014 in our new coding system as $X = 8$:

$$(\text{sales in 2014}) = 56.71 + 10.54(8)$$
$$= 141.03, \text{ or 141 generators}$$

We can estimate demand for 2015 by inserting $X = 9$ in the same equation:

$$(\text{sales in 2015}) = 56.71 + 10.54(9)$$
$$= 151.57, \text{ or 152 generators}$$

Program 5.4 provides output from Excel QM in Excel 2013. To run this model, from the Excel QM ribbon, select *Alphabetical* to see the techniques. Then select *Forecasting* and *Regression/ Trend Analysis*. When the input window opens, enter the number of past observations (7), and the spreadsheet is initialized allowing you to input the seven Y values and the seven X values as shown in Program 5.4.

PROGRAM 5.4

Output from Excel QM in Excel 2013 for Trend Line Example

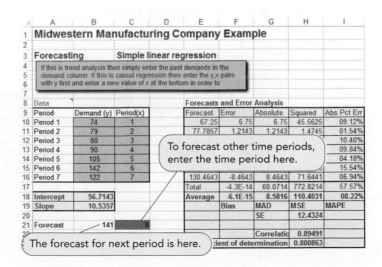

PROGRAM 5.5

Output from QM for Windows in Excel 2013 for Trend Line Example

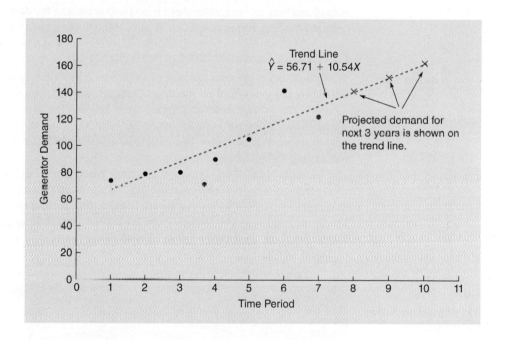

Measure		Future Period	Forecast
Error Measures		8	141
Bias (Mean Error)	0	9	151.536
MAD (Mean Absolute Deviation)	8.582	10	162.071
MSE (Mean Squared Error)	110.403	11	172.607
Standard Error (denom=n-2=5)	12.432	12	183.143
MAPE (Mean Absolute Percent	8.224%	13	193.679
Regression line		14	204.214
Demand(y) = 56.714		15	214.75
+ 10.536 * Time(x)		16	225.286
Statistics			235.822
Correlation coefficient			246.357
Coefficient of determination (r^2)			256.893
		20	267.429
		21	277.964

Midwestern Manufacturing Company Summary

Forecasts for future time periods are shown here.

The trend line is shown over two lines.

FIGURE 5.4

Generator Demand and Projections for Next Three Years Based on Trend Line

Trend Line
$\hat{Y} = 56.71 + 10.54X$

Projected demand for next 3 years is shown on the trend line.

This problem could also be solved using QM for Windows. To do this, select the *Forecasting* module, and then enter a new problem by selecting *New – Time Series Analysis*. When the next window opens, enter the number of observations (7) and press *OK*. Enter the values (Y) for the seven past observations when the input window opens. It is not necessary to enter the values for X (1, 2, 3, . . . , 7) because QM for Windows will automatically use these numbers. Then click *Solve* to see the results shown in Program 5.5.

Figure 5.4 provides a scatter diagram and a trend line for this data. The projected demand in each of the next three years is also shown on the trend line.

5.7 Adjusting for Seasonal Variations

Time-series forecasting such as that in the example of Midwestern Manufacturing involves looking at the *trend* of data over a series of time observations. Sometimes, however, recurring variations at certain seasons of the year make a *seasonal* adjustment in the trend line forecast necessary. Demand for coal and fuel oil, for example, usually peaks during cold winter months.

Demand for golf clubs or suntan lotion may be highest in summer. Analyzing data in monthly or quarterly terms usually makes it easy to spot seasonal patterns. A seasonal index is often used in multiplicative time-series forecasting models to make an adjustment in the forecast when a seasonal component exists. An alternative is to use an additive model such as a regression model that will be introduced in a later section.

Seasonal Indices

A **seasonal index** indicates how a particular season (e.g., month or quarter) compares with an average season. An index of 1 for a season would indicate that the season is average. If the index is higher than 1, the values of the time series in that season tend to be higher than average. If the index is lower than 1, the values of the time series in that season tend to be lower than average.

Seasonal indices are used with multiplicative forecasting models in two ways. First, each observation in a time series are divided by the appropriate seasonal index to remove the impact of seasonality. The resulting values are called **deseasonalized data**. Using these deseasonalized values, forecasts for future values can be developed using a variety of forecasting techniques. Once the forecasts of future deseasonalized values have been developed, they are multiplied by the seasonal indices to develop the final forecasts, which now include variations due to seasonality.

There are two ways to compute seasonal indices. The first method, based on an overall average, is easy and may be used when there is no trend present in the data. The second method, based on a centered-moving-average approach, is more difficult but it must be used when there is trend present.

Calculating Seasonal Indices with No Trend

An average season has an index of 1.

When no trend is present, the index can be found by dividing the average value for a particular season by the average of all the data. Thus, an index of 1 means the season is average. For example, if the average sales in January were 120 and the average sales in all months were 200, the seasonal index for January would be $120/200 = 0.60$, so January is below average. The next example illustrates how to compute seasonal indices from historical data and to use these in forecasting future values.

Monthly sales of one brand of telephone answering machine at Eichler Supplies are shown in Table 5.8, for the two most recent years. The average demand in each month is computed, and these values are divided by the overall average (94) to find the seasonal index for each month. We then use the seasonal indices from Table 5.8 to adjust future forecasts. For example, suppose we expected the third year's annual demand for answering machines to be 1,200 units, which is

TABLE 5.8

Answering Machine Sales and Seasonal Indices

MONTH	SALES DEMAND YEAR 1	SALES DEMAND YEAR 2	AVERAGE 2-YEAR DEMAND	MONTHLY DEMAND[a]	AVERAGE SEASONAL INDEX[b]
January	80	100	90	94	0.957
February	85	75	80	94	0.851
March	80	90	85	94	0.904
April	110	90	100	94	1.064
May	115	131	123	94	1.309
June	120	110	115	94	1.223
July	100	110	105	94	1.117
August	110	90	100	94	1.064
September	85	95	90	94	0.957
October	75	85	80	94	0.851
November	85	75	80	94	0.851
December	80	80	80	94	0.851

Total average demand = 1,128

[a] Average monthly demand $= \dfrac{1,128}{12 \text{ months}} = 94$

[b] Seasonal index $= \dfrac{\text{Average 2 year demand}}{\text{Average monthly demand}}$

100 per month. We would not forecast each month to have a demand of 100, but we would adjust these based on the seasonal indices as follows:

Jan. $\dfrac{1,200}{12} \times 0.957 = 96$ July $\dfrac{1,200}{12} \times 1.117 = 112$

Feb. $\dfrac{1,200}{12} \times 0.851 = 85$ Aug. $\dfrac{1,200}{12} \times 1.064 = 106$

Mar. $\dfrac{1,200}{12} \times 0.904 = 90$ Sept. $\dfrac{1,200}{12} \times 0.957 = 96$

Apr. $\dfrac{1,200}{12} \times 1.064 = 106$ Oct. $\dfrac{1,200}{12} \times 0.851 = 85$

May $\dfrac{1,200}{12} \times 1.309 = 131$ Nov. $\dfrac{1,200}{12} \times 0.851 = 85$

June $\dfrac{1,200}{12} \times 1.223 = 122$ Dec. $\dfrac{1,200}{12} \times 0.851 = 85$

Calculating Seasonal Indices with Trend

Centered moving averages are used to compute seasonal indices when there is trend.

When both trend and seasonal components are present in a time series, a change from one month to the next could be due to a trend, to a seasonal variation, or simply to random fluctuations. To help with this problem, the seasonal indices should be computed using a **centered moving average** (CMA) approach whenever trend is present. Using this approach prevents a variation due to trend from being incorrectly interpreted as a variation due to the season. Consider the following example.

Quarterly sales figures for Turner Industries are shown in Table 5.9. Notice that there is a definite trend as the total is increasing each year, and there is an increase for each quarter from one year to the next as well. The seasonal component is obvious as there is a definite drop from the fourth quarter of one year to the first quarter of the next. A similar pattern is observed in comparing the third quarters to the fourth quarters immediately following.

If a seasonal index for quarter 1 were computed using the overall average, the index would be too low and misleading, since this quarter has less trend than any of the others in the sample. If the first quarter of year 1 were omitted and replaced by the first quarter of year 4 (if it were available), the average for quarter 1 (and consequently the seasonal index for quarter 1) would be considerably higher. To derive an accurate seasonal index, we should use a CMA.

Consider quarter 3 of year 1 for the Turner Industries example. The actual sales in that quarter were 150. To determine the magnitude of the seasonal variation, we should compare this with an average quarter centered at that time period. Thus, we should have a total of four quarters (1 year of data) with an equal number of quarters before and after quarter 3 so the trend is averaged out. Thus, we need 1.5 quarters before quarter 3 and 1.5 quarters after it. To obtain the CMA, we take quarters 2, 3, and 4 of year 1, plus one-half of quarter 1 for year 1 and one-half of quarter 1 for year 2. The average will be

$$\text{CMA (quarter 3 of year 1)} = \frac{0.5(108) + 125 + 150 + 141 + 0.5(116)}{4} = 132.00$$

We compare the actual sales in this quarter to the CMA and we have the following seasonal ratio:

$$\text{Seasonal ratio} = \frac{\text{Sales in quarter 3}}{\text{CMA}} = \frac{150}{132.00} = 1.136$$

TABLE 5.9

Quarterly Sales ($1,000,000s) for Turner Industries

QUARTER	YEAR 1	YEAR 2	YEAR 3	AVERAGE
1	108	116	123	115.67
2	125	134	142	133.67
3	150	159	168	159.00
4	141	152	165	152.67
Average	131.00	140.25	149.50	140.25

TABLE 5.10

Centered Moving Averages and Seasonal Ratios for Turner Industries

YEAR	QUARTER	SALES ($1,000,000s)	CMA	SEASONAL RATIO
1	1	108		
	2	125		
	3	150	132.000	1.136
	4	141	134.125	1.051
2	1	116	136.375	0.851
	2	134	138.875	0.965
	3	159	141.125	1.127
	4	152	143.000	1.063
3	1	123	145.125	0.848
	2	142	147.875	0.960
	3	168		
	4	165		

Thus, sales in quarter 3 of year 1 are about 13.6% higher than an average quarter at this time. All of the CMAs and the seasonal ratios are shown in Table 5.10.

Since there are two seasonal ratios for each quarter, we average these to get the seasonal index. Thus,

$$\text{Index for quarter } 1 = I_1 = (0.851 + 0.848)/2 = 0.85$$
$$\text{Index for quarter } 2 = I_2 = (0.965 + 0.960)/2 = 0.96$$
$$\text{Index for quarter } 3 = I_3 = (1.136 + 1.127)/2 = 1.13$$
$$\text{Index for quarter } 4 = I_4 = (1.051 + 1.063)/2 = 1.06$$

The sum of these indices should be the number of seasons (4) since an average season should have an index of 1. In this example, the sum is 4. If the sum were not 4, an adjustment would be made. We would multiply each index by 4 and divide this by the sum of the indices.

Steps Used to Compute Seasonal Indices Based on CMAs

1. Compute a CMA for each observation (where possible).
2. Compute seasonal ratio = Observation/CMA for that observation.
3. Average seasonal ratios to get seasonal indices.
4. If seasonal indices do not add to the number of seasons, multiply each index by (Number of seasons)/(Sum of the indices).

The seasonal indices found using the CMAs will be used to remove the impact of seasonal so that the trend is easier to identify. Later, the seasonal indices will be used again to adjust the trend forecast based on the seasonal variations.

5.8   Forecasting Models—Trend, Seasonal, and Random Variations

When both trend and seasonal components are present in a time series, the forecasting model selected must address these. The decomposition method, which uses seasonal indices, is a very common approach. Multiple regression models are also common, with dummy variables used to adjust for seasonal variations in an additive time-series model.

The Decomposition Method

The process of isolating linear trend and seasonal factors to develop more accurate forecasts is called **decomposition**. The first step is to compute seasonal indices for each season as we have done with the Turner Industries data. Then, the data are deseasonalized by dividing each number

TABLE 5.11

Deseasonalized Data for Turner Industries

SALES ($1,000,000s)	SEASONAL INDEX	DESEASONALIZED SALES ($1,000,000s)
108	0.85	127.059
125	0.96	130.208
150	1.13	132.743
141	1.06	133.019
116	0.85	136.471
134	0.96	139.583
159	1.13	140.708
152	1.06	143.396
123	0.85	144.706
142	0.96	147.917
168	1.13	148.673
165	1.06	155.660

by its seasonal index, as shown in Table 5.11. Figure 5.5 provides a graph of the original data as well as a graph of the deseasonalized data. Notice how smooth the deseasonalized data is.

A trend line is then found using the deseasonalized data. Using computer software with this data, we have[*]

$$b_1 = 2.34$$
$$b_0 = 124.78$$

The trend equation is

$$\hat{Y} = 124.78 + 2.34X$$

where

$$X = \text{time}$$

FIGURE 5.5

Scatterplot of Turner Industries's Original Sales Data and Deseasonalized Data

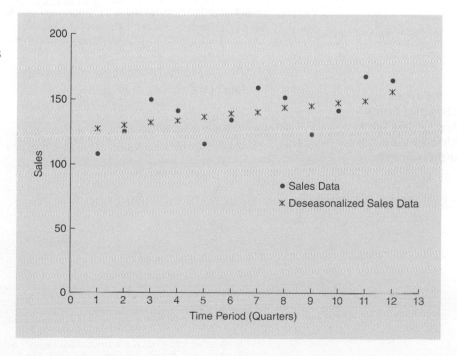

*If you do the calculations by hand, the numbers may differ slightly from these due to rounding.

TABLE 5.12 Turner Industry Forecasts for Four Quarters of Year 4

YEAR	QUARTER	TIME PERIOD (X)	TREND FORECAST $\hat{Y} = 124.78 + 2.34X$	SEASONAL INDEX	FINAL (ADJUSTED) FORECAST
4	1	13	155.20	0.85	131.92
	2	14	157.54	0.96	151.24
	3	15	159.88	1.13	180.66
	4	16	162.22	1.06	171.95

This equation is used to develop the forecast based on trend, and the result is multiplied by the appropriate seasonal index to make a seasonal adjustment. For the Turner Industries data, the forecast for the first quarter of year 4 (time period $X = 13$ and seasonal index $I_1 = 0.85$) would be found as follows:

$$\hat{Y} = 124.78 + 2.34X$$
$$= 124.78 + 2.34(13)$$
$$= 155.2 \text{ (forecast before adjustment for seasonality)}$$

We multiply this by the seasonal index for quarter 1 and we get

$$\hat{Y} \times I_1 = 155.2 \times 0.85 = 131.92$$

Using the same procedure, we find the forecasts for quarters 2, 3, and 4 of the next year. Table 5.12 shows the unadjusted forecast based on the trend line, for each of the four quarters of year 4. The last column of this table gives the final forecasts that were found by multiplying each trend forecast by the appropriate seasonal index. A scatter diagram showing the original data and the deseasonalized data as well as the unadjusted forecast and the final forecast for these next four quarters is provided in Figure 5.6.

Steps to Develop a Forecast Using the Decomposition Method

1. Compute seasonal indices using CMAs.
2. Deseasonalize the data by dividing each number by its seasonal index.
3. Find the equation of a trend line using the deseasonalized data.
4. Forecast for future periods using the trend line.
5. Multiply the trend line forecast by the appropriate seasonal index.

FIGURE 5.6

Scatterplot of Turner Industries Original Sales Data and Deseasonalized Data with Unadjusted and Adjusted Forecasts

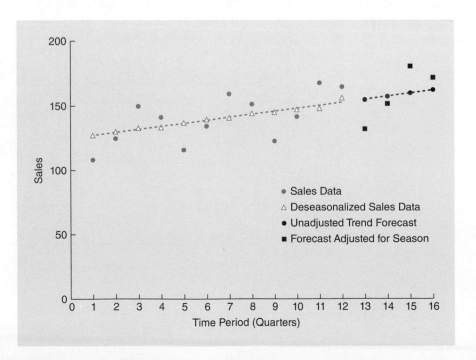

Most forecasting software, including Excel QM and QM for Windows, includes the decomposition method as one of the available techniques. This will automatically compute the CMAs, deseasonalize the data, develop the trend line, make the forecast using the trend equation, and adjust the final forecast for seasonality.

Software for Decomposition

Program 5.6A shows the QM for Windows input screen that appears after selecting the Forecasting Module, selecting New-Time Series, and specifying 12 past observations. The multiplicative decomposition method is selected, and you can see the inputs that are used for this problem. When this is solved, the output screen in Program 5.6B appears. Additional output is available by selecting details or graph from the Windows drop-down menu (not shown in Program 5.6B) that appears after the problem is solved. The forecasts are slightly different from the ones shown in Table 5.12 due to round-off error.

Excel QM can be used in Excel 2013 for this problem also. From the QM Ribbon, select the menus *By Chapter* and select *Chapter 5-Forecasting-Decomposition*. Specify there are 12 past observations, 4 seasons, and use a centered moving average.

PROGRAM 5.6A

QM for Windows Input Screen for Turner Industries Example

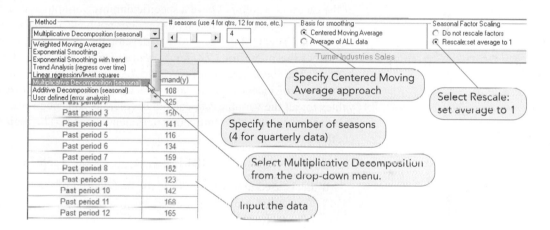

PROGRAM 5.6B

QM for Windows Output Screen for Turner Industries Example

Multiple regression can be used to develop an additive decomposition model.

Using Regression with Trend and Seasonal Components

Multiple regression may be used to forecast with both trend and seasonal components present in a time series. One independent variable is time, and other independent variables are dummy variables to indicate the season. If we forecast quarterly data, there are four categories (quarters) so we would use three dummy variables. The basic model is an additive decomposition model and is expressed as follows:

$$\hat{Y} = a + b_1X_1 + b_2X_2 + b_3X_3 + b_4X_4$$

where

$$X_1 = \text{time period}$$
$$X_2 = 1 \text{ if quarter 2}$$
$$= 0 \text{ otherwise}$$
$$X_3 = 1 \text{ if quarter 3}$$
$$= 0 \text{ otherwise}$$
$$X_4 = 1 \text{ if quarter 4}$$
$$= 0 \text{ otherwise}$$

If $X_2 = X_3 = X_4 = 0$, then the quarter would be quarter 1. It is an arbitrary choice as to which of the quarters would not have a specific dummy variable associated with it. The forecasts will be the same regardless of which quarter does not have a specific dummy variable.

Using Excel QM in Excel 2013 to develop the regression model, from the Excel QM ribbon, we select the menu for *Chapter 5—Forecasting*, and then choose the *Multiple Regression* method. The input screen in Program 5.7A appears, and the number of observations (12) and the number of independent variables (4) are entered. An initialized spreadsheet appears and the values for all the variables are entered in columns B through F as shown in Program 5.7B. Once this has been done, the regression coefficients appear. The regression equation (with rounded coefficients) is

$$\hat{Y} = 104.1 + 2.3X_1 + 15.7X_2 + 38.7X_3 + 30.1X_4$$

If this is used to forecast sales in the first quarter of the next year, we get

$$\hat{Y} = 104.1 + 2.3(13) + 15.7(0) + 38.7(0) + 30.1(0) = 134$$

For quarter 2 of the next year, we get

$$\hat{Y} = 104.1 + 2.3(14) + 15.7(1) + 38.7(0) + 30.1(0) = 152$$

Notice these are not the same values we obtained using the multiplicative decomposition method. We could compare the MAD or MSE for each method and choose the one that is better.

PROGRAM 5.7A

Excel QM Multiple Regression Initialization Screen for Turner Industries

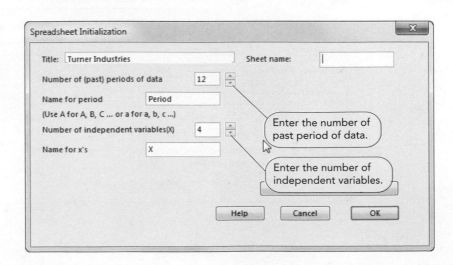

IN ACTION   Forecasting at Disney World

When the Disney chairman receives a daily report from his main theme parks in Orlando, Florida, the report contains only two numbers: the *forecast* of yesterday's attendance at the parks (Magic Kingdom, Epcot, Fort Wilderness, Hollywood Studios (formerly MGM Studios), Animal Kingdom, Typhoon Lagoon, and Blizzard Beach) and the actual attendance. An error close to zero (using MAPE as the measure) is expected. The chairman takes his forecasts very seriously.

The forecasting team at Disney World doesn't just do a daily prediction, however, and the chairman is not its only customer. It also provides daily, weekly, monthly, annual, and 5-year forecasts to the labor management, maintenance, operations, finance, and park scheduling departments. It uses judgmental models, econometric models, moving average models, and regression analysis. The team's annual forecast of total volume, conducted in 1999 for the year 2000, resulted in a MAPE of 0.

With 20% of Disney World's customers coming from outside the United States, its econometric model includes such variables as consumer confidence and the gross domestic product of seven countries. Disney also surveys one million people each year to examine their future travel plans and their experiences at the parks. This helps forecast not only attendance, but behavior at each ride (how long people will wait and how many times they will ride). Inputs to the monthly forecasting model include airline specials, speeches by the chair of the Federal reserve, and Wall Street trends. Disney even monitors 3,000 school districts inside and outside the United States for holiday/vacation schedules.

Source: Based on J. Newkirk and M. Haskell. "Forecasting in the Service Sector," presentation at the 12th Annual Meeting of the Production and Operations Management Society. April 1, 2001, Orlando, FL.

PROGRAM 5.7B

Excel QM Multiple Regression Output Screen for Turner Industries

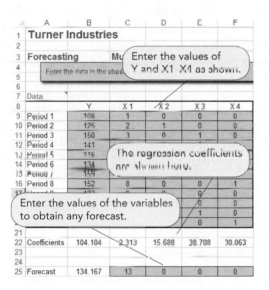

5.9   Monitoring and Controlling Forecasts

A tracking signal measures how well predictions fit actual data.

After a forecast has been completed, it is important that it not be forgotten. No manager wants to be reminded when his or her forecast is horribly inaccurate, but a firm needs to determine why the actual demand (or whatever variable is being examined) differed significantly from that projected.[*]

One way to monitor forecasts to ensure that they are performing well is to employ a **tracking signal**. A tracking signal is a measurement of how well the forecast is predicting actual values. As forecasts are updated every week, month, or quarter, the newly available demand data are compared to the forecast values.

---

[*]If the forecaster is accurate, he or she usually makes sure that everyone is aware of his or her talents. Very seldom does one read articles in *Fortune*, *Forbes*, or the *Wall Street Journal*, however, about money managers who are consistently off by 25% in their stock market forecasts.

The tracking signal is computed as the **running sum of the forecast errors (RSFE)** divided by the mean absolute deviation:

$$\text{Tracking signal} = \frac{\text{RSFE}}{\text{MAD}} \qquad (5\text{-}13)$$

$$= \frac{\sum(\text{forecast error})}{\text{MAD}}$$

where

$$\text{MAD} = \frac{\sum |\text{forecast error}|}{n}$$

as seen earlier in Equation 5-1.

Positive tracking signals indicate that demand is greater than the forecast. Negative signals mean that demand is less than forecast. A good tracking signal—that is, one with a low RSFE—has about as much positive error as it has negative error. In other words, small deviations are okay, but the positive and negative deviations should balance so that the tracking signal centers closely around zero.

Setting tracking limits is a matter of setting reasonable values for upper and lower limits.

When tracking signals are calculated, they are compared with predetermined control limits. When a tracking signal exceeds an upper or lower limit, a signal is tripped. This means that there is a problem with the forecasting method, and management may want to reevaluate the way it forecasts demand. Figure 5.7 shows the graph of a tracking signal that is exceeding the range of acceptable variation. If the model being used is exponential smoothing, perhaps the smoothing constant needs to be readjusted.

How do firms decide what the upper and lower tracking limits should be? There is no single answer, but they try to find reasonable values—in other words, limits not so low as to be triggered with every small forecast error and not so high as to allow bad forecasts to be regularly overlooked. George Plossl and Oliver Wight, two inventory control experts, suggested using maximums of ± 4 MADs for high-volume stock items and ± 8 MADs for lower-volume items.[*]

Other forecasters suggest slightly lower ranges. One MAD is equivalent to approximately 0.8 standard deviation, so that ± 2 MADs = 1.6 standard deviations, ± 3 MADs = 2.4 standard deviations, and ± 4 MADs = 3.2 standard deviations. This suggests that for a forecast to be "in control," 89% of the errors are expected to fall within ± 2 MADs, 98% within ± 3 MADs, or 99.9% within ± 4 MADs whenever the errors are approximately normally distributed.[**]

FIGURE 5.7
Plot of Tracking Signals

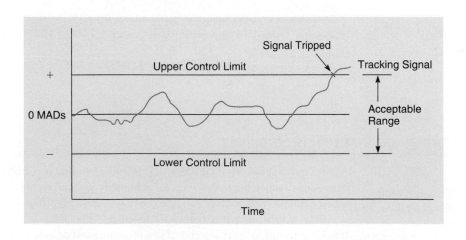

*See G. W. Plossl and O. W. Wight. *Production and Inventory Control.* Upper Saddle River, NJ: Prentice Hall, 1967.
**To prove these three percentages to yourself, just set up a normal curve for ± 1.6 standard deviations (Z values). Using the normal table in Appendix A, you find that the area under the curve is 0.89. This represents ± 2 MADs. Similarly, ± 3 MADs = 2.4 standard deviations encompasses 98% of the area, and so on for ± 4 MADs.

Here is an example that shows how the tracking signal and RSFE can be computed. Kimball's Bakery's quarterly sales of croissants (in thousands), as well as forecast demand and error computations, are in the following table. The objective is to compute the tracking signal and determine whether forecasts are performing adequately.

TIME PERIOD	FORECAST DEMAND	ACTUAL DEMAND	ERROR	RSFE	FORECAST ERROR	CUMULATIVE ERROR	MAD	TRACKING SIGNAL
1	100	90	−10	−10	10	10	10.0	−1
2	100	95	−5	−15	5	15	7.5	−2
3	100	115	+15	0	15	30	10.0	0
4	110	100	−10	−10	10	40	10.0	−1
5	110	125	+15	+5	15	55	11.0	+0.5
6	110	140	+30	+35	30	85	14.2	+2.5

In period 6, the calculations are

$$MAD = \frac{\Sigma \, |\text{forecast error}|}{n} = \frac{85}{6}$$

$$= 14.2$$

$$\text{Tracking signal} = \frac{\text{RSFE}}{\text{MAD}} = \frac{35}{14.2}$$

$$= 2.5 \text{ MADs}$$

This tracking signal is within acceptable limits. We see that it drifted from −2.0 MADs to +2.5 MADs.

Adaptive Smoothing

A lot of research has been published on the subject of adaptive forecasting. This refers to computer monitoring of tracking signals and self-adjustment if a signal passes its preset limit. In exponential smoothing, the α and β coefficients are first selected based on values that minimize error forecasts and are then adjusted accordingly whenever the computer notes an errant tracking signal. This is called **adaptive smoothing**.

Summary

Forecasts are a critical part of a manager's function. Demand forecasts drive the production, capacity, and scheduling systems in a firm and affect the financial, marketing, and personnel planning functions.

In this chapter we introduced three types of forecasting models: time series, causal, and qualitative. Moving averages, exponential smoothing, trend projection, and decomposition time-series models were developed. Regression and multiple regression models were recognized as causal models. Four qualitative models were briefly discussed. In addition, we explained the use of scatter diagrams and measures of forecasting accuracy. In future chapters you will see the usefulness of these techniques in determining values for the various decision-making models.

As we learned in this chapter, no forecasting method is perfect under all conditions. Even when management has found a satisfactory approach, it must still monitor and control its forecasts to make sure that errors do not get out of hand. Forecasting can often be a very challenging but rewarding part of managing.

Glossary

Adaptive Smoothing   The process of automatically monitoring and adjusting the smoothing constants in an exponential smoothing model.

Bias   A technique for determining the accuracy of a forecasting model by measuring the average error and its direction.

Causal Models   Models that forecast using variables and factors in addition to time.

Centered Moving Average   An average of the values centered at a particular point in time. This is used to compute seasonal indices when trend is present.

Cyclical Component   A component of a time series is a pattern in annual data that tends to repeat every several years.

Decision-Making Group   A group of experts in a Delphi technique that has the responsibility of making the forecast.

Decomposition   A forecasting model that decomposes a time series into its seasonal and trend components.

Delphi   A judgmental forecasting technique that uses decision makers, staff personnel, and respondents to determine a forecast.

Deseasonalized Data   Time-series data in which each value has been divided by its seasonal index to remove the effect of the seasonal component.

Deviation   A term used in forecasting for error.

Error   The difference between the actual value and the forecast value.

Exponential Smoothing   A forecasting method that is a combination of the last forecast and the last observed value.

Least Squares   A procedure used in trend projection and regression analysis to minimize the squared distances between the estimated straight line and the observed values.

Mean Absolute Deviation (MAD)   A technique for determining the accuracy of a forecasting model by taking the average of the absolute deviations.

Mean Absolute Percent Error (MAPE)   A technique for determining the accuracy of a forecasting model by taking the average of the absolute errors as a percentage of the observed values.

Mean Squared Error (MSE)   A technique for determining the accuracy of a forecasting model by taking the average of the squared error terms for a forecasting model.

Moving Average   A forecasting technique that averages past values in computing the forecast.

Naïve Model   A time-series forecasting model in which the forecast for next period is the actual value for the current period.

Qualitative Models   Models that forecast using judgments, experience, and qualitative and subjective data.

Random Component   The irregular, unpredictable variations in a time series.

Running Sum of Forecast Errors (RSFE)   Used to develop a tracking signal for time-series forecasting models, this is a running total of the errors and may be positive or negative.

Seasonal Component   A pattern of fluctuations in a time series above or below an average value that repeats at regular intervals.

Seasonal Index   An index number that indicates how a particular season compares with an average time period (with an index of 1 indicating an average season).

Smoothing Constant   A value between 0 and 1 that is used in an exponential smoothing forecast.

Time-series Model   A forecasting technique that predicts the future values of a variable by using only historical data on that one variable.

Tracking Signal   A measure of how well the forecast is predicting actual values.

Trend Component   The general upward or downward movement of the data in a time series over relatively long period of time.

Trend Projection   The use of a trend line to forecast a time-series with trend present. A linear trend line is a regression line with time as the independent variable.

Weighted Moving Average   A moving average forecasting method that places different weights on past values.

Key Equations

(5-1) $\text{MAD} = \dfrac{\Sigma |\text{forecast error}|}{n}$

A measure of overall forecast error called mean absolute deviation.

(5-2) $\text{MSE} = \dfrac{\Sigma (\text{error})^2}{n}$

A measure of forecast accuracy called mean squared error.

(5-3) $\text{MAPE} = \dfrac{\Sigma \left|\dfrac{\text{error}}{\text{actual}}\right|}{n} 100\%$

A measure of forecast accuracy called mean absolute percent error.

(5-4) $\text{Moving average forecast} = \dfrac{\text{Sum of demands in previous } n \text{ periods}}{n}$

An equation for computing a moving average forecast.

(5-5) $F_{t+1} = \dfrac{Y_t + Y_{t-1} + \cdots + Y_{t-n+1}}{n}$

A mathematical expression for a moving average forecast.

(5-6) $F_{t+1} = \dfrac{\Sigma(\text{Weight in period } i)(\text{Actual value in period } i)}{\Sigma(\text{Weights})}$

An equation for computing a weighted moving average forecast.

(5-7) $F_{t+1} = \dfrac{w_1 Y_t + w_2 Y_{t-1} + \cdots + w_n Y_{t-n+1}}{w_1 + w_2 + \cdots + w_n}$

A mathematical expression for a weighted moving average forecast.

(5-8) New forecast = Last period's forecast + α(Last period's actual demand − Last period's forecast)

An equation for computing an exponential smoothing forecast.

(5-9) $F_{t+1} = F_t + \alpha(Y_t - F_t)$

Equation 5-8 rewritten mathematically.

(5-10) $F_{t+1} = FIT_t + \alpha(Y_t - FIT_t)$

Equation to update the smoothed forecast (F_{t+1}) used in the trend-adjusted exponential smoothing model.

(5-11) $T_{t+1} = T_t + \beta(F_{t+1} - FIT_t)$

Equation to update the smoothed trend value (T_{t+1}) used in the trend-adjusted exponential smoothing model.

(5-12) $FIT_{t+1} = F_{t+1} + T_{t+1}$

Equation to develop forecast including trend (*FIT*) in the trend-adjusted exponential smoothing model.

(5-13) Tracking signal $= \dfrac{RSFE}{MAD}$

$= \dfrac{\Sigma(\text{forecast error})}{MAD}$

An equation for monitoring forecasts with a tracking signal.

Solved Problems

Solved Problem 5-1

Demand for patient surgery at Washington General Hospital has increased steadily in the past few years, as seen in the following table:

YEAR	OUTPATIENT SURGERIES PERFORMED
1	45
2	50
3	52
4	56
5	58
6	—

The director of medical services predicted six years ago that demand in year 1 would be 42 surgeries. Using exponential smoothing with a weight of $\alpha = 0.20$, develop forecasts for years 2 through 6. What is the MAD?

Solution

YEAR	ACTUAL	FORECAST (SMOOTHED)	ERROR	|ERROR|
1	45	42	+3	3
2	50	42.6 = 42 + 0.2(45 − 42)	+7.4	7.4
3	52	44.1 = 42.6 + 0.2(50 − 42.6)	+7.9	7.9
4	56	45.7 = 44.1 + 0.2(52 − 44.1)	+10.3	10.3
5	58	47.7 = 45.7 + 0.2(56 − 45.7)	+10.3	10.3
6	—	49.8 = 47.7 + 0.2(58 − 47.7)	—	—
				38.9

$$\text{MAD} = \frac{\Sigma|\text{errors}|}{n} = \frac{38.9}{5} = 7.78$$

Solved Problem 5-2

Quarterly demand for Jaguar XJ8 at a New York auto dealership is forecast with the equation

$$\hat{Y} = 10 + 3X$$

where

X = time period (quarter): quarter 1 of last year = 0

quarter 2 of last year = 1

quarter 3 of last year = 2

quarter 4 of last year = 3

quarter 1 of this year = 4, and so on

and

$$\hat{Y} = \text{predicted quarterly demand}$$

The demand for luxury sedans is seasonal, and the indices for quarters 1, 2, 3, and 4 are 0.80, 1.00, 1.30, and 0.90, respectively. Using the trend equation, forecast the demand for each quarter of next year. Then adjust each forecast to adjust for seasonal (quarterly) variations.

Solution

Quarter 2 of this year is coded $X = 5$; quarter 3 of this year, $X = 6$; and quarter 4 of this year, $X = 7$. Hence, quarter 1 of next year is coded $X = 8$; quarter 2, $X = 9$; and so on.

$\hat{Y}$ (next year quarter 1) = $10 + (3)(8) = 34$ Adjusted forecast = $(0.80)(34) = 27.2$

$\hat{Y}$ (next year quarter 2) = $10 + (3)(9) = 37$ Adjusted forecast = $(1.00)(37) = 37$

$\hat{Y}$ (next year quarter 3) = $10 + (3)(10) = 40$ Adjusted forecast = $(1.30)(40) = 52$

$\hat{Y}$ (next year quarter 4) = $10 + (3)(11) = 43$ Adjusted forecast = $(0.90)(43) = 38.7$

Self-Test

- Before taking the self-test, refer to the learning objectives at the beginning of the chapter, the notes in the margins, and the glossary at the end of the chapter.
- Use the key at the back of the book to correct your answers.
- Restudy pages that correspond to any questions that you answered incorrectly or material you feel uncertain about.

1. Qualitative forecasting models include
   a. regression analysis.
   b. Delphi.
   c. time-series models.
   d. trend lines.
2. A forecasting model that only uses historical data for the variable being forecast is called a
   a. time-series model.
   b. causal model.
   c. Delphi model.
   d. variable model.
3. One example of a causal model is
   a. exponential smoothing.
   b. trend projections.
   c. moving averages.
   d. regression analysis.
4. Which of the following is a time-series model?
   a. the Delphi model
   b. regression analysis

   c. exponential smoothing
   d. multiple regression
5. Which of the following is not a component of a time series?
   a. seasonality
   b. causal variations
   c. trend
   d. random variations
6. Which of the following may be negative?
   a. MAD
   b. bias
   c. MAPE
   d. MSE
7. When comparing several forecasting models to determine which one best fits a particular set of data, the model that should be selected is the one
   a. with the highest MSE.
   b. with the MAD closest to 1.
   c. with a bias of 0.
   d. with the lowest MAD.

8. In exponential smoothing, if you wish to give a significant weight to the most recent observations, then the smoothing constant should be
   a. close to 0.
   b. close to 1.
   c. close to 0.5.
   d. less than the error.

9. A trend equation is a regression equation in which
   a. there are multiple independent variables.
   b. the intercept and the slope are the same.
   c. the dependent variable is time.
   d. the independent variable is time.

10. Sales for a company are typically higher in the summer months than in the winter months. This variation would be called a
    a. trend.
    b. seasonal factor.
    c. random factor.
    d. cyclical factor.

11. An exponential smoothing forecast with a smoothing constant of 1 would result in the same forecast as
    a. a trend line forecast.
    b. an exponential smoothing forecast with a smoothing constant of 0.
    c. a naïve forecast.
    d. a 2-period moving average forecast.

12. If the seasonal index for January is 0.80, then
    a. January sales tend to be 80% higher than an average month.
    b. January sales tend to be 20% higher than an average month.
    c. January sales tend to be 80% lower than an average month.
    d. January sales tend to be 20% lower than an average month.

13. If both trend and seasonal components are present in a time-series, then the seasonal indices
    a. should be computed based on an overall average.
    b. should be computed based on CMAs.
    c. will all be greater than 1.
    d. should be ignored in developing the forecast.

14. Which of the following is used to alert the user of a forecasting model that a significant error occurred in one of the periods?
    a. a seasonal index
    b. a smoothing constant
    c. a tracking signal
    d. a regression coefficient

15. If the multiplicative decomposition model is used to forecast daily sales for a retail store, how many seasons will there be?
    a. 4
    b. 7
    c. 12
    d. 365

Discussion Questions and Problems

Discussion Questions

5-1 Describe briefly the steps used to develop a forecasting system.

5-2 What is a time-series forecasting model?

5-3 What is the difference between a causal model and a time-series model?

5-4 What is a qualitative forecasting model, and when is it appropriate?

5-5 What are some of the problems and drawbacks of the moving average forecasting model?

5-6 What effect does the value of the smoothing constant have on the weight given to the past forecast and the past observed value?

5-7 Describe briefly the Delphi technique.

5-8 What is MAD, and why is it important in the selection and use of forecasting models?

5-9 Explain how the number of seasons is determined when forecasting with a seasonal component.

5-10 A seasonal index may be less than one, equal to one, or greater than one. Explain what each of these values would mean.

5-11 How is the impact of seasonality removed from a time series?

5-12 In using the decomposition method, the forecast based on trend is found using the trend line. How is the seasonal index used to adjust this forecast based on trend?

5-13 Explain what would happen if the smoothing constant in an exponential smoothing model was equal to zero. Explain what would happen if the smoothing constant was equal to one.

5-14 Explain when a CMA (rather than an overall average) should be used in computing a seasonal index. Explain why this is necessary.

Problems

5-15 Develop a four-month moving average forecast for Wallace Garden Supply and compute the MAD. A three-month moving average forecast was developed in the section on moving averages in Table 5.2.

5-16 Using MAD, determine whether the forecast in Problem 5-15 or the forecast in the section concerning Wallace Garden Supply is more accurate.

Note: Ω means the problem may be solved with QM for Windows; ✗ means the problem may be solved with Excel QM; and ⚥ means the problem may be solved with QM for Windows and/or Excel QM.

5-17 Data collected on the yearly demand for 50-pound bags of fertilizer at Wallace Garden Supply are shown in the following table. Develop a 3-year moving average to forecast sales. Then estimate demand again with a weighted moving average in which sales in the most recent year are given a weight of 2 and sales in the other 2 years are each given a weight of 1. Which method do you think is best?

YEAR	DEMAND FOR FERTILIZER (1,000s OF BAGS)
1	4
2	6
3	4
4	5
5	10
6	8
7	7
8	9
9	12
10	14
11	15

5-18 Develop a trend line for the demand for fertilizer in Problem 5-17, using any computer software.

5-19 In Problems 5-17 and 5-18, three different forecasts were developed for the demand for fertilizer. These three forecasts are a 3-year moving average, a weighted moving average, and a trend line. Which one would you use? Explain your answer.

5-20 Use exponential smoothing with a smoothing constant of 0.3 to forecast the demand for fertilizer given in Problem 5-17. Assume that last period's forecast for year 1 is 5,000 bags to begin the procedure. Would you prefer to use, the exponential smoothing model or the weighted average model developed in Problem 5-17? Explain your answer.

5-21 Sales of Cool-Man air conditioners have grown steadily during the past 5 years:

YEAR	SALES
1	450
2	495
3	518
4	563
5	584
6	?

The sales manager had predicted, before the business started, that year 1's sales would be 410 air conditioners. Using exponential smoothing with a weight of $\alpha = 0.30$, develop forecasts for years 2 through 6.

5-22 Using smoothing constants of 0.6 and 0.9, develop forecasts for the sales of Cool-Man air conditioners (see Problem 5-21).

5-23 What effect did the smoothing constant have on the forecast for Cool-Man air conditioners? (See Problems 5-21 and 5-22.) Which smoothing constant gives the most accurate forecast?

5-24 Use a three-year moving average forecasting model to forecast the sales of Cool-Man air conditioners (see Problem 5-21).

5-25 Using the trend projection method, develop a forecasting model for the sales of Cool-Man air conditioners (see Problem 5-21).

5-26 Would you use exponential smoothing with a smoothing constant of 0.3, a 3-year moving average, or a trend to predict the sales of Cool-Man air conditioners? Refer to Problems 5-21, 5-24, and 5-25.

5-27 Sales of industrial vacuum cleaners at R. Lowenthal Supply Co. over the past 13 months are as follows:

SALES ($1,000s)	MONTH	SALES ($1,000s)	MONTH
11	January	14	August
14	February	17	September
16	March	12	October
10	April	14	November
15	May	16	December
17	June	11	January
11	July		

(a) Using a moving average with three periods, determine the demand for vacuum cleaners for next February.

(b) Using a weighted moving average with three periods, determine the demand for vacuum cleaners for February. Use 3, 2, and 1 for the weights of the most recent, second most recent, and third most recent periods, respectively. For example, if you were forecasting the demand for February, November would have a weight of 1, December would have a weight of 2, and January would have a weight of 3.

(c) Evaluate the accuracy of each of these methods.

(d) What other factors might R. Lowenthal consider in forecasting sales?

5-28 Passenger miles flown on Northeast Airlines, a commuter firm serving the Boston hub, are as follows for the past 12 weeks:

WEEK	ACTUAL PASSENGER MILES (1,000s)	WEEK	ACTUAL PASSENGER MILES (1,000s)
1	17	7	20
2	21	8	18
3	19	9	22
4	23	10	20
5	18	11	15
6	16	12	22

(a) Assuming an initial forecast for week 1 of 17,000 miles, use exponential smoothing to compute miles for weeks 2 through 12. Use $\alpha = 0.2$.

(b) What is the MAD for this model?

(c) Compute the RSFE and tracking signals. Are they within acceptable limits?

5-29 Emergency calls to Winter Park, Florida's 911 system, for the past 24 weeks are as follows:

WEEK	CALLS	WEEK	CALLS	WEEK	CALLS
1	50	9	35	17	55
2	35	10	20	18	40
3	25	11	15	19	35
4	40	12	40	20	60
5	45	13	55	21	75
6	35	14	35	22	50
7	20	15	25	23	40
8	30	16	55	24	65

(a) Compute the exponentially smoothed forecast of calls for each week. Assume an initial forecast of 50 calls in the first week and use $\alpha = 0.1$. What is the forecast for the 25th week?

(b) Reforecast each period using $\alpha = 0.6$.

(c) Actual calls during the 25th week were 85. Which smoothing constant provides a superior forecast?

5-30 How would the forecast for week 25 of the previous problem change if the initial forecast was 40 instead of 50? How would the forecast for week 25 change if the forecast for week 1 were assumed to be 60?

5-31 Consulting income at Kate Walsh Associates for the period February–July has been as follows:

MONTH	INCOME ($1,000s)
February	70.0
March	68.5
April	64.8
May	71.7
June	71.3
July	72.8

Use exponential smoothing to forecast August's income. Assume that the initial forecast for February is $65,000. The smoothing constant selected is $\alpha = 0.1$.

5-32 Resolve Problem 5-31 with $\alpha = 0.3$. Using MAD, which smoothing constant provides a better forecast?

5-33 A major source of revenue in Texas is a state sales tax on certain types of goods and services. Data are compiled and the state comptroller uses them to project future revenues for the state budget. One particular category of goods is classified as Retail Trade. Four years of quarterly data (in $millions) for one particular area of southeast Texas follow:

QUARTER	YEAR 1	YEAR 2	YEAR 3	YEAR 4
1	218	225	234	250
2	247	254	265	283
3	243	255	264	289
4	292	299	327	356

(a) Compute seasonal indices for each quarter based on a CMA.

(b) Deseasonalize the data and develop a trend line on the deseasonalized data.

(c) Use the trend line to forecast the sales for each quarter of year 5.

(d) Use the seasonal indices to adjust the forecasts found in part (c) to obtain the final forecasts.

5-34 Using the data in Problem 5-33, develop a multiple regression model to predict sales (both trend and seasonal components), using dummy variables to incorporate the seasonal factor into the model. Use this model to predict sales for each quarter of the next year. Comment on the accuracy of this model.

5-35 Trevor Harty, an avid mountain biker, always wanted to start a business selling top-of-the-line mountain bikes and other outdoor supplies. A little over 6 years ago, he and a silent partner opened a store called Hale and Harty Trail Bikes and Supplies. Growth was rapid in the first 2 years, but since that time, growth in sales has slowed a bit, as expected. The quarterly sales (in $1,000s) for the past 4 years are shown in the table below:

	YEAR 1	YEAR 2	YEAR 3	YEAR 4
QUARTER 1	274	282	282	296
QUARTER 2	172	178	182	210
QUARTER 3	130	136	134	158
QUARTER 4	162	168	170	182

(a) Develop a trend line using the data in the table. Use this to forecast sales for each quarter of year 5. What does the slope of this line indicate?

(b) Use the multiplicative decomposition model to incorporate both trend and seasonal components into the forecast. What does the slope of this line indicate?

(c) Compare the slope of the trend line in part (a) to the slope in the trend line for the decomposition model that was based on the deseasonalized sales figures. Discuss why these are so different and explain which one is best to use.

5-36 The unemployment rates in the United States during a 10-year period are given in the following table. Use exponential smoothing to find the best forecast for next year. Use smoothing constants of 0.2, 0.4, 0.6, and 0.8. Which one had the lowest MAD?

YEAR	1	2	3	4	5	6	7	8	9	10
Unemployment rate (%)	7.2	7.0	6.2	5.5	5.3	5.5	6.7	7.4	6.8	6.1

• **5-37** Management of Davis's Department Store has used time-series extrapolation to forecast retail sales for the next four quarters. The sales estimates are $100,000, $120,000, $140,000, and $160,000 for the respective quarters before adjusting for seasonality. Seasonal indices for the four quarters have been found to be 1.30, 0.90, 0.70, and 1.10, respectively. Compute a seasonalized or adjusted sales forecast.

⁙ 5-38   In the past, Judy Holmes's tire dealership sold an average of 1,000 radials each year. In the past two years, 200 and 250, respectively, were sold in fall, 350 and 300 in winter, 150 and 165 in spring, and 300 and 285 in summer. With a major expansion planned, Judy projects sales next year to increase to 1,200 radials. What will the demand be each season?

5-39   The following table provides the Dow Jones Industrial Average (DJIA) opening index value on the first working day of 1994–2013:

Develop a trend line and use it to predict the opening DJIA index value for years 2014, 2015, and 2016. Find the MSE for this model.

YEAR	DJIA	YEAR	DJIA
2013	13,104	2003	8,342
2012	12,392	2002	10,022
2011	11,577	2001	10,791
2010	10,431	2000	11,502
2009	8,772	1999	9,213
2008	13,262	1998	7,908
2007	12,460	1997	6,448
2006	10,718	1996	5,117
2005	10,784	1995	3,834
2004	10,453	1994	3,754

5-40   Using the DJIA data in Problem 5-39, use exponential smooth with trend adjustment to forecast the opening DJIA value for 2014. Use $\alpha = 0.8$ and $\beta = 0.2$. Compare the MSE for this technique with the MSE for the trend line.

5-41   Refer to the DJIA data in Problem 5-39.

(a) Use an exponential smoothing model with a smoothing constant of 0.4 to predict the opening DJIA index value for 2014. Find the MSE for this.

(b) Use QM for Windows or Excel and find the smoothing constant that would provide the lowest MSE.

5-42   The following table gives the average monthly exchange rate between the U.S. dollar and the euro for 2009. It shows that 1 euro was equivalent to 1.289 U.S. dollars in January 2009. Develop a trend line that could be used to predict the exchange rate for 2010. Use this model to predict the exchange rate for January 2010 and February 2010.

MONTH	EXCHANGE RATE
January	1.289
February	1.324
March	1.321
April	1.317
May	1.280
June	1.254
July	1.230
August	1.240
September	1.287
October	1.298
November	1.283
December	1.311

5-43   For the data in Problem 5-42, develop an exponential smoothing model with a smoothing constant of 0.3. Using the MSE, compare this with the model in Problem 5-42.

 Internet Homework Problems

See our Internet home page, at **www.pearsonhighered.com/render**, for additional homework problems, Problems 5-44 to 5-52.

Case Study

Forecasting Attendance at SWU Football Games

Southwestern University (SWU), a large state college in Stephenville, Texas, 30 miles southwest of the Dallas/Fort Worth metroplex, enrolls close to 20,000 students. In a typical town–gown relationship, the school is a dominant force in the small city, with more students during fall and spring than permanent residents.

A longtime football powerhouse, SWU is a member of the Big Eleven conference and is usually in the top 20 in college football rankings. To bolster its chances of reaching the elusive and long-desired number-one ranking, in 2008 SWU hired the legendary Billy Bob Taylor as its head coach. Although

the number-one ranking remained out of reach, attendance at the five Saturday home games each year increased. Prior to Taylor's arrival, attendance generally averaged 25,000 to 29,000 per game. Season ticket sales bumped up by 10,000 just with the announcement of the new coach's arrival. Stephenville and SWU were ready to move to the big time!

The immediate issue facing SWU, however, was not NCAA ranking. It was capacity. The existing SWU stadium, built in 1953, has seating for 54,000 fans. The following table indicates attendance at each game for the past six years.

One of Taylor's demands upon joining SWU had been a stadium expansion, or possibly even a new stadium. With attendance increasing, SWU administrators began to face the issue head-on. Taylor had wanted dormitories solely for his athletes in the stadium as an additional feature of any expansion.

SWU's president, Dr. Marty Starr, decided it was time for his vice president of development to forecast when the existing stadium would "max out." He also sought a revenue projection, assuming an average ticket price of $20 in 2014 and a 5% increase each year in future prices.

Discussion Questions

1. Develop a forecasting model, justify its selection over other techniques, and project attendance through 2015.
2. What revenues are to be expected in 2014 and 2015?
3. Discuss the school's options.

Southwestern University Football Game Attendance, 2008–2013

| GAME | 2008 | | 2009 | | 2010 | |
	ATTENDEES	OPPONENT	ATTENDEES	OPPONENT	ATTENDEES	OPPONENT
1	34,200	Baylor	36,100	Oklahoma	35,900	TCU
2*	39,800	Texas	40,200	Nebraska	46,500	Texas Tech
3	38,200	LSU	39,100	UCLA	43,100	Alaska
4**	26,900	Arkansas	25,300	Nevada	27,900	Arizona
5	35,100	USC	36,200	Ohio State	39,200	Rice

| GAME | 2011 | | 2012 | | 2013 | |
	ATTENDEES	OPPONENT	ATTENDEES	OPPONENT	ATTENDEES	OPPONENT
1	41,900	Arkansas	42,500	Indiana	46,900	LSU
2*	46,100	Missouri	48,200	North Texas	50,100	Texas
3	43,900	Florida	44,200	Texas A&M	45,900	Prairie View A&M
4**	30,100	Miami	33,900	Southern	36,300	Montana
5	40,500	Duke	47,800	Oklahoma	49,900	Arizona State

*Homecoming games

**During the fourth week of each season, Stephenville hosted a hugely popular southwestern crafts festival. This event brought tens of thousands of tourists to the town, especially on weekends, and had an obvious negative impact on game attendance.

Source: J. Heizer and B. Render. *Operations Management*, 11th ed. Upper Saddle River, NJ: Pearson, 2014, p. 148.

Case Study

Forecasting Monthly Sales

For years The Glass Slipper restaurant has operated in a resort community near a popular ski area of New Mexico. The restaurant is busiest during the first 3 months of the year, when the ski slopes are crowded and tourists flock to the area.

When James and Deena Weltee built The Glass Slipper, they had a vision of the ultimate dining experience. As the view of surrounding mountains was breathtaking, a high priority was placed on having large windows and providing a spectacular view from anywhere inside the restaurant. Special attention was also given to the lighting, colors, and overall ambiance, resulting in a truly magnificent experience for all who came to enjoy gourmet dining. Since its opening, The Glass Slipper has developed and maintained a reputation as one of the "must visit" places in that region of New Mexico.

While James loves to ski and truly appreciates the mountains and all that they have to offer, he also shares Deena's dream of retiring to a tropical paradise and enjoying a more relaxed lifestyle on the beach. After some careful analysis of their financial condition, they knew that retirement was many years away. Nevertheless, they were hatching a plan to bring them closer to their dream. They decided to sell The Glass Slipper and open a bed and breakfast on a beautiful beach in

TABLE 5.13
Monthly Revenue (in $1,000s)

MONTH	2011	2012	2013
January	438	444	450
February	420	425	438
March	414	423	434
April	318	331	338
May	306	318	331
June	240	245	254
July	240	255	264
August	216	223	231
September	198	210	224
October	225	233	243
November	270	278	289
December	315	322	335

Mexico. While this would mean that work was still in their future, they could wake up in the morning to the sight of the palm trees blowing in the wind and the waves lapping at the shore. They also knew that hiring the right manager would allow James and Deena the time to begin a semi-retirement in a corner of paradise.

To make this happen, James and Deena would have to sell The Glass Slipper for the right price. The price of the business would be based on the value of the property and equipment, as well as projections of future income. A forecast of sales for the next year is needed to help in the determination of the value of the restaurant. Monthly sales for each of the past 3 years are provided in Table 5.13.

Discussion Questions

1. Prepare a graph of the data. On this same graph, plot a 12-month moving average forecast. Discuss any apparent trend and seasonal patterns.
2. Use regression to develop a trend line that could be used to forecast monthly sales for the next year. Is the slope of this line consistent with what you observed in question 1? If not, discuss a possible explanation.
3. Use the multiplicative decomposition model on these data. Use this model to forecast sales for each month of the next year. Discuss why the slope of the trend equation with this model is so different from that of the trend equation in question 2.

Internet Case Study

See our Internet home page, at **www.pearsonhighered.com/render**, for the additional case study on **Akron Zoological Park**. This case involves forecasting attendance at Akron's zoo.

Bibliography

Billah, Baki, Maxwell L. King, Ralph D. Snyder, and Anne B. Koehler. "Exponential Smoothing Model Selection for Forecasting," *International Journal of Forecasting* 22, 2, (April–June 2006): 239–247.

Black, Ken. *Business Statistics: For Contemporary Decision Making*, 7th ed. John Wiley & Sons, Inc., 2012.

Diebold, F. X. *Elements of Forecasting*, 4th ed. Cincinnati: Cengage College Publishing, 2007.

Gardner, Everette Jr. "Exponential Smoothing: The State of the Art—Part II," *International Journal of Forecasting* 22, 4 (October 2006): 637–666.

Granger, Clive W., and J. M. Hashem Pesaran. "Economic and Statistical Measures of Forecast Accuracy," *Journal of Forecasting* 19, 7 (December 2000): 537–560.

Hanke, J. E., and D. W. Wichern. *Business Forecasting*, 9th ed. Upper Saddle River, NJ: Prentice Hall, 2009.

Heizer, J., and B. Render. *Operations Management*, 9th ed. Upper Saddle River, NJ: Prentice Hall, 2008.

Hyndman, Rob J. "The Interaction Between Trend and Seasonality," *International Journal of Forecasting* 20, 4 (October–December 2004): 561–563.

Hyndman, Rob J., and Anne B. Koehler. "Another Look at Measures of Forecast Accuracy," *International Journal of Forecasting* 22, 4 (October 2006): 679–688.

Levine, David M., David F. Stephan, and Kathryn A. Szabat. *Statistics for Managers Using Microsoft Excel,* 7th ed. Upper Saddle River, NJ: Pearson, 2014.

Meade, Nigel. "Evidence for the Selection of Forecasting Methods," *Journal of Forecasting* 19, 6 (November 2000): 515–535.

Snyder, Ralph D., and Roland G. Shami. "Exponential Smoothing of Seasonal Data: A Comparison," *Journal of Forecasting* 20, 3 (April 2001): 197–202.

Yurkiewicz, J. "Forecasting Software Survey," *OR/MS Today* 39, 3 (June 2012): 52–61.

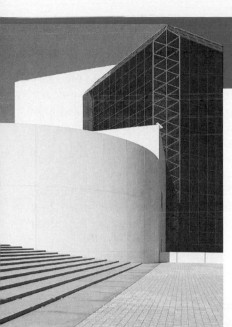

CHAPTER 6

Inventory Control Models

6.1 Introduction

Inventory is any stored resource that is used to satisfy a current or future need.

Inventory is one of the most expensive and important assets to many companies, representing as much as 50% of total invested capital. Managers have long recognized that good inventory control is crucial. On one hand, a firm can try to reduce costs by reducing on-hand inventory levels. On the other hand, customers become dissatisfied when frequent inventory outages, called **stockouts**, occur. Thus, companies must make the balance between low and high inventory levels. As you would expect, cost minimization is the major factor in obtaining this delicate balance.

Inventory is any stored resource that is used to satisfy a current or a future need. Raw materials, work-in-process, and finished goods are examples of inventory. Inventory levels for finished goods are a direct function of demand. When we determine the demand for completed clothes dryers, for example, it is possible to use this information to determine how much sheet metal, paint, electric motors, switches, and other raw materials and work-in-process are needed to produce the finished product.

All organizations have some type of inventory planning and control system. A bank has methods to control its inventory of cash. A hospital has methods to control blood supplies and other important items. State and federal governments, schools, and virtually every manufacturing and production organization are concerned with inventory planning and control. Studying how organizations control their inventory is equivalent to studying how they achieve their objectives by supplying goods and services to their customers. Inventory is the common thread that ties all the functions and departments of the organization together.

Figure 6.1 illustrates the basic components of an inventory planning and control system. The *planning* phase is concerned primarily with what inventory is to be stocked and how it is to be acquired (whether it is to be manufactured or purchased). This information is then used in *forecasting* demand for the inventory and in *controlling* inventory levels. The feedback loop in Figure 6.1 provides a way of revising the plan and forecast based on experiences and observation.

Through inventory planning, an organization determines what goods and/or services are to be produced. In cases of physical products, the organization must also determine whether to produce these goods or to purchase them from another manufacturer. When this has been determined, the next step is to forecast the demand. As discussed in Chapter 5, there are many mathematical techniques that can be used in forecasting demand for a particular product. The emphasis in this chapter is on inventory control, that is, how to maintain adequate inventory levels within an organization.

FIGURE 6.1

Inventory Planning and Control

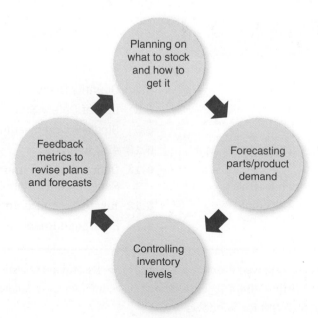

6.2   Importance of Inventory Control

Inventory control serves several important functions and adds a great deal of flexibility to the operation of the firm. Consider the following five uses of inventory:

1. The decoupling function
2. Storing resources
3. Irregular supply and demand
4. Quantity discounts
5. Avoiding stockouts and shortages

Decoupling Function

Inventory can act as a buffer.

One of the major functions of inventory is to decouple manufacturing processes within the organization. If you did not store inventory, there could be many delays and inefficiencies. For example, when one manufacturing activity has to be completed before a second activity can be started, it could stop the entire process. If, however, you have some stored inventory between processes, it could act as a buffer.

Storing Resources

Agricultural and seafood products often have definite seasons over which they can be harvested or caught, but the demand for these products is somewhat constant during the year. In these and similar cases, inventory can be used to store these resources.

Resources can be stored in work-in-process.

In a manufacturing process, raw materials can be stored by themselves, in work-in-process, or in the finished product. Thus, if your company makes lawn mowers, you might obtain lawn mower tires from another manufacturer. If you have 400 finished lawn mowers and 300 tires in inventory, you actually have 1,900 tires stored in inventory. Three hundred tires are stored by themselves, and 1,600 (1,600 = 4 tires per lawn mower × 400 lawn mowers) tires are stored in the finished lawn mowers. In the same sense, *labor* can be stored in inventory. If you have 500 subassemblies and it takes 50 hours of labor to produce each assembly, you actually have 25,000 labor hours stored in inventory in the subassemblies. In general, any resource, physical or otherwise, can be stored in inventory.

Irregular Supply and Demand

Inventory can alleviate irregular demand and supply patterns.

When the supply or demand for an inventory item is irregular, storing certain amounts in inventory can be important. If the greatest demand for Diet-Delight beverage is during the summer, you will have to make sure that there is enough supply to meet this irregular demand. This might require that you produce more of the soft drink in the winter than is actually needed to meet the winter demand. The inventory levels of Diet-Delight will gradually build up over the winter, but this inventory will be needed in the summer. The same is true for irregular *supplies.*

Quantity Discounts

Buying in bulk can be an economic advantage.

Another use of inventory is to take advantage of **quantity discounts**. Many suppliers offer discounts for large orders. For example, an electric jigsaw might normally cost $20 per unit. If you order 300 or more saws in one order, your supplier may lower the cost to $18.75. Purchasing in larger quantities can substantially reduce the cost of products. There are, however, some disadvantages of buying in larger quantities. You will have higher storage costs and higher costs due to spoilage, damaged stock, theft, insurance, and so on. Furthermore, by investing in more inventory, you will have less cash to invest elsewhere.

Avoiding Stockouts and Shortages

Carrying safety stock can increase customer satisfaction.

Another important function of inventory is to avoid shortages or stockouts. If you are repeatedly out of stock, customers are likely to go elsewhere to satisfy their needs. Lost goodwill can be an expensive price to pay for not having the right item at the right time.

6.3   Inventory Decisions

Even though there are literally millions of different types of products produced in our society, there are only two fundamental decisions that you have to make when controlling inventory:

1. How much to order
2. When to order

A major objective of all inventory models is to minimize inventory costs.

The purpose of all inventory models and techniques is to determine rationally how much to order and when to order. As you know, inventory fulfills many important functions within an organization. But as the inventory levels go up to provide these functions, the cost of storing and holding inventory also increases. Thus, you must reach a fine balance in establishing inventory levels. A major objective in controlling inventory is to minimize total inventory costs. Some of the most significant inventory costs follow:

1. Cost of the items (purchase cost or material cost)
2. Cost of ordering
3. Cost of carrying, or holding, inventory
4. Cost of stockouts

MODELING IN THE REAL WORLD   Managing Today's Energy Supply Chain

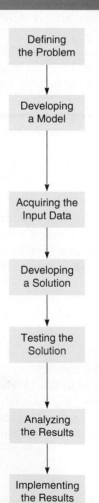

Defining the Problem

Managing today's energy supply chain is an ever increasing complex problem. Yet, to survive in today's marketplace, oil and gas companies must optimize their supply chains.

Developing a Model

Researchers from Portugal developed a uni-directional model of oil and gas products from refineries to distribution center. The model incorporated many different parameters including number of products, maximum storage capacities for each product, pipeline capacities, as well as the demand for each product among them.

Acquiring the Input Data

The input data consisted of the current inventory levels of specific oil and gas products at different points along the supply chain.

Developing a Solution

A large mixed integer-linear program (see Chapter 10 in this book) was developed as part of the solution procedure to optimize the supply chain.

Testing the Solution

All the problems that were solved by the Portuguese researchers were based on real data from Companhia Logistica Combustiveis, a large Portuguese oil and gas distribution company. Testing was done and the results were compared to real-world scenarios.

Analyzing the Results

Results obtained from the model were compared to the real-world operation. The results identified opportunities for marked improvements in flow rates and reductions in pumping costs.

Implementing the Results

As a result, oil and gas companies can better plan and manage their supply chains with less disruptions and lower overall costs.

Source: S. Relvas, S.N.B. Magatão, A.P.F.D. Barbosa-Póvoa, and F. Neves. "Integrated Scheduling and Inventory Management of an Oil Products Distribution System," *Omega* 41 (2013): 955–968.

TABLE 6.1 Inventory Cost Factors

ORDERING COST FACTORS	CARRYING COST FACTORS
Developing and sending purchase orders	Cost of capital
Processing and inspecting incoming inventory	Taxes
Bill paying	Insurance
Inventory inquiries	Spoilage
Utilities, phone bills, and so on for the purchasing department	Theft
Salaries and wages for purchasing department employees	Obsolescence
Supplies such as forms and paper for the purchasing department	Salaries and wages for warehouse employees
	Utilities and building costs for the warehouse
	Supplies such as forms and paper for the warehouse

The most common factors associated with ordering costs and holding costs are shown in Table 6.1. Notice that the ordering costs are generally independent of the size of the order, and many of these involve personnel time. An ordering cost is incurred each time an order is placed, whether the order is for 1 unit or 1,000 units. The time to process the paperwork, pay the bill, and so forth does not depend on the number of units ordered.

On the other hand, the holding cost varies as the size of the inventory varies. If 1,000 units are placed into inventory, the taxes, insurance, cost of capital, and other holding costs will be higher than if only 1 unit was put into inventory. Similarly, if the inventory level is low, there is little chance of spoilage and obsolescence.

The cost of the items, or the purchase cost, is what is paid to acquire the inventory. The stockout cost indicates the lost sales and goodwill (future sales) that result from not having the items available for the customers. This is discussed later in the chapter.

6.4 Economic Order Quantity: Determining How Much to Order

The **economic order quantity (EOQ)** is one of the oldest and most commonly known inventory control techniques. Research on its use dates back to a 1915 publication by Ford W. Harris. This technique is still used by a large number of organizations today. It is relatively easy to use, but it does make a number of assumptions. Some of the most important assumptions follow:

1. Demand is known and constant over time.
2. The lead time—that is, the time between the placement of the order and the receipt of the order—is known and constant.
3. The receipt of inventory is instantaneous. In other words, the inventory from an order arrives in one batch, at one point in time.
4. The purchase cost per unit is constant throughout the year. Quantity discounts are not possible.
5. The only variable costs are the cost of placing an order, *ordering cost*, and the cost of holding or storing inventory over time, *holding* or *carrying cost*. The holding cost per unit per year and the ordering cost per order are constant throughout the year.
6. Orders are placed so that stockouts or shortages are avoided completely.

When these assumptions are *not* met, adjustments must be made to the EOQ model. These are discussed later in this chapter.

The inventory usage curve has a sawtooth shape.

With these assumptions, inventory usage has a sawtooth shape, as in Figure 6.2. In Figure 6.2, Q represents the amount that is ordered. If this amount is 500 dresses, all 500 dresses arrive at one time when an order is received. Thus, the inventory level jumps from 0 to 500 dresses. In general, an inventory level increases from 0 to Q units when an order arrives.

Because demand is constant over time, inventory drops at a uniform rate over time. (Refer to the sloped lines in Figure 6.2.) Another order is placed such that when the inventory level reaches 0, the new order is received and the inventory level again jumps to Q units, represented by the vertical lines. This process continues indefinitely over time.

FIGURE 6.2
Inventory Usage over Time

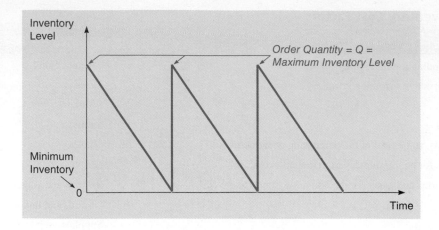

Inventory Costs in the EOQ Situation

The objective of the simple EOQ model is to minimize total inventory cost. The relevant costs are the ordering and holding costs.

The objective of most inventory models is to minimize the total costs. With the assumptions just given, the relevant costs are the ordering cost and the carrying, or holding cost. All other costs, such as the cost of the inventory itself (the purchase cost), are constant. Thus, if we minimize the sum of the ordering and carrying costs, we are also minimizing the total costs.

The **annual ordering cost** is simply the number of orders per year times the cost of placing each order. Since the inventory level changes daily, it is appropriate to use the average inventory level to determine annual holding or carrying cost. The **annual carrying cost** will equal the average inventory times the inventory carrying cost per unit per year. Again looking at Figure 6.2, we see that the maximum inventory is the order quantity (Q), and the **average inventory** will be one-half of that. Table 6.2 provides a numerical example to illustrate this. Notice that for this situation, if the order quantity is 10, the average inventory will be 5, or one-half of Q. Thus:

The average inventory level is one-half the maximum level.

$$\text{Average inventory level} = \frac{Q}{2} \tag{6-1}$$

Using the following variables, we can develop mathematical expressions for the annual ordering and carrying costs:

$$Q = \text{number of pieces of order}$$
$$\text{EOQ} = Q^* = \text{optimal number of pieces to order}$$
$$D = \text{annual demand in units for the inventory item}$$
$$C_o = \text{ordering cost of each order}$$
$$C_h = \text{holding or carrying cost per unit per year}$$

TABLE 6.2
Computing Average Inventory

DAY	INVENTORY LEVEL		
	BEGINNING	ENDING	AVERAGE
April 1 (order received)	10	8	9
April 2	8	6	7
April 3	6	4	5
April 4	4	2	3
April 5	2	0	1

Maximum level April 1 = 10 units
Total of daily averages = 9 + 7 + 5 + 3 + 1 = 25
Number of days = 5
Average inventory level = 25/5 = 5 units

IN ACTION Global Fashion Firm Fashions Inventory Management System

Founded in 1975, the Spanish retailer Zara currently has more than 1,600 stores worldwide, launches more than 10,000 new designs each year, and is recognized as one of the world's principal fashion retailers. Goods were shipped from two central warehouses to each of the stores, based on requests from individual store managers. These local decisions inevitably led to inefficient warehouse, shipping, and logistics operations when assessed on a global scale. Recent production overruns, inefficient supply chains, and an ever-changing marketplace (to say the least) caused Zara to tackle this problem.

A variety of operations research models were used in redesigning and implementing an entirely new inventory management system. The new centralized decision-making system replaced all store-level inventory decisions, thus providing results that were more globally optimal. Having the right products in the right places at the right time for customers has increased sales from 3% to 4% since implementation. This translated into an increase in revenue of over $230 million in 2007 and over $350 million in 2008. Talk about fashionistas!

Source: Based on F. Caro, J. Gallien, M. Díaz, J. García, J. M. Corredoira, M. Montes, J.A. Ramos, and J. Correa. "Zara Uses Operations Research to Re-engineer Its Global Distribution Process," *Interfaces* 40, 1 (January–February 2010): 71–84.

$$\text{Annual ordering cost} = (\text{Number of orders placed per year}) \times (\text{Ordering cost per order})$$

$$= \frac{\text{Annual demand}}{\text{Number of units in each order}} \times (\text{Ordering cost per order})$$

$$= \frac{D}{Q} C_o$$

$$\text{Annual holding or carrying cost} = (\text{Average inventory}) \times (\text{Carrying cost per unit per year})$$

$$= \frac{\text{Order quantity}}{2} \times (\text{Carrying cost per unit per year})$$

$$= \frac{Q}{2} C_h$$

A graph of the holding cost, the ordering cost, and the total of these two is shown in Figure 6.3. The lowest point on the total cost curves occurs where the ordering cost is equal to the carrying cost. Thus, to minimize total costs given this situation, the order quantity should occur where these two costs are equal.

FIGURE 6.3

Total Cost as a Function of Order Quantity

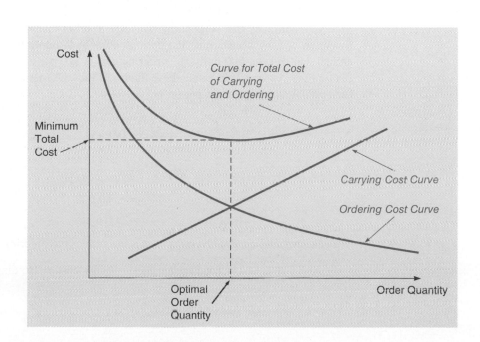

Finding the EOQ

When the EOQ assumptions are met, total cost is minimized when:

$$\text{Annual holding cost} = \text{Annual ordering cost}$$

$$\frac{Q}{2}C_h = \frac{D}{Q}C_o$$

Solving this for Q gives the optimal order quantity:

$$Q^2 C_h = 2DC_o$$

$$Q^2 = \frac{2DC_o}{C_h}$$

$$Q = \sqrt{\frac{2DC_o}{C_h}}$$

This optimal order quantity is often denoted by Q^*. Thus, the economic order quantity is given by the following formula:

$$\text{EOQ} = Q^* = \sqrt{\frac{2DC_o}{C_h}}$$

This EOQ formula is the basis for many more advanced models, and some of these are discussed later in this chapter.

Economic Order Quantity (EOQ) Model

$$\text{Annual ordering cost} = \frac{D}{Q}C_o \tag{6-2}$$

$$\text{Annual holding cost} = \frac{Q}{2}C_h \tag{6-3}$$

$$\text{EOQ} = Q^* = \sqrt{\frac{2DC_o}{C_h}} \tag{6-4}$$

Sumco Pump Company Example

Sumco, a company that sells pump housings to other manufacturers, would like to reduce its inventory cost by determining the optimal number of pump housings to obtain per order. The annual demand is 1,000 units, the ordering cost is $10 per order, and the average carrying cost per unit per year is $0.50. Using these figures, if the EOQ assumptions are met, we can calculate the optimal number of units per order:

$$Q^* = \sqrt{\frac{2DC_o}{C_h}}$$

$$= \sqrt{\frac{2(1,000)(10)}{0.50}}$$

$$= \sqrt{40,000}$$

$$= 200 \text{ units}$$

The relevant total annual inventory cost is the sum of the ordering costs and the carrying costs:

$$\text{Total annual cost} = \text{Order cost} + \text{Holding cost}$$

The total annual inventory cost is equal to ordering plus holding costs for the simple EOQ model.

In terms of the variables in the model, the total cost (TC) can now be expressed as

$$TC = \frac{D}{Q} C_o + \frac{Q}{2} C_h \tag{6-5}$$

The total annual inventory cost for Sumco is computed as follows:

$$TC = \frac{D}{Q} C_o + \frac{Q}{2} C_h$$

$$= \frac{1,000}{200} (10) + \frac{200}{2} (0.5)$$

$$= \$50 + \$50 = \$100$$

The number of orders per year (D/Q) is 5, and the average inventory ($Q/2$) is 100.

As you might expect, the ordering cost is equal to the carrying cost. You may wish to try different values for Q, such as 100 or 300 pumps. You will find that the minimum total cost occurs when Q is 200 units. The EOQ, Q^*, is 200 pumps.

USING EXCEL QM FOR BASIC EOQ INVENTORY PROBLEMS   The Sumco Pump Company example, and a variety of other inventory problems we address in this chapter, can be easily solved using Excel QM. Program 6.1A shows the input data for Sumco and the Excel formulas needed for the EOQ model. Program 6.1B contains the solution for this example, including the optimal order quantity, maximum inventory level, average inventory level, and the number of setups or orders.

Purchase Cost of Inventory Items

Sometimes the total inventory cost expression is written to include the actual cost of the material purchased. With the EOQ assumptions, the purchase cost does not depend on the particular order policy found to be optimal, because regardless of how many orders are placed each year, we still incur the same annual purchase cost of $D \times C$, where C is the purchase cost per unit and D is the annual demand in units.[*]

PROGRAM 6.1A

Input Data and Excel QM Formulas for the Sumco Pump Company Example

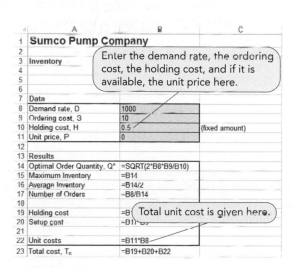

---

[*]Later in this chapter, we discuss the case in which price can affect order policy, that is, when quantity discounts are offered.

PROGRAM 6.1B

Excel QM Solution for the Sumco Pump Company Example

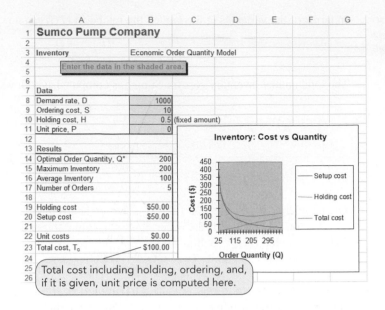

It is useful to know how to calculate the average inventory level in dollar terms when the price per unit is given. This can be done as follows. With the variable Q representing the quantity of units ordered, and assuming a unit cost of C, we can determine the average dollar value of inventory:

$$\text{Average dollar level} = \frac{(CQ)}{2} \tag{6-6}$$

This formula is analogous to Equation 6-1.

Inventory carrying costs for many businesses and industries are also often expressed as an annual percentage of the unit cost or price. When this is the case, a new variable is introduced. Let I be the annual inventory holding charge as a percent of unit price or cost. Then the cost of storing one unit of inventory for the year, C_h, is given by $C_h = IC$, where C is the unit price or cost of an inventory item. Q^* can be expressed, in this case, as

I is the annual carrying cost as a percentage of the cost per unit.

$$Q^* = \sqrt{\frac{2DC_o}{IC}} \tag{6-7}$$

Sensitivity Analysis with the EOQ Model

The EOQ model assumes that all input values are fixed and known with certainty. However, since these values are often estimated or may change over time, it is important to understand how the order quantity might change if different input values are used. Determining the effects of these changes is called **sensitivity analysis**.

The EOQ formula is given as follows:

$$EOQ = \sqrt{\frac{2DC_o}{C_h}}$$

Because of the square root in the formula, any changes in the inputs (D, C_o, C_h) will result in relatively minor changes in the optimal order quantity. For example, if C_o were to increase by a factor of 4, the EOQ would only increase by a factor of 2. Consider the Sumco example just presented. The EOQ for this company is as follows:

$$EOQ = \sqrt{\frac{2(1,000)(10)}{0.50}} = 200$$

If we increased C_o from \$10 to \$40,

$$EOQ = \sqrt{\frac{2(1,000)(40)}{0.50}} = 400$$

In general, the EOQ changes by the square root of a change in any of the inputs.

6.5   Reorder Point: Determining When to Order

The reorder point (ROP) determines when to order inventory. It is found by multiplying the daily demand times the lead time in days.

Now that we have decided how much to order, we look at the second inventory question: when to order. The time between the placing and receipt of an order, called the **lead time** or delivery time, is often a few days or even a few weeks. Inventory must be available to meet the demand during this time, and this inventory can either be on hand now or on order but not yet received. The total of these is called the **inventory position**. Thus, the *when to order* decision is usually expressed in terms of a **reorder point (ROP)**, the inventory position at which an order should be placed. The ROP is given as

$$ROP = (\text{Demand per day}) \times (\text{Lead time for a new order in days})$$
$$= d \times L \tag{6-8}$$

Figure 6.4 has two graphs showing the ROP. One of these has a relatively small lead time, while the other has a relatively large lead time. When the inventory position reaches the ROP, a new order should be placed. While waiting for that order to arrive, the demand will be met with either

FIGURE 6.4
Reorder Point Graphs

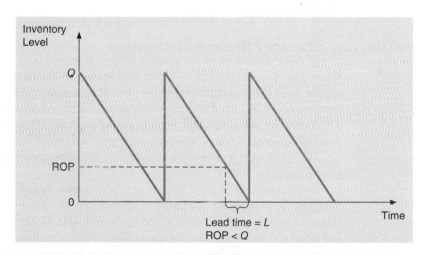

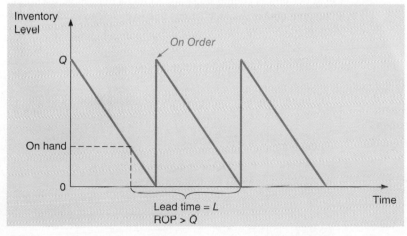

inventory currently on hand or with inventory that already has been ordered but will arrive when the on-hand inventory falls to zero. Let's look at an example.

PROCOMP'S COMPUTER CHIP EXAMPLE   Procomp's demand for computer chips is 8,000 per year. The firm has a daily demand of 40 units, and the order quantity is 400 units. Delivery of an order takes three working days. The reorder point for chips is calculated as follows:

$$\text{ROP} = d \times L = 40 \text{ units per day} \times 3 \text{ days}$$
$$= 120 \text{ units}$$

Hence, when the inventory stock of chips drops to 120, an order should be placed. The order will arrive three days later, just as the firm's stock is depleted to 0. Since the order quantity is 400 units, the ROP is simply the on-hand inventory. This is the situation in the first graph in Figure 6.4.

Suppose the lead time for Procomp Computer Chips was 12 days instead of 3 days. The reorder point would be:

$$\text{ROP} = 40 \text{ units per day} \times 12 \text{ days}$$
$$= 480 \text{ units}$$

Since the maximum on-hand inventory level is the order quantity of 400, an inventory position of 480 would be:

$$\text{Inventory position} = (\text{Inventory on hand}) + (\text{Inventory on order})$$
$$480 = 80 + 400$$

Thus, a new order would have to be placed when the on-hand inventory fell to 80 while there was one other order in-transit. The second graph in Figure 6.4 illustrates this type of situation.

6.6   EOQ Without the Instantaneous Receipt Assumption

The production run model eliminates the instantaneous receipt assumption.

When a firm receives its inventory over a period of time, a new model is needed that does not require the **instantaneous inventory receipt** assumption. This new model is applicable when inventory continuously flows or builds up over a period of time after an order has been placed or when units are produced and sold simultaneously. Under these circumstances, the daily demand rate must be taken into account. Figure 6.5 shows inventory levels as a function of time. Because this model is especially suited to the production environment, it is commonly called the **production run model**.

In this model, instead of having an ordering cost, there will be a *setup cost*. This is the cost of setting up the production facility to manufacture the desired product. It normally includes the salaries and wages of employees who are responsible for setting up the equipment, engineering and design costs of making the setup, paperwork, supplies, utilities, and so on. The carrying cost per unit is composed of the same factors as the traditional EOQ model, although the annual carrying cost equation changes due to a change in average inventory.

FIGURE 6.5

Inventory Control and the Production Process

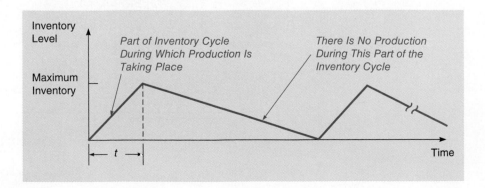

Solving the production run model involves setting setup costs equal to holding costs and solving for Q.

The optimal production quantity can be derived by setting setup costs equal to holding or carrying costs and solving for the order quantity. Let's start by developing the expression for carrying cost. You should note, however, that making setup cost equal to carrying cost does not always guarantee optimal solutions for models more complex than the production run model.

Annual Carrying Cost for Production Run Model

As with the EOQ model, the carrying costs of the production run model are based on the average inventory, and the average inventory is one-half the maximum inventory level. However, since the replenishment of inventory occurs over a period of time and demand continues during this time, the maximum inventory will be less than the order quantity Q. We can develop the annual carrying, or holding, cost expression using the following variables:

$$Q = \text{number of pieces per order, or production run}$$
$$C_s = \text{setup cost}$$
$$C_h = \text{holding or carrying cost per unit per year}$$
$$p = \text{daily production rate}$$
$$d = \text{daily demand rate}$$
$$t = \text{length of production run in days}$$

The maximum inventory level is as follows:

$$(\text{Total produced during the production run}) - (\text{Total used during production run})$$
$$= (\text{Daily production rate})(\text{Number of days of production})$$
$$- (\text{Daily demand})(\text{Number of days of production})$$
$$= (pt) - (dt)$$

Since

$$\text{total produced} = Q = pt,$$

we know that

$$t = \frac{Q}{p}$$

$$\text{Maximum inventory level} = pt - dt = p\frac{Q}{p} - d\frac{Q}{p} = Q\left(1 - \frac{d}{p}\right)$$

The maximum inventory level in the production model is less than Q.

Since the average inventory is one-half of the maximum, we have

$$\text{Average inventory} = \frac{Q}{2}\left(1 - \frac{d}{p}\right) \tag{6-9}$$

and

$$\text{Annual holding cost} = \frac{Q}{2}\left(1 - \frac{d}{p}\right)C_h \tag{6-10}$$

Annual Setup Cost or Annual Ordering Cost

When a product is produced over time, setup cost replaces ordering cost. Both of these are independent of the size of the order and the size of the production run. This cost is simply the number of orders (or production runs) times the ordering cost (setup cost). Thus,

$$\text{Annual setup cost} = \frac{D}{Q}C_s \tag{6-11}$$

and

$$\text{Annual ordering cost} = \frac{D}{Q}C_o \tag{6-12}$$

Determining the Optimal Production Quantity

When the assumptions of the production run model are met, costs are minimized when the setup cost equals the holding cost. We can find the optimal quantity by setting these costs equal and solving for Q. Thus,

$$\text{Annual holding cost} = \text{Annual setup cost}$$

$$\frac{Q}{2}\left(1 - \frac{d}{p}\right)C_h = \frac{D}{Q}C_s$$

Here is the formula for the optimal production quantity. Notice the similarity to the basic EOQ model.

Solving this for Q, we get the optimal production quantity (Q^*):

$$Q^* = \sqrt{\frac{2DC_s}{C_h\left(1 - \frac{d}{p}\right)}} \qquad (6\text{-}13)$$

It should be noted that if the situation does not involve production but rather involves the receipt of inventory gradually over a period of time, this same model is appropriate, but C_o replaces C_s in the formula.

Production Run Model

$$\text{Annual holding cost} = \frac{Q}{2}\left(1 - \frac{d}{p}\right)C_h$$

$$\text{Annual setup cost} = \frac{D}{Q}C_s$$

$$\text{Optimal production quantity } Q^* = \sqrt{\frac{2DC_s}{C_h\left(1 - \frac{d}{p}\right)}}$$

Brown Manufacturing Example

Brown Manufacturing produces commercial refrigeration units in batches. The firm's estimated demand for the year is 10,000 units. It costs about $100 to set up the manufacturing process, and the carrying cost is about 50 cents per unit per year. When the production process has been set up, 80 refrigeration units can be manufactured daily. The demand during the production period has traditionally been 60 units each day. Brown operates its refrigeration unit production area 167 days per year. How many refrigeration units should Brown Manufacturing produce in each batch? How long should the production part of the cycle shown in Figure 6.5 last? Here is the solution:

$$\text{Annual demand} = D = 10,000 \text{ units}$$

$$\text{Setup cost} = C_s = \$100$$

$$\text{Carrying cost} = C_h = \$0.50 \text{ per unit per day}$$

$$\text{Daily production rate} = p = 80 \text{ units daily}$$

$$\text{Daily demand rate} = d = 60 \text{ units daily}$$

1. $Q^* = \sqrt{\dfrac{2DC_s}{C_h\left(1 - \dfrac{d}{p}\right)}}$

2. $Q^* = \sqrt{\dfrac{2 \times 10,000 \times 100}{0.5\left(1 - \dfrac{60}{80}\right)}}$

   $= \sqrt{\dfrac{2,000,000}{0.5(^1/_4)}} = \sqrt{16,000,000}$

   $= 4,000 \text{ units}$

If $Q^* = 4,000$ units and we know that 80 units can be produced daily, the length of each production cycle will be $Q/p = 4,000/80 = 50$ days. Thus, when Brown decides to produce refrigeration units, the equipment will be set up to manufacture the units for a 50-day time span. The number of production runs per year will be $D/Q = 10,000/4,000 = 2.5$. This means that the average number of production runs per year is 2.5. There will be three production runs in one year with some inventory carried to the next year, so only two production runs are needed in the second year.

USING EXCEL QM FOR PRODUCTION RUN MODELS   The Brown Manufacturing production run model can also be solved using Excel QM. Program 6.2A contains the input data and the Excel formulas for this problem. Program 6.2B provides the solution results, including the optimal production quantity, maximum inventory level, average inventory level, and the number of setups.

PROGRAM 6.2A
Excel QM Formulas and Input Data for the Brown Manufacturing Problem

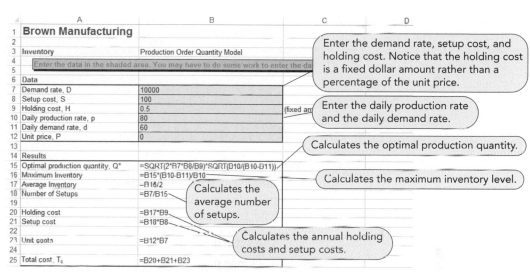

PROGRAM 6.2B
Excel QM Solutions for the Brown Manufacturing Problem

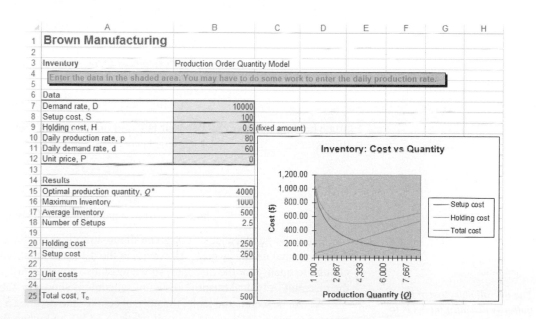

Most manufacturers of home appliances provide in-home repair of the appliances that are under warranty. One such Fortune 100 firm had about 70,000 different parts that were used in the repair of its appliances. The annual value of the parts inventory was over $7 million. The company had more than 1,300 service vehicles that were dispatched when service requests were received. Due to limited space on these vehicles, only about 400 parts were typically carried on each one. If a service person arrived to repair an appliance and did not have necessary part (i.e., a stockout occured), a special order was made to have the order delivered by air so that the repair person could return and fix the appliance as soon as possible.

Deciding which parts to carry was a particularly difficult problem. A project was begun to find a better way to forecast the demand for parts and identify which parts should be stocked on each vehicle. Initially, the intent was to reduce the parts inventory

on each truck as this represented a significant cost of holding the inventory. However, upon further analysis, it was decided that the goal should be to minimize the overall cost—including the costs of special deliveries of parts, revisiting the customer for the repair if the part was not initially available, and overall customer satisfaction.

The project team improved the forecasting system used to project the number of parts needed on each vehicle. As a result, the actual number of parts carried on each vehicle increased. However, the number of first-visit repairs increased from 86% to 90%. This resulted in a savings of $3 million per year in the cost of these repairs. It also improved customer satisfaction because the problem was fixed without the service person having to return a second time.

Source: Based on Michael F. Gorman and Sanjay Ahire. "A Major Appliance Manufacturer Rethinks Its Inventory Policies for Service Vehicles," *Interfaces* 36, 5 (September–October 2006): 407–419.

6.7 Quantity Discount Models

In developing the EOQ model, we assumed that quantity discounts were not available. However, many companies do offer quantity discounts. If such a discount is possible, and all of the other EOQ assumptions are met, it is possible to find the quantity that minimizes the total inventory cost by using the EOQ model and making some adjustments.

When quantity discounts are available, the purchase cost or material cost becomes a relevant cost, as it changes based on the order quantity. The total relevant costs are as follows:

$$\text{Total cost} = \text{Material cost} + \text{Ordering cost} + \text{Carrying cost}$$

$$\text{Total cost} = DC + \frac{D}{Q}C_o + \frac{Q}{2}C_h \qquad (6\text{-}14)$$

where

$$D = \text{annual demand in units}$$
$$C_o = \text{ordering cost of each order}$$
$$C = \text{cost per unit}$$
$$C_h = \text{holding or carrying cost per unit per year}$$

Since holding cost per unit per year is based on the cost of the items, it is convenient to express this as

$$C_h = IC$$

where

$$I = \text{holding cost as a percentage of the unit cost } (C)$$

For a specific purchase cost (C), given the assumptions we have made, ordering the EOQ will minimize total inventory costs. However, in the discount situation, this quantity may not be large enough to qualify for the discount, so we must also consider ordering this minimum quantity for the discount. A typical quantity discount schedule is shown in Table 6.3.

The overall objective of the quantity discount model is to minimize total inventory costs, which now include actual material costs.

As can be seen in the table, the normal cost for the item is $5. When 1,000 to 1,999 units are ordered at one time, the cost per unit drops to $4.80, and when the quantity ordered at one time is 2,000 units or more, the cost is $4.75 per unit. As always, management must decide when and how much to order. But with quantity discounts, how does the manager make these decisions?

TABLE 6.3

Quantity Discount Schedule

DISCOUNT NUMBER	DISCOUNT QUANTITY	DISCOUNT (%)	DISCOUNT COST ($)
1	0 to 999	0	5.00
2	1,000 to 1,999	4	4.80
3	2,000 and over	5	4.75

As with other inventory models discussed so far, the overall objective will be to minimize the total cost. Because the unit cost for the third discount in Table 6.3 is lowest, you might be tempted to order 2,000 units or more to take advantage of the lower material cost. Placing an order for that quantity with the greatest discount cost, however, might not minimize the total inventory cost. As the discount quantity goes up, the material cost goes down, but the carrying cost increases because the orders are large. Thus, the major trade-off when considering quantity discounts is between the reduced material cost and the increased carrying cost.

Figure 6.6 provides a graphical representation of the total cost for this situation. Notice the cost curve drops considerably when the order quantity reaches the minimum for each discount. With the specific costs in this example, we see that the EOQ for the second price category ($1,000 \leq Q \leq 1,999$) is less than 1,000 units. Although the total cost for this EOQ is less than the total cost for the EOQ with the cost in category 1, the EOQ is not large enough to obtain this discount. Therefore, the lowest possible total cost for this discount price occurs at the minimum quantity required to obtain the discount ($Q = 1,000$). The process for determining the minimum cost quantity in this situation is summarized in the following box.

Quantity Discount Model

1. For each discount price (C), compute EOQ $= \sqrt{\dfrac{2DC_o}{IC}}$.

2. If EOQ $<$ Minimum for discount, adjust the quantity to $Q =$ Minimum for discount.

3. For each EOQ or adjusted Q, compute Total cost $= DC + \dfrac{D}{Q}C_o + \dfrac{Q}{2}C_h$.

4. Choose the lowest-cost quantity.

FIGURE 6.6

Total Cost Curve for the Quantity Discount Model

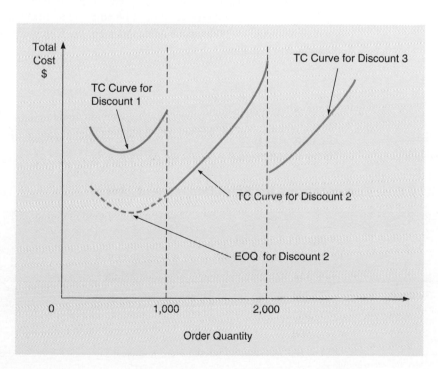

IN ACTION Intel Improves Inventory Operations

Faced with skyrocketing distribution costs, Intel turned to quantitative analysis to design, construct, and implement a multi-echelon inventory optimization (MEIO) system. The system spanned all of Intel's global supply chain and included suppliers, third party logistics (3PL) providers, dealers, and retailers among others. Because of the inherent complexities, designing and constructing the system took several years by itself.

However, as a result, Intel was able to optimize inventory levels worldwide. After one year of operation, the MEIO system reduced global inventory levels by approximately 11 percent without sacrificing delivery schedules, service levels improved by eight percentage points, and an order of magnitude reduction in the number of costly expedites was realized.

Source: Based on B. Wieland, P. Mastrantonio, S. Willems, and K.G. Kempf. "Optimizing Inventory Levels within Intel's Channel Supply Demand Operations," *Interfaces* 42, 6 (November–December 2012): 517–527.

Brass Department Store Example

Let's see how this procedure can be applied by showing an example. Brass Department Store stocks toy race cars. Recently, the store was given a quantity discount schedule for the cars; this quantity discount schedule is shown in Table 6.3. Thus, the normal cost for the toy race cars is $5. For orders between 1,000 and 1,999 units, the unit cost is $4.80, and for orders of 2,000 or more units, the unit cost is $4.75. Furthermore, the ordering cost is $49 per order, the annual demand is 5,000 race cars, and the inventory carrying charge as a percentage of cost, I, is 20% or 0.2. What order quantity will minimize the total inventory cost?

The first step is to compute EOQ for every discount in Table 6.3. This is done as follows:

$$EOQ_1 = \sqrt{\frac{(2)(5,000)(49)}{(0.2)(5.00)}} = 700 \text{ cars per order}$$

EOQ values are computed.

$$EOQ_2 = \sqrt{\frac{(2)(5,000)(49)}{(0.2)(4.80)}} = 714 \text{ cars per order}$$

$$EOQ_3 = \sqrt{\frac{(2)(5,000)(49)}{(0.2)(4.75)}} = 718 \text{ cars per order}$$

EOQ values are adjusted.

The second step is to adjust those quantities that are below the allowable discount range. Since EOQ_1 is between 0 and 999, it does not have to be adjusted. EOQ_2 is below the allowable range of 1,000 to 1,999, and therefore, it must be adjusted to 1,000 units. The same is true for EOQ_3; it must be adjusted to 2,000 units. After this step, the following order quantities must be tested in the total cost equation:

$$Q_1 = 700$$
$$Q_2 = 1,000$$
$$Q_3 = 2,000$$

The total cost is computed.

The third step is to use Equation 6-14 and compute a total cost for each of the order quantities. This is accomplished with the aid of Table 6.4.

TABLE 6.4 Total Cost Computations for Brass Department Store

DISCOUNT NUMBER	UNIT PRICE (C)	ORDER QUANTITY (Q)	ANNUAL MATERIAL COST ($) = DC	ANNUAL ORDERING COST ($) = $\frac{D}{Q}C_o$	ANNUAL CARRYING COST ($) = $\frac{Q}{2}C_h$	TOTAL ($)
1	$5.00	700	25,000	350.00	350.00	25,700.00
2	4.80	1,000	24,000	245.00	480.00	24,725.00
3	4.75	2,000	23,750	122.50	950.00	24,822.50

The fourth step is to select that order quantity with the lowest total cost. Looking at Table 6.4, you can see that an order quantity of 1,000 toy race cars minimizes the total cost. It should be recognized, however, that the total cost for ordering 2,000 cars is only slightly greater than the total cost for ordering 1,000 cars. Thus, if the third discount cost is lowered to $4.65, for example, this order quantity might be the one that minimizes the total inventory cost.

Q* is selected.

USING EXCEL QM FOR QUANTITY DISCOUNT PROBLEMS   As seen in the previous analysis, the quantity discount model is more complex than the inventory models discussed so far in this chapter. Fortunately, we can use the computer to simplify the calculations. Program 6.3A shows the Excel formulas and input data needed for Excel QM for the Brass Department Store problem. Program 6.3B provides the solution to this problem, including adjusted order quantities and total costs for each price break.

PROGRAM 6.3A

Excel QM Formulas and Input Data for the Brass Department Store Quantity Discount Problem

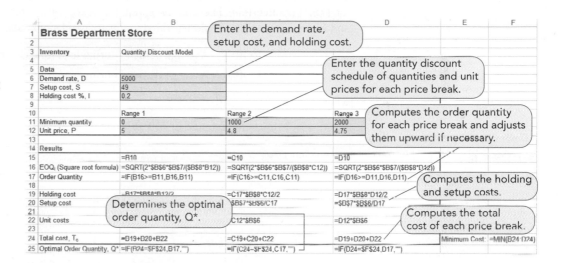

PROGRAM 6.3B

Excel QM Solutions for the Brass Department Store Quantity Discount Problem

	A	B	C	D	E	F
1	**Brass Department Store**					
2						
3	Inventory	Quantity Discount Model				
4						
5	Data					
6	Demand rate, D	5000				
7	Setup cost, S	49				
8	Holding cost %, I	20%				
9						
10		Range 1	Range 2	Range 3		
11	Minimum quantity	0	1000	2000		
12	Unit price, P	5	4.8	4.75		
13						
14	Results					
15		Range 1	Range 2	Range 3		
16	EOQ$_i$ (Square root formula)	700	714.4345083	718.1848466		
17	Order Quantity	700	1000	2000		
18						
19	Holding cost	$350.00	$480.00	$950.00		
20	Setup cost	$350.00	$245.00	$122.50		
21						
22	Unit costs	$25,000.00	$24,000.00	$23,750.00		
23						
24	Total cost, T$_c$	$25,700.00	$24,725.00	$24,822.50	Minimum Cost:	$24,725.00
25	Optimal Order Quantity, Q*		1000			

6.8 Use of Safety Stock

Safety stock helps in avoiding stockouts. It is extra stock kept on hand.

When the EOQ assumptions are met, it is possible to schedule orders to arrive so that stockouts are completely avoided. However, if the demand or the lead time is uncertain, the exact demand during the lead time (which is the ROP in the EOQ situation) will not be known with certainty. Therefore, to prevent stockouts, it is necessary to carry additional inventory called **safety stock**.

When demand is unusually high during the lead time, you dip into the safety stock instead of encountering a *stockout*. Thus, the main purpose of safety stock is to avoid stockouts when the demand is higher than expected. Its use is shown in Figure 6.7. Note that although stockouts can often be avoided by using safety stock, there is still a chance that they may occur. The demand may be so high that all the safety stock is used up, and thus there is still a stockout.

One of the best ways to implement a safety stock policy is to adjust the reorder point. In the EOQ situation where the demand and lead time are constant, the reorder point is simply the amount of inventory that would be used during the lead time (i.e., the daily demand times the lead time in days). This is assumed to be known with certainty, so there is no need to place an order when the inventory position is more than this. However, when the daily demand or the lead time fluctuate and are uncertain, the exact amount of inventory that will be used during the lead time is uncertain. The average inventory usage during the lead time should be computed and some safety stock should be added to this to avoid stockouts. The reorder point becomes

$$ROP = (Average\ demand\ during\ lead\ time) + (Safety\ stock)$$

$$ROP = (Average\ demand\ during\ lead\ time) + SS \tag{6-15}$$

where

$$SS = safety\ stock$$

FIGURE 6.7
Use of Safety Stock

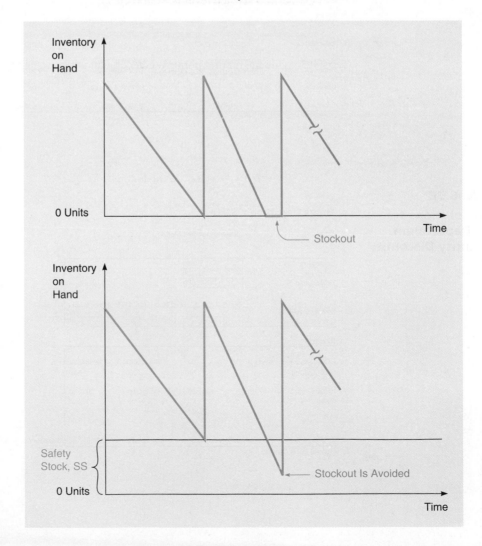

How to determine the correct amount of safety stock is the only remaining question. Two important factors in this decision are the stockout cost and the holding cost. The stockout cost usually involves lost sales and lost goodwill, which results in loss of future sales. If holding cost is low while stockout cost is high, a large amount of safety stock should be carried to avoid stockouts as it costs little to carry this, while stockouts are expensive. On the other hand, if stockout cost is low but holding cost is high, a lower amount of safety stock would be preferred, as having a stockout would cost very little, but too much safety stock will result in much higher annual holding costs.

How is the optimum stock level determined? If demand fluctuates while lead time is constant, and if both the stockout cost per unit and the holding cost per unit are known, the use of a payoff/cost table might be considered. With only a small number of possible demand values during the lead time, a cost table could be constructed in which the different possible demand levels would be the states of nature, and the different amounts of safety stock as the alternatives. Using the techniques discussed in Chapter 3, the expected cost could be calculated for each safety stock level, and the minimum cost solution could be found.

However, a more general approach is to determine what service level is desired and then to find the safety stock level that would accomplish this. A prudent manager will look at the holding cost and the stockout cost to help determine an appropriate service level. A **service level** indicates what percentage of the time customer demand is met. In other words, the service level is the percentage of time that stockouts are avoided. Thus,

$$\text{Service level} = 1 - \text{Probability of a stockout}$$

or

$$\text{Probability of a stockout} = 1 - \text{Service level}$$

Once the desired service level is established, the amount of safety stock to carry can be found using the probability distribution of demand during the lead time.

SAFETY STOCK WITH THE NORMAL DISTRIBUTION   Equation 6-15 provides the general formula for determining the reorder point. When demand during the lead time is normally distributed, the reorder point becomes

$$\text{ROP} = (\text{Average demand during lead time}) + Z\sigma_{d\text{LT}} \tag{6-16}$$

where

$$Z = \text{number of standard deviations for a given service level}$$
$$\sigma_{d\text{LT}} = \text{standard deviation of demand during the lead time}$$

Thus, the amount of safety stock is simply $Z\sigma_{d\text{LT}}$. The following example looks at how to determine the appropriate safety stock level when demand during the lead time is normally distributed and the mean and standard deviation are known.

HINSDALE COMPANY EXAMPLE   The Hinsdale Company carries a variety of electronic inventory items, and these are typically identified by SKU. One particular item, SKU A3378, has a demand that is normally distributed during the lead time, with a mean of 350 units and a standard deviation of 10. Hinsdale wants to follow a policy that results in stockouts occurring only 5% of the time on any order. How much safety stock should be maintained and what is the reorder point? Figure 6.8 helps visualize this example.

From the normal distribution table (Appendix A) we have $Z = 1.65$:

$$\text{ROP} = (\text{Average demand during lead time}) + Z\sigma_{d\text{LT}}$$
$$= 350 + 1.65(10)$$
$$= 350 + 16.5 = 366.5 \text{ units (or about 367 units)}$$

So the reorder point is 366.5, and the safety stock is 16.5 units.

CALCULATING LEAD TIME DEMAND AND STANDARD DEVIATION   If the mean and standard deviation of demand during the lead time are not known, they must be calculated from historical demand and lead time data. Once these are found, Equation 6-16 can be used to find the safety

FIGURE 6.8

Safety Stock and the Normal Distribution

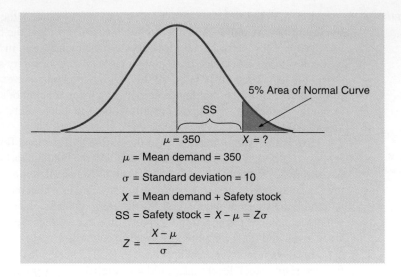

stock and reorder point. Throughout this section, we assume that lead time is in days, although the same procedure can be applied to weeks, months, or any other time period. We will also assume that if demand fluctuates, the distribution of demand each day is identical to and independent of demand on other days. If both daily demand and lead time fluctuate, they are also assumed to be independent.

There are three situations to consider. In each of the following ROP formulas, the average demand during the lead time is the first term and the safety stock $(Z\sigma_{dLT})$ is the second term.

1. Demand is variable but lead time is constant:

$$\text{ROP} = \bar{d}L + Z(\sigma_d\sqrt{L}) \tag{6-17}$$

where

$$\bar{d} = \text{average daily demand}$$
$$\sigma_d = \text{standard deviation of daily demand}$$
$$L = \text{lead time in days}$$

2. Demand is constant but lead time is variable:

$$\text{ROP} = d\bar{L} + Z(d\sigma_L) \tag{6-18}$$

where

$$\bar{L} = \text{average lead time}$$
$$\sigma_L = \text{standard deviation of lead time}$$
$$d = \text{daily demand}$$

3. Both demand and lead time are variable:

$$\text{ROP} = \bar{d}\bar{L} + Z(\sqrt{\bar{L}\sigma_d^2 + \bar{d}^2\sigma_L^2}) \tag{6-19}$$

Notice that the third situation is the most general case and the others can be derived from that. If either demand or lead time is constant, the standard deviation and variance for that would be 0, and the average would just equal the constant amount. Thus, the formula for ROP in situation 3 can be simplified to the ROP formula given for that situation.

HINSDALE COMPANY EXAMPLE, CONTINUED Hinsdale has decided to determine the safety stock and ROP for three other items: SKU F5402, SKU B7319, and SKU F9004.

For SKU F5402, the daily demand is normally distributed, with a mean of 15 units and a standard deviation of 3. Lead time is exactly 4 days. Hinsdale wants to maintain a 97% service level. What is the reorder point, and how much safety stock should be carried?

From Appendix A, for a 97% service level $Z = 1.88$. Since demand is variable but lead time is constant, we find

$$\text{ROP} = \bar{d}L + Z(\sigma_d \sqrt{L}) = 15(4) + 1.88(3\sqrt{4}) = 15(4) + 1.88(6)$$
$$= 60 + 11.28 = 71.28$$

So the average demand during the lead time is 60, and the safety stock is 11.28 units.

For SKU B7319, the daily demand is constant at 25 units per day, and the lead time is normally distributed, with a mean of 6 days and a standard deviation of 3. Hinsdale wants to maintain a 98% service level on this particular product. What is the reorder point?

From Appendix A, for a 98% service level $Z = 2.05$. Since demand is constant but lead time is variable, we find

$$\text{ROP} = d\bar{L} + Z(d\sigma_L) = 25(6) + 2.05(25)(3) = 150 + 2.05(75)$$
$$= 150 + 153.75 = 303.75$$

So the average demand during the lead time is 150, and the safety stock is 154.03 units.

For SKU F9004, the daily demand is normally distributed, with a mean of 20 units and a standard deviation of 4, and the lead time is normally distributed, with a mean of 5 days and a standard deviation of 2. Hinsdale wants to maintain a 94% service level on this particular product. What is the reorder point?

From Appendix A, for a 94% service level, $Z = 1.55$. Since both demand and lead time are variable, we find

$$\text{ROP} = \bar{d}\bar{L} + Z(\sqrt{\bar{L}\sigma_d^2 + \bar{d}^2\sigma_L^2}) = (20)(5) + 1.55(\sqrt{5(4)^2 + (20)^2(2)^2})$$
$$= 100 + 1.55\sqrt{1680}$$
$$= 100 + 1.55(40.99)$$
$$= 100 + 63.53$$
$$= 163.53$$

So the average demand during the lead time is 100, and the safety stock is 63.53 units.

A safety stock level is determined for each service level.

As the service level increases, the safety stock increases at an increasing rate. Table 6.5 illustrates how the safety stock level would change in the Hinsdale Company (SKU A3378) example for changes in the service level. As the amount of safety stock increases, the annual holding cost increases as well.

CALCULATING ANNUAL HOLDING COST WITH SAFETY STOCK   When the EOQ assumptions of constant demand and constant lead time are met, the average inventory is $Q/2$, and the annual holding cost is $(Q/2)C_h$. When safety stock is carried because demand fluctuates, the

TABLE 6.5

Safety Stock for SKU A3378 at Different Service Levels

SERVICE LEVEL (%)	Z VALUE FROM NORMAL CURVE TABLE	SAFETY STOCK (UNITS)
90	1.28	12.8
91	1.34	13.4
92	1.41	14.1
93	1.48	14.8
94	1.55	15.5
95	1.65	16.5
96	1.75	17.5
97	1.88	18.8
98	2.05	20.5
99	2.33	23.3
99.99	3.72	37.2

holding cost for this safety stock is added to the holding cost of the regular inventory to get the total annual holding cost. If demand during the lead time is normally distributed and safety stock is used, the average inventory on the order quantity (Q) is still $Q/2$, but the average amount of safety stock carried is simply the amount of the safety stock (SS) and not one-half this amount. Since demand during the lead time is normally distributed, there would be times when inventory usage during the lead time exceeded the expected amount and some safety stock would be used. But it is just as likely that the inventory usage during the lead time would be less than the expected amount and the order would arrive while some regular inventory remained in addition to all the safety stock. Thus, on the average, the company would always have this full amount of safety stock in inventory, and a holding cost would apply to all of this. From this we have

Total annual holding cost = Holding cost of regular inventory + Holding cost of safety stock

$$\text{THC} = \frac{Q}{2} C_h + (\text{SS})C_h \qquad \text{(6-20)}$$

where

$$
\begin{aligned}
\text{THC} &= \text{total annual holding cost} \\
Q &= \text{order quantity} \\
C_h &= \text{holding cost per unit per year} \\
\text{SS} &= \text{safety stock}
\end{aligned}
$$

Carrying cost increases at an increasing rate as the service level increases.

In the Hinsdale example for SKU A3378, let's assume that the holding cost is $2 per unit per year. The amount of safety stock needed to achieve various service levels is shown in Table 6.5. The holding cost for the safety stock would be these amounts times $2 per unit. As illustrated in Figure 6.9, this holding cost would increase extremely rapidly once the service level reached 98%.

USING EXCEL QM FOR SAFETY STOCK PROBLEMS To use Excel QM to determine the safety stock and reorder point, select *Excel QM* from the *Add-Ins* tab and select *Inventory—Reorder Point/Safety Stock (normal distribution)*. Enter a title when the input window appears and click

FIGURE 6.9

Service Level Versus Annual Carrying Costs

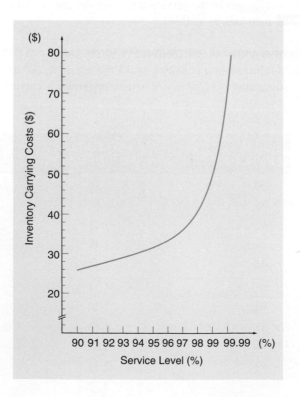

PROGRAM 6.4A
Excel QM Formulas and Input Data for the Hinsdale Safety Stock Problem

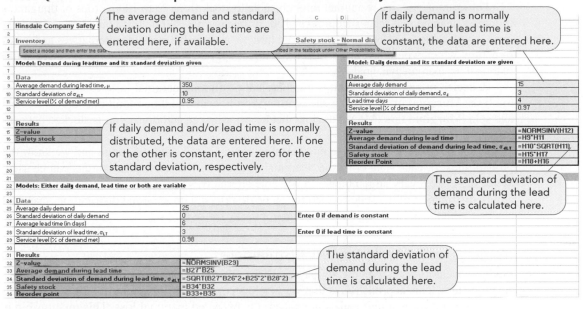

The average demand and standard deviation during the lead time are entered here, if available.

If daily demand is normally distributed but lead time is constant, the data are entered here.

If daily demand and/or lead time is normally distributed, the data are entered here. If one or the other is constant, enter zero for the standard deviation, respectively.

The standard deviation of demand during the lead time is calculated here.

The standard deviation of demand during the lead time is calculated here.

PROGRAM 6.4B
Excel QM Solutions for the Hinsdale Safety Stock Problem

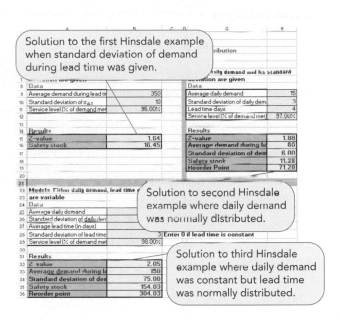

Solution to the first Hinsdale example when standard deviation of demand during lead time was given.

Solution to second Hinsdale example where daily demand was normally distributed.

Solution to third Hinsdale example where daily demand was constant but lead time was normally distributed.

OK. Program 6.4A shows the input screen and formulas for the first three Hinsdale Company examples. Program 6.4B shows the solution.

6.9 Single-Period Inventory Models

So far, we have considered inventory decisions in which demand continues in the future, and future orders will be placed for the same product. There are some products for which a decision to meet the demand for a single time period is made, and items that do not sell during this time period are of no value or have a greatly reduced value in the future. For example, a daily newspaper is worthless after the next paper is available. Other examples include weekly magazines, programs printed for athletic events, certain prepared foods that have a short life, and some seasonal clothes that have greatly reduced value at the end of the season. This type of problem is often called the news vendor problem or a single-period inventory model.

For example, a large restaurant might be able to stock from 20 to 100 cartons of doughnuts to meet a demand that ranges from 20 to 100 cartons per day. While this could be modeled using a payoff table (see Chapter 3), we would have to analyze 101 possible alternatives and states of nature, which would be quite tedious. A simpler approach for this type of decision is to use marginal, or incremental, analysis.

A decision-making approach using marginal profit and marginal loss is called **marginal analysis**. **Marginal profit (MP)** is the additional profit achieved if one additional unit is stocked and sold. **Marginal loss (ML)** is the loss that occurs when an additional unit is stocked but cannot be sold.

When there are a manageable number of alternatives and states of nature and we know the probabilities for each state of nature, marginal analysis with discrete distributions can be used. When there are a very large number of possible alternatives and states of nature and the probability distribution of the states of nature can be described with a normal distribution, marginal analysis with the normal distribution are appropriate.

Marginal Analysis with Discrete Distributions

Finding inventory level with the lowest cost is not difficult when we follow the marginal analysis procedure. This approach says that we would stock an additional unit only if the expected marginal profit for that unit equals or exceeds the expected marginal loss. This relationship is expressed symbolically as follows:

P = probability that demand will be greater than or equal to a given supply (or the probability of selling at least one additional unit)

$1 - P$ = probability that demand will be less than supply (or the probability that one additional unit will not sell)

The expected marginal profit is found by multiplying the probability that a given unit will be sold by the marginal profit, $P(MP)$. Similarly, the expected marginal loss is the probability of not selling the unit multiplied by the marginal loss, or $(1 - P)(ML)$.

The optimal decision rule is to stock the additional unit if

$$P(MP) \geq (1 - P)ML$$

With some basic mathematical manipulations, we can determine the level of P for which this relationship holds:

$$P(MP) \geq ML - P(ML)$$
$$P(MP) + P(ML) \geq ML$$
$$P(MP + ML) \geq ML$$

or

$$P \geq \frac{ML}{ML + MP} \tag{6-21}$$

In other words, as long as the probability of selling one more unit (P) is greater than or equal to $ML/(MP + ML)$, we would stock the additional unit.

Steps of Marginal Analysis with Discrete Distributions

1. Determine the value of $\dfrac{ML}{ML + MP}$ for the problem.
2. Construct a probability table and add a cumulative probability column.
3. Keep ordering inventory as long as the probability (P) of selling at least one additional unit is greater than $\dfrac{ML}{ML + MP}$.

TABLE 6.6

Café du Donut's Probability Distribution

DAILY SALES (CARTONS OF DOUGHNUTS)	PROBABILITY (*P*) THAT DEMAND WILL BE AT THIS LEVEL
4	0.05
5	0.15
6	0.15
7	0.20
8	0.25
9	0.10
10	0.10
	Total 1.00

Café du Donut Example

Café du Donut is a popular New Orleans dining spot on the edge of the French Quarter. Its specialty is coffee and doughnuts; it buys the doughnuts fresh daily from a large industrial bakery. The café pays $4 for each carton (containing two dozen doughnuts) delivered each morning. Any cartons not sold at the end of the day are thrown away, for they would not be fresh enough to meet the café's standards. If a carton of doughnuts is sold, the total revenue is $6. Hence, the marginal profit per carton of doughnuts is

$$MP = \text{Marginal profit} = \$6 - \$4 = \$2$$

The marginal loss is $ML - \$4$ since the doughnuts cannot be returned or salvaged at day's end.

From past sales, the café's manager estimates that the daily demand will follow the probability distribution shown in Table 6.6. The manager then follows the three steps to find the optimal number of cartons of doughnuts to order each day.

Step 1. Determine the value of $\dfrac{ML}{ML + MP}$ for the decision rule

$$P \geq \frac{ML}{ML + MP} = \frac{\$4}{\$4 + \$2} = \frac{4}{6} = 0.67$$

$$P \geq 0.67$$

So the inventory stocking decision rule is to stock an additional unit if $P \geq 0.67$.

Step 2. Add a new column to the table to reflect the probability that doughnut sales will be at each level or greater. This is shown in the right-hand column of Table 6.7. For example, the probability that demand will be 4 cartons or greater is $1.00 (= 0.05 + 0.15 + 0.15 + 0.20 + 0.25 + 0.10 + 0.10)$. Similarly, the probability that sales will be 8 cartons or greater is $0.45 (= 0.25 + 0.10 + 0.10)$: namely, the sum of probabilities for sales of 8, 9, or 10 cartons.

TABLE 6.7

Marginal Analysis for Café du Donut

DAILY SALES (CARTONS OF DOUGHNUTS)	PROBABILITY (*P*) THAT DEMAND WILL BE AT THIS LEVEL	PROBABILITY (*P*) THAT DEMAND WILL BE AT THIS LEVEL OR GREATER
4	0.05	$1.00 \geq 0.66$
5	0.15	$0.95 \geq 0.66$
6	0.15	$0.80 \geq 0.66$
7	0.20	0.65
8	0.25	0.45
9	0.10	0.20
10	0.10	0.10
	Total 1.00	

Step 3. Keep ordering additional cartons as long as the probability of selling at least one additional carton is greater than P, which is the indifference probability. If Café du Donut orders 6 cartons, marginal profits will still be greater than marginal loss since

$$P \text{ at 6 cartons} = 0.80 > 0.67$$

Marginal Analysis with the Normal Distribution

When product demand or sales follow a normal distribution, which is a common business situation, marginal analysis with the normal distribution can be applied. First, we need to find four values:

1. The average or mean sales for the product, μ
2. The standard deviation of sales, σ
3. The marginal profit for the product, MP
4. The marginal loss for the product, ML

Once these quantities are known, the process of finding the best stocking policy is somewhat similar to marginal analysis with discrete distributions. We let $X^* =$ optimal stocking level.

Steps of Marginal Analysis with the Normal Distribution

1. Determine the value of $\dfrac{\text{ML}}{\text{ML} + \text{MP}}$ for the problem.
2. Locate P on the normal distribution (Appendix A) and find the associated Z-value.
3. Find X^* using the relationship

$$Z = \frac{X^* - \mu}{\sigma}$$

to solve for the resulting stocking policy:

$$X^* = \mu + Z\sigma$$

Newspaper Example

Demand for copies of the *Chicago Tribune* newspaper at Joe's Newsstand is normally distributed and has averaged 60 papers per day, with a standard deviation of 10 papers. With a marginal loss of 20 cents and a marginal profit of 30 cents, what daily stocking policy should Joe follow?

Step 1. Joe should stock the *Chicago Tribune* as long as the probability of selling the last unit is at least $\text{ML}/(\text{ML} + \text{MP})$:

$$\frac{\text{ML}}{\text{ML} + \text{MP}} = \frac{20 \text{ cents}}{20 \text{ cents} + 30 \text{ cents}} = \frac{20}{50} = 0.40$$

Let $P = 0.40$.

Step 2. Figure 6.10 shows the normal distribution. Since the normal table has cumulative areas under the curve between the left side and any point, we look for 0.60 ($= 1.0 - 0.40$) in order to get the corresponding Z value:

$$Z = 0.25 \text{ standard deviations from the mean}$$

Step 3. In this problem, $\mu = 60$ and $\sigma = 10$, so

$$0.25 = \frac{X^* - 60}{10}$$

or

$$X^* = 60 + 0.25(10) = 62.5, \text{ or 62 newspapers.}$$

Thus, Joe should order 62 copies of the *Chicago Tribune* daily since the probability of selling 63 is slightly less than 0.40.

FIGURE 6.10

Joe's Stocking Decision for the *Chicago Tribune*

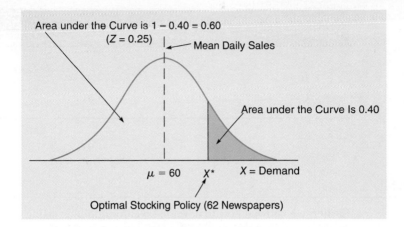

FIGURE 6.11

When P is greater than 0.50, the same basic procedure is used, although caution should be used when looking up the Z value. Let's say that Joe's Newsstand also stocks the *Chicago Sun-Times*, and its marginal loss is 40 cents and marginal profit is 10 cents. The daily sales have averaged 100 copies of the *Chicago Sun-Times*, with a standard deviation of 10 papers. The optimal stocking policy is as follows:

$$\frac{ML}{ML + MP} = \frac{40 \text{ cents}}{40 \text{ cents } + 10 \text{ cents}} = \frac{40}{50} = 0.80$$

The normal curve is shown in Figure 6.11. Since the normal curve is symmetrical, we find Z for an area under the curve of 0.80 and multiply this number by -1 since all values below the mean are associated with a negative Z value:

$$Z = -0.84 \text{ standard deviations from the mean for an area of } 0.80$$

With $\mu = 100$ and $\sigma = 10$,

$$-0.84 = \frac{X^* - 100}{10}$$

or

$$X^* = 100 - 0.84(10) = 91.6, \text{ or } 91 \text{ newspapers.}$$

So Joe should order 91 copies of the *Chicago Sun-Times* every day.

The optimal stocking policies in these two examples are intuitively consistent. When marginal profit is greater than marginal loss, we would expect X^* to be greater than the average demand, μ and when marginal profit is less than marginal loss, we would expect the optimal stocking policy, X^*, to be less than μ.

FIGURE 6.11

Joe's Stocking Decision for the *Chicago Sun-Times*

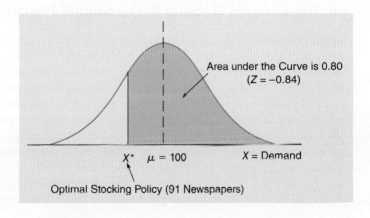

TABLE 6.8
Summary of ABC Analysis

INVENTORY GROUP	DOLLAR USAGE (%)	INVENTORY ITEMS (%)	ARE QUANTITATIVE CONTROL TECHNIQUES USED?
A	70	10	Yes
B	20	20	In some cases
C	10	70	No

6.10   ABC Analysis

Earlier, we showed how to develop inventory policies using quantitative techniques. There are also some very practical considerations that should be incorporated into the implementation of inventory decisions, such as **ABC analysis**.

The purpose of ABC analysis is to divide all of a company's inventory items into three groups (group A, group B, and group C) based on the overall inventory value of the items. A prudent manager should spend more time managing those items representing the greatest dollar inventory cost because this is where the greatest potential savings are. A brief description of each group follows, with general guidelines as to how to categorize items.

The inventory items in the A group account for a major portion of the inventory costs of the organization. As a result, their inventory levels must be monitored carefully. These items typically make up more than 70% of the company's business in dollars, but may consist of only 10% of all inventory items. In other words, a few inventory items are very costly to the company. Thus, great care should be taken in forecasting the demand and developing good inventory management policies for this group of items (refer to Table 6.8). Since there are relatively few of these, the time involved would not be excessive.

The items in the B group are typically moderately priced items and represent much less investment than the A items. Thus, it may not be appropriate to spend as much time developing optimal inventory policies for this group as with the A group since these inventory costs are much lower. Typically, the group B items represent about 20% of the company's business in dollars, and about 20% of the items in inventory.

The items in the C group are the very low-cost items that represent very little in terms of the total dollars invested in inventory. These items may constitute only 10% of the company's business in dollars, but they may consist of 70% of the items in inventory. From a cost–benefit perspective, it would not be good to spend as much time managing these items as the A and B items.

For the group C items, the company should develop a very simple inventory policy, and this may include a relatively large safety stock. Since the items cost very little, the holding cost associated with a large safety stock will also be very low. More care should be taken in determining the safety stock with the higher priced group B items. For the very expensive group A items, the cost of carrying the inventory is so high, it is beneficial to carefully analyze the demand for these so that safety stock is at an appropriate level. Otherwise, the company may have exceedingly high holding costs for the group A items.

6.11   Dependent Demand: The Case for Material Requirements Planning

In all the inventory models discussed earlier, we assume that the demand for one item is independent of the demand for other items. For example, the demand for refrigerators is usually independent of the demand for toaster ovens. Many inventory problems, however, are interrelated; the demand for one item is dependent on the demand for another item. Consider a manufacturer of small power lawn mowers. The demand for lawn mower wheels and spark plugs is dependent on the demand for lawn mowers. Four wheels and one spark plug are needed for each finished lawn mower. Usually when the demand for different items is dependent, the relationship between the items is known and constant. Thus, you should forecast the demand for the final products and compute the requirements for component parts.

As with the inventory models discussed previously, the major questions that must be answered are *how much to order* and *when to order*. But with dependent demand, inventory scheduling and planning can be very complex indeed. In these situations, **materials requirements palnning (MRP)** can be employed effectively. Some of the benefits of MRP follow:

1. Increased customer service and satisfaction
2. Reduced inventory costs
3. Better inventory planning and scheduling
4. Higher total sales
5. Faster response to market changes and shifts
6. Reduced inventory levels without reduced customer service

Although most MRP systems are computerized, the analysis is straightforward and similar from one computerized system to the next. Here is the typical procedure.

Material Structure Tree

Parents and components are identified in the material structure tree.

We begin by developing a **bill of materials (BOM)**. The BOM identifies the components, their descriptions, and the number required in the production of one unit of the final product. From the BOM, we develop a material structure tree. Let's say that demand for product A is 50 units. Each unit of A requires 2 units of B and 3 units of C. Now, each unit of B requires 2 units of D and 3 units of E. Furthermore, each unit of C requires 1 unit of E and 2 units of F. Thus, the demand for B, C, D, E, and F is completely dependent on the demand for A. Given this information, a material structure tree can be developed for the related inventory items (see Figure 6.12).

The structure tree has three levels: 0, 1, and 2. Items above any level are called *parents*, and items below any level are called *components*. There are three parents: A, B, and C. Each parent item has at least one level below it. Items B, C, D, E, and F are components because each item has at least one level above it. In this structure tree, B and C are both parents and components.

The material structure tree shows how many units are needed at every level of production.

Note that the number in the parentheses in Figure 6.12 indicates how many units of that particular item are needed to make the item immediately above it. Thus, B(2) means that it takes 2 units of B for every unit of A, and F(2) means that it takes 2 units of F for every unit of C.

After the material structure tree has been developed, the number of units of each item required to satisfy demand can be determined. This information can be displayed as follows:

Part B: 2 × number of A's = 2 × 50 = 100
Part C: 3 × number of A's = 3 × 50 = 150
Part D: 2 × number of B's = 2 × 100 = 200
Part E: 3 × number of B's + 1 × number of C's = 3 × 100 + 1 × 150 = 450
Part F: 2 × number of C's = 2 × 150 = 300

Thus, for 50 units of A we need 100 units of B, 150 units of C, 200 units of D, 450 units of E, and 300 units of F. Of course, the numbers in this table could have been determined directly from the material structure tree by multiplying the numbers along the branches times the

FIGURE 6.12

Material Structure Tree for Item A

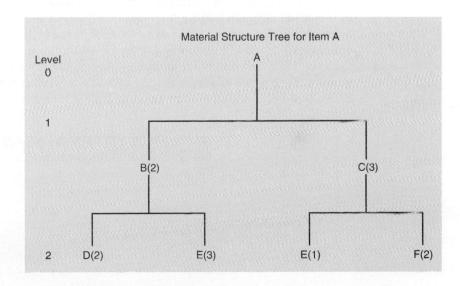

FIGURE 6.13

Gross Material Requirements Plan for 50 Units of A

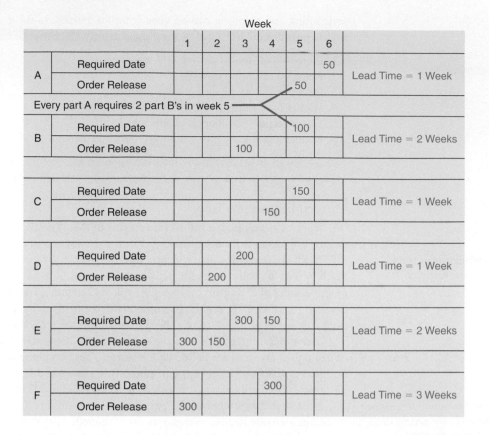

demand for A, which is 50 units for this problem. For example, the number of units of D needed is simply $2 \times 2 \times 50 = 200$ units.

Gross and Net Material Requirements Plan

Once the materials structure tree has been developed, we construct a gross material requirements plan. This is a time schedule that shows when an item must be ordered from suppliers when there is no inventory on hand, or when the production of an item must be started in order to satisfy the demand for the finished product at a particular date. Let's assume that all of the items are produced or manufactured by the same company. It takes one week to make A, two weeks to make B, one week to make C, one week to make D, two weeks to make E, and three weeks to make F. With this information, the gross material requirements plan can be constructed to reveal the production schedule needed to satisfy the demand of 50 units of A at a future date. (Refer to Figure 6.13.)

The interpretation of the material in Figure 6.13 is as follows: If you want 50 units of A at week 6, you must start the manufacturing process in week 5. Thus, in week 5 you need 100 units of B and 150 units of C. These two items take 2 weeks and 1 week to produce. (See the lead times.) Production of B should be started in week 3, and C should be started in week 4. (See the order release for these items.) Working backward, the same computations can be made for all the other items. The material requirements plan graphically reveals when each item should be started and completed in order to have 50 units of A at week 6. Now, a net requirements plan can be developed given the on-hand inventory in Table 6.9; here is how it is done.

Using on-hand inventory to compute net requirements.

TABLE 6.9

On-Hand Inventory

ITEM	ON-HAND INVENTORY
A	10
B	15
C	20
D	10
E	10
F	5

FIGURE 6.14

Net Material Requirements Plan for 50 Units of A

Item		Week 1	2	3	4	5	6	Lead Time
A	Gross						50	1
	On-Hand 10						10	
	Net						40	
	Order Receipt						40	
	Order Release					40		
B	Gross					80^A		2
	On-Hand 15					15		
	Net					65		
	Order Receipt					65		
	Order Release			65				
C	Gross					120^A		1
	On-Hand 20					20		
	Net					100		
	Order Receipt					100		
	Order Release				100			
D	Gross			130^B				1
	On-Hand 10			10				
	Net			120				
	Order Receipt			120				
	Order Release		120					
E	Gross			195^B	100^C			2
	On-Hand 10			10	0			
	Net			185	100			
	Order Receipt			185	100			
	Order Release	185	100					
F	Gross				200^C			3
	On-Hand 5				5			
	Net				195			
	Order Receipt				195			
	Order Release	195						

Using these data, we can develop a net material requirements plan that includes gross requirements, on-hand inventory, net requirements, planned-order receipts, and planned-order releases for each item. It is developed by beginning with A and working backward through the other items. Figure 6.14 shows a net material requirements plan for product A.

The net requirements plan is constructed like the gross requirements plan. Starting with item A, we work backward determining net requirements for all items. These computations are done by referring constantly to the structure tree and lead times. The gross requirements for A are 50 units in week 6. Ten items are on hand, and thus the net requirements and planned-order receipt are both 40 items in week 6. Because of the one-week lead time, the planned-order release is 40 items in week 5. (See the arrow connecting the order receipt and order release.) Look down column 5 and refer to the structure tree in Figure 6.13. Eighty (2×40) items of B and $120 = 3 \times 40$ items of C are required in week 5 in order to have a total of 50 items of A in week 6. The letter A in the upper-right corner for items B and C means that this demand for B and C was generated as a result of the demand for the parent, A. Now the same type of analysis is done for B and C to determine the net requirements for D, E, and F.

Two or More End Products

So far, we have considered only one end product. For most manufacturing companies, there are normally two or more end products that use some of the same parts or components. All of the end products must be incorporated into a single net material requirements plan.

In the MRP example just discussed, we developed a net material requirements plan for product A. Now, we show how to modify the net material requirements plan when a second end product is introduced. Let's call the second end product AA. The material structure tree for product AA is as follows:

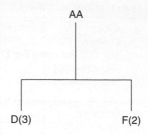

Let's assume that we need 10 units of AA. With this information we can compute the gross requirements for AA:

Part D: 3 × number of AA's = 3 × 10 = 30
Part F: 2 × number of AA's = 2 × 10 = 20

To develop a net material requirements plan, we need to know the lead time for AA. Let's assume that it is one week. We also assume that we need 10 units of AA in week 6 and that we have no units of AA on hand.

Now, we are in a position to modify the net material requirements plan for product A to include AA. This is done in Figure 6.15.

FIGURE 6.15

Net Material Requirements Plan, Including AA

Item	Inventory	Week 1	2	3	4	5	6	Lead Time
AA	Gross						10	1 Week
	On-Hand: 0						0	
	Net						10	
	Order Receipt						10	
	Order Release					10		
A	Gross						50	1 Week
	On-Hand: 10						10	
	Net						40	
	Order Receipt						40	
	Order Release					40		
B	Gross					80[A]		2 Weeks
	On-Hand: 15					15		
	Net					65		
	Order Receipt					65		
	Order Release			65				
C	Gross					120[A]		1 Week
	On-Hand: 20					20		
	Net					100		
	Order Receipt					100		
	Order Release				100			
D	Gross			130[B]		30[AA]		1 Week
	On-Hand: 10			10		0		
	Net			120		30		
	Order Receipt			120		30		
	Order Release		120		30			
E	Gross			195[B]	100[C]			2 Weeks
	On-Hand: 10			10	0			
	Net			185	100			
	Order Receipt			185	100			
	Order Release	185	100					
F	Gross				200[C]	20[AA]		3 Weeks
	On-Hand: 5				5	0		
	Net				195	20		
	Order Receipt				195	20		
	Order Release	195	20					

Look at the top row of the figure. As you can see, we have a gross requirement of 10 units of AA in week 6. We don't have any units of AA on hand, so the net requirement is also 10 units of AA. Because it takes one week to make AA, the order release of 10 units of AA is in week 5. This means that we start making AA in week 5 and have the finished units in week 6.

Because we start making AA in week 5, we must have 30 units of D and 20 units of F in week 5. See the rows for D and F in Figure 6.15. The lead time for D is one week. Thus, we must give the order release in week 4 to have the finished units of D in week 5. Note that there was no inventory on hand for D in week 5. The original 10 units of inventory of D were used in week 5 to make B, which was subsequently used to make A. We also need to have 20 units of F in week 5 to produce 10 units of AA by week 6. Again, we have no on-hand inventory of F in week 5. The original 5 units were used in week 4 to make C, which was subsequently used to make A. The lead time for F is three weeks. Thus, the order release for 20 units of F must be in week 2. (See the F row in Figure 6.15.)

This example shows how the inventory requirements of two products can be reflected in the same net material requirements plan. Some manufacturing companies can have more than 100 end products that must be coordinated in the same net material requirements plan. Although such a situation can be very complicated, the same principles we used in this example are employed. Remember that computer programs have been developed to handle large and complex manufacturing operations.

In addition to using MRP to handle end products and finished goods, MRP can also be used to handle spare parts and components. This is important because most manufacturing companies sell spare parts and components for maintenance. A net material requirements plan should also reflect these spare parts and components.

6.12   Just-In-Time Inventory Control

With JIT, inventory arrives just before it is needed.

During the past several decades, there has been a trend to make the manufacturing process more efficient. One objective is to have less in-process inventory on hand. This is known as **JIT inventory**. With this approach, inventory arrives just in time to be used during the manufacturing process to produce subparts, assemblies, or finished goods. One technique of implementing JIT is a manual procedure called **kanban**. *Kanban* in Japanese means "card." With a dual-card kanban system, there is a conveyance kanban, or C-kanban, and a production kanban, or P-kanban. The kanban system is very simple. Here is how it works.

Four Steps of Kanban

Arrow 1:   As shown in Figure 6.16, full containers along with their C-kanban card are taken from the storage area to a user area, typically on a manufacturing line (see arrow 1).

Arrow 2:   During the manufacturing process, parts in the container are used up by the user. When the container is empty, the empty container along with the same C-kanban card is taken back to the storage area (depicted by arrow number 2). Here the user picks up a new full container, detaches the P-kanban card from it, attaches his or her C-kanban card to it, and returns with it to the user area (depicted by arrow number 1 again).

Arrow 3:   This detached P-kanban card is then attached to an empty container in the storage area and then—and only then—is the empty container taken back to the upstream producer area (depicted by arrow number 3).

Arrow 4:   This empty container is then refilled with parts and taken with its P-kanban card back to the storage area (depicted by arrow number 4). This kanban process continuously cycles throughout the day. Kanban is sometimes known as a "pull" production system.

FIGURE 6.16

The Kanban System

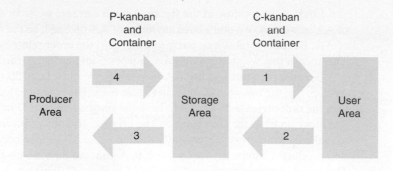

At a minimum, two containers are required using the kanban system. One container is used at the user area, and another container is being refilled for future use. In reality, there are usually more than two containers. This is how inventory control is accomplished. Inventory managers can introduce additional containers and their associated P-kanbans into the system. In a similar fashion, the inventory manager can remove containers and the P-kanbans to have tighter control over inventory buildups.

In addition to being a simple, easy-to-implement system, the kanban system can also be very effective in controlling inventory costs and in uncovering production bottlenecks. Inventory arrives at the user area or on the manufacturing line just before it is needed. Inventory does not build up unnecessarily, cluttering the production line or adding to unnecessary inventory expense. The kanban system reduces inventory levels and makes for a more effective operation. It is like putting the production line on an inventory diet. Like any diet, the inventory diet imposed by the kanban system makes the production operation more streamlined. Furthermore, production bottlenecks and problems can be uncovered. Many production managers remove containers and their associated P-kanban from the kanban system in order to "starve" the production line to uncover bottlenecks and potential problems.

In implementing a kanban system, a number of work rules or kanban rules are normally implemented. One typical kanban rule is that no containers are filled without the appropriate P-kanban. Another rule is that each container must hold exactly the specified number of parts or inventory items. These and similar rules make the production process more efficient. Only those parts that are actually needed are produced. The production department does not produce inventory just to keep busy. It produces inventory or parts only when they are needed in the user area or on an actual manufacturing line.

6.13   Enterprise Resource Planning

Over the years, MRP has evolved to include not only the materials required in production but also the labor hours, material cost, and other resources related to production. When approached in this fashion, the term MRP II is often used, and the word *resource* replaces the word *requirements*. As this concept evolved and sophisticated computer software programs were developed, these systems were called **enterprise resource planning (ERP)** systems.

The objective of an ERP system is to reduce costs by integrating all of the operations of a firm. This starts with the supplier of the materials needed and flows through the organization to include invoicing the customer of the final product. Data are entered once into a database, and then these data can be quickly and easily accessed by anyone in the organization. This benefits not only the functions related to planning and managing inventory but also other business processes such as accounting, finance, and human resources.

The benefits of a well-developed ERP system are reduced transaction costs and increased speed and accuracy of information. However, there are drawbacks as well. The software is expensive to buy and costly to customize. The implementation of an ERP system may require a company to change its normal operations, and employees are often resistant to change. Also, training employees on the use of the new software can be expensive.

There are many ERP systems available. The most common ones include SAP, Oracle, and PeopleSoft. Even small systems can cost hundreds of thousands of dollars. The larger systems can cost hundreds of millions of dollars.

Summary

This chapter introduces the fundamentals of inventory control theory. We show that the two most important problems are (1) how much to order and (2) when to order.

We investigate the economic order quantity, which determines how much to order, and the reorder point, which determines when to order. In addition, we explore the use of sensitivity analysis to determine what happens to computations when one or more of the values used in one of the equations changes.

The basic EOQ inventory model presented in this chapter makes a number of assumptions: (1) known and constant demand and lead times, (2) instantaneous receipt of inventory, (3) no quantity discounts, (4) no stockouts or shortages, and (5) the only variable costs are ordering costs and carrying costs. If these assumptions are valid, the EOQ inventory model provides optimal solutions. On the other hand, if these assumptions do not hold, the basic EOQ model does not apply. In these cases, more complex models are needed, including the production run, quantity discount, and safety stock models. When the inventory item is for use in a single time period, the marginal analysis approach is used. ABC analysis is used to determine which items represent the greatest potential inventory cost so these items can be more carefully managed.

When the demand for inventory is not independent of the demand for another product, a technique such as MRP is needed. MRP can be used to determine the gross and net material requirements for products. Computer software is necessary to implement major inventory systems including MRP systems successfully. Today, many companies are using ERP software to integrate all of the operations within a firm, including inventory, accounting, finance, and human resources.

JIT can lower inventory levels, reduce costs, and make a manufacturing process more efficient. Kanban, a Japanese word meaning "card," is one way to implement the JIT approach.

Glossary

ABC Analysis An analysis that divides inventory into three groups. Group A is more important than group B, which is more important than group C.

Annual Setup Cost The cost to set up the manufacturing or production process for the production run model.

Average Inventory The average inventory on hand. In this chapter the average inventory is $Q/2$ for the EOQ model.

Bill of Materials (BOM) A material structure tree of the components in a product, with a description and the quantity required to make one unit of that product.

Economic Order Quantity (EOQ) The amount of inventory ordered that will minimize the total inventory cost. It is also called the optimal order quantity, or Q^*.

Enterprise Resource Planning (ERP) A computerized information system that integrates and coordinates the operations of a firm.

Instantaneous Inventory Receipt A system in which inventory is received or obtained at one point in time and not over a period of time.

Inventory Position The amount of inventory on hand plus the amount in any orders that have been placed but not yet received.

Just-In-Time (JIT) Inventory An approach whereby inventory arrives just in time to be used in the manufacturing process.

Kanban A manual JIT system developed by the Japanese. Kanban means "card" in Japanese.

Lead Time The time it takes to receive an order after it is placed (called L in the chapter).

Marginal Analysis A decision-making technique that uses marginal profit and marginal loss in determining optimal decision policies. Marginal analysis is used when the number of alternatives and states of nature is large.

Marginal Loss The loss that would be incurred by stocking and not selling an additional unit.

Marginal Profit The additional profit that would be realized by stocking and selling one more unit.

Material Requirements Planning (MRP) An inventory model that can handle dependent demand.

Production Run Model An inventory model in which inventory is produced or manufactured over time instead of being ordered or purchased. This model eliminates the instantaneous receipt assumption.

Quantity Discount The cost per unit when large orders of an inventory item are placed.

Reorder Point (ROP) The number of units on hand when an order for more inventory is placed.

Safety Stock Extra inventory that is used to help avoid stockouts.

Sensitivity Analysis The process of determining how sensitive the optimal solution is to changes in the values used in the equations.

Service Level The chance, expressed as a percent, that there will not be a stockout. Service level $= 1 -$ Probability of a stockout.

Stockout A situation that occurs when there is no inventory on hand.

Key Equations

Equations 6-1 through 6-8 are associated with the economic order quantity (EOQ).

(6-1) Average inventory level $= \dfrac{Q}{2}$

(6-2) Annual ordering cost $= \dfrac{D}{Q} C_o$

(6-3) Annual holding cost $= \dfrac{Q}{2} C_h$

(6-4) $\text{EOQ} = Q^* = \sqrt{\dfrac{2DC_o}{C_h}}$

(6-5) $TC = \dfrac{D}{Q} C_o + \dfrac{Q}{2} C_h$

Total relevant inventory cost.

(6-6) Average dollar level $= \dfrac{(CQ)}{2}$

(6-7) $Q = \sqrt{\dfrac{2DC_o}{IC}}$

EOQ with C_h expressed as percentage of unit cost.

(6-8) $\text{ROP} = d \times L$

Reorder point: d is the daily demand and L is the lead time in days.

Equations 6-9 through 6-13 are associated with the production run model.

(6-9) Average inventory $= \dfrac{Q}{2}\left(1 - \dfrac{d}{p}\right)$

(6-10) Annual holding cost $= \dfrac{Q}{2}\left(1 - \dfrac{d}{p}\right)C_h$

(6-11) Annual setup cost $= \dfrac{D}{Q} C_s$

(6-12) Annual ordering cost $= \dfrac{D}{Q} C_o$

(6-13) $Q^* = \sqrt{\dfrac{2DC_s}{C_h\left(1 - \dfrac{d}{p}\right)}}$

Optimal production quantity.

Equation 6-14 is used for the quantity discount model.

(6-14) Total cost $= DC + \dfrac{D}{Q} C_o + \dfrac{Q}{2} C_h$

Total inventory cost (including purchase cost).

Equations 6-15 to 6-20 are used when safety stock is required.

(6-15) ROP $=$ (Average demand during lead time) $+$ SS

General reorder point formula for determining when safety stock (SS) is carried.

(6-16) ROP $=$ (Average demand during lead time) $+ Z\sigma_{d\text{LT}}$

Reorder point formula when demand during lead time is normally distributed with a standard deviation of $\sigma_{d\text{LT}}$.

(6-17) $\text{ROP} = \bar{d}L + Z(\sigma_d \sqrt{L})$

Formula for determining the reorder point when daily demand is normally distributed but lead time is constant, where $\bar{d}$ is the average daily demand, L is the constant lead time in days, and σ_d is the standard deviation of daily demand.

(6-18) $\text{ROP} = d\bar{L} + Z(d\sigma_L)$

Formula for determining the reorder point when daily demand is constant but lead time is normally distributed, where $\bar{L}$ is the average lead time in days, d is the constant daily demand, and σ_L is the standard deviation of lead time.

(6-19) $\text{ROP} = \bar{d}\,\bar{L} + Z(\sqrt{\bar{L}\sigma_d^2 + \bar{d}^2\sigma_L^2})$

Formula for determining reorder point when both daily demand and lead time are normally distributed; where $\bar{d}$ is the average daily demand, $\bar{L}$ is the average lead time in days, σ_L is the standard deviation of lead time, and σ_d is the standard deviation of daily demand.

(6-20) $\text{THC} = \dfrac{Q}{2} C_h + (\text{SS})C_h$

Total annual holding cost formula when safety stock is carried.

Equation 6-21 is used for marginal analysis.

(6-21) $P \geq \dfrac{\text{ML}}{\text{ML} + \text{MP}}$

Decision rule in marginal analysis for stocking additional units.

Solved Problems

Solved Problem 6-1

Patterson Electronics supplies microcomputer circuitry to a company that incorporates microprocessors into refrigerators and other home appliances. One of the components has an annual demand of 250 units, and this is constant throughout the year. Carrying cost is estimated to be $1 per unit per year, and the ordering cost is $20 per order.

a. To minimize cost, how many units should be ordered each time an order is placed?
b. How many orders per year are needed with the optimal policy?
c. What is the average inventory if costs are minimized?
d. Suppose the ordering cost is not $20, and Patterson has been ordering 150 units each time an order is placed. For this order policy to be optimal, what would the ordering cost have to be?

Solution

a. The EOQ assumptions are met, so the optimal order quantity is

$$\text{EOQ} = Q^* = \sqrt{\frac{2DC_o}{C_h}} = \sqrt{\frac{2(250)20}{1}} = 100 \text{ units}$$

b. Number of orders per year $= \dfrac{D}{Q} = \dfrac{250}{100} = 2.5$ orders per year

Note that this would mean in one year the company places three orders and in the next year it would only need two orders, since some inventory would be carried over from the previous year. It averages 2.5 orders per year.

c. Average inventory $= \dfrac{Q}{2} = \dfrac{100}{2} = 500$ units

d. Given an annual demand of 250, a carrying cost of $1, and an order quantity of 150, Patterson Electronics must determine what the ordering cost would have to be for the order policy of 150 units to be optimal. To find the answer to this problem, we must solve the traditional EOQ equation for the ordering cost. As you can see in the calculations that follow, an ordering cost of $45 is needed for the order quantity of 150 units to be optimal.

$$Q = \sqrt{\frac{2DC_o}{C_h}}$$

$$C_o = Q^2 \frac{C_h}{2D}$$

$$= \frac{(150)^2(1)}{2(250)}$$

$$= \frac{22,500}{500} = \$45$$

Solved Problem 6-2

Flemming Accessories produces paper slicers used in offices and in art stores. The minislicer has been one of its most popular items: Annual demand is 6,750 units and is constant throughout the year. Kristen Flemming, owner of the firm, produces the minislicers in batches. On average, Kristen can manufacture 125 minislicers per day. Demand for these slicers during the production process is 30 per day. The setup cost for the equipment necessary to produce the minislicers is $150. Carrying costs are $1 per minislicer per year. How many minislicers should Kristen manufacture in each batch?

Solution

The data for Flemming Accessories are summarized as follows:

$$D = 6{,}750 \text{ units}$$
$$C_s = \$150$$
$$C_h = \$1$$
$$d = 30 \text{ units}$$
$$p = 125 \text{ units}$$

This is a production run problem that involves a daily production rate and a daily demand rate. The appropriate calculations are shown here:

$$Q^* = \sqrt{\frac{2DC_s}{C_h(1 - d/p)}}$$

$$= \sqrt{\frac{2(6{,}750)(150)}{1(1 - 30/125)}}$$

$$= 1{,}632$$

Solved Problem 6-3

Dorsey Distributors has an annual demand for a metal detector of 1,400. The cost of a typical detector to Dorsey is $400. Carrying cost is estimated to be 20% of the unit cost, and the ordering cost is $25 per order. If Dorsey orders in quantities of 300 or more, it can get a 5% discount on the cost of the detectors. Should Dorsey take the quantity discount? Assume the demand is constant.

Solution

The solution to any quantity discount model involves determining the total cost of each alternative after quantities have been computed and adjusted for the original problem and every discount. We start the analysis with no discount:

$$\text{EOQ (no discount)} = \sqrt{\frac{2(1{,}400)(25)}{0.2(400)}}$$

$$= 29.6 \text{ units}$$

$$\text{Total cost (no discount)} = \text{Material cost} + \text{Ordering cost} + \text{Carrying cost}$$

$$= \$400(1{,}400) + \frac{1{,}400(\$25)}{29.6} + \frac{29.6(\$400)(0.2)}{2}$$

$$= \$560{,}000 + \$1{,}183 + \$1{,}183 = \$562{,}366$$

The next step is to compute the total cost for the discount:

$$\text{EOQ (with discount)} = \sqrt{\frac{2(1{,}400)(25)}{0.2(\$380)}}$$

$$= 30.3 \text{ units}$$

$$Q(\text{adjusted}) = 300 \text{ units}$$

Because this last economic order quantity is below the discounted price, we must adjust the order quantity to 300 units. The next step is to compute total cost:

$$\text{Total cost (with discount)} = \text{Material cost} + \text{Ordering cost} + \text{Carrying cost}$$

$$= \$380(1{,}400) + \frac{1{,}400(25)}{300} + \frac{300(\$380)(0.2)}{2}$$

$$= \$532{,}000 + \$117 + \$11{,}400 = \$543{,}517$$

The optimal strategy is to order 300 units at a total cost of $543,517.

Solved Problem 6-4

The F. W. Harris Company sells an industrial cleaner to a large number of manufacturing plants in the Houston area. An analysis of the demand and costs has resulted in a policy of ordering 300 units of this product every time an order is placed. The demand is constant, at 25 units per day. In an agreement with the supplier, F. W. Harris is willing to accept a lead time of 20 days since the supplier has provided an excellent price. What is the reorder point? How many units are actually in inventory when an order should be placed?

Solution

The reorder point is

$$ROP = dxL = 25(20) = 500 \text{ units}$$

This means that an order should be placed when the inventory position is 500. Since the ROP is greater than the order quantity, $Q = 300$, an order must have been placed already but not yet delivered. So the inventory position must be

$$\text{Inventory position} = (\text{Inventory on hand}) + (\text{Inventory on order})$$
$$500 = 200 + 300$$

There would be 200 units on hand and an order of 300 units in transit.

Solved Problem 6-5

The B. N. Thayer and D. N. Thaht Computer Company sells a desktop computer that is popular among gaming enthusiasts. In the past few months, demand has been relatively consistent, although it does fluctuate from day to day. The company orders the computer cases from a supplier. It places an order for 5,000 cases at the appropriate time to avoid stockouts. The demand during the lead time is normally distributed, with a mean of 1,000 units and a standard deviation of 200 units. The holding cost per unit per year is estimated to be $4. How much safety stock should the company carry to maintain a 96% service level? What is the reorder point? What would the total annual holding cost be if this policy is followed?

Solution

Using the table for the normal distribution, the Z value for a 96% service level is about 1.75. The standard deviation is 200. The safety stock is calculated as

$$SS = Z\sigma_{dLT} = 1.75(200) = 375 \text{ units}$$

For a normal distribution with a mean of 1,000, the reorder point is

$$ROP = (\text{Average demand during lead time}) + SS$$
$$= 1000 + 350 = 1,350 \text{ units}$$

The total annual holding cost is

$$THC = \frac{Q}{2} C_h + (SS)C_h = \frac{5,000}{2} 4 + (375)4 = \$11,500$$

Self-Test

- Before taking the self-test, refer to the learning objectives at the beginning of the chapter, the notes in the margins, and the glossary at the end of the chapter.
- Use the key at the back of the book to correct your answers.
- Restudy pages that correspond to any questions that you answered incorrectly or material you feel uncertain about.

1. Which of the following is a basic component of an inventory control system?
   a. planning what inventory to stock and how to acquire it
   b. forecasting the demand for parts and products
   c. controlling inventory levels
   d. developing and implementing feedback measurements for revising plans and forecasts
   e. all of the above are components of an inventory control system

2. Which of the following is a valid use of inventory?
   a. the decoupling function
   b. to take advantage of quantity discounts
   c. to avoid shortages and stockouts
   d. to smooth out irregular supply and demand
   e. all of the above are valid uses of inventory

3. Onc assumption necessary for the EOQ model is instantaneous replenishment. This means
   a. the lead time is zero.
   b. the production time is assumed to be zero.
   c. the entire order is delivered at one time.
   d. replenishment cannot occur until the on-hand inventory is zero.

4. If the EOQ assumptions are met and a company orders the EOQ each time an order is placed, then the
   a. total annual holding costs are minimized.
   b. total annual ordering costs are minimized.
   c. total of all inventory costs are minimized.
   d. order quantity will always be less than the average inventory.

5. If the EOQ assumptions are met and a company orders more than the economic order quantity, then
   a. total annual holding cost will be greater than the total annual ordering cost.
   b. total annual holding cost will be less than the total annual ordering cost.
   c. total annual holding cost will be equal to the total annual ordering cost.
   d. total annual holding cost will be equal to the total annual purchase cost.

6. The reorder point is
   a. the quantity that is reordered each time an order is placed.
   b. the amount of inventory that would be needed to meet demand during the lead time.
   c. equal to the average inventory when the EOQ assumptions are met.
   d. assumed to be zero if there is instantaneous replenishment.

7. If the EOQ assumptions are met, then
   a. annual stockout cost will be zero.
   b. total annual holding cost will equal total annual ordering cost.
   c. average inventory will be one-half the order quantity.
   d. all of the above are true.

8. In the production run model, the maximum inventory level will be
   a. greater than the production quantity.
   b. equal to the production quantity.
   c. less than the production quantity.
   d. equal to the daily production rate plus the daily demand.

9. Why is the annual purchase (material) cost not considered to be a relevant inventory cost if the EOQ assumptions are met?
   a. This cost will be zero.
   b. This cost is constant and not affected by the order quantity.
   c. This cost is insignificant compared with the other inventory costs.
   d. This cost is never considered to be an inventory cost.

10. A JIT system will usually result in
    a. a low annual holding cost.
    b. very few orders per year.
    c. frequent shutdowns in an assembly line.
    d. high levels of safety stock.

11. Manufacturers use MRP when
    a. the demand for one product is dependent on the demand for other products.
    b. the demand for each product is independent of the demand for other products.
    c. demand is totally unpredictable.
    d. purchase cost is extremely high.

12. In using marginal analysis, an additional unit should be stocked if
    a. $MP = ML$.
    b. the probability of selling that unit is greater than or equal to $MP/(MP + ML)$.
    c. the probability of selling that unit is less than or equal to $ML/(MP + ML)$.
    d. the probability of selling that unit is greater than or equal to $ML/(MP + ML)$.

13. In using marginal analysis with the normal distribution, if marginal profit is less than marginal loss, we expect the optimal stocking quantity to be
    a. greater than the standard deviation.
    b. less than the standard deviation.
    c. greater than the mean.
    d. less than the mean.

14. The inventory position is defined as
    a. the amount of inventory needed to meet the demand during the lead time.
    b. the amount of inventory on hand.
    c. the amount of inventory on order.
    d. the total of the on-hand inventory plus the on-order inventory.

Discussion Questions and Problems

Discussion Questions

6-1   Why is inventory an important consideration for managers?

6-2   What is the purpose of inventory control?

6-3   Under what circumstances can inventory be used as a hedge against inflation?

6-4   Why wouldn't a company always store large quantities of inventory to eliminate shortages and stockouts?

6-5   What are some of the assumptions made in using the EOQ?

6-6   Discuss the major inventory costs that are used in determining the EOQ.

6-7   What is the ROP? How is it determined?

6-8   If the ROP is greater than the order quantity, explain how the ROP is implemented. Can the ROP be more than twice the order quantity and, if so, how is such a situation handled?

6-9   Let the annual demand for an arbitrary commodity be 1,000 units per year and the associated EOQ be 400 units per order. Under this circumstance the number of orders per year would be $(D/Q) = 2.5$ orders per year. How can this be so?

6-10   What is the purpose of sensitivity analysis?

6-11   What assumptions are made in the production run model?

6-12   What happens to the production run model when the daily production rate becomes very large?

6-13   Briefly describe what is involved in solving a quantity discount model.

6-14   When using safety stock, how is the standard deviation of demand during the lead time calculated if daily demand is normally distributed but lead time is constant? How is it calculated if daily demand is constant but lead time is normally distributed? How is it calculated if both daily demand and lead time are normally distributed?

6-15   Briefly explain the marginal analysis approach to the single period inventory problem.

6-16   Briefly describe what is meant by ABC analysis. What is the purpose of this inventory technique?

6-17   What is the overall purpose of MRP?

6-18   What is the difference between the gross and net material requirements plan?

6-19   What is the objective of JIT?

Problems

6-20   Lila Battle has determined that the annual demand for number 6 screws is 100,000 screws. Lila, who works in her brother's hardware store, is in charge of purchasing. She estimates that it costs $10 every time an order is placed. This cost includes her wages, the cost of the forms used in placing the order, and so on. Furthermore, she estimates that the cost of carrying one screw in inventory for a year is one-half of 1 cent. Assume that the demand is constant throughout the year.

(a) How many number 6 screws should Lila order at a time if she wishes to minimize total inventory cost?

(b) How many orders per year would be placed? What would the annual ordering cost be?

(c) What would the average inventory be? What would the annual holding cost be?

6-21   It takes approximately 8 working days for an order of number 6 screws to arrive once the order has been placed. (Refer to Problem 6-20.) The demand for number 6 screws is fairly constant, and on the average, Lila has observed that her brother's hardware store sells 500 of these screws each day. Because the demand is fairly constant, Lila believes that she can avoid stockouts completely if she only orders the number 6 screws at the correct time. What is the ROP?

6-22   Lila's brother believes that she places too many orders for screws per year. He believes that an order should be placed only twice per year. If Lila follows her brother's policy, how much more would this cost every year over the ordering policy that she developed in Problem 6-20? If only two orders were placed each year, what effect would this have on the ROP?

6-23   Barbara Bright is the purchasing agent for West Valve Company. West Valve sells industrial valves and fluid control devices. One of the most popular valves is the Western, which has an annual demand of 4,000 units. The cost of each valve is $90, and the inventory carrying cost is estimated to be 10% of the cost of each valve. Barbara has made a study of the costs involved in placing an order for any of the valves that West Valve stocks, and she has concluded that the average ordering cost is $25 per order. Furthermore, it takes about two weeks for an order to arrive from the supplier, and during this time the demand per week for West valves is approximately 80.

(a) What is the EOQ?

(b) What is the ROP?

(c) Is the ROP greater than the EOQ? If so, how is this situation handled?

(d) What is the average inventory? What is the annual holding cost?

(e) How many orders per year would be placed? What is the annual ordering cost?

6-24   Ken Ramsing has been in the lumber business for most of his life. Ken's biggest competitor is Pacific Woods. Through many years of experience, Ken knows that the ordering cost for an order of plywood is $25 and that the carrying cost is 25% of the unit cost. Both Ken and Pacific Woods receive plywood in loads that cost $100 per load. Furthermore, Ken and Pacific Woods use the same supplier of plywood, and Ken was able to find out that Pacific Woods orders in quantities of 4,000 loads at a time. Ken also knows that 4,000 loads is the EOQ for Pacific Woods. What is the annual demand in loads of plywood for Pacific Woods?

6-25   Shoe Shine is a local retail shoe store located on the north side of Centerville. Annual demand for a popular sandal is 500 pairs, and John Dirk, the owner of Shoe Shine, has been in the habit of ordering 100 pairs at a time. John estimates that the ordering cost is $10 per order. The cost of the sandal is $5 per pair. For John's ordering policy to be correct, what would the carrying cost as a percentage of the unit cost have to be? If the carrying cost were 10% of the cost, what would the optimal order quantity be?

6-26 In Problem 6-20 you helped Lila Battle determine the optimal order quantity for number 6 screws. She had estimated that the ordering cost was $10 per order. At this time, though, she believes that this estimate was too low. Although she does not know the exact ordering cost, she believes that it could be as high as $40 per order. How would the optimal order quantity change if the ordering cost were $20, $30, and $40?

6-27 Ross White's machine shop uses 2,500 brackets during the course of a year, and this usage is relatively constant throughout the year. These brackets are purchased from a supplier 100 miles away for $15 each, and the lead time is 2 days. The holding cost per bracket per year is $1.50 (or 10% of the unit cost) and the ordering cost per order is $18.75. There are 250 working days per year.

(a) What is the EOQ?
(b) Given the EOQ, what is the average inventory? What is the annual inventory holding cost?
(c) In minimizing cost, how many orders would be made each year? What would be the annual ordering cost?
(d) Given the EOQ, what is the total annual inventory cost (including purchase cost)?
(e) What is the time between orders?
(f) What is the ROP?

6-28 Ross White (see Problem 6-27) wants to reconsider his decision of buying the brackets and is considering making the brackets in-house. He has determined that setup costs would be $25 in machinist time and lost production time, and 50 brackets could be produced in a day once the machine has been set up. Ross estimates that the cost (including labor time and materials) of producing one bracket would be $14.80. The holding cost would be 10% of this cost.

(a) What is the daily demand rate?
(b) What is the optimal production quantity?
(c) How long will it take to produce the optimal quantity? How much inventory is sold during this time?
(d) If Ross uses the optimal production quantity, what would be the maximum inventory level? What would be the average inventory level? What is the annual holding cost?
(e) How many production runs would there be each year? What would be the annual setup cost?
(f) Given the optimal production run size, what is the total annual inventory cost?
(g) If the lead time is one-half day, what is the ROP?

6-29 Upon hearing that Ross White (see Problems 6-27 and 6-28) is considering producing the brackets in-house, the vendor has notified Ross that the purchase price would drop from $15 per bracket to $14.50 per bracket if Ross will purchase the brackets in lots of 1,000. Lead times, however, would increase to 3 days for this larger quantity.

(a) What is the total annual inventory cost plus purchase cost if Ross buys the brackets in lots of 1,000 at $14.50 each?
(b) If Ross does buy in lots of 1,000 brackets, what is the new ROP?
(c) Given the options of purchasing the brackets at $15 each, producing them in-house at $14.80, and taking advantage of the discount, what is your recommendation to Ross White?

6-30 After analyzing the costs of various options for obtaining brackets, Ross White (see Problems 6.27 through 6.29) recognizes that although he knows that lead time is 2 days and demand per day averages 10 units, the demand during the lead time often varies. Ross has kept very careful records and has determined lead time demand is normally distributed with a standard deviation of 1.5 units.

(a) What Z value would be appropriate for a 98% service level?
(b) What safety stock should Ross maintain if he wants a 98% service level?
(c) What is the adjusted ROP for the brackets?
(d) What is the annual holding cost for the safety stock if the annual holding cost per unit is $1.50?

6-31 Douglas Boats is a supplier of boating equipment for the states of Oregon and Washington. It sells 5,000 White Marine WM-4 diesel engines every year. These engines are shipped to Douglas in a shipping container of 100 cubic feet, and Douglas Boats keeps the warehouse full of these WM-4 motors. The warehouse can hold 5,000 cubic feet of boating supplies. Douglas estimates that the ordering cost is $10 per order, and the carrying cost is estimated to be $10 per motor per year. Douglas Boats is considering the possibility of expanding the warehouse for the WM-4 motors. How much should Douglas Boats expand, and how much would it be worth for the company to make the expansion? Assume demand is constant throughout the year.

6-32 Northern Distributors is a wholesale organization that supplies retail stores with lawn care and household products. One building is used to store Neverfail lawn mowers. The building is 25 feet wide by 40 feet deep by 8 feet high. Anna Oldham, manager of the warehouse, estimates that about 60% of the warehouse can be used to store the Neverfail lawn mowers. The remaining 40% is used for walkways and a small office. Each Neverfail lawn mower comes in a box that is 5 feet by 4 feet by 2 feet high. The annual demand for these lawn mowers is 12,000, and the ordering cost for Northern Distributors is $30 per order. It is estimated that it costs Northern $2 per lawn mower per year for storage. Northern Distributors is thinking about increasing the size of the warehouse. The company can only do this by making the warehouse deeper. At the present time, the warehouse is 40 feet deep. How many feet of depth should be added on to the warehouse to minimize the annual inventory costs? How much should the company be willing to pay for this addition? Remember that only 60% of the total area can be used to store Neverfail lawn mowers. Assume all EOQ conditions are met.

6-33 Lisa Surowsky was asked to help in determining the best ordering policy for a new product. Currently, the demand for the new product has been projected to be about 1,000 units annually. To get a handle on the carrying and ordering costs, Lisa prepared a series of average inventory costs. Lisa thought that these costs would be appropriate for the new product. The results are summarized in the following table. These data were compiled for 10,000 inventory items that were carried or held during the year and were ordered 100 times during the past year. Help Lisa determine the EOQ.

COST FACTOR	COST ($)
Taxes	2,000
Processing and inspection	1,500
New product development	2,500
Bill paying	500
Ordering supplies	50
Inventory insurance	600
Product advertising	800
Spoilage	750
Sending purchasing orders	800
Inventory inquiries	450
Warehouse supplies	280
Research and development	2,750
Purchasing salaries	3,000
Warehouse salaries	2,800
Inventory theft	800
Purchase order supplies	500
Inventory obsolescence	300

6-34 Jan Gentry is the owner of a small company that produces electric scissors used to cut fabric. The annual demand is for 8,000 scissors, and Jan produces the scissors in batches. On the average, Jan can produce

150 scissors per day, and during the production process, demand for scissors has been about 40 scissors per day. The cost to set up the production process is $100, and it costs Jan 30 cents to carry one pair of scissors for one year. How many scissors should Jan produce in each batch?

6-35 Jim Overstreet, inventory control manager for Itex, receives wheel bearings from Wheel-Rite, a small producer of metal parts. Unfortunately, Wheel-Rite can only produce 500 wheel bearings per day. Itex receives 10,000 wheel bearings from Wheel-Rite each year. Since Itex operates 200 working days each year, its average daily demand for wheel bearings is 50. The ordering cost for Itex is $40 per order, and the carrying cost is 60 cents per wheel bearing per year. How many wheel bearings should Itex order from Wheel-Rite at one time? Wheel-Rite has agreed to ship the maximum number of wheel bearings that it produces each day to Itex when an order has been received.

6-36 North Manufacturing has a demand for 1,000 pumps each year. The cost of a pump is $50. It costs North Manufacturing $40 to place an order, and the carrying cost is 25% of the unit cost. If pumps are ordered in quantities of 200, North Manufacturing can get a 3% discount on the cost of the pumps. Should North Manufacturing order 200 pumps at a time and take the 3% discount?

6-37 Linda Lechner is in charge of maintaining hospital supplies at General Hospital. During the past year, the mean lead time demand for bandage BX-5 was 60. Furthermore, the standard deviation for BX-5 was 7. Linda would like to maintain a 90% service level. What safety stock level do you recommend for BX-5?

6-38 Linda Lechner has just been severely chastised for her inventory policy. (See Problem 6-37.) Sue Surrowski, her boss, believes that the service level should be either 95% or 98%. Compute the safety stock levels for a 95% and a 98% service level. Linda knows that the carrying cost of BX-5 is 50 cents per unit per year. Compute the carrying cost that is associated with a 90%, a 95%, and a 98% service level.

6-39 Ralph Janaro simply does not have time to analyze all of the items in his company's inventory. As a young manager, he has more important things to do. The following is a table of six items in inventory along with the unit cost and the demand in units.

(a) Find the total amount spent on each item during the year. What is the total investment for all of these?

(b) Find the percentage of the total investment in inventory that is spent on each item.

IDENTIFICATION CODE	UNIT COST ($)	DEMAND IN UNITS
XX1	5.84	1,200
B66	5.40	1,110
3CPO	1.12	896
33CP	74.54	1,104
R2D2	2.00	1,110
RMS	2.08	961

(c) Based on the percentages in part (b), which item(s) would be classified in categories A, B, and C using ABC analysis?

(d) Which item(s) should Ralph most carefully control using quantitative techniques?

6-40 Thaarugo, Inc., produces a GPS device that is becoming popular in parts of Scandinavia. When Thaarugo produces one of these, a printed circuit board (PCB) is used, and it is populated with several electronic components. Thaarugo determines that it needs about 16,000 of this type of PCB each year. Demand is relatively constant throughout the year, and the ordering cost is about $25 per order; the holding cost is 20% of the price of each PCB. Two companies are competing to become the dominant supplier of the PCBs, and both have now offered discounts, as shown in the following table. Which of the two suppliers should be selected if Thaarugo wishes to minimize total annual inventory cost? What would be the annual inventory cost?

SUPPLIER A		SUPPLIER B	
QUANTITY	PRICE	QUANTITY	PRICE
1–199	38.40	1–299	39.50
200–499	35.80	300–999	35.40
500 or more	34.70	1000 or more	34.60

6-41 Dillard Travey receives 5,000 tripods annually from Quality Suppliers to meet his annual demand. Dillard runs a large photographic outlet, and the tripods are used primarily with 35-mm cameras. The ordering cost is $15 per order, and the carrying cost is 50 cents per unit per year. Quality is starting a new option for its customers. When an order is placed, Quality will ship one-third of the order every week for three weeks instead of shipping the entire order at one time. Weekly demand over the lead time is 100 tripods.

(a) What is the order quantity if Dillard has the entire order shipped at one time?

(b) What is the order quantity if Dillard has the order shipped over three weeks using the new option from Quality Suppliers, Inc.? To simplify your calculations, assume that the average inventory is equal to one-half of the maximum inventory level for Quality's new option.

(c) Calculate the total cost for each option. What do you recommend?

6-42 Quality Suppliers, Inc., has decided to extend its shipping option. (Refer to Problem 6-41 for details.) Now, Quality Suppliers is offering to ship the amount ordered in five equal shipments, one each week. It will take five weeks for this entire order to be received. What are the order quantity and total cost for this new shipping option?

6-43 The Hardware Warehouse is evaluating the safety stock policy for all its items, as identified by the SKU code. For SKU M4389, the company always orders 80 units each time an order is placed. The daily demand is constant, at 5 units per day; the lead time is normally distributed, with a mean of 3 days and a standard deviation of 2. Holding cost is $3 per unit per year. A 95% service level is to be maintained.

(a) What is the standard deviation of demand during the lead time?

(b) How much safety stock should be carried, and what should be the reorder point?

(c) What is the total annual holding cost?

6-44 For SKU A3510 at the Hardware Warehouse, the order quantity has been set at 150 units each time an order is placed. The daily demand is normally distributed, with a mean of 12 units and a standard deviation of 4. It always takes exactly 5 days for an order of this item to arrive. Holding cost has been determined to be $10 per unit per year. Due to the large volume of this item sold, management wants to maintain a 99% service level.

(a) What is the standard deviation of demand during the lead time?

(b) How much safety stock should be carried, and what should be the reorder point?

(c) What is the total annual holding cost?

6-45 H & K Electronic Warehouse sells a 12-pack of AAA batteries, and this is a very popular item. Demand for this is normally distributed, with an average of 50 packs per day and a standard deviation of 16. The average delivery time is 5 days, with a standard deviation of 2 days. Delivery time has been found to be normally distributed. A 96% service level is desired.

(a) What is the standard deviation of demand during the lead time?

(b) How much safety stock should be carried, and what should be the reorder point?

6-46 Xemex has collected the following inventory data for the six items that it stocks:

ITEM CODE	UNIT COST ($)	ANNUAL DEMAND (UNITS)	ORDERING COST ($)	CARRYING COST AS A PERCENTAGE OF UNIT COST
1	10.60	600	40	20
2	11.00	450	30	25
3	2.25	500	50	15
4	150.00	560	40	15
5	4.00	540	35	16
6	4.10	490	40	17

Lynn Robinson, Xemex's inventory manager, does not feel that all of the items can be controlled. What ordered quantities do you recommend for which inventory product(s)?

6-47 Georgia Products offers the following discount schedule for its 4- by 8-foot sheets of good-quality plywood:

ORDER	UNIT COST ($)
9 sheets or less	18.00
10 to 50 sheets	17.50
More than 50 sheets	17.25

Home Sweet Home Company orders plywood from Georgia Products. Home Sweet Home has an ordering cost of $45. The carrying cost is 20%, and the annual demand is 100 sheets. What do you recommend?

6-48 Sunbright Citrus Products produces orange juice, grapefruit juice, and other citrus-related items. Sunbright obtains fruit concentrate from a cooperative in Orlando consisting of approximately 50 citrus growers. The cooperative will sell a minimum of 100 cans of fruit concentrate to citrus processors such as Sunbright. The cost per can is $9.90.

Last year, the cooperative developed the Incentive Bonus Program to give an incentive to their large customers to buy in quantity. It works like this: If 200 cans of concentrate are purchased, 10 cans of free concentrate are included in the deal. In addition, the names of the companies purchasing the concentrate are added to a drawing for a new personal computer. The personal computer has a value of about $3,000, and currently about 1,000 companies are eligible for this drawing. At 300 cans of concentrate, the cooperative will give away 30 free cans and will also place the company name in the drawing for the personal computer. When the quantity goes up to 400 cans of concentrate, 40 cans of concentrate will be given away free with the order. In addition, the company is also placed in a drawing for the personal computer and a free trip for two. The value of the trip for two is approximately $5,000. About 800 companies are expected to qualify and to be in the running for this trip.

Sunbright estimates that its annual demand for fruit concentrate is 1,000 cans. In addition, the ordering cost is estimated to be $10, while the carrying cost is estimated to be 10%, or about $1 per unit. The firm is intrigued with the incentive bonus plan. If the company decides that it will keep the free cans, the trip, or the computer if they are won, what should it do?

6-49 John Lindsay sells CDs that contain 25 software packages that perform a variety of financial functions, including net present value, internal rate of return, and other financial programs typically used by business students majoring in finance. Depending on the quantity ordered, John offers the following price discounts. The annual demand is 2,000 units on average. His setup cost to produce the CDs is $250. He estimates holding costs to be 10% of the price, or about $1 per unit per year.

PRICE RANGES	QUANTITY ORDERED		
	FROM	TO	PRICE
	1	500	$10.00
	501	1,000	9.95
	1,001	1,500	9.90
	1,500	2,000	9.85

(a) What is the optimal number of CDs to produce at a time?
(b) What is the impact of the following quantity price schedule on the optimal order quantity?

PRICE RANGES	QUANTITY ORDERED		
	FROM	TO	PRICE
	1	500	$10.00
	501	1,000	9.99
	1,001	1,500	9.98
	1,500	2,000	9.97

6-50 Teresa Granger is the manager of Chicago Cheese, which produces cheese spreads and other cheese-related products. E-Z Spread Cheese is a product that has always been popular. The probability of sales, in cases, is as follows:

DEMAND (CASES)	PROBABILITY
10	0.2
11	0.3
12	0.2
13	0.2
14	0.1

A case of E-Z Spread Cheese sells for $100 and has a cost of $75. Any cheese that is not sold by the end of the week is sold to a local food processor for $50. Teresa never sells cheese that is more than a week old. Use marginal analysis to determine how many cases of E-Z Spread Cheese to produce each week to maximize average profit.

6-51 Harry's Hardware does a brisk business during the year. During Christmas, Harry's Hardware sells Christmas trees for a substantial profit. Unfortunately, any trees not sold at the end of the season are totally worthless. Thus, the number of trees that are stocked for a given season is a very important decision. The following table reveals the demand for Christmas trees:

DEMAND FOR CHRISTMAS TREES	PROBABILITY
50	0.05
75	0.1
100	0.2
125	0.3
150	0.2
175	0.1
200	0.05

Harry sells trees for $80 each, but his cost is only $20.

(a) Use marginal analysis to determine how many trees Harry should stock at his hardware store.

(b) If the cost increased to $35 per tree and Harry continues to sell trees for $80 each, how many trees should Harry stock?

(c) Harry is thinking about increasing the price to $100 per tree. Assume that the cost per tree is $20. With the new price, it is expected that the probability of selling 50, 75, 100, or 125 trees will be 0.25 each. Harry does not expect to sell more than 125 trees with this price increase. What do you recommend?

6-52 In addition to selling Christmas trees during the Christmas holidays, Harry's Hardware sells all the ordinary hardware items (see Problem 6-51). One of the most popular items is Great Glue HH, a glue that is made just for Harry's Hardware. The selling price is $4 per bottle, but unfortunately, the glue gets hard and unusable after one month. The cost of the glue is $1.20. During the past several months, the mean sales of glue have been 60 units, and the standard deviation is 7. How many bottles of glue should Harry's Hardware stock? Assume that sales follow a normal distribution.

6-53 The marginal loss on Washington Reds, a brand of apples from the state of Washington, is $35 per case.

The marginal profit is $15 per case. During the past year, the mean sales of Washington Reds in cases was 45,000 cases, and the standard deviation was 4,450. How many cases of Washington Reds should be brought to market? Assume that sales follow a normal distribution.

6-54 Linda Stanyon has been the production manager for Plano Produce for over eight years. Plano Produce is a small company located near Plano, Illinois. One produce item, tomatoes, is sold in cases, with daily sales averaging 400 cases. Daily sales are assumed to be normally distributed. In addition, 85% of the time the sales are between 350 and 450 cases. Each case costs $10 and sells for $15. All cases that are not sold must be discarded.

(a) Using the information provided, estimate the standard deviation of sales.

(b) Using the standard deviation in part (a), determine how many cases of tomatoes Linda should stock.

6-55 Paula Shoemaker produces a weekly stock market report for an exclusive readership. She normally sells 3,000 reports per week, and 70% of the time her sales range from 2,900 to 3,100. The report costs Paula $15 to produce, but Paula is able to sell reports for $350 each. Of course, any reports not sold by the end of the week have no value. How many reports should Paula produce each week?

6-56 Emarpy Appliance produces all kinds of major appliances. Richard Feehan, the president of Emarpy, is concerned about the production policy for the company's best selling refrigerator. The demand for this has been relatively constant at about 8,000 units each year. The production capacity for this product is 200 units per day. Each time production starts, it costs the company $120 to move materials into place, reset the assembly line, and clean the equipment. The holding cost of a refrigerator is $50 per year. The current production plan calls for 400 refrigerators to be produced in each production run. Assume there are 250 working days per year.

(a) What is the daily demand of this product?

(b) If the company were to continue to produce 400 units each time production starts, how many days would production continue?

(c) Under the current policy, how many production runs per year would be required? What would the annual setup cost be?

(d) If the current policy continues, how many refrigerators would be in inventory when production stops? What would the average inventory level be?

(e) If the company produces 400 refrigerators at a time, what would the total annual setup cost and holding cost be?

6-57 Consider the Emarpy Appliance situation in Problem 6-56. If Richard Feehan wants to minimize the total annual inventory cost, how many refrigerators should be produced in each production run? How much would this save the company in inventory costs compared with the current policy of producing 400 in each production run?

6-58 This chapter presents a material structure tree for item A in Figure 6.12. Assume that it now takes 1 unit of item B to make every unit of item A. What impact does this have on the material structure tree and the number of items of D and E that are needed?

6-59 Given the information in Problem 6-58, develop a gross material requirements plan for 50 units of item A.

6-60 Using the data from Figures 6.12–6.14, develop a net material requirements plan for 50 units of item A assuming that it only takes 1 unit of item B for each unit of item A.

6-61 The demand for product S is 100 units. Each unit of S requires 1 unit of T and 0.5 ounce of U. Each unit of T requires 1 unit of V, 2 units of W, and 1 unit of X. Finally, each unit of U requires 0.5 ounce of Y and 3 units of Z. All items are manufactured by the same firm. It takes two weeks to make S, one week to make T, two weeks to make U, two weeks to make V, three weeks to make W, one week to make X, two weeks to make Y, and one week to make Z.

(a) Construct a material structure tree and a gross material requirements plan for the dependent inventory items.

(b) Identify all levels, parents, and components.

(c) Construct a net material requirements plan using the following on-hand inventory data:

ITEM	S	T	U	V	W	X	Y	Z
On-Hand Inventory	20	20	10	30	30	25	15	10

6-62 The Webster Manufacturing Company produces a popular type of serving cart. This product, the SL72, is made from the following parts: 1 unit of Part A, 1 unit of Part B, and 1 unit of Subassembly C. Each subassembly C is made up of 2 units of Part D, 4 units of Part E, and 2 units of Part F. Develop a material structure tree for this.

6-63 Blair H. Dodds, III, runs a medium-to-large-sized home eBay business dealing in vintage photographs. The annual demand for his photos is approximately 50,000. The annual overhead cost (excluding the purchase price) to buy the photographs is $4,000 per year. Given that this cost represents the optimal annual ordering cost and the optimal ordering quantity is 400 photographs at a time determine the ordering cost and the average inventory level.

6-64 The lead time for each of the parts in the SL72 (Problem 6-62) is one week, except for Part B, which has a lead time of two weeks. Develop a net materials requirements plan for an order of 800 SL72s. Assume that currently there are no parts in inventory.

6-65 Refer to Problem 6-64. Develop a net material requirements plan assuming that there are currently 150 units of Part A, 40 units of Part B, 50 units of Subassembly C, and 100 units of Part F currently in inventory.

Internet Homework Problems

See our Internet home page, at www.pearsonhighered.com/render, for additional homework problems, Problems 6-66 to 6-73.

Case Study

Martin-Pullin Bicycle Corporation

Martin-Pullin Bicycle Corp. (MPBC), located in Dallas, is a wholesale distributor of bicycles and bicycle parts. Formed in 1981 by cousins Ray Martin and Jim Pullin, the firm's primary retail outlets are located within a 400-mile radius of the distribution center. These retail outlets receive the order from Martin-Pullin within two days after notifying the distribution center, provided that the stock is available. However, if an order is not fulfilled by the company, no backorder is placed; the retailers arrange to get their shipment from other distributors, and MPBC loses that amount of business.

Demands for AirWing Model

MONTH	2009	2010	FORECAST FOR 2011
January	6	7	8
February	12	14	15
March	24	27	31
April	46	53	59
May	75	86	97
June	47	54	60
July	30	34	39
August	18	21	24
September	13	15	16
October	12	13	15
November	22	25	28
December	38	42	47
Total	343	391	439

The company distributes a wide variety of bicycles. The most popular model, and the major source of revenue to the company, is the AirWing. MPBC receives all the models from a single manufacturer overseas, and shipment takes as long as four weeks from the time an order is placed. With the cost of communication, paperwork, and customs clearance included, MPBC estimates that each time an order is placed, it incurs a cost of $65. The purchase price paid by MPBC, per bicycle, is roughly 60% of the suggested retail price for all the styles available, and the inventory carrying cost is 1% per month (12% per year) of the purchase price paid by MPBC. The retail price (paid by the customers) for the AirWing is $170 per bicycle.

MPBC is interested in making an inventory plan for 2011. The firm wants to maintain a 95% service level with its customers to minimize the losses on the lost orders. The data collected for the past two years are summarized in the following table. A forecast for AirWing model sales in the upcoming year 2011 has been developed and will be used to make an inventory plan for MPBC.

Discussion Questions

1. Develop an inventory plan to help MPBC.
2. Discuss ROPs and total costs.
3. How can you address demand that is not at the level of the planning horizon?

Source: Professor Kala Chand Seal, Loyola Marymount University.

Internet Case Studies

See our Internet home page, at **www.pearsonhighered.com/render**, for these additional case studies:

(1) **LaPlace Power and Light:** This case involves a public utility in Louisiana and its use of electric cables for connecting houses to power lines.

(2) **Western Ranchman Outfitters:** This case involves managing the inventory of a popular style of jeans when the delivery date is sometimes unpredictable.

(3) **Professional Video Management:** This case involves a videotape system in which discounts from suppliers are possible.

(4) **Drake Radio:** This case involves ordering FM tuners.

Bibliography

Anderson, Eric T., Gavan J. Fitzsimons, and Duncan Simester. "Measuring and Mitigating the Costs of Stockouts," *Management Science* 52, 11 (November 2006): 1751–1763.

Bradley, James R., and Richard W. Conway. "Managing Cyclic Inventories," *Production and Operations Management* 12, 4 (Winter 2003): 464–479.

Chan, Lap Mui Ann, David Simchi-Levi, and Julie Swann. "Pricing, Production, and Inventory Policies for Manufacturing with Stochastic Demand and Discretionary Sales," *Manufacturing & Service Operations Management* 8, 2 (Spring 2006): 149–168.

Chickering, David Maxwell, and David Heckerman. "Targeted Advertising on the Web with Inventory Management," *Interfaces* 33, 5 (September–October 2003): 71–77.

Chopra, Sunil, Gilles Reinhardt, and Maqbool Dada. "The Effect of Lead Time Uncertainty on Safety Stocks," *Decision Sciences* 35, 1 (Winter 2004): 1–24.

Desai, Preyas S., and Oded Koenigsberg. "The Role of Production Lead Time and Demand Uncertainty in Marketing Durable Goods," *Management Science* 53, 1 (January 2007): 150–158.

Jayaraman, Vaidyanathan, Cindy Burnett, and Derek Frank. "Separating Inventory Flows in the Materials Management Department of Hancock Medical Center," *Interfaces* 30, 4 (July–August 2000): 56–64.

Kapuscinski, Roman, Rachel Q. Zhang, Paul Carbonneau, Robert Moore, and Bill Reeves. "Inventory Decisions in Dell's Supply Chain," *Interfaces* 34, 3 (May–June 2004): 191–205.

Karabakal, Nejat, Ali Gunal, and Warren Witchie. "Supply-Chain Analysis at Volkswagen of America," *Interfaces* 30, 4 (July–August, 2000): 46–55.

Kök, A. Gürhan, and Kevin H. Shang. "Inspection and Replenishment Policies for Systems with Inventory Record Inaccuracy," *Manufacturing & Service Operations Management* 9, 2 (Spring 2007): 185–205.

Ramasesh, Ranga V. and Ram Rachmadugu. "Lot-Sizing Decision Under Limited-Time Price Reduction," *Decision Sciences* 32, 1 (Winter 2001): 125–143.

Ramdas, Kamalini and Robert E. Spekman. "Chain or Shackles: Understanding What Drives Supply-Chain Performance," *Interfaces* 30, 4 (July– August 2000): 3–21.

Rubin, Paul A., and W. C. Benton. "A Generalized Framework for Quantity Discount Pricing Schedules," *Decision Sciences* 34, 1 (Winter 2003): 173–188.

Shin, Hojung, and W. C. Benton. "Quantity Discount-Based Inventory Coordination: Effectiveness and Critical Environmental Factors," *Production and Operations Management* 13, 1 (Spring 2004): 63–76.

Appendix 6.1: Inventory Control with QM for Windows

A variety of inventory control models are covered in this chapter. Each model makes different assumptions and uses slightly different approaches. The use of QM for Windows is similar for these different types of inventory problems. As you can see in the inventory menu for QM for Windows, most of the inventory problems discussed in this chapter can be solved using your computer.

To demonstrate QM for Windows, we start with the basic EOQ model. Sumco, a manufacturing company discussed in the chapter, has an annual demand of 1,000 units, an ordering cost of $10 per unit, and a carrying cost of $0.50 per unit per year. With these data, we can use QM for Windows to determine the economic order quantity. The results are shown in Program 6.5.

The production run inventory problem, which requires the daily production and demand rate in addition to the annual demand, the ordering cost per order, and the carrying cost per unit per year, is also covered in this chapter. The Brown Manufacturing example is used in this chapter to show how the calculations can be made manually. We can use QM for Windows on these data. Program 6.6 shows the results.

PROGRAM 6.5

QM for Windows Results for EOQ Model

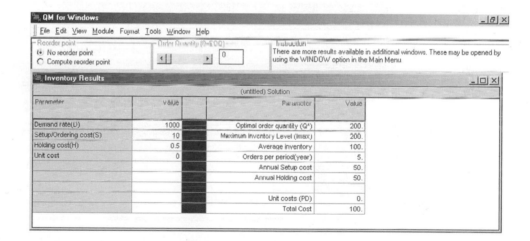

PROGRAM 6.6

QM for Windows Results for the Production Run Model

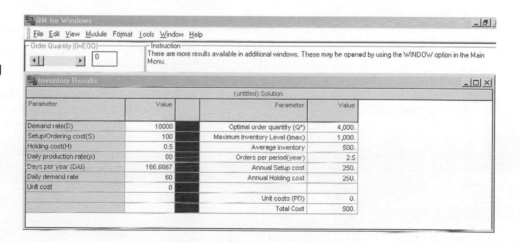

The quantity discount model allows the material cost to vary with the quantity ordered. In this case the model must consider and minimize material, ordering, and carrying costs by examining each price discount. Program 6.7 shows how QM for Windows can be used to solve the quantity discount model discussed in the chapter. Note that the program output shows the input data in addition to the results.

PROGRAM 6.7

QM for Windows Results for the Quantity Discount Model

When an organization has a large number of inventory items, ABC analysis is often used. As discussed in this chapter, total dollar volume for an inventory item is one way to determine if quantitative control techniques should be used. Performing the necessary calculations is done in Program 6.8, which shows how QM for Windows can be used to compute dollar volume and determine if quantitative control techniques are justified for each inventory item with this new example.

PROGRAM 6.8

QM for Windows Results for ABC Analysis

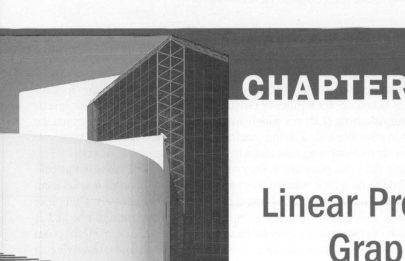

CHAPTER 7

Linear Programming Models: Graphical and Computer Methods

Summary • Glossary • Solved Problems • Self-Test • Discussion Questions and Problems • Internet Homework Problems • Case Study: Mexicana Wire Works • Internet Case Study • Bibliography

7.1   Introduction

Linear programming is a technique that helps in resource allocation decisions.

Many management decisions involve trying to make the most effective use of an organization's resources. Resources typically include machinery, labor, money, time, warehouse space, and raw materials. These resources may be used to make products (such as machinery, furniture, food, or clothing) or services (such as schedules for airlines or production, advertising policies, or investment decisions). **Linear programming (LP)** is a widely used mathematical modeling technique designed to help managers in planning and decision making relative to resource allocation. We devote this and the next chapter to illustrating how and why linear programming works.

Despite its name, LP and the more general category of techniques called **"mathematical" programming** have very little to do with computer programming. In the world of management science, *programming* refers to modeling and solving a problem mathematically. Computer programming has, of course, played an important role in the advancement and use of LP. Real-life LP problems are too cumbersome to solve by hand or with a calculator. So throughout the chapters on LP we give examples of how valuable a computer program can be in solving an LP problem.

7.2   Requirements of a Linear Programming Problem

In the past 60 years, LP has been applied extensively to military, industrial, financial, marketing, accounting, and agricultural problems. Even though these applications are diverse, all LP problems have several properties and assumptions in common.

Problems seek to maximize or minimize an objective.

All problems seek to *maximize* or *minimize* some quantity, usually profit or cost. We refer to this property as the **objective function** of an LP problem. The major objective of a typical manufacturer is to maximize dollar profits. In the case of a trucking or railroad distribution system, the objective might be to minimize shipping costs. In any event, this objective must be stated clearly and defined mathematically. It does not matter, by the way, whether profits and costs are measured in cents, dollars, or millions of dollars.

Constraints limit the degree to which the objective can be obtained.

The second property that LP problems have in common is the presence of restrictions, or **constraints**, that limit the degree to which we can pursue our objective. For example, deciding how many units of each product in a firm's product line to manufacture is restricted by available personnel and machinery. Selection of an advertising policy or a financial portfolio is limited by the amount of money available to be spent or invested. We want, therefore, to maximize or minimize a quantity (the objective function) subject to limited resources (the constraints).

There must be alternatives available.

There must be alternative courses of action to choose from. For example, if a company produces three different products, management may use LP to decide how to allocate among them its limited production resources (of personnel, machinery, and so on). Should it devote all manufacturing capacity to make only the first product, should it produce equal amounts of each product, or should it allocate the resources in some other ratio? If there were no alternatives to select from, we would not need LP.

Mathematical relationships are linear.

The objective and constraints in LP problems must be expressed in terms of *linear* equations or inequalities. Linear mathematical relationships just mean that all terms used in the objective function and constraints are of the first degree (i.e., not squared, or to the third or higher power, or appearing more than once). Hence, the equation $2A + 5B = 10$ is an acceptable linear function, while the equation $2A^2 + 5B^3 + 3AB = 10$ is not linear because the variable A is squared, the variable B is cubed, and the two variables appear again as a product of each other.

The term *linear* implies both proportionality and additivity. Proportionality means that if production of 1 unit of a product uses 3 hours, production of 10 units would use 30 hours. Additivity means that the total of all activities equals the sum of the individual activities. If the production of one product generated $3 profit and the production of another product generated $8 profit, the total profit would be the sum of these two, which would be $11.

We assume that conditions of *certainty* exist: that is, number in the objective and constraints are known with certainty and do not change during the period being studied.

We make the *divisibility* assumption that solutions need not be in whole numbers (integers). Instead, they are divisible and may take any fractional value. In production problems, we often define variables as the number of units produced per week or per month, and a fractional value

TABLE 7.1

LP Properties and Assumptions

PROPERTIES OF LINEAR PROGRAMS
1. One objective function
2. One or more constraints
3. Alternative courses of action
4. Objective function and constraints are linear—proportionality and divisibility
5. Certainty
6. Divisibility
7. Nonnegative variables

(e.g., 0.3 chair) would simply mean that there is work in process. Something that was started in one week can be finished in the next. However, in other types of problems, fractional values do not make sense. If a fraction of a product cannot be purchased (for example, one-third of a submarine), an integer programming problem exists. Integer programming is discussed in more detail in Chapter 10.

Finally, we assume that all answers or variables are *nonnegative*. Negative values of physical quantities are impossible; you simply cannot produce a negative number of chairs, shirts, lamps, or computers. However, there are some variables that can have negative values, such as profit, where a negative value indicates a loss. A simple mathematical operation can transform such a variable into two nonnegative variables, and that process can be found in books on linear programming. However, when working with linear programming in this book, we will only work with nonnegative variables. Table 7.1 summarizes these properties and assumptions.

7.3 Formulating LP Problems

Formulating a linear program involves developing a mathematical model to represent the managerial problem. Thus, in order to formulate a linear program, it is necessary to completely understand the managerial problem being faced. Once this is understood, we can begin to develop the mathematical statement of the problem. The steps in formulating a linear program follow:

1. Completely understand the managerial problem being faced
2. Identify the objective and the constraints.
3. Define the decision variables.
4. Use the decision variables to write mathematical expressions for the objective function and the constraints.

Product mix problems use LP to decide how much of each product to make, given a series of resource restrictions.

One of the most common LP applications is the **product mix problem**. Two or more products are usually produced using limited resources such as personnel, machines, raw materials, and so on. The profit that the firm seeks to maximize is based on the profit contribution per unit of each product. (Profit contribution, you may recall, is just the selling price per unit minus the variable cost per unit.[*]) The company would like to determine how many units of each product it should produce so as to maximize overall profit given its limited resources. A problem of this type is formulated in the following example.

Flair Furniture Company

The Flair Furniture Company produces inexpensive tables and chairs. The production process for each is similar in that both require a certain number of hours of carpentry work and a certain number of labor hours in the painting and varnishing department. Each table takes 4 hours of carpentry and 2 hours in the painting and varnishing shop. Each chair requires 3 hours in carpentry and 1 hour in painting and varnishing. During the current production period, 240 hours of carpentry time are available and 100 hours in painting and varnishing time are available. Each table sold yields a profit of $70; each chair produced is sold for a $50 profit.

---

[*]Technically, we maximize total contribution margin, which is the difference between unit selling price and costs that vary in proportion to the quantity of the item produced. Depreciation, fixed general expense, and advertising are excluded from calculations.

HISTORY The Beginning of Linear Programming

Prior to 1945, some conceptual problems regarding the allocation of scarce resources had been suggested by economists and others. Two of these people, Leonid Kantorovich and Tjalling Koopmans, shared the 1975 Nobel Prize in Economics for advancing the concepts of optimal planning in their work that began during the 1940s. In 1945, George Stigler proposed the "diet problem" which is now the name given to a major category of linear programming applications. However, Stigler relied on heuristic techniques to find a good solution to this problem as there was no method available to find the optimal solution.

Major progress in the field, however, took place in 1947 when George D. Dantzig, often called the "Father of Linear Programming," published his work on the solution procedure known as the simplex algorithm. Dantzig had been an Air Force

mathematician during World War II and was assigned to work on logistics problems. He saw that many problems involving limited resources and more than one demand could be set up in terms of a series of equations and inequalities, and he subsequently developed the simplex algorithm for solving these problems.

Although early applications of linear programming were military in nature, industrial applications rapidly became apparent with the widespread use of business computers. As problems became larger, research continued to find even better ways to solve linear programs. The work of Leonid Kachiyan in 1979 and Narendra Karmarkar in 1984 spurred others to study the use of interior point methods for solving linear programs, some of which are used today. However, the simplex algorithm developed by Dantzig is still the basis for much of the software used for solving linear programs today.

Flair Furniture's problem is to determine the best possible combination of tables and chairs to manufacture in order to reach the maximum profit. The firm would like this production mix situation formulated as an LP problem.

We begin by summarizing the information needed to formulate and solve this problem (see Table 7.2). This helps us understand the problem being faced. Next we identify the objective and the constraints. The objective is

Maximize profit

The constraints are

1. The hours of carpentry time used cannot exceed 240 hours per week.
2. The hours of painting and varnishing time used cannot exceed 100 hours per week.

The **decision variables** that represent the actual decisions we will make are defined as

$$T = \text{number of tables to be produced per week}$$
$$C = \text{number of chairs to be produced per week}$$

Now we can create the LP objective function in terms of T and C. The objective function is Maximize profit = $70T + \$50C$.

Our next step is to develop mathematical relationships to describe the two constraints in this problem. One general relationship is that the amount of a resource used is to be less than or equal to ($\leq$) the amount of resource *available*.

In the case of the carpentry department, the total time used is

$$(4 \text{ hours per table})(\text{Number of tables produced})$$
$$+ (3 \text{ hours per chair})(\text{Number of chairs produced})$$

TABLE 7.2

Flair Furniture Company Data

	HOURS REQUIRED TO PRODUCE 1 UNIT		
DEPARTMENT	(T) TABLES	(C) CHAIRS	AVAILABLE HOURS THIS WEEK
Carpentry	4	3	240
Painting and varnishing	2	1	100
Profit per unit	$70	$50	

The resource constraints put limits on the carpentry labor resource and the painting labor resource mathematically.

So the first constraint may be stated as follows:

$$\text{Carpentry time used} \leq \text{Carpentry time available}$$

$$4T + 3C \leq 240 \text{ (hours of carpentry time)}$$

Similarly, the second constraint is as follows:

$$\text{Painting and varnishing time used} \leq \text{Painting and varnishing time available}$$

$$\fbox{$②$}T + 1C \leq 100 \text{ (hours of painting and varnishing time)}$$

(This means that each table produced takes two hours of the painting and varnishing resource.)

Both of these constraints represent production capacity restrictions and, of course, affect the total profit. For example, Flair Furniture cannot produce 80 tables during the production period because if $T = 80$, both constraints will be violated. It also cannot make $T = 50$ tables and $C = 10$ chairs. Why? Because this would violate the second constraint that no more than 100 hours of painting and varnishing time be allocated.

To obtain meaningful solutions, the values for T and C must be nonnegative numbers. That is, all potential solutions must represent real tables and real chairs. Mathematically, this means that

$$T \geq 0 \text{ (number of tables produced is greater than or equal to 0)}$$

$$C \geq 0 \text{ (number of chairs produced is greater than or equal to 0)}$$

Here is a complete mathematical statement of the LP problem.

The complete problem may now be restated mathematically as

$$\text{Maximize profit} = \$70T + \$50C$$

subject to the constraints

$$4T + 3C \leq 240 \quad \text{(carpentry constraint)}$$
$$2T + 1C \leq 100 \quad \text{(painting and varnishing constraint)}$$
$$T \geq 0 \quad \text{(first nonnegativity constraint)}$$
$$C \geq 0 \quad \text{(second nonnegativity constraint)}$$

While the nonnegativity constraints are technically separate constraints, they are often written on a single line with the variables separated by commas. In this example, this would be written as

$$T, C \geq 0$$

7.4   Graphical Solution to an LP Problem

The graphical method works only when there are two decision variables, but it provides valuable insight into how larger problems are structured.

The easiest way to solve a small LP problem such as that of the Flair Furniture Company is with the graphical solution approach. The graphical procedure is useful only when there are two decision variables (such as number of tables to produce, T, and number of chairs to produce, C) in the problem. When there are more than two variables, it is not possible to plot the solution on a two-dimensional graph and we must turn to more complex approaches. But the graphical method is invaluable in providing us with insights into how other approaches work. For that reason alone, it is worthwhile to spend the rest of this chapter exploring graphical solutions as an intuitive basis for the chapters on mathematical programming that follow.

Graphical Representation of Constraints

To find the optimal solution to an LP problem, we must first identify a set, or region, of feasible solutions. The first step in doing so is to plot each of the problem's constraints on a graph. The variable T (tables) is plotted as the horizontal axis of the graph and the variable C (chairs) is plotted as the vertical axis. The notation (T, C) is used to identify the points on the graph. The

Nonnegativity constraints mean $T \geq 0$ and $C \geq 0$.

nonnegativity constraints mean that we are always working in the first (or northeast) quadrant of a graph (see Figure 7.1).

To represent the first constraint graphically, $4T + 3C \leq 240$, we must first graph the equality portion of this, which is

$$4T + 3C = 240$$

FIGURE 7.1

Quadrant Containing All Positive Values

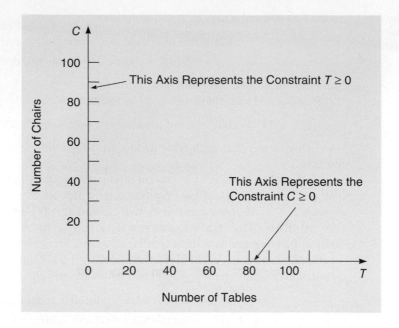

Plotting the first constraint involves finding points at which the line intersects the T *and* C *axes.*

As you may recall from elementary algebra, a linear equation in two variables is a straight line. The easiest way to plot the line is to find any two points that satisfy the equation, then draw a straight line through them.

The two easiest points to find are generally the points at which the line intersects the T and C axes.

When Flair Furniture produces no tables, namely $T = 0$, it implies that

$$4(0) + 3C = 240$$

or

$$3C = 240$$

or

$$C = 80$$

In other words, if *all* of the carpentry time available is used to produce chairs, 80 chairs *could* be made. Thus, this constraint equation crosses the vertical axis at 80.

To find the point at which the line crosses the horizontal axis, we assume that the firm makes no chairs, that is, $C = 0$. Then

$$4T + 3(0) = 240$$

or

$$4T = 240$$

or

$$T = 60$$

Hence, when $C = 0$, we see that $4T = 240$ and that $T = 60$.

The carpentry constraint is illustrated in Figure 7.2. It is bounded by the line running from point $(T = 0, C = 80)$ to point $(T = 60, C = 0)$.

Recall, however, that the actual carpentry constraint was the **inequality** $4T + 3C \leq 240$. How can we identify all of the solution points that satisfy this constraint? It turns out that there are three possibilities. First, we know that any point that lies on the line $4T + 3C = 240$ satisfies the constraint. Any combination of tables and chairs on the line will use up all 240 hours of carpentry time.* Now we must find the set of solution points that would use less than

*Thus, what we have done is to plot the constraint equation in its most binding position, that is, using all of the carpentry resource.

FIGURE 7.2

Graph of Carpentry Constraint Equation 4T + 3C = 240

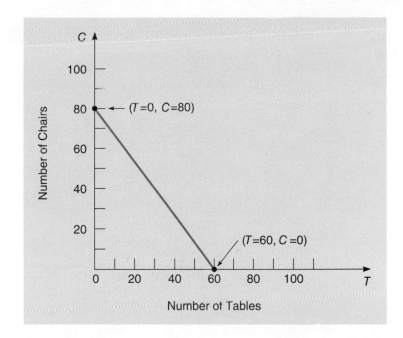

the 240 hours. The points that satisfy the $<$ portion of the constraint (i.e., $4T + 3C < 240$) will be all the points on one side of the line, while all the points on the other side of the line will not satisfy this condition. To determine which side of the line this is, simply choose any point on either side of the constraint line shown in Figure 7.2 and check to see if it satisfies this condition. For example, choose the point (30, 20), as illustrated in Figure 7.3:

$$4(30) + 3(20) - 180$$

Since $180 < 240$, this point satisfies the constraint, and all points on this side of the line will also satisfy the constraint. This set of points is indicated by the shaded region in Figure 7.3.

To see what would happen if the point did not satisfy the constraint, select a point on the other side of the line, such as (70, 40). This constraint would not be met at this point as

$$4(70) + 3(40) = 400$$

Since $400 > 240$, this point and every other point on that side of the line would not satisfy this constraint. Thus, the solution represented by the point (70, 40) would require more than the 240 hours that are available. There are not enough carpentry hours to produce 70 tables and 40 chairs.

FIGURE 7.3

Region That Satisfies the Carpentry Constraint

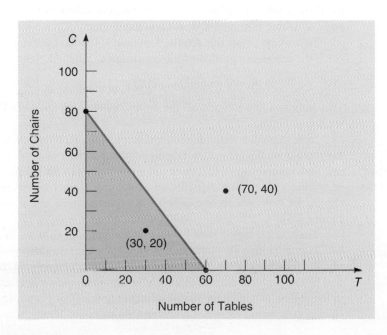

FIGURE 7.4

Region That Satisfies the Painting and Varnishing Constraint

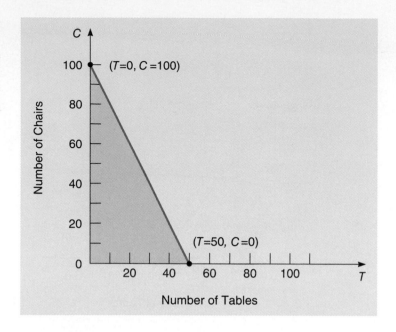

Next, let us identify the solution corresponding to the second constraint, which limits the time available in the painting and varnishing department. That constraint was given as $2T + 1C \leq 100$. As before, we start by graphing the equality portion of this constraint, which is

$$2T + 1C = 100$$

To find two points on the line, select $T = 0$ and solve for C:

$$2(0) + 1C = 100$$
$$C = 100$$

So, one point on the line is $(0, 100)$. To find the second point, select $C = 0$ and solve for T:

$$2T + 1(0) = 100$$
$$T = 50$$

The second point used to graph the line is $(50, 0)$. Plotting this point, $(50, 0)$, and the other point, $(0, 100)$, results in the line representing all the solutions in which exactly 100 hours of painting and varnishing time are used, as shown in Figure 7.4.

To find the points that require less than 100 hours, select a point on either side of this line to see if the inequality portion of the constraint is satisfied. Selecting $(0, 0)$ gives us

$$2(0) + 1(0) = 0 < 100$$

This indicates that this and all the points below the line satisfy the constraint, and this region is shaded in Figure 7.4.

Now that each individual constraint has been plotted on a graph, it is time to move on to the next step. We recognize that to produce a chair or a table, both the carpentry and painting and varnishing departments must be used. In an LP problem we need to find that set of solution points that satisfies all of the constraints *simultaneously*. Hence, the constraints should be redrawn on one graph (or superimposed one upon the other). This is shown in Figure 7.5.

In LP problems we are interested in satisfying all constraints at the same time.

The shaded region now represents the area of solutions that does not exceed either of the two Flair Furniture constraints. It is known by the term *area of feasible solutions* or, more simply, the **feasible region**. The feasible region in an LP problem must satisfy *all* conditions specified by the problem's constraints, and is thus the region where all constraints overlap. Any point in the region would be a **feasible solution** to the Flair Furniture problem; any point outside the shaded area would represent an **infeasible solution**. Hence, it would be feasible to manufacture

The feasible region is the set of points that satisfy all the constraints.

FIGURE 7.5

Feasible Solution Region for the Flair Furniture Company Problem

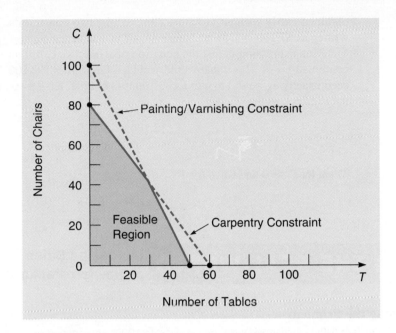

30 tables and 20 chairs ($T = 30, C = 20$) during a production period because both constraints are observed:

Carpentry constraint	$4T + 3C \leq 240$ hours available
	$(4)(30) + (3)(20) = 180$ hours used
Painting constraint	$2T + 1C \leq 100$ hours available
	$(2)(30) + (1)(20) = 80$ hours used

But it would violate both of the constraints to produce 70 tables and 40 chairs, as we see here mathematically:

Carpentry constraint	$4T + 3C \leq 240$ hours available
	$(4)(70) + (3)(40) = 400$ hours used
Painting constraint	$2T + 1C \leq 100$ hours available
	$(2)(70) + (1)(40) = 180$ hours used

Furthermore, it would also be infeasible to manufacture 50 tables and 5 chairs ($T = 50, C = 5$). Can you see why?

Carpentry constraint	$4T + 3C \leq 240$ hours available
	$(4)(50) + (3)(5) = 215$ hours used
Painting constraint	$2T + 1C \leq 100$ hours available
	$(2)(50) + (1)(5) = 105$ hours used

This possible solution falls within the time available in carpentry but exceeds the time available in painting and varnishing and thus falls outside the feasible region.

Isoprofit Line Solution Method

Now that the feasible region has been graphed, we may proceed to find the optimal solution to the problem. The optimal solution is the point lying in the feasible region that produces the highest profit. Yet there are many, many possible solution points in the region. How do we go about selecting the best one, the one yielding the highest profit?

The isoprofit method is the first method we introduce for finding the optimal solution.

There are a few different approaches that can be taken in solving for the optimal solution when the feasible region has been established graphically. The speediest one to apply is called the *isoprofit line method*.

We start the technique by letting profits equal some arbitrary but small dollar amount. For the Flair Furniture problem we may choose a profit of $2,100. This is a profit level that can be obtained easily without violating either of the two constraints. The objective function can be written as $2,100 = 70T + 50C$.

This expression is just the equation of a line; we call it an **isoprofit line**. It represents all combinations of (T, C) that would yield a total profit of $2,100$. To plot the profit line, we proceed exactly as we did to plot a constraint line. First, let $T = 0$ and solve for the point at which the line crosses the C axis:

$$\$2,100 = \$70(0) = \$50C$$

$$C = 42 \text{ chairs}$$

Then, let $C = 0$ and solve for T:

$$\$2,100 = \$70T + 50(0)$$

$$T = 30 \text{ tables}$$

MODELING IN THE REAL WORLD

Increasing Sales at Hewlett Packard

Defining the Problem

Developing a Model

Acquiring Input Data

Developing a Solution

Testing the Solution

Analyzing the Results

Implementing the Results

Defining the Problem

Hewlett Packard (HP) launched HPDirect.com in the late 1990s and opened online sales of HP products including computers, printers, accessories, and supplies. In 2008, the management of HPDirect.com were told that online sales had to grow 150% in the next three years, and this had to be done without exceeding marketing budgets. To do this, they had to attract more visitors to the site, they had to convert the visitors into customers by targeted marketing efforts, and they had to retain loyal customers by providing a satisfying experience in a cost-efficient manner.

Developing a Model

The massive nature of this project required the use of a variety of operations research models to achieve the objectives. Multiple regression was used to identify the key drivers of online visitors, and it was combined with time-series models (which identified seasonality and trend) to forecast the number of visits across all Web pages as well as the sales of the large variety of products. Bayesian models and Markov models were used to help predict the likelihood of a making a purchase. Linear programming was used to determine which marketing channels to use for different customers and to optimize these decisions.

Acquiring Input Data

Data was collected over a 2-year period not only on visitors to the website and their behavior, but also on sales and marketing activities over this same 2-year period. The data was separated into two groups: a training set to develop the model and a test set to validate the model.

Developing a Solution

The training set of data was used to develop the models that would be used in this project, including the linear programs to optimally allocate the marketing budget.

Testing the Solution

The data in the test set was then used to validate the models to make sure that the models were working as planned. When the different parts of the project were implemented, a test group of customers received customized marketing material based on their segment profile, while a control group received generic material.

Analyzing the Results

The test group performed better than the control group on all key metrics, including average order size, conversion rate, and total sales per dollar spent on marketing. During one particular period, the conversion rate of the targeted group was 58% higher than for the control group and dollar sales per marketing item up 33%.

Implementing the Results

At the beginning of each quarter, the models are run to help the marketing team plan efforts for that quarter. The models themselves are refreshed every quarter. Since 2009, the models have been credited with increasing incremental revenue by $117 million, increasing order size, and reducing overall inventory cost.

Source: Based on R. Randon et al., "Hewlett Packard: Delivering Profitable Growth for HPDirect.com Using Operations Research," *Interfaces* 43, 1 (January–February 2013): 48–61.

FIGURE 7.6

Profit Line of $2,100 Plotted for the Flair Furniture Company

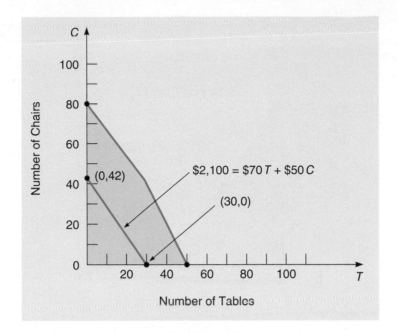

We can now connect these two points with a straight line. This profit line is illustrated in Figure 7.6. All points on the line represent feasible solutions that produce a profit of $2,100.*

Isoprofit involves graphing parallel profit lines.

Now, obviously, the isoprofit line for $2,100 does not produce the highest possible profit to the firm. In Figure 7.7 we try graphing two more lines, each yielding a higher profit. The middle equation, $2,800 = $70T + $50C, was plotted in the same fashion as the lower line. When $T = 0$,

$$\$2,800 = \$70(0) + \$50C$$
$$C = 56$$

When $C = 0$,

$$\$2,800 = \$70T + \$50(C)$$
$$T = 40$$

FIGURE 7.7

Four Isoprofit Lines Plotted for the Flair Furniture Company

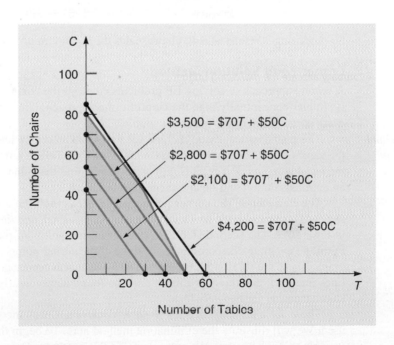

---

*Iso means "equal" or "similar." Thus, an isoprofit line represents a line with all profits the same, in this case $2,100.

FIGURE 7.8

Optimal Solution to the Flair Furniture Problem

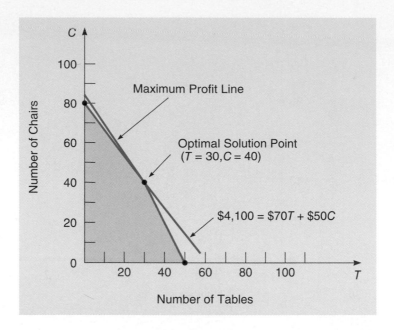

We draw a series of parallel isoprofit lines until we find the highest isoprofit line, that is, the one with the optimal solution.

Again, any combination of tables (T) and chairs (C) on this isoprofit line produces a total profit of $2,800. Note that the third line generates a profit of $3,500, even more of an improvement. The farther we move from the origin, the higher our profit will be. Another important point is that these isoprofit lines are parallel. We now have two clues as to how to find the optimal solution to the original problem. We can draw a series of parallel lines (by carefully moving our ruler in a plane parallel to the first profit line). The highest profit line that still touches some point of the feasible region pinpoints the optimal solution. Notice that the fourth line ($4,200) is too high to be considered.

The last point that an isoprofit line would touch in this feasible region is the corner point where the two constraint lines intersect, so this point will result in the maximum possible profit. To find the coordinates of this point, solve the two equations simultaneously (as detailed in the next section). This results in the point (30, 40) as shown in Figure 7.8. Calculating the profit at this point, we get

$$\text{Profit} = 70T + 50C = 70(30) + 50(40) = \$4,100$$

So producing 30 tables and 40 chairs yields the maximum profit of $4,100.

Corner Point Solution Method

A second approach to solving LP problems employs the **corner point method**. This technique is simpler conceptually than the isoprofit line approach, but it involves looking at the profit at every corner point of the feasible region.

The mathematical theory behind LP is that the optimal solution must lie at one of the corner points in the feasible region.

The mathematical theory behind LP states that an optimal solution to any problem (that is, the values of T, C that yield the maximum profit) will lie at a **corner point**, or **extreme point**, of the feasible region. Hence, it is only necessary to find the values of the variables at each corner; an optimal solution will lie at one (or more) of them.

The first step in the corner point method is to graph the constraints and find the feasible region. This was also the first step in the isoprofit method, and the feasible region is shown again in Figure 7.9. The second step is to find the corner points of the feasible region. For the Flair Furniture example, the coordinates of three of the corner points are obvious from observing the graph. These are (0, 0), (50, 0), and (0, 80). The fourth corner point is where the two constraint lines intersect, and the coordinates must be found algebraically by solving the two equations simultaneously for two variables.

There are a number of ways to solve equations simultaneously, and any of these may be used. We will illustrate the elimination method here. To begin the elimination method, select a variable to be eliminated. We will select T in this example. Then multiply or divide one equation

FIGURE 7.9

Four Corner Points of the Feasible Region

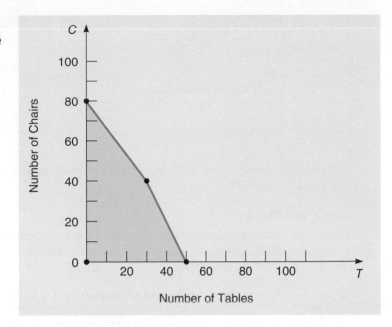

by a number so that the coefficient of that variable (T) in one equation will be the negative of the coefficient of that variable in the other equation. The two constraint equations are

$$4T + 3C = 240 \quad \text{(carpentry)}$$
$$2T + 1C = 100 \quad \text{(painting)}$$

To eliminate T, we multiply the second equation by -2:

$$-2(2T + 1C = 100) = -4T - 2C = -200$$

and then add it to the first equation:

$$+4T + 3C = 240$$
$$+ 1C = 40$$

or

$$C = 40$$

Doing this has enabled us to eliminate one variable, T, and to solve for C. We can now substitute 40 for C in either of the original equations and solve for T. Let's use the first equation. When $C = 40$, then

$$4T + (3)(40) = 240$$
$$4T + 120 = 240$$

or

$$4T = 120$$
$$T = 30$$

Thus, the last corner point is (30, 40).

The next step is to calculate the value of the objective function at each of the corner points. The final step is to select the corner with the best value, which would be the highest profit in this example. Table 7.3 lists these corners points with their profits. The highest profit is found to be $4,100, which is obtained when 30 tables and 40 chairs are produced. This is exactly what was obtained using the isoprofit method.

Table 7.4 provides a summary of both the isoprofit method and the corner point method. Either of these can be used when there are two decision variables. If a problem has more than

TABLE 7.3

Feasible Corner Points and Profits for Flair Furniture

NUMBER OF TABLES (T)	NUMBER OF CHAIRS (C)	Profit $= \$70T + \$50C$
0	0	$0
50	0	$3,500
0	80	$4,000
30	40	$4,100

two decision variables, we must rely on the computer software or use the simplex algorithm discussed in Module 7.

Slack and Surplus

The term slack is associated with ≤ constraints.

In addition to knowing the optimal solution to a linear program, it is helpful to know whether all of the available resources are being used. The term **slack** is used for the amount of a resource that is not used. For a less-than-or-equal to constraint,

$$\text{Slack} = (\text{Amount of resource available}) - (\text{Amount of resource used})$$

In the Flair Furniture example, there were 240 hours of carpentry time available. If the company decided to produce 20 tables and 25 chairs instead of the optimal solution, the amount of carpentry time used ($4T + 3C$) would be $4(20) + 3(25) = 155$. So,

$$\text{Slack time in carpentry} = 240 - 155 = 85$$

For the optimal solution $(30, 40)$ to the Flair Furniture problem, the slack is 0 since all 240 hours are used.

The term surplus is associated with ≥ constraints.

The term **surplus** is used with greater-than-or-equal-to constraints to indicate the amount by which the right-hand side of a constraint is exceeded. For a greater-than-or-equal-to constraint,

$$\text{Surplus} = (\text{Actual amount}) - (\text{Minimum amount})$$

Suppose there had been a constraint in the example that required the total number of tables and chairs combined to be at least 42 units (i.e., $T + C \geq 42$), and the company decided to produce 20 tables and 25 chairs. The total amount produced would be $20 + 25 = 45$, so the surplus would be

$$\text{Surplus} = 45 - 42 = 3$$

meaning that 3 units more than the minimum were produced. For the optimal solution $(30, 40)$ in the Flair Furniture problem, if this constraint had been in the problem, the surplus would be $70 - 42 = 28$.

TABLE 7.4

Summaries of Graphical Solution Methods

ISOPROFIT METHOD
1. Graph all constraints and find the feasible region.
2. Select a specific profit (or cost) line and graph it to find the slope.
3. Move the objective function line in the direction of increasing profit (or decreasing cost) while maintaining the slope. The last point it touches in the feasible region is the optimal solution.
4. Find the values of the decision variables at this last point and compute the profit (or cost).

CORNER POINT METHOD
1. Graph all constraints and find the feasible region.
2. Find the corner points of the feasible region.
3. Compute the profit (or cost) at each of the feasible corner points.
4. Select the corner point with the best value of the objective function found in step 3. This is the optimal solution.

So the slack and surplus represent the difference between the left-hand side (LHS) and the right-hand side (RHS) of a constraint. The term *slack* is used when referring to less-than-or-equal-to constraints, and the term *surplus* is used when referring to greater-than-or-equal-to constraints. Most computer software for linear programming will provide the amount of slack and surplus that exist for each constraint in the optimal solution.

A constraint that has zero slack or surplus for the optimal solution is called a **binding constraint**. A constraint with positive slack or surplus for the optimal solution is called a **nonbinding constraint**. Some computer outputs will specify whether a constraint is binding or nonbinding.

7.5 Solving Flair Furniture's LP Problem Using QM for Windows, Excel 2013, and Excel QM

Almost every organization has access to computer programs that are capable of solving enormous LP problems. Although each computer program is slightly different, the approach each takes toward handling LP problems is basically the same. The format of the input data and the level of detail provided in output results may differ from program to program and computer to computer, but once you are experienced in dealing with computerized LP algorithms, you can easily adjust to minor changes.

Using QM for Windows

Let us begin by demonstrating QM for Windows on the Flair Furniture Company problem. To use QM for Windows, select the Linear Programming module. Then specify the number of constraints (other than the nonnegativity constraints, as it is assumed that the variables must be nonnegative), the number of variables, and whether the objective is to be maximized or minimized. For the Flair Furniture Company problem, there are two constraints and two variables. Once these numbers are specified, the input window opens as shown in Program 7.1A. Then you can enter the coefficients for the objective function and the constraints. Placing the cursor over the X1 or X2 and typing a new name such as *T* and *C* will change the variable names. The constraint names can be similarly modified. Program 7.1B shows the QM for Windows screen after the data has been input and before the problem is solved. When you click the *Solve* button, you get the output shown in Program 7.1C.

PROGRAM 7.1A

QM for Windows Linear Programming Input Screen

The equations will automatically appear as you enter the coefficients in the other columns.

Type over X1 and X2 to change the names of the Variables.

Flair Furniture Company

	X1	X2		RHS	Equation form
Maximize	0	0			Max
Constraint 1	0	0	<=	0	<= 0
Constraint 2	0	0	<=	0	<= 0

Input the coefficients in the appropriate columns.

PROGRAM 7.1B

QM for Windows Data Input for Flair Furniture Problem

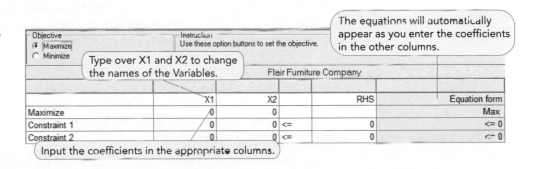

Click here to change the type of constraint.

Click Solve after entering the data.

Flair Furniture Company

	T	C		RHS	Equation form
Maximize	70	50			Max 70T + 50C
Constraint 1	4	3	<=	240	4T + 3C <= 240
Constraint 2	2	1	<=	100	2T + C <= 100

PROGRAM 7.1C

QM for Windows Output and Graph for Flair Furniture Problem

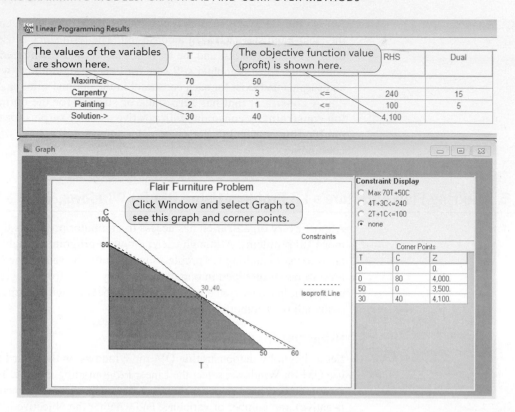

Once the problem has been solved, a graph may be displayed by selecting *Window—Graph* from the menu bar in QM for Windows. Program 7.1C shows the output for the graphical solution. Notice that in addition to the graph, the corner points and the original problem are also shown. Later we return to see additional information related to sensitivity analysis that is provided by QM for Windows.

Using Excel's Solver Command to Solve LP Problems

Excel 2013 (as well as earlier versions) has an add-in called Solver that can be used to solve linear programs. If this add-in doesn't appear on the Data tab in Excel 2013, it has not been activated. See Appendix F for details on how to activate it.

PREPARING THE SPREADSHEET FOR SOLVER The spreadsheet must be prepared with data and formulas for certain calculations before Solver can be used. Excel QM can be used to simplify this process (see Appendix 7.1). We will briefly describe the steps, and further discussion and suggestions will be provided when the Flair Furniture example is presented. Here is a summary of the steps to prepare the spreadsheet:

1. Enter the problem data. The problem data consist of the coefficients of the objective function and the constraints, plus the RHS values for each of the constraints. It is best to organize this in a logical and meaningful way. The coefficients will be used when writing formulas in steps 3 and 4, and the RHS will be entered into Solver.
2. Designate specific cells for the values of the decision variables. Later, these cell addresses will be input into Solver.
3. Write a formula to calculate the value of the objective function, using the coefficients for the objective function (from step 1) that you have entered and the cells containing the values of the decision variables (from step 2). Later, this cell address will be input into Solver.
4. Write a formula to calculate the value of the LHS of each constraint, using the coefficients for the constraints (from step 1) that you have entered and the cells containing the values of the decision variables (from step 2). Later, these cell addresses and the cell addresses for the corresponding RHS value will be input into Solver.

PROGRAM 7.2A

Excel Data Input for Flair Furniture Example

> These cells are selected to contain the values of the decision variables. Solver will enter the optimal solution here, but you may enter numbers here also.

> The signs for the constraints are entered here for reference only.

	A	B	C	D	E	F
1	Flair Furniture					
2						
3	Variables	T (Tables)	C (Chairs)			
4	Units Produced			Profit		
5	Objective function	70	50	0		
6						
7	Constraints			LHS (Hours used)		RHS
8	Carpentry	4	3	0	≤	240
9	Painting	2	1	0	≤	100

PROGRAM 7.2B

Formulas for Flair Furniture Example

	D
4	Profit
5	=SUMPRODUCT($B$4:$C$4,B5:C5)
6	
7	LHS (Hours used)
8	=SUMPRODUCT($B$4:$C$4,B8:C8)
9	=SUMPRODUCT($B$4:$C$4,B9:C9)

PROGRAM 7.2C

Excel Spreadsheet for Flair Furniture Example

> Because there is a 1 in each of these cells, the LHS values can be calculated very easily to see if a mistake has been made.

> You can change these values to see how the profit and resource utilization change.

	A	B	C	D	E	F
1	Flair Furniture					
2						
3	Variables	T (Tables)	C (Chairs)			
4	Units Produced	1	1	Profit		
5	Objective function	70	50	120		
6						
7	Constraints			LHS (Hours used)		RHS
8	Carpentry	4	3	7	≤	240
9	Painting	2	1	3	≤	100

These four steps must be completed in some way with all linear programs in Excel. Additional information may be put into the spreadsheet for clarification purposes. Let's illustrate these with an example.

1. Program 7.2A provides the input data for the Flair Furniture example. You should enter the numbers in the cells shown. The words can be any description that you choose. The "≤" symbols are entered for reference only. They are not specifically used by Excel Solver.
2. The cells designated for the values of the variables are B4 for T (tables) and C4 for C (chairs). These cell addresses will be entered into Solver as the *By Changing Variable Cells*. Solver will change the values in these cells to find the optimal solution. It is sometimes helpful to enter a 1 in each of these to help identify any obvious errors when the formulas for the objective and the constraints are written.
3. A formula is written in Excel for the objective function (D5), and this is displayed in Program 7.2B. The Sumproduct function is very helpful, although there are other ways to write this. This cell address will be entered into Solver as the *Set Objective* location.
4. The hours used in carpentry (the LHS of the carpentry constraint) is calculated with the formula in cell D8, while cell D9 calculates the hours used in painting as illustrated in Program 7.2B. These cells and the cells containing the RHS values will be used when the constraints are entered into Solver.

The problem is now ready for the use of Solver. However, even if the optimal solution is not found, this spreadsheet has benefits. You can enter different values for *T* and *C* into cells B4 and C4 just to see how the resource utilization (LHS) and profit change.

PROGRAM 7.2D

Starting Solver in Excel 2013

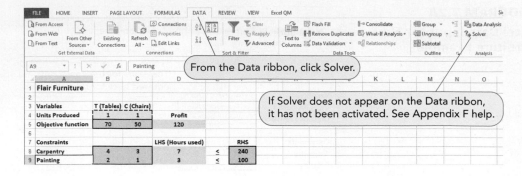

PROGRAM 7.2E   Solver Parameters Dialog Box

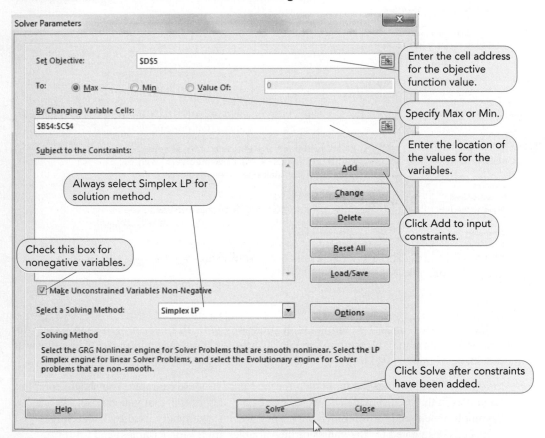

USING SOLVER   To begin using Solver, go to the *Data* tab in Excel 2013 and click *Solver*, as shown in Program 7.2D. If Solver does not appear on the Data tab, see Appendix F for instructions on how to activate this add-in. Once you click Solver, the Solver Parameters dialog box opens, as shown in Program 7.2E, and the following inputs should be entered, although the order is not important:

1. In the *Set Objective* box, enter the cell address for the total profit (D5).
2. In the *By Changing Variable Cells* box, enter the cell addresses for the variable values (B4:C4). Solver will allow the values in these cells to change while searching for the best value in the Set Objective cell reference.

PROGRAM 7.2F

Solver Add Constraint Dialog Box

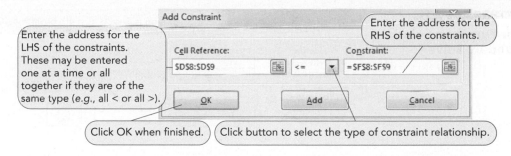

3. Click *Max* for a maximization problem and *Min* for a minimization problem.
4. Check the box for *Make Unconstrained Variables Non-Negative* since the variables *T* and *C* must be greater than or equal to zero.
5. Click the *Select Solving Method* button and select *Simplex LP* from the menu that appears.
6. Click *Add* to add the constraints. When you do this, the dialog box shown in Program 7.2F appears.
7. In the *Cell Reference* box, enter the cell references for the LHS values (D8:D9). Click the button to open the drop-down menu to select <=, which is for ≤ constraints. Then enter the cell references for the RHS values (F8:F9). Since these are all less-than- or-equal-to constraints, they can all be entered at one time by specifying the ranges. If there were other types of constraints, such as ≥ constraints, you could click *Add* after entering these first constraints, and the Add Constraint dialog box would allow you to enter additional constraints. When preparing the spreadsheet for Solver, it is easier if all the ≤ constraints are together and the ≥ constraints are together. After entering all the constraints, click *OK*. The Add Constraint dialog box closes, and the Solver Parameters dialog box reopens.
8. Click *Solve* on the Solver Parameters dialog box, and the solution is found. The Solver Results dialog box opens and indicates that a solution was found, as shown in Program 7.2G. In situations where there is no feasible solution, this box will indicate this. Additional information may be obtained from the Reports section of this as will be seen later. Program 7.2H shows the results of the spreadsheet with the optimal solution.

Using Excel QM

Using the Excel QM add-in can help you easily solve linear programming problems. Not only are all formulas automatically created by Excel QM, the spreadsheet preparation for the use of

PROGRAM 7.2G

Solver Results Dialog Box

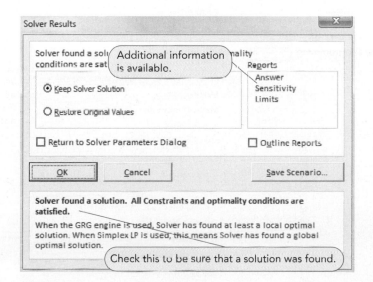

PROGRAM 7.2H

Flair Furniture Solution Found by Solver

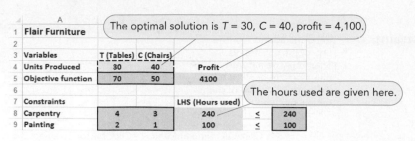

the Solver add-in is also automatically performed. We will illustrate this using the Flair Furniture example.

To begin, from the Excel QM ribbon in Excel 2013, click the *Alphabetical* menu and then select *Linear, Integer & Mixed Integer Programming* from the drop-down menu, as shown in Program 7.3A. The Excel QM Spreadsheet Initialization window opens, and in it you enter the problem title, the number of variables, and the number of constraints (do not count the nonnegativity constraints). Specify whether the problem is a maximization or minimization problem, and then click *OK*. When the initialization process is finished, a spreadsheet is prepared for data input, as shown in Program 7.3B. In this worksheet, enter the data in the section labeled Data. Specify the type of constraint (less-than, greater-than, or equal-to) and change the variable names and the constraint names, if desired. You do not have to write any formulas.

Once the data have been entered, from the *Data* tab, select *Solver*. The Solver Parameters window opens (refer back to Program 7.2E to see what input is normally required in a typical Solvers Parameters window), and you will see that Excel QM has made all the necessary inputs and selections. You do not enter any information, and you simply click *Solve* to find the solution. The solution is displayed in Program 7.3C.

Program 7.3A   Using Excel QM in Excel 2013 for the Flair Furniture Example

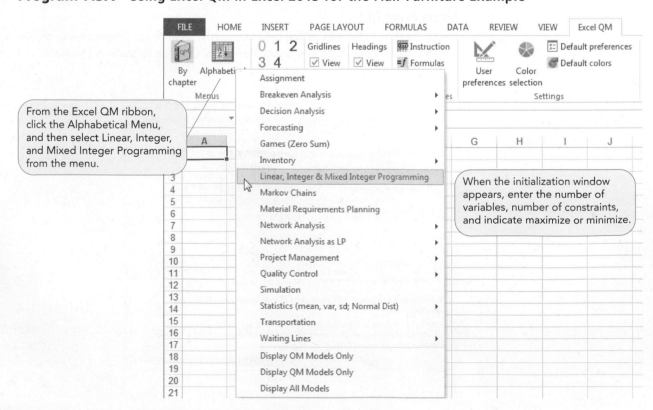

PROGRAM 7.3B Excel QM Data Input for the Flair Furniture Example

After entering the problem, click the Data tab and select Solver from the Data ribbon. When the window for Solver opens, simply click Solve as all the necessary inputs have been entered by Excel QM.

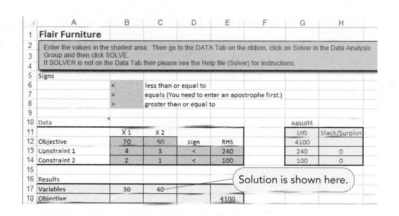

PROGRAM 7.3C

Excel QM Output for the Flair Furniture Example

7.6 Solving Minimization Problems

Many LP problems involve minimizing an objective such as cost instead of maximizing a profit function. A restaurant, for example, may wish to develop a work schedule to meet staffing needs while minimizing the total number of employees. A manufacturer may seek to distribute its products from several factories to its many regional warehouses in such a way as to minimize total shipping costs. A hospital may want to provide a daily meal plan for its patients that meets certain nutritional standards while minimizing food purchase costs.

Minimization problems with only two variables can be solved graphically by first setting up the feasible solution region and then using either the corner point method or an isocost line approach (which is analogous to the isoprofit approach in maximization problems) to find the values of the decision variables (e.g., X_1 and X_2) that yield the minimum cost. Let's take a look at a common LP problem referred to as the diet problem. This situation is similar to the one that the hospital faces in feeding its patients at the least cost.

Holiday Meal Turkey Ranch

The Holiday Meal Turkey Ranch is considering buying two different brands of turkey feed and blending them to provide a good, low-cost diet for its turkeys. Each feed contains, in varying proportions, some or all of the three nutritional ingredients essential for fattening turkeys. Each pound of brand 1 purchased, for example, contains 5 ounces of ingredient A, 4 ounces of ingredient B, and 0.5 ounce of ingredient C. Each pound of brand 2 contains 10 ounces of ingredient A,

TABLE 7.5
Holiday Meal Turkey Ranch Data

INGREDIENT	COMPOSITION OF EACH POUND OF FEED (OZ.)		MINIMUM MONTHLY REQUIREMENT PER TURKEY (OZ.)
	BRAND 1 FEED	BRAND 2 FEED	
A	5	10	90
B	4	3	48
C	0.5	0	1.5
Cost per pound	2 cents	3 cents	

3 ounces of ingredient B, but no ingredient C. The brand 1 feed costs the ranch 2 cents a pound, while the brand 2 feed costs 3 cents a pound. The owner of the ranch would like to use LP to determine the lowest-cost diet that meets the minimum monthly intake requirement for each nutritional ingredient.

Table 7.5 summarizes the relevant information. If we let

$$X_1 = \text{number of pounds of brand 1 feed purchased}$$
$$X_2 = \text{number of pounds of brand 2 feed purchased}$$

then we may proceed to formulate this linear programming problem as follows:

$$\text{Minimize cost (in cents)} = 2X_1 + 3X_2$$

subject to these constraints:

$$5X_1 + 10X_2 \geq 90 \text{ ounces} \quad \text{(ingredient A constraint)}$$
$$4X_1 + 3X_2 \geq 48 \text{ ounces} \quad \text{(ingredient B constraint)}$$
$$0.5\,X_1 \geq 1.5 \text{ ounces} \quad \text{(ingredient C constraint)}$$
$$X_1 \geq 0 \quad \text{(nonnegativity constraint)}$$
$$X_2 \geq 0 \quad \text{(nonnegativity constraint)}$$

Before solving this problem, we want to be sure to note three features that affect its solution. First, you should be aware that the third constraint implies that the farmer *must* purchase enough brand 1 feed to meet the minimum standards for the C nutritional ingredient. Buying only brand 2 would not be feasible because it lacks C. Second, as the problem is formulated, we will be solving for the best blend of brands 1 and 2 to buy per turkey per month. If the ranch houses 5,000 turkeys in a given month, it need simply multiply the X_1 and X_2 quantities by 5,000 to decide how much feed to order overall. Third, we are now dealing with a series of greater-than-or-equal-to constraints. These cause the feasible solution area to be above the constraint lines in this example.

We plot the three constraints to develop a feasible solution region for the minimization problem.

Note that minimization problems often have unbounded feasible regions.

USING THE CORNER POINT METHOD ON A MINIMIZATION PROBLEM To solve the Holiday Meal Turkey Ranch problem, we first construct the feasible solution region. This is done by plotting each of the three constraint equations as in Figure 7.10. Note that the third constraint, $0.5\,X_1 \geq 1.5$, can be rewritten and plotted as $X_1 \geq 3$. (This involves multiplying both sides of the inequality by 2 but does not change the position of the constraint line in any way.) Minimization problems are often unbounded outward (i.e., on the right side and on top), but this causes no difficulty in solving them. As long as they are bounded inward (on the left side and the bottom), corner points may be established. The optimal solution will lie at one of the corners as it would in a maximization problem.

In this case, there are three corner points: a, b, and c. For point a, we find the coordinates at the intersection of the ingredient C and B constraints, that is, where the line $X_1 = 3$ crosses the line $4X_1 + 3X_2 = 48$. If we substitute $X_1 = 3$ into the B constraint equation, we get

$$4(3) + 3X_2 = 48$$

or

$$X_2 = 12$$

Thus, point a has the coordinates ($X_1 = 3, X_2 = 12$).

FIGURE 7.10

Feasible Region for the
Holiday Meal Turkey
Ranch Problem

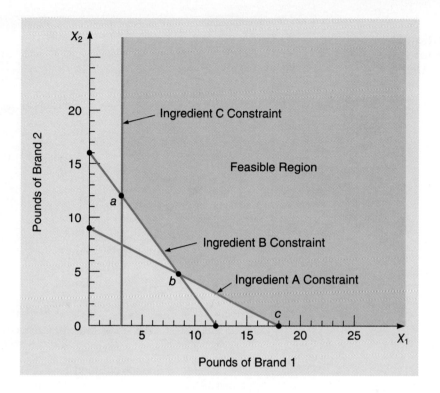

To find the coordinates of point *b* algebraically, we solve the equations $4X_1 + 3X_2 = 48$ and $5X_1 + 10X_2 = 90$ simultaneously. This yields $(X_1 = 8.4, X_2 = 4.8)$.

The coordinates at point *c* are seen by inspection to be $(X_1 = 18, X_2 = 0)$. We now evaluate the objective function at each corner point, and we get

$$Cost = 2X_1 + 3X_2$$

$$\text{Cost at point } a = 2(3) + 3(12) = 42$$

$$\text{Cost at point } b = 2(8.4) + 3(4.8) = 31.2$$

$$\text{Cost at point } c = 2(18) + 3(0) = 36$$

Hence, the minimum cost solution is to purchase 8.4 pounds of brand 1 feed and 4.8 pounds of brand 2 feed per turkey per month. This will yield a cost of 31.2 cents per turkey.

IN ACTION

NBC Uses Linear, Integer, and Goal Programming in Selling Advertising Slots

The National Broadcasting Company (NBC) sells over $4 billion in television advertising each year. About 60% to 80% of the air time for an upcoming season is sold in a 2- to 3-week period in late May. The advertising agencies approach the networks to purchase advertising time for their clients. Included in each request are the dollar amount, the demographic (e.g., age of the viewing audience) in which the client is interested, the program mix, weekly weighting, unit-length distribution, and a negotiated cost per 1,000 viewers. NBC must then develop detailed sales plans to meet these requirements. Traditionally, NBC developed these plans manually, and this required several hours per plan. These usually had to be reworked due to the complexity involved. With more than 300 such plans to be developed and reworked in a 2- to 3-week period, this was very time intensive and did not necessarily result in the maximum possible revenue.

In 1996, a project in the area of yield management was begun. Through this effort, NBC was able to create plans that more accurately meet customers' requirements, respond to customers more quickly, make the most profitable use of its limited inventory of advertising time slots, and reduce rework. The success of this system led to the development of a full-scale optimization system based on linear, integer, and goal programming. It is estimated that sales revenue between the years 1996 and 2000 increased by over $200 million due largely to this effort. Improvements in rework time, sales force productivity, and customer satisfaction were also benefits of this system.

Source: Based on Srinivas Bollapragada, et al. "NBC's Optimization Systems Increase Revenues and Productivity," *Interfaces* 32, 1 (January–February 2002): 47–60.

FIGURE 7.11

Graphical Solution to the Holiday Meal Turkey Ranch Problem Using the Isocost Line

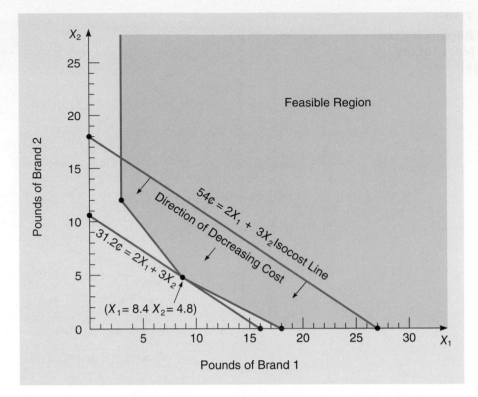

The isocost line method is analogous to the isoprofit line method we used in maximization problems.

ISOCOST LINE APPROACH As mentioned before, the **isocost line** approach may also be used to solve LP minimization problems such as that of the Holiday Meal Turkey Ranch. As with isoprofit lines, we need not compute the cost at each corner point, but instead draw a series of parallel cost lines. The lowest cost line (i.e., the one closest toward the origin) to touch the feasible region provides us with the optimal solution corner.

For example, we start in Figure 7.11 by drawing a 54-cent cost line, namely $54 = 2X_1 + 3X_2$. Obviously, there are many points in the feasible region that would yield a lower total cost. We proceed to move our isocost line toward the lower left, in a plane parallel to the 54-cent solution line. The last point we touch while still in contact with the feasible region is the same as corner point b of Figure 7.10. It has the coordinates $(X_1 = 8.4, X_2 = 4.8)$ and an associated cost of 31.2 cents.

This could be solved using QM for Windows by selecting the *Linear Programming* Module and selecting *New* problem. Specify that there are 2 variables and 3 constraints. When the input window opens, enter the data and click *Solve*. The output is shown in Program 7.4.

To solve this in Excel 2013, determine the cells where the solution will be, enter the coefficients from the objective function and the constraints, and write formulas for the total cost and the total of each ingredient (constraint). The input values and solution are shown in Program 7.5A, with Column D containing the formulas. These formulas are shown in Program 7.5B. When the Solver Parameters window opens, the *Set Objective* cell is D5; the *By Changing Variable Cells* are B4:C4; the Simplex LP method is used; the box for variables to be nonnegative is checked; and Min is selected because this is a minimization problem.

PROGRAM 7.4

Solution to the Holiday Meal Turkey Ranch Problem in QM for Windows

Linear Programming Results					
Holiday Meal Solution					
	X1	X2		RHS	Dual
Minimize	2	3			
Ingredient A	5	10	>=	90	-0.24
Ingredient B	4	3	>=	48	-0.2
Ingredient C	0.5	0	>=	1.5	0
Solution->	8.4	4.8		31.2	

PROGRAM 7.5A

Excel 2013 Solution for Holiday Meal Turkey Ranch Problem

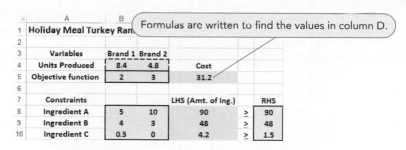

Formulas are written to find the values in column D.

	A	B			
1	Holiday Meal Turkey Ran				
2					
3	Variables	Brand 1	Brand 2		
4	Units Produced	8.4	4.8	Cost	
5	Objective function	2	3	31.2	
6					
7	Constraints			LHS (Amt. of Ing.)	RHS
8	Ingredient A	5	10	90	≥	90
9	Ingredient B	4	3	48	≥	48
10	Ingredient C	0.5	0	4.2	≥	1.5

PROGRAM 7.5B

Excel 2013 Formulas for Holiday Meal Turkey Ranch Problem

	D
4	Cost
5	=SUMPRODUCT($B$4:$C$4,B5:C5)
6	
7	LHS (Amt. of Ing.)
8	=SUMPRODUCT($B$4:$C$4,B8:C8)
9	=SUMPRODUCT($B$4:$C$4,B9:C9)
10	=SUMPRODUCT($B$4:$C$4,B10:C10)

7.7   Four Special Cases in LP

Four special cases and difficulties arise at times when using the graphical approach to solving LP problems: (1) infeasibility, (2) unboundedness, (3) redundancy, and (4) alternate optimal solutions.

No Feasible Solution

Lack of a feasible solution region can occur if constraints conflict with one another.

When there is no solution to an LP problem that satisfies all of the constraints given, then no feasible solution exists. Graphically, it means that no feasible solution region exists—a situation that might occur if the problem was formulated with conflicting constraints. This, by the way, is a frequent occurrence in real-life, large-scale LP problems that involve hundreds of constraints. For example, if one constraint is supplied by the marketing manager who states that at least 300 tables must be produced (namely, $X_1 \geq 300$) to meet sales demand, and a second restriction is supplied by the production manager, who insists that no more than 220 tables be produced (namely, $X_1 \leq 220$) because of a lumber shortage, no feasible solution region results. When the operations research analyst coordinating the LP problem points out this conflict, one manager or the other must revise his or her inputs. Perhaps more raw materials could be procured from a new source, or perhaps sales demand could be lowered by substituting a different model table to customers.

As a further graphic illustration of this, let us consider the following three constraints:

$$X_1 + 2X_2 \leq 6$$
$$2X_1 + X_2 \leq 8$$
$$X_1 \geq 7$$

As seen in Figure 7.12, there is no feasible solution region for this LP problem because of the presence of conflicting constraints.

Unboundedness

When the profit in a maximization problem can be infinitely large, the problem is unbounded and is missing one or more constraints.

Sometimes a linear program will not have a finite solution. This means that in a maximization problem, for example, one or more solution variables, and the profit, can be made infinitely large without violating any constraints. If we try to solve such a problem graphically, we will note that the feasible region is open ended.

FIGURE 7.12

A Problem with No Feasible Solution

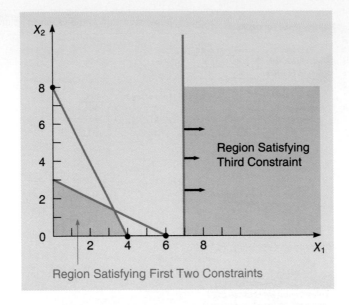

Region Satisfying Third Constraint

Region Satisfying First Two Constraints

Let us consider a simple example to illustrate the situation. A firm has formulated the following LP problem:

$$\text{Maximize profit} = \$3X_1 + \$5X_2$$

$$\text{subject to} \qquad X_1 \qquad\quad \geq 5$$

$$X_2 \leq 10$$

$$X_1 + 2X_2 \geq 10$$

$$X_1, X_2 \geq 0$$

As you see in Figure 7.13, because this is a maximization problem and the feasible region extends infinitely to the right, there is **unboundedness**, or an unbounded solution. This implies that the problem has been formulated improperly. It would indeed be wonderful for the company to be able to produce an infinite number of units of X_1 (at a profit of \$3 each!), but obviously no firm has infinite resources available or infinite product demand.

Redundancy

A redundant constraint is one that does not affect the feasible solution region.

The presence of redundant constraints is another common situation that occurs in large LP formulations. **Redundancy** causes no major difficulties in solving LP problems graphically, but you should be able to identify its occurrence. A redundant constraint is simply one that does

FIGURE 7.13

A Feasible Region That Is Unbounded to the Right

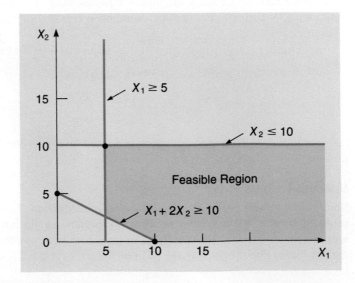

$X_1 \geq 5$

$X_2 \leq 10$

Feasible Region

$X_1 + 2X_2 \geq 10$

FIGURE 7.14

Example of a Redundant Constraint

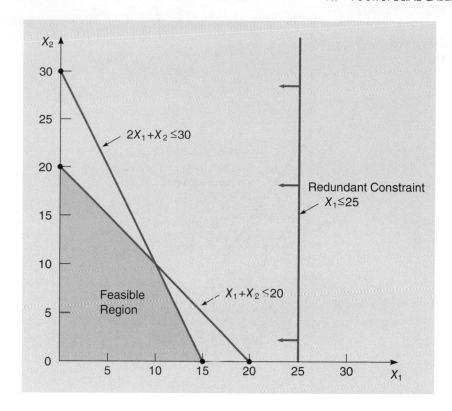

not affect the feasible solution region. In other words, other constraints may be more binding or restrictive than the redundant constraint.

Let's look at the following example of an LP problem with three constraints:

$$\text{Maximize profit} = \$1X_1 + \$2X_2$$

$$\text{subject to} \qquad X_1 + \quad X_2 \leq 20$$
$$2X_1 + \quad X_2 \leq 30$$
$$X_1 \qquad \leq 25$$
$$X_1, X_2 \geq 0$$

The third constraint, $X_1 \leq 25$, is less binding but the first two constraints are indeed more restrictive constraints (see Figure 7.14).

Alternate Optimal Solutions

Multiple optimal solutions are possible in LP problems.

An LP problem may, on occasion, have two or more **alternate optimal solutions**. Graphically, this is the case when the objective function's isoprofit or isocost line runs perfectly parallel to one of the problem's constraints—in other words, when they have the same slope.

Management of a firm noticed the presence of more than one optimal solution when they formulated this simple LP problem:

$$\text{Maximize profit} = \$3X_1 + \$2X_2$$

$$\text{subject to} \qquad 6X_1 + \quad 4X_2 \leq 24$$
$$X_1 \qquad \leq 3$$
$$X_1, X_2 \geq 0$$

As we see in Figure 7.15, our first isoprofit line of $8 runs parallel to the first constraint equation. At a profit level of $12, the isoprofit line will rest directly on top of the segment of the first constraint line. This means that any point along the line between A and B provides an optimal X_1 and X_2 combination. Far from causing problems, the existence of more than one optimal solution

FIGURE 7.15

Example of Alternate Optimal Solutions

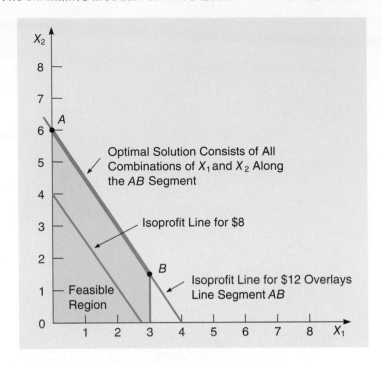

allows management great flexibility in deciding which combination to select. The profit remains the same at each alternate solution.

7.8   Sensitivity Analysis

Optimal solutions to LP problems have thus far been found under what are called *deterministic assumptions*. This means that we assume complete certainty in the data and relationships of a problem—namely, prices are fixed, resources known, time needed to produce a unit exactly set. But in the real world, conditions are dynamic and changing. How can we handle this apparent discrepancy?

How sensitive is the optimal solution to changes in profits, resources, or other input parameters?

One way we can do so is by continuing to treat each particular LP problem as a deterministic situation. However, when an optimal solution is found, we recognize the importance of seeing just how *sensitive* that solution is to model assumptions and data. For example, if a firm realizes that profit per unit is not $5 as estimated but instead is closer to $5.50, how will the final solution mix and total profit change? If additional resources, such as 10 labor hours or 3 hours of machine time, should become available, will this change the problem's answer? Such analyses are used to examine the effects of changes in three areas: (1) contribution rates for each variable, (2) technological coefficients (the numbers in the constraint equations), and (3) available resources (the right-hand-side quantities in each constraint). This task is alternatively called **sensitivity analysis**, *postoptimality analysis*, *parametric programming*, or *optimality analysis*.

An important function of sensitivity analysis is to allow managers to experiment with values of the input parameters.

Sensitivity analysis also often involves a series of what-if? questions. What if the profit on product 1 increases by 10%? What if less money is available in the advertising budget constraint? What if workers each stay one hour longer every day at 1½-time pay to provide increased production capacity? What if new technology will allow a product to be wired in one-third the time it used to take? So we see that sensitivity analysis can be used to deal not only with errors in estimating input parameters to the LP model but also with management's experiments with possible future changes in the firm that may affect profits.

There are two approaches to determining just how sensitive an optimal solution is to changes. The first is simply a trial-and-error approach. This approach usually involves resolving the entire problem, preferably by computer, each time one input data item or parameter is changed. It can take a long time to test a series of possible changes in this way.

Postoptimality analysis means examining changes after the optimal solution has been reached.

The approach we prefer is the analytic postoptimality method. After an LP problem has been solved, we attempt to determine a range of changes in problem parameters that will not affect the optimal solution or change the variables in the solution. This is done without resolving the whole problem.

Let's investigate sensitivity analysis by developing a small production mix problem. Our goal will be to demonstrate graphically and through the simplex tableau how sensitivity analysis can be used to make linear programming concepts more realistic and insightful.

High Note Sound Company

The High Note Sound Company manufactures quality speakers and stereo receivers. Each of these products requires a certain amount of skilled artisanship, of which there is a limited weekly supply. The firm formulates the following LP problem in order to determine the best production mix of speakers (X_1) and receivers (X_2):

$$\text{Maximize profit} = \$50X_1 + \$120X_2$$

$$\text{subject to} \quad 2X_1 + 4X_2 \leq 80 \quad \text{(hours of electricians' time available)}$$

$$3X_1 + 1X_2 \leq 60 \quad \text{(hours of audio technicians' time available)}$$

$$X_1, X_2 \geq 0$$

The solution to this problem is illustrated graphically in Figure 7.16. Given this information and deterministic assumptions, the firm should produce only stereo receivers (20 of them), for a weekly profit of $2,400.

For the optimal solution, $(0, 20)$, the electrician hours used are

$$2X_1 + 4X_2 = 2(0) + 4(20) = 80$$

and this equals the amount available, so there is 0 slack for this constraint. Thus, it is a binding constraint. If a constraint is binding, obtaining additional units of that resource will usually result in higher profits. The audio technician hours used for the optimal solution $(0, 20)$ are

$$3X_1 + 1X_2 = 3(0) + 1(20) = 20$$

but the hours available are 60. Thus, there is a slack of $60 - 20 = 40$ hours. Because there are extra hours available that are not being used, this is a nonbinding constraint. For a nonbinding constraint, obtaining additional units of that resource will not result in higher profits and will only increase the slack.

FIGURE 7.16

High Note Sound Company Graphical Solution

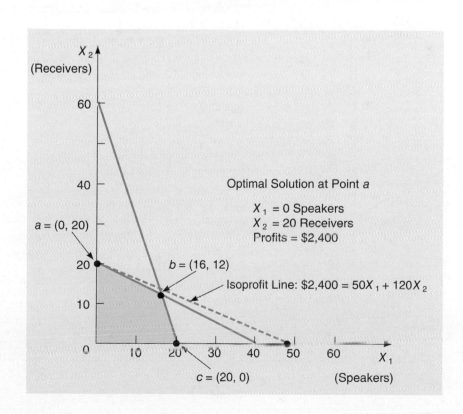

Changes in the Objective Function Coefficient

Changes in contribution rates are examined first.

In real-life problems, contribution rates (usually profit or cost) in the objective functions fluctuate periodically, as do most of a firm's expenses. Graphically, this means that although the feasible solution region remains exactly the same, the slope of the isoprofit or isocost line will change. It is easy to see in Figure 7.17 that the High Note Sound Company's profit line is optimal at point a. But what if a technical breakthrough just occurred that raised the profit per stereo receiver (X_2) from $120 to $150? Is the solution still optimal? The answer is definitely yes, for in this case the slope of the profit line accentuates the profitability at point a. The new profit is $3,000 = 0(\$50) + 20(\$150)$.

On the other hand, if X_2's profit coefficient was overestimated and should only have been $80, the slope of the profit line changes enough to cause a new corner point (b) to become optimal. Here the profit is $1,760 = 16(\$50) + 12(\$80)$.

A new corner point becomes optimal if an objective function coefficient is decreased or increased too much.

This example illustrates a very important concept about changes in objective function coefficients. We can increase or decrease the objective function coefficient (profit) of any variable, and the current corner point may remain optimal if the change is not too large. However, if we increase or decrease this coefficient by too much, then the optimal solution would be at a different corner point. How much can the objective function coefficient change before another corner point becomes optimal? Both QM for Windows and Excel provide the answer.

QM for Windows and Changes in Objective Function Coefficients

The current solution remains optimal unless an objective function coefficient is increased to a value above the upper bound or decreased to a value below the lower bound.

The QM for Windows input for the High Note Sound Company example is shown in Program 7.6A. When the solution has been found, selecting *Window* and *Ranging* allows us to see additional information on sensitivity analysis. Program 7.6B provides the output related to sensitivity analysis.

From Program 7.6B, we see the profit on speakers was $50, which is indicated as the original value in the output. This objective function coefficient has a lower bound of negative infinity

Figure 7.17   Changes in the Receiver Contribution Coefficients

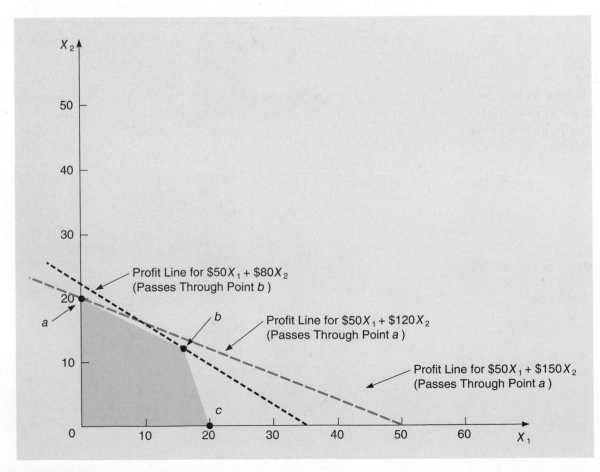

PROGRAM 7.6A

Input to QM for Windows High Note Sound Company Data

Objective		Instruction				
⦿ Maximize		Use these option buttons to set the objective.				
○ Minimize						

High Note Sound Company						
	X1	X2		RHS	Equation form	
Maximize	50	120			Max 50X1 + 120X2	
Electrician hours	2	4	<=	80	2X1 + 4X2 <= 80	
Audio technician hours	3	1	<=	60	3X1 + X2 <= 60	

PROGRAM 7.6B

High Note Sound Company Sensitivity Analysis Output

⬦ Ranging					▭ ▭

High Note Sound Company Solution					
Variable	Value	Reduced Cost	Original Val	Lower Bound	Upper Bound
X1	0	10	50	-Infinity	60
X2	20	0	120	100	Infinity
Constraint	Dual Value	Slack/Surplus	Original Val	Lower Bound	Upper Bound
Electrician hours	30	0	80	0	240
Audio technician hours	0	40	60	20	Infinity

and an upper bound of $60. This means that the current corner point solution remains optimal as long as the profit on speakers does not go above $60. If it equals $60, there would be two optimal solutions as the objective function would be parallel to the first constraint. The points (0, 20) and (16, 12) would both give a profit of $2,400. The profit on speakers may decrease any amount as indicated by the negative infinity, and the optimal corner point does not change. This negative infinity is logical because currently there are no speakers being produced because the profit is too low. Any decrease in the profit on speakers would make them less attractive relative to the receivers, and we certainly would not produce any speakers because of this.

The profit on receivers has an upper bound of infinity (it may increase by any amount) and a lower bound of $100. If this profit equaled $100, then the corner points (0, 20) and (16, 12) would both be optimal. The profit at each of these would be $2,000.

The upper and lower bounds relate to changing only one coefficient at a time.

In general, a change can be made to one (and only one) objective function coefficient, and the current optimal corner point remains optimal as long as the change is between the Upper and Lower Bounds. If two or more coefficients are changed simultaneously, then the problem should be solved with the new coefficients to determine whether or not this current solution remains optimal.

Excel Solver and Changes in Objective Function Coefficients

Program 7.7A illustrates how the Excel 2013 spreadsheet for this example is set up for Solver. When *Solver* is selected from the *Data* tab, the appropriate inputs are made, and *Solve* is clicked in the Solver dialog box, the solution and the Solver Results window will appear as in Program 7.7B. Selecting *Sensitivity* from the reports area of this window will provide a Sensitivity Report on a new worksheet, with results as shown in Program 7.7C. Note how the cells are named based on the text from Program 7.7A. Notice that Excel does not provide lower bounds and upper bounds for the objective function coefficients. Instead, it gives the allowable increases

PROGRAM 7.7A

Excel 2013 Spreadsheet for High Note Sound Company

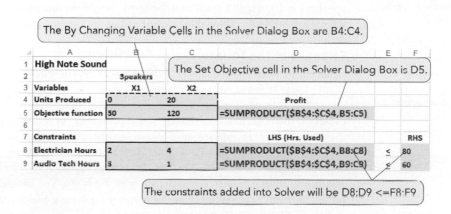

The By Changing Variable Cells in the Solver Dialog Box are B4:C4.

The Set Objective cell in the Solver Dialog Box is D5.

	A	B	C	D	E	F
1	High Note Sound					
2		Speakers				
3	Variables	X1	X2			
4	Units Produced	0	20	Profit		
5	Objective function	50	120	=SUMPRODUCT($B$4:$C$4,B5:C5)		
6						
7	Constraints			LHS (Hrs. Used)		RHS
8	Electrician Hours	2	4	=SUMPRODUCT($B$4:$C$4,B8:C8)	≤	80
9	Audio Tech Hours	3	1	=SUMPRODUCT($B$4:$C$4,B9:C9)	≤	60

The constraints added into Solver will be D8:D9 <=F8:F9

PROGRAM 7.7B   Excel 2013 Solution and Solver Results Window for High Note Sound Company

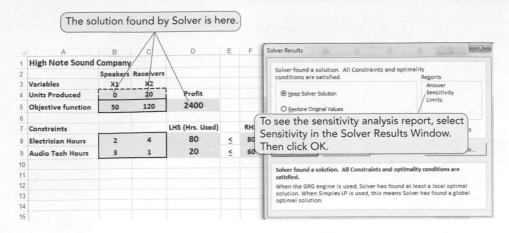

The solution found by Solver is here.

To see the sensitivity analysis report, select Sensitivity in the Solver Results Window. Then click OK.

PROGRAM 7.7C

Excel 2013 Sensitivity Report for High Note Sound Company

The names presented in the Sensitivity Report combine the text in column A and the text above the data, unless the cells have been named using the Name Manager from the Formulas tab.

The profit on speakers may change by these amounts and the current corner point will remain optimal.

Variable Cells

Cell	Name	Final Value	Reduced Cost	Objective Coefficient	Allowable Increase	Allowable Decrease
$B$4	Units Produced X1	0	-10	50	10	1E+30
$C$4	Units Produced X2	20	0	120	1E+30	20

Constraints

Cell	Name	Final Value	Shadow Price	Constraint R.H. Side	Allowable Increase	Allowable Decrease
$D$8	Electrician Hours LHS (Hrs. Used)	80	30	80	160	80
$D$9	Audio Tech Hours LHS (Hrs. Used)	20	0	60	1E+30	40

The resources used are here. The RHS can change by these amounts, and the shadow price will still be relevant.

Excel solver gives allowable increases and decreases rather than upper and lower bounds.

and decreases for these. By adding the allowable increase to the current value, we may obtain the upper bound. For example, the allowable increase on the profit (objective coefficient) for speakers is 10, which means that the upper bound on this profit is $50 + $10 = $60. Similarly, we may subtract the allowable decrease from the current value to obtain the lower bound.

Changes in the Technological Coefficients

Changes in technological coefficients affect the shape of the feasible solution region.

Changes in what are called the **technological coefficients** often reflect changes in the state of technology. If fewer or more resources are needed to produce a product such as a speaker or stereo receiver, coefficients in the constraint equations will change. These changes will have no effect on the objective function of an LP problem, but they can produce a significant change in the shape of the feasible solution region, and hence in the optimal profit or cost.

Figure 7.18 illustrates the original High Note Sound Company graphical solution as well as two separate changes in technological coefficients. In Figure 7.18, Part (a), we see that the optimal solution lies at point a, which represents $X_1 = 0, X_2 = 20$. You should be able to prove to yourself that point a remains optimal in Figure 7.18, Part (b) despite a constraint change from $3X_1 + 1X_2 \leq 60$ to $2X_1 + 1X_2 \leq 60$. Such a change might take place when the firm discovers that it no longer demands three hours of audio technicians' time to produce a speaker, but only two hours.

FIGURE 7.18 Change in the Technological Coefficients for the High Note Sound Company

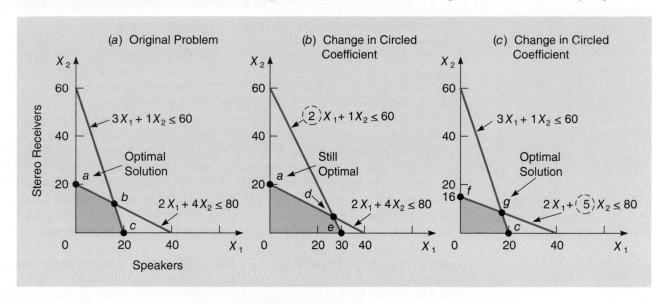

In Figure 7.18, Part (c), however, a change in the other constraint changes the shape of the feasible region enough to cause a new corner point (*g*) to become optimal. Before moving on, see if you reach an objective function value of $1,954 profit at point *g* (versus a profit of $1,920 at point *f*).[*]

Changes in the Resources or Right-Hand-Side Values

The right-hand-side values of the constraints often represent resources available to the firm. The resources could be labor hours or machine time or perhaps money or production materials available. In the High Note Sound Company example, the two resources are hours available of electricians' time and hours of audio technicians' time. If additional hours were available, a higher

IN ACTION Swift & Company Uses LP to Schedule Production

Based in Greeley, Colorado, Swift & Company has annual sales over $8 billion, with beef and related products making up the vast majority of this. Swift has five processing plants, which handle over 6 billion pounds of beef each year. Each head of beef is cut into two sides, which yield the chuck, the brisket, the loins, the ribs, the round, the plate, and the flank. With some cuts in greater demand than others, the customer service representatives (CSRs) try to meet the demand for customers while providing discounts when necessary to clear out some cuts that might be in excess supply. It is important that the CSRs have accurate information on product availability in close to real time so they can react quickly to changing demand.

With the cost of raw material being as high as 85%, and with a very thin profit margin, it is essential that the company operate efficiently. Swift started a project in March 2001 to develop a mathematical programming model that would optimize the

supply chain. Ten full-time employees worked with four operations research consultants from Aspen Technology on what was called Project Phoenix. At the heart of the final model are 45 integrated LP models that enable the company to dynamically schedule its operations in real time as orders are received.

With Project Phoenix, not only did profit margins increase, but the improvements in forecasting, cattle procurement, and manufacturing improved relations with customers and enhanced the reputation of Swift & Company in the marketplace. The company is better able to deliver products according to customer specification. While the model cost over $6 million to develop, in the first year of operation, it generated a benefit of $12.7 million.

Source: Based on Ann Bixby, Brian Downs, and Mike Self. "A Scheduling and Capable-to-Promise Application for Swift & Company," *Interfaces* 36, 1 (January–February 2006): 69–86.

---

[*]Note that the values of X_1 and X_2 at point *g* are fractions. Although the High Note Sound Company cannot produce 0.67, 0.75, or 0.90 of a speaker or stereo, we can assume that the firm can *begin* a unit one week and complete it the next. As long as the production process is fairly stable from week to week, this raises no major problems. If solutions *must* be whole numbers each period, refer to our discussion of integer programming in Chapter 10 to handle the situation.

total profit could be realized. How much should the company be willing to pay for additional hours? Is it profitable to have some electricians work overtime? Should we be willing to pay for more audio technician time? Sensitivity analysis about these resources will help us answer these questions.

If the right-hand side of a constraint is changed, the feasible region will change (unless the constraint is redundant), and often the optimal solution will change. In the High Note Sound Company example, there were 80 hours of electrician time available each week and the maximum possible profit was $2,400. There is no slack for this constraint, so it is a binding constraint. If the available electricians' hours are increased to 100 hours, the new optimal solution seen in Figure 7.19, part (a) is (0, 25) and the profit is $3,000. Thus, the extra 20 hours of time resulted in an increase in profit of $600 or $30 per hour. If the hours were decreased to 60 hours as shown in Figure 7.19, part (b), the new optimal solution is (0, 15) and the profit is $1,800.

The value of one additional unit of a scarce resource may be found from the dual price.

Thus, reducing the hours by 20 results in a decrease in profit of $600 or $30 per hour. This $30 per hour change in profit that resulted from a change in the hours available is called the dual price or dual value. The **dual price** for a constraint is the improvement in the objective function value that results from a one-unit increase in the right-hand side of the constraint.

The dual price of $30 per hour of electrician time tells us we can increase profit if we have more electrician hours. However, there is a limit to this as there is limited audio technician time. If the total hours of electrician time were 240 hours, the optimal solution would be (0, 60) as shown in Figure 7.19, part (c) and the profit would be $7,200. Again, this is an increase of $30 profit per hour (the dual price) for each of the 160 hours that were added to the original amount. If the number of hours increased beyond 240, then profit would no longer increase and the optimal solution would still be (0, 60) as shown in Figure 7.19, part (c). There would simply be excess (slack) hours of electrician time and all of the audio technician time would be used. Thus, the dual price is relevant only within limits. Both QM for Windows and Excel Solver provide these limits.

QM for Windows and Changes in Right-Hand-Side Values

The QM for Windows sensitivity analysis output was shown in Program 7.6B. The dual value for the electrician hours constraint is given as 30, and the lower bound is zero while the upper bound is 240. This means that each additional hour of electrician time, up to a total of 240 hours, will increase the maximum possible profit by $30. Similarly, if the available electrician time is decreased, the maximum possible profit will decrease by $30 per hour until the available time is decreased to the lower bound of 0. If the amount of electrician time (the right-hand-side value for this constraint) is outside this range (0 to 240), then the dual value is no longer relevant and the problem should be resolved with the new right-hand-side value.

Dual prices will change if the amount of the resource (the right-hand side of the constraint) goes above the upper bound or below the lower bound given in the Ranging section of the QM for Windows output.

In Program 7.6B, the dual value for audio technician hours is shown to be $0 and the slack is 40, so it is a nonbinding constraint. There are 40 hours of audio technician time that are not being used despite the fact that they are currently available. If additional hours were made available they would not increase profit but would simply increase the amount of slack. This dual value of zero is relevant as long as the right-hand side does not go below the lower bound of 20. The upper limit is infinity indicating that adding more hours would simply increase the amount of slack.

Excel Solver and Changes in Right-Hand-Side Values

The Sensitivity report from Excel Solver was shown in Program 7.7C. Notice that Solver gives the shadow price instead of the dual price. A **shadow price** is the change in the objective function value (e.g., profit or cost) that results from a one-unit increase in the right-hand-side of a constraint.

The shadow price is the same as the dual price in maximization problems.

Since an improvement in the objective function value in a maximization problem is the same as a positive change (increase), the dual price and the shadow price are exactly the same for maximization problems. For a minimization problem, an improvement in the objective function value is a decrease, which is a negative change. So for minimization problems, the shadow price will be the negative of the dual price.

FIGURE 7.19

Changes in the Electricians' Time Resource for the High Note Sound Company

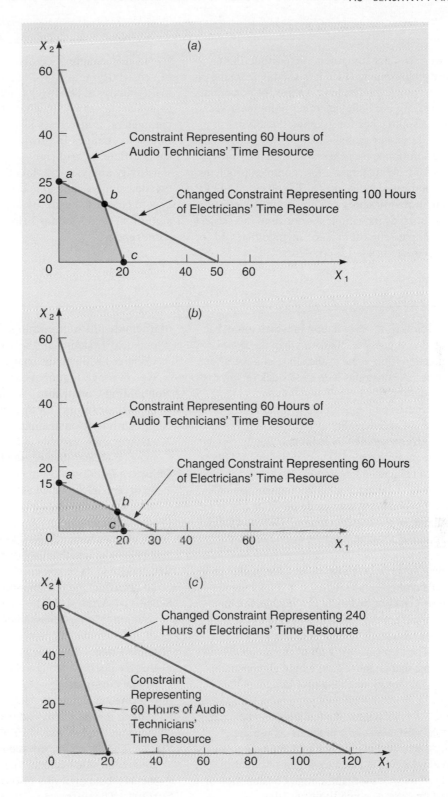

The Allowable Increase and Allowable Decrease for the right-hand side of each constraint is provided, and the shadow price is relevant for changes within these limits. For the electrician hours, the right-hand-side value of 80 may be increased by 160 (for a total of 240) or decreased by 80 (for a total of 0) and the shadow price remains relevant. If a change is made that exceeds these limits, then the problem should be resolved to find the impact of the change.

Summary

In this chapter, we introduce a mathematical modeling technique called linear programming (LP). It is used in reaching an optimum solution to problems that have a series of constraints binding the objective. We use both the corner point method and the isoprofit/isocost approaches for graphically solving problems with only two decision variables.

The graphical solution approaches of this chapter provide a conceptual basis for tackling larger, more complex problems, some of which are addressed in Chapter 8. To solve real-life LP problems with numerous variables and constraints, we need a solution procedure such as the simplex algorithm, the subject of Module 7. The simplex algorithm is the method that QM for Windows and Excel use to tackle LP problems.

In this chapter, we also present the important concept of sensitivity analysis. Sometimes referred to as postoptimality analysis, sensitivity analysis is used by management to answer a series of what-if? questions about LP model parameters. It also tests just how sensitive the optimal solution is to changes in profit or cost coefficients, technological coefficients, and right-hand-side resources. We explored sensitivity analysis graphically (i.e., for problems with only two decision variables) and with computer output, but to see how to conduct sensitivity algebraically through the simplex algorithm, read Module 7 (located at **www.pearsonhighered .com/render**).

Glossary

Alternate Optimal Solution   A situation in which more than one optimal solution is possible. It arises when the slope of the objective function is the same as the slope of a constraint.

Binding Constraint   A constraint with zero slack or surplus for the optimal solution.

Constraint   A restriction on the resources available to a firm (stated in the form of an inequality or an equation).

Corner Point, or **Extreme Point**   A point that lies on one of the corners of the feasible region. This means that it falls at the intersection of two constraint lines.

Corner Point Method   The method of finding the optimal solution to an LP problem by testing the profit or cost level at each corner point of the feasible region. The theory of LP states that the optimal solution must lie at one of the corner points.

Decision Variable   A variable whose value may be chosen by the decision maker.

Dual Price (value)   The improvement in the objective function value that results from a one-unit increase in the right-hand side of that constraint.

Feasible Region   The area satisfying all of the problem's resource restrictions; that is, the region where all constraints overlap. All possible solutions to the problem lie in the feasible region.

Feasible Solution   A point lying in the feasible region. Basically, it is any point that satisfies all of the problem's constraints.

Inequality   A mathematical expression containing a greater-than-or-equal-to relation ($\geq$) or a less-than-or-equal-to relation ($\leq$) used to indicate that the total consumption of a resource must be $\geq$ or $\leq$ some limiting value.

Infeasible Solution   Any point lying outside the feasible region. It violates one or more of the stated constraints.

Isocost Line   A straight line representing all combinations of X_1 and X_2 for a particular cost level.

Isoprofit Line   A straight line representing all nonnegative combinations of X_1 and X_2 for a particular profit level.

Linear Programming (LP)   A mathematical technique used to help management decide how to make the most effective use of an organization's resources.

Mathematical Programming   The general category of mathematical modeling and solution techniques used to allocate resources while optimizing a measurable goal. LP is one type of programming model.

Nonbinding Constraint   A constraint with a positive amount of slack or surplus for the optimal solution.

Nonnegativity Constraints   A set of constraints that requires each decision variable to be nonnegative; that is, each X_i must be greater than or equal to 0.

Objective Function   A mathematical statement of the goal of an organization, stated as an intent to maximize or to minimize some important quantity such as profits or costs.

Product Mix Problem   A common LP problem involving a decision as to which products a firm should produce given that it faces limited resources.

Redundancy   The presence of one or more constraints that do not affect the feasible solution region.

Sensitivity Analysis   The study of how sensitive an optimal solution is to model assumptions and to data changes. It is often referred to as postoptimality analysis.

Shadow Price   The increase in the objective function value that results from a one-unit increase in the right-hand side of that constraint.

Simultaneous Equation Method   The algebraic means of solving for the intersection point of two or more linear constraint equations.

Slack   The difference between the left-hand side and the right-hand side of a less-than-or-equal-to constraint. Often this is the amount of a resource that is not being used.

Surplus   The difference between the left-hand side and the right-hand side of a greater-than-or-equal-to constraint. Often this represents the amount by which a minimum quantity is exceeded.

Technological Coefficients   Coefficients of the variables in the constraint equations. The coefficients represent the amount of resources needed to produce one unit of the variable.

Unboundedness   A condition that exists when a solution variable and the profit can be made infinitely large without violating any of the problem's constraints in a maximization process.

Solved Problems

Solved Problem 7-1

Personal Mini Warehouses is planning to expand its successful Orlando business into Tampa. In doing so, the company must determine how many storage rooms of each size to build. Its objective and constraints follow:

$$\text{Maximize monthly earnings} = 50X_1 + 20X_2$$

$$\text{subject to} \qquad 20X_1 + 40X_2 \le 4{,}000 \qquad \text{(advertising budget available)}$$

$$100X_1 + 50X_2 \le 8{,}000 \qquad \text{(square footage required)}$$

$$X_1 \qquad\quad \le 60 \qquad \text{(rental limit expected)}$$

$$X_1, X_2 \ge 0$$

where

X_1 = number of large spaces developed

X_2 = number of small spaces developed

Solution

An evaluation of the five corner points of the accompanying graph indicates that corner point C produces the greatest earnings. Refer to the graph and table.

CORNER POINT	VALUES OF X_1, X_2	OBJECTIVE FUNCTION VALUE ($)
A	(0, 0)	0
B	(60, 0)	3,000
C	(60, 40)	3,800
D	(40, 80)	3,600
E	(0, 100)	2,000

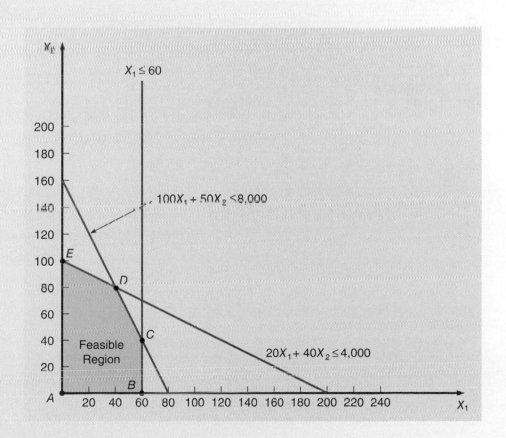

Solved Problem 7-2

The solution obtained with QM for Windows for Solved Problem 7-1 is given in the following program. Use this to answer the following questions.

a. For the optimal solution, how much of the advertising budget is spent?
b. For the optimal solution, how much square footage will be used?
c. Would the solution change if the budget were only $3,000 instead of $4,000?
d. What would the optimal solution be if the profit on the large spaces were reduced from $50 to $45?
e. How much would earnings increase if the square footage requirement were increased from 8,000 to 9,000?

Linear Programming Results

Solved Problem 7-2 Solution

	X1	X2		RHS	Dual
Maximize	50	20			
Constraint 1	20	40	<=	4,000	0
Constraint 2	100	50	<=	8,000	0.4
Constraint 3	1	0	<=	60	10
Solution->	60	40		3,800	

Ranging

Solved Problem 7-2 Solution

Variable	Value	Reduced	Original Val	Lower Bound	Upper Bound
X1	60	0	50	40	Infinity
X2	40	0	20	0	25
Constraint	Dual Value	Slack/Surplus	Original Val	Lower Bound	Upper Bound
Constraint 1	0	1,200	4,000	2,800	Infinity
Constraint 2	0.4	0	8,000	6,000	9,500
Constraint 3	10	0	60	40	80

Solution

a. In the optimal solution, $X_1 = 60$ and $X_2 = 40$. Using these values in the first constraint gives us

$$20X_1 + 40X_2 = 20(60) + 40(40) = 2,800$$

Another way to find this is by looking at the slack:

Slack for constraint 1 = 1,200 so the amount used is $4,000 - 1,200 = 2,800$

b. For the second constraint we have

$$100X_1 + 50X_2 = 100(60) + 50(40) = 8,000 \text{ square feet}$$

Instead of computing this, you may simply observe that the slack is 0, so all of the 8,000 square feet will be used.

c. No, the solution would not change. The dual price is 0 and there is slack available. The value 3,000 is between the lower bound of 2,800 and the upper bound of infinity. Only the slack for this constraint would change.

d. Since the new coefficient for X_1 is between the lower bound (40) and the upper bound (infinity), the current corner point remains optimal. So $X_1 = 60$ and $X_2 = 40$, and only the monthly earnings change.

$$\text{Earnings} = 45(60) + 20(40) = \$3,500$$

e. The dual price for this constraint is 0.4, and the upper bound is 9,500. The increase of 1,000 units will result in an increase in earnings of $1,000(0.4 \text{ per unit}) = \$400$.

Solved Problem 7-3

Solve the following LP formulation graphically, using the isocost line approach:

$$\text{Minimize costs} = 24X_1 + 28X_2$$
$$\text{subject to} \qquad 5X_1 + 4X_2 \leq 2,000$$
$$X_1 \qquad\qquad \geq 80$$
$$X_1 + X_2 \geq 300$$
$$X_2 \geq 100$$
$$X_1, X_2 \geq 0$$

Solution

A graph of the four constraints follows. The arrows indicate the direction of feasibility for each constraint. The next graph illustrates the feasible solution region and plots of two possible objective function cost lines. The first, $10,000, was selected arbitrarily as a starting point. To find the optimal corner point, we need to move the cost line in the direction of lower cost, that is, down and to the left. The last point where a cost line touches the feasible region as it moves toward the origin is corner point D. Thus D, which represents $X_1 = 200$, $X_2 = 100$, and a cost of $7,600, is optimal.

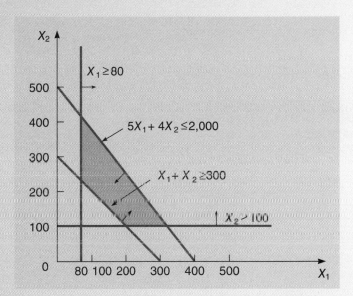

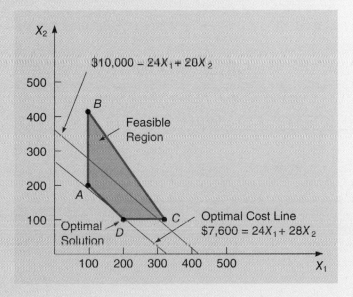

Solved Problem 7-4

Solve the following problem, using the corner point method. For the optimal solution, how much slack or surplus is there for each constraint?

$$\text{Maximize profit} = 30X_1 + 40X_2$$
$$\text{subject to} \qquad 4X_1 + 2X_2 \leq 16$$
$$2X_1 - X_2 \geq 2$$
$$X_2 \leq 2$$
$$X_1, X_2 \geq 0$$

Solution

The graph appears next with the feasible region shaded.

CORNER POINT	COORDINATES	PROFIT ($)
A	$X_1 = 1, X_2 = 0$	30
B	$X_1 = 4, X_2 = 0$	120
C	$X_1 = 3, X_2 = 2$	170
D	$X_1 = 2, X_2 = 2$	140

The optimal solution is (3, 2). For this point,

$$4X_1 + 2X_2 = 4(3) + 2(2) = 16$$

Therefore, slack = 0 for constraint 1. Also,

$$2X_1 - 1X_2 = 2(3) - 1(2) = 4 > 2$$

Therefore, surplus = 4 − 2 = 2 for constraint 2. Also,

$$X_2 = 2$$

Therefore, slack = 0 for constraint 3.

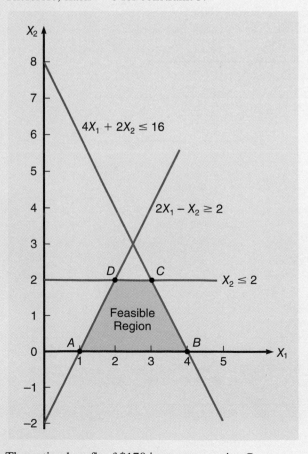

The optimal profit of $170 is at corner point C.

Self-Test

- Before taking the self-test, refer to the learning objectives at the beginning of the chapter, the notes in the margins, and the glossary at the end of the chapter.
- Use the key at the back of the book to correct your answers.
- Restudy pages that correspond to any questions that you answered incorrectly or material you feel uncertain about.

1. When using a graphical solution procedure, the region bounded by the set of constraints is called the
   a. solution.
   b. feasible region.
   c. infeasible region.
   d. maximum profit region.
   e. none of the above.

2. In an LP problem, at least one corner point must be an optimal solution if an optimal solution exists.
   a. True
   b. False

3. An LP problem has a bounded feasible region. If this problem has an equality ($=$) constraint, then
   a. this must be a minimization problem.
   b. the feasible region must consist of a line segment.
   c. the problem must be degenerate.
   d. the problem must have more than one optimal solution.

4. Which of the following would cause a change in the feasible region?
   a. Increasing an objective function coefficient in a maximization problem
   b. Adding a redundant constraint
   c. Changing the right-hand side of a nonredundant constraint
   d. Increasing an objective function coefficient in a minimization problem

5. If a nonredundant constraint is removed from an LP problem, then
   a. the feasible region will get larger.
   b. the feasible region will get smaller.
   c. the problem would become nonlinear.
   d. the problem would become infeasible.

6. In the optimal solution to a linear program, there are 20 units of slack for a constraint. From this we know that
   a. the dual price for this constraint is 20.
   b. the dual price for this constraint is 0.
   c. this constraint must be redundant.
   d. the problem must be a maximization problem.

7. A linear program has been solved and sensitivity analysis has been performed. The ranges for the objective function coefficients have been found. For the profit on X_1, the upper bound is 80, the lower bound is 60, and the current value is 75. Which of the following must be true if the profit on this variable is lowered to 70 and the optimal solution is found?
   a. A new corner point will become optimal.
   b. The maximum possible total profit may increase.
   c. The values for all the decision variables will remain the same.
   d. All of the above are possible.

8. A graphical method should only be used to solve an LP problem when
   a. there are only two constraints.
   b. there are more than two constraints.
   c. there are only two variables.
   d. there are more than two variables.

9. In LP, variables do not have to be integer valued and may take on any fractional value. This assumption is called
   a. proportionality.
   b. divisibility.
   c. additivity.
   d. certainty.

10. In solving a linear program, no feasible solution exists. To resolve this problem we might
    a. add another variable.
    b. add another constraint.
    c. remove or relax a constraint.
    d. try a different computer program.

11. If the feasible region gets larger due to a change in one of the constraints, the optimal value of the objective function
    a. must increase or remain the same for a maximization problem.
    b. must decrease or remain the same for a maximization problem.
    c. must increase or remain the same for a minimization problem.
    d. cannot change.

12. When alternate optimal solutions exist in an LP problem, then
    a. the objective function will be parallel to one of the constraints.
    b. one of the constraints will be redundant.
    c. two constraints will be parallel.
    d. the problem will also be unbounded.

13. If a linear program is unbounded, the problem probably has not been formulated correctly. Which of the following would most likely cause this?
    a. A constraint was inadvertently omitted.
    b. An unnecessary constraint was added to the problem.
    c. The objective function coefficients are too large.
    d. The objective function coefficients are too small.

14. A feasible solution to an LP problem
    a. must satisfy all of the problem's constraints simultaneously.
    b. need not satisfy all of the constraints, only some of them.
    c. must be a corner point of the feasible region.
    d. must give the maximum possible profit.

Discussion Questions and Problems

Discussion Questions

7-1   Discuss the similarities and differences between minimization and maximization problems using the graphical solution approaches of LP.

7-2   It is important to understand the assumptions underlying the use of any quantitative analysis model. What are the assumptions and requirements for an LP model to be formulated and used?

7-3   It has been said that each LP problem that has a feasible region has an infinite number of solutions. Explain.

7-4   You have just formulated a maximization LP problem and are preparing to solve it graphically. What criteria should you consider in deciding whether it would be easier to solve the problem by the corner point method or the isoprofit line approach?

7-5   Under what condition is it possible for an LP problem to have more than one optimal solution?

7-6   Develop your own set of constraint equations and inequalities and use them to illustrate graphically each of the following conditions:

(a) an unbounded problem
(b) an infeasible problem
(c) a problem containing redundant constraints

7-7   The production manager of a large Cincinnati manufacturing firm once made the statement, "I would like to use LP, but it's a technique that operates under conditions of certainty. My plant doesn't have that certainty; it's a world of uncertainty. So LP can't be used here." Do you think this statement has any merit? Explain why the manager may have said it.

7-8   The mathematical relationships that follow were formulated by an operations research analyst at the Smith–Lawton Chemical Company. Which ones are invalid for use in an LP problem, and why?

$$\text{Maximize profit} = 4X_1 + 3X_1X_2 + 8X_2 + 5X_3$$

$$\text{subject to} \quad 2X_1 \quad\quad + X_2 + 2X_3 \le 50$$
$$X_1 \quad\quad - 4X_2 \quad\quad \ge 6$$
$$1.5X_1^2 + 6X_2 + 3X_3 \ge 21$$
$$19X_2 - 0.35X_3 = 17$$
$$5X_1 \quad\quad + 4X_2 + 3\sqrt{X_3} \le 80$$
$$-X_1 \quad\quad - X_2 + X_3 = 5$$

7-9   Discuss the role of sensitivity analysis in LP. Under what circumstances is it needed, and under what conditions do you think it is not necessary?

7-10   A linear program has the objective of maximizing profit $= 12X + 8Y$. The maximum profit is $8,000. Using a computer we find the upper bound for profit on X is 20 and the lower bound is 9. Discuss the changes to the optimal solution (the values of the variables and the profit) that would occur if the profit on X were increased to $15. How would the optimal solution change if the profit on X were increased to $25?

7-11   A linear program has a maximum profit of $600. One constraint in this problem is $4X + 2Y \le 80$. Using a computer we find the dual price for this constraint is 3, and there is a lower bound of 75 and an upper bound of 100. Explain what this means.

7-12   Develop your own original LP problem with two constraints and two real variables.

(a) Explain the meaning of the numbers on the right-hand side of each of your constraints.
(b) Explain the significance of the technological coefficients.
(c) Solve your problem graphically to find the optimal solution.
(d) Illustrate graphically the effect of increasing the contribution rate of your first variable (X_1) by 50% over the value you first assigned it. Does this change the optimal solution?

7-13   Explain how a change in a technological coefficient can affect a problem's optimal solution. How can a change in resource availability affect a solution?

Problems

⚖• 7-14   The Electrocomp Corporation manufactures two electrical products: air conditioners and large fans. The assembly process for each is similar in that both require a certain amount of wiring and drilling. Each air conditioner takes 3 hours of wiring and 2 hours of drilling. Each fan must go through 2 hours of wiring and 1 hour of drilling. During the next production period, 240 hours of wiring time are available and up to 140 hours of drilling time may be used. Each air conditioner sold yields a profit of $25. Each fan assembled may be sold for a $15 profit. Formulate and solve this LP production mix situation to find the best combination of air conditioners and fans that yields the highest profit. Use the corner point graphical approach.

⚖• 7-15   Electrocomp's management realizes that it forgot to include two critical constraints (see Problem 7-14). In particular, management decides that there should be a minimum number of air conditioners produced in order to fulfill a contract. Also, due to an oversupply of fans in the preceding period, a limit should be placed on the total number of fans produced.

(a) If Electrocomp decides that at least 20 air conditioners should be produced but no more than 80 fans should be produced, what would be the optimal solution? How much slack or surplus is there for each of the four constraints?

(b) If Electrocomp decides that at least 30 air conditioners should be produced but no more than 50 fans should be produced, what would be the optimal solution? How much slack or surplus is there for each of the four constraints at the optimal solution?

7-16 A candidate for mayor in a small town has allocated $40,000 for last-minute advertising in the days preceding the election. Two types of ads will be used: radio and television. Each radio ad costs $200 and reaches an estimated 3,000 people. Each television ad costs $500 and reaches an estimated 7,000 people. In planning the advertising campaign, the campaign manager would like to reach as many people as possible, but she has stipulated that at least 10 ads of each type must be used. Also, the number of radio ads must be at least as great as the number of television ads. How many ads of each type should be used? How many people will this reach?

7-17 The Outdoor Furniture Corporation manufactures two products, benches and picnic tables, for use in yards and parks. The firm has two main resources: its carpenters (labor force) and a supply of redwood for use in the furniture. During the next production cycle, 1,200 hours of labor are available under a union agreement. The firm also has a stock of 3,500 board feet of good-quality redwood. Each bench that Outdoor Furniture produces requires 4 labor hours and 10 board feet of redwood; each picnic table takes 6 labor hours and 35 board feet of redwood. Completed benches will yield a profit of $9 each, and tables will result in a profit of $20 each. How many benches and tables should Outdoor Furniture produce to obtain the largest possible profit? Use the graphical LP approach.

7-18 The dean of the Western College of Business must plan the school's course offerings for the fall semester. Student demands make it necessary to offer at least 30 undergraduate and 20 graduate courses in the term. Faculty contracts also dictate that at least 60 courses be offered in total. Each undergraduate course taught costs the college an average of $2,500 in faculty wages, and each graduate course costs $3,000. How many undergraduate and graduate courses should be taught in the fall so that total faculty salaries are kept to a minimum?

7-19 MSA Computer Corporation manufactures two models of minicomputers, the Alpha 4 and the Beta 5. The firm employs five technicians, working 160 hours each per month, on its assembly line. Management insists that full employment (i.e., *all* 160 hours of time) be maintained for each worker during next month's operations. It requires 20 labor hours to assemble each Alpha 4 computer and 25 labor hours to assemble each Beta 5 model. MSA wants to see at least 10 Alpha 4s and at least 15 Beta 5s produced during the production period. Alpha 4s generate $1,200 profit per unit, and Beta 5s yield $1,800 each. Determine the most profitable number of each model of minicomputer to produce during the coming month.

7-20 A winner of the Texas Lotto has decided to invest $50,000 per year in the stock market. Under consideration are stocks for a petrochemical firm and a public utility. Although a long-range goal is to get the highest possible return, some consideration is given to the risk involved with the stocks. A risk index on a scale of 1–10 (with 10 being the most risky) is assigned to each of the two stocks. The total risk of the portfolio is found by multiplying the risk of each stock by the dollars invested in that stock.

The following table provides a summary of the return and risk:

STOCK	ESTIMATED RETURN	RISK INDEX
Petrochemical	12%	9
Utility	6%	4

The investor would like to maximize the return on the investment, but the average risk index of the investment should not be higher than 6. How much should be invested in each stock? What is the average risk for this investment? What is the estimated return for this investment?

7-21 Referring to the Texas Lotto situation in Problem 7-20, suppose the investor has changed his attitude about the investment and wishes to give greater emphasis to the risk of the investment. Now the investor wishes to minimize the risk of the investment as long as a return of at least 8% is generated. Formulate this as an LP problem and find the optimal solution. How much should be invested in each stock? What is the average risk for this investment? What is the estimated return for this investment?

7-22 Solve the following LP problem using the corner point graphical method. At the optimal solution, calculate the slack for each constraint:

$$\text{Maximize profit} = 4X + 4Y$$
$$\text{subject to} \quad 3X + 5Y \le 150$$
$$X - 2Y \le 10$$
$$5X + 3Y \le 150$$
$$X, Y \ge 0$$

⚡: 7-23 Consider this LP formulation:

$$\text{Minimize cost} = \$X + 2Y$$
$$\text{subject to} \quad X + 3Y \geq 90$$
$$8X + 2Y \geq 160$$
$$3X + 2Y \geq 120$$
$$Y \leq 70$$
$$X, Y \geq 0$$

Graphically illustrate the feasible region and apply the isocost line procedure to indicate which corner point produces the optimal solution. What is the cost of this solution?

⚡: 7-24 The stock brokerage firm of Blank, Leibowitz, and Weinberger has analyzed and recommended two stocks to an investors' club of college professors. The professors were interested in factors such as short-term growth, intermediate growth, and dividend rates. These data on each stock are as follows:

FACTOR	STOCK ($)	
	LOUISIANA GAS AND POWER	**TRIMEX INSULATION COMPANY**
Short-term growth potential, per dollar invested	0.36	0.24
Intermediate growth potential (over next three years), per dollar invested	1.67	1.50
Dividend rate potential	4%	8%

Each member of the club has an investment goal of (1) an appreciation of no less than $720 in the short term, (2) an appreciation of at least $5,000 in the next three years, and (3) a dividend income of at least $200 per year. What is the smallest investment that a professor can make to meet these three goals?

⚡: 7-25 Woofer Pet Foods produces a low-calorie dog food for overweight dogs. This product is made from beef products and grain. Each pound of beef costs $0.90, and each pound of grain costs $0.60. A pound of the dog food must contain at least 9 units of Vitamin 1 and 10 units of Vitamin 2. A pound of beef contains 10 units of Vitamin 1 and 12 units of Vitamin 2. A pound of grain contains 6 units of Vitamin 1 and 9 units of Vitamin 2. Formulate this as an LP problem to minimize the cost of the dog food. How many pounds of beef and grain should be included in each pound of dog food? What is the cost and vitamin content of the final product?

⚡: 7-26 The seasonal yield of olives in a Piraeus, Greece, vineyard is greatly influenced by a process of branch pruning. If olive trees are pruned every two weeks, output is increased. The pruning process, however, requires considerably more labor than permitting the olives to grow on their own and results in a smaller size olive. It also, though, permits olive trees to be spaced closer together. The yield of 1 barrel of olives by pruning requires 5 hours of labor and 1 acre of land. The production of a barrel of olives by the normal process requires only 2 labor hours but takes 2 acres of land. An olive grower has 250 hours of labor available and a total of 150 acres for growing. Because of the olive size difference, a barrel of olives produced on pruned trees sells for $20, whereas a barrel of regular olives has a market price of $30. The grower has determined that because of uncertain demand, no more than 40 barrels of pruned olives should be produced. Use graphical LP to find

(a) the maximum possible profit.
(b) the best combination of barrels of pruned and regular olives.
(c) the number of acres that the olive grower should devote to each growing process.

⚡: 7-27 Consider the following four LP formulations. Using a graphical approach, determine

(a) which formulation has more than one optimal solution.
(b) which formulation is unbounded.
(c) which formulation has no feasible solution.
(d) which formulation is correct as is.

Formulation 1

$$\text{Maximize } 10X_1 + 10X_2$$
$$\text{subject to} \quad 2X_1 \quad\quad \leq 10$$
$$2X_1 + 4X_2 \leq 16$$
$$4X_2 \leq 8$$
$$X_1 \quad\quad = 6$$

Formulation 2

$$\text{Maximize } X_1 + 2X_2$$
$$\text{subject to } X_1 \quad\quad \leq 1$$
$$2X_2 \leq 2$$
$$X_1 + 2X_2 \leq 2$$

Formulation 3

$$\text{Maximize } 3X_1 + 2X_2$$
$$\text{subject to} \quad X_1 + X_2 \geq 5$$
$$X_1 \quad\quad \geq 2$$
$$2X_2 \geq 8$$

Formulation 4

$$\text{Maximize } 3X_1 + 3X_2$$
$$\text{subject to } 4X_1 + 6X_2 \leq 48$$
$$4X_1 + 2X_2 \leq 12$$
$$3X_2 \geq 3$$
$$2X_1 \quad\quad \geq 2$$

⚡• 7-28 Graph the following LP problem and indicate the optimal solution point:

$$\text{Maximize profit} = \$3X + \$2Y$$
$$\text{subject to} \quad 2X + Y \leq 150$$
$$2X + 3Y \leq 300$$

(a) Does the optimal solution change if the profit per unit of X changes to $4.50?
(b) What happens if the profit function should have been $3X + $3Y?

7-29 Graphically analyze the following problem:

$$\text{Maximize profit} = \$4X + \$6Y$$

subject to
$$X + 2Y \le 8 \text{ hours}$$
$$6X + 4Y \le 24 \text{ hours}$$

(a) What is the optimal solution?
(b) If the first constraint is altered to $X + 3Y \le 8$, does the feasible region or optimal solution change?

7-30 Examine the LP formulation in Problem 7-29. The problem's second constraint reads

$$6X + 4Y \le 24 \text{ hours}\quad\text{(time available on machine 2)}$$

If the firm decides that 36 hours of time can be made available on machine 2 (namely, an additional 12 hours) at an additional cost of $10, should it add the hours?

7-31 Consider the following LP problem:

$$\text{Maximize profit} = 5X + 6Y$$

subject to
$$2X + Y \le 120$$
$$2X + 3Y \le 240$$
$$X, Y \ge 0$$

(a) What is the optimal solution to this problem? Solve it graphically.
(b) If a technical breakthrough occurred that raised the profit per unit of X to $8, would this affect the optimal solution?
(c) Instead of an increase in the profit coefficient X to $8, suppose that profit was overestimated and should only have been $3. Does this change the optimal solution?

7-32 Consider the LP formulation given in Problem 7-31. If the second constraint is changed from $2X + 3Y \le 240$ to $2X + 4Y \le 240$, what effect will this have on the optimal solution?

7-33 The computer output given below is for Problem 7-31. Use this to answer the following questions.

(a) How much could the profit on X increase or decrease without changing the values of X and Y in the optimal solution?
(b) If the right-hand side of constraint 1 were increased by 1 unit, how much would the profit increase?
(c) If the right-hand side of constraint 1 were increased by 10 units, how much would the profit increase?

7-34 The computer output on the next page is for a product mix problem in which there are two products and three resource constraints. Use the output to help you answer the following questions. Assume that you wish to maximize profit in each case.

(a) How many units of product 1 and product 2 should be produced?
(b) How much of each of the three resources is being used? How much slack is there for each constraint? Which of the constraints are binding, and which are nonbinding?
(c) What are the dual prices for each resource?
(d) If you could obtain more of one of the resources, which one should you obtain? How much should you be willing to pay for this?
(e) What would happen to profit if, with the original output, management decided to produce one more unit of product 2?

7-35 Graphically solve the following problem:

$$\text{Maximize profit} = 8X_1 + 5X_2$$

subject to
$$X_1 + X_2 \le 10$$
$$X_1 \le 6$$
$$X_1, X_2 \ge 0$$

(a) What is the optimal solution?
(b) Change the right-hand side of constraint 1 to 11 (instead of 10) and resolve the problem. How much did the profit increase as a result of this?

Linear Programming Results

Problem 33 Solution

	X	Y		RHS	Dual
Maximize	5	6			
const 1	2	1	<=	120	0.75
const 2	2	3	<=	240	1.75
Solution->	30	60		510	

Ranging

Problem 33 Solution

Variable	Value	Reduced Cost	Original Val	Lower Bound	Upper Bound
X	30	0	5	4	12
Y	60	0	6	2.5	7.5
Constraint	Dual Value	Slack/Surplus	Original Val	Lower Bound	Upper Bound
const 1	0.75	0	120	80	240
const 2	1.75	0	240	120	360

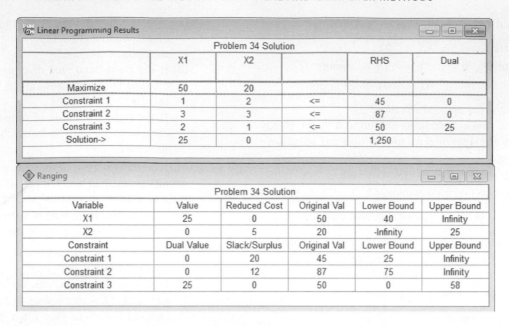

Linear Programming Results

Problem 34 Solution

	X1	X2		RHS	Dual
Maximize	50	20			
Constraint 1	1	2	<=	45	0
Constraint 2	3	3	<=	87	0
Constraint 3	2	1	<=	50	25
Solution->	25	0		1,250	

Ranging

Problem 34 Solution

Variable	Value	Reduced Cost	Original Val	Lower Bound	Upper Bound
X1	25	0	50	40	Infinity
X2	0	5	20	-Infinity	25
Constraint	Dual Value	Slack/Surplus	Original Val	Lower Bound	Upper Bound
Constraint 1	0	20	45	25	Infinity
Constraint 2	0	12	87	75	Infinity
Constraint 3	25	0	50	0	58

Linear Programming Results

Problem 35 Solution

	X1	X2		RHS	Dual
Maximize	8	5			
Constraint 1	1	1	<=	10	5
Constraint 2	1	0	<=	6	3
Solution->	6	4		68	

Ranging

Problem 35 Solution

Variable	Value	Reduced	Original Val	Lower Bound	Upper Bound
X1	6	0	8	5	Infinity
X2	4	0	5	0	8
Constraint	Dual Value	Slack/Surplus	Original Val	Lower Bound	Upper Bound
Constraint 1	5	0	10	6	Infinity
Constraint 2	3	0	6	0	10

(c) Change the right-hand side of constraint 1 to 6 (instead of 10) and resolve the problem. How much did the profit decrease as a result of this? Looking at the graph, what would happen if the right-hand-side value were to go below 6?

(d) Change the right-hand-side value of constraint 1 to 5 (instead of 10) and resolve the problem. How much did the profit decrease from the original profit as a result of this?

(e) Using the computer output on this page, what is the dual price of constraint 1? What is the lower bound on this?

(f) What conclusions can you draw from this regarding the bounds of the right-hand-side values and the dual price?

7-36 **Serendipity***

The three princes of Serendip
Went on a little trip.
They could not carry too much weight;
More than 300 pounds made them hesitate.
They planned to the ounce. When they returned to Ceylon
They discovered that their supplies were just about gone
When, what to their joy, Prince William found
A pile of coconuts on the ground.
"Each will bring 60 rupees," said Prince Richard with a grin

---

*The word *serendipity* was coined by the English writer Horace Walpole after a fairy tale titled *The Three Princes of Serendip*. Source of problem is unknown.

As he almost tripped over a lion skin.

"Look out!" cried Prince Robert with glee

As he spied some more lion skins under a tree.

"These are worth even more—300 rupees each

If we can just carry them all down to the beach."

Each skin weighed fifteen pounds and each coconut, five,

But they carried them all and made it alive.

The boat back to the island was very small

15 cubic feet baggage capacity—that was all.

Each lion skin took up one cubic foot

While eight coconuts the same space took.

With everything stowed they headed to sea

And on the way calculated what their new wealth might be.

"Eureka!" cried Prince Robert, "Our worth is so great

That there's no other way we could return in this state.

Any other skins or nut that we might have brought

Would now have us poorer. And now I know what—

I'll write my friend Horace in England, for surely

Only he can appreciate our serendipity."

Formulate and solve **Serendipity** by graphical LP in order to calculate "what their new wealth might be."

:7-37 Bhavika Investments, a group of financial advisors and retirement planners, has been requested to provide advice on how to invest $200,000 for one of its clients. The client has stipulated that the money must be put into either a stock fund or a money market fund, and the annual return should be at least $14,000. Other conditions related to risk have also

been specified, and the following linear program was developed to help with this investment decision:

Minimize risk $= 12S + 5M$

subject to

$$S + M = 200,000 \quad \text{total investment is } \$200,000$$

$$0.10S + 0.05M \geq 14,000 \quad \text{return must be at least } \$14,000$$

$$M \geq 40,000 \quad \text{at least } \$40,000 \text{ must be in money market fund}$$

$$S, M \geq 0$$

where

S = dollars invested in stock fund

M = dollars invested in money market fund

The QM for Windows output is shown below.

(a) How much money should be invested in the money market fund and the stock fund? What is the total risk?

(b) What is the total return? What rate of return is this?

(c) Would the solution change if risk measure for each dollar in the stock fund were 14 instead of 12?

(d) For each additional dollar that is available, how much does the risk change?

(e) Would the solution change if the amount that must be invested in the money market fund were changed from $40,000 to $50,000?

:7-38 Refer to the Bhavika Investments (Problem 7-37) situation once again. It has been decided that, rather than minimize risk, the objective should be to maximize return while placing restriction on the amount

Linear Programming Results

Problem 37 Solution					
	S	M		RHS	Dual
Minimize	12	5			
Constraint 1	1	1	=	200,000	2
Constraint 2	0.1	0.05	>=	14,000	-140
Constraint 3	0	1	>=	40,000	0
Solution->	80,000	120,000.0		1,560,000	

Ranging

Problem 37 Solution					
Variable	Value	Reduced Cost	Original Val	Lower Bound	Upper Bound
S	80,000	0	12	5	Infinity
M	120,000.0	0	5	-Infinity	12
Constraint	Dual Value	Slack/Surplus	Original Val	Lower Bound	Upper Bound
Constraint 1	2	0	200,000	160,000	280,000
Constraint 2	-140	0	14,000	10,000	18,000
Constraint 3	0	80,000.01	40,000	-Infinity	120,000.0

Linear Programming Results

Problem 38 Solution

	S	M		RHS	Dual
Maximize	0.1	0.05			
Constraint 1	1	1	=	200,000	0.1
Constraint 2	12	5	<=	2,200,000	0
Constraint 3	0	1	>=	40,000	-0.05
Solution->	160,000	40,000		18,000	

Ranging

Problem 38 Solution

Variable	Value	Reduced Cost	Original Val	Lower Bound	Upper Bound
S	160,000	0	0.1	0.05	Infinity
M	40,000	0	0.05	-Infinity	0.1
Constraint	Dual Value	Slack/Surplus	Original Val	Lower Bound	Upper Bound
Constraint 1	0.1	0	200,000	40,000	206,666.7
Constraint 2	0	80,000	2,200,000	2,120,000	Infinity
Constraint 3	-0.05	0	40,000	28,571.43	200,000

of risk. The average risk should be no more than 11 (with a total risk of 2,200,000 for the $200,000 invested). The linear program was reformulated, and the QM for Windows output is shown above.

(a) How much money should be invested in the money market fund and the stock fund? What is the total return? What rate of return is this?

(b) What is the total risk? What is the average risk?

(c) Would the solution change if return for each dollar in the stock fund were 0.09 instead of 0.10?

(d) For each additional dollar that is available, what is the marginal rate of return?

(e) How much would the total return change if the amount that must be invested in the money market fund were changed from $40,000 to $50,000?

Problems 7-39 to 7-44 test your ability to formulate LP problems that have more than two variables. They cannot be solved graphically but will give you a chance to set up a larger problem.

7-39 The Feed 'N Ship Ranch fattens cattle for local farmers and ships them to meat markets in Kansas City and Omaha. The owners of the ranch seek to determine the amounts of cattle feed to buy so that minimum nutritional standards are satisfied, and at the same time total feed costs are minimized. The feed mix can be made up of the three grains that contain the following ingredients per pound of feed:

	FEED (OZ.)		
INGREDIENT	STOCK X	STOCK Y	STOCK Z
A	3	2	4
B	2	3	1
C	1	0	2
D	6	8	4

The cost per pound of stocks X, Y, and Z are $2, $4, and $2.50, respectively. The minimum requirement per cow per month is 4 pounds of ingredient A, 5 pounds of ingredient B, 1 pound of ingredient C, and 8 pounds of ingredient D.

The ranch faces one additional restriction: it can only obtain 500 pounds of stock Z per month from the feed supplier regardless of its need. Because there are usually 100 cows at the Feed 'N Ship Ranch at any given time, this means that no more than 5 pounds of stock Z can be counted on for use in the feed of each cow per month.

(a) Formulate this as an LP problem.

(b) Solve using LP software.

7-40 The Weinberger Electronics Corporation manufactures four highly technical products that it supplies to aerospace firms that hold NASA contracts. Each of the products must pass through the following departments before they are shipped: wiring, drilling, assembly, and inspection. The time requirement in hours for each unit produced and its corresponding profit value are summarized in the following table:

	DEPARTMENT				UNIT PROFIT ($)
PRODUCT	WIRING	DRILLING	ASSEMBLY	INSPECTION	
XJ201	0.5	0.3	0.2	0.5	9
XM897	1.5	1	4	1	12
TR29	1.5	2	1	0.5	15
BR788	1	3	2	0.5	11

The production available in each department each month, and the minimum monthly production requirement to fulfill contracts, are as follows:

DEPARTMENT	CAPACITY (HOURS)	PRODUCT	MINIMUM PRODUCTION LEVEL
Wiring	15,000	XJ201	150
Drilling	17,000	XM897	100
Assembly	26,000	TR29	300
Inspection	12,000	BR788	400

The production manager has the responsibility of specifying production levels for each product for the coming month. Help him by formulating (that is, setting up the constraints and objective function) Weinberger's problem using LP.

7-41 Outdoor Inn, a camping equipment manufacturer in southern Utah, is developing a production schedule for a popular type of tent, the Double Inn. Orders have been received for 180 of these to be delivered at the end of this month, 220 to be delivered at the end of next month, and 240 to be delivered at the end of the month after that. This tent may be produced at a cost of $120, and the maximum number of tents that can be produced in a month is 230. The company may produce some extra tents in one month and keep them in storage until the next month. The cost for keeping these in inventory for 1 month is estimated to be $6 per tent for each tent left at the end of the month. Formulate this as an LP problem to minimize cost while meeting demand and not exceeding the monthly production capacity. Solve it using any computer software. (*Hint:* Define variables to represent the number of tents left over at the end of each month.)

7-42 Outdoors Inn (see Problem 7-41) expanded its tent-making operations later in the year. While still making the Double Inn tent, it is also making a larger tent, the Family Rolls, which has four rooms. The company can produce up to a combined total of 280 tents per month. The following table provides the demand that must be met and the production costs for the next 3 months. Note that the costs will increase in month 2. The holding cost for keeping a tent in inventory at the end of the month for use in the next month is estimated to be $6 per tent for the Double Inn and $8 per tent for the Family Rolls. Develop a linear program to minimize the total cost. Solve it using any computer software.

MONTH	DEMAND FOR DOUBLE INN	COST TO PRODUCE DOUBLE INN	DEMAND FOR FAMILY ROLLS	COST TO PRODUCE FAMILY ROLLS
1	185	$120	60	$150
2	205	$130	70	$160
3	225	$130	65	$160

7-43 Modem Corporation of America (MCA) is the world's largest producer of modem communication devices for microcomputers. MCA sold 9,000 of the regular model and 10,400 of the smart ("intelligent") model this September. Its income statement for the month is shown in the Table for Problem 7-43. Costs presented are typical of prior months and are expected to remain at the same levels in the near future.

The firm is facing several constraints as it prepares its November production plan. First, it has experienced a tremendous demand and has been unable to keep any significant inventory in stock. This situation is not expected to change. Second, the firm is located in a small Iowa town from which additional labor is not readily available. Workers can be shifted from production of one modem to another, however. To produce the 9,000 regular modems in September required 5,000 direct labor hours. The 10,400 intelligent modems absorbed 10,400 direct labor hours.

Third, MCA is experiencing a problem affecting the intelligent modems model. Its component supplier is able to guarantee only 8,000 microprocessors for November delivery. Each intelligent modem requires one of these specially made microprocessors. Alternative suppliers are not available on short notice.

TABLE FOR PROBLEM 7-43

MCA Income Statement Month Ended September 30

	REGULAR MODEMS	INTELLIGENT MODEMS
Sales	$450,000	$640,000
Less: Discounts	10,000	15,000
Returns	12,000	9,500
Warranty replacements	4,000	2,500
Net sales	$424,000	$613,000
Sales costs		
Direct labor	60,000	76,800
Indirect labor	9,000	11,520
Materials cost	90,000	128,000
Depreciation	40,000	50,800
Cost of sales	$199,000	$267,120
Gross profit	$225,000	$345,880
Selling and general expenses		
General expenses—variable	30,000	35,000
General expenses—fixed	36,000	40,000
Advertising	28,000	25,000
Sales commissions	31,000	60,000
Total operating cost	$125,000	$160,000
Pretax income	$100,000	$185,880
Income taxes (25%)	25,000	46,470
Net income	$ 75,000	$139,410

MCA wants to plan the optimal mix of the two modem models to produce in November to maximize profits for MCA.

(a) Formulate, using September's data, MCA's problem as a linear program.
(b) Solve the problem graphically.
(c) Discuss the implications of your recommended solution.

 7-44 Working with chemists at Virginia Tech and George Washington Universities, landscape contractor Kenneth Golding blended his own fertilizer, called "Golding-Grow." It consists of four chemical compounds, C-30, C-92, D-21, and E-11. The cost per pound for each compound is indicated as follows:

CHEMICAL COMPOUND	COST PER POUND ($)
C-30	0.12
C-92	0.09
D-21	0.11
E-11	0.04

The specifications for Golding-Grow are as follows: (1) E-11 must constitute at least 15% of the blend; (2) C-92 and C-30 must together constitute at least 45% of the blend; (3) D-21 and C-92 can together constitute no more than 30% of the blend; and (4) Golding-Grow is packaged and sold in 50-pound bags.

(a) Formulate an LP problem to determine what blend of the four chemicals will allow Golding to minimize the cost of a 50-pound bag of the fertilizer.
(b) Solve using a computer to find the best solution.

7-45 Raptor Fuels produces three grades of gasoline—Regular, Premium, and Super. All of these are produced by blending two types of crude oil—Crude A and Crude B. The two types of crude contain specific ingredients which help in determining the octane rating of gasoline. The important ingredients and the costs are contained in the following table:

	CRUDE A	CRUDE B
Cost per gallon	$0.42	$0.47
Ingredient 1	40%	52%
Other ingredients	60%	48%

In order to achieve the desired octane ratings, at least 41% of Regular gasoline should be Ingredient 1; at least 44% of Premium gasoline must be Ingredient 1, and at least 48% of Super gasoline must be Ingredient 1. Due to current contract commitments, Raptor Fuels must produce as least 20,000 gallons of Regular, at least 15,000 gallons of Premium, and at least 10,000 gallons of Super. Formulate a linear program that could be used to determine how much of Crude A and Crude B should be used in each of the gasolines to meet the demands at the minimum cost. What is the minimum cost? How much of Crude A and Crude B are used in each gallon of the different types of gasoline?

Internet Homework Problems

See our Internet home page, at **www.pearsonhighered.com/render**, for additional homework problems, Problems 7-46 to 7-50.

Case Study

Mexicana Wire Works

Ron Garcia felt good about his first week as a management trainee at Mexicana Wire Winding, Inc. He had not yet developed any technical knowledge about the manufacturing process, but he had toured the entire facility, located in the suburbs of Mexico City, and had met many people in various areas of the operation.

Mexicana, a subsidiary of Westover Wire Works, a Texas firm, is a medium-sized producer of wire windings used in making electrical transformers. José Arroyo, the production control manager, described the windings to Garcia as being of standardized design. Garcia's tour of the plant, laid out by process type (see Figure 7.20), followed the manufacturing sequence for the windings: drawing, extrusion, winding, inspection, and packaging. After inspection, good product is packaged and sent to finished product storage; defective product is stored separately until it can be reworked.

On March 8, Vivian Espania, Mexicana's general manager, stopped by Garcia's office and asked him to attend a staff meeting at 1:00 P.M.

"Let's get started with the business at hand," Vivian said, opening the meeting. "You all have met Ron Garcia, our new management trainee. Ron studied operations management in his MBA program in southern California, so I think he is competent to help us with a problem we have been discussing for a long time without resolution. I'm sure that each of you on my staff will give Ron your full cooperation."

FIGURE 7.20
Mexicana Wire Winding, Inc.

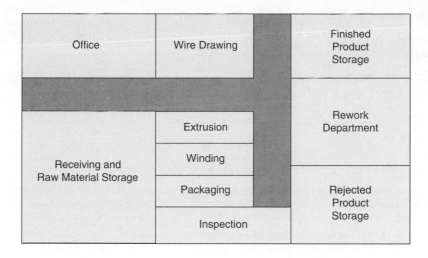

Vivian turned to José Arroyo, production manager. "José, why don't you describe the problem we are facing?"

"Well," José said, "business is very good right now. We are booking more orders than we can fill. We will have some new equipment on line within the next several months, which will take care of our capacity problems, but that won't help us in April. I have located some retired employees who used to work in the drawing department, and I am planning to bring them in as temporary employees in April to increase capacity there. Because we are planning to refinance some of our long-term debt, Vivian wants our profits to look as good as possible in April. I'm having a hard time figuring out which orders to run and which to back order so that I can make the bottom line look as good as possible. Can you help me with this?"

Garcia was surprised and apprehensive to receive such an important, high-profile assignment so early in his career. Recovering quickly, he said, "Give me your data and let me work with it for a day or two."

April Orders

Product W0075C	1,400 units
Product W0033C	250 units
Product W0005X	1,510 units
Product W0007X	1,116 units

Note: Vivian Espania has given her word to a key customer that we will manufacture 600 units of product W0007X and 150 units of product W0075C for him during April

Standard Cost

PRODUCT	MATERIAL	LABOR	OVERHEAD	SELLING PRICE
W0075C	$33.00	$ 9.90	$23.10	$100.00
W0033C	25.00	7.50	17.50	80.00
W0005X	35.00	10.50	24.50	130.00
W0007X	75.00	11.25	63.75	175.00

Selected Operating Data

Average output per month = 2,400 units

Average machine utilization = 63%

Average percentage of production set to rework department = 5% (mostly from Winding Department)

Average no. of rejected units awaiting rework = 850 (mostly from Winding Department)

Plant Capacity (Hours)

DRAWING	EXTRUSION	WINDING	PACKAGING
4,000	4,200	2,000	2,300

Note: Inspection capacity is not a problem; we can work overtime, as necessary, to accommodate any schedule.

Bill of Labor (Hours/Unit)

PRODUCT	DRAWING	EXTRUSION	WINDING	PACKAGING
W0075C	1.0	1.0	1.0	1.0
W0033C	2.0	1.0	3.0	0.0
W0005X	0.0	4.0	0.0	3.0
W0007X	1.0	1.0	0.0	2.0

Discussion Questions

1. What recommendations should Ron Garcia make, with what justification? Provide a detailed analysis with charts, graphs, and computer printouts included.
2. Discuss the need for temporary workers in the drawing department.
3. Discuss the plant layout.

Source: Professor Victor E. Sower, Sam Houston State University. This case material is based on an actual situation, with names and data altered for confidentiality.

Internet Case Study

See our Internet home page, at **www.pearsonhighered.com/render**, for this additional case study: **Agri Chem Corporation**. This case involves a company's response to an energy shortage.

Bibliography

Bassamboo, Achal, J. Michael Harrison, and Assaf Zeevi. "Design and Control of a Large Call Center: Asymptotic Analysis of an LP-Based Method," *Operations Research* 54, 3 (May–June 2006): 419–435.

Behjat, Laleh, Anthony Vannelli, and William Rosehart. "Integer Linear Programming Model for Global Routing," *INFORMS Journal on Computing* 18, 2 (Spring 2006): 137–150.

Bixby, Robert E. "Solving Real-World Linear Programs: A Decade and More of Progress," *Operations Research* 50, 1 (January–February 2002): 3–15.

Bodington, C. E., and T. E. Baker. "A History of Mathematical Programming in the Petroleum Industry," *Interfaces* 20, 4 (July–August 1990): 117–132.

Boros, E., L. Fedzhora, P. B. Kantor, K. Saeger, and P. Stroud. "A Large-Scale Linear Programming Model For Finding Optimal Container Inspection Strategies," *Naval Research Logistics* 56, 5 (August 2009): 404–420.

Chakravarti, N. "Tea Company Steeped in OR," *OR/MS Today* 27, 2 (April 2000): 32–34.

Ching, Wai-Ki, Wai-On Yuen, Michael K. Ng, and Shu-Qin Zhang. "A Linear Programming Approach for Determining Optimal Advertising Policy," *IMA Journal of Management Mathematics* 17, 1 (2006): 83–96.

Dantzig, George B. "Linear Programming Under Uncertainty," *Management Science* 50, 12 (December 2004): 1764–1769.

Degbotse, Alfred, Brian T. Denton, Kenneth Fordyce, R. John Milne, Robert Orzell, and Chi-Tai Wang. "IBM Blends Heuristics and Optimization to Plan Its Semiconductor Supply Chain," *Interfaces* 43 (March/April 2013): 130–141.

Gass, Saul I. "The First Linear-Programming Shoppe," *Operations Research* 50, 1 (January–February 2002): 61–68.

Greenberg, H. J. "How to Analyze the Results of Linear Programs—Part 1: Preliminaries," *Interfaces* 23, 4 (July–August 1993): 56–68.

Greenberg, H. J. "How to Analyze the Results of Linear Programs—Part 3: Infeasibility Diagnosis," *Interfaces* 23, 6 (November–December 1993): 120–139.

Hafizoğlu, A. B., and M Azizoğlu. "Linear Programming Based Approaches for the Discrete Time/Cost Trade-off Problem in Project Networks," *Journal of the Operational Research Society* 61 (April 2010): 676–685.

Higle, Julia L., and Stein W. Wallace. "Sensitivity Analysis and Uncertainty in Linear Programming," *Interfaces* 33, 4 (July–August 2003): 53–60.

Marszalkowski, Jakub and Drozdowski Maciej. "Optimization of Column Width in Website Layout for Advertisement Fit," *European Journal of Operational Research* 226, 3 (May 2013): 592–601.

Murphy, Frederic H. "ASP, the Art and Science of Practice: Elements of a Theory of the Practice of Operations Research: Expertise in Practice," Interfaces 35, 4 (July–August 2005): 313–322.

Orden, A. "LP from the '40s to the '90s," *Interfaces* 23, 5 (September–October 1993): 2–12.

Pazour, Jennifer A. and Lucas C. Neubert. "Routing and Scheduling of Cross-Town Drayage Operations at J.B. Hunt Transport," *Interfaces* 43, (March/April 2013): 117–129.

Romeijn, H. Edwin, Ravindra K. Ahuja, James F. Dempsey, and Arvind Kumar. "A New Linear Programming Approach to Radiation Therapy Treatment Planning Problems," *Operations Research* 54, 2 (March–April 2006): 201–216.

Rubin, D. S., and H. M. Wagner. "Shadow Prices: Tips and Traps for Managers and Instructors," *Interfaces* 20, 4 (July–August 1990): 150–157.

Wendell, Richard E. "Tolerance Sensitivity and Optimality Bounds in Linear Programming," *Management Science* 50, 6 (June 2004) 797–803.

CHAPTER 8

Linear Programming Applications

LEARNING OBJECTIVES

After completing this chapter, students will be able to:

1. Model a wide variety of medium to large LP problems.

2. Understand major application areas, including marketing, production, labor scheduling, fuel blending, and finance.

3. Gain experience in solving LP problems with Excel Solver software.

Summary • Self-Test • Problems • Internet Homework Problems • Case Study: Cable & Moore • Bibliography

8.1   Introduction

The graphical method of linear programming (LP) discussed in Chapter 7 is useful for understanding how to formulate and solve small LP problems. The purpose of this chapter is to go one step further and show how a large number of real-life problems can be modeled using LP. We do this by presenting examples of models in the areas of marketing research, media selection, production mix, labor scheduling, production scheduling, ingredient mix, and financial portfolio selection. We will solve many of these LP problems using Excel's Solver and QM for Windows.

Although some of these models are relatively small numerically, the principles developed here are definitely applicable to larger problems. Moreover, this practice in "paraphrasing" LP model formulations should help develop your skills in applying the technique to other, less common applications.

8.2   Marketing Applications

Media Selection

Media selection problems can be approached with LP from two perspectives. The objective can be to maximize audience exposure or to minimize advertising costs.

Linear programming models have been used in the advertising field as a decision aid in selecting an effective media mix. Sometimes the technique is employed in allocating a fixed or limited budget across various media, which might include radio or television commercials, newspaper ads, direct mailings, magazine ads, and so on. In other applications, the objective is the maximization of audience exposure. Restrictions on the allowable media mix might arise through contract requirements, limited media availability, or company policy. An example follows.

The Win Big Gambling Club promotes gambling junkets from a large Midwestern city to casinos in the Bahamas. The club has budgeted up to $8,000 per week for local advertising. The money is to be allocated among four promotional media: TV spots, newspaper ads, and two types of radio advertisements. Win Big's goal is to reach the largest possible high-potential audience through the various media. The following table presents the number of potential gamblers reached by making use of an advertisement in each of the four media. It also provides the cost per advertisement placed and the maximum number of ads that can be purchased per week.

MEDIUM	AUDIENCE REACHED PER AD	COST PER AD ($)	MAXIMUM ADS PER WEEK
TV spot (1 minute)	5,000	800	12
Daily newspaper (full-page ad)	8,500	925	5
Radio spot (30 seconds, prime time)	2,400	290	25
Radio spot (1 minute, afternoon)	2,800	380	20

Win Big's contractual arrangements require that at least five radio spots be placed each week. To ensure a broad-scoped promotional campaign, management also insists that no more than $1,800 be spent on radio advertising every week.

In formulating this as an LP, the first step is to completely understand the problem. Sometimes asking "what if" questions will help understand the situation. In this example, what would happen if exactly five ads of each type were used? What would this cost? How many people would it reach? Certainly the use of a spreadsheet for the calculations can help with this since formulas can be written to calculate the cost and the number of people reached. Once the situation is understood, the objective and the constraints are stated:

Objective:

Maximize number of people (audience) reached

Constraints:

(1) No more than 12 TV ads can be used. (2) No more than 5 newspaper ads can be used. (3) No more than 25 of the 30-second radio ads can be used. (4) No more than 20 of the 1-minute radio ads can be used. (5) Total amount spent cannot exceed $8,000. (6) Total number of radio ads must be at least 5. (7) Total amount spent on radio ads must not exceed $1,800.

Next, define the decision variables. The decisions being made here are the number of ads of each type to use. Once these are known, they can be used to calculate the amount spent and the number of people reached. Let

$$X_1 = \text{number of 1-minute TV spots taken each week}$$
$$X_2 = \text{number of full-page daily newspaper ads taken each week}$$
$$X_3 = \text{number of 30-second prime-time radio spots taken each week}$$
$$X_4 = \text{number of 1-minute afternoon radio spots taken each week}$$

Next, using these variables, write the mathematical expression for the objective and the constraint that were identified. The nonnegativity constraints are also explicitly stated.

Objective:

$$\text{Maximize audience coverage} = 5,000X_1 + 8,500X_2 + 2,400X_3 + 2,800X_4$$

subject to	$X_1 \leq 12$	(maximum TV spots/week)
	$X_2 \leq 5$	(maximum newspaper ads/week)
	$X_3 \leq 25$	(maximum 30-second radio spots/week)
	$X_4 \leq 20$	(maximum 1-minute radio spots/week)
$800X_1 + 925X_2 + 290X_3 + 380X_4 \leq \$8,000$		(weekly advertising budget)
	$X_3 + X_4 \geq 5$	(minimum radio spots contracted)
$290X_3 + 380X_4 \leq \$1,800$		(maximum dollars spent on radio)
	$X_1, X_2, X_3, X_4 \geq 0$	

The solution to this can be found using Excel's Solver. Program 8.1 gives the inputs to the Solver Parameter dialog box, the formula that must be written in the cell for the objective function value, and the cells where this formula should be copied. The results are shown in the spreadsheet. This solution is

$$X_1 = 1.97 \quad \text{TV spots}$$
$$X_2 = 5 \quad \text{newspaper ads}$$
$$X_3 = 6.2 \quad \text{30-second radio spots}$$
$$X_4 = 0 \quad \text{one-minute radio spots}$$

This produces an audience exposure of 67,240 contacts. Because X_1 and X_3 are fractional, Win Big would probably round them to 2 and 6, respectively. Problems that demand all-integer solutions are discussed in detail in Chapter 10.

Marketing Research

Linear programming has also been applied to marketing research problems and the area of consumer research. The next example illustrates how statistical pollsters can reach strategy decisions with LP.

Management Sciences Associates (MSA) is a marketing and computer research firm based in Washington, D.C., that handles consumer surveys. One of its clients is a national press service that periodically conducts political polls on issues of widespread interest. In a survey for the press service, MSA determines that it must fulfill several requirements in order to draw statistically valid conclusions on the sensitive issue of new U.S. immigration laws:

1. Survey at least 2,300 U.S. households in total.
2. Survey at least 1,000 households whose heads are 30 years of age or younger.

PROGRAM 8.1

Win Big Solution in Excel 2013

	A	B	C	D	E	F	G	H
1	Win Big Gambling Club							
2				Radio	Radio			
3		TV	Newspaper	30 sec.	1 min.			
4	Variables	X1	X2	X3	X4			
5	Solution	1.9688	5	6.2069	0	Total Audience		
6	Audience per ad	5000	8500	2400	2800	67240.3017		
7								
8	Constraints					LHS		RHS
9	Max. TV	1				1.9688	≤	12
10	Max. Newspaper		1			5	≤	5
11	Max. 30-sec. radio			1		6.2069	≤	25
12	Max. 1 min. radio				1	0	≤	20
13	Cost	800	925	290	380	8000	≤	8000
14	Radio dollars			290	380	1800	≤	1800
15	Radio spots			1	1	6.2069	≥	5

Solver Parameter Inputs and Selections

Set Objective: F6

By Changing cells: B5:E5

To: Max

Subject to the Constraints:

   F9:F14 <= H9:H14

   F15 >= H15

Solving Method: Simplex LP

☑   Make Variables Non-Negative

Key Formulas

	F
5	Total Audience
6	=SUMPRODUCT($B$5:$E$5,B6:E6)

Copy F6 to F9:F15

3. Survey at least 600 households whose heads are between 31 and 50 years of age.
4. Ensure that at least 15% of those surveyed live in a state that borders on Mexico.
5. Ensure that no more than 20% of those surveyed who are 51 years of age or over live in a state that borders on Mexico.

MSA decides that all surveys should be conducted in person. It estimates that the costs of reaching people in each age and region category are as follows:

	COST PER PERSON SURVEYED ($)		
REGION	AGE ≤ 30	AGE 31–50	AGE ≥ 51
State bordering Mexico	$7.50	$6.80	$5.50
State not bordering Mexico	$6.90	$7.25	$6.10

MSA would like to meet the five sampling requirements at the least possible cost.

In formulating this as an LP, the objective is to minimize cost. The five requirements about the number of people to be sampled with specific characteristics result in five constraints. The decision variables come from the decisions that must be made, which are the number of people sampled from each of the two regions in each of the three age categories. Thus, the six variables are

X_1 = number surveyed who are 30 or younger and live in a border state

X_2 = number surveyed who are 31–50 and live in a border state

X_3 = number surveyed who are 51 or older and live in a border state

X_4 = number surveyed who are 30 or younger and do not live in a border state

X_5 = number surveyed who are 31–50 and do not live in a border state

X_6 = number surveyed who are 51 or older and do not live in a border state

Objective function:

$$\text{Minimize total interview costs} = \$7.50X_1 + \$6.80X_2 + \$5.50X_3$$
$$+ \$6.90X_4 + \$7.25X_5 + \$6.10X_6$$

subject to

$$X_1 + X_2 + X_3 + X_4 + X_5 + X_6 \geq 2{,}300 \quad \text{(total households)}$$
$$X_1 + X_4 \geq 1{,}000 \quad \text{(households 30 or younger)}$$
$$X_2 + X_5 \geq 600 \quad \text{(households 31–50 in age)}$$
$$X_1 + X_2 + X_3 \geq 0.15(X_1 + X_2 + X_3 + X_4 + X_5 + X_6) \quad \text{(border states)}$$
$$X_3 \leq 0.2(X_3 + X_6) \quad \text{(limit on age group 51+ who live in border state)}$$
$$X_1, X_2, X_3, X_4, X_5, X_6 \geq 0$$

The computer solution to MSA's problem costs $15,166 and is presented in the following table and in Program 8.2, which presents the input and output from Excel 2013. Note that the variables in the constraints are moved to the left-hand side of the inequality.

REGION	AGE ≤ 30	AGE 31–50	AGE ≥ 51
State bordering Mexico	0	600	140
State not bordering Mexico	1,000	0	560

PROGRAM 8.2

MSA Solution in Excel 2013

	A	B	C	D	E	F	G	H	I	J
1	Management Science Associates									
2										
3	Variable	X1	X2	X3	X4	X5	X6			
4	Solution	0	600	140	1000	0	560	Total Cost		
5	Min. Cost	7.5	6.8	5.5	6.9	7.25	6.1	15166		
6										
7	Constraints							LHS		RHS
8	Total Households	1	1	1	1	1	1	2300	≥	2,300
9	30 and Younger	1	0	0	1	0	0	1000	≥	1,000
10	31 50	0	1	0	0	1	0	600	≥	600
11	Border States	0.85	0.85	0.85	0.15	-0.15	-0.15	395	≥	0
12	51+ Border States	0	0	0.8	0	0	-0.2	0	≤	0

Solver Parameter Inputs and Selections

Set Objective: H5

By Changing cells: B4:G4

To: Min

Subject to the Constraints:

H8:H11 <= J8:J11

H12 >= J12

Solving Method: Simplex LP

☑ Make Variables Non-Negative

Key Formulas

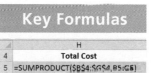

	H
4	Total Cost
5	=SUMPRODUCT($B$4:$G$4,B5:G5)

Copy H5 to H8:H12

8.3   Manufacturing Applications

Production Mix

A fertile field for the use of LP is in planning for the optimal mix of products to manufacture. A company must meet a myriad of constraints, ranging from financial concerns to sales demand to material contracts to union labor demands. Its primary goal is to generate the largest profit possible.

Fifth Avenue Industries, a nationally known manufacturer of menswear, produces four varieties of ties. One is an expensive, all-silk tie; one is an all-polyester tie; one is a blend of polyester and cotton; and one is a blend of silk and cotton. The following table illustrates the cost and availability (per monthly production planning period) of the three materials used in the production process:

MATERIAL	COST PER YARD ($)	MATERIAL AVAILABLE PER MONTH (YARDS)
Silk	24	1,200
Polyester	6	3,000
Cotton	9	1,600

The firm has fixed contracts with several major department store chains to supply ties. The contracts require that Fifth Avenue Industries supply a minimum quantity of each tie but allow for a larger demand if Fifth Avenue chooses to meet that demand. (Most of the ties are not shipped with the name Fifth Avenue on their label, incidentally, but with "private stock" labels supplied by the stores.) Table 8.1 summarizes the contract demand for each of the four styles of ties, the selling price per tie, and the fabric requirements of each variety. Fifth Avenue's goal is to maximize its monthly profit. It must decide upon a policy for product mix.

In formulating this problem, the objective is to maximize profit. There are three constraints (one for each material) indicating that the amount of silk, polyester, and cotton cannot exceed the amount that is available. There are four constraints (one for each type of tie) that specify that the number of all silk ties, all polyester ties, poly–silk ties, and silk–cotton ties produced must be at least the minimum contract amount. There are four more constraints (one for each type of tie) that indicate that the number of each of these ties produced cannot exceed the monthly demand. The variables are defined as

$$X_1 = \text{number of all-silk ties produced per month}$$
$$X_2 = \text{number of polyester ties}$$
$$X_3 = \text{number of blend 1 poly–cotton ties}$$
$$X_4 = \text{number of blend 2 silk–cotton ties}$$

TABLE 8.1   Data for Fifth Avenue Industries

VARIETY OF TIE	SELLING PRICE PER TIE ($)	MONTHLY CONTRACT MINIMUM	MONTHLY DEMAND	MATERIAL REQUIRED PER TIE (YARDS)	MATERIAL REQUIREMENTS
All silk	19.24	5,000	7,000	0.125	100% silk
All polyester	8.70	10,000	14,000	0.08	100% polyester
Poly–cotton blend 1	9.52	13,000	16,000	0.10	50% polyester–50% cotton
Silk–cotton blend 2	10.64	5,000	8,500	0.11	60% silk–40% cotton

But first the firm must establish the profit per tie:

1. Each all-silk tie (X_1) requires 0.125 yard of silk, at a cost of $24.00 per yard. Therefore, the material cost per tie is $3.00. The selling price is $19.24, leaving a net profit of $16.24 per silk tie.
2. Each all-polyester tie (X_2) requires 0.08 yard of polyester, at a cost of $6 per yard. Therefore, the material cost per tie is $0.48. The selling price is $8.70, leaving a net profit of $8.22 per polyester tie.
3. Each poly–cotton (blend 1) tie (X_3) requires 0.05 yard of polyester, at a cost of $6 per yard, and 0.05 yard of cotton, at $9 per yard, for a cost of $0.30 + $0.45 = $0.75 per tie. The selling price is $9.52, leaving a net profit of $8.77 per poly–cotton tie.
4. Performing similar calculations will show that each silk–cotton (blend 2) tie (X_4) has a material cost per tie of $1.98 and a profit of $8.66.

The objective function may now be stated as

$$\text{Maximize profit} = \$16.24X_1 + \$8.22X_2 + \$8.77X_3 + \$8.66X_4$$

subject to

$$0.125X_1 + 0.066X_4 \leq 1,200 \quad \text{(yards of silk)}$$
$$0.08X_2 + 0.05X_3 \leq 3,000 \quad \text{(yards of polyester)}$$
$$0.05X_3 + 0.044X_4 \leq 1,600 \quad \text{(yards of cotton)}$$
$$X_1 \geq 5,000 \quad \text{(contract minimum for all silk)}$$
$$X_1 \leq 7,000 \quad \text{(contract maximum)}$$
$$X_2 \geq 10,000 \quad \text{(contract minimum for all polyester)}$$
$$X_2 \leq 14,000 \quad \text{(contract maximum)}$$
$$X_3 \geq 13,000 \quad \text{(contract minimum for blend 1)}$$
$$X_3 \leq 16,000 \quad \text{(contract maximum)}$$
$$X_4 \geq 5,000 \quad \text{(contract minimum for blend 2)}$$
$$X_4 \leq 8,500 \quad \text{(contract maximum)}$$
$$X_1, X_2, X_3, X_4 \geq 0$$

Using Excel and its Solver command, the computer-generated solution is to produce 5,112 all-silk ties each month; 14,000 all-polyester ties; 16,000 poly–cotton blend 1 ties; and 8,500 silk–cotton blend 2 ties. This produces a profit of $412,028 per production period. See Program 8.3 for details.

Production Scheduling

Setting a low-cost production schedule over a period of weeks or months is a difficult and important management problem in most plants. The production manager has to consider many factors: labor capacity, inventory and storage costs, space limitations, product demand, and labor relations. Because most companies produce more than one product, the scheduling process is often quite complex.

Basically, the problem resembles the product mix model for each period in the future. The objective is either to maximize profit or to minimize the total cost (production plus inventory) of carrying out the task.

Production scheduling is amenable to solution by LP because it is a problem that must be solved on a regular basis. When the objective function and constraints for a firm are established, the inputs can easily be changed each month to provide an updated schedule.

An example of production scheduling: Greenberg Motors

Greenberg Motors, Inc., manufactures two different electrical motors for sale under contract to Drexel Corp., a well-known producer of small kitchen appliances. Its model GM3A is found in many Drexel food processors, and its model GM3B is used in the assembly of blenders.

Three times each year, the procurement officer at Drexel contacts Irwin Greenberg, the founder of Greenberg Motors, to place a monthly order for each of the coming four months. Drexel's demand for motors varies each month based on its own sales forecasts, production capacity, and financial position. Greenberg has just received the January–April order and must begin his own four-month production plan. The demand for motors is shown in Table 8.2.

PROGRAM 8.3

Fifth Avenue Solution in Excel 2013

	A	B	C	D	E	F	G	H
1	Fifth Avenue Industries							
2								
3		All silk	All poly.	Blend 1	Blend 2			
4	Variables	X1	X2	X3	X4			
5	Values	5112	14000	16000	8500	Total Profit		
6	Profit	16.24	8.22	8.77	8.66	412028.88		
7								
8	Constraints					LHS		RHS
9	Silk available	0.125			0.066	1200	≤	1200
10	Polyester available		0.08	0.05		1920	≤	3000
11	Cotton available			0.05	0.044	1174	≤	1600
12	Maximum silk	1				5112	≤	7000
13	Maximum polyester		1			14000	≤	14000
14	Maximum blend 1			1		16000	≤	16000
15	Maximum blend 2				1	8500	≤	8500
16	Minimum silk	1				5112	≥	5000
17	Minimum polyester		1			14000	≥	10000
18	Minimum blend 1			1		16000	≥	13000
19	Minimum blend 2				1	8500	≥	5000

Solver Parameter Inputs and Selections

Set Objective: F6

By Changing cells: B5:E5

To: Max

Subject to the Constraints:

　　F9:F15 <= H9:H15

　　F16:F19 >= H16:H19

Solving Method: Simplex LP

☑　**Make Variables Non-Negative**

Key Formulas

	F
5	Total Profit
6	=SUMPRODUCT($B$5:$E$5,B6:E6)

Copy F6 to F9:F19

TABLE 8.2

Four-Month Order Schedule for Electrical Motors

MODEL	JANUARY	FEBRUARY	MARCH	APRIL
GM3A	800	700	1,000	1,100
GM3B	1,000	1,200	1,400	1,400

Production planning at Greenberg Motors must consider several factors:

1. The company must meet the demand for each of the two products in each of the four months (see Table 8.2). Also, the company would like to have 450 units of the GM3A and 300 units of the GM3B in inventory at the end of April, as demand in May is expected to be somewhat higher than demand in the previous months.
2. There is a carrying, or holding, cost for any inventory left at the end of the month. So producing too many extra units of either product may not be desirable. The carrying cost assigned to the GM3A is $0.36 per unit per month, while the carrying cost for the GM3B is $0.26 per unit per month.
3. The company has been able to maintain a no-layoff policy, and it would like to continue with this. This is easier if the labor hours used do not fluctuate too much from month to month. Maintaining a production schedule that would require from 2,240 to 2,560 labor hours per month is desired. The GM3A requires 1.3 labor hours per unit, while the GM3B requires only 0.9 labor hours.

4. Warehouse limitations cannot be exceeded without great additional costs. There is room at the end of the month for only 3,300 units of the GM3A and GM3B combined.

Although these factors sometimes conflict, Greenberg has found that linear programming is an effective tool in setting up a production schedule that will minimize total cost. Production costs are currently $20 per unit for the GM3A and $15 per unit for the GM3B. However, each of these is due to increase by 10% on March 1 as a new labor agreement goes into effect.

In formulating this as a linear program, it is important to understand how all the important factors are related, how the costs are calculated, how the labor hours per month are calculated, and how demand is met with both production and inventory on hand. To help with understanding this, try to determine the number of labor hours used, the number of units left in inventory at the end of each month for each product, and the total cost if exactly 1,000 of the GM3A and exactly 1,200 of the GM3B were produced each month.

To begin formulating the linear program for the Greenberg production problem, the objective and the constraints are:

Objective:

Minimize total cost (production cost plus carrying cost)

Constraints:

4 demand constraints (1 constraint for each of 4 months) for GM3A

4 demand constraints (1 constraint for each of 4 months) for GM3B

2 constraints (1 for GM3A and 1 for GM3B) for the inventory at the end of April

4 constraints for minimum labor hours (1 constraint for each month)

4 constraints for maximum labor hours (1 constraint for each month)

4 constraints for inventory storage capacity each month

The decisions involve determining how many units of each of 2 products to produce in each of 4 months, so there will be 8 variables. But, since the objective is to minimize cost and there are costs associated not only with the units produced each month but also with the number of units of each left in inventory, it would be best to define variables for these also. Let

A_i = number of units of GM3A produced in month i (i = 1, 2, 3, 4 for January–April)

B_i = number of units of GM3B produced in month i (i = 1, 2, 3, 4 for January–April)

IA_i = units of GM3A left in inventory at end of month i (i = 1, 2, 3, 4 for January–April)

IB_i = units of GM3B left in inventory at end of month i (i = 1, 2, 3, 4 for January–April)

The objective function in the LP model is

$$\text{Minimize cost} = 20A_1 + 20A_2 + 22A_3 + 22A_4 + 15B_1 + 15B_2 + 16.50B_3$$
$$+ 16.50B_4 + 0.36IA_1 + 0.36IA_2 + 0.36IA_3 + 0.36IA_4$$
$$+ 0.26IB_1 + 0.26IB_2 + 0.26IB_3 + 0.26IR_4$$

Inventory constraints set the relationship between closing inventory this month, closing inventory last month, this month's production, and sales this month.

In setting up the constraints, we must recognize the relationship between last month's ending inventory, the current month's production, and the sales to Drexel this month. The inventory at the end of a month is

$$\begin{pmatrix} \text{Inventory} \\ \text{at the} \\ \text{end of} \\ \text{this month} \end{pmatrix} = \begin{pmatrix} \text{Inventory} \\ \text{at the} \\ \text{end of} \\ \text{last month} \end{pmatrix} + \begin{pmatrix} \text{Current} \\ \text{month's} \\ \text{production} \end{pmatrix} - \begin{pmatrix} \text{Sales} \\ \text{to Drexel} \\ \text{this month} \end{pmatrix}$$

While the constraints could be written in this form, inputting the problem into the computer requires all variables to be on the left-hand side of the constraint. Rearranging the terms to do this results in

$$\begin{pmatrix} \text{Inventory} \\ \text{at the} \\ \text{end of} \\ \text{last month} \end{pmatrix} + \begin{pmatrix} \text{Current} \\ \text{month's} \\ \text{production} \end{pmatrix} - \begin{pmatrix} \text{Inventory} \\ \text{at the} \\ \text{end of} \\ \text{this month} \end{pmatrix} = \begin{pmatrix} \text{Sales} \\ \text{to Drexel} \\ \text{this month} \end{pmatrix}$$

Using this, the demand constraints are:

$$\begin{array}{ll} A_1 - IA_1 = 800 & \text{(demand for GM3A in January)} \\ IA_1 + A_2 - IA_2 = 700 & \text{(demand for GM3A in February)} \\ IA_2 + A_3 - IA_3 = 1{,}000 & \text{(demand for GM3A in March)} \\ IA_3 + A_4 - IA_4 = 1{,}100 & \text{(demand for GM3A in April)} \\ B_1 - IB_1 = 1{,}000 & \text{(demand for GM3B in January)} \\ IB_1 + B_2 - IB_2 = 1{,}200 & \text{(demand for GM3B in February)} \\ IB_2 + B_3 - IB_3 = 1{,}400 & \text{(demand for GM3B in March)} \\ IB_3 + B_4 - IB_4 = 1{,}400 & \text{(demand for GM3B in April)} \\ IA_4 = 450 & \text{(inventory of GM3A at end of April)} \\ IB_4 = 300 & \text{(inventory of GM3B at end of April)} \end{array}$$

Employment constraints are set for each month.

The constraints for the minimum and maximum number of labor hours each month are:

$$\begin{array}{ll} 1.3A_1 + 0.9B_1 \geq 2{,}240 & \text{(minimum labor hours in January)} \\ 1.3A_2 + 0.9B_2 \geq 2{,}240 & \text{(minimum labor hours in February)} \\ 1.3A_3 + 0.9B_3 \geq 2{,}240 & \text{(minimum labor hours in March)} \\ 1.3A_4 + 0.9B_4 \geq 2{,}240 & \text{(minimum labor hours in April)} \\ 1.3A_1 + 0.9B_1 \leq 2{,}560 & \text{(maximum labor hours in January)} \\ 1.3A_2 + 0.9B_2 \leq 2{,}560 & \text{(maximum labor hours in February)} \\ 1.3A_3 + 0.9B_3 \leq 2{,}560 & \text{(maximum labor hours in March)} \\ 1.3A_4 + 0.9B_4 \leq 2{,}560 & \text{(maximum labor hours in April)} \end{array}$$

The storage capacity constraints are:

$$\begin{array}{ll} IA_1 + IB_1 \leq 3{,}300 & \text{(storage capacity in January)} \\ IA_2 + IB_2 \leq 3{,}300 & \text{(storage capacity in February)} \\ IA_3 + IB_3 \leq 3{,}300 & \text{(storage capacity in March)} \\ IA_4 + IB_4 \leq 3{,}300 & \text{(storage capacity in April)} \\ \text{All variables} \geq 0 & \text{(nonnegativity constraints)} \end{array}$$

The solution was obtained using Solver in Excel 2013, as shown in Program 8.4. Some of the variables are not integers, but this is not a problem because work in process can be carried over from one month to the next. Table 8.3 summarizes the solution with the values rounded. The total cost is about \$169,295. Greenberg can use this model to develop production schedules again in the future by letting the subscripts on the variables represent new months and making minor changes to the problem. The only things in the model that would have to be changed are the RHS values for the demand constraints (and inventory desired at the end of the fourth month) and the objective function coefficients (costs) if they should change.

PROGRAM 8.4

Greenberg Motors Solution in Excel 2013

Greenberg Motors

Variable	A1	A2	A3	A4	B1	B2	B3	B4	IA1	IA2	IA3	IA4	IB1	IB2	IB3	IB4		LHS	Sign	RHS
Solution	1276.9	223.1	1757.7	792.3	1000	2522.2	77.8	1700	476.9	0	757.7	450	0	1322.2	0	300	Total Cost			
Min. Cost	20	20	22	22	15	15	16.5	16.5	0.36	0.36	0.36	0.36	0.26	0.26	0.26	0.26	169294.9			
Demand Constraints																		LHS	Sign	RHS
Jan. GM3A	1								-1									800	=	800
Feb. GM3A		1							1	-1								700	=	700
Mar. GM3A			1							1	-1							1000	=	1000
Apr. GM3A				1							1	-1						1100	=	1100
Jan. GM3B					1								-1					1000	=	1000
Feb. GM3B						1							1	-1				1200	=	1200
Mar. GM3B							1							1	-1			1400	=	1400
Apr. GM3B								1							1	-1		1400	=	1400
Inv.GM3A Apr.												1						450	=	450
Inv.GM3B Apr.																1		300	=	300
Labor Hour Constraints																				
Hrs Min. Jan.	1.3				0.9													2560	≥	2240
Hrs Min. Feb.		1.3				0.9												2560	≥	2240
Hrs Min. Mar.			1.3				0.9											2355	≥	2240
Hrs Min. Apr.				1.3				0.9										2560	≥	2240
Hrs Max. Jan.	1.3				0.9													2560	≤	2560
Hrs Max. Feb.		1.3				0.9												2560	≤	2560
Hrs Max.Mar.			1.3				0.9											2355	≤	2560
Hrs Max. Apr.				1.3				0.9										2560	≤	2560
Storage Constraints																				
Jan. Inv. Limit									1				1					476.92	≤	3300
Feb. Inv. Limit										1				1				1322.22	≤	3300
Mar. Inv. Limit											1				1			757.69	≤	3300
Apr. Inv. Limit												1				1		750	≤	3300

Solver Parameter Inputs and Selections

Set Objective: F5

By Changing cells: B4:Q4

To: Min

Subject to the Constraints:

R19:R22 >= T19:T22

R23:R26 <= T23:T26

R28:R31 <= T28:T31

R8:R17 = T8:T17

Solving Method: Simplex LP

☑ Make Variables Non-Negative

Key Formulas

	R
4	Total Cost
5	=SUMPRODUCT($B$4:$Q$4,B5:Q5)

Copy formula in R5 to R8:R17
Copy formula in R5 to R19:R26
Copy formula in R5 to R28:R31

TABLE 8.3

Solution to Greenberg Motors Problem

PRODUCTION SCHEDULE	JANUARY	FEBRUARY	MARCH	APRIL
Units of GM3A produced	1,277	223	1,758	792
Units of GM3B produced	1,000	2,522	78	1,700
Inventory of GM3A carried	477	0	758	450
Inventory of GM3B carried	0	1,322	0	300
Labor hours required	2,560	2,560	2,355	2,560

8.4 Employee Scheduling Applications

Labor Planning

Labor planning problems address staffing needs over a specific time period. They are especially useful when managers have some flexibility in assigning workers to jobs that require overlapping or interchangeable talents. Large banks frequently use LP to tackle their labor scheduling.

TABLE 8.4

Hong Kong Bank of Commerce and Industry

TIME PERIOD	NUMBER OF TELLERS REQUIRED
9 A.M.–10 A.M.	10
10 A.M.–11 A.M.	12
11 A.M.–Noon	14
Noon–1 P.M.	16
1 P.M.–2 P.M.	18
2 P.M.–3 P.M.	17
3 P.M.–4 P.M.	15
4 P.M.–5 P.M.	10

Hong Kong Bank of Commerce and Industry is a busy bank that has requirements for between 10 and 18 tellers, depending on the time of day. The lunch time, from noon to 2 P.M., is usually heaviest. Table 8.4 indicates the workers needed at various hours that the bank is open.

The bank now employs 12 full-time tellers, but many people are on its roster of available part-time employees. A part-time employee must put in exactly four hours per day but can start anytime between 9 A.M. and 1 P.M. Part-timers are a fairly inexpensive labor pool, since no retirement or lunch benefits are provided for them. Full-timers, on the other hand, work from 9 A.M. to 5 P.M. but are allowed 1 hour for lunch. (Half of the full-timers eat at 11 A.M., the other half at noon.) Full-timers thus provide 35 hours per week of productive labor time.

By corporate policy, the bank limits part-time hours to a maximum of 50% of the day's total requirement. Part-timers earn $8 per hour (or $32 per day) on average, and full-timers earn $100 per day in salary and benefits, on average. The bank would like to set a schedule that would minimize its total personnel costs. It will release one or more of its full-time tellers if it is profitable to do so.

In formulating this as an LP, the objective is to minimize cost. There is a constraint for each hour of the day, stating that the number of people working at the bank during that hour should be at least the minimum number shown in Table 8.4, so there are eight of these constraints. Another constraint will limit the total number of full-time workers to be no more than 12. The last constraint will specify that the number of part-time hours must not exceed 50% of the total hours.

The bank must decide how many full-time tellers to use, so there will be one decision variable for that. Similarly, the bank must decide about using part-time tellers, but this is more complex as the part-time workers can start at different times of the day while all full-time workers start at the beginning of the day. Thus, there must be a variable indicating the number of part-time workers starting at each hour of the day from 9 A.M. until 1 P.M. Any worker who starts at 1 P.M. will work until closing, so there is no need to consider having any part-time workers start after that. Let

$$F = \text{full-time tellers}$$
$$P_1 = \text{part-timers starting at 9 A.M (leaving at 1 P.M.)}$$
$$P_2 = \text{part-timers starting at 10 A.M (leaving at 2 P.M.)}$$
$$P_3 = \text{part-timers starting at 11 A.M (leaving at 3 P.M.)}$$
$$P_4 = \text{part-timers starting at noon (leaving at 4 P.M.)}$$
$$P_5 = \text{part-timers starting at 1 P.M (leaving at 5 P.M.)}$$

Objective function:

$$\text{Minimize total daily personnel cost} = \$100F + \$32(P_1 + P_2 + P_3 + P_4 + P_5)$$

Constraints:

For each hour, the available labor hours must be at least equal to the required labor hours.

$$
\begin{array}{lll}
F + P_1 & \geq 10 & \text{(9 A.M.–10 A.M. needs)} \\
F + P_1 + P_2 & \geq 12 & \text{(10 A.M.–11 A.M. needs)} \\
0.5F + P_1 + P_2 + P_3 & \geq 14 & \text{(11 A.M.–noon needs)} \\
0.5F + P_1 + P_2 + P_3 + P_4 & \geq 16 & \text{(noon–1 P.M. needs)} \\
F \quad\ + P_2 + P_3 + P_4 + P_5 & \geq 18 & \text{(1 P.M.–2 P.M. needs)} \\
F \qquad\quad + P_3 + P_4 + P_5 & \geq 17 & \text{(2 P.M.–3 P.M. needs)} \\
F \qquad\qquad\quad + P_4 + P_5 & \geq 15 & \text{(3 P.M.–4 P.M. needs)} \\
F \qquad\qquad\qquad\quad + P_5 & \geq 10 & \text{(4 P.M.–5 P.M. needs)}
\end{array}
$$

Only 12 full-time tellers are available, so

$$F \leq 12$$

Part-time worker hours cannot exceed 50% of total hours required each day, which is the sum of the tellers needed each hour:

$$4(P_1 + P_2 + P_3 + P_4 + P_5) \leq 0.50(10 + 12 + 14 + 16 + 18 + 17 + 15 + 10)$$

or

$$4P_1 + 4P_2 + 4P_3 + 4P_4 + 4P_5 \leq 0.50(112)$$
$$F, P_1, P_2, P_3, P_4, P_5 \geq 0$$

Alternate optimal solutions are common in many LP problems. The sequence in which you enter the constraints into QM for Windows can affect the solution found.

Program 8.5 gives the solution to this, found using Solver in Excel 2013. There are several alternate optimal schedules that Hong Kong Bank can follow. The first is to employ only 10 full-time tellers ($F = 10$) and to start 7 part-timers at 10 A.M. ($P_2 = 7$), 2 part-timers at 11 A.M. ($P_3 = 2$), and 5 part-timers at noon ($P_4 = 5$). No part-timers would begin at 9 A.M. or 1 P M.

A second solution also employs 10 full-time tellers, but starts 6 part-timers at 9 A.M. ($P_1 = 6$), 1 part-timer at 10 A.M. ($P_2 = 1$), 2 part-timers at 11 A.M. and 5 at noon ($P_3 = 2$ and $P_4 = 5$), and 0 part-timers at 1 P.M. ($P_5 = 0$). The cost of either of these two policies is $1,448 per day.

8.5 Financial Applications

Portfolio Selection

Maximizing return on investment subject to a set of risk constraints is a popular financial application of LP.

A problem frequently encountered by managers of banks, mutual funds, investment services, and insurance companies is the selection of specific investments from among a wide variety of alternatives. The manager's overall objective is usually to maximize expected return on investment, given a set of legal, policy, or risk restraints.

For example, the International City Trust (ICT) invests in short-term trade credits, corporate bonds, gold stocks, and construction loans. To encourage a diversified portfolio, the board of directors has placed limits on the amount that can be committed to any one type of investment. ICT has $5 million available for immediate investment and wishes to do two things: (1) maximize the return on the investments made over the next six months and (2) satisfy the diversification requirements as set by the board of directors.

PROGRAM 8.5

Labor Planning Solution
in Excel 2013

	A	B	C	D	E	F	G	H	I	J
1	Labor Planning Example									
2										
3										
4	Variables	F	P1	P2	P3	P4	P5			
5	Values	10	0	7	2	5	0	Total Cost		
6	Cost	100	32	32	32	32	32	1448		
7										
8	Constraints							LHS	Sign	RHS
9	9 a.m. - 10 a.m.	1	1					10	≥	10
10	10 a.m. - 11 a.m.	1	1	1				17	≥	12
11	11 a.m. - noon	0.5	1	1	1			14	≥	14
12	noon - 1 p.m.	0.5	1	1	1	1		19	≥	16
13	1 p.m. - 2 p.m.	1		1	1	1	1	24	≥	18
14	2 p.m. - 3 p.m.	1			1	1	1	17	≥	17
15	3 p.m. - 4 p.m.	1				1	1	15	≥	15
16	4 p.m. - 5 p.m.	1					1	10	≥	10
17	Max. Full time	1						10	≤	12
18	Total PT hours		4	4	4	4	4	56	≤	56

Solver Parameter Inputs and Selections

Set Objective: H6

By Changing cells: B5:G5

To: Min

Subject to the Constraints:

H9:H16 >= J9:J16

H17:H18 <= J17:J18

Solving Method: Simplex LP

☑   Make Variables Non-Negative

Key Formulas

	H
5	Total Cost
6	=SUMPRODUCT($B$5:$G$5,B6:G6)

Copy H6 to H9:H18

The specifics of the investment possibilities are as follows:

INVESTMENT	INTEREST RETURN	MAXIMUM INVESTMENT ($ MILLIONs)
Trade credit	7%	1.0
Corporate bonds	11%	2.5
Gold stocks	19%	1.5
Construction loans	15%	1.8

In addition, the board specifies that at least 55% of the funds invested must be in gold stocks and construction loans, and that no less than 15% be invested in trade credit.

In formulating this as an LP, the objective is to maximize the return. There are four separate constraints limiting the maximum amount in each investment option to the maximum given in the table. The fifth constraint specifies that the total amount in gold stocks and construction loans must be at least 55% of the total amount invested, and the next constraint specifies that the total amount in trade credit must be at least 15% of the total amount invested. The final constraint stipulates that the total amount invested cannot exceed $5 million (it could be less). Define the variables as

$$X_1 = \text{dollars invested in trade credit}$$
$$X_2 = \text{dollars invested in corporate bonds}$$
$$X_3 = \text{dollars invested in gold stocks}$$
$$X_4 = \text{dollars invested in construction loans}$$

The total amount invested is $X_1 + X_2 + X_3 + X_4$, which may be less than $5 million. This is important when calculating 55% of the total amount invested and 15% of the total amount invested in two of the constraints.

Objective:

$$\text{Maximize dollars of interest earned} = 0.07X_1 + 0.11X_2 + 0.19X_3 + 0.15X_4$$
$$\text{subject to} \quad X_1 \qquad\qquad\qquad\qquad \leq 1{,}000{,}000$$
$$X_2 \qquad\qquad\quad \leq 2{,}500{,}000$$
$$X_3 \quad\quad \leq 1{,}500{,}000$$
$$X_4 \leq 1{,}800{,}000$$
$$X_3 + X_4 \geq 0.55(X_1 + X_2 + X_3 + X_4)$$
$$X_1 \qquad\qquad\qquad\quad \geq 0.15(X_1 + X_2 + X_3 + X_4)$$
$$X_1 + X_2 + X_3 + X_4 \leq 5{,}000{,}000$$
$$X_1, X_2, X_3, X_4 \geq 0$$

 IN ACTION Optimization at UPS

On an average day, UPS delivers 13 million packages to almost 8 million customers in 200 countries and territories. Deliveries are classified as same-day air, next-day air, and second-day air. The next-day air operations average more than 1.1 million packages per day and generate annual revenue of over $5 billion. The company has 256 aircraft and many more on order. During the busiest time of year, between Thanksgiving and New Year's Day, the company leases additional aircraft to meet the demand. The size of its fleet makes UPS the 9th-largest commercial airline in the United States and the 11th-largest commercial airline in the world.

In the next-day delivery operation, the pickup and delivery of packages by UPS involves several stages. Packages are carried by truck to ground centers. From there, the packages are taken to the airport, and then they are flown to one of the airport hubs with at most one stop at another airport to pick up more packages. At the hub, the packages are sorted and loaded onto planes and flown to the destination. Packages are then loaded on large trucks and taken to ground centers. At the ground centers, additional sorting is done, packages are put on smaller trucks, and the packages are delivered to their final destinations before 10:30 A.M. The same aircraft are used in the second-day

deliveries as well, so these two types of operations must be coordinated.

A team from UPS and Massachusetts Institute of Technology worked together to develop an optimization-based planning system called VOLCANO (Volume, Location, and Aircraft Network Optimizer) that is used for planning and managing operations. This group developed optimization methods to minimize overall cost (ownership and operating) while meeting capacity and service standard constraints. Mathematical models are used to determine the minimum cost set of routes, fleet assignments, and package flows. Constraints include the number of aircraft, landing restrictions at airports, and aircraft operating characteristics (such as speed, capacity, and range).

The VOLCANO system is credited with saving over $87 million from late in 2000 to the end of 2002. It is expected that $189 million will be saved over the next decade. This optimizer is also used to identify the needed fleet composition and recommend future aircraft acquisitions.

Source: Based on Andrew P. Armacost, Cynthia Barnhart, Keith A. Ware, and Alysia M. Wilson. "UPS Optimizes Its Air Network," *Interfaces* 34, 1 (January–February 2004): 15–25.

PROGRAM 8.6

ICT Portfolio Solution
in Excel 2013

	A	B	C	D	E	F	G	H
1	ICT Portfolio Selection							
2								
3	Variable	X1	X2	X3	X4			
4	Solution	750000	950000	1500000	1800000	Total Return		
5	Max. Return	0.07	0.11	0.19	0.15	712000		
6								
7						LHS		RHS
8	Trade	1				750000	≤	1,000,000
9	Bonds		1			950000	≤	2,500,000
10	Gold			1		1500000	≤	1,500,000
11	Construction				1	1800000	≤	1,800,000
12	Min. Gold+Const	-0.55	-0.55	0.45	0.45	550000	≥	0
13	Min. Trade	0.85	-0.15	-0.15	-0.15	0	≥	0
14	Total Invested	1	1	1	1	5000000	≤	5000000

Solver Parameter Inputs and Selections

Set Objective: F5

By Changing cells: B4:E4

To: Min

Subject to the Constraints:

  F8:F11 <= H8:H11

  F12:F13 >= H12:H13

  F14 <= H14

Solving Method: Simplex LP

☑ Make Variables Non-Negative

Key Formulas

	F
4	Total Return
5	=SUMPRODUCT($B$4:$E$4,B5:E5)

Copy F5 to F8:F14

Program 8.6 shows the solution found using Solver in Excel. ICT maximizes its interest earned by making the following investment: $X_1 = \$750,000$, $X_2 = \$950,000$, $X_3 = \$1,500,000$, and $X_4 = \$1,800,000$, and the total interest earned is $712,000.

Truck Loading Problem

The truck loading problem involves deciding which items to load on a truck so as to maximize the value of a load shipped. As an example, we consider Goodman Shipping, an Orlando firm owned by Steven Goodman. One of his trucks, with a capacity of 10,000 pounds, is about to be loaded.* Awaiting shipment are the following items:

ITEM	VALUE ($)	WEIGHT (POUNDS)
1	22,500	7,500
2	24,000	7,500
3	8,000	3,000
4	9,500	3,500
5	11,500	4,000
6	9,750	3,500

---

*Adapted from an example in S. L. Savage. *What's Best*! Oakland, CA: General Optimization, Inc., and Holden-Day, 1985.

Each of these six items, we see, has an associated dollar value and weight.

The objective is to maximize the total value of the items loaded onto the truck without exceeding the truck's weight capacity. We let X_i be the proportion of each item i loaded on the truck:

$$\text{Maximize load value} = \$22{,}500X_1 + \$24{,}000X_2 + \$8{,}000X_3 + \$9{,}500X_4$$
$$+ \$11{,}500X_5 + \$9{,}750X_6$$

$$\text{subject to} \quad 7{,}500X_1 + 7{,}500X_2 + 3{,}000X_3 + 3{,}500X_4 + 4{,}000X_5$$
$$+3{,}500X_6 \leq 10{,}000 \text{ lb capacity}$$

$$X_1 \leq 1$$
$$X_2 \leq 1$$
$$X_3 \leq 1$$
$$X_4 \leq 1$$
$$X_5 \leq 1$$
$$X_6 \leq 1$$
$$X_1, X_2, X_3, X_4, X_5, X_6 \geq 0$$

These final six constraints reflect the fact that at most one "unit" of an item can be loaded onto the truck. In effect, if Goodman can load a *portion* of an item (say, item 1 is a batch of 1,000 folding chairs, not all of which need be shipped together), the X_is will all be proportions ranging from 0 (nothing) to 1 (all of that item loaded).

To solve this LP problem, we turn to Excel's Solver. Program 8.7 shows Goodman's Excel formulation, input data, and the solution, which yields a total load value of $31,500.

The answer leads us to an interesting issue that we deal with in detail in Chapter 10. What does Goodman do if fractional values of items cannot be loaded? For example, if luxury cars were the items being loaded, we clearly cannot ship one-third of a Maserati.

PROGRAM 8.7

Goodman Truck Loading Solution in Excel

	A	B	C	D	E	F	G	H	I	J
1	Goodman Shipping									
2										
3	Variables	X1	X2	X3	X4	X5	X6			
4	Values	0.3333	1	0	0	0	0	Total Value		
5	Load Value $	22500	24000	8000	9500	11500	9750	31500		
6										
7	Constraints							LHS	Sign	RHS
8	Total weight	7500	7500	3000	3500	4000	3500	10000	≤	10000
9	% Item 1	1						0.3333333	≤	1
10	% Item 2		1					1	≤	1
11	% Item 3			1				0	≤	1
12	% Item 4				1			0	≤	1
13	% Item 5					1		0	≤	1
14	% Item 6						1	0	≤	1

Solver Parameter Inputs and Selections

Set Objective: H5

By Changing cells: B4:G4

To: Min

Subject to the Constraints:

H8:H14 <= J8:J14

Solving Method: Simplex LP

☑ **Make Variables Non-Negative**

Key Formulas

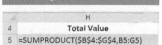

	H
4	Total Value
5	=SUMPRODUCT($B$4:$G$4,B5:G5)

Copy H5 to H8:H14

If the proportion of item 1 was rounded up to 1.00, the weight of the load would increase to 15,000 pounds. This would violate the 10,000 pounds maximum weight constraint. Therefore, the fraction of item 1 must be rounded down to zero. This would drop the value of the load to 7,500 pounds, leaving 2,500 pounds of the load capacity unused. Because no other item weighs less than 2,500 pounds, the truck cannot be filled up further.

Thus, we see that by using regular LP and rounding the fractional weights, the truck would carry only item 2, for a load weight of 7,500 pounds and a load value of $24,000.

QM for Windows and spreadsheet optimizers such as Excel's Solver are capable of dealing with *integer programming* problems as well; that is, LP problems requiring integer solutions. Using Excel, the integer solution to Goodman's problem is to load items 3, 4, and 6, for a total weight of 10,000 pounds and load value of $27,250.

8.6   Ingredient Blending Applications

Diet Problems

The diet problem, one of the earliest applications of LP, was originally used by hospitals to determine the most economical diet for patients. Known in agricultural applications as the feed mix problem, the diet problem involves specifying a food or feed ingredient combination that satisfies stated nutritional requirements at a minimum cost level.

The Whole Food Nutrition Center uses three bulk grains to blend a natural cereal that it sells by the pound. The cost of each bulk grain and the protein, riboflavin, phosphorus, and magnesium units per pound of each are shown in Table 8.5.

On the packaging for each of its products, Whole Food indicates the nutritional content in each bowl of cereal when eaten with 0.5 cup of milk. The USRDA (U.S. Recommended Dietary Allowance) and the more recent DRI (Dietary Reference Intake) were consulted to establish recommended amounts of certain vitamins and minerals for an average adult. Based on these figures and the desired amounts for labeling on the package, Whole Food has determined that each 2-ounce serving of the cereal should contain 3 units of protein, 2 units of riboflavin, 1 unit of phosphorous, and 0.425 unit of magnesium.

In modeling this as an LP, the objective is to minimize cost. There will be four constraints (one each for protein, riboflavin, phosphorous, and magnesium) stipulating that the number of units must be at least the minimum amount specified. Since these requirements are for each 2 ounce serving, the last constraint must say that the total amount of the grains used will be 2 ounces, or 0.125 pound.

In defining the variables, notice that the cost is expressed per pound of the three grains. Thus, in order to calculate the total cost, we must know the number of pounds of the grains used in one serving of the cereal. Also, the numbers in Table 8.5 are expressed in units per pound of grain, so defining variables as the number of pounds of the grains makes it easier to calculate the amounts of protein, riboflavin, phosphorous, and magnesium. We let

$$X_A = \text{pounds of grain A in one 2-ounce serving of cereal}$$

$$X_B = \text{pounds of grain B in one 2-ounce serving of cereal}$$

$$X_C = \text{pounds of grain C in one 2-ounce serving of cereal}$$

TABLE 8.5   Whole Food's Natural Cereal Requirements

GRAIN	COST PER POUND (CENTS)	PROTEIN (UNITS/LB)	RIBOFLAVIN (UNITS/LB)	PHOSPHORUS (UNITS/LB)	MAGNESIUM (UNITS/LB)
A	33	22	16	8	5
B	47	28	14	7	0
C	38	21	25	9	6

Objective function:

Minimize total cost of mixing a 2-ounce serving $= \$0.33X_A + \$0.47X_B + \$0.38X_C$
subject to

$$22X_A + 28X_B + 21X_C \geq 3 \qquad \text{(protein units)}$$
$$16X_A + 14X_B + 25X_C \geq 2 \qquad \text{(riboflavin units)}$$
$$8X_A + 7X_B + 9X_C \geq 1 \qquad \text{(phosphorus units)}$$
$$5X_A + 0X_B + 6X_C \geq 0.425 \quad \text{(magnesium units)}$$
$$X_A + X_B + X_C = 0.125 \quad \text{(total mix is 2 ounces or 0.125 pound)}$$
$$X_A, X_B, X_C \geq 0$$

The solution to this problem requires mixing together 0.025 lb of grain A, 0.050 lb of grain B, and 0.050 lb of grain C. Another way of stating the solution is in terms of the proportion of the 2-ounce serving of each grain, namely, 0.4 ounce of grain A, 0.8 ounce of grain B, and 0.8 ounce of grain C in each serving. The cost per serving is $0.05. Program 8.8 illustrates this solution using Solver in Excel 2013.

Ingredient Mix and Blending Problems

Diet and feed mix problems are actually special cases of a more general class of LP problems known as *ingredient* or *blending problems*. Blending problems arise when a decision must be made regarding the blending of two or more resources to produce one or more products. Resources, in this case, contain one or more essential ingredients that must be blended so that each final product contains specific percentages of each ingredient. The following example deals with an application frequently seen in the petroleum industry, the blending of crude oils to produce refinable gasoline.

PROGRAM 8.8

Whole Food Diet Solution in Excel 2013

⊿	A	B	C	D	E	F	G
1	Whole Foods Nutrition Problem						
2							
3		Grain A	Grain B	Grain C			
4	Variable	Xa	Xb	Xc			
5	Solution	0.025	0.05	0.05	Total Cost		
6	Minimize	0.33	0.47	0.38	0.05075		
7							
8	Constraints				LHS	Sign	RHS
9	Protein	22	28	21	3	≥	3
10	Riboflavin	16	14	25	2.35	≥	2
11	Phosphorus	8	7	9	1	≥	1
12	Magnesium	5	0	6	0.425	≥	0.425
13	Total Weight	1	1	1	0.125	=	0.125

Solver Parameter Inputs and Selections

Set Objective: E6

By Changing cells: B5:D5

To: Min

Subject to the Constraints:

E9:E12 <= G9:G12

E13 = G13

Solving Method: Simplex LP

☑ Make Variables Non-Negative

Key Formulas

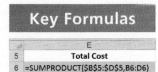

⊿	E
5	Total Cost
6	=SUMPRODUCT($B$5:$D$5,B6:D6)

Copy E6 to E9:E13

Major oil refineries all use LP for blending crude oils to produce gasoline grades.

The Low Knock Oil Company produces two grades of cut-rate gasoline for industrial distribution. The grades, regular and economy, are produced by refining a blend of two types of crude oil, type X100 and type X220. Each crude oil differs not only in cost per barrel, but in composition as well. The following table indicates the percentage of crucial ingredients found in each of the crude oils and the cost per barrel for each:

CRUDE OIL TYPE	INGREDIENT A (%)	INGREDIENT B (%)	COST/BARREL ($)
X100	35	55	30.00
X220	60	25	34.80

Weekly demand for the regular grade of Low Knock gasoline is at least 25,000 barrels, and demand for the economy is at least 32,000 barrels per week. *At least* 45% of each barrel of regular must be ingredient A. *At most* 50% of each barrel of economy should contain ingredient B. While the gasoline yield from one barrel of crude depends on the type of crude and the type of processing used, we will assume for the sake of this example that one barrel of crude oil will yield one barrel of gasoline.

The Low Knock management must decide how many barrels of each type of crude oil to buy each week for blending to satisfy demand at minimum cost. In modeling this as an LP, the objective is to minimize cost. Each of the two types of gasoline has a demand constraint, and each of the two types of gasoline has a constraint restricting the amount of the ingredients. Thus, there are four constraints. The decisions involve the amount of each type of crude to use in each type of gasoline, so these will be the decision variables. Let

$$X_1 = \text{barrels of crude X100 blended to produce the refined regular}$$
$$X_2 = \text{barrels of crude X100 blended to produce the refined economy}$$
$$X_3 = \text{barrels of crude X220 blended to produce the refined regular}$$
$$X_4 = \text{barrels of crude X220 blended to produce the refined economy}$$

This problem can be formulated as follows:

Objective:

$$\text{Minimize cost} = \$30X_1 + \$30X_2 + \$34.80X_3 + \$34.80X_4$$

subject to

$$X_1 + X_3 \geq 25,000 \quad \text{(demand for regular)}$$
$$X_2 + X_4 \geq 32,000 \quad \text{(demand for economy)}$$

At least 45% of each barrel of regular must be ingredient A:

$$(X_1 + X_3) = \text{total amount of crude blended to produce the refined regular}$$
$$\text{gasoline demand}$$

Thus,

$$0.45(X_1 + X_3) = \text{minimum amount of ingredient A required}$$

But

$$0.35X_1 + 0.60X_3 = \text{amount of ingredient A in refined regular gas}$$

So

$$0.35X_1 + 0.60X_3 \geq 0.45X_1 + 0.45X_3$$

or

$$-0.10X_1 + 0.15X_3 \geq 0 \quad \text{(ingredient A in regular constraint)}$$

Similarly, at most 50% of each barrel of economy should be ingredient B:

$$X_2 + X_4 = \text{total amount of crude blended to produce the refined economy}$$
$$\text{gasoline demanded}$$

Thus,

$$0.50(X_2 + X_4) = \text{maximum amount of ingredient B allowed}$$

But

$$0.55X_2 + 0.25X_4 = \text{amount of ingredient B in refined economy gas}$$

So

$$0.55X_2 + 0.25X_4 \leq 0.50X_2 + 0.50X_4$$

or

$$0.05X_2 - 0.25X_4 \leq 0 \,(\text{ingredient B in economy constraint})$$

Here is the entire LP formulation:

$$\text{Minimize cost} = 30X_1 + 30X_2 + 34.80X_3 + 34.80X_4$$

$$
\begin{array}{llll}
\text{subject to} & X_1 & + X_3 & \geq 25{,}000 \\
& X_2 + & X_4 & \geq 32{,}000 \\
& -0.10X_1 & + 0.15X_3 & \geq 0 \\
& 0.05X_2 & - 0.25X_4 & \leq 0 \\
& X_1, X_2, X_3, X_4 & \geq 0
\end{array}
$$

Using Excel, the solution to Low Knock Oil's formulation was found to be

$$X_1 = 15{,}000 \text{ barrels of X100 into regular}$$
$$X_2 = 26{,}666.67 \text{ barrels of X100 into economy}$$
$$X_3 = 10{,}000 \text{ barrels of X220 into regular}$$
$$X_4 = 5{,}333.33 \text{ barrels of X220 into economy}$$

The cost of this mix is $1,783,600. Refer to Program 8.9 for details.

8.7 Other Linear Programming Applications

There are many other types of linear programming applications. One particular application was first developed and used by American Airlines in the early 1990s, and it is called revenue management. This was designed to use differential pricing for seats so that additional revenue could be obtained. Some customers who were willing to book with certain restrictions, such as 14-day advance purchase or with a stay over a Saturday night, would receive lower fares. However, if all seats are sold at this reduced cost, then higher paying passengers, often business travelers who might try to book seats at the last minute, would not be able to do so. The extra revenue generated from these passengers is then lost. A revenue management system was developed to determine how many seats to make available to each type of passenger. Linear programs would have an objective of maximizing the total revenue, while constraints would be based on the number of total seats available on the plane and the number of seats allocated to each category. Companies have reported dramatic increases in revenues as a result of this.

Given the success of revenue management systems in the airlines industry, similar systems were also adopted by many hotel chains. The airline industry and the hotel industry have products with similar characteristics—a limited inventory of a very perishable

PROGRAM 8.9

Low Knock Oil Solution in Excel 2013

	A	B	C	D	E	F	G	H
1	Low Knock Oil Company							
2								
3		X100 Reg	X100 Econ	X220 Reg	X220 Econ			
4	Variable	X1	X2	X3	X4			
5	Solution	15000	26666.67	10000	5333.33	Total Cost		
6	Cost	30	30	34.8	34.8	1783600		
7								
8	Constraints					LHS	Sign	RHS
9	Demand Regular	1		1		25000	≥	25000
10	Demand Economy		1		1	32000	≥	32000
11	Ing. A in Regular	-0.1		0.15		0	≥	0
12	Ing. B in Economy		0.05		-0.25	0	≤	0

Solver Parameter Inputs and Selections

Set Objective: F6

By Changing cells: B5:E5

To: Min

Subject to the Constraints:

   F9:F11 >= H9:H11

   F12 <= H12

Solving Method: Simplex LP

☑ **Make Variables Non-Negative**

Key Formulas

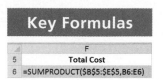

	F
5	Total Cost
6	=SUMPRODUCT($B$5:$E$5,B6:E6)

Copy F6 to F9:F12

product. A plane has a limited number of seats, and when the plane takes off, any empty seats can no longer be sold and the revenue is lost. A hotel has a limited number of rooms, and once a particular date has passed, an empty room on that date cannot be sold and the revenue is lost.

Another common type of application is data envelopment analysis (DEA). This is sometimes used to measure the efficiency of several similar operating units such as hospitals or schools. It is often used with nonprofit entities where measuring the success of a particular unit is difficult as there is no single objective, such as profit, that is to be optimized. In developing the LP, the inputs and outputs of the particular system must be identified. For a hospital system, the inputs might be the number of doctors working, the number of nurses working, the number of bed-day available per year, and the total payroll. The outputs might be the number of patient-days in the hospital, the number of nurses trained, the number of surgeries performed, the number of outpatient procedures performed, and the number of doctors trained. Constraints are developed for each of these inputs and outputs for each unit in the system. The objective is basically to minimize the resources needed to generate specific levels of output. The results indicate whether fewer resources could have been used to generate the same level of outputs when compared to a typical unit in the system. Efforts can then be made to identify specific areas that are deemed to be potentially inefficient, and improvements can be targeted for these areas.

Transportation problems, transshipment problems, and assignment problems are very widely used in business. These are so common that special purpose algorithms have been developed to solve these more quickly than the current procedures used for other type of linear programming problems. These applications will be presented in the next chapter.

IN ACTION

Harrah's Cherokee Casino Uses Linear Programming for Revenue Management

Identifying the customers who would generate the most revenue is usually very difficult, but Harrah's Cherokee Casino has benefited from a unique way of placing customers into particular market segments based on spending habits. Harrah's encourages casino customers to join their Total Rewards club. Points in this club are earned each time the member plays a casino game or spends money in a restaurant, spa, gift shop, or hotel facility. Earning points entitles players to receive benefits such as free or discounted rooms, meals, show tickets, and other things. Tracking the size of the bets as well as the number of bets allows Harrah's to place the players in segments based on the amount that they typically play when visiting the casinos. The best revenue generators are guests who typically gamble more money during each day of their stay. When a player tries to reserve a room, a low-spending player might be told there are no rooms available, while a high-spending customer will get to reserve the room. To promote goodwill, the customer in the lower-spending segment might be offered a free room at a nearby hotel. The additional revenue that will be obtained by reserving the room for a high-roller will more than offset this cost.

An LP is used to maximize the revenue generated subject to the total number of rooms available and the total number of rooms that are allocated to each segment of customers. The variables include the number of rooms to make available for each segment. The shadow prices of the constraints indicate how much extra revenue will be generated if one additional room is made available to the different segments. The model is frequently updated based on the number of rooms still available, the number of days remaining until the date of the reservation, and other factors. Based on results from this model, marketing efforts are targeted for very specific Total Rewards members when it appears that hotel traffic might be light on a particular day.

While revenue management implementations typically increase revenue by 3–7%, Harrah's has experienced a 15% increase in revenues from the revenue management systems throughout its many hotels and casinos. At Harrah's Cherokee Casino, the hotel opened with the system already in place so there is no basis for comparison. However, the profit margin of this particular property is 60% on gross revenue, which is twice the industry average.

Source: Based on Metters, Richard, et al. "The 'Killer Application' of Revenue Management: Harrah's Cherokee Casino & Hotel," *Interfaces* 38, 3 (May–June 2008): 161–175.

Summary

In this chapter we continued our discussion of linear programming models. The basic steps for formulating a linear program were followed for a variety of problems. These included applications in marketing, production scheduling, finance, and ingredient blending. Attention was paid to understanding the problem, identifying the objective and the constraints, defining the decision variables, and developing the mathematical model from these.

In future chapters, additional applications of linear programming will be presented. The transportation problem will be discussed in Chapter 9, along with two other closely related applications: the assignment problem and the transshipment problem.

Self-Test

- Before taking the self-test, refer to the learning objectives at the beginning of the chapter, the notes in the margins, and the glossary at the end of the chapter.
- Use the key at the back of the book to correct your answers.
- Restudy pages that correspond to any questions that you answered incorrectly or material you feel uncertain about.

1. Linear programming can be used to select effective media mixes, allocate fixed or limited budgets across media, and maximize audience exposure.
   a. True
   b. False
2. Using LP to maximize audience exposure in an advertising campaign is an example of the type of LP application known as
   a. marketing research.
   b. media selection.
   c. portfolio assessment.
   d. media budgeting.
   e. all of the above.
3. Which of the following *does not* represent a factor manager might consider when employing LP for production scheduling:
   a. labor capacity
   b. space limitations
   c. product demand
   d. risk assessment
   e. inventory costs

4. When applying LP to diet problems, the objective function is usually designed to
   a. maximize profits from blends of nutrients.
   b. maximize ingredient blends.
   c. minimize production losses.
   d. maximize the number of products to be produced.
   e. minimize the costs of nutrient blends.
5. The diet problem is
   a. also called the feed mix problem in agriculture.
   b. a special case of the ingredient mix problem.

c. a special case of the blending problem.
d. all of the above.
6. The selection of specific investments from among a wide variety of alternatives is the type of LP problem known as
   a. the product mix problem.
   b. the investment banker problem.
   c. the portfolio selection problem.
   d. the Wall Street problem.
   e. none of the above.

Problems

8-1 *(Production problem)* Winkler Furniture manufactures two different types of china cabinets: a French Provincial model and a Danish Modern model. Each cabinet produced must go through three departments: carpentry, painting, and finishing. The table below contains all relevant information concerning production times per cabinet produced and production capacities for each operation per day, along with net revenue per unit produced. The firm has a contract with an Indiana distributor to produce a minimum of 300 of each cabinet per week (or 60 cabinets per day). Owner Bob Winkler would like to determine a product mix to maximize his daily revenue.
(a) Formulate as an LP problem.
(b) Solve using an LP software program or spreadsheet.

8-2 *(Investment decision problem)* The Heinlein and Krampf Brokerage firm has just been instructed by one of its clients to invest $250,000 of her money obtained recently through the sale of land holdings in Ohio. The client has a good deal of trust in the investment house, but she also has her own ideas about the distribution of the funds being invested. In particular, she requests that the firm select whatever stocks and bonds they believe are well rated, but within the following guidelines:

(a) Municipal bonds should constitute at least 20% of the investment.
(b) At least 40% of the funds should be placed in a combination of electronic firms, aerospace firms, and drug manufacturers.
(c) No more than 50% of the amount invested in municipal bonds should be placed in a high-risk, high-yield nursing home stock.

Subject to these restraints, the client's goal is to maximize projected return on investments. The analysts at Heinlein and Krampf, aware of these guidelines, prepare a list of high-quality stocks and bonds and their corresponding rates of return:

INVESTMENT	PROJECTED RATE OF RETURN (%)
Los Angeles municipal bonds	5.3
Thompson Electronics, Inc.	6.8
United Aerospace Corp.	4.9
Palmer Drugs	8.4
Happy Days Nursing Homes	11.8

(a) Formulate this portfolio selection problem using LP.
(b) Solve this problem.

Data for Problem 8-1

CABINET STYLE	CARPENTRY (HOURS/ CABINET)	PAINTING (HOURS/ CABINET)	FINISHING (HOURS/ CABINET)	NET REVENUE/ CABINET ($)
French Provincial	3	1.5	0.75	28
Danish Modern	2	1	0.75	25
Department capacity (hours)	360	200	125	

Note: ⍭ means the problem may be solved with QM for Windows; ✖ means the problem may be solved with Excel; and ⍭ means the problem may be solved with QM for Windows and/or Excel.

⚖: 8-3 (*Restaurant work scheduling problem*). The famous Y. S. Chang Restaurant is open 24 hours a day. Waiters and busboys report for duty at 3 A.M., 7 A.M., 11 A.M., 3 P.M., 7 P.M., or 11 P.M., and each works an 8-hour shift. The following table shows the minimum number of workers needed during the six periods into which the day is divided. Chang's scheduling problem is to determine how many waiters and busboys should report for work at the start of each time period to minimize the total staff required for one day's operation. (*Hint:* Let X_i equal the number of waiters and busboys beginning work in time period i, where $i = 1, 2, 3, 4, 5, 6.$)

PERIOD	TIME	NUMBER OF WAITERS AND BUSBOYS REQUIRED
1	3 A.M.–7 A.M.	3
2	7 A.M.–11 A.M.	12
3	11 A.M.–3 P.M.	16
4	3 P.M.–7 P.M.	9
5	7 P.M.–11 P.M.	11
6	11 P.M.–3 A.M.	4

⚖: 8-4 (*Animal feed mix problem*) The Battery Park Stable feeds and houses the horses used to pull tourist-filled carriages through the streets of Charleston's historic waterfront area. The stable owner, an ex-racehorse trainer, recognizes the need to set a nutritional diet for the horses in his care. At the same time, he would like to keep the overall daily cost of feed to a minimum.

The feed mixes available for the horses' diet are an oat product, a highly enriched grain, and a mineral product. Each of these mixes contains a certain amount of five ingredients needed daily to keep the average horse healthy. The table on this page shows these minimum requirements, units of each ingredient per pound of feed mix, and costs for the three mixes.

In addition, the stable owner is aware that an overfed horse is a sluggish worker. Consequently, he determines that 6 pounds of feed per day are the most that any horse needs to function properly. Formulate this problem and solve for the optimal daily mix of the three feeds.

⚖: 8-5 The Kleenglass Corporation makes a dishwasher that has excellent cleaning power. This dishwasher uses less water than most competitors, and it is extremely quiet. Orders have been received from several retails stores for delivery at the end of each of the next 3 months, as shown below:

MONTH	NUMBER OF UNITS
June	195
July	215
August	205

Due to limited capacity, only 200 of these can be made each month on regular time, and the cost is $300 each. However, an extra 15 units per month can be produced if overtime is used, but the cost goes up to $325 each. Also, if there are any dishwashers produced in a month that are not sold in that month, there is a $20 cost to carry this item to the next month. Use linear programming to determine how many units to produce in each month on regular time and on overtime to minimize the total cost while meeting the demands.

⚖: 8-6 Eddie Kelly is running for reelection as mayor of a small town in Alabama. Jessica Martinez, Kelly's campaign manager during this election, is planning the marketing campaign, and there is some stiff competition. Martinez has selected four ways to advertise: television ads, radio ads, billboards,

Data for Problem 8-4

	FEED MIX			
DIET REQUIREMENT (INGREDIENTS)	OAT PRODUCT (UNITS/LB)	ENRICHED GRAIN (UNITS/LB)	MINERAL PRODUCT (UNITS/LB)	MINIMUM DAILY REQUIREMENT (UNITS)
A	2	3	1	6
B	0.5	1	0.5	2
C	3	5	6	9
D	1	1.5	2	8
E	0.5	0.5	1.5	5
Cost/lb	$0.09	$0.14	$0.17	

and newspaper ads. The costs of these, the audience reached by each type of ad, and the maximum number available is shown in the following table:

TYPE OF AD	COST PER AD	AUDIENCE REACHED/AD	MAXIMUM NUMBER
TV	$800	30,000	10
Radio	$400	22,000	10
Billboards	$500	24,000	10
Newspapers	$100	8,000	10

In addition, Martinez has decided that there should be at least six ads on TV or radio or some combination of those two. The amount spent on billboards and newspapers together must not exceed the amount spent on TV ads. While fundraising is still continuing, the monthly budget for advertising has been set at $15,000. How many ads of each type should be placed to maximize the total number of people reached?

8-7 *(Media selection problem)* The advertising director for Diversey Paint and Supply, a chain of four retail stores on Chicago's North Side, is considering two media possibilities. One plan is for a series of half-page ads in the Sunday *Chicago Tribune* newspaper, and the other is for advertising time on Chicago TV. The stores are expanding their lines of do-it-yourself tools, and the advertising director is interested in an exposure level of at least 40% within the city's neighborhoods and 60% in northwest suburban areas.

The TV viewing time under consideration has an exposure rating per spot of 5% in city homes and 3% in the northwest suburbs. The Sunday newspaper has corresponding exposure rates of 4% and 3% per ad. The cost of a half-page *Tribune* advertisement is $925; a television spot costs $2,000.

Diversey Paint would like to select the least costly advertising strategy that would meet desired exposure levels.
(a) Formulate using LP.
(b) Solve the problem.

8-8 *(Automobile leasing problem)* Sundown Rent-a-Car, a large automobile rental agency operating in the Midwest, is preparing a leasing strategy for the next six months. Sundown leases cars from an automobile manufacturer and then rents them to the public on a daily basis. A forecast of the demand for Sundown's cars in the next six months follows:

MONTH	MARCH	APRIL	MAY	JUNE	JULY	AUGUST
Demand	420	400	430	460	470	440

Cars may be leased from the manufacturer for either three, four, or five months. These are leased on the first day of the month and are returned on the last day of the month. Every six months the automobile manufacturer is notified by Sundown about the number of cars needed during the next six months. The automobile manufacturer has stipulated that at least 50% of the cars leased during a six-month period must be on the five-month lease. The cost per month on each of the three types of leases are $420 for the three-month lease, $400 for the four-month lease, and $370 for the five-month lease.

Currently, Sundown has 390 cars. The lease on 120 cars expires at the end of March. The lease on another 140 cars expires at the end of April, and the lease on the rest of these expires at the end of May.

Use LP to determine how many cars should be leased in each month on each type of lease to minimize the cost of leasing over the six-month period. How many cars are left at the end of August?

8-9 Management of Sundown Rent-a-Car (see Problem 8-8) has decided that perhaps the cost during the six-month period is not the appropriate cost to minimize because the agency may still be obligated to additional months on some leases after that time. For example, if Sundown had some cars delivered at the beginning of the sixth month, Sundown would still be obligated for two additional months on a three-month lease. Use LP to determine how many cars should be leased in each month on each type of lease to minimize the cost of leasing over the entire life of these leases.

8-10 *(High school busing problem)* The Arden County, Maryland, superintendent of education is responsible for assigning students to the *three* high schools in his county. He recognizes the need to bus a certain number of students, for several sectors of the county are beyond walking distance to a school. The superintendent partitions the county into *five* geographic sectors as he attempts to establish a plan that will minimize the total number of student miles traveled by bus. He also recognizes that if a student happens to live in a certain sector and is assigned to the high school in that sector, there is no need to bus that student because he or she can walk to school. The three schools are located in sectors B, C, and E.

The following table reflects the number of high-school-age students living in each sector and the busing distance in miles from each sector to each school:

	DISTANCE TO SCHOOL			
SECTOR	SCHOOL IN SECTOR B	SCHOOL IN SECTOR C	SCHOOL IN SECTOR E	NUMBER OF STUDENTS
A	5	8	6	700
B	0	4	12	500
C	4	0	7	100
D	7	2	5	800
E	12	7	0	400
				2,500

Each high school has a capacity of 900 students. Set up the objective function and constraints of this problem using LP so that the total number of student miles traveled by bus is minimized. Then solve the problem.

≗: 8-11 (*Pricing and marketing strategy problem*) The I. Kruger Paint and Wallpaper Store is a large retail distributor of the Supertrex brand of vinyl wallcoverings. Kruger will enhance its citywide image in Miami if it can outsell other local stores in total number of rolls of Supertrex next year. It is able to estimate the demand function as follows:

Number of rolls of Supertrex sold = 20 × Dollars spent on advertising + 6.8 × Dollars spent on in-store displays + 12 × Dollars invested in on-hand wallpaper inventory − 65,000 × Percentage markup taken above wholesale cost of a roll

The store budgets a total of $17,000 for advertising, in-store displays, and on-hand inventory of Supertrex for next year. It decides it must spend at least $3,000 on advertising; in addition, at least 5% of the amount invested in on-hand inventory should be devoted to displays. Markups on Supertrex seen at other local stores range from 20% to 45%. Kruger decides that its markup had best be in this range as well.
(a) Formulate as an LP problem.
(b) Solve the problem.
(c) What is the difficulty with the answer?
(d) What constraint would you add?

≗: 8-12 (*College meal selection problem*) Kathy Roniger, campus dietitian for a small Idaho college, is responsible for formulating a nutritious meal plan for students. For an evening meal, she feels that the following five meal-content requirements should be met: (1) between 900 and 1,500 calories; (2) at least 4 milligrams of iron; (3) no more than 50 grams of fat; (4) at least 26 grams of protein; and (5) no more than 50 grams of carbohydrates. On a particular day, Roniger's food stock includes seven items that can be prepared and served for supper to meet these requirements. The cost per pound for each food item and the contribution to each of the five nutritional requirements are given in the table below.

What combination and amounts of food items will provide the nutrition Roniger requires at the least total food cost?
(a) Formulate as an LP problem.
(b) What is the cost per meal?
(c) Is this a well-balanced diet?

≗: 8-13 (*High-tech production problem*) Quitmeyer Electronics Incorporated manufactures the following six microcomputer peripheral devices: internal modems, external modems, graphics circuit boards, CD drives, hard disk drives, and memory expansion boards. Each of these technical products requires time, in minutes, on three types of electronic testing equipment, as shown in the table below.

The first two test devices are available 120 hours per week. The third (device 3) requires more preventive maintenance and may be used only

Data for Problem 8-12

TABLE OF FOOD VALUES AND COSTS

FOOD ITEM	CALORIES/ LB	IRON (MG/LB)	FAT (GM/LB)	PROTEIN (GM/LB)	CARBOHYDRATES (GM/LB)	COST/ LB ($)
Milk	295	0.2	16	16	22	0.60
Ground meat	1216	0.2	96	81	0	2.35
Chicken	394	4.3	9	74	0	1.15
Fish	358	3.2	0.5	83	0	2.25
Beans	128	3.2	0.8	7	28	0.58
Spinach	118	14.1	1.4	14	19	1.17
Potatoes	279	2.2	0.5	8	63	0.33

Source: Pennington, Jean A. T., and Judith S. Douglass. Bowes and Church's Food Values of Portions Commonly Used, 18th ed., Philadelphia. Lippincott Williams & Wilkins, 2004, pp. 100–130.

Data for Problem 8-13

	INTERNAL MODEM	EXTERNAL MODEM	CIRCUIT BOARD	CD DRIVES	HARD DRIVES	MEMORY BOARDS
Test device 1	7	3	12	6	18	17
Test device 2	2	5	3	2	15	17
Test device 3	5	1	3	2	9	2

100 hours each week. The market for all six computer components is vast, and Quitmeyer Electronics believes that it can sell as many units of each product as it can manufacture. The table that follows summarizes the revenues and material costs for each product:

DEVICE	REVENUE PER UNIT SOLD ($)	MATERIAL COST PER UNIT ($)
Internal modem	200	35
External modem	120	25
Graphics circuit board	180	40
CD drive	130	45
Hard disk drive	430	170
Memory expansion board	260	60

In addition, variable labor costs are $15 per hour for test device 1, $12 per hour for test device 2, and $18 per hour for test device 3. Quitmeyer Electronics wants to maximize its profits.

(a) Formulate this problem as an LP model.
(b) Solve the problem by computer. What is the best product mix?
(c) What is the value of an additional minute of time per week on test device 1? Test device 2? Test device 3? Should Quitmeyer Electronics add more test device time? If so, on which equipment?

8-14 *(Nuclear plant staffing problem)* South Central Utilities has just announced the August 1 opening of its second nuclear generator at its Baton Rouge, Louisiana, nuclear power plant. Its personnel department has been directed to determine how many nuclear technicians need to be hired and trained over the remainder of the year.

The plant currently employs 350 fully trained technicians and projects the following personnel needs:

MONTH	PERSONNEL HOURS NEEDED
August	40,000
September	45,000
October	35,000
November	50,000
December	45,000

By Louisiana law, a reactor employee can actually work no more than 130 hours per month. (Slightly over 1 hour per day is used for check-in and check-out, recordkeeping, and daily radiation health scans.) Policy at South Central Utilities also dictates that layoffs are not acceptable in those months when the nuclear plant is overstaffed. So, if more trained employees are available than are needed in any month, each worker is still fully paid, even though he or she is not required to work the 130 hours.

Training new employees is an important and costly procedure. It takes one month of one-on-one classroom instruction before a new technician is permitted to work alone in the reactor facility. Therefore, South Central must hire trainees one month before they are actually needed. Each trainee teams up with a skilled nuclear technician and requires 90 hours of that employee's time, meaning that 90 hours less of the technician's time are available that month for actual reactor work.

Personnel department records indicate a turnover rate of trained technicians at 5% per month. In other words, about 5% of the skilled employees at the start of any month resign by the end of that month. A trained technician earns an average monthly salary of $2,000 (regardless of the number of hours worked, as noted earlier). Trainees are paid $900 during their one month of instruction.

(a) Formulate this staffing problem using LP.
(b) Solve the problem. How many trainees must begin each month?

8-15 *(Agricultural production planning problem)* Margaret Black's family owns five parcels of farmland broken into a southeast sector, north sector, northwest sector, west sector, and southwest sector. Margaret is involved primarily in growing wheat, alfalfa, and barley crops and is currently preparing her production plan for next year. The Pennsylvania Water Authority has just announced its yearly water allotment, with the Black farm receiving 7,400 acre-feet. Each parcel can only tolerate a specified amount of irrigation per growing season, as specified in the following table:

PARCEL	AREA (ACRES)	WATER IRRIGATION LIMIT (ACRE-FEET)
Southeast	2,000	3,200
North	2,300	3,400
Northwest	600	800
West	1,100	500
Southwest	500	600

Each of Margaret's crops needs a minimum amount of water per acre, and there is a projected limit on sales of each crop. Crop data follow:

CROP	MAXIMUM SALES	WATER NEEDED PER ACRE (ACRE-FEET)
Wheat	110,000 bushels	1.6
Alfalfa	1,800 tons	2.9
Barley	2,200 tons	3.5

Margaret's best estimate is that she can sell wheat at a net profit of $2 per bushel, alfalfa at $40 per ton, and barley at $50 per ton. One acre of land yields an average of 1.5 tons of alfalfa and 2.2 tons of barley. The wheat yield is approximately 50 bushels per acre.

(a) Formulate Margaret's production plan.

(b) What should the crop plan be, and what profit will it yield?

(c) The Water Authority informs Margaret that for a special fee of $6,000 this year, her farm will qualify for an additional allotment of 600 acre-feet of water. How should she respond?

8-16 (*Material blending problem*) Amalgamated Products has just received a contract to construct steel body frames for automobiles that are to be produced at the new Japanese factory in Tennessee. The Japanese auto manufacturer has strict quality control standards for all of its component subcontractors and has informed Amalgamated that each frame must have the following steel content:

MATERIAL	MINIMUM PERCENTAGE	MAXIMUM PERCENTAGE
Manganese	2.1	2.3
Silicon	4.3	4.6
Carbon	5.05	5.35

Amalgamated mixes batches of eight different available materials to produce one ton of steel used in the body frames. The table on this page details these materials.

Formulate and solve the LP model that will indicate how much each of the eight materials should be blended into a 1-ton load of steel so that Amalgamated meets its requirements while minimizing costs.

8-17 Refer to Problem 8-16. Find the cause of the difficulty and recommend how to adjust it. Then solve the problem again.

8-18 (*Hospital expansion problem*) Mt. Sinai Hospital in New Orleans is a large, private, 600-bed facility, complete with laboratories, operating rooms, and x-ray equipment. In seeking to increase revenues, Mt. Sinai's administration has decided to make a 90-bed addition on a portion of adjacent land currently used for staff parking. The administrators feel that the labs, operating rooms, and x-ray department are not being fully utilized at present and do not need to be expanded to handle additional patients. The addition of 90 beds, however, involves deciding how many beds should be allocated to the medical staff for medical patients and how many to the surgical staff for surgical patients.

The hospital's accounting and medical records departments have provided the following pertinent information. The average hospital stay for a medical patient is 8 days, and the average medical patient generates $2,280 in revenues. The average surgical patient is in the hospital 5 days and receives a $1,515 bill. The laboratory is capable of handling 15,000 tests per year more than it was handling. The average medical patient requires 3.1 lab tests and the average surgical patient takes 2.6 lab tests. Furthermore, the average medical patient uses one x-ray, whereas the average surgical patient requires two x-rays. If the hospital was expanded by 90 beds, the x-ray department could handle up to 7,000 x-rays without significant additional cost. Finally, the administration estimates that up to 2,800 additional operations could be performed in existing operating room facilities. Medical patients, of course, do not require surgery, whereas each surgical patient generally has one surgery performed.

Formulate this problem so as to determine how many medical beds and how many surgical beds should be added to maximize revenues. Assume that the hospital is open 365 days a year. Then solve the problem.

8-19 Prepare a written report to the CEO of Mt. Sinai Hospital in Problem 8-18 on the expansion of the hospital. Round off your answers to the nearest *integer*. The format of presentation of results is important. The CEO is a busy person and wants to be able

Data for Problem 8-16

MATERIAL AVAILABLE	MANGANESE (%)	SILICON (%)	CARBON (%)	POUNDS AVAILABLE	COST PER POUND ($)
Alloy 1	70.0	15.0	3.0	No limit	0.12
Alloy 2	55.0	30.0	1.0	300	0.13
Alloy 3	12.0	26.0	0	No limit	0.15
Iron 1	1.0	10.0	3.0	No limit	0.09
Iron 2	5.0	2.5	0	No limit	0.07
Carbide 1	0	24.0	18.0	50	0.10
Carbide 2	0	25.0	20.0	200	0.12
Carbide 3	0	23.0	25.0	100	0.09

to find your optimal solution quickly in your report. Cover all the areas given in the following sections, but do not mention any variables or shadow prices.

(a) What is the maximum revenue per year, how many medical patients/year are there, and how many surgical patients/year are there? How many medical beds and how many surgical beds of the 90-bed addition should be added?

(b) Are there any empty beds with this optimal solution? If so, how many empty beds are there? Discuss the effect of acquiring more beds if needed.

(c) Are the laboratories being used to their capacity? Is it possible to perform more lab tests/year? If so, how many more? Discuss the effect of acquiring more lab space if needed.

(d) Is the x-ray facility being used to its maximum? Is it possible to do more x-rays/year? If so, how many more? Discuss the effect of acquiring more x-ray facilities if needed.

(e) Is the operating room being used to capacity? Is it possible to do more operations/year? If so, how many more? Discuss the effect of acquiring more operating room facilities if needed. (**Source:** Professor Chris Vertullo.)

8-20 In the Low Knock Oil Company blending problem, it was assumed that one barrel of crude would result in one barrel of gasoline as the final product. In processing one barrel of crude, a typical gasoline yield is about 0.46 barrels, although it could be higher or lower than this, depending on the particular crude and processing used. However, other products such as diesel, jet fuel, home fuel oil, and asphalt also come from that same barrel. Assuming that only 46% of the crude turns into gasoline, modify the Low Knock Oil Company linear programming example to account for this. Solve the resulting LP problem, using any computer software.

8-21 A paper mill produces rolls of paper that are 10 inches wide and 100 feet long. These rolls are used for creating narrower rolls of paper that are used in cash registers, automatic teller machines (ATMs), and other devices. The narrower widths (2, 2.5, and 3 inches) needed for these devices are obtained by cutting the 10-inch rolls using pre-specified cutting patterns. Cutting pattern #1 will cut the 10-inch roll into four rolls that are 2.5 inches each. Cutting pattern #2 results in three rolls that are each 3 inches wide (leaving 1 inch of waste on the end). Cutting pattern #3 results in one roll that is 3 inches wide and two rolls that are 3.5 inches wide. Cutting pattern #4 results in one of the 2.5-inch rolls, one of the 3-inch rolls, and one of the 3.5-inch rolls (leaving 1 inch of waste). Cutting pattern #5 results in 1 roll that is 2.5 inches wide and two rolls that are 3.5 inches wide (leaving 0.5 inches of waste on the end). An order has been received for 2,000 of the 2.5-inch rolls,

4,000 of the 3-inch rolls, and 5,000 of the 3.5 inch rolls. How many rolls should be cut on each pattern if the company wants to minimize the total number of 10-inch rolls used? How many rolls should be cut on each pattern if the company wants to minimize the total waste?

8-22 (*Portfolio selection problem*) Daniel Grady is the financial advisor for a number of professional athletes. An analysis of the long-term goals for many of these athletes has resulted in a recommendation to purchase stocks with some of their income that is set aside for investments. Five stocks have been identified as having very favorable expectations for future performance. Although the expected return is important in these investments, the risk, as measured by the beta of the stock, is also important. (A high value of beta indicates that the stock has a relatively high risk.) The expected return and the betas for five stocks are as follows:

STOCK	1	2	3	4	5
Expected return (%)	11.0	9.0	6.5	15.0	13.0
Beta	1.20	0.85	0.55	1.40	1.25

Daniel would like to minimize the beta of the stock portfolio (calculated using a weighted average of the amounts put into the different stocks) while maintaining an expected return of at least 11%. Since future conditions may change, Daniel has decided that no more than 35% of the portfolio should be invested in any one stock.

(a) Formulate this as a linear program. (*Hint*: Define the variables to be the proportion of the total investment that would be put in each stock. Include a constraint that restricts the sum of these variables to be 1.)

(b) Solve this problem. What are the expected return and beta for this portfolio?

8-23 (*Airline fuel problem*) Coast-to-Coast Airlines is investigating the possibility of reducing the cost of fuel purchases by taking advantage of lower fuel costs in certain cities. Since fuel purchases represent a substantial portion of operating expenses for an airline, it is important that these costs be carefully monitored. However, fuel adds weight to an airplane, and consequently, excess fuel raises the cost of getting from one city to another. In evaluating one particular flight rotation, a plane begins in Atlanta, flies from Atlanta to Los Angeles, from Los Angeles to Houston, from Houston to New Orleans, and from New Orleans to Atlanta. When the plane arrives in Atlanta, the flight rotation is said to have been completed, and then it starts again. Thus, the fuel on board when the flight arrived in Atlanta must be taken into consideration when the flight begins.

Data for Problem 8-23

LEG	MINIMUM FUEL REQUIRED (1,000 GAL.)	MAXIMUM FUEL ALLOWED (1,000 GAL.)	REGULAR FUEL CONSUMPTION (1,000 GAL.)	FUEL PRICE PER GALLON
Atlanta–Los Angeles	24	36	12	$4.15
Los Angeles–Houston	15	23	7	$4.25
Houston–New Orleans	9	17	3	$4.10
New Orleans–Atlanta	11	20	5	$4.18

Along each leg of this route, there is a minimum and a maximum amount of fuel that may be carried. This and additional information is provided in the table above.

The regular fuel consumption is based on the plane carrying the minimum amount of fuel. If more than this is carried, the amount of fuel consumed is higher. Specifically, for each 1,000 gallons of fuel above the minimum, 5% (or 50 gallons per 1,000 gallons of extra fuel) is lost due to excess fuel consumption. For example, if 25,000 gallons of fuel were on board when the plane takes off from Atlanta, the fuel consumed on this route would be $12 + 0.05 = 12.05$ thousand gallons. If 26 thousand gallons were on board, the fuel consumed would be increased by another 0.05 thousand, for a total of 12.1 thousand gallons.

Formulate this as an LP problem to minimize the cost. How many gallons should be purchased in each city? What is the total cost of this?

 Internet Homework Problems

See our Internet home page, at **www.pearsonhighered.com/render**, for additional homework problems, Problems 8-24 to 8-26.

Case Study

Cable & Moore

With the company expanding into several new markets in the coming months, Cable & Moore was anticipating a large increase in sales revenue. The future looked bright for this provider of television, telephone, and Internet services. However, management of Cable & Moore was well aware of the importance of customer service in new markets. If the public had problems with new service and could not quickly and efficiently have their problems solved, demand would quickly erode and it might take years to recover from the bad publicity. Therefore, management was adamant that there would be enough well-trained customer service representatives to handle the calls from new customers and from potential customers.

Based on experience in other markets, the anticipated number of phone calls to customer service was projected. Given the average call-length, the number of hours of customer-service time from April to August was projected and is shown in the table below.

MONTH	APRIL	MAY	JUNE	JULY	AUGUST
Hours needed	21,600	24,600	27,200	28,200	29,700

Through experience, management knew that training a new employee well was essential. Each new employee was put through a 1-month training program, and was assigned to an existing employee for an entire month. Normally an existing employee would work 160 hours per month. However, when an employee was assigned to perform training of a new-hire, the productive work hours for that employee dropped to 80 hours per month.

During the training period, the trainee was paid $2,000 for the month. At the end of that time, the monthly salary increases to the standard salary for a regular customer service representative which is $3,000 per month. In the past, the company lost about 5% of the trained customer service representatives per month due to attrition. While the company is looking to improve upon this, for the next several months it is anticipated that this will continue. There will be 150 trained employees at the beginning of April. Management of the company would like to develop a schedule of hiring new employees so that there are sufficient customer service representatives to meet the demand, but this is to be done at the lowest possible cost.

Discussion Questions

1. Develop a schedule for hiring new employees. What is the total cost of this schedule?
2. Discuss any limitations that exist for this solution.
3. How would the schedule change if the attrition rate could be lowered to 3% per month instead of 5%? What would be the impact on the cost?

Internet Case Study

See out Internet home page, at **www.pearsonhighered.com/render**, for this additional case study: **Chase Manhattan Bank**. This case is about scheduling employees at a bank.

Bibliography

See the Bibliography at the end of Chapter 7.

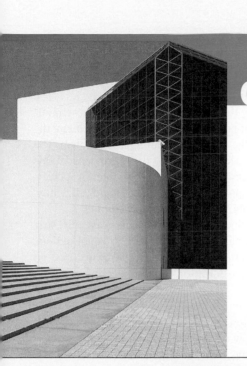

CHAPTER 9

Transportation, Assignment, and Network Models

LEARNING OBJECTIVES

After completing this chapter, students will be able to:

1. Structure LP problems for the transportation, transshipment, and assignment models.
2. Solve facility location and other application problems with transportation models.

3. Use LP to model shortest-route and maximal-flow problems.
4. Solve minimal-spanning tree problems.

CHAPTER OUTLINE

9.1   Introduction

Chapter 8 provided examples of a number of managerial problems that could be modeled using linear programming (LP), and this chapter will provide even more such examples. However, all of the problems in this chapter can be modeled as networks as well as linear programs. The use of networks helps in visualizing and understanding the managerial problem. These models include the transportation problem, the transshipment problem, the assignment problem, the maximal-flow problem, the shortest-route problem, and the minimal-spanning tree problem. The use of linear programming software will be the primary means of solving these problems in this chapter. However, to take advantage of the unique structure of some of these problems, specialized algorithms have been developed to solve very large problems more quickly and efficiently. These algorithms are presented on the Companion Website for this textbook in Module 8.

The basic transportation problem is concerned with finding the best (usually least cost) way to distribute goods from sources such as factories, to final destinations such as retail outlets. If there are intermediate points, such as regional distribution centers, where the items must go before being shipped to the final destination, then the transportation problem becomes a transshipment problem. The assignment problem involves finding the best (usually least cost) way to assign individuals or pieces of equipment to projects or jobs on a one-to-one basis. In other words, each person is assigned to only one job, and each job only needs one person assigned to it.

The maximal-flow technique finds the maximum flow of any quantity or substance through a network. This technique can determine, for example, the maximum number of vehicles (cars, trucks, and so forth) that can go through a network of roads from one location to another. The shortest-route technique can find the shortest path through a network. For example, this technique can find the shortest route from one city to another through a network of roads. The minimal-spanning tree technique determines the path through the network that connects all the points while minimizing total distance. When the points represent houses in a subdivision, the minimal-spanning tree technique can be used to determine how to connect all of the houses to electrical power, water systems, and so on, in a way that minimizes the total distance or length of power lines or water pipes.

The circles in the networks are called nodes. *The lines connecting them are called* arcs.

While there are many different types of examples in this chapter, some terminology is common to all of the network models. The points on the network are referred to as **nodes** and the lines on the network that connect these nodes are called **arcs**. Typically nodes are presented as circles, although sometimes squares or rectangles are used for the nodes.

IN ACTION   Improving Package Delivery

TNT Express is one of the world's largest delivery companies. The 77,000 employees of the company handle over 4 million packages each week, using about 30,000 trucks and other road vehicles and about 50 aircraft. Trying to maintain a high level of customer service while keeping costs low through efficient operations is a daunting task. In 2005, the director of operations for TNT Express turned to the use of operations research models to improve the road network of deliveries in Italy. A decrease in costs of over 6% caused the company to incorporate the use of optimization models into every aspect of their supply chain.

Several initiatives were developed to improve their supply chain. The Global Optimization (GO) Academy was established to teach employees the principles of optimization. Communities of practice (CoPs) were developed and key employees met three times a year to discuss and share their best practices with

their suppliers and academia members. In addition to developing optimization models and improving efficiency, the company taught employees the basic concepts of operations management and management science so that everyone would recognize opportunities for improvement through the use of these techniques.

The result of TNT Express implementing these practices was a cost savings of 207 million Euros from 2008 to 2011. Other benefits include the reduction of CO_2 emissions from their vehicles by 283 million kilograms, improved networking with other employees of the company, and a feeling of empowerment as workers now feel they can obtain support from colleagues outside their own operating units or even outside their own country. Optimization models truly delivered for TNT Express.

Source: Based on H. Fleuren, C. Goossens, M. Hendricks, M.-L. Lombard, and J. Poppelaars. "Supply Chain Wide Optimization at TNT Express," *Interfaces* 43, 1 (January/February 2013): 5–20.

9.2 The Transportation Problem

The **transportation problem** deals with the distribution of goods from several points of supply (*origins* or **sources**) to a number of points of demand (**destinations**). Usually we are given a capacity (supply) of goods at each source, a requirement (demand) for goods at each destination, and the shipping cost per unit from each source to each destination. An example is shown in Figure 9.1. The objective of such a problem is to schedule shipments so that total transportation costs are minimized. At times, production costs are also included.

Transportation models can also be used when a firm is trying to decide where to locate a new facility. Before opening a new warehouse, factory, or sales office, it is good practice to consider a number of alternative sites. Good financial decisions concerning the facility location also attempt to minimize total transportation and production costs for the entire system.

Linear Program for the Transportation Example

The Executive Furniture Corporation is faced with the transportation problem shown in Figure 9.1. The company would like to minimize the transportation costs while meeting the demand at each destination and not exceeding the supply at each source. In formulating this as a linear program, there are three supply constraints (one for each source) and three demand constraints (one for each destination). The decisions to be made are the number of units to ship on each route, so there is one decision variable for each arc (arrow) in the network. Let

$$X_{ij} = \text{number of units shipped from source } i \text{ to destination } j$$

where

$$i = 1, 2, 3, \text{ with } 1 = \text{Des Moines, } 2 = \text{Evansville, and } 3 = \text{Fort Lauderdale}$$
$$j = 1, 2, 3, \text{ with } 1 = \text{Albuquerque, } 2 = \text{Boston, and } 3 = \text{Cleveland}$$

The LP formulation is

$$\text{Minimize total cost} = 5X_{11} + 4X_{12} + 3X_{13} + 8X_{21} + 4X_{22}$$
$$+ 3X_{23} + 9X_{31} + 7X_{32} + 5X_{33}$$

subject to

$$X_{11} + X_{12} + X_{13} \leq 100 \quad (\text{Des Moines supply})$$
$$X_{21} + X_{22} + X_{23} \leq 300 \quad (\text{Evansville supply})$$
$$X_{31} + X_{32} + X_{33} \leq 300 \quad (\text{Fort Lauderdale supply})$$
$$X_{11} + X_{21} + X_{31} = 300 \quad (\text{Albuquerque demand})$$
$$X_{12} + X_{22} + X_{32} = 200 \quad (\text{Boston demand})$$
$$X_{13} + X_{23} + X_{33} = 200 \quad (\text{Cleveland demand})$$
$$X_{ij} \geq 0 \text{ for all } i \text{ and } j$$

The solution is found using computer software, and the optimal shipping schedule is the following:

100 units from Des Moines to Albuquerque

200 units from Evansville to Boston

100 units from Evansville to Cleveland

200 units from Ft. Lauderdale to Albuquerque

100 units from Ft. Lauderdale to Cleveland

The total cost is $3,900. The following section will illustrate how this solution was found.

Solving Transportation Problems Using Computer Software

The solution to this transportation problem modeled as an LP problem could be found by using Solver in Excel 2013 as illustrated in Chapter 7, by using QM for Windows, or by using Excel QM in Excel 2013. When using Excel 2013 and Solver, the constraints could be entered in rows as discussed in Chapter 7. However, the special structure for this problem allows for an

FIGURE 9.1

Network Representation of a Transportation Problem, with Costs, Demands, and Supplies

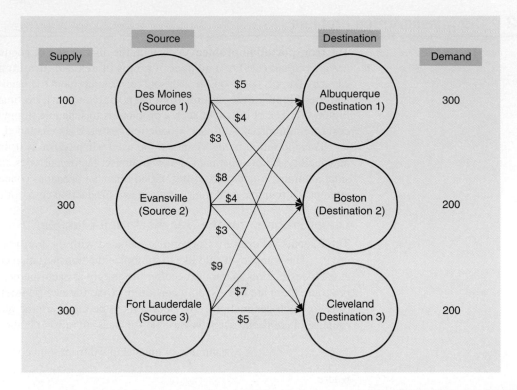

easier and more intuitive input in Excel 2013 with Solver, and Excel QM will be used for this example to illustrate this.

Program 9.1 provides the input data and the solution for this example. Click the *Excel QM* tab and select the *Alphabetical* Menu from the Excel QM ribbon. When the menu appears, scroll down and select *Transportation*. In the input window that opens, enter the number of Origins or sources (3 in this example), the number of Destinations (3 in this example), select *Minimize*, and click *OK*. A worksheet appears and you enter the costs, supplies, and demands shown in the data table. Then click the *Data* tab, select *Solver* from the Data ribbon, and click *Solve* in the Solver input window. You do not have to write any formulas or change any of the parameters.

A General LP Model for Transportation Problems

In this example, there were 3 sources and 3 destinations. The LP had $3 \times 3 = 9$ variables and $3 + 3 = 6$ constraints. In general, for a transportation problem with m sources and n destination, the number of variables is mn, and the number of constraints is $m + n$. For example, if

PROGRAM 9.1

Executive Furniture Corporation Solution in Excel 2013 Using Excel QM

1	**Exe**	From Excel QM ribbon, select Menu (Alphabetical or By Chapter). Select Transportation from the drop-down menu, and then input 3 Origins (sources) and 3 Destination.		From the Data tab, select Solver and then click Solve.	
2					
3	Tran				
4	En			ab on the ribbon, click on Solver in the	
5	Da			for instructions.	
6	If S				
7					
8	Data				
9	COSTS	Albuquerque	Boston	Cleveland	Supply
10	Des Moines	5	4	3	100
11	Evansville	8	4	3	300
12	Ft. Lauderdale	9	7	5	300
13	Demand	300	200	200	700 \ 700
14					
15	Shipments				
16	Shipments	Albuquerque	Boston	Cleveland	
17	Des Moines	100			100
18	Evansville		200	100	300
19	Ft. Lauderdale	200		100	300
20	Column Total	300	200	200	700 \ 700
21					
22	Total Cost	3900			

Fill in the table with the costs, supplies, and demands.

The solution is shown here.

The number of variables and constraints for a typical transportation problem can be found from the number of sources and destinations.

there are 5 (i.e., $m = 5$) constraints and 8 (i.e., $n = 8$) variables, the linear program would have $5(8) = 40$ variables and $5 + 8 = 13$ constraints.

The use of the double subscripts on the variables makes the general form of the linear program for a transportation problem with m sources and n destinations easy to express. Let

$$x_{ij} = \text{number of units shipped from source } i \text{ to destination } j$$
$$c_{ij} = \text{cost of one unit from source } i \text{ to destination } j$$
$$s_i = \text{supply at source } i$$
$$d_j = \text{demand at destination } j$$

The linear programming model is

$$\text{Minimize cost} = \sum_{j=1}^{n} \sum_{i=1}^{m} c_{ij} x_{ij}$$

subject to

$$\sum_{j=1}^{n} x_{ij} \leq s_i \qquad i = 1, 2, \ldots, m$$
$$\sum_{i=1}^{m} x_{ij} = d_j \qquad j = 1, 2, \ldots, n$$
$$x_{ij} \geq 0 \qquad \text{for all } i \text{ and } j$$

Facility Location Analysis

The transportation method has proved to be especially useful in helping a firm decide where to locate a new factory or warehouse. Since a new location is an issue of major financial importance to a company, several alternative locations must ordinarily be considered and evaluated. Even though a wide variety of subjective factors are considered, including quality of labor supply, presence of labor unions, community attitude and appearance, utilities, and recreational and educational facilities for employees, a final decision also involves minimizing total shipping and production costs. This means that each alternative facility location should be analyzed within the framework of one *overall* distribution system.

Locating a new facility within one overall distribution system is aided by the transportation method.

To determine which of two locations should be selected for a new production facility, linear programming models will be developed for two transportation problems—one for each location. If three or more locations were being considered, a transportation problem modeled as a linear programming model would be developed for each of these. The existing sources and destinations would be used in each of these, and one new source would be included as well. This will find the minimum cost for the distribution system if that one source is added to the system. This would be repeated for the second source, and the minimum costs for these two problems will be compared to find which one is better. This will be illustrated in the following example.

The Hardgrave Machine Company produces computer components at its plants in Cincinnati, Salt Lake City, and Pittsburgh. These plants have not been able to keep up with demand for orders at Hardgrave's four warehouses in Detroit, Dallas, New York, and Los Angeles. As a result, the firm has decided to build a new plant to expand its productive capacity. The two sites being considered are Seattle and Birmingham; both cities are attractive in terms of labor supply, municipal services, and ease of factory financing.

Table 9.1 presents the production costs and output requirements for each of the three existing plants, demand at each of the four warehouses, and estimated production costs of the new proposed plants. Transportation costs from each plant to each warehouse are summarized in Table 9.2.

The important question that Hardgrave now faces is this: Which of the new locations will yield the lowest cost for the firm in combination with the existing plants and warehouses? Note that the cost of each individual plant-to-warehouse route is found by adding the shipping costs (in the body of Table 9.2) to the respective unit production costs (from Table 9.1). Thus, the total production plus shipping cost of one computer component from Cincinnati to Detroit is $73 ($25 for shipping plus $48 for production).

We solve two transportation problems to find the new plant with lowest system cost.

To determine which new plant (Seattle or Birmingham) shows the lowest total systemwide cost of distribution and production, we solve two transportation problems—one for each of the

TABLE 9.1

Hardgrave's Demand and Supply Data

WAREHOUSE	MONTHLY DEMAND (UNITS)	PRODUCTION PLANT	MONTHLY SUPPLY	COST TO PRODUCE ONE UNIT ($)
Detroit	10,000	Cincinnati	15,000	48
Dallas	12,000	Salt Lake City	6,000	50
New York	15,000	Pittsburgh	14,000	52
Los Angeles	9,000		35,000	
	46,000			

Supply needed from new plant = 46,000 − 35,000 = 11,000 units per month

ESTIMATED PRODUCTION COST PER UNIT AT PROPOSED PLANTS	
Seattle	$53
Birmingham	$49

TABLE 9.2

Hardgrave's Shipping Costs

FROM \ TO	DETROIT	DALLAS	NEW YORK	LOS ANGELES
CINCINNATI	$25	$55	$40	$60
SALT LAKE CITY	35	30	50	40
PITTSBURGH	36	45	26	66
SEATTLE	60	38	65	27
BIRMINGHAM	35	30	41	50

two possible combinations. The first linear program will be for the Seattle location, and the second will be for Birmingham. To evaluate the Seattle location, the variables are defined as follows:

$$X_{ij} = \text{number of units shipped from source } i \text{ to destination } j$$

where

$i = 1, 2, 3, 4$ with 1 = Cincinnati, 2 = Salt Lake City, 3 = Pittsburgh, and 4 = Seattle

$j = 1, 2, 3, 4$ with 1 = Detroit, 2 = Dallas, 3 = New York, and 4 = Los Angeles

The linear program formulation has an objective of minimizing the total cost—transportation cost plus production cost.

Minimize total cost = $73X_{11} + 103X_{12} + 88X_{13} + 108X_{14} + 85X_{21} + 80X_{22} + 100X_{23}$
$+ 90X_{24} + 88X_{31} + 97X_{32} + 78X_{33} + 118X_{34} + 113X_{41} + 91X_{42} + 118X_{43} + 80X_{44}$

subject to

$$X_{11} + X_{21} + X_{31} + X_{41} = 10,000 \quad \text{Detroit Demand}$$
$$X_{12} + X_{22} + X_{32} + X_{42} = 12,000 \quad \text{Dallas Demand}$$
$$X_{13} + X_{23} + X_{33} + X_{43} = 15,000 \quad \text{New York Demand}$$
$$X_{14} + X_{24} + X_{34} + X_{44} = 9,000 \quad \text{Los Angeles Demand}$$
$$X_{11} + X_{12} + X_{13} + X_{14} \leq 15,000 \quad \text{Cincinnati Supply}$$
$$X_{21} + X_{22} + X_{23} + X_{24} \leq 6,000 \quad \text{Salt Lake City Supply}$$
$$X_{31} + X_{32} + X_{33} + X_{34} \leq 14,000 \quad \text{Pittsburgh Supply}$$
$$X_{41} + X_{42} + X_{43} + X_{44} \leq 11,000 \quad \text{Seattle Supply}$$

All variables ≥ 0

When this is solved, the total cost with the Seattle location is found to be $3,704,000.

For the second transportation model, the linear program is modified and the Birmingham location replaces the Seattle location. Now in the linear program, $i = 4$ represents Birmingham instead of Seattle, the last constraint is for Birmingham instead of Seattle, and the costs for these four variables in the objective function are now 84 for X_{41}, 79 for X_{42}, 90 for X_{43}, and 99 for X_{44}. Nothing else in the problem changes. When this is solved, the total cost with the Birmingham location is $3,741,000. Thus, the Seattle location results in an overall lower cost and would be the preferred location based on cost.

Excel QM will be used for this example, and Program 9.2 provides the solution for the problem with the Seattle location. To enter the problem, click the *Excel QM* tab, select the *Alphabetical* Menu from the Excel QM ribbon, and when the menu appears, scroll down to select *Transportation*. An input window opens and you simply enter the number of Origins (sources), the number of Destinations, select *Minimize*, and click *OK*. A worksheet is then developed and you enter the numbers for the costs, the supplies, and the demands shown in the Data table in Program 9.2. Once all inputs have been entered, click the *Data* tab, select *Solver*, and click *Solve* from the Solver input window. No other input for Solver is necessary. The shipments for the optimal solution are shown in the Shipments table. Program 9.3 provides the Excel QM results for the Birmingham location.

PROGRAM 9.2

Facility Location (Seattle) Solution in Excel 2013 Using Excel QM

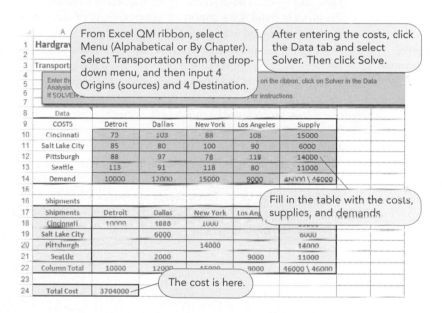

PROGRAM 9.3

Facility Location (Birmingham) Solution in Excel 2013 Using Excel QM

	A	B	C	D	E	F	G	H
1	Hardgrave Machine							
2								
3	Transportation							
4								
5	Enter the transportation data in the shaded area. Then go to the DATA Tab on the ribbon, click on Solver in the Data							
6	Analysis Group and then click SOLVE. If SOLVER is not on the Data Tab then please see the Help file (Solver) for instructions.							
7								
8	Data							
9	COSTS	Detroit	Dallas	New York	Los Angeles	Supply		
10	Cincinnati	73	103	88	108	15000		
11	Salt Lake City	85	80	100	90	6000		
12	Pittsburgh	88	97	78	118	14000		
13	Birmingham	84	79	90	99	11000		
14	Demand	10000	12000	15000	9000	46000 \ 46000		
15								
16	Shipments							
17	Shipments	Detroit	Dallas	New York	Los Angeles	Row Total		
18	Cincinnati	10000		1000	4000	15000		
19	Salt Lake City		1000		5000	6000		
20	Pittsburgh			14000		14000		
21	Birmingham		11000			11000		
22	Column Total	10000	12000	15000	9000	46000 \ 46000		
23			The cost is here.					
24	Total Cost	3741000						

9.3   The Assignment Problem

The **assignment problem** refers to the class of LP problem that involves determining the most efficient assignment of people to projects, sales people to territories, auditors to companies for audits, contracts to bidders, jobs to machines, heavy equipment (such as cranes) to construction jobs, and so on. The objective is most often to minimize total costs or total time of performing the tasks at hand. One important characteristic of assignment problems is that only one job or worker is assigned to one machine or project.

An assignment problem is equivalent to a transportation problem with each supply and demand equal to 1.

Figure 9.2 provides a network representation of an assignment problem. Notice that this network is very similar to the network for the transportation problem. In fact, an assignment problem may be viewed as a special type of transportation problem in which the supply at each source and the demand at each destination must equal one. Each person may only be assigned to one job or project, and each job only needs one person.

Linear Program for Assignment Example

The network in Figure 9.2 represents a problem faced by the Fix-It Shop, which has just received three new repair projects that must be completed quickly: (1) a radio, (2) a toaster oven, and (3) a coffee table. Three repair persons, each with different talents, are available to do the jobs. The shop owner estimates the cost in wages if the workers are assigned to each of the three projects. The costs differ due to the talents of each worker on each of the jobs. The owner wishes

FIGURE 9.2

Example of an Assignment Problem in a Transportation Network Format

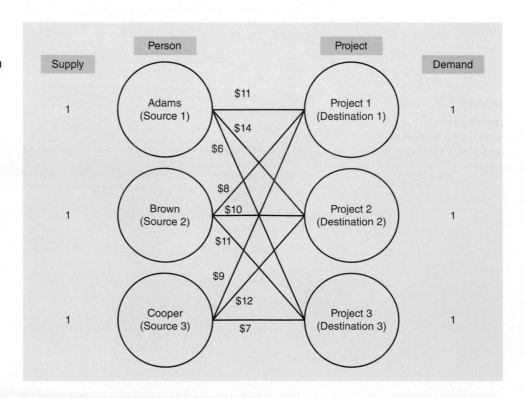

to assign the jobs so that total cost is minimized and each job must have one person assigned to it, and each person can only be assigned to one job.

In formulating this as a linear program, the general LP form of the transportation problem can be used. In defining the variables, let

Special variables 0-1 are used with the assignment model.

$$X_{ij} = \begin{cases} 1 \text{ if person } i \text{ is assigned to project } j \\ 0 \text{ otherwise} \end{cases}$$

where

$$i = 1, 2, 3, \text{ with } 1 = \text{Adams}, 2 = \text{Brown, and } 3 = \text{Cooper}$$
$$j = 1, 2, 3, \text{ with } 1 = \text{Project 1}, 2 = \text{Project 2, and } 3 = \text{Project 3}$$

The LP formulation is

$$\text{Minimize total cost} = 11X_{11} + 14X_{12} + 6X_{13} + 8X_{21} + 10X_{22}$$
$$+ 11X_{23} + 9X_{31} + 12X_{32} + 7X_{33}$$

subject to

$$X_{11} + X_{12} + X_{13} \leq 1$$
$$X_{21} + X_{22} + X_{23} \leq 1$$
$$X_{31} + X_{32} + X_{33} \leq 1$$
$$X_{11} + X_{21} + X_{31} = 1$$
$$X_{12} + X_{22} + X_{32} = 1$$
$$X_{13} + X_{23} + X_{33} = 1$$
$$x_{ij} = 0 \text{ or } 1 \text{ for all } i \text{ and } j$$

The solution is shown in Program 9.4. From this, $x_{13} = 1$, so Adams is assigned to project 3; $x_{22} = 1$, so Brown is assigned to project 2; and $x_{31} = 1$, so Cooper is assigned to project 1. All other variables are 0. The total cost is $25.

This problem could be input into Excel, Excel QM, or QM for Windows as a linear program, or it could be input as a transportation problem with all supplies and demands equal to 1. However, both Excel QM and QM for Windows have a module for this assignment problem. In Excel QM, from the *Alphabetical* Menu on the Excel QM ribbon, select *Assignment*. The initialization window opens and you enter the number of assignments and select *Minimization*. Click *OK* and a worksheet opens for you to enter the costs as shown in the data table in Program 9.4. Then select *Solver* from the *Data* ribbon, and click *Solve* in the Solver input window. The results are shown in Program 9.4.

PROGRAM 9.4

Mr. Fix-It Shop Assignment Solution in Excel 2013 Using Excel QM

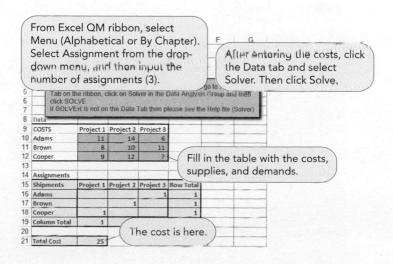

From Excel QM ribbon, select Menu (Alphabetical or By Chapter). Select Assignment from the drop-down menu, and then input the number of assignments (3).

After entering the costs, click the Data tab and select Solver. Then click Solve.

Fill in the table with the costs, supplies, and demands.

The cost is here.

The software for the assignment problem assumes that the problem is balanced, which means that the number of sources (or people) is equal to the number of destinations (or jobs). If the problem is not balanced, a dummy source or a dummy destination is added to the problem to make it balanced. In some cases, more than one dummy source or destination is used. Because this dummy is not a real assignment and only indicates which source or destination will be lacking an assignment, all costs are zero. Solved Problem 9-2 at the end of the chapter will illustrate this.

In the assignment problem, the variables are required to be either 0 or 1. Due to the special structure of this problem with the constraint coefficients as 0 or 1 and all the right-hand-side values equal to 1, the problem can be solved as a linear program. The solution to such a problem (if one exists) will always have the variables equal to 0 or 1. There are other types of problems where the use of such 0–1 variables is desired, but the solution to such problems using normal linear programming methods will not necessarily have only zeros and ones. In such cases, special methods must be used to force the variables to be either 0 or 1, and this will be discussed as a special type of integer programming problem which will be seen in Chapter 10.

9.4 The Transshipment Problem

A transportation problem with intermediate points is a transshipment problem.

In a transportation problem, if the items being transported must go through an intermediate point (called a *transshipment point*) before reaching a final destination, the problem is called a *transshipment problem*. For example, a company might be manufacturing a product at several factories to be shipped to a set of regional distribution centers. From these centers, the items are shipped to retail outlets that are the final destinations. Figure 9.3 provides a network representation of a transshipment problem. In this example, there are two sources, two transshipment points, and three final destinations.

Linear Program for Transshipment Example

Frosty Machines manufactures snow blowers in factories located in Toronto and Detroit. These are shipped to regional distribution centers in Chicago and Buffalo, where they are delivered to the supply houses in New York, Philadelphia, and St. Louis, as illustrated in Figure 9.3.

The available supplies at the factories, the demands at the final destination, and shipping costs are shown in the Table 9.3. Notice that snow blowers may not be shipped directly from Toronto or Detroit to any of the final destinations but must first go to either Chicago or Buffalo. This is why Chicago and Buffalo are listed not only as destinations but also as sources.

Frosty would like to minimize the transportation costs associated with shipping sufficient snow blowers to meet the demands at the three destinations while not exceeding the supply at each factory. Thus, we have supply and demand constraints similar to the transportation problem, but we also have one constraint for each transshipment point indicating that anything

FIGURE 9.3

Network Representation of Transshipment Example

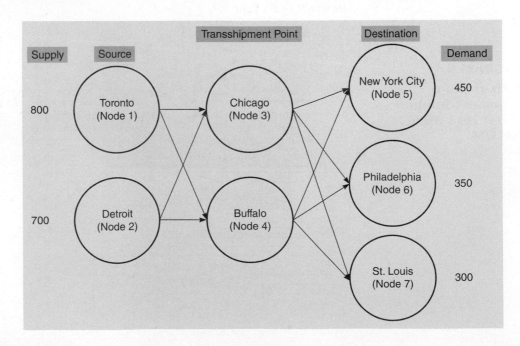

TABLE 9.3 Frosty Machine Transshipment Data

FROM	CHICAGO	BUFFALO	NEW YORK CITY	PHILADELPHIA	ST. LOUIS	SUPPLY
Toronto	$4	$7	—	—	—	800
Detroit	$5	$7	—	—	—	700
Chicago	—	—	$6	$4	$5	—
Buffalo	—	—	$2	$3	$4	—
Demand	—	—	450	350	300	

shipped from these to a final destination must have been shipped into that transshipment point from one of the sources. The verbal statement of this problem would be as follows:

Minimize cost

subject to

1. The number of units shipped from Toronto is not more than 800
2. The number of units shipped from Detroit is not more than 700
3. The number of units shipped to New York is 450
4. The number of units shipped to Philadelphia is 350
5. The number of units shipped to St. Louis is 300
6. The number of units shipped out of Chicago is equal to the number of units shipped into Chicago
7. The number of units shipped out of Buffalo is equal to the number of units shipped into Buffalo

Special transshipment constraints are used in the linear program.

The decision variables should represent the number of units shipped from each source to each transshipment point and the number of units shipped from each transshipment point to each final destination, as these are the decisions management must make. The decision variables are

$$X_{ij} = \text{number of units shipped from location (node) } i \text{ to location (node) } j$$

where

$$i = 1, 2, 3, 4$$
$$j = 3, 4, 5, 6, 7$$

The numbers are the nodes shown in Figure 9.3, and there is one variable for each arc (route) in the figure.

The LP model is

$$\text{Minimize total cost} = 4X_{13} + 7X_{14} + 5X_{23} + 7X_{24} + 6X_{35} + 4X_{36}$$
$$+ 5X_{37} + 2X_{45} + 3X_{46} + 4X_{47}$$

subject to

$X_{13} + X_{14} \leq 800$	(Supply at Toronto [node 1])
$X_{23} + X_{24} \leq 700$	(Supply at Detroit [node 2])
$X_{35} + X_{45} = 450$	(Demand at New York City [node 5])
$X_{36} + X_{46} = 350$	(Demand at Philadelphia [node 6])
$X_{37} + X_{47} = 300$	(Demand at St. Louis [node 7])
$X_{13} + X_{23} = X_{35} + X_{36} + X_{37}$	(Shipping through Chicago [node 3])
$X_{14} + X_{24} = X_{45} + X_{46} + X_{47}$	(Shipping through Buffalo [node 4])
$x_{ij} \geq 0 \text{ for all } i \text{ and } j$	

The solution found using Solver in Excel 2013 and Excel QM is shown in Program 9.5. The total cost is $9,550 by shipping 650 units from Toronto to Chicago, 150 units from Toronto to Buffalo, 300 units from Detroit to Buffalo, 350 units from Chicago to Philadelphia, 300 units from Chicago to St. Louis, and 450 units from Buffalo to New York City.

PROGRAM 9.5

Excel QM Solution to Frosty Machine Transshipment Problem in Excel 2013

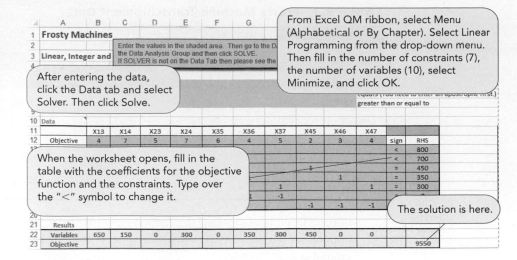

When the worksheet opens, fill in the table with the coefficients for the objective function and the constraints. Type over the "<" symbol to change it.

After entering the data, click the Data tab and select Solver. Then click Solve.

From Excel QM ribbon, select Menu (Alphabetical or By Chapter). Select Linear Programming from the drop-down menu. Then fill in the number of constraints (7), the number of variables (10), select Minimize, and click OK.

The solution is here.

	X13	X14	X23	X24	X35	X36	X37	X45	X46	X47	sign	RHS
Objective	4	7	5	7	6	4	5	2	3	4		
											<	800
											<	700
						1					=	450
							1				=	350
					1			1		1	=	300
	1				-1							
						-1		-1	-1	-1		
Results												
Variables	650	150	0	300	0	350	300	450	0	0		
Objective												9550

MODELING IN THE REAL WORLD   Moving Sugar Cane in Cuba

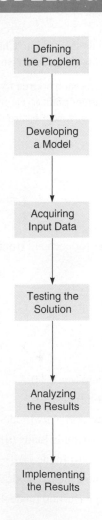

Defining the Problem

Developing a Model

Acquiring Input Data

Testing the Solution

Analyzing the Results

Implementing the Results

Defining the Problem

The sugar market has been in a crisis for over a decade. Low sugar prices and decreasing demand have added to an already unstable market. Sugar producers needed to minimize costs. They targeted the largest unit cost in the manufacturing of raw sugar contributor—namely, sugar cane transportation costs.

Developing a Model

To solve this problem, researchers developed a linear program with some integer decision variables (e.g., number of trucks) and some continuous (linear) variables and linear decision variables (e.g., tons of sugar cane).

Acquiring Input Data

In developing the model, the inputs gathered were the operating demands of the sugar mills involved, the capacities of the intermediary storage facilities, the per-unit transportation costs per route, and the production capacities of the various sugar cane fields.

Testing the Solution

The researchers involved first tested a small version of their mathematical formulation using a spreadsheet. After noting encouraging results, they implemented the full version of their model on a large capacity computer. Results were obtained for this very large and complex model (on the order of 40,000 decision variables and 10,000 constraints) in just a few milliseconds.

Analyzing the Results

The solution obtained contained information on the quantity of cane delivered to each sugar mill, the field where cane should be collected, and the means of transportation (by truck, by train, etc.), and several other vital operational attributes.

Implementing the Results

While solving such large problems with some integer variables might have been impossible only a decade ago, solving these problems now is certainly possible. To implement these results, the researchers worked to develop a more user-friendly interface so that managers would have no problem using this model to help make decisions.

Source: Based on E. L. Milan, S. M. Fernandez, and L. M. Pla Aragones. "Sugar Cane Transportation in Cuba: A Case Study," *European Journal of Operational Research*, 174, 1 (2006): 374–386.

9.5 Maximal-Flow Problem

The **maximal-flow problem** involves determining the maximum amount of material that can flow from one point (the **source**) to another (the **sink**) in a network. Examples of this type of problem include determining the maximum number of cars that can flow through a highway system, the maximum amount of a liquid that can flow through a series of pipes, the maximum number of cell-phone calls that can pass through a series of cell towers, and the maximum amount of data that can flow through a computer network.

To find the maximal flow from the source or start of a network to the sink or finish of that network, two common methods are used: linear programming and the maximal-flow technique. We will begin by presenting an example and demonstrating the use of linear programming for this type of problem.

Example

Waukesha, a small town in Wisconsin, is in the process of developing a road system for the downtown area. Bill Blackstone, one of the city planners, would like to determine the maximum number of cars that can flow through the town from west to east. The road network is shown in Figure 9.4. The streets are indicated by their respective arcs. For example, the arc from node 1 to node 2 is arc 1–2. The arc in the reverse direction (from node 2 to node 1) is arc 2–1. The numbers by the nodes indicate the maximum number of cars (in hundreds of cars per hour) that can flow from the various nodes along the respective arcs. The maximum flow along arc 1–2 is 3, while the flow along arc 1–3 is 10. The city planners would like to know the capacity of the current road system in the west to east direction.

The maximal-flow problem can be modeled as a linear program. This type of problem may be viewed as a special type of transshipment problem with one source, one destination, and a number of transshipment points. The number shipped through the network would be called the flow. The objective is to maximize the flow through the network. There are two types of constraints. The first set of constraints restricts the amount of flow on any arc to the capacity of that arc. The second set of constraints indicates that the amount of flow out of a node will equal the amount of flow into that node. These are the same as the transshipment constraints in the transshipment problem.

The variables are defined as:

$$X_{ij} - \text{flow from node } i \text{ to node } j$$

One additional arc will be added to the network, and this arc will go from the sink (node 6) back to the source (node 1). The flow along this arc represents the total flow in the network. The first set of constraints in the linear program are the maximum flows along each arc in each direction. They are grouped together based on the node from which the flow originates. The last six

FIGURE 9.4

Road Network for Waukesha Maximal-Flow Example

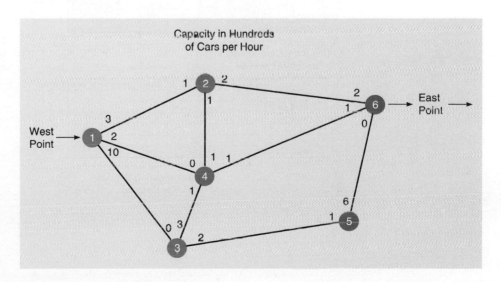

constraints are restricting the flow out of a node to equal the flow into a node (i.e., the flow into a node minus the flow out of that node must equal zero). The linear program is

Maximize flow $= X_{61}$

subject to

$X_{12} \leq 3$	$X_{13} \leq 10$	$X_{14} \leq 2$	Capacities for arcs from node 1
$X_{21} \leq 1$	$X_{24} \leq 1$	$X_{26} \leq 2$	Capacities for arcs from node 2
$X_{34} \leq 3$	$X_{35} \leq 2$		Capacities for arcs from node 3
$X_{42} \leq 1$	$X_{43} \leq 1$	$X_{46} \leq 1$	Capacities for arcs from node 4
$X_{53} \leq 1$	$X_{56} \leq 1$		Capacities for arcs from node 5
$X_{62} \leq 2$	$X_{64} \leq 1$		Capacities for arcs from node 6

$$(X_{21} + X_{61}) - (X_{12} + X_{13} + X_{14}) = 0 \qquad \text{Flows into} = \text{flows out of node 1}$$
$$(X_{12} + X_{42} + X_{62}) - (X_{21} + X_{24} + X_{26}) = 0 \qquad \text{Flows into} = \text{flows out of node 2}$$
$$(X_{13} + X_{43} + X_{53}) - (X_{34} + X_{35}) = 0 \qquad \text{Flows into} = \text{flows out of node 3}$$
$$(X_{14} + X_{24} + X_{34} + X_{64}) - (X_{42} + X_{43} + X_{46}) = 0 \qquad \text{Flows into} = \text{flows out of node 4}$$
$$(X_{35}) - (X_{56} + X_{53}) = 0 \qquad \text{Flows into} = \text{flows out of node 5}$$
$$(X_{26} + X_{46} + X_{56}) - (X_{61} + X_{62} + X_{64}) = 0 \qquad \text{Flows into} = \text{flows out of node 6}$$
$$X_{ij} \geq 0$$

The problem is now ready to solve using the linear programming module QM for Windows or using Solver in Excel 2013. However, Program 9.6 illustrates the solution found using Excel QM. To obtain this, from the Excel QM ribbon, select *Network Analysis as LP* and then choose *Maximal Flow*. In the initialization window that opens, you enter the number of nodes (6) and click *OK*. A worksheet is developed as seen in Program 9.6. Enter the data for the arc capacities, and then click *Solver* from the *Data* ribbon. Click *Solve* from the Solver input window, and the results (flows) are put into the worksheet.

PROGRAM 9.6

Waukesha Maximal-Flow Solution in Excel 2013 Using Excel QM

Callout: From Excel QM ribbon, select Menu (Alphabetical or By Chapter). Select Network Analysis as LP and Maximal Flow from the drop-down menu. Then fill in the number of branches or arcs (6). Click OK.

	A						
1	Waukesha						
2							
3	Maximal Flow						
4	Enter the flow capac...						
5	the sink must be set...						
6	Data Analysis Group...						
7							
8	**Data - Arc capacities**						
9	From\to	Node 1	Node 2	Node 3	Node 4	Node 5	Node 6
10	Node 1	0	3	10	2	0	0
11	Node 2	1	0	0	1	0	2
12	Node 3	0	0	0	3	2	0
13	Node 4	0	1	1	0	0	1
14	Node 5	0	0	1	0	0	6
15	Node 6	999999	2	0	1	0	0
16							

Callout: When the worksheet opens, enter the flows in the table.

Callout: This is entered already and is used by Excel QM.

	From\to	Node 1	Node 2	Node 3	Node 4	Node 5	Node 6	Outflow
20	From\to	Node 1	Node 2	Node 3	Node 4	Node 5	Node 6	Outflow
21	Node 1			2				2
22	Node 2						2	2
23	Node 3				2			2
24	Node 4						1	1
25	Node 5						2	2
26	Node 6	2	2		1			5
27	Inflow	2	2	2	1	2	5	
28	Outflow	2	2					
29								
30								
31	Max Flow	5						

Callout: After entering the data, click the Data tab and select Solver. Then click Solve.

9.6 Shortest-Route Problem

The objective of the **shortest-route problem** is to find the shortest distance from one location to another. In a network, this often involves determining the shortest route from one node to each of the other nodes. This problem can be modeled as a linear program with 0–1 variables, or it could be modeled and solved using a specialized algorithm that is presented in Module 8. The following example is a typical shortest-route problem

Every day, Ray Design, Inc., must transport beds, chairs, and other furniture items from the factory to the warehouse. This involves going through several cities, and there are no direct interstate highways to make the delivery easier. Ray would like to find the route with the shortest distance. The road network is shown in Figure 9.5.

The shortest-route problem may be viewed as a special type of transshipment problem with one source having a supply of 1, one destination with a demand of 1, and a number of transshipment points. This type of problem can be modeled as a linear program with 0–1 variables. Ray is trying to decide which of the routes (arcs) to choose to be a part of the delivery system. Therefore, the decision variables will indicate whether a particular arc is chosen to be a part of the route taken. For the Ray Design, Inc., example, the objective is to minimize the total distance (cost) from the start to the finish. The constraints will specify that the number of units (either 0 or 1) going into a node must equal the number going out of that node. The variables are defined as

$$X_{ij} = 1 \text{ if arc from node } i \text{ to node } j \text{ is selected and } X_{ij} = 0 \text{ otherwise}$$

Since the starting point is node 1, we will not include variables going from node 2 or 3 back to node 1. Similarly, since node 6 is the final destination, we will not include any variable that starts at node 6. Viewing this as a transshipment problem, the origin node (node 1) must have one unit shipped out of it. This would be

$$X_{12} + X_{13} = 1$$

The final destination node (node 6) must have one unit shipped to it, and this is written as

$$X_{46} + X_{56} = 1$$

Each intermediate node will have a constraint requiring the amount coming into the node to equal the amount going out of that node (i.e., the flow into a node minus the flow out of a node must equal zero). For node 2 this would be

$$X_{12} + X_{32} = X_{23} + X_{24} + X_{25}$$

This simplifies to

$$X_{12} + X_{32} - X_{23} - X_{24} - X_{25} = 0$$

The other constraints would be constructed in a similar manner. The linear program is

Minimize distance $= 100X_{12} + 200X_{13} + 50X_{23} + 50X_{32} + 200X_{24} + 200X_{42} + 100X_{25}$
$+ 100X_{52} + 40X_{35} + 40X_{53} + 150X_{45} + 150X_{54} + 100X_{46} + 100X_{56}$

subject to

$$
\begin{array}{ll}
X_{12} + X_{13} = 1 & \text{Node 1} \\
X_{12} + X_{32} - X_{23} - X_{24} - X_{25} = 0 & \text{Node 2} \\
X_{13} + X_{23} - X_{32} - X_{35} = 0 & \text{Node 3} \\
X_{24} + X_{54} - X_{42} - X_{45} - X_{46} = 0 & \text{Node 4} \\
X_{25} + X_{35} + X_{45} - X_{52} - X_{53} - X_{54} - X_{56} = 0 & \text{Node 5} \\
X_{46} + X_{56} = 1 & \text{Node 6} \\
\end{array}
$$

All variables $= 0$ or 1

FIGURE 9.5

Roads from Ray's Plant to Warehouse

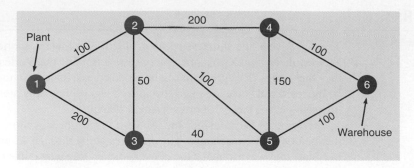

PROGRAM 9.7

Ray Designs, Inc. Solution in Excel 2013 Using Excel QM

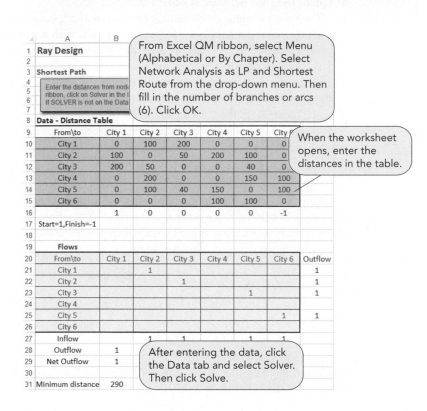

While this problem could be solved as a linear program, using Excel QM is the easiest to obtain the solutions. To solve a *shortest-route* problem, from the Excel QM ribbon select *Network Analysis as LP* and then choose *Shortest Path*. In the initialization window that opens, you enter the number of nodes (6) and click *OK*. A worksheet is developed as seen in Program 9.7. Enter the data for the distances, and then click *Solver* from the *Data* ribbon. Click *Solve* from the Solver input window, and the results (flows) are put into the worksheet. From Program 9.7 we see that

$$X_{12} = X_{23} = X_{35} = X_{56} = 1$$

So Ray will travel from city 1 to city 2, then to city 3, then to city 5, and from there to the final destination city 6. The total distance is 290 miles.

9.7 Minimal-Spanning Tree Problem

The **minimal-spanning tree problem** involves connecting all points of a network together while minimizing the total distance of these connections. Some common examples include telephone or cable companies trying to connect houses in a neighborhood, and network administrators trying to minimize the cable required to hard-wire computers in a network. While a linear programming model has been used for this, there are certain properties of this problem that make this quite complex. Fortunately, there is another method for finding the solution to such a problem that is very easy, and that will be presented here. The minimal-spanning tree technique problem will be presented using the following example.

Let us consider the Lauderdale Construction Company, which is currently developing a luxurious housing project in Panama City Beach, Florida. Melvin Lauderdale, owner and president of Lauderdale Construction, must determine the least expensive way to provide water and power to each house. The network of houses is shown in Figure 9.6.

As seen in Figure 9.6, there are eight houses on the gulf. The distance between each house in hundreds of feet is shown on the network. The distance between houses 1 and 2, for example, is 300 feet. (The number 3 is between nodes 1 and 2.) Now, the minimal-spanning tree technique is used to determine the minimal distance that can be used to connect all of the nodes. The approach is outlined as follows:

There are four steps for the minimal-spanning tree problem.

Steps for the Minimal-Spanning Tree Technique

1. Select any node in the network.
2. Connect this node to the nearest node that minimizes the total distance.
3. Considering all of the nodes that are now connected, find and connect the nearest node that is not connected. If there is a tie for the nearest node, select one arbitrarily. A tie suggests there may be more than one optimal solution.
4. Repeat the third step until all nodes are connected.

Step 1: We select node 1.
Step 2: We connect node 1 to node 3.

Now, we solve the network in Figure 9.6 for Melvin Lauderdale. We start by arbitrarily selecting node 1. Since the nearest node is the third node at a distance of 2 (200 feet), we connect node 1 to node 3. This is shown in Figure 9.7.

Considering nodes 1 and 3, we look for the next-nearest node. This is node 4, which is the closest to node 3. The distance is 2 (200 feet). Again, we connect these nodes (see Figure 9.8, part (a)).

We continue, looking for the nearest unconnected node to nodes 1, 3, and 4. This is node 2 or node 6, each at a distance of 3 from node 3. We will pick node 2 and connect it to node 3 (see Figure 9.8, part (b)).

FIGURE 9.6
Network for Lauderdale Construction

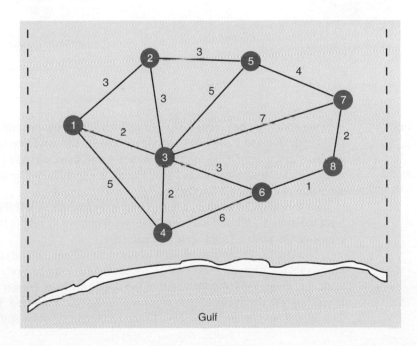

Gulf

FIGURE 9.7
First Iteration for Lauderdale Construction

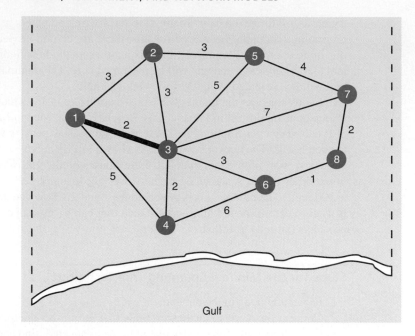

Gulf

FIGURE 9.8   Second and Third Iterations

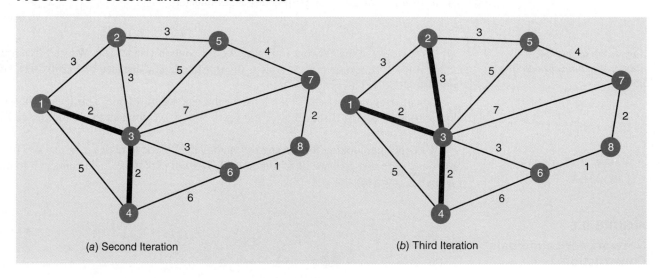

(a) Second Iteration

(b) Third Iteration

Step 3: We connect the next nearest node.

Step 4: We repeat the process.

We continue the process. There is another tie for the next iteration with a minimum distance of 3 (node 2–node 5 and node 3–node 6). You should note that we do not consider node 1–node 2 with a distance of 3 because both nodes 1 and 2 are already connected. We arbitrarily select node 5 and connect it to node 2 (see Figure 9.9, part (a)). The next nearest node is node 6, and we connect it to node 3 (see Figure 9.9, part (b)).

At this stage, we have only two unconnected nodes left. Node 8 is the nearest to node 6, with a distance of 1 and we connect it (see Figure 9.9, part (c)). Then the remaining node 7 is connected to node 8 (see Figure 9.9, part (d)).

The final solution can be seen in the seventh and final iteration. Nodes 1, 2, 4, and 6 are all connected to node 3. Node 2 is connected to node 5. Node 6 is connected to node 8, and node 8 is connected to node 7. All of the nodes are now connected. The total distance is found by adding the distances for the arcs used in the spanning tree. In this example, the distance is 2 + 2 + 3 + 3 + 3 + 1 + 2 = 16 (or 1,600 feet). This is summarized in Table 9.4.

FIGURE 9.9 Last Four Iterations for Lauderdale Construction

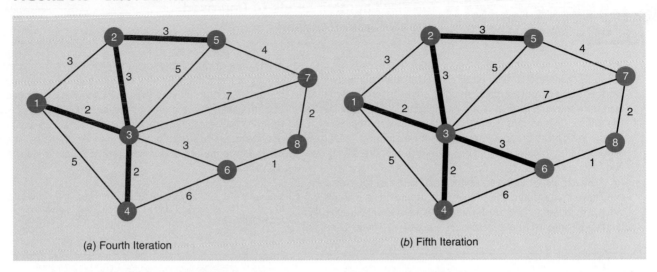

(a) Fourth Iteration

(b) Fifth Iteration

(c) Sixth Iteration

(d) Seventh Iteration

The minimal-spanning tree problem can be solved with Excel QM or QM for Windows. Using Excel QM in Excel 2013, select *Alphabetical* Menu from the ribbon, scroll down to *Network Analysis*, and select *Minimal Spanning Tree*. In the spreadsheet initialization window that opens, enter the number of branches or arcs (13 in this example). When the worksheet opens, for each

TABLE 9.4 Summary of Steps in Lauderdale Construction Minimal-Spanning Tree Problem

STEP	CONNECTED NODES	UNCONNECTED NODES	CLOSEST UNCONNECTED NODE	ARC SELECTED	ARC LENGTH	TOTAL DISTANCE
1	1	2, 3, 4, 5, 6, 7, 8	3	1–3	2	2
2	1, 3	2, 4, 5, 6, 7, 8	4	3–4	2	4
3	1, 3, 4	2, 5, 6, 7, 8	2 or 6	3–2	3	7
4	1, 2, 3, 4	5, 6, 7, 8	5 or 6	2–5	3	10
5	1, 2, 3, 4, 5	6, 7, 8	6	3–6	3	13
6	1, 2, 3, 4, 5, 6	7, 8	8	6–8	1	14
7	1, 2, 3, 4, 5, 6, 8	7	7	8–7	2	16

IN ACTION Facility Location Leads to Improved Supply-Chain Reliability

Supply chains are, at their physical level, an interconnected network of delivery routes (roads, bridges, shipping lanes, etc.) that lead from multiple sources (warehouse, factories, refineries, etc.) to multiple destinations (stores, outlets, other warehouses, etc.) along which products and commodities travel. In most cases, the allocation of particular destinations to particular sources is known and fairly constant.

Researchers, in trying to help companies plan for emergencies, have investigated the problem of supply-chain disruption. What would happen if one of the sources were to catastrophically fail due to an earthquake, a tornado, or worse? The answer lies

in the area of the facility location problem: Which warehouses should deliver to which stores addresses this issue. Analyzing the transportation problem with current sources eliminated one by one, the analysts were able to measure the impact of such disruption. The researchers concluded that "backup assignments" of warehouses to stores should be planned ahead of time to help mitigate the impact of possible catastrophes. It always pays to plan ahead!

Source: Based on L. Snyder and M. Daskin. "Reliability Models for Facility Location: The Expected Failure Cost Case," *Transportation Science* 39, 3 (2005): 400–416.

PROGRAM 9.8

Lauderdale Construction Minimal-Spanning Tree Example

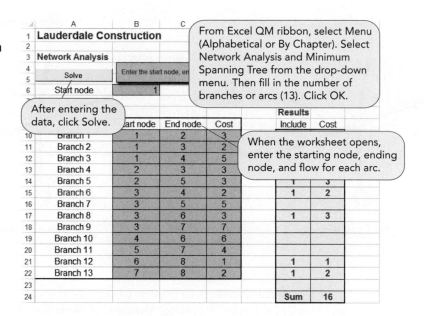

arc enter the beginning node, the ending node, and the distance between the two (i.e., the length of the arc) as shown in Program 9.8. Click the *Solve* button that appears in the spreadsheet, and the solution will be displayed as in Program 9.8. The problem could also be solved in QM for Windows by selecting the networks module and entering a new problem as a minimal-spanning tree. The input is very similar to the Excel QM input.

Summary

In this chapter we explored several problems that are commonly modeled as networks, with nodes and arcs representing a variety of situations. These problems were the transportation, assignment, transshipment, maximal-flow, shortest-route, and minimal-spanning tree problems. Linear programming models

were developed for all but the minimal-spanning tree, highlighting the fact that linear programming can be beneficial in many different areas. Computer software that takes advantage of the special structure of these problems can help solve large network problems very efficiently.

Glossary

Arc   A line in a network that may represent a path or route. An arc or branch is used to connect the nodes in a network.

Assignment Problem   A special type of network problem in which costs are minimized while assigning people to jobs (or other such assignments) on a one-to-one basis.

Destination   A demand location in a transportation problem.

Facility Location Analysis   An application of the transportation method to help a firm decide where to locate a new factory, warehouse, or other facility.

Maximal-Flow Problem   A network problem with the objective of determining the maximum amount that may flow from the origin or source to the final destination or sink.

Minimal-Spanning Tree Problem   A network problem with the objective of minimizing the total distance or cost required to connect all the nodes in the network.

Node   A point in a network, often represented by a circle, that is at the beginning or end of an arc.

Shortest-Route Problem   A network problem with the objective of finding the shortest distance from one location to another while passing through intermediate nodes.

Sink   The final node or destination in a network.

Source   An origin or supply location in a transportation problem. Also, the origin or beginning node in a maximal-flow network.

Transportation Problem   A specific case of LP concerned with scheduling shipments from sources to destinations so that total transportation costs are minimized.

Solved Problems

Solved Problem 9-1

Don Yale, president of Hardrock Concrete Company, has plants in three locations and is currently working on three major construction projects, located at different sites. The shipping cost per truckload of concrete, plant capacities, and project requirements are provided in the accompanying table.

Formulate Hardrock's transportation problem as a linear program and solve using software.

TO / FROM	PROJECT A	PROJECT B	PROJECT C	PLANT CAPACITIES
PLANT 1	$10	$4	$11	70
PLANT 2	$12	$5	$8	50
PLANT 3	$9	$7	$6	30
PROJECT REQUIREMENTS	40	50	60	150

Solution

Define the variables as

$$X_{ij} = \text{number of units shipped from Plant } i \text{ to Project } j$$

where

$i = 1, 2, 3$ with $1 =$ Plant 1, $2 =$ Plant 2, and $3 =$ Plant 3

$j = 1, 2, 3$ with $1 =$ Project A, $2 =$ Project B, and $3 =$ Project C

The linear program formulation is

Minimize total cost $= 10X_{11} + 4X_{12} + 11X_{13} + 12X_{21} + 5X_{22} + 8X_{23} + 9X_{31} + 7X_{32} + 6X_{33}$

subject to

$X_{11} + X_{21} + X_{31} = 40$	Project A requirements
$X_{12} + X_{22} + X_{32} = 50$	Project B requirements
$X_{13} + X_{23} + X_{33} = 60$	Project C requirements
$X_{11} + X_{12} + X_{13} \leq 70$	Plant 1 capacity
$X_{21} + X_{22} + X_{23} \leq 50$	Plant 2 capacity
$X_{31} + X_{32} + X_{33} \leq 30$	Plant 3 capacity
All variables ≥ 0	

The computer output found using Excel QM gives the optimal solution. From Plant 1 Ship 20 units to Project A and 50 units to Project B. From Plant 2 Ship 50 units to Project C. From Plant 3 Ship 20 units to Project A and 10 units to Project B. The total cost of this solution is $1,040. While not shown in the computer output, there are alternate optimal solutions to this problem.

Program for Solved Problem 9-1

	A	B	C	D	E	F	G	H
1	Solved Problem 9-1							
2								
3	Transportation							
4								
5	Enter the transportation data in the shaded area. Then go to the DATA Tab on the ribbon, click on Solver							
6	in the Data Analysis Group and then click SOLVE.							
7	If SOLVER is not on the Data Tab then please see the Help file (Solver) for instructions.							
8	Data							
9	COSTS	Project 1	Project 2	Project 3	Supply			
10	Plant 1	10	4	11	70			
11	Plant 2	12	5	8	50			
12	Plant 3	9	7	6	30			
13	Demand	40	50	60	150 \ 150			
14								
15	Shipments							
16	Shipments	Project 1	Project 2	Project 3	Row Total			
17	Plant 1	20	50		70			
18	Plant 2			50	50			
19	Plant 3	20		10	30			
20	Column Total	40	50	60	150 \ 150			
21								
22	Total Cost	1040						

Solved Problem 9-2

Prentice Hall, Inc., a publisher headquartered in New Jersey, wants to assign three recently hired college graduates, Jones, Smith, and Wilson to regional sales districts in Omaha, Dallas, and Miami. But the firm also has an opening in New York and would send one of the three there if it were more economical than a move to Omaha, Dallas, or Miami. It will cost $1,000 to relocate Jones to New York, $800 to relocate Smith there, and $1,500 to move Wilson. What is the optimal assignment of personnel to offices?

HIREE \ OFFICE	OMAHA	MIAMI	DALLAS
JONES	$800	$1,100	$1,200
SMITH	$500	$1,600	$1,300
WILSON	$500	$1,000	$2,300

Because there are three new hires and four offices when New York is included, the problem is not balanced. It is impossible for all four cities to have a person assigned (i.e., there is no feasible solution). Therefore, a dummy source (new hire) is added, and the costs are zero for this dummy. Thus, the variables could be omitted from the objective function, but they are included for the sake of completeness.

Define the variables as

$X_{ij} = 1$ if new hire i is assigned to office j

where

$i = 1, 2, 3, 4$ with $1 =$ Jones, $2 =$ Smith, $3 =$ Wilson, and $4 =$ Dummy hire

$j = 1, 2, 3, 4$ with $1 =$ Omaha, $2 =$ Miami, $3 =$ Dallas, and $4 =$ New York

The linear program formulation is

$$\text{Minimize total cost} = 800X_{11} + 1100X_{12} + 1200X_{13} + 1000X_{14} + 500X_{21} + 1600X_{22} + 1300X_{23} + 800X_{24} + 500X_{31} + 1000X_{32} + 2300X_{33} + 1500X_{34} + 0X_{41} + 0X_{42} + 0X_{43} + 0X_{44}$$

subject to

$$X_{11} + X_{21} + X_{31} + X_{41} \le 1 \quad \text{Omaha Office}$$
$$X_{12} + X_{22} + X_{32} + X_{42} \le 1 \quad \text{Miami Office}$$
$$X_{13} + X_{23} + X_{33} + X_{43} \le 1 \quad \text{Dallas Office}$$
$$X_{14} + X_{24} + X_{34} + X_{44} \le 1 \quad \text{New York Office}$$
$$X_{11} + X_{12} + X_{13} + X_{14} = 1 \quad \text{Jones}$$
$$X_{21} + X_{22} + X_{23} + X_{24} = 1 \quad \text{Smith}$$
$$X_{31} + X_{32} + X_{33} + X_{34} = 1 \quad \text{Wilson}$$
$$X_{41} + X_{42} + X_{43} + X_{44} = 1 \quad \text{Dummy hire}$$
$$\text{All variables} \ge 0$$

The solution found using Excel QM is shown below, and it provides the optimal solution: Jones is assigned to Miami ($X_{12} = 1$), Smith is assigned to New York ($X_{24} = 1$), Wilson is assigned to Omaha ($X_{31} = 1$), and no one (the dummy) is assigned to Dallas ($X_{43} = 1$). The total cost is $2,400.

Program for Solved Problem 9-2

	A	B	C	D	E	F	G
1	Solved Problem 9-2						
2							
3	Assignment						
4	Enter the assignment costs in the shaded area. Then go to the DATA Tab on the						
5	ribbon, click on Solver in the Data Analysis Group and then click SOLVE.						
6	If SOLVER is not on the Data Tab then please see the Help file (Solver) for						
7	instructions.						
8	Data						
9	COSTS	Omaha	Miami	Dallas	NY		
10	Jones	800	1100	1200	1000		
11	Smith	500	1600	1300	800		
12	Wilson	500	1000	2300	1500		
13	Dummy	0	0	0	0		
14							
15	Assignments						
16	Shipments	Omaha	Miami	Dallas	NY	Row Total	
17	Jones		1			1	
18	Smith				1	1	
19	Wilson	1				1	
20	Dummy			1		1	
21	Column Total	1	1	1	1	4	
22							
23	Total Cost	2400					

Self-Test

- Before taking the self-test, refer to the learning objectives at the beginning of the chapter, the notes in the margins, and the glossary at the end of the chapter.
- Use the key at the back of the book to correct your answers.
- Restudy pages that correspond to any questions that you answered incorrectly or material you feel uncertain about.

1. If a transportation problem has 4 sources and 5 destinations, the linear program for this will have
   a. 4 variables and 5 constraints.
   b. 5 variable and 4 constraints.
   c. 9 variables and 20 constraints.
   d. 20 variables and 9 constraints.

2. An assignment problem may be viewed as a transportation problem with
   a. a cost of $1 for all shipping routes.
   b. all supplies and demands equal to 1.
   c. only demand constraints.
   d. only supply constraints.

3. A company is considering opening one new production facility, and three locations are being considered. For this facility location problem, how many transportation models must be developed and solved?
   a. 1
   b. 2
   c. 3
   d. 4

4. Four cranes are being assigned to five construction jobs. One of the jobs will be delayed until one of the cranes becomes available after finishing the first job. An assignment model will be used. To allow specialized software to find a solution to this problem,
   a. nothing special must be done to this problem.
   b. one dummy crane must be used in the model.
   c. one dummy job must be used in the model.
   d. both a dummy job and a dummy crane must be used in the model.

5. Which network model is used to determine how to connect all points of a network together while minimizing the total distance between them?
   a. The assignment model.
   b. The maximal-flow model.
   c. The shortest-route model.
   d. The minimal-spanning tree model.

6. In a typical shortest-route model, the objective is to
   a. minimize the number of nodes in the route.
   b. minimize the time or distance to get from one point to another.
   c. minimize the number of arcs in the route.
   d. travel through all nodes in the best way possible.

7. A large city is planning for the Olympic Games which will be coming in a few years. The transportation system is being evaluated to determine what expansion is needed to handle the large number of visitors to the games. Which of the following models would most likely help the city planners determine the capacity of the current system?
   a. The transportation model.
   b. The maximal-flow model.
   c. The shortest-route model.
   d. The minimal-spanning tree model.

8. The computing center of a large university is installing fiber-optic cables to fifteen building on campus. Which of the following models could be used to determine the least amount of cable required to connect all the buildings?
   a. The transportation model.
   b. The maximal-flow model.
   c. The shortest-route model.
   d. The minimal-spanning tree model.

Discussion Questions and Problems

Discussion Questions

9-1 Is the transportation model an example of decision making under certainty or decision making under uncertainty? Why?

9-2 Explain how to determine the number of variables and constraints that would be in a transportation problem simply by knowing the number of sources and the number of destinations.

9-3 Explain what it means for an assignment model to be balanced.

9-4 Explain the purpose of the transshipment constraints in the linear program for a transshipment model.

9-5 Describe a problem that can be solved by using the shortest-route model.

9-6 Explain how the maximal-flow model might be viewed as a transshipment model.

Problems*

9-7 The management of the Executive Furniture Corporation decided to expand the production capacity at its Des Moines factory and to cut back production at its other factories. It also recognizes a shifting market for its desks and revises the requirements at its three warehouses.

The table below provides the requirements at each of the warehouses, the capacities at each of the factories, and the shipping cost per unit to ship from each factory to each warehouse. Find the least cost way to meet the requirements given the capacity at each factory.

9-8 The Hardrock Concrete Company has plants in three locations and is currently working on three major construction projects, each located at a different site. The shipping cost per truckload of concrete, daily

TO FROM	ALBUQUERQUE	BOSTON	CLEVELAND	CAPACITY
DES MOINES	$5	$4	$3	300
EVANSVILLE	8	4	3	150
FORT LAUDERDALE	9	7	5	250
REQUIREMENTS	200	200	300	

Note: ⚲ means the problem may be solved with QM for Windows; ✖ means the problem may be
solved with Excel QM; and ⚲ means the problem may be solved with QM for Windows and/or Excel QM.

plant capacities, and daily project requirements are provided in the table below.

Formulate this as a linear program to determine the least cost way to meet the requirements. Solve using any computer software.

9-9 Hardrock Concrete's owner has decided to increase the capacity at his smallest plant (see Problem 9-8). Instead of producing 30 loads of concrete per day at plant 3, that plant's capacity is doubled to 60 loads. Does this change the schedule developed previously?

9-10 The Saussy Lumber Company ships pine flooring to three building supply houses from its mills in Pineville, Oak Ridge, and Mapletown. Determine the best transportation schedule for the data given in the table below.

9-11 The Krampf Lines Railway Company specializes in coal handling. On Friday, April 13, Krampf had empty cars at the following towns in the quantities indicated:

TOWN	SUPPLY OF CARS
Morgantown	35
Youngstown	60
Pittsburgh	25

By Monday, April 16, the following towns will need coal cars as follows:

TOWN	DEMAND FOR CARS
Coal Valley	30
Coaltown	45
Coal Junction	25
Coalsburg	20

Using a railway city-to-city distance chart, the dispatcher constructs a mileage table for the preceding towns. The result is shown in the table below. Minimizing total miles over which cars are moved to new locations, compute the best shipment of coal cars.

9-12 An air conditioning manufacturer produces room air conditioners at plants in Houston, Phoenix, and Memphis. These are sent to regional distributors in Dallas, Atlanta, and Denver. The shipping costs vary, and the company would like to find the least-cost way to meet the demands at each of the distribution centers. Dallas needs to receive 800 air conditioners per month, Atlanta needs 600, and Denver needs 200. Houston has 850 air conditioners available each month, Phoenix has 650, and Memphis has 300. The

Table for Problem 9-8

TO / FROM	PROJECT A	PROJECT B	PROJECT C	CAPACITY
PLANT 1	$10	$4	$11	70
PLANT 2	12	5	8	50
PLANT 3	9	7	6	30
REQUIREMENTS	40	50	60	

Table for Problem 9-10

TO / FROM	SUPPLY HOUSE 1	SUPPLY HOUSE 2	SUPPLY HOUSE 3	MILL CAPACITY (TONS)
PINEVILLE	$3	$3	$2	25
OAK RIDGE	4	2	3	40
MAPLETOWN	3	2	3	30
SUPPLY HOUSE DEMAND	30	30	35	

Table for Problem 9-11

TO / FROM	COAL VALLEY	COALTOWN	COAL JUNCTION	COALSBURG
MORGANTOWN	50	30	60	70
YOUNGSTOWN	20	80	10	90
PITTSBURGH	100	40	80	30

shipping cost per unit from Houston to Dallas is $8, to Atlanta is $12, and to Denver is $10. The cost per unit from Phoenix to Dallas is $10, to Atlanta is $14, and to Denver is $9. The cost per unit from Memphis to Dallas is $11, to Atlanta is $8, and to Denver is $12. How many units should be shipped from each plant to each regional distribution center? What is the total cost for this?

9-13 Finnish Furniture manufactures tables in facilities located in three cities—Reno, Denver, and Pittsburgh. The tables are then shipped to three retail stores located in Phoenix, Cleveland, and Chicago. Management wishes to develop a distribution schedule that will meet the demands at the lowest possible cost. The shipping cost per unit from each of the sources to each of the destinations is shown in the following table:

TO FROM	PHOENIX	CLEVELAND	CHICAGO
RENO	10	16	19
DENVER	12	14	13
PITTSBURGH	18	12	12

The available supplies are 120 units from Reno, 200 from Denver, and 160 from Pittsburgh. Phoenix has a demand of 140 units, Cleveland has a demand of 160 units, and Chicago has a demand of 180 units. How many units should be shipped from each manufacturing facility to each of the retail stores if cost is to be minimized? What is the total cost?

9-14 The state of Missouri has three major power-generating companies (A, B, and C). During the months of peak demand, the Missouri Power Authority authorizes these companies to pool their excess supply and to distribute it to smaller independent power companies that do not have generators large enough to handle the demand. Excess supply is distributed on the basis of cost per kilowatt hour transmitted. The following table shows the demand and supply in millions of kilowatt hours and the cost per kilowatt hour of transmitting electric power to four small companies in cities W, X, Y, and Z:

TO FROM	W	X	Y	Z	EXCESS SUPPLY
A	12¢	4¢	9¢	5¢	55
B	8¢	1¢	6¢	6¢	45
C	1¢	12¢	4¢	7¢	30
UNFILLED POWER DEMAND	40	20	50	20	

Find the least-cost distribution system.

9-15 The three blood banks in Franklin County are coordinated through a central office that facilitates blood delivery to four hospitals in the region. The cost to ship a standard container of blood from each bank to each hospital is shown in the table below. Also given are the biweekly number of containers available at each bank and the biweekly number of containers of blood needed at each hospital. How many shipments should be made biweekly from each blood bank to each hospital so that total shipment costs are minimized?

9-16 The B. Hall Real Estate Investment Corporation has identified four small apartment buildings in which it would like to invest. Mrs. Hall has approached three savings and loan companies regarding financing.

Table for Problem 9-15

TO FROM	HOSPITAL 1	HOSPITAL 2	HOSPITAL 3	HOSPITAL 4	SUPPLY
BANK 1	$8	$9	$11	$16	50
BANK 2	12	7	5	8	80
BANK 3	14	10	6	7	120
DEMAND	90	70	40	50	

Table for Problem 9-16

SAVINGS AND LOAN COMPANY	PROPERTY (INTEREST RATES) (%)				MAXIMUM CREDIT LINE ($)
	HILL ST.	BANKS ST.	PARK AVE.	DRURY LANE	
FIRST HOMESTEAD	8	8	10	11	80,000
COMMONWEALTH	9	10	12	10	100,000
WASHINGTON FEDERAL	9	11	10	9	120,000
LOAN REQUIRED TO PURCHASE BUILDING	$60,000	$40,000	$130,000	$70,000	

Because Hall has been a good client in the past and has maintained a high credit rating in the community, each savings and loan company is willing to consider providing all or part of the mortgage loan needed on each property. Each loan officer has set differing interest rates on each property (rates are affected by the neighborhood of the apartment building, condition of the property, and desire by the individual savings and loan to finance various-size buildings), *and* each loan company has placed a maximum credit ceiling on how much it will lend Hall in total. This information is summarized in the table on the previous page.

Each apartment building is equally attractive as an investment to Hall, so she has decided to purchase all buildings possible at the lowest total payment of interest. From which savings and loan companies should she borrow to purchase which buildings? More than one savings and loan can finance the same property.

9-17 The J. Mehta Company's production manager is planning for a series of 1-month production periods for stainless steel sinks. The demand for the next 4 months is as follows:

MONTH	DEMAND FOR STAINLESS STEEL SINKS
1	120
2	160
3	240
4	100

The Mehta firm can normally produce 100 stainless steel sinks in a month. This is done during regular production hours at a cost of $100 per sink. If demand in any 1 month cannot be satisfied by regular

production, the production manager has three other choices: (1) He can produce up to 50 more sinks per month in overtime but at a cost of $130 per sink; (2) he can purchase a limited number of sinks from a friendly competitor for resale (the maximum number of outside purchases over the 4-month period is 450 sinks, at a cost of $150 each); or (3) he can fill the demand from his on-hand inventory. The inventory carrying cost is $10 per sink per month. Back orders are not permitted. Inventory on hand at the beginning of month 1 is 40 sinks. Set up this "production smoothing" problem as a transportation problem to minimize cost.

9-18 Ashley's Auto Top Carriers currently maintains plants in Atlanta and Tulsa that supply major distribution centers in Los Angeles and New York. Because of an expanding demand, Ashley has decided to open a third plant and has narrowed the choice to one of two cities—New Orleans or Houston. The pertinent production and distribution costs, as well as the plant capacities and distribution demands, are shown in the table below.

Which of the new possible plants should be opened?

9-19 Marc Smith, vice president for operations of HHN, Inc., a manufacturer of cabinets for telephone switches, is constrained from meeting the 5-year forecast by limited capacity at the existing three plants. These three plants are Waterloo, Pusan, and Bogota. You, as his able assistant, have been told that because of existing capacity constraints and the expanding world market for HHN cabinets, a new plant is to be added to the existing three plants. The real estate department has advised Marc that two sites seem particularly good because of a stable political situation and tolerable exchange rate: Dublin, Ireland, and Fontainebleau, France. Marc suggests that you should be able to take the data on the next page and determine where the fourth plant should be

Data for Problem 9-18

FROM PLANTS \ TO DISTRIBUTION CENTERS	LOS ANGELES	NEW YORK	NORMAL PRODUCTION	UNIT PRODUCTION COST ($)
ATLANTA	$8	$5	600	6
TULSA	4	7	900	5
NEW ORLEANS	5	6	500	4 (anticipated)
HOUSTON	4	6	500	3 (anticipated)
FORECAST DEMAND	800	1,200	2,000	

Existing plants: ATLANTA, TULSA
Proposed locations: NEW ORLEANS, HOUSTON

Indicates distribution cost (shipping, handling, storage) will be $6 per carrier if sent from Houston to New York

Data for Problem 9-19

MARKET AREA	WATERLOO	PUSAN	BOGOTA	FONTAINEBLEAU	DUBLIN
			PLANT LOCATION		
Canada					
Demand 4,000					
Production cost	$50	$30	$40	$50	$45
Transportation cost	10	25	20	25	25
South America					
Demand 5,000					
Production cost	50	30	40	50	45
Transportation cost	20	25	10	30	30
Pacific Rim					
Demand 10,000					
Production cost	50	30	40	50	45
Transportation cost	25	10	25	40	40
Europe					
Demand 5,000					
Production cost	50	30	40	50	45
Transportation cost	25	40	30	10	20
Capacity	8,000	2,000	5,000	9,000	9,000

located on the basis of production costs and transportation costs. Which location is better?

9-20 Don Levine Corporation is considering adding an additional plant to its three existing facilities in Decatur, Minneapolis, and Carbondale. Both St. Louis and East St. Louis are being considered. Evaluating only the transportation costs per unit as shown in the tables below, which site is best?

	FROM EXISTING PLANTS			
TO	DECATUR	MINNEAPOLIS	CARBONDALE	DEMAND
Blue Earth	$20	$17	$21	250
Ciro	25	27	20	200
Des Moines	22	25	22	350
Capacity	300	200	150	

	FROM PROPOSED PLANTS	
TO	EAST ST. LOUIS	ST. LOUIS
Blue Earth	$29	$27
Ciro	30	28
Des Moines	30	31
Capacity	150	150

9-21 Using the data from Problem 9-20 plus the unit production costs shown in the following table, which locations yield the lowest cost?

LOCATION	PRODUCTION COSTS
Decatur	$50
Minneapolis	60
Carbondale	70
East St. Louis	40
St. Louis	50

9-22 In a job shop operation, four jobs may be performed on any of four machines. The hours required for each job on each machine are presented in the following table. The plant supervisor would like to assign jobs so that total time is minimized. Find the best solution. Which assignments should be made?

JOB	MACHINE			
	W	X	Y	Z
A12	10	14	16	13
A15	12	13	15	12
B2	9	12	12	11
B9	14	16	18	16

9-23 Four automobiles have entered Bubba's Repair Shop for various types of work, ranging from a transmission overhaul to a brake job. The experience level of the mechanics is quite varied, and Bubba would like to minimize the time required to complete all of the jobs. He has estimated the time in minutes for each mechanic to complete each job. Billy can complete job 1 in 400 minutes, job 2 in 90 minutes, job 3 in 60 minutes, and job 4 in 120 minutes. Taylor will finish job 1 in 650 minutes, job 2 in 120 minutes, job 3 in 90 minutes, and job 4 in 180 minutes. Mark will finish job 1 in 480 minutes, job 2 in 120 minutes, job 3 in 80 minutes, and job 4 in 180 minutes. John will complete job 1 in 500 minutes, job 2 in 110 minutes, job 3 in 90 minutes, and job 4 in 150 minutes. Each mechanic should be assigned to just one of these jobs. What is the minimum total time required to finish the four jobs? Who should be assigned to each job?

9-24 Baseball umpiring crews are currently in four cities where three-game series are beginning. When these are finished, the crews are needed to work games in four different cities. The distances (miles) from each of the cities where the crews are currently working to the cities where the new games will begin are shown in the following table:

	TO			
FROM	**KANSAS CITY**	**CHICAGO**	**DETROIT**	**TORONTO**
Seattle	1,500	1,730	1,940	2,070
Arlington	460	810	1,020	1,270
Oakland	1,500	1,850	2,080	X
Baltimore	960	610	400	330

The X indicates that the crew in Oakland cannot be sent to Toronto. Determine which crew should be sent to each city to minimize the total distance traveled. How many miles will be traveled if these assignments are made?

9-25 In Problem 9-24, the minimum travel distance was found. To see how much better this solution is than the assignments that might have been made, find the assignments that would give the maximum distance traveled. Compare this total distance with the distance found in Problem 9-24.

9-26 Roscoe Davis, chairman of a college's business department, has decided to apply a new method in assigning professors to courses next semester. As a criterion for judging who should teach each course, Professor Davis reviews the past two years' teaching evaluations (which were filled out by students). Since each of the four professors taught each of the four courses at one time or another during the two-year period, Davis is able to record a course rating for each instructor. These ratings are shown in the table at top of next column. Find the best assignment of professors to courses to maximize the overall teaching rating.

	COURSE			
PROFESSOR	**STATISTICS**	**MANAGEMENT**	**FINANCE**	**ECONOMICS**
Anderson	90	65	95	40
Sweeney	70	60	80	75
Williams	85	40	80	60
McKinney	55	80	65	55

9-27 The hospital administrator at St. Charles General must appoint head nurses to four newly established departments: urology, cardiology, orthopedics, and obstetrics. In anticipation of this staffing problem, she had hired four nurses: Hawkins, Condriac, Bardot, and Hoolihan. Believing in the quantitative analysis approach to problem solving, the administrator has interviewed each nurse, considered his or her background, personality, and talents, and developed a cost scale ranging from 0 to 100 to be used in the assignment. A 0 for Nurse Bardot being assigned to the cardiology unit implies that she would be perfectly suited to that task. A value close to 100, on the other hand, would imply that she is not at all suited to head that unit. The accompanying table gives the complete set of cost figures that the hospital administrator felt represented all possible assignments. Which nurse should be assigned to which unit?

	DEPARTMENT			
NURSE	**UROLOGY**	**CARDIOLOGY**	**ORTHOPEDICS**	**OBSTETRICS**
Hawkins	28	18	15	75
Condriac	32	48	23	38
Bardot	51	36	24	36
Hoolihan	25	38	55	12

9-28 The Gleaming Company has just developed a new dishwashing liquid and is preparing for a national television promotional campaign. The firm has decided to schedule a series of 1-minute commercials during the peak homemaker audience viewing hours of 1 P.M. to 5 P.M. To reach the widest possible audience, Gleaming wants to schedule one commercial on each of four networks and to have one commercial appear during each of the four 1-hour time blocks. The exposure ratings for each hour, which represent the number of viewers per $1,000 spent, are presented in the following table. Which network should be scheduled each hour to provide the maximum audience exposure?

	NETWORK			
VIEWING HOURS	**A**	**B**	**C**	**INDEPENDENT**
1–2 P.M.	27.1	18.1	11.3	9.5
2–3 P.M.	18.9	15.5	17.1	10.6
3–4 P.M.	19.2	18.5	9.9	7.7
4–5 P.M.	11.5	21.4	16.8	12.8

Data for Problem 9-29

MEDICAL DEVICES	PLANT							
	1	2	3	4	5	6	7	8
C53	$0.10	$0.12	$0.13	$0.11	$0.10	$0.06	$0.16	$0.12
C81	0.05	0.06	0.04	0.08	0.04	0.09	0.06	0.06
D5	0.32	0.40	0.31	0.30	0.42	0.35	0.36	0.49
D44	0.17	0.14	0.19	0.15	0.10	0.16	0.19	0.12
E2	0.06	0.07	0.10	0.05	0.08	0.10	0.11	0.05
E35	0.08	0.10	0.12	0.08	0.09	0.10	0.09	0.06
G99	0.55	0.62	0.61	0.70	0.62	0.63	0.65	0.59

9-29 The Patricia Garcia Company is producing seven new medical products. Each of Garcia's eight plants can add one more product to its current line of medical devices. The unit manufacturing costs for producing the different parts at the eight plants are shown in the table above. How should Garcia assign the new products to the plants to minimize manufacturing costs?

9-30 Haifa Instruments, an Israeli producer of portable kidney dialysis units and other medical products, develops an 8-month aggregate plan. Demand and capacity (in units) are forecast as shown in the table below.

The cost of producing each dialysis unit is $1,000 on regular time, $1,300 on overtime, and $1,500 on a subcontract. Inventory carrying cost is $100 per unit per month. There is no beginning or ending inventory in stock.

(a) Set up a production plan, using the transportation model, that minimizes cost. What is this plan's cost?

(b) Through better planning, regular time production can be set at exactly the same value, 275 per month. Does this alter the solution?

(c) If overtime costs rise from $1,300 to $1,400, does this change your answer to part (a)? What if they fall to $1,200?

9-31 NASA's astronaut crew currently includes 10 mission specialists who hold a doctoral degree in either astrophysics or astromedicine. One of these specialists will be assigned to each of the 10 flights scheduled for the upcoming nine months. Mission specialists are responsible for carrying out scientific and medical experiments in space or for launching, retrieving, or repairing satellites. The chief of astronaut personnel, himself a former crew member with three missions under his belt, must decide who should be assigned and trained for each of the very different missions. Clearly, astronauts with medical educations are more suited to missions involving biological or medical experiments, whereas those with engineering- or physics-oriented degrees are best suited to other types of missions. The chief assigns each astronaut a rating on a scale of 1 to 10 for each possible mission, with a 10 being a perfect match for the task at hand and a 1 being a mismatch. Only one specialist is assigned to each flight, and none is reassigned until all others have flown at least once.

(a) Who should be assigned to which flight?

(b) NASA has just been notified that Anderson is getting married in February and has been granted a highly sought publicity tour in Europe that month. (He intends to take his wife and let the trip double as a honeymoon.) How does this change the final schedule?

(c) Certo has complained that he was misrated on his January missions. Both ratings should be 10s, he claims to the chief, who agrees and

Data for Problem 9-30

CAPACITY SOURCE	JAN.	FEB.	MAR.	APR.	MAY	JUNE	JULY	AUG.
Labor								
Regular time	235	255	290	300	300	290	300	290
Overtime	20	24	26	24	30	28	30	30
Subcontract	12	15	15	17	17	19	19	20
Demand	255	294	321	301	330	320	345	340

Data for Problem 9-31

ASTRONAUT	JAN. 12	JAN. 27	FEB. 5	FEB. 26	MAR. 26	APR. 12	MAY 1	JUN. 9	AUG. 20	SEP. 19
					MISSION					
Vincze	9	7	2	1	10	9	8	9	2	6
Veit	8	8	3	4	7	9	7	7	4	4
Anderson	2	1	10	10	1	4	7	6	6	7
Herbert	4	4	10	9	9	9	1	2	3	4
Schatz	10	10	9	9	8	9	1	1	1	1
Plane	1	3	5	7	9	7	10	10	9	2
Certo	9	9	8	8	9	1	1	2	2	9
Moses	3	2	7	6	4	3	9	7	7	9
Brandon	5	4	5	9	10	10	5	4	9	8
Drtina	10	10	9	7	6	7	5	4	8	8

recomputes the schedule. Do any changes occur over the schedule set in part (b)?

(d) What are the strengths and weaknesses of this approach to scheduling?

9-32 The XYZ Corporation is expanding its market to include Texas. Each salesperson is assigned to potential distributors in one of five different areas. It is anticipated that the salesperson will spend about three to four weeks in their assigned area. A statewide marketing campaign will begin once the product has been delivered to the distributors. The five sales people who will be assigned to these areas (one person for each area) have rated the areas on the desirability of the assignment as shown in the following table. The scale is 1 (least desirable) to 5 (most desirable). Which assignments should be made if the total of the ratings is to be maximized?

9-33 Bechtold Construction is in the process of installing power lines to a large housing development. Steve Bechtold wants to minimize the total length of wire used, which will minimize his costs. The housing development is shown as a network. Each house has been numbered, and the distances between houses are given in hundreds of feet. What do you recommend?

Table for Problem 9-32

	AUSTIN/SAN ANTONIO	DALLAS/FT. WORTH	EL PASO/WEST TEXAS	HOUSTON/ GALVESTON	CORPUS CHRISTI/RIO GRANDE VALLEY
Erica	5	3	2	3	4
Louis	3	4	4	2	2
Maria	4	5	4	3	3
Paul	2	4	3	4	3
Orlando	4	5	3	5	4

Network for Problem 9-33

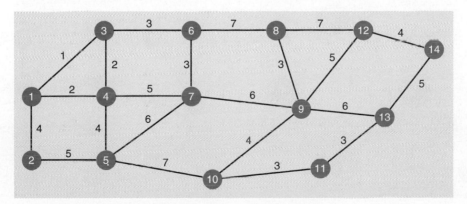

Network for Problem 9-34

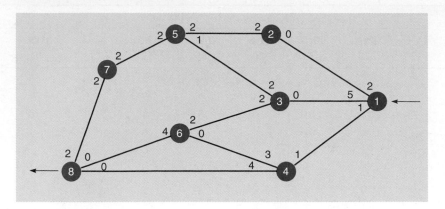

9-34 The city of New Berlin is considering making several of its streets one-way (see the network provided). Also, due to increased property taxes and an aggressive road development plan, the city of New Berlin has been considering increasing the road capacity of two of its roads. If this is done, traffic along road 1–2 (from node 1 to node 2) will be increased from 2 to 5, and traffic capacity along road 1–4 will increase from 1 to 3. What is the maximum number of cars per hour that can travel from east to west with the current road system? If the increases in capacity for road 1–2 and 2–5 were both made, how would that change the number of cars per hour that can travel from east to west?

9-35 The director of security wants to connect security video cameras to the main control site from five potential trouble locations. Ordinarily, cable would simply be run from each location to the main control site. However, because the environment is potentially explosive, the cable must be run in a special conduit that is continually air purged. This conduit is very expensive but large enough to handle five cables (the maximum that might be needed). Use the minimal-spanning tree technique to find a minimum distance route for the conduit between the locations noted in the figure. (Note that it makes no difference which one is the main control site.)

9-36 The road system around the hotel complex on International Drive (node 1) to Disney World (node 11) in Orlando, Florida, is shown in the network. The numbers by the nodes represent the traffic flow in hundreds of cars per hour. What is the maximum flow of cars from the hotel complex to Disney World?

Network for Problem 9-36

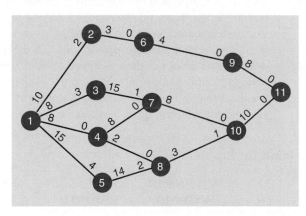

9-37 The numbers in the network below represent thousands of gallons per hour as they flow through a chemical processing plant. Two terminals in the chemical processing plant, represented by nodes 6

Network for Problem 9-35

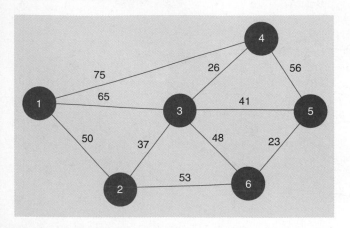

Network for Problem 9-37

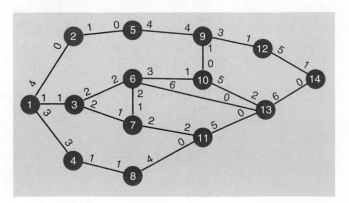

and 7, have had problems recently, and repairs on these are being considered. However, these repairs would require that these terminals (nodes) be shut down for a significant amount of time, and no material could flow into or out of these nodes until the repairs are finished. What impact would closing these nodes have on the capacity of the network?

9-38 The German towns around the Black Forest are represented by nodes in the network below. The distances between towns is shown in kilometers. Find the shortest route from city 1 to city 16. If flooding in cities 7 and 8 force closure of all roads leading into or coming out of those cities, how would that impact the shortest route?

Network for Problem 9-38

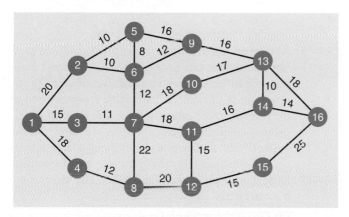

9-39 Grey Construction would like to determine the least expensive way of connecting houses it is building with cable TV. It has identified 11 possible branches or routes that could be used to connect the houses. The cost in hundreds of dollars and the branches are summarized in the following table.

(a) What is the least expensive way to run cable to the houses?

BRANCH	START NODE	END NODE	COST ($100s)
Branch 1	1	2	5
Branch 2	1	3	6
Branch 3	1	4	6
Branch 4	1	5	5
Branch 5	2	6	7
Branch 6	3	7	5
Branch 7	4	7	7
Branch 8	5	8	4
Branch 9	6	7	1
Branch 10	7	9	6
Branch 11	8	9	2

(b) After reviewing cable and installation costs, Grey Construction would like to alter the costs for installing cable TV between its houses. The first branches need to be changed. The changes are summarized in the following table. What is the impact on total costs?

BRANCH	START NODE	END NODE	COST ($100s)
Branch 1	1	2	5
Branch 2	1	3	1
Branch 3	1	4	1
Branch 4	1	5	1
Branch 5	2	6	7
Branch 6	3	7	5
Branch 7	4	7	7
Branch 8	5	8	4
Branch 9	6	7	1
Branch 10	7	9	6
Branch 11	8	9	2

9-40 In going from Quincy to Old Bainbridge, there are 10 possible roads that George Olin can take. Each road can be considered a branch in the shortest-route problem.

(a) Determine the best way to get from Quincy (node 1) to Old Bainbridge (node 8) that will minimize total distance traveled. All distances are in hundreds of miles.

BRANCH	START NODE	END NODE	DISTANCE (IN HUNDREDS OF MILES)
Branch 1	1	2	3
Branch 2	1	3	2
Branch 3	2	4	3
Branch 4	3	5	3
Branch 5	4	5	1
Branch 6	4	6	4
Branch 7	5	7	2
Branch 8	6	7	2
Branch 9	6	8	3
Branch 10	7	8	6

(b) George Olin made a mistake in estimating the distances from Quincy to Old Bainbridge. The new distances are in the following table. What impact does this have on the shortest route from Quincy to Old Bainbridge?

BRANCH	START NODE	END NODE	DISTANCE (IN HUNDREDS OF MILES)
Branch 1	1	2	3
Branch 2	1	3	2
Branch 3	2	4	3
Branch 4	3	5	1
Branch 5	4	5	1
Branch 6	4	6	4
Branch 7	5	7	2
Branch 8	6	7	2
Branch 9	6	8	3
Branch 10	7	8	6

9-41 South Side Oil and Gas, a new venture in Texas, has developed an oil pipeline network to transport oil from exploration fields to the refinery and other locations. There are 10 pipelines (branches) in the network. The oil flow in hundreds of gallons and the network of pipelines is given in the following table.

(a) What is the maximum that can flow through the network?

BRANCH	START NODE	END NODE	CAPACITY	REVERSE CAPACITY	FLOW
Branch 1	1	2	10	4	10
Branch 2	1	3	8	2	5
Branch 3	2	4	12	1	10
Branch 4	2	5	6	6	0
Branch 5	3	5	8	1	5
Branch 6	4	6	10	2	10
Branch 7	5	6	10	10	0
Branch 8	5	7	5	5	5
Branch 9	6	8	10	1	10
Branch 10	7	8	10	1	5

(b) South Side Oil and Gas needs to modify its pipeline network flow patterns. The new data is in the following table. What impact does this have on the maximum flow through the network?

BRANCH	START NODE	END NODE	CAPACITY	REVERSE CAPACITY	FLOW
Branch 1	1	2	10	4	10
Branch 2	1	3	8	2	5
Branch 3	2	4	12	1	10
Branch 4	2	5	0	0	0
Branch 5	3	5	8	1	5
Branch 6	4	6	10	2	10
Branch 7	5	6	10	10	0
Branch 8	5	7	5	5	5
Branch 9	6	8	10	1	10
Branch 10	7	8	10	1	5

9-42 The following table represents a network with the arcs identified by their starting and ending nodes. Draw the network and use the minimal-spanning tree to find the minimum distance required to connect these nodes.

ARC	DISTANCE
1–2	12
1–3	8
2–3	7
2–4	10
3–4	9
3–5	8
4–5	8
4–6	11
5–6	9

9-43 Northwest University is in the process of completing a computer bus network that will connect computer facilities throughout the university. The prime objective is to string a main cable from one end of the campus to the other (nodes 1–25) through underground conduits. These conduits are shown in the network; the distance between them is in hundreds of feet. Fortunately, these underground conduits have remaining capacity through which the bus cable can be placed.

(a) Given the network for this problem, how far (in hundreds of feet) is the shortest route from node 1 to node 25?

(b) In addition to the computer bus network, a new phone system is also being planned. The phone system would use the same underground conduits. If the phone system were installed, the following paths along the conduit would be at capacity and would not be available for the computer bus network: 6–11, 7–12, and 17–20. What changes (if any) would you have to make to the path used for the computer bus if the phone system were installed?

Network for Problem 9-43

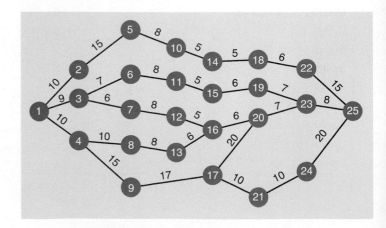

(c) The university *did* decide to install the new phone system before the cable for the computer network. Because of unexpected demand for computer networking facilities, an additional cable is needed for node 1 to node 25. Unfortunately, the cable for the first or original network has completely used up the capacity along its path. Given this situation, what is the best path for the second network cable?

 Internet Homework Problems

See our Internet home page, at **www.pearsonhighered.com/render**, for additional problems, Problems 9-44 through 9-50.

Case Study

Andrew–Carter, Inc.

Andrew–Carter, Inc. (A–C), is a major Canadian producer and distributor of outdoor lighting fixtures. Its fixture is distributed throughout North America and has been in high demand for several years. The company operates three plants that manufacture the fixture and distribute it to five distribution centers (warehouses).

During the present recession, A–C has seen a major drop in demand for its fixture as the housing market has declined. Based on the forecast of interest rates, the head of operations feels that demand for housing and thus for its product will remain depressed for the foreseeable future. A–C is considering closing one of its plants, as it is now operating with a forecasted excess capacity of 34,000 units per week. The forecasted weekly demands for the coming year are

Warehouse 1	9,000 units
Warehouse 2	13,000 units
Warehouse 3	11,000 units
Warehouse 4	15,000 units
Warehouse 5	8,000 units

The plant capacities in units per week are

Plant 1, regular time	27,000 units
Plant 1, on overtime	7,000 units
Plant 2, regular time	20,000 units
Plant 2, on overtime	5,000 units
Plant 3, regular time	25,000 units
Plant 3, on overtime	6,000 units

If A–C shuts down any plants, its weekly costs will change, as fixed costs are lower for a nonoperating plant. Table 9.4 shows production costs at each plant, both variable at regular time and overtime, and fixed when operating and shut down. Table 9.5 shows distribution costs from each plant to each warehouse (distribution center).

Discussion Questions

1. Evaluate the various configurations of operating and closed plants that will meet weekly demand. Determine which configuration minimizes total costs.
2. Discuss the implications of closing a plant.

Source: Professor Michael Ballot, University of the Pacific.

TABLE 9.5

Andrew–Carter, Inc., Variable Costs and Fixed Production Costs per Week

PLANT	VARIABLE COST	FIXED COST PER WEEK	
		OPERATING	NOT OPERATING
No. 1, regular time	$2.80/unit	$14,000	$6,000
No. 1, overtime	3.52		
No. 2, regular time	2.78	12,000	5,000
No. 2, overtime	3.48		
No. 3, regular time	2.72	15,000	7,500
No. 3, overtime	3.42		

TABLE 9.6
Andrew–Carter, Inc.,
Distribution Costs
per Unit

	TO DISTRIBUTION CENTER				
FROM PLANT	W1	W2	W3	W4	W5
No. 1	$0.50	$0.44	$0.49	$0.46	$0.56
No. 2	0.40	0.52	0.50	0.56	0.57
No. 3	0.56	0.53	0.51	0.54	0.35

Case Study

Northeastern Airlines

Northeastern Airlines is a regional airline serving nine cities in the New England states as well as cities in New York, New Jersey, and Pennsylvania. While nonstop flights are available for some of the routes, connecting flights are often necessary. The network shows the cities served and profit in U.S. dollars per passenger along each of these routes. The routes from Boston-to-Providence and from Providence-to-Boston make only $9 per passenger profit after all expenses. To service these cities, Northeastern operates a fleet of sixteen 122-passenger Embraer E-195 jets. These jets, which were first introduced by Embraer in late 2004, have helped Northeastern Airlines remain profitable for a number of years. However, in recent years, the profit margins have been falling, and Northeastern is facing the prospect of downsizing their operations.

Management at Northeastern Airlines has considered several options to reduce cost and increase profitability. Due to Federal Aviation Administration regulations, the company must continue to serve each of the nine cities. How they serve these cities, however, is up to the management at Northeastern. One suggestion has been made to provide fewer direct flights, which would mean that a city served by Northeastern might only have direct flights to one other city. The company plans to hire a marketing analytics consultant to determine how demand would be impacted by longer flights with more connections, and to forecast the demand along each of the routes based on a modified flight operations map. Before hiring the consultant, the company would like to first determine the most profitable (on a profit per passenger basis) way to continue serving all of the cities.

Discussion Questions

1. Develop a flight operations map that still serves each of the nine cities, but maximizes the company's profit per passenger (*Hint:* Find the *maximal*-spanning tree)
2. Comment on how the 16 jets should be assigned.

Thanks to Professor Faizul Huq, College of Business, Ohio University, for providing this case.

**Northeastern Airlines
Service Area**

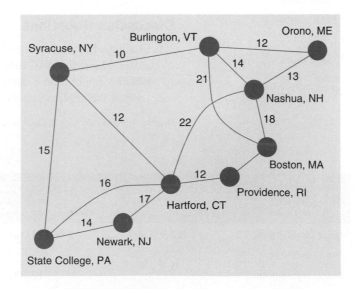

Case Study

Southwestern University Traffic Problems

Southwestern University (SWU), located in the small town of Stephenville, Texas, is experiencing increased interest in its football program now that a big-name coach has been hired. The increase in season ticket sales for the upcoming season means additional revenues, but it also means increased complaints due to the traffic problems associated with the football games. When a new stadium is built, this will only get worse. Marty Starr, SWU's president, has asked the University Planning Committee to look into this problem.

Based on traffic projections, Dr. Starr would like to have sufficient capacity so that 35,000 cars per hour could travel from the stadium to the interstate highway. To alleviate the anticipated traffic problems, some of the current streets leading from the university to the interstate highway are being considered for widening to increase the capacity. The current street capacities with the number of cars (in 1,000s) per hour are shown below. Since the major problem will be after the game, only the flows away from the stadium are indicated. These flows include some streets closest to the stadium being transformed into one-way streets for a short period after each game with police officers directing traffic.

Alexander Lee, a member of the University Planning Committee, has said that a quick check of the road capacities in the diagram indicates that the total number of cars per hour that may leave the stadium (node 1) is 33,000. The number of cars that may pass through nodes 2, 3, and 4 is 35,000 per hour, and the number of cars that may pass through nodes 5, 6, and 7 is even greater. Therefore, Dr. Lee has suggested that the current

capacity is 33,000 cars per hour. He has also suggested that a recommendation be made to the city manager for expansion of one of the routes from the stadium to the highway to permit an additional 2,000 cars per hour. He recommends expanding whichever route is cheapest. If the city chooses not to expand the roads, it is felt that the traffic problem would be a nuisance but would be manageable.

Based on past experience, it is believed that as long as the street capacity is within 2,500 cars per hour of the number that leave the stadium, the problem is not too severe. However, the severity of the problem grows dramatically for each additional 1,000 cars that are added to the streets.

Discussion Questions

1. If there is no expansion, what is the maximum number of cars that may actually travel from the stadium to the interstate per hour? Why is this number not equal to 33,000, as Dr. Lee suggested?
2. If the cost for expanding a street were the same for each street, which street(s) would you recommend expanding to increase the capacity to 33,000? Which streets would you recommend expanding to get the total capacity of the system to 35,000 per hour?

Roads from Stadium to Interstate

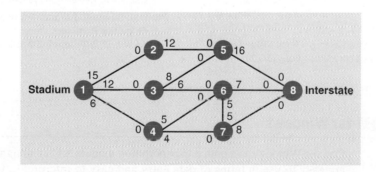

Internet Case Studies

See our Internet home page, at **www.pearsonhighered.com/render**, for these additional case studies:

(1) **Northwest General Hospital:** This case involves improving the food distribution system in a hospital to reduce the chances of food getting cold before it is delivered to the patients.

(2) **Custom Vans, Inc:** This case involves finding the best location for a plant that will manufacture showers used in customized vans.

(3) **Ranch Development Project:** This case involves finding the least-cost way to provide water and sewer services to homes in a new housing development.

(4) **Old Oregon Wood Store:** This case involves determining the best way to assign employees to jobs in a small manufacturing company.

(5) **Binder's Beverage:** This case is about finding the shortest route from a plant to a warehouse.

Bibliography

Adlakha, V., and K. Kowalski. "Simple Algorithm for the Source-Induced Fixed-Charge Transportation Problem," *Journal of the Operational Research Society* 55, 12 (2004): 1275–1280.

Bowman, E. "Production Scheduling by the Transportation Method of Linear Programming," *Operations Research* 4 (1956).

Dawid, Herbert, Johannes Konig, and Christine Strauss. "An Enhanced Rostering Model for Airline Crews," *Computers and Operations Research* 28, 7 (June 2001): 671–688.

Hezarkhani, Behzad, and Wieslaw Kubiak. "A Coordinating Contract for Transshipment In a Two-Company Supply Chain," *European Journal of Operational Research* 207, 1 (2010): 232–237.

Jacobs, T., B. Smith, and E. Johnson. "Incorporating Network Flow Effects into the Airline Fleet Assignment Process," *Transportation Science* 42, 4(2008): 514–529.

Johnsonbaugh, Richard. *Discrete Mathematics*, 5th ed. Upper Saddle River, NJ: Prentice Hall, 2001.

Kawatra, R., and D. Bricker. "A Multiperiod Planning Model for the Capacitated Minimal Spanning Tree Problem," *European Journal of Operational Research* 121, 2 (2000): 412–419.

Koksalan, Murat, and Haldun Sural. "Efes Beverage Group Makes Location and Distribution Decisions for Its Malt Plants," *Interfaces* 29, 2 (March–April, 1999): 89–103.

Liu, Jinming, and Fred Rahbar. "Project Time–Cost Trade-off Optimization by Maximal Flow Theory," *Journal of Construction Engineering & Management* 130, 4 (July/August 2004): 607–609.

Liu, Shiang-Tai. "The Total Cost Bounds of the Transportation Problem with Varying Demand and Supply," *Omega* 31, 4 (2003): 247–251.

Martello, Silvano. "Jeno Egervary: From the Origins of the Hungarian Algorithm to Satellite Communication," *Central European Journal of Operations Research* 18, 1 (2010): 47–58.

McKeown, P., and B. Workman. "A Study in Using Linear Programming to Assign Students to Schools," *Interfaces* 6, 4 (August 1976).

Render, B., and R. M. Stair. *Introduction to Management Science*. Boston: Allyn & Bacon, Inc., 1992.

Sancho, N. G. F. "On the Maximum Expected Flow in a Network," *Journal of Operational Research Society* 39 (May 1988): 481–485.

Sedeño-Noda, Antonio, Carlos González-Martín, and Sergio Alonso. "A Generalization of the Scaling Max-Flow Algorithm," *Computers & Operations Research* 31, 13 (November 2004): 2183–2198.

Troutt, M. D., and G. P White. "Maximal Flow Network Modeling of Production Bottleneck Problems," *Journal of the Operational Research Society* 52, 2 (February 2001): 182–187.

Appendix 9.1: Using QM for Windows

QM for Windows has both a transportation module and an assignment module in its menu. Both are easy to use in terms of data entry and easy to interpret in terms of output. Program 9.9A shows the input screen for the Executive Furniture transportation example. The starting solution technique may be specified. The results are shown in Program 9.9B. Program 9.10A provides the input screen for the Fix-It Shop assignment example. Simply enter the costs and then *click Solve*. Program 9.10B gives the solution to this.

PROGRAM 9.9A

QM for Windows Input for Executive Furniture Transportation Example

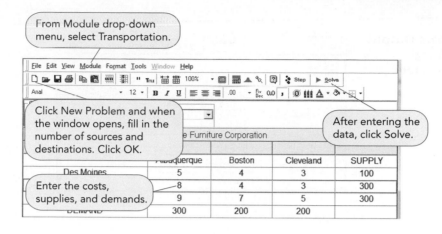

From Module drop-down menu, select Transportation.

Click New Problem and when the window opens, fill in the number of sources and destinations. Click OK.

After entering the data, click Solve.

Enter the costs, supplies, and demands.

	Albuquerque	Boston	Cleveland	SUPPLY
Des Moines	5	4	3	100
	8	4	3	300
	9	7	5	300
DEMAND	300	200	200	

PROGRAM 9.9B

QM for Windows Solution for Executive Furniture Transportation Example

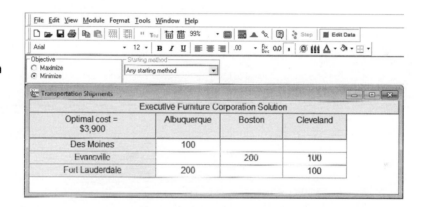

Optimal cost = $3,900	Albuquerque	Boston	Cleveland
Des Moines	100		
Evansville		200	100
Fort Lauderdale	200		100

Executive Furniture Corporation Solution

PROGRAM 9.10A

QM for Windows Input for the Fix-It Shop Assignment Example

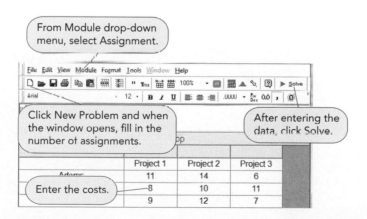

From Module drop-down menu, select Assignment.

Click New Problem and when the window opens, fill in the number of assignments.

After entering the data, click Solve.

Enter the costs.

	Project 1	Project 2	Project 3
Adams	11	14	6
	8	10	11
	9	12	7

PROGRAM 9.10B

QM for Windows Output for the Fix-It Shop Assignment Example

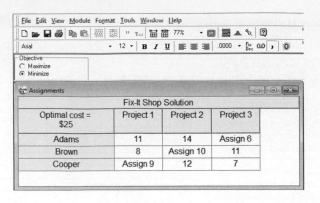

CHAPTER 10

Integer Programming, Goal Programming, and Nonlinear Programming

10.1 Introduction

Integer programming is the extension of LP that solves problems requiring integer solutions.

This chapter presents a series of other important mathematical programming models that arise when some of the basic assumptions of LP are made more or less restrictive. For example, one assumption of LP is that decision variables can take on fractional values such as $X_1 = 0.33$, $X_2 = 1.57$, or $X_3 = 109.4$. Yet a large number of business problems can be solved only if variables have *integer* values. When an airline decides how many Boeing 757s or Boeing 777s to purchase, it can't place an order for 5.38 aircraft; it must order 4, 5, 6, 7, or some other integer amount. In this chapter we present the general topic of integer programming, and we specifically consider the use of special variables that must be either 0 or 1.

Goal programming is the extension of LP that permits more than one objective to be stated.

A major limitation of LP is that it forces the decision maker to state one objective only. But what if a business has several objectives? Management may indeed want to maximize profit, but it might also want to maximize market share, maintain full employment, and minimize costs. Many of these goals can be conflicting and difficult to quantify. South States Power and Light, for example, wants to build a nuclear power plant in Taft, Louisiana. Its objectives are to maximize power generated, reliability, and safety, and to minimize cost of operating the system and the environmental effects on the community. Goal programming is an extension to LP that can permit multiple objectives such as these.

Nonlinear programming is the case in which objectives or constraints are nonlinear.

Linear programming can, of course, be applied only to cases in which the constraints and objective function are linear. Yet in many situations this is not the case. The price of various products, for example, may be a function of the number of units produced. As more units are produced, the price per unit decreases. Hence an objective function may read as follows:

$$\text{Maximize profit} = 25X_1 - 0.4X_1{}^2 + 30X_2 - 0.5X_2{}^2$$

Because of the squared terms, this is a nonlinear programming problem.

Let's examine each of these extensions of LP—integer, goal, and nonlinear programming—one at a time.

10.2 Integer Programming

Solution values must be whole numbers in integer programming.

An **integer programming** model is a model that has constraints and an objective function identical to that formulated by LP. The only difference is that one or more of the decision variables has to take on an integer value in the final solution. There are three types of integer programming problems:

There are three types of integer programs: pure integer programming; mixed-integer programming; and 0–1 integer programming.

1. Pure integer programming problems are cases in which all variables are required to have integer values.
2. Mixed-integer programming problems are cases in which some, but not all, of the decision variables are required to have integer values.
3. Zero–one integer programming problems are special cases in which all the decision variables must have integer solution values of 0 or 1.

Solving an integer programming problem is much more difficult than solving an LP problem. The solution time required to solve some of these may be excessive even on the fastest computer.

Harrison Electric Company Example of Integer Programming

The Harrison Electric Company, located in Chicago's Old Town area, produces two products popular with home renovators: old-fashioned chandeliers and ceiling fans. Both the chandeliers and fans require a two-step production process involving wiring and assembly. It takes about 2 hours to wire each chandelier and 3 hours to wire a ceiling fan. Final assembly of the chandeliers and fans requires 6 and 5 hours, respectively. The production capability is such that only 12 hours of wiring time and 30 hours of assembly time are available. If each chandelier produced nets the firm $7 and each fan $6, Harrison's production mix decision can be formulated using LP as follows:

$$\text{Maximize profit} = \$7X_1 + \$6X_2$$

$$\text{subject to} \qquad 2X_1 + 3X_2 \leq 12 \quad \text{(wiring hours)}$$
$$6X_1 + 5X_2 \leq 30 \quad \text{(assembly hours)}$$
$$X_1, X_2 \geq 0$$

where

X_1 = number of chandeliers produced

X_2 = number of ceiling fans produced

Although enumeration is feasible for some small integer programming problems, it can be difficult or impossible for large ones.

With only two variables and two constraints, Harrison's production planner, Wes Wallace, employed the graphical LP approach (see Figure 10.1) to generate the optimal solution of $X_1 = 3.75$ chandeliers and $X_2 = 1.5$ ceiling fans during the production cycle. Recognizing that the company could not produce and sell a fraction of a product, Wes decided that he was dealing with an integer programming problem.

Rounding off is one way to reach integer solution values, but it often does not yield the best solution.

It seemed to Wes that the simplest approach was to round off the optimal fractional solutions for X_1 and X_2 to integer values of $X_1 = 4$ chandeliers and $X_2 = 2$ ceiling fans. Unfortunately, rounding can produce two problems. First, the new integer solution may not be in the feasible region and thus is not a practical answer. This is the case if we round to $X_1 = 4, X_2 = 2$. Second, even if we round off to a feasible solution, such as $X_1 = 4, X_2 = 1$, it may not be the *optimal* feasible integer solution.

Listing all feasible solutions and selecting the one with the best objective function value is called the *enumeration* method. Obviously this can be quite tedious for even small problems, and it is virtually impossible for large problems as the number of feasible integer solutions is extremely large.

FIGURE 10.1
Harrison Electric Problem

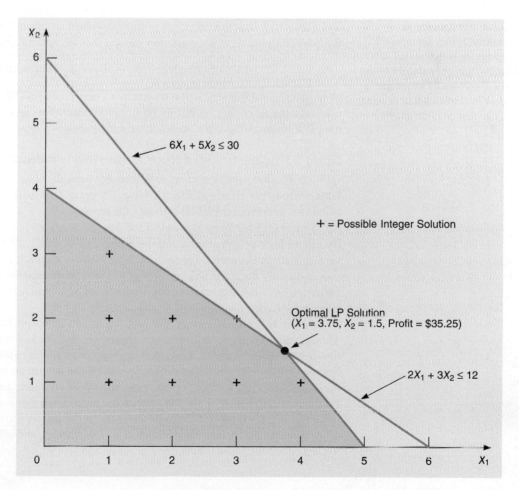

TABLE 10.1

Integer Solutions to the Harrison Electric Company Problem

CHANDELIERS (X_1)	CEILING FANS (X_2)	PROFIT $(\$7X_1 + \$6X_2)$	
0	0	$0	
1	0	7	
2	0	14	
3	0	21	
4	0	28	
5	0	35	← Optimal solution to integer programming problem
0	1	6	
1	1	13	
2	1	20	
3	1	27	
4	1	34	← Solution if rounding is used
0	2	12	
1	2	19	
2	2	26	
3	2	33	
0	3	18	
1	3	25	
0	4	24	

An important concept to understand is that an integer programming solution can never be better than the solution to the same LP problem. The integer problem is usually worse in terms of higher cost or lower profit.

Table 10.1 lists the entire set of integer-valued solutions to the Harrison Electric problem. By inspecting the right-hand column, we see that the optimal *integer* solution is

$$X_1 = 5 \text{ chandeliers, } X_2 = 0 \text{ ceiling fans, with a profit} = \$35$$

Note that this integer restriction results in a lower profit level than the original optimal LP solution. As a matter of fact, an integer programming solution can *never* produce a greater profit than the LP solution to the same problem; *usually*, it means a lesser value.

Using Software to Solve the Harrison Integer Programming Problem

QM for Windows and Excel spreadsheets are capable of handling integer programming problems such as the Harrison Electric case. Program 10.1A illustrates the input data to QM for Windows, and Program 10.1B provides the results.

To use QM for Windows, select the *Integer & Mixed Integer Programming* module. Specify the number of constraints and the number of variables. Program 10.1A provides the input screen, with data entered for the Harrison Electric example. The last row of the table allows you to classify each variable according to the type of variable (Integer, Real, or 0/1). Once all variables have been correctly specified, click *Solve*, and you will see the output as shown in Program 10.1B.

Solver in Excel 2013 can also be used to solve this problem, as shown in Program 10.2. The Solver parameters and selections are shown, and the key formulas are displayed. To specify that the variables must be integers, a special constraint is entered in Solver. After opening the Solver Parameters window, select *Add* just as you would do to enter other constraints. When the Add Constraint window opens, enter the range containing the solution values, as shown in Program 10.2. Then click the tab to open the drop-down menu and then change the type of constraint to int, for integer. Click *OK* to return to the Solver Parameters window. Then enter the other constraints, specify the parameters and selections, and click *Solve*. The solution is shown to be 5 chandeliers and 0 fans, for a profit of $35.

PROGRAM 10.1A

QM for Windows Input Screen for Harrison Electric Problem

Objective
○ Maximize
○ Minimize

Maximum number of iterations: 1000

Maximum level (depth) in procedure: 50

Harrison Electric Integer Programming Problem

	X1	X2		RHS	Equation form
Maximize	7	6			Max 7X1 + 6X2
Constraint 1	2	3	<=	12	2X1 + 3X2 <= 12
Constraint 2	6	5	<=	30	6X1 + 5X2 <= 30
Variable type	Integ ▼	Integer			

Integer
Real
0/1

PROGRAM 10.1B

QM for Windows Solution Screen for Harrison Electric Problem

Objective
○ Maximize
○ Minimize

Maximum number of iterations: 1000

Integer & Mixed Integer Programming Results

Variable	Type	Value
X1	Integer	5
X2	Integer	0
Solution value		35

PROGRAM 10.2

Excel 2013 Solver Solution for Harrison Electric Problem

	A	B	C	D
1	Harrison Electric Integer Programming Analysis			
2		Chandeliers	Fans	
3	Variables	X1	X2	
4	Values	5	0	Total Profit
5	Profit	7	6	35
6				
7	Constraints			LHS
8	Wiring hours	2	3	10
9	Assembly hours	6	5	30

(Sign / RHS columns)

LHS	Sign	RHS
10	≤	12
30	≤	30

Change Constraint

Cell Reference: $B$4:$C$4   =   Constraint: integer

<= = >= int bin dif

OK   Cancel

Solver Parameter Inputs and Selections

Set Objective: D5

By Changing cells: B4:C4

To: Max

Subject to the Constraints:

  D8:D9 <= F8:F9

  B4:C4 = integer

Solving Method: Simplex LP

☑ Make Variables Non-Negative

Key Formulas

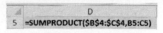

	D
5	=SUMPRODUCT($B$4:$C$4,B5:C5)

Copy D5 to D8:D9

Mixed-Integer Programming Problem Example

Although the Harrison Electric example was a pure integer problem, there are many situations in which some of the variables are restricted to be integers and others are not. The following is an example of such a mixed-integer programming problem.

Bagwell Chemical Company, in Jackson, Mississippi, produces two industrial chemicals. The first product, xyline, must be produced in 50-pound bags; the second, hexall, is sold by the pound in dry bulk and hence can be produced in any quantity. Both xyline and hexall are composed of three ingredients—*A, B,* and *C*—as follows:

AMOUNT PER 50-POUND BAG OF XYLINE (LB)	AMOUNT PER POUND OF HEXALL (LB)	AMOUNT OF INGREDIENTS AVAILABLE
30	0.5	2,000 lb—ingredient *A*
18	0.4	800 lb—ingredient *B*
2	0.1	200 lb—ingredient *C*

Bagwell sells 50-pound bags of xyline for $85 and hexall in any weight for $1.50 per pound.

MODELING IN THE REAL WORLD: Integer Programming at the USPS

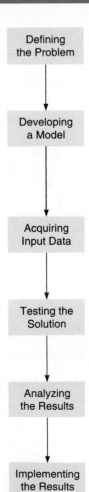

Defining the Problem

Defining the Problem

The U.S. Postal Service (USPS) operates one of the largest transportation networks in the world, delivering one-fifth of a trillion items every year. The inherent transportation-related problems are, obviously, very large. Nevertheless, USPS's problem is how to deliver mail in the most cost-efficient manner possible.

Developing a Model

Developing a Model

A large-scale integer program known as the Highway Corridor Analytical Program (HCAP) was developed to help solve the problem. More specifically, the HCAP solves a Vehicle Routing Problem (VRP) with known pickup and delivery locations. That is, the model takes into account all the different modes of transportation, the capacities inherent to the system, all the pickup locations, and all the delivery locations and then assigns trucks to routes as the (binary) decision variable of interest.

Acquiring Input Data

Acquiring Input Data

Geographic information system (GIS) data of all the pickup and delivery locations is integrated into the model. Realistic time and distance constraints were placed on the model to prevent drivers from being assigned a pickup in one area and a delivery in an area too far away.

Testing the Solution

Testing the Solution

The model was loaded into a large-scale mathematical programming solver. Several versions and models were tested.

Analyzing the Results

Analyzing the Results

Decision makers found improvements in several areas. For example, one of the model outputs resulted in a 20% reduction in redundant trips.

Implementing the Results

Implementing the Results

USPS has already realized over $5 million in transportation savings due to its implementation of the HCAP integer programming optimization model. Efforts are under way to seek out additional efficiencies through the use of HCAP.

Source: Based on A. Pajunas, E. J. Matto, M. Trick, and L.F. Zuluaga. "Optimizing Highway Transportation at the United States Postal Service," *Interfaces* 37, 6 (2007): 515–525.

If we let X = number of 50-pound bags of xyline produced and Y = number of pounds of hexall (in dry bulk) mixed, Bagwell's problem can be described with mixed-integer programming:

$$\text{Maximize profit} = \$85X + \$1.50Y$$
$$\text{subject to} \quad 30X + 0.5Y \le 2{,}000$$
$$18X + 0.4Y \le 800$$
$$2X + 0.1Y \le 200$$
$$X, Y \ge 0 \text{ and } X \text{ integer.}$$

Note that Y represents bulk weight of hexall and is not required to be integer valued.

USING QM FOR WINDOWS AND EXCEL TO SOLVE BAGWELL'S INTEGER PROGRAMMING MODEL The solution to Bagwell's problem is to produce 44 bags of xyline and 20 pounds of hexall, yielding a profit of $3,770. (The optimal linear solution, by the way, is to produce 44.444 bags of xyline and 0 pounds of hexall, yielding a profit of $3,777.78.) This is first illustrated in Program 10.3, which uses the Mixed Integer Programming module in QM for Windows. Note that variable X is identified as Integer, while Y is Real in Program 10.3.

In Program 10.4, we use Excel to provide an alternative solution method.

PROGRAM 10.3

QM for Windows Solution for Bagwell Chemical Problem

Objective	Maximum number of iterations		Maximum level [depth] in procedure		Ins Oth
⦿ Maximize		1000		50	
○ Minimize					

Limits are used, and the best solution available after a certain time is presented.

Bagwell Chemical Company Solution	X	Y		RHS
Ma	85	1.5		
Cons...	30	0.5	<=	2000
Constraint 2	18	0.4	<=	800
Constraint 3	2	0.1	<=	200
Variable type	Integer	Real		
Solution->	44	20	Optimal Σ->	3770

Notice that only X must be integer, while Y may be any real number.

IN ACTION | **Mixed-Integer Programming in the IBM Supply Chain**

The manufacture of semiconductors is a very expensive operation, often requiring investments in the billions of dollars. The IBM Systems and Technology Group has used mixed-integer programming (MIP) along with other operations research techniques to plan and optimize its semiconductor supply chain. The business of supply-chain optimization (SCO) has been deemed business critical and must incorporate a variety of planning criteria and constraints.

IBM uses a central planning engine (CPE) to balance the supply chain's resources against the semiconductor demand. The MIP is an important part of this CPE. The MIP model is a cost-minimization problem with constraints related to material flows and other aspect of the supply chain.

Some of the models involved in SCO include sourcing among multiple plants, the logistics of interplant shipping, and the development of production plans for all the plants within the system. They may involve a planning horizon of a few days, a few months, or even a few years, depending on the specific type of application. While LP is commonly used in supply-chain modeling, it is necessary to use models in which some of the variables are required to be integers. The resulting MIP models are so large (millions of variables) that they cannot be solved with even the fastest computers. Therefore, the IBM Systems and Technology Group developed heuristic methods to solve the optimization models as part of the company's advanced planning systems.

The benefits of the CPE are many. The on-time deliveries improved by 15%. A 25% to 30% reduction in inventory was observed as a result of the model. The company also observed an improvement in asset allocation of between 2% and 4% of costs. This model allowed "what-if" questions to be quickly answered—a process that was not possible in the past. Strategic planning was also facilitated by the CPE. IBM benefited greatly from the use of MIP in managing the semiconductor supply chain.

Source: Based on Brian. T. Denton, John Forrest, and R. John Milne. "IBM Solves a Mixed-Integer Program to Optimize Its Semiconductor Supply Chain," *Interfaces* 36, 5 (September–October 2006): 386–399.

PROGRAM 10.4
Excel 2013 Solver Solution for Bagwell Chemical Problem

	A	B	C	D	E	F
1	Bagwell Chemical Company					
2		Xyline (bags)	Hexall (lbs)			
3	Variables	X	Y			
4	Values	44	20	Total Profit		
5	Profit	85	1.5	3770		
6						
7	Constraints			LHS	sign	RHS
8	Ingredient A	30	0.5	1330	≤	2000
9	Ingredient B	18	0.4	800	≤	800
10	Ingredient C	2	0.1	90	≤	200

Solver Parameter Inputs and Selections

Set Objective: D5

By Changing cells: B4:C4

To: Max

Subject to the Constraints:

  D8:D10 <= F8:F10

    B4 = integer

Solving Method: Simplex LP

☑ Make Variables Non-Negative

Key Formulas

	D
5	=SUMPRODUCT($B$4:$C$4,B5:C5)

Copy D5 to D8:D10

10.3 Modeling with 0–1 (Binary) Variables

In this section we demonstrate how 0–1 variables can be used to model several diverse situations. Typically a 0–1 variable is assigned a value of 0 if a certain condition is not met and 1 if the condition is met. Another name for a 0–1 variable is a *binary variable*. A common problem of this type, the assignment problem, involves deciding which individuals to assign to a set of jobs. (This is discussed in Chapter 9.) In this assignment problem, a value of 1 indicates a person is assigned to a specific job, and a value of 0 indicates the assignment was not made. We present other types of 0–1 problems to show the wide applicability of this modeling technique.

Capital Budgeting Example

A common capital budgeting decision involves selecting from a set of possible projects when budget limitations make it impossible to select all of these. A separate 0–1 variable can be defined for each project. We will see this in the following example.

Quemo Chemical Company is considering three possible improvement projects for its plant: a new catalytic converter, a new software program for controlling operations, and expanding the warehouse used for storage. Capital requirements and budget limitations in the next 2 years prevent the firm from undertaking all of these at this time. The net present value (the future value of the project discounted back to the present time) of each of the projects, the capital requirements, and the available funds for the next 2 years are given in Table 10.2.

To formulate this as an integer programming problem, we identify the objective function and the constraints as follows:

Maximize net present value of projects undertaken

subject to Total funds used in year 1 ≤ $20,000

Total funds used in year 2 ≤ $16,000

TABLE 10.2

Quemo Chemical Company Information

PROJECT	NET PRESENT VALUE	YEAR 1	YEAR 2
Catalytic Converter	$25,000	$8,000	$7,000
Software	$18,000	$6,000	$4,000
Warehouse Expansion	$32,000	$12,000	$8,000
Available Funds		$20,000	$16,000

We define the decision variables as

$$X_1 = \begin{cases} 1 \text{ if catalytic converter project is funded} \\ 0 \text{ otherwise} \end{cases}$$

$$X_2 = \begin{cases} 1 \text{ if software project is funded} \\ 0 \text{ otherwise} \end{cases}$$

$$X_3 = \begin{cases} 1 \text{ if warehouse expansion project is funded} \\ 0 \text{ otherwise} \end{cases}$$

The mathematical statement of the integer programming problem becomes

$$\text{Maximize NPV} = 25,000X_1 + 18,000X_2 + 32,000X_3$$

$$\text{subject to} \quad 8,000X_1 + 6,000X_2 + 12,000X_3 \le 20,000$$

$$7,000X_1 + 4,000X_2 + 8,000X_3 \le 16,000$$

$$X_1, X_2, X_3 = 0 \text{ or } 1$$

Program 10.5 provides the Solver solution in Excel 2013. You specify the variables to be binary (0–1) by selecting bin from the Add Constraint window. The optimal solution is $X_1 = 1$,

PROGRAM 10.5

Excel 2013 Solver Solution for Quemo Chemical Problem

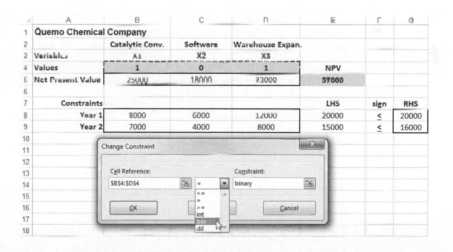

Solver Parameter Inputs and Selections

Set Objective: E5

By Changing cells: B4:D4

To: Max

Subject to the Constraints:

    E8:E9 <= G8:G9

    B4:D4 = binary

Solving Method: Simplex LP

☑ **Make Variables Non-Negative**

Key Formulas

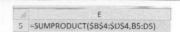

	E
5	=SUMPRODUCT($B$4:$D$4,B5:D5)

Copy E5 to E8:E9

$X_2 = 0, X_3 = 1$ with an objective function value of 57,000. This means that Quemo should fund the catalytic converter project and the warehouse expansion project but not the new software project. The net present value of these investments will be $57,000.

Limiting the Number of Alternatives Selected

One common use of 0–1 variables involves limiting the number of projects or items that are selected from a group. Suppose that in the Quemo Chemical Company example, the company is required to select no more than two of the three projects *regardless* of the funds available. This could be modeled by adding the following constraint to the problem:

$$X_1 + X_2 + X_3 \leq 2$$

If we wished to force the selection of *exactly* two of the three projects for funding, the following constraint should be used:

$$X_1 + X_2 + X_3 = 2$$

This forces exactly two of the variables to have values of 1, whereas the other variable must have a value of 0.

Dependent Selections

At times the selection of one project depends in some way upon the selection of another project. This situation can be modeled with the use of 0–1 variables. Now suppose in the Quemo Chemical problem that the new catalytic converter could be purchased only if the software was also purchased. The following constraint would force this to occur:

$$X_1 \leq X_2$$

or, equivalently,

$$X_1 - X_2 \leq 0$$

Thus, if the software is not purchased, the value of X_2 is 0, and the value of X_1 must also be 0 because of this constraint. However, if the software is purchased ($X_2 = 1$), then it is possible that the catalytic converter could also be purchased ($X_1 = 1$), although this is not required.

If we wished for the catalytic converter and the software projects to either both be selected or both not be selected, we should use the following constraint:

$$X_1 = X_2$$

or, equivalently,

$$X_1 - X_2 = 0$$

Thus, if either of these variables is equal to 0, the other must also be 0. If either of these is equal to 1, the other must also be 1.

Fixed-Charge Problem Example

Often businesses are faced with decisions involving a fixed charge that will affect the cost of future operations. Building a new factory or entering into a long-term lease on an existing facility would involve a fixed cost that might vary depending upon the size of the facility and the location. Once a factory is built, the variable production costs will be affected by the labor cost in the particular city where it is located. An example follows.

Sitka Manufacturing is planning to build at least one new plant, and three cities are being considered: Baytown, Texas; Lake Charles, Louisiana; and Mobile, Alabama. Once the plant or plants have been constructed, the company wishes to have sufficient capacity to produce at least 38,000 units each year. The costs associated with the possible locations are given in Table 10.3.

In modeling this as an integer program, the objective function is to minimize the total of the fixed cost and the variable cost. The constraints are: (1) total production capacity is at least 38,000; (2) number of units produced at the Baytown plant is 0 if the plant is not built, and it is no more than 21,000 if the plant is built; (3) number of units produced at the Lake Charles plant is 0 if the plant is not built, and it is no more than 20,000 if the plant is built; (4) number of units

TABLE 10.3
Fixed and Variable Costs for Sitka Manufacturing

SITE	ANNUAL FIXED COST	VARIABLE COST PER UNIT	ANNUAL CAPACITY
Baytown, TX	$340,000	$32	21,000
Lake Charles, LA	$270,000	$33	20,000
Mobile, AL	$290,000	$30	19,000

produced at the Mobile plant is 0 if the plant is not built, and it is no more than 19,000 if the plant is built.

Then, we define the decision variables as

$$X_1 = \begin{cases} 1 \text{ if factory is built in Baytown} \\ 0 \text{ otherwise} \end{cases}$$

$$X_2 = \begin{cases} 1 \text{ if factory is built in Lake Charles} \\ 0 \text{ otherwise} \end{cases}$$

$$X_2 = \begin{cases} 1 \text{ if factory is built in Mobile} \\ 0 \text{ otherwise} \end{cases}$$

The number of units produced must be 0 if the plant is not built.

X_4 = number of units produced at Baytown plant

X_5 = number of units produced at Lake Charles plant

X_6 = number of units produced at Mobile plant

The integer programming problem formulation becomes

$$\text{Minimize cost} = 340{,}000X_1 + 270{,}000X_2 + 290{,}000X_3 + 32X_4 + 33X_5 + 30X_6$$
$$\text{subject to} \quad X_4 + X_5 + X_6 \geq 38{,}000$$
$$X_4 \leq 21{,}000X_1$$
$$X_5 \leq 20{,}000X_2$$
$$X_6 \leq 19{,}000X_3$$
$$X_1, X_2, X_3 = 0 \text{ or } 1; X_4, X_5, X_6 \geq 0 \text{ and integer}$$

PROGRAM 10.6
Excel 2013 Solver Solution for Sitka Manufacturing Problem

	A	B	C	D	E	F	G	H	I	J
1	Sitka Manufacturing Company									
2		Baytown	Lake Charles	Mobile	Baytown units	L. Charles units	Mobile units			
3	Variables	X1	X2	X3	X4	X5	X6			
4	Values	0	1	1	0	19000	19000	Cost		
5	Cost	340000	270000	290000	32	33	30	1757000		
6										
7	Constraints							LHS	Sign	RHS
8	Minimum capacity				1	1	1	38000	≥	38000
9	Maximum in Baytown	-21000			1			0	≤	0
10	Maximum in L. C.		-20000			1		-1000	≤	0
11	Maximum in Mobile			-19000			1	0	≤	0

Solver Parameter Inputs and Selections

Set Objective: H5

By Changing cells: B4:G4

To: Min

Subject to the Constraints:

H8 >= J8

H9:H11 <= J9:J11

B4:D4 = binary

E4:G4 = integer

Solving Method: Simplex LP

☑ Make Variables Non-Negative

Key Formulas

	H
5	=SUMPRODUCT($B$4:$G$4,B5:G5)

Copy H5 to H8:H11

TABLE 10.4

Oil Investment Opportunities

STOCK	COMPANY NAME	EXPECTED ANNUAL RETURN ($1,000s)	COST FOR BLOCK OF SHARES ($1,000s)
1	Trans-Texas Oil	50	480
2	British Petroleum	80	540
3	Dutch Shell	90	680
4	Houston Drilling	120	1,000
5	Texas Petroleum	110	700
6	San Diego Oil	40	510
7	California Petro	75	900

Notice that if $X_1 = 0$ (meaning Baytown plant is not built), then X_4 (number of units produced at Baytown plant) must also equal zero due to the second constraint. If $X_1 = 1$, then X_4 may be any integer value less than or equal to the limit of 21,000. The third and fourth constraints are similarly used to guarantee that no units are produced at the other locations if the plants are not built. The optimal solution, shown in Program 10.6, is

$$X_1 = 0, \quad X_2 = 1, \quad X_3 = 1, \quad X_4 = 0, \quad X_5 = 19,000, \quad X_6 = 19,000$$
$$\text{Objective function value} = 1,757,000$$

This means that factories will be built at Lake Charles and Mobile. Each of these will produce 19,000 units each year, and the total annual cost will be $1,757,000.

Financial Investment Example

Here is an example of stock portfolio analysis with 0–1 programming.

Numerous financial applications exist with 0–1 variables. A very common type of problem involves selecting from a group of investment opportunities. The following example illustrates this application.

The Houston-based investment firm of Simkin, Simkin, and Steinberg specializes in recommending oil stock portfolios for wealthy clients. One such client has made the following specifications: (1) at least two Texas oil firms must be in the portfolio, (2) no more than one investment can be made in foreign oil companies, (3) one of the two California oil stocks must be purchased. The client has up to $3 million available for investments and insists on purchasing large blocks of shares of each company that he invests in. Table 10.4 describes various stocks that Simkin considers. The objective is to maximize annual return on investment subject to the constraints.

To formulate this as a 0–1 integer programming problem, Simkin lets X_i be a 0–1 integer variable, where $X_i = 1$ if stock i is purchased and $X_i = 0$ if stock i is not purchased:

$$\text{Maximize return} = 50X_1 + 80X_2 + 90X_3 + 120X_4 + 110X_5 + 40X_6 + 75X_7$$

$$\text{subject to} \quad X_1 + X_4 + X_5 \geq 2 \quad \text{(Texas constraint)}$$
$$X_2 + X_3 \leq 1 \quad \text{(foreign oil constraint)}$$
$$X_6 + X_7 = 1 \quad \text{(California constraint)}$$
$$480X_1 + 540X_2 + 680X_3 + 1,000X_4 + 700X_5 + 510X_6 + 900X_7 \leq 3,000$$
$$\text{($3 million limit)}$$

$$X_i = 0 \text{ or } 1 \text{ for all } i$$

The solution from using Solver in Excel 2013 is shown is Program 10.7

10.4 Goal Programming

Firms usually have more than one goal.

In today's business environment, profit maximization or cost minimization are not always the only objectives that a firm sets forth. Often, maximizing total profit is just one of several goals, including such contradictory objectives as maximizing market share, maintaining full employment, providing quality ecological management, minimizing noise level in the neighborhood, and meeting numerous other noneconomic goals.

PROGRAM 10.7

Excel 2013 Solver Solution for Financial Investment Problem

	A	B	C	D	E	F	G	H	I	J	K
1	Simkin, Simkin and Steinberg										
2											
3	Variables	X1	X2	X3	X4	X5	X6	X7			
4	Values	0	0	1	1	1	1	0	Return		
5	Return ($1,000s)	50	80	90	120	110	40	75	360		
6	Constraints								LHS	Sign	RHS
7	Texas	1			1	1			2	≥	2
8	Foreign Oil		1	1					1	≤	1
9	California					1	1		1	=	1
10	$3 Million	480	540	680	1000	700	510	900	2890	≤	3000

Solver Parameter Inputs and Selections

Set Objective: I5

By Changing cells: B4:H4

To: Max

Subject to the Constraints:

　　　I7 >= K7

　　　I8 <= K8

　　　I9 = K9

　　　I10 <= K10

　　　B4:H4 = binary

Solving Method: Simplex LP

☑　Make Variables Non-Negative

Key Formulas

	I
5	=SUMPRODUCT($B$4:$H$4,B5:H5)

Copy I5 to I7:I10

The shortcoming of mathematical programming techniques such as linear and integer programming is that their objective function is measured in one dimension only. It's not possible for LP to have *multiple goals* unless they are all measured in the same units (such as dollars), a highly unusual situation. An important technique that has been developed to supplement LP is called **goal programming**.

Goal programming permits multiple goals.

IN ACTION

Continental Airlines Saves $40 Million Using CrewSolver

Airlines use state-of-the-art processes and automated tools to develop schedules that maximize profit. These schedules will assign aircraft to specific routes, and then schedule pilots and flight attendant crews to each of these aircraft. When disruptions occur, planes and personnel are often left in positions where they are unable to adhere to the next day's assignments. Airlines face schedule disruptions from a variety of unexpected reasons such as bad weather, mechanical problems, and crew unavailability.

In 1993, Continental Airlines began an effort to develop a system of dealing with disruptions in real time. Working with CALEB Technologies, Continental developed the CrewSolver and OptSolver systems (based on 0–1 integer programming models) to produce comprehensive recovery solutions for both aircraft and crews. These solutions retain revenue and promote customer satisfaction by reducing flight cancellations and minimizing delays. These crew recovery solutions are low cost while maintaining a high quality of life for pilots and flight attendants.

In late 2000 and throughout 2001, Continental and other airlines experienced four major disruptions. The first two were due to severe snowstorms in early January and in March 2001. The Houston floods caused by Tropical Storm Allison closed a major hub in June 2001 and left aircraft in locations where they were not scheduled to be. The terrorist attacks of September 11, 2001 left aircraft and crews scattered about and totally disrupted the flight schedules. The CrewSolver system provided a faster and more efficient recovery than had been possible in the past. It is estimated that the CrewSolver system saved approximately $40 million for these major disruptions in 2001. This system also saved additional money and made recovery much easier when there were minor disruptions due to local weather problems at other times throughout the year.

Source: Based on Gang Yu, Michael Arguello, Gao Song, Sandra M. McCowan, and Anna White. "A New Era for Crew Recovery at Continental Airlines," *Interfaces* 33, (January–February 2003): 5–22.

Goal programming is capable of handling decision problems involving multiple goals. It began with the work of Charnes and Cooper in 1961 and was refined and extended by Lee and Ignizio in the 1970s and 1980s (see the Bibliography).

In typical decision-making situations, the goals set by management can be achieved only at the expense of other goals. It is necessary to establish a hierarchy of importance among these goals so that lower-priority goals are tackled only after higher-priority goals are satisfied. Since it is not always possible to achieve every goal to the extent the decision maker desires, goal programming attempts to reach a satisfactory level of multiple objectives. This, of course, differs from LP, which tries to find the best possible outcome for a *single* objective. Nobel laureate Herbert A. Simon, of Carnegie-Mellon University, states that modern managers may not be able to optimize, but may instead have to "**satisfice**" or "come as close as possible" to reaching goals. This is the case with models such as goal programming.

How, specifically, does goal programming differ from LP? The objective function is the main difference. Instead of trying to maximize or minimize the objective function directly, with goal programming we try to minimize *deviations* between set goals and what we can actually achieve within the given constraints. In the LP simplex approach, such deviations are called slack and surplus variables. Because the coefficient for each of these in the objective function is zero, slack and surplus variables do not have an impact on the optimal solution. In goal programming, the deviational variables are typically the only variables in the objective function, and the objective is to minimize the total of these **deviational variables**.

When the goal programming model is formulated, the computational algorithm is almost the same as a minimization problem solved by the simplex method.

Goal programming "satisfices," as opposed to LP, which tries to "optimize." This means coming as close as possible to reaching goals.

The objective function is the main difference between goal programming and LP.

In goal programming we want to minimize deviational variables, which are the only terms in the objective function.

Example of Goal Programming: Harrison Electric Company Revisited

To illustrate the formulation of a goal programming problem, let's look back at the Harrison Electric Company case presented earlier in this chapter as an integer programming problem. That problem's LP formulation, you recall, is

$$\text{Maximize profit} = \$7X_1 + \$6X_2$$
$$\text{subject to} \quad 2X_1 + 3X_2 \le 12 \quad \text{(wiring hours)}$$
$$6X_1 + 5X_2 \le 30 \quad \text{(assembly hours)}$$
$$X_1, X_2 \ge 0$$

where

X_1 = number of chandeliers produced

X_2 = number of ceiling fans produced

We saw that if Harrison's management had a single goal, say profit, LP could be used to find the optimal solution. But let's assume that the firm is moving to a new location during a particular production period and feels that maximizing profit is not a realistic goal. Management sets a profit level, which would be satisfactory during the adjustment period, of $30. We now have a goal programming problem in which we want to find the production mix that achieves this goal as closely as possible, given the production time constraints. This simple case will provide a good starting point for tackling more complicated goal programs.

We first define two deviational variables:

$$d_1^- = \text{underachievement of the profit target}$$
$$d_1^+ = \text{overachievement of the profit target}$$

Now we can state the Harrison Electric problem as a *single-goal* programming model:

$$\text{Minimize under or overachievement of profit target} = d_1^- + d_1^+$$
$$\text{subject to} \quad \$7X_1 + \$6X_2 + d_1^- - d_1^+ = \$30 \quad \text{(profit goal constraint)}$$
$$2X_1 + 3X_2 \qquad\qquad \le 12 \quad \text{(wiring hours constraint)}$$
$$6X_1 + 5X_2 \qquad\qquad \le 30 \quad \text{(assembly hours constraint)}$$
$$X_1, X_2, d_1^-, d_1^+ \ge 0$$

Note that the first constraint states that the profit made, $7X_1 + 6X_2$, plus any underachievement of profit minus any overachievement of profit has to equal the target of $30. For example, if $X_1 = 3$ chandeliers and $X_2 = 2$ ceiling fans, then $33 profit has been made. This exceeds $30 by $3, so d_1^+ must be equal to 3. Since the profit goal constraint was *overachieved*, Harrison did not underachieve and d_1^- will clearly be equal to zero. This problem is now ready for solution by a goal programming algorithm.

Deviational variables are zero if a goal is exactly obtained.

If the target profit of $30 is exactly achieved, we see that both d_1^+ and d_1^- are equal to zero. The objective function will also be minimized at zero. If Harrison's management was only concerned with *underachievement* of the target goal, how would the objective function change? It would be as follows: minimize underachievement $= d_1^-$. This is also a reasonable goal since the firm would probably not be upset with an overachievement of its target.

In general, once all goals and constraints are identified in a problem, management should analyze each goal to see if underachievement or overachievement of that goal is an acceptable situation. If overachievement is acceptable, the appropriate d^+ variable can be eliminated from the objective function. If underachievement is okay, the d^- variable should be dropped. If management seeks to attain a goal exactly, both d^- and d^+ must appear in the objective function.

Extension to Equally Important Multiple Goals

We need a clear definition of deviational variables, such as these.

Let's now look at the situation in which Harrison's management wants to achieve several goals, each equal in priority.

Goal 1: to produce profit of $30 if possible during the production period

Goal 2: to fully utilize the available wiring department hours

Goal 3: to avoid overtime in the assembly department

Goal 4: to meet a contract requirement to produce at least seven ceiling fans

The deviational variables can be defined as follows:

$$d_1^- = \text{underachievement of the profit target}$$
$$d_1^+ = \text{overachievement of the profit target}$$
$$d_2^- = \text{idle time in the wiring department (underutilization)}$$
$$d_2^+ = \text{overtime in the wiring department (overutilization)}$$
$$d_3^- = \text{idle time in the assembly department (underutilization)}$$
$$d_3^+ = \text{overtime in the assembly department (overutilization)}$$
$$d_4^- = \text{underachievement of the ceiling fan goal}$$
$$d_4^+ = \text{overachievement of the ceiling fan goal}$$

Management is unconcerned about whether there is overachievement of the profit goal, overtime in the wiring department, idle time in the assembly department, or more than seven ceiling fans are produced: hence, d_1^+, d_2^+, d_3^-, and d_4^+ may be omitted from the objective function. The new objective function and constraints are

$$\text{Minimize total deviation} = d_1^- + d_2^- + d_3^+ + d_4^-$$
$$\text{subject to } 7X_1 + 6X_2 + d_1^- - d_1^+ = 30 \quad \text{(profit constraint)}$$
$$2X_1 + 3X_2 + d_2^- - d_2^+ = 12 \quad \text{(wiring hours constraint)}$$
$$6X_1 + 5X_2 + d_3^- - d_3^+ = 30 \quad \text{(assembly constraint)}$$
$$X_2 + d_4^- - d_4^+ = 7 \quad \text{(ceiling fan constraint)}$$
$$\text{All } X_i, d_i \text{ variables} \geq 0.$$

Ranking Goals with Priority Levels

A key idea in goal programming is that one goal is more important than another. Priorities are assigned to each deviational variable.

In most goal programming problems, one goal will be more important than another, which in turn will be more important than a third. The idea is that goals can be ranked with respect to their importance in management's eyes. Lower-order goals are considered only after higher-order goals are met. Priorities (P_is) are assigned to each deviational variable—with the ranking that P_1 is the most important goal, P_2 the next most important, then P_3, and so on.

Let's say Harrison Electric sets the priorities shown in the following table:

GOAL	PRIORITY
Reach a profit as much above $30 as possible	P_1
Fully use wiring department hours available	P_2
Avoid assembly department overtime	P_3
Produce at least seven ceiling fans	P_4

Priority 1 is infinitely more important than Priority 2, which is infinitely more important than the next goal, and so on.

This means, in effect, that the priority of meeting the profit goal (P_1) is infinitely more important than the wiring goal (P_2), which is, in turn, infinitely more important than the assembly goal (P_3), which is infinitely more important than producing at least seven ceiling fans (P_4).

With ranking of goals considered, the new objective function becomes

$$\text{Minimize total deviation} = P_1 d_1^- + P_2 d_2^- + P_3 d_3^+ + P_4 d_4^-$$

The constraints remain identical to the previous ones.

Goal Programming with Weighted Goals

When priority levels are used in goal programming, any goal in the top priority level is infinitely more important than the goals in lower priority levels. However, there may be times when one goal is more important than another goal, but it may be only two or three times as important. Instead of placing these goals in different priority levels, they would be placed in the same priority level but with different weights. When using weighted goal programming, the coefficients in the objective function for the deviational variables include both the priority level and the weight. If all goals are in the same priority level, then simply using the weights as objective function coefficients is sufficient.

Consider the Harrison Electric example, in which the least important goal is goal 4 (produce at least seven ceiling fans). Suppose Harrison decides to add another goal of producing at least two chandeliers. The goal of seven ceiling fans is considered twice as important as this goal, so both of these should be in the same priority level. The goal of 2 chandeliers is assigned a weight of 1, while the 7 ceiling fan goal will be given a weight of 2. Both of these will be in priority level 4. A new constraint (goal) would be added:

$$X_1 + d_5^- - d_5^+ = 2 \quad \text{(chandeliers)}$$

 IN ACTION **The Use of Goal Programming for Tuberculosis Drug Allocation in Manila**

Allocation of resources is critical when applied to the health industry. It is a matter of life and death when neither the right supply nor the correct quantity is available to meet patient demand. This was the case faced by the Manila (Philippines) Health Center, whose drug supply to patients afflicted with Category I tuberculosis (TB) was not being efficiently allocated to its 45 regional health centers. When the TB drug supply does not reach patients on time, the disease becomes worse and can result in death. Only 74% of TB patients were being cured in Manila, 11% short of the 85% target cure rate set by the government. Unlike other diseases, TB can only be treated with four medicines and cannot be cured by alternative drugs.

Researchers at the Mapka Institute of Technology set out to create a model, using goal programming, to optimize the allocation of resources for TB treatment while considering supply constraints. The objective function of the model was to meet the target cure rate of 85% (which is the equivalent of minimizing the underachievement in the allocation of anti-TB drugs to the 45 centers). Four goal constraints considered the interrelationships among variables in the distribution system. Goal 1 was to satisfy the medication requirement (a 6-month regimen) for each patient. Goal 2 was to supply each health center with the proper allocation. Goal 3 was to satisfy the cure rate of 85%. Goal 4 was to satisfy the drug requirements of each health center.

The goal programming model successfully dealt with all of these goals and raised the TB cure rate to 88%, a 13% improvement in drug allocation over the previous distribution approach. This means that 335 lives per year were saved through this thoughtful use of goal programming.

Source: Based on G. J. C. Esmeria. "An Application of Goal Programming in the Allocation of Anti-TB Drugs in Rural Health Centers in the Philippines," *Proceedings of the 12th Annual Conference of the Production and Operations Management Society* (March 2001), Orlando, FL: 50.

PROGRAM 10.8A

Harrison Electric's Goal
Programming Analysis
Using QM for Windows:
Inputs

	Wt(d+)	Prty(d+)	Wt(d-)	Prty(d-)	X1	X2		RHS
					Harrison Electric Company			
Constraint 1	0	0	1	1	7	6	=	30
Constraint 2	0	0	1	2	2	3	=	12
Constraint 3	1	3	0	0	6	5	=	30
Constraint 4	0	0	1	4	0	1	=	7

PROGRAM 10.8B

Summary Solution
Screen for Harrison
Electric's Goal
Programming Problem
Using QM for Windows

Harrison Electric Company Solution			
Item			
Decision variable analysis	Value		
X1	0.		
X2	6.		
Priority analysis	Nonachievement		
Priority 1	0.		
Priority 2	0.		
Priority 3	0.		
Priority 4	1.		
Constraint Analysis	RHS	d+ (row i)	d- (row i)
Constraint 1	30.	6.	0.
Constraint 2	12.	6.	0.
Constraint 3	30.	0.	0.
Constraint 4	7.	0	1.

The new objective function value would be

$$\text{Minimize total deviation} = P_1 d_1^- + P_2 d_2^- + P_3 d_3^+ + P_4(2d_4^-) + P_4 d_5^-$$

Note that the ceiling fan goal has a weight of 2. The weight for the chandelier goal is 1. Technically all of the goals in the other priority levels are assigned weights of 1 also.

USING QM FOR WINDOWS TO SOLVE HARRISON'S PROBLEM   QM for Windows goal programming module is illustrated in Programs 10.8A and 10.8B. The input screen is shown first, in Program 10.8A. Note in this first screen that there are two priority level columns for each constraint. For this example, the priority for either the positive or the negative deviation will be zero since the objective function does not contain both types of deviational variables for any of these goals. If a problem had a goal with both deviational variables in the objective function, both priority level columns for this goal (constraint) would contain values other than zero. Also, the weight for each deviational variable contained in the objective function is listed as 1. (It is 0 if the variable is not appearing in the objective function.) If different weights are used, they would be placed in the appropriate weight column within one priority level.

The solution with an analysis of deviations and goal achievement is shown in Program 10.8B. We see that the first two constraints have negative deviational variables equal to 0, indicating full achievement of those goals. In fact, the positive deviational variables both have values of 6, indicating overachievement of these goals by 6 units each. Goal (constraint) 3 has both deviational variables equal to 0, indicating complete achievement of that goal, whereas goal 4 has a negative deviational variable equal to 1, indicating underachievement by 1 unit.

10.5   Nonlinear Programming

Linear, integer, and goal programming all assume that a problem's objective function and constraints are linear. That means that they contain no nonlinear terms such as X_1^3, $1/X_2$, $\log X_3$, or $5X_1X_2$. Yet in many mathematical programming problems, the objective function and/or one or more of the constraints are nonlinear.

Unlike with linear programming methods, computational procedures for solving many nonlinear programming (NLP) problems do not always yield an optimal solution. In many NLP problems, a particular solution may be better than any other point nearby, but it may not be the overall best point. This is called a **local optimum**, and the overall best solution is called the **global optimum**. Thus, for a particular problem, a solution technique may indicate that an optimum solution has been found, but it is only a local optimum, so there may be a global optimum that is better. The mathematics involved in solving these problems is beyond the scope of this text. We will rely on Solver in Excel to solve the nonlinear problems presented in this section.

In this section, we examine three categories of NLP problems and illustrate how Excel can be used to search for the solution to these problems. In Solved Problem 10–3, we will see how NLP in Excel can help find the best parameter to use in an exponential smoothing forecasting model.

Nonlinear Objective Function and Linear Constraints

Here is an example of a nonlinear objective function.

The Great Western Appliance Company sells two models of toaster ovens, the Microtoaster (X_1) and the Self-Clean Toaster Oven (X_2). The firm earns a profit of \$28 for each Microtoaster regardless of the number sold. Profits for the Self-Clean model, however, increase as more units are sold because of fixed overhead. Profit on this model may be expressed as $21X_2 + 0.25X_2^2$.

Hence the firm's objective function is nonlinear:

$$\text{Maximize profit} = 28X_1 + 21X_2 + 0.25X_2^2$$

Great Western's profit is subject to two linear constraints on production capacity and sales time available:

$$X_1 + X_2 \leq 1,000 \quad \text{(units of production capacity)}$$
$$0.5X_1 + 0.4X_2 \leq 500 \quad \text{(hours of sales time available)}$$
$$X_1, X_2 \geq 0$$

Quadratic programming contains squared terms in the objective function.

When an objective function contains squared terms (such as $0.25X_2^2$) and the problem's constraints are linear, it is called a *quadratic programming* problem. A number of useful problems in the field of portfolio selection fall into this category. Quadratic programs can be solved by a modified method of the simplex method. Such work is outside the scope of this book but can be found in sources listed in the Bibliography.

The solution to the Great Western Appliance nonlinear programming problem is shown in Program 10.9. This was found using Solver in Excel 2013, and there are two important features of this spreadsheet that are different from the previous linear and integer programming examples. First, the *solving method* used for this in Solver is GRG Nonlinear instead of Simplex LP. The second change involves the objective function and the changing cells. For the sake of consistency, values for both X_2 (cell C4) and X_2^2 (cell D7) are shown in Program 10.9. However, cell D7 is simply cell C4 squared. Thus, when cell C4 changes, D7 will automatically change, and the Changing cells specified in Solver are B4:C4, while D7 is not included.

Both Nonlinear Objective Function and Nonlinear Constraints

An example in which the objective and constraints are both nonlinear.

The annual profit at a medium-sized (200–400 beds) Hospicare Corporation–owned hospital depends on the number of medical patients admitted (X_1) and the number of surgical patients admitted (X_2). The nonlinear objective function for Hospicare is

$$\text{Maximize profit} = \$13X_1 + \$6X_1X_2 + \$5X_2 + \$1/X_2$$

An example of nonlinear constraints.

The corporation identifies three constraints, two of which are also nonlinear, that affect operations. They are

$$2X_1^2 + 4X_2 \leq 90 \quad \text{(nursing capacity, in thousands of labor–days)}$$
$$X_1 + X_2^3 \leq 75 \quad \text{(x–ray capacity, in thousands)}$$
$$8X_1 - 2X_2 \leq 61 \quad \text{(marketing budget limit, in thousands of \$)}$$

Excel's Solver is capable of formulating such a problem. The optimal solution is provided in Program 10.10.

PROGRAM 10.9

Excel 2013 Solver Solution for Great Western Appliance NLP Problem

	A	B	C	D	E	F	G
1	Great Western Appliance						
2		Micro	Self-Clean				
3	Variables	X1	X2				
4	Values	0	1000				
5							
6	Terms	X1	X2	X2^2			
7	Calculated Values	0	1000	1000000	Profit		
8	Profit	28	21	0.25	271000		
9							
10	Constraints				LHS	Sign	RHS
11	Capacity	1	1		1000	≤	1000
12	Hours Available	0.5	0.4		400	≤	500

Solver Parameter Inputs and Selections

Set Objective: E8

By Changing cells: B4:C4

To: Max

Subject to the Constraints:

    E11:E12 <= G11:G12

Solving Method: GRG Nonlinear

☑ Make Variables Non-Negative

Key Formulas

	E
8	=SUMPRODUCT($B$7:$D$7,B8:D8)
9	
10	LHS
11	=SUMPRODUCT($B$4:$C$4,B11:C11)
12	=SUMPRODUCT($B$4:$C$4,B12:C12)

	B	C	D
7	=B4	=C4	=C4^2

PROGRAM 10.10

Excel 2013 Solution to the Hospicare NLP Problem

	A	B	C	D	E	F	G	H	I	J
1	Hospicare Corp									
2										
3	Variables	X1	X2							
4	Values	6.0663	4.1003							
5										
6	Terms	X1	X1^2	X1*X2	X2	X2^3	1/X2			
7	Calculated Values	6.0663	36.7993	24.8732	4.1003	68.9337	0.2439	Total Profit		
8	Profit	13	0	6	5		1	248.8457		
9										
10	Constraints							LHS	Sign	RHS
11	Nursing		2		4			90.00	≤	90
12	X-Ray	1				1		75.00	≤	75
13	Budget	8			-2			40.33	≤	61

Solver Parameter Inputs and Selections

Set Objective: H8

By Changing cells: B4:C4

To: Max

Subject to the Constraints:

    H11:H13 <= J11:J13

Solving Method: GRG Nonlinear

☑ Make Variables Non-Negative

Key Formulas

	H
8	=SUMPRODUCT($B$7:$G$7,B8:G8)

Copy H8 to H11:H13

	B	C	D	E	F	G
7	=B4	=B4^2	=B4*C4	=C4	=C4^3	=1/C4

Linear Objective Function with Nonlinear Constraints

Thermlock Corp. produces massive rubber washers and gaskets like the type used to seal joints on the NASA Space Shuttles. To do so, it combines two ingredients: rubber (X_1) and oil (X_2). The cost of the industrial-quality rubber used is $5 per pound and the cost of the high-viscosity oil is $7 per pound. Two of the three constraints Thermlock faces are nonlinear. The firm's objective function and constraints are

$$\text{Minimize costs} = \$5X_1 + \$7X_2$$

$$\text{subject to} \qquad 3X_1 + 0.25X_1^2 + 4X_2 + 0.3X_2^2 \geq 125 \quad \text{(hardness contraint)}$$
$$13X_1 + X_1^3 \geq 80 \quad \text{(tensile strength)}$$
$$0.7X_1 + X_2 \geq 17 \quad \text{(elasticity)}$$

To solve this nonlinear programming, we turn again to Excel. The output is provided in Program 10.11.

PROGRAM 10.11

Excel 2013 Solution to the Thermlock NLP Problem

	A	B	C	D	E	F	G	H	I
1	**Thermlock Gaskets**								
2									
3	Variables	**X1**	**X2**						
4	Values	3.325	14.672	Total Cost					
5	Cost	5	7	119.333					
6									
7		**X1**	**X1²**	**X1³**	**X2**	**X2²**			
8	Value	3.325	11.058	36.771	14.672	215.276			
9	Constraints						LHS	Sign	RHS
10	Hardness	3	0.25		4	0.3	136.012	≥	125
11	Tensile Strengt	13		1			80	≥	80
12	Elasticity	0.7			1		17	≥	17

Solver Parameter Inputs and Selections

Set Objective: D5

By Changing cells: B4:C4

To: Min

Subject to the Constraints:

    G10:G12 >= I10:I12

Solving Method: GRG Nonlinear

☑ **Make Variables Non-Negative**

Key Formulas

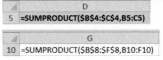

	D
5	=SUMPRODUCT($B$4:$C$4,B5:C5)

	G
10	=SUMPRODUCT($B$8:$F$8,B10:F10)

Copy G10 to G11:G12

	B	C	D	E	F
8	=B4	=B4^2	=B4^3	=C4	=C4^2

Summary

This chapter addresses three special types of LP problems. The first, integer programming, examines LP problems that cannot have fractional answers. We also note that there are three types of integer programming problems: (1) pure or all-integer programs, (2) mixed problems, in which *some* solution variables need not be integer, and (3) 0–1 problems, in which all solutions are either 0 or 1. We also demonstrate how 0–1 variables can be used to model special situations such as fixed-charge problems. QM for Windows and Excel are used to illustrate computer approaches to these problems.

The latter part of the chapter deals with goal programming. This extension of LP allows problems to have multiple goals. Again, software such as QM for Windows is a powerful tool in solving this offshoot of LP. Finally, the advanced topic of NLP is introduced as a special mathematical programming problem. Excel is seen to be a useful tool in solving simple NLP models.

However, it is important to remember that the solution found for an NLP problem might be a local optimum and not a global optimum.

Glossary

Deviational Variables   Terms that are minimized in a goal programming problem. Like slack variables in LP, they are real. They are the only terms in the objective function.

Global Optimum   The overall best solution to a nonlinear programming problem.

Goal Programming   A mathematical programming technique that permits decision makers to set and prioritize multiple objectives.

Integer Programming   A mathematical programming technique that produces integer solutions to linear programming problems.

Local Optimum   A solution to a nonlinear programming problem which is better than any nearby point, but which may not be the global optimum.

Nonlinear Programming   A category of mathematical programming techniques that allows the objective function and/or constraints to be nonlinear.

Satisficing   The process of coming as close as possible to reaching your set of objectives.

0–1 Integer Programming   Problems in which all decision variables must have integer values of 0 or 1. This is also called a binary variable.

Solved Problems

Solved Problem 10-1

Consider the 0–1 integer programming problem that follows:

$$\text{Maximize} \quad 50X_1 + 45X_2 + 48X_3$$
$$\text{subject to} \quad 19X_1 + 27X_2 + 34X_3 \le 80$$
$$22X_1 + 13X_2 + 12X_3 \le 40$$
$$X_1, X_2, X_3 \text{ must be either 0 or 1}$$

Now reformulate this problem with additional constraints so that no more than two of the three variables can take on a value equal to 1 in the solution. Further, make sure that if $X_1 = 1$, then $X_2 = 1$ also. Then solve the new problem using Excel.

Solution
Excel can handle all-integer, mixed-integer, and 0–1 integer problems. Program 10.12 below shows two new constraints to handle the reformulated problem. These constraints are

$$X_1 + X_2 + X_3 \le 2$$

and

$$X_1 - X_2 \quad \le 0$$

The optimal solution is $X_1 = 1, X_2 = 1, X_3 = 0$, with an objective function value of 95.

PROGRAM 10.12

Excel 2013 Solution for Solved Problem 10-1

	A	B	C	D	E	F	G
1	Solved Problem 10-1						
2							
3	Variables	X1	X2	X3			
4	Values	1	1	0	Total		
5	Maximize	50	45	48	95		
6							
7	Constraints				LHS	Sign	RHS
8	Constraint 1	19	27	34	46	≤	80
9	Constraint 2	22	13	12	35	≤	40
10	Constraint 3	1	1	1	2	≤	2
11	Constraint 4	1	-1	0	0	≤	0

Solver Parameter Inputs and Selections

Set Objective: E5

By Changing cells: B4:D4

To: Max

Subject to the Constraints:

   E8:E11 <= G8:G11

   B4:D4 = binary

Solving Method: Simples LP

☑ Make Variables Non-Negative

Key Formulas

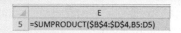

	E
5	=SUMPRODUCT($B$4:$D$4,B5:D5)

Copy E5 to E8:E11

Solved Problem 10-2

Recall the Harrison Electric Company goal programming problem seen in Section 10.4. Its LP formulation was

$$\text{Maximize profit} = \$7X_1 + \$6X_2$$
$$\text{subject to} \qquad 2X_1 + 3X_2 \leq 12 \quad \text{(wiring hours)}$$
$$6X_1 + 5X_2 \leq 30 \quad \text{(assembly hours)}$$
$$X_1, X_2 \geq 0$$

where

   X_1 = number of chandeliers produced
   X_2 = number of ceiling fans produced

Reformulate Harrison Electrical as a goal programming model with the following goals:

Priority 1: Produce at least 4 chandeliers and 3 ceiling fans.
Priority 2: Limit overtime in the assembly department to 10 hours and in the wiring department to 6 hours.
Priority 3: Maximize profit.

Solution

$$\text{Minimize } P_1(d_1^- + d_2^-) + P_2(d_3^+ + d_4^+) + P_3 d_5^-$$
$$\text{subject to} \quad X_1 + d_1^- - d_1^+ = 4 \left. \vphantom{\begin{matrix}1\\1\end{matrix}} \right\} \text{Priority 1}$$
$$X_2 + d_2^- - d_2^+ = 3$$
$$2X_1 + 3X_2 + d_3^- - d_3^+ = 18 \left. \vphantom{\begin{matrix}1\\1\end{matrix}} \right\} \text{Priority 2}$$
$$6X_1 + 5X_2 + d_4^- - d_4^+ = 40$$
$$7X_1 + 6X_2 + d_5^- - d_5^+ = 99{,}999 \} \text{ Priority 3}$$

In the priority 3 goal constraint, the 99,999 represents an unrealistically high profit. It is just a mathematical trick to use as a target so that we can get as close as possible to the maximum profit.

Solved Problem 10-3

In Chapter 5, the exponential smoothing method for forecasting time series was presented. Program 10.13A provides an example of this, with the smoothing constant (α) selected to be 0.1. The forecast in time period 1 is assumed to be perfect, so the error and the absolute value of the error are both 0. The mean absolute deviation (MAD) is the measure of accuracy, and the first time period error is not used in computing this since it was simply assumed to be perfect. The MAD is very dependent on the value of α. Use Excel to find the value of α that will minimize the MAD. *Hint:* Instead of writing the entire objective function, simply use the cell already developed in Excel for the MAD. Remember, α must be between 0 and 1.

Solution

The MAD is a nonlinear function, so Solver in Excel can be used to solve this. There is only one constraint: The smoothing constant, α, must be less than or equal to 1. This can be entered directly into the *Add Constraint* window in Solver, with a 1 entered on the right-hand side of the inequality. Program 10.13B provides the information and the final solution for this. The value for α that minimizes the MAD is 0.3478, and this yields an MAD of 16.70.

Note: Solver can be used in a similar manner to find the best weights to use in a weighted moving average forecast.

PROGRAM 10.13A   Excel 2013 Spreadsheet for Solved Problem 10-3

	A	B	C	D	E
1	Forecasting - Exponential Smoothing				
2					
3	$\alpha =$	0.1000	$F_{t+1} = F_t + \alpha(Y_t - F_t)$		
4	Time Period (t)	Demand (Y_t)	Forecast (F_t)	Error $= Y_t - F_t$	|error|
5	1	110	110	0	-
6	2	156	110	46.000	46.000
7	3	126	114.6	11.400	11.400
8	4	138	115.74	22.260	22.260
9	5	124	117.966	6.034	6.034
10	6	125	118.5694	6.431	6.431
11	7	160	119.21246	40.788	40.788
12	8		123.291214	MAD=	22.152
13					
14	F_1 is assumed to be a perfect forecast.				
15	MAD is based on time periods 2 through 7				

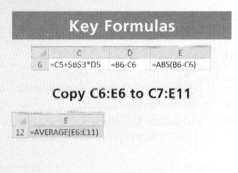

Key Formulas

	C	D	E
6	=C5+$B$3*D5	=B6-C6	=ABS(B6-C6)

Copy C6:E6 to C7:E11

	E
12	=AVERAGE(E6:E11)

PROGRAM 10.13B

Excel 2013 Spreadsheet Solution for Solved Problem 10-3

	A	B	C	D	E
1	Forecasting - Exponential Smoothing				
2					
3	α =	0.3478	$F_{t+1} = F_t + \alpha(Y_t - F_t)$		
4	Time Period (t)	Demand (Y_t)	Forecast (F_t)	Error = Y_t - F_t	|error|
5	1	110	110	0	-
6	2	156	110	46.000	46.000
7	3	126	125.9999998	0.000	0.000
8	4	138	125.9999999	12.000	12.000
9	5	124	130.1739129	-6.174	6.174
10	6	125	128.026465	-3.026	3.026
11	7	160	126.9737815	33.026	33.026
12	8		138.4611617	MAD=	16.704
13					
14	F_1 is assumed to be a perfect forecast.				
15	MAD is based on time periods 2 through 7				

Solver Parameter Inputs and Selections

Set Objective: E12

By Changing cells: B3

To: Min

Subject to the Constraints:

    B3 <= 1

Solving Method: GRG Nonlinear

☑ **Make Variables Non-Negative**

Key Formulas

	C	D	E
6	=C5+$B$3*D5	=B6-C6	=ABS(B6-C6)

Copy C6:E6 to C7:E11

	E
12	=AVERAGE(E6:E11)

Self-Test

- Before taking the self-test, refer to the learning objectives at the beginning of the chapter, the notes in the margins, and the glossary at the end of the chapter.
- Use the key at the back of the book to correct your answers.
- Restudy pages that correspond to any questions that you answered incorrectly or material you feel uncertain about.

1. If all of the decision variables require integer solutions, the problem is
   a. a pure integer programming type of problem.
   b. a simplex method type of problem.
   c. a mixed-integer programming type of problem.
   d. a Gorsky type of problem.

2. In a mixed-integer programming problem
   a. some integers must be even and others must be odd.
   b. some decision variables must require integer results only and some variables must allow for continuous results.
   c. different objectives are mixed together even though they sometimes have relative priorities established.

3. A model containing a linear objective function and linear constraints but requiring that one or more of the decision variables take on an integer value in the final solution is called
   a. an integer programming problem.
   b. a goal programming problem.
   c. a nonlinear programming problem.
   d. a multiple objective LP problem.

4. An integer programming solution can never produce a greater profit than the LP solution to the same problem.
   a. True
   b. False

5. In goal programming, if all the goals are achieved, the value of the objective function will always be zero.
   a. True
   b. False

6. The objective in a goal programming problem with one priority level is to maximize the sum of the deviational variables.
   a. True
   b. False

7. Nobel Laureate Herbert A. Simon of Carnegie-Mellon University says that modern managers should always optimize, not satisfice.
   a. True
   b. False

8. The fixed-charge problem is typically classified as
   a. a goal programming problem.
   b. a 0–1 integer problem.

c. a quadratic programming problem.

d. an assignment problem.

9. The 0–1 integer programming problem

   a. requires the decision variables to have values between 0 and 1.

   b. requires that the constraints all have coefficients between 0 and 1.

   c. requires that the decision variables have coefficients between 0 and 1.

   d. requires the decision variables to be equal to 0 or 1.

10. Goal programming

   a. requires only that you know whether the goal is direct profit maximization or cost minimization.

   b. allows you to have multiple goals.

c. is an algorithm with the goal of a quicker solution to the pure integer programming problem.

d. is an algorithm with the goal of a quicker solution to the mixed-integer programming problem.

11. Nonlinear programming includes problems

   a. in which the objective function is linear but some constraints are not linear.

   b. in which the constraints are linear but the objective function is not linear.

   c. in which both the objective function and all of the constraints are not linear.

   d. solvable by quadratic programming.

   e. all of the above.

Discussion Questions and Problems

Discussion Questions

10-1 Compare the similarities and differences of linear and goal programming.

10-2 A linear programming problem was developed, and the feasible region was found. If the additional restriction that all variables must be integers were added to the problem, how would the size of the feasible region change? How would the optimal value of the objective function change?

10-3 List the advantages and disadvantages of solving integer programming problems by (a) rounding off and (b) enumeration.

10-4 What is the difference between the three types of integer programming problems? Which do you think is most common, and why?

10-5 What is meant by "satisficing," and why is the term often used in conjunction with goal programming?

10-6 What are deviational variables? How do they differ from decision variables in traditional LP problems?

10-7 If you were the president of the college you are attending and were employing goal programming to assist in decision making, what might your goals be? What kinds of constraints would you include in your model?

10-8 What does it mean to rank goals in goal programming? How does this affect the problem's solution?

10-9 Which of the following are NLP problems, and why?

   (a) Maximize profit $= 3X_1 + 5X_2 + 99X_3$

        subject to $X_1 \geq 10$

                    $X_2 \leq 5$

                    $X_3 \geq 18$

   (b) Maximize cost $= 25X_1 + 30X_2 + 8X_1X_2$

        subject to $X_1 \qquad\qquad \geq 8$

                    $X_1 + \quad X_2 \geq 12$

               $0.0005X_1 - \quad X_2 = 11$

   (c) Maximize $Z = P_1d_1^- + P_2d_2^+ + P_3^+$

        subject to $X_1 + X_2 + d_1^- - d_1^+ = 300$

                      $X_2 + d_2^- - d_2^+ = 200$

            $X_1 + \qquad d_3^- - d_3^+ = 100$

   (d) Maximize profit $= 3X_1 + 4X_2$

        subject to $X_1^2 - 5X_2 \geq 8$

                     $3X_1 + 4X_2 \geq 12$

   (e) Minimize cost $= 18X_1 + 5X_2 + X_2^2$

        subject to $4X_1 - 3X_2 \geq 8$

                    $X_1 + \quad X_2 \geq 18$

   Are any of these quadratic programming problems?

Problems*

:10-10 Elizabeth Bailey is the owner and general manager of Princess Brides, which provides a wedding planning service in Southwest Louisiana. She uses radio advertising to market her business. Two types of ads are available—those during prime time hours and those at other times. Each prime time ad costs $390 and reaches 8,200 people, while the offpeak ads each cost $240 and reach 5,100 people. Bailey has budgeted $1,800 per week for advertising. Based on comments from her customers, Bailey wants to have

---

Note: means the problem may be solved with QM for Windows;   means the problem may be solved with Excel; and   means the problem may be solved with QM for Windows and/or Excel.

at least 2 prime time ads and no more than 6 off peak ads.

(a) Formulate this as a linear program.

(b) Find a good or optimal integer solution for part (a) by rounding off or making an educated guess at the answer.

(c) Solve this as an integer programming problem using a computer.

:10-11 A group of college students is planning a camping trip during the upcoming break. The group must hike several miles through the woods to get to the campsite, and anything that is needed on this trip must be packed in a knapsack and carried to the campsite. One particular student, Tina Shawl, has identified eight items that she would like to take on the trip, but the combined weight is too great to take all of them. She has decided to rate the utility of each item on a scale of 1 to 100, with 100 being the most beneficial. The item weights in pounds and their utility values are given below.

ITEM	1	2	3	4	5	6	7	8
WEIGHT	8	1	7	6	3	12	5	14
UTILITY	80	20	50	55	50	75	30	70

Recognizing that the hike to the campsite is a long one, a limit of 35 pounds has been set as the maximum total weight of the items to be carried.

(a) Formulate this as a 0–1 programming problem to maximize the total utility of the items carried. Solve this knapsack problem using a computer.

(b) Suppose item number 3 is an extra battery pack, which may be used with several of the other items. Tina has decided that she will only take item number 5, a CD player, if she also takes item number 3. On the other hand, if she takes item number 3, she may or may not take item number 5. Modify this problem to reflect this and solve the new problem.

:10-12 Student Enterprises sells two sizes of wall posters, a large 3- by 4-foot poster and a smaller 2- by 3-foot poster. The profit earned from the sale of each large poster is $3; each smaller poster earns $2. The firm, although profitable, is not large; it consists of one art student, Jan Meising, at the University of Kentucky. Because of her classroom schedule, Jan has the following weekly constraints: (1) up to three large posters can be sold, (2) up to five smaller posters can be sold, (3) up to 10 hours can be spent on posters during the week, with each large poster requiring 2 hours of work and each small one taking 1 hour. With the semester almost over, Jan plans on taking a three-month summer vacation to England

and doesn't want to leave any unfinished posters behind. Find the integer solution that will maximize her profit.

•10-13 An airline owns an aging fleet of Boeing 737 jet airplanes. It is considering a major purchase of up to 17 new Boeing model 787 and 767 jets. The decision must take into account numerous cost and capability factors, including the following: (1) the airline can finance up to $1.6 billion in purchases; (2) each Boeing 787 will cost $80 million, and each Boeing 767 will cost $110 million; (3) at least one-third of the planes purchased should be the longer-range 787; (4) the annual maintenance budget is to be no more than $8 million; (5) the annual maintenance cost per 787 is estimated to be $800,000, and it is $500,000 for each 767 purchased; and (6) each 787 can carry 125,000 passengers per year, whereas each 767 can fly 81,000 passengers annually. Formulate this as an integer programming problem to maximize the annual passenger-carrying capability. What category of integer programming problem is this? Solve this problem.

:10-14 Trapeze Investments is a venture capital firm that is currently evaluating six different investment opportunities. There is not sufficient capital to invest in all of these, but more than one will be selected. A 0–1 integer programming model is planned to help determine which of the six opportunities to choose. Variables X_1, X_2, X_3, X_4, X_5, and X_6 represent the six choices. For each of the following situations, write a constraint (or several constraints) that would be used.

(a) At least 3 of these choices are to be selected.

(b) Either investment 1 or investment 4 must be undertaken, but not both.

(c) If investment 4 is selected, then investment 6 must also be selected. However, if investment 4 is not selected, it is still possible to select number 6.

(d) Investment 5 cannot be selected unless both investments 2 and 3 are also selected.

(e) Investment 5 must be selected if both investments 2 and 3 are also selected.

:10-15 Horizon Wireless, a cellular telephone company, is expanding into a new era. Relay towers are necessary to provide wireless telephone coverage to the different areas of the city. A grid is superimposed on a map of the city to help determine where the towers should be located. The grid consists of 8 areas labeled A through H. Six possible tower locations (numbered 1–6) have been identified, and each location could serve several areas. The following table indicates the areas served by each of the towers.

TOWER LOCATION	1	2	3	4	5	6
AREAS SERVED	A, B, D	B, C, G	C, D, E, F	E, F, H	E, G, H	A, D, F

Formulate this as a 0–1 programming model to minimize the total number of towers required to cover all the areas. Solve this using a computer.

•10-16 Innis Construction Company specializes in building moderately priced homes in Cincinnati, Ohio. Tom Innis has identified eight potential locations to construct new single-family dwellings, but he cannot put up homes on all of the sites because he has only $300,000 to invest in all projects. The accompanying table shows the cost of constructing homes in each area and the expected profit to be made from the sale of each home. Note that the home-building costs differ considerably due to lot costs, site preparation, and differences in the models to be built. Note also that a fraction of a home cannot be built.

LOCATION	COST OF BUILDING AT THIS SITE ($)	EXPECTED PROFIT ($)
Clifton	60,000	5,000
Mt. Auburn	50,000	6,000
Mt. Adams	82,000	10,000
Amberly	103,000	12,000
Norwood	50,000	8,000
Covington	41,000	3,000
Roselawn	80,000	9,000
Eden Park	69,000	10,000

(a) Formulate Innis's problem using 0–1 integer programming.
(b) Solve with QM for Windows or Excel.

:10-17 A real estate developer is considering three possible projects: a small apartment complex, a small shopping center, and a mini-warehouse. Each of these requires different funding over the next two years, and the net present value of the investments also varies. The following table provides the required investment amounts (in $1,000s) and the net present value (NPV) of each (also expressed in $1,000s):

		INVESTMENT	
	NPV	YEAR 1	YEAR 2
Apartment	18	40	30
Shopping center	15	30	20
Mini-warehouse	14	20	20

The company has $80,000 to invest in year 1 and $50,000 to invest in year 2.

(a) Develop an integer programming model to maximize the NPV in this situation.
(b) Solve the problem in part (a) using computer software. Which of the three projects would be undertaken if NPV is maximized? How much money would be used each year?

:10-18 Refer to the real estate investment situation in Problem 10-17.

(a) Suppose that the shopping center and the apartment would be on adjacent properties, and the shopping center would only be considered if the apartment were also built. Formulate the constraint that would stipulate this.
(b) Formulate a constraint that would force exactly two of the three projects to be undertaken.

:10-19 Triangle Utilities provides electricity for three cities. The company has four electric generators that are used to provide electricity. The main generator operates 24 hours per day, with an occasional shutdown for routine maintenance. Three other generators (1, 2, and 3) are available to provide additional power when needed. A startup cost is incurred each time one of these generators is started. The startup costs are $6,000 for 1, $5,000 for 2, and $4,000 for 3. These generators are used in the following ways: A generator may be started at 6:00 A.M. and run for either 8 hours or 16 hours, or it may be started at 2:00 P.M. and run for 8 hours (until 10:00 P.M.). All generators except the main generator are shut down at 10:00 P.M. Forecasts indicate the need for 3,200 megawatts more than provided by the main generator before 2:00 P.M., and this need goes up to 5,700 megawatts between 2:00 and 10:00 P.M. Generator 1 may provide up to 2,400 megawatts, generator 2 may provide up to 2,100 megawatts, and generator 3 may provide up to 3,300 megawatts. The cost per megawatt used per eight hour period is $8 for 1, $9 for 2, and $7 for 3.

(a) Formulate this problem as an integer programming problem to determine the least-cost way to meet the needs of the area.
(b) Solve using computer software.

•10-20 The campaign manager for a politician who is running for reelection to a political office is planning the campaign. Four ways to advertise have been selected: TV ads, radio ads, billboards, and newspaper ads. The cost of these are $900 for each TV ad, $500 for each radio ad, $600 for a billboard for one month, and $180 for each newspaper ad. The audience reached by each type of advertising has been estimated to be 40,000 for each TV ad, 32,000 for each radio ad, 34,000 for each billboard, and 17,000 for each newspaper ad. The total monthly advertising budget is $16,000. The following goals have been established and ranked:

1. The number of people reached should be at least 1,500,000.
2. The total monthly advertising budget should not be exceeded.
3. Together, the number of ads on either TV or radio should be at least 6.
4. No more than 10 ads of any one type of advertising should be used.

(a) Formulate this as a goal programming problem.
(b) Solve this using computer software.
(c) Which goals are exactly met and which of them are not?

Q•10-21 Geraldine Shawhan is president of Shawhan File Works, a firm that manufactures two types of metal file cabinets. The demand for her two-drawer model is up to 600 cabinets per week; demand for a three-drawer cabinet is limited to 400 per week. Shawhan File Works has a weekly operating capacity of 1,300 hours, with the two-drawer cabinet taking 1 hour to produce and the three-drawer cabinet requiring 2 hours. Each two-drawer model sold yields a $10 profit, and the profit for the large model is $15. Shawhan has listed the following goals in order of importance:

1. Attain a profit as close to $11,000 as possible each week.
2. Avoid underutilization of the firm's production capacity.
3. Sell as many two- and three-drawer cabinets as the demand indicates.

Set this up as a goal programming problem.

10-22 Solve Problem 10-21. Are any goals unachieved in this solution? Explain.

Q•10-23 Hilliard Electronics produces specially coded computer chips for laser surgery in 64MB, 256MB, and 512MB sizes. (1MB means that the chip holds 1 million bytes of information.) To produce a 64MB chip requires 8 hours of labor, a 256MB chip takes 13 hours, and a 512MB chip requires 16 hours. Hilliard's monthly production capacity is 1,200 hours. Mr. Blank, the firm's sales manager, estimates that the maximum monthly sales of the 64MB, 256MB, and 512MB chips are 40, 50, and 60, respectively. The company has the following goals (ranked in order from most important to least important):

1. Fill an order from the best customer for thirty 64MB chips and thirty-five 256MB chips.
2. Provide sufficient chips to at least equal the sales estimates set by Mr. Blank.
3. Avoid underutilization of the production capacity.

Formulate this problem using goal programming.

Q‡10-24 An Oklahoma manufacturer makes two products: speaker telephones (X_1) and pushbutton telephones (X_2). The following goal programming model has been formulated to find the number of each to produce each day to meet the firm's goals:

$$\text{Minimize} \quad P_1 d_1^- + P_2 d_2^- + P_3 d_3^+ + P_4 d_1^+$$

$$\text{subject to} \quad 2X_1 + 4X_2 + d_1^- - d_1^+ = 80$$
$$8X_1 + 10X_2 + d_2^- - d_2^+ = 320$$
$$8X_1 + 6X_2 + d_3^- - d_3^+ = 240$$
$$\text{all } X_i, d_i \geq 0$$

Find the optimal solution using a computer.

Q•10-25 Major Bill Bligh, director of the Army War College's new 6-month attaché training program, is concerned about how the 20 officers taking the course spend their precious time while in his charge. Major Bligh recognizes that there are 168 hours per week and thinks that his students have been using them rather inefficiently. Bligh lets

X_1 = number of hours of sleep needed per week

X_2 = number of personal hours (eating, personal hygiene, handling laundary, and so on)

X_3 = number of hours of class and studying

X_4 = number of hours of social time off base (dating, sports, family visits, and so on)

He thinks that students should study 30 hours a week to have time to absorb material. This is his most important goal. Bligh feels that students need at most 7 hours sleep per night on average and that this goal is number 2. He believes that goal number 3 is to provide at least 20 hours per week of social time.

(a) Formulate this as a goal programming problem.
(b) Solve the problem using computer software.

Q‡10-26 Mick Garcia, a certified financial planner (CFP) has been asked by a client to invest $250,000. This money may be placed in stocks, bonds, or a mutual fund in real estate. The expected return on investment is 13% for stocks, 8% for bonds, and 10% for real estate. While the client would like a very high expected return, she would be satisfied with a 10% expected return on her money. Due to risk considerations, several goals have been established to keep the risk at an acceptable level. One goal is to put at least 30% of the money in bonds. Another goal is that the amount of money in real estate should not exceed 50% of the money invested in stocks and bonds combined. In addition to these goals, there is one absolute restriction. Under no circumstances should more than $150,000 be invested in any one area.

(a) Formulate this as a goal programming problem. Assume that all of the goals are equally important.

(b) Use any available software to solve this problem. How much money should be put in each of the investment options? What is the total return? Which of the goals are not met?

✗:10-27 Hinkel Rotary Engine, Ltd., produces four- and six-cylinder models of automobile engines. The firm's profit for each four-cylinder engine sold during its quarterly production cycle is $1,800 - $50X_1$, where X_1 is the number sold. Hinkel makes $2,400 - $70X_2$ for each of the larger engines sold, with X_2 equal to the number of six-cylinder engines sold. There are 5,000 hours of production time available during each production cycle. A four-cylinder engine requires 100 hours of production time, whereas six-cylinder engines take 130 hours to manufacture. Formulate this production planning problem for Hinkel.

✗:10-28 Motorcross of Wisconsin produces two models of snowmobiles, the XJ6 and the XJ8. In any given production-planning week Motorcross has 40 hours available in its final testing bay. Each XJ6 requires 1 hour to test and each XJ8 takes 2 hours. The revenue (in $1,000s) for the firm is nonlinear and is stated as (Number of XJ6s)(4 - 0.1 number of XJ6s) + (Number of XJ8s)(5 - 0.2 number of XJ8s).

(a) Formulate this problem.
(b) Solve using Excel.

✗:10-29 During the busiest season of the year, Green-Gro Fertilizer produces two types of fertilizers. The standard type (X) is just fertilizer, and the other type (Y) is a special fertilizer and weed-killer combination. The following model has been developed to determine how much of each type should be produced to maximize profit subject to a labor constraint:

Maximize profit $= 12X - 0.04X^2 + 15Y - 0.06Y^2$
subject to $\quad\quad 2X + 4Y \leq 160$ hours
$$X, Y \geq 0$$

Find the optimal solution to this problem.

✗:10-30 Pat McCormack, a financial advisor for Investors R Us, is evaluating two stocks in a particular industry. He wants to minimize the variance of a portfolio consisting of these two stocks, but he wants to have an expected return of at least 9%. After obtaining historical data on the variance and returns, he develops the following nonlinear program:

Minimize portfolio variance $= 0.16X^2 + 0.2XY + 0.09Y^2$
subject to $\quad\quad X + Y = 1$ (all funds must be invested)
$\quad\quad 0.11X + 0.08Y > 0.09$ (return on the investment)
$$X, Y \geq 0$$

where

$X =$ proportion of money invested in stock 1
$Y =$ proportion of money invested in stock 2

Solve this using Excel and determine how much to invest in each of the two stocks. What is the return for this portfolio? What is the variance of this portfolio?

✗:10-31 Summertime Tees sells two very popular styles of embroidered shirts in southern Florida: a tank top and a regular T-shirt. The cost of the tank top is $6, and the cost of the T-shirt is $8. The demand for these is sensitive to the price, and historical data indicate that the weekly demands are given by

$$X_1 = 500 - 12P_1$$
$$X_2 = 400 - 15P_2$$

where

$X_1 =$ demand for tank top
$P_1 =$ price for tank top
$X_2 =$ demand for regular T-shirt
$P_2 =$ price for regular T-shirt

(a) Develop an equation for the total profit.
(b) Use Excel to find the optimal solution to the following nonlinear program. Use the profit function developed in part (a).

Maximize profit

subject to $\quad\quad X_1 = 500 - 12P_1$
$\quad\quad\quad\quad\quad\quad X_2 = 400 - 15P_2$
$\quad\quad\quad\quad\quad\quad P_1 \leq 20$
$\quad\quad\quad\quad\quad\quad P_2 \leq 25$
$\quad\quad X_1, P_1, X_2, P_2 \geq 0$

≗10-32 The integer programming problem on the following page has been developed to help First National Bank decide where, out of 10 possible sites, to locate four new branch offices:

where X_i represents Winter Park, Maitland, Osceola, Downtown, South Orlando, Airport, Winter Garden, Apopka, Lake Mary, Cocoa Beach, for i equals 1 to 10, respectively.

(a) Where should the four new sites be located, and what will be the expected return?
(b) If at least one new branch *must* be opened in Maitland or Osceola, will this change the answers? Add the new constraint and rerun.
(c) The expected return at Apopka was overestimated. The correct value is $160,000 per year (i.e., 160). Using the original assumptions (namely, ignoring (b)), does your answer to part (a) change?

✗:10-33 In Solved Problem 10-3, nonlinear programming was used to find the best value for the smoothing constant, α, in an exponential smoothing forecasting problem. To see how much the MAD can vary due to the selection of the smoothing constant, use Excel and the data in Program 10.13A to find the value of the smoothing constant that would maximize the MAD. Compare this MAD to the minimum MAD found in the solved problem.

:10-34 Using the data in Solved Problem 10-3, develop a spreadsheet for a 2-period weighted moving average forecast with weights of 0.6 (w_1) for the most recent period and 0.4 (w_2) for the other period.

Note these weights sum to 1, so the forecast is simply

$$\text{Forecast for next period} = w_1(\text{Value in current period}) + w_2(\text{Value in last period.})$$

Find the weights for this 2-period weighted moving average that would minimize the MAD. (*Hint:* The weights must sum to 1.)

IP for Problem 10-32

$$\text{Maximize expected returns} = 120X_1 + 100X_2 + 110X_3 + 140X_4 + 155X_5 + 128X_6 + 145X_7 + 190X_8 + 170X_9 + 150X_{10}$$

subject to

$$20X_1 + 30X_2 + 20X_3 + 25X_4 + 30X_5 + 30X_6 + 25X_7 + 20X_8 + 25X_9 + 30X_{10} \le 110$$
$$15X_1 + 5X_2 + 20X_3 + 20X_4 + 5X_5 + 5X_6 + 10X_7 + 20X_8 + 5X_9 + 20X_{10} \le 50$$
$$X_2 + \qquad\qquad X_6 + X_7 + \qquad X_9 + X_{10} \le 3$$
$$X_2 + X_3 + \qquad X_5 + \qquad\qquad X_8 + X_9 \qquad\qquad \ge 2$$
$$X_1 + \qquad X_3 + \qquad\qquad\qquad\qquad\qquad\qquad X_{10} \ge 1$$
$$X_1 + X_2 + X_3 + X_4 + X_5 + X_6 + X_7 + X_8 + X_9 + X_{10} \le 4$$

all $X_i = 0$ or 1

---

www Internet Homework Problems

See our Internet home page, at **www.pearsonhighered.com/render**, for additional homework problems 10-35 to 10-40.

Case Study

Schank Marketing Research

Schank Marketing Research has just signed contracts to conduct studies for four clients. At present, three project managers are free for assignment to the tasks. Although all are capable of handling each assignment, the times and cost to complete the studies depend on the experience and knowledge of each manager. Using his judgment, John Schank, the president, has been able to establish a cost for each possible assignment. These costs, which are really the salaries each manager would draw on each task, are summarized in the table on the next page.

Schank is very hesitant about neglecting NASA, which has been an important customer in the past. (NASA has employed the firm to study the public's attitude toward the Space Shuttle and proposed Space Station.) In addition, Schank has promised to try to provide Ruth a salary of at least $3,000 on his next assignment. From previous contracts, Schank also knows that Gardener does not get along well with the management at CBT Television, so he hopes to avoid assigning her to CBT. Finally, as Hines Corporation is also an old and

valued client, Schank feels that it is twice as important to assign a project manager immediately to Hines's task as it is to provide one to General Foundry, a brand-new client. Schank wants to minimize the total costs of all projects while considering each of these goals. He feels that all of these goals are important, but if he had to rank them, he would put his concern about NASA first, his worry about Gardener second, his need to keep Hines Corporation happy third, his promise to Ruth fourth, and his concern about minimizing all costs last.

Each project manager can handle, at most, one new client.

Discussion Questions

1. If Schank were not concerned about noncost goals, how would he formulate this problem so that it could be solved quantitatively?

2. Develop a formulation that will incorporate all five objectives.

PROJECT MANAGER	CLIENT			
	HINES CORP.	NASA	GENERAL FOUNDRY	CBT TELEVISION
Gardener	$3,200	$3,000	$2,800	$2,900
Ruth	2,700	3,200	3,000	3,100
Hardgraves	1,900	2,100	3,300	2,100

Case Study

Oakton River Bridge

The Oakton River had long been considered an impediment to the development of a certain medium-sized metropolitan area in the southeast. Lying to the east of the city, the river made it difficult for people living on its eastern bank to commute to jobs in and around the city and to take advantage of the shopping and cultural attractions that the city had to offer. Similarly, the river inhibited those on its western bank from access to the ocean resorts lying one hour to the east. The bridge over the Oakton River had been built prior to World War II and was grossly inadequate to handle the existing traffic, much less the increased traffic that would accompany the forecasted growth in the area. A congressional delegation from the state prevailed upon the federal government to fund a major portion of a new toll bridge over the Oakton River and the state legislature appropriated the rest of the needed monies for the project.

Progress in construction of the bridge has been in accordance with what was anticipated at the start of construction. The state highway commission, which will have operational jurisdiction over the bridge, has concluded that the opening of the bridge for traffic is likely to take place at the beginning of the next summer, as scheduled. A personnel task force has been established to recruit, train, and schedule the workers needed to operate the toll facility.

The personnel task force is well aware of the budgetary problems facing the state. They have taken as part of their mandate the requirement that personnel costs be kept as low as possible. One particular area of concern is the number of toll collectors that will be needed. The bridge is scheduling three shifts of collectors: shift A from midnight to 8 A.M., shift B from 8 A.M. to 4 P.M., and shift C from 4 P.M. to midnight. Recently, the state employees union negotiated a contract with the state which requires that all toll collectors be permanent, full-time employees. In addition, all collectors must work a five-on, two-off schedule on the same shift. Thus, for example, a worker could be assigned to work Tuesday, Wednesday, Thursday, Friday, and Saturday on shift A, followed by Sunday and Monday off. An employee could not be scheduled to work, say, Tuesday on shift A followed by Wednesday, Thursday, Friday, and Saturday on shift B or on any other mixture of shifts during a 5-day block. The

employees would choose their assignments in order of their seniority.

The task force has received projections of traffic flow on the bridge by day and hour. These projections are based on extrapolations of existing traffic patterns—the pattern of commuting, shopping, and beach traffic currently experienced with growth projections factored in. Standards data from other state-operated toll facilities have allowed the task force to convert these traffic flows into toll collector requirements, that is, the minimum number of collectors required per shift, per day, to handle the anticipated traffic load. These toll collector requirements are summarized in the following table:

Minimum Number of Toll Collectors Required per Shift

SHIFT	SUN.	MON.	TUE.	WED.	THU.	FRI.	SAT.
A	8	13	12	12	13	13	15
B	10	10	10	10	10	13	15
C	15	13	13	12	12	13	8

The numbers in the table include one or two extra collectors per shift to fill in for collectors who call in sick and to provide relief for collectors on their scheduled breaks. Note that each of the eight collectors needed for shift A on Sunday, for example, could have come from any of the A shifts scheduled to begin on Wednesday, Thursday, Friday, Saturday, or Sunday.

Discussion Questions

1. Determine the minimum number of toll collectors that would have to be hired to meet the requirements expressed in the table.
2. The union had indicated that it might lift its opposition to the mixing of shifts in a 5-day block in exchange for additional compensation and benefits. By how much could the number of toll collectors required be reduced if this is done?

Source: Based on B. Render, R. M. Stair, and I. Greenberg. *Cases and Readings In Management Science*, 2nd ed., 1990, pp. 55–56. Reprinted by permission of Prentice Hall, Upper Saddle River, NJ.

Bibliography

Aköz, Onur, and Dobrila Petrovic. "A Fuzzy Goal Programming Method with Imprecise Goal Hierarchy," *European Journal of Operational Research* 181, 3 (September 2007): 1427–1433.

Araz, Ceyhun, Pinar Mizrak Ozfirat, and Irem Ozkarahan. "An Integrated Multicriteria Decision-Making Methodology for Outsourcing Management," *Computers & Operations Research* 34, 12 (December 2007): 3738–3756.

Bertsimas, Dimitris, Christopher Darnell, and Robert Soucy. "Portfolio Construction through Mixed-Integer Programming at Grantham, Mayo, Van Otterloo and Company," *Interfaces* 29, 1 (January 1999): 49–66.

Chang, Ching-Ter. "Multi-Choice Goal Programming," *Omega* 25, 4 (August 2007): 389–396.

Charnes, A., and W. W. Cooper. *Management Models and Industrial Applications of Linear Programming*, Vols. I and II. New York: John Wiley & Sons, Inc.1961.

Dawid, Herbert, Johannes König, and Christine Strauss. "An Enhanced Rostering Model for Airline Crews," *Computers & Operations Research* 28, 7 (June 2001): 671–688.

Drees, Lawrence David, and Wilbert E. Wilhelm. "Scheduling Experiments on a Nuclear Reactor Using Mixed Integer Programming," *Computers & Operations Research* 28, 10 (September 2001): 1013–1037.

Hueter, Jackie, and William Swart. "An Integrated Labor-Management System for Taco Bell," *Interfaces* 28, 1 (January–February 1998): 75–91.

Ignizio, James P. *Introduction to Linear Goal Programming*. Beverly Hills: Sage Publications, 1985.

Katok, Elena, and Dennis Ott. "Using Mixed-Integer Programming to Reduce Label Changes in the Coors Aluminum Can Plant," *Interfaces* 30, 2 (March 2000): 1–12.

Land, Alisa, and Susan Powell. "A Survey of the Operational Use of ILP Models," *Annals of Operations Research* 149, 1 (2007): 147–156.

Lee, Sang M., and Marc J. Schniederjans. "A Multicriterial Assignment Problem: A Goal Programming Approach," *Interfaces* 13, 4 (August 1983): 75–79.

Pati, Rupesh Kumar, Prem Vrat, and Pradeep Kumar. "A Goal Programming Model for a Paper Recycling System," *Omega* 36, 3 (June 2008): 405–417.

Reyes, Pedro M., and Gregory V. Frazier. "Goal Programming Model for Grocery Shelf Space Allocation," *European Journal of Operational Research* 181, 2 (September 2007): 634–644.

Wadhwa, Vijay, and A. Ravi Ravindran. "Vendor Selection in Outsourcing," *Computers & Operations Research* 34, 12 (December 2007): 3725–3737.

Zangwill, W. I. *Nonlinear Programming: A Unified Approach*. Upper Saddle River, NJ: Prentice Hall, 1969.

CHAPTER 11

Project Management

11.1   Introduction

Project management can be used to manage complex projects.

Most realistic projects that organizations like Microsoft, General Motors, or the U.S. Defense Department undertake are large and complex. A builder putting up an office building, for example, must complete thousands of activities costing millions of dollars. NASA must inspect countless components before it launches a rocket. The Bath Iron Works shipyard on the Kennebec River in Bath, Maine, must manage and coordinate thousands of complex activities simultaneously. Almost every industry worries about how to manage similar large-scale, complicated projects effectively. It is a difficult problem, and the stakes are high. Millions of dollars in cost overruns have been wasted due to poor planning of projects. Unnecessary delays have occurred due to poor scheduling. How can such problems be solved?

The first step in planning and scheduling a project is to develop the **work breakdown structure (WBS)**. This involves identifying the activities that must be performed in the project. An **activity** is a job or task that is a part of a project. The beginning or end of an activity is called an **event**. There may be varying levels of detail, and each activity may be broken into its most basic components. The time, cost, resource requirements, predecessors, and person(s) responsible are identified for each activity. When this has been done, a schedule for the project can be developed.

The **program evaluation and review technique (PERT)** and the **critical path method (CPM)** are two popular quantitative analysis techniques that help managers plan, schedule, monitor, and control large and complex projects. They were developed because there was a critical need for a better way to manage (see the History box).

PERT is probabilistic, whereas CPM is deterministic.

When they were first developed, PERT and CPM were similar in their basic approach, but they differed in the way activity times were estimated. For every PERT activity, three time estimates are combined to determine the expected activity completion time. Thus, PERT is a probabilistic technique. On the other hand, CPM is a deterministic method since it is assumed that the times are known with certainty. While these differences are still noted, the two techniques are so similar that the term PERT/CPM is often used to describe the overall approach. This reference is used in this chapter, and differences are noted where appropriate.

HISTORY   How PERT and CPM Started

Managers have been planning, scheduling, monitoring, and controlling large-scale projects for hundreds of years, but it has only been in the past 50 years that QA techniques have been applied to major projects. One of the earliest techniques was the *Gantt chart*. This type of chart shows the start and finish times of one or more activities, as shown in the accompanying chart.

In 1958, the Special Projects Office of the U.S. Navy developed the program evaluation and review technique (PERT) to plan and control the Polaris missile program. This project involved the coordination of thousands of contractors. Today PERT is still used to monitor countless government contract schedules. At about the same time (1957), the critical path method (CPM) was developed by J. E. Kelley, Jr. of Remington Rand and M. R. Walker of DuPont. Originally, CPM was used to assist in the building and maintenance of chemical plants at DuPont.

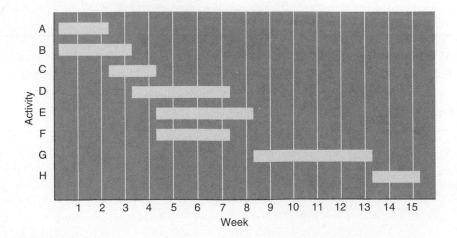

There are six steps common to both PERT and CPM. The procedure follows:

Six Steps of PERT/CPM

1. Define the project and all of its significant activities or tasks.
2. Develop the relationships among the activities. Decide which activities must precede others.
3. Draw the **network** connecting all of the activities.
4. Assign time and/or cost estimates to each activity.
5. Compute the longest time path through the network; this is called the **critical path**.
6. Use the network to help plan, schedule, monitor, and control the project.

The critical path is important because activities on the critical path can delay the entire project.

Finding the critical path is a major part of controlling a project. The activities on the critical path represent tasks that will delay the entire project if they are delayed. Managers derive flexibility by identifying noncritical activities and replanning, rescheduling, and reallocating resources such as personnel and finances.

11.2   PERT/CPM

Almost any large project can be subdivided into a series of smaller activities or tasks that can be analyzed with PERT/CPM. When you recognize that projects can have thousands of specific activities, you see why it is important to be able to answer questions such as the following:

Questions answered by PERT.

1. When will the entire project be completed?
2. What are the *critical* activities or tasks in the project, that is, the ones that will delay the entire project if they are late?
3. Which are the *noncritical* activities, that is, the ones that can run late without delaying the entire project's completion?
4. If there are three time estimates, what is the probability that the project will be completed by a specific date?
5. At any particular date, is the project on schedule, behind schedule, or ahead of schedule?
6. On any given date, is the money spent equal to, less than, or greater than the budgeted amount?
7. Are there enough resources available to finish the project on time?

General Foundry Example of PERT/CPM

General Foundry, Inc., a metalworks plant in Milwaukee, has long been trying to avoid the expense of installing air pollution control equipment. The local environmental protection group has recently given the foundry 16 weeks to install a complex air filter system on its main smokestack. General Foundry was warned that it will be forced to close unless the device is installed in the allotted period. Lester Harky, the managing partner, wants to make sure that installation of the filtering system progresses smoothly and on time.

The first step is to define the project and all project activities.

When the project begins, the building of the internal components for the device (activity *A*) and the modifications that are necessary for the floor and roof (activity *B*) can be started. The construction of the collection stack (activity *C*) can begin once the internal components are completed, and pouring of the new concrete floor and installation of the frame (activity *D*) can be completed as soon as the roof and floor have been modified. After the collection stack has been constructed, the high-temperature burner can be built (activity *E*), and the installation of the pollution control system (activity *F*) can begin. The air pollution device can be installed (activity *G*) after the high-temperature burner has been built, the concrete floor has been poured and the frame has been installed (activity *D*). Finally, after the control system and pollution device have been installed, the system can be inspected and tested (activity *H*).

All of these activities seem rather confusing and complex until they are placed in a network. First, all of the activities must be listed. This information is shown in Table 11.1. We see in the table that before the collection stack can be constructed (activity *C*), the internal components

TABLE 11.1

Activities and Immediate Predecessors for General Foundry, Inc.

ACTIVITY	DESCRIPTION	IMMEDIATE PREDECESSORS
A	Build internal components	—
B	Modify roof and floor	—
C	Construct collection stack	A
D	Pour concrete and install frame	B
E	Build high-temperature burner	C
F	Install control system	C
G	Install air pollution device	D, E
H	Inspect and test	F, G

MODELING IN THE REAL WORLD

PERT Helps Change the Face of British Airways

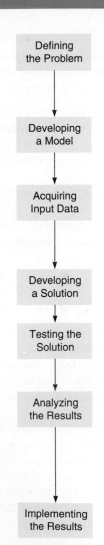

Defining the Problem

Developing a Model

Acquiring Input Data

Developing a Solution

Testing the Solution

Analyzing the Results

Implementing the Results

Defining the Problem

British Airways (BA) wanted to rejuvenate its image using international design consultants to help develop a new identity. The "makeover" was to be completed in all areas of BA's public image as quickly as possible.

Developing a Model

Using a computerized project management package—PERTMASTER from Abex Software—a BA team constructed a PERT model of all tasks involved.

Acquiring Input Data

Data were collected from each department involved. Printers were asked to develop time estimates for new company stationery, tickets, timetables, and baggage tags; clothing suppliers for uniforms; and Boeing Corp. for all the tasks involved in remaking the inside and outside of BA's jets.

Developing a Solution

All the data were entered into PERTMASTER for a schedule and critical path.

Testing the Solution

The resulting schedule did not please BA management. Boeing could not prepare a huge 747 in time for a December 4 gala launch date. Uniform designs were also going to delay the entire project.

Analyzing the Results

An analysis of the earliest possible date that all items for a refurbished airplane could be ready (new paint, upholstery, carpets, trim, and so on) revealed that there were just sufficient materials to totally convert a smaller Boeing 737 that was available in the Seattle plant. Critical path analysis also showed that uniforms—the work of British designer Roland Klein—would have to be launched six months later in a separate ceremony.

Implementing the Results

The smaller 737 was outfitted just in time for a brilliant light show in an auditorium specially built in a Heathrow Airport hangar. Ground vehicles were also prepared in time.

Source: Based on *Industrial Management and Data Systems* (March–April 1986): 6–7.

FIGURE 11.1

Network for General Foundry, Inc.

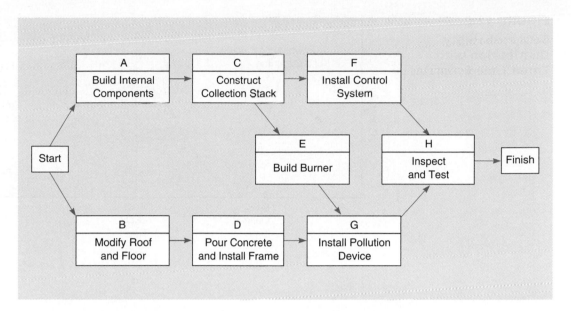

Immediate predecessors are determined in the second step.

must be built (activity A). Thus, activity A is the **immediate predecessor** of activity C. Similarly, both activities D and E must be performed just prior to installation of the air pollution device (activity G).

Drawing the PERT/CPM Network

Activities and events are drawn and connected in the third step.

Once the activities have all been specified (step 1 of the PERT procedure) and management has decided which activities must precede others (step 2), the network can be drawn (step 3).

There are two common techniques for drawing PERT networks. The first is called **activity-on-node (AON)** because the nodes represent the activities. The second is called **activity-on-arc (AOA)** because the arcs are used to represent the activities. In this book, we present the AON technique, as this is easier and is often used in commercial software.

In constructing an AON network, there should be one node representing the start of the project and one node representing the finish of the project. There will be one node (represented as a rectangle in this chapter) for each activity. Figure 11.1 gives the entire network for General Foundry. The arcs (arrows) are used to show the predecessors for the activities. For example, the arrows leading into activity G indicate that both D and E are immediate predecessors for G.

Activity Times

The next step in both CPM and PERT is to assign estimates of the time required to complete each activity. For some projects, such as construction projects, the time to complete each activity may be known with certainty. The developers of CPM assigned just one time estimate to each activity. These times are then used to find the critical path, as described in the sections that follow.

The fourth step is to assign activity times.

However, for one-of-a-kind projects or for new jobs, providing **activity time estimates** is not always an easy task. Without solid historical data, managers are often uncertain about the activity times. For this reason, the developers of PERT employed a probability distribution based on three time estimates for each activity. A weighted average of these times is used with PERT in place of the single time estimate used with CPM, and these averages are used to find the critical path. The time estimates in PERT are

Optimistic time (a) = time an activity will take if everything goes as well as possible. There should be only a small probability (say, $1/100$) of this occurring.

Pessimistic time (b) = time an activity would take assuming very unfavorable conditions. There should also be only a small probability that the activity will really take this long.

Most likely time (m) = most realistic time estimate to complete the activity.

The beta probability distribution is often used.

PERT often assumes that time estimates follow the **beta probability distribution** (see Figure 11.2). This continuous distribution has been found to be appropriate, in many cases, for determining an expected value and variance for activity completion times.

FIGURE 11.2
Beta Probability Distribution with Three Time Estimates

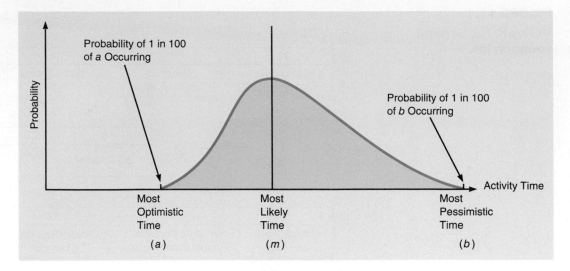

To find the **expected activity time** (t), the beta distribution weights the estimates as follows:

$$t = \frac{a + 4m + b}{6} \qquad (11\text{-}1)$$

To compute the dispersion or **variance of activity completion time**, we use this formula:*

$$\text{Variance} = \left(\frac{b - a}{6}\right)^2 \qquad (11\text{-}2)$$

Table 11.2 shows General Foundry's optimistic, most likely, and pessimistic time estimates for each activity. It also reveals the expected time (t) and variance for each of the activities, as computed with Equations 11-1 and 11-2.

How to Find the Critical Path

Once the expected completion time for each activity has been determined, we accept it as the actual time of that task. Variability in times will be considered later.

Although Table 11.2 indicates that the total expected time for all eight of General Foundry's activities is 25 weeks, it is obvious in Figure 11.3 that several of the tasks can be taking place simultaneously. To find out just how long the project will take, we perform the critical path analysis for the network.

The fifth step is to compute the longest path through the network—the critical path.

The *critical path* is the longest time path route through the network. If Lester Harky wants to reduce the total project time for General Foundry, he will have to reduce the length of some activity on the critical path. Conversely, any delay of an activity on the critical path will delay completion of the entire project.

To find the critical path, we need to determine the following quantities for each activity in the network:

1. **Earliest start (ES) time**: the earliest time an activity can begin without violation of immediate predecessor requirements
2. **Earliest finish (EF) time**: the earliest time at which an activity can end
3. **Latest start (LS) time**: the latest time an activity can begin without delaying the entire project
4. **Latest finish (LF) time**: the latest time an activity can end without delaying the entire project

---

*This formula is based on the statistical concept that from one end of the beta distribution to the other are 6 standard deviations (± 3 standard deviations from the mean). Because $b - a$ is 6 standard deviations, 1 standard deviation is $(b - a)/6$. Thus, the variance is $[(b - a)/6]^2$.

TABLE 11.2 Time Estimates (Weeks) for General Foundry, Inc.

ACTIVITY	OPTIMISTIC, a	MOST LIKELY, m	PESSIMISTIC, b	EXPECTED TIME, $t = [(a + 4m + b)/6]$	VARIANCE, $[(b - a)/6]^2$
A	1	2	3	2	$\left(\dfrac{3 - 1}{6}\right)^2 = \dfrac{4}{36}$
B	2	3	4	3	$\left(\dfrac{4 - 2}{6}\right)^2 = \dfrac{4}{36}$
C	1	2	3	2	$\left(\dfrac{3 - 1}{6}\right)^2 = \dfrac{4}{36}$
D	2	4	6	4	$\left(\dfrac{6 - 2}{6}\right)^2 = \dfrac{16}{36}$
E	1	4	7	4	$\left(\dfrac{7 - 1}{6}\right)^2 = \dfrac{36}{36}$
F	1	2	9	3	$\left(\dfrac{9 - 1}{6}\right)^2 = \dfrac{64}{36}$
G	3	4	11	5	$\left(\dfrac{11 - 3}{6}\right)^2 = \dfrac{64}{36}$
H	1	2	3	$\underline{2}$	$\left(\dfrac{3 - 1}{6}\right)^2 = \dfrac{4}{36}$
				25	

In the network, we represent these times as well as the activity times (t) in the nodes, as seen here:

ACTIVITY	t
ES	EF
LS	LF

We first show how to determine the earliest times. When we find these, the latest times can be computed.

FIGURE 11.3

General Foundry's Network with Expected Activity Times

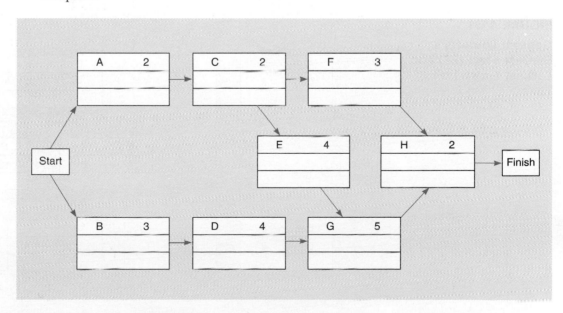

EARLIEST TIMES   There are two basic rules to follow when computing ES and EF times. The first rule is for the earliest finish time, which is computed as follows:

$$\text{Earliest finish time} = \text{Earliest start time} + \text{Expected activity time}$$
$$EF = ES + t \tag{11-3}$$

Also, before any activity can be started, all of its predecessor activities must be completed. In other words, we search for the largest EF for all of the immediate predecessors in determining ES. The second rule is for the earliest start time, which is computed as follows:

The ES is the largest EF of the immediate predecessors.

$$\text{Earliest start} = \text{Largest of the earliest finish times of immediate predecessors}$$
$$ES = \text{Largest EF of immediate predecessors}$$

The start of the whole project will be set at time zero. Therefore, any activity that has no predecessors will have an earliest start time of zero. So ES = 0 for both *A* and *B* in the General Foundry problem, as seen here:

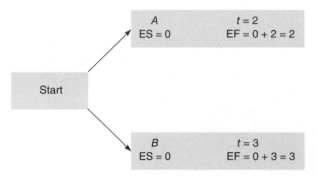

The earliest times are found by beginning at the start of the project and making a forward pass through the network.

The rest of the earliest times for General Foundry are shown in Figure 11.4. These are found using a **forward pass** through the network. At each step, EF = ES + *t*, and ES is the largest EF of the predecessors. Notice that activity *G* has an earliest start time of 8, since both *D* (with EF = 7) and *E* (with EF = 8) are immediate predecessors. Activity *G* cannot start until both predecessors are finished, and so we choose the larger of the earliest finish times for these. Thus, *G* has ES = 8. The finish time for the project will be 15 weeks, which is the EF for activity *H*.

LATEST TIMES   The next step in finding the critical path is to compute the latest start (LS) time and the latest finish (LF) time for each activity. We do this by making a **backward pass** through the network, that is, starting at the finish and working backward.

FIGURE 11.4

General Foundry's Earliest Start (ES) and Earliest Finish (EF) Times

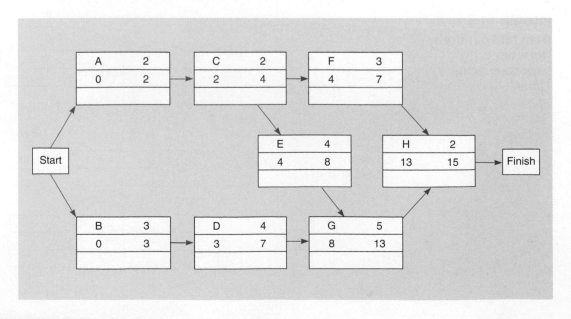

FIGURE 11.5

General Foundry's Latest Start (LS) and Latest Finish (LF) Times

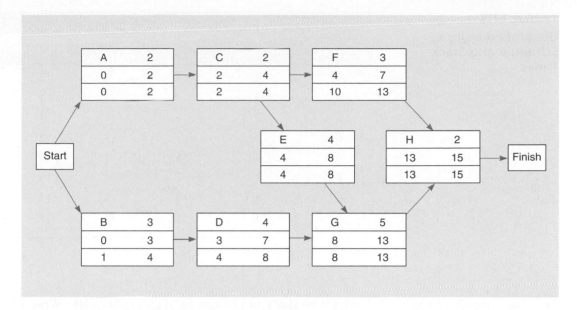

There are two basic rules to follow when computing the latest times. The first rule involves the latest start time, which is computed as

The latest times are found by beginning at the finish of the project and making a backward pass through the network.

$$\text{Latest start time} = \text{Latest finish time} - \text{Activity time}$$
$$\text{LS} = \text{LF} - t \tag{11-4}$$

Also, since all immediate predecessors must be finished before an activity can begin, the latest start time for an activity determines the latest finish time for its immediate predecessors. If an activity is the immediate predecessor for two or more activities, it must be finished so that all following activities can begin by their latest start times. Thus, the second rule involves the latest finish time, which is computed as

The LF is the smallest LS of the activities that immediately follow.

$$\text{Latest finish time} = \text{Smallest of latest start times for following activities, or}$$
$$\text{LF} = \text{Smallest LS of following activities}$$

To compute the latest times, we start at the finish and work backwards. Since the finish time for the General Foundry project is 15, activity *H* has LF = 15. The latest start for activity *H* is

$$\text{LS} = \text{LF} - t = 15 - 2 = 13 \text{ weeks}$$

Continuing to work backward, this latest start time of 13 becomes the latest finish time for immediate predecessors *F* and *G*. All of the latest times are shown in Figure 11.5. Notice that for activity *C*, which is the immediate predecessor for two activities (*E* and *F*), the latest finish time is the smaller of the latest start times (4 and 10) for activities *E* and *F*.

IN ACTION   Project Management In an Office-Less, Cloud-Based Work Environment

Stillwater Associates is an energy supply chain consulting company with a unique characteristic: They are an *office-less* company. They do not have a building, per se. All of their associates are scattered across the country. Needless to say, in some ways, not having a "brick and mortar" office helped Stillwater. For example, Stillwater's overhead costs are extremely low when compared to their competition. In other ways, however, not having an office hindered the company . . . especially in the area of project management. Employees were duplicating effort and experienced trouble communicating. As a result, schedules slipped, budgets busted, and clients became irritated.

Stillwater turned to Project Insight, a software tool by Metafuse, Inc. Project Insight allowed Stillwater employees to "log-in" to particular projects from any work site and from any platform. As soon as Stillwater Associates' employees logged in, the software kept track of their hours on any task, on any project, from anywhere.

As a result, Stillwater Associates budget overruns became a thing of the past, allowing their employees to more effectively respond to their client's needs.

Source: Project Insight Drives Budget Management Success at Stillwater Associates, *Wall Street Journal*, May 21, 2013, <online.wsj.com>

TABLE 11.3
General Foundry's Schedule and Slack Times

ACTIVITY	EARLIEST START, ES	EARLIEST FINISH, EF	LATEST START, LS	LATEST FINISH, LF	SLACK, LS − ES	ON CRITICAL PATH?
A	0	2	0	2	0	Yes
B	0	3	1	4	1	No
C	2	4	2	4	0	Yes
D	3	7	4	8	1	No
E	4	8	4	8	0	Yes
F	4	7	10	13	6	No
G	8	13	8	13	0	Yes
H	13	15	13	15	0	Yes

Slack time is free time for an activity.

CONCEPT OF SLACK IN CRITICAL PATH COMPUTATIONS When ES, LS, EF, and LF have been determined, it is a simple matter to find the amount of **slack time**, or free time, that each activity has. Slack is the length of time an activity can be delayed without delaying the whole project. Mathematically,

$$\text{Slack} = \text{LS} - \text{ES}, \quad \text{or} \quad \text{Slack} = \text{LF} - \text{EF} \quad (11\text{-}5)$$

Table 11.3 summarizes the ES, EF, LS, LF, and slack times for all of General Foundry's activities. Activity B, for example, has 1 week of slack time since LS − ES = 1 − 0 = 1 (or, similarly, LF − EF = 4 − 3 = 1). This means that it can be delayed up to 1 week without causing the project to run any longer than expected.

Critical activities have no slack time.

On the other hand, activities A, C, E, G, and H have *no* slack time; this means that none of them can be delayed without delaying the entire project. Because of this, they are called *critical activities* and are said to be on the *critical path*. Lester Harky's critical path is shown in network form in Figure 11.6. The total project completion time (T), 15 weeks, is seen as the largest number in the EF or LF columns of Table 11.3. Industrial managers call this a boundary timetable.

FIGURE 11.6
General Foundry's Critical Path (A–C–E–G–H)

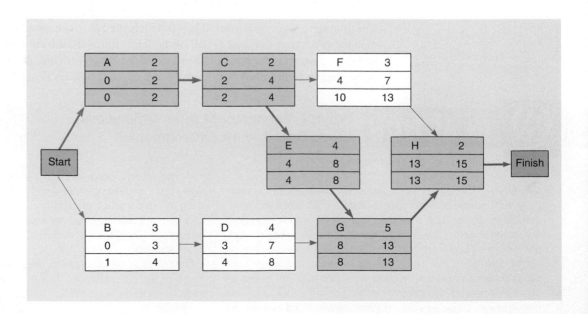

Probability of Project Completion

The **critical path analysis** helped us determine that the foundry's expected project completion time is 15 weeks. Harky knows, however, that if the project is not completed in 16 weeks, General Foundry will be forced to close by environmental controllers. He is also aware that there is significant variation in the time estimates for several activities. Variation in activities that are on the critical path can affect overall project completion—possibly delaying it. This is one occurrence that worries Harky considerably.

Computing project variance is done by summing activity variances along the critical path.

PERT uses the variance of critical path activities to help determine the variance of the overall project. If the activity times are statistically independent, the project variance is computed by summing the variances of the critical activities:

$$\text{Project variance} = \sum \text{variances of activities on the critical path} \qquad (11\text{-}6)$$

From Table 11.2 we know that

CRITICAL ACTIVITY	VARIANCE
A	$4/36$
C	$4/36$
E	$36/36$
G	$64/36$
H	$4/36$

Hence, the project variance is

$$\text{Project variance} = {}^4/_{36} + {}^4/_{36} + {}^{36}/_{36} + {}^{64}/_{36} + {}^4/_{36} = {}^{112}/_{36} = 3.111$$

We know that the standard deviation is just the square root of the variance, so

Computing the standard deviation.

$$\text{Project standard deviation} = \sigma_T = \sqrt{\text{Project variance}}$$
$$= \sqrt{3.111} = 1.76 \text{ weeks}$$

How can this information be used to help answer questions regarding the probability of finishing the project on time? In addition to assuming that the activity times are independent, we also assume that total project completion time follows a normal probability distribution. With

PERT has two assumptions.

these assumptions, the bell-shaped curve shown in Figure 11.7 can be used to represent project

FIGURE 11.7

Probability Distribution for Project Completion Times

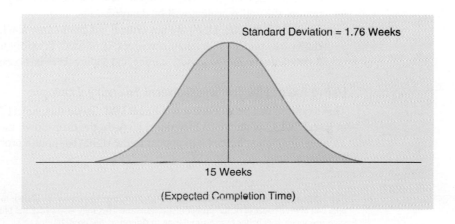

Standard Deviation = 1.76 Weeks

15 Weeks

(Expected Completion Time)

FIGURE 11.8

Probability of General Foundry's Meeting the 16-Week Deadline

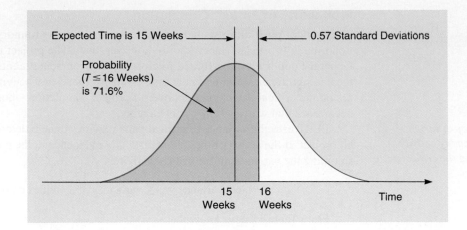

completion dates. It also means that there is a 50% chance that the entire project will be completed in less than the expected 15 weeks and a 50% chance that it will exceed 15 weeks.*

For Harky to find the probability that his project will be finished on or before the 16-week deadline, he needs to determine the appropriate area under the normal curve. The standard normal equation can be applied as follows:

Computing the probability of project completion.

$$Z = \frac{\text{Due date} - \text{Expected date of completion}}{\sigma_T} \tag{11-7}$$

$$= \frac{16 \text{ weeks} - 15 \text{ weeks}}{1.76 \text{ weeks}} = 0.57$$

where

Z is the number of standard deviations the due date or target date lies from the mean or expected completion date.

Referring to the normal table in Appendix *A*, we find a probability of 0.71566. Thus, there is a 71.6% chance that the pollution control equipment can be put in place in 16 weeks or less. This is shown in Figure 11.8.

What PERT Was Able to Provide

PERT has thus far been able to provide Lester Harky with several valuable pieces of management information:

The sixth and final step is to monitor and control the project using the information provided by PERT.

1. The project's expected completion date is 15 weeks.
2. There is a 71.6% chance that the equipment will be in place within the 16-week deadline. PERT can easily find the probability of finishing by any date Harky is interested in.
3. Five activities (*A, C, E, G, H*) are on the critical path. If any one of them is delayed for any reason, the entire project will be delayed.
4. Three activities (*B, D, F*) are not critical but have some slack time built in. This means that Harky can borrow from their resources, if needed, possibly to speed up the entire project.
5. A detailed schedule of activity starting and ending dates has been made available (see Table 11.3).

Using Excel QM for the General Foundry Example

This example can be worked using Excel QM. To do this, select *Excel QM* from the *Add-Ins* tab in Excel 2013, as shown in Program 11.1A. In the drop-down menu, put the cursor over *Project Management*, and choices will appear to the right. To input a problem that is presented in a table

---

*You should be aware that noncritical activities also have variability (as shown in Table 11.2). In fact, a different critical path can evolve because of the probabilistic situation. This may also cause the probability estimates to be unreliable. In such instances, it is better to use simulation to determine the probabilities.

PROGRAM 11.1A

Excel QM Initialization Screen for General Foundry Example with 3 Time Estimate

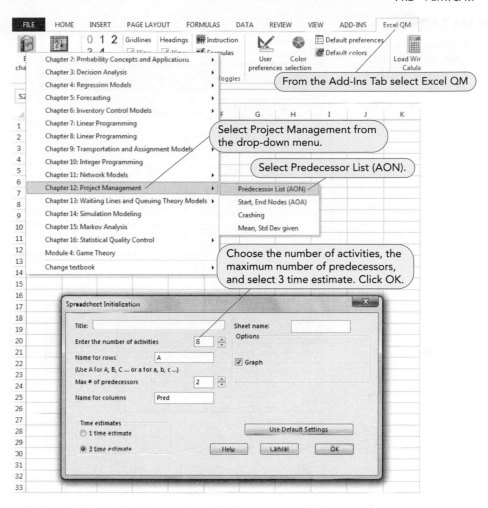

with the immediate predecessors and three time estimates, select *Predecessor List (AON)*, and the initialization window will appear. Specify the number of activities, the maximum number of immediate predecessors for the activities, and select the *3 Time Estimate* option. If you wish to see a Gantt chart, check *Graph*. Click *OK* when finished, and a spreadsheet will appear, with all the necessary rows and columns labeled. For this example, enter the three time estimates in cells B8:D15 and then enter the immediate predecessors in cells C18:D25, as shown in Program 11.1B. No other inputs or steps are required.

As these data are being entered, Excel QM calculates the expected times and variances for all activities, and a table will automatically display the earliest, latest, and slack times for all the activities. A **Gantt chart** is displayed, and this chart shows the critical path and slack time for the activities.

Sensitivity Analysis and Project Management

During any project, the time required to complete an activity can vary from the projected or expected time. If the activity is on the critical path, the total project completion time will change, as discussed previously. In addition to having an impact on the total project completion time, there is also an impact on the earliest start, earliest finish, latest start, latest finish, and slack times for other activities. The exact impact depends on the relationship between the various activities.

In previous sections we define an *immediate predecessor* activity as an activity that comes immediately before a given activity. In general, a *predecessor activity* is one that must be completed before the given activity can be started. Consider activity G (install pollution device) for

PROGRAM 11.1B

Excel QM Input Screen and Solution for General Foundry Example with 3 Time Estimates

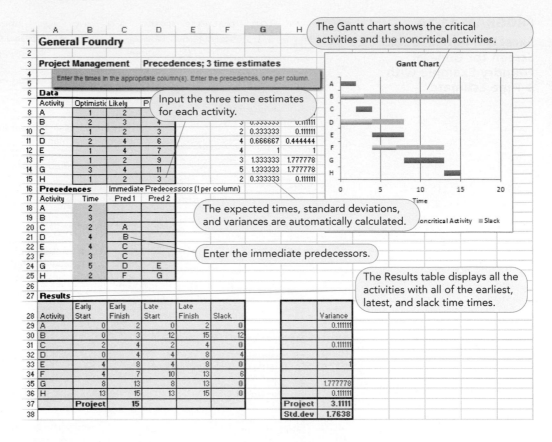

The Gantt chart shows the critical activities and the noncritical activities.

Input the three time estimates for each activity.

The expected times, standard deviations, and variances are automatically calculated.

Enter the immediate predecessors.

The Results table displays all the activities with all of the earliest, latest, and slack time times.

the General Foundry example. As seen previously, this activity is on the critical path. Predecessor activities are *A, B, C, D,* and *E*. All of these activities must be completed before activity *G* can be started. A *successor activity* is an activity that can be started only after the given activity is finished. Activity *H* is the only successor activity for activity *G*. A *parallel activity* is an activity that does not directly depend on the given activity. Again consider activity *G*. Are there any parallel activities for this activity? Looking at the network for General Foundry, it can be seen that activity *F* is a parallel activity of activity *G*.

After predecessor, successor, and parallel activities have been defined, we can explore the impact that an increase (decrease) in an activity time for a critical path activity would have on other activities in the network. The results are summarized in Table 11.4. If the time it takes to complete activity *G* increases, there will be an increase in the earliest start, earliest finish, latest start, and latest finish times for all successor activities. Because these activities follow activity *G*, these times will also increase. Because slack time is equal to latest finish time minus the earliest finish time (or the latest start time minus earliest start time; LF − EF or LS − ES), there will be no change in the slack for successor activities. Because activity *G*

TABLE 11.4

Impact of an Increase (Decrease) in an Activity Time for a Critical Path Activity

ACTIVITY TIME	SUCCESSOR ACTIVITY	PARALLEL ACTIVITY	PREDECESSOR ACTIVITY
Earliest start	Increase (decrease)	No change	No change
Earliest finish	Increase (decrease)	No change	No change
Latest start	Increase (decrease)	Increase (decrease)	No change
Latest finish	Increase (decrease)	Increase (decrease)	No change
Slack	No change	Increase (decrease)	No change

is on the critical path, an increase in activity time will increase the total project competition time. This would mean that the latest finish, latest start, and slack time will also increase for all parallel activities. You can prove this to yourself by completing a backward pass through the network using a higher total project competition time. There are no changes for predecessor activities.

11.3 PERT/Cost

Using PERT/Cost to plan, schedule, monitor, and control project cost helps accomplish the sixth and final step of PERT.

Although PERT is an excellent method of monitoring and controlling project length, it does not consider another very important factor, project *cost*. **PERT/Cost** is a modification of PERT that allows a manager to plan, schedule, monitor, and control cost as well as time.

We begin this section by investigating how costs can be planned and scheduled. Then we see how costs can be monitored and controlled.

Planning and Scheduling Project Costs: Budgeting Process

The overall approach in the budgeting process of a project is to determine how much is to be spent every week or month. This is accomplished as follows:

Four Steps of the Budgeting Process

1. Identify all costs associated with each of the activities. Then add these costs together to get one estimated cost or budget for each activity.
2. If you are dealing with a large project, several activities can be combined into larger work packages. A work *package* is simply a logical collection of activities. Since the General Foundry project we have been discussing is small, each activity will be a work package.
3. Convert the budgeted cost per activity into a cost per time period. To do this, we assume that the cost of completing any activity is spent at a uniform rate over time. Thus, if the budgeted cost for a given activity is $48,000 and the activity's expected time is four weeks, the budgeted cost per week is $12,000 ($=$48,000/4$ weeks).
4. Using the earliest and latest start times, find out how much money should be spent during each week or month to finish the project by the date desired.

BUDGETING FOR GENERAL FOUNDRY Let us apply this budgeting process to the General Foundry problem. The Gantt chart for this problem, shown in Figure 11.9, illustrates this process. In this chart, a horizontal bar shows when each activity will be performed based on the earliest times. To develop a budget schedule, we will determine how much will be spent on each activity during each week and fill these amounts into the chart in place of the bars. Lester Harky has carefully computed the costs associated with each of his eight activities. He has also divided the total budget for each activity by the activity's expected completion time to determine the weekly

FIGURE 11.9

Gantt Chart for General Foundry Example

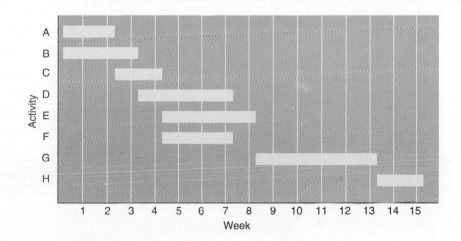

California Needs Project Management for $25 Billion Water Project

The budget crunch in California has affected many lives. Amidst the turmoil, a new project to divert water from the Sacramento River via two enormous tunnels routed to the southern part of the state. The project would take 10 years to finish and is expected to have 50 years of useful life.

Advocates say the water project would improve the water quality, improve sustainability, increase earthquake robustness, minimize overall exports, and decrease demand from existing fish-killing water facilities in the southern part of California. The biggest challenge for the proposed massive double-tunnel, water diversion project will be the coordination of state and federal agencies, administration of the construction and excavation contractors, and the supervision of the overall expenses . . . in other words, the management of the project.

The state of California has estimated that building the two tunnels will cost $14.5 billion, the net present value of the operation and maintenance of the two tunnels over their 50 year useful life equivocates to $4.8 billion, and the ensuing habit restoration would require another $4.1 billion. In this case, sound project management is not just a nicety ... it is a necessity.

Source: California plan to overhaul water system hub to cost $25 billion, *Los Angeles Times*, May 29, 2013, <articles.latimes.com>

budget for the activity. The budget for activity A, for example, is $22,000 (see Table 11.5). Since its expected time (t) is 2 weeks, $11,000 is spent each week to complete the activity. Table 11.5 also provides two pieces of data we found earlier using PERT: the earliest start time (ES) and latest start time (LS) for each activity.

Looking at the total of the budgeted activity costs, we see that the entire project will cost $308,000. Finding the weekly budget will help Harky determine how the project is progressing on a week-to-week basis.

A budget is computed using ES.

The weekly budget for the project is developed from the data in Table 11.5. The earliest start time for activity A, for example, is 0. Because A takes 2 weeks to complete, its weekly budget of $11,000 should be spent in weeks 1 and 2. For activity B, the earliest start time is 0, the expected completion time is 3 weeks, and the budgeted cost per week is $10,000. Thus, $10,000 should be spent for activity B in each of weeks 1, 2, and 3. Using the earliest start time, we can find the exact weeks during which the budget for each activity should be spent. These weekly amounts can be summed for all activities to arrive at the weekly budget for the entire project. This is shown in Table 11.6. Notice the similarities between this chart and the Gantt chart shown in Figure 11.9.

Do you see how the weekly budget for the project (total per week) is determined in Table 11.6? The only two activities that can be performed during the first week are activities A and B because their earliest start times are 0. Thus, during the first week, a total of $21,000

TABLE 11.5 Activity Cost for General Foundry, Inc.

ACTIVITY	EARLIEST START TIME, ES	LATEST START TIME, LS	EXPECTED TIME, t	TOTAL BUDGETED COST ($)	BUDGETED COST PER WEEK ($)
A	0	0	2	22,000	11,000
B	0	1	3	30,000	10,000
C	2	2	2	26,000	13,000
D	3	4	4	48,000	12,000
E	4	4	4	56,000	14,000
F	4	10	3	30,000	10,000
G	8	8	5	80,000	16,000
H	13	13	2	16,000	8,000
				Total 308,000	

TABLE 11.6 Budgeted Cost (Thousands of Dollars) for General Foundry, Inc., Using Earliest Start Times

	WEEK															
ACTIVITY	1	2	3	4	5	6	7	8	9	10	11	12	13	14	15	TOTAL
A	11	11														22
B	10	10	10													30
C			13	13												26
D				12	12	12	12									48
E					14	14	14	14								56
F					10	10	10									30
G									16	16	16	16	16			80
H														8	8	16
																308
Total per week	21	21	23	25	36	36	36	14	16	16	16	16	16	8	8	
Total to date	21	42	65	90	126	162	198	212	228	244	260	276	292	300	308	

should be spent. Because activities A and B are still being performed in the second week, a total of $21,000 should also be spent during that period. The earliest start time for activity C is at the end of week 2 (ES = 2 for activity C). Thus, $13,000 is spent on activity C in both weeks 3 and 4. Because activity B is also being performed during week 3, the total budget in week 3 is $23,000. Similar computations are done for all activities to determine the total budget for the entire project for each week. Then these weekly totals can be added to determine the total amount that should be spent to date (total to date). This information is displayed in the bottom row of the table.

Another budget is computed using LS.

Those activities along the critical path must spend their budgets at the times shown in Table 11.6. The activities that are *not* on the critical path, however, can be started at a later date. This concept is embodied in the latest starting time, LS, for each activity. Thus, if *latest starting times* are used, another budget can be obtained. This budget will delay the expenditure of funds until the last possible moment. The procedures for computing the budget when LS is used are the same as when ES is used. The results of the new computations are shown in Table 11.7.

TABLE 11.7 Budgeted Cost (Thousands of Dollars) for General Foundry, Inc., Using Latest Start Times

ACTIVITY	1	2	3	4	5	6	7	8	9	10	11	12	13	14	15	TOTAL
A	11	11														22
B		10	10	10												30
C			13	13												26
D					12	12	12	12								48
E					14	14	14	14								56
F											10	10	10			30
G									16	16	16	16	16			80
H														8	8	16
																308
Total per week	11	21	23	23	26	26	26	26	16	16	26	26	26	8	8	
Total to date	11	32	55	78	104	130	156	182	198	214	240	266	292	300	308	

FIGURE 11.10

Budget Ranges for General Foundry

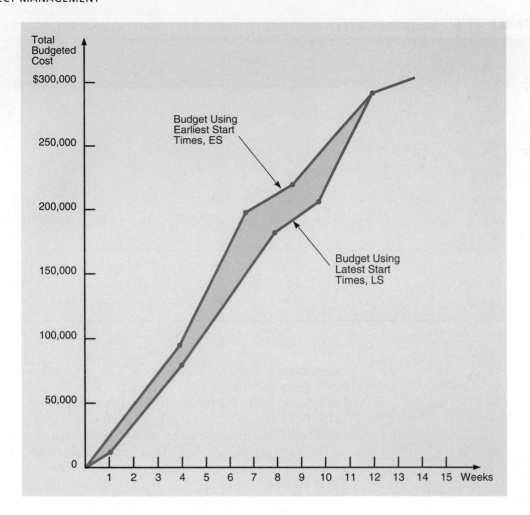

Compare the budgets given in Tables 11.6 and 11.7. The amount that should be spent to date (total to date) for the budget in Table 11.7 uses fewer financial resources in the first few weeks. This is because this budget is prepared using the latest start times. Thus, the budget in Table 11.7 shows the *latest* possible time that funds can be expended and still finish the project on time. The budget in Table 11.6 reveals the *earliest* possible time that funds can be expended. Therefore, a manager can choose any budget that falls between the budgets presented in these two tables. These two tables form feasible budget ranges. This concept is illustrated in Figure 11.10.

The budget ranges for General Foundry were established by plotting the total-to-date budgets for ES and LS. Lester Harky can use any budget between these feasible ranges and still complete the air pollution project on time. Budgets like the ones shown in Figure 11.10 are normally developed before the project is started. Then, as the project is being completed, funds expended should be monitored and controlled.

Although there are cash flow and money management advantages to delaying activities until their latest start times, such delays can create problems with finishing the project on schedule. If an activity is not started until its latest start time, there is no slack remaining. Any subsequent delays in this activity will delay the project. For this reason, it may not be desirable to schedule all activities to start at the latest start time.

Is the project on schedule and within its budget?

Monitoring and Controlling Project Costs

The purpose of monitoring and controlling project costs is to ensure that the project is progressing on schedule and that cost overruns are kept to a minimum. The status of the entire project should be checked periodically.

Lester Harky wants to know how his air pollution project is going. It is now the sixth week of the 15-week project. Activities *A, B,* and *C* have been finished. These activities incurred costs of $20,000, $36,000, and $26,000, respectively. Activity *D* is only 10% completed and so far the cost expended has been $6,000. Activity *E* is 20% completed with an incurred cost of $20,000,

TABLE 11.8 Monitoring and Controlling Budgeted Cost

ACTIVITY	TOTAL BUDGETED COST ($)	PERCENT OF COMPLETION	VALUE OF WORK COMPLETED ($)	ACTUAL COST ($)	ACTIVITY DIFFERENCE ($)
A	22,000	100	22,000	20,000	−2,000
B	30,000	100	30,000	36,000	6,000
C	26,000	100	26,000	26,000	0
D	48,000	10	4,800	6,000	1,200
E	56,000	20	11,200	20,000	8,800
F	30,000	20	6,000	4,000	−2,000
G	80,000	0	0	0	0
H	16,000	0	0	0	0
		Total	100,000	112,000	12,000
					Overrun

and activity *F* is 20% completed with an incurred cost of $4,000. Activities *G* and *H* have not been started. Is the air pollution project on schedule? What is the value of work completed? Are there any cost overruns?

The value of work completed, or the budgeted cost to date for any activity, can be computed as follows:

$$\text{Value of work completed} = (\text{Percentage of work completed}) \times (\text{Total activity budget}) \quad (11\text{-}8)$$

The activity difference is also of interest:

$$\text{Activity difference} = \text{Actual cost} - \text{Value of work completed} \quad (11\text{-}9)$$

If an activity difference is negative, there is a cost underrun, but if the number is positive, there has been a cost overrun.

Compute the value of work completed by multiplying budgeted cost times percent of completion.

Table 11.8 provides this information for General Foundry. The second column contains the total budgeted cost (from Table 11.6), and the third column contains the percent of completion. With these data and the actual cost expended for each activity, we can compute the value of work completed and the overruns or underruns for every activity.

One way to measure the value of the work completed is to multiply the total budgeted cost times the percent of completion for every activity.* Activity *D*, for example, has a value of work completed of $4,800 (=$48,000 times 10%). To determine the amount of overrun or underrun for any activity, the value of work completed is subtracted from the actual cost. These differences can be added to determine the overrun or underrun for the project. As you see, at week 6 there is a $12,000 cost overrun. Furthermore, the value of work completed is only $100,000, and the actual cost of the project to date is $112,000. How do these costs compare with the budgeted costs for week 6? If Harky had decided to use the budget for earliest start times (see Table 11.6) we can see that $162,000 should have been spent. Thus, the project is behind schedule and there are cost overruns. Harky needs to move faster on this project to finish on time, and he must control future costs carefully to try to eliminate the current cost overrun of $12,000. To monitor and control costs, the budgeted amount, the value of work completed, and the actual costs should be computed periodically.

In the next section we see how a project can be shortened by spending additional money. The technique is called crashing and is part of the critical path method (CPM).

---

*The percentage of completion for each activity can be measured in other ways as well. For example, one might examine the ratio of labor hours expended to total labor hours estimated.

IN ACTION   Small Companies Utilize Project Management in Five Phases

Recently, small companies have incorporated project management tools into their workplaces. For small companies, proprietors and managers assign activities in the project to employees, including themselves. Researchers have identified five basic phases of a project to help small businesses. These five are conception, planning and design, execution, control, and closing.

Conception
During conception, small business decision makers integrate their ideas and align them with the company's goals. The decision to go forward with the project is made during this phase.

Planning and Design
The second phase involves determining the tasks and milestones that need to happen for the project to be successful. It also involves the assignment of activities to departments and preparing the PERT network.

Execution
Beginning at the project's start is the execution phase. Managers direct employees to perform tasks and make note of their completion times.

Control
The control phase can overlap the execution phase above and involves ensuring deadlines and milestones are met on time and on budget. Resources may need to be re-allocated during this phase.

Closing
This phase is aptly named as presentations are performed, analyses are finished, and reports are filed.

Source: Major Activities in Project Management Phases, *Houston Chronicle*, May 21, 2013, <smallbusiness.chron.com>

11.4   Project Crashing

Shortening a project is called crashing.

At times, projects have deadlines that may be impossible to meet using the normal procedures for completion of the project. However, by using overtime, working weekends, hiring extra workers, or using extra equipment, it may be possible to finish a project in less time than is normally required. However, the cost of the project will usually increase as a result. When CPM was developed, the possibility of reducing the project completion time was recognized; this process is called **crashing**.

When crashing a project, the *normal time* for each activity is used to find the critical path. The *normal cost* is the cost for completing the activity using normal procedures. If the project completion time using normal procedures meets the deadline that has been imposed, there is no problem. However, if the deadline is before the normal project completion time, some extraordinary measures must be taken. Another set of times and costs is then developed for each activity. The *crash time* is the shortest possible activity time, and this requires the use of additional resources. The *crash cost* is the price of completing the activity in an earlier-than-normal time. If a project must be crashed, it is desirable to do this at the least additional cost.

Project crashing with CPM involves four steps:

Four Steps of Project Crashing

1. Find the normal critical path and identify the critical activities.
2. Compute the crash cost per week (or other time period) for all activities in the network. This process uses the following formula:*

$$\text{Crash cost/Time period} = \frac{\text{Crash cost} - \text{Normal cost}}{\text{Normal time} - \text{Crash time}} \qquad (11\text{-}10)$$

3. Select the activity on the critical path with the smallest crash cost per week. Crash this activity to the maximum extent possible or to the point at which your desired deadline has been reached.
4. Check to be sure that the critical path you were crashing is still critical. Often, a reduction in activity time along the critical path causes a noncritical path or paths to become critical. If the critical path is still the longest path through the network, return to step 3. If not, find the new critical path and return to step 3.

*This formula assumes that crash costs are linear. If they are not, adjustments must be made.

TABLE 11.9 Normal and Crash Data for General Foundry, Inc.

ACTIVITY	TIME (WEEKS)		COST ($)		CRASH COST PER WEEK ($)	CRITICAL PATH?
	NORMAL	CRASH	NORMAL	CRASH		
A	2	1	22,000	23,000	1,000	Yes
B	3	1	30,000	34,000	2,000	No
C	2	1	26,000	27,000	1,000	Yes
D	4	3	48,000	49,000	1,000	No
E	4	2	56,000	58,000	1,000	Yes
F	3	2	30,000	30,500	500	No
G	5	2	80,000	86,000	2,000	Yes
H	2	1	16,000	19,000	3,000	Yes

General Foundry Example

Suppose that General Foundry had been given 14 weeks instead of 16 weeks to install the new pollution control equipment or face a court-ordered shutdown. Or suppose that there was a bonus on the line for Lester if the equipment is installed in 12 weeks or less. As you recall, the length of Lester Harky's critical path was 15 weeks. What can he do? We see that Harky cannot possibly meet the deadline unless he is able to shorten some of the activity times.

General Foundry's normal and crash times and normal and crash costs are shown in Table 11.9. Note, for example, that activity B's normal time is 3 weeks (this estimate was also used for PERT) and its crash time is 1 week. This means that the activity can be shortened by 2 weeks if extra resources are provided. The normal cost is $30,000, and the crash cost is $34,000. This implies that crashing activity B will cost General Foundry an additional $4,000. Crash costs are assumed to be linear. As shown in Figure 11.11, activity B's crash cost per week is $2,000. Crash costs for all other activities can be computed in a similar fashion. Then steps 3 and 4 can be applied to reduce the project's completion time.

FIGURE 11.11

Crash and Normal Times and Costs for Activity B

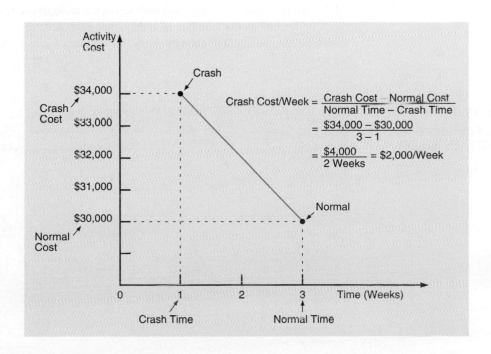

Activities A, C, and E are on the critical path, and each have a minimum crash cost per week of $1,000. Harky can crash activity A by 1 week to reduce the project completion time to 14 weeks. The cost is an additional $1,000.

There are now two critical paths.

At this stage, there are two critical paths. The original critical path consists of activities A, C, E, G, and H, with a total completion time of 14 weeks. The new critical path consists of activities B, D, G, and H, also with a total completion time of 14 weeks. Any further crashing must be done to both critical paths. For example, if Harky wants to reduce the project completion time by an additional 2 weeks, both paths must be reduced. This can be done by reducing activity G, which is on both critical paths, by two weeks for an additional cost of $2,000 per week. The total completion time would be 12 weeks, and total crashing cost would be $5,000 ($1,000 to reduce activity A by one week and $4,000 to reduce activity G by two weeks).

For small networks, such as General Foundry's, it is possible to use the four-step procedure to find the least cost of reducing the project completion dates. For larger networks, however, this approach is difficult and impractical, and more sophisticated techniques, such as linear programming, must be employed.

Project Crashing with Linear Programming

Linear programming (see Chapters 7 and 8) is another approach to finding the best project crashing schedule. We illustrate its use on General Foundry's network. The data needed are derived from Table 11.9 and Figure 11.12.

The first step is to define decision variables for the linear program.

We begin by defining the decision variables. If X is the earliest finish time for an activity, then

$$X_A = \text{EF for activity } A$$
$$X_B = \text{EF for activity } B$$
$$X_C = \text{EF for activity } C$$
$$X_D = \text{EF for activity } D$$
$$X_E = \text{EF for activity } E$$
$$X_F = \text{EF for activity } F$$
$$X_G = \text{EF for activity } G$$
$$X_H = \text{EF for activity } H$$
$$X_{\text{start}} = \text{start time for project (usually 0)}$$
$$X_{\text{finish}} = \text{earliest finish time for the project}$$

Although the starting node has a variable (X_{start}) associated with it, this is not necessary since it will be given a value of 0, and this could be used instead of the variable.

Y is defined as the number of weeks that each activity is crashed. Y_A is the number of weeks we decide to crash activity A, Y_B the amount of crash time used for activity B, and so on, up to Y_H.

FIGURE 11.12

General Foundry's Network with Activity Times

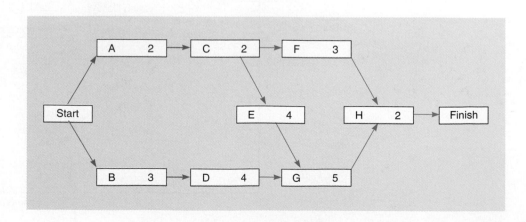

The next step is to determine the objective function.

OBJECTIVE FUNCTION Since the objective is to minimize the cost of crashing the total project, our LP objective function is

$$\text{Minimize crash cost} = 1{,}000Y_A + 2{,}000Y_B + 1{,}000Y_C + 1{,}000Y_D + 1{,}000Y_E$$
$$+ 500Y_F + 2{,}000Y_G + 3{,}000Y_H$$

(These cost coefficients were drawn from the sixth column of Table 11.9.)

Crash constraints are determined next.

CRASH TIME CONSTRAINTS Constraints are required to ensure that each activity is not crashed more than its maximum allowable crash time. The maximum for each Y variable is the difference between the normal time and the crash time (from Table 11.9):

$$Y_A \leq 1$$
$$Y_B \leq 2$$
$$Y_C \leq 1$$
$$Y_D \leq 1$$
$$Y_E \leq 2$$
$$Y_F \leq 1$$
$$Y_G \leq 3$$
$$Y_H \leq 1$$

The final step is to determine event constraints.

PROJECT COMPLETION CONSTRAINT This constraint specifies that the last event must take place before the project deadline date. If Harky's project must be crashed down to 12 weeks, then

$$X_{\text{finish}} \leq 12$$

CONSTRAINTS DESCRIBING THE NETWORK The final set of constraints describes the structure of the network. Every activity will have one constraint for each of its predecessors. The form of these constraints is

$$\text{Earliest finish time} \geq \text{Earliest finish time for predecessor} + \text{Activity time}$$
$$EF \geq EF_{\text{predecessor}} + (t - Y)$$

or
$$X \geq X_{\text{predecessor}} + (t - Y)$$

The activity time is given as $t - Y$, or the normal activity time minus the time saved by crashing. We know $EF = ES + \text{Activity time}$, and $ES = \text{Largest EF of predecessors}$.

We begin by setting the start of the project to time zero: $X_{\text{start}} = 0$.

For activity A,

$$X_A \geq X_{\text{start}} + (2 - Y_A)$$

or
$$X_A - X_{\text{start}} + Y_A \geq 2$$

For activity B,

$$X_B \geq X_{\text{start}} + (3 - Y_B)$$

or
$$X_B - X_{\text{start}} + Y_B \geq 3$$

For activity C,

$$X_C \geq X_A + (2 - Y_C)$$

or
$$X_C - X_A + Y_C \geq 2$$

For activity D,

$$X_D \geq X_B + (4 - Y_D)$$

or
$$X_D - X_B + Y_D \geq 4$$

For activity E,

$$X_E \geq X_C + (4 - Y_E)$$

or

$$X_E - X_C + Y_E \geq 4$$

For activity F,

$$X_F \geq X_C + (3 - Y_F)$$

or

$$X_F - X_C + Y_F \geq 3$$

For activity G, we need two constraints since there are two predecessors. The first constraint for activity G is

$$X_G \geq X_D + (5 - Y_G)$$

or

$$X_G - X_D + Y_G \geq 5$$

The second constraint for activity G is

$$X_G \geq X_E + (5 - Y_G)$$

or

$$X_G - X_E + Y_G \geq 5$$

For activity H we need two constraints since there are two predecessors. The first constraint for activity H is

$$X_H \geq X_F + (2 - Y_H)$$

or

$$X_H - X_F + Y_H \geq 2$$

The second constraint for activity H is

$$X_H \geq X_G + (2 - Y_H)$$

or

$$X_H - X_G + Y_H \geq 2$$

To indicate the project is finished when activity H is finished, we have

$$X_{\text{finish}} \geq X_H$$

After adding nonnegativity constraints, this LP problem can be solved for the optimal Y values. This can be done with QM for Windows or Excel QM. Program 11.2 provides the Excel QM solution to this problem.

PROGRAM 11.2

Solution to Crashing Problem via Solver in Excel

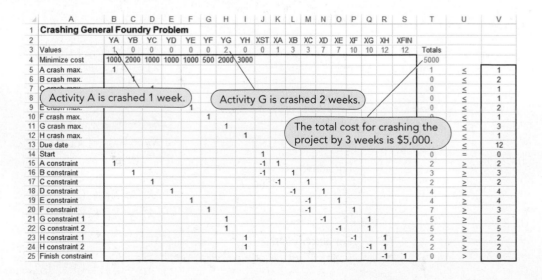

11.5   Other Topics in Project Management

We have seen how to schedule a project and develop budget schedules. However, there are other things that are important and helpful to a project manager. We now briefly introduce these.

Subprojects

For extremely large projects, an activity may be made of several smaller subactivities. Each activity might be viewed as a smaller project or a subproject of the original project. The person in charge of the activity might wish to create a PERT/CPM chart for managing this subproject. Many software packages have the ability to include several levels of subprojects.

Milestones

Major events in a project are often referred to as **milestones**. These are often reflected in Gantt charts and PERT charts to highlight the importance of reaching these events.

Resource Leveling

In addition to managing the time and costs involved in a project, a manager must also be concerned with the resources used in a project. These resources might be equipment or people. In planning a project (and often as part of the work breakdown structure), a manager must identify which resources are needed with each activity. For example, in a construction project there may be several activities requiring the use of heavy equipment such as a crane. If the construction company has only one such crane, then conflicts will occur if two activities requiring the use of this crane are scheduled for the same day. To alleviate problems such as this, **resource leveling** is employed. This means that one or more activities are moved from the earliest start time to another time (no later than the latest start time) so that the resource utilization is more evenly distributed over time. If the resources are construction crews, this is very beneficial in that the crews are kept busy and overtime is minimized.

Software

There are numerous project management software packages on the market for both mainframe computers and personal computers. There are numerous project management software packages on the market. Some are hosted locally while others are cloud-based. Some of them include Microsoft Project, Clarizen (cloud-based), OmniPlan, and OpenProj. They can be used to develop budget schedules, automatically adjust future start times based on the actual start times for prior activities, and level the resource utilization.

Good software for personal computers ranges in price from a few hundred dollars to several thousand dollars. For mainframe computers, software may cost considerably more. Companies have paid several hundred thousand dollars for project management software and support because it helps management make better decisions and keep track of things that would otherwise be unmanageable.

Summary

The fundamentals of PERT and CPM are presented in this chapter. Both of these techniques are excellent for controlling large and complex projects.

PERT is probabilistic and allows three time estimates for each activity. These estimates are used to compute the project's expected completion time, variance, and the probability that the project will be completed by a given date. PERT/Cost, an extension of standard PERT, can be used to plan, schedule, monitor, and control project costs. Using PERT/Cost, it is possible to determine if there are cost overruns or underruns at any point in time. It is also possible to determine whether the project is on schedule.

CPM, although similar to PERT, has the ability to crash projects by reducing their completion time through additional resource expenditures. Finally, we see that linear programming can also be used to crash a network by a desired amount at a minimum cost.

Glossary

Activity A time-consuming job or task that is a key subpart of the total project.

Activity-on-Arc (AOA) A network in which the activities are represented by arcs.

Activity-on-Node (AON) A network in which the activities are represented by nodes. This is the model illustrated in our book.

Activity Time Estimates Three time estimates that are used in determining the expected completion time and variance for an activity in a PERT network.

Backward Pass A procedure that moves from the end of the network to the beginning of the network. It is used in determining the latest finish and latest start times.

Beta Probability Distribution A probability distribution that is often used in computing the expected activity completion times and variances in networks.

CPM Critical path method. A deterministic network technique that is similar to PERT but allows for project crashing.

Crashing The process of reducing the total time that it takes to complete a project by expending additional funds.

Critical Path The series of activities that have zero slack. It is the longest time path through the network. A delay for any activity that is on the critical path will delay the completion of the entire project.

Critical Path Analysis An analysis that determines the total project completion time, the critical path for the project, slack, ES, EF, LS, and LF for every activity.

Earliest Finish Time (EF) The earliest time that an activity can be finished without violation of precedence requirements.

Earliest Start Time (ES) The earliest time that an activity can start without violation of precedence requirements.

Event A point in time that marks the beginning or ending of an activity.

Expected Activity Time The average time that it should take to complete an activity. $t = (a + 4m + b)/6$.

Forward Pass A procedure that moves from the beginning of a network to the end of the network. It is used in determining earliest activity start times and earliest finish times.

Gantt Chart A bar chart indicating when the activities (represented by bars) in a project will be performed.

Immediate Predecessor An activity that must be completed before another activity can be started.

Latest Finish Time (LF) The latest time that an activity can be finished without delaying the entire project.

Latest Start Time (LS) The latest time that an activity can be started without delaying the entire project.

Milestone A major event in a project.

Most Likely Time (m) The amount of time that you would expect it would take to complete the activity.

Network A graphical display of a project that contains both activities and events.

Optimistic Time (a) The shortest amount of time that could be required to complete the activity.

PERT Program evaluation and review technique. A network technique that allows three time estimates for each activity in a project.

PERT/Cost A technique that allows a decision maker to plan, schedule, monitor, and control project *cost* as well as project time.

Pessimistic Time (b) The greatest amount of time that could be required to complete the activity.

Resource Leveling The process of smoothing out the utilization of resources in a project.

Slack Time The amount of time that an activity can be delayed without delaying the entire project. Slack is equal to the latest start time minus the earliest start time, or the latest finish time minus the earliest finish time.

Variance of Activity Completion Time A measure of dispersion of the activity completion time. Variance $= [(b - a)/6]^2$.

Work Breakdown Structure (WBS) A list of the activities that must be performed in a project.

Key Equations

(11-1) $t = \dfrac{a + 4m + b}{6}$

Expected activity completion time for activity.

(11-2) Variance $= \left(\dfrac{b - a}{6}\right)^2$

Activity variance.

(11-3) $EF = ES + t$

Earliest finish time.

(11-4) $LS = LF - t$

Latest start time.

(11-5) Slack $= LS - ES$ *or* Slack $= LF - EF$

Slack time in an activity.

(11-6) Project variance $= \Sigma$ variances of activities on critical path

(11-7) $Z = \dfrac{\text{Due date} - \text{Expected date of completion}}{\sigma_T}$

Number of standard deviations the target date lies from the expected date, using the normal distribution.

(11-8) Value of work completed $=$ (Percentage of work completed) $\times$ (Total activity budget)

(11-9) Activity difference $=$ Actual cost $-$ Value of work completed

(11-10) Crash cost/Time period $= \dfrac{\text{Crash cost} - \text{Normal cost}}{\text{Normal time} - \text{Crash time}}$

The cost in CPM of reducing an activity's length per time period.

Solved Problems

Solved Problem 11-1

To complete the wing assembly for an experimental aircraft, Scott DeWitte has laid out the major steps and seven activities involved. These activities have been labeled A through G in the following table, which also shows their estimated completion times (in weeks) and immediate predecessors. Determine the expected time and variance for each activity.

ACTIVITY	a	m	b	IMMEDIATE PREDECESSORS
A	1	2	3	—
B	2	3	4	—
C	4	5	6	A
D	8	9	10	B
E	2	5	8	C, D
F	4	5	6	B
G	1	2	3	E

Solution

Although not required for this problem, a diagram of all the activities can be useful. A PERT diagram for the wing assembly is shown in Figure 11.13.

FIGURE 11.13

PERT Diagram for Scott DeWitte (Solved Problem 11-1)

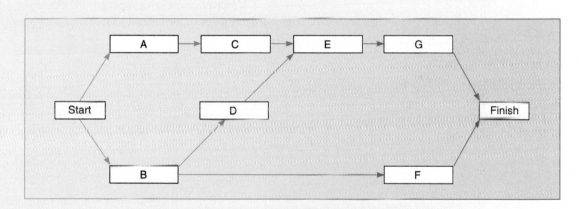

Expected times and variances can be computed using the formulas presented in the chapter. The results are summarized in the following table:

ACTIVITY	EXPECTED TIME (IN WEEKS)	VARIANCE
A	2	$\frac{1}{9}$
B	3	$\frac{1}{9}$
C	5	$\frac{1}{9}$
D	9	$\frac{1}{9}$
E	5	1
F	5	$\frac{1}{9}$
G	2	$\frac{1}{9}$

Solved Problem 11-2

Referring to Solved Problem 11-1, now Scott would like to determine the critical path for the entire wing assembly project as well as the expected completion time for the total project. In addition, he would like to determine the earliest and latest start and finish times for all activities.

Solution

The critical path, earliest start times, earliest finish times, latest start times, and latest finish times can be determined using the procedures outlined in the chapter. The results are shown in Figure 11.14 and are summarized in the following table:

ACTIVITY	ES	EF	LS	LF	SLACK
	ACTIVITY TIME				
A	0	2	5	7	5
B	0	3	0	3	0
C	2	7	7	12	5
D	3	12	3	12	0
E	12	17	12	17	0
F	3	8	14	19	11
G	17	19	17	19	0

Expected project length = 19 weeks
Variance of the critical path = 1.333
Standard deviation of the critical path = 1.155 weeks

FIGURE 11.14

Completed PERT Diagram for Scott DeWitte (Solved Problem 11-2)

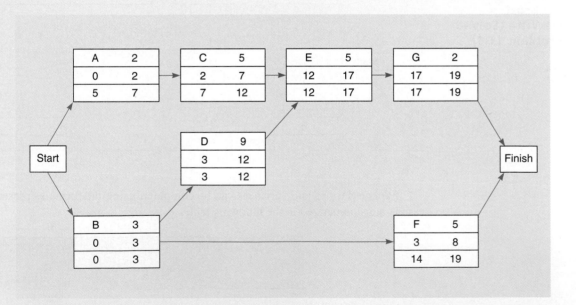

The activities along the critical path are *B, D, E,* and *G*. These activities have zero slack, as shown in the table. The expected project completion time is 19 weeks. The earliest and latest start and finish times are shown in the table.

Self-Test

- Before taking the self-test, refer to the learning objectives at the beginning of the chapter, the notes in the margins, and the glossary at the end of the chapter.
- Use the key at the back of the book to correct your answers.
- Restudy pages that correspond to any questions that you answered incorrectly or material you feel uncertain about.

1. Network models such as PERT and CPM are used
   a. to plan large and complex projects.
   b. to schedule large and complex projects.
   c. to monitor large and complex projects.
   d. to control large and complex projects.
   e. for all of the above.
2. The primary difference between PERT and CPM is that
   a. PERT uses one time estimate.
   b. CPM has three time estimates.
   c. PERT has three time estimates.
   d. with CPM, it is assumed that all activities can be performed at the same time.
3. The earliest start time for an activity is equal to
   a. the largest EF of the immediate predecessors.
   b. the smallest EF of the immediate predecessors.
   c. the largest ES of the immediate predecessors.
   d. the smallest ES of the immediate predecessors.
4. The latest finish time for an activity is found during the backward pass through the network. The latest finish time is equal to
   a. the largest LF of the activities for which it is an immediate predecessor.
   b. the smallest LF of the activities for which it is an immediate predecessor.
   c. the largest LS of the activities for which it is an immediate predecessor.
   d. the smallest LS of the activities for which it is an immediate predecessor.
5. When PERT is used and probabilities are found, one of the assumptions that is made is that
   a. all activities are on the critical path.
   b. activity times are independent.
   c. all activities have the same variance.
   d. the project variance is equal to the sum of the variances of all activities in the project.
   e. all of the above.
6. In PERT, the time estimate b represents
   a. the most optimistic time.
   b. the most likely time.
   c. the most pessimistic time.
   d. the expected time.
   e. none of the above.
7. In PERT, slack time equals
   a. ES + t.
   b. LS − ES.
   c. 0.
   d. EF − ES.
   e. none of the above.

8. The standard deviation for the PERT project is approximately
   a. the square root of the sum of the variances along the critical path.
   b. the sum of the critical path activity standard deviations.
   c. the square root of the sum of the variances of the project activities.
   d. all of the above.
   e. none of the above.
9. The critical path is the
   a. shortest path in a network.
   b. longest path in a network.
   c. path with the smallest variance.
   d. path with the largest variance.
   e. none of the above.
10. If the project completion time is normally distributed and the due date for the project is greater than the expected completion time, then the probability that the project will be finished by the due date is
    a. less than 0.50.
    b. greater than 0.50.
    c. equal to 0.50.
    d. undeterminable without more information.
11. If activity A is not on the critical path, then the slack for A will equal
    a. LF − EF.
    b. EF − ES.
    c. 0.
    d. all of the above.
12. If a project is to be crashed at the minimum possible additional cost, then the first activity to be crashed must be
    a. on the critical path.
    b. the one with the shortest activity time.
    c. the one with the longest activity time.
    d. the one with the lowest cost.
13. _____ activities are ones that will delay the entire project if they are late or delayed.
14. PERT stands for _____.
15. Project crashing can be performed using a _____.
16. PERT can use three estimates for activity time. These three estimates are _____, _____, and _____.
17. The latest start time minus the earliest start time is called the _____ time for any activity.
18. The percent of project completion, value of work completed, and actual activity costs are used to _____ projects.

Discussion Questions and Problems

Discussion Questions

11-1 What are some of the questions that can be answered with PERT and CPM?

11-2 What are the major differences between PERT and CPM?

11-3 What is an activity? What is an event? What is an immediate predecessor?

11-4 Describe how expected activity times and variances can be computed in a PERT network.

11-5 Briefly discuss what is meant by critical path analysis. What are critical path activities, and why are they important?

11-6 What are the earliest activity start time and latest activity start time? How are they computed?

11-7 Describe the meaning of slack and discuss how it can be determined.

11-8 How can we determine the probability that a project will be completed by a certain date? What assumptions are made in this computation?

11-9 Briefly describe PERT/Cost and how it is used.

11-10 What is crashing, and how is it done by hand?

11-11 Why is linear programming useful in CPM crashing?

Problems*

: 11-12 Sid Davidson is the personnel director of Babson and Willcount, a company that specializes in consulting and research. One of the training programs that Sid is considering for the middle-level managers of Babson and Willcount is leadership training. Sid has listed a number of activities that must be completed before a training program of this nature could be conducted. The activities and immediate predecessors appear in the following table:

ACTIVITY	IMMEDIATE PREDECESSORS
A	—
B	—
C	—
D	B
E	A, D
F	C
G	E, F

Develop a network for this problem.

Q: 11-13 Sid Davidson was able to determine the activity times for the leadership training program. He would

like to determine the total project completion time and the critical path. The activity times appear in the following table (see Problem 11-12):

ACTIVITY	TIME (DAYS)
A	2
B	5
C	1
D	10
E	3
F	6
G	8
	35

•11-14 Jean Walker is making plans for spring break at the beaches in Florida. In applying techniques she learned in her quantitative methods class, she has identified the activities that are necessary to prepare for her trip. The following table lists the activities and the immediate predecessors. Draw the network for this project.

ACTIVITY	IMMEDIATE PREDECESSORS
A	—
B	—
C	A
D	B
E	C, D
F	A
G	E, F

Q: 11-15 The following are the activity times for the project in Problem 11-14. Find the earliest, latest, and slack times for each activity. Then find the critical path.

ACTIVITY	TIME (DAYS)
A	3
B	7
C	4
D	2
E	5
F	6
G	3

---

*Note: Q means the problem may be solved with QM for Windows; ✖ means the problem may be solved with Excel QM; and ⚮ means the problem may be solved with QM for Windows and/or Excel.

•11-16 Monohan Machinery specializes in developing weed-harvesting equipment that is used to clear small lakes of weeds. George Monohan, president of Monohan Machinery, is convinced that harvesting weeds is far better than using chemicals to kill weeds. Chemicals cause pollution, and the weeds seem to grow faster after chemicals have been used. George is contemplating the construction of a machine that would harvest weeds on narrow rivers and waterways. The activities that are necessary to build one of these experimental weed-harvesting machines are listed in the following table. Construct a network for these activities.

ACTIVITY	IMMEDIATE PREDECESSORS
A	—
B	—
C	A
D	A
E	B
F	B
G	C, E
H	D, F

Q:11-17 After consulting with Butch Radner, George Monohan was able to determine the activity times for constructing the weed-harvesting machine to be used on narrow rivers. George would like to determine ES, EF, LS, LF, and slack for each activity. The total project completion time and the critical path should also be determined. (See Problem 11-16 for details.) The activity times are shown in the following table:

ACTIVITY	TIME (WEEKS)
A	6
B	5
C	3
D	2
E	4
F	6
G	10
H	7

Q:11-18 A project was planned using PERT with three time estimates. The expected completion time of the project was determined to be 40 weeks. The variance of the critical path is 9.

(a) What is the probability that the project will be finished in 40 weeks or less?

(b) What is the probability that the project takes longer than 40 weeks?

(c) What is the probability that the project will be finished in 46 weeks or less?

(d) What is the probability that the project will take longer than 46 weeks?

(e) The project manager wishes to set the due date for the completion of the project so that there is a 90% chance of finishing on schedule. Thus, there would only be a 10% chance the project would take longer than this due date. What should this due date be?

Q:11-19 Tom Schriber, a director of personnel of Management Resources, Inc., is in the process of designing a program that its customers can use in the job-finding process. Some of the activities include preparing resumés, writing letters, making appointments to see prospective employers, researching companies and industries, and so on. Some of the information on the activities is shown in the following table:

ACTIVITY	DAYS a	m	b	IMMEDIATE PREDECESSORS
A	8	10	12	—
B	6	7	9	—
C	3	3	4	—
D	10	20	30	A
E	6	7	8	C
F	9	10	11	B, D, E
G	6	7	10	B, D, E
H	14	15	16	F
I	10	11	13	F
J	6	7	8	G, H
K	4	7	8	I, J
L	1	2	4	G, H

(a) Construct a network for this problem.

(b) Determine the expected time and variance for each activity.

(c) Determine ES, EF, LS, LF, and slack for each activity.

(d) Determine the critical path and project completion time.

(e) Determine the probability that the project will be finished in 70 days or less.

(f) Determine the probability that the project will be finished in 80 days or less.

(g) Determine the probability that the project will be finished in 90 days or less.

Q:11-20 Using PERT, Ed Rose was able to determine that the expected project completion time for the construction of a pleasure yacht is 21 months and the project variance is 4.

(a) What is the probability that the project will be completed in 17 months or less?

(b) What is the probability that the project will be completed in 20 months or less?

(c) What is the probability that the project will be completed in 23 months or less?

(d) What is the probability that the project will be completed in 25 months or less?

:11-21 The air pollution project discussed in the chapter has progressed over the past several weeks, and it is now the end of week 8. Lester Harky would like to know the value of the work completed, the amount of any cost overruns or underruns for the project, and the extent to which the project is ahead of or behind schedule by developing a table like Table 11.8. The revised cost figures are shown in the following table:

ACTIVITY	PERCENT OF COMPLETION	ACTUAL COST ($)
A	100	20,000
B	100	36,000
C	100	26,000
D	100	44,000
E	50	25,000
F	60	15,000
G	10	5,000
H	10	1,000

:11-22 Fred Ridgeway has been given the responsibility of managing a training and development program. He knows the earliest start time, the latest start time, and the total costs for each activity. This information is given in the following table.

(a) Using earliest start times, determine Fred's total monthly budget.

(b) Using latest start times, determine Fred's total monthly budget.

ACTIVITY	ES	LS	t	TOTAL COST ($1,000s)
A	0	0	6	10
B	1	4	2	14
C	3	3	7	5
D	4	9	3	6
E	6	6	10	14
F	14	15	11	13
G	12	18	2	4
H	14	14	11	6
I	18	21	6	18
J	18	19	4	12
K	22	22	14	10
L	22	23	8	16
M	18	24	6	18

:11-23 General Foundry's project crashing data are shown in Table 11.9. Crash this project to 13 weeks using CPM. What are the final times for each activity after crashing?

:11-24 Bowman Builders manufactures steel storage sheds for commercial use. Joe Bowman, president of Bowman Builders, is contemplating producing sheds for home use. The activities necessary to build an experimental model and related data are given in the accompanying table.

(a) What is the project completion date?

(b) Formulate an LP problem to crash this project to 10 weeks.

ACTIVITY	NORMAL TIME	CRASH TIME	NORMAL COST ($)	CRASH COST ($)	IMMEDIATE PREDECESSORS
A	3	2	1,000	1,600	—
B	2	1	2,000	2,700	—
C	1	1	300	300	—
D	7	3	1,300	1,600	A
E	6	3	850	1,000	B
F	2	1	4,000	5,000	C
G	4	2	1,500	2,000	D, E

:11-25 The Bender Construction Co. is involved in constructing municipal buildings and other structures that are used primarily by city and state municipalities. This requires developing legal documents, drafting feasibility studies, obtaining bond ratings, and so forth. Recently, Bender was given a request to submit a proposal for the construction of a municipal building. The first step is to develop legal documents and to perform all steps necessary before the construction contract is signed. This requires more than 20 separate activities that must be completed. These activities, their immediate predecessors, and time requirements are given in Table 11.10 on the next page.

As you can see, optimistic (a), most likely (m), and pessimistic (b) time estimates have been given for all of the activities described in the table. Using the data, determine the total project completion time for this preliminary step, the critical path, and slack time for all activities involved.

:11-26 Getting a degree from a college or university can be a long and difficult task. Certain courses must be completed before other courses may be taken. Develop a network diagram, in which every activity is a particular course that must be taken for a given degree program. The immediate predecessors will

TABLE 11.10   Data for Problem 11-25, Bender Construction Company

ACTIVITY	TIME REQUIRED (WEEKS)			DESCRIPTION OF ACTIVITY	IMMEDIATE PREDECESSORS
	a	m	b		
1	1	4	5	Draft of legal documents	—
2	2	3	4	Preparation of financial statements	—
3	3	4	5	Draft of history	—
4	7	8	9	Draft demand portion of feasibility study	—
5	4	4	5	Review and approval of legal documents	1
6	1	2	4	Review and approval of history	3
7	4	5	6	Review of feasibility study	4
8	1	2	4	Draft final financial portion of feasibility study	7
9	3	4	4	Draft facts relevant to the bond transaction	5
10	1	1	2	Review and approval of financial statements	2
11	18	20	26	Receive firm price of project	—
12	1	2	3	Review and completion of financial portion of feasibility study	8
13	1	1	2	Completion of draft statement	6, 9, 10, 11, 12
14	.10	.14	.16	All material sent to bond rating services	13
15	.2	.3	.4	Statement printed and distributed to all interested parties	14
16	1	1	2	Presentation to bond rating services	14
17	1	2	3	Bond rating received	16
18	3	5	7	Marketing of bonds	15, 17
19	.1	.1	.2	Purchase contract executed	18
20	.1	.14	.16	Final statement authorized and completed	19
21	2	3	6	Purchase contract	19
22	.1	.1	.2	Bond proceeds available	20
23	0	.2	.2	Sign construction contract	21, 22

be course prerequisites. Don't forget to include all university, college, and departmental course requirements. Then try to group these courses into semesters or quarters for your particular school. How long do you think it will take you to graduate? Which courses, if not taken in the proper sequence, could delay your graduation?

Q:11-27 Dream Team Productions was in the final design phases of its new film, *Killer Worms*, to be released next summer. Market Wise, the firm hired to coordinate the release of *Killer Worms* toys, identified 16 critical tasks to be completed before the release of the film.

(a) How many weeks in advance of the film release should Market Wise start its marketing campaign? What are the critical path activities? The tasks are as follows:

Table for Problem 11-27

ACTIVITY	IMMEDIATE PREDECESSORS	OPTIMISTIC TIME	MOST LIKELY TIME	PESSIMISTIC TIME
Task 1	—	1	2	4
Task 2	—	3	3.5	4
Task 3	—	10	12	13
Task 4	—	4	5	7
Task 5	—	2	4	5
Task 6	Task 1	6	7	8
Task 7	Task 2	2	4	5.5
Task 8	Task 3	5	7.7	9
Task 9	Task 3	9.9	10	12
Task 10	Task 3	2	4	5
Task 11	Task 4	2	4	6
Task 12	Task 5	2	4	6
Task 13	Tasks 6, 7, 8	5	6	6.5
Task 14	Tasks 10, 11, 12	1	1.1	2
Task 15	Tasks 9, 13	5	7	8
Task 16	Task 14	5	7	9

(b) If Tasks 9 and 10 were not necessary, what impact would this have on the critical path and the number of weeks needed to complete the marketing campaign?

⚌:11-28 The estimated times (in weeks) and immediate predecessors for the activities in a project are given in the following table. Assume that the activity times are independent.

ACTIVITY	IMMEDIATE PREDECESSORS	a	m	b
A	—	9	10	11
B	—	4	10	16
C	A	9	10	11
D	B	5	8	11

(a) Calculate the expected time and variance for each activity.
(b) What is the expected completion time of the critical path? What is the expected completion time of the other path in the network?
(c) What is the variance of the critical path? What is the variance of the other path in the network?
(d) If the time to complete path A–C is normally distributed, what is the probability that this path will be finished in 22 weeks or less?
(e) If the time to complete path B–D is normally distributed, what is the probability that this path will be finished in 22 weeks or less?
(f) Explain why the probability that the critical path will be finished in 22 weeks or less is not necessarily the probability that the project will be finished in 22 weeks or less.

⚌:11-29 The following costs have been estimated for the activities in a project:

ACTIVITY	IMMEDIATE PREDECESSORS	TIME	COST ($)
A	—	8	8,000
B	—	4	12,000
C	A	3	6,000
D	B	5	15,000
E	C, D	6	9,000
F	C, D	5	10,000
G	F	3	6,000

(a) Develop a cost schedule based on earliest start times.
(b) Develop a cost schedule based on latest start times.
(c) Suppose that it has been determined that the $6,000 for activity G is not evenly spread over the three weeks. Instead, the cost for the first week is $4,000, and the cost is $1,000 per week for each of the last two weeks. Modify the cost schedule based on earliest start times to reflect this situation.

⚌:11-30 The Scott Corey accounting firm is installing a new computer system. Several things must be done to make sure the system works properly before all the accounts are put into the new system. The following table provides information about this project. How long will it take to install the system? What is the critical path?

ACTIVITY	IMMEDIATE PREDECESSORS	TIME (WEEKS)
A	—	3
B	—	4
C	A	6
D	B	2
E	A	5
F	C	2
G	D, E	4
H	F, G	5

⚌:11-31 The managing partner of the Scott Corey accounting firm (see Problem 11-30) has decided that the system must be up and running in 16 weeks. Consequently, information about crashing the project was put together and is shown in the following table:

ACTIVITY	IMMEDIATE PREDECESSORS	NORMAL TIME (WEEKS)	CRASH TIME (WEEKS)	NORMAL COST ($)	CRASH COST ($)
A	—	3	2	8,000	9,800
B	—	4	3	9,000	10,000
C	A	6	4	12,000	15,000
D	B	2	1	15,000	15,500
E	A	5	3	5,000	8,700
F	C	2	1	7,500	9,000
G	D, E	4	2	8,000	9,400
H	F, G	5	3	5,000	6,600

(a) If the project is to be finished in 16 weeks, which activity or activities should be crashed to do this at the least additional cost? What is the total cost of this?
(b) List all the paths in this network. After the crashing in part (a) has been done, what is the time required for each path? If the project completion time must be reduced another week so that the total time is 15 weeks, which activity or activities should be crashed? Solve this by inspection. Note that it is sometimes better to crash an activity that is not the least cost for crashing if it is on several paths rather than to crash several activities on separate paths when there is more than one critical path.

✖:11-32 The L. O. Gystics Corporation is in need of a new regional distribution center. The planning is in the early stages of this project, but the activities have been identified along with their predecessors and their activity times in weeks. The table below provides this information. Develop a linear program that could be used to determine the length of the critical path (i.e., the minimum time required to complete the project). Solve this linear program to find the critical path and the time required to complete the project.

ACTIVITY	IMMEDIATE PREDECESSORS	TIME (WEEKS)
A	—	4
B	—	8
C	A	5
D	B	11
E	A, B	7
F	C, E	10
G	D	16
H	F	6

11-33 The Laurenster Corporation needs to perform the following tasks in weeks.

ACTIVITY	IMMEDIATE PREDECESSORS	OPTIMISTIC TIME	MOST LIKELY TIME	PESSIMISTIC TIME
A		2	3	4
B		4	6	8
C		2	5	8
D	A	3	4	5
E	B	6	7	8
F	C	4	7	10
G	A	1	5	9
H	B	2	5	8
I	C	3	5	7
J	D, G	2	2	2
K	E, H	4	4	4
L	F, I	3	3	3

Determine the associated PERT network diagram and determine the probability that the project will be complete in 16 weeks or less.

11-34 The Laurenster Corporation has determined the client will pay them a $10,000 bonus if they complete the project in Problem 11-33 in 14 weeks or less. The associated normal times and costs as well as the crash times and costs are shown below.

ACTIVITY	NORMAL TIME	CRASH TIME	NORMAL COST ($)	CRASH COST ($)
A	3	2	600	1,200
B	6	4	1,200	2,400
C	5	2	1,200	2,400
D	4	3	1,200	1,800
E	7	6	1,200	1,800
F	7	4	1,200	3,000
G	5	1	2,400	4,800
H	5	2	1,200	3,000
I	5	3	1,800	2,400
J	2	2	300	300
K	4	4	300	300
L	3	3	300	300

Considering the costs involved to crash the project, determine if the Laurenster Corporation should crash the project to 14 weeks to receive the bonus.

Internet Homework Problems

See our Internet home page, at **www.pearsonhighered.com/render**, for additional homework problems, Problems 11–35 to 11–42.

Case Study

Southwestern University Stadium Construction

After six months of study, much political arm wrestling, and some serious financial analysis, Dr. Martin Starr, president of Southwestern University, had reached a decision. To the delight of its students, and to the disappointment of its athletic boosters, SWU would not be relocating to a new football site but would expand the capacity at its on-campus stadium.

Adding 21,000 seats, including dozens of luxury skyboxes, would not please everyone. The influential football coach, Billy Bob Taylor, had long argued the need for a first-class stadium, one with built-in dormitory rooms for his players and a palatial office appropriate for the coach of a future NCAA champion

TABLE 11.11   Southwestern University Stadium Project

			TIME ESTIMATES (DAYS)			
ACTIVITY	DESCRIPTION	PREDECESSORS	OPTIMISTIC	MOST LIKELY	PESSIMISTIC	CRASH COST/DAY($)
A	Bonding, insurance, tax structuring	—	20	30	40	1,500
B	Foundation, concrete footings for boxes	A	20	65	80	3,500
C	Upgrading skyboxes, stadium seating	A	50	60	100	4,000
D	Upgrading walkways, stairwells, elevators	C	30	50	100	1,900
E	Interior wiring, lathes	B	25	30	35	9,500
F	Inspection approvals	E	1	1	1	0
G	Plumbing	D, E	25	30	35	2,500
H	Painting	G	10	20	30	2,000
I	Hardware/air conditioning/ metal workings	H	20	25	60	2,000
J	Tile/carpeting/windows	H	8	10	12	6,000
K	Inspection	J	1	1	1	0
L	Final detail work/ cleanup	I, K	20	25	60	4,500

Source: Adapted from J. Heizer and B. Render. *Operations Management*, 6th ed. Upper Saddle River, NJ: Prentice Hall, 2000: 693–694.

team. But the decision was made, and *everyone*, including the coach, would learn to live with it.

The job now was to get construction going immediately after the current season ended. This would allow exactly 270 days until the upcoming season opening game. The contractor, Hill Construction (Bob Hill being an alumnus, of course), signed the contract. Bob Hill looked at the tasks his engineers had outlined and looked President Starr in the eye. "I guarantee the team will be able to take the field on schedule next year," he said with a sense of confidence. "I sure hope so," replied Starr. "The contract penalty of $10,000 per day for running late is nothing compared to what Coach Bill Bob Taylor will do to you if our opening game with Penn State is delayed or cancelled." Hill, sweating slightly, did not respond. In football-crazy Texas, Hill Construction would be *mud* if the 270-day target were missed.

Back in his office, Hill again reviewed the data. (See Table 11.11 and note that optimistic time estimates can be used as crash times.) He then gathered his foremen. "People, if we're not 75% sure we'll finish this stadium in less than 270 days, I want this project crashed! Give me the cost figures for a target date of 250 days—also for 240 days. I want to be *early*, not just on time!"

Discussion Questions

1. Develop a network drawing for Hill Construction and determine the critical path. How long is the project expected to take?
2. What is the probability of finishing in 270 days?
3. If it were necessary to crash to 250 or 240 days, how would Hill do so, and at what costs? As noted in the case, assume that optimistic time estimates can be used as crash times.

Case Study

Family Planning Research Center of Nigeria

Dr. Adinombe Watage, deputy director of the Family Planning Research Center in Nigeria's Over-the-River Province, was assigned the task of organizing and training five teams of field workers to perform educational and outreach activities as part of a large project to demonstrate acceptance of a new method of birth control. These workers already had training in family planning education but must receive specific training regarding

the new method of contraception. Two types of materials must also be prepared: (1) those for use in training the workers, and (2) those for distribution in the field. Training faculty must be brought in and arrangements made for transportation and accommodations for the participants.

Dr. Watage first called a meeting of his office staff. Together they identified the activities that must be carried out,

TABLE 11.12 Family Planning Research Center Activities

ACTIVITY	MUST FOLLOW	TIME (DAYS)	STAFFING NEEDED
A. Identify faculty and their schedules	—	5	2
B. Arrange transport to base	—	7	3
C. Identify and collect training materials	—	5	2
D. Arrange accommodations	A	3	1
E. Identify team	A	7	4
F. Bring in team	B, E	2	1
G. Transport faculty to base	A, B	3	2
H. Print program material	C	10	6
I. Have program materials delivered	H	7	3
J. Conduct training program	D, F, G, I	15	0
K. Perform fieldwork training	J	30	0

TABLE 11.13 Family Planning Research Center Costs

ACTIVITY	NORMAL		MINIMUM		AVERAGE COST PER DAY SAVED ($)
	TIME	COST ($)	TIME	COST ($)	
A. Identify faculty	5	400	2	700	100
B. Arrange transport	7	1,000	4	1,450	150
C. Identify materials	5	400	3	500	50
D. Make accommodations	3	2,500	1	3,000	250
E. Identify team	7	400	4	850	150
F. Bring team in	2	1,000	1	2,000	1,000
G. Transport faculty	3	1,500	2	2,000	500
H. Print materials	10	3,000	5	4,000	200
I. Deliver materials	7	200	2	600	80
J. Train team	15	5,000	10	7,000	400
K. Do fieldwork	30	10,000	20	14,000	400

their necessary sequences, and the time that they would require. Their results are displayed in Table 11.12.

Louis Odaga, the chief clerk, noted that the project had to be completed in 60 days. Whipping out his solar-powered calculator, he added up the time needed. It came to 94 days. "An impossible task, then," he noted. "No," Dr. Watage replied, "some of these tasks can go forward in parallel." "Be careful, though," warned Mr. Oglagadu, the chief nurse, "there aren't that many of us to go around. There are only 10 of us in this office."

"I can check whether we have enough heads and hands once I have tentatively scheduled the activities," Dr. Watage responded. "If the schedule is too tight, I have permission from the Pathminder Fund to spend some funds to speed it up, just so long as I can prove that it can be done at the least cost necessary. Can you help me prove that? Here are the costs for the activities with the elapsed time that we planned and the costs and times if we shorten them to an absolute minimum." Those data are given in Table 11.13.

Discussion Questions

1. Some of the tasks in this project can be done in parallel. Prepare a diagram showing the required network of tasks and define the critical path. What is the length of the project without crashing?

2. At this point, can the project be done given the personnel constraint of 10 persons?

3. If the critical path is longer than 60 days, what is the least amount that Dr. Watage can spend and still achieve this schedule objective? How can he prove to Pathminder Foundation that this is the minimum-cost alternative?

Source: Professor Curtis P. McLaughlin, Kenan-Flagler Business School, University of North Carolina at Chapel Hill.

Internet Case Studies

See our Internet home page, at **www.pearsonhighered.com/render**, for these additional case studies:

(1) **Alpha Beta Gamma Record:** This case involves publishing a monthly magazine for a fraternity.

(2) **Bay Community Hospital:** This case involves the acquisition and installation of equipment to be used in a new medical procedure.

(3) **Cranston Construction Company:** This case involves the construction of a new building at a university.

(4) **Haygood Brothers Construction Company:** This case involves planning the construction of a house.

(5) **Shale Oil Company:** This case involves planning the shutdown of a petrochemical plant for routine maintenance.

Bibliography

Ahuja, V., and V. Thiruvengadam. "Project Scheduling and Monitoring: Current Research Status," *Construction Innovation* 4, 1 (2004): 19–31.

Griffith, Andrew F. "Scheduling Practices and Project Success," *Cost Engineering* 48, 9 (2006): 24–30.

Herroelen, Willy, and Roel Leus. "Project Scheduling Under Uncertainty: Survey and Research Potentials," *European Journal of Operational Research* 165, 2 (2005): 289–306.

Jorgensen, Trond, and Stein W. Wallace. "Improving Project Cost Estimation by Taking into Account Managerial Flexibility," *European Journal of Operational Research* 127, 2 (2000): 239–251.

Lancaster, John, and Mustafa Ozbayrak. "Evolutionary Algorithms Applied to Project Scheduling Problems—A Survey of the State-of-the-art," *International Journal of Production Research* 45, 2 (2007): 425–450.

Lu, Ming, and Heng Li. "Resource-Activity Critical-Path Method for Construction Planning," *Journal of Construction Engineering & Management* 129, 4 (2003): 412–420.

Mantel, Samuel J., Jack R. Meredith, Scott M. Shafer, and Margaret M. Sutton. *Project Management in Practice.* New York: John Wiley & Sons, Inc., 2001.

Premachandra, I. M. "An Approximation of the Activity Duration Distribution in PERT," *Computers and Operations Research* 28, 5 (April 2001): 443–452.

Roe, Justin. "Bringing Discipline to Project Management," *Harvard Business Review* (April 1998): 153–160.

Sander, Wayne. "The Project Manager's Guide," *Quality Progress* (January 1998): 109.

Vaziri, Kabeh, Paul G. Carr, and Linda K. Nozick. "Project Planning for Construction under Uncertainty with Limited Resources," *Journal of Construction Engineering & Management* 133, 4 (2007): 268–276.

Walker II, Edward D. "Introducing Project Management Concepts Using a Jewelry Store Robbery," *Decision Sciences Journal of Innovative Education* 2, 1 (2004): 65–69.

Appendix 11.1: Project Management with QM for Windows

PERT is one of the most popular project management techniques. In this chapter, we explore the General Foundry, Inc., example. When expected times and variances have been computed for each activity, we can use the data to determine slack, the critical path, and the total project completion time. Program 11.3A shows the QM for Windows input screen for the General Foundry problem. By selecting the precedence list as the type of network, the data can be input without even constructing the network. The method indicated is for three time estimates, although this can be changed to a single time estimate, crashing, or cost budgeting. Program 11.3B provides the output for the General Foundry problem. The critical path consists of the activities with zero slack.

In addition to basic project management, QM for Windows also allows for project crashing, in which additional resources are used to reduce project completion time. Program 11.4A shows the input screen for the General Foundry data from Table 11.9. The output is shown in Program 11.4B. This indicates that the normal time is 15 weeks, but the project may be finished in 7 weeks if necessary; it may be finished in any number of weeks between 7 and 15. Selecting *Windows—Crash Schedule* provides additional information regarding these other times.

Monitoring and controlling projects is always an important aspect of project management. In this chapter we demonstrate how to construct budgets using the earliest and latest start times. Programs 11.5 and 11.6 show how QM for Windows can be used to develop budgets using earliest and latest starting times for a project. The data come from the General Foundry example in Tables 11.6 and Table 11.7.

PROGRAM 11.3A

QM for Windows Input Screen for General Foundry, Inc.

File Edit View Module Format Tools Window Help

Network type
- Immediate predecessor list
- Start/end node numbers

Method
Triple time estimate

	PERT Example				
Activity	Optimistic time	Most Likely time	Pessimistic time	Predecessor 1	Predecessor 2
A	1	2	3		
B	2	3	4		
C	1	2	3	A	
D	2	4	6	B	
E	1	4	7	C	
F	1	2	9	C	
G	3	4	11	D	E
H	1	2	3	F	G

PROGRAM 11.3B

QM for Windows Solution Screen for General Foundry, Inc.

File Edit View Module Format Tools Window Help

Network type
- Immediate predecessor list
- Start/end node numbers

Method
Triple time estimate

Project Management (PERT/CPM) Results

	PERT Example Solution						
Activity	Activity time	Early Start	Early Finish	Late Start	Late Finish	Slack	Standard Deviation
Project	15						1.76
A	2	0	2	0	2	0	0.33
B	3	0	3	1	4	1	0.33
C	2	2	4	2	4	0	0.33
D	4	3	7	4	8	1	0.67
E	4	4	8	4	8	0	1
F	3	4	7	10	13	6	1.33
G	5	8	13	8	13	0	1.33
H	2	13	15	13	15	0	0.33

PROGRAM 11.4A

QM for Windows Input Screen for Crashing General Foundry Example

Network type
- Immediate predecessor list
- Start/end node numbers

Method
Crashing

	General Foundry					
Activity	Normal time	Crash time	Normal Cost	Crash Cost	Predecessor 1	Predecessor 2
A	2	1	22,000	23,000		
B	3	1	30,000	34,000		
C	2	1	26,000	27,000	A	
D	4	3	48,000	49,000	B	
E	4	2	56,000	58,000	C	
F	3	2	30,000	30,500	C	
G	5	2	80,000	86,000	D	E
H	2	1	16,000	19,000	F	G

PROGRAM 11.4B

QM for Windows Output Screen for Crashing General Foundry Example

Network type
○ Immediate predecessor list
○ Start/end node numbers

Method
Crashing

Project Management (PERT/CPM) Results

General Foundry Solution

Activity	Normal time	Crash time	Normal Cost	Crash Cost	Crash cost/pd	Crash by	Crashing cost
Project	15	7					
A	2	1	22,000	23,000	1,000	1	1,000
B	3	1	30,000	34,000	2,000	2	4,000
C	2	1	26,000	27,000	1,000	1	1,000
D	4	3	48,000	49,000	1,000	1	1,000
E	4	2	56,000	58,000	1,000	2	2,000
F	3	2	30,000	30,500	500	0	0
G	5	2	80,000	86,000	2,000	3	6,000
H	2	1	16,000	19,000	3,000	1	3,000
TOTALS			308,000				18,000

PROGRAM 11.5

QM for Windows for Budgeting with Earliest Start Times for General Foundry

Early Start Budget

General Foundry Solution

	Period 1	Period 2	Period 3	Period 4	Period 5	Period 6	Period 7	Period 8	Period 9	Period 10	Period 11	Period 12	Period 13	Period 14	Period 15
A	11	11													
B	10	10	10												
C			13	13											
D				12	12	12	12								
E					14	14	14	14							
F					10	10	10								
G									16	16	16	16	16		
H														8	8
Total in Period	21	21	23	25	36	36	36	14	16	16	16	16	16	8	8
Cumulative from	21	42	65	90	126	162	198	212	228	244	260	276	292	300	308

PROGRAM 11.6

QM for Windows for Budgeting with Latest Start Times for General Foundry

Late Start Budget

General Foundry Solution

	Period 1	Period 2	Period 3	Period 4	Period 5	Period 6	Period 7	Period 8	Period 9	Period 10	Period 11	Period 12	Period 13	Period 14	Period 15
A	11	11													
B		10	10	10											
C			13	13											
D					12	12	12	12							
E					14	14	14	14							
F											10	10	10		
G									16	16	16	16	16		
H														8	8
Total in Period	11	21	23	23	26	26	26	26	16	16	26	26	26	8	8
Cumulative from	11	32	55	78	104	130	156	182	198	214	240	266	292	300	308

CHAPTER 12

Waiting Lines and Queuing Theory Models

LEARNING OBJECTIVES

After completing this chapter, students will be able to:

1. Describe the trade-off curves for cost-of-waiting time and cost of service.
2. Understand the three parts of a queuing system: the calling population, the queue itself, and the service facility.
3. Describe the basic queuing system configurations.
4. Understand the assumptions of the common models dealt with in this chapter.
5. Analyze a variety of operating characteristics of waiting lines.

CHAPTER OUTLINE

Summary • Glossary • Key Equations • Solved Problems • Self-Test • Discussion Questions and Problems • Internet Homework Problems • Case Study: New England Foundry ♦ Case Study: Winter Park Hotel • Internet Case Study • Bibliography

Appendix 12.1: Using QM for Windows

12.1 Introduction

The study of *waiting lines*, called **queuing theory**, is one of the oldest and most widely used quantitative analysis techniques. Waiting lines are an everyday occurrence, affecting people shopping for groceries, buying gasoline, making a bank deposit, or waiting on the telephone for the first available airline reservationist to answer. Queues,* another term for waiting lines, may also take the form of machines waiting to be repaired, trucks in line to be unloaded, or airplanes lined up on a runway waiting for permission to take off. The three basic components of a queuing process are arrivals, service facilities, and the actual waiting line.

In this chapter we discuss how analytical models of waiting lines can help managers evaluate the cost and effectiveness of service systems. We begin with a look at waiting line costs and then describe the characteristics of waiting lines and the underlying mathematical assumptions used to develop queuing models. We also provide the equations needed to compute the operating characteristics of a service system and show examples of how they are used. Later in the chapter, you will see how to save computational time by applying queuing tables and by running waiting line computer programs.

12.2 Waiting Line Costs

One of the goals of queuing analysis is finding the best level of service for an organization.

Most **waiting line** problems are centered on the question of finding the ideal level of services that a firm should provide. Supermarkets must decide how many cash register checkout positions should be opened. Gasoline stations must decide how many pumps should be opened and how many attendants should be on duty. Manufacturing plants must determine the optimal number of mechanics to have on duty each shift to repair machines that break down. Banks must decide how many teller windows to keep open to serve customers during various hours of the day. In most cases, this level of service is an option over which management has control. An extra teller, for example, can be borrowed from another chore or can be hired and trained quickly if demand warrants it. This may not always be the case, though. A plant may not be able to locate or hire skilled mechanics to repair sophisticated electronic machinery.

When an organization *does* have control, its objective is usually to find a happy medium between two extremes. On the one hand, a firm can retain a large staff and provide *many* service facilities. This may result in excellent customer service, with seldom more than one or two customers in a queue. Customers are kept happy with the quick response and appreciate the convenience. This, however, can become expensive.

The other extreme is to have the *minimum* possible number of checkout lines, gas pumps, or teller windows open. This keeps the **service cost** down but may result in customer dissatisfaction. How many times would you return to a large discount department store that had only one cash register open during the day you shop? As the average length of the queue increases and poor service results, customers and goodwill may be lost.

Managers must deal with the trade-off between the cost of providing good service and the cost of customer waiting time. The latter may be hard to quantify.

Most managers recognize the trade-off that must take place between the cost of providing good service and the cost of customer waiting time. They want queues that are short enough so that customers don't become unhappy and either storm out without buying or buy but never return. But they are willing to allow some waiting in line if it is balanced by a significant savings in service costs.

One means of evaluating a service facility is thus to look at a *total expected cost*, a concept illustrated in Figure 12.1. Total expected cost is the sum of expected *service costs* plus expected **waiting costs**.

HISTORY   How Queuing Models Began

Queuing theory had its beginning in the research work of a Danish engineer named A. K. Erlang. In 1909, Erlang experimented with fluctuating demand in telephone traffic. Eight years later, he published a report addressing the delays in automatic dialing equipment. At the end of World War II, Erlang's early work was extended to more general problems and to business applications of waiting lines.

---

*The word *queue* is pronounced like the letter *Q*, that is, "kew."

FIGURE 12.1

Queuing Costs and Service Levels

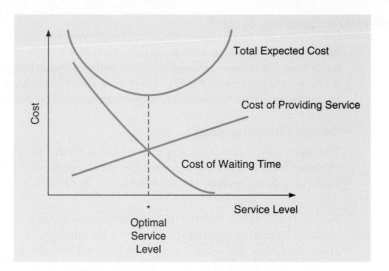

Total expected cost is the sum of service plus waiting costs.

Service costs are seen to increase as a firm attempts to raise its level of service. For example, if three teams of stevedores, instead of two, are employed to unload a cargo ship, service costs are increased by the additional price of wages. As service improves in speed, however, the cost of time spent waiting in lines decreases. This waiting cost may reflect lost productivity of workers while their tools or machines are awaiting repairs or may simply be an estimate of the costs of customers lost because of poor service and long queues.

Three Rivers Shipping Company Example

As an illustration, let's look at the case of the Three Rivers Shipping Company. Three Rivers runs a huge docking facility located on the Ohio River near Pittsburgh. Approximately five ships arrive to unload their cargoes of steel and ore during every 12-hour work shift. Each hour that a ship sits idle in line waiting to be unloaded costs the firm a great deal of money, about $1,000 per hour. From experience, management estimates that if one team of stevedores is on duty to handle the unloading work, each ship will wait an average of 7 hours to be unloaded. If two teams are working, the average waiting time drops to 4 hours; for three teams, it's 3 hours; and for four teams of stevedores, only 2 hours. But each additional team of stevedores is also an expensive proposition, due to union contracts.

The goal is to find the service level that minimizes total expected cost.

Three Rivers's superintendent would like to determine the optimal number of teams of stevedores to have on duty each shift. The objective is to minimize total expected costs. This analysis is summarized in Table 12.1. To minimize the sum of service costs and waiting costs, the firm makes the decision to employ two teams of stevedores each shift.

TABLE 12.1 Three Rivers Shipping Company Waiting Line Cost Analysis

	NUMBER OF TEAMS OF STEVEDORES WORKING			
	1	2	3	4
(a) Average number of ships arriving per shift	5	5	5	5
(b) Average time each ship waits to be unloaded (hours)	7	4	3	2
(c) Total ship hours lost per shift $(a \times b)$	35	20	15	10
(d) Estimated cost per hour of idle ship time	$1,000	$1,000	$1,000	$1,000
(e) Value of ship's lost time or waiting cost $(c \times d)$	$35,000	$20,000	$15,000	$10,000
(f) Stevedore team salary,* or service cost	$6,000	$12,000	$18,000	$24,000
(g) Total expected cost $(e + f)$	$41,000	$32,000	$33,000	$34,000

→ ($32,000) ⌐ Optimal cost

*Stevedore team salaries are computed as the number of people in a typical team (assumed to be 50), times the number of hours each person works per day (12 hours), times an hourly salary of $10 per hour. If two teams are employed, the rate is just doubled.

12.3 Characteristics of a Queuing System

In this section we take a look at the three parts of a queuing system: (1) the arrivals or inputs to the system (sometimes referred to as the **calling population**), (2) the queue or the waiting line itself, and (3) the service facility. These three components have certain characteristics that must be examined before mathematical queuing models can be developed.

Arrival Characteristics

The input source that generates arrivals or customers for the service system has three major characteristics. It is important to consider the *size* of the calling population, the *pattern* of arrivals at the queuing system, and the *behavior* of the arrivals.

Unlimited (or infinite) calling populations are assumed for most queuing models.

SIZE OF THE CALLING POPULATION   Population sizes are considered to be either **unlimited** (essentially *infinite*) or **limited** (*finite*). When the number of customers or arrivals on hand at any given moment is just a small portion of potential arrivals, the calling population is considered unlimited. For practical purposes, examples of unlimited populations include cars arriving at a highway tollbooth, shoppers arriving at a supermarket, or students arriving to register for classes at a large university. Most queuing models assume such an infinite calling population. When this is not the case, modeling becomes much more complex. An example of a finite population is a shop with only eight machines that might break down and require service.

Arrivals are random when they are independent of one another and cannot be predicted exactly.

PATTERN OF ARRIVALS AT THE SYSTEM   Customers either arrive at a service facility according to some known schedule (e.g., one patient every 15 minutes or one student for advising every half hour) or else they arrive *randomly*. Arrivals are considered random when they are independent of one another and their occurrence cannot be predicted exactly. Frequently in queuing problems, the number of arrivals per unit of time can be estimated by a probability distribution known as the **Poisson distribution**. See Section 2.11 for details about this distribution.

The concepts of balking and reneging.

BEHAVIOR OF THE ARRIVALS   Most queuing models assume that an arriving customer is a patient customer. Patient customers are people or machines that wait in the queue until they are served and do not switch between lines. Unfortunately, life and quantitative analysis are complicated by the fact that people have been known to balk or renege. **Balking** refers to customers who refuse to join the waiting line because it is too long to suit their needs or interests. **Reneging** customers are those who enter the queue but then become impatient and leave without completing their transaction. Actually, both of these situations just serve to accentuate the need for queuing theory and waiting line analysis. How many times have you seen a shopper with a basket full of groceries, including perishables such as milk, frozen food, or meats, simply abandon the shopping cart before checking out because the line was too long? This expensive occurrence for the store makes managers acutely aware of the importance of service-level decisions.

Waiting Line Characteristics

The waiting line itself is the second component of a queuing system. The length of a line can be either *limited* or *unlimited*. A queue is limited when it cannot, by law of physical restrictions, increase to an infinite length. This may be the case in a small restaurant that has only 10 tables and can serve no more than 50 diners an evening. Analytic queuing models are treated in this chapter under an assumption of **unlimited queue length**. A queue is unlimited when its size is unrestricted, as in the case of the tollbooth serving arriving automobiles.

The models in this chapter assume unlimited queue length.

A second waiting line characteristic deals with **queue discipline**. This refers to the rule by which customers in the line are to receive service. Most systems use a queue discipline known as the **first-in, first-out** (**FIFO**) rule. In a hospital emergency room or an express checkout line at a supermarket, however, various assigned priorities may preempt FIFO. Patients who are critically injured will move ahead in treatment priority over patients with broken fingers or noses. Shoppers with fewer than 10 items may be allowed to enter the express checkout queue but are *then* treated as first come, first served. Computer programming runs are another example of queuing systems that operate under priority scheduling. In most large companies, when

Most queuing models use the FIFO rule. This is obviously not appropriate in all service systems, especially those dealing with emergencies.

computer-produced paychecks are due out on a specific date, the payroll program has highest priority over other runs.*

Service Facility Characteristics

The third part of any queuing system is the service facility. It is important to examine two basic properties: (1) the configuration of the service system and (2) the pattern of service times.

Number of service channels in a queuing system is the number of servers.

BASIC QUEUING SYSTEM CONFIGURATIONS Service systems are usually classified in terms of their number of channels, or number of servers, and number of phases, or number of service stops, that must be made. A **single-channel system**, with one server, is typified by the drive-in bank that has only one open teller, or by the type of drive-through fast-food restaurant that has become so popular in the United States. If, on the other hand, the bank had several tellers on duty and each customer waited in one common line for the first available teller, we would have a **multichannel system** at work. Many banks today are multichannel service systems, as are most large barber shops and many airline ticket counters.

Single-phase means the customer receives service at only one station before leaving the system. Multiphase implies two or more stops before leaving the system.

A **single-phase system** is one in which the customer receives service from only one station and then exits the system. A fast-food restaurant in which the person who takes your order also brings you the food and takes your money is a single-phase system. So is a driver's license agency in which the person taking your application also grades your test and collects the license fee. But if the restaurant requires you to place your order at one station, pay at a second, and pick up the food at a third service stop, it becomes a **multiphase system**. Similarly, if the driver's license agency is large or busy, you will probably have to wait in a line to complete the application (the first service stop), then queue again to have the test graded (the second service stop), and finally go to a third service counter to pay the fee. To help you relate the concepts of channels and phases, Figure 12.2 presents four possible configurations.

Service times often follow the negative exponential distribution.

SERVICE TIME DISTRIBUTION Service patterns are like arrival patterns in that they can be either constant or random. If service time is constant, it takes the same amount of time to take care of each customer. This is the case in a machine-performed service operation such as an automatic car wash. More often, service times are randomly distributed. In many cases it can be assumed that random service times are described by the **negative exponential probability distribution**. See Section 2.10 for details about this distribution.

It is important to confirm that the queuing assumptions of Poisson arrivals and exponential services are valid before applying the model.

The exponential distribution is important to the process of building mathematical queuing models because many of the models' theoretical underpinnings are based on the assumption of Poisson arrivals and exponential services. Before they are applied, however, the quantitative analyst can and should observe, collect, and plot service time data to determine if they fit the exponential distribution.

Identifying Models Using Kendall Notation

D. G. Kendall developed a notation that has been widely accepted for specifying the pattern of arrivals, the service time distribution, and the number of channels in a queuing model. This notation is often seen in software for queuing models. The basic three-symbol **Kendall notation** is in the form

Arrival distribution/Service time distribution/Number of service channels open

where specific letters are used to represent probability distributions. The following letters are commonly used in Kendall notation:

M = Poisson distribution for number of occurrences (or exponential times)

D = constant (deterministic) rate

G = general distribution with mean and variance known

---

*The term *FIFS* (*first in, first served*) is often used in place of FIFO. Another discipline, LIFS (*last in, first served*), is common when material is stacked or piled and the items on top are used first.

FIGURE 12.2 **Four Basic Queuing System Configurations**

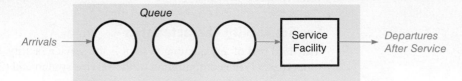

Single-Channel, Single-Phase System

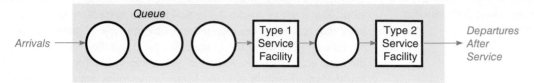

Single-Channel, Multiphase System

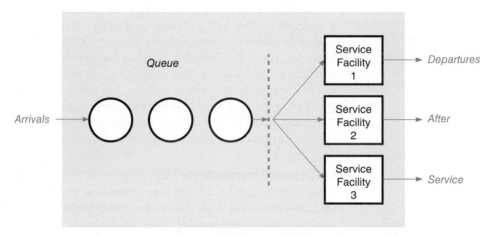

Multichannel, Single-Phase System

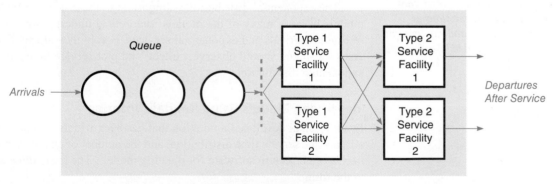

Multichannel, Multiphase System

Thus, a single-channel model with Poisson arrivals and exponential service times would be represented by

$$M/M/1$$

*An **M/M/2** model has Poisson arrivals, exponential service times, and two channels.*

When a second channel is added, we would have

$$M/M/2$$

If there are *m* distinct service channels in the queuing system with Poisson arrivals and exponential service times, the Kendall notation would be *M/M/m*. A three-channel system with Poisson arrivals and constant service time would be identified as *M/D/3*. A four-channel system with Poisson arrivals and service times that are normally distributed would be identified as *M/G/4*.

MODELING IN THE REAL WORLD
Montgomery County's Public Health Services

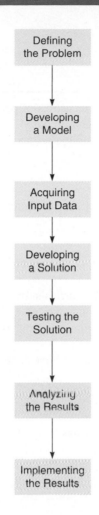

Defining the Problem

Developing a Model

Acquiring Input Data

Developing a Solution

Testing the Solution

Analyzing the Results

Implementing the Results

Defining the Problem

In 2002, the Centers for Disease Control and Prevention began to require that public health departments create plans for smallpox vaccinations. A county must be prepared to vaccinate every person in an infected area in a few days. This was of particular concern after the terrorist attack of September 11, 2001.

Developing a Model

Queuing models for capacity planning and discrete event simulation models were developed through a joint effort of the Montgomery County (Maryland) Public Health Service and the University of Maryland, College Park.

Acquiring Input Data

Data were collected on the time required for the vaccinations to occur or for medicine to be dispensed. Clinical exercises were used for this purpose.

Developing a Solution

The models indicate the number of staff members needed to achieve specific capacities to avoid congestion in the clinics.

Testing the Solution

The smallpox vaccination plan was tested using a simulation of a mock vaccination clinic in a full-scale exercise involving residents going through the clinic. This highlighted the need for modifications in a few areas. A computer simulation model was then developed for additional testing.

Analyzing the Results

The results of the capacity planning and queuing model provide very good estimates of the true performance of the system. Clinic planners and managers can quickly estimate capacity and congestion as the situation develops.

Implementing the Results

The results of this study are available on a Web site for public health professionals to download and use. The guidelines include suggestions for workstation operations. Improvements to the process are continuing.

Source: Based on Kay Aaby, et al. "Montgomery County's Public Health Service Operations Research to Plan Emergency Mass Dispensing and Vaccination Clinics," *Interfaces* 36, 6 (November–December 2006): 569–579.

 IN ACTION Slow Down the Ski Lift to Get Shorter Lines

At a small, five-lift ski resort, management was worried that lift lines were getting too long. While this is sometimes a nice problem to have because it means business is booming, it is a problem that can backfire. If word spreads that a ski resort's lift lines are too long, customers may choose to ski elsewhere, where lines are shorter.

Because building new ski lifts requires significant financial investment, management decided to hire an external consultant with queuing system experience to study the problem. After several weeks of investigating the problem, collecting data, and measuring the length of the lift lines at various times, the consultant presented recommendations to the ski resort's management.

Surprisingly, instead of building new ski lifts, the consultant proposed that management slow down its five ski lifts at the resort to half their current speed and to double the number of chairs on each of the lifts. This meant, for example, that instead of 40 feet between lift chairs, there would be only 20 feet between lift chairs, but because they were moving more slowly, there was still the same amount of time for customers to board the lift. So if a particular lift previously took 4 minutes to get to the top, it would now take 8 minutes. It was reasoned that skiers wouldn't notice the difference in time because they were on the lifts and enjoying the view on the way to the top; this proved to be a valid assumption. Moreover, at any given time, twice as many people could actually be on the ski lifts, and fewer people were in the lift lines. The problem was solved!

There is a more detailed notation with additional terms that indicate the maximum number in the system and the population size. When these are omitted, it is assumed there is no limit to the queue length or the population size. Most of the models we study here will have those properties.

12.4   Single-Channel Queuing Model with Poisson Arrivals and Exponential Service Times (*M/M/*1)

In this section we present an analytical approach to determine important measures of performance in a typical service system. After these numeric measures have been computed, it will be possible to add in cost data and begin to make decisions that balance desirable service levels with waiting line service costs.

Assumptions of the Model

These seven assumptions must be met if the single-channel, single-phase model is to be applied.

The single-channel, single-phase model considered here is one of the most widely used and simplest queuing models. It involves assuming that seven conditions exist:

1. Arrivals are served on a FIFO basis.
2. Every arrival waits to be served regardless of the length of the line; that is, there is no balking or reneging.
3. Arrivals are independent of preceding arrivals, but the average number of arrivals (the arrival rate) does not change over time.
4. Arrivals are described by a Poisson probability distribution and come from an infinite or very large population.
5. Service times also vary from one customer to the next and are independent of one another, but their average rate is known.
6. Service times occur according to the negative exponential probability distribution.
7. The average service rate is greater than the average arrival rate.

When these seven conditions are met, we can develop a series of equations that define the queue's **operating characteristics**. The mathematics used to derive each equation is rather complex and outside the scope of this book, so we will just present the resulting formulas here.

Queuing Equations

We let

$$\lambda = \text{mean number of arrivals per time period (e.g., per hour)}$$
$$\mu = \text{mean number of people or items served per time period}$$

When determining the arrival rate (λ) and the service rate (μ), the same time period must be used. For example, if λ is the average number of arrivals per hour, then μ must indicate the average number that could be served per hour.

The queuing equations follow.

These seven queuing equations for the single-channel, single-phase model describe the important operating characteristics of the service system.

1. The average number of customers or units in the system, L, that is, the number in line plus the number being served:

$$L = \frac{\lambda}{\mu - \lambda} \tag{12-1}$$

2. The average time a customer spends in the system, W, that is, the time spent in line plus the time spent being served:

$$W = \frac{1}{\mu - \lambda} \tag{12-2}$$

3. The average number of customers in the queue, L_q:

$$L_q = \frac{\lambda^2}{\mu(\mu - \lambda)} \qquad (12\text{-}3)$$

4. The average time a customer spends waiting in the queue, W_q:

$$W_q = \frac{\lambda}{\mu(\mu - \lambda)} \qquad (12\text{-}4)$$

5. The **utilization factor** for the system, ρ (the Greek lowercase letter rho), that is, the probability that the service facility is being used:

$$\rho = \frac{\lambda}{\mu} \qquad (12\text{-}5)$$

6. The percent idle time, P_0, that is, the probability that no one is in the system:

$$P_0 = 1 - \frac{\lambda}{\mu} \qquad (12\text{-}6)$$

7. The probability that the number of customers in the system is greater than k, $P_{n>k}$:

$$P_{n>k} = \left(\frac{\lambda}{\mu}\right)^{k+1} \qquad (12\text{-}7)$$

Arnold's Muffler Shop Case

We now apply these formulas to the case of Arnold's Muffler Shop in New Orleans. Arnold's mechanic, Reid Blank, is able to install new mufflers at an average rate of 3 per hour, or about 1 every 20 minutes. Customers needing this service arrive at the shop on the average of 2 per hour. Larry Arnold, the shop owner, studied queuing models in an MBA program and feels that all seven of the conditions for a single-channel model are met. He proceeds to calculate the numerical values of the preceding operating characteristics:

$\lambda = 2$ cars arriving per hour

$\mu = 3$ cars serviced per hour

$L = \dfrac{\lambda}{\mu - \lambda} = \dfrac{2}{3 - 2} = \dfrac{2}{1} = 2$ cars in the system on the average

$W = \dfrac{1}{\mu - \lambda} = \dfrac{1}{3 - 2} = 1$ hour that an average car spends in the system

$L_q = \dfrac{\lambda^2}{\mu(\mu - \lambda)} = \dfrac{2^2}{3(3 - 2)} = \dfrac{4}{3(1)} = \dfrac{4}{3} = 1.33$ cars waiting in line on the average

$W_q = \dfrac{\lambda}{\mu(\mu - \lambda)} = \dfrac{2}{3(3 - 2)} = \dfrac{2}{3}$ hour $= 40$ minutes $=$ average waiting time per car

Note that W and W_q are in *hours*, since λ was defined as the number of arrivals per *hour*.

$\rho = \dfrac{\lambda}{\mu} = \dfrac{2}{3} = 0.67 = $ percentage of time mechanic is busy, or the probability that the server is busy

$P_0 = 1 - \dfrac{\lambda}{\mu} = 1 - \dfrac{2}{3} = 0.33 = $ probability that there are 0 cars in the system

Probability of More Than k Cars in the System

k	$P_{n>k} = \left(\frac{2}{3}\right)^{k+1}$	
0	0.667	← Note that this is equal to $1 - P_0 = 1 - 0.33 = 0.667$.
1	0.444	
2	0.296	
3	0.198	← Implies that there is a 19.8% chance that more than 3 cars are in the system.
4	0.132	
5	0.088	
6	0.058	
7	0.039	

USING EXCEL QM ON THE ARNOLD'S MUFFLER SHOP QUEUE To use Excel QM for this problem, from the Excel QM menu, select *Waiting Lines - Single Channel (M/M/1)*. When the spreadsheet appears, enter the arrival rate (2) and service rate (3). All the operating characteristic will automatically be computed, as demonstrated in Program 12.1.

INTRODUCING COSTS INTO THE MODEL Now that the characteristics of the queuing system have been computed, Arnold decides to do an economic analysis of their impact. The waiting line model was valuable in predicting potential waiting times, queue lengths, idle times, and so on. But it did not identify optimal decisions or consider cost factors. As stated earlier, the solution to a queuing problem may require management to make a trade-off between the increased cost of providing better service and the decreased waiting costs derived from providing that service. These two costs are called the waiting cost and the service cost.

The total service cost is

$$\text{Total service cost} = (\text{Number of channels})(\text{Cost per channel})$$

$$\text{Total service cost} = mC_s \tag{12-8}$$

Conducting an economic analysis is the next step. It permits cost factors to be included.

PROGRAM 12.1

Excel QM Solution to Arnold's Muffler Shop

	A	B	C	D	E
1	**Arnold's Muffler Shop**				
2					
3	**Waiting Lines**		**M/M/1 (Single Server Model)**		
4	The arrival RATE and service RATE both must be rates and use the same time unit. Given a				
5	time such as 10 minutes, convert it to a rate such as 6 per hour.				
6	**Data**			**Results**	
7	Arrival rate (λ)	2		Average server utilization(ρ)	0.666667
8	Service rate (μ)	3		Average number of customers in the queue(L_q)	1.333333
9				Average number of customers in the system(L_s)	2
10				Average waiting time in the queue(W_q)	0.666667
11				Average time in the system(W_s)	1
12				Probability (% of time) system is empty (P_0)	0.333333
13					
14					
15	**Probabilities**				
16	**Number**	Probability	Cumulative Probability		
17	0	0.333333	0.333333		
18	1	0.222222	0.555556		
19	2	0.148148	0.703704		
20	3	0.098765	0.802469		
21	4	0.065844	0.868313		
22	5	0.043896	0.912209		
23	6	0.029264	0.941472		
24	7	0.019509	0.960982		

where

$$m = \text{number of channels}$$
$$C_s = \text{service cost (labor cost) of each channel}$$

The waiting cost when the waiting time cost is based on time in the system is

$$\text{Total waiting cost} = (\text{Total time spent waiting by all arrivals})(\text{Cost of waiting})$$
$$= (\text{Number of arrivals})(\text{Average wait per arrival})C_w$$

so,

$$\text{Total waiting cost} = (\lambda W)C_w \tag{12-9}$$

If the waiting time cost is based on time in the queue, this becomes

$$\text{Total waiting cost} = (\lambda W_q)C_w \tag{12-10}$$

These costs are based on whatever time units (often hours) are used in determining λ. Adding the total service cost to the total waiting cost, we have the total cost of the queuing system. When the waiting cost is based on the time in the system, this is

$$\text{Total cost} = \text{Total service cost} + \text{Total waiting cost}$$
$$\text{Total cost} = mC_s + \lambda WC_w \tag{12-11}$$

When the waiting cost is based on time in the queue, the total cost is

$$\text{Total cost} = mC_s + \lambda W_q C_w \tag{12-12}$$

At times we may wish to determine the daily cost, and then we simply find the total number of arrivals per day. Let us consider the situation for Arnold's Muffler Shop.

Customer waiting time is often considered the most important factor.

Arnold estimates that the cost of customer waiting time, in terms of customer dissatisfaction and lost goodwill, is $50 per hour of time spent *waiting* in line. (After customers' cars are actually being serviced on the rack, customers don't seem to mind waiting.) Because on the average a car has a $^2/_3$ hour wait and there are approximately 16 cars serviced per day (2 per hour times 8 working hours per day), the total number of hours that customers spend waiting for mufflers to be installed each day is $^2/_3 \times 16 = {}^{32}/_3$, or $10\,^2/_3$ hours. Hence, in this case,

$$\text{Total daily waiting cost} = (8 \text{ hours per day})\lambda W_q C_w = (8)(2)(^2/_3)(\$50) = \$533.33$$

The only other cost that Larry Arnold can identify in this queuing situation is the pay rate of Reid Blank, the mechanic. Blank is paid $15 per hour:

$$\text{Total daily service cost} = (8 \text{ hours per day})mC_s = 8(1)(\$15) = \$120$$

Waiting cost plus service cost equal total cost.

The total daily cost of the system as it is currently configured is the total of the waiting cost and the service cost, which gives us

$$\text{Total daily cost of the queuing system} = \$533.33 + \$120 = \$653.33$$

Now comes a decision. Arnold finds out through the muffler business grapevine that the Rusty Muffler, a cross-town competitor, employs a mechanic named Jimmy Smith who can efficiently install new mufflers at the rate of 4 per hour. Larry Arnold contacts Smith and inquires as to his interest in switching employers. Smith says that he would consider leaving the Rusty Muffler but only if he were paid a $20 per hour salary. Arnold, being a crafty businessman, decides that it may be worthwhile to fire Blank and replace him with the speedier but more expensive Smith.

He first recomputes all the operating characteristics using a new service rate of 4 mufflers per hour:

$$\lambda = 2 \text{ cars arriving per hour}$$

$$\mu = 4 \text{ cars serviced per hour}$$

$$L = \frac{\lambda}{\mu - \lambda} = \frac{2}{4 - 2} = 1 \text{ car in the system on the average}$$

$$W = \frac{1}{\mu - \lambda} = \frac{1}{4 - 2} = \frac{1}{2} \text{ hour in the system on the average}$$

$$L_q = \frac{\lambda^2}{\mu(\mu - \lambda)} = \frac{2^2}{4(4 - 2)} = \frac{4}{8} = \frac{1}{2} \text{ car waiting in line on the average}$$

$$W_q = \frac{\lambda}{\mu(\mu - \lambda)} = \frac{2}{4(4 - 2)} = \frac{2}{8} = \frac{1}{4} \text{ hour} = 15 \text{ minutes average waiting time per car in the queue}$$

$$\rho = \frac{\lambda}{\mu} = \frac{2}{4} = 0.5 = \text{percentage of time mechanic is busy}$$

$$P_0 = 1 - \frac{\lambda}{\mu} = 1 - 0.5 = 0.5 = \text{probability that there are 0 cars in the system}$$

Probability of More Than k Cars in the System

k	$P_{n>k} = \left(\frac{2}{4}\right)^{k+1}$
0	0.500
1	0.250
2	0.125
3	0.062
4	0.031
5	0.016
6	0.008
7	0.004

It is quite evident that Smith's speed will result in considerably shorter queues and waiting times. For example, a customer would now spend an average of $\frac{1}{2}$ hour in the system and $\frac{1}{4}$ hour waiting in the queue, as opposed to 1 hour in the system and $\frac{2}{3}$ hour in the queue with Blank as mechanic. The total daily waiting time cost with Smith as the mechanic will be

$$\text{Total daily waiting cost} = (8 \text{ hours per day})\lambda W_q C_w = (8)(2)\left(\frac{1}{4}\right)(\$50) = \$200 \text{ per day}$$

Notice that the total time spent waiting for the 16 customers per day is now

$$(16 \text{ cars per day}) \times (\tfrac{1}{4} \text{ hour per car}) = 4 \text{ hours}$$

instead of 10.67 hours with Blank. Thus, the waiting is much less than half of what it was, even though the service rate only changed from 3 per hour to 4 per hour.

Here is a comparison for total costs using the two different mechanics.

The service cost will go up due to the higher salary, but the overall cost will decrease, as we see here:

$$\text{Service cost of Smith} = 8 \text{ hours/day} \times \$20/\text{hour} = \$160 \text{ per day}$$

$$\text{Total expected cost} = \text{Waiting cost} + \text{Service cost} = \$200 + \$160$$
$$= \$360 \text{ per day}$$

IN ACTION

Ambulances in Chile Evaluate and Improve Performance Metrics Through Queuing Theory

Researchers in Chile turned to queuing theory to evaluate and improve ambulance services. They investigated the key performance indicators that are of value to an ambulance company manager (e.g., number of ambulances deployed, ambulance base locations, operating costs) and the key performance indicators that are of value to a customer (e.g., waiting time until service, queue prioritization system).

The somewhat surprising result that the researchers brought to light was that seemingly simple metrics such as waiting time in queue, W_q, were of the most value for ambulance operations. Reducing wait times saves the ambulance company money in gasoline and transportation costs, and, more importantly, it can save lives for its customers. In other words, sometimes simpler is better.

Source: Based on Marcos Singer and Patricio Donoso. "Assessing an Ambulance Service with Queuing Theory," *Computers & Operations Research* 35, 8 (2008): 2549–2560.

Because the total daily expected cost with Blank as mechanic was $653.33, Arnold may very well decide to hire Smith and reduce costs by $653.33 − $360 = $293.33 per day.

Enhancing the Queuing Environment

Although reducing the waiting time is an important factor in reducing the waiting time cost of a queuing system, a manager might find other ways to reduce this cost. The total waiting time cost is based on the total amount of time spent waiting (based on W or W_q) and the cost of waiting (C_w). Reducing either of these will reduce the overall cost of waiting. Enhancing the queuing environment by making the wait less unpleasant may reduce C_w as customers will not be as upset by having to wait. There are magazines in the waiting room of doctors' offices for patients to read while waiting. There are tabloids on display by the checkout lines in grocery stores, and customers read the headlines to pass time while waiting. Music is often played while telephone callers are placed on hold. At major amusement parks there are video screens and televisions in some of the queue lines to make the wait more interesting. For some of these, the waiting line is so entertaining that it is almost an attraction itself.

All of these things are designed to keep the customer busy and to enhance the conditions surrounding the waiting so that it appears that time is passing more quickly than it actually is. Consequently, the cost of waiting (C_w) becomes lower and the total cost of the queuing system is reduced. Sometimes, reducing the total cost in this way is easier than reducing the total cost by lowering W or W_q. In the case of Arnold's Muffler Shop, Arnold might consider putting a television in the waiting room and remodeling this room so customers feel more comfortable while waiting for their cars to be serviced.

12.5 Multichannel Queuing Model with Poisson Arrivals and Exponential Service Times (*M/M/m*)

The next logical step is to look at a *multichannel queuing system,* in which two or more servers or channels are available to handle arriving customers. Let us still assume that customers awaiting service form one single line and then proceed to the first available server. An example of such a multichannel, single-phase waiting line is found in many banks today. A common line is formed and the customer at the head of the line proceeds to the first free teller (Refer to Figure 12.2 for a typical multichannel configuration.)

The multichannel model also assumes Poisson arrivals and exponential service times.

The multiple-channel system presented here again assumes that arrivals follow a Poisson probability distribution and that service times are distributed exponentially. Service is first come, first served, and all servers are assumed to perform at the same rate. Other assumptions listed earlier for the single-channel model apply as well.

Equations for the Multichannel Queuing Model

If we let

$$m = \text{number of channels open,}$$
$$\lambda = \text{average arrival rate, and}$$
$$\mu = \text{average service rate at each channel}$$

the following formulas may be used in the waiting line analysis:

1. The probability that there are zero customers or units in the system:

$$P_0 = \frac{1}{\left[\sum_{n=0}^{n=m-1} \frac{1}{n!}\left(\frac{\lambda}{\mu}\right)^n\right] + \frac{1}{m!}\left(\frac{\lambda}{\mu}\right)^m \frac{m\mu}{m\mu - \lambda}} \quad \text{for } m\mu > \lambda \tag{12-13}$$

2. The average number of customers or units in the system:

$$L = \frac{\lambda\mu(\lambda/\mu)^m}{(m-1)!(m\mu - \lambda)^2}P_0 + \frac{\lambda}{\mu} \tag{12-14}$$

3. The average time a unit spends in the waiting line or being serviced (namely, in the system):

$$W = \frac{\mu(\lambda/\mu)^m}{(m-1)!(m\mu - \lambda)^2}P_0 + \frac{1}{\mu} = \frac{L}{\lambda} \tag{12-15}$$

4. The average number of customers or units in line waiting for service:

$$L_q = L - \frac{\lambda}{\mu} \tag{12-16}$$

5. The average time a customer or unit spends in the queue waiting for service:

$$W_q = W - \frac{1}{\mu} = \frac{L_q}{\lambda} \tag{12-17}$$

6. Utilization rate:

$$\rho = \frac{\lambda}{m\mu} \tag{12-18}$$

These equations are obviously more complex than the ones used in the single-channel model, yet they are used in exactly the same fashion and provide the same type of information as did the simpler model.

Arnold's Muffler Shop Revisited

For an application of the multichannel queuing model, let's return to the case of Arnold's Muffler Shop. Earlier, Larry Arnold examined two options. He could retain his current mechanic, Reid Blank, at a total expected cost of $653 per day; or he could fire Blank and hire a slightly more expensive but faster worker named Jimmy Smith. With Smith on board, service system costs could be reduced to $360 per day.

The muffler shop considers opening a second muffler service channel that operates at the same speed as the first one.

A third option is now explored. Arnold finds that at minimal after-tax cost he can open a *second* garage bay in which mufflers can be installed. Instead of firing his first mechanic, Blank, he would hire a second worker. The new mechanic would be expected to install mufflers at the same rate as Blank—about $\mu = 3$ per hour. Customers, who would still arrive at the rate of $\lambda = 2$ per hour, would wait in a single line until one of the two mechanics is free. To find out

TABLE 12.2 Effect of Service Level on Arnold's Operating Characteristics

OPERATING CHARACTERISTIC	LEVEL OF SERVICE		
	ONE MECHANIC (REID BLANK) $\mu = 3$	TWO MECHANICS $\mu = 3$ FOR EACH	ONE FAST MECHANIC (JIMMY SMITH) $\mu = 4$
Probability that the system is empty (P_0)	0.33	0.50	0.50
Average number of cars in the system (L)	2 cars	0.75 car	1 car
Average time spent in the system (W)	60 minutes	22.5 minutes	30 minutes
Average number of cars in the queue (L_q)	1.33 cars	0.083 car	0.50 car
Average time spent in the queue (W_q)	40 minutes	2.5 minutes	15 minutes

how this option compares with the old single-channel waiting line system, Arnold computes several operating characteristics for the $m = 2$ channel system:

$$P_0 = \cfrac{1}{\left[\displaystyle\sum_{n=0}^{1}\frac{1}{n!}\left(\frac{2}{3}\right)^n\right] + \frac{1}{2!}\left(\frac{2}{3}\right)^2\left(\frac{2(3)}{2(3) - 2}\right)}$$

$$= \cfrac{1}{1 + \frac{2}{3} + \frac{1}{2}\left(\frac{4}{9}\right)\left(\frac{6}{6 - 2}\right)} = \cfrac{1}{1 + \frac{2}{3} + \frac{1}{3}} = \frac{1}{2} = 0.5$$

$$= \text{probability of 0 cars in the system}$$

$$L = \left(\frac{(2)(3)(\frac{2}{3})^2}{1![2(3) - 2]^2}\right)\left(\frac{1}{2}\right) + \frac{2}{3} = \frac{\frac{8}{3}}{16}\left(\frac{1}{2}\right) + \frac{2}{3} = \frac{3}{4} = 0.75$$

$$= \text{average number of cars in the system}$$

$$W = \frac{L}{\lambda} = \frac{\frac{3}{4}}{2} = \frac{3}{8}\text{ hour} = 22\frac{1}{2}\text{ minutes}$$

$$= \text{average time a car spends in the system}$$

$$L_q = L - \frac{\lambda}{\mu} = \frac{3}{4} - \frac{2}{3} = \frac{1}{12} = 0.083$$

$$= \text{average number of cars in the queue}$$

$$W_q = \frac{L_q}{\lambda} = \frac{0.083}{2} = 0.0417\text{ hour} = 2\frac{1}{2}\text{ minutes}$$

$$= \text{average time a car spends in the queue}$$

Dramatically lower waiting time results from opening the second service bay.

These data are compared with earlier operating characteristics in Table 12.2. The increased service from opening a second channel has a dramatic effect on almost all characteristics. In particular, time spent waiting in line drops from 40 minutes with one mechanic (Blank) or 15 minutes with Smith down to only $2\frac{1}{2}$ minutes! Similarly, the average number of cars in the queue falls to 0.083 (about $\frac{1}{12}$ of a car).* But does this mean that a second bay should be opened?

To complete his economic analysis, Arnold assumes that the second mechanic would be paid the same as the current one, Blank, namely, $15 per hour. The daily waiting cost now will be

$$\text{Total daily waiting cost} = (8\text{ hours per day})\lambda W_q C_w = (8)(2)(0.0417)(\$50) = \$33.36$$

---

*You might note that adding a second mechanic does not cut queue waiting time and length just in half, but makes it even smaller. This is because of the *random* arrival and service processes. When there is only one mechanic and two customers arrive within a minute of each other, the second will have a long wait. The fact that the mechanic may have been idle for 30 to 40 minutes before they both arrive does not change this average waiting time. Thus, single-channel models often have higher wait times relative to multichannel models.

PROGRAM 12.2

Excel QM Solution to Arnold's Muffler Multichannel Example

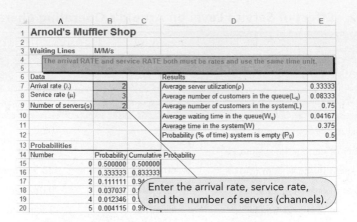

Notice that the total waiting time for the 16 cars per day is $(16 \text{ cars/day}) \times (0.0415 \text{ hour/car})$ $= 0.664$ hours per day instead of the 10.67 hours with only one mechanic.

The service cost is doubled, as there are two mechanics, so this is

$$\text{Total daily service cost} = (8 \text{ hours per day})mC_s = (8)2(\$15) = \$240$$

The total daily cost of the system as it is currently configured is the total of the waiting cost and the service cost, which is

$$\text{Total daily cost of the queuing system} = \$33.20 + \$240 = \$273.20$$

As you recall, total cost with just Blank as mechanic was found to be $653 per day. Cost with just Smith was just $360. Opening a second service bay will save about $380 per day compared to the current system, and it will save about $87 per day compared to the system with the faster mechanic. Thus, because the after-tax cost of a second bay is very low, Arnold's decision is to open a second service bay and hire a second worker who is paid the same as Blank. This may have additional benefits because word may spread about the very short waits at Arnold's Muffler Shop, and this may increase the number of customers who choose to use Arnold's.

USING EXCEL QM FOR ANALYSIS OF ARNOLD'S MULTICHANNEL QUEUING MODEL   To use Excel QM for this problem, from the Excel QM menu, select *Waiting Lines - Multiple Channel Model (M/M/s)*. When the spreadsheet appears, enter the arrival rate (2), service rate (3), and number of servers (2). Once these are entered, the solution shown in Program 12.2 will be displayed.

12.6   Constant Service Time Model (*M/D/1*)

Constant service rates speed the process compared to exponentially distributed service times with the same value of μ.

Some service systems have constant service times instead of exponentially distributed times. When customers or equipment are processed according to a fixed cycle, as in the case of an automatic car wash or an amusement park ride, constant service rates are appropriate. Because constant rates are certain, the values for L_q, W_q, L, and W are always less than they would be in the models we have just discussed, which have variable service times. As a matter of fact, both the average queue length and the average waiting time in the queue are *halved* with the constant service rate model.

Equations for the Constant Service Time Model
Constant service model formulas follow:

1. Average length of the queue:

$$L_q = \frac{\lambda^2}{2\mu(\mu - \lambda)} \tag{12-19}$$

2. Average waiting time in the queue:

$$W_q = \frac{\lambda}{2\mu(\mu - \lambda)} \tag{12-20}$$

IN ACTION   Queuing at the Polls

The long lines at the polls in recent presidential elections have caused some concern. In 2000, some voters in Florida waited in line over 2 hours to cast their ballots. The final tally favored the winner by 527 votes of the almost 6 million votes cast in that state. Some voters growing tired of waiting and simply leaving the line without voting may have affected the outcome. A change of 0.01% could have caused different results. In 2004, there were reports of voters in Ohio waiting in line 10 hours to vote. If as few as 19 potential voters at each precinct in the 12 largest counties in Ohio got tired of waiting and left without voting, the outcome of the election may have been different. There were obvious problems with the number of machines available in some of the precincts. One precinct needed 13 machines but had only 2. Inexplicably, there were 68 voting machines in warehouses that were not even used. Other states had some long lines as well.

The basic problem stems from not having enough voting machines in many of the precincts, although some precincts had sufficient machines and no problems. Why was there such a problem in some of the voting precincts? Part of the reason is related to poor forecasting of the voter turnout in various precincts. Whatever the cause, the misallocation of voting machines among the precincts seems to be a major cause of the long lines in the national elections. Queuing models can help provide a scientific way to analyze the needs and anticipate the voting lines based on the number of machines provided.

The basic voting precinct can be modeled as a multichannel queuing system. By evaluating a range of values for the forecast number of voters at the different times of the day, a determination can be made on how long the lines will be, based on the number of voting machines available. While there still could be some lines if the state does not have enough voting machines to meet the anticipated need, the proper distribution of these machines will help to keep the waiting times reasonable.

Source: Based on Alexander S. Belenky and Richard C. Larson. "To Queue or Not to Queue," *OR/MS Today* 33, 3 (June 2006): 30–34.

3. Average number of customers in the system:

$$L = L_q + \frac{\lambda}{\mu} \qquad (12\text{-}21)$$

4. Average time in the system:

$$W = W_q + \frac{1}{\mu} \qquad (12\text{-}22)$$

Garcia-Golding Recycling, Inc.

Garcia-Golding Recycling, Inc., collects and compacts aluminum cans and glass bottles in New York City. Its truck drivers, who arrive to unload these materials for recycling, currently wait an average of 15 minutes before emptying their loads. The cost of the driver and truck time wasted while in queue is valued at $60 per hour. A new automated compactor can be purchased that will process truck loads at a constant rate of 12 trucks per hour (i.e., 5 minutes per truck). Trucks arrive according to a Poisson distribution at an average rate of 8 per hour. If the new compactor is put in use, its cost will be amortized at a rate of $3 per truck unloaded. A summer intern from a local college did the following analysis to evaluate the costs versus benefits of the purchase:

Cost analysis for the recycling example.

$$\textit{Current} \text{ waiting cost/trip} = \left(\tfrac{1}{4} \text{ hour waiting now}\right)(\$60/\text{hour cost})$$
$$= \$15/\text{trip}$$
$$\textit{New} \text{ system: } \lambda = 8 \text{ trucks/hour arriving}$$
$$\mu = 12 \text{ trucks/hour served}$$
$$\text{Average waiting time in queue} = W_q = \frac{\lambda}{2\mu(\mu - \lambda)} = \frac{8}{2(12)(12 - 8)}$$
$$= \frac{1}{12} \text{ hour}$$
$$\text{Waiting cost/trip with new compactor} = \left(\tfrac{1}{12} \text{ hour wait}\right)(\$60/\text{hour cost}) = \$5/\text{trip}$$
$$\text{Savings with new equipment} = \$15 \text{ (current system)} - \$5 \text{ (new system)}$$
$$= \$10/\text{trip}$$
$$\text{Cost of new equipment amortized} = \underline{\$3/\text{trip}}$$
$$\text{Net savings} = \$7/\text{trip}$$

PROGRAM 12.3

Excel QM Solution for Constant Service Time Model for Garcia-Golding Recycling Example

	A	B	C	D	E
1	Garcia-Golding Recycling				
2					
3	Waiting Lines			M/D/1 (Constant Service Times)	
4	The arrival RATE and service RATE both must be rates and use the same time unit. Given a time such				
5	as 10 minutes, convert it to a rate such as 6 per hour.				
6	Data			Results	
7	Arrival rate (λ)	8		Average server utilization(ρ)	0.66667
8	Service rate (μ)	12		Average number of customers in the queue(L_q)	0.66667
9				Average number of customers in the system(L_s)	1.33333
10				Average waiting time in the queue(W_q)	0.08333
11				Average time in the system(W_s)	0.16667
12				Probability (% of time) system is empty (P_0)	0.33333

USING EXCEL QM FOR GARCIA-GOLDING'S CONSTANT SERVICE TIME MODEL   To use Excel QM for this problem, from the Excel QM menu, select *Waiting Lines - Constant Service Time Model (M/D/1)*. When the spreadsheet appears, enter the arrival rate (8) and the service rate (12). Once these are entered, the solution shown in Program 12.3 will be displayed.

12.7   Finite Population Model (*M/M/1* with Finite Source)

When there is a limited population of potential customers for a service facility, we need to consider a different queuing model. This model would be used, for example, if you were considering equipment repairs in a factory that has five machines, if you were in charge of maintenance for a fleet of 10 commuter airplanes, or if you ran a hospital ward that has 20 beds. The limited population model permits any number of repair people (servers) to be considered.

The reason this model differs from the three earlier queuing models is that there is now a *dependent* relationship between the length of the queue and the arrival rate. To illustrate the extreme situation, if your factory had five machines and all were broken and awaiting repair, the arrival rate would drop to zero. In general, as the waiting line becomes longer in the limited population model, the arrival rate of customers or machines drops lower.

In this section, we describe a finite calling population model that has the following assumptions:

1. There is only one server.
2. The population of units seeking service is finite.*
3. Arrivals follow a Poisson distribution, and service times are exponentially distributed.
4. Customers are served on a first-come, first-served basis.

Equations for the Finite Population Model

Using

$$\lambda = \text{mean arrival rate}, \mu = \text{mean service rate}, N = \text{size of the population}$$

the operating characteristics for the finite population model with a single channel or server on duty are as follows:

1. Probability that the system is empty:

$$P_0 = \frac{1}{\sum_{n=0}^{N} \frac{N!}{(N-n)!}\left(\frac{\lambda}{\mu}\right)^n} \tag{12-23}$$

---

*Although there is no definite number that we can use to divide finite from infinite populations, the general rule of thumb is this: If the number in the queue is a significant proportion of the calling population, use a finite queuing model. *Finite Queuing Tables*, by L. G. Peck and R. N. Hazelwood (New York: John Wiley & Sons, Inc., 1958), eliminate much of the mathematics involved in computing the operating characteristics for such a model.

2. Average length of the queue:

$$L_q = N - \left(\frac{\lambda + \mu}{\lambda}\right)(1 - P_0) \qquad (12\text{-}24)$$

3. Average number of customers (units) in the system:

$$L = L_q + (1 - P_0) \qquad (12\text{-}25)$$

4. Average waiting time in the queue:

$$W_q = \frac{L_q}{(N - L)\lambda} \qquad (12\text{-}26)$$

5. Average time in the system:

$$W = W_q + \frac{1}{\mu} \qquad (12\text{-}27)$$

6. Probability of *n* units in the system:

$$P_n = \frac{N!}{(N - n)!}\left(\frac{\lambda}{\mu}\right)^n P_0 \quad \text{for } n = 0, 1, \ldots, N \qquad (12\text{-}28)$$

Department of Commerce Example

Past records indicate that each of the five high-speed "page" printers at the U.S. Department of Commerce, in Washington, D.C., needs repair after about 20 hours of use. Breakdowns have been determined to be Poisson distributed. The one technician on duty can service a printer in an average of 2 hours, following an exponential distribution.

To compute the system's operation characteristics we first note that the mean arrival rate is $\lambda = \frac{1}{20} = 0.05$ printer/hour. The mean service rate is $\mu = \frac{1}{2} = 0.50$ printer/hour. Then

1. $P_0 = \dfrac{1}{\displaystyle\sum_{n=0}^{5} \dfrac{5!}{(5 - n)!}\left(\dfrac{0.05}{0.5}\right)^n} = 0.564$ (we leave these calculations for you to confirm)

2. $L_q = 5 - \left(\dfrac{0.05 + 0.5}{0.05}\right)(1 - P_0) = 5 - (11)(1 - 0.564) = 5 - 4.8$

    $= 0.2$ printer

3. $L = 0.2 + (1 - 0.564) = 0.64$ printer

4. $W_q = \dfrac{0.2}{(5 - 0.64)(0.05)} = \dfrac{0.2}{0.22} = 0.91$ hour

5. $W = 0.91 + \dfrac{1}{0.50} = 2.91$ hours

If printer downtime costs $120 per hour and the technician is paid $25 per hour, we can also compute the total cost per hour:

$$
\begin{aligned}
\text{Total hourly cost} &= (\text{Average number of printers down})(\text{Cost per downtime hour}) \\
&\quad + \text{Cost per technician hour} \\
&= (0.64)(\$120) + \$25 = \$76.80 + \$25.00 = \$101.80
\end{aligned}
$$

SOLVING THE DEPARTMENT OF COMMERCE FINITE POPULATION MODEL WITH EXCEL QM To use Excel QM for this problem, from the Excel QM menu, select *Waiting Lines - Limited Population Model (M/M/s)*. When the spreadsheet appears, enter the arrival rate (8), service rate (12), number of servers, and population size. Once these are entered, the solution shown in Program 12.4 will be displayed. Additional output is also available.

PROGRAM 12.4

Excel QM solution for Finite Population Model for Department of Commerce Example

	A	B	C	D	E
1	Department of Commerce				
2					
3	Waiting Lines		M/M/s with a finite population		
4	The arrival rate is for each member of the population. If they go for service every 20				
5	minutes then enter 3 (per hour).				
6	Data			Results	
7	Arrival rate (λ) per customer	0.05		Average server utilization(ρ)	0.43605
8	Service rate (μ)	0.5		Average number of customers in the queue(L_q)	0.20347
9	Number of servers	1		Average number of customers in the system(L_s)	0.63952
10	Population size (N)	5		Average waiting time in the queue(W_q)	0.93326
11				Average time in the system(W_s)	2.93326
12				Probability (% of time) system is empty (P_0)	0.56395
13				Effective arrival rate	0.21802

12.8 Some General Operating Characteristic Relationships

A steady state is the normal operating condition of the queuing system.

A queuing system is in a transient state before the steady state is reached.

Certain relationships exist among specific operating characteristics for any queuing system in a **steady state**. A steady state condition exists when a queuing system is in its normal stabilized operating condition, usually after an initial or **transient state** that may occur (e.g., having customers waiting at the door when a business opens in the morning). Both the arrival rate and the service rate should be stable in steady state. John D. C. Little is credited with the first two of these relationships, and hence they are called **Little's Flow Equations**:

$$L = \lambda W \ (\text{or } W = L/\lambda) \tag{12-29}$$

$$L_q = \lambda W_q \ (\text{or } W_q = L_q/\lambda) \tag{12-30}$$

A third condition that must always be met is

Average time in system = average time in queue + average time receiving service

$$W = W_q + 1/\mu \tag{12-31}$$

The advantage of these formulas is that once one of these four characteristics is known, the other characteristics can easily be found. This is important because for certain queuing models, one of these may be much easier to determine than the others. These are applicable to all of the queuing systems discussed in this chapter except the finite population model.

12.9 More Complex Queuing Models and the Use of Simulation

Many practical waiting line problems that occur in production and operations service systems have characteristics like those of Arnold's Muffler Shop, Garcia-Golding Recycling Inc., or the Department of Commerce. This is true when the situation calls for single- or multichannel waiting lines, with Poisson arrivals and exponential or constant service times, an infinite calling population, and FIFO service.

Often, however, *variations* of this specific case are present in an analysis. Service times in an automobile repair shop, for example, tend to follow the normal probability distribution instead of the exponential. A college registration system in which seniors have first choice of courses and hours over all other students is an example of a first-come, first-served model with a preemptive priority queue discipline. A physical examination for military recruits is an example of a multiphase system—one that differs from the single-phase models discussed in this chapter. A recruit first lines up to have blood drawn at one station, then waits to take an eye exam at the next station, talks to a psychiatrist at the third, and is examined by a doctor for medical problems at the fourth. At each phase, the recruit must enter another queue and wait for his or her turn.

More sophisticated models exist to handle variations of basic assumptions, but when even these do not apply we can turn to computer simulation, the topic of Chapter 13.

Models to handle these cases have been developed by operations researchers. The computations for the resulting mathematical formulations are somewhat more complex than the ones covered in this chapter,* and many real-world queuing applications are too complex to be modeled analytically at all. When this happens, quantitative analysts usually turn to *computer simulation*.

---

*Often, the *qualitative* results of queuing models are as useful as the quantitative results. Results show that it is inherently more efficient to pool resources, use central dispatching, and provide single multiple-server systems rather than multiple single-server systems.

Simulation, the topic of Chapter 13, is a technique in which random numbers are used to draw inferences about probability distributions (such as arrivals and services). Using this approach, many hours, days, or months of data can be developed by a computer in a few seconds. This allows analysis of controllable factors, such as adding another service channel, without actually doing so physically. Basically, whenever a standard analytical queuing model provides only a poor approximation of the actual service system, it is wise to develop a simulation model instead.

Summary

Waiting lines and service systems are important parts of the business world. In this chapter we describe several common queuing situations and present mathematical models for analyzing waiting lines following certain assumptions. Those assumptions are that (1) arrivals come from an infinite or very large population, (2) arrivals are Poisson distributed, (3) arrivals are treated on a FIFO basis and do not balk or renege, (4) service times follow the negative exponential distribution or are constant, and (5) the average service rate is faster than the average arrival rate.

The models illustrated in this chapter are for single-channel, single-phase and multichannel, single-phase problems. After a series of operating characteristics are computed, total expected costs are studied. As shown graphically in Figure 12.1, total cost is the sum of the cost of providing service plus the cost of waiting time.

Key operating characteristics for a system are shown to be (1) utilization rate, (2) percent idle time, (3) average time spent waiting in the system and in the queue, (4) average number of customers in the system and in the queue, and (5) probabilities of various numbers of customers in the system.

The chapter emphasizes that a variety of queuing models exist that do not meet all of the assumptions of the traditional models. In these cases we use more complex mathematical models or turn to a technique called computer simulation. The application of simulation to problems of queuing systems, inventory control, machine breakdown, and other quantitative analysis situations is the topic discussed in Chapter 13.

Glossary

Balking   The case in which arriving customers refuse to join the waiting line.

Calling Population   The population of items from which arrivals at the queuing system come.

FIFO   A queue discipline (meaning first-in, first-out) in which the customers are served in the strict order of arrival.

Kendall Notation   A method of classifying queuing systems based on the distribution of arrivals, the distribution of service times, and the number of service channels.

Limited, or Finite, Population   A case in which the number of customers in the system is a significant proportion of the calling population.

Limited Queue Length   A waiting line that cannot increase beyond a specific size.

Little's Flow Equations   A set of relationships that exist for any queuing system in a steady state.

M/D/1   Kendall notation for the constant service time model.

M/M/1   Kendall notation for the single-channel model with Poisson arrivals and exponential service times.

M/M/m   Kendall notation for the multichannel queuing model (with *m* servers) and Poisson arrivals and exponential service times.

Multichannel Queuing System   A system that has more than one service facility, all fed by the same single queue.

Multiphase System   A system in which service is received from more than one station, one after the other.

Negative Exponential Probability Distribution   A probability distribution that is often used to describe random service times in a service system.

Operating Characteristics   Descriptive characteristics of a queuing system, including the average number of customers in a line and in the system, the average waiting times in a line and in the system, and percent idle time.

Poisson Distribution   A probability distribution that is often used to describe random arrivals in a queue.

Queue Discipline   The rule by which customers in a line receive service.

Queuing Theory   The mathematical study of waiting lines or queues.

Reneging   The case in which customers enter a queue but then leave before being serviced.

Service Cost   The cost of providing a particular level of service.

Single-Channel Queuing System   A system with one service facility fed by one queue.

Single-Phase System   A queuing system in which service is received at only one station.

Steady State   The normal, stabilized operating condition of a queuing system.

Transient State   The initial condition of a queuing system before a steady state is reached.

Unlimited, or Infinite, Population A calling population that is very large relative to the number of customers currently in the system.

Unlimited Queue Length A queue that can increase to an infinite size.

Utilization Factor (ρ) The proportion of the time that service facilities are in use.

Waiting Cost The cost to the firm of having customers or objects waiting to be serviced in the queue or in the system.

Waiting Line (Queue) One or more customers or objects waiting to be served.

Key Equations

λ = mean number of arrivals per time period

μ = mean number of people or items served per time period

Equations 12-1 through 12-7 describe operating characteristics in the single-channel model that has Poisson arrival and exponential service rates.

(12-1) L = average number of units (customers) in the system

$$= \frac{\lambda}{\mu - \lambda}$$

(12-2) W = average time a unit spends in the system (Waiting time + Service time)

$$= \frac{1}{\mu - \lambda}$$

(12-3) L_q = average number of units in the queue

$$= \frac{\lambda^2}{\mu(\mu - \lambda)}$$

(12-4) W_q = average time a unit spends waiting in the queue

$$= \frac{\lambda}{\mu(\mu - \lambda)}$$

(12-5) ρ = utilization factor for the system $= \dfrac{\lambda}{\mu}$

(12-6) P_0 = probability of 0 units in the system (i.e., the service unit is idle)

$$= 1 - \frac{\lambda}{\mu}$$

(12-7) $P_{n>k}$ = probability of more than k units in the system

$$= \left(\frac{\lambda}{\mu}\right)^{k+1}$$

Equations 12-8 through 12-12 are used for finding the costs of a queuing system.

(12-8) Total service cost $= mC_s$

where

m = number of channels

C_s = service cost (labor cost) of each channel

(12-9) Total waiting cost per time period $= (\lambda W)C_w$

C_w = cost of waiting

Waiting time cost based on time in the system.

(12-10) Total waiting cost per time period $= (\lambda W_q)C_w$

Waiting time cost based on time in the queue.

(12-11) Total cost $= mC_s + \lambda W C_w$

Waiting time cost based on time in the system.

(12-12) Total cost $= mC_s + \lambda W_q C_w$

Waiting time cost based on time in the queue.

Equations 12-13 through 12-18 describe operating characteristics in multichannel models that have Poisson arrival and exponential service rates, where m = *the number of open channels.*

(12-13) $$P_0 = \frac{1}{\left[\displaystyle\sum_{n=0}^{n=m-1} \frac{1}{n!}\left(\frac{\lambda}{\mu}\right)^n\right] + \frac{1}{m!}\left(\frac{\lambda}{\mu}\right)^m \frac{m\mu}{m\mu - \lambda}}$$

for $m\mu > \lambda$

Probability that there are no people or units in the system.

(12-14) $$L = \frac{\lambda\mu(\lambda/\mu)^m}{(m-1)!(m\mu - \lambda)^2}P_0 + \frac{\lambda}{\mu}$$

Average number of people or units in the system.

(12-15) $$W = \frac{\mu(\lambda/\mu)^m}{(m-1)!(m\mu - \lambda)^2}P_0 + \frac{1}{\mu} = \frac{L}{\lambda}$$

Average time a unit spends in the waiting line or being serviced (namely, in the system).

(12-16) $$L_q = L - \frac{\lambda}{\mu}$$

Average number of people or units in line waiting for service.

(12-17) $$W_q = W - \frac{1}{\mu} = \frac{L_q}{\lambda}$$

Average time a person or unit spends in the queue waiting for service.

(12-18) $$\rho = \frac{\lambda}{m\mu}$$

Utilization rate.

Equations 12-19 through 12-22 describe operating characteristics in single-channel models that have Poisson arrivals and
constant service rates.

$$(12\text{-}19)\ L_q = \frac{\lambda^2}{2\mu(\mu - \lambda)}$$

Average length of the queue.

$$(12\text{-}20)\ W_q = \frac{\lambda}{2\mu(\mu - \lambda)}$$

Average waiting time in the queue.

$$(12\text{-}21)\ L = L_q + \frac{\lambda}{\mu}$$

Average number of customers in the system.

$$(12\text{-}22)\ W = W_q + \frac{1}{\mu}$$

Average waiting time in the system.

Equations 12-23 through 12-28 describe operating characteristics in single-channel models that have Poisson arrivals and
exponential service rates and a finite calling population.

$$(12\text{-}23)\ P_0 = \frac{1}{\displaystyle\sum_{n=0}^{N} \frac{N!}{(N-n)!}\left(\frac{\lambda}{\mu}\right)^n}$$

Probability that the system is empty.

$$(12\text{-}24)\ L_q = N - \left(\frac{\lambda + \mu}{\lambda}\right)(1 - P_0)$$

Average length of the queue.

$$(12\text{-}25)\ L = L_q + (1 - P_0)$$

Average number of units in the system.

$$(12\text{-}26)\ W_q = \frac{L_q}{(N - L)\lambda}$$

Average time in the queue.

$$(12\text{-}27)\ W = W_q + \frac{1}{\mu}$$

Average time in the system.

$$(12\text{-}28)\ P_n = \frac{N!}{(N - n)!}\left(\frac{\lambda}{\mu}\right)^n P_0 \quad \text{for } n = 0, 1, \dots, N$$

Probability of n units in the system.

Equations 12-29 to 12-31 are Little's Flow Equations, which
can be used when a steady state condition exists.

$$(12\text{-}29)\ L = \lambda W$$

$$(12\text{-}30)\ L_q = \lambda W_q$$

$$(12\text{-}31)\ W = W_q + 1/\mu$$

Solved Problems

Solved Problem 12-1

The Maitland Furniture store gets an average of 50 customers per shift. The manager of Maitland wants
to calculate whether she should hire 1, 2, 3, or 4 salespeople. She has determined that average waiting
times will be 7 minutes with 1 salesperson, 4 minutes with 2 salespeople, 3 minutes with 3 salespeople,
and 2 minutes with 4 salespeople. She has estimated the cost per minute that customers wait at $1. The
cost per salesperson per shift (including benefits) is $70.
     How many salespeople should be hired?

Solution

The manager's calculations are as follows:

	NUMBER OF SALESPEOPLE			
	1	2	3	4
(a) Average number of customers per shift	50	50	50	50
(b) Average waiting time per customer (minutes)	7	4	3	2
(c) Total waiting time per shift ($a \times b$) (minutes)	350	200	150	100
(d) Cost per minute of waiting time (estimated)	$1.00	$1.00	$1.00	$1.00
(e) Value of lost time ($c \times d$) per shift	$ 350	$ 200	$ 150	$ 100
(f) Salary cost per shift	$ 70	$ 140	$ 210	$ 280
(g) Total cost per shift	$ 420	$ 340	$ 360	$ 380

Because the minimum total cost per shift relates to two salespeople, the manager's optimum strategy is
to hire 2 salespeople.

Solved Problem 12-2

Marty Schatz owns and manages a chili dog and soft drink store near the campus. Although Marty can service 30 customers per hour on the average (μ), he only gets 20 customers per hour (λ). Because Marty could wait on 50% more customers than actually visit his store, it doesn't make sense to him that he should have any waiting lines.

Marty hires you to examine the situation and to determine some characteristics of his queue. After looking into the problem, you find this to be an $M/M/1$ system. What are your findings?

Solution

$$L = \frac{\lambda}{\mu - \lambda} = \frac{20}{30 - 20} = 2 \text{ customers in the system on the average}$$

$$W = \frac{1}{\mu - \lambda} = \frac{1}{30 - 20} = 0.1 \text{ hour (6 minutes) that the average customer spends in the total system}$$

$$L_q = \frac{\lambda^2}{\mu(\mu - \lambda)} = \frac{20^2}{30(30 - 20)} = 1.33 \text{ customers waiting for service in line on the average}$$

$$w_q = \frac{\lambda}{\mu(\mu - \lambda)} = \frac{20}{30(30 - 20)} = {}^1/_{15} \text{ hour} = (4 \text{ minutes}) = \text{average waiting time of a customer in the queue awaiting service}$$

$$\rho = \frac{\lambda}{\mu} = \frac{20}{30} = 0.67 = \text{percentage of the time that Marty is busy waiting on customers}$$

$$P_0 = 1 - \frac{\lambda}{\mu} = 1 - \rho = 0.33 = \text{probability that there are no customers in the system (being waited on or waiting in the queue) at any given time}$$

**Probability of k or More Customers
Waiting in Line and/or Being Waited On**

k	$P_{n>k} = \left(\frac{\lambda}{\mu}\right)^{k+1}$
0	0.667
1	0.444
2	0.296
3	0.198

Solved Problem 12-3

Refer to Solved Problem 12-2. Marty agreed that these figures seemed to represent his approximate business situation. You are quite surprised at the length of the lines and elicit from him an estimated value of the customer's waiting time (in the queue, not being waited on) at 10 cents per minute. During the 12 hours that he is open he gets $(12 \times 20) = 240$ customers. The average customer is in a queue 4 minutes, so the total customer waiting time is $(240 \times 4 \text{ minutes}) = 960$ minutes. The value of 960 minutes is $(\$0.10)(960 \text{ minutes}) = \$96$. You tell Marty that not only is 10 cents per minute quite conservative, but he could probably save most of that $96 of customer ill will if he hired another salesclerk. After much haggling, Marty agrees to provide you with all the chili dogs you can eat during a week-long period in exchange for your analysis of the results of having two clerks wait on the customers.

Assuming that Marty hires one additional salesclerk whose service rate equals Marty's rate, complete the analysis.

Solution

With two people working, the system becomes two channel, or $m = 2$. The computations yield

$$P_0 = \cfrac{1}{\left[\displaystyle\sum_{n=0}^{n=m-1} \frac{1}{n!}\left[\frac{20}{30}\right]^n\right] + \frac{1}{2!}\left[\frac{20}{30}\right]^2\left[\frac{2(30)}{2(30) - 20}\right]}$$

$$= \frac{1}{(1)(2/3)^0 + (1)(2/3)^1 + (1/2)(4/9)(6/4)} = 0.5$$

$= $ probability of no customers in the system

$$L = \left[\frac{(20)(30)(20/30)^2}{(2 - 1)![(2)(30 - 20)]^2}\right]0.5 + \frac{20}{30} = 0.75 \text{ customer in the system on the average}$$

$$W = \frac{L}{\lambda} = \frac{3/4}{20} = \frac{3}{80} \text{ hour} = 2.25 \text{ minutes that the average customer spends in the total system}$$

$$L_q = L - \frac{\lambda}{\mu} = \frac{3}{4} - \frac{20}{30} = \frac{1}{12} = 0.083 \text{ customer waiting for service in line on the average}$$

$$W_q = \frac{L_q}{\lambda} = \frac{^1\!/_2}{20} = \frac{1}{240} \text{ hour} = \frac{1}{4} \text{ minute} = \begin{array}{l} \text{average waiting time of a customer in the queue} \\ \text{itself (not being serviced)} \end{array}$$

$$\rho = \frac{\lambda}{m\mu} = \frac{20}{2(30)} = \frac{1}{3} = 0.33 = \text{utilization rate}$$

You now have $(240 \text{ customers}) \times (1/240 \text{ hour}) = 1$ hour total customer waiting time per day.

Total cost of 60 minutes of customer waiting time is $(60 \text{ minutes})(\$0.10 \text{ per minute}) = \$6$.

Now you are ready to point out to Marty that the hiring of one additional clerk will save $\$96 - \$6 = \$90$ of customer ill will per 12-hour shift. Marty responds that the hiring should also reduce the number of people who look at the line and leave as well as those who get tired of waiting in line and leave. You tell Marty that you are ready for two chili dogs, extra hot.

Solved Problem 12-4

Vacation Inns is a chain of hotels operating in the southwestern part of the United States. The company uses a toll-free telephone number to take reservations for any of its hotels. The average time to handle each call is 3 minutes, and an average of 12 calls are received per hour. The probability distribution that describes the arrivals is unknown. Over a period of time it is determined that the average caller spends 6 minutes either on hold or receiving service. Find the average time in the queue, the average time in the system, the average number in the queue, and the average number in the system.

Solution

The probability distributions are unknown, but we are given the average time in the system (6 minutes). Thus, we can use Little's Flow Equations:

$$W = 6 \text{ minutes} = 6/60 \text{ hour} = 0.1 \text{ hour}$$
$$\lambda = 12 \text{ per hour}$$
$$\mu = 60/3 = 20 \text{ per hour}$$

Average time in queue $= W_q = W - 1/\mu = 0.1 - 1/20 = 0.1 - 0.05 = 0.05 \text{ hour}$

Average number in system $= L = \lambda W = 12(0.1) = 1.2 \text{ callers}$

Average number in queue $= L_q = \lambda W_q = 12(0.05) = 0.6 \text{ caller}$

Self-Test

- Before taking the self-test, refer to the learning objectives at the beginning of the chapter, the notes in the margins, and the glossary at the end of the chapter.
- Use the key at the back of the book to correct your answers.
- Restudy pages that correspond to any questions that you answered incorrectly or material you feel uncertain about.

1. Most systems use the queue discipline known as the FIFO rule.
   a. True
   b. False
2. Before using exponential distributions to build queuing models, the quantitative analyst should determine if the service time data fit the distribution.
   a. True
   b. False
3. In a multichannel, single-phase queuing system, the arrival will pass through at least two different service facilities.
   a. True
   b. False
4. Which of the following is *not* an assumption in $M/M/1$ models?
   a. Arrivals come from an infinite or very large population.
   b. Arrivals are Poisson distributed.
   c. Arrivals are treated on a FIFO basis and do not balk or renege.
   d. Service times follow the exponential distribution.
   e. The average arrival rate is faster than the average service rate.
5. A queuing system described as $M/D/2$ would have
   a. exponential service times.
   b. two queues.
   c. constant service times.
   d. constant arrival rates.
6. Cars enter the drive-through of a fast-food restaurant to place an order, and then they proceed to pay for the food and pick up the order. This is an example of
   a. a multichannel system.
   b. a multiphase system.
   c. a multiqueue system.
   d. none of the above.
7. The utilization factor for a system is defined as
   a. mean number of people served divided by the mean number of arrivals per time period.
   b. the average time a customer spends waiting in a queue.
   c. proportion of the time the service facilities are in use.
   d. the percentage of idle time.
   e. none of the above.

8. Which of the following would not have a FIFO queue discipline?
   a. Fast-food restaurant
   b. Post office
   c. Checkout line at grocery store
   d. Emergency room at a hospital
9. A company has one computer technician who is responsible for repairs on the company's 20 computers. As a computer breaks, the technician is called to make the repair. If the repairperson is busy, the machine must wait to be repaired. This is an example of
   a. a multichannel system.
   b. a finite population system.
   c. a constant service rate system.
   d. a multiphase system.
10. In performing a cost analysis of a queuing system, the waiting time cost (C_w) is sometimes based on the time in the queue and sometimes based on the time in the system. The waiting cost should be based on time in the system for which of the following situations?
    a. Waiting in line to ride an amusement park ride
    b. Waiting to discuss a medical problem with a doctor
    c. Waiting for a picture and an autograph from a rock star
    d. Waiting for a computer to be fixed so it can be placed back in service
11. Customers enter the waiting line at a cafeteria on a first-come, first-served basis. The arrival rate follows a Poisson distribution, and service times follow an exponential distribution. If the average number of arrivals is 6 per minute and the average service rate of a single server is 10 per minute, what is the average number of customers in the system?
    a. 0.6
    b. 0.9
    c. 1.5
    d. 0.25
    e. none of the above
12. In the standard queuing model, we assume that the queue discipline is _____.
13. The service *time* in the $M/M/1$ queuing model is assumed to be _____.
14. When managers find standard queuing formulas inadequate or the mathematics unsolvable, they often resort to _____ to obtain their solutions.

Discussion Questions and Problems

Discussion Questions

12-1 What is the waiting line problem? What are the components in a waiting line system?

12-2 What are the assumptions underlying common queuing models?

12-3 Describe the important operating characteristics of a queuing system.

12-4 Why must the service rate be greater than the arrival rate in a single-channel queuing system?

12-5 Briefly describe three situations in which the FIFO discipline rule is not applicable in queuing analysis.

12-6 Provide examples of four situations in which there is a limited, or finite, population.

12-7 What are the components of the following systems? Draw and explain the configuration of each.
   (a) Barbershop
   (b) Car wash
   (c) Laundromat
   (d) Small grocery store

12-8 Give an example of a situation in which the waiting time cost would be based on waiting time in the queue. Give an example of a situation in which the waiting time cost would be based on waiting time in the system.

12-9 Do you think the Poisson distribution, which assumes independent arrivals, is a good estimation of arrival rates in the following queuing systems? Defend your position in each case.
   (a) Cafeteria in your school
   (b) Barbershop
   (c) Hardware store
   (d) Dentist's office
   (e) College class
   (f) Movie theater

Problems*

:12-10 The Schmedley Discount Department Store has approximately 300 customers shopping in its store between 9 A.M. and 5 P.M. on Saturdays. In deciding how many cash registers to keep open each Saturday, Schmedley's manager considers two factors: customer waiting time (and the associated waiting cost) and the service costs of employing additional checkout clerks. Checkout clerks are paid an average of $8 per hour. When only one is on duty, the waiting time per customer is about 10 minutes (or $\frac{1}{6}$ hour); when two clerks are on duty, the average checkout

time is 6 minutes per person; 4 minutes when three clerks are working; and 3 minutes when four clerks are on duty.

Schmedley's management has conducted customer satisfaction surveys and has been able to estimate that the store suffers approximately $10 in lost sales and goodwill for every *hour* of customer time spent waiting in checkout lines. Using the information provided, determine the optimal number of clerks to have on duty each Saturday to minimize the store's total expected cost.

•12-11 The Rockwell Electronics Corporation retains a service crew to repair machine breakdowns that occur on an average of $\lambda = 3$ per day (approximately Poisson in nature).

The crew can service an average of $\mu = 8$ machines per day, with a repair time distribution that resembles the exponential distribution.
   (a) What is the utilization rate of this service system?
   (b) What is the average downtime for a machine that is broken?
   (c) How many machines are waiting to be serviced at any given time?
   (d) What is the probability that more than one machine is in the system? Probability that more than two are broken and waiting to be repaired or being serviced? More than three? More than four?

•12-12 From historical data, Harry's Car Wash estimates that dirty cars arrive at the rate of 10 per hour all day Saturday. With a crew working the wash line, Harry figures that cars can be cleaned at the rate of one every 5 minutes. One car at a time is cleaned in this example of a single-channel waiting line.

Assuming Poisson arrivals and exponential service times, find the
   (a) average number of cars in line.
   (b) average time a car waits before it is washed.
   (c) average time a car spends in the service system.
   (d) utilization rate of the car wash.
   (e) probability that no cars are in the system.

:12-13 Mike Dreskin manages a large Los Angeles movie theater complex called Cinema I, II, III, and IV. Each of the four auditoriums plays a different film; the schedule is set so that starting times are staggered to avoid the large crowds that would occur if all four movies started at the same time. The theater has a single ticket booth and a cashier who can maintain an average service rate of 280 movie patrons per hour. Service times are assumed to follow an exponential distribution. Arrivals on a typically active day are Poisson distributed and average 210 per hour.

To determine the efficiency of the current ticket operation, Mike wishes to examine several queue operating characteristics.

(a) Find the average number of moviegoers waiting in line to purchase a ticket.

(b) What percentage of the time is the cashier busy?

(c) What is the average time that a customer spends in the system?

(d) What is the average time spent waiting in line to get to the ticket window?

(e) What is the probability that there are more than two people in the system? More than three people? More than four?

12-14 A university cafeteria line in the student center is a self-serve facility in which students select the food items they want and then form a single line to pay the cashier. Students arrive at the cashier at a rate of about four per minute according to a Poisson distribution. The single cashier ringing up sales takes about 12 seconds per customer, following an exponential distribution.

(a) What is the probability that there are more than two students in the system? More than three students? More than four?

(b) What is the probability that the system is empty?

(c) How long will the average student have to wait before reaching the cashier?

(d) What is the expected number of students in the queue?

(e) What is the average number in the system?

(f) If a second cashier is added (who works at the same pace), how will the operating characteristics computed in parts (b), (c), (d), and (e) change? Assume that customers wait in a single line and go to the first available cashier.

12-15 The wheat harvesting season in the American Midwest is short, and most farmers deliver their truckloads of wheat to a giant central storage bin within a two-week span. Because of this, wheat-filled trucks waiting to unload and return to the fields have been known to back up for a block at the receiving bin. The central bin is owned cooperatively, and it is to every farmer's benefit to make the unloading/storage process as efficient as possible. The cost of grain deterioration caused by unloading delays, the cost of truck rental, and idle driver time are significant concerns to the cooperative members. Although farmers have difficulty quantifying crop damage, it is easy to assign a waiting and unloading cost for truck and driver of $18 per hour. The storage bin is open and operated 16 hours per day, 7 days per week, during the harvest season and is capable of unloading 35 trucks per hour according to an exponential distribution. Full trucks arrive all day long (during the hours the bin is open) at a rate of about 30 per hour, following a Poisson pattern.

To help the cooperative get a handle on the problem of lost time while trucks are waiting in line or unloading at the bin, find the

(a) average number of trucks in the unloading system.

(b) average time per truck in the system.

(c) utilization rate for the bin area.

(d) probability that there are more than three trucks in the system at any given time.

(e) total daily cost to the farmers of having their trucks tied up in the unloading process.

The cooperative, as mentioned, uses the storage bin only two weeks per year. Farmers estimate that enlarging the bin would cut unloading costs by 50% next year. It will cost $9,000 to do so during the off-season. Would it be worth the cooperative's while to enlarge the storage area?

12-16 Ashley's Department Store in Kansas City maintains a successful catalog sales department in which a clerk takes orders by telephone. If the clerk is occupied on one line, incoming phone calls to the catalog department are answered automatically by a recording machine and asked to wait. As soon as the clerk is free, the party that has waited the longest is transferred and answered first. Calls come in at a rate of about 12 per hour. The clerk is capable of taking an order in an average of 4 minutes. Calls tend to follow a Poisson distribution, and service times tend to be exponential. The clerk is paid $10 per hour, but because of lost goodwill and sales, Ashley's loses about $50 per hour of customer time spent waiting for the clerk to take an order.

(a) What is the average time that catalog customers must wait before their calls are transferred to the order clerk?

(b) What is the average number of callers waiting to place an order?

(c) Ashley's is considering adding a second clerk to take calls. The store would pay that person the same $10 per hour. Should it hire another clerk? Explain.

12-17 Automobiles arrive at the drive-through window at a post office at the rate of 4 every 10 minutes. The average service time is 2 minutes. The Poisson distribution is appropriate for the arrival rate and service times are exponentially distributed.

(a) What is the average time a car is in the system?

(b) What is the average number of cars in the system?

(c) What is the average time cars spend waiting to receive service?

(d) What is the average number of cars in line *behind* the customer receiving service?

(e) What is the probability that there are no cars at the window?

(f) What percentage of the time is the postal clerk busy?

(g) What is the probability that there are exactly two cars in the system?

12-18 For the post office in Problem 12-17, a second drive-through window is being considered. A single line would be formed and as a car reached the front of the line it would go to the next available clerk. The clerk at the new window works at the same rate as the current one.

(a) What is the average time a car is in the system?

(b) What is the average number of cars in the system?

(c) What is the average time cars spend waiting to receive service?

(d) What is the average number of cars in line *behind* the customer receiving service?

(e) What is the probability that there are no cars in the system?

(f) What percentage of the time are the clerks busy?

(g) What is the probability that there are exactly two cars in the system?

12-19 Juhn and Sons Wholesale Fruit Distributors employ one worker whose job is to load fruit on outgoing company trucks. Trucks arrive at the loading gate at an average of 24 per day, or 3 per hour, according to a Poisson distribution. The worker loads them at a rate of 4 per hour, following approximately the exponential distribution in service times.

Determine the operating characteristics of this loading gate problem. What is the probability that there will be more than three trucks either being loaded or waiting? Discuss the results of your queuing model computation

12-20 Juhn believes that adding a second fruit loader will substantially improve the firm's efficiency. He estimates that a two-person crew, still acting like a single-server system, at the loading gate will double the loading rate from 4 trucks per hour to 8 trucks per hour. Analyze the effect on the queue of such a change and compare the results with those found in Problem 12-19.

12-21 Truck drivers working for Juhn and Sons (see Problems 12-19 and 12-20) are paid a salary of $20 per hour on average. Fruit loaders receive about $12 per hour. Truck drivers waiting in the queue or at the loading gate are drawing a salary but are productively idle and unable to generate revenue during that time. What would be the *hourly* cost savings to the firm associated with employing two loaders instead of one?

12-22 Juhn and Sons Wholesale Fruit Distributors (of Problem 12-19) are considering building a second platform or gate to speed the process of loading their fruit trucks. This, they think, will be even more efficient than simply hiring another loader to help out the first platform (as in Problem 12-20).

Assume that workers at each platform will be able to load 4 trucks per hour each and that trucks will continue to arrive at the rate of 3 per hour. Find the waiting line's new operating conditions. Is this new approach indeed speedier than the other two considered?

12-23 Bill First, general manager of Worthmore Department Store, has estimated that every hour of customer time spent waiting in line for a sales clerk to become available costs the store $100 in lost sales and goodwill. Customers arrive at the checkout counter at the rate of 30 per hour, and the average service time is 3 minutes. The Poisson distribution describes the arrivals and the service times are exponentially distributed. The number of sales clerks can be 2, 3, or 4, with each one working at the same rate. Bill estimates the salary and benefits for each clerk to be $10 per hour. The store is open 10 hours per day.

(a) Find the average time in the line if 2, 3, and 4 clerks are used.

(b) What is the total time spent waiting in line each day if 2, 3, and 4 clerks are used?

(c) Calculate the total of the daily waiting cost and the service cost if 2, 3, and 4 clerks are used. What is the minimum total daily cost?

12-24 Billy's Bank is the only bank in a small town in Arkansas. On a typical Friday, an average of 10 customers per hour arrive at the bank to transact business. There is one single teller at the bank, and the average time required to transact business is 4 minutes. It is assumed that service times can be described by the exponential distribution. Although this is the only bank in town, some people in the town have begun using the bank in a neighboring town about 20 miles away. If a single teller at Billy's is used, find

(a) the average time in the line.

(b) the average number in the line.

(c) the average time in the system.

(d) the average number in the system.

(e) the probability that the bank is empty.

12-25 Refer to the Billy's Bank situation in Problem 12-24. Billy is considering adding a second teller (who would work at the same rate as the first) to reduce the waiting time for customers, and he assumes that this will cut the waiting time in half. A single line would be used, and the customer at the front of the line would go to the first available bank teller. If a second teller is added, find

(a) the average time in the line.

(b) the average number in the line.

(c) the average time in the system.

(d) the average number in the system.

(e) the probability that the bank is empty.

12-26 For the Billy's Bank situation in Problems 12-24 and 12-25, the salary and benefits for a teller would be $12 per hour. The bank is open 8 hours each day.

It has been estimated that the waiting time cost per hour is $25 per hour in the line.

(a) How many customers would enter the bank on a typical day?

(b) How much total time would the customers spend waiting in line during the entire day if one teller were used? What is the total daily waiting time cost?

(c) How much total time would the customers spend waiting in line during the entire day if two tellers were used? What is the total waiting time cost?

(d) If Billy wishes to minimize the total waiting time and personnel cost, how many tellers should be used?

•12-27 Customers arrive at an automated coffee vending machine at a rate of 4 per minute, following a Poisson distribution. The coffee machine dispenses a cup of coffee in exactly 10 seconds.

(a) What is the average number of people waiting in line?

(b) What is the average number in the system?

(c) How long does the average person wait in line before receiving service?

12-28 The average number of customers in the system in the single-channel, single-phase model described in Section 12.4 is

$$L = \frac{\lambda}{\mu - \lambda}$$

Show that for $m = 1$ server, the multichannel queuing model in Section 12.5,

$$L = \frac{\lambda\mu\left(\frac{\lambda}{\mu}\right)^m}{(m - 1)!(m\mu - \lambda)^2} P_0 + \frac{\lambda}{\mu}$$

is identical to the single-channel system. Note that the formula for P_0 (Equation 12-13) must be utilized in this highly algebraic exercise.

:12-29 One mechanic services 5 drilling machines for a steel plate manufacturer. Machines break down on an average of once every 6 working days, and breakdowns tend to follow a Poisson distribution. The mechanic can handle an average of one repair job per day. Repairs follow an exponential distribution.

(a) How many machines are waiting for service, on average?

(b) How many are in the system, on average?

(c) How many drills are in running order, on average?

(d) What is the average waiting time in the queue?

(e) What is the average wait in the system?

12-30 A technician monitors a group of five computers that run an automated manufacturing facility. It takes an average of 15 minutes (exponentially distributed) to adjust a computer that develops a problem. The computers run for an average of 85 minutes (Poisson distributed) without requiring adjustments. What is the

(a) average number of computers waiting for adjustment?

(b) average number of computers not in working order?

(c) probability the system is empty?

(d) average time in the queue?

(e) average time in the system?

:12-31 The typical subway station in Washington, D.C., has 6 turnstiles, each of which can be controlled by the station manager to be used for either entrance or exit control—but never for both. The manager must decide at different times of the day just how many turnstiles to use for entering passengers and how many to be set up to allow exiting passengers.

At the Washington College Station, passengers enter the station at a rate of about 84 per minute between the hours of 7 and 9 A.M. Passengers exiting trains at the stop reach the exit turnstile area at a rate of about 48 per minute during the same morning rush hours. Each turnstile can allow an average of 30 passengers per minute to enter or exit. Arrival and service times have been thought to follow Poisson and exponential distributions, respectively. Assume riders form a common queue at both entry and exit turnstile areas and proceed to the first empty turnstile.

The Washington College Station manager does not want the average passenger at his station to have to wait in a turnstile line for more than 6 seconds, nor does he want more than 8 people in any queue at any average time.

(a) How many turnstiles should be opened in each direction every morning?

(b) Discuss the assumptions underlying the solution of this problem using queuing theory.

•12-32 The Clear Brook High School band is holding a car wash as a fundraiser to buy new equipment. The average time to wash a car is 4 minutes, and the time is exponentially distributed. Cars arrive at a rate of one every 5 minutes (or 12 per hour), and the number of arrivals per time period is described by the Poisson distribution.

(a) What is the average time for cars waiting in the line?

(b) What is the average number of cars in the line?

(c) What is the average number of cars in the system?

(d) What is the average time in the system?

(e) What is the probability there are more than three cars in the system?

12-33 When additional band members arrived to help at the car wash (see Problem 12-32), it was decided that two cars should be washed at a time instead of just the one. Both work crews would work at the same rate.

(a) What is the average time for cars waiting in the line?

(b) What is the average number of cars in the line?

(c) What is the average number of cars in the system?

(d) What is the average time in the system?

 :12-34 Upon arrival at the Sunkist Gate at Naval Base Ventura County in Port Hueneme, California, there are two security guards, each assigned to one of the two vehicular lanes that lead up to the gate, to check the identification (i.e., the military Common Access Cards) of people in the vehicles going on to the base. In the morning, when the gate is the busiest, cars arrive every 12 seconds and randomly get into one of the two clearly marked "No-Lane-Change" lanes. Once a car is at the beginning of their particular line, it takes the guard about 20 seconds, on the average, to check the IDs of everyone in every car. Usually that means just one person. However, some people carpool and there may be as many as six or seven in any particular vehicle. Given that the vehicular arrivals follow a Poisson distribution and

the time to check IDs follows a negative exponential distribution, determine the average number of cars and the average waiting time in each of the queues.

:12-35 Ye Olde Creamery, a popular ice cream store on campus, has one line for its tasty treats. Students arrive at the Creamery about one every minute. Because of the new automated "Wave N Pay" payment system, it only takes about 40 seconds, on the average, to place and then pay for an order as students need only hold their cell phones over the "Wave N Pay" device and the system automatically deducts the cost of the ice cream cone from their account. However, the "Wave N Pay" system is finicky and is often offline, causing students to pay with cash. This causes the average order and pay times to double and a long line to form, forcing Ye Olde Creamery to open another order and pay station. Having two order and pay stations open (with just one line) costs the Creamery an extra $12.00 an hour while upgrading the "Wave N Pay" system to never go offline would cost $1200. Assuming Poisson arrivals and negative exponential service times, compare the operation of Ye Olde Creamery with the two different configurations. Given the additional costs involved, what should the management of Ye Olde Creamery do?

Internet Homework Problems

See our Internet home page, at **www.pearsonhighered.com/render**, for additional homework problems, Problems 12-36 to 12-40.

Case Study

New England Foundry

For more than 75 years, New England Foundry, Inc., has manufactured wood stoves for home use. In recent years, with increasing energy prices, George Mathison, president of New England Foundry, has seen sales triple. This dramatic increase in sales has made it even more difficult for George to maintain quality in all the wood stoves and related products.

Unlike other companies manufacturing wood stoves, New England Foundry is *only* in the business of making stoves and stove-related products. Their major products are the Warmglo I, the Warmglo II, the Warmglo III, and the Warmglo IV. The Warmglo I is the smallest wood stove, with a heat output of 30,000 Btu, and the Warmglo IV is the largest, with a heat output of 60,000 Btu. In addition, New England Foundry, Inc., produces a large array of products that have been designed to be used with one of their four stoves, including warming shelves, surface thermometers, stovepipes, adaptors, stove gloves, trivets, mitten racks, andirons, chimneys, and heat

shields. New England Foundry also publishes a newsletter and several paperback books on stove installation, stove operation, stove maintenance, and wood sources. It is George's belief that its wide assortment of products was a major contributor to the sales increases.

The Warmglo III outsells all the other stoves by a wide margin. The heat output and available accessories are ideal for the typical home. The Warmglo III also has a number of outstanding features that make it one of the most attractive and heat-efficient stoves on the market. Each Warmglo III has a thermostatically controlled primary air intake valve that allows the stove to adjust itself automatically to produce the correct heat output for varying weather conditions. A secondary air opening is used to increase the heat output in case of very cold weather. The internal stove parts produce a horizontal flame path for more efficient burning, and the output gases are forced to take an S-shaped path through the stove. The S-shaped path allows more complete combustion of the gases and better heat

Figure 12.3 Overview of Factory

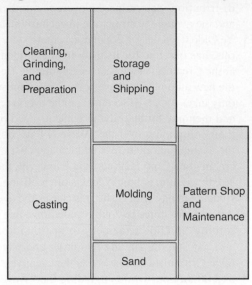

Figure 12.4 Overview of Factory After Changes

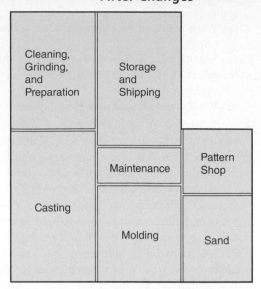

transfer from the fire and gases through the cast iron to the area to be heated. These features, along with the accessories, resulted in expanding sales and prompted George to build a new factory to manufacture Warmglo III stoves. An overview diagram of the factory is shown in Figure 12.3.

The new foundry uses the latest equipment, including a new Disamatic that helps in manufacturing stove parts. Regardless of new equipment or procedures, casting operations have remained basically unchanged for hundreds of years. To begin with, a wooden pattern is made for every cast-iron piece in the stove. The wooden pattern is an exact duplication of the cast-iron piece that is to be manufactured. New England Foundry has all of its patterns made by Precision Patterns, Inc., and these patterns are stored in the pattern shop and maintenance room. Then a specially formulated sand is molded around the wooden pattern. There can be two or more sand molds for each pattern. Mixing the sand and making the molds are done in the molding room. When the wooden pattern is removed, the resulting sand molds form a negative image of the desired casting. Next, the molds are transported to the casting room, where molten iron is poured into the molds and allowed to cool. When the iron has solidified, the molds are moved into the cleaning, grinding, and preparation room. The molds are dumped into large vibrators that shake most of the sand from the casting. The rough castings are then subjected to both sandblasting to remove the rest of the sand and grinding to finish some of the surfaces of the castings. The castings are then painted with a special heat-resistant paint, assembled into workable stoves, and inspected for manufacturing defects that may have gone undetected thus far. Finally, the finished stoves are moved to storage and shipping, where they are packaged and shipped to the appropriate locations.

At present, the pattern shop and the maintenance department are located in the same room. One large counter is used by both maintenance personnel to get tools and parts and by sand molders that need various patterns for the molding operation. Peter Nawler and Bob Bryan, who work behind the counter, are able to service a total of 10 people per hour (or about 5 per hour each). On the average, 4 people from maintenance and 3 people from the molding department arrive at the counter per hour. People from the molding department and from maintenance arrive randomly, and to be served they form a single line. Pete and Bob have always had a policy of first come, first served. Because of the location of the pattern shop and maintenance department, it takes about 3 minutes for a person from the maintenance department to walk to the counter, and it takes about 1 minute for a person to walk from the molding department to the pattern and maintenance room.

After observing the operation of the pattern shop and maintenance room for several weeks, George decided to make some changes to the layout of the factory. An overview of these changes is shown in Figure 12.4.

Separating the maintenance shop from the pattern shop had a number of advantages. It would take people from the maintenance department only 1 minute instead of 3 to get to the new maintenance department counter. Using time and motion studies, George was also able to determine that improving the layout of the maintenance department would allow Bob to serve 6 people from the maintenance department per hour, and improving the layout of the pattern department would allow Pete to serve 7 people from the molding shop per hour.

Discussion Questions

1. How much time would the new layout save?
2. If maintenance personnel were paid $9.50 per hour and molding personnel were paid $11.75 per hour, how much could be saved per hour with the new factory layout?

Case Study

Winter Park Hotel

Donna Shader, manager of the Winter Park Hotel, is considering how to restructure the front desk to reach an optimum level of staff efficiency and guest service. At present, the hotel has five clerks on duty, each with a separate waiting line, during the peak check-in time of 3:00 P.M. to 5:00 P.M. Observation of arrivals during this time show that an average of 90 guests arrive each hour (although there is no upward limit on the number that could arrive at any given time). It takes an average of 3 minutes for each front-desk clerk to register each guest.

Donna is considering three plans for improving guest service by reducing the length of time guests spend waiting in line. The first proposal would designate one employee as a quick-service clerk for guests registering under corporate accounts, a market segment that fills about 30% of all occupied rooms. Because corporate guests are preregistered, their registration takes just 2 minutes. With these guests separated from the rest of the clientele, the average time for registering a typical guest would climb to 3.4 minutes. Under plan 1, noncorporate guests would choose any of the remaining four lines.

The second plan is to implement a single-line system. All guests could form a single waiting line to be served by whichever of five clerks became available. This option would require sufficient lobby space for what could be a substantial queue.

The third proposal involves using an automatic teller machine (ATM) for check-ins. This ATM would provide approximately the same service rate as a clerk would. Given that initial use of this technology might be minimal, Shader estimated that 20% of customers, primarily frequent guests, would be willing to use the machines. (This might be a conservative estimate if the guests perceive direct benefits from using the ATM, as bank customers do. Citibank reports that some 95% of its Manhattan customers use its ATMs.) Donna would set up a single queue for customers who prefer human check-in clerks. This would be served by the five clerks, although Donna is hopeful that the machine will allow a reduction to four.

Discussion Questions

1. Determine the average amount of time that a guest spends checking in. How would this change under each of the stated options?
2. Which option do you recommend?

Internet Case Study

See our Internet home page, at **www.pearsonhighered.com/render**, for this additional case study: **Pantry Shopper**. This case involves providing better service in a grocery store.

Bibliography

Baldwin, Rusty O., Nathaniel J. Davis IV, Scott F. Midkiff, and John E. Kobza. "Queueing Network Analysis: Concepts, Terminology, and Methods," *Journal of Systems & Software* 66, 2 (2003): 99–118.

Barron, K. "Hurry Up and Wait," *Forbes* (October 16, 2000): 158–164.

Cayirli, Tugba, and Emre Veral. "Outpatient Scheduling in Health Care: A Review of Literature," *Production and Operations Management* 12, 4 (2003): 519–549.

Cooper, R. B. *Introduction to Queuing Theory*, 2nd ed. New York: Elsevier—North Holland, 1980.

de Bruin, Arnoud M., A. C. van Rossum, M. C. Visser, and G. M. Koole. "Modeling the Emergency Cardiac Inpatient Flow: An Application of Queuing Theory," *Health Care Management Science* 10, 2 (2007): 125–137.

Derbala, Ali. "Priority Queuing in an Operating System," *Computers & Operations Research* 32, 2 (2005): 229–238.

Grassmann, Winfried K. "Finding the Right Number of Servers in Real-World Queuing Systems," *Interfaces* 18, 2 (March–April 1988): 94–104.

Janic, Milan. "Modeling Airport Congestion Charges," *Transportation Planning & Technology* 28, 1 (2005): 1–26.

Katz, K., B. Larson, and R. Larson. "Prescription for the Waiting-in-Line Blues," *Sloan Management Review* (Winter 1991): 44–53.

Koizumi, Naoru, Eri Kuno, and Tony E. Smith. "Modeling Patient Flows Using a Queuing Network with Blocking," *Health Care Management Science* 8, 1 (2005): 49–60.

Larson, Richard C. "Perspectives on Queues: Social Justice and the Psychology of Queuing," *Operations Research* 35, 6 (November–December 1987): 895–905.

Murtojärvi, Mika, et al. "Determining the Proper Number and Price of Software Licenses," *IEEE Transactions on Software Engineering* 33, 5 (2007): 305–315.

Prabhu, N. U. *Foundations of Queuing Theory*. Norwell, MA: Kluwer Academic Publishers, 1997.

Regattieri, A., R. Gamberini, F. Lolli, and R. Manzini. "Designing Production and Service Systems Using Queuing Theory: Principles and Application to an Airport Passenger Security Screening System," *International Journal of Services and Operations Management* 6, 2 (2010): 206–225.

Tarko, A. P. "Random Queues in Signalized Road Networks," *Transportation Science* 34, 4 (November 2000): 415–425.

Appendix 12.1: Using QM for Windows

For all these problems, from the Module menu, select *Waiting Lines* and then select *New* to enter a new problem. Then select the type of model you want to use from the ones that appear.

This appendix illustrates the ease of use of the QM for Windows in solving queuing problems. Program 12.5 represents the Arnold's Muffler Shop analysis with 2 servers. The only required inputs are selection of the proper model, a title, whether to include costs, the time units being used for arrival and service rates (hours in this example), the arrival rate (2 cars per hour), the service rate (3 cars per hour), and the number of servers (2). Because the time units are specified as hours, W and W_q are given in hours, but they are also converted into minutes and seconds, as seen in Program 12.5.

Program 12.6 reflects a constant service time model, illustrated in the chapter by Garcia-Golding Recycling, Inc. The other queuing models can also be solved by QM for Windows, which additionally provides cost/economic analysis.

PROGRAM 12.5

Using QM for Windows to Solve a Multichannel Queuing Model (Arnold Muffler Shop Data)

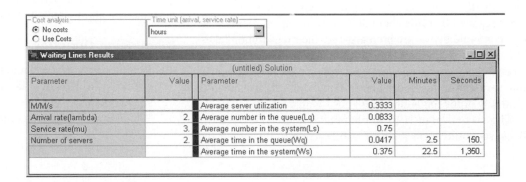

Parameter	Value		Parameter	Value	Minutes	Seconds
M/M/s			Average server utilization	0.3333		
Arrival rate(lambda)	2.		Average number in the queue(Lq)	0.0833		
Service rate(mu)	3.		Average number in the system(Ls)	0.75		
Number of servers	2.		Average time in the queue(Wq)	0.0417	2.5	150.
			Average time in the system(Ws)	0.375	22.5	1,350.

PROGRAM 12.6

Using QM for Windows to Solve a Constant Service Time Model (Garcia-Golding Data)

Garcia-Golding Recycling, Inc. Solution

Parameter	Value		Parameter	Value	Minutes	Seconds
Constant service times			Average server utilization	0.6667		
Arrival rate(lambda)	8.		Average number in the queue(Lq)	0.6667		
Service rate(mu)	12.		Average number in the system(Ls)	1.3333		
Number of servers	1.		Average time in the queue(Wq)	0.0833	5.	300.
			Average time in the system(Ws)	0.1667	10.	600.

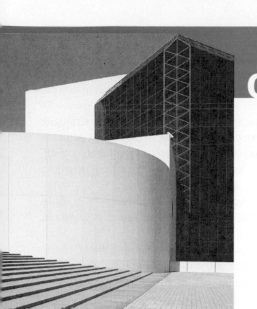

CHAPTER 13

Simulation Modeling

After completing this chapter, students will be able to:

1. Tackle a wide variety of problems using simulation.
2. Understand the seven steps of conducting a simulation.
3. Explain the advantages and disadvantages of simulation.

4. Develop random number intervals and use them to generate outcomes.
5. Understand alternative computer simulation packages available.

CHAPTER OUTLINE

13.1 Introduction
13.2 Advantages and Disadvantages of Simulation
13.3 Monte Carlo Simulation
13.4 Simulation and Inventory Analysis

13.5 Simulation of a Queuing Problem
13.6 Simulation Model for a Maintenance Policy
13.7 Other Simulation Issues

Summary • Glossary • Solved Problems • Self-Test • Discussion Questions and Problems • Internet Homework Problems • Case Study: Alabama Airlines ◆ Case Study: Statewide Development Corporation ◆ Case Study: FB Badpoore Aerospace ◆ Internet Case Studies • Bibliography

13.1 Introduction

We are all aware to some extent of the importance of simulation models in our world. Boeing Corporation and Airbus Industries, for example, commonly build **simulation** models of their proposed jet aircraft and then test the aerodynamic properties of the models. Your local civil defense organization may carry out rescue and evacuation practices as it simulates the natural disaster conditions of a hurricane or tornado. The U.S. Army simulates enemy attacks and defense strategies in war games played on a computer. Business students take courses that use management games to simulate realistic competitive business situations. And thousands of business, government, and service organizations develop simulation models to assist in making decisions concerning inventory control, maintenance scheduling, plant layout, investments, and sales forecasting.

As a matter of fact, simulation is one of the most widely used quantitative analysis tools. Various surveys of the largest U.S. corporations reveal that over half use simulation in corporate planning.

Simulation sounds like it may be the solution to all management problems. This is, unfortunately, by no means true. Yet we think you may find it one of the most flexible and fascinating of the quantitative techniques in your studies. Let's begin our discussion of simulation with a simple definition.

To *simulate* is to try to duplicate the features, appearance, and characteristics of a real system. In this chapter we show how to simulate a business or management system by building a *mathematical model* that comes as close as possible to representing the reality of the system. We won't build any *physical* models, as might be used in airplane wind tunnel simulation tests. But just as physical model airplanes are tested and modified under experimental conditions, our mathematical models are used to experiment and to estimate the effects of various actions. The idea behind simulation is to imitate a real-world situation mathematically, then to study its properties and operating characteristics, and, finally, to draw conclusions and make action decisions based on the results of the simulation. In this way, the real-life system is not touched until the advantages and disadvantages of what may be a major policy decision are first measured on the system's model.

The idea behind simulation is to imitate a real-world situation with a mathematical model that does not affect operations. The seven steps of simulation are illustrated in Figure 13.1.

Using simulation, a manager should (1) define a problem, (2) introduce the variables associated with the problem, (3) construct a simulation model, (4) set up possible courses of action for testing, (5) run the simulation experiment, (6) consider the results (possibly deciding to modify the model or change data inputs), and (7) decide what course of action to take. These steps are illustrated in Figure 13.1.

The problems tackled by simulation can range from very simple to extremely complex, from bank teller lines to an analysis of the U.S. economy. Although very small simulations can be conducted by hand, effective use of this technique requires some automated means of calculation, namely, a computer. Even large-scale models, simulating perhaps years of business decisions, can be handled in a reasonable amount of time by computer. Though simulation is one of the oldest

FIGURE 13.1
Process of Simulation

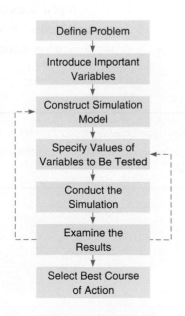

The explosion of personal computers has created a wealth of computer simulation languages and broadened the use of simulation. Now, even spreadsheet software can be used to conduct fairly complex simulations.

quantitative analysis tools (see the History below), it was not until the introduction of computers in the mid-1940s and early 1950s that it became a practical means of solving management and military problems.

We begin this chapter with a presentation of the advantages and disadvantages of simulation. An explanation of the Monte Carlo method of simulation follows. Three sample simulations, in the areas of inventory control, queuing, and maintenance planning, are presented. Other simulation models besides the Monte Carlo approach are also discussed briefly. Finally, the important role of computers in simulation is illustrated.

13.2 Advantages and Disadvantages of Simulation

These eight advantages of simulation make it one of the most widely used quantitative analysis techniques in corporate America.

Simulation is a tool that has become widely accepted by managers for several reasons:

1. It is relatively straightforward and flexible. It can be used to compare many different scenarios side-by-side.
2. Recent advances in software make some simulation models very easy to develop.
3. It can be used to analyze large and complex real-world situations that cannot be solved by conventional quantitative analysis models. For example, it may not be possible to build and solve a mathematical model of a city government system that incorporates important economic, social, environmental, and political factors. Simulation has been used successfully to model urban systems, hospitals, educational systems, national and state economies, and even world food systems.
4. Simulation allows what-if? types of questions. Managers like to know in advance what options are attractive. With a computer, a manager can try out several policy decisions within a matter of minutes.
5. Simulations do not interfere with the real-world system. It may be too disruptive, for example, to experiment with new policies or ideas in a hospital, school, or manufacturing plant. With simulation, experiments are done with the model, not on the system itself.
6. Simulation allows us to study the interactive effect of individual components or variables to determine which ones are important.
7. "Time compression" is possible with simulation. The effect of ordering, advertising, or other policies over many months or years can be obtained by computer simulation in a short time.
8. Simulation allows for the inclusion of real-world complications that most quantitative analysis models cannot permit. For example, some queuing models require exponential or Poisson distributions; some inventory and network models require normality. But simulation can use *any* probability distribution that the user defines; it does not require any particular distribution.

HISTORY | Simulation

The history of simulation dates back over 5,000 years to Chinese war games called *weich'i*. Around 1780, the Prussians used simulation to help train their army. Since then all major military powers have used war games to test out military strategies under simulated environments.

From military gaming arose a new concept called *Monte Carlo simulation*. It was developed during the 1940s as a quantitative analysis technique by Drs. John von Neumann, Stan Ulam, and Nicholas Metropolis at Los Alamos National Laboratory (LANL; see www.lanl.gov) to solve physics problems that were too complex or too expensive to solve by hand. The first application of Monte Carlo simulation was to study neutron behavior

in fissionable materials. Because their research at LANL was Top Secret, the scientists needed a code name for their new tool. The scientists came up with "Monte Carlo" because the behavior of the neutrons reminded them of a roulette wheel and Dr. Ulam's uncle spent a lot of time gambling in Monte Carlo, Monaco.

With the advent and use of computers in the 1950s, simulation grew as a management tool. Specialized computer programming languages (e.g., GPSS and SIMSCRIPT) were developed in the 1960s to handle large-scale problems more effectively. In the 1980s, pre-written, object oriented simulation programs came onto the scene that could handle situations ranging from weather forecasting to auto parts factory analysis to ski resort design. These programs had names like SLAM, SIMAN, and Witness.

The main disadvantages of simulation are:

1. Good simulation models for complex situations can be very expensive. It is often a long, complicated process to develop a model. A corporate planning model, for example, may take months or even years to develop.
2. Simulation does not generate optimal solutions to problems as do other quantitative analysis techniques such as economic order quantity, linear programming, or PERT. It is a trial-and-error approach that can produce different solutions in repeated runs.
3. Managers must generate all of the conditions and constraints for solutions that they want to examine. The simulation model does not produce answers by itself.
4. Each simulation model is unique. Its solutions and inferences are not usually transferable to other problems.

13.3   Monte Carlo Simulation

When a system contains elements that exhibit chance in their behavior, the *Monte Carlo method* of simulation can be applied.

The basic idea in **Monte Carlo simulation** is to generate values for the variables making up the model being studied. There are a lot of variables in real-world systems that are probabilistic in nature and that we might want to simulate. A few examples of these variables follow:

Variables we may want to simulate abound in business problems because very little in life is certain.

1. Inventory demand on a daily or weekly basis
2. Lead time for inventory orders to arrive
3. Times between machine breakdowns
4. Times between arrivals at a service facility
5. Service times
6. Times to complete project activities
7. Number of employees absent from work each day

Some of these variables, such as the daily demand and the number of employees absent, are discrete and must be integer valued. For example, the daily demand can be 0, 1, 2, 3, and so forth. But daily demand cannot be 4.7362 or any other noninteger value. Other variables, such as those related to time, are continuous and are not required to be integers because time can be any value. When selecting a method to generate values for the random variable, this characteristic of the random variable should be considered. Examples of both will be given in the following sections.

The basis of Monte Carlo simulation is experimentation on the chance (or probabilistic) elements through random sampling. The technique breaks down into five simple steps:

Five Steps of Monte Carlo Simulation

The Monte Carlo method can be used with variables that are probabilistic.

1. Establishing probability distributions for important input variables
2. Building a cumulative probability distribution for each variable in step 1
3. Establishing an interval of random numbers for each variable
4. Generating random numbers
5. Simulating a series of trials

We will examine each of these steps and illustrate them with the following example.

Harry's Auto Tire Example

Harry's Auto Tire sells all types of tires, but a popular radial tire accounts for a large portion of Harry's overall sales. Recognizing that inventory costs can be quite significant with this product, Harry wishes to determine a policy for managing this inventory. To see what the demand would look like over a period of time, he wishes to simulate the daily demand for a number of days.

Step 1: Establishing Probability Distributions.   One common way to establish a *probability distribution* for a given variable is to examine historical outcomes. The probability, or relative frequency, for each possible outcome of a variable is found by dividing the frequency of observation

TABLE 13.1

Historical Daily Demand for Radial Tires at Harry's Auto Tire and Probability Distribution

DEMAND FOR TIRES	FREQUENCY (DAYS)	PROBABILITY OF OCCURRENCE
0	10	$10/200 = 0.05$
1	20	$20/200 = 0.10$
2	40	$40/200 = 0.20$
3	60	$60/200 = 0.30$
4	40	$40/200 = 0.20$
5	30	$30/200 = 0.15$
	200	$200/200 = 1.00$

To establish a probability distribution for tires we assume that historical demand is a good indicator of future outcomes.

by the total number of observations. The daily demand for radial tires at Harry's Auto Tire over the past 200 days is shown in Table 13.1. We can convert these data to a probability distribution, if we assume that past demand rates will hold in the future, by dividing each demand frequency by the total demand, 200.

Probability distributions, we should note, need not be based solely on historical observations. Often, managerial estimates based on judgment and experience are used to create a distribution. Sometimes, a sample of sales, machine breakdowns, or service rates is used to create probabilities for those variables. And the distributions themselves can be either empirical, as in Table 13.1, or based on the commonly known normal, binomial, Poisson, or exponential patterns.

Step 2: Building a Cumulative Probability Distribution for Each Variable.   The conversion from a regular probability distribution, such as in the right-hand column of Table 13.1, to a *cumulative distribution* is an easy job. A cumulative probability is the probability that a variable (demand) will be less than or equal to a particular value. A cumulative distribution lists all of the possible values and the probabilities. In Table 13.2 we see that the cumulative probability for each level of demand is the sum of the number in the probability column (middle column) added to the previous cumulative probability (rightmost column). The cumulative probability, graphed in Figure 13.2, is used in step 3 to help assign random numbers.

Step 3: Setting Random Number Intervals.   After we have established a cumulative probability distribution for each variable included in the simulation, we must assign a set of numbers to represent each possible value or outcome. These are referred to as **random number intervals**. Random numbers are discussed in detail in step 4. Basically, a **random number** is a series of digits (say, two digits from 01, 02, ..., 98, 99, 00) that have been selected by a totally random process.

If there is a 5% chance that demand for a product (such as Harry's radial tires) is 0 units per day, we want 5% of the random numbers available to correspond to a demand of 0 units. If a total of 100 two-digit numbers is used in the simulation (think of them as being numbered chips in a bowl), we could assign a demand of 0 units to the first five random numbers: 01, 02, 03, 04, and 05.* Then

TABLE 13.2

Cumulative Probabilities for Radial Tires

Cumulative probabilities are found by summing all the previous probabilities up to the current demand.

DAILY DEMAND	PROBABILITY	CUMULATIVE PROBABILITY
0	0.05	0.05
1	0.10	0.15
2	0.20	0.35
3	0.30	0.65
4	0.20	0.85
5	0.15	1.00

*Alternatively, we could have assigned the random numbers 00, 01, 02, 03, 04 to represent a demand of 0 units. The two digits 00 can be thought of as either 0 or 100. As long as 5 numbers out of 100 are assigned to the 0 demand, it doesn't make any difference which 5 they are.

FIGURE 13.2

Graphical Representation of the Cumulative Probability Distribution for Radial Tires

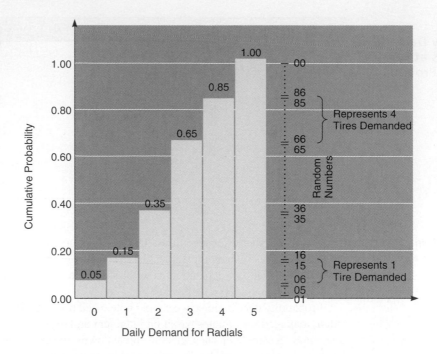

Random numbers can actually be assigned in many different ways—as long as they represent the correct proportion of the outcomes.

The relation between intervals and cumulative probability is that the top end of each interval is equal to the cumulative probability percentage.

There are several ways to pick random numbers—random number generators (which are a built-in feature in spreadsheets and many computer languages), tables (such as Table 13.4), a roulette wheel, and so on.

a simulated demand for 0 units would be created every time one of the numbers 01 to 05 was drawn. If there is also a 10% chance that demand for the same product is 1 unit per day, we could let the next 10 random numbers (06, 07, 08, 09, 10, 11, 12, 13, 14, and 15) represent that demand—and so on for other demand levels.

In general, using the cumulative probability distribution computed and graphed in step 2, we can set the interval of random numbers for each level of demand in a very simple fashion. You will note in Table 13.3 that the interval selected to represent each possible daily demand is very closely related to the cumulative probability on its left. The top end of each interval is always equal to the cumulative probability percentage.

Similarly, we can see in Figure 13.2 and in Table 13.3 that the length of each interval on the right corresponds to the probability of one of each of the possible daily demands. Hence, in assigning random numbers to the daily demand for three radial tires, the range of the random number interval (36 to 65) corresponds *exactly* to the probability (or proportion) of that outcome. A daily demand for three radial tires occurs 30% of the time. Any of the 30 random numbers greater than 35 up to and including 65 are assigned to that event.

Step 4: Generating Random Numbers. Random numbers may be generated for simulation problems in several ways. If the problem is very large and the process being studied involves thousands of simulation trials, computer programs are available to generate the random numbers needed.

If the simulation is being done by hand, as in this book, the numbers may be selected by the spin of a roulette wheel that has 100 slots, by blindly grabbing numbered chips out of a hat, or

TABLE 13.3

Assignment of Random Number Intervals for Harry's Auto Tire

DAILY DEMAND	PROBABILITY	CUMULATIVE PROBABILITY	INTERVAL OF RANDOM NUMBERS
0	0.05	0.05	01 to 05
1	0.10	0.15	06 to 15
2	0.20	0.35	16 to 35
3	0.30	0.65	36 to 65
4	0.20	0.85	66 to 85
5	0.15	1.00	86 to 00

by any method that allows you to make a random selection.* The most commonly used means is to choose numbers from a table of random digits such as Table 13.4.

Table 13.4 was itself generated by a computer program. It has the characteristic that every digit or number in it has an equal chance of occurring. In a very large random number table, 10% of digits would be 1s, 10% 2s, 10% 3s, and so on. Because *everything* is random, we can select numbers from anywhere in the table to use in our simulation procedures in step 5.

Step 5: Simulating the Experiment. We can simulate outcomes of an experiment by simply selecting random numbers from Table 13.4. Beginning anywhere in the table, we note the interval in Table 13.3 or Figure 13.2 into which each number falls. For example, if the random number chosen is 81 and the interval 66 to 85 represents a daily demand for four tires, we select a demand of four tires.

We now illustrate the concept further by simulating 10 days of demand for radial tires at Harry's Auto Tire (see Table 13.5). We select the random numbers needed from Table 13.4, starting in the upper left-hand corner and continuing down the first column.

TABLE 13.4

Table of Random Numbers

52	06	50	88	53	30	10	47	99	37	66	91	35	32	00	84	57	07
37	63	28	02	74	35	24	03	29	60	74	85	90	73	59	55	17	60
82	57	68	28	05	94	03	11	27	79	90	87	92	41	09	25	36	77
69	02	36	49	71	99	32	10	75	21	95	90	94	38	97	71	72	49
98	94	90	36	06	78	23	67	89	85	29	21	25	73	69	34	85	76
96	52	62	87	49	56	59	23	78	71	72	90	57	01	98	57	31	95
33	69	27	21	11	60	95	89	68	48	17	89	34	09	93	50	44	51
50	33	50	95	13	44	34	62	64	39	55	29	30	64	49	44	30	16
88	32	18	50	62	57	34	56	62	31	15	40	90	34	51	95	26	14
90	30	36	24	69	82	51	74	30	35	36	85	01	55	92	64	09	85
50	48	61	18	85	23	08	54	17	12	80	69	24	84	92	16	49	59
27	88	21	62	69	64	48	31	12	73	02	68	00	16	16	46	13	85
45	14	46	32	13	49	66	62	74	41	86	98	92	98	84	54	33	40
81	02	01	78	82	74	97	37	45	31	94	99	42	49	27	64	89	42
66	83	14	74	27	76	03	33	11	97	59	81	72	00	64	61	13	52
74	05	81	82	93	09	96	33	52	78	13	06	28	30	94	23	37	39
30	34	87	01	74	11	46	82	59	94	25	34	32	23	17	01	58	73
59	55	72	33	62	13	74	68	22	44	42	09	32	46	71	79	45	89
67	09	80	98	99	25	77	50	03	32	36	63	65	75	94	19	95	88
60	77	46	63	71	69	44	22	03	85	14	48	69	13	30	50	33	24
60	08	19	29	36	72	30	27	50	64	85	72	75	29	87	05	75	01
80	45	86	99	02	34	87	08	86	84	49	76	24	08	01	86	29	11
53	84	49	63	26	65	72	84	85	63	26	02	75	26	92	62	40	67
69	84	12	94	51	36	17	02	15	29	16	52	56	43	26	22	08	62
37	77	13	10	02	18	31	19	32	85	31	94	81	43	31	58	33	51

Source: Excerpted from *A Million Random Digits with 100,000 Normal Deviates* (New York: The Free Press, 1955), p. 7, with permission of the RAND Corporation.

*One more method of generating random numbers is called the von Neumann midsquare method, developed in the 1940s. Here's how it works: (1) select any arbitrary number with *n* digits (e.g., *n* = 4 digits), (2) square the number, (3) extract the middle *n* digits as the next random number. As an example of a four-digit arbitrary number, use 3,614. The square of 3,614 is 13,060,996. The middle four digits of this new number are 0609. Thus, 0609 is the next random number and steps 2 and 3 are repeated. The midsquare method is simple and easily programmed, but sometimes the numbers repeat quickly and are *not* random. For example, try using the method starting with 6,100 as your first arbitrary number!

IN ACTION

Simulating GM's OnStar System to Evaluate Strategic Alternatives

General Motors (GM) has a two-way vehicle communication system, OnStar, that is the leader in the telematics business of providing communications services to automobiles. Communication can be by an automated system (a virtual advisor) or with a human advisor via a cell-phone connection. This is used for such things as crash notification, navigation, Internet access, and traffic information. OnStar answers thousands of emergency calls each month, and many lives have been saved by providing a rapid emergency response.

In developing the new business model for OnStar, GM used an integrated simulation model to analyze the new telematics industry. Six factors were considered in this model—customer acquisition, customer choice, alliances, customer service, financial dynamics, and societal results. The team responsible for this model reported that an aggressive strategy would be the best

way to approach this new industry. This included installation of OnStar in every GM vehicle and free first year subscription service. This eliminated the high cost of dealer installation, but it carried with it a cost that was not recoverable if the buyer chose not to renew the OnStar subscription.

The implementation of this business strategy and subsequent growth progressed as indicated by the model. As of fall 2001, OnStar had an 80% market share with more than two million subscribers, and this number was growing rapidly. Update: As of the first quarter of 2013, OnStar is estimated to have over six million subscribers worldwide, revenues of $1.5 billion per year, and profit margins of over 30%.

Sources: Based on "A Multimethod Approach for Creating New Business Models: The General Motors OnStar Project," *Interfaces*, 32, 1 (January–February 2002): 20–34.
Based on General Motors quarterly earnings report released on May 2, 2013.

Simulated results can differ from analytical results in a short simulation.

It is interesting to note that the average demand of 3.9 tires in this 10-day simulation differs significantly from the *expected* daily demand, which we can compute from the data in Table 13.2:

$$\text{Expected daily demand} = \sum_{i=0}^{5} (\text{Probability of } i \text{ tires}) \times (\text{Demand of } i \text{ tires})$$

$$= (0.05)(0) + (0.10)(1) + (0.20)(2) + (0.30)(3)$$

$$+ (0.20)(4) + (0.15)(5)$$

$$= 2.95 \text{ tires}$$

If this simulation were repeated hundreds or thousands of times, it is much more likely that the average *simulated* demand would be nearly the same as the *expected* demand.

Naturally, it would be risky to draw any hard and fast conclusions regarding the operation of a firm from only a short simulation. However, this simulation by hand demonstrates the important principles involved. It helps us to understand the process of Monte Carlo simulation that is used in computerized simulation models.

TABLE 13.5

Ten-Day Simulation of Demand for Radial Tires

DAY	RANDOM NUMBER	SIMULATED DAILY DEMAND
1	52	3
2	37	3
3	82	4
4	69	4
5	98	5
6	96	5
7	33	2
8	50	3
9	88	5
10	90	5

39 = total 10-day demand

3.9 = average daily demand for tires

PROGRAM 13.1

QM for Windows Output Screen for Simulation of Harry's Auto Tire Example

Number of trials	1000	Seed	0

Simulation Results

Harry's Auto Tire Shop Solution

Category name	Value	Frequency	Probability	Cumulative Probability	Value * Frequency	Occurrences	Percentage	Occurences * Value
Category 1	0	10	0.05	0.05	0	53	0.05	0
Category 2	1	20	0.1	0.15	0.1	113	0.11	113
Category 3	2	4_	_	0.4	213	0.21	426
Category 4	3	6_	_	0.9	_			3
Category 5	4	40	0.2	0.85	0.8			4
Category 6	5	30	0.15	1	0.75	134	0.13	670
Total		200	1	Expected	2.95	1000	1	2866
							Average	2.87

The expected value is calculated mathematically.

This is the output for this individual simulation run.

The simulation for Harry's Auto Tire involved only one variable. The true power of simulation is seen when several random variables are involved and the situation is more complex. In Section 13.4 we see a simulation of an inventory problem in which both the demand and the lead time may vary.

As you might expect, the computer can be a very helpful tool in carrying out the tedious work in larger simulation undertakings. In the next two sections, we demonstrate how QM for Windows and Excel can both be used for simulation.

Using QM for Windows for Simulation

Program 13.1 is a Monte Carlo simulation using the QM for Windows software. Inputs to this model are the possible values for the variable, the number of trials to be generated, and either the

PROGRAM 13.2

Using Excel 2013 to Simulate Tire Demand for Harry's Auto Tire Shop

	A	B	C	D	E	F	G	H	I
1	**Harry's Tire Shop**								
2		Probability	Probability Range (Lower)	Cumulative Probability	Tires Demand		Day	Random Number	Simulated Demand
3		0.05	0	0.05	0		1	0.437221	3
4		0.1	0.05	0.15	1		2	0.798398	4
5		0.2	0.15	0.35	2		3	0.187351	2
6		0.3	0.35	0.65	3		4	0.711124	4
7		0.2	0.65	0.85	4		5	0.348322	2
8		0.15	0.85	1	5		6	0.406072	3
9							7	0.750798	4
10							8	0.076279	4
11							9	0.592743	3
12							10	0.189257	2
13								Average	3.1
14		Results (Frequency table)							
15		Tires Demanded	Frequency	Percentage	Cum %				
16		0	0	0%	0%				
17		1	0	0%	0%				
18		2	3	30%	30%				
19		3	3	30%	60%				
20		4	4	40%	100%				
21		5	0	0%	100%				
22			10						

Key Formulas

	I
13	=AVERAGE(I3:I12)

	C
22	=SUM(C16:C21)

	H	I
3	=RAND()	=VLOOKUP(H3,$C$3:$E$8,3,TRUE)

Copy H3:I3 to H4:I12

	C	D
3	0	=B3
4	=D3	=D3+B4

Copy C4:D4 to C5:D8

	C
16	=FREQUENCY($I$3:$I$12,$B$16:$B$21)

This entered as an array. Highlight C16:C21, type this formula, then press Ctrl-Shift-Enter.

	D	E
16	=C16/$C$22	=D16
17	=C17/$C$22	=E16+D17

Copy D17:E17 to D18:E21

associated frequency or the probability for each value. If frequencies are input, QM for Windows will compute the probabilities as well as the cumulative probability distribution. We see that the expected value (2.95) is computed mathematically, and we can compare the actual sample average (2.87) with this. If another simulation is performed, the sample average may change.

Simulation with Excel Spreadsheets

The ability to generate random numbers and then "look up" these numbers in a table in order to associate them with a specific event makes spreadsheets excellent tools for conducting simulations. Program 13.2 illustrates an Excel simulation for Harry's Auto Tire.

The RAND( ) function is used to generate a random number between 0 and 1. The VLOOKUP function looks up the random number in the leftmost column of the defined lookup table ($C$3:$E$8). It moves downward through this column until it finds a cell that is bigger than the random number. It then goes to the previous row and gets the value from column E of the table.

In Program 13.2, for example, the first random number shown is 0.437. Excel looked down the left-hand column of the lookup table ($C$3:$E$8) of Program 13.2 until it found 0.65. From the previous row it retrieved the value in column E, which is 3. Pressing the F9 function key recalculates the random numbers and the simulation.

MODELING IN THE REAL WORLD   Simulating Chips

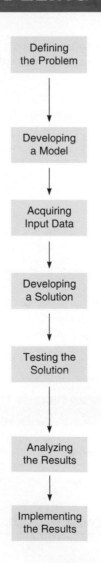

Defining the Problem:

The world's largest semiconductor manufacturer, Intel Corporation, has gross annual sales of over fifty billion dollars. To stay competitive, Intel spends over five billion dollars a year on new semiconductor fabrication equipment. Increasing lead times of fabrication equipment coupled with increasing variability in the global semiconductor chip market led to board room quandaries in capital equipment purchasing.

Developing a Model:

Analysts at Intel built a simulation model of the ordering, shipping, and installation of their capital equipment business process.

Acquiring Input Data:

These same analysts modeled and analyzed the current capital equipment procurement practices at Intel for several years.

Developing a Solution:

A two mode simulation model was developed. The model was named the Dual Mode Equipment Procedure (DMEP).

Testing the Solution:

In the first mode of DMEP, capital equipment was procured according to standard contracts and standard lead times. In the second mode, new capital equipment is purchased at slightly higher costs but with reduced lead times. The idea was that the reduced lead times in equipment meant Intel would reap the benefits of being the first to market with new products.

Analyzing the Results:

The DMEP model integrated common forecasting techniques with Monte Carlo simulation to procure capital equipment at higher costs but with shorter lead times as outlined above.

Implementing the Results:

Once implemented and in place, the DMEP decision engine saved Intel Corporation hundreds of millions of dollars.

Source: Based on K. G. Kempf, F. Erhun, E. F. Hertzler, T. R. Rosenberg, and C. Peng. "Optimizing Capital Investment Decisions at Intel Corporation," *Interfaces* 43, 1 (January–February 2013): 62–78.

The FREQUENCY function in Excel (column C in Program 13.2) is used to tabulate how often a value occurs in a set of data. This is an array function, so special procedures are required to enter it. First, highlight the entire range where this is to be located (C16:C21 in this example). Then enter the function, as illustrated in cell C16, and press Ctrl + Shift + Enter. This causes the formula to be entered as an array into all the cells that were highlighted (cells C16:C21).

Many problems exist in which the variable to be simulated is normally distributed and thus is a continuous variable. A function (NORMINV) in Excel makes generating normal random numbers very easy, as seen in Program 13.3. The mean is 40 and the standard deviation is 5. The format is

$$= \text{NORMINV}\,(probability,\ mean,\ standard\_deviation)$$

In Program 13.3, the 200 simulated values for the normal random variable are generated in Column A. A chart (cells C3:E19) was developed to show the distribution of the randomly generated numbers.

Excel QM has a simulation module that is very easy to use. When *Simulation* is selected from the Excel QM menu, an initialization window opens, and you enter the number of categories and the number of simulation trials you want to run. A spreadsheet will be developed, and you then enter the values and the frequencies, as shown in Program 13.4. The actual random numbers and their associated demand values are also displayed in the output, but they are not shown in Program 13.4.

PROGRAM 13.3

Generating Normal Random Numbers in Excel

	A	B	C	D	E
1	Generating Normal Random Numbers				
2					
3	Random number		Value	Frenquency	Percentage
4	48.33642948		26	1	0.5%
5	36.21820631		28	0	0.0%
6	34.78432388		30	1	0.5%
7	46.61361129		32	6	3.0%
8	38.63662756		34	9	4.5%
9	44.22026912		36	21	10.5%
10	41.97911359		38	24	12.0%
11	34.25168722		40	31	15.5%
12	41.25648029		42	30	15.0%
13	40.70042594		44	31	15.5%
14	40.04584085		46	17	8.5%
15	38.50150643		48	15	7.5%
16	39.84624169		50	8	4.0%
17	46.11687306		52	3	1.5%
18	48.01731698		54	2	1.0%
19	35.86007936		56	1	0.5%
20	38.18663076			200	
201	35.96608863	Rows 21-200 are hidden			
202	36.45899378				
203	45.67207291				

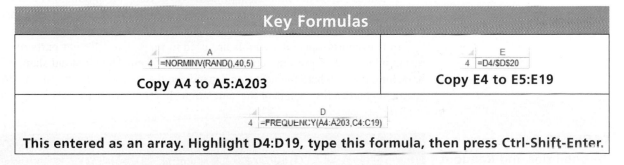

Key Formulas

	A
4	=NORMINV(RAND(),40,5)

Copy A4 to A5:A203

	E
4	=D4/$D$20

Copy E4 to E5:E19

	D
4	=FREQUENCY(A4:A203,C4:C19)

This entered as an array. Highlight D4:D19, type this formula, then press Ctrl-Shift-Enter.

PROGRAM 13.4

Excel QM Simulation of Harry's Auto Tire Example

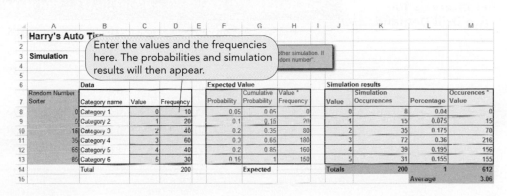

	A	B	C	D	E	F	G	H	I	J	K	L	M
1	Harry's Auto Tire												
2													
3	Simulation												
4													
5													
6		Data					Expected Value				Simulation results		
7	Random Number Sorter	Category name	Value	Frequency			Probability	Cumulative Probability	Value * Frequency		Value	Simulation Occurrences	Percentage	Occurrences * Value
8	0	Category 1	0	10			0.05	0.05	0		0	8	0.04	0
9	5	Category 2	1	20			0.1	0.15	20		1	15	0.075	15
10	15	Category 3	2	40			0.2	0.35	80		2	35	0.175	70
11	35	Category 4	3	60			0.3	0.65	180		3	72	0.36	216
12	65	Category 5	4	40			0.2	0.85	160		4	39	0.195	156
13	85	Category 6	5	30			0.15	1	150		5	31	0.155	155
14		Total		200				Expected			Totals	200	1	612
15													Average	3.06

Enter the values and the frequencies here. The probabilities and simulation results will then appear.

13.4   Simulation and Inventory Analysis

Simulation is useful when demand and lead time are probabilistic—in this case the inventory models like economic order quantity (of Chapter 6) can't be used.

In Chapter 6, we introduced the subject of "deterministic" inventory models. These commonly used models are based on the assumption that both product demand and reorder lead time are known, constant values. In many real-world inventory situations, though, demand and lead time are variables, and accurate analysis becomes extremely difficult to handle by any means other than simulation.

In this section we present an inventory problem with two decision variables and two probabilistic components. The owner of the hardware store described in the next section would like to establish *order quantity* and *reorder point* decisions for a particular product that has probabilistic (uncertain) daily demand and reorder lead time. He wants to make a series of simulation runs, trying out various order quantities and reorder points, to minimize his total inventory cost for the item. Inventory costs in this case include an ordering, holding, and stockout cost.

Simkin's Hardware Store

Mark Simkin, owner and general manager of Simkin Hardware, wants to find a good, low-cost inventory policy for one particular product: the Ace model electric drill. Due to the complexity of this situation, he has decided to use simulation to help with this. The first step in the simulation process seen in Figure 13.1 is to define the problem. Simkin specifies this to be finding a good inventory policy for the Ace electric drill.

In the second step of this process, Simkin identifies two types of variables: the controllable and uncontrollable inputs. The controllable inputs (or decision variables) are the order quantity and the reorder point. Simkin must specify the values that he wishes to consider. The other important variables are the uncontrollable inputs: the fluctuating daily demand and the variable lead time. Monte Carlo simulation is used to simulate the values for both of these.

Daily demand for the Ace model drill is relatively low but subject to some variability. Over the past 300 days, Simkin has observed the sales shown in column 2 of Table 13.6. He converts this historical frequency data into a probability distribution for the variable daily demand (column 3). A cumulative probability distribution is formed in column 4. Finally, Simkin establishes an interval of random numbers to represent each possible daily demand (column 5).

When Simkin places an order to replenish his inventory of Ace electric drills, there is a delivery lag of one to three days. This means that lead time can also be considered a probabilistic variable. The number of days it took to receive the past 50 orders is presented in Table 13.7. In a fashion similar to that for the demand variable, Simkin establishes a probability distribution for the lead time variable (column 3 of Table 13.7), computes the cumulative distribution (column 4), and assigns random number intervals for each possible time (column 5).

The third step in the simulation process is to develop the simulation model. A **flow diagram, or flowchart**, is helpful in the logical coding procedures for programming this simulation process (see Figure 13.3).

In flowcharts, special symbols are used to represent different parts of a simulation. The rectangular boxes represent actions that must be taken. The diamond shaped figures represent branching points where the next step depends on the answer to the question in the diamond. The beginning and ending points of the simulation are represented as ovals or rounded rectangles.

TABLE 13.6

Probabilities and Random Number Intervals for Daily Ace Drill Demand

(1) DEMAND FOR ACE DRILL	(2) FREQUENCY (DAYS)	(3) PROBABILITY	(4) CUMULATIVE PROBABILITY	(5) INTERVAL OF RANDOM NUMBERS
0	15	0.05	0.05	01 to 05
1	30	0.10	0.15	06 to 15
2	60	0.20	0.35	16 to 35
3	120	0.40	0.75	36 to 75
4	45	0.15	0.90	76 to 90
5	30	0.10	1.00	91 to 00
	300	1.00		

TABLE 13.7

Probabilities and Random Number Intervals for Reorder Lead Time

(1) LEAD TIME (DAYS)	(2) FREQUENCY (ORDERS)	(3) PROBABILITY	(4) CUMULATIVE PROBABILITY	(5) RANDOM NUMBER INTERVAL
1	10	0.20	0.20	01 to 20
2	25	0.50	0.70	21 to 70
3	15	0.30	1.00	71 to 00
	50	1.00		

FIGURE 13.3

Flow Diagram for Simkin's Inventory Example

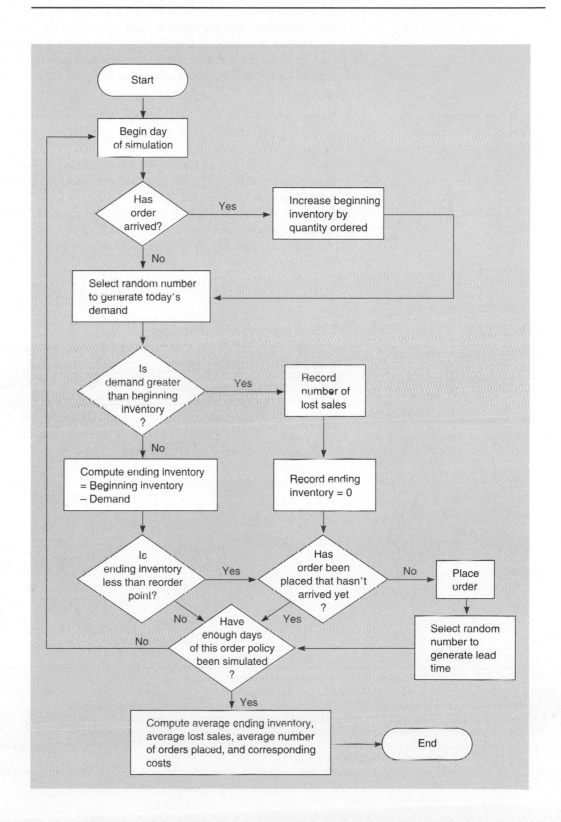

A delivery lag is the lead time in receiving an order—the time it was placed until it was received.

The fourth step of this simulation is to specify the values of the variables that we wish to test.

The first inventory policy that Simkin Hardware wants to simulate is an order quantity of 10 with a reorder point of 5. That is, every time the on-hand inventory level at the end of the day is 5 or less, Simkin will call his supplier and place an order for 10 more drills. If the lead time is one day, by the way, the order will not arrive the next morning but at the beginning of the following working day.

The fifth step of the simulation process is to actually conduct the simulation, and the Monte Carlo method is used for this. The entire process is simulated for a 10-day period in Table 13.8. We can assume that beginning inventory is 10 units on day 1. (Actually, it makes little difference in a long simulation what the initial inventory level is. Since we would tend in real life to simulate hundreds or thousands of days, the beginning values will tend to be averaged out.) Random numbers for Simkin's inventory problem are selected from the second column of Table 13.4.

Table 13.8 is filled in by proceeding one day (or line) at a time, working from left to right. It is a four-step process:

Here is how we simulated the Simkin Hardware example.

1. Begin each simulated day by checking whether any ordered inventory has just arrived (column 2). If it has, increase the current inventory (in column 3) by the quantity ordered (10 units, in this case).
2. Generate a daily demand from the demand probability distribution in Table 13.6 by selecting a random number. This random number is recorded in column 4. The demand simulated is recorded in column 5.
3. Compute the ending inventory every day and record it in column 6. Ending inventory equals beginning inventory minus demand. If on-hand inventory is insufficient to meet the day's demand, satisfy as much as possible and note the number of lost sales (in column 7).

TABLE 13.8 Simkin Hardware's First Inventory Simulation

	ORDER QUANTITY = 10 UNITS			REORDER POINT = 5 UNITS					
(1) DAY	(2) UNITS RECEIVED	(3) BEGINNING INVENTORY	(4) RANDOM NUMBER	(5) DEMAND	(6) ENDING INVENTORY	(7) LOST SALES	(8) ORDER	(9) RANDOM NUMBER	(10) LEAD TIME
1	...	10	06	1	9	0	No		
2	0	9	63	3	6	0	No		
3	0	6	57	3	3[a]	0	Yes	02[b]	1
4	0	3	94[c]	5	0	2	No[d]		
5	10[e]	10	52	3	7	0	No		
6	0	7	69	3	4	0	Yes	33	2
7	0	4	32	2	2	0	No		
8	0	2	30	2	0	0	No		
9	10[f]	10	48	3	7	0	No		
10	0	7	88	4	3	0	Yes	14	1
					Total 41	2			

[a]This is the first time inventory dropped below the reorder point of 5 drills. Because no prior order was outstanding, an order is placed.

[b]The random number 02 is generated to represent the first lead time. It was drawn from column 2 of Table 13.4 as the next number in the list being used. A separate column could have been used to draw lead time random numbers from if we had wanted to do so, but in this example we did not do so.

[c]Again, notice that the random digits 02 were used for lead time (see footnote b). So the next number in the column is 94.

[d]No order is placed on day 4 because there is one outstanding from the previous day that has not yet arrived.

[e]The lead time for the first order placed is one day, but as noted in the text, an order does not arrive the next morning but at the beginning of the following working day. Thus, the first order arrives at the start of day 5.

[f]This is the arrival of the order placed at the close of business on day 6. Fortunately for Simkin, no lost sales occurred during the 2-day lead time until the order arrived.

4. Determine whether the day's ending inventory has reached the reorder point (5 units). If it has and if there are no outstanding orders, place an order (column 8). Lead time for a new order is simulated by first choosing a random number from Table 13.4 and recording it in column 9. (We can continue down the same string of the random number table that we were using to generate numbers for the demand variable.) Finally, we convert this random number into a lead time by using the distribution set in Table 13.7.

Analyzing Simkin's Inventory Costs

Now that the simulation results have been generated, Simkin is ready to proceed to step 6 of this process—examining the results. Since the objective is to find a low-cost solution, Simkin must determine, given these results, what the costs would be. In doing this, Simkin finds some interesting results. The average daily ending inventory is

$$\text{Average ending inventory} = \frac{41 \text{ total units}}{10 \text{ days}} = 4.1 \text{ units per day}$$

We also note the average lost sales and number of orders placed per day:

$$\text{Average lost sales} = \frac{2 \text{ sales lost}}{10 \text{ days}} = 0.2 \text{ unit per day}$$

$$\text{Average number of orders placed} = \frac{3 \text{ orders}}{10 \text{ days}} = 0.3 \text{ order per day}$$

These data are useful in studying the inventory costs of the policy being simulated.

Simkin Hardware is open for business 200 days per year. Simkin estimates that the cost of placing each order for Ace drills is $10. The cost of holding a drill in stock is $6 per drill per year, which can also be viewed as 3 cents per drill per day (over a 200-day year). Finally, Simkin estimates that the cost of each shortage, or lost sale, is $8. What is Simkin's total daily inventory cost for the ordering policy of order quantity, $Q = 10$ and reorder point, ROP = 5?

Let us examine the three cost components:

$$\text{Daily order cost} = (\text{Cost of placing one order})$$
$$\times (\text{Number of orders placed per day})$$
$$= \$10 \text{ per order} \times 0.3 \text{ order per day} = \$3$$

$$\text{Daily holding cost} = (\text{Cost of holding one unit for one day})$$
$$\times (\text{Average ending inventory})$$
$$= \$0.03 \text{ per unit per day} \times 4.1 \text{ units per day}$$
$$= \$0.12$$

$$\text{Daily stockout cost} = (\text{Cost per lost sale})$$
$$\times (\text{Average number of lost sales per day})$$
$$= \$8 \text{ per lost sale} \times 0.2 \text{ lost sale per day}$$
$$= \$1.60$$

$$\text{Total Daily inventory cost} = \text{Daily order cost} + \text{Daily holding cost}$$
$$+ \text{Daily stockout cost} = \$4.72$$

Thus, the total daily inventory cost for this simulation is $4.72. Annualizing this daily figure to a 200-day working year suggests that this inventory policy's cost is approximately $944.

It is important to remember that the simulation should be conducted for many, many days before it is legitimate to draw any solid conclusions.

Now once again we want to emphasize something very important. This simulation should be extended many more days before we draw any conclusions as to the cost of the inventory policy being tested. If a hand simulation is being conducted, 100 days would provide a better representation. If a computer is doing the calculations, 1,000 days would be helpful in reaching accurate cost estimates.

IN ACTION   Federal Aviation Administration Uses Simulation to Solve Assignment Problem

The Federal Aviation Administration (FAA) is responsible for managing transportation in the air. This typically involves the assignment of airline flights to particular air-traffic routes in real time. On the surface, this problem may seem rather mundane. However, as air traffic demand has grown in recent years, the number of available air-traffic routes has diminished at any given time. This can make the associated assignment problem very hard. Confounding the problem is the weather, as thunderstorms can wreak havoc on the availability of air-traffic routes at any given time.

In 2005, the FAA developed a simulation decision-making tool known as the Airspace Flow Program (AFP) at a total cost

of about $5 million. The AFP integrates upcoming and current flight data with impending storm weather data and simulates several different possible assignment decisions. All of these "look-ahead" simulations are then analyzed, allowing FAA decision makers to "pre-pick" a robust set of assignment solutions that minimize system-wide flight delays. The result is faster, more efficient flights for the traveler and hundreds of millions of dollars of annual savings for the airlines.

Source: Based on V. Sud, M. Tanino, J. Wetherly, M. Brennan, M. Lehky, K. Howard, and R. Oiesen. "Reducing Flight Delays Through Better Traffic Management," *Interfaces* 39, 1 (2009): 35–45.

Let's say that Simkin *does* complete a 1,000-day simulation of the policy that order quantity = 10 drills, reorder point = 5 drills. Does this complete his analysis? The answer is *no*—this is just the beginning! We should now verify that the model is correct and validate that the model truly represents the situation on which it is based. As indicated in Figure 13.1, once the results of the model are examined, we may want to go back and modify the model that we have developed. If we are satisfied that the model performed as we expected, then we can specify other values of the variables. Simkin must now compare *this* potential strategy to other possibilities. For example, what about $Q = 10$, ROP = 4; or $Q = 12$, ROP = 6; or $Q = 14$, ROP = 5? Perhaps every combination of values of Q from 6 to 20 drills and ROP from 3 to 10 should be simulated. After simulating all reasonable combinations of order quantities and reorder points, Simkin would go to step 7 of the simulation process and probably select the pair that yields the lowest total inventory cost.

13.5 Simulation of a Queuing Problem

An important area of simulation application has been in the analysis of waiting line problems. As mentioned earlier, the assumptions required for solving queuing problems analytically are quite restrictive. For most realistic queuing systems, simulation may actually be the only approach available. This section illustrates the simulation at a large unloading dock and its associated queue.

Port of New Orleans

Barge arrivals and unloading rates are both probabilistic variables. Unless they follow the queuing probability distributions of Chapter 12, we must turn to a simulation approach.

Fully loaded barges arrive at night in New Orleans following their long trips down the Mississippi River from industrial midwestern cities. The number of barges docking on any given night ranges from 0 to 5. The probability of 0, 1, 2, 3, 4, or 5 arrivals is displayed in Table 13.9. In the same table, we establish cumulative probabilities and corresponding random number intervals for each possible value.

A study by the dock superintendent reveals that because of the nature of their cargo, the number of barges unloaded also tends to vary from day to day. The superintendent provides information from which we can create a probability distribution for the variable *daily unloading rate* (see Table 13.10). As we just did for the arrival variable, we can set up an interval of random numbers for the unloading rates.

Barges are unloaded on a first-in, first-out basis. Any barges that are not unloaded the day of arrival must wait until the following day. Tying up a barge in dock is an expensive proposition, and the superintendent cannot ignore the angry phone calls from barge line owners reminding him that "time is money!" He decides that before going to the Port of New Orleans's controller to request additional unloading crews, a simulation study of arrivals, unloadings, and delays should be conducted. A 100-day simulation would be ideal, but for purposes of illustration, the superintendent begins with a shorter 15-day analysis. Random numbers are drawn from the top row of Table 13.4 to generate daily arrival rates. They are drawn from the second row of Table 13.4 to create daily unloading rates. Table 13.11 shows the day-by-day port simulation.

TABLE 13.9
Overnight Barge Arrival Rates and Random Number Intervals

NUMBER OF ARRIVALS	PROBABILITY	CUMULATIVE PROBABILITY	RANDOM NUMBER INTERVAL
0	0.13	0.13	01 to 13
1	0.17	0.30	14 to 30
2	0.15	0.45	31 to 45
3	0.25	0.70	46 to 70
4	0.20	0.90	71 to 90
5	0.10	1.00	91 to 00

TABLE 13.10
Unloading Rates and Random Number Intervals

DAILY UNLOADING RATE	PROBABILITY	CUMULATIVE PROBABILITY	RANDOM NUMBER INTERVAL
1	0.05	0.05	01 to 05
2	0.15	0.20	06 to 20
3	0.50	0.70	21 to 70
4	0.20	0.90	71 to 90
5	0.10	1.00	91 to 00
	1.00		

TABLE 13.11 Queuing Simulation of Port of New Orleans Barge Unloadings

(1) DAY	(2) NUMBER DELAYED FROM PREVIOUS DAY	(3) RANDOM NUMBER	(4) NUMBER NIGHTLY ARRIVALS	(5) TOTAL TO BE UNLOADED	(6) RANDOM NUMBER	(7) NUMBER UNLOADED
1	—[a]	52	3	3	37	3
2	0	06	0	0	63	0[b]
3	0	50	3	3	28	3
4	0	88	4	4	02	1
5	3	53	3	6	74	4
6	2	30	1	3	35	3
7	0	10	0	0	24	0[c]
8	0	47	3	3	03	1
9	2	99	5	7	29	3
10	4	37	2	6	60	3
11	3	66	3	6	74	4
12	2	91	5	7	85	4
13	3	35	2	5	90	4
14	1	32	2	3	73	3[d]
15	0	00	5	5	59	3
	20		41			39
	Total delays		Total arrivals			Total unloadings

[a]We can begin with no delays from the previous day. In a long simulation, even if we started with 5 overnight delays, that initial condition would be averaged out.
[b]Three barges *could* have been unloaded on day 2. But because there were no arrivals and no backlog existed, zero unloadings took place.
[c]The same situation as noted in footnote b takes place.
[d]This time 4 barges could have been unloaded, but since only 3 were in the queue, the number unloaded is recorded as 3.

The superintendent will probably be interested in at least three useful and important pieces of information:

Here are the simulation results regarding average barge delays, average nightly arrivals, and average unloadings.

$$\text{Average number of barges delayed to the next day} = \frac{20 \text{ delays}}{15 \text{ days}}$$

$$= 1.33 \text{ barges delayed per day}$$

$$\text{Average number of nightly arrivals} = \frac{41 \text{ arrivals}}{15 \text{ days}} = 2.73 \text{ arrivals}$$

$$\text{Average number of barges unloaded each day} = \frac{39 \text{ unloadings}}{15 \text{ days}} = 2.60 \text{ unloadings}$$

When these data are analyzed in the context of delay costs, idle labor costs, and the cost of hiring extra unloading crews, it will be possible for the dock superintendent and port controller to make a better staffing decision. They may even elect to resimulate the process assuming different unloading rates that would correspond to increased crew sizes. Although simulation is a tool that cannot guarantee an optimal solution to problems such as this, it can be helpful in recreating a process and identifying good decision alternatives.

Using Excel to Simulate the Port of New Orleans Queuing Problem

Excel has been used to simulate the Port of New Orleans example, and the results are shown in Program 13.5. The VLOOKUP function is used as it was used in previous Excel simulations. Ten days of operation were simulated, and the results are displayed in rows 4 to 13 of the spreadsheet.

PROGRAM 13.5

Excel Model for Port of New Orleans Queuing Simulation

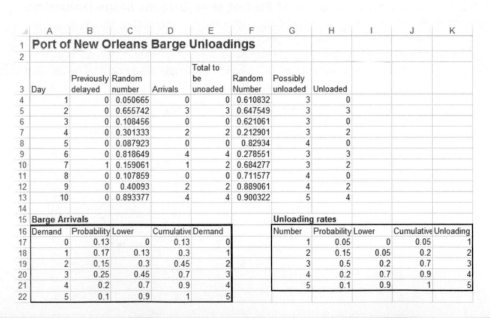

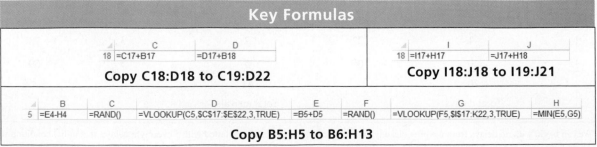

13.6 Simulation Model for a Maintenance Policy

Maintenance problems are an area in which simulation is widely used.

Simulation is a valuable technique for analyzing various maintenance policies before actually implementing them. A firm can decide whether to add more maintenance staff based on machine downtime costs and costs of additional labor. It can simulate replacing parts that have not yet failed in exploring ways to prevent future breakdowns. Many companies use computerized simulation models to decide if and when to shut down an entire plant for maintenance activities. This section provides an example of the value of simulation in setting maintenance policy.

Three Hills Power Company

The Three Hills Power Company provides electricity to a large metropolitan area through a series of almost 200 hydroelectric generators. Management recognizes that even a well-maintained generator will have periodic failures or breakdowns. Energy demands over the past three years have been consistently high, and the company is concerned over downtime of generators. It currently employs four highly skilled repairpersons at $30 per hour. Each works every fourth 8-hour shift. In this way there is a repairperson on duty 24 hours a day, 7 days a week.

As expensive as the maintenance staff salaries are, breakdown expenses are even more costly. For each hour that one of its generators is down, Three Hills loses approximately $75. This amount is the charge for reserve power that Three Hills must "borrow" from the neighboring utility company.

Stephanie Robbins has been assigned to conduct a management analysis of the break down problem. She determines that simulation is a workable tool because of the probabilistic nature of this problem. Stephanie decides her objective is to determine (1) the service maintenance cost, (2) the simulated machine breakdown cost, and (3) the total of these breakdown and maintenance costs (which gives the total cost of this system). Since the total downtime of the machines is needed to compute the breakdown cost, Stephanie must know when each machine breaks and when each machine returns to service. Therefore, a next event step simulation model must be used. In planning for this simulation, a flowchart, as seen in Figure 13.4, is developed.

Stephanie identifies two important maintenance system components. First, the time between successive generator breakdowns varies historically from as little as one-half hour to as much as three hours. For the past 100 breakdowns Stephanie tabulates the frequency of various times between machine failures (see Table 13.12). She also creates a probability distribution and assigns random number intervals to each expected time range.

Robbins then notes that the people who do repairs log their maintenance time in one-hour time blocks. Because of the time it takes to reach a broken generator, repair times are generally rounded to one, two, or three hours. In Table 13.13 she performs a statistical analysis of past repair times, similar to that conducted for breakdown times.

Robbins begins conducting the simulation by selecting a series of random numbers to generate simulated times between generator breakdowns and a second series to simulate repair times required. A simulation of 15 machine failures is presented in Table 13.14. We now examine the elements in the table, one column at a time.

Column 1: Breakdown Number. This is just the count of breakdowns as they occur, going from 1 to 15.

Column 2: Random Number for Breakdowns. This is a number used to simulate time between breakdowns. The numbers in this column have been selected from Table 13.4, from the second column from the right-hand side of the table.

Column 3: Time Between Breakdowns. This number is generated from column 2 random numbers and the random number intervals defined in Table 13.12. The first random number, 57, falls in the interval 28 to 60, implying a time of 2 hours since the prior breakdown.

FIGURE 13.4
Three Hills Flow Diagram

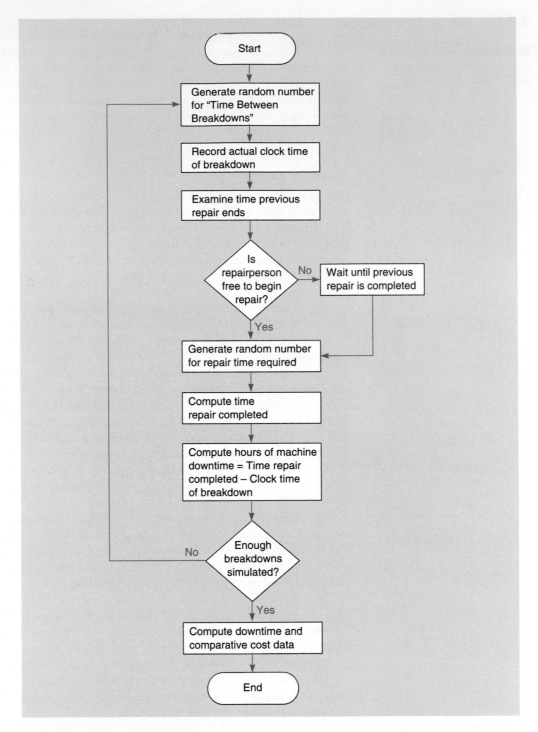

Column 4: Time of Breakdown.   This converts the data in column 3 into an actual time of day for each breakdown. This simulation assumes that the first day begins at midnight (00:00 hours). Since the time between zero breakdowns and the first breakdown is 2 hours, the first recorded machine failure is at 02:00 on the clock. The second breakdown, you note, occurs 1.5 hours later, at a calculated clock time of 03:30 (or 3:30 A.M.).

Column 5: Time Repairperson Is Free to Begin Repair.   This is 02:00 hours for the first breakdown if we assume that the repairperson began work at 00:00 hours and was not tied up from a previous generator failure. Before recording this time on the second and all subsequent lines, however,

TABLE 13.12

Time Between Generator Breakdown at Three Hills Power

TIME BETWEEN RECORDED MACHINE FAILURES (HOURS)	NUMBER OF TIMES OBSERVED	PROBABILITY	CUMULATIVE PROBABILITY	RANDOM NUMBER INTERVAL
0.5	5	0.05	0.05	01 to 05
1.0	6	0.06	0.11	06 to 11
1.5	16	0.16	0.27	12 to 27
2.0	33	0.33	0.60	28 to 60
2.5	21	0.21	0.81	61 to 81
3.0	19	0.19	1.00	82 to 00
Total	100	1.00		

TABLE 13.13

Generator Repair Times Required

REPAIR TIME REQUIRED (HOURS)	NUMBER OF TIMES OBSERVED	PROBABILITY	CUMULATIVE PROBABILITY	RANDOM NUMBER INTERVAL
1	28	0.28	0.28	01 to 28
2	52	0.52	0.80	29 to 80
3	20	0.20	1.00	81 to 00
Total	100	1.00		

we must check column 8 to see what time the repairperson finishes the previous job. Look, for example, at the seventh breakdown. The breakdown occurs at 15:00 hours (or 3:00 P.M.). But the repairperson does not complete the previous job, the sixth breakdown, until 16:00 hours. Hence, the entry in column 5 is 16:00 hours.

One further assumption is made to handle the fact that each repairperson works only an 8-hour shift: When each person is replaced by the next shift, he or she simply hands the tools over to the new worker. The new repairperson continues working on the same broken generator until the job is completed. There is no lost time and no overlap of workers. Hence, labor costs for each 24-hour day are exactly 24 hours × $30 per hour = $720.

Column 6: Random Number for Repair Time. This is a number selected from the rightmost column of Table 13.4. It helps simulate repair times.

Column 7: Repair Time Required. This is generated from column 6's random numbers and Table 13.13's repair time distribution. The first random number, 07, represents a repair time of 1 hour since it falls in the random number interval 01 to 28.

Column 8: Time Repair Ends. This is the sum of the entry in column 5 (time repairperson is free to begin) plus the required repair time from column 7. Since the first repair begins at 02:00 and takes one hour to complete, the time repair ends is recorded in column 8 as 03:00.

Column 9: Number of Hours the Machine Is Down. This is the difference between column 4 (time of breakdown) and column 8 (time repair ends). In the case of the first breakdown, that difference is 1 hour (03:00 minus 02:00). In the case of the tenth breakdown, the difference is 23:00 hours minus 19:30 hours, or 3.5 hours.

Cost Analysis of the Simulation

The simulation of 15 generator breakdowns in Table 13.14 spans a time of 34 hours of operation. The clock began at 00:00 hours of day 1 and ran until the final repair at 10:00 hours of day 2.

TABLE 13.14 Simulation of Generator Breakdowns and Repairs

(1) BREAKDOWN NUMBER	(2) RANDOM NUMBER FOR BREAKDOWNS	(3) TIME BETWEEN BREAKDOWNS	(4) TIME OF BREAKDOWN	(5) TIME REPAIRPERSON IS FREE TO BEGIN THIS REPAIR	(6) RANDOM NUMBER FOR REPAIR TIME	(7) REPAIR TIME REQUIRED	(8) TIME REPAIR ENDS	(9) NUMBER OF HOURS MACHINE DOWN
1	57	2	02:00	02:00	07	1	03:00	1
2	17	1.5	03:30	03:30	60	2	05:30	2
3	36	2	05:30	05:30	77	2	07:30	2
4	72	2.5	08:00	08:00	49	2	10:00	2
5	85	3	11:00	11:00	76	2	13:00	2
6	31	2	13:00	13:00	95	3	16:00	3
7	44	2	15:00	16:00	51	2	18:00	3
8	30	2	17:00	18:00	16	1	19:00	2
9	26	1.5	18:30	19:00	14	1	20:00	1.5
10	09	1	19:30	20:00	85	3	23:00	3.5
11	49	2	21:30	23:00	59	2	01:00	3.5
12	13	1.5	23:00	01:00	85	3	04:00	5
13	33	2	01:00	04:00	40	2	06:00	5
14	89	3	04:00	06:00	42	2	08:00	4
15	13	1.5	05:30	08:00	52	2	10:00	4.5
								Total 44

IN ACTION Simulating Jackson Memorial Hospital's Operating Rooms

Miami's Jackson Memorial Hospital, Florida's largest hospital, with 1,576 inpatient beds, is also one of the finest hospitals in the United States. In June 1996, it received the highest accreditation score of any public-sector hospital in the country. Jackson's Department of Management Systems Engineering is constantly seeking ways of increasing hospital efficiency, and the construction of new operating rooms (ORs) prompted the development of a simulation of the existing 31 ORs.

The OR boundary includes the Holding Area and the Recovery Area, both of which were experiencing problems due to ineffective scheduling of OR services. A simulation study, modeled using the ARENA software package, sought to maximize the current use of OR rooms and staff. Inputs to the model included (1) the amount of time a patient waits in holding, (2) the specific process

the patient undergoes, (3) the staff schedule, (4) room availability, and (5) time of day.

The first hurdle that the research team had to deal with at Jackson was the vast number of records to scour to extract data for the probabilistic simulation model. The second hurdle was the *quality* of the data. A thorough analysis of the records determined which were good and which had to be discarded. In the end, Jackson's carefully screened databases led to a good set of model inputs. The simulation model then successfully developed five measures of OR performance: (1) number of procedures a day, (2) average case time, (3) staff utilization, (4) room utilization, and (5) average waiting time in the holding area.

Source: Based on M. A. Centeno, et al. "Challenges of Simulating Hospital Facilities," *Proceedings of the 12th Annual Conference of the Production and Operations Management Society*, Orlando, FL (March 2001): 50.

The critical factor that interests Robbins is the total number of hours that generators are out of service (from column 9). This is computed to be 44 hours. She also notes that toward the end of the simulation period, a backlog is beginning to appear. The thirteenth breakdown occurred at 01:00 hours but could not be worked on until 04:00 hours. The fourteenth and fifteenth breakdowns experienced similar delays. Robbins is determined to write a computer program to carry out a few hundred more simulated breakdowns but first wants to analyze the data she has collected thus far.

She measures her objectives as follows:

$$\text{Service maintenance cost} = 34 \text{ hours of worker service time} \times \$30 \text{ per hour}$$
$$= \$1,020$$

$$\text{Simulated machine breakdown cost} = 44 \text{ total hours of breakdown}$$
$$\times \$75 \text{ lost per hour of downtime}$$
$$= \$3,300$$

$$\text{Total simulated maintenance cost of the current system} = \text{Service cost} + \text{Breakdown cost}$$
$$= \$1,020 + \$3,300$$
$$= \$4,320$$

A total cost of $4,320 is reasonable only when compared with other more attractive or less attractive maintenance options. Should, for example, the Three Hills Power Company add a second full-time repairperson to each shift? Should it add just one more worker and let him or her come on duty every fourth shift to help catch up on any backlogs? These are two alternatives that Robbins may choose to consider through simulation. You can help by solving Problem 13-25 at the end of the chapter.

As mentioned at the outset of this section, simulation can also be used in other maintenance problems, including the analysis of *preventive maintenance*. Perhaps the Three Hills Power Company should consider strategies for replacing generator motors, valves, wiring, switches, and other miscellaneous parts that typically fail. It could (1) replace all parts after a certain type when one fails on any generator, or (2) repair or replace all parts after a certain length of service based on an estimated average service life. This would again be done by setting probability distributions for failure rates, selecting random numbers, and simulating past failures and their associated costs.

Preventive maintenance policies can also be simulated.

BUILDING AN EXCEL SIMULATION MODEL FOR THREE HILLS POWER COMPANY Program 13.6 provides an Excel spreadsheet approach to simulating the Three Hills Power maintenance problem.

PROGRAM 13.6

Excel Model for Three Hills Power Company Maintenance Problem

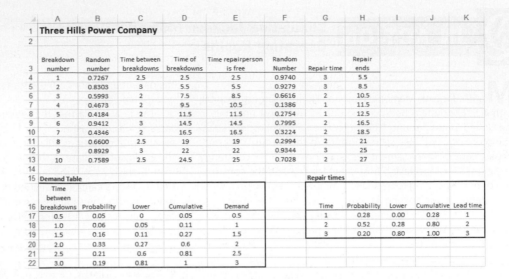

	Breakdown number	Random number	Time between breakdowns	Time of breakdowns	Time repairperson is free	Random Number	Repair time	Repair ends
4	1	0.7267	2.5	2.5	2.5	0.9740	3	5.5
5	2	0.8303	3	5.5	5.5	0.9279	3	8.5
6	3	0.5993	2	7.5	8.5	0.6616	2	10.5
7	4	0.4673	2	9.5	10.5	0.1386	1	11.5
8	5	0.4184	2	11.5	11.5	0.2754	1	12.5
9	6	0.9412	3	14.5	14.5	0.7995	2	16.5
10	7	0.4346	2	16.5	16.5	0.3224	2	18.5
11	8	0.6600	2.5	19	19	0.2994	2	21
12	9	0.8929	3	22	22	0.9344	3	25
13	10	0.7589	2.5	24.5	25	0.7028	2	27

Demand Table

Time between breakdowns	Probability	Lower	Cumulative	Demand
0.5	0.05	0	0.05	0.5
1.0	0.06	0.05	0.11	1
1.5	0.16	0.11	0.27	1.5
2.0	0.33	0.27	0.6	2
2.5	0.21	0.6	0.81	2.5
3.0	0.19	0.81	1	3

Repair times

Time	Probability	Lower	Cumulative	Lead time
1	0.28	0.00	0.28	1
2	0.52	0.28	0.80	2
3	0.20	0.80	1.00	3

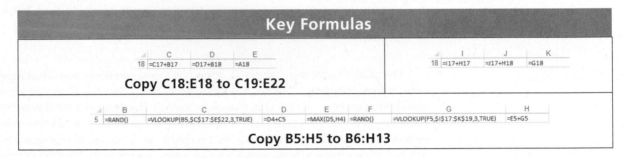

Key Formulas

	C	D	E
18	=C17+B17	=D17+B18	=A18

Copy C18:E18 to C19:E22

	I	J	K
18	=I17+H17	=J17+H18	=G18

	B	C	D	E	F	G	H
5	=RAND()	=VLOOKUP(B5,$C$17:$E$22,3,TRUE)	=D4+C5	=MAX(D5,H4)	=RAND()	=VLOOKUP(F5,$I$17:$K$19,3,TRUE)	=E5+G5

Copy B5:H5 to B6:H13

13.7 Other Simulation Issues

Simulation is one of the most widely used tools in business. As we have seen in the earlier parts of this chapter, applications abound, as we are not restricted by the assumptions in some of the mathematical models discussed in earlier chapters. In this section, we look at a few other issues related to simulation, including some of the software tools available.

Two Other Types of Simulation Models

Simulation models are often broken into three categories. The first, the Monte Carlo method just discussed, uses the concepts of probability distribution and random numbers to evaluate system responses to various policies. The other two categories are operational gaming and systems simulation. Although in theory the three methods are distinctly different, the growth of computerized simulation has tended to create a common basis in procedures and blur these differences.*

OPERATIONAL GAMING   **Operational gaming** refers to simulation involving two or more competing players. The best examples are military games and business games. Both allow participants to match their management and decision-making skills in hypothetical situations of conflict.

Military games are used worldwide to train a nation's top military officers, to test offensive and defensive strategies, and to examine the effectiveness of equipment and armies. Business games, first developed by the firm Booz, Allen, and Hamilton in the 1950s, are popular with both executives and business students. They provide an opportunity to test business skills and decision-making ability in a competitive environment. The person or team that performs best

---

*Theoretically, random numbers are used only in Monte Carlo simulation. However, in some complex gaming or systems simulation problems in which all relationships cannot be defined exactly, it may be necessary to use the probability concepts of the Monte Carlo method.

in the simulated environment is rewarded by knowing that his or her company has been most successful in earning the largest profit, grabbing a high market share, or perhaps increasing the firm's trading value on the stock exchange.

During each period of competition, be it a week, month, or quarter, teams respond to market conditions by coding their latest management decisions with respect to inventory, production, financing, investment, marketing, and research. The competitive business environment is simulated by computer, and a new printout summarizing current market conditions is presented to players. This allows teams to simulate years of operating conditions in a matter of days, weeks, or a semester.

SYSTEMS SIMULATION   **Systems simulation** is similar to business gaming in that it allows users to test various managerial policies and decisions to evaluate their effect on the operating environment. This variation of simulation models the dynamics of large *systems*. Such systems include corporate operations,* the national economy, a hospital, or a city government system.

Econometric models are huge simulations involving thousands of regression equations tied together by economic factors. They use what-if? questions to test out various policies.

In a *corporate operating system*, sales, production levels, marketing policies, investments, union contracts, utility rates, financing, and other factors are all related in a series of mathematical equations that are examined by simulation. In a simulation of an *urban government*, systems simulation can be employed to evaluate the impact of tax increases, capital expenditures for roads and buildings, housing availability, new garbage routes, immigration and out-migration, locations of new schools or senior citizen centers, birth and death rates, and many more vital issues. Simulations of *economic systems*, often called econometric models, are used by government agencies, bankers, and large organizations to predict inflation rates, domestic and foreign money supplies, and unemployment levels. Inputs and outputs of a typical economic system simulation are illustrated in Figure 13.5.

The value of systems simulation lies in its allowance of what-if? questions to test the effects of various policies. A corporate planning group, for example, can change the value of any input, such as an advertising budget, and examine the impact on sales, market share, or short-term costs. Simulation can also be used to evaluate different research and development projects or to determine long-range planning horizons.

Verification and Validation

In the development of a simulation model, it is important that the model be checked to see that it is working properly and providing a good representation of the real world situation. The **verification** process involves determining that the computer model is internally consistent and following the logic of the conceptual model.

Validation is the process of comparing a model to the real system that it represents to make sure that it is accurate. The assumptions of the model should be checked to see that the appropriate probability distribution is being used. An analysis of the inputs and outputs should be made to see that the results are reasonable. If we know what the actual outputs are for a specific set of inputs, we could use those inputs in the computer model to see that the outputs of the simulation are consistent with the real world system.

Verification relates to building the model right. Validation relates to building the right model.

It has been said that verification answers the question "Did we build the model right?" On the other hand, validation answers the question "Did we build the right model?" Only after we are convinced that the model is good should we feel comfortable in using the results.

FIGURE 13.5

Inputs and Outputs of a Typical Economic System Simulation

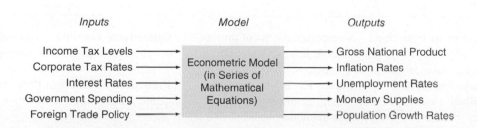

---

*This is sometimes referred to as *industrial dynamics*, a term coined by Jay Forrester. Forrester's goal was to find a way "to show how policies, decisions, structure, and delays are interrelated to influence growth and stability" in industrial systems. See J. W. Forrester. *Industrial Dynamics* (Cambridge, MA: MIT Press, 1961).

IN ACTION   Simulating a Tiger

What does it take to beat Tiger Woods on the golf course? Quantitative analysts studied that very question using a simulation model.

The simulation model was quite extensive. It was essentially a simulation based estimate of relative tournament difficulty. It included variables such as individual player skill, strength of the field (how good are the players at any particular tournament), depth of field (how many players are at any particular tournament), along with random variation in individual scoring. The model noted that when Tiger Woods wins, he wins by an average of 2.84 strokes per tournament.

This difference suggested that Tiger Woods wasn't just lucky and was, in fact, significantly better than everyone else in the field. Indeed, from the moment he became a professional golfer in 1996 he won 71 of the ensuing 239 PGA TOUR events that he entered. That's a staggering 29.7% winning percentage!

Source: Based on R. A. Connolly and R. J. Rendleman, Jr. "What It Takes to Win on the PGA TOUR (If Your Name Is "Tiger" or If It Isn't".) *Interfaces*, 42, 6 (November–December 2012): 554–576.

Role of Computers in Simulation

We recognize that computers are critical in simulating complex tasks. They can generate random numbers, simulate thousands of time periods in a matter of seconds or minutes, and provide management with reports that make decision making easier. As a matter of fact, a computer approach is almost a necessity for us to draw valid conclusions from a simulation. Because we require a very large number of simulations, it would be a real burden to rely on pencil and paper alone.

While general-purpose programming languages can be used for simulation, some special **simulation software tools** have been developed that make the simulation process much easier. Some of these tools are Arena, ProModel, SIMUL8, ExtendSim, Proof 5, and numerous others.* In addition to these stand-alone tools, there are several Excel add-ins, such as @Risk, Crystal Ball, RiskSim, and XLSim, which can make simulating with Excel very easy.

Summary

The purpose of this chapter is to discuss the concept and approach of simulation as a problem-solving tool. Simulation involves building a mathematical model that attempts to describe a real-world situation. The model's goal is to incorporate important variables and their interrelationships in such a way that we can study the impact of managerial changes on the total system. The approach has many advantages over other quantitative analysis techniques and is especially useful when a problem is too complex or difficult to solve by other means.

The Monte Carlo method of simulation is developed through the use of probability distributions and random numbers. Random number intervals are established to represent possible outcomes for each probabilistic variable in the model. Random numbers are then either selected from a random number table or generated by computer to simulate variable outcomes. The simulation procedure is conducted for many time periods to evaluate the long-term impact of each policy value being studied. Monte Carlo simulation by hand is illustrated on problems of inventory control, queuing, and machine maintenance.

Operational gaming and systems simulation, two other categories of simulation, are also presented in this chapter. The chapter concludes with a discussion of the important role of the computer in the simulation process.

Glossary

Flow Diagram, or Flowchart   A graphical means of presenting the logic of a simulation model. It is a tool that helps in writing a simulation computer program.

Monte Carlo Simulation   Simulations that experiment with probabilistic elements of a system by generating random numbers to create values for those elements.

Operational Gaming   The use of simulation in competitive situations such as military games and business or management games.

Prewritten Simulation Programs   Graphical programs that are prestructured to handle a variety of situations.

---

*For a list of simulation software products, see James J. Swain. "To Boldly Go," *OR/MS Today* 36, 5 (October 2009): 50–61.

Random Number   A number whose digits are selected completely at random.

Random Number Interval   A range of random numbers assigned to represent a possible simulation outcome.

Simulation   A quantitative analysis technique that involves building a mathematical model that represents a real-world situation. The model is then experimented with to estimate the effects of various actions and decisions.

Simulation Software Tools   Programming languages especially designed to be efficient in handling simulation problems.

Systems Simulation   Simulation models that deal with the dynamics of large organizational or governmental systems.

Validation   The process of comparing a model to the real system that it represents to make sure that it is accurate.

Verification   The process of determining that the computer model is internally consistent and follows the logic of the conceptual model.

Solved Problems

Solved Problem 13-1

Higgins Plumbing and Heating maintains a stock of 30-gallon hot water heaters that it sells to homeowners and installs for them. Owner Jerry Higgins likes the idea of having a large supply on hand to meet customer demand, but he also recognizes that it is expensive to do so. He examines hot water heater sales over the past 50 weeks and notes the following:

HOT WATER HEATER SALES PER WEEK	NUMBER OF WEEKS THIS NUMBER WAS SOLD
4	6
5	5
6	9
7	12
8	8
9	7
10	3
	Total 50

a. If Higgins maintains a constant supply of 8 hot water heaters in any given week, how many times will he be out of stock during a 20-week simulation? We use random numbers from the seventh column of Table 13.4, beginning with the random digits 10.

b. What is the average number of sales per week (including stockouts) over the 20-week period?

c. Using an analytic nonsimulation technique, what is the expected number of sales per week? How does this compare with the answer in part (b)?

Solution

The variable of interest is the number of sales per week.

HEATER SALES	PROBABILITY	RANDOM NUMBER INTERVALS
4	0.12	01 to 12
5	0.10	13 to 22
6	0.18	23 to 40
7	0.24	41 to 64
8	0.16	65 to 80
9	0.14	81 to 94
10	0.06	95 to 00
	1.00	

a.

WEEK	RANDOM NUMBER	SIMULATED SALES	WEEK	RANDOM NUMBER	SIMULATED SALES
1	10	4	11	08	4
2	24	6	12	48	7
3	03	4	13	66	8
4	32	6	14	97	10
5	23	6	15	03	4
6	59	7	16	96	10
7	95	10	17	46	7
8	34	6	18	74	8
9	34	6	19	77	8
10	51	7	20	44	7

With a supply of 8 heaters, Higgins will be out of stock three times during the 20-week period (in weeks 7, 14, and 16).

b. Average sales by simulation $= \dfrac{\text{Total sales}}{20 \text{ weeks}} = \dfrac{135}{20} = 6.75$ per week.

c. Using expected value,

$$E(\text{sales}) = 0.12(4 \text{ heaters}) + 0.10(5) + 0.18(6) + 0.24(7)$$
$$+ 0.16(8) + 0.14(9) + 0.06(10)$$
$$= 6.88 \text{ heaters}$$

With a longer simulation, these two approaches will lead to even closer values.

Solved Problem 13-2

The manager of a bank in Greensboro, North Carolina, is attempting to determine how many tellers are needed at the drive-in window during peak times. As a general policy, the manager wishes to offer service such that average customer waiting time does not exceed 2 minutes. Given the existing service level, as shown in the following data, does the drive-in window meet this criterion?

DATA FOR SERVICE TIME			
SERVICE TIME (MINUTES)	PROBABILITY (FREQUENCY)	CUMULATIVE PROBABILITY	RANDOM NUMBER INTERVAL
0	0.00	0.00	(impossible)
1.0	0.25	0.25	01 to 25
2.0	0.20	0.45	26 to 45
3.0	0.40	0.85	46 to 85
4.0	0.15	1.00	86 to 00

	DATA FOR CUSTOMER ARRIVALS		
TIME BETWEEN SUCCESSIVE CUSTOMER ARRIVALS	PROBABILITY (FREQUENCY)	CUMULATIVE PROBABILITY	RANDOM NUMBER INTERVAL
0	0.10	0.10	01 to 10
1.0	0.35	0.45	11 to 45
2.0	0.25	0.70	46 to 70
3.0	0.15	0.85	71 to 85
4.0	0.10	0.95	86 to 95
5.0	0.05	1.00	96 to 00

Solution

Average waiting time is a variable of concern.

(1) CUSTOMER NUMBER	(2) RANDOM NUMBER	(3) INTERVAL TO ARRIVAL	(4) TIME OF ARRIVAL	(5) RANDOM NUMBER	(6) SERVICE TIME	(7) START SERVICE	(8) END SERVICE	(9) WAIT TIME	(10) IDLE TIME
1	50	2	9:02	52	3	9:02	9:05	0	2
2	28	1	9:03	37	2	9:05	9:07	2	0
3	68	2	9:05	82	3	9:07	9:10	2	0
4	36	1	9:06	69	3	9:10	9:13	4	0
5	90	4	9:10	98	4	9:13	9:17	3	0
6	62	2	9:12	96	4	9:17	9:21	5	0
7	27	1	9:13	33	2	9:21	9:23	8	0
8	50	2	9:15	50	3	9:23	9:26	8	0
9	18	1	9:16	88	4	9:26	9:30	10	0
10	36	1	9:17	90	4	9:30	9:34	13	0
11	61	2	9:19	50	3	9:34	9:37	15	0
12	21	1	9:20	27	2	9:37	9:39	17	0
13	46	2	9:22	45	2	9:39	9:41	17	0
14	01	0	9:22	81	3	9:41	9:44	19	0
15	14	1	9:23	66	3	9:44	9:47	21	0

Read the data as in the following example for the first row:

Column 1: Number of customer.

Column 2: From third column of random number Table 13.4.

Column 3: Time interval corresponding to random number (random number of 50 implies a 2-minute interval).

Column 4: Starting at 9 A.M. the first arrival is at 9:02.

Column 5: From the first column of the random number Table 13.4.

Column 6: Teller time corresponding to random number 52 is 3 minutes.

Column 7: Teller is available and can start at 9:02.

Column 8: Teller completes work at 9:05 (9:02 + 0:03).

Column 9: Wait time for customer is 0 as the teller was available.

Column 10: Idle time for the teller was 2 minutes (9:00 to 9:02).

The drive-in window clearly does not meet the manager's criteria for an average wait time of 2 minutes. As a matter of fact, we can observe an increasing queue buildup after only a few customer simulations. This observation can be confirmed by expected value calculations on both arrival and service rates.

Self-Test

- Before taking the self-test, refer to the learning objectives at the beginning of the chapter, the notes in the margins, and the glossary at the end of the chapter.
- Use the key at the back of the book to correct your answers.
- Restudy pages that correspond to any questions that you answered incorrectly or material you feel uncertain about.

1. Simulation is a technique usually reserved for studying only the simplest and most straightforward of problems.
   a. True
   b. False
2. A simulation model is designed to arrive at a single specific numerical answer to a given problem.
   a. True
   b. False
3. Simulation typically requires a familiarity with statistics to evaluate the results.
   a. True
   b. False
4. The verification process involves making sure that
   a. the model adequately represents the real-world system.
   b. the model is internally consistent and logical.
   c. the correct random numbers are used.
   d. enough trial runs are simulated.
5. The validation process involves making sure that
   a. the model adequately represents the real-world system.
   b. the model is internally consistent and logical.
   c. the correct random numbers are used.
   d. enough trial runs are simulated.
6. Which of the following is an *advantage* of simulation?
   a. It allows time compression.
   b. It is always relatively simple and inexpensive.
   c. The results are usually transferable to other problems.
   d. It will always find the optimal solution to a problem.
7. Which of the following is a *disadvantage* of simulation?
   a. It is inexpensive even for the most complex problem.
   b. It always generates the optimal solution to a problem.
   c. The results are usually transferable to other problems.
   d. Managers must generate all of the conditions and constraints for solutions that they wish to examine.
8. A meteorologist was simulating the number of days that rain would occur in a month. The random number interval from 01 to 30 was used to indicate that rain occurred on a particular day, and the interval 31–00 indicated that rain did not occur. What is the probability that rain did occur?
   a. 0.30
   b. 0.31
   c. 1.00
   d. 0.70
9. Simulation is best thought of as a technique to
   a. give concrete numerical answers.
   b. increase understanding of a problem.
   c. provide rapid solutions to relatively simple problems.
   d. provide optimal solutions to complex problems.
10. When simulating the Monte Carlo experiment, the average simulated demand over the long run should approximate the
    a. real demand.
    b. expected demand.
    c. sample demand.
    d. daily demand.
11. The idea behind simulation is to
    a. imitate a real-world situation.
    b. study the properties and operating characteristics of a real-world situation.
    c. draw conclusions and make action decisions based on simulation results.
    d. all of the above.
12. Using simulation for a queuing problem would be appropriate if
    a. the arrival rate follows a Poisson distribution.
    b. the service rate is constant.
    c. the FIFO queue discipline is assumed.
    d. there is a 10% chance an arrival would leave before receiving service.
13. A probability distribution has been developed, and the probability of 2 arrivals in the next hour is 0.20. A random number interval is to be assigned to this. Which of the following would *not* be an appropriate interval?
    a. 01–20
    b. 21–40
    c. 00–20
    d. 00–19
    e. All of the above would be appropriate.
14. In a Monte Carlo simulation, a variable that we might want to simulate is
    a. lead time for inventory orders to arrive.
    b. times between machine breakdowns.
    c. times between arrivals at a service facility.
    d. number of employees absent from work each day.
    e. all of the above.
15. Use the following random numbers to simulate *yes* and *no* answers to 10 questions by starting in the first *row* and letting
    a. the double-digit numbers 00–49 represent *yes*, and 50–99 represent *no*.
    b. the double-digit even numbers represent *yes*, and the odd numbers represent *no*.
    Random numbers: 52 06 50 88 53 30 10 47 99 37 66 91 35 32 00 84 57 00

Discussion Questions and Problems

Discussion Questions

13-1 What are the advantages and limitations of simulation models?

13-2 Why might a manager be forced to use simulation instead of an analytical model in dealing with a problem of
(a) inventory ordering policy?
(b) ships docking in a port to unload?
(c) bank teller service windows?
(d) the U.S. economy?

13-3 What types of management problems can be solved more easily by quantitative analysis techniques other than simulation?

13-4 What are the major steps in the simulation process?

13-5 What is Monte Carlo simulation? What principles underlie its use, and what steps are followed in applying it?

13-6 List three ways in which random numbers may be generated for use in a simulation.

13-7 Discuss the concepts of verification and validation in simulation.

13-8 Give two examples of random variables that would be continuous and give two examples of random variables that would be discrect.

13-9 In the simulation of an order policy for drills at Simkin's Hardware, would the results (Table 13.8) change significantly if a longer period were simulated? Why is the 10-day simulation valid or invalid?

13-10 Why is a computer necessary in conducting a real world simulation?

13-11 What is operational gaming? What is systems simulation? Give examples of how each may be applied.

13-12 Do you think the application of simulation will increase strongly in the next 10 years? Why or why not?

13-13 List five of the simulation software tools that are available today.

Problems*

The problems that follow involve simulations that are to be done by hand. You are aware that to obtain accurate and meaningful results, long periods must be simulated. This is usually handled by computer. If you are able to program some of the problems using a spreadsheet, or QM for Windows, we suggest that you try to do so. If not, the hand simulations will still help you in understanding the simulation process.

•13-14 Clark Property Management is responsible for the maintenance, rental, and day-to-day operation of a large apartment complex on the east side of New Orleans. George Clark is especially concerned about the cost projections for replacing air conditioner compressors. He would like to simulate the number of compressor failures each year over the next 20 years. Using data from a similar apartment building he manages in a New Orleans suburb, Clark establishes a table of relative frequency of failures during a year as shown in the following table:

NUMBER OF A.C. COMPRESSOR FAILURES	PROBABILITY (RELATIVE FREQUENCY)
0	0.06
1	0.13
2	0.25
3	0.28
4	0.20
5	0.07
6	0.01

He decides to simulate the 20-year period by selecting two-digit random numbers from the third column of Table 13.4, starting with the random number 50.

Conduct the simulation for Clark. Is it common to have three or more consecutive years of operation with two or fewer compressor failures per year?

•13-15 The number of cars arriving per hour at Lundberg's Car Wash during the past 200 hours of operation is observed to be the following:

NUMBER OF CARS ARRIVING	FREQUENCY
3 or fewer	0
4	20
5	30
6	50
7	60
8	40
9 or more	0
	Total 200

(a) Set up a probability and cumulative probability distribution for the variable of car arrivals.
(b) Establish random number intervals for the variable.

---

*Note: ♀ means the problem may be solved with QM for Windows; ✘ means the problem may be solved with Excel; and ♀✘ means the problem may be solved with QM for Windows and/or Excel.

(c) Simulate 15 hours of car arrivals and compute the average number of arrivals per hour. Select the random numbers needed from the first column of Table 13.4, beginning with the digits 52.

• 13-16 Compute the expected number of cars arriving in Problem 13-15 using the expected value formula. Compare this with the results obtained in the simulation.

• 13-17 Refer to the data in Solved Problem 13-1, which deals with Higgins Plumbing and Heating. Higgins has now collected 100 weeks of data and finds the following distribution for sales:

HOT WATER HEATER SALES PER WEEK	NUMBER OF WEEKS THIS NUMBER WAS SOLD
3	2
4	9
5	10
6	15
7	25
8	12
9	12
10	10
11	5

(a) Resimulate the number of stockouts incurred over a 20-week period (assuming Higgins maintains a constant supply of 8 heaters).

(b) Conduct this 20-week simulation two more times and compare your answers with those in part (a). Did they change significantly? Why or why not?

(c) What is the new expected number of sales per week?

• 13-18 An increase in the size of the barge unloading crew at the Port of New Orleans (see Section 13.5) has resulted in a new probability distribution for daily unloading rates. In particular, Table 13.10 may be revised as shown here:

DAILY UNLOADING RATE	PROBABILITY
1	0.03
2	0.12
3	0.40
4	0.28
5	0.12
6	0.05

(a) Resimulate 15 days of barge unloadings and compute the average number of barges delayed, average number of nightly arrivals, and average number of barges unloaded each day. Draw

random numbers from the leftmost value of the bottom row of Table 13.4 to generate daily arrivals and from the second-from-the-bottom row to generate daily unloading rates.

(b) How do these simulated results compare with those in the chapter?

13-19 Every home football game for the past eight years at Eastern State University has been sold out. The revenues from ticket sales are significant, but the sale of food, beverages, and souvenirs has contributed greatly to the overall profitability of the football program. One particular souvenir is the football program for each game. The number of programs sold at each game is described by the following probability distribution:

NUMBER (IN 100s) OF PROGRAMS SOLD	PROBABILITY
23	0.15
24	0.22
25	0.24
26	0.21
27	0.18

Historically, Eastern has never sold fewer than 2,300 programs or more than 2,700 programs at one game. Each program costs $0.80 to produce and sells for $2.00. Any programs that are not sold are donated to a recycling center and do not produce any revenue.

(a) Simulate the sales of programs at 10 football games. Use the last column in the random number table (Table 13.4) and begin at the top of the column.

(b) If the university decided to print 2,500 programs for each game, what would the average profits be for the 10 games simulated in part (a)?

(c) If the university decided to print 2,600 programs for each game, what would the average profits be for the 10 games simulated in part (a)?

13-20 Refer to Problem 13-19. Suppose the sale of football programs described by the probability distribution in that problem only applies to days when the weather is good. When poor weather occurs on the day of a football game, the crowd that attends the game is only half of capacity. When this occurs, the sales of programs decreases, and the total sales are given in the following table:

NUMBER (IN 100s) OF PROGRAMS SOLD	PROBABILITY
12	0.25
13	0.24
14	0.19
15	0.17
16	0.15

Programs must be printed two days prior to game day. The university is trying to establish a policy for determining the number of programs to print based on the weather forecast.

(a) If the forecast is for a 20% chance of bad weather, simulate the weather for ten games with this forecast. Use column 4 of Table 13.4.

(b) Simulate the demand for programs at 10 games in which the weather is bad. Use column 5 of the random number table (Table 13.4) and begin with the first number in the column.

(c) Beginning with a 20% chance of bad weather and an 80% chance of good weather, develop a flowchart that would be used to prepare a simulation of the demand for football programs for 10 games.

(d) Suppose there is a 20% chance of bad weather, and the university has decided to print 2,500 programs. Simulate the total profits that would be achieved for 10 football games.

✕:13-21 Dumoor Appliance Center sells and services several brands of major appliances. Past sales for a particular model of refrigerator have resulted in the following probability distribution for demand:

DEMAND PER WEEK	0	1	2	3	4
Probability	0.20	0.40	0.20	0.15	0.05

The lead time, in weeks, is described by the following distribution:

LEAD TIME (WEEKS)	1	2	3
Probability	0.15	0.35	0.50

Based on cost considerations as well as storage space, the company has decided to order 10 of these each time an order is placed. The holding cost is $1 per week for each unit that is left in inventory at the end of the week. The stockout cost has been set at $40 per stockout. The company has decided to place an order whenever there are only two refrigerators left at the end of the week. Simulate 10 weeks of operation for Dumoor Appliance assuming there are currently 5 units in inventory. Determine what the weekly stockout cost and weekly holding cost would be for the problem.

✕:13-22 Repeat the simulation in Problem 13-21, assuming that the reorder point is 4 units rather than 2. Compare the costs for these two situations.

✕·13-23 Simkin's Hardware Store simulated an inventory ordering policy for Ace electric drills that involved an order quantity of 10 drills with a reorder point of 5. The first attempt to develop a cost-effective ordering strategy is illustrated in Table 13.8. The brief simulation resulted in a total daily inventory cost of $4.72. Simkin would now like to compare this strategy with

one in which he orders 12 drills, with a reorder point of 6. Conduct a 10-day simulation for him and discuss the cost implications.

:13-24 Draw a flow diagram to represent the logic and steps of simulating barge arrivals and unloadings at the Port of New Orleans (see Section 13.5). For a refresher in flowcharts, see Figure 13.3.

✕:13-25 Stephanie Robbins is the Three Hills Power Company management analyst assigned to simulate maintenance costs. In Section 13.6 we describe the simulation of 15 generator breakdowns and the repair times required when one repairperson is on duty per shift. The total simulated maintenance cost of the current system is $4,320.

Robbins would now like to examine the relative cost-effectiveness of adding one more worker per shift. Each new repairperson would be paid $30 per hour, the same rate as the first is paid. The cost per breakdown hour is still $75. Robbins makes one vital assumption as she begins—that repair times with two workers will be exactly one-half the times required with only one repairperson on duty per shift. Table 13.13 can then be restated as follows:

REPAIR TIME REQUIRED (HOURS)	PROBABILITY
0.5	0.28
1	0.52
1.5	0.20
	1.00

(a) Simulate this proposed maintenance system change over a 15-generator breakdown period. Select the random numbers needed for time between breakdowns from the second-from-the-bottom row of Table 13.4 (beginning with the digits 69). Select random numbers for generator repair times from the last row of the table (beginning with 37).

(b) Should Three Hills add a second repairperson each shift?

✕:13-26 The Brennan Aircraft Division of TLN Enterprises operates a large number of computerized plotting machines. For the most part, the plotting devices are used to create line drawings of complex wing airfoils and fuselage part dimensions. The engineers operating the automated plotters are called loft lines engineers.

The computerized plotters consist of a mini-computer system connected to a 4- by 5-foot flat table with a series of ink pens suspended above it. When a sheet of clear plastic or paper is properly placed on the table, the computer directs a series of horizontal and vertical pen movements until the desired figure is drawn.

The plotting machines are highly reliable, with the exception of the four sophisticated ink pens that are built in. The pens constantly clog and jam in a raised or lowered position. When this occurs, the plotter is unusable.

Currently, Brennan Aircraft replaces each pen as it fails. The service manager has, however, proposed replacing all four pens every time one fails. This should cut down the frequency of plotter failures. At present, it takes one hour to replace one pen. All four pens could be replaced in two hours. The total cost of a plotter being unusable is $50 per hour. Each pen costs $8.

If only one pen is replaced each time a clog or jam occurs, the following breakdown data are thought to be valid:

HOURS BETWEEN PLOTTER FAILURES IF ONE PEN IS REPLACED DURING A REPAIR	PROBABILITY
10	0.05
20	0.15
30	0.15
40	0.20
50	0.20
60	0.15
70	0.10

Based on the service manager's estimates, if all four pens are replaced each time one pen fails, the probability distribution between failures is as follows:

HOURS BETWEEN PLOTTER FAILURES IF ALL FOUR PENS ARE REPLACED DURING A REPAIR	PROBABILITY
100	0.15
110	0.25
120	0.35
130	0.20
140	0.00

(a) Simulate Brennan Aircraft's problem and determine the best policy. Should the firm replace one pen or all four pens on a plotter each time a failure occurs?

(b) Develop a second approach to solving this problem, this time without simulation. Compare the results. How does it affect Brennan's policy decision using simulation?

13-27 Dr. Mark Greenberg practices dentistry in Topeka, Kansas. Greenberg tries hard to schedule appointments so that patients do not have to wait beyond their appointment time. His October 20 schedule is shown in the following table.

SCHEDULED APPOINTMENT AND TIME		EXPECTED TIME NEEDED
Adams	9:30 A.M.	15
Brown	9:45 A.M.	20
Crawford	10:15 A.M.	15
Dannon	10:30 A.M.	10
Erving	10:45 A.M.	30
Fink	11:15 A.M.	15
Graham	11:30 A.M.	20
Hinkel	11:45 A.M.	15

Unfortunately, not every patient arrives exactly on schedule, and expected times to examine patients are just that—*expected*. Some examinations take longer than expected, and some take less time.

Greenberg's experience dictates the following:

(a) 20% of the patients will be 20 minutes early.
(b) 10% of the patients will be 10 minutes early.
(c) 40% of the patients will be on time.
(d) 25% of the patients will be 10 minutes late.
(e) 5% of the patients will be 20 minutes late.

He further estimates that

(a) 15% of the time he will finish in 20% less time than expected.
(b) 50% of the time he will finish in the expected time.
(c) 25% of the time he will finish in 20% more time than expected.
(d) 10% of the time he will finish in 40% more time than expected.

Dr. Greenberg has to leave at 12:15 P.M. on October 20 to catch a flight to a dental convention in New York. Assuming that he is ready to start his workday at 9:30 A.M. and that patients are treated in order of their scheduled exam (even if one late patient arrives after an early one), will he be able to make the flight? Comment on this simulation.

13-28 The Pelnor Corporation is the nation's largest manufacturer of industrial-size washing machines. A main ingredient in the production process is 8- by 10-foot sheets of stainless steel. The steel is used for both interior washer drums and outer casings.

Steel is purchased weekly on a contractual basis from the Smith-Layton Foundry, which, because of limited availability and lot sizing, can ship either 8,000 or 11,000 square feet of stainless steel each week. When Pelnor's weekly order is placed, there is a 45% chance that 8,000 square feet will arrive and a 55% chance of receiving the larger size order.

Pelnor uses the stainless steel on a stochastic (nonconstant) basis. The probabilities of demand each week follow:

STEEL NEEDED PER WEEK (SQ FT)	PROBABILITY
6,000	0.05
7,000	0.15
8,000	0.20
9,000	0.30
10,000	0.20
11,000	0.10

Pelnor has a capacity to store no more than 25,000 square feet of steel at any time. Because of the contract, orders *must* be placed each week regardless of the on-hand supply.

(a) Simulate stainless steel order arrivals and use for 20 weeks. (Begin the first week with a starting inventory of 0 stainless steel.) If an end-of-week inventory is ever negative, assume that back orders are permitted and fill the demand from the next arriving order.

(b) Should Pelnor add more storage area? If so, how much? If not, comment on the system.

13-29 Milwaukee's General Hospital has an emergency room that is divided into six departments: (1) the initial exam station, to treat minor problems or make diagnoses; (2) an x-ray department; (3) an operating room; (4) a cast-fitting room; (5) an observation room for recovery and general observation before final diagnoses or release; and (6) an out-processing department where clerks check patients out and arrange for payment or insurance forms.

The probabilities that a patient will go from one department to another are presented in the table below:

(a) Simulate the trail followed by 10 emergency room patients. Proceed one patient at a time from each one's entry at the initial exam station until he or she leaves through out-processing. You should be aware that a patient can enter the same department more than once.

(b) Using your simulation data, what are the chances that a patient enters the x-ray department twice?

13-30 Management of the First Syracuse Bank is concerned about a loss of customers at its main office downtown. One solution that has been proposed is to add one or more drive-through teller stations to make it easier for customers in cars to obtain quick service without parking. Chris Carlson, the bank president, thinks the bank should only risk the cost of installing one drive-through. He is informed by his staff that the cost (amortized over a 20-year period) of building a drive-through is $12,000 per year. It also costs $16,000 per year in wages and benefits to staff each new teller window.

The director of management analysis, Beth Shader, believes that the following two factors encourage the immediate construction of two drive-through stations, however. According to a recent article in *Banking Research* magazine, customers who wait in long lines for drive-through teller service will cost banks an average of $1 per minute in loss of goodwill. Also, adding a second drive-through will cost an additional $16,000 in staffing, but amortized construction costs can be cut to a total of $20,000 per year if two drive-throughs are

Table for Problem 13-29

FROM	TO	PROBABILITY
Initial exam at emergency room entrance	X-ray department	0.45
	Operating room	0.15
	Observation room	0.10
	Out-processing clerk	0.30
X-ray department	Operating room	0.10
	Cast-fitting room	0.25
	Observation room	0.35
	Out-processing clerk	0.30
Operating room	Cast-fitting room	0.25
	Observation room	0.70
	Out-processing clerk	0.05
Cast-fitting room	Observation room	0.55
	X-ray department	0.05
	Out-processing clerk	0.40
Observation room	Operating room	0.15
	X-ray department	0.15
	Out-processing clerk	0.70

installed together instead of one at a time. To complete her analysis, Shader collected one month's arrival and service rates at a competing downtown bank's drive-through stations. These data are shown as observation analyses 1 and 2 in the following tables.

(a) Simulate a 1-hour time period, from 1 P.M. to 2 P.M., for a single-teller drive-through.
(b) Simulate a 1-hour time period, from 1 P.M. to 2 P.M., for a single line of people waiting for next available teller in a two-teller system.
(c) Conduct a cost analysis of the two options. Assume that the bank is open 7 hours per day and 200 days per year.

OBSERVATION ANALYSIS 2: CUSTOMER SERVICE TIME FOR 1,000 CUSTOMERS	
SERVICE TIME (MINUTES)	NUMBER OF OCCURRENCES
1	100
2	150
3	350
4	150
5	150
6	100

OBSERVATION ANALYSIS 1: INTERARRIVAL TIMES FOR 1,000 OBSERVATIONS	
TIME BETWEEN ARRIVALS (MINUTES)	NUMBER OF OCCURRENCES
1	200
2	250
3	300
4	150
5	100

Internet Homework Problems

See our Internet home page, at www.pearsonhighered.com/render, for additional homework problems 13-31 to 13-37.

Case Study

Alabama Airlines

Alabama Airlines opened its doors in June 1995 as a commuter service with its headquarters and only hub located in Birmingham. A product of airline deregulation, Alabama Air joined the growing number of successful short-haul, point-to-point airlines, including Lone Star, Comair, Atlantic Southeast, Skywest, and Business Express.

Alabama Air was started and managed by two former pilots, David Douglas (who had been with the defunct Eastern Airlines) and Savas Ozatalay (formerly with Pan Am). It acquired a fleet of 12 used prop-jet planes and the airport gates vacated by the 1994 downsizing of Delta Air Lines.

With business growing quickly, Douglas turned his attention to Alabama Air's toll-free reservations system. Between midnight and 6:00 A.M., only one telephone reservations agent had been on duty. The time between incoming calls during this period is distributed as shown in Table 13.15. Douglas carefully observed and timed the agent and estimated that the time

taken to process passenger inquiries is distributed as shown in Table 13.16.

All customers calling Alabama Air go on hold and are served in the order of the calls unless the reservations agent is

TABLE 13.15 Incoming Call Distribution

TIME BETWEEN CALLS (MINUTES)	PROBABILITY
1	0.11
2	0.21
3	0.22
4	0.20
5	0.16
6	0.10

TABLE 13.16 Service Time Distribution

TIME TO PROCESS CUSTOMER INQUIRIES (MINUTES)	PROBABILITY
1	0.20
2	0.19
3	0.18
4	0.17
5	0.13
6	0.10
7	0.03

TABLE 13.17 Incoming Call Distribution

TIME BETWEEN CALLS (MINUTES)	PROBABILITY
1	0.22
2	0.25
3	0.19
4	0.15
5	0.12
6	0.07

available for immediate service. Douglas is deciding whether a second agent should be on duty to cope with customer demand. To maintain customer satisfaction, Alabama Air does not want a customer on hold for more than 3 to 4 minutes and also wants to maintain a "high" operator utilization.

Further, the airline is planning a new TV advertising campaign. As a result, it expects an increase in toll-free-line phone inquiries. Based on similar campaigns in the past, the incoming call distribution from midnight to 6 A.M. is expected to be as shown in Table 13.17. (The same service time distribution will apply.)

Discussion Questions

1. What would you advise Alabama Air to do for the current reservation system based on the original call distribution? Create a simulation model to investigate the scenario. Describe the model carefully and justify the duration of the simulation, assumptions, and measures of performance.
2. What are your recommendations regarding operator utilization and customer satisfaction if the airline proceeds with the advertising campaign?

Source: Professor Zbigniew H. Przasnyski, Loyola Marymount University.

Case Study

Statewide Development Corporation

Statewide Development Corporation has built a very large apartment complex in Gainesville, Florida. As part of the student-oriented marketing strategy that has been developed, it is stated that if any problems with plumbing or air conditioning are experienced, a maintenance person will begin working on the problem within one hour. If a tenant must wait more than one hour for the repairperson to arrive, a $10 deduction from the monthly rent will be made for each additional hour of time waiting. An answering machine will take the calls and record the time of the call if the maintenance person is busy. Past experience at other complexes has shown that during the week when most occupants are at school, there is little difficulty in meeting the one hour guarantee. However, it is observed that weekends have been particularly troublesome during the summer months.

A study of the number of calls to the office on weekends concerning air conditioning and plumbing problems has resulted in the following distribution:

TIME BETWEEN CALLS (MINUTES)	PROBABILITY
30	0.15
60	0.30
90	0.30
120	0.25

The time required to complete a service call varies according to the difficulty of the problem. Parts needed for most repairs are kept in a storage room at the complex. However, for certain types of unusual problems, a trip to a local supply house is necessary. If a part is available on site, the maintenance person finishes one job before checking on the next complaint. If the part is not available on site and any other calls have been received, the maintenance person will stop by the other apartment(s) before going to the supply house. It takes approximately one hour to drive to the supply house, pick up a part, and return to the apartment complex. Past records indicate that, on approximately 10% of all calls, a trip must be made to the supply house.

The time required to resolve a problem if the part is available on site varies according to the following:

TIME FOR REPAIR (MINUTES)	PROBABILITY
30	0.45
60	0.30
90	0.20
120	0.05

It takes approximately 30 minutes to diagnose difficult problems for which parts are not on site. Once the part has been obtained from a supply house, it takes approximately one hour to install the new part. If any new calls have been recorded while the maintenance person has been away picking up a new part, these new calls will wait until the new part has been installed.

The cost of salary and benefits for a maintenance person is $20 per hour. Management would like to determine whether two maintenance people should be working on weekends instead of just one. It can be assumed that each person works at the same rate.

Discussion Questions

1. Use simulation to help you analyze this problem. State any assumptions that you are making about this situation to help clarify the problem.
2. On a typical weekend day, how many tenants would have to wait more than an hour, and how much money would the company have to credit these tenants?

Case Study

FB Badpoore Aerospace

FB Badpoore Aerospace makes carbon brake discs for large airplanes with a proprietary "cross weave" of the carbon fibers. The brake discs are 4 feet in diameter but weigh significantly less than conventional ceramic brake discs making them attractive for airplane manufacturers as well as commercial airliners.

Processing the discs at FB Badpoore requires heat treating the discs in a sequence of 12 electric, high pressure, industrial grade furnaces (simply called Furnace A, Furnace B, Furnace C, . . . , Furnace L) each of them fed with a proprietary mixture of chemicals. All brake discs visit each of the 12 furnaces in the same order, Furnace A through Furnace L. These dozen furnaces each follow their own very specific set of simultaneous temperature and pressure profiles. An example of one such profile is depicted in Figure 13.6. All profiles are 12 hours in duration.

All 12 furnaces are top loading. Additionally, each of them are cylindrical in shape, 15 feet in diameter, and about 10 feet in depth. They are arranged in an "egg-carton-like" array (six on one side and six on the other), loaded and unloaded via their top facing round ends by three overhead ten ton bridge cranes, and located in part of the factory known as the *furnace deck*.

Each furnace can process seven stacks of 20 discs at a time. This equates to a batch size of 140 discs. Each batch is loaded onto a ceramic *furnace shelf* that is sturdy, round, and 14 feet in diameter. The furnace deck is said to be *fully loaded* when all 12 furnaces are processing discs.

Loading and unloading the discs is a labor intensive process requiring high level coordination of the three overhead bridge cranes. Bridge crane Alpha (BC-A) serves the incoming area, furnaces A, B, K, L, as well as the outgoing area where discs are stored when they have finished processing in all 12 furnaces. Bridge crane Beta (BC-B) serves furnaces C, D, I, and J while bridge crane Gamma (BC-G) serves furnaces E, F, G, and H. When discs travel within a service area, they are moved by the crane assigned to that area. When discs have to travel between service areas, they are first deposited in a waiting area before moved into the next service area. For example, discs being moved from Furnace D to Furnace E would be unloaded from Furnace D by BC-B, which would deposit them in the waiting area. Then BC-G would pick up the batch and load it into (an already empty) Furnace E.

Due to energy restrictions by the local electric utility company, all furnace processing must be performed at night between 8:00 P.M. and 10:00 A.M. daily. This, in turn, requires all loading and unloading operations to be performed during the day. Indeed, the main shift is from 1:00 P.M. (allowing the discs to cool after processing and before unloading) and 9:00 P.M. (allowing the shift to end by starting up all 12 furnaces after 8:00 P.M.).

FIGURE 13.6

Temperature and
Pressure Profile Example

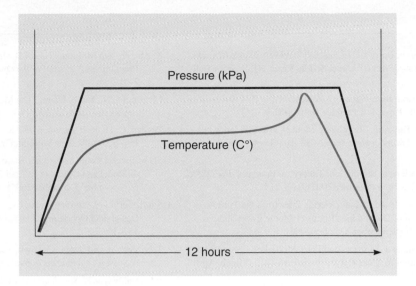

Each furnace has a known yield rate with no noticeable variation according to the following:

FURNACE	A	B	C	D	E	F	G	H	I	J	K	L
Yield	0.95	0.975	0.975	0.975	0.975	0.975	0.975	0.995	0.995	0.995	0.995	0.999

That is to say, one in twenty batches fail at Furnace A and must be scrapped whereas only one in a thousand fail at Furnace L. As one might expect, upstream batch failures are very disruptive to the downstream operations. Scrapping batches causes downstream furnaces to sit idle under the current "zero in queue" work in process (WIP) inventory policy as they wait for good batches to arrive from upstream operations.

Design, build, and perform a 1000 day simulation model study of the system described above in Excel incorporating the random number generator function, RAND(). Start your simulation with a fully loaded furnace deck.

Discussion Questions

1. Determine and comment on the overall yield (the number of batches that make it all the way through Furnace L divided by the number that started at Furnace A) of disc brakes at FB Badpoore.
2. Determine the utilization of Furnace L.
3. Suggest improvements to the system.

Internet Case Studies

See our Internet home page, at **www.pearsonhighered.com/render**, for these additional case studies:

(1) **Abjar Transport Company:** This case involves a trucking company in Saudi Arabia.
(2) **Biales Waste Disposal:** Simulation is used to help a German company evaluate the profitability of a customer in Italy.
(3) **Buffalo Alkali and Plastics:** This case involves determining a good maintenance policy for a soda ash plant.

Bibliography

Banks, Jerry, John S. Carson, Barry L. Nelson, and David M. Nicol. *Discrete-Event System Simulation*, 4th ed. Upper Saddle River, NJ: Prentice Hall, 2005.

Evans, J. R., and D. L. Olson. *Introduction to Simulation and Risk Analysis*, 2nd ed. Upper Saddle River, NJ: Prentice Hall, 2002.

Fishman, G. S., and V. G. Kulkarni. "Improving Monte Carlo Efficiency by Increasing Variance," *Management Science* 38, 10 (October 1992): 1432–1444.

Fu, Michael C. "Optimization for Simulation: Theory vs. Practice," *INFORMS Journal on Computing* 14, 3 (Summer 2002): 192–215.

Gass, Saul I., and Arjang A. Assad. "Model World: Tales from the Time Line—The Definition of OR and the Origins of Monte Carlo Simulation," *Interfaces* 35, 5 (September–October 2005): 429–435.

Gavirneni, Srinagesh, Douglas J. Morrice, and Peter Mullarkey. "Simulation Helps Maxager Shorten Its Sales Cycle," *Interfaces* 34, 2 (March–April 2004): 87–96.

Hartvigsen, David. *SimQuick: Process Simulation with Excel*, 2nd ed. Upper Saddle River, NJ: Prentice Hall, 2004.

Lee, Dong-Eun. "Probability of Project Completion Using Stochastic Project Scheduling Simulation," *Journal of Construction Engineering & Management* 131, 3 (2005): 310–318.

Melão, N., and M. Pidd. "Use of Business Process Simulation: A Survey of Practitioners," *Journal of the Operational Research Society* 54, 1 (2003): 2–10.

Metropolis, N., and S. Ulam. "The Monte Carlo Method," *Journal of American Statistical Association* 44, 247 (1949): 335–341.

Pegden, C. D., R. E. Shannon, and R. P. Sadowski. *Introduction to Simulation Using SIMAN*. New York: McGraw-Hill, 1995.

Sabuncuoglu, Ihsan, and Ahmet Hatip. "The Turkish Army Uses Simulation to Model and Optimize Its Fuel-Supply System," *Interfaces* 35, 6 (November–December 2005): 474–482.

Smith, Jeffrey S. "Survey on the Use of Simulation for Manufacturing System Design and Operation," *Journal of Manufacturing Systems* 22, 2 (2003): 157–171.

Terzi, Sergio, and Sergio Cavalieri. "Simulation in the Supply Chain Context: A Survey," *Computers in Industry* 53, 1 (2004): 3–16.

Winston, Wayne L. *Simulation Modeling Using @Risk*. Pacific Grove, CA: Duxbury, 2001.

Zhang, H., C. M. Tam, and Jonathan J. Shi. "Simulation-Based Methodology for Project Scheduling," *Construction Management & Economics* 20, 8 (2002): 667–668.

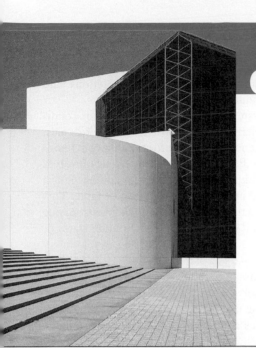

CHAPTER 14

Markov Analysis

14.1   Introduction

Markov analysis is a technique that deals with the probabilities of future occurrences by analyzing presently known probabilities.* The technique has numerous applications in business, including market share analysis, bad debt prediction, university enrollment predictions, and determining whether a machine will break down in the future.

Markov analysis makes the assumption that the system starts in an initial state or condition. For example, two competing manufacturers might have 40% and 60% of the market sales, respectively, as initial states. Perhaps in two months the market shares for the two companies will change to 45% and 55% of the market, respectively. Predicting these future states involves knowing the system's likelihood or probability of changing from one state to another. For a particular problem, these probabilities can be collected and placed in a matrix or table. This **matrix of transition probabilities** shows the likelihood that the system will change from one time period to the next. This is the Markov process, and it enables us to predict future states or conditions.

The matrix of transition probabilities shows the likelihood of change.

Like many other quantitative techniques, Markov analysis can be studied at any level of depth and sophistication. Fortunately, the major mathematical requirements are just that you know how to perform basic matrix manipulations and solve several equations with several unknowns. If you are not familiar with these techniques, you may wish to review Module 5 (on the Companion Website for this book) which covers matrices and other useful mathematical tools, before you begin this chapter.

There are four assumptions of Markov analysis.

Because the level of this course prohibits a detailed study of Markov mathematics, we limit our discussion to Markov processes that follow four assumptions:

1. There are a limited or finite number of possible states.
2. The probability of changing states remains the same over time.
3. We can predict any future state from the previous state and the matrix of transition probabilities.
4. The size and makeup of the system (e.g., the total number of manufacturers and customers) do not change during the analysis.

14.2   States and State Probabilities

States are used to identify all possible conditions of a process or a system. For example, a machine can be in one of two states at any point in time. It can be either functioning correctly or not functioning correctly. We can call the proper operation of the machine the first state, and we can call the incorrect functioning the second state. Indeed, it is possible to identify specific states for many processes or systems. If there are only three grocery stores in a small town, a resident can be a customer of any one of the three at any point in time. Therefore, there are three states corresponding to the three grocery stores. If students can take one of three specialties in the management area (let's say management science, management information systems, or general management), each of these areas can be considered a state.

Collectively exhaustive and mutually exclusive states are two additional assumptions of Markov analysis.

In Markov analysis we also assume that the states are both *collectively exhaustive* and *mutually exclusive*. Collectively exhaustive means that we can list all of the possible states of a system or process. Our discussion of Markov analysis assumes that there is a finite number of states for any system. Mutually exclusive means that a system can be in only one state at any point in time. A student can be in only one of the three management specialty areas and *not* in two or more areas at the same time. It also means that a person can only be a customer of *one* of the three grocery stores at any point in time.

---

*The founder of the concept was A. A. Markov, whose 1905 studies of the sequence of experiments connected in a chain were used to describe the principle of Brownian motion.

After the states have been identified, the next step is to determine the probability that the system is in this state. Such information is then placed into a **vector of state probabilities**.

$$\pi(i) = \text{vector of state probabilities for period } i \qquad \text{(14-1)}$$
$$= (\pi_1, \pi_2, \pi_3, \ldots, \pi_n)$$

where

$$n = \text{number of states}$$
$$\pi_1, \pi_2, \ldots, \pi_n = \text{probability of being in state1, state 2}, \ldots, \text{state } n$$

In some cases, in which we are only dealing with one item, such as one machine, it is possible to know with complete certainty what state this item is in. For example, if we are investigating only one machine, we may know that at this point in time the machine is functioning correctly. Then the vector of states can be represented as follows:

$$\pi(1) = (1, 0)$$

where

$$\pi(1) = \text{vector of states for the machine in period 1}$$
$$\pi_1 = 1 = \text{probability of being in the first state}$$
$$\pi_2 = 0 = \text{probability of being in the second state}$$

This shows that the probability the machine is functioning correctly, state 1, is 1, and the probability that the machine is functioning incorrectly, state 2, is 0 for the first period. In most cases, however, we are dealing with more than one item.

The Vector of State Probabilities for Three Grocery Stores Example

Let's look at the vector of states for people in the small town with the three grocery stores. There could be a total of 100,000 people that shop at the three grocery stores during any given month. Forty thousand people may be shopping at American Food Store, which will be called state 1. Thirty thousand people may be shopping at Food Mart, which will be called state 2, and 30,000 people may be shopping at Atlas Foods, which will be called state 3. The probability that a person will be shopping at one of these three grocery stores is as follows:

State 1—American Food Store:	$40,000/100,000 = 0.40 = 40\%$
State 2—Food Mart:	$30,000/100,000 = 0.30 = 30\%$
State 3—Atlas Foods:	$30,000/100,000 = 0.30 = 30\%$

These probabilities can be placed in the vector of state probabilities shown as follows:

$$\pi(1) = (0.4, 0.3, 0.3)$$

where

$$\pi(1) = \text{vector of state probabilities for the three grocery stores for period 1}$$
$$\pi_1 = 0.4 = \text{probability that a person will shop at American Food, state 1}$$
$$\pi_2 = 0.3 = \text{probability that a person will shop at Food Mart, state 2}$$
$$\pi_3 = 0.3 = \text{probability that a person will shop at Atlas Foods, state 3}$$

The vector of state probabilities represents market shares.

You should also notice that the probabilities in the vector of states for the three grocery stores represent the **market shares** for these three stores for the first period. Thus, American Food has 40% of the market, Food Mart has 30%, and Atlas Foods has 30% of the market in period 1. When we are dealing with market shares, the market shares can be used in place of probability values.

Management of these three groceries should be interested in how their market shares change over time. Customers do not always remain with one store, but they may go to a different store for their next purchase. In this example, a study has been performed to determine how loyal the

FIGURE 14.1

Tree Diagram for Three Grocery Stores Example

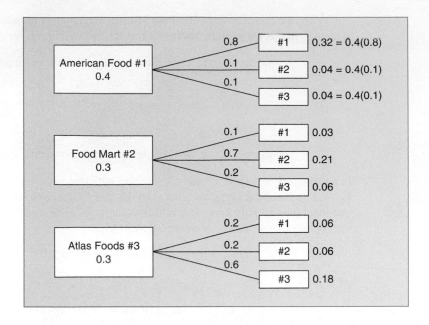

customers have been. It is determined that 80% of the customers who shop at American Food Store one month will return to that store next month. However, of the other 20% of American's customers, 10% will switch to Food Mart, and the other 10% will switch to Atlas Foods for their next purchase. For customers who shop this month at Food Mart, 70% will return, 10% will switch to American Food Store, and 20% will switch to Atlas Foods. Of the customers who shop this month at Atlas Foods, 60% will return, but 20% will go to American Food Store and 20% will switch to Food Mart.

Figure 14.1 provides a tree diagram to illustrate this situation. Notice that of the 40% market share for American Food Store this month, 32% ($0.40 \times 0.80 = 0.32$) will return, 4% will shop at Food Mart, and 4% will shop at Atlas Foods. To find the market share for American next month, we can add this 32% of returning customers to the 3% that leave Food Mart to come to American and the 6% that leave Atlas Foods to come to American. Thus, American Food Store will have a 41% market share next month.

Although a tree diagram and the calculations just illustrated could be used to find the state probabilities for the next month and the month after that, the tree would soon get very large. Rather than use a tree diagram, it is easier to use a matrix of transition probabilities. This matrix is used along with the current state probabilities to predict the future conditions.

14.3 Matrix of Transition Probabilities

The matrix of transition probabilities allows us to get from a current state to a future state.

The concept that allows us to get from a current state, such as market shares, to a future state is the *matrix of transition probabilities.* This is a matrix of conditional probabilities of being in a future state given a current state. The following definition is helpful:

Let P_{ij} = conditional probability of being in state j in the future given the current state of i

For example, P_{12} is the probability of being in state 2 in the future given the event was in state 1 in the period before:

Let P = matrix of transition probabilities

$$P = \begin{bmatrix} P_{11} & P_{12} & P_{13} & \cdots & P_{1n} \\ P_{21} & P_{22} & P_{23} & \cdots & P_{2n} \\ \vdots & & & & \vdots \\ P_{m1} & & \cdots & & P_{mn} \end{bmatrix} \quad (14\text{-}2)$$

Individual P_{ij} values are usually determined empirically. For example, if we have observed over time that 10% of the people currently shopping at store 1 (or state 1) will be shopping at store 2 (state 2) next period, then we know that $P_{12} = 0.1$ or 10%.

Transition Probabilities for the Three Grocery Stores

We used historical data with the three grocery stores to determine what percentage of the customers would switch each month. We put these transitional probabilities into the following matrix:

$$P = \begin{bmatrix} 0.8 & 0.1 & 0.1 \\ 0.1 & 0.7 & 0.2 \\ 0.2 & 0.2 & 0.6 \end{bmatrix}$$

Recall that American Food represents state 1, Food Mart is state 2, and Atlas Foods is state 3. The meaning of these probabilities can be expressed in terms of the various states as follows:

Row 1

$0.8 = P_{11} =$ probability of being in state 1 after being in state 1 the preceding period
$0.1 = P_{12} =$ probability of being in state 2 after being in state 1 the preceding period
$0.1 = P_{13} =$ probability of being in state 3 after being in state 1 the preceding period

Row 2

$0.1 = P_{21} =$ probability of being in state 1 after being in state 2 the preceding period
$0.7 = P_{22} =$ probability of being in state 2 after being in state 2 the preceding period
$0.2 = P_{23} =$ probability of being in state 3 after being in state 2 the preceding period

Row 3

$0.2 = P_{31} =$ probability of being in state 1 after being in state 3 the preceding period
$0.2 = P_{32} =$ probability of being in state 2 after being in state 3 the preceding period
$0.6 = P_{33} =$ probability of being in state 3 after being in state 3 the preceding period

The probability values for any row must sum to 1.

Note that the three probabilities in the top row sum to 1. The probabilities for any row in a matrix of transition probabilities will also sum to 1.

After the state probabilities have been determined along with the matrix of transition probabilities, it is possible to predict future state probabilities.

14.4 Predicting Future Market Shares

One of the purposes of Markov analysis is to predict the future. Given the vector of state probabilities and the matrix of transition probabilities, it is not very difficult to determine the state probabilities at a future date. With this type of analysis, we are able to compute the probability that a person will be shopping at one of the grocery stores in the future. Because this probability is equivalent to market share, it is possible to determine future market shares for American Food, Food Mart, and Atlas Foods. When the current period is 0, calculating the state probabilities for the next period (period 1) can be accomplished as follows:

Computing future market shares.

$$\pi(1) = \pi(0)P \tag{14-3}$$

Furthermore, if we are in any period n, we can compute the state probabilities for period $n + 1$ as follows:

$$\pi(n + 1) = \pi(n)P \tag{14-4}$$

Equation 14-3 can be used to answer the question of next period's market shares for the grocery stores. The computations are

$$\pi(1) = \pi(0)P$$

$$= (0.4, 0.3, 0.3) \begin{bmatrix} 0.8 & 0.1 & 0.1 \\ 0.1 & 0.7 & 0.2 \\ 0.2 & 0.2 & 0.6 \end{bmatrix}$$

$$= [(0.4)(0.8) + (0.3)(0.1) + (0.3)(0.2), (0.4)(0.1) \\ + (0.3)(0.7) + (0.3)(0.2), (0.4)(0.1) + (0.3)(0.2) + (0.3)(0.6)]$$

$$= (0.41, 0.31, 0.28)$$

As you can see, the market share for American Food and Food Mart has increased while the market share for Atlas Foods has decreased. Will this trend continue in the next period and the one after that? From Equation 14-4, we can derive a model that will tell us what the state probabilities will be in any time period in the future. Consider two time periods from now:

$$\pi(2) = \pi(1)P$$

Since we know that

$$\pi(1) = \pi(0)P$$

we have

$$\pi(2) = [\pi(1)]P = [\pi(0)P]P = \pi(0)PP = \pi(0)P^2$$

In general,

$$\pi(n) = \pi(0)P^n \tag{14-5}$$

Thus, the state probabilities for n periods in the future can be obtained from the current state probabilities and the matrix of transition probabilities.

In the three grocery stores example, we saw that American Food and Food Mart had increased market shares in the next period, while Atlas Food had lost market share. Will Atlas eventually lose its entire market share? Or will all three groceries reach a stable condition? Although Equation 14-5 provides some help in determining this, it is better to discuss this in terms of equilibrium or steady state conditions. To help introduce the concept of equilibrium, we present a second application of Markov analysis: machine breakdowns.

14.5   Markov Analysis of Machine Operations

Paul Tolsky, owner of Tolsky Works, has recorded the operation of his milling machine for several years. Over the past two years, 80% of the time the milling machine functioned correctly during the current month if it had functioned correctly in the preceding month. This also means that only 20% of the time did the machine not function correctly for a given month when it was functioning correctly during the preceding month. In addition, it has been observed that 90% of the time the machine remained incorrectly adjusted for any given month if it was incorrectly adjusted the preceding month. Only 10% of the time did the machine operate correctly in a given month when it did *not* operate correctly during the preceding month. In other words, this machine *can* correct itself when it has not been functioning correctly in the past, and this happens 10% of the time. These values can now be used to construct the matrix of transition probabilities. Again, state 1 is a situation in which the machine is functioning correctly, and state 2 is a situation in which the machine is not functioning correctly. The matrix of transition probabilities for this machine is

$$P = \begin{bmatrix} 0.8 & 0.2 \\ 0.1 & 0.9 \end{bmatrix}$$

where

$P_{11} = 0.8 =$ probability that the machine will be *correctly* functioning this month given it was *correctly* functioning last month

$P_{12} = 0.2 =$ probability that the machine will *not* be correctly functioning this month given it was *correctly* functioning last month

$P_{21} = 0.1 =$ probability that the machine will be functioning *correctly* this month given it was *not* correctly functioning last month

$P_{22} = 0.9 =$ probability that the machine will *not* be correctly functioning this month given it was *not* correctly functioning last month

The row probabilities must sum to 1 because the events are mutually exclusive and collectively exhaustive.

Look at this matrix for the machine. The two probabilities in the top row are the probabilities of functioning correctly and not functioning correctly given that the machine was functioning correctly in the last period. Because these are mutually exclusive and collectively exhaustive, the row probabilities again sum to 1.

What is the probability that Tolsky's machine will be functioning correctly one month from now? What is the probability that the machine will be functioning correctly in two months? To answer these questions, we again apply Equation 14-3:

$$\pi(1) = \pi(0)P$$

$$= (1, 0)\begin{bmatrix} 0.8 & 0.2 \\ 0.1 & 0.9 \end{bmatrix}$$

$$= [(1)(0.8) + (0)(0.1), (1)(0.2) + (0)(0.9)]$$

$$= (0.8, 0.2)$$

Therefore, the probability that the machine will be functioning correctly one month from now, given that it is now functioning correctly, is 0.80. The probability that it will *not* be functioning correctly in one month is 0.20. Now we can use these results to determine the probability that the machine will be functioning correctly two months from now. The analysis is exactly the same:

$$\pi(2) = \pi(1)P$$

$$= (0.8, 0.2)\begin{bmatrix} 0.8 & 0.2 \\ 0.1 & 0.9 \end{bmatrix}$$

$$= [(0.8)(0.8) + (0.2)(0.1), (0.8)(0.2) + (0.2)(0.9)]$$

$$= (0.66, 0.34)$$

This means that two months from now there is a probability of 0.66 that the machine will still be functioning correctly. The probability that the machine will not be functioning correctly is 0.34. Of course, we could continue this analysis as many times as we want in computing state probabilities for future months.

14.6   Equilibrium Conditions

Looking at the Tolsky machine example, it is easy to think that eventually all market shares or state probabilities will be either 0 or 1. This is usually not the case. *Equilibrium share* of the market values or probabilities are normally encountered. The probabilities are called **steady-state probabilities**, or **equilibrium probabilities**.

One way to compute the equilibrium share of the market is to use Markov analysis for a large number of periods. It is possible to see if the future values are approaching a stable value. For example, it is possible to repeat Markov analysis for 15 periods for Tolsky's machine. This is not too difficult to do by hand. The results for this computation appear in Table 14.1.

The machine starts off functioning correctly (in state 1) in the first period. In period 5, there is only a 0.4934 probability that the machine is still functioning correctly, and by period 10, this probability is only 0.360235. In period 15, the probability that the machine is still functioning correctly is about 0.34. The probability that the machine will be functioning correctly at a future period is decreasing—but it is decreasing at a decreasing rate. What would you expect in the long run? If we made these calculations for 100 periods, what would happen? Would there be an equilibrium in this case? If the answer is *yes*, what would it be? Looking at Table 14.1, it appears that there will be an equilibrium at 0.333333, or 1/3. But how can we be sure?

Equilibrium conditions exist if state probabilities do not change after a large number of periods.

By definition, an **equilibrium condition** exists if the state probabilities or market shares do not change after a large number of periods. Thus, at equilibrium, the state probabilities for a future period must be the same as the state probabilities for the current period. This fact is the key to solving for the steady state probabilities. This relationship can be expressed as follows:

From Equation 14-4 it is always true that

$$\pi(\text{next period}) = \pi(\text{this period})P$$

or

$$\pi(n + 1) = \pi(n)P$$

TABLE 14.1

State Probabilities for the Machine Example for 15 Periods

PERIOD	STATE 1	STATE 2
1	1.000000	0.000000
2	0.800000	0.200000
3	0.660000	0.340000
4	0.562000	0.438000
5	0.493400	0.506600
6	0.445380	0.554620
7	0.411766	0.588234
8	0.388236	0.611763
9	0.371765	0.628234
10	0.360235	0.639754
11	0.352165	0.647834
12	0.346515	0.653484
13	0.342560	0.657439
14	0.339792	0.660207
15	0.337854	0.662145

At equilibrium, we know that

$$\pi(n + 1) = \pi(n)$$

Therefore, at equilibrium,

$$\pi(n + 1) = \pi(n)P = \pi(n)$$

So

$$\pi(n) = \pi(n)P$$

or, dropping the n term,

$$\pi = \pi P \tag{14-6}$$

At equilibrium, state probabilities for the next period equal the state probabilities for this period.

Equation 14-6 states that at equilibrium, the state probabilities for the *next* period are the same as the state probabilities for the *current* period. For Tolsky's machine, this can be expressed as follows:

$$\pi = \pi P$$

$$(\pi_1, \pi_2) = (\pi_1, \pi_2)\begin{bmatrix} 0.8 & 0.2 \\ 0.1 & 0.9 \end{bmatrix}$$

Using matrix multiplication, we get

$$(\pi_1, \pi_2) = [(\pi_1)(0.8) + (\pi_2)(0.1), (\pi_1)(0.2) + (\pi_2)(0.9)]$$

The *first term* on the left-hand side, π_1, is equal to the *first term* on the right-hand side $(\pi_1)(0.8) + (\pi_2)(0.1)$. In addition, the *second term* on the left-hand side, π_2, is equal to the *second term* on the right-hand side $(\pi_1)(0.2) + (\pi_2)(0.9)$. This gives us the following:

$$\pi_1 = 0.8\pi_1 + 0.1\pi_2 \tag{a}$$

$$\pi_2 = 0.2\pi_1 + 0.9\pi_2 \tag{b}$$

We also know that the state probabilities, π_1 and π_2 in this case, must sum to 1. (Looking at Table 14.1, you note that π_1 and π_2 sum to 1 for all 15 periods.) We can express this property as follows:

$$\pi_1 + \pi_2 + \cdots + \pi_n = 1 \tag{c}$$

For Tolsky's machine, we have

$$\pi_1 + \pi_2 = 1 \qquad \textbf{(d)}$$

We drop one equation in solving for equilibrium conditions.

Now, we have three equations for the machine (**a**, **b**, and **d**). We know that Equation **d** must hold. Thus, we can drop either Equation **a** or **b** and solve the remaining two equations for π_1 and π_2. It is necessary to drop one of the equations so that we end up with two unknowns and two equations. If we were solving for equilibrium conditions that involved three states, we would end up with four equations. Again, it would be necessary to drop one of the equations so that we end up with three equations and three unknowns. In general, when solving for equilibrium conditions, it will always be necessary to drop one of the equations such that the total number of equations is the same as the total number of variables for which we are solving. The reason that we can drop one of the equations is that they are interrelated mathematically. In other words, one of the equations is redundant in specifying the relationships between the various equilibrium equations.

Let us arbitrarily drop Equation **a**. Thus, we will be solving the following two equations:

$$\pi_2 = 0.2\pi_1 + 0.9\pi_2$$
$$\pi_1 + \pi_2 = 1$$

Rearranging the first equation, we get

$$0.1\pi_2 = 0.2\pi_1$$

or

$$\pi_2 = 2\pi_1$$

Substituting this into Equation **d**, we have

$$\pi_1 + \pi_2 = 1$$

or

$$\pi_1 + 2\pi_1 = 1$$

or

$$3\pi_1 = 1$$
$$\pi_1 = 1/3 = 0.33333333$$

Thus,

$$\pi_2 = 2/3 = 0.66666667$$

Initial-state probability values do not influence equilibrium conditions.

Compare these results with Table 14.1. As you can see, the steady-state probability for state 1 is 0.33333333, and the equilibrium state probability for state 2 is 0.66666667. These values are what you would expect by looking at the tabled results. This analysis indicates that it is only necessary to know the matrix of transition probabilities in determining the equilibrium market shares. The initial values for the state probabilities or the market shares do not influence the equilibrium state probabilities. The analysis for determining equilibrium state probabilities or market shares is the same when there are more states. If there are three states (as in the grocery store example), we have to solve three equations for the three equilibrium states; if there are four states, we have to solve four simultaneous equations for the four unknown equilibrium values, and so on.

You may wish to prove to yourself that the equilibrium states we have just computed are, in fact, equilibrium states. This can be done by multiplying the equilibrium states by the original matrix of transition probabilities. The results will be the same equilibrium states. Performing this analysis is also an excellent way to check your answers to end-of-chapter problems or examination questions.

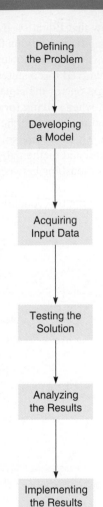

MODELING IN THE REAL WORLD

Airline Uses Markov Analysis to Reduce Marketing Costs

Defining the Problem

Finnair, a major European airline, was experiencing very low customer loyalty. The company's numbers for repeat business were much lower than industry averages.

Developing a Model

Analysts at IBM tackled the problem using Markov analysis to model customer behavior. Three states of the system were identified, and each customer was listed as either (1) an occasional flyer (OF), or (2) a repeat purchaser (RP), or (3) a loyal customer (LC).

Acquiring Input Data

Data were collected on each customer so that transition probabilities could be developed. These probabilities indicated the likelihood of a customer moving from one state to another. Most important were the probabilities of going from OF to RP and from RP to LC.

Testing the Solution

The analysts built a tool called Customer Equity Loyalty Management (CELM). CELM tracked customer responses by customer type (OF, RP, and LC) and by the associated marketing efforts.

Analyzing the Results

The results were nothing short of astounding. By targeting its marketing efforts based upon the *type* of customer, Finnair was able to reduce its overall marketing costs by 20% while simultaneously increasing its customer response rate by over 10%.

Implementing the Results

Finnair uses CELM as an integral part of its in-house frequent flyer program.

Source: Based on A. Labbi and C. Berrospi. "Optimizing Marketing Planning and Budgeting Using Markov Decision Processes: An Airline Case Study," *IBM Journal of Research and Development* 51, 3 (2007): 421–431.

14.7 Absorbing States and the Fundamental Matrix: Accounts Receivable Application

In the examples discussed thus far, we assume that it is possible for the process or system to go from one state to any other state between any two periods. In some cases, however, if you are in a state, you cannot go to another state in the future. In other words, when you are in a given state, you are "absorbed" by it, and you will remain in that state. Any state that has this property is called an **absorbing state**. An example of this is the accounts receivable application.

If you are in an absorbing state, you cannot go to another state in the future.

An accounts receivable system normally places debts or receivables from its customers into one of several categories or states depending on how overdue the oldest unpaid bill is. Of course, the exact categories or states depend on the policy set by each company. Four typical states or categories for an accounts receivable application follow:

State 1 (π_1): paid, all bills

State 2 (π_2): bad debt, overdue more than three months

State 3 (π_3): overdue less than one month

State 4 (π_4): overdue between one and three months

At any given period, in this case one month, a customer can be in one of these four states.* For this example it will be assumed that if the oldest unpaid bill is over three months due, it is automatically placed in the bad debt category. Therefore, a customer can be paid in full (state 1), have the oldest unpaid bill overdue less than one month (state 3), have the oldest unpaid bill overdue between one and three months inclusive (state 4), or have the oldest unpaid bill overdue more than three months, which is a bad debt (state 2).

As in any other Markov process, we can set up a matrix of transition probabilities for these four states. This matrix will reflect the propensity of customers to move among the four accounts receivable categories from one month to the next. The probability of being in the paid category for any item or bill in a future month, given that a customer is in the paid category for a purchased item this month, is 100% or 1. It is impossible for a customer to completely pay for a product one month and to owe money on it in a future month. Another absorbing state is the bad debts state. If a bill is not paid in three months, we are assuming that the company will completely write it off and not try to collect it in the future. Thus, once a person is in the bad debt category, that person will remain in that category forever. For any absorbing state, the probability that a customer will be in this state in the future is 1, and the probability that a customer will be in any other state is 0.

If a person is in an absorbing state now, the probability of being in an absorbing state in the future is 100%.

These values will be placed in the matrix of transition probabilities. But before we construct this matrix, we need to know the future probabilities for the other two states—a debt of less than one month and a debt that is between one and three months old. For a person in the less than one month category, there is a 0.60 probability of being in the paid category, a 0 probability of being in the bad debt category, a 0.20 probability of remaining in the less than one month category, and a probability of 0.20 of being in the one to three month category in the next month. Note that there is a 0 probability of being in the bad debt category the next month because it is impossible to get from state 3, less than one month, to state 2, more than three months overdue, in just one month. For a person in the one to three month category, there is a 0.40 probability of being in the paid category, a 0.10 probability of being in the bad debt category, a 0.30 probability of being in the less than one month category, and a 0.20 probability of remaining in the one to three month category in the next month.

How can we get a probability of 0.30 of being in the one to three month category for one month, and in the one month or less category in the next month? Because these categories are determined by the oldest unpaid bill, it is possible to pay one bill that is one to three months old and still have another bill that is one month or less old. In other words, any customer may have more than one outstanding bill at any point in time. With this information, it is possible to construct the matrix of transition probabilities of the problem.

THIS MONTH	NEXT MONTH			
	PAID	BAD DEBT	<1 MONTH	1 TO 3 MONTHS
Paid	1	0	0	0
Bad debt	0	1	0	0
Less than 1 month	0.6	0	0.2	0.2
1 to 3 months	0.4	0.1	0.3	0.2

---

*You should also be aware that the four states can be placed in any order you choose. For example. It might seem more natural to order this problem with the states:

1. Paid
2. Overdue less than one month
3. Overdue one to three months
4. Overdue more than three months; bad debt

This is perfectly legitimate, and the only reason this ordering is not used is to facilitate some matrix manipulations you will see shortly.

Thus,

$$P = \begin{bmatrix} 1 & 0 & 0 & 0 \\ 0 & 1 & 0 & 0 \\ 0.6 & 0 & 0.2 & 0.2 \\ 0.4 & 0.1 & 0.3 & 0.2 \end{bmatrix}$$

If we know the fraction of the people in each of the four categories or states for any given period, we can determine the fraction of the people in these four states or categories for any future period. These fractions are placed in a vector of state probabilities and multiplied times the matrix of transition probabilities. This procedure was described in Section 14.5.

In the long run, everyone will be either in the paid or bad debt category.

Even more interesting are the equilibrium conditions. Of course, in the long run, everyone will be either in the paid or bad debt category. This is because the categories are absorbing states. But how many people, or how much money, will be in each of these categories? Knowing the total amount of money that will be in either the paid or bad debt category will help a company manage its bad debts and cash flow. This analysis requires the use of the **fundamental matrix**.

To obtain the fundamental matrix, it is necessary to *partition* the matrix of transition probabilities, P. This can be done as follows:

$$
\begin{array}{cc}
I & 0 \\
\downarrow & \downarrow
\end{array}
$$

$$P = \left[\begin{array}{cc:cc} 1 & 0 & 0 & 0 \\ 0 & 1 & 0 & 0 \\ \hdashline 0.6 & 0 & 0.2 & 0.2 \\ 0.4 & 0.1 & 0.3 & 0.2 \end{array} \right] \qquad \text{(14-7)}$$

$$
\begin{array}{cc}
\uparrow & \uparrow \\
A & B
\end{array}
$$

$$I = \begin{bmatrix} 1 & 0 \\ 0 & 1 \end{bmatrix} \qquad 0 = \begin{bmatrix} 0 & 0 \\ 0 & 0 \end{bmatrix}$$

$$A = \begin{bmatrix} 0.6 & 0 \\ 0.4 & 0.1 \end{bmatrix} \qquad B = \begin{bmatrix} 0.2 & 0.2 \\ 0.3 & 0.2 \end{bmatrix}$$

where

I = an identity matrix (i.e., a matrix with 1s on the diagonal and 0s everyplace else)

0 = a matrix with all 0s

The fundamental matrix can be computed as follows:

$$F = (I - B)^{-1} \qquad \text{(14-8)}$$

F *is the fundamental matrix.*

In Equation 14-8, $(I - B)$ means that we subtract matrix B from matrix I. The superscript -1 means that we take the inverse of the result of $(I - B)$. Here is how we can compute the fundamental matrix for the accounts receivable application:

$$F = (I - B)^{-1}$$

or

$$F = \left(\begin{bmatrix} 1 & 0 \\ 0 & 1 \end{bmatrix} - \begin{bmatrix} 0.2 & 0.2 \\ 0.3 & 0.2 \end{bmatrix} \right)^{-1}$$

Subtracting B from I, we get

$$F = \begin{bmatrix} 0.8 & -0.2 \\ -0.3 & 0.8 \end{bmatrix}^{-1}$$

Taking the inverse of a large matrix involves several steps, as described in Module 5 on the Companion Website for this book. Appendix 14.2 shows how this inverse can be found using

Excel. However, for a matrix with two rows and two columns, the computations are relatively simple, as shown here:

The inverse of the matrix $\begin{bmatrix} a & b \\ c & d \end{bmatrix}$ is

$$\begin{bmatrix} a & b \\ c & d \end{bmatrix}^{-1} = \begin{bmatrix} \dfrac{d}{r} & \dfrac{-b}{r} \\ \dfrac{-c}{r} & \dfrac{a}{r} \end{bmatrix} \tag{14-9}$$

where

$$r = ad - bc$$

To find the matrix F in the accounts receivable example, we first compute

$$r = ad - bc = (0.8)(0.8) - (-0.2)(-0.3) = 0.64 - 0.06 = 0.58$$

With this we have

$$F = \begin{bmatrix} 0.8 & -0.2 \\ -0.3 & 0.8 \end{bmatrix}^{-1} = \begin{bmatrix} \dfrac{0.8}{0.58} & \dfrac{-(-0.2)}{0.58} \\ \dfrac{-(-0.3)}{0.58} & \dfrac{0.8}{0.58} \end{bmatrix} = \begin{bmatrix} 1.38 & 0.34 \\ 0.52 & 1.38 \end{bmatrix}$$

Now we are in a position to use the fundamental matrix in computing the amount of bad debt money that we could expect in the long run. First we need to multiply the fundamental matrix, F, times the matrix A. This is accomplished as follows:

$$FA = \begin{bmatrix} 1.38 & 0.34 \\ 0.52 & 1.38 \end{bmatrix} \times \begin{bmatrix} 0.6 & 0 \\ 0.4 & 0.1 \end{bmatrix}$$

or

$$FA = \begin{bmatrix} 0.97 & 0.03 \\ 0.86 & 0.14 \end{bmatrix}$$

The FA matrix indicates the probability that an amount will end up in an absorbing state.

The new FA matrix has an important meaning. It indicates the probability that an amount in one of the nonabsorbing states will end up in one of the absorbing states. The top row of this matrix indicates the probabilities that an amount in the less than one month category will end up in the paid and the bad debt category. The probability that an amount that is less than one month overdue will be paid is 0.97, and the probability that an amount that is less than one month overdue will end up as a bad debt is 0.03. The second row has a similar interpretation for the other nonabsorbing state, which is the one to three month category. Therefore, 0.86 is the probability that an amount that is one to three months overdue will eventually be paid, and 0.14 is the probability that an amount that is one to three months overdue will never be paid but will become a bad debt.

The matrix M represents the money in the absorbing states—paid or bad debt.

This matrix can be used in a number of ways. If we know the amount of the less than one month category and the one to three month category, we can determine the amount of money that will be paid and the amount of money that will become bad debts. We let the matrix M represent the amount of money that is in each of the nonabsorbing states as follows:

$$M = (M_1, M_2, M_3, \ldots, M_n)$$

where

n = number of nonabsorbing states
M_1 = amount in the first state or category
M_2 = amount in the second state or category
M_n = amount in the nth state or category

IN ACTION Markovian Volleyball!

Volleyball coaches turned to Markovian analysis to rank five basic volleyball skills (passing, setting, digging, serving, or attacking) in high-level volleyball. In other words, the coaches wanted to know which skill had the highest probability of leading to a point on any given play, which skill had the second highest probability of leading to a point on any given play, and so on.

For an entire season, data were collected from all matches and all individual skill performances (e.g., a serve) in each match were rated based on a simple rubric. For example, a set that was in perfect position (3–5 feet away from the net) was given 3 performance points while a set that was 5–8 feet away from the net was given just 1 performance point. The end result of each skill (a point for the visiting team, the rally continued, or a point for the home team) was also recorded.

A rather large 36 × 36 transition matrix was developed and a mix of empirical and Bayesian methods (see chapter 2) were employed to arrive at the individual transition probabilities, P_{ij}s. State transitions that were impossible (e.g., a perfectly positioned set followed by a service error) were assigned a probability of zero.

The ensuing Markovian analysis led analysts to one overarching conclusion: Whereas the most important skills in men's volleyball are (by a large margin over the others) serving and attacking, the most important skills in women's volleyball are (again by large margin over the others) passing, setting, and digging. Can you dig it?

Source: M.A. Miskin, G.W. Fellingham, and L.W. Florence. "Skill Importance in Women's Volleyball," *Journal of Quantitative Analysis in Sport* 6 (2010): Article 5.

Assume that there is $2,000 in the less than one month category and $5,000 in the one to three month category. Then *M* would be represented as follows:

$$M = (2,000, 5,000)$$

The amount of money that will end up as being paid and the amount that will end up as bad debts can be computed by multiplying the matrix *M* times the *FA* matrix that was computed previously. Here are the computations:

$$\text{Amount paid and amount in bad debts} = MFA$$

$$= (2,000, 5,000)\begin{bmatrix} 0.97 & 0.03 \\ 0.86 & 0.14 \end{bmatrix}$$

$$= (6,240, 760)$$

Thus, out of the total of $7,000 ($2,000 in the less than one month category and $5,000 in the one to three month category), $6,240 will be eventually paid, and $760 will end up as bad debts.

Summary

Markov analysis can be very helpful in predicting future states. The equilibrium conditions are determined to indicate how the future will look if things continue as in the past. In this chapter, the existence of absorbing states was presented, and the equilibrium conditions were determined when one or more of these were present.

However, it is important to remember that the future conditions found using Markov analysis are based on the assumption that the transition probabilities do not change. When using Markov analysis to predict market shares, as in the Three Grocery Store example, it should be noted that companies are constantly trying to change these probabilities so that their own market shares increase. This was illustrated in the *Modeling in the Real World* vignette about Finnair, which was using Markov analysis to help measure its success in retaining customers. When one company succeeds in changing the transition probabilities, other companies will respond and try to move the probabilities in a direction more favorable to them.

At times, new companies enter the market and this changes the dynamics (and probabilities) as well.

In the accounts receivable example on absorbing states, future revenues were predicted based on existing probabilities. However, things can certainly change due to factors that are controllable as well as factors that are not controllable. The financial crisis throughout the United States in 2007–2009 is a good example of this. Some banks and other lending institutions had been making loans that were less secure than the ones they had made in the past. Many mortgages, which were reliable sources of income for the banks when housing prices were rapidly rising, were becoming problematic when housing prices began to fall. The economy as a whole was in decline, and individuals who became unemployed were having trouble repaying their loans. Thus, the future conditions (and revenues) that were expected if probabilities did not change were never realized. It is important to remember the assumptions behind all these models.

Glossary

Absorbing State A state that, when entered, cannot be left. The probability of going from an absorbing state to any other state is 0.

Equilibrium Condition A condition that exists when the state probabilities for a future period are the same as the state probabilities for a previous period.

Fundamental Matrix A matrix that is the inverse of the I minus B matrix. It is needed to compute equilibrium conditions when absorbing states are involved.

Market Share The fraction of the population that shops at a particular store or market. When expressed as a fraction, market shares can be used in place of state probabilities.

Markov Analysis A type of analysis that allows us to predict the future by using the state probabilities and the matrix of transition probabilities.

Matrix of Transition Probabilities A matrix containing all transition probabilities for a certain process or system.

State Probability The probability of an event occurring at a point in time. Examples include the probability that a person will be shopping at a given grocery store during a given month.

Steady-State Probability A state probability when the equilibrium condition has been reached. Also called equilibrium probability.

Transition Probability The conditional probability that we will be in a future state given a current or existing state.

Vector of State Probabilities A collection or vector of all state probabilities for a given system or process. The vector of state probabilities could be the initial state or future state.

Key Equations

(14-1) $\pi(i) = (\pi_1, \pi_2, \pi_3, \ldots, \pi_n)$

Vector of state probabilities for period i.

(14-2) $P = \begin{bmatrix} P_{11} & P_{12} & P_{13} & \cdots & P_{1n} \\ P_{21} & P_{22} & P_{23} & \cdots & P_{2n} \\ \vdots & & & & \vdots \\ P_{m1} & & \cdots & & P_{mn} \end{bmatrix}$

Matrix of transition probabilities, that is, the probability of going from one state into another.

(14-3) $\pi(1) = \pi(0)P$

Formula for calculating the state 1 probabilities, given state 0 data.

(14-4) $\pi(n + 1) = \pi(n)P$

Formula for calculating the state probabilities for the period $n + 1$ if we are in period n.

(14-5) $\pi(n) = \pi(0)P^n$

Formula for computing the state probabilities for period n if we are in period 0.

(14-6) $\pi = \pi P$

Equilibrium state equation used to derive equilibrium probabilities.

(14-7) $P = \begin{bmatrix} I & O \\ \hline A & B \end{bmatrix}$

Partition of the matrix of transition for absorbing state analysis.

(14-8) $F = (I - B)^{-1}$

Fundamental matrix used in computing probabilities ending up in an absorbing state.

(14-9) $\begin{bmatrix} a & b \\ c & d \end{bmatrix}^{-1} = \begin{bmatrix} \dfrac{d}{r} & \dfrac{-b}{r} \\ \dfrac{-c}{r} & \dfrac{a}{r} \end{bmatrix}$ where $r = ad - bc$

Inverse of a matrix with 2 rows and 2 columns.

Solved Problems

Solved Problem 14-1

George Walls, president of Bradley School, is concerned about declining enrollments. Bradley School is a technical college that specializes in training computer programmers and computer operators. Over the years, there has been a lot of competition among Bradley School, International Technology, and Career Academy. The three schools compete in providing education in the areas of programming, computer operations, and basic secretarial skills.

To gain a better understanding of which of these schools is emerging as a leader, George decided to conduct a survey. His survey looked at the number of students who transferred from one school to the other during their academic careers. On the average, Bradley School was able to retain 65% of those students it originally enrolled. Twenty percent of the students originally enrolled transferred to Career

Academy, and 15% transferred to International Technology. Career Academy had the highest retention rate: 90% of its students remained at Career Academy for their full academic program. George estimated that about half the students who left Career Academy went to Bradley School, and the other half went to International Technology. International Technology was able to retain 80% of its students after they enrolled. Ten percent of the originally enrolled students transferred to Career Academy, and the other 10% enrolled in Bradley School.

Currently, Bradley School has 40% of the market. Career Academy, a much newer school, has 35% of the market. The remaining market share—25%—consists of students attending International Technology. George would like to determine the market share for Bradley for the next year. What are the equilibrium market shares for Bradley School, International Technology, and Career Academy?

Solution

The data for this problem are summarized as follows:

State 1 initial share = 0.40—Bradley School

State 2 initial share = 0.35—Career Academy

State 3 initial share = 0.25—International Technology

The transition matrix values are

	TO		
	1	2	3
FROM	**BRADLEY**	**CAREER**	**INTERNATIONAL**
1 BRADLEY	0.65	0.20	0.15
2 CAREER	0.05	0.90	0.05
3 INTERNATIONAL	0.10	0.10	0.80

For George to determine market share for Bradley School for next year, he has to multiply the current market shares times the matrix of transition probability. Here is the overall structure of these calculations:

$$(0.40 \quad 0.35 \quad 0.25) \begin{bmatrix} 0.65 & 0.20 & 0.15 \\ 0.05 & 0.90 & 0.05 \\ 0.10 & 0.10 & 0.80 \end{bmatrix}$$

Thus, the market shares for Bradley School, International Technology, and Career Academy can be computed by multiplying the current market shares times the matrix of transition probabilities as shown. The result will be a new matrix with three numbers, each representing the market share for one of the schools. The detailed matrix computations follow:

$$\text{Market share for Bradley School} = (0.40)(0.65) + (0.35)(0.05) + (0.25)(0.10)$$
$$= 0.303$$

$$\text{Market share for Career Academy} = (0.40)(0.20) + (0.35)(0.90) + (0.25)(0.10)$$
$$= 0.420$$

$$\text{Market share for International Technology} = (0.40)(0.15) + (0.35)(0.05) + (0.25)(0.80)$$
$$= 0.278$$

Now George would like to compute the equilibrium market shares for the three schools. At equilibrium conditions, the future market share is equal to the existing or current market share times the matrix of transition probabilities. By letting the variable X represent various market shares for these three schools, it is possible to develop a general relationship that will allow us to compute equilibrium market shares.

Let

$$X_1 = \text{market share for Bradley School}$$

$$X_2 = \text{market share for Career Academy}$$

$$X_3 = \text{market share for International Technology}$$

At equilibrium,

$$(X_1, X_2, X_3) = (X_1, X_2, X_3) \begin{bmatrix} 0.65 & 0.20 & 0.15 \\ 0.05 & 0.90 & 0.05 \\ 0.10 & 0.10 & 0.80 \end{bmatrix}$$

The next step is to make the appropriate multiplications on the right-hand side of the equation. Doing this will allow us to obtain three equations with the three unknown X values. In addition, we know that the sum of the market shares for any particular period must equal 1. Thus, we are able to generate four equations, which are now summarized:

$$X_1 = 0.65X_1 + 0.05X_2 + 0.10X_3$$

$$X_2 = 0.20X_1 + 0.90X_2 + 0.10X_3$$

$$X_3 = 0.15X_1 + 0.05X_2 + 0.80X_3$$

$$X_1 + X_2 + X_3 = 1$$

Because we have four equations and only three unknowns, we are able to delete one of the top three equations, which will give us three equations and three unknowns. These equations can then be solved using standard algebraic procedures to obtain the equilibrium market share values for Bradley School, International Technology, and Career Academy. The results of these calculations are shown in the following table:

SCHOOL	MARKET SHARE
X_1 (Bradley)	0.158
X_2 (Career)	0.579
X_3 (International)	0.263

Solved Problem 14-2

Central State University administers computer competency examinations every year. These exams allow students to "test out" of the introductory computer class held at the university. Results of the exams can be placed in one of the following four states:

State 1: pass all of the computer exams and be exempt from the course
State 2: do not pass all of the computer exams on the third attempt and be required to take the course
State 3: fail the computer exams on the first attempt
State 4: fail the computer exams on the second attempt

The course coordinator for the exams has noticed the following matrix of transition probabilities:

$$P = \begin{bmatrix} 1 & 0 & 0 & 0 \\ 0 & 1 & 0 & 0 \\ 0.8 & 0 & 0.1 & 0.1 \\ 0.2 & 0.2 & 0.4 & 0.2 \end{bmatrix}$$

Currently, there are 200 students who did not pass all of the exams on the first attempt. In addition, there are 50 students who did not pass on the second attempt. In the long run, how many students will be exempted from the course by passing the exams? How many of the 250 students will be required to take the computer course?

Solution

The transition matrix values are summarized as follows:

	TO			
FROM	**1**	**2**	**3**	**4**
1	1	0	0	0
2	0	1	0	0
3	0.8	0	0.1	0.1
4	0.2	0.2	0.4	0.2

The first step in determining how many students will be required to take the course and how many will be exempt from it is to partition the transition matrix into four matrices. These are the I, 0, A, and B matrices:

$$I = \begin{bmatrix} 1 & 0 \\ 0 & 1 \end{bmatrix}$$

$$0 = \begin{bmatrix} 0 & 0 \\ 0 & 0 \end{bmatrix}$$

$$A = \begin{bmatrix} 0.8 & 0 \\ 0.2 & 0.2 \end{bmatrix}$$

$$B = \begin{bmatrix} 0.1 & 0.1 \\ 0.4 & 0.2 \end{bmatrix}$$

The next step is to compute the fundamental matrix, which is represented by the letter F. This matrix is determined by subtracting the B matrix from the I matrix and taking the inverse of the result:

$$F = (I - B)^{-1} = \begin{bmatrix} 0.9 & -0.1 \\ -0.4 & 0.8 \end{bmatrix}^{-1}$$

We first find

$$r = ad - bc = (0.9)(0.8) - (-0.1)(-0.4) = 0.72 - 0.04 = 0.68$$

$$F = \begin{bmatrix} 0.9 & -0.1 \\ -0.4 & 0.8 \end{bmatrix}^{-1} = \begin{bmatrix} \dfrac{0.8}{0.68} & \dfrac{-(-0.1)}{0.68} \\ \dfrac{-(-0.4)}{0.68} & \dfrac{0.9}{0.68} \end{bmatrix} = \begin{bmatrix} 1.176 & 0.147 \\ 0.588 & 1.324 \end{bmatrix}$$

Now multiply the F matrix by the A matrix. This step is needed to determine how many students will be exempt from the course and how many will be required to take it. Multiplying the F matrix times the A matrix is fairly straightforward:

$$FA = \begin{bmatrix} 1.176 & 0.147 \\ 0.588 & 1.324 \end{bmatrix} \begin{bmatrix} 0.8 & 0 \\ 0.2 & 0.2 \end{bmatrix}$$

$$= \begin{bmatrix} 0.971 & 0.029 \\ 0.735 & 0.265 \end{bmatrix}$$

The final step is to multiply the results from the FA matrix by the M matrix, as shown here:

$$MFA = (200 \quad 50) \begin{bmatrix} 0.971 & 0.029 \\ 0.735 & 0.265 \end{bmatrix}$$

$$= (231 \quad 19)$$

As you can see, the MFA matrix consists of two numbers. The number of students who will be exempt from the course is 231. The number of students who will eventually have to take the course is 19.

Self-Test

- Before taking the self-test, refer to the learning objectives at the beginning of the chapter, the notes in the margins, and the glossary at the end of the chapter.
- Use the key at the back of the book to correct your answers.
- Restudy pages that correspond to any questions that you answered incorrectly or material you feel uncertain about.

1. If the states in a system or process are such that the system can only be in one state at a time, then the states are
   a. collectively exhaustive.
   b. mutually exclusive.
   c. absorbing.
   d. disappearing.
2. The product of a vector of state probabilities and the matrix of transition probabilities will yield
   a. another vector of state probabilities.
   b. a meaningless mess.
   c. the inverse of the equilibrium state matrix.
   d. all of the above.
   e. none of the above.
3. In the long run, the state probabilities will be 0 and 1
   a. in no instances.
   b. in all instances.
   c. in some instances.
4. To find equilibrium conditions,
   a. the first vector of state probabilities must be known.
   b. the matrix of transition probabilities is unnecessary.
   c. the general terms in the vector of state probabilities are used on two occasions.
   d. the matrix of transition probabilities must be squared before it is inverted.
   e. none of the above.
5. Which of the following is not one of the assumptions of Markov analysis?
   a. There is a limited number of possible states.
   b. There is a limited number of possible future periods.
   c. A future state can be predicted from the previous state and the matrix of transition probabilities.
   d. The size and makeup of the system do not change during the analysis.
   e. All of the above are assumptions of Markov analysis.

6. In Markov analysis, the state probabilities must
   a. sum to 1.
   b. be less than 0.
   c. be less than 0.01.
   d. be greater than 1.
   e. be greater than 0.01.
7. If the state probabilities do not change from one period to the next, then
   a. the system is in equilibrium.
   b. each state probability must equal 0.
   c. each state probability must equal 1.
   d. the system is in its fundamental state.
8. In the matrix of transition probabilities,
   a. the sum of the probabilities in each row will equal 1.
   b. the sum of the probabilities in each column will equal 1.
   c. there must be at least one 0 in each row.
   d. there must be at least one 0 in each column.
9. It is necessary to use the fundamental matrix
   a. to find the equilibrium conditions when there are no absorbing states.
   b. to find the equilibrium conditions when there is one or more absorbing states.
   c. to find the matrix of transition probabilities.
   d. to find the inverse of a matrix.
10. In Markov analysis, the _____ allows us to get from a current state to a future state.
11. In Markov analysis, we assume that the state probabilities are both _____ and _____.
12. The _____ is the probability that the system is in a particular state.

Discussion Questions and Problems

Discussion Questions

14-1 List the assumptions that are made in Markov analysis.

14-2 What are the vector of state probabilities and the matrix of transition probabilities, and how can they be determined?

14-3 Describe how we can use Markov analysis to make future predictions.

14-4 What is an equilibrium condition? How do we know that we have an equilibrium condition, and how can we compute equilibrium conditions given the matrix of transition probabilities?

14-5 What is an absorbing state? Give several examples of absorbing states.

14-6 What is the fundamental matrix, and how is it used in determining equilibrium conditions?

Problems*

•14-7 Find the inverse of each of the following matrices:

(a) $\begin{bmatrix} 0.9 & -0.1 \\ -0.2 & 0.7 \end{bmatrix}$

(b) $\begin{bmatrix} 0.8 & -0.1 \\ -0.3 & 0.9 \end{bmatrix}$

(c) $\begin{bmatrix} 0.7 & -0.2 \\ -0.2 & 0.9 \end{bmatrix}$

(d) $\begin{bmatrix} 0.8 & -0.2 \\ -0.1 & 0.7 \end{bmatrix}$

⚲• 14-8 Ray Cahnman is the proud owner of a 1955 sports car. On any given day, Ray never knows whether his car will start. Ninety percent of the time it will start if it started the previous morning, and 70% of the time it will not start if it did not start the previous morning.
   (a) Construct the matrix of transition probabilities.
   (b) What is the probability that it will start tomorrow if it started today?
   (c) What is the probability that it will start tomorrow if it did *not* start today?

⚲• 14-9 Alan Resnik, a friend of Ray Cahnman, bet Ray $5 that Ray's car would not start five days from now (see Problem 14-8).
   (a) What is the probability that it will not start five days from now if it started today?
   (b) What is the probability that it will not start five days from now if it did not start today?
   (c) What is the probability that it will start in the long run if the matrix of transition probabilities does not change?

⚲:14-10 Over any given month, Dress-Rite loses 10% of its customers to Fashion, Inc., and 20% of its market to Luxury Living. But Fashion, Inc., loses 5% of its market to Dress-Rite and 10% of its market to Luxury Living each month; and Luxury Living loses 5% of its market to Fashion, Inc., and 5% of its market to Dress-Rite. At the present time, each of these clothing stores has an equal share of the market. What do you think the market shares will be next month? What will they be in three months?

• 14-11 Draw a tree diagram to illustrate what the market shares would be next month for Problem 14-10.

⚲:14-12 Goodeating Dog Chow Company produces a variety of brands of dog chow. One of their best values is the 50-pound bag of Goodeating Dog Chow. George Hamilton, president of Goodeating, uses a very old machine to load 50 pounds of Goodeating Chow automatically into each bag. Unfortunately, because the machine is old, it occasionally over- or under-fills the bags. When the machine is *correctly* placing 50 pounds of dog chow into each bag, there is a 0.10 probability that the machine will only put 49 pounds in each bag the following day, and there is a 0.20 probability that 51 pounds will be placed in each bag the next day. If the machine is currently placing 49 pounds of dog chow in each bag, there is a 0.30 probability that it will put 50 pounds in each bag tomorrow and a 0.20 probability that it will put 51 pounds in each bag tomorrow. In addition, if the machine is placing 51 pounds in each bag today, there is a 0.40 probability that it will place 50 pounds in each bag tomorrow and a 0.10 probability that it will place 49 pounds in each bag tomorrow.
   (a) If the machine is loading 50 pounds in each bag today, what is the probability that it will be placing 50 pounds in each bag tomorrow?
   (b) Resolve part (a) when the machine is only placing 49 pounds in each bag today.
   (c) Resolve part (a) when the machine is placing 51 pounds in each bag today.

⚲:14-13 Resolve Problem 14-12 (Goodeating Dog Chow) for five periods.

⚲:14-14 The University of South Wisconsin has had steady enrollments over the past five years. The school has its own bookstore, called University Book Store, but there are also three private bookstores in town: Bill's Book Store, College Book Store, and Battle's Book Store. The university is concerned about the large number of students who are switching to one of the private stores. As a result, South Wisconsin's president, Andy Lange, has decided to give a student three hours of university credit to look into the problem. The following matrix of transition probabilities was obtained:

	UNIVERSITY	BILL'S	COLLEGE	BATTLE'S
UNIVERSITY	0.6	0.2	0.1	0.1
BILL'S	0	0.7	0.2	0.1
COLLEGE	0.1	0.1	0.8	0
BATTLE'S	0.05	0.05	0.1	0.8

At the present time, each of the four bookstores has an equal share of the market. What will the market shares be for the next period?

⚲:14-15 Andy Lange, president of the University of South Wisconsin, is concerned with the declining business at the University Book Store. (See Problem 14-14 for details.) The students tell him that the prices are simply too high. Andy, however, has decided not to lower the prices. If the same conditions exist, what long-run market shares can Andy expect for the four bookstores?

Q:14-16 Hervis Rent-A-Car has three car rental locations in the greater Houston area: the Northside branch, the West End branch, and the Suburban branch. Customers can rent a car at any of these places and return it to any of the others without any additional fees. However, this can create a problem for Hervis if too many cars are taken to the popular Northside branch. For planning purposes, Hervis would like to predict where the cars will eventually be. Past data indicate that 80% of the cars rented at the Northside branch will be returned there, and the rest will be evenly distributed between the other two. For the West End branch, about 70% of the cars rented there will be returned there, and 20% will be returned to the Northside branch and the rest will go to the Suburban branch. Of the cars rented at the Suburban branch, 60% are returned there, 25% are returned to the Northside branch, and the other 15% are dropped off at the West End. If there are currently 100 cars being rented from Northside, 80 from West End, and 60 from the Suburban branch, how many of these will be dropped off at each of the car rental locations?

Q:14-17 A study of accounts receivables at the A&W Department Store indicates that bills are either current, one month overdue, two months overdue, written off as bad debts, or paid in full. Of those that are current, 80% are paid that month, and the rest become one month overdue. Of the one month overdue bills, 90% are paid, and the rest become two months overdue. Those that are two months overdue will either be paid (85%) or be listed as bad debts. If the sales each month average $150,000, determine how much the company expects to receive of this amount. How much will become bad debts?

Q:14 18 The cellular phone industry is very competitive. Two companies in the greater Lubbock area, Horizon and Local Cellular, are constantly battling each other in an attempt to control the market. Each company has a one-year service agreement. At the end of each year, some customers will renew, while some will switch to the other company. Horizon customers tend to be loyal, and 80% renew, while 20% switch. About 70% of the Local Cellular customers renew with them and about 30% switch to Horizon. If there are currently 100,000 Horizon customers this year, and 80,000 Local Cellular customers, how many would we expect each company to have next year?

Q:14-19 The personal computer industry is very fast moving and technology provides motivation for customers to upgrade with new computers every few years. Brand loyalty is very important and companies try to do things to keep their customers happy. However, some current customers will switch to a different company. Three particular brands, Doorway, Bell, and Kumpaq, hold the major shares of the market. People who own Doorway computers will buy another Doorway in their next purchase 80% of the

time, while the rest will switch to the other companies in equal proportions. Owners of Bell computers will buy Bell again 90% of the time, while 5% will buy Doorway and 5% will buy Kumpaq. About 70% of the Kumpaq owners will make Kumpaq their next purchase while 20% will buy Doorway and the rest will buy Bell. If each brand currently has 200,000 customers who plan to buy a new computer in the next year, how many computers of each type will be purchased?

14-20 In Section 14.7, we investigated an accounts receivable problem. How would the paid category and the bad debt category change with the following matrix of transition probabilities?

$$P = \begin{bmatrix} 1 & 0 & 0 & 0 \\ 0 & 1 & 0 & 0 \\ 0.7 & 0 & 0.2 & 0.1 \\ 0.4 & 0.2 & 0.2 & 0.2 \end{bmatrix}$$

14-21 Professor Green gives two-month computer programming courses during the summer term. Students must pass a number of exams to pass the course, and each student is given three chances to take the exams. The following states describe the possible situations that could occur:

1. *State 1:* pass all of the exams and pass the course
2. *State 2:* do not pass all of the exams by the third attempt and flunk the course
3. *State 3:* fail an exam in the first attempt
4. *State 4:* fail an exam in the second attempt

After observing several classes, Professor Green was able to obtain the following matrix of transition probabilities:

$$P = \begin{bmatrix} 1 & 0 & 0 & 0 \\ 0 & 1 & 0 & 0 \\ 0.6 & 0 & 0.1 & 0.3 \\ 0.3 & 0.3 & 0.2 & 0.2 \end{bmatrix}$$

At the present time, there are 50 students who did not pass all exams on the first attempt, and there are 30 students who did not pass all remaining exams on the second attempt. How many students in these two groups will pass the course, and how many will fail the course?

14-22 Hicourt Industries is a commercial printing outfit in a medium-sized town in central Florida. Its only competitors are the Printing House and Gandy Printers. Last month, Hicourt Industries had approximately 30% of the market for the printing business in the area. The Printing House had 50% of the market, and Gandy Printers had 20% of the market. The association of printers, a locally run association, had recently determined how these three printers and smaller printing operations not involved in the commercial market were able to retain their customer base. Hicourt was the most successful in keeping its customers. Eighty percent of its customers for any one month remained customers for the next month. The Printing House, on the other hand, had only a 70% retention rate. Gandy Printers was in the worst condition. Only 60% of the customers for any one month remained with the firm. In one month, the market share had significantly changed. This was very exciting to George Hicourt, president of Hicourt Industries. This month, Hicourt Industries was able to obtain a 38% market share. The Printing House, on the other hand, lost market share. This month, it only had 42% of the market share. Gandy Printers remained the same; it kept its 20% of the market. Just looking at market share, George concluded that he was able to take 8% per month away from the Printing House. George estimated that in a few short months, he could basically run the Printing House out of business. His hope was to capture 80% of the total market, representing his original 30% along with the 50% share that the Printing House started off with. Will George be able to reach his goal? What do you think the long-term market shares will be for these three commercial printing operations? Will Hicourt Industries be able to run the Printing House completely out of business?

14-23 John Jones of Bayside Laundry has been providing cleaning and linen service for rental condominiums on the Gulf coast for over 10 years. Currently, John is servicing 26 condominium developments. John's two major competitors are Cleanco, which currently services 15 condominium developments, and Beach Services, which performs laundry and cleaning services for 11 condominium developments.

Recently, John contacted Bay Bank about a loan to expand his business operations. To justify the loan, John has kept detailed records of his customers and the customers that he received from his two major competitors. During the past year, he was able to keep 18 of his original 26 customers. During the same period, he was able to get 1 new customer from Cleanco and 2 new customers from Beach Services. Unfortunately, John lost 6 of his original customers to Cleanco and 2 of his original customers to Beach Services during the same year. John has also learned that Cleanco has kept 80% of its current customers. He also knows that Beach Services will keep at least 50% of its customers. For John to get the loan from Bay Bank, he needs to show the loan officer that he will maintain an adequate share of the market. The officers of Bay Bank are concerned about the recent trends for market share, and they have decided not to give John a loan unless he will keep at least 35% of the market share in the long run. What types of equilibrium market shares can John expect? If you were an officer of Bay Bank, would you give John a loan?

14-24 Set up both the vector of state probabilities and the matrix of transition probabilities given the following information:

Store 1 currently has 40% of the market; store 2 currently has 60% of the market.

In each period, store 1 customers have an 80% chance of returning; 20% of switching to store 2.

In each period, store 2 customers have a 90% chance of returning; 10% of switching to store 1.

14-25 Find $\pi(2)$ for Problem 14-24.

14-26 Find the equilibrium conditions for Problem 14-24. Explain what it means.

14-27 As a result of a recent survey of students at the University of South Wisconsin, it was determined that the university owned bookstore currently has 40% of the market. (See Problem 14-14.) The other three bookstores, Bill's, College, and Battle's, each split the remaining initial market share. Given that the state probabilities are the same, what is the market share for the next period given the initial market shares? What impact do the initial market shares have on each store next period? What is the impact on the steady state market shares?

14-28 Sandy Sprunger is part owner in one of the largest quick-oil-change operations for a medium-sized city in the Midwest. Currently, the firm has 60% of the market. There are a total of 10 quick lubrication shops in the area. After performing some basic marketing research, Sandy has been able to capture the initial probabilities, or market shares, along with the matrix of transition, which represents probabilities that customers will switch from one quick lubrication shop to another. These values are shown in the table on the next page:

Initial probabilities, or market share, for shops 1 through 10 are 0.6, 0.1, 0.1, 0.1, 0.05, 0.01, 0.01, 0.01, 0.01, and 0.01.

(a) Given these data, determine market shares for the next period for each of the 10 shops.

(b) What are the equilibrium market shares?

(c) Sandy believes that the original estimates for market shares were wrong. She believes that shop 1 has 40% of the market, and shop 2 has 30%. All other values are the same. If this is the case, what is the impact on market shares for next-period and equilibrium shares?

(d) A marketing consultant believes that shop 1 has tremendous appeal. She believes that this shop will retain 99% of its current market share; 1% may switch to shop 2. If the consultant is correct, will shop 1 have 90% of the market in the long run?

14-29 During a recent trip to her favorite restaurant, Sandy (owner of shop 1) met Chris Talley (owner of shop 7) (see Problem 14-28). After an enjoyable lunch, Sandy and Chris had a heated discussion about market share for the quick-oil-change operations in their city. Here is their conversation:

Data for Problem 14-28

FROM	TO									
	1	2	3	4	5	6	7	8	9	10
1	0.60	0.10	0.10	0.10	0.05	0.01	0.01	0.01	0.01	0.01
2	0.01	0.80	0.01	0.01	0.01	0.10	0.01	0.01	0.01	0.03
3	0.01	0.01	0.70	0.01	0.01	0.10	0.01	0.05	0.05	0.05
4	0.01	0.01	0.01	0.90	0.01	0.01	0.01	0.01	0.01	0.02
5	0.01	0.01	0.01	0.10	0.80	0.01	0.03	0.01	0.01	0.01
6	0.01	0.01	0.01	0.01	0.01	0.91	0.01	0.01	0.01	0.01
7	0.01	0.01	0.01	0.01	0.01	0.10	0.70	0.01	0.10	0.04
8	0.01	0.01	0.01	0.01	0.01	0.10	0.03	0.80	0.01	0.01
9	0.01	0.01	0.01	0.01	0.01	0.10	0.01	0.10	0.70	0.04
10	0.01	0.01	0.01	0.01	0.01	0.10	0.10	0.05	0.00	0.70

Sandy: My operation is so superior that after someone changes oil at one of my shops, they will never do business with anyone else. On second thought, maybe 1 person out of 100 will try your shop after visiting one of my shops. In a month, I will have 99% of the market, and you will have 1% of the market.

Chris: You have it completely reversed. In a month, I will have 99% of the market, and you will only have 1% of the market. In fact, I will treat you to a meal at a restaurant of your choice if you are right. If I am right, you will treat me to one of those big steaks at David's Steak House. Do we have a deal?

Sandy: Yes! Get your checkbook or your credit card. You will have the privilege of paying for two very expensive meals at Anthony's Seafood Restaurant.

(a) Assume that Sandy is correct about customers visiting one of her quick-oil-change shops. Will she win the bet with Chris?

(b) Assume that Chris is correct about customers visiting one of his quick-oil-change shops. Will he win the bet?

(c) Describe what would happen if both Sandy and Chris are correct about customers visiting their quick-oil-change operations.

:14-30 The first quick-oil-change store in Problem 14-28 retains 73% of its market share. This represents a probability of 0.73 in the first row and first column of the matrix of transition probabilities. The other probability values in the first row are equally distributed across the other stores (namely, 3% each). What

impact does this have on the steady-state market shares for the quick-oil-change stores?

14-31 The following digraph represents the changes in weather from one day to the next in Erie, Pennsylvania.

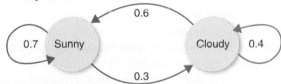

Determine the associated transition matrix and the probability that it will be cloudy in three days given that it is cloudy today.

14-32 The following digraph represents the changes in weather from one day to the next in Lowell, Massachusetts.

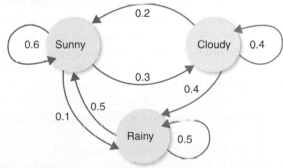

Determine the associated transition matrix and the overall percentage of sunny days.

Internet Homework Problems

See our Internet home page, at **www.pearsonhighered.com/render**, for additional homework problems, Problems 14-33 to 14-36.

Case Study

Rentall Trucks

Jim Fox, an executive for Rentall Trucks, could not believe it. He had hired one of the town's best law firms, Folley, Smith, and Christensen. Their fee for drawing up the legal contracts was over $50,000. Folley, Smith, and Christensen had made one important omission from the contracts, and this blunder would more than likely cost Rentall Trucks millions of dollars. For the hundredth time, Jim carefully reconstructed the situation and pondered the inevitable.

Rentall Trucks was started by Robert (Bob) Renton more than 10 years ago. It specialized in renting trucks to businesses and private individuals. The company prospered, and Bob increased his net worth by millions of dollars. Bob was a legend in the rental business and was known all over the world for his keen business abilities.

Only a year and a half ago, some of the executives of Rentall and some additional outside investors offered to buy Rentall from Bob. Bob was close to retirement, and the offer was unbelievable. His children and their children would be able to live in high style off the proceeds of the sale. Folley, Smith, and Christensen developed the contracts for the executives of Rentall and other investors, and the sale was made.

Being a perfectionist, it was only a matter of time until Bob was marching down to the Rentall headquarters, telling everyone the mistakes that Rentall was making and how to solve some of their problems. Pete Rosen, president of Rentall, became extremely angry about Bob's constant interference, and in a brief 10-minute meeting, Pete told Bob never to enter the Rentall offices again. It was at this time that Bob decided to re-read the contracts, and it was also at this time that Bob and his lawyer discovered that there was no clause in the contracts that prevented Bob from competing directly with Rentall.

The brief 10-minute meeting with Pete Rosen was the beginning of Rentran. In less than six months, Bob Renton had lured some of the key executives away from Rentall and into his new business, Rentran, which would compete directly with Rentall Trucks in every way. After a few months of operation, Bob estimated that Rentran had about 5% of the total national market for truck rentals. Rentall had about 80% of the market, and another company, National Rentals, had the remaining 15% of the market.

Rentall's Jim Fox was in total shock. In a few months, Rentran had already captured 5% of the total market. At this rate, Rentran might completely dominate the market in a few short years. Pete Rosen even wondered if Rentall could maintain 50% of the market in the long run. As a result of these concerns, Pete hired a marketing research firm that analyzed a random sample of truck rental customers. The sample consisted of 1,000 existing or potential customers. The marketing research firm was very careful to make sure that the sample represented the true market conditions. The sample, taken in August, consisted of 800 customers of Rentall, 60 customers of Rentran, and the remainder National customers. The same sample was then analyzed the next month concerning the customers'

propensity to switch companies. Of the original Rentall customers, 200 switched to Rentran, and 80 switched to National. Rentran was able to retain 51 of their original customers. Three customers switched to Rentall, and 6 customers switched to National. Finally, 14 customers switched from National to Rentall, and 35 customers switched from National to Rentran.

The board of directors meeting was only two weeks away, and there would be some difficult questions to answer—what happened, and what can be done about Rentran? In Jim Fox's opinion, nothing could be done about the costly omission made by Folley, Smith, and Christensen. The only solution was to take immediate corrective action that would curb Rentran's ability to lure customers away from Rentall.

After a careful analysis of Rentran, Rentall, and the truck rental business in general, Jim concluded that immediate changes would be needed in three areas: rental policy, advertising, and product line. Regarding rental policy, a number of changes were needed to make truck rental both easier and faster. Rentall could implement many of the techniques used by Hertz and other car rental agencies. In addition, changes in the product line were needed. Rentall's smaller trucks had to be more comfortable and easier to drive. Automatic transmission, comfortable bucket seats, air conditioners, quality radio and tape stereo systems, and cruise control should be included. Although expensive and difficult to maintain, these items could make a significant difference in market shares. Finally, Jim knew that additional advertising was needed. The advertising had to be immediate and aggressive. Television and journal advertising had to be increased, and a good advertising company was needed. If these new changes were implemented now, there would be a good chance that Rentall would be able to maintain close to its 80% of the market. To confirm Jim's perceptions, the same marketing research firm was employed to analyze the effect of these changes, using the same sample of 1,000 customers.

The marketing research firm, Meyers Marketing Research, Inc., performed a pilot test on the sample of 1,000 customers. The results of the analysis revealed that Rentall would only lose 100 of its original customers to Rentran and 20 to National if the new policies were implemented. In addition, Rentall would pick up customers from both Rentran and National. It was estimated that Rentall would now get 9 customers from Rentran and 28 customers from National.

Discussion Questions

1. What will the market shares be in one month if these changes are made? If no changes are made?
2. What will the market shares be in three months with the changes?
3. If market conditions remain the same, what market share would Rentall have in the long run? How does this compare with the market share that would result if the changes were not made?

Internet Case Studies

See our Internet home page, at www.pearsonhighered.com/render, for these additional case studies:

(1) **St. Pierre Salt Company:** This case involves the selection of centrifuges that are used to separate recrystallized salt from brine solution.

(2) **University of Texas–Austin:** This case involves doctoral students at different stages of their graduate programs.

Bibliography

Aviv, Yossi, and Amit Pazgal. "A Partially Observed Markov Decision Process for Dynamic Pricing," *Management Science* 51, 9 (September 2005): 1400–1416.

Çelikyurt, U., and S. Özekici. "Multiperiod Portfolio Optimization Models in Stochastic Markets Using the Mean–Variance Approach," *European Journal of Operational Research* 179, 1 (2007): 186–202.

Deslauriers, Alexandre, et al. "Markov Chain Models of a Telephone Call Center with Call Blending," *Computers & Operations Research* 34, 6 (2007): 1616–1645.

Freedman, D. *Markov Chains*. San Francisco: Holden-Day, Inc., 1971.

Juneja, Sandeep, and Perwez Shahabuddin. "Fast Simulation of Markov Chains with Small Transition Probabilities," *Management Science* 47, 4 (April 2001): 547–562.

Lim, Gino J., and Sumeet S Desai. "Markov Decision Process Approach for Multiple Objective Hazardous Material Transportation Route Selection

Problem," *International Journal of Operational Research* 7, 4 (2010): 506–529.

Matalycki, M.A., and A.V. Pańkow. "Research of Markov Queuing Network with Central System and Incomes," *Informatyka Teoretyczna i Stosowana* 4, 7 (2004): 23–32.

Park, Yonil, and John L. Spouge. "Searching for Multiple Words in a Markov Sequence," *INFORMS Journal on Computing* 16, 4 (Fall 2004): 341–347.

Renault, Jérôme. "The Value of Markov Chain Games with Lack of Information on One Side," *Mathematics of Operations Research* 31, 3 (August 2006): 490–512.

Tsao, H.-Y., P.-C. Lin, L. Pitt, and C. Campbell. "The Impact of Loyalty and Promotion Effects on Retention Rate," *Journal of the Operational Research Society* (2009) 60, 5: 646–651.

Zhu, Quanxin, and Xianping Guo, "Markov Decision Processes with Variance Minimization: A New Condition and Approach," *Stochastic Analysis and Applications* 25, 3 (2007): 577–592.

Appendix 14.1: Markov Analysis with QM for Windows

Markov analysis can be used for a variety of practical problems, including market share, equilibrium conditions, and tracing patients through a medical system. The grocery store example is used to show how Markov analysis can be used to determine future market-share conditions. Programs 14.1A and 14.1B reveal how QM for Windows is used to compute market share and equilibrium conditions. Note that the initial conditions and the ending market share (probabilities) are also displayed.

PROGRAM 14.1A

QM for Windows Input Screen for Market Share Example

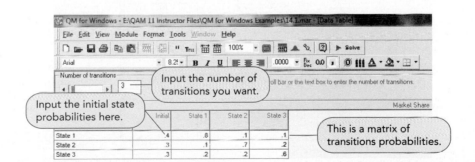

PROGRAM 14.1B

QM for Windows Output Screen for Market Share Example

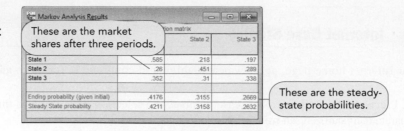

Absorbing state analysis is also discussed in this chapter using a bill-paying example. Programs 14.2A and 14.2B show how QM for Windows is used to compute the amount paid and the amount of bad debt using absorbing state analysis.

PROGRAM 14.2A

QM for Windows Input Screen for Absorbing State Example

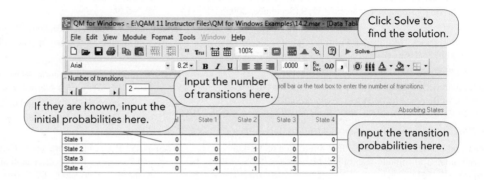

PROGRAM 14.2B

QM for Windows Output Screen for Absorbing State Example

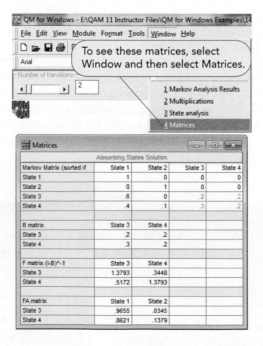

Appendix 14.2: Markov Analysis With Excel

Performing the Markov analysis matrix operations is very easy with Excel, although the input process is different from most Excel operations. The two Excel functions that are most helpful with matrices are MMULT for matrix multiplication and MINVERSE for finding the inverse of the matrix. However, special procedures are used when these are entered in the spreadsheet. Matrix addition and subtraction is also easy in Excel using special procedures.

Using Excel to Predict Future Market Shares

In using Markov analysis to predict future market shares or future states, matrices are multiplied. To multiply matrices in Excel, we use MMULT as follows:

1. Highlight all the cells that will contain the resulting matrix.
2. Type = MMULT(*matrix*1, *matrix*2), where *matrix 1* and *matrix 2* are the cell ranges for the two matrices being multiplied.
3. Instead of just pressing Enter, hold down the Ctrl and Shift keys and then press Enter.

Pressing Ctrl + Shift + Enter is used to indicate that a matrix operation is being performed so that all cells in the matrix are changed accordingly.

Program 14.3A shows the formulas for the three grocery store example from Section 14.2. We have entered the time period in column A for reference only, as we will be computing the state probabilities through time period 6. The state probabilities (cells B6 through D6) and the matrix of transition probabilities (cells E6 through G8) are entered as shown. We then use matrix multiplication to find the state probabilities for the next period. Highlight cells B7, C7, and D7 (this is where the resulting matrix will be) and type = MMULT(B6:D6,E6:G8), as shown in the table. Then press Ctrl + Shift + Enter (all at one time), and this formula is put in each of the three cells that were highlighted. When you have done this, Excel places { } around this formula in the box at the top of the screen (not shown). We then copy cells B7, C7, and D7 to rows 8 through 12 as shown. Program 14.3B shows the result and the state probabilities for the next six time periods.

PROGRAM 14.3A

Excel Input and Formulas, for Three Grocery Store Example

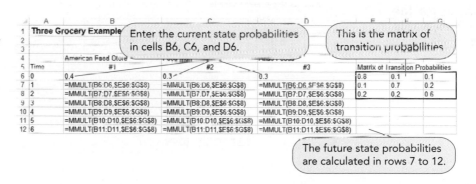

PROGRAM 14.3B

Excel Output for Three Grocery Store Example

	A	B	C	D	E	F	G
1	Three Grocery Example						
2							
3			State Probabilities				
4	Time	American Food Store #1	Food Mart #2	Atlas Foods #3	Matrix of Transition Probabilities		
5							
6	0	0.4	0.3	0.3	0.8	0.1	0.1
7	1	0.41	0.31	0.28	0.1	0.7	0.2
8	2	0.415	0.314	0.271	0.2	0.2	0.6
9	3	0.4176	0.3155	0.2669			
10	4	0.41901	0.31599	0.265			
11	5	0.419807	0.316094	0.264099			
12	6	0.4202748	0.3160663	0.2636589			

Using Excel to Find the Fundamental Matrix and Absorbing States

Excel can be used to find the fundamental matrix that is used to predict future conditions when absorbing states exist. The MINVERSE function is used in the accounts receivable example from Section 14.7 of this chapter. Program 14.4A shows the formulas, and Program 14.4B provides the results. Remember that the entire range of the matrix (D12 through E13) is highlighted before the MINVERSE function is entered. Also remember to press Ctrl + Shift + Enter all at once.

Matrix addition and subtraction can be handled in a fashion similar to the methods just described. In Program 14.4A, the $I - B$ matrix was computed using a matrix method. First we highlighted the cells D9 through E10 (where the result is to be). Then we typed the formula seen in these cells and pressed Ctrl + Shift + Enter (all at once), causing this formula to be entered in each of these cells. Excel then computes the appropriate values as shown in Program 14.4B.

PROGRAM 14.4A

Excel Input and Formulas for the Accounts Receivable Example

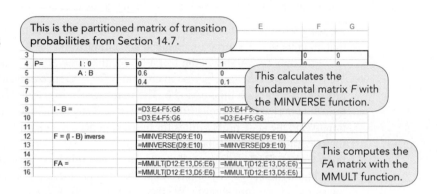

This is the partitioned matrix of transition probabilities from Section 14.7.

This calculates the fundamental matrix F with the MINVERSE function.

This computes the FA matrix with the MMULT function.

			E	F	G
3			1	0	0	0
4 P=	I : 0	=	0	1	0	0
5	A : B		0.6	0		
6			0.4	0.1		
7						
8						
9	I - B =		=D3:E4-F5:G6	=D3:E4-F5:G6		
10			=D3:E4-F5:G6	=D3:E4-F5:G6		
11						
12	F = (I - B) inverse		=MINVERSE(D9:E10)	=MINVERSE(D9:E10)		
13			=MINVERSE(D9:E10)	=MINVERSE(D9:E10)		
14						
15	FA =		=MMULT(D12:E13,D5:E6)	=MMULT(D12:E13,D5:E6)		
16			=MMULT(D12:E13,D5:E6)	=MMULT(D12:E13,D5:E6)		

PROGRAM 14.4B

Excel Output for the Accounts Receivable Example

	A	B	C	D	E	F	G
1	Accounts Receivable Example						
2							
3				1	0	0	0
4	P=	I : 0	=	0	1	0	0
5		A : B		0.6	0	0.2	0.2
6				0.4	0.1	0.3	0.2
7							
8							
9		I - B =		0.8	-0.2		
10				-0.3	0.8		
11							
12		F = (I - B) inverse		1.37931034	0.34482759		
13				0.51724138	1.37931034		
14							
15		FA =		0.96551724	0.03448276		
16				0.86206897	0.13793103		

CHAPTER 15

Statistical Quality Control

15.1   Introduction

For almost every product or service, there is more than one organization trying to make a sale. Price may be a major issue in whether a sale is made or lost, but another factor is *quality*. In fact, quality is often the major issue; and poor quality can be very expensive for both the producing firm and the customer.

Consequently, firms employ quality management tactics. Quality management, or as it is more commonly called, *quality control* (QC), is critical throughout the organization. One of the manager's major roles is to ensure that his or her firm can deliver a quality product at the right place, at the right time, and at the right price. Quality is not just of concern for manufactured products either; it is also important in services, from banking to hospital care to education.

Statistical process control uses statistical and probability tools to help control processes and produce consistent goods and services.

We begin this chapter with an attempt to define just what quality really is. Then we deal with the most important statistical methodology for quality management: *statistical process control* (SPC). SPC is the application of the statistical tools we discussed in Chapter 2 to the control of processes that result in products or services.

15.2   Defining Quality and TQM

The quality of a product or service is the degree to which the product or service meets specifications.

To some people, a high-quality product is one that is stronger, will last longer, is built heavier, and is, in general, more durable than other products. In some cases this is a good definition of a quality product, but not always. A good circuit breaker, for example, is *not* one that lasts longer during periods of high current or voltage. So the **quality** *of a product* or *service* is the degree to which the product or service meets specifications. Increasingly, definitions of *quality* include an added emphasis on meeting the customer's needs. As you can see in Table 15.1, the first and second ones are similar to our definition.

Total quality management encompasses the whole organization.

Total quality management (TQM) refers to a quality emphasis that encompasses the entire organization, from supplier to customer. TQM emphasizes a commitment by management to have a companywide drive toward excellence in all aspects of the products and services that are important to the customer. Meeting the customer's expectations requires an emphasis on TQM if the firm is to compete as a leader in world markets.

This emphasis on quality means that the company will seek continuous improvement in every aspect of the delivery of products and services.

TABLE 15.1

Several Definitions of Quality

"Quality is the degree to which a specific product conforms to a design or specification."

H. L. Gilmore. "Product Conformance Cost," *Quality Progress* (June 1974): 16.

"Quality is the totality of features and characteristics of a product or service that bears on its ability to satisfy stated or implied needs."

Ross Johnson and William O. Winchell. *Production and Quality.* Milwaukee, WI: American Society of Quality Control, 1989, p. 2.

"Quality is fitness for use."

J. M. Juran, ed. *Quality Control Handbook*, 3rd ed. New York: McGraw-Hill, 1974, p. 2.

"Quality is defined by the customer; customers want products and services that, throughout their lives, meet customers' needs and expectations at a cost that represents value."

Ford's definition, as presented in William W. Scherkenbach. *Deming's Road to Continual Improvement.* Knoxville, TN: SPC Press, 1991, p. 161.

"Even though quality cannot be defined, you know what it is."

R. M. Pirsig. *Zen and the Art of Motorcycle Maintenance.* New York: Bantam Books, 1974, p. 213.

HISTORY How Quality Control Has Evolved

In the early nineteenth century an individual skilled artisan started and finished a whole product. With the Industrial Revolution and the factory system, semiskilled workers, each making a small portion of the final product, became common. With this, responsibility for the quality of the final product tended to shift to supervisors, and pride of workmanship declined.

As organizations became larger in the twentieth century, inspection became more technical and organized. Inspectors were often grouped together; their job was to make sure that bad lots were not shipped to customers. Starting in the 1920s, major statistical QC tools were developed. W. Shewhart introduced control charts in 1924, and in 1930, H. F. Dodge and H. G. Romig designed acceptance sampling tables. Also at that time the important role of QC in all areas of the company's performance became recognized.

During and after World War II, the importance of quality grew, often with the encouragement of the U.S. government. Companies recognized that more than just inspection was needed to make a quality product. Quality needed to be built into the production process.

After World War II, an American, W. Edwards Deming, went to Japan to teach statistical QC concepts to the devastated Japanese manufacturing sector. A second pioneer, J. M. Juran, followed Deming to Japan, stressing top management support and involvement in the quality battle. In 1961 A. V. Feigenbaum wrote his classic book *Total Quality Control*, which delivered a fundamental message: Make it right the first time! In 1979, Philip Crosby published *Quality Is Free*, stressing the need for management and employee commitment to the battle against poor quality. In 1988, the U.S. government presented its first awards for quality improvement. These are known as the Malcolm Baldrige National Quality Awards.

A method of quality management called Six Sigma was developed in the electronics industry. The goal of Six Sigma is continuous improvement in performance to reduce and eliminate defects. Technically, to achieve Six Sigma quality, there would have to be fewer than 3.4 defects per million opportunities. This approach to quality has been credited with achieving significant cost savings for a number of companies. General Electric estimated savings of $12 billion over a 5-year period, and other firms have reported savings in the hundreds of millions of dollars.

Today, companies strive to be ISO 9000 certified as this is an international quality standard that is recognized worldwide. ISO 9000 was developed by the International Organization for Standardization (ISO), the world's largest developer and publisher of international standards.

15.3 Statistical Process Control

Statistical process control helps set standards. It can also monitor, measure, and correct quality problems.

Statistical process control involves establishing standards, monitoring standards, taking measurements, and taking corrective action as a product or service is being produced. Samples of process outputs are examined; if they are within acceptable limits, the process is permitted to continue. If they fall outside certain specific ranges, the process is stopped and, typically, the assignable cause is located and removed.

A control chart is a graphic way of presenting data over time.

Control charts are graphs that show upper and lower limits for the process we want to control. A **control chart** is a graphic presentation of data over time. Control charts are constructed in such a way that new data can quickly be compared with past performance. Upper and lower limits in a control chart can be in units of temperature, pressure, weight, length, and so on. We take samples of the process output and plot the averages of these samples on a chart that has the limits on it.

Figure 15.1 graphically reveals the useful information that can be portrayed in control charts. When the averages of the samples fall within the upper and lower control limits and no discernible pattern is present, the process is said to be in control; otherwise, the process is out of control or out of adjustment.

Variability in the Process

All processes are subject to a certain degree of variability. Walter Shewhart of Bell Laboratories, while studying process data in the 1920s, made the distinction between the common and special causes of variation. The key is keeping variations under control. So we now look at how to build control charts that help managers and workers develop a process that is capable of producing within established limits.

BUILDING CONTROL CHARTS When building control charts, averages of small samples (often of five items or parts) are used, as opposed to data on individual parts. Individual pieces tend to be too erratic to make trends quickly visible. The purpose of control charts is to help distinguish between **natural variations** and *variations due to assignable causes*.

FIGURE 15.1

Patterns to Look for in Control Charts

(**Source:** Bertrand L. Hansen, *Quality Control: Theory and Applications,* © 1963, renewed 1991, p. 65. Reprinted by permission of Prentice Hall, Upper Saddle River, NJ.)

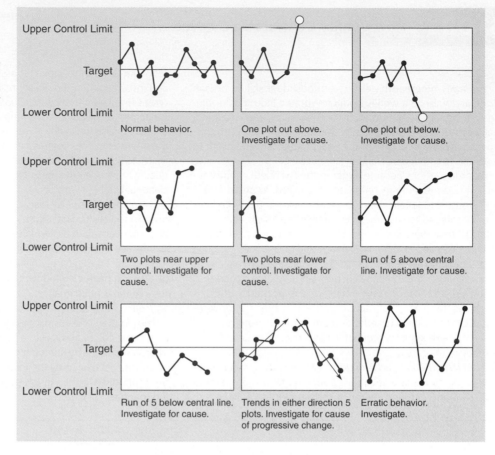

IN ACTION **Bank of America Uses Statistics to Combat Pecuniary Corruption**

Banks and similar financial institutions have good reason to help law enforcement fight fiscal improprieties. Debit card fraud alone costs the banking industry over $2.75 billion annually! In their fight against fraud, analysts at Bank of America use statistical *outlier analysis* to help detect suspicious fiscal activities. Bank of America specifically targets money laundering and retail banking fraud in its analysis. The company tracks characteristics such as where, when, and how much money is involved in each transaction for every customer. Then it performs statistical analyses to see if the activity falls within usual activity boundaries for that particular customer. For you as a customer, that means nothing more than that the bank knows how much money you typically withdraw from an ATM and which ATM you normally use.

The bank analysts are on the lookout for *outliers*, which are unusual events that have a very small probability of occurring. For example, if you normally use one particular ATM and then use a different ATM, the transaction at the unusual location may raise a small flag, but the transaction would likely proceed without interference. However, if you try to cash a very large third-party check at an out-of-state location, several flags will be raised, as this is very unusual behavior for you. The teller may require several forms of identification and then get approval from the branch manager before completing the transaction.

Source: Based on A. Sudjianto, S. Nair, M. Yuan, A. Zhang, D. Ker, and F. Cela-Díaz. "Statistical Methods for Fighting Financial Crimes," *Technometrics* 52, 1 (2010): 5–19.

Natural variations are sources of variation in a process that is statistically in control.

NATURAL VARIATIONS Natural variations affect almost every production or service process and are to be expected. These variations are random and uncontrollable. *Natural variations* are the many sources of variation within a process that is in statistical control. They behave like a constant system of chance causes. Although individual measured values are all different, as a group they form a pattern that can be described as a distribution. When these distributions are *normal*, they are characterized by two parameters:

1. Mean, μ (the measure of central tendency, in this case, the average value)
2. Standard deviation, σ (variation, an indication of the average amount by which the values differ from the mean)

As long as the distribution (output precision) remains within specified limits, the process is said to be "in control," and the modest variations are tolerated.

Assignable variations in a process can be traced to a specific problem.

ASSIGNABLE VARIATIONS When a process is not in control, we must detect and eliminate special (*assignable*) causes of *variation*. These variations are not random and can be controlled when the cause of the variation is determined. Factors such as machine wear, misadjusted equipment, fatigued or untrained workers, or new batches of raw material are all potential sources of **assignable variations**. Control charts such as those illustrated in Figure 15.1 help the manager pinpoint where a problem may lie.

The ability of a process to operate within statistical control is determined by the total variation that comes from natural causes—the minimum variation that can be achieved after all assignable causes have been eliminated. The objective of a process control system, then, is *to provide a statistical signal when assignable causes of variation are present*. Such a signal can quicken appropriate action to eliminate assignable causes.

15.4 Control Charts for Variables

x̄-charts measure central tendency of a process.

Control charts for the mean, $\bar{x}$, and the range, R, are used to monitor processes that are measured in continuous units. Examples of these would be weight, height, and volume. The **x̄-chart** (x-bar chart) tells us whether changes have occurred in the central tendency of a process. This might be due to such factors as tool wear, a gradual increase in temperature, a different method used on the second shift, or new and stronger materials. The **R-chart** values indicate that a gain or loss in uniformity has occurred. Such a change might be due to worn bearings, a loose tool part, an erratic flow of lubricants to a machine, or sloppiness on the part of a machine operator. The two types of charts go hand in hand when monitoring variables.

R-charts measure the range between the biggest (or heaviest) and smallest (or lightest) items in a random sample.

The Central Limit Theorem

The central limit theorem says that the distribution of sample means will be approximately normally distributed.

The statistical foundation for $\bar{x}$-charts is the **central limit theorem**. In general terms, this theorem states that regardless of the distribution of the population of all parts or services, the distribution of $\bar{x}$'s (each of which is a mean of a sample drawn from the population) will tend to follow a normal curve as the sample size grows large. Fortunately, even if n is fairly small (say 4 or 5), the distributions of the averages will still roughly follow a normal curve. The theorem also states that (1) the mean of the distribution of the $\bar{x}$s (called $\mu_{\bar{x}}$) will equal the mean of the overall population (called μ); and (2) the standard deviation of the sampling distribution, $\sigma_{\bar{x}}$, will be the population deviation, σ_x, divided by the square root of the sample size, n. In other words,

$$\mu_{\bar{x}} = \mu \quad \text{and} \quad \sigma_{\bar{x}} = \frac{\sigma_x}{\sqrt{n}}$$

Although there may be times when we may know $\mu_{\bar{x}}$ (and μ), often we must estimate this with the average of all the sample means (written as $\bar{\bar{x}}$).

Figure 15.2 shows three possible population distributions, each with its own mean, μ, and standard deviation, σ_x. If a series of random samples ($\bar{x}_1, \bar{x}_2, \bar{x}_3, \bar{x}_4$, and so on) each of size n is drawn from any one of these, the resulting distribution of $\bar{x}_i$s will appear as in the bottom graph of that figure. Because this is a normal distribution (as discussed in Chapter 2), we can state that

1. 99.7% of the time, the sample averages will fall within $\pm 3\sigma_{\bar{x}}$ of the population mean if the process has only random variations.
2. 95.5% of the time, the sample averages will fall within $\pm 2\sigma_{\bar{x}}$ of the population mean if the process has only random variations.

If a point on the control chart falls outside the $\pm 3\sigma_{\bar{x}}$ control limits, we are 99.7% sure that the process has changed. This is the theory behind control charts.

FIGURE 15.2
Population and Sampling Distributions

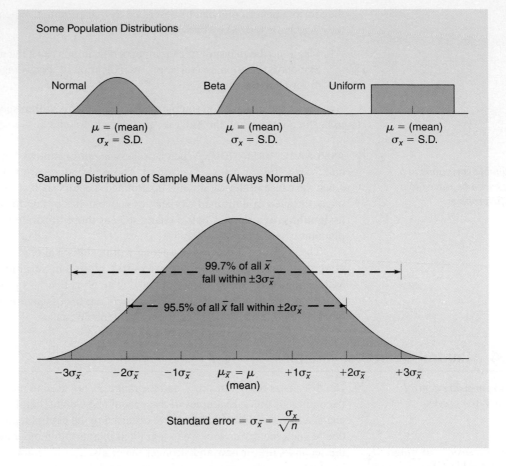

Setting $\bar{x}$-Chart Limits

If we know through historical data the standard deviation of the process population, σ_x, we can set upper and lower control limits by these formulas:

$$\text{Upper control limit (UCL)} = \bar{\bar{x}} + z\sigma_{\bar{x}} \qquad (15\text{-}1)$$

$$\text{Lower control limit (LCL)} = \bar{\bar{x}} - z\sigma_{\bar{x}} \qquad (15\text{-}2)$$

where

$\bar{\bar{x}}$ = mean of the sample means

z = number of normal standard deviations (2 for 95.5% confidence, 3 for 99.7%)

$\sigma_{\bar{x}}$ = standard deviation of the sampling distribution of the sample means $= \dfrac{\sigma_x}{\sqrt{n}}$

BOX-FILLING EXAMPLE Let us say that a large production lot of boxes of cornflakes is sampled every hour. To set control limits that include 99.7% of the sample means, 36 boxes are randomly selected and weighed. The standard deviation of the overall population of boxes is estimated, through analysis of old records, to be 2 ounces. The average mean of all samples taken is 16 ounces. We therefore have $\bar{\bar{x}} = 16$ ounces, $\sigma_x = 2$ ounces, $n = 36$, and $z = 3$. The control limits are

$$\text{UCL}_{\bar{x}} = \bar{\bar{x}} + z\sigma_{\bar{x}} = 16 + 3\left(\frac{2}{\sqrt{36}}\right) = 16 + 1 = 17 \text{ ounces}$$

$$\text{LCL}_{\bar{x}} = \bar{\bar{x}} - z\sigma_{\bar{x}} = 16 - 3\left(\frac{2}{\sqrt{36}}\right) = 16 - 1 = 15 \text{ ounces}$$

MODELING IN THE REAL WORLD

Hospital Uses Quality Control Analytics to Improve Business Process

Defining the Problem

Developing a Model

Acquiring Input Data

Developing a Solution

Testing the Solution

Analyzing the Results

Implementing the Results

Defining the Problem

The billing process at a medium-sized hospital was taking far too long. The long cycle times from care performed to payment received was identified as the root cause of missed payments, upset patients, and headaches for the accounts receivable department of the hospital.

Developing a Model

Hospital management turned to quality control analytics to reduce the cycle times. In particular, they looked to a Six Sigma technique known as Define-Measure-Analyze-Improve-Control (DMAIC).

Acquiring Input Data

A project team was formed and they began to work on the problem. They first modeled the "as-is" business process of patient billing with a flow chart. This allowed the team to see where potential bottlenecks in the process were. Average times for each task in the flow chart were captured and examined.

Developing a Solution

Team members developed alternative processes for some existing ones (e.g., email instead of hard copy), eliminated some existing procedures (e.g., deleting unnecessary approval signatures on forms), and redesigned the entire process from care performed to payment received.

Testing the Solution

A critical path analysis was performed on the "as-is" billing process as well as the newly designed "to-be" billing process. This allowed the team to test their solution alongside the existing one.

Analyzing the Results

The critical path analysis also led the team to identify a task within the process (i.e., price acquisition) that had no immediate predecessors but was the cause of many long billing cycles. The team was able to "move" this task to the beginning of the process.

Implementing the Results

Hospital management installed the new business process. The result was a billing process that was an entire month shorter and saved the hospital some 390,000 euros annually.

Source: Based on M. Schoonhoven, C. Lubbers, and R.J.M.M. Does. "Quality Quandaries: Shortening the Throughput Time of a Hospital's Billing Process," *Quality Engineering* 25 (2013), 188–193.

If the process standard deviation is not available or is difficult to compute, which is usually the case, these equations become impractical. In practice, the calculation of control limits is based on the average *range* rather than on standard deviations. We can use the equations

Control chart limits can be found using the range rather than the standard deviation.

$$\text{UCL}_{\bar{x}} = \bar{\bar{x}} + A_2 \bar{R} \qquad (15\text{-}3)$$
$$\text{LCL}_{\bar{x}} = \bar{\bar{x}} - A_2 \bar{R} \qquad (15\text{-}4)$$

where

$\bar{R}$ = average of the samples
A_2 = value found in Table 15.2 (which assumes that $z = 3$)
$\bar{\bar{x}}$ = mean of the sample means

USING EXCEL QM FOR BOX FILLING EXAMPLE The upper and lower limits for this example can be found using Excel QM, as shown in Program 15.1. From the Excel QM menu, select *Quality Control* and specify the *X-Bar* and *R Charts* option. Enter the number of samples (1) and select *Standard Deviation* in the initialization window. When the spreadsheet is initialized, enter the sample size (36), the standard deviation (2), and the mean of the sample (16). The upper and lower limits are immediately displayed.

TABLE 15.2

Factors for Computing Control Chart Limits when $z = 3$

SAMPLE SIZE, n	MEAN FACTOR, A_2	UPPER RANGE, D_4	LOWER RANGE, D_3
2	1.880	3.268	0
3	1.023	2.574	0
4	0.729	2.282	0
5	0.577	2.114	0
6	0.483	2.004	0
7	0.419	1.924	0.076
8	0.373	1.864	0.136
9	0.337	1.816	0.184
10	0.308	1.777	0.223
12	0.266	1.716	0.284
14	0.235	1.671	0.329
16	0.212	1.636	0.364
18	0.194	1.608	0.392
20	0.180	1.586	0.414
25	0.153	1.541	0.459

Source: Reprinted by permission of the American Society for Testing and Materials, copyright 1951. Taken from Special Technical Publication 15-C, "Quality Control of Materials," pp. 63 and 72.

PROGRAM 15.1

Excel QM Solution for Box Filling Example

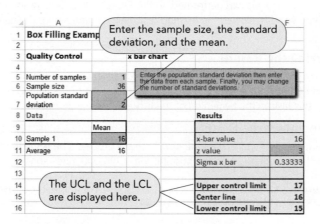

SUPER COLA EXAMPLE Super Cola bottles soft drinks labeled "net weight 16 ounces." An overall process average of 16.01 ounces has been found by taking several batches of samples, in which each sample contained five bottles. The average range of the process is 0.25 ounce. We want to determine the upper and lower control limits for averages for this process.

Looking in Table 15.2 for a sample size of 5 in the mean factor A_2 column, we find the number 0.577. Thus, the upper and lower control chart limits are

$$\text{UCL}_{\bar{x}} = \bar{\bar{x}} + A_2 \bar{R}$$
$$= 16.01 + (0.577)(0.25)$$
$$= 16.01 + 0.144$$
$$= 16.154$$
$$\text{LCL}_{\bar{x}} = \bar{\bar{x}} - A_2 \bar{R}$$
$$= 16.01 - 0.144$$
$$= 15.866$$

The upper control limit is 16.154, and the lower control limit is 15.866.

PROGRAM 15.2

Excel QM Solution for Super Cola Example

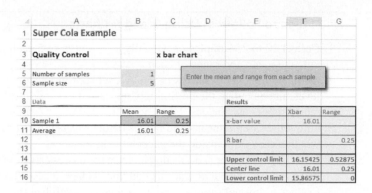

USING EXCEL QM FOR SUPER COLA EXAMPLE The upper and lower limits for this example can be found using Excel QM, as shown in Program 15.2. From the Excel QM menu, select *Quality Control* and specify the *X-Bar* and *R Charts* option. Enter the number of samples (1) and select *Range* in the initialization window. The sample size (5) can be entered in this initialization window or in the spreadsheet. When the spreadsheet is initialized, enter the range (0.25) and the mean of the sample (16.01). The upper and lower limits are immediately displayed.

Setting Range Chart Limits

Dispersion or variability is also important. The central tendency can be under control, but ranges can be out of control.

We just determined the upper and lower control limits for the process *average*. In addition to being concerned with the process average, managers are interested in the *dispersion* or *variability*. Even though the process average is under control, the variability of the process may not be. For example, something may have worked itself loose in a piece of equipment. As a result, the average of the samples may remain the same, but the variation within the samples could be entirely too large and the x-bar charts could be unreliable. For this reason it is necessary to find a control chart for *ranges* in order to monitor the process variability. The theory behind the control charts for ranges is the same for the process average. Limits are established that contain ± 3 standard deviations of the distribution for the average range $\bar{R}$. With a few simplifying assumptions, we can set the upper and lower control limits for ranges:

$$\text{UCL}_R = D_4 \bar{R} \tag{15-5}$$

$$\text{LCL}_R = D_3 \bar{R} \tag{15-6}$$

where

$$\text{UCL}_R = \text{upper control chart limit for the range}$$
$$\text{LCL}_R = \text{lower control chart limit for the range}$$
$$D_4 \text{ and } D_3 = \text{values from Table 15.2}$$

RANGE EXAMPLE As an example, consider a process in which the average *range* is 53 pounds. If the sample size is 5, we want to determine the upper and lower control chart limits.

Looking in Table 15.2 for a sample size of 5, we find that $D_4 = 2.114$ and $D_3 = 0$. The range control chart limits are

$$\text{UCL}_R = D_4 \bar{R}$$
$$= (2.114)(53 \text{ pounds})$$
$$= 112.042 \text{ pounds}$$
$$\text{LCL}_R = D_3 \bar{R}$$
$$= (0)(53 \text{ pounds})$$
$$= 0$$

A summary of the steps used for creating and using control charts for the mean and the range.

Five Steps to Follow in Using $\bar{x}$ and R-Charts

1. Collect 20 to 25 samples of typically $n = 4$ or $n = 5$ each from a stable process and compute the mean and range of each.
2. Compute the overall means ($\bar{\bar{x}}$ and $\bar{R}$), set appropriate control limits, usually at the 99.7% level, and calculate the preliminary upper and lower control limits. If the process is not currently stable, use the desired mean, μ, instead of $\bar{\bar{x}}$ to calculate limits.
3. Graph the sample means and ranges on their respective control charts and determine whether they fall outside the acceptable limits.
4. Investigate points or patterns that indicate the process is out of control. Try to find an assignable cause for the out of control condition, address it accordingly, and then resume the process.
5. Collect additional samples and, if necessary, revalidate the control limits using the new data.

15.5   Control Charts for Attributes

Sampling attributes differ from sampling variables.

Control charts for $\bar{x}$ and R do not apply when we are sampling *attributes*, which are typically classified as defective or nondefective. Measuring defectives involves counting them (e.g., number of bad lightbulbs in a given lot, or number of letters or data entry records typed with errors). There are two kinds of attribute control charts: (1) those that measure the percent defective in a sample, called *p-charts*, and (2) those that count the number of defects, called *c-charts*.

p-Charts

p-chart limits are based on the binomial distribution and are easy to compute.

p-charts are the principal means of controlling attributes. Although attributes that are either good or bad follow the binomial distribution, the normal distribution can be used to calculate p-chart limits when sample sizes are large. The procedure resembles the $\bar{x}$-chart approach, which is also based on the central limit theorem.

The formulas for p-chart upper and lower control limits follow:

$$\text{UCL}_p = \bar{p} + z\sigma_p \tag{15-7}$$

$$\text{LCL}_p = \bar{p} - z\sigma_p \tag{15-8}$$

where

$\bar{p}$ = mean proportion or fraction defective in the sample

z = number of standard deviations ($z = 2$ for 95.5% limits; $z = 3$ for 99.7% limits)

σ_p = standard deviation of the sampling distribution

σ_p is estimated by $\hat{\sigma}_p$, which is

$$\hat{\sigma}_p = \sqrt{\frac{\bar{p}(1 - \bar{p})}{n}} \tag{15-9}$$

where n is the size of each sample.

ARCO p-CHART EXAMPLE Using a popular database software package, data-entry clerks at ARCO key in thousands of insurance records each day. Samples of the work of 20 clerks are shown in the following table. One hundred records entered by each clerk were carefully examined to determine if they contained any errors; the fraction defective in each sample was then computed.

IN ACTION   Safer Drinking Water Through SPC

Nitrate (NO_3^-) contamination levels of groundwater has risen to alarming levels in recent years. The United States Environmental Protection Agency limits nitrate contamination levels to 45 mg per liter. Early detection of rising contamination levels is critical in providing safe drinking water.

An environmental research team utilized a statistical process control (SPC) chart to monitor nitrate levels in groundwater. In particular, the team used a special SPC chart known as an "autoregressive integrated moving average" (ARIMA) chart. This chart integrates elements from the x-bar chart of this chapter as well as moving averages which were studied in Chapter 5 of this book.

After collecting data from several different aquifers, the researchers built the statistical process control charts and checked them for out-of-control conditions. The environmental research team paid careful attention to increasing trends of five points (one of the out-of-control conditions specified in Figure 15.1) on the control chart. Fortunately, no out-of-control conditions were identified. However, the team now had a tool that improved early detections of rising nitrate levels by several days. That's a lot of water!

Source: Based on J. C. García-Díaz "Monitoring and Forecasting Nitrate Concentration in the Ground Water Using Statistical Process Control and Time Series Analysis: A Case Study," *Stochastic Environmental Research and Risk Assessment* 25 (2011), 331–339.

SAMPLE NUMBER	NUMBER OF ERRORS	FRACTION DEFECTIVE	SAMPLE NUMBER	NUMBER OF ERRORS	FRACTION DEFECTIVE
1	6	0.06	11	6	0.06
2	5	0.05	12	1	0.01
3	0	0.00	13	8	0.08
4	1	0.01	14	7	0.07
5	4	0.04	15	5	0.05
6	2	0.02	16	4	0.04
7	5	0.05	17	11	0.11
8	3	0.03	18	3	0.03
9	3	0.03	19	0	0.00
10	2	0.02	20	4	0.04
				80	

We want to set control limits that include 99.7% of the random variation in the entry process when it is in control. Thus, $z = 3$.

$$\bar{p} = \frac{\text{Total number of errors}}{\text{Total number of records examined}} = \frac{80}{(100)(20)} = 0.04$$

$$\hat{\sigma}_p = \sqrt{\frac{(0.04)(1 - 0.04)}{100}} = 0.02$$

(*Note:* 100 *is the size of each sample* = n)

$$UCL_p = \bar{p} + z\hat{\sigma}_p = 0.04 + 3(0.02) = 0.10$$

$$LCL_p = \bar{p} - z\hat{\sigma}_p = 0.04 - 3(0.02) = 0 \longleftarrow$$

(since we cannot have a negative percentage defective)

When we plot the control limits and the sample fraction defectives, we find that only one data-entry clerk (number 17) is out of control. The firm may wish to examine that person's work a bit more closely to see whether a serious problem exists (see Figure 15.3).

FIGURE 15.3
p-Chart for Data Entry
for ARCO

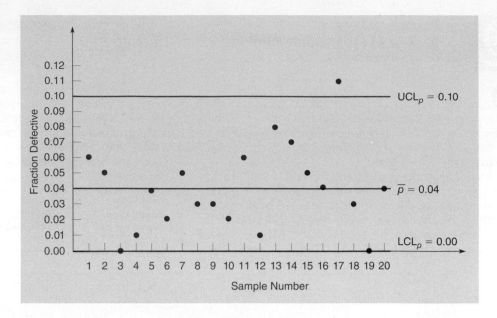

USING EXCEL QM FOR *p*-CHARTS Excel QM can be used to develop the limits for a *p*-chart, determine which samples exceed the limits, and develop the graph. Program 15.3 provides the output for the ARCO example, with the graph. To use Excel QM, from the Add-Ins tab select *Excel QM*. From the drop-down menu, select *Quality Control* and specify the *p Charts* option. Enter the number of samples (20), input a title if desired, and select *Graph* if you wish to view the *p*-chart. When the spreadsheet is initialized, enter the size of each sample (100) and the number of defects in each of the 20 samples. One of the 20 samples (sample number 17) is identified as a sample that exceeds the limits.

c-Charts

c-charts count the number of defects, whereas p-charts track the percentage defective.

In the ARCO example discussed previously, we counted the number of defective database records entered. A defective record is one that was not exactly correct. A bad record may contain more than one defect, however. We use **c-charts** to control the *number* of defects per unit of output (or per insurance record in this case).

PROGRAM 15.3
**Excel QM Solution for
ARCO *p*-Chart Example**

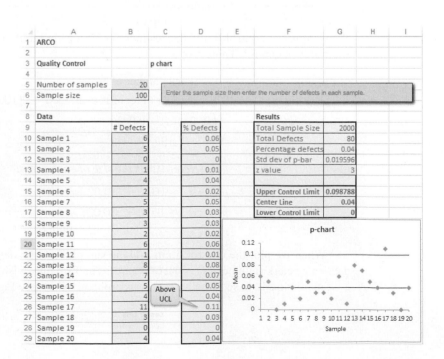

Control charts for defects are helpful for monitoring processes in which a large number of potential errors can occur but the actual number that do occur is relatively small. Defects may be mistyped words in a newspaper, blemishes on a table, or missing pickles on a fast-food hamburger.

The Poisson probability distribution, which has a variance equal to its mean, is the basis for c-charts. Since $\bar{c}$ is the mean number of defects per unit, the standard deviation is equal to $\sqrt{\bar{c}}$. To compute 99.7% control limits for c, we use the formula

$$\bar{c} \pm 3\sqrt{\bar{c}} \tag{15-10}$$

Here is an example.

RED TOP CAB COMPANY c-CHART EXAMPLE Red Top Cab Company receives several complaints per day about the behavior of its drivers. Over a nine-day period (in which days are the units of measure), the owner received the following number of calls from irate passengers: 3, 0, 8, 9, 6, 7, 4, 9, 8, for a total of 54 complaints.

To compute 99.7% control limits, we take

$$\bar{c} = \frac{54}{9} = 6 \text{ complaints per day}$$

Thus,

$$\text{UCL}_c = \bar{c} + 3\sqrt{\bar{c}} = 6 + 3\sqrt{6} = 6 + 3(2.45) = 13.35$$
$$\text{LCL}_c = \bar{c} - 3\sqrt{\bar{c}} = 6 - 3\sqrt{6} = 6 - 3(2.45) = 0 \longleftarrow$$

(because we cannot have a negative control limit) ⟶

After the owner plotted a control chart summarizing these data and posted it prominently in the drivers' locker room, the number of calls received dropped to an average of 3 per day. Can you explain why this may have occurred?

USING EXCEL QM FOR c-CHARTS Excel QM can be used to develop the limits for a c-chart, determine which samples exceed the limits, and develop the graph. Program 15.4 provides the output for the Red Top Cab Company example, with the graph. To use Excel QM, from the Add Ins tab select *Excel QM*. From the drop-down menu, select *Quality Control* and specify the *c Charts* option. Enter the number of samples (9 days, in this example), input a title if desired, and select *Graph* if you wish to view the c-chart. When the spreadsheet is initialized, enter the number of complaints (i.e., defects) in each of the 9 samples.

PROGRAM 15.4

Excel QM Solution for Red Top Cab Company c-Chart Example

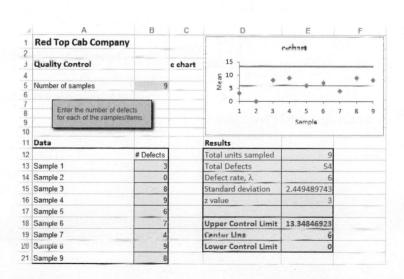

Summary

To the manager of a firm producing goods or services, quality is the degree to which the product meets specifications. Quality control has become one of the most important precepts of business.

The expression "quality cannot be inspected into a product" is a central theme of organizations today. More and more world-class companies are following the ideas of total quality management (TQM), which emphasizes the entire organization, from supplier to customer.

Statistical aspects of quality control date to the 1920s but are of special interest in our global marketplaces of this new century. Statistical process control tools described in this chapter include the $\bar{x}$- and R-charts for variable sampling and the p- and c-charts for attribute sampling.

Glossary

Assignable Variation Variation in the production process that can be traced to specific causes.

c-Chart A quality control chart that is used to control the number of defects per unit of output.

Central Limit Theorem The theoretical foundation for $\bar{x}$-charts. It states that regardless of the distribution of the population of all parts or services, the distribution of $\bar{x}$s will tend to follow a normal curve as the sample size grows.

Control Chart A graphic presentation of process data over time.

Natural Variations Variabilities that affect almost every production process to some degree and are to be expected; also known as common causes.

p-Chart A quality control chart that is used to control attributes.

Quality The degree to which a product or service meets the specifications set for it.

R-Chart A process control chart that tracks the "range" within a sample; indicates that a gain or loss of uniformity has occurred in a production process.

Total Quality Management (TQM) An emphasis on quality that encompasses the entire organization.

x-Chart A quality control chart for variables that indicates when changes occur in the central tendency of a production process.

Key Equations

(15-1) Upper control limit (UCL) $= \bar{\bar{x}} + z\sigma_{\bar{x}}$
Upper limit for an $\bar{x}$-chart using standard deviations.

(15-2) Lower control limit (LCL) $= \bar{\bar{x}} - z\sigma_{\bar{x}}$
Lower control limit for an $\bar{x}$-chart using standard deviations.

(15-3) $\text{UCL}_{\bar{x}} = \bar{\bar{x}} + A_2\bar{R}$
Upper control limit for an $\bar{x}$-chart using tabled values and ranges.

(15-4) $\text{LCL}_{\bar{x}} = \bar{\bar{x}} - A_2\bar{R}$
Lower control limit for an $\bar{x}$-chart using tabled values and ranges.

(15-5) $\text{UCL}_R = D_4\bar{R}$
Upper control limit for a range chart.

(15-6) $\text{LCL}_R = D_3\bar{R}$
Lower control limit for a range chart.

(15-7) $\text{UCL}_p = \bar{p} + z\sigma_p$
Upper control unit for a p-chart.

(15-8) $\text{LCL}_p = \bar{p} - z\sigma_p$
Lower control limit for a p-chart.

(15-9) $\hat{\sigma}_p = \sqrt{\dfrac{\bar{p}(1 - \bar{p})}{n}}$

Estimated standard deviation of a binomial distribution.

(15-10) $\bar{c} \pm 3\sqrt{\bar{c}}$
Upper and lower limits for a c-chart.

Solved Problems

Solved Problem 15-1

The manufacturer of precision parts for drill presses produces round shafts for use in the construction of drill presses. The average diameter of a shaft is 0.56 inch. The inspection samples contain six shafts each. The average range of these samples is 0.006 inch. Determine the upper and lower control chart limits.

Solution

The mean factor A_2 from Table 15.2, where the sample size is 6, is seen to be 0.483. With this factor, you can obtain the upper and lower control limits:

$$UCL_{\bar{x}} = 0.56 + (0.483)(0.006)$$
$$= 0.56 + 0.0029 = 0.5629$$
$$LCL_{\bar{x}} = 0.56 - 0.0029$$
$$= 0.5571$$

Solved Problem 15-2

Nocaf Drinks, Inc., a producer of decaffeinated coffee, bottles Nocaf. Each bottle should have a net weight of 4 ounces. The machine that fills the bottles with coffee is new, and the operations manager wants to make sure that it is properly adjusted. The operations manager takes a sample of $n = 8$ bottles and records the average and range in ounces for each sample. The data for several samples are given in the following table. Note that every sample consists of 8 bottles.

SAMPLE	SAMPLE RANGE	SAMPLE AVERAGE	SAMPLE	SAMPLE RANGE	SAMPLE AVERAGE
A	0.41	4.00	E	0.56	4.17
B	0.55	4.16	F	0.62	3.93
C	0.44	3.99	G	0.54	3.98
D	0.48	4.00	H	0.44	4.01

Is the machine properly adjusted and in control?

Solution

We first find that $\bar{\bar{x}} = 4.03$ and $\bar{R} = 0.51$. Then, using Table 15.2, we find

$$UCL_{\bar{x}} = \bar{\bar{x}} + A_2\bar{R} = 4.03 + (0.373)(0.51) = 4.22$$
$$LCL_{\bar{x}} = \bar{\bar{x}} - A_2\bar{R} = 4.03 - (0.373)(0.51) = 3.84$$
$$UCL_R = D_4\bar{R} = (1.864)(0.51) = 0.95$$
$$LCL_R = D_3\bar{R} = (0.136)(0.51) = 0.07$$

It appears that the process average and range are both in control.

Solved Problem 15-3

Crabill Electronics, Inc., makes resistors, and among the last 100 resistors inspected, the percentage defective has been 0.05. Determine the upper and lower limits for this process for 99.7% confidence.

Solution

$$UCL_p = \bar{p} + 3\sqrt{\frac{\bar{p}(1 - \bar{p})}{n}} = 0.05 + 3\sqrt{\frac{(0.05)(1 - 0.05)}{100}}$$
$$= 0.05 + 3(0.0218) = 0.1154$$
$$LCL_p = \bar{p} - 3\sqrt{\frac{\bar{p}(1 - \bar{p})}{n}} = 0.05 - 3(0.0218)$$
$$= 0.05 - 0.0654 = 0 \text{ (since percent defective cannot be negative)}$$

Self-Test

- Before taking the self-test, refer to the learning objectives at the beginning of the chapter, the notes in the margins, and the glossary at the end of the chapter.
- Use the key at the back of the book to correct your answers.
- Restudy pages that correspond to any questions that you answered incorrectly or material you feel uncertain about.

1. The degree to which the product or service meets specifications is one definition of
   a. sigma.
   b. quality.
   c. range.
   d. process variability.

2. A control chart for monitoring processes in which values are measured in continuous units such as weight or volume is called a control chart for
   a. attributes.
   b. measurements.
   c. variables.
   d. quality.

3. The type of chart used to control the number of defects per unit of output is the
   a. $\bar{x}$-chart.
   b. R-chart.
   c. p-chart.
   d. c-chart.

4. Control charts for attributes are
   a. p-charts.
   b. m-charts.
   c. R-charts.
   d. $\bar{x}$-charts.

5. The Poisson distribution is often used with
   a. R-charts.
   b. p-charts.
   c. c-charts.
   d. x-charts.

6. A type of variability that indicates that a process is out of control is called
   a. natural variation.
   b. assignable variation.
   c. random variation.
   d. average variation.

7. A company is implementing a new quality control program. Items are sampled and classified as being defective or nondefective. The type of control chart that should be used is
   a. an R-chart.
   b. a control chart for variables.
   c. a control chart for attributes.
   d. a control limit chart.

8. After a control chart (for means) has been developed, samples are taken and the average is computed for each sample. The process could be considered out of control if
   a. one of the sample means is above the upper control limit.
   b. one of the sample means is below the lower control limit.
   c. five consecutive sample means show a consistent trend (either increasing or decreasing).
   d. all of the above were true.

9. A machine is supposed to fill soft drink cans to 12 ounces. It appears that although the average amount in the cans is about 12 ounces (based on sample means), there is a great deal of variability in each of the individual cans. The type of chart that would best detect this problem would be
   a. a p-chart.
   b. an R-chart.
   c. a c-chart.
   d. an attribute chart.

10. If a process only has random variations (it is in control), then 95.5% of the time the sample averages will fall within
   a. 1 standard deviation of the population mean.
   b. 2 standard deviations of the population mean.
   c. 3 standard deviations of the population mean.
   d. 4 standard deviations of the population mean.

Discussion Questions and Problems

Discussion Questions

15-1 Why is the central limit theorem so important in quality control?

15-2 Why are $\bar{x}$- and R-charts usually used hand in hand?

15-3 Explain the difference between control charts for variables and control charts for attributes.

15-4 Explain the difference between c-charts and p-charts.

15-5 When using a control chart, what are some patterns that would indicate that the process is out of control?

15-6 What might cause a process to be out of control?

15-7 Explain why a process can be out of control even though all the samples fall within the upper and lower control limits.

Problems*

15-8 Shader Storage Technologies produces refrigeration units for food producers and retail food establishments. The overall average temperature that these units maintain is 46° Fahrenheit. The average range is 2° Fahrenheit. Samples of 6 are taken to monitor the process. Determine the upper and lower control chart limits for averages and ranges for these refrigeration units.

15-9 When set at the standard position, Autopitch can throw hard balls toward a batter at an average speed of 60 mph. Autopitch devices are made for both major- and minor-league teams to help them improve their batting averages. Autopitch executives take samples of 10 Autopitch devices at a time to monitor these devices and to maintain the highest quality. The average range is 3 mph. Using control-chart techniques, determine control-chart limits for averages and ranges for Autopitch.

15-10 Zipper Products, Inc., produces granola cereal, granola bars, and other natural food products. Its natural granola cereal is sampled to ensure proper weight. Each sample contains eight boxes of cereal. The overall average for the samples is 17 ounces. The range is only 0.5 ounce. Determine the upper and lower control-chart limits for averages for the boxes of cereal.

15-11 Small boxes of NutraFlakes cereal are labeled "net weight 10 ounces." Each hour, random samples of size $n = 4$ boxes are weighed to check process control. Five hours of observations yielded the following:

		WEIGHT		
TIME	BOX 1	BOX 2	BOX 3	BOX 4
9 A.M.	9.8	10.4	9.9	10.3
10 A.M.	10.1	10.2	9.9	9.8
11 A.M.	9.9	10.5	10.3	10.1
Noon	9.7	9.8	10.3	10.2
1 P.M.	9.7	10.1	9.9	9.9

Using these data, construct limits for $\bar{x}$- and R-Charts. Is the process in control? What other steps should the QC department follow at this point?

15-12 Sampling four pieces of precision-cut wire (to be used in computer assembly) every hour for the past 24 hours has produced the following results:

HOUR	$\bar{x}$	R	HOUR	$\bar{x}$	R
1	3.25"	0.71"	13	3.11"	0.85"
2	3.10	1.18	14	2.83	1.31
3	3.22	1.43	15	3.12	1.06
4	3.39	1.26	16	2.84	0.50
5	3.07	1.17	17	2.86	1.43
6	2.86	0.32	18	2.74	1.29
7	3.05	0.53	19	3.41	1.61
8	2.65	1.13	20	2.89	1.09
9	3.02	0.71	21	2.65	1.08
10	2.85	1.33	22	3.28	0.46
11	2.83	1.17	23	2.94	1.58
12	2.97	0.40	24	2.64	0.97

Develop appropriate control limits and determine whether there is any cause for concern in the cutting process.

15-13 Due to the poor quality of various semiconductor products used in their manufacturing process, Microlaboratories has decided to develop a QC program. Because the semiconductor parts they get from suppliers are either good or defective, Milton Fisher has decided to develop control charts for attributes. The total number of semiconductors in every sample is 200. Furthermore, Milton would like to determine the upper control chart limit and the lower control chart limit for various values of the fraction defective ($\bar{p}$) in the sample taken. To allow more flexibility, he has decided to develop a table that lists values for $\bar{p}$, UCL, and LCL. The values for $\bar{p}$ should range from 0.01 to 0.10, incrementing by 0.01 each time. What are the 10 UCLs and the LCLs for 99.7% confidence?

15-14 For the past two months, Suzan Shader has been concerned about machine number 5 at the West Factory. To make sure that the machine is operating correctly, samples are taken, and the average and range for each sample is computed. Each sample consists of 12 items produced from the machine. Recently, 12 samples were taken, and for each, the sample range and average were computed. The sample range and sample average were 1.1 and 46 for the first sample, 1.31 and 45 for the second sample, 0.91 and 46 for the third sample, and 1.1 and 47 for the fourth sample. After the fourth sample, the sample averages increased. For the fifth sample, the range was 1.21, and the average was 48; for sample number 6, it was 0.82 and 47; for sample number 7, it was 0.86 and 50; and for the eighth sample, it was 1.11 and 49. After the eighth sample, the sample average continued to increase, never getting below 50. For sample number 9, the range and average were 1.12 and 51; for sample number 10, they were 0.99 and 52; for sample number 11, they were 0.86 and 50; and for sample number 12, they were 1.2 and 52.

Although Suzan's boss wasn't overly concerned about the process, Suzan was. During installation, the supplier set a value of 47 for the process average with an average range of 1.0. It was Suzan's feeling that something was definitely wrong with machine number 5. Do you agree?

:15-15 Kitty Products caters to the growing market for cat supplies, with a full line of products, ranging from litter to toys to flea powder. One of its newer products, a tube of fluid that prevents hair balls in long-haired cats, is produced by an automated machine that is set to fill each tube with 63.5 grams of paste.

To keep this filling process under control, four tubes are pulled randomly from the assembly line every 4 hours. After several days, the data shown in the following table resulted. Set control limits for this process and graph the sample data for both the $\bar{x}$- and R-charts.

:15-16 Colonel Electric is a large company that produces lightbulbs and other electrical products. One particular lightbulb is supposed to have an average life of about 1,000 hours before it burns out. Periodically the company will test 5 of these and measure the average time before these burn out. The following table gives the results of 10 such samples:

SAMPLE NO.	$\bar{x}$	R	SAMPLE NO.	$\bar{x}$	R	SAMPLE NO.	$\bar{x}$	R
1	63.5	2.0	10	63.5	1.3	18	63.6	1.8
2	63.6	1.0	11	63.3	1.8	19	63.8	1.3
3	63.7	1.7	12	63.2	1.0	20	63.5	1.6
4	63.9	0.9	13	63.6	1.8	21	63.9	1.0
5	63.4	1.2	14	63.3	1.5	22	63.2	1.8
6	63.0	1.6	15	63.4	1.7	23	63.3	1.7
7	63.2	1.8	16	63.4	1.4	24	64.0	2.0
8	63.3	1.3	17	63.5	1.1	25	63.4	1.5
9	63.7	1.6						

SAMPLE	1	2	3	4	5	6	7	8	9	10
Mean	979	1087	1080	934	1072	1007	952	986	1063	958
Range	50	94	57	65	135	134	101	98	145	84

(a) What is the overall average of these means? What is the average range?

(b) What are the upper and lower control limits for a 99.7% control chart for the mean?

(c) Does this process appear to be in control? Explain.

•15-17 For Problem 15-16, develop upper and lower control limits for the range. Do these samples indicate that the process is in control?

:15-18 Kate Drew has been hand-painting wooden Christmas ornaments for several years. Recently, she has hired some friends to help her increase the volume of her business. In checking the quality of the work, she notices that some slight blemishes occasionally are apparent. A sample of 20 pieces of work resulted in the following number of blemishes on each piece: 0, 2, 1, 0, 0, 3, 2, 0, 4, 1, 2, 0, 0, 1, 2, 1, 0, 0, 0, 1. Develop upper and lower control limits for the number of blemishes on each piece.

:15-19 A new president at Big State University has made student satisfaction with the enrollment and registration process one of her highest priorities. Students must see an advisor, sign up for classes, obtain a parking permit, pay tuition and fees, and buy textbooks and other supplies. During one registration period, 10 students every hour are sampled and asked about satisfaction with each of these areas. Twelve different groups of students were sampled, and the number in each group who had at least one complaint are as follows: 0, 2, 1, 0, 0, 1, 3, 0, 1, 2, 2, 0.

Develop upper and lower control limits (99.7%) for the proportion of students with complaints.

15-20 Cybersecurity is an area of increasing concern. The National Security Agency (NSA) monitors the number of hits at sensitive Web sites. When the number of hits is much larger than normal, there is cause for concern and further investigation is warranted. For the past twelve months the number of hits at one such Web site has been: 181, 162, 172, 169, 185, 212, 190, 168, 190, 191, 197, and 204. Determine the upper and lower control limits (99.7%) for the associated c-chart. Using the upper control limit as your reference, at what point should the NSA take action?

15-21 V. S. Industries in Parkersburg, West Virginia is a small manufacturer of military grade hybrid microcircuits. One of the many quality assurance procedures required by Military Standard 883J (MIL-STD-883J) for hybrid microcircuits is known as nondestructive bond pull (method number 2023.7 in MIL-STD-883J). The procedure involves pulling on a random sample of wires within the hybrid microcircuit with a prespecified amount of force. If the wire tears, breaks, or separates in any way from the circuit it fails the test and is considered defective and scrapped. In a recent batch of 1000 devices 13 failed the pull test. Determine upper and lower control limits for the associated p-chart.

Internet Homework Problems

See our Internet home page, at **www.pearsonhighered.com/render**, for additional homework problems, Problems 15-22 to 15-25.

Internet Case Study

See our Internet home page, at **www.pearsonhighered.com/render**, for this additional case study: **Bayfield Mud Company**. This case involes bags of mud-treating agents used in drilling for oil and natural gas.

Bibliography

Crosby, P. B. *Quality Is Free. New* York: McGraw-Hill, 1979.

Deming, W. E. *Out of the Crisis.* Cambridge, MA: MIT Center for Advanced Engineering Study, 1986.

Foster, S. Thomas. *Managing Quality*, 2nd ed. Upper Saddle River, NJ: Prentice Hall, 2004.

Foster, S. Thomas. *Managing Quality: Integrating the Supply Chain* , 3rd ed. Upper Saddle River, NJ: Prentice Hall, 2007.

Goetsch, David, and Stanley Davis. *Quality Management*, 5th ed. Upper Saddle River, NJ: Prentice Hall, 2006.

Juran, Joseph M., and A. Blanton Godfrey. *Juran's Quality Handbook*, 5th ed. New York: McGraw-Hill, 1999.

Naveh, Eitan, and Miriam Erez. "Innovation and Attention to Detail in the Quality Improvement Paradigm," *Management Science* 50, 11 (November 2004): 1576–1586.

Ravichandran, T. "Swiftness and Intensity of Administrative Innovation Adoption: An Empirical Study of TQM in Information Systems," *Decision Sciences* 31, 3 (Summer 2000): 691–724.

Smith, Gerald. *Statistical Process Control and Quality Improvement*, 5th ed. Upper Saddle River, NJ: Prentice Hall, 2004.

Summers, Donna. *Quality*, 4th ed. Upper Saddle River, NJ: Prentice Hall, 2006.

Tarí, Juan José, José Francisco Molina, and Juan Luis Castejón. "The Relationship between Quality Management Practices and Their Effects on Quality Outcomes," *European Journal of Operational Research* 183, 2 (December 2007): 483–501.

Wilson, Darryl D., and David A. Collier. "An Empirical Investigation of the Malcolm Baldrige National Quality Award Casual Model," *Decision Sciences* 31, 2 (Spring 2000): 361–390,

Witte, Robert D. "Quality Control Defined," *Contract Management* 47, 5 (May 2007): 51–53.

Zhu, Kaijie, Rachel Q. Zhang, and Fugee Tsung. "Pushing Quality Improvement Along Supply Chains," *Management Science* 53, 3 (March 2007): 421–436.

Appendix 15.1: Using QM for Windows for SPC

The QM for Windows Quality Control module can compute most of the SPC control charts and limits introduced in this chapter. Once the module is selected, we select *New* and indicate which type of chart (p-chart, x-bar chart, or c-chart). Program 15.5A displays the different possible choices in QM for Windows. When the p-chart is selected for the ARCO example, the initialization window opens, as displayed in Program 15.5B. We enter a title and the number of samples (20 in this example), and then click *OK*. An input window opens, and we enter the 20 sample values (number of errors or defects in the sample) and specify the sample size (100). We click *Solve*, and the output window opens, as illustrated in Program 15.5C. The original input data and the sample size are displayed, as are the results. While this problem has been set to use the 3 standard deviation (sigma) limits, other values are possible, also. QM for Windows computes the average proportion $(\overline{p})$, standard deviation, and upper and lower control limits. From this screen, we can select *Window* and select *Control Chart* to actually view the chart and look for patterns which might indicate that the process is out of control.

PROGRAM 15.5A

Using *p*-Charts from the Quality Control Module in QM for Windows

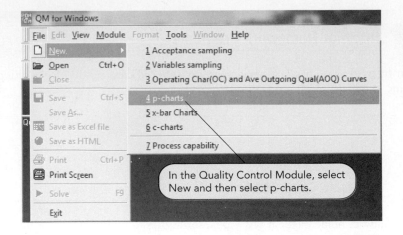

In the Quality Control Module, select New and then select p-charts.

PROGRAM 15.5B

QM for Windows Initialization Window for *p*-Charts with ARCO Insurance

Create data set for Quality Control/p-charts

Title: ARCO Insurance Records   Modify default title

Number of Samples   20

Enter a title and specify the number of samples.

Row names | Column names | Overview

- Sample 1, Sample 2, Sample 3,...
- a, b, c, d, e, ...
- A, B, C, D, E, ...
- 1, 2, 3, 4, 5, ...
- January, February, March, April, ...
  Click here to set start month
- Other

Cancel   Help   OK

PROGRAM 15.5C

QM for Windows Solution for ARCO Insurance Records Example

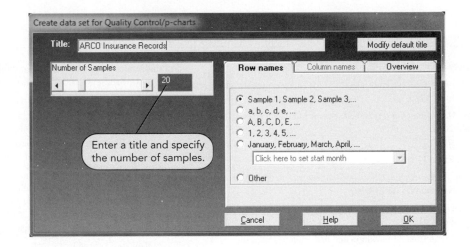

Program 15.5 Solution

Sample	Number of Defects	Fraction Defective		3 sigma (99.73%)
Sample 1	6	.06	Total Defects	80
Sample 2	5	.05	Total units sampled	2,000
Sample 3	0	0	Defect rate (pbar)	.04
Sample 4	1	.01	Std dev of proportions	.0196
Sample 5	4	.04		
Sample 6	2	.02	UCL (Upper control limit)	.0988
Sample 7	5	.05	CL (Center line)	.04
Sample 8	3	.03	LCL (Lower Control Limit)	0
Sample 9	3	.03		
Sample 10				
Sample 11				
Sample 12				
Sample 13				
Sample 14				
Sample 15	5	.05		
Sample 16	4	.04		
Sample 17	11	.11		
Sample 18	3	.03		
Sample 19	0	0		
Sample 20	4	.04		

Once the data has been input, put the number of defects in this column and specify the size of each of the 20 samples. Then click Solve and this final screen appears.

Appendices

Appendix A: Areas Under the Standard Normal Curve

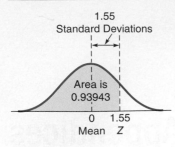

1.55
Standard Deviations

Area is
0.93943

0   1.55
Mean Z

Example: To find the area under the normal curve, you must know how many standard deviations that point is to the right of the mean. Then the area under the normal curve can be read directly from the normal table. For example, the total area under the normal curve for a point that is 1.55 standard deviations to the right of the mean is 0.93943.

	0.00	0.01	0.02	0.03	0.04	0.05	0.06	0.07	0.08	0.09
0.0	0.50000	0.50399	0.50798	0.51197	0.51595	0.51994	0.52392	0.52790	0.53188	0.53586
0.1	0.53983	0.54380	0.54776	0.55172	0.55567	0.55962	0.56356	0.56749	0.57142	0.57535
0.2	0.57926	0.58317	0.58706	0.59095	0.59483	0.59871	0.60257	0.60642	0.61026	0.61409
0.3	0.61791	0.62172	0.62552	0.62930	0.63307	0.63683	0.64058	0.64431	0.64803	0.65173
0.4	0.65542	0.65910	0.66276	0.66640	0.67003	0.67364	0.67724	0.68082	0.68439	0.68793
0.5	0.69146	0.69497	0.69847	0.70194	0.70540	0.70884	0.71226	0.71566	0.71904	0.72240
0.6	0.72575	0.72907	0.73237	0.73565	0.73891	0.74215	0.74537	0.74857	0.75175	0.75490
0.7	0.75804	0.76115	0.76424	0.76730	0.77035	0.77337	0.77637	0.77935	0.78230	0.78524
0.8	0.78814	0.79103	0.79389	0.79673	0.79955	0.80234	0.80511	0.80785	0.81057	0.81327
0.9	0.81594	0.81859	0.82121	0.82381	0.82639	0.82894	0.83147	0.83398	0.83646	0.83891
1.0	0.84134	0.84375	0.84614	0.84849	0.85083	0.85314	0.85543	0.85769	0.85993	0.86214
1.1	0.86433	0.86650	0.86864	0.87076	0.87286	0.87493	0.87698	0.87900	0.88100	0.88298
1.2	0.88493	0.88686	0.88877	0.89065	0.89251	0.89435	0.89617	0.89796	0.89973	0.90147
1.3	0.90320	0.90490	0.90658	0.90824	0.90988	0.91149	0.91309	0.91466	0.91621	0.91774
1.4	0.91924	0.92073	0.92220	0.92364	0.92507	0.92647	0.92785	0.92922	0.93056	0.93189
1.5	0.93319	0.93448	0.93574	0.93699	0.93822	0.93943	0.94062	0.94179	0.94295	0.94408
1.6	0.94520	0.94630	0.94738	0.94845	0.94950	0.95053	0.95154	0.95254	0.95352	0.95449
1.7	0.95543	0.95637	0.95728	0.95818	0.95907	0.95994	0.96080	0.96164	0.96246	0.96327
1.8	0.96407	0.96485	0.96562	0.96638	0.96712	0.96784	0.96856	0.96926	0.96995	0.97062
1.9	0.97128	0.97193	0.97257	0.97320	0.97381	0.97441	0.97500	0.97558	0.97615	0.97670
2.0	0.97725	0.97778	0.97831	0.97882	0.97932	0.97982	0.98030	0.98077	0.98124	0.98169
2.1	0.98214	0.98257	0.98300	0.98341	0.98382	0.98422	0.98461	0.98500	0.98537	0.98574
2.2	0.98610	0.98645	0.98679	0.98713	0.98745	0.98778	0.98809	0.98840	0.98870	0.98899
2.3	0.98928	0.98956	0.98983	0.99010	0.99036	0.99061	0.99086	0.99111	0.99134	0.99158
2.4	0.99180	0.99202	0.99224	0.99245	0.99266	0.99286	0.99305	0.99324	0.99343	0.99361
2.5	0.99379	0.99396	0.99413	0.99430	0.99446	0.99461	0.99477	0.99492	0.99506	0.99520
2.6	0.99534	0.99547	0.99560	0.99573	0.99585	0.99598	0.99609	0.99621	0.99632	0.99643
2.7	0.99653	0.99664	0.99674	0.99683	0.99693	0.99702	0.99711	0.99720	0.99728	0.99736
2.8	0.99744	0.99752	0.99760	0.99767	0.99774	0.99781	0.99788	0.99795	0.99801	0.99807
2.9	0.99813	0.99819	0.99825	0.99831	0.99836	0.99841	0.99846	0.99851	0.99856	0.99861
3.0	0.99865	0.99869	0.99874	0.99878	0.99882	0.99886	0.99889	0.99893	0.99896	0.99900
3.1	0.99903	0.99906	0.99910	0.99913	0.99916	0.99918	0.99921	0.99924	0.99926	0.99929
3.2	0.99931	0.99934	0.99936	0.99938	0.99940	0.99942	0.99944	0.99946	0.99948	0.99950

	0.00	0.01	0.02	0.03	0.04	0.05	0.06	0.07	0.08	0.09
3.3	0.99952	0.99953	0.99955	0.99957	0.99958	0.99960	0.99961	0.99962	0.99964	0.99965
3.4	0.99966	0.99968	0.99969	0.99970	0.99971	0.99972	0.99973	0.99974	0.99975	0.99976
3.5	0.99977	0.99978	0.99978	0.99979	0.99980	0.99981	0.99981	0.99982	0.99983	0.99983
3.6	0.99984	0.99985	0.99985	0.99986	0.99986	0.99987	0.99987	0.99998	0.99988	0.99989
3.7	0.99989	0.99990	0.99990	0.99990	0.99991	0.99991	0.99992	0.99992	0.99992	0.99992
3.8	0.99993	0.99993	0.99993	0.99994	0.99994	0.99994	0.99994	0.99995	0.99995	0.99995
3.9	0.99995	0.99995	0.99996	0.99996	0.99996	0.99996	0.99996	0.99996	0.99997	0.99997

Appendix B: Binomial Probabilities

Probability of exactly r successes in n trials

n	r	0.05	0.10	0.15	0.20	0.25	0.30	0.35	0.40	0.45	0.50
1	0	0.9500	0.9000	0.8500	0.8000	0.7500	0.7000	0.6500	0.6000	0.5500	0.5000
	1	0.0500	0.1000	0.1500	0.2000	0.2500	0.3000	0.3500	0.4000	0.4500	0.5000
2	0	0.9025	0.8100	0.7225	0.6400	0.5625	0.4900	0.4225	0.3600	0.3025	0.2500
	1	0.0950	0.1800	0.2550	0.3200	0.3750	0.4200	0.4550	0.4800	0.4950	0.5000
	2	0.0025	0.0100	0.0225	0.0400	0.0625	0.0900	0.1225	0.1600	0.2025	0.2500
3	0	0.8574	0.7290	0.6141	0.5120	0.4219	0.3430	0.2746	0.2160	0.1664	0.1250
	1	0.1354	0.2430	0.3251	0.3840	0.4219	0.4410	0.4436	0.4320	0.4084	0.3750
	2	0.0071	0.0270	0.0574	0.0960	0.1406	0.1890	0.2389	0.2880	0.3341	0.3750
	3	0.0001	0.0010	0.0034	0.0080	0.0156	0.0270	0.0429	0.0640	0.0911	0.1250
4	0	0.8145	0.6561	0.5220	0.4096	0.3164	0.2401	0.1785	0.1296	0.0915	0.0625
	1	0.1715	0.2916	0.3685	0.4096	0.4219	0.4116	0.3845	0.3456	0.2995	0.2500
	2	0.0135	0.0486	0.0975	0.1536	0.2109	0.2646	0.3105	0.3456	0.3675	0.3750
	3	0.0005	0.0036	0.0115	0.0256	0.0469	0.0756	0.1115	0.1536	0.2005	0.2500
	4	0.0000	0.0001	0.0005	0.0016	0.0039	0.0081	0.0150	0.0256	0.0410	0.0625
5	0	0.7738	0.5905	0.4437	0.3277	0.2373	0.1681	0.1160	0.0778	0.0503	0.0313
	1	0.2036	0.3281	0.3915	0.4096	0.3955	0.3602	0.3124	0.2592	0.2059	0.1563
	2	0.0214	0.0729	0.1382	0.2048	0.2637	0.3087	0.3364	0.3456	0.3369	0.3125
	3	0.0011	0.0081	0.0244	0.0512	0.0879	0.1323	0.1811	0.2304	0.2757	0.3125
	4	0.0000	0.0005	0.0022	0.0064	0.0146	0.0284	0.0488	0.0768	0.1128	0.1563
	5	0.0000	0.0000	0.0001	0.0003	0.0010	0.0024	0.0053	0.0102	0.0185	0.0313
6	0	0.7351	0.5314	0.3771	0.2621	0.1780	0.1176	0.0754	0.0467	0.0277	0.0156
	1	0.2321	0.3543	0.3993	0.3932	0.3560	0.3025	0.2437	0.1866	0.1359	0.0938
	2	0.0305	0.0984	0.1762	0.2458	0.2966	0.3241	0.3280	0.3110	0.2780	0.2344
	3	0.0021	0.0146	0.0415	0.0819	0.1318	0.1852	0.2355	0.2765	0.3032	0.3125
	4	0.0001	0.0012	0.0055	0.0154	0.0330	0.0595	0.0951	0.1382	0.1861	0.2344
	5	0.0000	0.0001	0.0004	0.0015	0.0044	0.0102	0.0205	0.0369	0.0609	0.0938
	6	0.0000	0.0000	0.0000	0.0001	0.0002	0.0007	0.0018	0.0041	0.0083	0.0156
7	0	0.6983	0.4783	0.3206	0.2097	0.1335	0.0824	0.0490	0.0280	0.0152	0.0078
	1	0.2573	0.3720	0.3960	0.3670	0.3115	0.2471	0.1848	0.1306	0.0872	0.0547
	2	0.0406	0.1240	0.2097	0.2753	0.3115	0.3177	0.2985	0.2613	0.2140	0.1641
	3	0.0036	0.0230	0.0617	0.1147	0.1730	0.2269	0.2679	0.2903	0.2918	0.2734
	4	0.0002	0.0026	0.0109	0.0287	0.0577	0.0972	0.1442	0.1935	0.2388	0.2734
	5	0.0000	0.0002	0.0012	0.0043	0.0115	0.0250	0.0466	0.0774	0.1172	0.1641
	6	0.0000	0.0000	0.0001	0.0004	0.0013	0.0036	0.0084	0.0172	0.0320	0.0547
	7	0.0000	0.0000	0.0000	0.0000	0.0001	0.0002	0.0006	0.0016	0.0037	0.0078
8	0	0.6634	0.4305	0.2725	0.1678	0.1001	0.0576	0.0319	0.0168	0.0084	0.0039
	1	0.2793	0.3826	0.3847	0.3355	0.2670	0.1977	0.1373	0.0896	0.0548	0.0313
	2	0.0515	0.1488	0.2376	0.2936	0.3115	0.2965	0.2587	0.2090	0.1569	0.1094

						P					
n	*r*	0.05	0.10	0.15	0.20	0.25	0.30	0.35	0.40	0.45	0.50
	3	0.0054	0.0331	0.0839	0.1468	0.2076	0.2541	0.2786	0.2787	0.2568	0.2188
	4	0.0004	0.0046	0.0185	0.0459	0.0865	0.1361	0.1875	0.2322	0.2627	0.2734
	5	0.0000	0.0004	0.0026	0.0092	0.0231	0.0467	0.0808	0.1239	0.1719	0.2188
	6	0.0000	0.0000	0.0002	0.0011	0.0038	0.0100	0.0217	0.0413	0.0703	0.1094
	7	0.0000	0.0000	0.0000	0.0001	0.0004	0.0012	0.0033	0.0079	0.0164	0.0313
	8	0.0000	0.0000	0.0000	0.0000	0.0000	0.0001	0.0002	0.0007	0.0017	0.0039
9	0	0.6302	0.3874	0.2316	0.1342	0.0751	0.0404	0.0207	0.0101	0.0046	0.0020
	1	0.2985	0.3874	0.3679	0.3020	0.2253	0.1556	0.1004	0.0605	0.0339	0.0176
	2	0.0629	0.1722	0.2597	0.3020	0.3003	0.2668	0.2162	0.1612	0.1110	0.0703
	3	0.0077	0.0446	0.1069	0.1762	0.2336	0.2668	0.2716	0.2508	0.2119	0.1641
	4	0.0006	0.0074	0.0283	0.0661	0.1168	0.1715	0.2194	0.2508	0.2600	0.2461
	5	0.0000	0.0008	0.0050	0.0165	0.0389	0.0735	0.1181	0.1672	0.2128	0.2461
	6	0.0000	0.0001	0.0006	0.0028	0.0087	0.0210	0.0424	0.0743	0.1160	0.1641
	7	0.0000	0.0000	0.0000	0.0003	0.0012	0.0039	0.0098	0.0212	0.0407	0.0703
	8	0.0000	0.0000	0.0000	0.0000	0.0001	0.0004	0.0013	0.0035	0.0083	0.0176
	9	0.0000	0.0000	0.0000	0.0000	0.0000	0.0000	0.0001	0.0003	0.0008	0.0020
10	0	0.5987	0.3487	0.1969	0.1074	0.0563	0.0282	0.0135	0.0060	0.0025	0.0010
	1	0.3151	0.3874	0.3474	0.2684	0.1877	0.1211	0.0725	0.0403	0.0207	0.0098
	2	0.0746	0.1937	0.2759	0.3020	0.2816	0.2335	0.1757	0.1209	0.0763	0.0439
	3	0.0105	0.0574	0.1298	0.2013	0.2503	0.2668	0.2522	0.2150	0.1665	0.1172
	4	0.0010	0.0112	0.0401	0.0881	0.1460	0.2001	0.2377	0.2508	0.2384	0.2051
	5	0.0001	0.0015	0.0085	0.0264	0.0584	0.1029	0.1536	0.2007	0.2340	0.2461
	6	0.0000	0.0001	0.0012	0.0055	0.0162	0.0368	0.0689	0.1115	0.1596	0.2051
	7	0.0000	0.0000	0.0001	0.0008	0.0031	0.0090	0.0212	0.0425	0.0746	0.1172
	8	0.0000	0.0000	0.0000	0.0001	0.0004	0.0014	0.0043	0.0106	0.0229	0.0439
	9	0.0000	0.0000	0.0000	0.0000	0.0000	0.0001	0.0005	0.0016	0.0042	0.0098
	10	0.0000	0.0000	0.0000	0.0000	0.0000	0.0000	0.0000	0.0001	0.0003	0.0010
15	0	0.4633	0.2059	0.0874	0.0352	0.0134	0.0047	0.0016	0.0005	0.0001	0.0000
	1	0.3658	0.3432	0.2312	0.1319	0.0668	0.0305	0.0126	0.0047	0.0016	0.0005
	2	0.1348	0.2669	0.2856	0.2309	0.1559	0.0916	0.0476	0.0219	0.0090	0.0032
	3	0.0307	0.1285	0.2184	0.2501	0.2252	0.1700	0.1110	0.0634	0.0318	0.0139
	4	0.0049	0.0428	0.1156	0.1876	0.2252	0.2186	0.1792	0.1268	0.0780	0.0417
	5	0.0006	0.0105	0.0449	0.1032	0.1651	0.2061	0.2123	0.1859	0.1404	0.0916
	6	0.0000	0.0019	0.0132	0.0430	0.0917	0.1472	0.1906	0.2066	0.1914	0.1527
	7	0.0000	0.0003	0.0030	0.0138	0.0393	0.0811	0.1319	0.1771	0.2013	0.1964
	8	0.0000	0.0000	0.0005	0.0035	0.0131	0.0348	0.0710	0.1181	0.1647	0.1964
	9	0.0000	0.0000	0.0001	0.0007	0.0034	0.0116	0.0298	0.0612	0.1048	0.1527
	10	0.0000	0.0000	0.0000	0.0001	0.0007	0.0030	0.0096	0.0245	0.0515	0.0916
	11	0.0000	0.0000	0.0000	0.0000	0.0001	0.0006	0.0024	0.0074	0.0191	0.0417
	12	0.0000	0.0000	0.0000	0.0000	0.0000	0.0001	0.0004	0.0016	0.0052	0.0139
	13	0.0000	0.0000	0.0000	0.0000	0.0000	0.0000	0.0001	0.0003	0.0010	0.0032
	14	0.0000	0.0000	0.0000	0.0000	0.0000	0.0000	0.0000	0.0000	0.0001	0.0005
	15	0.0000	0.0000	0.0000	0.0000	0.0000	0.0000	0.0000	0.0000	0.0000	0.0000

		P									
n	r	0.05	0.10	0.15	0.20	0.25	0.30	0.35	0.40	0.45	0.50
20	0	0.3585	0.1216	0.0388	0.0115	0.0032	0.0008	0.0002	0.0000	0.0000	0.0000
	1	0.3774	0.2702	0.1368	0.0576	0.0211	0.0068	0.0020	0.0005	0.0001	0.0000
	2	0.1887	0.2852	0.2293	0.1369	0.0669	0.0278	0.0100	0.0031	0.0008	0.0002
	3	0.0596	0.1901	0.2428	0.2054	0.1339	0.0716	0.0323	0.0123	0.0040	0.0011
	4	0.0133	0.0898	0.1821	0.2182	0.1897	0.1304	0.0738	0.0350	0.0139	0.0046
	5	0.0022	0.0319	0.1028	0.1746	0.2023	0.1789	0.1272	0.0746	0.0365	0.0148
	6	0.0003	0.0089	0.0454	0.1091	0.1686	0.1916	0.1712	0.1244	0.0746	0.0370
	7	0.0000	0.0020	0.0160	0.0545	0.1124	0.1643	0.1844	0.1659	0.1221	0.0739
	8	0.0000	0.0004	0.0046	0.0222	0.0609	0.1144	0.1614	0.1797	0.1623	0.1201
	9	0.0000	0.0001	0.0011	0.0074	0.0271	0.0654	0.1158	0.1597	0.1771	0.1602
	10	0.0000	0.0000	0.0002	0.0020	0.0099	0.0308	0.0686	0.1171	0.1593	0.1762
	11	0.0000	0.0000	0.0000	0.0005	0.0030	0.0120	0.0336	0.0710	0.1185	0.1602
	12	0.0000	0.0000	0.0000	0.0001	0.0008	0.0039	0.0136	0.0355	0.0727	0.1201
	13	0.0000	0.0000	0.0000	0.0000	0.0002	0.0010	0.0045	0.0146	0.0366	0.0739
	14	0.0000	0.0000	0.0000	0.0000	0.0000	0.0002	0.0012	0.0049	0.0150	0.0370
	15	0.0000	0.0000	0.0000	0.0000	0.0000	0.0000	0.0003	0.0013	0.0049	0.0148
	16	0.0000	0.0000	0.0000	0.0000	0.0000	0.0000	0.0000	0.0003	0.0013	0.0046
	17	0.0000	0.0000	0.0000	0.0000	0.0000	0.0000	0.0000	0.0000	0.0002	0.0011
	18	0.0000	0.0000	0.0000	0.0000	0.0000	0.0000	0.0000	0.0000	0.0000	0.0002
	19	0.0000	0.0000	0.0000	0.0000	0.0000	0.0000	0.0000	0.0000	0.0000	0.0000
	20	0.0000	0.0000	0.0000	0.0000	0.0000	0.0000	0.0000	0.0000	0.0000	0.0000

		P									
n	r	0.55	0.60	0.65	0.70	0.75	0.80	0.85	0.90	0.95	
1	0	0.4500	0.4000	0.3500	0.3000	0.2500	0.2000	0.1500	0.1000	0.0500	
	1	0.5500	0.6000	0.6500	0.7000	0.7500	0.8000	0.8500	0.9000	0.9500	
2	0	0.2025	0.1600	0.1225	0.0900	0.0625	0.0400	0.0225	0.0100	0.0025	
	1	0.4950	0.4800	0.4550	0.4200	0.3750	0.3200	0.2550	0.1800	0.0950	
	2	0.3025	0.3600	0.4225	0.4900	0.5625	0.6400	0.7225	0.8100	0.9025	
3	0	0.0911	0.0640	0.0429	0.0270	0.0156	0.0080	0.0034	0.0010	0.0001	
	1	0.3341	0.2880	0.2389	0.1890	0.1406	0.0960	0.0574	0.0270	0.0071	
	2	0.4084	0.4320	0.4436	0.4410	0.4219	0.3840	0.3251	0.2430	0.1354	
	3	0.1664	0.2160	0.2746	0.3430	0.4219	0.5120	0.6141	0.7290	0.8574	
4	0	0.0410	0.0256	0.0150	0.0081	0.0039	0.0016	0.0005	0.0001	0.0000	
	1	0.2005	0.1536	0.1115	0.0756	0.0469	0.0256	0.0115	0.0036	0.0005	
	2	0.3675	0.3456	0.3105	0.2646	0.2109	0.1536	0.0975	0.0486	0.0135	
	3	0.2995	0.3456	0.3845	0.4116	0.4219	0.4096	0.3685	0.2916	0.1715	
	4	0.0915	0.1296	0.1785	0.2401	0.3164	0.4096	0.5220	0.6561	0.8145	
5	0	0.0185	0.0102	0.0053	0.0024	0.0010	0.0003	0.0001	0.0000	0.0000	
	1	0.1128	0.0768	0.0488	0.0283	0.0146	0.0064	0.0022	0.0004	0.0000	
	2	0.2757	0.2304	0.1811	0.1323	0.0879	0.0512	0.0244	0.0081	0.0011	
	3	0.3369	0.3456	0.3364	0.3087	0.2637	0.2048	0.1382	0.0729	0.0214	
	4	0.2059	0.2592	0.3124	0.3602	0.3955	0.4096	0.3915	0.3280	0.2036	
	5	0.0503	0.0778	0.1160	0.1681	0.2373	0.3277	0.4437	0.5905	0.7738	

						P				
n	r	0.55	0.60	0.65	0.70	0.75	0.80	0.85	0.90	0.95
6	0	0.0083	0.0041	0.0018	0.0007	0.0002	0.0001	0.0000	0.0000	0.0000
	1	0.0609	0.0369	0.0205	0.0102	0.0044	0.0015	0.0004	0.0001	0.0000
	2	0.1861	0.1382	0.0951	0.0595	0.0330	0.0154	0.0055	0.0012	0.0001
	3	0.3032	0.2765	0.2355	0.1852	0.1318	0.0819	0.0415	0.0146	0.0021
	4	0.2780	0.3110	0.3280	0.3241	0.2966	0.2458	0.1762	0.0984	0.0305
	5	0.1359	0.1866	0.2437	0.3025	0.3560	0.3932	0.3993	0.3543	0.2321
	6	0.0277	0.0467	0.0754	0.1176	0.1780	0.2621	0.3771	0.5314	0.7351
7	0	0.0037	0.0016	0.0006	0.0002	0.0001	0.0000	0.0000	0.0000	0.0000
	1	0.0320	0.0172	0.0084	0.0036	0.0013	0.0004	0.0001	0.0000	0.0000
	2	0.1172	0.0774	0.0466	0.0250	0.0115	0.0043	0.0012	0.0002	0.0000
	3	0.2388	0.1935	0.1442	0.0972	0.0577	0.0287	0.0109	0.0026	0.0002
	4	0.2918	0.2903	0.2679	0.2269	0.1730	0.1147	0.0617	0.0230	0.0036
	5	0.2140	0.2613	0.2985	0.3177	0.3115	0.2753	0.2097	0.1240	0.0406
	6	0.0872	0.1306	0.1848	0.2471	0.3115	0.3670	0.3960	0.3720	0.2573
	7	0.0152	0.0280	0.0490	0.0824	0.1335	0.2097	0.3206	0.4783	0.6983
8	0	0.0017	0.0007	0.0002	0.0001	0.0000	0.0000	0.0000	0.0000	0.0000
	1	0.0164	0.0079	0.0033	0.0012	0.0004	0.0001	0.0000	0.0000	0.0000
	2	0.0703	0.0413	0.0217	0.0100	0.0038	0.0011	0.0002	0.0000	0.0000
	3	0.1719	0.1239	0.0808	0.0467	0.0231	0.0092	0.0026	0.0004	0.0000
	4	0.2627	0.2322	0.1875	0.1361	0.0865	0.0459	0.0185	0.0046	0.0004
	5	0.2568	0.2787	0.2786	0.2541	0.2076	0.1468	0.0839	0.0331	0.0054
	6	0.1569	0.2090	0.2587	0.2965	0.3115	0.2936	0.2376	0.1488	0.0515
	7	0.0548	0.0896	0.1373	0.1977	0.2670	0.3355	0.3847	0.3826	0.2793
	8	0.0084	0.0168	0.0319	0.0576	0.1001	0.1678	0.2725	0.4305	0.6634
9	0	0.0008	0.0003	0.0001	0.0000	0.0000	0.0000	0.0000	0.0000	0.0000
	1	0.0083	0.0035	0.0013	0.0004	0.0001	0.0000	0.0000	0.0000	0.0000
	2	0.0407	0.0212	0.0098	0.0039	0.0012	0.0003	0.0000	0.0000	0.0000
	3	0.1160	0.0743	0.0424	0.0210	0.0087	0.0028	0.0006	0.0001	0.0000
	4	0.2128	0.1672	0.1181	0.0735	0.0389	0.0165	0.0050	0.0008	0.0000
	5	0.2600	0.2508	0.2194	0.1715	0.1168	0.0661	0.0283	0.0074	0.0006
	6	0.2119	0.2508	0.2716	0.2668	0.2336	0.1762	0.1069	0.0446	0.0077
	7	0.1110	0.1612	0.2162	0.2668	0.3003	0.3020	0.2597	0.1722	0.0629
	8	0.0339	0.0605	0.1004	0.1556	0.2253	0.3020	0.3679	0.3874	0.2985
	9	0.0046	0.0101	0.0207	0.0404	0.0751	0.1342	0.2316	0.3874	0.6302
10	0	0.0003	0.0001	0.0000	0.0000	0.0000	0.0000	0.0000	0.0000	0.0000
	1	0.0042	0.0016	0.0005	0.0001	0.0000	0.0000	0.0000	0.0000	0.0000
	2	0.0229	0.0106	0.0043	0.0014	0.0004	0.0001	0.0000	0.0000	0.0000
	3	0.0746	0.0425	0.0212	0.0090	0.0031	0.0008	0.0001	0.0000	0.0000
	4	0.1596	0.1115	0.0689	0.0368	0.0162	0.0055	0.0012	0.0001	0.0000
	5	0.2340	0.2007	0.1536	0.1029	0.0584	0.0264	0.0085	0.0015	0.0001
	6	0.2384	0.2508	0.2377	0.2001	0.1460	0.0881	0.0401	0.0112	0.0010
	7	0.1665	0.2150	0.2522	0.2668	0.2503	0.2013	0.1298	0.0574	0.0105
	8	0.0763	0.1209	0.1757	0.2335	0.2816	0.3020	0.2759	0.1937	0.0746
	9	0.0207	0.0403	0.0725	0.1211	0.1877	0.2684	0.3474	0.3874	0.3151
	10	0.0025	0.0060	0.0135	0.0282	0.0563	0.1074	0.1969	0.3487	0.5987

							P				
n	r	0.55	0.60	0.65	0.70	0.75	0.80	0.85	0.90	0.95	
15	0	0.0000	0.0000	0.0000	0.0000	0.0000	0.0000	0.0000	0.0000	0.0000	
	1	0.0001	0.0000	0.0000	0.0000	0.0000	0.0000	0.0000	0.0000	0.0000	
	2	0.0010	0.0003	0.0001	0.0000	0.0000	0.0000	0.0000	0.0000	0.0000	
	3	0.0052	0.0016	0.0004	0.0001	0.0000	0.0000	0.0000	0.0000	0.0000	
	4	0.0191	0.0074	0.0024	0.0006	0.0001	0.0000	0.0000	0.0000	0.0000	
	5	0.0515	0.0245	0.0096	0.0030	0.0007	0.0001	0.0000	0.0000	0.0000	
	6	0.1048	0.0612	0.0298	0.0116	0.0034	0.0007	0.0001	0.0000	0.0000	
	7	0.1647	0.1181	0.0710	0.0348	0.0131	0.0035	0.0005	0.0000	0.0000	
	8	0.2013	0.1771	0.1319	0.0811	0.0393	0.0138	0.0030	0.0003	0.0000	
	9	0.1914	0.2066	0.1906	0.1472	0.0917	0.0430	0.0132	0.0019	0.0000	
	10	0.1404	0.1859	0.2123	0.2061	0.1651	0.1032	0.0449	0.0105	0.0006	
	11	0.0780	0.1268	0.1792	0.2186	0.2252	0.1876	0.1156	0.0428	0.0049	
	12	0.0318	0.0634	0.1110	0.1700	0.2252	0.2501	0.2184	0.1285	0.0307	
	13	0.0090	0.0219	0.0476	0.0916	0.1559	0.2309	0.2856	0.2669	0.1348	
	14	0.0016	0.0047	0.0126	0.0305	0.0668	0.1319	0.2312	0.3432	0.3658	
	15	0.0001	0.0005	0.0016	0.0047	0.0134	0.0352	0.0874	0.2059	0.4633	
20	0	0.0000	0.0000	0.0000	0.0000	0.0000	0.0000	0.0000	0.0000	0.0000	
	1	0.0000	0.0000	0.0000	0.0000	0.0000	0.0000	0.0000	0.0000	0.0000	
	2	0.0000	0.0000	0.0000	0.0000	0.0000	0.0000	0.0000	0.0000	0.0000	
	3	0.0002	0.0000	0.0000	0.0000	0.0000	0.0000	0.0000	0.0000	0.0000	
	4	0.0013	0.0003	0.0000	0.0000	0.0000	0.0000	0.0000	0.0000	0.0000	
	5	0.0049	0.0013	0.0003	0.0000	0.0000	0.0000	0.0000	0.0000	0.0000	
	6	0.0150	0.0049	0.0012	0.0002	0.0000	0.0000	0.0000	0.0000	0.0000	
	7	0.0366	0.0146	0.0045	0.0010	0.0002	0.0000	0.0000	0.0000	0.0000	
	8	0.0727	0.0355	0.0136	0.0039	0.0008	0.0001	0.0000	0.0000	0.0000	
	9	0.1185	0.0710	0.0336	0.0120	0.0030	0.0005	0.0000	0.0000	0.0000	
	10	0.1593	0.1171	0.0686	0.0308	0.0099	0.0020	0.0002	0.0000	0.0000	
	11	0.1771	0.1597	0.1158	0.0654	0.0271	0.0074	0.0011	0.0001	0.0000	
	12	0.1623	0.1797	0.1614	0.1144	0.0609	0.0222	0.0046	0.0004	0.0000	
	13	0.1221	0.1659	0.1844	0.1643	0.1124	0.0545	0.0160	0.0020	0.0000	
	14	0.0746	0.1244	0.1712	0.1916	0.1686	0.1091	0.0454	0.0089	0.0003	
	15	0.0365	0.0746	0.1272	0.1789	0.2023	0.1746	0.1028	0.0319	0.0022	
	16	0.0139	0.0350	0.0738	0.1304	0.1897	0.2182	0.1821	0.0898	0.0133	
	17	0.0040	0.0123	0.0323	0.0716	0.1339	0.2054	0.2428	0.1901	0.0596	
	18	0.0008	0.0031	0.0100	0.0278	0.0669	0.1369	0.2293	0.2852	0.1887	
	19	0.0001	0.0005	0.0020	0.0068	0.0211	0.0576	0.1368	0.2702	0.3774	
	20	0.0000	0.0000	0.0002	0.0008	0.0032	0.0115	0.0388	0.1216	0.3585	

Appendix C: Values of $e^{-\lambda}$ for Use in the Poisson Distribution

λ	$e^{-\lambda}$	λ	$e^{-\lambda}$
0.0	1.0000	3.1	0.0450
0.1	0.9048	3.2	0.0408
0.2	0.8187	3.3	0.0369
0.3	0.7408	3.4	0.0334
0.4	0.6703	3.5	0.0302
0.5	0.6065	3.6	0.0273
0.6	0.5488	3.7	0.0247
0.7	0.4966	3.8	0.0224
0.8	0.4493	3.9	0.0202
0.9	0.4066	4.0	0.0183
1.0	0.3679	4.1	0.0166
1.1	0.3329	4.2	0.0150
1.2	0.3012	4.3	0.0136
1.3	0.2725	4.4	0.0123
1.4	0.2466	4.5	0.0111
1.5	0.2231	4.6	0.0101
1.6	0.2019	4.7	0.0091
1.7	0.1827	4.8	0.0082
1.8	0.1653	4.9	0.0074
1.9	0.1496	5.0	0.0067
2.0	0.1353	5.1	0.0061
2.1	0.1225	5.2	0.0055
2.2	0.1108	5.3	0.0050
2.3	0.1003	5.4	0.0045
2.4	0.0907	5.5	0.0041
2.5	0.0821	5.6	0.0037
2.6	0.0743	5.7	0.0033
2.7	0.0672	5.8	0.0030
2.8	0.0608	5.9	0.0027
2.9	0.0550	6.0	0.0025
3.0	0.0498		

Appendix D: *F* Distribution Values

F distribution table for the upper 5% probability ($\alpha = 0.05$).

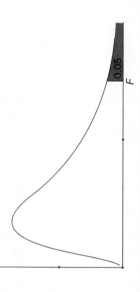

df2	1	2	3	4	5	6	7	8	9	10	12	15	20	24	30	120	∞
1	161.4	199.5	215.7	224.6	230.2	234.0	236.8	238.9	240.5	241.9	243.9	245.9	248.0	249.0	250.1	253.3	254.3
2	18.51	19.00	19.16	19.25	19.30	19.33	19.35	19.37	19.38	19.40	19.41	19.43	19.45	19.45	19.46	19.49	19.50
3	10.13	9.55	9.28	9.12	9.01	8.94	8.89	8.85	8.81	8.79	8.74	8.70	8.66	8.64	8.62	8.55	8.53
4	7.71	6.94	6.59	6.39	6.26	6.16	6.09	6.04	6.00	5.96	5.91	5.86	5.80	5.77	5.75	5.66	5.63
5	6.61	5.79	5.41	5.19	5.05	4.95	4.88	4.82	4.77	4.74	4.68	4.62	4.56	4.53	4.50	4.40	4.36
6	5.99	5.14	4.76	4.53	4.39	4.28	4.21	4.15	4.10	4.06	4.00	3.94	3.87	3.84	3.81	3.70	3.67
7	5.59	4.74	4.35	4.12	3.97	3.87	3.79	3.73	3.68	3.64	3.57	3.51	3.44	3.41	3.38	3.27	3.23
8	5.32	4.46	4.07	3.84	3.69	3.58	3.50	3.44	3.39	3.35	3.28	3.22	3.15	3.12	3.08	2.97	2.93
9	5.12	4.26	3.86	3.63	3.48	3.37	3.29	3.23	3.18	3.14	3.07	3.01	2.94	2.90	2.86	2.75	2.71
10	4.96	4.10	3.71	3.48	3.33	3.22	3.14	3.07	3.02	2.98	2.91	2.85	2.77	2.74	2.70	2.58	2.54
11	4.84	3.98	3.59	3.36	3.20	3.09	3.01	2.95	2.90	2.85	2.79	2.72	2.65	2.61	2.57	2.45	2.40
12	4.75	3.89	3.49	3.26	3.11	3.00	2.91	2.85	2.80	2.75	2.69	2.62	2.54	2.51	2.47	2.34	2.30
13	4.67	3.81	3.41	3.18	3.03	2.92	2.83	2.77	2.71	2.67	2.60	2.53	2.46	2.42	2.38	2.25	2.21
14	4.60	3.74	3.34	3.11	2.96	2.85	2.76	2.70	2.65	2.60	2.53	2.46	2.39	2.35	2.31	2.18	2.13
15	4.54	3.68	3.29	3.06	2.90	2.79	2.71	2.64	2.59	2.54	2.48	2.40	2.33	2.29	2.25	2.11	2.07
16	4.49	3.63	3.24	3.01	2.85	2.74	2.66	2.59	2.54	2.49	2.42	2.35	2.28	2.24	2.19	2.06	2.01
17	4.45	3.59	3.20	2.96	2.81	2.70	2.61	2.55	2.49	2.45	2.38	2.31	2.23	2.19	2.15	2.01	1.96
18	4.41	3.55	3.16	2.93	2.77	2.66	2.58	2.51	2.46	2.41	2.34	2.27	2.19	2.15	2.11	1.97	1.92
19	4.38	3.52	3.13	2.90	2.74	2.63	2.54	2.48	2.42	2.38	2.31	2.23	2.16	2.11	2.07	1.93	1.88
20	4.35	3.49	3.10	2.87	2.71	2.60	2.51	2.45	2.39	2.35	2.28	2.20	2.12	2.08	2.04	1.90	1.84
24	4.26	3.40	3.01	2.78	2.62	2.51	2.42	2.36	2.30	2.25	2.18	2.11	2.03	1.98	1.94	1.79	1.73
30	4.17	3.32	2.92	2.69	2.53	2.42	2.33	2.27	2.21	2.16	2.09	2.01	1.93	1.89	1.84	1.68	1.62
40	4.08	3.23	2.84	2.61	2.45	2.34	2.25	2.18	2.12	2.08	2.00	1.92	1.84	1.79	1.74	1.58	1.51
60	4.00	3.15	2.76	2.53	2.37	2.25	2.17	2.10	2.04	1.99	1.92	1.84	1.75	1.70	1.65	1.47	1.39
120	3.92	3.07	2.68	2.45	2.29	2.18	2.09	2.02	1.96	1.91	1.83	1.75	1.66	1.61	1.55	1.35	1.25
∞	3.84	3.00	2.60	2.37	2.21	2.10	2.01	1.94	1.88	1.83	1.75	1.67	1.57	1.52	1.46	1.22	1.00

df1

F distribution table for the upper 1% probability ($\alpha = 0.01$).

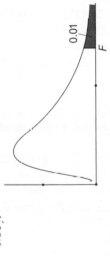

df2	1	2	3	4	5	6	7	8	9	10	12	15	20	24	30	120	∞
1	4052	5000	5403	5625	5764	5859	5928	5982	6022.5	6056	6106	6157	6209	6235	6261	6339	6366
2	98.50	99.00	99.17	99.25	99.30	99.33	99.36	99.37	99.39	99.40	99.42	99.43	99.45	99.46	99.47	99.49	99.50
3	34.12	30.82	29.46	28.71	28.24	27.91	27.67	27.49	27.35	27.23	27.05	26.87	26.69	26.60	26.50	26.22	26.13
4	21.20	18.00	16.69	15.98	15.52	15.21	14.98	14.80	14.66	14.55	14.37	14.20	14.02	13.93	13.84	13.56	13.46
5	16.26	13.27	12.06	11.39	10.97	10.67	10.46	10.29	10.16	10.05	9.89	9.72	9.55	9.47	9.38	9.11	9.02
6	13.75	10.92	9.78	9.15	8.75	8.47	8.26	8.10	7.98	7.87	7.72	7.56	7.40	7.31	7.23	6.97	6.88
7	12.25	9.55	8.45	7.85	7.46	7.19	6.99	6.84	6.72	6.62	6.47	6.31	6.16	6.07	5.99	5.74	5.65
8	11.26	8.65	7.59	7.01	6.63	6.37	6.18	6.03	5.91	5.81	5.67	5.52	5.36	5.28	5.20	4.95	4.86
9	10.56	8.02	6.99	6.42	6.06	5.80	5.61	5.47	5.35	5.26	5.11	4.96	4.81	4.73	4.65	4.40	4.31
10	10.04	7.56	6.55	5.99	5.64	5.39	5.20	5.06	4.94	4.85	4.71	4.56	4.41	4.33	4.25	4.00	3.91
11	9.65	7.21	6.22	5.67	5.32	5.07	4.89	4.74	4.63	4.54	4.40	4.25	4.10	4.02	3.94	3.69	3.60
12	9.33	6.93	5.95	5.41	5.06	4.82	4.64	4.50	4.39	4.30	4.16	4.01	3.86	3.78	3.70	3.45	3.36
13	9.07	6.70	5.74	5.21	4.86	4.62	4.44	4.30	4.19	4.10	3.96	3.82	3.66	3.59	3.51	3.25	3.17
14	8.86	6.51	5.56	5.04	4.69	4.46	4.28	4.14	4.03	3.94	3.80	3.66	3.51	3.43	3.35	3.09	3.00
15	8.68	6.36	5.42	4.89	4.56	4.32	4.14	4.00	3.89	3.80	3.67	3.52	3.37	3.29	3.21	2.96	2.87
16	8.53	6.23	5.29	4.77	4.44	4.20	4.03	3.89	3.78	3.69	3.55	3.41	3.26	3.18	3.10	2.84	2.75
17	8.40	6.11	5.18	4.67	4.34	4.10	3.93	3.79	3.68	3.59	3.46	3.31	3.16	3.08	3.00	2.75	2.65
18	8.29	6.01	5.09	4.58	4.25	4.01	3.84	3.71	3.60	3.51	3.37	3.23	3.08	3.00	2.92	2.66	2.57
19	8.18	5.93	5.01	4.50	4.17	3.94	3.77	3.63	3.52	3.43	3.30	3.15	3.00	2.92	2.84	2.58	2.49
20	8.10	5.85	4.94	4.43	4.10	3.87	3.70	3.56	3.46	3.37	3.23	3.09	2.94	2.86	2.78	2.52	2.42
24	7.82	5.61	4.72	4.22	3.90	3.67	3.50	3.36	3.26	3.17	3.03	2.89	2.74	2.66	2.58	2.31	2.21
30	7.56	5.39	4.51	4.02	3.70	3.47	3.30	3.17	3.07	2.98	2.84	2.70	2.55	2.47	2.39	2.11	2.01
40	7.31	5.18	4.31	3.83	3.51	3.29	3.12	2.99	2.89	2.80	2.66	2.52	2.37	2.29	2.20	1.92	1.80
60	7.08	4.98	4.13	3.65	3.34	3.12	2.95	2.82	2.72	2.63	2.50	2.35	2.20	2.12	2.03	1.73	1.60
120	6.85	4.79	3.95	3.48	3.17	2.96	2.79	2.66	2.56	2.47	2.34	2.19	2.03	1.95	1.86	1.53	1.38
∞	6.63	4.61	3.78	3.32	3.02	2.80	2.64	2.51	2.41	2.32	2.18	2.04	1.88	1.79	1.70	1.32	1.00

df1

Appendix E: Using POM-QM for Windows

Welcome to POM-QM for Windows. Along with its companion Excel QM (see Appendix F), it makes available to you the most user-friendly software available for the field of quantitative analysis/ quantitative methods (QA/QM). This software may also be used for the field of production/ operations management (POM). It is possible to display all of the modules, only the QM modules, or only the POM modules. Because this book is about quantitative methods, only the QM modules are shown throughout the textbook, and this software is referenced as QM for Windows. QM for Windows is a package that has been designed to help you to better learn and understand this field. The software can be used to either solve problems or check answers that have been derived by hand. You will find that this software is exceptionally friendly due to the following features:

- Anyone familiar with any standard spreadsheet or word processor in Windows will easily be able to use QM for Windows. All modules have help screens that can be accessed at any time.
- The screens for every module are consistent, so that when you become accustomed to using one module, you will have an easy time with the other modules.
- The spreadsheet-type data editor allows full screen editing.
- Files are opened and saved in the usual Windows fashion, and in addition, files are named by module, which makes it easy to find files saved previously.
- It is easy to change from one solution method to another to compare methods and answers.
- Graphs are easily displayed and printed.

Installing POM-QM for Windows

Go to the Companion Website for this book to download and install the POM-QM for Windows software. Instructions are provided on how to download, install, and register the software.

After the installation and registration is complete, you will have a program group added to your Program Manager. The group will be called POM-QM for Windows 3. In addition, a shortcut to the program will be placed on the desktop. To use the QM for Windows program, double-click on the shortcut on the desktop or use Start, POM-QM for Windows 3, POM-QM for Windows.

When you use QM for Windows for the first time, you should select Help from the menu bar, and then select PDF Manual or Word Manual to obtain complete instructions on using the software. Brief instructions will be provided in this appendix.

The first screen that is displayed in QM for Windows (see Program 1.1 in Chapter 1) contains the assorted components that are available on most screens. The top of that screen is the standard Windows title bar. Below the title bar is a standard Windows menu bar. The details of the eight menu options File, Edit, View, Module, Format, Tools, Window, and Help are explained in this appendix. Upon starting QM for Windows, some of the menu options such as Edit and Format may not be available. They will become available when a module is selected or when a problem is entered.

Below the menu are two toolbars: a standard toolbar and a format toolbar. The toolbars contain standard shortcuts for several of the menu commands. If you move the mouse over the button for about two seconds, an explanation of the button will be displayed on the screen.

The next bar contains an instruction. There is always an instruction here trying to help you to figure out what to do or what to enter. Currently, the instruction indicates to select a module or open a file. When data are to be entered into the data table, this instruction will explain what type of data (integer, real, positive, etc.) are to be entered.

In Program 1.1 in Chapter 1, we show the module list after clicking on Module. We selected to show only the QM modules.

Creating a New Problem

To enter a new problem, select Module to see the list of available techniques. Click the module you wish to use based on the type of problem to be solved. Next you either click the icon to enter a new problem or open a previously saved problem, or you select **File** and then **New** or **Open**. In some modules, when New is selected, there will be a menu of submodules. Where this is the case, one of these must be selected before the problem is entered.

The top line of the creation screen contains a text box in which the title of the problem can be entered. For many modules it is necessary to enter the number of rows in the problem. Rows will

Solving a problem
There are several ways to solve a problem. The easiest way is to press the Solve button on the standard toolbar. Alternatively, the function key F9 may be used. Finally, if you press the enter key after the last piece of data is entered, the problem will be solved. After solving a problem, to return to editing the data press the Edit button, which has replaced the Solve button on the standard toolbar, or use F9.

have different names depending on the modules. For example, in linear programming, rows are constraints, whereas in forecasting, rows are past periods. The number of rows can be chosen with either the scroll bar or the text box.

POM-QM for Windows has the capability to allow you different options for the default row and column names. Select one of the radio buttons to indicate which style of default naming should be used. In most modules the row names are not used for computations, but you should be careful because in some modules (most notably, Project Management) the names might relate to precedences.

Many modules require you to enter the number of columns. This is given in the same way as the number of rows. All row and column names can be changed in the data table.

Some modules will have an extra option box, such as for choosing minimize or maximize or selecting whether distances are symmetric. Select one of these options. In most cases this option can later be changed on the data screen.

When you are satisfied with your choices, click on the **OK** button or press the **Enter** key. At this point, a blank data screen will be displayed. Screens will differ from module to module.

Entering and Editing Data

Enter
This key moves from cell to cell in the order from left to right, from top to bottom, skipping the first column (which usually contains names). Therefore, when entering a table of data, if you start at the upper left and work your way to the lower right row by row, this key is exceptionally useful.

After a new data set has been created or an existing data set has been loaded, the data can be edited. Every entry is in a row and column position. You navigate through the spreadsheet using the cursor movement keys. These keys function in a regular way with one exception—the **Enter** key.

The instruction bar on the screen will contain a brief instruction describing what is to be done. There are essentially three types of cells in the data table. One type is a regular data cell into which you enter either a name or a number. A second type is a cell that cannot be changed. A third type is a cell that contains a drop-down box. For example, the signs in a linear programming constraint are chosen from this type of box. To see all of the options, press the box with the arrow.

There is one more aspect to the data screen that needs to be considered. Some modules need extra data above that in the table. In most of these cases the data are contained in text/scrollbar combinations that appear on top of the data table.

Solution Displays

Numerical Formatting
Formatting is handled by the program automatically. For example, in most cases the number 1000 will automatically be formatted as 1,000. Do not type the comma. The program will prevent you from doing so!

At this point you can press the **Solve** button to begin the solution process. A new screen will be displayed.

An important thing to notice is that there is more solution information available. This can be seen by the icons given at the bottom. Click on these to view the information. Alternatively, notice that the Window option in the main menu is now enabled. It is always enabled at solution time. Even if the icons are covered by a window, the Window option will always allow you to view the other solution windows.

Now that we have examined how to create and solve a problem we explain all of the Menu options that are available.

File

File contains the usual options that one finds in Windows:

New   As demonstrated before, this is chosen to begin a new problem/file.

Open   This is used to open/load a previously saved file. File selection is the standard Windows common dialog type. Notice that the extension for files in the QM for Windows system is given by the first three letters of the module name. For example, all linear programming files have the extension *.lin. When you go to the open dialog, the default value is for the program to look for files of the type in this module. This can be changed at the bottom left where it says "Files of Type."

Deleting Files
It is not possible to delete a file using QM for Windows. Use the Windows file manager to do so.

The names that are legal are standard file names. Case (upper or lower) does not matter. You may type them in as uppercase, lowercase, or mixed. In all of the examples, QM for Windows will add the three-letter extension to the end of the file name. For example, linear programming problem will become *linear programming problem.lin* (assuming that it is indeed a linear programming problem).

Save   Save will replace the file without asking you if you care about overwriting the previous version of this file. If you try to save and have not previously named the file, you will be asked to name this file.

Save as   Save as will prompt you for a file name before saving. This option is very similar to the option to load a data file. When you choose this option, the Save As Dialog Box for Files will be displayed.

Save as Excel File   Save as Excel File saves a file as an Excel file with both the data and appropriate formulas for the solutions and is available for some but not all of the modules.

Save as HTML   Save as HTML saves the tables as an HTML formatted file that can immediately be placed on the Internet.

Print   Print will display a print menu screen with four tabs. The Information tab allows you to select which of the output tables should be printed. The Page Header tab allows you to control the information displayed at the top of the page. The Layout tab controls the printing style. Information may be printed as plain ASCII text or as a table (grid) resembling the table on the screen. Try both types of printing and see which one you/your instructor prefers. The Print tab allows certain print settings to be changed.

Exit the Program   The last option on the File menu is Exit. This will exit the program if you are on the data screen or exit the solution screen and return to the data screen if you are on the solution screen. This can also be achieved by pressing the Edit command button on the solution screen.

Edit

The commands under Edit have three purposes. The first four commands are used to insert or delete rows or columns. The next command is used to copy an entry from one cell to all cells below it in the column. This is not often useful, but when it is useful it saves a great deal of work. The last two entries can be used to copy the data table to other Windows programs.

View

View has several options that enable you to customize the appearance of the screen. The toolbar can be displayed or not. The Instruction bar can be displayed at its default location above the data or below the data, as a floating window, or not at all. The status bar can be displayed or not.

Colors can be set to monochrome (black and white) or from this state to their original colors.

Module

Module is shown in Chapter 1 as Program 1.1. The module selection contains a list of programs available with this book.

Format

Format also has several options for the display. The colors for the entire screen can be set, and the font type and size for the table can be set. Zeros can be set to display as blanks rather than zeros. The problem title that is displayed in the data table and was created at the creation screen can be changed. The table can be squeezed or expanded. That is, the column widths can be decreased or increased. The input can be checked or not.

Tools

The Tools menu option is an area available to annotate problems. If you want to write a note to yourself about the problem, select annotation; the note will be saved with the file if you save the file.

A calculator is available for simple calculations, including square root. There is a normal distribution calculator that can be used for finding confidence intervals and the like.

A normal distribution calculator is found in the Tools menu option.

Window

The Window menu option is enabled only at the solution screen. Additional output is available under Window. The type of output depends on the module being used.

Help

The Help menu option provides information about the software in general as well as about the individual modules. The first time you run POM-QM for Windows, you should select Help and choose Program Update to ensure that your software has the latest updates.

Help also contains a manual with further details about the program, a link to a program update and a link for e-mail support. If you send mail, be sure to include the name of the program (POM-QM for Windows), the version of the program (from Help, About), the module in which the problem is occurring, and a detailed explanation of the problem, and to attach the data file for which the problem occurs.

Appendix F: Using Excel QM and Excel Add-Ins

Excel QM

Excel QM has been designed to help you to better learn and understand both quantitative analysis and Excel. Even though the software contains many modules and submodules, the screens for every module are consistent and easy to use. The modules are illustrated in Program 1.3.

Excel QM is an add-in to Excel, so you must have Excel on your PC. To install Excel QM, go to the Companion Website for instructions and the free download. An Excel QM icon will be placed on your desktop.

To run Excel QM, click the icon on the desktop and Excel will start with the Excel QM add-in available. In addition to the usual Excel tabs, a tab for Excel QM will appear. Click this to see the Excel QM ribbon. There are two items on this ribbon that can be used to access the available techniques. The first way is to select **By Chapter**, which will show the techniques arranged by chapter number. The second way is to select **Alphabetical**, which will display the techniques in alphabetical order. Using either of these, select the appropriate technique based on the problem you want to enter. A window will open for you to input information about the problem, such as the number of variables or the number of observations. When you click **OK**, a spreadsheet that has been initialized will appear. Instructions are included in a text box that appears just below the title that has been given to that problem. These instructions typically indicate what you must enter on the worksheet and, for certain methods, what other steps are necessary to obtain the final solution. For many of the modules, no further steps are necessary. For others, such as linear programming, Excel QM will have provided the inputs and made the necessary selections for the use of Solver.

Excel QM serves two purposes in the learning process. First, it can simply help you solve homework problems. You enter the appropriate data, and the program provides numerical solutions. QM for Windows operates on the same principle. But Excel QM allows for a second approach, that is, noting the Excel *formulas* used to develop solutions and modifying them to deal with a wider variety of problems. This "open" approach allows you to observe, understand, and even change the formulas underlying the Excel calculations, conveying Excel's power as a quantitative analysis tool.

Technical Support for Excel QM

If you have technical problems with either POM-QM for Windows or Excel QM that your instructor cannot answer, send an e-mail to the address found at the www.prenhall.com/weiss website. If you send e-mail, be sure to include the name of the program (POM-QM for Windows or Excel QM), the version of the program (from Help, About in POM-QM for Windows; from QM About in Excel QM), the module in which the problem is occurring, and a detailed explanation of the problem, and to attach the data file for which the problem occurs (if appropriate).

Activating Excel Add-Ins in Excel 2013 and 2010

Two important Excel add-ins are Solver and Analysis ToolPak. Both of these are a part of Excel but must be activated or loaded before you can use them the first time. To load these add-ins, follow these steps:

1. For Excel 2013 and 2010, click the **File** tab, click **Options**, and then click **Add-Ins**.
2. In the Manage box, select **Excel Add-Ins** and click **Go**.
3. Check the boxes next to Analysis ToolPak and Solver Add-In, and then click **OK**.

The Data tab now displays Solver and Data Analysis every time Excel is started. Instructions on using Data Analysis for regression are provided in Chapter 4.

Appendix G: Solutions to Selected Problems

Chapter 1

1-16 BEP = 5 units

1-18 BEP = 700 units

1-20 BEP = 160 per week; Total revenue = $6,400

1-22 $s = 45$

1-24 (a) BEP = 25   (b) BEP = 18.333

Chapter 2

2-14 0.30

2-16 (a) 0.10   (b) 0.04   (c) 0.25   (d) 0.40

2-18 (a) 0.20   (b) 0.09   (c) 0.31   (d) dependent

2-20 (a) 0.3   (b) 0.3   (c) 0.8   (d) 0.49   (e) 0.24   (f) 0.27

2-22 0.719

2-24 (a) 0.08   (b) 0.84   (c) 0.44   (d) 0.92

2-26 (a) 0.995   (b) 0.885   (c) Assumed events are independent

2-28 0.78

2-30 2.85

2-32 (a) 0.1172   (b) 0.0439   (c) 0.0098
(d) 0.0010   (e) 0.1719

2-34 0.328, 0.590

2-36 0.776

2-38 (a) 0.0548   (b) 0.6554   (c) 0.6554   (d) 0.2119

2-40 1829.27

2-42 (a) 0.5   (b) 0.27425   (c) 48.2

2-44 0.7365

2-46 0.162

Chapter 3

3-18 Maximin criterion; Texan

3-20 (a) Stock market   (b) $21,500

3-22 (b) CD

3-24 (b) Medium

3-26 8 cases

3-30 (b) Very large   (c) Small   (c) Very large   (d) Very large   (f) Very large

3-32 Minimax regret decision: Option 2; Minimum EOL decision: Option 2

3-34 −$0.526

3-36 Construct the clinic (EMV = 30,000)

3-40 Do not gather information; build quadplex

3-42 0.533; 0.109

3-44 (c) Conduct the survey. If the survey is favorable, produce razor; if not favorable, don't produce razor.

3-46 (a) 0.923, 0.077, 0.25, 0.75   (b) 0.949, 0.051, 0.341, 0.659

3-48 Do not use study. Risk avoiders.

3-50 (a) Broad   (b) Expressway   (c) Risk avoider

Chapter 4

4-10 (b) SST = 29.5 SSE = 12 SSR = 17.5 $\hat{Y} = 6 + 0.1X$
(c) $\hat{Y} = 10$

4-12 (a) $\hat{Y} = 6 + 0.1X$

4-16 (a) $149,542   (b) The model predicts the average price for a house this size.   (c) Age, number of bedrooms, lot size   (d) 0.3969

4-18 For $X = 1200$, $\hat{Y} = 2.35$ for $X = 2400$, $\hat{Y} = 3.67$

4-22 The model with just *age* is best because it has the highest r^2 (0.70).

4-24 (a) $\hat{Y} = 91,446.49 + 29.86X_1 + 2,116.86X_2 - 1,504.77X_3 = 142,465.16$.

4-26 The model with horsepower is: $\hat{Y} = 53.87 - 0.269X_1$; $r^2 = 0.77$
The model with weight is: $\hat{Y} = 57.53 - 0.01X_2$; $r^2 = 0.73$.

4-30 $\hat{Y} = 77.190 + 0.047X$

4-32 (a) $\hat{Y} = 42.43 + 0.0004X$;
(b) $\hat{Y} = -31.54 + 0.0058X$

Chapter 5

5-16 MAD = 6.48 for 3-month moving average; MAD = 7.78 for 4-month moving average

5-18 $Y = 2.22 + 1.05X$

5-20 Forecast for year 12 is 11.789; MAD = 2.437

5-22 Forecasts for year 6 are 565.6 and 581.4

5-24 Forecast for year 6 is 555

5-26 MAD = 5.6 for trend line; MAD = 74.56 for exponential smoothing; MAD = 67 for moving average

5-28 (b) MAD = 2.60; RSFE = 5.11 at week 10

5-32 MAD = 3.34

5-36 $F_{11} = 6.26$; MAD = 0.58 for $\alpha = 0.8$ is lowest.

5-38 270, 390, 189, 351

Chapter 6

6-20 (a) 20,000   (b) 50   (c) 50

6-22 $45 more. ROP = 4,000

6-24 8 million

6-26 28,284; 34,641; 40,000

6-28 (a) 10   (b) 324.92   (c) 6.5 days; 65 units
(d) maximum = 259.94 average = 129.97
(e) 7.694 runs;   (f) $192.35; $37,384.71   (g) 5

6-30 (a) $Z = 2.05$ (b) 3.075   (c) 23.075   (d) $4.61

6-32 Add 160 feet. $1,920

6-34 2,697

6-36 Take the discount. Cost = $49,912.50

6-38 $4.50; $6.00; $7.50

6-46 Item 4 EOQ = 45

6-48 Order 200 units

Chapter 7

7-14 40 air conditioners, 60 fans, profit = $1,900

7-16 175 radio ads, 10 TV ads

7-18 40 undergraduate, 20 graduate, $160,000

7-20 $20,000 Petrochemical; $30,000 Utilities; return = $4,200; risk = 6

7-22 $X = 18.75$, $Y = 18.75$, profit = $150

7-24 (1358.7, 1820.6), $3,179.30

7-26 (a) profit = $2,375   (b) 25 barrels pruned, 62.5 barrels regular   (c) 25 acres pruned, 125 acres regular

7-28 (a) Yes   (b) Doesn't change

7-34 (a) 25 units product 1, 0 units product 2   (b) 25 units of resource 1 is used, slack $= 20$; 75 units of resource 2 is used, slack $= 12$; 50 units of resource 3 is used, slack $= 0$; constraint 3 is binding and others are not. (c) 0, 0, and 25   (d) Resource 3. Up to $25 (dual price)   (e) Total profit would decrease by 5 (value of reduced cost).

7-36 24 coconuts, 12 skins; profit $= 5,040$ rupees

7-42 Use 7.5 lb of C-30, 15 lb of C-92, 0 lb of D-21, and 27.5 lb of E-11; cost $=$ \$3.35 per lb

Chapter 8

8-2 (b) $50,000 in LA bonds, $175,000 in Palmer Drugs, $25,000 in Happy Days

8-4 1.33 pounds of oat product per horse, 0 pounds of grain, 3.33 pounds of mineral product

8-6 6.875 TV ads; 10 radio ads; 9 billboard ads; 10 newspaper ads

8-8 Use 30 of the 5-month leases starting in March, 100 5-month leases starting in April, 170 5-month leases starting in May, 160 5-month leases starting in June, and 10 5-month leases starting in July.

8-10 Send 400 students from sector A to school B, 300 from A to school E, 500 from B to school B, 100 from C to school C, 800 from D to school C, and 400 from E to school E.

8-12 (b) 0.499 lb of ground meat, 0.173 lb of chicken, 0.105 lb of spinach, and 0.762 lb of potatoes. Total cost $=$ \$1.75.

8-14 13.7 trainees begin in August, and 72.2 begin in October.

Chapter 9

9-8 Des Moines to Albuquerque 200, Des Moines to Boston 50, Des Moines to Cleveland 50, Evansville to Boston 150, Ft. Lauderdale to Cleveland 250. Cost $=$ \$3,200.

9-10 25 units from Pineville to 3; 30 units from Oak Ridge to 2; 10 units from Oakville to 3; 30 units from Mapletown to 1. Cost $=$ \$230. Multiple optimal solutions

9-12 Total cost $=$ \$14,700

9-14 Total cost $=$ \$635.

9-18 New Orleans' systems cost $=$ \$20,000; Houston's is $19,500, so Houston should be selected.

9-20 Optimal cost using East St. Louis: $17,400. Optimal cost using St. Louis: $17,250

9-22 Job A12 to machine W; Job A15 to machine Z; Job B2 to machine Y; Job B9 to machine X. Time $= 50$ hours

9-24 4,580 miles

9-26 Total rating $= 335$

9-28 Maximum total rating $= 75.5$

9-30 (a) $2,591,200   (b) $2,640,400   (c) $2,610,100 and $2,572,100

9-34 200 on path 1–2–5–7–8, 200 on path 1–3–6–8, and 100 on path 1–4–8. Total $= 500$. This increases to 700 with the changes.

9-36 Total flow $= 13$

9-38 Shortest path is 1–3–7–11–14–16. Total distance is 74.

9-40 (a) 1,200 miles   (b) 1,000 miles

9-42 Total distance $= 40$

Chapter 10

10-10 (a) 2 prime-time ads per week, 4.25 off-peak ads per week, audience $= 38,075$ (b) 2 prime-time ads per week, 4 off-peak ads per week, audience $= 36,800$ (c) 4 prime-time ads per week, 1 off-peak ads per week, audience $= 37,900$

10-12 3 large posters and 4 small posters

10-16 Build at Mt. Auburn, Mt. Adams, Norwood, Covington, and Eden Park.

10-18 (a) $X_1 \geq X_2$ (b) $X_1 + X_2 + X_3 = 2$

10-20 (b) 0 TV, 0.73 radio, 0 billboard, and 88.86 newspaper ads

10-24 $X_1 = 15$, $X_2 = 20$

10-28 18.3 XJ6 and 10.8 XJ8; Revenue $= 70,420$.

10-30 0.333 in stock 1 and 0.667 in stock 2; variance $= 0.102$; return $= 0.09$

Chapter 11

11-18 (a) 0.50   (b) 0.50   (c) 0.97725   (d) 0.02275 (e) 43.84

11-20 (a) 0.0228   (b) 0.3085   (c) 0.8413   (d) 0.9772

11-24 14

11-28 (b) Critical path A–C takes 20 weeks; path B–D takes 18 weeks   (c) 0.222 for A–C; 5 for B–D   (d) 1.00 (e) 0.963   (f) path B–D has more variability and has higher probability of exceeding 22 weeks.

11-34 Yes. The cost to crash is $2,200.

Chapter 12

12-10 Total costs for 1, 2, 3, and 4 clerks are $564, $428, $392, and $406, respectively.

12-12 (a) 4.167 cars   (b) 0.4167 hours   (c) 0.5 hours (d) 0.8333   (e) 0.1667

12-14 (a) 0.512, 0.410, 0.328   (b) 0.2   (c) 0.8 minutes (d) 3.2   (e) 4   (f) 0.429, 0.038 minutes, 0.15, 0.95

12-16 (a) 0.2687 hours   (b) 3.2 (c) Yes. Savings $=$ \$142.50 per hour.

12-18 (a) 0.0397 hours   (b) 0.9524   (c) 0.006 hours (d) 0.1524   (e) 0.4286   (f) 0.4   (g) 0.137

12-20 With one person, $L = 3$, $W = 1$ hour, $L_q = 2.25$, and $W_q = 0.75$ hour. With two people, $L = 0.6$, $W = 0.2$ hour, $L_q = 2.225$, and $W_q = 0.075$ hour.

12-22 No

12-24 (a) 0.1333 hours   (b) 1.333   (c) 0.2 hour   (d) 2 (e) 0.333

12-26 (a) 80 customers per day   (b) 10.66 hours, $266.50 (c) 0.664, $16.60   (d) 2 tellers, $208.60

12-30 (a) 0.576   (b) 1.24   (c) 0.344   (d) 0.217 hour (e) 0.467 hour

12-32 (a) 0.27 hour   (b) 3.2   (c) 4   (d) 0.33 hour (e) 0.4096

Chapter 13

13-14 No

13-16 Expected value 6.35 (using formula). The average number is 7 in Problem 13-15.

13-18 (b) Average number delayed $= 0.40$. Average number of arrivals $= 2.07$.

13-26 (a) Cost/hour is generally more expensive replacing 1 pen each time.
(b) Expected cost/hour with 1 pen policy = $1.38 (or $58/breakdown); expected cost/hour with 4-pen policy = $1.12 (or $132/breakdown).

Chapter 14

14-8 (b) 90%   (c) 30%

14-10 Next month, 4/15, 5/15, 6/15. Three months, 0.1952, 0.3252, 0.4796

14-12 (a) 70%   (b) 30%   (c) 40%

14-14 25% for Battles; 18.75% for University; 26.25% for Bill's; 30% for College

14-16 111 at Northside, 75 at West End, and 54 at Suburban

14-18 Horizon will have 104,000 customers, and Local will have 76,000.

14-20 New MFA=(5,645.16, 1,354.84)

14-22 50% Hicourt, 30% Printing House, and 20% Gandy

14-26 Store 1 will have one-third of the customers, and store 2 will have two-thirds.

Chapter 15

15-8 45.034 to 46.966 for $\bar{x}$
0 to 4.008 for R

15-10 16.814 to 17.187 for $\bar{x}$.
0.068 to 0.932 for R

15-12 2.236 to 3.728 for $\bar{x}$
0 to 2.336 for R
In control

15-16 (a) 1011.8 for $\bar{x}$ and 96.3 for R (b) 956.23 to 1067.37
(c) Process is out of control.

15-18 LCL = 0, UCL = 4

Module 1

M1-4 SUN − 0.80

M1-6 Lambda = 3.0445, Value of
CI = 0.0223, RI = 0.58, CR = 0.0384

M1-8 Car 1, 0.4045

M1-10 University B has highest weighted average = 0.4995

Module 2

M2-6 1–2–6–7, with a total distance of 10 miles.

M2-8 Shortest route is 1–2–6–7, with a total distance of 14 miles.

M2-10 Shortest route is 1–2–5–8–9. Distance = 19 miles.

M2-12 4 units of item 1, 1 unit of item 2, and no units of items 3 and 4.

M2-14 Ship 6 units of item 1, 1 unit of item 2, and 1 unit of item 3.

M2-16 The shortest route is 1–3–6–11–15–17–19–20.

Module 3

M3-6 (a) OL = $8(20,000 − X)$ for $X \leq 20,000$; OL = 0 otherwise   (b) $0.5716   (c) $0.5716   (d) 99.99%
(e) Print the book

M3-8 (a) BEP = 1,500   (b) Expected profit = $8,000

M3-10 (a) OL = $10(30 − X)$ for $X \leq 30$; OL = 0 otherwise   (b) EOL = $59.34   (c) EVPI = $59.34

M3-12 (a) Use new process. New EMV = $283,000.
(b) Increase selling price. New EMV = $296,000.

M3-14 BEP = 4,955

M3-16 EVPI = $249.96

M3-18 EVPI = $51.24

Module 4

M4-8 Strategy for $X:X_2$; strategy for $Y:Y_1$; value of the game = 6

M4-10 $X_1 = {}^{35}/_{57}$; $X_2 = {}^{22}/_{57}$; $Y_1 = {}^{32}/_{57}$; $Y_2 = {}^{25}/_{57}$; value of game = 66.70

M4-12 (b) $Q = 41/72$, $1 − Q = 31/72$; $P = 55/72$. $1 − P = 17/72$

M4-14 Value of game = 9.33

M4-16 Saddle point exists. Shoe Town should invest $15,000 in advertising and Fancy Foot should invest $20,000 in advertising.

M4-18 Eliminate dominated strategy X_2. Then Y_3 is dominated and may be eliminated. The value of the game is 6.

M4-20 Always play strategy A_{14}. $3 million.

Module 5

M5-8 $X = {}^{-3}/_2$, $Y = {}^1/_2$; $Z = {}^7/_2$

M5-16 $\begin{pmatrix} {}^{-48}/_{60} & {}^6/_{60} & {}^{32}/_{60} \\ {}^6/_{60} & {}^{-12}/_{60} & {}^6/_{60} \\ {}^{12}/_{60} & {}^6/_{60} & {}^{-8}/_{60} \end{pmatrix}$

M5-18 $0X_1 + 4X_2 + 3X_3 = 28$; $1X_1 + 2X_2 + 2X_3 = 16$

Module 6

M6-6 (a) $Y'' = 12X − 6$ (b) $Y'' = 80X^3 + 12X$
(c) $Y'' = 6/X^4$ (d) $Y'' = 500/X^6$

M6-8 (a) $Y'' = 30X^4 − 1$ (b) $Y'' = 60X^2 + 24$
(c) $Y'' = 24/X^5$ (d) $Y'' = 250/X^6$

M6-10 $X = 5$ is point of inflection.

M6-12 $Q = 2,400$, $TR = 1,440,000$

M6-14 $P = 5.48$

Module 7

M7-18 (b) $14X_1 + 4X_2 \leq 3,360$; $10X_1 + 12X_2 \leq 9,600$
(d) $S_1 = 3,360$, $S_2 = 9,600$ (e) X_2 (f) S_2
(g) 800 units of X_2 (h) 1,200,000

M7-20 $X_1 = 2$, $X_2 = 6$, $S_1 = 0$, $S_2 = 0$, $P = $36

M7-22 $X_1 = 14$, $X_2 = 33$, $C = $221

M7-24 Unbounded

M7-26 Degeneracy; $X_1 = 27$, $X_2 = 5$, $X_3 = 0$, $P = $177

M7-28 (a) Min. $C = 9X_1 + 15X_2$
$X_1 + 2X_2 \geq 30$
$X_1 + 4X_2 \geq 40$
(b) $X_1 = 0$, $X_2 = 20$, $C = $300

M7-30 8 coffee tables, 2 bookcases, profit = 96

M7-34 (a) 7.5 to infinity   (b) Negative infinity to $40
(c) $20   (d) $0

M7-36 (a) 18 Model 102, 4 Model H23
(b) S_1 = slack time for soldering
S_2 = slack time for inspection   (c) Yes—shadow price is $4   (d) No—shadow price is less than $1.75.

M7-38 (a) Negative infinity to $6 for phosphate; $5 to infinity for potassium

(b) Basis won't change; but X_1, X_2, and S_2 will change.

M7-40 max $P = 50\,U_1 + 4U_2$

$12U_1 + 1U_2 \leq 120$

$20U_1 + 3U_2 \leq 250$

Module 8

M8-14 Total cost remains unchanged at $1,040.

M8-16 Total cost is $230.

M8-18 Total cost is $14,700.

M8-20 Unbalanced, total cost $= $5,310

M8-22 Total cost $= $28,300

M8-24 Job A12 to machine W; Job A15 to machine Z; Job B2 to machine Y; Job B9 to machine X; Time $= 50$ hours

M8-26 (a) 4,580   (b) 6.040

M8-28 Total $= 86$

M8-32 Total cars per hour $= 5$

M8-34 Total distance $= 430$

M8-38 Total $= 167$ per day

M8-40 (a) The shortest path is 1–3–7–11–14–16 with a distance of 74.   (b) The distance increases by 2.

M8-42 (a) 1,200 miles   (b) 1,000 miles

Appendix H: Solutions to Self-Tests

Chapter 1

1. c
2. d
3. b
4. b
5. c
6. c
7. d
8. c
9. d
10. a
11. a
12. c

Chapter 2

1. c
2. b
3. a
4. d
5. b
6. c
7. a
8. c
9. b
10. d
11. b
12. a
13. a
14. b
15. a

Chapter 3

1. b
2. c
3. c
4. a
5. c
6. b
7. a
8. c
9. a
10. d
11. b
12. c
13. c
14. a
15. c
16. b

Chapter 4

1. b
2. c
3. d
4. b
5. b
6. c

7. b
8. c
9. a
10. b
11. b
12. c

Chapter 5

1. b
2. a
3. d
4. c
5. b
6. b
7. d
8. b
9. d
10. b
11. c
12. d
13. b
14. c
15. b

Chapter 6

1. e
2. e
3. c
4. c
5. a
6. b
7. d
8. c
9. b
10. a
11. a
12. d
13. d
14. d

Chapter 7

1. b
2. a
3. b
4. c
5. a
6. b
7. c
8. c
9. b
10. c
11. a
12. a
13. a
14. a

Chapter 8

1. a
2. b
3. d
4. e
5. d
6. c

Chapter 9

1. d
2. b
3. c
4. b
5. d
6. b
7. b
8. d

Chapter 10

1. a
2. b
3. a
4. a
5. a
6. b
7. b
8. b
9. d
10. b
11. e

Chapter 11

1. e
2. c
3. a
4. d
5. b
6. c
7. b
8. a
9. b
10. b
11. a
12. a
13. Critical path (or critical)
14. program evaluation and review technique
15. linear programming model
16. optimistic, most likely, pessimistic
17. slack
18. monitor and control

Chapter 12

1. a
2. a

3. b
4. e
5. c
6. b
7. c
8. d
9. b
10. d
11. c
12. first-come, first-served
13. negative exponentially distributed
14. simulation

Chapter 13

1. b
2. b
3. a
4. b
5. a
6. a
7. d
8. a
9. b
10. b
11. d
12. d
13. c
14. e
15. (a) no, yes, no, no, no, yes, yes, yes, no, yes
    (b) yes, yes, yes, yes, no, yes, yes, no, no, no

Chapter 14

1. b
2. a
3. c
4. c
5. b
6. a
7. a
8. a
9. b
10. matrix of transition probabilities
11. collectively exhaustive, mutually exclusive
12. vector of state probabilities

Chapter 15

1. b
2. c

3. d
4. a
5. c
6. b
7. c
8. d
9. b
10. b

Module 1

1. a
2. d
3. b
4. b
5. c
6. b
7. b
8. b

Module 2

1. c
2. b
3. e
4. c
5. b
6. a
7. c
8. e
9. a
10. a
11. c
12. c
13. b
14. b

Module 3

1. c
2. d
3. b
4. a
5. b
6. b
7. c

Module 4

1. b
2. a
3. c
4. b
5. b
6. b
7. a

Module 5

1. c
2. a
3. b
4. c
5. b
6. a
7. e
8. d

Module 6

1. a
2. d
3. a
4. b
5. c
6. d
7. d

Module 7

1. a
2. d
3. d
4. a
5. a
6. d
7. a
8. d
9. b
10. a
11. a
12. b
13. c
14. c
15. d
16. a
17. b

Module 8

1. c
2. b
3. b
4. a
5. b
6. b
7. a
8. b
9. a
10. b
11. b
12. b
13. b

Index